Practical JavaScript™, DOM Scripting, and Ajax Projects

Frank W. Zammetti

Practical JavaScript™, DOM Scripting, and Ajax Projects

Copyright © 2007 by Frank W. Zammetti

ISBN-13 (pbk): 978-1-59059-816-0

ISBN-10 (pbk): 1-59059-816-4

Printed and bound in the United States of America 9 8 7 6 5 4 3 2 1

Lead Editor: Matthew Moodie

Technical Reviewer: Herman van Rosmalen

Editorial Board: Steve Anglin, Ewan Buckingham, Gary Cornell, Jason Gilmore, Jonathan Gennick, Jonathan Hassell, James Huddleston, Chris Mills, Matthew Moodie, Jeff Pepper, Paul Sarknas, Dominic Shakeshaft, Jim Sumser, Matt Wade

Project Manager: Tracy Brown Collins

Copy Edit Manager: Nicole Flores

Copy Editor: Marilyn Smith

Assistant Production Director: Kari Brooks-Copony

Production Editor: Laura Esterman

Compositor: Susan Glinert

Proofreaders: Lori Bring and April Eddy

Indexer: Broccoli Information Management

Cover Designer: Kurt Krames

Manufacturing Director: Tom Debolski

Distributed to the book trade worldwide by Springer-Verlag New York, Inc., 233 Spring Street, 6th Floor, New York, NY 10013. Phone 1-800-SPRINGER, fax 201-348-4505, e-mail orders-ny@springer-sbm.com, or visit http://www.springeronline.com.

For information on translations, please contact Apress directly at 2560 Ninth Street, Suite 219, Berkeley, CA 94710. Phone 510-549-5930, fax 510-549-5939, e-mail info@apress.com, or visit http://www.apress.com.

The source code for this book is available to readers at http://www.apress.com in the Source Code/Download section.

Dedicated to all the animals I've eaten over the years, without whom I most certainly would have died a long time ago due to starvation. Well, I suppose I could have been a vegan, but then I'd have to dedicate this to all the plants I've eaten, and that would just be silly because very few plants can read.

To all my childhood friends who provided me with cool stories to tell: Joe, Thad, Meenie, Kenny, Franny, Tubby, Stubby, Kenway, JD, dVoot, Corey, and Francine.

To Denny Crane, for raising awareness of Mad Cow disease.

Hmm, who am I forgetting? Oh yeah, and to my wife and kids. You guys make life worth living.

Contents at a Glance

PART 1 ■■■ Say Hello to My Little Friend: JavaScript!

PART 2 ■■■ The Projects

Contents

PART 1 ■■■ Say Hello to My Little Friend: JavaScript!

PART 2 ■■■ **The Projects**

CHAPTER 7   JSDigester: Taking the Pain Out of Client-Side XML 231

CHAPTER 8   Get It Right, Bub: A JavaScript Validation Framework 261

CHAPTER 9   Widget Mania: Using a GUI Widget Framework 305

About the Author

FRANK W. ZAMMETTI is a web architect specialist for a leading worldwide financial company by day, and a PocketPC and open source developer by night. He is the founder and chief software architect of Omnytex Technologies, a PocketPC development house.

Frank has more than 13 years of "professional" experience in the IT field, and over 12 more of "amateur" experience. He began his nearly lifelong love of computers at age 7, when he became one of four students chosen to take part in the school district's pilot computer program. A year later, he was the only participant left! The first computer Frank owned was a Timex Sinclair 1000, in 1982, on which he wrote a program to look up movie times for all of Long Island (and without the 16kb expansion module!). After that, he moved on to an Atari computer, and then a Commodore 64, where he spent about four years doing nothing but assembly programming (games mostly). He finally got his first IBM-compatible PC in 1987, and began learning the finer points of programming (as they existed at that time!).

Frank has primarily developed web-based applications for about eight years. Before that, he developed Windows-based client/server applications in a variety of languages. Frank holds numerous certifications, including SCJP, MCSD, CNA, i-Net+, A+, CIW Associate, MCP, and numerous BrainBench certifications. He is a contributor to a number of open source projects, including DataVision, Struts, PocketFrog, and Jakarta Commons. In addition, Frank has started two projects: Java Web Parts and The Struts Web Services Enablement Project. He also was one of the founding members of a project that created the first fully functioning Commodore 64 emulator for PocketPC devices (PocketHobbit).

Frank has authored various articles on topics that range from integrating DataVision into web applications to using Ajax in Struts-based applications, as well as a book on Ajax for Apress. He is currently working on a new application framework specifically geared to creating next-generation web applications.

Frank lives in the United States with his wife Traci, his two kids Andrew and Ashley, and his dog Belle. And an assortment of voices in his head, but the pills are supposed to stop that.

About the Technical Reviewer

HERMAN VAN ROSMALEN works as a developer/software architect for De Nederlandsche Bank N.V., the central bank of the Netherlands. He has more than 20 years of experience in developing software applications in a variety of programming languages. Herman has been involved in building mainframe, PC, and client/server applications. For the past six years, however, he has been involved mainly in building J2EE web-based applications. After working with Struts (pre-1.0) for years, he got interested in Ajax and joined the Java Web Parts open source project in 2005.

Herman lives in a small town, Pijnacker, in the Netherlands, with his wife Liesbeth and their children, Barbara, Leonie, and Ramon.

About the Illustrator

ANTHONY VOLPE did the illustrations for this book and the K&G Arcade game. He has worked on several video games with author Frank Zammetti, including Invasion Trivia!, Io Lander, and Ajax Warrior. Anthony lives in Collegeville, Pennsylvania, and works as a graphic designer and front-end web developer. His hobbies include recording music, writing fiction, making video games, and going to karaoke bars to make a spectacle of himself.

Acknowledgments

Many people helped make this book a reality in one form or another, and some of them may not even realize it! I'll try to remember them all here, but chances are I haven't, and I apologize in advance.

First and foremost, I would like to thank everyone at Apress who made this book a reality. This is my second go-round with you folks, and it was just as pleasurable an experience this time as the first. Chris, Matt, Tracy, Marilyn, Laura, Tina, and all the rest, thank you!

A great deal of thanks goes to Herman van Rosmalen, one of my partners in crime on the Java Web Parts project (http://javawebparts.sourceforge.net) project, and technical reviewer for this book. I know you put in a lot of time and effort in keeping me honest, and I can't tell you how much I appreciate it! Now, let's get back to work on JWP!

A big thanks must also go to Anthony Volpe, the fine artist who did the illustrations for this book. He and I have been friends for about ten years now, and we have collaborated on a number of projects, including three PocketPC games (check 'em out: http://www.omnytex.com), as well as a couple of Flash games (http://www.planetvolpe.com/crackhead) and some web cartoons (http://www.planetvolpe.com/du). He is a fantastic artist, as I'm sure you can see for yourself, an incredibly creative person, and a good friend to boot.

I would also like to thank those that built some of the libraries used in this book, including all the folks working on Dojo, Sam Stephenson (Prototype), Aaron Newton, Christophe Beyls, and Valerio Proietti of the Mootools team; Bob Ippolito of MochiKit fame; all the YUI developers; and everyone working on script.aculo.us and Rico.

Last but most definitely not least, I would like to thank everyone who bought this book! I sincerely hope you have as much fun reading it as I did writing it, and I hope that you find it to be worth your hard-earned dollars and that it proves to be an educational and eye-opening experience.

As I said, I know I am almost certainly forgetting a boatload of people, so how about I just thank the entire world and be done with it?!? In fact, if I had the technology, I'd be like Wowbagger the Infinitely Prolonged, only with "Thanks!" instead of insults.

And on that note, let's get to some code!

Introduction

So there I was, just minding my own business, when along came a publisher asking me if I'd be interested in writing a book on JavaScript. It seemed like a good thing to do at the time, so I said yes.

I'm just kidding. No one asked me, I just showed up one day on the doorstep of Apress with a manuscript and some puppy-dog eyes. I'm just kidding again.

Seriously though, JavaScript is one of those kids we all knew when we were young who start out really ugly, but whom everyone wants as their beautiful date to the prom years later. Then they go on to Yale, become a district attorney, and suddenly everyone realizes that they really want to be with that person. Fortunately, unlike the DA, JavaScript doesn't involve crimes and misdemeanors, since you know you don't have a chance any other way with the DA!

JavaScript has quickly become one of the most important topics in web development, one that any self-respecting web developer can't do without. With the advent of Ajax, which I'll talk about in this book, JavaScript has very quickly gone from something that can enhance a web site a little to something used to build very serious, professional-quality applications. It's no longer a peripheral player; it's a main focus nowadays.

There are plenty of books on JavaScript and plenty of how-to articles strewn across the intrawebs, any of which can be of great help to you. Far harder to come by though are real, substantial examples. Oh, you can get a lot of simplistic, artificial examples to be sure, but it's more difficult to find full-blown, real-world applications that you can examine. Many developers learn best by tearing apart code, messing around with it a bit, and generally getting their hands dirty with real, working bits. That's why I wrote this book: to fill that gap.

In this book, you will find two chapters on some general JavaScript topics, including a brief history of JavaScript, good coding habits, debugging techniques, tools, and more. From then on, it's ten chapters of nothing but projects! Each chapter will present a different application, explain its inner workings, and offer some suggested exercises you can do to sharpen your skills and further your learning. The projects run the gamut from generally useful (an extensible calculator) to current ideas (a mashup) to just plain fun (a JavaScript game).

In the process, you will learn about a wide variety of topics, including debugging techniques, various JavaScript libraries, and a few somewhat unique and useful approaches to coding. I believe you will also find this to be an entertaining book, and in fact, one of the exercises I suggest from the beginning is to try to pick out all the pop-culture references scattered all over the place (try to place them without looking at the footnotes that accompany most, but not all!). I tried to make this book like an episode of *Gilmore Girls* in that regard (and if you aren't familiar with the show, there's your first pop-culture reference!).

So, enough babbling (for the time being anyway). You know what's coming, so let's stop dropping hints about numbers, Dharma, and bizarre connections between characters (pop-culture reference number 2!), and get on with the good stuff. Let's get on with the show!

An Overview of This Book

This book is divided into two main parts. Part 1, "Say Hello to My Little Friend: JavaScript!," contains two chapters:

- Chapter 1 is a brief history of JavaScript, from its humble beginning to its current state of acceptance.

- Chapter 2 goes into the techniques and approaches employed by modern-day "professional" JavaScript developers.

Part 2, "The Projects," contains ten chapters:

- Chapter 3 starts you off with the first project: an extensible, packaged collection of utility functions.

- Chapter 4 develops an extensible calculator and introduces the first JavaScript library, Rico.

- Chapter 5 introduces the concept of a mashup, one of the hottest topics going today, by way of a working example using the very popular script.aculo.us library.

- Chapter 6 uses the Dojo library to deal with an issue that comes up frequently in JavaScript development, that of client-side data persistence.

- Chapter 7 explores the very useful JSDigester component of the Java Web Parts project, which allows you to parse XML and create JavaScript objects from it without tedious coding on your part.

- Chapter 8 develops an extensible validation framework for doing client-side form validation in a purely declarative fashion.

- Chapter 9 introduces the Yahoo! User Interface Library and uses it to create a handy little contact manager application.

- Chapter 10 uses the MochiKit library to develop a drag-and-drop shopping cart for e-commerce applications.

- Chapter 11 is where we get into the fun stuff: a JavaScript game! And not a simple little Tetris clone or tile-matching game, but something a fair bit more substantial.

- Chapter 12 is where we have an in-depth look at Ajax, perhaps the biggest reason JavaScript has taken on a whole new level of importance in recent years, using the relatively new Mootools library.

Obtaining This Book's Source Code

All the examples in this book are freely available from the Source Code section of the Apress web site. In fact, due to the nature of this book, you will absolutely *have* to download the source code before you begin Chapter 3. To do so, visit http://www.apress.com, click the Source Code link, and find *Practical JavaScript, DOM Scripting, and Ajax Projects* in the list. From this book's home page, you can download the source code as a zip file. The source code is organized by chapter.

Obtaining Updates for This Book

Writing a book is a big endeavor—quite a bit bigger than many people think! Contrary to what I claim in private to my friends, I am not perfect. I make my mistakes like everyone else. Not in this book of course. Oh no, none at all.

Ahem . . .

Let me apologize in advance for any errors you may find in this book. Rest assured that everyone involved has gone to extremes to ensure there are none, but let's be real here. We've all read technical books before, and we know that the cold, sharp teeth of reality bite every now and again. I'm sorry, I'm sorry, I'm sorry!

A current errata list is available from this book's home page on the Apress web site (http://www.apress.com) along with information about how to notify us of any errors you may find. This will usually involve some sort of telepathy, but my understanding is that Windows Vista Service Pack 1 will include this feature, so rest easy my friends.

Contacting the Author

I very much would like to hear your questions and comments regarding this book's content and source code examples. Please do feel free to email me directly at fzammetti@omnytex.com (spammers *will* be hunted down by Sentinels and disposed of). I will reply to your inquiries as soon as I can, but please remember, I do have a life (no, really, I do . . . OK, no I don't), so I may not be able to reply immediately.

Lastly, and most important, thank you for buying this book! I thank you, my wife thanks you, my kids thank you, my kids' orthodontist thanks you, my dog's veterinarian thanks you, my roofing contractor thanks you . . .

PART 1

■■■

Say Hello to My Little Friend: JavaScript!

Eaten any good books lately?

Q (to Worf) in the *Star Trek: The Next Generation* episode, "Deja-Q"

The Internet? Is that thing still around?

Homer Simpson

Programming today is a race between software engineers striving to build bigger and better idiot-proof programs, and the Universe trying to produce bigger and better idiots. So far, the Universe is winning.

Rich Cook

The first 90% of the code accounts for the first 10% of the development time. The remaining 10% of the code accounts for the other 90% of the development time.

Tom Cargill

There are only two kinds of programming languages: those people always bitch about and those nobody uses.

Bjarne Stroustrup

There are only two industries that refer to their customers as 'users.'

Edward Tufte

CHAPTER 1

∎∎∎

A Brief History of JavaScript

I can only hope Stephen Hawking doesn't mind me paraphrasing his book title as the title of this chapter![1] Just as in his book *A Brief History of Time*, we are about to begin an exploration of a universe of sorts, from its humble beginnings to its current state of being.

In this chapter, we will explore the genesis of JavaScript. More than providing a mere history lesson though, in the tradition of Mr. Hawking himself, I'll give you a deeper look and show what's below the surface. In the process, you'll gain an understanding of the problems inherent in early JavaScript development and how those flaws have largely been overcome. By the end of our journey, you'll have a good understanding of the pitfalls to avoid and start to know how to overcome them (the rest of that knowledge will be revealed in subsequent chapters). So, let's get ready for an adventure, and let's do Mr. Hawking proud!

How JavaScript Came to Exist

The year was 1995, and the Web was still very much in its infancy. It's fair to say that the vast majority of computer users couldn't tell you what a web site was at that point, and most developers couldn't build one without doing some research and learning first. Microsoft was really just beginning to realize that the Internet was going to matter. And *Google* was still just a made-up term from an old Little Rascals episode.[2]

Netscape ruled the roost at that point, with its Navigator browser as the primary method for most people to get on the Web. A new feature at the time, Java applets, was making people stand up and take notice. However, one of the things they were noticing is that Java wasn't as accessible to many developers as some (specifically, Sun Microsystems, the creator of Java) had hoped. Netscape needed something more.

---

1. *A Brief History of Time* is the title of one of the most famous books on physics and cosmology ever written, and is the obvious, ahem, inspiration, for the title of this chapter. Its author, Professor Stephen Hawking of the University of Cambridge, is considered one of the world's best theoretical physicists. His book brought many of the current theories about the universe to the layman, and those of us that pretend we actually know what we're talking about when discussing things like superstrings, supersymmetry, and quantum singularities (outside a *Star Trek* episode, that is!). For more information, see http://en.wikipedia.org/wiki/Stephen_Hawking.

2. The word *google* was first used in the 1927 Little Rascals silent film *Dog Heaven*, to refer to having a drink of water. See http://experts.about.com/e/g/go/Google.htm. Although this reference does not state it was the first use of the word, numerous other sources on the Web indicate it was. I wouldn't bet all my money on this if I ever made it to the finals of *Jeopardy*, but it should be good enough for polite party conversation!

Enter Brendan Eich, formerly of MicroUnity Systems Engineering, a new hire at Netscape. Brendan was given the task of leading development of a new, simple, lightweight language for non-Java developers to use. Many of the growing legions of web developers, who often didn't have a full programming background, found Java's object-oriented nature, compilation requirements, and package and deployment requirements a little too much to tackle. Brendan quickly realized that to make a language accessible to these developers, he would need to make certain decisions. Among them, he decided that this new language should be loosely typed and very dynamic by virtue of it being interpreted.

The language he created was initially called LiveWire, but its name was pretty quickly changed to LiveScript, owing to its dynamic nature. However, as is all too often the case, some marketing drones got hold of it and decided to call it JavaScript, to ride the coattails of Java. This change was actually implemented before the end of the Navigator 2.0 beta cycle.[3] So for all intents and purposes, JavaScript was known as JavaScript from the beginning. At least the marketing folks were smart enough to get Sun involved. On December 4, 1995, both Netscape and Sun jointly announced JavaScript, terming it "complementary" to both HTML and Java (one of the initial reasons for its creation was to help web designers manipulate Java applets easier, so this actually made some sense). The shame of all this is that for years to come, JavaScript and Java would be continually confused on mailing lists, message boards, and in general by developers and the web-surfing public alike!

It didn't take long for JavaScript to become something of a phenomenon, although tellingly on its own, rather than in the context of controlling applets. Web designers were just beginning to take the formerly static Web and make it more dynamic, more reactive to the user, and more multimedia. People were starting to try to create interactive and sophisticated (relatively speaking) user interfaces, and JavaScript was seen as a way to do that. Seemingly simple things like swapping images on mouse events, which before then would have required a bulky browser plug-in of some sort, became commonplace. In fact, this single application of JavaScript—flipping images in response to user mouse events—was probably the most popular usage of JavaScript for a long time. Manipulating forms, and, most usually, validating them, was a close second in terms of early JavaScript usage. Document Object Model (DOM) manipulation took a little bit longer to catch on for the most part, mostly because the early DOM level 0, as it came to be known, was relatively simplistic, with form, link, and anchor manipulation as the primary goals.

In early 1996, shortly after its creation, JavaScript was submitted to the European Computer Manufacturers Association (ECMA) for standardization. ECMA (http://www.ecma-international.org) produced the specification called ECMAScript, which covered the core JavaScript syntax, and a subset of DOM level 0. ECMAScript still exists today, and most browsers implement that specification in one form or another. However, it is rare to hear people talk about ECMAScript in place of JavaScript. The name has simply stuck in the collective consciousness for too long to be replaced. And, of course, this book itself is about *JavaScript*, not ECMAScript. But do be clear about it: they are the same thing!

What made JavaScript so popular so fast? Probably most important was the very low barrier to entry. All you had to do was open any text editor, type in some code, save it, and load that file in a browser, and it worked! You didn't need to go through a compilation cycle or package and

---

3. As a historical aside, you might be interested to know that version 2.0 of Netscape Navigator introduced not one but two noteworthy features. Aside from JavaScript, frames were also introduced. Of course, one of these has gained popularity, while the other tends to be shunned by the web developer community at large, but that's a story for another book!

deploy it—none of that complex "programming" stuff. And no complicated integrated development environment (IDE) was involved. It was really just as easy as saving a quick note to yourself.

Another important reason for JavaScript's early success was its seeming simplicity. You didn't have to worry about data types, because it was (and still is) a loosely typed language. It wasn't object-oriented, so you didn't have to think about class hierarchies and the like. In fact, you didn't even have to deal with functions if you didn't want to (and wanted your script to execute immediately upon page loading). There was no multithreading to worry about or generic collections classes to learn. In fact, the intrinsic JavaScript objects were very limited, and thus quickly picked up by anyone with even just an inkling of programming ability. It was precisely this seeming simplicity that lead to a great many of the early problems.

Unfortunately, JavaScript's infancy wasn't all roses by any stretch. A number of highly publicized security flaws hurt its early reputation considerably. A flood of books aimed squarely at nonprogrammers had the effect of getting a lot of people involved in writing code who probably shouldn't have been doing so (at least, not as publicly as a web site tends to be).

Probably the biggest problem, however, was the frankly elitist attitude of many "real" programmers. They saw JavaScript's lack of development tools (IDEs, debuggers, and so on), its inability to be developed outside a browser (in some sort of test environment), and apparent simplicity as indications that it was a "script kiddie" language—something that would be used only by amateurs, beginners, and/or hacks. For a long time, JavaScript was very much the "ugly duckling" of the programming world. It was the Christina Crawford,[4] forever being berated by her metaphorical mother, the "real" programmers of the world.

Poor javascript—other languages can be so cruel!

---

4. Christina Crawford was the daughter of Jane Crawford, and her story is told in the classic movie *Mommy Dearest* (http://www.imdb.com/title/tt0082766). Even if you don't remember the movie, you almost certainly remember the phrase "No more wire hangers!" uttered by Jane to Christina in what was probably the most memorable scene in the movie.

This attitude blinded programmers to the amazing potential that lay just below the surface, and that would become apparent as both JavaScript and the skill of those using it matured. This attitude also kept away a lot of excellent developers, who could have been helping accelerate that maturation process instead of stunting it. But JavaScript was destined for greatness, no matter what anyone else said!

The Evolution of JavaScript: Teething Pains

While it's true that JavaScript wasn't given a fair shake early on by programmers, some of their criticisms were, without question, true. JavaScript was far from perfect in its first few iterations— a fact I doubt that Netscape or Brendan Eich would dispute! As you'll see, some of it was a simple consequence of being a new technology that needed a few revisions to get right (the same problem Microsoft is so often accused of having), and some of it was, well, something else.

So, what were the issues that plagued early JavaScript? Several of them tend to stand out above the rest: browser incompatibilities, memory, and performance. Also, there was the true reason JavaScript wasn't embraced by everyone from the get-go: developers themselves! Let's explore these areas in some detail, because in order to understand where we are now, it helps to understand where we were not so very long ago.

But It's the Same Code: Browser Incompatibilities

To better understand the discussion to follow, and in the interest of those who prefer the graphical representation of information to the textual, let's look at two timelines. Figure 1-1 shows the somewhat simplified release history of Netscape's Navigator browser, and in lockstep, versions of JavaScript. Figure 1-2 shows the same basic information for Microsoft's Internet Explorer (IE) and its JScript implementation of JavaScript. While these data points are accurate, I have probably left out a point release here and there. And I haven't carried these timelines to the current day, because from the point where they end, we've been in the realm of ECMAScript and largely compatible implementations across browsers.

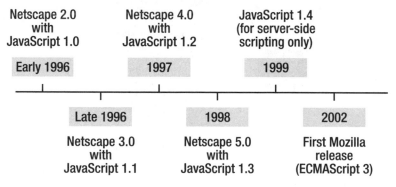

Figure 1-1. *The quick-and-dirty history of Netscape Navigator and JavaScript*

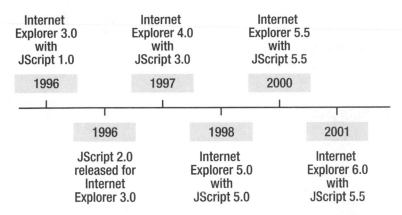

Figure 1-2. *The quick-and-dirty history of Internet Explorer and JScript*

When JavaScript came out, Microsoft developers realized they had a problem on their hands. Despite whatever issues may have existed with JavaScript early on, it was clear that this was something web developers were going to want. How could it be otherwise? For the first time, static pages could come alive.[5]

Microsoft found an answer for this situation. In fact, it had two! First, it created VBScript, which was at least syntactically modeled after its Visual Basic product. Second, and most important for the discussion in this section, Microsoft also created JScript, which was a (mostly) compatible version of JavaScript. It's that "mostly" part that caused problems.

One of the biggest perceived problems with JavaScript for a long time—really, until just two or three years ago—was incompatibilities among different browser versions. Most of this problem was caused by Microsoft's implementation coming into the picture. Logically, had Netscape remained the dominant browser, there likely would not have been any compatibility issues to speak of! On the gripping hand,[6] when Microsoft released JScript 1.0, it was actually quite compatible with JavaScript 1.0—close enough that cross-browser development could begin. It wasn't until Netscape released JavaScript 1.1 that compatibility issues really began. So, if you're a Microsoft booster, you can feel free to bash Netscape. If you're a Micro$oft hater, then it was clearly at fault!

From the point when Netscape released JavaScript 1.1 with Navigator 3.0 on, Microsoft's JScript implementation was at least one point release behind Netscape's at any given time, and

---

5. Well, not really the first time, but the first time without cumbersome, not to mention often buggy, plug-ins that required extra download time. Remember that this was years before broadband came into play, back in the days when a 56kbps modem that never quite performed up to spec was the predominant technology for connecting to the Internet.

6. "On the gripping hand" is a phrase used in the science-fiction book *The Mote in God's Eye*, written by Larry Niven and Jerry Ournelle, and also in *The Gripping Hand*, the sequel. It is used to describe the third choice sometimes available to us. For example, when you say, "We could do A . . . ; on the other hand, we could do B," you can also say ". . . on the gripping hand, we could do C." The phrase stems from the fact that the alien race the book deals with, the Moties, are asymmetrical in terms of their appendage layout; they have two arms on one side! It also happened to usually be the strongest of the three arms possessed by these creatures. These are excellent books, and if you are into science fiction and haven't read them yet, I highly recommend picking them up! They are considered classic works by most (so how you could call yourself a sci-fi fan without having read them?).

this condition persisted for quite some time. So, as one example, while image rollovers were becoming commonplace in Netscape browsers, this ability was not yet present in IE (around the IE 3.0 timeframe). To handle the differences, using "browser-sniffing" code to enable or disable bits of functionality became commonplace. This code would look something like that shown in Listing 1-1.

Listing 1-1. *An Old Browser-Sniffer Routine*

```
function Redirect()    {
  var WhatBrowser;
  var WhatVersion;
  WhatBrowser = navigator.appName.toUpperCase();
  WhatVersion = navigator.appVersion.toUpperCase();
  if (WhatBrowser.indexOf("MICROSOFT") >= 0) {
    if (WhatVersion.indexOf("3") >= 0) {
      top.location = "MainPage.html";
    } else {
      top.location = "BadVersion.html";
    }
  }
  if (WhatBrowser.indexOf("NETSCAPE") >= 0) {
    if (WhatVersion.indexOf("2") >= 0) {
      top.location = "MainPage.html";
    } else {
      top.location = "BadVersion.html";
    }
  }
}
```

In this code, if the browser version detected is not 3.*x* or higher for IE, or 2.*x* for Netscape, users are directed to BadVersion.html, which presumably tells them their browser is not compatible. They wind up at MainPage.html if the version meets these minimum requirements. This is obviously very flawed code for a number of reasons, which I'll leave as an exercise for you to find.

The important point here is that this "sniffing" of browser versions (and type, in some cases) was commonplace for a long time. In fact, you would often find two different versions of the same page: one designed for IE and the other for Netscape. This was clearly not an optimal situation! But for a long time, it was really the only way, because a piece of code would simply not work as expected in one browser vs. another. Often, it was more a matter of one browser supporting some feature that the other did not—sometimes because of proprietary extensions, and sometimes because one browser implemented an earlier version of JavaScript. Other times, it was outright differences in the way things worked.

It wasn't just enough to test for browser type and version though, because Microsoft had designed things such that the browser and the JScript language were separate entities. They could upgrade one without touching the other, because JScript was just a dynamic link library (DLL, a library of code linked to by another program at runtime). When IE 3.0 shipped, it did so with the first version of the JScript DLL. A short while later, when IE 3.0 was still the most current shipping version of the browser, Microsoft updated JScript to version 2.0. Microsoft did provide two functions, ScriptEngineMajorVersion() and ScriptEngineMinorVersion(), but aside from those functions not being supported by anything other than IE, they also were not available in JScript 1.0! So dealing with them was often more trouble than they were worth. Still, they tended to be the best answer, because you sometimes needed the information to branch your code accordingly.

As an example of some of the sorts of incompatibilities you had to deal with back in the day, the split() method of the String class allowed for an optional limitInteger parameter, which would restrict the number of items converted into an array element. However, this parameter was recognized only by Navigator 4. As another example, Netscape did not support the typeof operator until Navigator 3, while Microsoft introduced it with JScript 1.0 (this is one of those proprietary extensions that proved so useful it was added to the ECMAScript 1.0 specification). For one more example, check out this simple snippet:

```
var d = new Date();
alert(d);
```

Something this simple would have been a problem early on because the toString() method of the Date object, which was intrinsically present in Netscape's implementation of the Date object, was not present in JScript until version 2.0!

Various problems like these would arise, and seemingly always at the most inopportune time! A tight deadline and a substring() function that doesn't treat negative values quite the same in IE as it does in Navigator are a sure recipe for disaster![7] That's why browser sniffing was so common for so long, even though we all knew it wasn't a good idea.

If that had been the only real problem with JavaScript though, I suspect developers would have griped and muttered under their breaths, but would have worked around it and gotten used to it. Unfortunately, it wasn't the only strike against JavaScript.

Of Snails and Elephants: JavaScript Performance and Memory Issues

JavaScript can be slow. There, I said it! Even today, you can easily write code that performs quite poorly. One trivial example is shown in Listing 1-2.

Listing 1-2. *An Example of Poor JavaScript Performance (and How to Fix It)*

```
<html>
  <head>
    <title>Listing 1-2</title>
    <script>

      function badTest() {
        var startTime = new Date().valueOf();
        var s = "";
        for (var i = 0; i < 10000; i++) {
          s += "This is a test string";
        }
```

---

7. I remember something like this being an issue, but I frankly couldn't pull anything out of Google to substantiate it. So, I offer it purely anecdotally, with the hope that my memory isn't failing *quite* this early in life!

```
      return new Date().valueOf() - startTime;
    }

    function goodTest() {
      var startTime = new Date().valueOf();
      var stringBuffer = new Array();
      for (var i = 0; i < 10000; i++) {
        stringBuffer.push("This is a test string");
      }
      var s = stringBuffer.join("");
      return new Date().valueOf() - startTime;
    }

    function betterTest() {
      var startTime = new Date().valueOf();
      var stringBuffer = new Array();
      for (var i = 0; i < 10000; i++) {
        stringBuffer[stringBuffer.length] = "This is a test string";
      }
      var s = stringBuffer.join("");
      return new Date().valueOf() - startTime;
    }

    function doTests() {
      var htm = "";
      htm += "Time badTest took: " + badTest() + "<br>";
      htm += "Time goodTest took: " + goodTest() + "<br>";
      htm += "Time betterTest took: " + betterTest();
      document.getElementById("result").innerHTML = htm;
    }

  </script>

 </head>

 <body>
   <a href="javascript:void(0);" onClick="doTests();">Click here to test</a>
   <br><br>
   <div id="result"> </div>
 </body>

</html>
```

As the caption for Listing 1-2 says, this example also gives you a free bonus: an optimization that you can definitely use in the real world! This example does the same (admittedly contrived) thing in three different ways:

- It constructs a string that consists of the string "This is a test string" 10,000 times ("This is a test stringThis is a test stringThis is a test string" and so on 10,000 times). It does a simple string concatenation using the + operator.

- It creates an array and uses the push() method to add "This is a string" to the array 10,000 times, and then finally uses the join() method of the Array class with a blank character, which returns a string formed by combining all the elements of the array together, separated by essentially nothing.

- It does this same array trick, but instead of using push(), it sets each element of the array explicitly, making use of the fact that if you try to set an element of an array whose index equals the length of the array, the array will grow by one.

Figure 1-3 shows how long each approach took in Firefox. You can see that none of them took an especially long time. The Mozilla developers have done an excellent job of optimizing their JavaScript engine, and this is especially evident in the simple + concatenation test case taking the least amount of time. This wasn't the case just a short while ago!

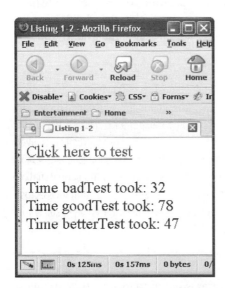

Figure 1-3. *The speed test results in Firefox (1.5.0.6, latest as of this writing)*

Now look at the same speed test results in IE, shown in Figure 1-4. The array tests are actually a little faster than in Firefox, although certainly not drastically so. But obviously string concatenation is a big no-no in IE. It's a whooping 95 times slower than Firefox!

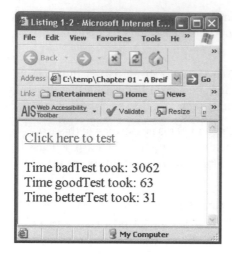

Figure 1-4. *The speed test results in Internet Explorer (6.0.2900.2180, latest as of this writing)*

Lest anyone think something fishy is going on, these speed tests were run on the same PC, without virtual machines or anything like that. So the difference is attributable to the browsers almost entirely. It's possible that differences at runtime in the operating system itself could have had an impact. But I actually went so far as to reboot before running each test and didn't load anything else, so it was roughly as close to identical at runtime as could reasonably be expected.

Note I ran the same speed test on Maxthon, version 1.5.6 build 4.2, latest as of this writing. Maxthon tends to be my preferred browser for day-to-day browsing. It is a wrapper around IE that extends it with all sorts of features and fixes, putting it, in my opinion, on par with Firefox and most other browsers, while still using the IE rendering engine (some will say this is a bad thing, but most sites tend to work correctly in IE even if they don't in Firefox). The results were very surprising: 19141 for the bad test, 141 for the good test, and 93 for the better test. I have no explanation why it should be that much slower, especially the string concatenation approach. I don't mean this as a criticism of Maxthon, but it does illustrate the point that performance across different browsers, even where it seems that logically there should be no appreciable difference, is still something to be aware of when doing your work.

None of this is meant to persuade you that one browser is better than any other. In fact, a great many web developers will tell you that Firefox is superior, yet here we can see that in two out of three approaches to the same thing, it's a little slower than IE. The point is to illustrate the following:

- The same piece of JavaScript executed in one browser won't necessarily perform the same as in another browser, and sometimes the difference can be drastic.

- Performance of modern JavaScript engines still, in some cases, leaves a lot to be desired.

That's the situation today. It used to be much worse. As an example, Figure 1-5 shows the results of the same example in IE 4.0, which shipped with Windows 98.

Figure 1-5. *The speed test results in Internet Explorer 4.0*

Wow, the IE development team has clearly been busy! The simple bad test, using the + operator, is something on the order of 13 times faster now than it was with IE 4.0! The better test is about twice as fast. Note that the good test could not be run because the push() method was not available on the Array object in this iteration of JScript. I think we can reasonably surmise that it also would have been significantly slower back then.

The same tests on Netscape 3.01 yield even worse results. In fact, the bad test was taking so long, and was eating up so many system resources, that I had to kill the process! Suffice it to say the test more than validated my point about performance having improved markedly over the years.

Netscape 3.0 also demonstrates the other common failing of early JavaScript implementations: they were not efficient with memory. This inefficiency can largely be attributed to the simple evolution that occurs for virtually all software over time. You write something, you see what the flaws are, and you correct them for the next version. A JavaScript engine is no different.

Even just a few years ago, it was not uncommon to find that relatively simple pieces of code could cause the browser to use much more memory than it really needed. Memory leaks were not uncommon. Although they tended to be caused by developers doing things incorrectly, there were times when the engine and browser themselves caused such leaks. Remember, too, that JavaScript, like Java, is a memory-managed language with a garbage collector task running in the background. If the JavaScript interpreter may have had flaws, is it so crazy to imagine that the garbage collector implementation might have had its own set of flaws?

The speed and memory factors lent to the impression that JavaScript was slow and bloated. It was just in its early stages of development, and like all (relatively) complex pieces of software, it wasn't perfect out of the gate. That isn't to say that some problems don't exist to this day, because they do (just look at that first example). But the problems are far less frequent. In fact, I would dare say they are rare, except when caused by something the developer does. The problems also tend to not be as drastic as they once might have been. For example, unless you do something truly stupid, you won't usually kill the browser, as my test on Netscape 3.01 did.

And speaking of developers and doing something stupid . . .

The Root of All Evil: *Developers*!

As I talked about in the previous section, there were legitimate problems with early JavaScript implementations. It is also true that while you may find some problems today, they are few and far between. The one constant has been developers. Simply put, JavaScript is a tremendously powerful language, yet it is also easy to mess up. It is easy to write slow, bloated, error-prone code without trying very hard.

Like the language itself, developers had to evolve. They needed to learn what worked and what didn't, and they had to fight their own urges to take the easy way out. JavaScript is very flexible and dynamic, and this leads many developers to do things that in a more rigid language they would know not to do. For instance, consider the example in the previous section. If you were working in Java, you would almost certainly know that doing string concatenations is a Bad Thing™ and that the string buffer is your friend! But there is no string buffer in JavaScript, so many developers simply assume that string concatenation must be the way to go. In Firefox, that likely won't kill you, as the example showed, but in IE, you're just asking for trouble!

Another example is passing parameters to a function. Look at the code in Listing 1-3.

Listing 1-3. *An Example of Inefficient Coding*

```html
<html>
  <head>
    <title>Listing 1-3</title>
    <script>

      function Person1(firstName, lastName) {
        this.firstName = firstName;
        this.lastName = lastName;
        this.toString = function() {
          return this.firstName + " " + this.lastName;
        }
      }

      function Person2(attrs) {
        this.firstName = attrs["firstName"]
        this.lastName = attrs["lastName"];
        this.toString = function() {
          return this.firstName + " " + this.lastName;
        }
      }

      function showPerson() {
        var p1 = new Person1("Frank", "Zammetti");
        var p2 = new Person2({"firstName":"Frank","lastName":"Zammetti"});
        document.getElementById("divPerson").innerHTML = p1 + "<br><br>" + p2;
      }
```

```
    </script>
  </head>
  <body onLoad="showPerson();">
    <div id="divPerson"> </div>
  </body>
</html>
```

Here, we have two different classes representing a person: Person1 and Person2. Person1's constructor accepts two parameters, firstName and lastName. Person2 accepts a single parameter, attrs, which is an array of attributes. The showPerson() function creates two identical people, one using Person1 and the other using Person2. What happens when we want to have other attributes to help describe a person? For Person1, we need to modify the constructor to accept more parameters. For Person2, it's just a matter of adding the appropriate field set lines. The call to the constructor has to change for both, so that's a wash. But what does the Person1 call tell us?

```
    var p1 = new Person1("Frank", "Zammetti");
```

You cannot deduce the meaning of the parameters just by looking at this call. How do we know that Zammetti isn't actually my first name? Or that Frank isn't the name of my father (which it just happens to be)? Clearly, the call syntax for Person2 is better in terms of code clarity. The code is also a bit more easily extensible with that approach.

This is a relatively minor point, but it is an element of style that has only in the past few years come into the minds of JavaScript developers. Early on, you would rarely have seen the approach used in Person2. You would have instead seen function calls with oodles of arguments. But if you asked C++ developers how they would have coded this, you almost certainly would hear an answer involving some sort of collection, maybe a value object being passed in, or something along those lines.

Another problem that was prevalent for a long time was variable scoping. *Everything* was in the global scope, which is counter to most every other language out there, where variables are generally scoped only at the level they are required. Another thing that tripped up a lot of people for a long time, and sometimes still does, is the lack of block scope. Take a look at Listing 1-4.

Listing 1-4. *An Example of JavaScript's Lack of Block-Level Scoping*

```
<html>
  <head>
    <title>Listing 1-4</title>
    <script>
      function test() {
        var i = 1;
        if (1) {
          var i = 2;
          if (1) {
            var i = 3;
            alert(i);
          }
```

```
            alert(i);
        }
        alert(i);
    }
    </script>
  </head>
  <body onLoad="test();"></body>
</html>
```

In just about every other language on the planet, you would get the alerts 3, 2, 1, in that order. In JavaScript, however, you'll get the alerts 3, 3, 3. The variable i is allocated just once, the first time it is encountered, and overrides any declarations at a lower scope level.

One of the bigger changes is the drive toward more proper object-orientation. For many years, JavaScript developers—ones who seemed to know their stuff pretty well—didn't even realize that JavaScript was object-oriented! They tended to just write collections of functions, and that was that (for a long time, externalizing JavaScript wasn't even a common practice, which is another way in which developers have evolved). But if you look at most modern JavaScript libraries, such as Dojo and script.aculo.us, you will find a very clean, object-oriented design.

Another one of the early criticisms of JavaScript—something of a self-fulfilling prophecy— was that developers using JavaScript were somehow amateurs and didn't know their stuff. Unfortunately, as with most unpleasant generalizations, it started with a grain of truth. As previously discussed, the barrier to getting started with JavaScript is very low. You just need to throw together an HTML page, put some script in it, and point your browser at it. No compilation is required, and no development kit needs to be installed. Just Notepad and a reference web site somewhere would do the trick. Because of this, everyone and their mothers (literally, in some cases) started coding scripts. All of a sudden, you had forms being validated client-side, which was cool, but then the validations were not performed server-side, because the JavaScript coder didn't have the experience to know that's a Good Thing™ to do. You had image rollovers that didn't preload the images, so that each mouse event resulted in spurious network traffic, not to mention seemingly unresponsive user interfaces. You had the bane of all web surfers: pop-up ads!

All of these (except maybe pop-up ads, which are just the result of some evil marketing suits muscling their way into the technological side of the Web) are really just things that inexperienced developers do because they don't yet know any better. None were the fault of JavaScript per se, because it's likely that something else would have come along in its place anyway and caused all the same problems. Still, like our hairy ancestors before us, we had some evolving to do!

DHTML—The Devil's Buzzword

One more element to the "evil developers" story has to do with Dynamic HTML (DHTML). Although the label DHTML still correctly applies to effects used today, a certain connotation that goes along with that term makes people not want to use it any longer. The connotation is that while there was plenty of sizzle early on, there was very little steak.

Early JavaScript developers discovered that they could do all sorts of whiz-bang tricks— from fading the background color of a page when it loaded to having a colorful trail follow the cursor around the page. You could see various types of scrolling text all over the place, as well as different page-transition effects, such as wipes and the like. While some of these effects may look rather cool, they serve virtually no purpose other than as eye candy for the user. Now, don't get me wrong here—eye candy is great! There's nothing I like more than checking out a new screen saver or a new utility that adds effects to my Windows shell. It's fun! But I always find myself removing those things later on, not only because they hurt system performance, but also because they pretty quickly become annoying and distracting.

Early JavaScript developers were huge purveyors of such muck, and it got old pretty fast. I don't think it is going too far to say that some people began to question whether the Web was worth it or not, based entirely on the perception that it was a playground and not something for serious business. A web site that annoys visitors with visual spam is not one they will likely use again. And if you're trying to make a living with that site and your company's revenues depend on it, that's going to lead to bad news real fast!

This obviously was not a failing of the technology. Just because we have nuclear weapons doesn't mean we should be flinging them all over the place! I suppose equating nuclear war to an annoying flashing thing on a web page is a bit of hyperbole, but the parallel is that just because a technology exists and allows you to do something doesn't necessarily mean you should go off and do it.[8]

Here's a quick test: if you are using Microsoft Windows, take a quick look at the Performance options for your PC (accessed by right-clicking My Computer, selecting Properties, clicking the Advanced tab, and clicking the Settings button under the Performance group). Did you turn off the expanding and collapsing of windows when minimized and maximized? Did you turn off shadows under the cursor? Did you disable the growing and shrinking of taskbar buttons when applications close? Many of us make it a habit to turn this stuff off, not only because it makes our system snappier (or at least gives that perception), but also because some of it just gets in the way. Seeing my windows fly down to the taskbar when I minimize them is pretty pointless. Now, you may argue that it depends on the implementation, because the effects on a Macintosh are better and not as annoying, and to a certain extent I would agree. But you still have to ask yourself whether the effect is helping you get work done. Is it making you more productive? I dare say the answer is no for virtually anyone. So while there may be degrees of annoyance and obtrusiveness, certain things are still generally annoying, obtrusive, and pointless. Unfortunately, this is what DHTML means to many people, and while I wish it weren't so, it isn't at all an undeserved connotation to carry.

So, part of the evolution of the JavaScript developer was in starting to recognize when the super-cool, neat-o, whiz-bang eye candy should be put aside. Developers began to realize that what they were doing was actually counterproductive, since it was distracting and annoying in many cases. Instead, a wave of responsibility has been spreading over the past few years. Some will say this is the single most important part of JavaScript's overall evolution towards acceptance.

You can still find just as many nifty-keen effects out there today as in the past—perhaps even more so. But they tend to truly enhance the experience for the user. For example, with the yellow fade effect (originated by 37signals, http://www.37signals.com), changes on a page are highlighted briefly upon page reload and then quickly fade to their usual state. Spotting changes after a page reload is often difficult, and so this technique helps focus the users on those changes. It enhances their ability to work effectively. This is the type of responsible eye candy that is in vogue today, and to virtually everyone, it is better than what came before.

---

8. I remember a television commercial where a bunch of web developers were showing their newly created site to their boss. The boss says there needs to be more flash, like a flaming logo. The developers look at him a little funny, and proceed to put a flaming logo on the page. It was pretty obvious to anyone watching the commercial that the flaming logo served no useful purpose, and in fact, had the opposite effect as was intended in that it made the site look amateurish. It's so easy to abuse eye candy it's not even funny!

■**Tip** To see an example of the positive usage of the yellow fade effect, take a peek at the contact form for ClearLeft at `http://clearleft.com/contact/`. Just click the submit button without entering anything and see what happens. You can also see the effect all over the place in the 37signals BaseCamp product at `http://www.basecamphq.com/` (you'll need to sign up for a free account to play around). You can get a good sense of where and why this seemingly minor (and relatively simple technically) technique has gained a great deal of attention. Other 37signals products make use of this technique, too, so by all means explore— it's always good to learn from those near the top! And if you would like to go straight to the source, check Matthew Linderman's blog entry at `http://www.37signals.com/svn/archives/000558.php`.

So, when you hear the term DHTML, don't automatically recoil in fear, as some do, because it still accurately describes what we're doing today from a purely technical definition. However, you should, at the same time, recognize that the term does have a well-earned negative connotation, brought on by the evils of early JavaScript developers.[9]

The Evolution Continues: Approaching Usability

After the initial wave of relatively inexperienced developers using JavaScript, and many times doing so poorly, the next iteration began to emerge. Certain common mistakes were recognized and began to be rectified.

Perhaps most important of all, the more experienced programmers who had initially shunned JavaScript began to see its power and brought their talents to bear on it. Those with true computer science backgrounds began to take a look and point out the mistakes and the ways to fix them. With that input came something akin to the Renaissance. Ideas began to flow, and improvements started to be made. It wasn't the final destination, but an important port of call along the way.

Javascript developers: out of the trees and onto the Web!

---

9. I'm not only the hair club president, but I'm also a client. I have some old web sites in my archives (thankfully, none are still live) with some really horrendous things on them! I certainly was not immune to the DHTML whiz-bang disease. I had my share of flaming logos, believe me. I like to think I've learned from my mistakes (and so would my boss).

Building a Better Widget: Code Structure

It may not sound like much, but simply structuring code in a clean, efficient way makes that code easier to follow, comprehend, and maintain months or years down the road. How many times have you run into something like the following code?

```
1:  function f(
2:  p1, p2)
3:  {
4:  p2 =
5:    p2.toUpperCase();
6:  s = ""
7:  for (i = 0; i < 10; i++) { s = s + p1;
8:      s += p2 + '-' + i
9:  }
10: if (p1 == "y") s += '<br>' + s
11:     if (p2 == 'n')
12: {
13:     s = s + "<br><br>"; }
14: }
```

Do yourself a favor and don't try to figure out what it's supposed to do. It's nonsense (I just threw some gibberish together). But it is syntactically correct and does execute, even if it does nothing intelligible. The point of the example is the structure of the code. It stinks, doesn't it? Let's try to spot the problems with it, in no particular order:

- Indentation is either nonexistent on some lines (line 2) or inconsistent between lines (two spaces on line 5 and four spaces on line 8).

- The argument names are not descriptive.

- Quotes are used inconsistently (single quotes vs. double quotes).

- Some lines end with semicolons; some do not.

- Some code blocks are surrounded by braces (the for loop in lines 7 through 9); some are not (the if on line 10).

- No checking is done before the call toUpperCase() on p2. If only one parameter were passed in, or the second parameter were passed as null, this would throw an error.

- Sometimes the code uses the Sun standard of an opening brace at the end of the line starting the block (line 7); other times it's on its own line (line 3). Sometimes the closing brace is on its own line (line 14); sometimes it's at the end of the block (line 13).

- Sometimes the += operator is used; other times the expanded s = s + form is used.

- The function itself doesn't have a meaningful name.

- There's not a single comment throughout the entire function, or before it.

- Characters that could cause problems, namely the < and > characters, are not escaped.

You may argue that most of this stuff, save maybe the null check of the incoming parameters, is simply sloppy coding. The problem is that this type of sloppy programming was prevalent for a long time in the JavaScript world. As more seasoned developers got involved, this problem started to go away. Anyone who programs for a living probably maintains code for a living, too (their own or someone else's), and seemingly little things like those in the example just won't fly. That isn't to say that you won't still see garbage code like this from time to time, and not just in JavaScript either, but it tends to be a lot less frequent nowadays.

Even the use of functions, as seen in the previous bad code example, isn't required in JavaScript. Indeed, early on, you could often find whole pages that didn't use functions at all, or used them only sparingly. You would find `<script>` blocks strewn throughout the page, executed as they were encountered as the page was parsed. This is still valid, and sometimes the best way to accomplish some goals, but in a whole page like this, it's not generally a good idea! So, developers started learning that functions were a good way to organize their code. The use of the `onLoad` page event to call setup functions, which previously would have just been anonymous `<script>` blocks somewhere on the page, became commonplace.

Another relatively important change was the notion of externalizing JavaScript. This is one of the tenants of unobtrusive JavaScript, which will be discussed in the next chapter. Externalizing your script tends to make your pages easier to follow, because you can concentrate on the markup and then refer to the code as required. It also leads to reusability, something else that was severely lacking early on.[10] Externalizing script tends to make you think in terms of reusability a little more. Another benefit of externalizing scripts is that it can lead to some performance gains. The browser can then cache a `.js` file, and if you happen to reuse it on another page, that's one less request the browser needs to make. Another possibly less obvious advantage is that others can easily use your scripts and see how they work. If you've ever tried to dig a couple lines of JavaScript out of a 200kb web page to see how the developers did some neat trick, you'll know exactly what I'm talking about. It can be a pain to find what you're looking for amidst all the markup and other script (and probably style sheets, too, since if they didn't externalize their scripts, they probably didn't externalize their style sheets either). Modern browser tools make this a lot less difficult, but it can still be an unpleasant experience, and it was certainly less pleasant in the not-too-distant past.

Relearning Good Habits

While a lot of the early problems with JavaScript undoubtedly did come from less experienced programmers getting into the mix, certainly that didn't account for everything. Overnight, thousands of otherwise good, experienced programmers got stupid all at once!

As I mentioned earlier, working on JavaScript was almost too easy in a sense—throw some code in a file, fire up a browser, and off you go! In most other languages, you have a compile cycle, which tends to ferret out a lot of problems. Then you often have static code analysis tools, which find even more things to fix. You may even have a code formatter involved to enforce the appropriate coding standards. None of this is (typically) present when working

---

10. Reusability is often hard! It's frequently—maybe even usually—easier to write code specific to the task at hand. It takes effort to think generically enough that the code can be applied to other similar situations later, but specific enough to solve the problem at hand. Programmers are often lazy beasts (I know because I am one!) and like to take the easy road. Just as anger, fear, and aggression are the path to the dark side of the Force, laziness is the path to code that can't (easily) be reused. Of course, not knowing better also has something to do with it.

with JavaScript. I put *typically* in parentheses because modern development tools now exist to give you all of this (well, generally not the compile part).

Maybe "the bubble" had something to do with it, too. I'm referring to that period when everyone thought he had the sure-fire way to make a buck off the Web, and when the public was just starting to get online and figure out how cool a place the Web was. There were 80-hour work weeks, powered by Jolt cola, jelly donuts, and the incessant chant of some flower shirt-wearing, Segway-riding (OK, Segway wasn't out then, but work with me here!) recent college grad with an MBA, who promised us all those stock options would be worth more than we could count. Maybe that caused everyone to just slap the code together so it at least *appeared* to work, in a pointless attempt to implement the business plan, and is really what caused all the trouble.

Yeah, you're right, probably not. Ahem.

The good habits that developers had learned over time—like code formatting, commenting, and logical code structure—had to essentially be relearned in the context of JavaScript. And, of course, those who hadn't done much programming before had to learn it all anew. But learn they did, and from that point, JavaScript started to become something "professional" developers didn't thumb their noses at as a reflex act. Now it could start to become a first-class citizen, with the knowledge of how to do it right.

Of course, the last step was yet to come.

The Final Evolution: Professional JavaScript at Last!

We've arrived at the present time, meaning the past two to three years. JavaScript has really come into its own.

The whole Ajax movement has certainly been the biggest catalyst for getting JavaScript on a more solid footing, but even a bit before then, things were starting to come around. The desire to build fancier, more reactive, user-friendly, and ultimately fat-client-like web applications drove the need and desire to do more on the client. Performance considerations certainly played a role, too, but I suspect a lot smaller one than many people tend to think.

The bottom line is that JavaScript has moved pretty quickly into the realm of first-class citizen, the realm of "professional" development. Perhaps the best evidence of this is that you can now find terms like *JavaScript engineer*, *JavaScript lead*, and *senior JavaScript developer* used to describe job offerings on most job search sites. And people now say them with a straight face during an interview!

So, aside from Ajax, what are the reasons for this relatively current trend toward respectability that JavaScript seems to have earned? Let's have a look.

Javascript: finally getting the respect it deserves!

The Browsers Come Around

Over the past few years, the major browsers, and even the more minor ones, have come to a point of relative equilibrium where their JavaScript implementations are mostly compatible. You can still find discrepancies here and there, but they have become what they always should have been: the exceptions to the rules. Today, it's relatively rare that you need to write branching code for different browsers, and it's virtually unheard of to do browser-sniffing to redirect to a browser-specific version of a page.

If you write ECMAScript-compliant code these days, you'll find that it works correctly in the vast majority of client browsers. That isn't to say that you won't need to do some performance tuning for a browser. The example in Listing 1-3 is a good example. The code is compatible across browsers, but you still need to accommodate the performance of IE if you initially did string concatenations.

Indeed, the major problem you find today is not at all about the JavaScript implementation, because all the big players have been based on ECMAScript for a few versions now. The problem that still crops up in terms of compatibility is actually the DOM.

DOM is the in-memory representation of the current page. Each item on the page is a node in a tree—the tree formed by the relationship between the elements on the page. JavaScript has been standardized as ECMAScript for some time now, but the DOM was not standardized for a while after JavaScript was released. This led to the major browser vendors doing things in sometimes drastically different ways.

Just as one example, let's consider handling keypresses in IE vs. Firefox. Let's say we want to hook the keyDown event for the current document. We can do this like so:

```
document.onkeydown=keyDown;
```

That will work just fine in IE, but in Firefox, you also have to do this:

```
document.captureEvents(Event.KEYDOWN);
```

The basic keyDown() function signature for either browser is this:

```
function keyDown(e) { }
```

In Firefox, the parameter e will be an event object passed in that describes the keypress event. In IE, however, this parameter is not passed in at all because IE uses an event model called *event bubbling*. To get a reference to the event object in IE, you need to reference the event property of the window object. This isn't a difference in JavaScript itself; this is a difference in the event-handling model in the DOM of each browser.

To take the example further, once you have a reference to the event object, you will quite likely want to figure out which key was actually pressed. Again, there are DOM differences to overcome. In IE, the event object exposes a keyCode property. In Firefox, the corresponding property is called charCode. So, you will necessarily have some branching code to obtain the key code properly. You will usually wind up with code along these lines:

```
document.onkeydown = keyDown;
if (document.layers) {
  document.captureEvents(Event.KEYDOWN);
}
function keyDown(e) {
  var ev = (e) ? e : (window.event) ? window.event : null;
  if (ev) {
    return (ev.charCode) ? ev.charCode:
      ((ev.keyCode) ? ev.keyCode : ((ev.which) ? ev.which : null));
  }
  return -1;
}
```

This code should work in any browser. The first if check in the second line will be true only in non-IE browsers, where the layers attribute of the document object is present. In that case, the captureEvents() call is made. Then, inside keyDown() itself, the first line will set ev to the passed-in argument e, if e was passed in. If it wasn't, then window.event is used. But if window.event is itself not defined, then ev is set to null (this can happen in certain situations, so it must be checked). Then, if ev is set, the code of the key is discovered by determining if charCode or keyCode is present in the event object. If ev was null, then –1 is returned.

Code like this is becoming less and less necessary, as the browsers begin to converge on their implementations of not only JavaScript, but the DOM specification as well. You may still need to do it occasionally, but it's a far better situation than it used to be!

The other improvements that the browser vendors made were in the areas of performance and memory utilization. While still interpreted, JavaScript performs much better in modern browsers than it did in earlier ones. Optimizations have come fast and furious. Each successive JavaScript release has improved optimization by leaps and bounds. Probably the biggest reason is simply that usage patterns began to emerge over time. For instance, DOM manipulation is without question the most common use of JavaScript, so a lot of work has gone into making that as efficient as possible.

Likewise, the garbage collection algorithms have improved greatly, resulting in less memory utilization over a given period of time. The JavaScript engines themselves are better written these days, so they intrinsically take up less memory. The code has been tightened up, too. Memory leaks are nearly always caused by developer mistakes nowadays; the browser and JavaScript engine are virtually never the culprits anymore.

Finally, crashes are infrequent in any current implementation. It used to be that you might occasionally see some random crashes here and there—the browser just "disappearing" and things like that. This was sometimes caused by the JavaScript engine (usually because the developer did something that wasn't too smart, but still, the engine should have been able to cope). This was never a huge problem, but even it has improved, so the browsers get credit for it anyway!

Object-Oriented JavaScript

The life of most JavaScript developers changes the day they discover the prototype. Once they realize that every JavaScript object can be extended via its prototype, and that this also allows them to create custom classes, things are never the same again. For instance, take a look at this code:

```
var answer = 0;
function addNumbers(num1, num2) {
  answer = num1 + num2;
}
function subtractNumbers(num1, num2) {
  answer = num1 - num2;
}
function multiplyNumbers(num1, num2) {
  answer = num1 * num2;
}
function divideNumbers(num1, num2) {
  if (num2 != 0) {
    answer = num1 / num2;
  } else {
    answer = 0;
  }
}
```

Now, there isn't anything *technically* wrong with that code. It will work just fine. But is it organized especially well? Not really. The answer variable being in global scope is a code smell, and each of the functions is just that: a stand-alone function, which also happens to be in the global scope. One of the things I'll talk about in the next chapter that contributes to a more professional style of JavaScript is not "polluting" the global scope.

Using global variables in most other languages is considered a bad practice because their nonlocality means they can be modified from any part of the program, thereby creating the potential for mutual dependencies and difficult-to-locate problems (which are often transient and therefore even more insidious). The same is true in JavaScript. Functions in the global scope are a little less bothersome, although the lack of structure means that there is no inherent relationship among the functions and no logical groups to make sense of it all at a higher level.

In contrast, let's see the code rewritten with a more object-oriented twist:

```
function NumberFunctions() {
  var answer = 0;
}
NumberFunctions.prototype.addNumbers = function(num1, num2) {
  this.answer = num1 + num2;
}
NumberFunctions.prototype.subtractNumbers = function(num1, num2) {
  this.answer = num1 - num2;
}
NumberFunctions.prototype.multiplyNumbers = function(num1, num2) {
  this.answer = num1 * num2;
}
NumberFunctions.prototype.divideNumbers = function(num1, num2) {
  if (num2 != 0) {
    this.answer = num1 / num2;
  } else {
    this.answer = 0;
  }
}
NumberFunctions.prototype.toString = function() {
  return this.answer;
}
```

To use this code, we would do something like this:

```
var nf = new NumberFunctions();
nf.addNumbers(2, 1);
alert(nf);
nf.subtractNumbers(10, 3);
alert(nf);
nf.multiplyNumbers(4, 5);
alert(nf);
nf.divideNumbers(12, 6);
alert(nf);
```

This version of the code has a few advantages:

- There is no pollution of the global scope, save the fact that NumberFunctions is there. This is most important in terms of the answer variable. Because it is declared using the var keyword, it is not accessible from outside the class, so only functions of NumberFunctions can change it.

- All the functions are clearly related by virtue of being members of the NumberFunctions class.

- Basic object-orientation: the data and the function that operates on it are encapsulated nicely.

None of this is anything special or unusual in most other modern languages, but it took a while to find its way into JavaScript.

Object-orientation isn't the final word in JavaScript's evolution to the modern day, however. A few others concepts come into play.

"Responsible" JavaScript: Signs and Portents

Responsibility may seem like an odd term to use with regard to a programming language. We're not dealing with handguns or nuclear weapons after all! But it is indeed a very important concept that, until recently, was severely lacking in JavaScript circles.

You probably have heard the term *graceful degradation*. This is the idea that a web page designed for a certain version of a browser should degrade gracefully in older versions, and still be usable, if not optimal. The same guiding principle can, and should, be applied to JavaScript as well.

A somewhat more recent term is *unobtrusive JavaScript*. This is graceful degradation in a more refined form, but it also covers other areas such as making pages that use JavaScript still accessible for those with handicaps, creating future-proofed code, and keeping your script separate from the markup and style of the page.

Another factor that frequently comes into play is making JavaScript an enhancement to the browsing experience, but something you barely notice (this, too, is one of the meanings of *unobtrusiveness* as applied to JavaScript). Users expect a certain level of interaction and power in modern web user interfaces, and JavaScript definitely helps enable them. But any time users notice any of this, and most especially if it gets in their way, your code has probably intruded on their experience. There is a very fine line between a whiz-bang feature that your users will feel empowers them and an annoying feature that they dread.

Proper error handling is also a tenet of responsible JavaScript. Error handling in JavaScript used to amount to not much more than letting the browser display whatever error messages it needed to! After a while, people discovered that they could hook into the error-handling mechanism and present their own error messages, but it still amounted to little more than a message to the user saying, "Sorry, something went wrong. You're boinked." Modern JavaScript implementations provide better ways to handle errors, using mechanisms built in to the language to allow your code to continue and recover in the face of exceptions. Doing so makes your code more robust and pleasant for the user.

Lastly, although not strictly speaking functions of JavaScript itself, modern development tools far exceed those available in the past. All sorts of browser plug-ins and extensions now make developing JavaScript, if not a pleasant experience, at least a far less painful one. Even more powerful commercial tools offer whole environments dedicated to JavaScript. Most modern IDEs support JavaScript natively, as a first-class citizen.

If it seems like I've glossed over these points, it's because I have! The next chapter will go into these topics in much greater detail, I promise! This last section is just my way of whetting your appetite a bit, giving you a heads-up about what is to come. Stick around—it's going to be a fun ride!

Summary

This chapter covered the genesis of JavaScript—how it evolved in terms of usage from its not so spectacular early days to the current professional-quality JavaScript. We looked at some of the problems faced by early JavaScript developers and how they began to overcome them. You then got a glimpse of the ways in which JavaScript is now being used so it is much cleaner, less intrusive, and just generally better! In the next chapter, we'll look at what goes into working with JavaScript in a more mature way than used to be the case.

CHAPTER 2

The Seven Habits of Highly Successful JavaScript Developers

In this chapter, we'll continue the discussion began in Chapter 1 and look in more detail at the art of making JavaScript a first-class language. We'll look at object-oriented techniques, as well as some of the latest buzzwords such as *unobtrusive JavaScript* and *graceful degradation*. We'll talk about how to make your web applications accessible, even with JavaScript involved (no easy task!). We'll look at error-handling and debugging techniques, since things sometimes (OK, *frequently!*) don't go right. We'll also take a look at some of the tools available to you that will make working with JavaScript a much more pleasant experience. Lastly, we'll do a quick survey of some of the most popular JavaScript libraries out there today, and discuss why you really, honestly, and truly want to be using them! That's a lot to cover, so let's get to it!

JavaScript: reach divinity in the eyes of your users by doing it right!

More on Object-Oriented JavaScript

When many JavaScript programmers start out, they often do not even realize that the language offers some object orientation. Indeed, JavaScript does not require the use of objects at all.[1]

There is more than one way to skin a cat, and likewise, there is more than one way to create objects in JavaScript.

Simple Object Creation

Perhaps the easiest way to create an object is to start with a new Object, and then add to it. To create a new Object, you simply do this:

```
var newObject = new Object();
```

The variable newObject now points to an instance of Object, which is the base class of all objects in JavaScript. To add elements to it, say a property named firstName, all you need to do is this:

```
newObject.firstName = "frank";
```

From that point on in the code, newObject.firstName will have the value "frank", unless it's changed later. You can add functions just as easily:

```
newObject.sayName = function() {
 alert(this.firstName);
}
```

A call to newObject.sayName() now results in an alert message showing "frank." Unlike most full-blown object-oriented languages, in JavaScript, you do not necessarily need to create a class, or blueprint, for an object instance. You can instead create it on the fly, as shown here. You can do this throughout the life of the object. On a web page, that means that you can add properties and methods to the object at any time.

JavaScript actually implements all objects as nothing but associative arrays. It then puts a façade over that array to make the syntax look more like Java, or C++, using dot notation. To emphasize this point, note that you could retrieve the value of the firstName field of newObject like so:

```
var theFirstName = newObject["firstName"];
```

Likewise, the sayName() function could be called like so:

```
newObject["sayName"]();
```

This simple fact can be the basis for a lot of power. For instance, what if you wanted to call a method of an object based on some bit of logic? Well, you can do this:

---

1. Well, implicitly it does, since you use built-in objects in many cases, but your code itself doesn't have to be object-oriented.

```
var whatFunction;
if (whatVolume ==1) {
  whatFunction = "sayName";
}
if (whatVolume == 2) {
  whatFunction = "sayLoudly";
}
newObject[whatFunction]();
```

Assume that we had the function sayLoudly() added to newObject, which called toUpperCase() on the firstName field before the alert(). Then we could have that object saying the name loudly (all caps) or softly (all lowercase, as shown), and do this based on the value of a variable.

When adding functions to an object, you can also use existing functions. Let's go ahead and add that sayLoudly() function now as an example:

```
function sayLoudly() {
  alert(this.firstName.toUpperCase());
}
newObject.sayLoudly = sayLoudly;
```

Note the use of the this keyword here. The object it refers to will be dynamically calculated, so to speak, at runtime. Therefore, in this case, it will point to the object the sayLoudly() function is a member of, newObject in this case. What's interesting to note is that when sayLoudly() is part of another object entirely, the keyword this will then reference that other object. This runtime binding is another very powerful feature of JavaScript's object-oriented implementation, since it allows for sharing of code, and, in essence, a form of inheritance.

Object Creation with JSON

Because JavaScript Object Notation (JSON) has recently been getting a great deal of attention with its use in Ajax requests, many people are aware of it. However, many people are still not aware that JSON is actually a core part of the JavaScript specification, and it was designed even before Ajax came onto the scene. Its original goal was for quickly and easily defining complex object graphs; that is, instances where objects are nested within others. Even in its simplest form though, it allows for another way to create objects.

Recall that objects in JavaScript are just associative arrays under the covers. This fact is what allows JSON to work. Let's see how to create the previous example's newObject with JSON:

```
function sayLoudly() {
  alert(this.firstName.toUpperCase());
}
var newObject = {
  firstName : "frank",
  sayName : function() { alert(this.firstName); },
  sayLoudly : sayLoudly
};
```

Using JSON is very similar to defining an array, except that you use curly braces instead of square brackets. Note that functions can be defined inline or can reference external functions. (It may be a little confusing to see sayLoudly : sayLoudly, but JavaScript understands that the first sayLoudly is to be a member of the object, while the second sayLoudly is a reference to an existing object.)

You can nest object definitions as much as you like in JSON to create a hierarchy of objects. For instance, let's add an object into newObject named LastName:

```
function sayLoudly() {
  alert(this.firstName.toUpperCase());
}
var newObject = {
  firstName : "frank",
  sayName : function() { alert(this.firstName); },
  sayLoudly : sayLoudly,
  LastName : {
    lastName : "Zammetti",
    sayName : function() { alert(this.lastName); }
  }
};
```

You can then display the last name by calling the following:

```
newObject.LastName.sayName();
```

Class Definition

In JavaScript, virtually everything is an object. This is true with only a few exceptions, such as some built-in primitives. Most important for this discussion, functions themselves are objects! You've seen how you can create instances of Object and add properties and methods to it, but that means that every time you want a new instance of that object, you essentially need to construct it from scratch. Certainly there must be a better way, right? Of course there is: create a class!

A class in JavaScript is actually nothing more than a function. This function also serves as the constructor of the class. So, for example, let's write that newObject as a class, renamed newClass:

```
function newClass() {
  alert("constructor");
  this.firstName = "frank";
  this.sayName = function() {
    alert(this.firstName);
  }
}
var nc = new newClass();
nc.sayName();
```

When this code is executed, you see two alerts in sequence: first, one saying "constructor" when the line var nc = new newClass(); executes, and then one saying "frank" when the line nc.sayName(); executes. You can create as many instances of newClass as you want, and they will have the same properties and methods. Upon creation, they will generate the same alert, and firstName will have the same starting value. In short, you have created a blueprint for creating newClass objects. You have defined a class!

However, one problem that arises from this is that each instance of newClass has a copy of firstName and a copy of the sayName() method, so every instance adds more memory usage. Each copy of newClass having its own copy of firstName is probably what you want, but wouldn't it be great if all instances could share the same copy of sayName(), thereby saving memory? Clearly, in this instance, we're not talking about a big deal in terms of memory, but you can easily imagine a more substantial piece of code where it would make a much bigger difference. Fortunately, there is a way to do that.

Prototypes

Every single object in JavaScript has a prototype property associated with it. There is no real equivalent to prototype in any other language that I am aware of, but it can be seen as a simplistic form of inheritance. Basically, the way it works is that when you construct a new instance of an object, all the properties and methods defined in the prototype of the object are attached to the new instance at runtime.

I realize this can be a bit bizarre to comprehend at first blush, but fortunately, it is simple enough to demonstrate:

```
function newClass() {
  this.firstName = "frank";
}
newClass.prototype.sayName = function() {
  alert(this.firstName);
}
var nc = new newClass();
nc.sayName();
```

When executed, this code results in the familiar alert saying "frank." What makes this different from the previous example is that no matter how many instances of newClass you create, only a single instance of the sayName() function will be in memory. This method will essentially be attached to each of those instances, and the this keyword will again be calculated at runtime, so that it always refers to the specific instance of newClass to which it belongs. For example, if you have two instances of newClass named nc1 and nc2, then a call to nc1.sayName() results in this pointing to nc1, and a call to nc2.sayName() results in this pointing to nc2.

Which Approach Should You Use?

Each of the preceding approaches has its own pluses and minuses, and I doubt there is any real consensus anywhere about when one approach should be used over another. They are all *functionally* equivalent, so it's largely a matter of how you prefer your code to look. That being said, I think there are a few general guidelines to making your decision.

Probably the biggest one is that if you are creating a class that is rather large and you know there may be multiple instances of it, you almost certainly want to use the prototype approach. This will lead to the best memory efficiency, which is always an important goal.

If you are creating a singleton class—something that you know there will be only one instance of—I personally would opt for defining a class. To me, the code is the most logical and the most similar to the more fully object-oriented languages, and so will probably tend to be easier to comprehend for new developers on a project.

The JSON approach is probably a good choice if (a) your object hierarchy is going to be highly nested and/or (b) you need to define the object in a dynamic fashion (as the result of logic code). JSON is also pretty clearly the best choice if you need to serialize an object and transmit it over the wire. This is also true if you need to reconstitute an object sent from a server. I doubt there are many easier ways than JSON for this, and that is in no small part because that's largely what it was designed for!

Benefits of Object-Orientation

Whatever approach you choose, object-orienting your code has a lot of benefits. One important benefit is that each object is essentially a namespace. You can simulate Java and C# packaging this way, as you will see in the next chapter.

Another benefit is that you can hide data using objects. Consider the following:

```
function newClass() {
  this.firstName = "Frank";
  lastName = "Zammetti";
}
var nc = new newClass();
alert(nc.firstName);
alert(nc.lastName);
```

Executing this code results in two alerts: the first saying "Frank" and the second saying "undefined." That is because the lastName field is *not* accessible outside an instance of newClass. Note the difference in how the fields are defined. Any fields defined with the this keyword, as firstName is, will be accessible outside the class. Any defined without this will be accessible only inside the class. This goes for methods as well.

Also, don't forget that the built-in JavaScript objects can be extended using their prototype. In fact, the JavaScript library named Prototype does exactly this, as you will see in the "JavaScript Libraries" section later in this chapter. However, you can really mess up things if you're not careful, so extend built-in objects with caution!

You can also "borrow" functions from other objects and add them to your own. For instance, let's say you want to be able to display the firstName field of newClass simply by outputting newClass itself. To do this, you implement the toString() function. Let's further say you want to always use the toUpperCase() function from the String object on it. You can do all that easy enough:

```
function newClass() {
  this.firstName = "frank";
  this.toUC = String.toUpperCase;
  this.toString = function() {
    return this.toUC(this.firstName);
  }
}
var nc = new newClass();
alert(nc);
```

Executing this code results in an alert saying "FRANK." Note that `toString()` was called, but *not* as a method of the `firstName String` object. Instead, it was called via the reference to it included as part of `newClass` under the property named `toUC()`. This is a handy capability, especially when you create your own objects and later decide to create new ones that leverage code you have already written. You don't need to copy, cut, and paste. You just reference the existing methods of other classes, and you're all set.

Graceful Degradation and Unobtrusive JavaScript

Unobtrusive JavaScript is a term that has come onto the scene relatively recently. It is, in simplest terms, a trend where JavaScript on web pages is done in such a way that it doesn't, well, intrude on the page.

The basic tenets of unobtrusive JavaScript are pretty simple and can be easily summarized:

- Keep JavaScript separate.

- Generally, allow graceful degradation.

- Never use browser-sniffing scripts to determine the capabilities of a browser.

- Never, under any circumstances, create JavaScript that is not cross-browser, or more specifically, code that is dialect-specific.

- Properly scope variables.

- For accessibility, avoid triggering required events as the result of mouse events.

However, the term *unobtrusive JavaScript* can have different meanings to different people. Some like to extend the rules a bit further and make it more rigid. Others try to trim the rules back a bit and make it more flexible. The key point is to implement JavaScript in such a way that we learn from some of our past mistakes.

Let's now look at each of the basic tenets in a little more detail.

Keep JavaScript Separate

The idea is to treat JavaScript as a layer of your application, and try to make it as separate as possible, with well-defined interaction points. For instance, always import JavaScript from external files. None of this JavaScript embedded in HTML stuff!

This is one of those rules that can be a little flexible, in my opinion. For instance, a few configuration variables on the main page wouldn't upset me much, but others may tell you to externalize even those. But the basic idea is sound: keep scripts separate to the largest extent possible.

Think of Cascading Style Sheets (CSS). You're in the habit of externalizing style sheets, right? Look at JavaScript in the same way! This will logically break up the pieces that compose your page, making it easier to quickly home in on what you're actually interested in working on. It will also lead you down a path of reuse. Scripts that are externalized stand a much better chance of being used on other pages, other sites, and other projects. It doesn't guarantee it of course, but it tends to help.

Some people even advocate adding event handlers via scripts. The usual reasons given for doing this are to keep scripts out of markup entirely and to avoid having to modify code in many places if the function names change. I do not entirely agree with this directive, mainly because of the argument that an event handler is specific to a given element, so why shouldn't it be directly attached to the element? To me, if I need to change an event handler, it is easier to go directly to the element than to figure out which external .js file contains the code. An exception is if the handler will be shared (used by more than one element); in that case, I *would* externalize it.

I leave you to reach your own conclusion on what is best for you. However, I do encourage you to keep your event handlers as small as possible, regardless of where you put them. They should generally do little more than call some larger piece of code or execute one or two statements. This is an especially good idea if you do decide to have the handlers in-line with the elements.

Allow Graceful Degradation

A page should work, even if in a degraded form, without JavaScript. A good example is form validation. Don't have a plain button that calls a function that submits the form, as the form will be unsubmittable without JavaScript. For example, try the code in Listing 2-1 and see what happens if JavaScript is disabled.

Listing 2-1. *Form Submission That Doesn't Degrade*

```
<html>
  <head>
    <script>

      function doSubmit(inForm) {
        if (inForm.firstName.value == "") {
          alert("You must enter a first name");
          return false;
        }
        if (inForm.lastName.value == "") {
          alert("You must enter a last name");
          return false;
        }
        inForm.submit();
        return true;
      }

    </script>

  </head>
  <body>

    <form name="test" action="#" method="post">
      First name: <input type="test" name="firstName">
      <br>
      Last name: <input type="test" name="lastName">
```

```
      <br>
      <input type="button" onClick="doSubmit(this.form);" value="Submit">
    </form>

  </body>
</html>
```

If you run Listing 2-1 with JavaScript disabled, you'll see that nothing happens, because the form submission depends on the JavaScript executing. This is clearly bad.

Instead of this approach, validate in response to the onSubmit event. That way, if JavaScript is enabled, users get the benefit of the client-side validations. But if JavaScript is turned off, the form can still be submitted. Listing 2-2 shows how this works.

Listing 2-2. *Form Submission That Gracefully Degrades*

```
<html>
  <head>
    <script>

      function doSubmit(inForm) {
        if (inForm.firstName.value == "") {
          alert("You must enter a first name");
          return false;
        }
        if (inForm.lastName.value == "") {
          alert("You must enter a last name");
          return false;
        }
        inForm.submit();
        return true;
      }

    </script>

  </head>
  <body>

    <form name="test" action="#" method="post"
      onSubmit="return doSubmit(this);">
      First name: <input type="test" name="firstName">
      <br>
      Last name: <input type="test" name="lastName">
      <br>
      <input type="submit" value="Submit">
    </form>

  </body>
</html>
```

By the way, one cardinal sin is using purely client-side validation and assuming any data coming from the client is good. In fact, your systems should always be designed to assume the data coming from the client is *bad*. It's perfectly acceptable to do client-side validation. But it's virtually never acceptable for that to be the *only* validation your system performs.

Now for some opinion. Some people believe that graceful degradation, and some of the other tenets of unobtrusiveness and accessibility, should apply to *any* web application. I do not agree with that view, and moreover, I believe it is a view that is untenable.

Take a web-based game like the project in Chapter 11—can you imagine one being written without requiring JavaScript? That would be akin to saying Electronic Arts should write the next version of Madden Football using Logo, or that Bungie should write the next version of Halo in HTML, or that Microsoft should create a version of Windows based on any programming language that doesn't supply logic branching, looping, variables, or data structures.

The point is that a game requires executable code, as you'll see in Chapter 11 (go ahead, feed your curiosity and take a quick peek—I'll still be here when you return!). Do you think graceful degradation in such a project is a reasonable goal? Aside from degrading to a page that says something like, "Sorry, you can't play without JavaScript," I certainly can't. Should JavaScript be optional in such an application? I don't doubt that someone, somewhere, has written a web-based game that requires just straight HTML and/or degrades gracefully in the absence of JavaScript. But I also don't doubt that such a creation is an exceedingly rare exception.

We are in an era when Rich Internet Applications (RIAs) are beginning to rule the roost. Google, for instance, is now in the early stages of putting a full office suite on the Web for all to use.[2] Do you think the developers will attempt to make a version that adheres to all the tenets of unobtrusiveness, degrades gracefully (beyond a certain minimum level), and is fully accessible? Almost certainly not, because it is a nearly impossible task in such advanced applications. Let me be clear: *most* of what unobtrusiveness is all about as described here is still perfectly doable in an RIA world. It's just that some of it probably isn't.

This is where the distinction between a web *site* and a web *application* comes into play. A web site is something that primarily has the goal of disseminating information. It has limited requirements in terms of user interaction; usually, simple HTML forms suffice nicely. In a web site, all of the rules described here should almost certainly be followed, and more important, the rules *can* be followed. Web applications, on the other hand, are more complex and require more advanced user interactions. They are meant to replace fat clients, applications that users have become accustomed to over the years. They expect a dynamic user interface (UI) that is powerful and yet simple, bells and whistles, and features that simply can't be done without code—and some of that code will have to wind up on the client. In these situations, my opinion is that following all these rules is simply not reasonable and will lead to a lot of failed projects.

However, for anything that is for public consumption on the Web, you should without question strive for perfect accessibility, graceful degradation, and all the other unobtrusive JavaScript goals. For the places you don't achieve those goals, you should have very clear and solid reasons for not doing so, and you should be utterly convinced that you can't meet the goals of your application while at the same time adhering to these rules.

---

2. Google's application is called Google Docs & Spreadsheets. You can play with it by going to `http://docs.google.com`.

So, in short, I believe you should examine what you're doing and what your goals are, and decide which of these guidelines to follow. Make no mistake, I do believe you should be trying to follow them all! But that will not always be possible in my estimation. Again, this is one man's opinion. Please do form your own opinion based on your own best judgment.

Don't Use Browser-Sniffing Routines

Rather than using browser-sniffing scripts to determine the capabilities of a browser, check for object existence and capabilities. As an extension to this, JavaScript errors that occur simply because the developer was lazy, and didn't check whether a given object existed before accessing it, are obtrusive and not good.

As an example, look at the following code:

```
function setContent(inObj, inContent {
  inObject.innerHTML = inContent;
}
```

Here, if the object inObj does not support innerHTML, which is possible since innerHTML is not a standard part of the DOM (although, in practice, I don't know of any browser that fails to implement it), an error will occur. Rewriting this to avoid the error is trivial:

```
function setContent(inObj, inContent {
  if (inObj.innerHTML) {
    inObject.innerHTML = inContent;
  }
}
```

While checks like this are good practice in general, the real point is to determine whether a browser supports a certain capability. One of the best examples of this is basic Ajax programming, where you need an instance of the XMLHttpRequest object. Unfortunately, various browsers support this in different ways (Ajax will be discussed in Chapter 12, so don't worry about the details if this is new to you). However, you can check for various objects, and based on their existence or nonexistence, branch your code accordingly, like so:

```
var xhr = null;
if (window.XMLHttpRequest) {
  xhr = new XMLHttpRequest();
} else if (window.ActiveXObject) {
  xhr = new ActiveXObject("Microsoft.XMLHTTP");
}
```

It's always better to write code that doesn't need to branch at all, of course, but that just isn't always possible. Browser-sniffing is a bad idea because, as many developers have learned over the years, you always need to worry about keeping the sniffing code up-to-date and able to recognize new browsers. Object-existence checks are much less brittle and don't generally require reworking to handle new browsers, so this technique is preferred over browser-sniffing.

Don't Create Browser-Specific or Dialect-Specific JavaScript

You shouldn't ever, under any circumstances, create JavaScript that is not cross-browser, or more specifically, code that is dialect-specific—well, unless there is an exceptionally good reason!

This is one rule that should be obvious to anyone who has done even relatively trivial JavaScript coding. The simple fact is that JavaScript in modern browsers is pretty close to 100% compatible anyway. There are still exceptions here and there, but you will find that the vast majority of the differences are actually in regard to DOM differences and how to work with the DOM in a particular browser. So, while this guideline refers to cross-browser JavaScript, in reality, it probably has more to do with DOM access.

As a trivial example, you should no longer need to check for things like `document.layers` or `document.all` to determine how to properly access an element on a page. Almost all modern browsers will support `document.getElementById()`, which is the spec-compliant way to do it, and that's what you should be using. Any time you find yourself coding to a specific dialect of JavaScript, or for a specific browser, ask yourself (a) is there a spec-compliant way to accomplish this? and (b) will it work across all browsers I'm interested in supporting? When you find those exceptions, clearly note via comments in the code why you did it. That will save you a lot of mental anguish down the road, and will also remind you which parts of your code to check later to see if you can update to standards-compliancy.

Properly Scope Variables

Variables should be local unless they are truly meant as globals. In particular, be careful when working with Ajax, because global variables in an asynchronous world can be the cause of many difficult-to-debug problems.

As an example of bad scoping, take a look at the code in Listing 2-3.

Listing 2-3. *Bad Variable Scoping*

```
<html>
  <head>

    <script>

      var fauxConstant = "123";

      function badFunction() {
        fauxConstant = "456";
      }

      function goodFunction() {
       var fauxConstant = "456";
      }
```

```
      function testIt() {
        alert(fauxConstant);
        goodFunction();
        alert(fauxConstant);
        badFunction();
        alert(fauxConstant);
      }

  </script>

</head>

<body>
  Three alerts will follow... the first should and does say "123."
  The second should and does say "123" again. And the third should say
  "123" but instead says "456."
  <br><hr>
  <input type="button" value="Click to test scoping" onClick="testIt();">

</body>
</html>
```

In this example, notice how the last value displayed is not correct because of how the variables are scoped. The idea is that both goodFunction() and badFunction() will create a variable with the same name as the global variable, and then use it locally, but *not* change the value of the global version. badFunction(), as you can guess, doesn't work that way; it touches the global version. Had fauxConstant been declared locally in badFunction(), the problem would be avoided, as is the case in goodFunction(). If the intent were to actually have a global variable, then goodFunction() would be wrong, since it declares a local variable. However, the name *faux*Constant should be a hint that the value is not expected to be changed after it is declared and initialized. Since there are no true constants in JavaScript, we can only fake it—hence the name *faux*Constant. In short, scope your variables locally whenever possible.

One other point to remember is that any JavaScript variable declared inside a function without the var keyword will continue to exist outside that function. This can often lead to difficult-to-diagnose problems, so do yourself a favor and always use the var keyword unless you specifically know you have a reason not to!

Don't Use Mouse Events to Trigger Required Events

For accessibility, you should avoid triggering required events as the result of mouse events. onChange, while not strictly speaking a mouse event, is often misused. For instance, we've all seen sites with a <select> that, when changed, navigates to a new page, as in the example in Listing 2-4. This is generally bad because the page cannot properly be used without a mouse, which means it will be difficult, or even impossible, for those with certain disabilities to use your site.

Listing 2-4. *Inaccessible Page Change*

```html
<html>
  <head>
  </head>
  <body>
    <select onChange="alert('Change to page ' + this.value);">
      <option value="page1.htm"></option>
      <option value="page1.htm">Page 1</option>
      <option value="page2.htm">Page 2</option>
    </select>
  </body>
</html>
```

Instead, rely on events that can be activated with the keyboard, as in Listing 2-5.

Listing 2-5. *A More Accessible Page Change*

```html
<html>
  <head>
  </head>
  <body>
    <select id="theSelect">
      <option value="page1.htm"></option>
      <option value="page1.htm">Page 1</option>
      <option value="page2.htm">Page 2</option>
    </select>
    <br>
    <input type="button" value="Click to change pages"
      onClick=
      "alert('Change to page ' + document.getElementById('theSelect').value);">
  </body>
</html>
```

This example places a button beside the <select>, and the button is what activates the page change. This can easily be activated with the mouse as well as the keyboard, greatly enhancing the accessibility of your page.

It's Not All Just for Show: Accessibility Concerns

Accessibility for the disabled in modern RIAs, especially those using Ajax techniques, is a very difficult problem. Anyone who says differently is probably trying to sell you a solution you probably don't want! The fact is that accessibility is a growing problem, not a diminishing one, and this is due to the nature of "modern" web applications.

Accessibility generally boils down to two main concerns: helping the vision-impaired and helping those with motor dysfunctions. Those with hearing problems tend to have fewer issues with web applications, although with more multimedia-rich applications coming online each day, this may be increasingly less true. Those with motor disorders will be concerned with things like keyboard shortcuts, since they tend to be easier to work with than mouse movements (and are generally easier than mouse movements for specialized devices to implement).

Often overlooked is another kind of vision impairment: color blindness. Web developers usually do a good job of helping the blind, but they typically don't give as much attention to those who are color-blind. It is important to understand that color-blind people do not usually see the world in only black and white.[3] Color blindness, or rather color deficiencies, is a failing of one of the three pigments that work in conjunction with the cone cells in your eyes. Each of the three pigments, as well as the cones, is sensitive to one of the three wavelengths of light: red, green, or blue. Normal eyesight, and therefore normal functioning of these pigments and cone cells, allows people to see very subtle differences in shades of the colors that can be made by mixing red, green, and blue. Someone with color blindness cannot distinguish these subtle shading differences as well as someone with normal color vision can, and sometimes cannot distinguish such differences at all. To someone with color blindness, a field of blue dots with subtle red ones mixed in will appear as a field of dots all the same color, just as one example. A page that demonstrates the effects of color deficiencies to someone with normal vision can be found at `http://colorvisiontesting.com/what%20colorblind%20people%20see.htm`.

When Life Gives You Grapes, Make Wine: Error Handling

A soberingly short time ago, error/exception handling in JavaScript amounted to little more than hoping the browser would display a not too unpleasant message to the user when something went wrong. Most "real" languages had rather sophisticated exception-handling mechanisms, but JavaScript was not one of them. Java had `try . . . catch` blocks. So did C++, even before Java did. Heck, even the much maligned Visual Basic had `On Error`, which was considered "unstructured" exception handling (as opposed to `try . . . catch`, which is considered "structured"), but even *that* was better than what JavaScript had to offer for a long time!

At some point, a clever JavaScript coder discovered that you could hook into the browser's exception-handling mechanism. So now, instead of a plain-old browser error message, like the one shown in Figure 2-1, you could put in your own (slightly) more pleasant version, as in Figure 2-2.

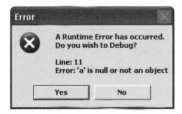

Figure 2-1. *A plain JavaScript error message from Internet Explorer*

---

3. Seeing only in black, gray, and white is termed *monochromasy* and is actually quite rare. Monochromasy would actually be easier to deal with than the typical forms of color blindness.

Figure 2-2. *A custom JavaScript error message*

The code for a custom error handler is pretty trivial, but it is still often a very useful capability to have in your toolbox. Listing 2-6 shows the code for the page with the handler that generated the message in Figure 2-2, along with the error-generating code to test it. In general, errors can often be handled by structured exception handling instead, but there are still times when a true last-resort error handler such as this is a good idea. In fact, it isn't too hard to convince yourself that a handler like this should *always* be present, even if you make every attempt to avoid it ever being activated, which you should, of course!

Listing 2-6. *An Example of an Error Handler and Test Code*

```html
<html>
  <head>

    <script>

      window.onerror = handleError;
      var s = null;
      s.toString();

      function handleError(desc, page, line) {
        s = "An unexpected JavaScript error has occurred.  ";
        s += "We apologize unreservedly!\n\n";
        s += "Page 'test.htm', line " + line + "\n";
        s += "Description: " + desc + "\n\n";
        s += "Please contact customer support at 555-123-4567.";
        alert(s);
      }

    </script>

  </head>

  <body>
  </body>

</html>
```

■**Note** The difference between an *error* and an *exception* is something that many developers tend to ignore, but it's a fairly important distinction when designing your code. An error is a condition that you do not expect to happen and usually will, and even arguably *should*, lead to a program crash (or, at best, an error message saying the program cannot continue). On the other hand, an exception is a situation you expect can and might happen, and the program should be able to handle it in some way and continue. You will often find that an error is really an exception in disguise; that is, if you think about it a bit and plan accordingly, you can handle it just like any other exception. It may require more work on your part, but that's one of the tickets to writing more robust code!

So, what is this structured exception handling I refer to, in the context of JavaScript? Like Java, C++, and many other languages, the try . . . catch construct is at the heart of it. Listing 2-7 shows a simple example of try . . . catch in action.

Listing 2-7. *JavaScript Exception Handling in Action*

```
<html>
  <head>

    <script>

      function test(inVal) {
        try {
          inVal = inVal.toLowerCase();
        } catch(error) {
          alert("An error has occurred.  Error was:\n\n" + error.message);
        }
      }

    </script>

  </head>

  <body>
    <input type="button" value="Test" onClick="test(null);">
  </body>

</html>
```

The exception in this code should be pretty easy to spot: it tries to call toLowerCase() on a string that was passed in as null. This is the type of thing that may not be caught by a developer at design time, because the conditions that call the test() function may be dependent on various factors (here, obviously the developer *should* catch this, since null is passed specifically, but you know what I mean!). Exceptions tend to be things that wouldn't occur until runtime based on some user-generated condition. Even still, this demonstrates how try . . . catch works.

In short, some condition that you, as the developer, know could throw an exception is enclosed in try { }. This is followed by a catch { } block, which will be executed if an exception occurs in the try { } block. In the example in Listing 2-7, the exception-handling code does nothing more than pop up an alert message, which sometimes is all you can really do anyway.

When It Doesn't Go Quite Right: Debugging Techniques

Let's face facts folks: we developers are like baseball players in that we probably get it right maybe only three out of every ten tries, and that actually makes us pretty good! What I mean is that the modern development model is quite different from the old days.

I admit I wasn't around for the period when programming was an exercise in patience, but I've heard all about it. Programmers would spend all day writing out programs on special paper, thinking every last detail through as best they could. They then sent those papers down to another department, which entered the program into a machine that spit out punch cards. The next day, the programmer (or a whole other department sometimes) would feed those punch cards into the computer (and I'm not even going to mention the times someone would trip while bringing the box of punch cards somewhere, and then frantically try to reorder hundreds or thousands of cards before his boss noticed!). Then the programmer sat around, waiting for some output somewhere to verify his program was correct, or whether he had to start all over again.

Today, things are quite considerably better. We generally get immediate feedback about the correctness of our programs. In fact, we often get earlier hints about mistakes we've made. Correcting them is a simple matter of typing in some new code and clicking a button. Yes, we definitely have it good compared to just a few (relatively speaking) years ago.

Even so, how many times do you write more than a handful of code and have it work perfectly the first run? It's a pretty rare thing. There's a reason the saying "Programmers curse a lot, but only at inanimate objects" was invented!

In the world of JavaScript, things are getting better at a breakneck speed. That being said, debugging JavaScript in a modern web application is usually not the most pleasant of experiences. It is not as bad as the punch card days, but generally not as nice as working in modern fourth-generation languages (4GLs). IDEs have only relatively recently begun to support JavaScript fully in terms of debugging capabilities and static code analysis capabilities. So, we still need to develop our own debugging techniques and learn to put them to good use. Of course, a proper debugger is no longer as rare as it was two to three years ago, and so some of the techniques are beginning to give way to using debuggers.

Perhaps the earliest debugging technique, if one can really call it that, was "alert debugging." This amounts to sprinkling alert() calls throughout your code to display various messages. For instance, let's say you need to debug the code in Listing 2-8.

Listing 2-8. *Using alert() Debugging*

```
<html>
  <head>

    <script>

      function test() {
        var a = 0;
        alert("checkpoint 1");
        a = a + 1;
        alert("checkpoint 2");
        a = a - 1;
        alert("checkpoint 3");
        a = a.toLowerCase();
        alert("checkpoint 4");
      }

    </script>

  </head>

  <body>
    <input type="button" value="Test" onClick="test(null);">
  </body>

</html>
```

In this example, you know you are seeing an error somewhere in the function. So, you sprinkle some alert() calls throughout, showing some checkpoint messages. When you view this page and click the Test button, you'll get a series of pop-ups, and eventually the error will occur. You now know that the error occurs between the pop-up showing "checkpoint 3" and "checkpoint 4." In effect, you've created a rudimentary "step-into" debugging facility of a sort. Now, this certainly can get the job done, and I often find myself doing it simply because I've gotten so quick and efficient at it. That being said, it clearly isn't the best answer. What if there were a loop involved in this code that iterated 300 times? Do I really want to be clicking through 300 alert pop-ups? Heck no!

What are the alternatives? Well, if you do your development in Firefox, you have access to a great tool call Firebug, which I'll discuss in more detail in the next section. As a preview though, Firebug offers logging to a console. So, the code from Listing 2-8 can be changed to that in Listing 2-9.

Listing 2-9. *Firebug Console Logging*

```html
<html>
  <head>

    <script>

      function test() {
        var a = 0;
        console.log("checkpoint 1");
        a = a + 1;
        console.log("checkpoint 2");
        a = a - 1;
        console.log("checkpoint 3");
        a = a.toLowerCase();
        console.log("checkpoint 4");
      }

    </script>

  </head>

  <body>
    <input type="button" value="Test" onClick="test(null);">
  </body>

</html>
```

Now, instead of a bunch of pop-ups, if you look in the Firebug console, you'll see the messages displayed there. Sweet! Note, however, that trying to run this in IE will result in errors, because the console object isn't known to IE. If you wanted to work in IE, you could create the following code and add it to the page (as a script import most likely):

```javascript
function Console() {
  this.log = function(inText) {
    alert(inText);
  }
}
console = new Console();
```

Of course that goes back to logging to an alert() popup, so you would probably instead want to write out to a <div> that is on the page. But the basic idea is to somehow emulate the console object, and this does the trick, if not perfectly.

But, what if you don't work in Firefox or don't have Firebug installed? What if you need to send the code to a client's site, and you can't assume that client has Firefox and Firebug? Well, one option is to write your own simple message logger. This is actually part of the project in Chapter 3, so I'll save it for then, but suffice it to say that it's a relatively trivial exercise.

At the end of the day though, a logger is really just a less annoying implementation of alert() debugging, isn't it? "What about a proper debugger?" I hear you ask. You have it in your IDE of choice when doing development in C/C++, Java, Visual Basic, or just about any other language you use, right? If JavaScript is going to play with the big boys, it has to come to the party well equipped. Well, guess what? *JavaScript debugger* used to be almost an oxymoron, but no more! There are now quite a few options—some better than others, some free, and some not, but they most certainly exist. Let's talk about those debuggers and some other tools that all JavaScript coders should have in their toolbox.

Browser Extensions That Make Life Better

The web browser isn't just for rendering markup any more! Modern web browsers are really their own runtime platform for running other bits of software. Some are better than others, but all offer some extensibility in the form of extensions. In this section, we will look at a just a few of my personal favorites that I find help me do my day-to-day development work. Of course, I can only hope to scratch the surface in terms of what is available. I believe I've covered probably the most useful in each browser (for a developer I mean), but explore on your own, because there are plenty more out there!

Firefox Extensions

Whether you use IE, Firefox, Opera, or some other browser on a day-to-day basis, I very much recommend doing your primary development in Firefox. The reason is twofold. First, Firefox tends to be a bit more standards-compliant than other browsers, most notably IE, so your code and markup developed in Firefox will tend to be more standards-compliant. Second, Firefox has some of the best client-side development tools available today, and nearly all of them are totally free!

You can find all sorts of Firefox extensions (or *add-ons*, which is another term for the same thing) by opening Firefox, clicking the Tools menu, and selecting Add-ons. A sidebar will open, and there you will see an icon that looks like a little gray gear with a black down arrow next to it. Click the gear to open a menu that lists Firefox Add-ons near the bottom. Click that item, and you'll be taken to the Firefox Add-ons page. Alternatively, you can simply navigate to https://addons.mozilla.org/firefox/extensions. On the Add-ons page, you can browse through all the available extensions.

Now I'll talk about a few of the extensions I personally find to be the most useful, but I very much recommend taking some time to browse for yourself, because there is plenty more where these come from!

Venkman

It is truly amazing to think that something as powerful as the Venkman debugger is 100% free! All your favorite debugging tricks are available here, including call stack navigation, the ability to watch the values of specified variables, breakpoints in code, and real-time changing of variable values to see how the code reacts. As you can see from Figure 2-3, Venkman looks a whole lot like any of the debuggers you've probably used on the server side of things.

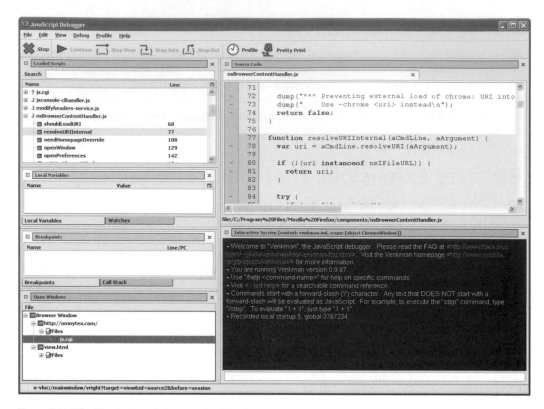

Figure 2-3. *The Venkman debugger for Firefox*

Firebug

Firebug has very quickly garnered the reputation as one of the most popular developer extensions for Firefox in existence today. In fact, a great many of us have taken to using almost nothing but Firebug for our client-side development efforts. Little else seems necessary!

Firebug offers a number of different capabilities all rolled into one nice, neat package. For instance, the Console tab, which you can see in Figure 2-4, shows errors and warning of various kinds, with filtering capabilities. A really nice thing about it is that when an error occurs, you can expand the error and see the full stack trace. Each item in that list is clickable and brings you directly to the offending line. Also, this console is accessible to your applications by simply doing this:

```
console.log("message");
```

This is exceedingly handy!

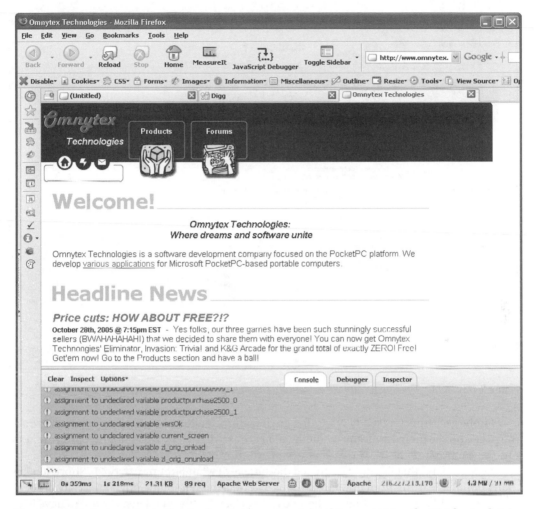

Figure 2-4. *Firebug: perhaps the single most important developer extension for Firefox to date!*

Firebug registers Ajax requests, which few other extensions I've seen do. You can expand the request and see the parameters that were passed, the POST body, the response, and so on. If you're doing Ajax work, this is absolutely invaluable.

Firebug also provides a debugger that shows full stack traces, as well as the ability to change values in real time and set breakpoints. The debugger is shown in Figure 2-5.

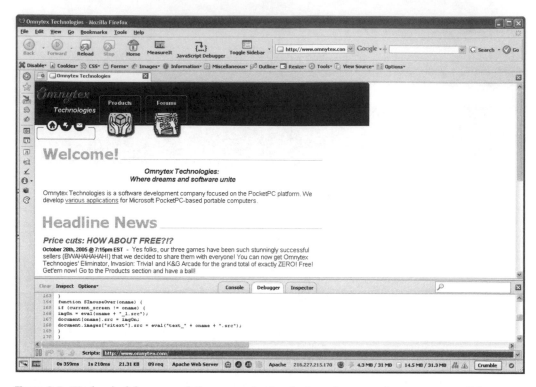

Figure 2-5. *Firebug's debugger, while extremely simple, is at the same time very powerful.*

Firebug's Inspector facility is another great feature. It allows you to hover over items on the page and see their definition, including their styles, where they were inherited from, and so on. You can explore the DOM tree at any point, digging down as far as you like.

Keep in mind that I've only scratched the surface of what Firebug can do! In short, it takes many popular features from other extensions and rolls them into one tidy, powerful package. By the way, you can put Firebug on the side rather than the bottom; I just choose to have it at the bottom, as reflected in Figures 2-4 and 2-5.

If you primarily do your development in Firefox, which I recommend, and if you install no other extension, install Firebug!

Page Info

Page Info is an immensely useful, yet immensely simple, Firefox tool, as shown in Figure 2-6. Page Info actually comes with Firefox, and is accessible from the browser's Tools menu.

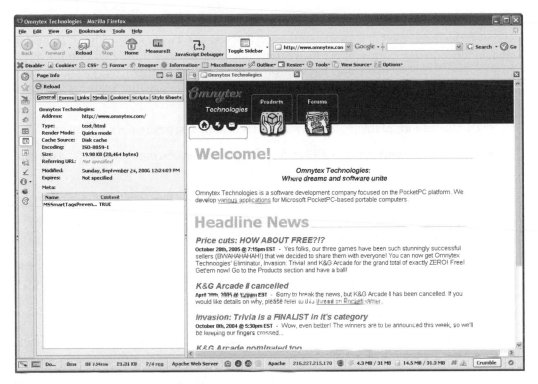

Figure 2-6. *Page Info, another invaluable Firefox tool*

Page Info displays, as its name clearly states, information about the current page, such as the following:

- The render mode the page uses

- A list of all the forms on the page and all the pertinent information about them

- A list of all the links on the page

- Links to all the images and other media resources on the page (plus dimensions for images and other information about each)

- A list of cookies the page uses (with the ability to remove each one or all of them together)

- A list of scripts and style sheets used on the page (with the ability to open each separately)

- A tree view of all the page's dependencies (images, scripts, applets, and so on)

- All the HTTP headers for both the request of the page and the response, and security-related information for the page

If this sounds like an absolute treasure trove of information to you, then you've definitely gotten the right picture!

Web Developer

The Web Developer toolbar is another extension that you won't want to do without! This extension, in the form of a toolbar, offers such a tremendous wealth of features that I simply can't cover even a quarter of them. So, I'll just throw out a list of some things it lets you do, in no particular order. But keep in mind, and I can't emphasis this enough, the following is a very small portion of what it offers:

- Disable all sorts of things, like JavaScript, meta redirects, page colors, and so on.

- View cookie information, as well as clear individual cookies, or all cookies for a domain, and so on.

- Edit CSS used on the page, disable CSS entirely, or just view style sheets that were imported.

- Change the method of a form, make disabled form fields writable, change `<select>` elements to text fields, and so on.

- Manipulate images in a number of ways, as well as get all sorts of information about them.

- Get virtually any piece of information about a page you can imagine.

- Make locked frames resizable.

- Outline virtually any type of page elements you want, so you can see tables, `<div>` elements, forms . . . whatever you wish, clearly.

- Resize the window, as well as automatically resize it to any of the most common window sizes (great to see what your page looks like on a 640-by-480 monitor, for example).

- Get quick access to numerous online validators, as well as the JavaScript and Java consoles.

- View generated source, an absolutely invaluable aid!

You may by now realize that this toolbar has a great deal of overlap with the Page Info tool. However, Page Info presents it in a more well-organized manner, and makes it a little easier to access. Either one will do the trick, though.

Five minutes with this toolbar is probably enough to convince you of its merit, so I suggest taking those five minutes now and having a look. Go ahead, I'll wait.

Back already? OK, let's move on to some IE extensions.

IE Extensions

When you compare the landscape of browser extensions available in Firefox vs. IE, at least as far as developer tools go, you quickly conclude that Firefox has the edge. Heck, just putting Firebug against most of what is available for IE is a win for Firefox! However, that isn't to say that there aren't some excellent tools available for IE.

HttpWatch

HttpWatch (`http://www.httpwatch.com`), shown in Figure 2-7, offers the ability to capture requests and responses between the browser and a remote system. And when I say capture them, I mean *capture* them! Every available detail is recorded for your analysis, and better still, it is organized very well, making it easy to get the information you need. One of the best features is that it shows you the raw HTTP data stream that was sent or retrieved. This can help a great deal in debugging some tricky issues.

Figure 2-7. *In the world of Internet Explorer, HttpWatch is unmatched.*

The unfortunate thing about HttpWatch is that it isn't free, and it isn't especially cheap for an individual. That being said, it's a truly helpful tool that will pay for itself in short order. Grab the demo and have a look!

Web Accessibility Toolbar

The Web Accessibility Toolbar (http://www.visionaustralia.org.au/ais/toolbar) is a great aid in making sure your site is accessible, and it offers other useful features. It is akin to the Web

Developer toolbar in Firefox, but not quite as feature-rich (which is to be expected, since this toolbar has a bit narrower focus). Here are some of the features it offers:

- The ability to resize the window to common window sizes

- Quick and easy access to a large number of online validators

- Manipulation of and information about images on the page

- Color contrast analysis

- All sorts of page structure analyses (to help ensure your page is properly readable by screen readers)

- The ability to simulate various disabilities, including color blindness and cataracts

- Tons of page information displays

Accessibility can be difficult to implement—sometimes nearly impossible with modern RIAs. This toolbar will give you a good leg up on that difficult task, and even if for some reason you have no concern about accessibility, this would still be a great tool. It's free, so I can't think of a single good reason not to add it to you repertoire.

IEDocMon

IEDocMon (`http://www.cheztabor.com/IEDocMon/index.htm`) is another one of those tools that makes you wonder how someone released it for free! This IE extension allows you to view the page's DOM tree, expanding down to the point you need, as shown in Figure 2-8. It can highlight the element on the page from the tree, so you can be sure you are looking at the right thing. It can show you the snippet of HTML representing the current element, so you can find precisely what you're looking for (a huge help when you're trying to figure out how some clever developer pulled off a specific trick!). Moreover, it can do the same thing with scripts, so you can focus in on the precise bit of script that performs a given task.

One of IEDocMon's best features is its ability to monitor events for selected elements. Say you have a `<div>`, and you have it changing colors when you mouse over it, but it doesn't seem to be working. With IEDocMon, you can select the `<div>` from the DOM tree, and you will see every event that occurs for that element. Especially in a complex RIA, this is a capability that is worth its weight in gold, and I frankly haven't found many other extensions, for any browser, that can do it.

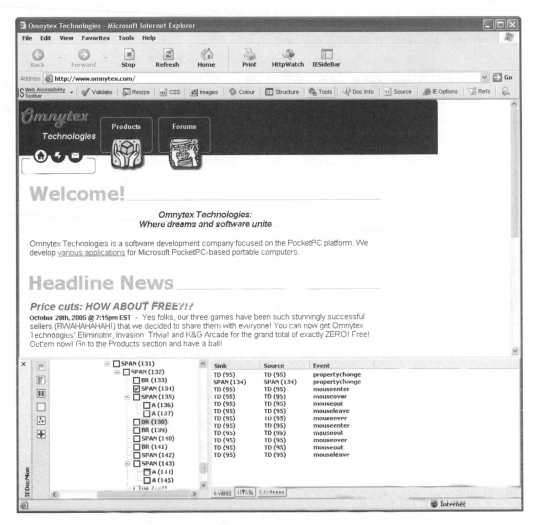

Figure 2-8. *IEDocMon: anyone who says free isn't good hasn't seen this!*

Visual Studio Script Debugger

The Microsoft Visual Studio Script Debugger, a part of Visual Studio, is a full-fledged just-in-time debugger, as shown in Figure 2-9. It can intercept errors on the page in IE and pop up to show you the offending line and allow you to manipulate the code on the fly.

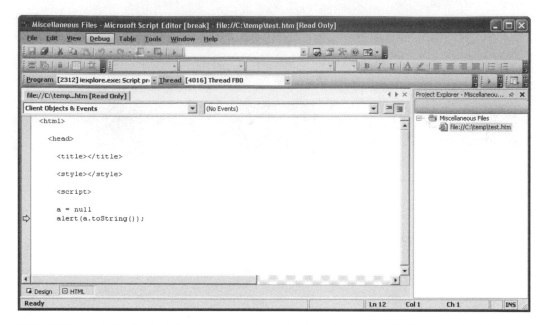

Figure 2-9. *Visual Studio Script Debugger makes debugging in Internet Explorer a tolerable experience.*

As a part of Visual Studio, this debugger is not only not free, it also is fairly heavyweight. If you are fortunate enough to have a subscription to MSDN, or already have Visual Studio, this debugger can be a big help when working in IE.

Unfortunately, there aren't many debuggers for IE in the first place, so your choices are somewhat limited. If you must use IE, this debugger will serve you pretty well, as long as you aren't looking for something particularly svelte and sprightly.

Microsoft Script Debugger

Not to be confused with the Visual Studio Script Debugger, there is also a separate Microsoft Script Debugger. This debugger is not as full-featured as the Visual Studio Script Debugger. Although it is more lightweight, it can still be quite useful. Once installed, it exposes itself via a new Script Debugger menu in IE.

If you have access to Visual Studio, you will want to use that debugger. Otherwise, have a peek at the Microsoft Script Debugger at http://www.microsoft.com/downloads/details.aspx? FamilyID=2f465be0-94fd-4569-b3c4-dffdf19ccd99&DisplayLang=en.

Microsoft Internet Explorer Developer Toolbar

Microsoft recently released a new developer's toolbar for IE that is very much along the lines of the Web Developer toolbar for Firefox. It isn't quite as extensive yet, but it is, as of this writing, a beta release, so it certainly could be expanded in the future. Here are a few of its features:

- The ability to outline tables, images, selected tags, and other items

- The ability to resize the browser window to a specified size

- A full-featured design ruler (to help align and measure items)

- The ability to explore the DOM of the current page in a tree view

If you would like to check this out for yourself, you can do so at this (rather long and unwieldy) address: `http://www.microsoft.com/downloads/details.aspx?familyid=e59c3964-672d-4511-bb3e-2d5e1db91038&displaylang=en`.

Maxthon Extension: DevArt

Maxthon is my day-to-day browser of choice. It is a wrapper around IE that provides many of the more advanced features IE is lacking, but keeps the underlying IE rendering engine intact. This means I rarely, if ever, have to worry about a site not working for me. It also deals with many of the security flaws IE tends to have, so it's safer than "naked" IE to boot. But we're not here to talk about which browser is better or more secure, we're talking about developer tools!

Like Firefox, Maxthon (`http://www.maxthon.com`) has a much more robust extension architecture than does IE. One of those extensions is DevArt (`http://forum.maxthon.com/index.php?showtopic=14885`), which provides a number of very handy developer features, as shown in Figure 2-10.

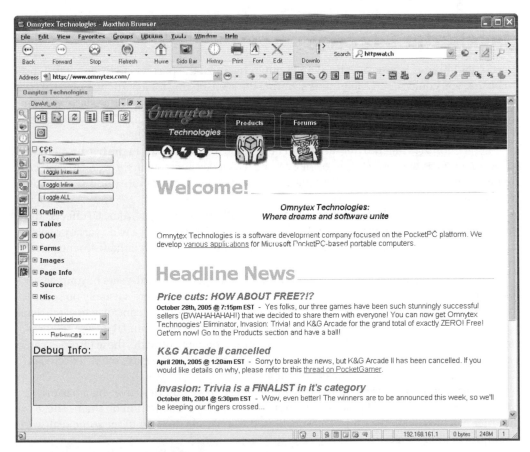

Figure 2-10. *DevArt, an excellent extension for Maxthon*

DevArt provides the following capabilities:

- Toggle style sheets on and off.

- Put outlines around tables, images, and <div> elements.

- Remove tables.

- Display DOM trees.

- Show hidden input fields on forms and show the values of input fields.

- Display the sources of all images on a page as well as their dimensions.

- Show response headers for the current page.

- View the generated source for the page (that is, what the browser actually used to render the page).

- Validate the current page in various ways.

All of this makes DevArt a must-have for developers if you use Maxthon. DevArt comes in two flavors: a toolbar and a sidebar.

JavaScript Libraries

JavaScript libraries have grown leaps and bounds over just the past two to three years. It used to be that you could spend a few hours scouring the Web looking for a particular piece of code, and you would eventually find it. Often, you might have to, ahem, appropriate it from some web site. Many times, you could find it on one of a handful of "script sites" that were there expressly to supply developers with JavaScript snippets for their own use.

Larger libraries that provide all sorts of bells and whistles, as exist in the big-brother world of Java, C++, PHP, and other languages, are a more recent development in the world of JavaScript. In many ways, we are now in a golden age, and you will find almost more options than you would want!

Some libraries out there focus on one area or another: GUI widgets, Ajax, UI effects, and so on. Other libraries try to be the proverbial jack-of-all-trades, covering a wide variety of areas such as client-side storage, widgets, Ajax, collections, basic JavaScript enhancements, and security.

The one thing they all have in common is that their quality is light-years beyond what came before, and they all will make your life considerably easier! There's usually no sense in reinventing the wheel. If you are doing Ajax, unless you need absolute control over every detail, I can't think of a good reason not to use a library for it. If you know your UI design requires some more advanced widgets that the browser doesn't natively provide, these libraries can be invaluable. Do you need to store some data client side and want to use Flash scope (covered in Chapter 6)? Let a library handle the details for you!

In this section, I'll introduce you to some representative libraries, give you a basic overview of what they offer, and point you to more expansive documentation on them. These libraries will be used in the projects throughout the book, so you'll get to see some real-world examples of their usage.

No point in reinventing the wheel, so USE THOSE LIBRARIES, lest you wind up like Tor!

There are oodles of libraries out there today, and it would be impossible to cover more than just a handful here, and even these will not be covered in excruciating detail. So, please don't look at this as the definitive reference on these libraries. I'm offering a brief introduction to whet your appetite. I'm confident that once you read this section, and look at the usage of these libraries in the projects to follow, you will want to check them out yourself in much more detail! Until you explore them on your own, I guarantee you won't get the full feel for the benefits they offer.

Prototype

Some libraries focus squarely on Ajax; others are concerned with GUI widgets; still others provide all sorts of whiz-bang effects you can easily add to your pages. Prototype is something that exists at a layer below most of that, as evidenced by the fact that many libraries are actually built *on top* of Prototype.

Prototype (http://prototype.conio.net) can, in a sense, be viewed as an extension to JavaScript itself. On a more technical level, it works a lot of its magic by quite literally extending some of the built-in JavaScript objects.

As is the case with most of these libraries, the only way to really get your brain wrapped around Prototype is to explore it and use it. That's one of the points of the projects in this book, which begin in the next chapter. However, I want to highlight a few of the more notable things Prototype provides:

- Prototype includes a number of shorthand utility functions, including $(),$(), which is a shortcut to writing document.getElementById(). Likewise, $F() returns the value of any form field. There are others, but these are the two I find to be the most useful.

- Prototype offers relatively basic Ajax support via its Ajax object. One of its most useful features is Ajax.Updater, which provides a quick and easy way to fill an existing page element with the response from the server, assumed to be HTML. This is by far the most common thing to do in the realm of Ajax.

- The `PeriodicalExecuter` object provides a simple way to set up a piece of code to be executed repeatedly at a known interval. This saves you from having to set up timeouts and such.

- Prototype extends the built-in `Array` object to provide some excellent added value, such as an `Enumerable` interface so that you can iterate over an array very cleanly, without having to set up a `for` loop using the length of the array.

Some people have an aversion to Prototype because of the way it extends built-in objects, which can cause some subtle problems. There are those who will not touch Prototype, or any library that uses it, because of this. My take—from my own experience with Prototype, as well as a lot of reading on the issues—is that while the problems are not to be ignored, they are not enough to stop me from using Prototype. Still, you should be aware of the potential issues in case they do come up.

Dojo

Dojo (`http://dojotoolkit.org`) is probably one of the fastest growing and most popular libraries out there today. It has a massive scope, seeking to provide just about everything you need to effectively do modern client-side development.

In my previous book on Ajax (*Practical Ajax Projects with Java Technology*), I said that Dojo had one problem at that point: lack of documentation and good examples. I said that using Dojo means fending for yourself, often having to look over the source to figure out how to do things. While I can't yet reverse that opinion, I can back off of it a little. Dojo has improved a good bit in all these regards. The documentation is coming along nicely, and you can find more examples now. This is the logical progression you would expect from a library that is obviously run by people who know what they're doing, as is the case with Dojo.

Also, IBM, Sun, and some other vendors have pledged support for Dojo, and one of the primary areas they talk about helping with is documentation. So, there is every reason to believe that this evolution will continue, and perhaps even quicken, in short order. Until then, I still do highly suggest you sign up for the Dojo mailing list if you intend to use this library. Plenty of helpful people will do their best to answer your questions. However, please do bring a good dose of patience with you, because it often does take a day or two to get a useful response. But the responses usually *will* come, and that's what counts!

So, what does Dojo have to offer? Tons! As I mentioned, Dojo has a very wide scope, but here are a few things that I find to be of immense interest:

- The widgets! Dojo is, I think it's fair to say, best known for its many widgets. Some are definitely better than others, but that's to be expected. They all extend from the same basic widget framework, so they expose a similar set of baseline functionality. This makes working with them fairly easy for the most part. Some of the more noteworthy widgets include the following:

  - The Fisheye, which emulates the Apple launcher bar, with its expanding icons as you mouse over them

  - The tree widget, which gives you an expanding/collapsing tree interface similar to Windows Explorer's folder list

- A very nice slideshow widget

- A widget for inserting Google maps into your pages

- Analogies to most of the basic HTML form elements, as well as expanded form elements, such as buttons with arrows to open a drop-down list, a rich text editor, a date picker, a color picker, and combo box

- Dojo's support of Ajax is very, very good. I can't go so far as to say it's the best, but you can't go wrong with it.

- Dojo provides most of the commonly used effects, such as wipes and fades, and makes it very easy to do them.

- Dojo provides drag-and-drop support that is drop-dead easy to use.

- The storage support Dojo provides is unique as far as I can see. It offers the ability to use durable client-side data stores such as Flash storage (this is essentially cookies on steroids, provided by the Adobe Flash plug-in).

- Dojo contains a number of collection implementations and other commonly used data structures that can make your JavaScript code much more robust and more akin to what you write on the server side of things.

- A number of "core" libraries are part of Dojo. They provide things like advanced string manipulations, simplified DOM manipulation, functions to make JavaScript itself easier and more powerful, and functions specifically for manipulating HTML.

- Dojo contains some basic cryptography functionality and some more powerful math-related functionality.

Although serious improvements have been made to Dojo since I wrote about it in my Ajax book, I still feel it necessary to put up a slight caution sign: Dojo will occasionally give you fits. I am currently using it on a very complex project, and while it cooperates and makes life better the vast majority of the time, there are still days when I have to fight with it a bit. Now, to be fair about it, some of that (maybe even most of that) is due to me not being an expert in it. I'm learning about all Dojo has to offer and how it works, right along with everyone else! However, I have found definite bugs here and there, and have found things that could probably work a little better. All that this means is that you should be prepared to take the initiative when working with Dojo. Don't just expect that it will be plug-and-play, even though you'll find more and more that is indeed the case. You will have questions, and some of them won't be answered by any existing documentation. Google will help sometimes, but often you will find you need to ask someone, which is where the mailing list comes into play.

At the end of the day, Dojo, in my opinion, offers so much that it is ultimately a no-brainer in terms of whether it's worth it or not. It is! Any problems you may encounter and have to overcome will be more than balanced by how powerful it is and by how much time and effort it ultimately saves you. Dojo has a tremendously bright future, and even in the year since I first wrote about it, I have clearly seen the improvements. Give it a shot—it's getting a lot of press for very good reason!

Java Web Parts

Java Web Parts (http://javawebparts.sourceforge.net) is a project that is geared toward Java developers, but provides some JavaScript functionality as well. The way it provides this functionality is a bit unique: it is part of a component called JSTags, which is a tag library that emits JavaScript. A number of useful functions can be found there, including the following:

- JSDigester, a client-side implementation of the popular Jakarta Commons Digester component

- A function to convert a form to XML

- Functions for working with cookies

- A function for validating string input

- A function for disabling right-click functionality

If you're not a Java developer, you can steal the JavaScript the tags emit and use it independently. If you're a Java developer though, the tag library will make your life easier.

Also of note is another tag library in Java Web Parts: UI Widgets, which provides a couple of good widgets, including a pop-up calendar and a swapper.

Finally, the AjaxParts Taglib (APT) is, I believe, one of the best Ajax libraries around. This is one you won't be able to use unless you are a Java developer, but if you are a Java developer, prepare to have Ajax become as easy as pie! APT allows you to add Ajax by doing nothing but adding tags to your page and configuring some XML. Every Ajax function that occurs on your page is defined in an XML configuration file—there is *zero* JavaScript to write yourself! All the most common Ajax functions are built in, which should cover your needs probably 95% of the time. For the other 5%, APT is extensible in a very simple and logical manner. So, if you need to do something more advanced, you can do so, and only have to write the basic JavaScript that your particular case needs; you still will not need to write the underlying Ajax code. All of this makes APT an excellent choice for those doing Java web development.

Script.aculo.us

Script.aculo.us (http://script.aculo.us) is one of those libraries built on top of Prototype. Script.aculo.us offers functionality in a couple of areas, but frankly, it's best at one thing: effects. If you're looking for fades, wipes, animations, and that sort of thing, script.aculo.us is one of the first libraries you should consider. Here are some of the items it offers:

- Five core effects: opacity, scale, moveBy, highlight, and parallel. Parallel is an effect that allows you to combine effects, which leads to the next item.

- Combination effects, which can be thought of as more advanced effects, created by combining more than one core effect. Examples of these are shakes, pulsate, slideDown, and squish.

- A few controls, such as an auto-complete input box and in-place editing of content.

- The Builder object, which makes it easier to build DOM fragments in JavaScript.

Script.aculo.us also offers capabilities in the areas of unit testing and functional testing, which is pretty unique among libraries. If you've ever used JUnit, this support will look rather familiar!

I strongly suggest cruising over to the script.aculo.us page and spending some time looking at the various demos there, especially if the effects mentioned earlier piqued your interest. Seeing them in action is the best way to appreciate what this library has to offer. Don't ignore the other stuff, though. You'll find some good features that have nothing to do with effects! But if effects are your game, than script.aculo.us is your name (uh, or something like that!).

Yahoo! User Interface Library

The Yahoo! User Interface Library (`http://developer.yahoo.com/yui`), or YUI Library, as it is often called, has garnered a lot of attention since its introduction earlier this year. It provides a collection of UI widgets and a collection of commonly needed JavaScript functions, all in a very clean, well-documented package. While the YUI Library isn't as eye-catching as some other libraries out there, the widgets it offers are simple, easy to use, and relatively lightweight, as is the entire library. The following are some of the items it provides:

- Simple cross-browser logging

- An `Event` component, which allows you to do things like attach events to elements, execute code when a DOM element is detected, and fully abstract the browser event model from your code, among a host of other event-related things

- The `ConnectionManager` object, which provides Ajax functionality in a clean and simple way

- Some utility functions for manipulating DOM, such as a handy feature that lets you get the viewport width and height in a cross-browser fashion (something that can be quite tricky!)

- Basic animation support, including motion along a curve and scrolling

- A fairly rich drag-and-drop utility (actually one of the more robust drag-and-drop implementations I've seen, providing a great number of events to hook into)

- UI widgets, including a calendar, a drop-down menu, a slider, a tree view, and a number of containers for organizing your UIs

The YUI Library is a little odd in the sense that when you first look at it, you may not see its true power. Take some time and explore the documentation, which is excellent, as well as the examples. After a few minutes, I suspect you'll begin to see how good and useful it really is.

MochiKit

"MochiKit makes JavaScript suck less." That's the site's tagline, and who am I to disagree? Indeed, some of the features offered by MochiKit (`http://www.mochikit.com`) most certainly do exactly as the tagline says.

Have you ever tried to do rounded corners on tables? Have you looked it up and seen exactly how many tricks and techniques there are to do this? There are tons, and it's surprisingly difficult to do well and in a cross-browser fashion at the same time. MochiKit does it for you! It may not seem like much, but rounded corners can really make a page look a lot better when used properly.

MochiKit has a neat feature that displays the source of the current page in a very nicely formatted way. While I agree this may not be the most useful feature in terms of end users, it can be a great thing for developers!

MochiKit also provides a client-side sortable table widget and a cross-browser key event-handling mechanism. On the demo page of the MochiKit site, you'll also find some neat examples, such as a live regular expression evaluator and a minimal JavaScript interpreter. All of this shows that MochiKit has some very interesting capabilities to explore.

Rico

Next up on our parade of libraries is Rico (http://openrico.org), which bills itself simply enough as "JavaScript for Rich Internet Applications." Rico offers functionality in four key areas: Ajax, drag-and-drop, cinematic effects, and behaviors. It has a fairly limited focus, so you would expect it to cover these areas pretty well, and indeed it does. Here is a brief summation of what it provides:

- In the Ajax department, Rico offers a nifty feature to populate form elements automatically from an Ajax request. It also provides the prototypical innerHTML change from an Ajax request and does so in a simple way.

- In the drag-and-drop department, the basics are covered well. It also offers some more advanced features, such as customized drop zones and custom draggability for elements.

- In the cinematics department, Rico offers the ability to move and resize elements easily, as well as the ability to easily round the corners of a section.

- In the behaviors department, you'll find things like accordion, which allows you to turn a collection of <div> elements into an excellent accordion. Also present is the live grid, which takes an ordinary HTML table and hooks it up to an Ajax data source, allowing for real-time loading and sorting of data, among other things.

I was particularly impressed with the accordion behavior and the ability to round the corners of arbitrary sections. Both of these are top-notch implementations and things I intend to use in my own work quite a bit. That isn't to shortchange the rest of what Rico offers, but in pointing out highlights, those things stand above the rest for me.

Mootools

As the saying goes, last but not least, we have Mootools (http://mootools.net/). Mootools is a library I discovered late in the process of writing this book, but I thought it was definitely something I wanted to include. Mootools is a very lightweight and modular library with a number of pieces that can be included or not included at your discretion. It is a fully object-oriented library and designed to be developer-extensible. Its various modules cover a wide range of needs, including the following:

- A JavaScript chain of responsibility (CoR) pattern implementation[4]

- Tons of effects, transitions, and effects-related utility functions

- Ajax functionality (not too different from most other libraries, but a nice, simple, clean implementation makes using it a breeze)

- Functions to work with cookies, create and consume JSON, work with the browser window, and helpful string utilities

One especially cool thing about Mootools is actually outside the library itself, and that's its download page! Rather than the typical "download this and that" type page, it instead presents the list of modules offered, from which you select what you want. Your download is then generated on the fly based on your selections, including compression! You can create your own custom Mootools library quickly and easily with this handy tool.

Summary

Whew! This chapter has been quite a whirlwind of topics! We opened up by discussing object-oriented techniques in JavaScript a bit more beyond what was discussed in Chapter 1. We then looked at the relatively new term *unobtrusive JavaScript* and discussed what it means and when and why it should be applied. Tied in with that was the concept of graceful degradation, and how it still applies today as much as ever. We then discussed accessibility concerns and some ways to keep our sites accessible to those with disabilities. Next, we took a look at more robust error handling in JavaScript than used to be possible. After that came a tour of debugging techniques and tools available to us nowadays. Lastly, we looked at some browser plug-ins that make our lives easier, as well as some of the popular JavaScript libraries out there that save us time and effort in spades.

Armed with this knowledge, the next chapter will begin the barrage of projects that form the core of this book. Let's have some fun, shall we?

---

4. You can argue that it isn't technically a CoR implementation, and to be clear, this is my description of what it is, not the Mootools team's description. But this is basically what it does, and it's something unique to Mootools as far as I am aware. For more information on the CoR pattern in general, see http://en.wikipedia.org/wiki/Chain-of-responsibility_pattern.

PART 2

■■■

The Projects

The important thing is not to stop questioning.

Albert Einstein

The dumbest people I know are those who know it all.

Malcolm Forbes

Human beings, who are almost unique in having the ability to learn from the experience of others, are also remarkable for their apparent disinclination to do so.

Douglas Adams

A computer lets you make more mistakes faster than any invention in human history—with the possible exceptions of handguns and tequila.

Mitch Ratliffe

Creativity is the sudden cessation of stupidity.

Edwin Land

Never trust a computer you can't throw out a window.

Steve Wozniak

CHAPTER 3

Hodgepodge: Building an Extensible JavaScript Library

No, we aren't talking about the rabbit[1] here. Programmers who have been coding for any length of time have invariably built up their own little private library of handy bits of code that they reuse from project to project. JavaScript is certainly no different in this regard. In this chapter, you'll put together such a library for yourself—a library you'll find numerous uses for in the projects to follow.

This chapter will take the form of a question-and-answer session between an imaginary junior developer and his senior mentor who is, shall we say, a bit on the eccentric side. Not only will you put together a batch of handy functions, but you'll also see how to organize it in a pseudo-package structure to avoid namespace collisions and make it easier to find what you want, and also to make it look a bit more like a "real" language, *à la* Java. Oh yeah, the tongue-in-cheek structure of this chapter is a bit fun, too! Now it's time to do a *Wayne's World*[2] flashback fade and have at it!

Bill the n00b Starts the Day

"Geez, 11:30 a.m., and they expect me to start coding right away? I hate this place."

Gilbert had been working at Initech[3] for all of five years (he was exceptionally loyal for a developer!), and he still couldn't quite get the hang of getting up "early." Gilbert rolled out of bed at around 10:45 a.m., showered (usually), and then hopped in the car for the 15-minute drive to work. Fortunately, he was a phenomenal developer, and everyone knew it, so he was cut perhaps more than his fair share of slack.

---

1. Hodge-Podge was the name of the rabbit in the comic strip *Bloom County* by Berke Breathed.
2. *Wayne's World* was a 1992 movie starring Mike Myers, Dana Carvey, and Tia Carrere, in which two slacker friends (Myers and Carvey) try to promote their public-access cable television show called "Wayne's World." As you might expect, madness way above and beyond that simple plot quickly ensues. At least one scene involves a flashback by one of the characters, which is preceded by a transition effect where the screen begins to wobble as the scene dissolves to the flashback scene (and Myers and Carvey accompany the waving with hilarious hand motions and sound effects). Still not ringing a bell? Take a cruise over to YouTube (http://www.youtube.com) and search for it; you're bound to find a clip in no time!
3. Initech is the name of the imaginary company where the main characters in the movie *Office Space* worked.

But today he was facing a challenge he had never encountered before—a horror so grave that he could barely comprehend how he would do it, let alone at this ungodly hour of the morning.

Today was Bill's third day of work. Bill was a n00b[4] of the highest order.

Hence, Gilbert was extremely unenthusiastic. Even by his standards.

"Uh, Gilbert, sir?" Bill asked timidly.

"What offering do you have for me today?" Gilbert replied.

"Two cans of Jolt cola, some gummy worms, and a jug of Dunkin' Donuts coffee."

Gilbert was pleased with his young apprentice. "You may approach and converse."

"Well, umm . . . Jack, the senior architect . . ."

"Do not speak the beast's name in my presence!" exclaimed Gilbert.

Bill had been afraid of this. He knew Gilbert didn't think too highly of people who sat around all day just writing "thesis papers," as he put it, and never actually twiddled bits anymore. Bill had indeed been prepared, though.

"I realize the beast is not on your level my master, but he is my superior, and I must therefore acquiesce to his will."

Gilbert considered his young apprentice for a moment. "That is true. He is superior to you. Few aren't. You may proceed."

"Well," Bill continued, "He asked me to add some functions to the online accounting system, and I have some questions I was hoping you could answer for me, as only you can." That last part, Bill knew, would score him some points with Gilbert. Indeed, he looked pleased.

"You may ask your questions, n00b, so that you may receive my wisdom."

And with that, Bill began.

Whoa, back to reality for just a minute. Yes, this is the voice of your author! I just wanted to make sure I haven't lost you here. What we'll do now is build up a library of JavaScript functions and also learn how to put it in something of a pseudo-package structure reminiscent of Java or C# packages. Many (but probably not all) of these functions will be used in later projects, and should give you a nice start on your own little library. You should absolutely add your own code to build up this library, and you'll find it to be a very handy tool in your future work!

Overall Code Organization

In this section, we will look at how to organize JavaScript in a clean, logical way that will also make it a little safer in terms of avoiding naming conflicts.

Question: How can I organize JavaScript code to avoid naming conflicts and generally group related functions together cleanly?

I want to make sure I organize my code well and that I don't risk naming anything I add in such a way that it conflicts with code that's already in the system.

Answer: In JavaScript, you can, to a certain degree, emulate the packaging system you use in Java, C#, or most other modern languages. All you need to do is create a new class, and then make all your utility functions members of that class.

For example, let's say you want to create a package that will contain a bunch of functions for displaying various predefined alert messages. You can do this by writing the following code:

---

4. n00b is short for newbie in Leetspeak (1337). A newbie is someone who is new at something. Leetspeak is a way of speaking, or more precisely, writing words, usually associated with the computer "underground" (software pirates, hackers, crackers, hardcore gamers, and so on).

```
jscript = function() { }
jscript.ui = function() { }
jscript.ui.alerts = new function() { }
jscript.ui.alerts.showErrorAlert = function() { }
```

What happens when this executes? Simply put, you will have an object named `jscript`, which is a reference to a function. Remember that in JavaScript, a function is an object, and you can therefore have a variable that references the object (similar to how in C you can have a pointer to a function). Within this object will be a member named `ui`, which is itself a function. Then within that object is another object named `alerts`, again a function. Finally, within that object is another object named `showErrorAlert`, which is once again a function.

We are essentially building up a hierarchy of objects, nested within the parent object `jscript`. This is the root of our package. Each subsequent line adds a member to that object, representing a new subpackage.

We can then reference any member (subpackage) of `jscript` or any object down in its hierarchy of child objects (in other words, functions or fields defined in a given subpackage). If you have ever worked in Java or C#, you will recognize that this gives us the appearance of packages. I say "appearance" because, in truth, you have a series of objects that you can actually instantiate individually. For instance, you can do this.

```
var v = new jscript.ui.alerts();
```

Clearly, you can't do that with a Java package, for instance, but you can do it here. There is really no way to stop this either, because each function is, in effect, the constructor of a class, not the mechanism by which an instance is created. In other words, it is tempting to try this:

```
jscript = new function() {
  return null;
}
var v = new jscript();
```

It might seem reasonable to suspect that the value of v would be null, but, in fact, that is not its value. This is because the function that `jscript` points to is returned, not the result of that function being executed.

The function that you are instantiating in this case *will* execute (remember that it's essentially a constructor), but as in Java, there is no return type, which is why returning null doesn't do what we might expect. However, this *does* allow us to do something like this:

```
jscript = new function() {
  alert("Do not instantiate me!");
}
```

Clearly, this isn't as good as making instantiation impossible in the first place, but it's better than nothing.

Now, moving on, what if you want to have a method that displays an alert when an error occurs, and you want it to be a part of this package? That's easy enough. You just write this:

```
jscript = function() { }
jscript.ui = function() { }
jscript.ui.alerts = new function() { }
jscript.ui.alerts.showErrorAlert = function() {
  alert("An error occurred");
}
```

Now, you can call this:

```
jscript.ui.alerts.showErrorAlert();
```

This will pop up the alert "An error occurred," just as you would expect.

Bill interrupted Gilbert's explanation at this point and asked, "But what if I want to have a class in that alerts package, just like I can do in Java, to display a specific message, for instance?" Gilbert smiled at the attentiveness of his pupil and replied, "Not a problem . . ."

```
jscript.ui.alerts.MessageDisplayer = function(inMsg) {
  this.msg = inMsg;
  this.toString = function() {
    return "msg=" + this.msg;
  }
}
var v = new jscript.ui.alerts.MessageDisplayer("Hello!");
alert(v);
```

This effectively creates a class named MessageDisplayer in the jscript.ui.alerts package. When the last two lines are executed, a new instance of MessageDisplayer will be created, and the string "Hello!" is passed to the constructor. Then when we call alert(), passing the variable that points to that instance, the toString() function is called, and we get the expected alert pop-up that says "msg=Hello!."

"That's pretty cool!" exclaimed Bill, clearly excited with his new knowledge. "Let me see if I can put it all together." Bill hacked away at the keyboard for a few moments and finally produced the code shown in Listing 3-1.

Listing 3-1. *A Complete Example of Pseudo-Packaging in JavaScript*

```
<html>
  <head>
    <title>JavaScript Packaging Example</title>
    <script>
      jscript = function() { }
      jscript.ui = function() { }
      jscript.ui.alerts = new function() { }
      jscript.ui.alerts.showErrorAlert = function() {
        alert("An error occurred");
      }
```

```
      jscript.ui.alerts.MessageDisplayer = function(inMsg) {
        this.msg = inMsg;
        this.toString = function() {
          return "msg=" + this.msg;
        }
      }
      function test() {
        jscript.ui.alerts.showErrorAlert()
        var v = new jscript.ui.alerts.MessageDisplayer ("Hello!!");
        alert(v);
      }
    </script>
  </head>
  <body>
    <input type="button" value="Test Alert"
      onclick="test();">
  </body>
</html>
```

Gilbert examined Bill's code, tried it out, and saw that it worked as expected. He was pleased.

"Only one thing could make this better," Gilbert said. "Do you have any idea what it might be?" Bill thought for a moment, and then suddenly realized what Gilbert was getting at. "Yes, something along the lines of import!" Bill exclaimed. "Exactly," Gilbert replied, "And you know what? It's not even that hard."

Let's say we want to have a package named jscript.string, and we want to be able to import this package separately from any other that may exist in jscript. We'll create a file like so:

```
if (typeof jscript == 'undefined') {
  jscript = function() { }
}

jscript.string = function() { }

jscript.string.sampleFunction = function(inMsg) {
  alert(inMsg);
}
```

Now, to "import" this into a page, we simply do this:

```
<script src="jscript.string.js"></script>
```

If this is the only import, then we wind up with a jscript object, which contains a string function, which finally contains the sampleFunction function, all in a hierarchy, forming our pseudo-package. Even better, if we have other packages under jscript and we import them, the if check seen here will ensure we always have only one copy of each package object. One last benefit: if we want to extend our packages later, say, add a jscript.string.format package, all we need to do is add a new jscript.string.format.js file, use the same check, and also add one to check whether jscript.string is defined and instantiate if it is not defined.

If we really wanted to go nuts, we could place each function, or each object, from every single package, in its own .js file. That way, just like in Java or C#, you can import only the specific classes you want (here, we are essentially equating stand-alone functions to classes). As it stands now, you basically can do only the equivalent of wildcard imports, which is probably sufficient, but I wanted to point out that you could have class-specific imports as well, if you wish.

Keep in mind, however, that unlike Java imports, which don't affect the size of the final class if you wind up not using something you imported, the size of the page the user downloads *will* be affected by what you import here, whether or not you use it. So, it is important to import only those packages you actually need. Remember, too, that it isn't only a matter of size. Each .js file imported will require another trip to the server to retrieve the resources (ignoring caching, which should, in many cases, eliminate the request, but not the first time, for sure!).

"You have more questions, my young apprentice?" Bill half expected Gilbert to pull out a light saber. He was acting even more bizarre than usual today. Bill did indeed have many more questions though, so he pressed on.

Creating the Packages

Now that we know how the packages will be structured, we're ready to begin building the JavaScript library itself. The library will contain a diverse collection of useful functions, many of which you'll use throughout this book. Let's get to it!

Building the jscript.array Package

In this section, we will write some code that will help us work with arrays, and start to create our first package, jscript.array.

Question: How can I copy the contents of one array into another?

Well, here's another scenario Jack is bringing up: when the application is first accessed, it builds up an array of categories, but the user can add to that array later. I'd like to take the array of entries by the user and append them to the existing array.

Answer: Are you kidding? Is that all? Take a peek at Listing 3-2.

Listing 3-2. *The copyArray() Function*

```
jscript.array.copyArray = function(inSrcArray, inDestArray) {

  var i;
  for (i = 0; i < inSrcArray.length; i++) {
    inDestArray.push(inSrcArray[i]);
  }
  return inDestArray;

} // End copyArray().
```

It's literally nothing more than looping through inSrcArray, and pushing each element into inDestArray. The result is that inDestArray will be expanded by *X* elements, where *X* is the length of inSrcArray, and will then include the contents of inSrcArray.

Question: How can I search for a specific element in an array?

Let's say we let the user enter a series of values on a page. It seems reasonable that we might want to put them into an array. What if later on we need to find if a specific value is present in the array? Can JavaScript do that for us intrinsically?

Answer: No, it can't. We'll have to throw some bits together to make that happen. Listing 3-3 shows those bits.

Listing 3-3. *The findInArray() Function*

```
jscript.array.findInArray = function(inArray, inValue) {

  var i;
  for (i = 0; i < inArray.length; i++) {
    if (inArray[i] == inValue) {
      return i;
    }
  }
  return -1;

} // Fnd findInArray().
```

Just iterate over inArray, and check each element to see if it matches inValue, the value to find. If we find it, we'll return the index we found it at because, presumably, you may want to actually do something with the value once it is found. If it isn't found, we'll return –1, which is, at this point, almost the universal return value for "nope, not found" in any type of search.

Question: Assuming I have an array of numeric values, how can I calculate the average of all the elements in the array?

Jack is also asking me to add the capability to calculate an average of all the expense items the user has entered. Naturally, he has specified this happens on the client side. How?!?

Answer: You know how to calculate an average in general, right? Well, doing it on an array of numbers is the same thing, as shown in Listing 3-4.

Listing 3-4. *The arrayAverage() Function*

```
jscript.array.arrayAverage = function(inArray) {

  var accumulator = 0;
  var i;
  for (i = 0; i < inArray.length; i++) {
    accumulator += inArray[i];
  }
  return accumulator / inArray.length;

} // End arrayAverage().
```

Begin by iterating over inArray, and adding up all the values you find. Then divide that accumulated result by the length of inArray, and you have your average!

Building the jscript.browser Package

This section will begin a package of code that deals with the web browser as a whole, independent of any specific page that might be loaded at the time.

Question: How can I get identification information on the browser accessing the application?

Currently, the accounting application supports only IE. Jack would like me to rectify this, and I believe the first step is simply to be able to display some identification information about the browser client accessing the web site. How do I do that?

Answer: Check out Listing 3-5.

Listing 3-5. *The getBrowserIdentity() Function*

```
jscript.browser.getBrowserIdentity = function() {

  return navigator.appName + " " + navigator.appVersion;

} // End getBrowserIdentity().
```

This code will return a string consisting of the browser name and version, such as:

```
Microsoft Internet Explorer 4.0 (compatible; MSIE 6.0; Windows NT 5.1; SV1; Maxthon;
WebCloner ; .NET CLR 1.1.4322; .NET CLR 2.0.50727; InfoPath.1)
```

The `Microsoft Internet Explorer` portion is the result of `navigator.appName()`. The rest is the result of `navigator.appVersion()`.

Building the jscript.datetime Package

This section deals with code that helps work with dates and times, and puts it all in a new package in our ever-growing package structure.

Question: How can I easily determine how many days are in a given month without having to remember that stupid poem?

I need to validate that a user-entered date is allowed for a given month. For example, if they enter 31, I need to be sure the entered month has 31 days.

Answer: Well, most kids learn a poem[5] to remember that:

30 days has September, April, June, and November

Teaching a computer to understand poetry might prove just a tad difficult, but fortunately, the "algorithm" to match this poem, such as it is, turns out to be very simple, as Listing 3-6 shows.

---

5. I could frankly never remember it, but here is what most people seem to have learned early in school: http://www.kidport.com/Grade1/TAL/G1-TAL-Rhymes.htm.

Listing 3-6. *The getNumberDaysInMonth() Function*

```
jscript.datetime.getNumberDaysInMonth = function(inMonth, inYear) {

  inMonth = inMonth - 1;
  var leap_year = this.isLeapYear(inYear);
  if (leap_year) {
    leap_year = 1;
  } else {
    leap_year = 0;
  }
  if (inMonth == 3 || inMonth == 5 || inMonth == 8 || inMonth == 10) {
    return 30;
  } else if (inMonth == 1) {
    return 28 + leap_year;
  } else {
    return 31;
  }

} // End getNumberDaysInMonth().
```

First, we need to determine if the specified inYear is a leap year. To do that, we'll be writing another function called isLeapYear() that does that check. We need to do this because we know that in a leap year, February has 29 days, and in nonleap years, it has only 28 days. Once we do that, we check to see if the inMonth is April (3), June (5), September (8), or November (10), and if it is, we return 30.

Note that the first step is to subtract 1 from the incoming month. The caller uses a value of 1 for January and 12 for December, as is most logical. But in order to make the leap year calculation easy, internally we subtract 1 so that January becomes 0 and December becomes 11. That's why the values for April, June, September, and November seem off by 1. If inMonth is February (1), then we return 28 plus 1 if it is a leap year, resulting in 29, or 28 plus 0 if it isn't a leap year, resulting in 28. If it is any other month, we return 31.

Question: How can I determine if a given year is a leap year?

It's funny you mention leap years, Gilbert, because Jack identified a flaw in the system when February is used in a leap year. So, I need to be able to determine if a specified year is a leap year to correct that flaw.

Answer: Here, we have to play with some math, but it's still relatively simple, as Listing 3-7 shows.

Listing 3-7. *The isLeapYear() Function*

```
jscript.datetime.isLeapYear = function(inYear) {

  if ((inYear % 4 == 0 && !(inYear % 100 == 0)) || inYear % 400 == 0) {
    return true;
  } else {
    return false;
  }

} // End isLeapYear().
```

The algorithm is basically this: if the year is evenly divisible by 4, and if it isn't evenly divisible by 100, or if it's evenly divisible by 400, then it's a leap year!

Building the jscript.debug Package

Our `jscript` package continues to grow in this section as we introduce a new package that will contain code to help us debug our JavaScript.

Question: How can I display all the properties, and their values, of an arbitrary object?

You know, Gilbert, I often find that when debugging JavaScript, I have some object, and it would be helpful to see its current state—all its properties and their values. I know I can use a debugger to do this, but sometimes a simple alert would be sufficient. Is there any way to do that?

Answer: Well, of course, there is, Bill! Listing 3-8 shows how.

Listing 3-8. *The enumProps() Function*

```
jscript.debug.enumProps = function(inObj) {

  var props = "";
  var i;
  for (i in inObj) {
    props += i + " = " + inObj[i] + "\n";
  }
  alert(props);

} // End enumProps().
```

We use the `for . . . in` loop style to iterate over the properties of `inObj`. For each, we add its name (the value of `i`) and its value (using array notation to access the member) to a string. At the end, we pass this string to `alert()`, and we've achieved your goal.

Question: How can I implement a somewhat robust logging mechanism, something similar to Jakarta Commons Logging, for instance?

I often find that I'd like to put logging messages in my code. But I'm not sure how to do it in JavaScript as I would in, say, Java with the Jakarta Commons Logging package, where I can create some object, a logger for example, and pass it messages to write to a log without having to know the details of the underlying logging implementation. Got any thoughts, Gilbert?

Answer: Well, if by "somewhat robust," you mean something that gives you the ability to log or not log messages based on a severity level, and not a whole lot more, then sure, we can do that. Check out Listing 3-9.

Listing 3-9. *The DivLogger Class Function*

```
jscript.debug.DivLogger = function() {


  /**
   * The following are faux constants that define the various levels a log
   * instance can be set to output.
   */
```

```
this.LEVEL_TRACE = 1;
this.LEVEL_DEBUG = 2;
this.LEVEL_INFO  = 3;
this.LEVEL_WARN  = 4;
this.LEVEL_ERROR = 5;
this.LEVEL_FATAL = 6;


/**
 * These are the font colors for each logging level.
 */
this.LEVEL_TRACE_COLOR = "a0a000";
this.LEVEL_DEBUG_COLOR = "64c864";
this.LEVEL_INFO_COLOR  = "000000";
this.LEVEL_WARN_COLOR  = "0000ff";
this.LEVEL_ERROR_COLOR = "ff8c00";
this.LEVEL_FATAL_COLOR = "ff0000";


/**
 * logLevel determines the minimum message level the instance will show.
 */
this.logLevel = 3;


/**
 * targetDIV is the DIV object to output to.
 */
this.targetDiv = null;


/**
 * This function is used to set the minimum level a log instance will show.
 *
 * @param inLevel One of the level constants.  Any message at this level
 *                or a higher level will be displayed, others will not.
 */
this.setLevel = function(inLevel) {

  this.logLevel = inLevel;

} // End setLevel().
```

```
/**
 * This function is used to set the target DIV that all messages are
 * written to.  Note that when you call this, the DIV's existing contents
 * are cleared out.
 *
 * @param inTargetDiv The DIV object that all messages are written to.
 */
this.setTargetDiv = function(inTargetDiv) {

  this.targetDiv = inTargetDiv;
  this.targetDiv.innerHTML = "";

} // End setTargetDiv().


/**
 * This function is called to determine if a particular message meets or
 * exceeds the current level of the log instance and should therefore be
 * logged.
 *
 * @param inLevel The level of the message being checked.
 */
this.shouldBeLogged = function(inLevel) {

  if (inLevel >= this.logLevel) {
    return true;
  } else {
    return false;
  }

} // End shouldBeLogged().


/**
 * This function logs messages at TRACE level.
 *
 * @param inMessage The message to log.
 */
this.trace = function(inMessage) {

  if (this.shouldBeLogged(this.LEVEL_TRACE) && this.targetDiv) {
    this.targetDiv.innerHTML +=
    "<div style='color:#" + this.LEVEL_TRACE_COLOR + ";'>" +
    "[TRACE] " + inMessage + "</div>";
  }
```

```
} // End trace().


} // End DivLogger().
```

Note that after the trace() function would actually be a couple more: debug(), info(), warn(), error(), and fatal()—one for each logging level. I left them out just to save some space here, but they are essentially identical to the trace() method, except that trace is replaced with debug, info, error, or fatal, as appropriate.

To use this, you instantiate a DivLogger, like so:

```
var log = new jscript.debug.DivLogger();
```

The one other required thing for this particular logger is to call setTargetDiv(), passing it a reference to the <div> element to which all log output should be written. From then on out, you simply call log.xxxx(yyyy), where xxxx is the severity (trace, debug, info, warn, error, or fatal) and yyyy is the message to log. You can also call log.setLevel() to set the level of messages to be logged. If, for instance, you did this:

```
log.setLevel(log.LEVEL_ERROR);
```

then from that point on, only messages of severity LEVEL_ERROR or LEVEL_FATAL would be logged.

This is a very simple logger that just appends a message to the target <div>, and it also color-codes the log messages to make it easier to see messages of a certain type while browsing the log output. You could easily write another implementation to make an Ajax call to write the message to a database on the server, or whatever you like. The basic skeleton would be the same, although you may or may not need the targetDiv stuff or the color-coding stuff.

Building the jscript.dom Package

In this section, we add a new package of functions that will aid us in manipulating the DOM.

Question: How can I center an arbitrary DOM element?

Gilbert, at present, the application shows a "please wait" pop-up when a form is being submitted. It's just a <div> with a z-index set to a high number so it is on top of everything else. Unfortunately, the contractor that wrote the code didn't know how to center the <div>, so it's always in the upper-left corner, and Jack isn't thrilled with this. How can I center it?

Answer: I have code lying around to do that. Interestingly, it was written a long time ago, as evidenced by the fact that it uses the term *layer*, which is an old Netscape term. That doesn't really matter, because it still works. Listing 3-10 shows how to center an element horizontally.

Listing 3-10. *The layerCenterH() Function*

```
jscript.dom.layerCenterH = function(inObj) {

  var lca;
  var lcb;
  var lcx;
  var iebody;
  var dsocleft;
```

```
  if (window.innerWidth) {
    lca = window.innerWidth;
  } else {
    lca = document.body.clientWidth;
  }
  lcb = inObj.offsetWidth;
  lcx = (Math.round(lca / 2)) - (Math.round(lcb / 2));
  iebody = (document.compatMode &&
    document.compatMode != "BackCompat") ?
    document.documentElement : document.body;
  dsocleft = document.all ? iebody.scrollLeft : window.pageXOffset;
  inObj.style.left = lcx + dsocleft + "px";

} // End layerCenterH().
```

This will actually center any element that has a left style property exposed, which is most elements, not just <div> elements. It works by first getting the size of the browser window—the area that the content actually fills. This is done differently, depending on which browser it is executing in: either by getting the innerWidth property of the window or by getting the body's clientWidth property. Next, we get the width of the object by getting its offsetWidth property. Then it's a simple bit of math to calculate what the *X* location should be to center the object (it's basically subtracting half the element's width from half the window's size).

There is one more bit of calculation to do, and that's taking the amount that the page may be horizontally scrolled into account. Once again, there is a different method to get this value depending on which browser is in use, and what's worse, there is a different method depending on which rendering mode IE is in! When rendering in compatibility mode but *not* BackCompat mode, we need to go after the document.documentElement element; otherwise, it's the document.body element. Next, we see if the document.all element is present in the DOM. If it is, then we're running in IE, and we request the scrollLeft property of the object we previously determined we needed. If document.all is not present, we're not running in IE, so we need the window's pageXOffset property. In either case, we now have the amount the page is scrolled horizontally, so we add that to the value we calculated to center the element, and *voilà*, we've got it centered on the page as it is currently displayed!

You probably noticed this would only center horizontally. What about vertically? Well, the code is nearly identical. It's just a matter of making some replacements: width with height, style.left with style.top, scrollLeft with scrollTop, and pageXOffset with pageYOffset. Listing 3-11 shows what this modified code would look like, and as I said, it's basically the same.

Listing 3-11. *The layerCenterV() Function*

```
jscript.dom.layerCenterV = function(inObj) {

  var lca;
  var lcb;
  var lcy;
  var iebody;
  var dsoctop;
```

```
if (window.innerHeight) {
  lca = window.innerHeight;
} else {
  lca = document.body.clientHeight;
}
lcb = inObj.offsetHeight;
lcy = (Math.round(lca / 2)) - (Math.round(lcb / 2));
iebody = (document.compatMode &&
  document.compatMode != "BackCompat") ?
  document.documentElement : document.body;
dsoctop = document.all ? iebody.scrollTop : window.pageYOffset;
inObj.style.top = lcy + dsoctop + "px";

} // End layerCenterV().
```

I made it two separate functions because you may sometimes want to center one way, but not the other. Now you have that ability.

Note In Listings 3-10 and 3-11, you may have noticed that I broke one of my own rules from Chapter 1: self-describing variable names. lca, lcb, lcx, lcy—what exactly do those mean? Well, you're right to slap my hand with a ruler next time you see me! However, what good are rules unless you can break them occasionally? The reason it's probably acceptable here is that we're talking about very short-lived variables whose context you can easily see on a single screen. Furthermore, these are used as intermediate parts of a calculation, so they don't have any sustained meaning. Think of them as you would loop counter variables, for which people frequently use just single letters, which generally doesn't bother anyone. So, while I certainly stand by the original rule, there are times where breaking it is OK. Just use your best judgment!

Question: When I make an Ajax request, I get a chunk of text back. If that chunk of text has some <script> blocks in it, how can I execute them?

I'm actually a bit amazed by this, given how backwards the application seems to be, but it is actually using Ajax for updating parts of a couple of screens. Unfortunately, Jack discovered that it isn't working fully (the consultants are at it again!) because the returned text from the server contains some <script> blocks that are not being executed. Is there a way to execute them?

Answer: Well, of course there is, Bill, and this is a somewhat common problem when doing Ajax. Take a gander at Listing 3-12 to see how it's done.

Listing 3-12. *The execScripts() Function*

```
jscript.dom.execScripts = function (inText) {

  var si = 0;
  while (true) {
    // Finding opening script tag.
    var ss = inText.indexOf("<" + "script" + ">", si);
```

```
    if (ss == -1) {
      return;
    }
    // Find closing script tag.
    var se = inText.indexOf("<" + "/" + "script" + ">", ss);
    if (se == -1) {
      return;
    }
    // Jump ahead 9 characters, after the closing script tag.
    si = se + 9;
    // Get the content in between and execute it.
    var sc = inText.substring(ss + 8, se);
    eval(sc);
  }

} // End execScripts().
```

I'm sure there are other ways to write this code—some fancy regular expression probably—but sometimes I like the simple things in life, so I went with the straightforward approach. We take in a string of text as inText, and we then begin to scan through it, looking for <script> blocks (and note that it literally must be <script>—<script type="text/javascript">, for instance, won't be detected. Do you sense a suggested enhancement?). If we find one, we then find its corresponding closing </script> tag. Once we have that, we take the substring in between those tags and eval() it. We then take care to set the location after the closing </script> tag we just found, and we do it again. At whatever point no more <script> tags are found, our work is done.

Question: How can I get a reference to an arbitrary number of DOM elements?

I know I can use document.getElementById() to get a reference to a DOM element—that's no problem. But if I want to get a reference to a batch of elements, it gets a little onerous to write all those calls. Is there a simpler way?

Answer: Sure, a relatively simple wrapper function can save you a lot of time and effort. Check out Listing 3-13.

Listing 3-13. *The getDOMElements() Function*

```
jscript.dom.getDOMElements = function() {

  if (arguments.length == 0) {
    return null;
  }
  if (arguments.length == 1) {
    return document.getElementById(arguments[0]);
  }
  var elems = new Array();
  for (var i = 0; i < arguments.length; i++) {
    elems.push(document.getElementById(arguments[i]));
  }
  return elems;

} // End getDOMElements().
```

This function will accept a variable number of arguments, which are presumed to be DOM element IDs. Remember that every JavaScript function inherently has reference to an `arguments` array, which is an array of all the arguments (parameters) that were passed into it. So, if no arguments are passed in, this function returns null, which is essentially an invalid call. If just one argument is passed in, we do the typical `document.getElementById()` and return it, and that's that. When the number of arguments is more than one though, that's when it gets fun! We loop through the `arguments` array, and for each, we do `document.getElementById()`. We push the return from that call onto a new array we created, and when we're finished, we return that array. Each element in the array is now a reference to one of the DOM IDs passed in. Then you can do whatever you want with that array, and you didn't have to write all the calls to `document.getElementById()` yourself!

Building the jscript.form Package

In the `jscript.form` package, which we are about to begin building, we will introduce some code that helps us work with HTML forms and form elements.

Question: How can I generate XML from an HTML form?

Jack has asked me to create a simple web service interface to the application. To test it, I'd like to take the HTML form on one page of the application, convert it to XML, and submit it to a specified URL. The only part I'm stuck on is the conversion to XML.

Answer: This is one of those tasks that kind of sounds like it should be difficult, but it's actually pretty easy. I've put the code in Listing 3-14 together to show you.

Listing 3-14. *The formToXML() Function*

```
jscript.form.formToXML = function(inForm, inRootElement) {

  if (inForm == null) {
    return null;
  }
  if (inRootElement == null) {
    return null;
  }
  var outXML = "<" + inRootElement + ">";
  var i;
  for (i = 0; i < inForm.length; i++) {
    var ofe = inForm[i];
    var ofeType = ofe.type.toUpperCase();
    var ofeName = ofe.name;
    var ofeValue = ofe.value;
    if (ofeType == "TEXT" || ofeType == "HIDDEN" ||
      ofeType == "PASSWORD" || ofeType == "SELECT-ONE" ||
      ofeType == "TEXTAREA") {
      outXML += "<" + ofeName + ">" + ofeValue + "</" + ofeName + ">"
    }
    if (ofeType == "RADIO" && ofe.checked == true) {
      outXML += "<" + ofeName + ">" + ofeValue + "</" + ofeName + ">"
    }
```

```
      if (ofeType == "CHECKBOX") {
        if (ofe.checked == true) {
          cbval = "true";
        } else {
          cbval = "false";
        }
        outXML = outXML + "<" + ofeName + ">" + cbval + "</" + ofeName + ">"

      }
      outXML += "";
    }
    outXML += "</" + inRootElement + ">";
    return outXML;

} // End formToXML().
```

Let's say we have the following HTML form:

```
<form>
  <input type="text" name="firstName"><br>
  <input type="hidden" name="lastName"><br>
  <input type="password" name="password"><br>
  <textarea name="notes"></textarea><br>
  <select name="gender">
    <option value="male">Male</option>
    <option value="female">Female</option>
  </select>
  <input type="radio" name="married" value="yes">Yes<br>
  <input type="radio" name="married" value="no">No<br>
  <input type="checkbox" name="haveKids">Check if you have kids</input><br>
</form>
```

This function will accept a reference to a form as inForm, and also a string inRootElement, which is the name of the root element of the XML document to create. After we check the input values to make sure they are good, we begin to build up the string outXML by first adding the root element to it.

Then we start iterating over the children of the form. For each, we get its type, name, and value. Next, we see what its type is. If it's a text, hidden, password, select-one, or textarea field, we simply add an element to our XML string with the name of the element as the tag, and then the value of the field in between the opening and closing tags. select-one, by the way, is the value that you see in the type attribute for a <select> field, when it's not multi-enabled (this code won't handle multiple selection fields—something for you to extend, I think!). For radio fields, we'll actually examine each of them, even if they are all in the same group. Of course, since only one can be selected at a time, this isn't a problem. The XML string is generated similarly as for the other element types. Finally, for checkbox fields, we will send the value "true" or "false", depending on whether or not it is checked.

So, assuming we passed in Person as the root element, and assuming the entries in the form fields are Frank, Zammetti, myPassword, Hello, Male, and Yes, and haveKids is checked, the following XML would be generated:

```
<Person>
  <firstName>Frank</firstName>
  <lastName>Zammetti</lastName>
  <password>myPassword</password>
  <notes>Hello</notes>
  <gender>male</gender>
  <married>yes</married>
  <haveKids>true</haveKids>
</Person>
```

This is returned as a string, for the caller to handle as desired, such as submit via POST body to a web service endpoint, as you suggested, Bill.

Question: How can I find, and optionally select, a specified option in a <select> **field?**

When one of the pages of the accounting application is first shown, there is a <select> field with some options, and initially, one of those options will be selected, depending on various criteria. How can I select a given option? Also, what if I just wanted to find it and not select it?

Answer: You can simply take the brute-force approach, Bill. Also, although you didn't mention it, I think it would be handy to be able to determine if case will matter during the search. Listing 3-15 does all of this.

Listing 3-15. *The selectLocateOption() Function*

```
jscript.form.selectLocateOption = function(inSelect, inValue, inJustFind,
  inCaseInsensitive) {

  if (inSelect == null ||
    inValue == null || inValue == "" ||
    inCaseInsensitive == null ||
    inJustFind == null) {
    return;
  }
  if (inCaseInsensitive) {
    inValue = inValue.toLowerCase();
  }
  var found = false;
  var i;
  for (i = 0; (i < inSelect.length) && !found; i++) {
    var nextVal = inSelect.options[i].value;
    if (inCaseInsensitive) {
      nextVal = nextVal.toLowerCase();
    }
    if (nextVal == inValue) {
      found = true;
```

```
      if (!inJustFind) {
        inSelect.options[i].selected = true;
      }
    }
  }
  return found;

} // End selectLocateOption().
```

After the usual trivial rejections, we start iterating over the options in the specified <select> element as passed in as inSelect. For each option, we examine its value. If it matches inValue, which is the value we are looking for, then we set the found flag to true, which will then be the return value from the function. Also, we check the value of inCaseInsensitive. If its value is true, then the match will ignore case. If it is false, then the case must match exactly. Once we find the option, or run out of options to check, we see if the caller requested the option be selected via the value of the inJustFind parameter. If the value is true, then we don't have anything further to do, but if it is false, we need to select the option as well. Lastly, we return the value of found, which will be true if the option was found (regardless of whether it was selected or not) and false if not.

Question: How can I provide the ability to select all the options in a <select>?

Gilbert, Jack has asked me to give the users the ability to select all the options in a <select> on one screen, at one time. Is there an easy way to do it?

Answer: There is, indeed. Direct your gaze to Listing 3-16.

Listing 3-16. *The selectSelectAll() Function*

```
jscript.form.selectSelectAll = function(inSelect) {

  if (inSelect == null || !inSelect.options || inSelect.options.length == 0) {
    return;
  }
  var i;
  for (i = 0; i < inSelect.options.length; i++) {
    inSelect.options[i].selected = true;
  }

} // End selectSelectAll().
```

inSelect is a reference to the <select> you want to manipulate. Then you simply iterate over the collection of options it contains, and set selected on each one to true. That's really it!

I'm sure you'll also want a selectUnselectAll() function. Well, to do that, simply change the line:

```
inSelect.options[i].selected = true;
```

to:

```
inSelect.options[i].selected = false;
```

and you've done it!

You may want to consider combining it and making it one function, where you pass in a boolean parameter. But for now you can keep them separate—no real harm.

Building the jscript.lang Package

In this section, we'll build the `jscript.lang` package, which will contain code that helps us work with JavaScript at a fundamental language level.

Question: How can I take the properties of one object and copy them into another object?

In a couple of instances, I've had a JavaScript object that I basically want to combine with another object. In other words, I want to copy all the properties of one into another. Can you show me how to do that, Gilbert?

Answer: Ask and ye shall receive. Listing 3-17 is your blessing, Bill.

Listing 3-17. *The copyProperties() Function*

```
jscript.lang.copyProperties = function(inSrcObj, inDestObj, inOverride){

  var prop;
  for (prop in inSrcObj) {
    if (inOverride || !inDestObj[prop]) {
      inDestObj[prop] = inSrcObj[prop];
    }
  }
  return inDestObj;

} // End copyProperties().
```

Using the for . . . in loop style, we iterate over the properties of inSrcObj. For each property, we check to see if it already exists in inDestObj, and if it does, we see if the caller told us to override existing properties by passing true as the value of the inOverride parameter. If it exists and we are overriding, or if it didn't already exist, we use array notation to set the value of the property on inDestObj. This has the effect of adding the property if is wasn't there, or changing the value to that found in inSrcObj if the property already existed. We then return inDestObj, and our work here is complete.

Building the jscript.math Package

Now we'll create some code to help perform some mathematical functions (well, OK, just one actually), and we'll stick it in a new package, appropriately named jscript.math.

Question: How can I generate a random number in a specified range?

OK, Gilbert, I admit this one isn't something Jack asked me about because, after all, random numbers in an accounting system would probably be a bad thing! But I'm working on a little JavaScript game on the side, and I'd like to know how to generate a random number in a given range.

Answer: Ah, well, far be it for me to get in the way of your slackery, Bill! As you've probably discovered, random number generation in JavaScript doesn't give you this feature for free, so I'll show you how to do it. Please review Listing 3-18 now.

Listing 3-18. *The genRandomNumber() Function*

```
jscript.math.genRandomNumber = function(inMin, inMax) {

  if (inMin > inMax) {
    return 0;
  }
  return inMin + (inMax - inMin) * Math.random();

} // End genRandomNumber().
```

First, we do a quick trivial rejection: if the `inMin` value (the start of the range) is greater than `inMax` (the end of the range), then we just return zero, content in the knowledge that the caller did something stupid and we didn't blow up because of it! Once that's out of the way, we use the basic formula seen in the `return` statement, which will always result in a number in the specified range.

Building the jscript.page Package

The `jscript.page` package will contain code that deals with the current web page as a whole. Let's go build it!

Question: How can I programmatically initiate printing of the current page?

Jack asked me to add a Print button to the final report page. I know that the user can just click the browser's Print button, but he insists!

Answer: Well, you can call `window.print()` at any time, but that's only on more recent browsers. And also note that even with the function I'm about to show you, the user will still get the usual print dialog box. There's no way to simply initiate printing without user intervention (which is probably a good thing—imagine all the trees you could kill with the right hack!). So, a little wrapping function is in order. Check out Listing 3-19.

Listing 3-19. *The printPage() Function*

```
jscript.page.printPage = function() {

  if (parseInt(navigator.appVersion) >= 4) {
    window.print()
  }

} // End printPage().
```

We just do a quick version check to ensure the browser will support the `window.print()` call, and that's it. There's really not much to say about this one, Bill.

Question: How can I access parameters that were passed to a page?

You know, Gilbert, sometimes I try to prototype something locally using just plain HTML pages. If I want to submit a form, and I want to submit it to another HTML page, is there any way I can access the parameters?

Answer: Yes, Bill, there certainly is. Listing 3-20 shows how.

Listing 3-20. *The getParameter() Function*

```
jscript.page.getParameter = function(inParamName) {

  var retVal = null;
  var varvals = unescape(location.search.substring(1));
  if (varvals) {
    var search_array = varvals.split("&");
    var temp_array = new Array();
    var j = 0;
    var i = 0;
    for (i = 0; i < search_array.length; i++) {
      temp_array = search_array[i].split("=");
      var pName = temp_array[0];
      var pVal = temp_array[1];
      if (inParamName == null) {
        if (retVal == null) {
          retVal = new Array();
        }
        retVal[j] = pName;
        retVal[j + 1] = pVal;
        j = j + 2;
      } else {
        if (pName == inParamName) {
          retVal = pVal;
          break;
        }
      }
    }
  }
  return retVal;

} // End getParameters().
```

This function actually allows you to get a specific parameter by name, or an array of all parameters. If inParamName is passed in, then a parameter with the specified name will be returned (or null will be returned if it isn't found). If null is passed as the value of inParamName, then an array of all parameters will be returned.

location.search.substring(1) is the way we get a reference to the query string. By starting with the second character of the URL, which is what the (1) parameter does, we are removing the leading question mark, leaving just the parameters themselves. After that, we simply call split() on that string, splitting on the ampersand character (&) that separates each parameter, which gives us an array. Then that array is iterated over, and each element is further split on an equal sign, since each parameter is a name=value pair.

After that, it's a simple matter to see if a specific parameter was requested or all of them will be returned. In the latter case, we instantiate a new array the first time through, and add the parameter to the array, and the value after it, so the array winds up being in the form *name, value*, *name*, *value*, and so on. Once we run out of parameters, we return the array. In the case of a specific parameter being requested, as soon as we find it, we return its value.

Question: How can I break out of a frameset via JavaScript?

Jack didn't ask for this, but I noticed it on my own. We have that home page where all our users start, and it has links to all of our applications, including this accounting application. Unfortunately, that home page is built with frames, and when you go to any application, you are still within that frameset. This isn't good most of the time, so I'd like to provide a way for the applications to break out of the frameset.

Answer: You know how many people truly hate frames these days? It seems like no self-respecting web developer uses frames anymore. I, however, do not suffer the opinions of fools and therefore I don't mind frames, when used properly. But I digress. To answer your question, I have provided Listing 3-21.

Listing 3-21. *The breakOutOfFrames() Function*

```
jscript.page.breakOutOfFrames = function() {

  if (self != top) {
    top.location = self.location;
  }

} // End breakOutOfFrames().
```

Breaking out of frames is a simple matter of making sure that the document in the browser is also the top, which means, if it were a frameset, it would be the parent frameset document. If the document isn't the top document, then we set the location of the top document to the location of the current document, which basically causes any frameset to be overwritten with the new document (as a result of a new retrieval from the server).

Building the jscript.storage Package

Client-side storage isn't really all that complex, but we could do with some utility functions to make it that much easier, and that's exactly what we'll put together now, in the jscript.storage package.

Question: How do I create a cookie and store it on the client?

Jack pointed out this one part of the application where we store user preferences on the server. He thinks, and I agree, that it would be more efficient to store it on the client. I know storage on the client is a bit limited with JavaScript, but cookies would seem to be a good fit here. How do I create one?

Answer: You're right, cookies are perfect for things like this: small bits of data stored per web site on the client. Let's make Cookie Monster happy and create a cookie, as shown in Listing 3-22.

Listing 3-22. *The setCookie() Function*

```
jscript.storage.setCookie = function(inName, inValue, inExpiry) {

  if (typeof inExpiry == "Date") {
    inExpiry = inExpiry.toGMTString();
  }
  document.cookie = inName + "=" + escape(inValue) + "; expires=" + inExpiry;

} // End setCookie().
```

Each cookie has a name and a value, obviously, as well as an expiration date. Therefore, this function accepts all three as inName, inValue, and inExpiry. The date must be in the form of a GMT date string, so we'll allow inExpiry to be either an actual Date object or a presumably properly formatted GMT date string. If it is a Date object, we call its toGMTString() method to get the proper format. After that, we set document.cookie equal to a string in the form of *xxxx=yyyy;expires=zzzz*, where *xxxx* is the name of the cookie, *yyyy* is the value, and *zzzz* is the date string. It might seem a little weird to you to be setting the property of document to a cookie—after all, wouldn't that mean that if you tried to set another cookie, the first cookie would be overwritten? But don't worry, because the browser properly deals with that. It's just a bit of syntactical weirdness, probably left over from the Netscape days.

Question: How can I get the value of a specified cookie?
Setting a cookie is easy! How about getting its value later?
Answer: That's also not difficult, Bill. Examine Listing 3-23.

Listing 3-23. *The getCookie() Function*

```
jscript.storage.getCookie = function(inName) {

  var docCookies = document.cookie;
  var cIndex = docCookies.indexOf(inName + "=");
  if (cIndex == -1) {
    return null;
  }
  cIndex = docCookies.indexOf("=", cIndex) + 1;
  var endStr = docCookies.indexOf(";", cIndex);
  if (endStr == -1) {
    endStr = docCookies.length;
  }
  return unescape(docCookies.substring(cIndex, endStr));

} // End getCookie().
```

When you retrieve the value of document.cookie, what you get is a giant string with all the cookies applicable for that page. So, the easiest way to find the cookie you are interested in is just to look for the substring *xxxx=*, where *xxxx* is the name of the cookie you want.

If we get back –1 from the call to indexOf(),(), then the cookie is not present, so we just return null. If it is found, then we need to find the end of it. Since all cookies will have the ;expires=*zzzz* string after it, we can look for the semicolon. Once we have the start and end location of the cookie we want, we return only the substring, making sure to unescape() it, since it is stored as a URL-encoded string, and the caller is happy.

Question: How can I delete a cookie?

OK, Gilbert, so I can create and retrieve cookies. Only one thing remains: how do I delete them?

Answer: Well, strictly speaking, you can't actually delete a cookie outright. However, you can retrieve the cookie, change its expiration date to something that has already passed, and set it again. That will overwrite the existing cookie, and the browser will immediately see that it has already expired, and will go ahead and delete it. See Listing 3-24 for the details.

Listing 3-24. *The deleteCookie() Function*

```
jscript.storage.deleteCookie = function(inName) {

  if (this.getCookie(inName)) {
    this.setCookie(inName, null, "Thu, 01-Jan-1970 00:00:01 GMT");
  }

} // End deleteCookie().
```

We use the getCookie() function we built earlier, and then pass what it returns along to setCookie(),(), as we saw earlier. We also pass in a string with an expiration date of January 1, 1970. Unless the system clock is pretty severely messed up, the cookie will be set, overwriting the one that's there already. It will then immediately expire and be deleted by the browser. A bit of trickery I suppose, but it works!

Building the jscript.string Package

Now we come to the final package we will build for our library, the jscript.string package. I'm sure you can guess its purpose: to help us work with strings!

Question: How can I count how many times a substring appears in a string?

One of the features Jack is requesting is the ability to check some free-form text that the user can enter and see how many times certain keywords appear, so we can flag the input as suspicious. How can I count how many times a given substring appears in a given string?

Answer: Not a big deal really. Check out Listing 3-25.

Listing 3-25. *The substrCount() Function*

```
jscript.string.substrCount = function(inStr, inSearchStr) {

  if (inStr == null || inStr == "" ||
    inSearchStr == null || inSearchStr == "") {
    return 0;
  }
  var splitChars = inStr.split(inSearchStr);
  return splitChars.length - 1;

} // End substrCount().
```

We can call this function, and pass it the string to search (inStr) and the string to search for (inSearchStr). First, the function does some trivial rejections to be sure the input parameters are valid. It will return zero if either is not. After that, it uses a handy method of the JavaScript String object called split(). This is essentially like StringTokenizer in Java. It splits the string into pieces, breaking it on a specified substring. So, in other words, if we have the string Sally sells seashells by the seashore on this dreary day, and we want to split it on the substring ea, it would break like this: Sally sells s̲e̲ashells by the s̲e̲ashore on this dr̲e̲ary day. The result is four pieces: Sally sells s, shells by the s, shore on this dr, and ry day.

What actually is returned by the call to split() is an array, which, in this case, contains four elements, as stated. So, all we need to do is return the length of the array minus one, and we have our answer. "Why minus one?" you ask. Think about splitting the string XYZ on Y. The length of the array would be 2, with X and Z as the elements. But we want to know how many times Y occurs, and that is always the length of the resultant array from the call to split(), minus 1! And if the element we're looking for isn't found, the array returned by split() still has a single element: the string we were trying to split. So, subtracting 1 from the length of that array still gives the correct answer: 0.

"That makes sense?" asked Gilbert. "Oh yes, completely!" replied Bill, "But I have more," he added.

Question: How can I strip certain characters from a string, or alternatively, strip any characters *except* certain ones from a string?

Jack also wants me to modify the code on the page where the user enters expense categories. It seems that, currently, the user can enter anything, even though only numbers are valid entries. I think I should write the function to be able to strip any characters that aren't in a list of allowed characters, as well as be able to strip only characters that appear in a disallowed list, just to be sure I cover all my bases for the future.

Answer: Neither of these goals is especially difficult. Both basically boil down to scanning through a source string and examining each character. If it matches any character from another string, then either copy it or don't copy it to a new string. You could write two separate functions to do this, but a single one should do the trick. Listing 3-26 shows the function that does both types of stripping.

Listing 3-26. *The stripChars() Function*

```
jscript.string.stripChars = function(inStr, inStripOrAllow, inCharList) {

  if (inStr == null || inStr == "" ||
    inCharList == null || inCharList == "" ||
    inStripOrAllow == null || inStripOrAllow == "") {
    return "";
  }
  inStripOrAllow = inStripOrAllow.toLowerCase();
  var outStr = "";
  var i;
  var j;
  var nextChar;
  var keepChar;
```

```
  for (i = 0; i < inStr.length; i++) {
    nextChar = inStr.substr(i, 1);
    if (inStripOrAllow == "allow") {
      keepChar = false;
    } else {
      keepChar = true;
    }
    for (j = 0; j < inCharList.length; j++) {
      checkChar = inCharList.substr(j, 1);
      if (inStripOrAllow == "allow" && nextChar == checkChar) {
        keepChar = true;
      }
      if (inStripOrAllow == "strip" && nextChar == checkChar) {
        keepChar = false;
      }
    }
    if (keepChar == true) {
      outStr = outStr + nextChar;
    }
  }
  return outStr;

} // End stripChars().
```

After a quick trivial rejection is done, just to be sure we have valid input values, we start scanning through the source string inStr. For each character, we scan through the list of allowed (or disallowed) values, which is also passed in as inCharList. For each, we check the value of the inStripOrAllow parameter, which is either allow or strip. If it's allow, and the character in inStr we are currently checking appears in inCharList, then we are keeping the character. If inStripOrAllow is strip, and the current character appears in inCharList, then in this case we are removing that character. To understand that, note the way keepChar is set before the inner loop begins.

When we are checking for allowed characters, the assumption is that the character will *not* be allowed *unless* it is found in the list. Conversely, when we are stripping characters, the assumption is that the character *will* be allowed *unless* it is found in the list. Finally, every character we keep in either case is added to outStr, which is returned at the end. So, that returned string will be less any characters as specified.

Question: What if I don't want to actually alter the string, but I just want to test if it contains only valid characters, or alternatively, contains any invalid characters?

stripChars() is indeed handy, but I'm thinking I may at some point just want to do a test to see if a given string contains only valid characters, or even just to see if it contains any invalid characters.

Answer: This is also not a big deal, and is quite similar to stripChars(), but I think we can do it a bit more efficiently, as shown in Listing 3-27.

Listing 3-27. *The strContentValid() Function*

```
jscript.string.strContentValid = function(inString, inCharList, inFromExcept) {

  if (inString == null || inCharList == null || inFromExcept == null ||
    inString == "" || inCharList == "") {
    return false;
  }
  inFromExcept = inFromExcept.toLowerCase();
  var i;
  if (inFromExcept == "from_list") {
    for (i = 0; i < inString.length; i++) {
      if (inCharList.indexOf(inString.charAt(i)) == -1) {
        return false;
      }
    }
    return true;
  }
  if (inFromExcept == "not_from_list") {
    for (i = 0; i < inString.length; i++) {
      if (inCharList.indexOf(inString.charAt(i)) != -1) {
        return false;
      }
    }
    return true;
  }

} // End strContentValid().
```

Again, we start with a trivial rejection, which is usually a good idea, by the way! After that, we again scan the input string inString. This time, though, our job is a little easier because we don't really need to go through the entire string. All we need to do is determine if the current character is not present in inCharList in the case of inFromExcept being from_list, and if it isn't, return false. In the case of inFromExcept being not_from_list, we check to be sure the current character *does not* appear in inCharList, and if it does, we again return false. If we make it all the way through inString, we return true.

Question: How can I replace *all* occurrences of a substring in a string?

I know that the String object in JavaScript has a replace() method that lets you replace a substring in a string with another substring. However, what if I want to replace *all* occurrences of a substring in a string?

Answer: You are observant to notice this shortcoming of the built-in replace() method, Bill. Fortunately, handling all occurrences, even though it requires some work on our part, isn't a big deal either. Listing 3-28 shows how to do it.

Listing 3-28. *The replace() Function*

```
jscript.string.replace = function(inSrc, inOld, inNew) {

  if (inSrc == null || inSrc == "" || inOld == null || inOld == "" ||
    inNew == null || inNew == "") {
    return "";
  }
  while (inSrc.indexOf(inOld) > -1) {
    inSrc = inSrc.replace(inOld, inNew);
  }
  return inSrc;

} // End replace().
```

Yes, that's really it! It's a simple matter of looping, looking for inOld in inSrc, and each time, replacing it with inNew. Just keep doing this in a loop until inOld doesn't appear in inSrc anymore, and we're finished. Couldn't be easier!

Question: How can I trim spaces from the start of a string?

I notice that in most other languages, the string class has methods to trim spaces from the beginning of a string, usually leftTrim() or something like that. JavaScript doesn't. How can I do that?

Answer: Oh, come on now, Bill, can't you challenge me a bit more? Listing 3-29 is your answer.

Listing 3-29. *The leftTrim() Function*

```
jscript.string.leftTrim = function(inStr) {

  if (inStr == null || inStr == "") {
    return null;
  }
  var j;
  for (j = 0; inStr.charAt(j) == " "; j++) { }
  return inStr.substring(j, inStr.length);

} // End leftTrim().
```

It's just a matter of finding where the first nonspace character is in the string, and we do that by iterating over the characters in inStr as long as we encounter a space. Then we just use the built-in substring() function and return the string starting from the value of the loop variable at the end (which, remember, is the first nonspace character) until the end of the string.

Oh yeah, and before you ask, you can easily make a rightTrim() function, too, as shown in Listing 3-30.

Listing 3-30. *The rightTrim() Function*

```
jscript.string.rightTrim = function(inStr) {

  if (inStr == null || inStr == "") {
    return null;
  }
  var j;
  for (j = inStr.length - 1; inStr.charAt(j) == " "; j--) { }
  return inStr.substring(0, j + 1);

} // End rightTrim().
```

It's the same basic logic, except that, this time, we iterate backwards over the string, since we're looking for the *last* nonspace character this time. Then we just return the substring starting from the beginning of the string until that last nonspace character.

I know what you're going to ask next: what about trimming both at the same time? Certainly, you could just call both of these on the source string, but why not make it a little more convenient? Listing 3-31 shows the fullTrim() method, which provides that convenience.

Listing 3-31. *The fullTrim() Function*

```
jscript.string.fullTrim = function(inStr) {

  if (inStr == null || inStr == "") {
    return "";
  }
  inStr = this.leftTrim(inStr);
  inStr = this.rightTrim(inStr);
  return inStr;

} // End fullTrim().
```

Might as well use what we've already developed, right? So, just call leftTrim() and then rightTrim() on the input inStr, and we're good to go.

Question: How can I take a string and break it into pieces of a specified length?

One last thing with regard to strings, Gilbert. We have a free-form text entry area for notes about an expense, and Jack wants me to store it in a number of database fields, each of which is 100 characters long. How can I break up what the user enters into 100-character chunks?

Answer: While breaking up a string like that isn't hard, one thing you didn't mention was making sure you don't break up the string in the middle of words. Certainly, Jack wouldn't like that, right? So, we have to take that into account. Listing 3-32 shows one of probably many ways you can pull this off.

Listing 3-32. *The breakLine() Function*

```
jscript.string.breakLine = function(inText, inSize) {

  if (inText == null || inText == "" || inSize <= 0) {
    return inText;
  }
  if (inText.length <= inSize) {
    return inText;
  }
  var outArray = new Array();
  var str = inText;
  while (str.length > inSize) {
    var x = str.substring(0, inSize);
    var y = x.lastIndexOf(" ");
    var z = x.lastIndexOf("\n");
    if (z != -1) {
      y = z;
    }
    if (y == -1) {
      y = inSize;
    }
    outArray.push(str.substring(0, y));
    str = str.substring(y);
  }
  outArray.push(str);
  return outArray;

} // End breakLine().
```

First things first: make sure we have a string to break up, and also make sure the specified size is greater than or equal to 1, since anything else wouldn't make much sense. Also, we check to see if the size of inText is less than or equal to the specified size. If it is, we just return inText, and we're finished!

After those checks, we copy inText to a variable named, creatively enough, str, and we begin a loop that will continue until str is longer than the specified size. See, with each loop iteration, we're going to reduce str, so that eventually it will be shorter than inSize, and the loop will end. So, in the loop, we get a substring whose size equals inSize. We then find the last space and line break in the string. If either is found, we set the variable y to its location. If neither is found, y gets set to the size of the string. We then finally push the substring into our outArray, and cut str down by the chunk we just removed, and then the loop begins again. Finally, we return outArray, which contains inText, broken up into chunks of the appropriate size (or slightly smaller, depending on where the breaks wound up falling).

"Well," said Bill, "That was quite a ride! I learned a ton today. Thank you, Gilbert!"

"Eh, it's all in a day's work," came the smug reply from Gilbert. "I'll make a good c0dr out of you yet."

"Well, with all you've taught me here, I should be able to fulfill all of Jack's requests, and then some," said Bill. "I should be able to impress him greatly, and soon he'll give *me* that promotion that *you've* been after! Oh yeah, who's the C00l D00D with the M4d 5KiLL2 now, huh? I R0><0R, j00'r3 0\/\/l\l3D, ll4l\/l4!"

(For the secret decoder ring you'll need to understand that mess, visit `http://www.learnleetspeak.com`.)

Gilbert sat in stunned silence, looking at the grinning face of Bill, the realization of what just happened sinking in. Gilbert opened his mouth, trying to prepare a smart-ass comeback on the fly, but before he could utter a syllable, Bill turned and left the room, a new bounce in his step obvious to anyone who was looking.

Gilbert looked at his Dilbert mug, his wall of IT certifications, his 1:100 scale models of the Enterprise NCC-1701D and E, and his Darth Maul mask from last Halloween, and realized he would have to pack up all this stuff pretty soon.

And for the first time in the five years Gilbert worked at Initech, just as he was realizing his days were likely numbered, he was smug and arrogant no more!

Testing All the Pieces

OK, back to reality, this time to stay!

The source code presented in this book is available for download from the Source Code/Download area of the Apress web site (`http://www.apress.com`). One of the downloadable items for this chapter, which does not actually appear in the chapter itself, is a test HTML document that exercises all the functions we have built here. This also doubles as a form of documentation, since it shows basic usages of all the functions. I highly recommend grabbing that source code and taking a look to see how all of this fits together and works. Go ahead, Gilbert won't mind! In fact, you will really *need* the source in front of you in later chapters. If you grab everything now, you'll be able to move through the rest of the chapters smoothly.

Just as a quick example of what you'll see when you run this application, Figure 3-1 shows the tests available for the `jscript.array` package, and the pop-up shows the result of the `findInArray()` function specifically.

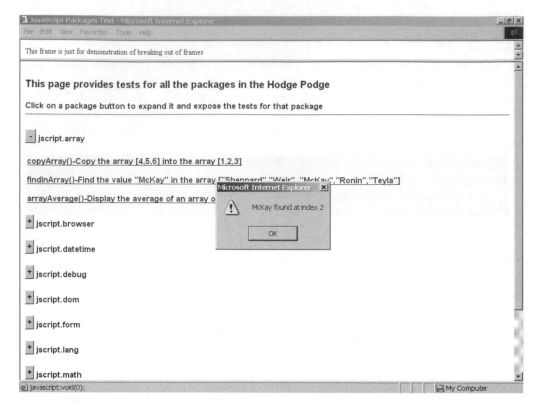

Figure 3-1. *Some tests for the jscript.array package, and the pop-up showing the result of testing the findInArray() function*

As another example to whet your appetite, Figure 3-2 shows the jscript.debug package test group, specifically, the DivLogger in action. (Unfortunately, you cannot discern the color-coding in the screenshot here, but trust me, each message is color-coded!)

One other important aspect that this test page demonstrates is how to use this as a library. All you actually need to do is have the various package source files that you intend to use available to your pages, and then "import," via the appropriate <script> tag, those packages. There are no packaging requirements aside from that—no building a DLL or anything along those lines. However, it is reasonable to set aside a directory for just these source files. Then when you want to include the library in another project, it's just a matter of copying that single directory.

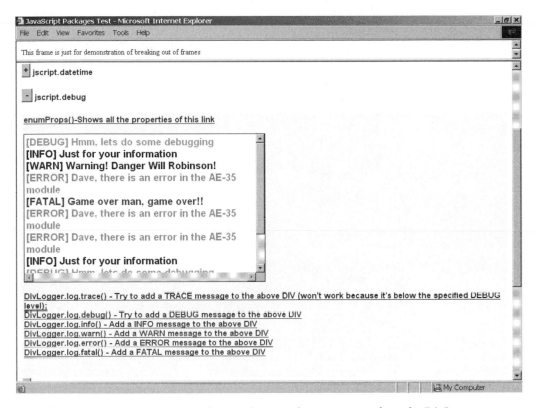

Figure 3-2. *The tests for the jscript.debug package, with some output from the DivLogger*

Suggested Exercises

A chapter like this makes is rather easy to suggest exercises because really one suggestion covers them all: go add some stuff! I suggest adding various functions to the existing packages—whatever you think will come in handy. I also suggest adding a package or two, just to see that it works. You may want to add a whole new package under jscript, as well as add a new subpackage to an existing package, maybe something like jscript.dom.effects, if you want to add some functions to do various effects. The possibilities are unlimited!

Summary

In this chapter, we put together a nice little library of functions that you should find a great deal of use for later. You have also seen how to create a rudimentary package structure that helps avoid namespace collisions and having a lot of global variables and functions all over the place.

More than likely, not all the functions will be used in this book's projects. (I wrote this chapter before writing the code for the projects to follow, so some of my guesses may have been off). That doesn't really matter though, because they are useful functions nonetheless and should serve you down the road.

CHAPTER 4

■■■

CalcTron 3000:
A JavaScript Calculator

From Dustin Hoffman to Russell Crowe,[1] calculators have played an important role in the everyday lives of humans ever since the Babylonians first put stones on some lines in the sand (or was it the Chinese, as some pundits claim—I'm no historian, so I'll leave that debate to more qualified folks). Why not bring the idea into the modern age and build one in JavaScript for ourselves?

Along with the simple add, subtract, multiply, and divide functions, our calculator (dubbed CalcTron) will include some other common functions, such as percentages, square roots, and, since we're programmers, base conversions. Of course, those won't be quite enough to make a geek happy, so we'll make this a fully extensible calculator, to which we can add functions at will. We'll also do our best to make the interface a bit fancy, using some styles and cool effects. We can then see if adding enough features later allows it to gain sentience and take over the world, but one thing at a time!

Calculator Project Requirements and Goals

A calculator isn't fundamentally a complex project, as long as you don't try to include every bit of functionality possible. At the same time, it should be a good project to get some exposure to JavaScript concepts and make you think a bit. Let's throw some requirements out there that will help to fulfill that goal:

- CalcTron should present a relatively flexible interface that can morph as we add new features. Specifically, we'll allow CalcTron to be switched into a number of modes, each with its own defined layout (within some predefined constraints). Let's allow these layouts to be specified in JSON.

- A calculator isn't fundamentally the most visually exciting project, so to alleviate our boredom, we'll put some special effects and visual flair into it where possible. We'll do this with a library to save ourselves as much effort as possible.

- CalcTron should be extensible, allowing us to plug in new functions as required.

---

1. In the movie *Rain Man*, Dustin Hoffman played Raymond Babbitt, who was an autistic man with some startling mathematical abilities. In the movie *A Beautiful Mind*, Russell Crowe played John Nash, a brilliant mathematician.

That's a fairly short list, I admit. However, once we get into the code of things, you'll see that a project that seems minimal on the outside isn't necessarily that simplistic on the inside.

A Preview of CalcTron

We'll begin by having a look at CalcTron, and said look commences with Figure 4-1.

Figure 4-1. *CalcTron in Standard mode*

CalcTron provides two modes of operation out of the box: Standard mode, as shown in Figure 4-1, and BaseCalc (base calculations) mode, as shown in Figure 4-2.

Figure 4-2. *CalcTron in BaseCalc mode*

When you click the Mode button, you are presented with a pop-up that flies onto the screen and allows you to choose a new mode of operation for the calculator, as shown in Figure 4-3. The pop-up is pretty simple, but it's an integral part of making CalcTron extensible.

What you cannot see in a screenshot is the fact that the pop-up flies to the center of the browser content area from one of the four corners randomly. This flying is accomplished with the help of a library named Rico. In addition to the flying pop-up, Rico does the rounding of the corners of the calculator itself. Let's take a quick peek at what Rico has to offer.

Figure 4-3. *Mode change pop-up*

Rico Features

I introduced Rico with some of the other representative JavaScript libraries in Chapter 2. Rico (http://openrico.org) is a smallish library (as compared to something like Dojo, for example) that covers relatively few topics, but does so quite well. Rico provides functionality in four key areas: Ajax, drag-and-drop management, cinematic effects, and behaviors.

Rico is one of the many libraries that is built on top of the Prototype library. Rico itself is housed in one relatively small (88kb) JavaScript file. Add the 46kb of Prototype (depending on version), and you can see it's not very big at all. As they say though, it packs a pretty good punch.

Rico provides two Ajax functions: one designed for updating the innerHTML of a target element, and one for updating multiple elements via an XML response. Both of these use an interesting model where you register a given Ajax request with the Ajax engine Rico provides and give it an ID. You can then reuse this request in different circumstances and at different times by referencing its ID. The latter expects an XML response from the server, and then uses it to populate elements on the screen. If you jump over to the Rico web site and check out the demos, which you can get to by clicking the Demos link, you'll see some good examples of this (as well as everything else I'm describing here).

Rico also offers some nifty drag-and-drop support. In addition to being able to make arbitrary elements (<div> elements usually) draggable, it also allows you to define drop zones. This means that you can, for instance, have a <div> that is draggable, and have another <div> defined as a drop zone. When you drag the first <div> onto the second, it becomes a child of the drop zone. The Rico demos page shows this, as well as another example of a custom swap box that is drag-and-drop-enabled (that is, there is a list of items on the left, and you can drag those items into the list box on the right). Coding all this yourself would be a real hassle. Rico makes it very easy (a few lines of code in most cases).

In the area of cinematic effects, Rico offers functionality such as the ability to animate the position of an element, animate the size of an element, animate both the size and position of an element, fade elements in and out, and round shapes. Rounding shapes and animating size and position are two effects that you'll be seeing in action in CalcTron.

Another area of functionality Rico provides is called *behaviors*. Behaviors are what most other libraries call *widgets*; at least, that's true of what's in Rico now (it might not always be this way). Behaviors are generally combinations of cinematic effects and/or Ajax that create a unique component of functionality (a widget). Here are some of the behaviors Rico currently offers:

Accordion: Microsoft Outlook has a sidebar where you can click a category and have it expand into view. This is roughly what the accordion behavior is. Basically, you have a bunch of <div> elements running down the screen. You then specify that they form an accordion. When you click one of them, Rico will expand it, while shrinking any other that is showing. The effect is really quite impressive. Other libraries offer similar functionality, but I have to say, Rico's is the simplest, most straightforward, and cleanest looking implementation I've seen.

Weather: This is the typical show-me-the-weather-in-my-area widget. This makes use of some effects, the accordion behavior, and Ajax to make calls to a remote server to get the weather information. Once again, I highly recommend checking out the demos page on the Rico web site, because this is a really impressive behavior to see in action.

LiveGrid: This is the typical data grid with Ajax connectivity, buffering, and compression strategies to aid in performance. You've probably seen a number of different versions of this idea, and while Rico's is nice, it's not especially remarkable. It is definitely useful, but just OK in my opinion.

As you can see, Rico isn't about covering every last requirement a JavaScript and RIA developer might have. It's about a handful of targeted areas only, but it covers them rather well. The drag-and-drop support especially stands out to me as one of the best implementations I've seen. In Chapter 10's project, we'll use MochiKit for drag-and-drop support. While that library also offers pretty good drag-and-drop features, if I had to do it all over again, to be quite honest, I would choose Rico for this functionality. That's not meant as a slap against MochiKit at all. You'll see that it's a good library as well. I'm just emphasizing how good Rico's feature set is in this area.

I also feel that the accordion behavior is a real standout. I thought of ways I could shoehorn it into CalcTron, but decided not to force the issue.

■**Tip** I've said it a couple of times now, but it's worth repeating: spend some time on the Rico demos page to see all of this in action. I think you'll really like what you see there.

Now that you've seen CalcTron and Rico, and understand some of our goals and expectations for this project (and I hope you've played with CalcTron a bit by now, too), we can begin our exploration of what makes it tick.

Dissecting the CalcTron Solution

To get a grasp on how CalcTron is put together, let's examine the directory structure of the application, as shown in Figure 4-4.

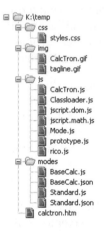

Figure 4-4. *Directory structure for the CalcTron project*

The solution consists of the following:

- calctron.htm: In the root directory is our starting point. The calctron.htm file defines the basic layout of the application, includes all the required JavaScript, and begins executing the application.

- css: This directory is home to the styles.css file, which is the style information CalcTron uses to define its display.

- img: This directory is where the images are stored. Only two images are used in CalcTron: the title graphic and the tag line underneath it.

- js: This directory contains a number of JavaScript files. These files are what literally make up CalcTron. Also found here are some support libraries that the application uses.

- modes: This directory houses a JavaScript file, as well as a JSON file, for each mode the calculator has.

Not really much to it, is there? With that brief overview, we can get down to brass tacks and dive straight into some code.

Writing calctron.htm

CalcTron begins by importing its style sheet, which we'll look at next, as well as all of the JavaScript source files it needs:

```
<link rel="StyleSheet" href="css/styles.css" type="text/css">

<script src="js/prototype.js" type="text/javascript"></script>
<script src="js/rico.js" type="text/javascript"></script>
<script src="js/jscript.math.js" type="text/javascript"></script>
<script src="js/Mode.js" type="text/javascript"></script>
<script src="js/Classloader.js" type="text/javascript"></script>
<script src="js/CalcTron.js" type="text/javascript"></script>
```

Prototype is imported first, and then Rico, which needs Prototype (we'll also be using a function from Prototype directly). Next is one of the packages we built in Chapter 3, the jscript.math package. The math package is needed because the code will be making a random determination of which corner the mode-change pop-up will fly in from, and the math package includes the random number generation function. After that is the import of the Mode class, the Classloader class, and the CalcTron class. We'll get to those shortly.

After these imports comes a single line of JavaScript that is actually key to making everything work:

```
<script>
  var calcTron = new CalcTron();
</script>
```

This single line of code creates an instance of the CalcTron class and assigns it to the variable calcTron. The CalcTron class is the core of the application, but let's not get ahead of ourselves; there's more to calctron.htm than this.

Since calctron.htm is the file the user loads, what happens on load is important:

```
<body onLoad="calcTron.init();">
```

The init() method of the CalcTron class is responsible for all application-level initialization, and hence is called in response to the page's onLoad event.

The body of calctron.htm is the basic structure of the page, as shown earlier in Figures 4-1, 4-2, and 4-3. The first element we encounter is a <div>:

```
<div id="divMode" class="cssDivMode">
  <br/>
  <center>
    Select mode here
    <br/><br/>
    <input type="button" value="Standard"
      onClick="calcTron.setMode('Standard');">
    <br/>
```

```
      <input type="button" value="BaseCalc"
        onClick="calcTron.setMode('BaseCalc');">
    </center>
  </div>
```

This <div> is the mode-change pop-up. It's pretty straightforward; in fact, the onClick event handler is the only interesting thing about it. As discussed in previous chapters, you generally want to avoid in-line JavaScript like this. However, I don't view it as an egregious breach to do so when it is just a function call, as is the case here. As the name implies, the setMode() method of the calcTron object sets the mode as specified. We'll get into those details soon enough (in the "Writing CalcTron.js" section), so please allow this explanation to suffice for the time being.

After this <div> is another one with the ID mainContainer, which is where the actual calculator structure is housed. Within it is a table, where each cell is one of the buttons of the calculator, preceded by the results, and followed by the information area at the bottom. This is a somewhat large chunk of frankly rather mundane HTML, so I won't list it all here. However, let's look at it in brief. First is the results section:

```
      <tr>
        <td nowrap colspan="10" align="right" valign="middle">
          <div style="height:16px;" id="divResults"></div>
        </td>
      </tr>
```

There's nothing unusual here. That being said, note that the <div> inside the cell with the ID divResults is where the results (or the number the user is currently entering) are displayed by altering its innerHTML property.

Following this is the top row of command buttons (the calculator has five command buttons on top and five below, with the input buttons in between):

```
<tr>
  <td nowrap colspan="2" align="center" valign="middle"> ➥
    <input type="button" class="cssInputCommandButton" id="commandButton0" ➥
      onClick="calcTron.currentMode.commandButton0();"> ➥
  </td>
  <td nowrap colspan="2" align="center" valign="middle"> ➥
    <input type="button" class="cssInputCommandButton" id="commandButton1" ➥
    onClick="calcTron.currentMode.commandButton1();"> ➥
  </td>
  <td nowrap colspan="2" align="center" valign="middle"> ➥
    <input type="button" class="cssInputCommandButton" id="commandButton2" ➥
    onClick="calcTron.currentMode.commandButton2();"> ➥
  </td>
  <td nowrap colspan="2" align="center" valign="middle"> ➥
    <input type="button" class="cssInputCommandButton" id="commandButton3" ➥
    onClick="calcTron.currentMode.commandButton3();"> ➥
  </td>
```

```
<td nowrap colspan="2" align="center" valign="middle"> ➡
  <input type="button" class="cssInputCommandButton" id="commandButton4" ➡
  onClick="calcTron.currentMode.commandButton4();"> ➡
</td>
</tr>
```

I've broken the lines here so they'll fit on the page. In the actual code you execute, each of the cells is on a single line of code. Unfortunately, IE does not always ignore whitespace as it is supposed to, and so this code would not display properly if it were actually entered as it is here.

Once again, you see a single function call in the onClick event handler. Note that none of the buttons has a value (a label), because one is added dynamically when a calculator mode is selected, as you'll see in a bit. Also note that the bottom row of command buttons looks basically the same as this, except for the last button, which is always the mode-change button. It looks like this:

```
<td nowrap colspan="2" align="center" valign="middle">
  <input type="button" class="cssInputCommandButton" style="display:block;"
    value="Mode" onClick="calcTron.changeModePopup();">
</td>
```

As you can see, a value is given here, and the onClick handler is different. Otherwise, it's nothing special

In between the top and bottom row of command buttons are five rows of input buttons. Let's take a look at a single row:

```
<tr>
  <td nowrap align="center" valign="middle">
    <input type="button" class="cssInputButton" id="button0_0"
      onClick="calcTron.currentMode.button0_0();">
  </td>
  <td nowrap align="center" valign="middle">
    <input type="button" class="cssInputButton" id="button0_1"
      onClick="calcTron.currentMode.button0_1();">
  </td>
  <td nowrap align="center" valign="middle">
    <input type="button" class="cssInputButton" id="button0_2"
      onClick="calcTron.currentMode.button0_2();">
  </td>
  <td nowrap align="center" valign="middle">
    <input type="button" class="cssInputButton" id="button0_3"
      onClick="calcTron.currentMode.button0_3();">
  </td>
  <td nowrap align="center" valign="middle">
    <input type="button" class="cssInputButton" id="button0_4"
      onClick="calcTron.currentMode.button0_4();">
  </td>
```

```
<td nowrap align="center" valign="middle">
  <input type="button" class="cssInputButton" id="button0_5"
    onClick="calcTron.currentMode.button0_5();">
</td>
<td nowrap align="center" valign="middle">
  <input type="button" class="cssInputButton" id="button0_6"
    onClick="calcTron.currentMode.button0_6();">
</td>
<td nowrap align="center" valign="middle">
  <input type="button" class="cssInputButton" id="button0_7"
    onClick="calcTron.currentMode.button0_7();">
</td>
<td nowrap align="center" valign="middle">
  <input type="button" class="cssInputButton" id="button0_8"
    onClick="calcTron.currentMode.button0_8();">
</td>
<td nowrap align="center" valign="middle">
  <input type="button" class="cssInputButton" id="button0_9"
    onClick="calcTron.currentMode.button0_9();">
</td>
</tr>
```

These are substantially similar to the command buttons; only the functions called in the onClick handlers differ, as well as the style class applied to them. The other four rows are the same, differing only in the id of each button.

Following the buttons is the information area:

```
<td nowrap colspan="10" align="center" valign="middle">
  <div style="height:16px;" id="divInfo"></div>
</td>
```

This is pretty much the same as the result area, with just a different style. And with that, we've examined calctron.htm pretty much in its entirety. I never said it was rocket science.

Writing styles.css

styles.css is, naturally enough, the main style sheet used by CalcTron. You've already seen a number of the styles it contains in our examination of calctron.htm, so let's see if there's anything else of interest. The entire style sheet is shown in Listing 4-1.

Listing 4-1. *The styles.css File for CalcTron*

```
/* Style applied to all elements */
* {
  font-family    : arial;
  font-size      : 10pt;
  font-weight    : bold;
}
```

```css
/* Style applied to the outer calculator container */
.cssCalculatorOuter {
  position         : absolute;
  background-color : #c6c3de;
}

/* Style applied to the table cell where command buttons are placed */
.cssSpanCB {
  width            : 110px;
}

/* Style applied to the table cell where input buttons are placed */
.cssSpanB {
  width            : 60px;
}

/* Style applied to input buttons */
.cssInputButton {
  width            : 50px;
  display          : none;
}

/* Style applied to command buttons */
.cssInputCommandButton {
  width            : 100px;
  display          : none;
}

/* Style applied to the mode switch popup DIV */
.cssDivMode {
  display          : none;
  z-index          : 100;
  position         : absolute;
  border           : 2px solid #000000;
  background-color : #efefef;
}
```

Let's look at each selector in turn:

- The first selector is somewhat interesting. It applies to all elements on the page, and is kind of a catchall style. The nice thing about it is that it cascades down into tables and cells and such, which usually isn't the case, so it really does cover *everything*. This style sets the font to Arial, 10pt, and makes it all bold.

- The next style is applied to the outer <div>. We set it to a purple-blue color and position it absolutely, which is required so we can center it.

- Next, two styles are applied to the cells that contain the command buttons and input buttons, respectively. They ensure each cell is sized for a button to fit nicely, with a little padding.

- After that, two styles are applied to the command and input buttons. These ensure that all the buttons have a consistent size. They also ensure that all the buttons start out hidden, which avoids any unnecessary and ugly flickering when the application loads and the initial mode initiates.

- Finally, a style is applied to the mode-change pop-up. We set its z-index to ensure it floats over the calculator itself, and give it a solid color and a border. Like the outer <div> style, it is positioned absolutely, which is the only way we could make it fly in from a corner and center it.

Writing CalcTron.js

As mentioned earlier, CalcTron is the main class that powers this application—its core. It contains fields describing the overall state of the calculator, as well as initialization code, and the code that deals with switching modes. For all it does, and as central to the application as it is, it really isn't that big or complicated at all, as the UML diagram in Figure 4-5 illustrates.

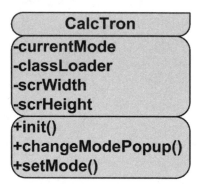

Figure 4-5. *UML diagram of the CalcTron class*

A mere four fields and three methods are all it takes. Let's begin by looking at those four fields:

- currentMode: This field stores the id, which is really the name, of CalcTron's current mode. As it stands, CalcTron has two modes: Standard and BaseCalc, and those are the only two values you would find in this field (not counting its initial null value).

- classLoader: This field is a reference to an instance of the Classloader class, which is described in the next section. In brief, this class is responsible for loading a class that contains the functions needed for a given mode. It also verifies the class meets certain interface requirements, which will generally mean the class is a valid CalcTron Mode class.

- scrWidth and scrHeight: These fields store the width and height of the browser window at startup. This information is used to center the calculator itself, and also for various calculations dealing with the mode-change pop-up.

Moving along to the methods of the CalcTron class, we first encounter init(). This is the method called by the onLoad of the calctron.htm file, and its task is to initialize a number of things to get CalcTron ready for user interaction. The init() function is as follows:

```
this.init = function() {

  // Figure out how wide the browser content area is.
  if (window.innerWidth) {
    this.scrWidth = window.innerWidth;
  } else {
    this.scrWidth = document.body.clientWidth;
  }

  // Figure out how high the browser content area is.
  if (window.innerHeight) {
    this.scrHeight = window.innerHeight;
  } else {
    this.scrHeight = document.body.clientHeight;
  }

  // Round the corners of the main content div.
  new Rico.Effect.Round(null, "cssCalculatorOuter");

  // Set initial mode to standard.
  this.setMode("Standard");

} // End init().
```

First, the function determines the width of the content area of the browser window. Some browsers present this information via the innerWidth attribute of the window object, while others present it via the clientWidth attribute of the document.body object, so a little branching action is in order, followed by virtually identical code for determining the height of the browser content area.

Following that is our first exposure to Rico in this application. As mentioned in the earlier look at Rico, one of the neat features it offers is the ability to round arbitrary elements, so we can have some nice, soft, round corners around our calculator instead of the usual sharp, square corners. The code instantiates a new Rico.Effect.Round object, passing it the name of a style sheet. The first argument to Round() is actually an element to round, and the second is a class name. I decided to use the class name because, initially, I wasn't sure if there might be other shapes to round, and using the class means that I can round any object that uses the same style class.

■**Tip** You can pass a third argument to Round() to define the rounding further. For example, if for the third parameter you pass { corners : 'tl br' }, you are saying that only the top-left and bottom-right corners are to be rounded. See the Rico documentation and examples for further explanations of what is possible with these options.

Once the rounding is done, one important piece of business remains, and that's to set the initial mode of CalcTron. This is done with the following statement:

```
this.setMode("Standard");
```

Standard is our starting mode, just as with the built-in Windows calculator (which CalcTron was roughly modeled after, at least as far as the Standard mode goes). Once that's complete, CalcTron is ready for the user.

The next method in CalcTron is the changeModePopup() method. This is called when the Mode button is clicked. Although it's a bit longer than init(), it's still a pretty simple animal:

```
this.changeModePopup = function() {

  // This is the width and height of the div as it should ultimately appear.
  var divWidth = 150;
  var divHeight = 150;

  // Get reference to mode change div and reset it to begin animation. It's
  // going to randomly come flying from one of the corners of the screen,
  // so first choose which corner, then set the top and left attributes
  // accordingly.
  var modeDiv = $("divMode");
  modeDiv.style.width = "0px";
  modeDiv.style.height = "0px";

  // What corner does it fly from?
  var whatCorner = jscript.math.genRandomNumber(1, 4)

  // Set the starting coordinates accordingly.
  switch (whatCorner) {
    case 1:
      modeDiv.style.left = "0px";
      modeDiv.style.top = "0px";
    break;
    case 2:
      modeDiv.style.left = this.scrWidth - divWidth;
      modeDiv.style.top = "0px";
    break;
    case 3:
      modeDiv.style.left = "0px";
      modeDiv.style.top = this.scrHeight - divHeight;
    break;
    case 4:
      modeDiv.style.left = this.scrWidth - divWidth;
      modeDiv.style.top = this.scrHeight - divHeight;
    break;
  }
```

```
// Calculate the final left and top position for the div so it's centered
// in the browser content area.
var left = (this.scrWidth - divWidth) / 2;
var top = (this.scrHeight - divHeight) / 2;

// Show the div so the animation can begin.  Since its width and height are
// zero, it won't actually be visible just yet.
$("divMode").style.display = "block";

// Ask Rico to do the animation for us.
new Rico.Effect.SizeAndPosition("divMode", left, top, divWidth, divHeight,
  400, 25, null
);

} // End changeMode().
```

First, we have two variables, divWidth and divHeight, which define how wide and how tall the mode change pop-up is. These are needed for calculations to come shortly.

We begin the real work by getting a reference to divMode. This is accomplished by using the $() function, which is actually part of Prototype, not Rico. $() is, in simplest terms, shorthand for the ubiquitous document.getElementById(), although it adds the ability to get a reference to multiple objects at the same time. Once we have a reference to the <div>, we set its width and height to zero. Not only does the mode-change pop-up fly in from one of the four corners of the browser content area, but it also grows as it flies in. So, it needs to start out as small as possible to make the effect work correctly.

Next, we see a call to the jscript.math.genRandomNumber() function introduced in Chapter 3. It generates a random number between 1 and 4, inclusive, which determines from which corner the pop-up will fly in.

After that, we see a switch on this value. Depending on which corner was chosen, the left and top attributes of divMode are set to start it out in the proper corner.

Following that are two lines that calculate the final location of the pop-up. These statements make use of the scrWidth and scrHeight we calculated in init(), as well as divWidth and divHeight, as set at the beginning of this function. Taking the difference between those two values and dividing by two, for both width and height, results in the proper coordinates required for the pop-up to be centered in the content area.

Finally, we see our next usage of Rico, the Rico.Effect.SizeAndPosition object. This object is fed the name of the <div> to manipulate (divMode), the final X and Y (left and top, respectively) location where it should end up, the width and height it should wind up, how many milliseconds the whole thing should take (400), and how many steps there should be (25). This means that Rico will take divMode and move it from its current location to the location specified by the left and top variables, and at the same time, will expand it from its current size to the size specified by divWidth and divHeight. It will do this over 25 steps in 400 milliseconds (which means that each step will take 16 milliseconds). Isn't it cool that we can get all that action from one function call?

The final method of CalcTron is setMode(), which is called when one of the buttons on the mode-change pop-up is clicked. It's actually an interesting little function because it gets called not once, but *twice* when modes are switched, and it does something a little different each time. Let's have a look at this method first:

```
this.setMode = function(inVal) {

  // First time through: should have been passed a string naming the mode
  // to switch to. We simply pass it to the classloader to load it for us.
  if (typeof inVal == "string") {

    $("divMode").style.display = "none";
    this.classloader.load(inVal);

  } else {

    // Second time through, inVal is an instance of a class descending from
    // Mode. In that case, we ask the classloader to verify it for us,
    // and assumimg it's valid, we store a reference to it and ask it to
    // initialize itself.
    if (this.classloader.verify(inVal, new Mode())) {
      this.currentMode = inVal;
      this.currentMode.init();
    } else {
      alert("Not a valid mode class");
    }

  }

} // End setMode().
```

OK, so it's fairly diminutive, but interesting nonetheless. The first time it's called, immediately when a mode-selection button is clicked, it's passed the name of the mode to switch to. So, the first check is if the incoming parameter is a string. If it is, the mode-change pop-up is hidden, and the Classloader instance is called with the value that was passed to setMode().

The Classloader loads the class, and when it completes, setMode() is called again (you'll see exactly how in just a bit). However, at this point, what is passed in is *not* a string, but is instead a class descending from Mode. That's where the else clause comes into play. Here, we ask the Classloader to verify the class, and if it doesn't pass, we just pop up an alert, since there's not much we can do about it. If it is verified though, we set the currentMode field of CalcTron to point to this class that was passed in, and we then call the init() method on it.

And that sums up CalcTron.js. A couple of points probably are not quite clear to you yet, so let's commence clearing those things up now. We'll begin by looking at this Classloader class I've referenced a couple of times.

Writing Classloader.htm

As I've noted, CalcTron is designed to be extensible; that is, you can add modes to it with little difficulty. Each mode is implemented as a class extending the Mode class. We'll be looking at these implementation classes next, but before we do, let's talk about how those classes are loaded.

Java has a fairly complex mechanism called the *classloader*. Its job, as I'm sure you'll be unsurprised to learn, is to . . . wait for it . . . load classes. It does more than that, however. It is also responsible for verifying classes, checking them for security violations, making sure they aren't corrupt, and so on.

JavaScript doesn't offer anything that fancy, but that has never stopped us from doing it ourselves. What would a JavaScript classloader offer? Well, security isn't really a concern, since JavaScript executes in a relatively secure sandbox to begin with, so we can skip that. Could we check for a corrupt class? Perhaps, but beyond ensuring we didn't get an error from the server the class is being loaded from, there isn't much to be done there either.

One operation we can perform is to verify that the class meets a certain public interface. Each of the mode implementation classes must implement certain functions for CalcTron to be able to use it. We can verify that a loaded class does so.

But perhaps we should discuss the idea of how exactly to load a JavaScript class in the first place, since even that simple concept isn't native to JavaScript. Before we even do *that*, however, let's take a look at the UML diagram for the `Classloader` class, as shown in Figure 4-6.

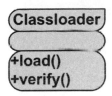

Figure 4-6. *UML diagram of the Classloader class*

Heck, we might as well look at the code, too. There isn't a whole lot to it, so the entire `Classloader` code is listed in Listing 4-2.

Listing 4-2. *The Classloader.js File*

```javascript
function Classloader() {


  /**
   * Load a named class.
   *
   * @param inClassName The name of the class to load.  We assume it's a
   *                    calculator mode class, so it's always in the modes
   *                    subdirectory.
   */
  this.load = function(inClassName) {

    // Dynamically create a new script tag, point it at the mode source file,
    // and append it to the document's head section, thereby loading and
    // parsing it automatically.
    var scriptTag = document.createElement("script");
    scriptTag.src = "modes/" + inClassName + ".js";
    var headTag = document.getElementsByTagName("head").item(0);
    headTag.appendChild(scriptTag);
```

```
  } // End load().


  /**
   * This function verifies that a given class matches another. In other
   * words, it ensures that all the functions of inBaseClass are found in
   * inClass, which means they have the same public interface. It also
   * checks that the id field is present, which is required by code outside
   * a mode class (note that all other non-function fields are ignored, since
   * they do not contribute to the public interface).
   *
   * @param  inClass      The class to verify.
   * @param  inBaseClass  The class to verify against.
   * @return              True if inClass is "valid", false if not.
   */
  this.verify = function(inClass, inBaseClass) {

    var isValid = true;
    for (i in inBaseClass) {
      if (i != "resultsCurrent" && i != "resultsPrevious" &&
        i != "resultsCurrentNegated" && i != "resultsPreviousNegated" &&
        !inClass[i]) {
        isValid = false;
      }
    }
    return isValid;

  } // End verify().


} // End Classloader class.
```

With those preliminaries out of the way, let's see how this all works.

The first step is a call to the load() method. This method accepts the name of the class to be loaded. This name must match exactly, including case, the name of the JavaScript source file that contains it. Since this Classloader is specific to loading Mode classes, it assumes the source file is found in the modes subdirectory. Here's the load() method:

```
  this.load = function(inClassName) {

    // Dynamically create a new script tag, point it at the mode source file,
    // and append it to the document's head section, thereby loading and
    // parsing it automatically.
    var scriptTag = document.createElement("script");
    scriptTag.src = "modes/" + inClassName + ".js";
    var headTag = document.getElementsByTagName("head").item(0);
    headTag.appendChild(scriptTag);

  } // End load().
```

LOADING REMOTE CONTENT VIA A DYNAMIC SCRIPT TAG

Tangent alert! One of the problems with most Ajax techniques is that they do not work across domains. All current browsers implement a security restriction that says you can make Ajax requests only to the domain that served the original page. This makes many sorts of things much more difficult than they need to be. A number of solutions exist to get around this restriction, and one of the most useful is the dynamic `<script>` tag trick.

Basically, if you create a new `<script>` tag and insert it into the DOM, the browser goes off and loads the source file and evaluates it, just as it does for a `<script>` tag on the page at load time. Since a `<script>` tag does not have a domain restriction, you can do cross-domain calls. Now, if the content that is the source of the `<script>` tag adheres to a special rule, you can essentially do Ajax in this manner. What is that special rule? Simply that the response must contain a JavaScript call to some callback function.

So, when the `<script>` tag is inserted, the browser loads the source file it specifies. This source file contains a call to some JavaScript function that already exists on the page. The browser evaluates this source file, which executes the call to that function. This is akin to the callback function in Ajax, except that it is called only once in this case, as opposed to many times for an Ajax call. In other words, the source of a `<script>` tag *doesn't have to be script*. Well, not in the usual sense anyway; it still is JavaScript.

What I mean by this is best illustrated with a simple example. Let's say we want to retrieve a list of URLs from a remote server that we want to display in an `alert()` box when the user clicks a button. Why we would want to do this is beyond me, but that's why they invented contrived examples. Anyway, let's say we want to do this. Let's further say that the file `js_book_ch4_url_list.txt` exists on the Omnytex web server (which it does, so yes, all of this will work if you try it, but if it should fail for some reason, just create a file with this name and the contents shown next, and place it on some web server somewhere, and change the target URL accordingly). So, when we access `http://www.omnytex.com/js_book_ch4_url_list.txt`, we get the following response:

```
showURLs("www.microsoft.com", "www.omnytex.com", "www.apress.com");
```

Here's the code to do what we want:

```
<html>
<head>
<script>
  function testIt() {
    var scriptTag = document.createElement("script");
    scriptTag.src = "http://www.omnytex.com/js_book_ch4_url_list.txt";
    var headTag = document.getElementsByTagName("head").item(0);
    headTag.appendChild(scriptTag);
  }
  function showURLs() {
    var s = "";
    for (var i = 0; i < showURLs.arguments.length; i++) {
      s += showURLs.arguments[i] + "\n";
    }
    alert(s);
  }
```

```
</script>
</head>
<body>
  <input type="button" value="Click here to display URLs" onClick="testIt();">
</body>
</html>
```

Let's walk through this. The user clicks the button, which calls `testIt()`. In `testIt()`, we create a new `<script>` tag, setting its `src` attribute to point to our remote URL file. This new `<script>` tag is appended to the document's `<head>` element. The browser then goes off and loads the remote file, and evaluates it. This evaluation causes the call to `showURLs()`, which is contained in the remote file, to execute. `showURLs()` executes, and it iterates over the collection of arguments passed to it, which can be none to as many as we want. For each, it appends it to a string, breaking the line after each one. Finally, it pops up an `alert()` showing the string. Blink and you missed it.

Now take another look at the `load()` method in the `Classloader.js` file. Doesn't that look familiar? It's the exact same code, but with a different URL for the `src` attribute.

Once a class has been loaded via the load() method, the verify() method is called. This method accepts the class that was loaded and another class that it is to be verified against. verify() iterates over the properties contained in the class to verify against, and for each, it ensures that the property is present in the class to be verified. If the property isn't present, verify() sets the isValid flag to false. This flag is the return value of the method, so true will be returned if all properties are found. Note that this method checks only for functions. It ignores data fields, except for id, which is a required part of the public interface of a Mode-descendant class. All the other data fields do not contribute to the public interface, so they are ignored.

It is often said that a picture is worth a thousand words, and in the spirit of that statement, Figure 4-7 is a flow diagram showing all the steps involved in loading a class in CalcTron.

This flow is slightly different for the BaseCalc mode. In that case, everything is the same up until the step "JSON includes call to init() of Mode object, JSON is passed to it." This still occurs, but in the case of the BaseCalc class, the init() method is overridden, so it does some work, then calls init() on the superclass (which, in case you are unfamiliar with the term, means the same thing as parent class), namely the Mode class. The rest of the flow after that is again the same. Don't worry if this didn't quite make sense. We haven't looked at the Mode class or the classes for the two calculator modes, so this is kind of jumping the gun just a bit. Let's get to that stuff now to put this all in the proper context.

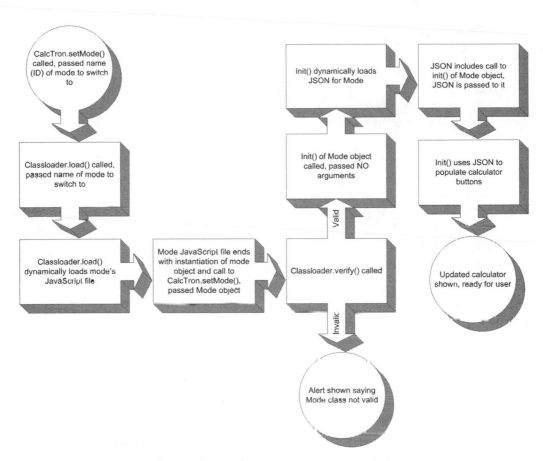

Figure 4-7. *Flow diagram of the steps involved in loading a class*

Writing Mode.js

Every mode that CalcTron supports, including the Standard and BaseCalc modes that come with it, is implemented in a class that extends from the Mode class. The Mode class itself contains some fields that are commonly needed by all calculator modes, and it also includes stub methods for all the methods any calculator mode is expected to implement. Together, these methods form the public interface a Mode implementation class must expose for CalcTron to be able to properly interact with it. You can see the overall structure of the Mode class in the UML diagram in Figure 4-8.

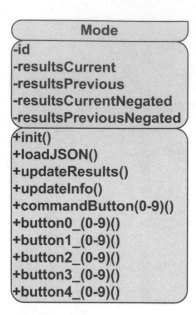

Figure 4-8. *UML diagram of the Mode class*

The first property, id, is actually part of the public interface as well, as this is needed by other code outside a class extending from Mode. However, the others—resultsCurrent, resultsPrevious, resultsCurrentNegated, and resultsPreviousNegated—are *not* considered part of the public interface, because they are needed only within the class itself.

The methods begin with init(), which as you saw during the discussion of the class-loading cycle, is called after the class is loaded and verified to initialize the calculator mode. Most of the time, the implementation of this method in the Mode class suffices, so let's look at that code now:

```
this.init = function(inVal) {

  if (inVal) {

    var mainDiv = $("mainContainer");

    // Size width and height as specified.
    mainDiv.style.width = inVal.mainWidth + "px";
    mainDiv.style.height = inVal.mainHeight + "px";

    // Center the main content div in the browser content area.
    mainDiv.style.left = (calcTron.scrWidth - parseInt(inVal.mainWidth)) / 2;
    mainDiv.style.top = (calcTron.scrHeight - parseInt(inVal.mainHeight)) / 2;

    // Command buttons (10 of them, numbered 0-8).
    for (var i = 0; i < 9; i++) {
      var btn = $("commandButton" + i);
```

```
      if (inVal.commandButtons[i].enabled == "true") {
        btn.style.display = "block";
        btn.value = inVal.commandButtons[i].caption;
      } else {
        btn.style.display = "none";
      }
    }

    // Buttons (50 of them, 10 in a row numbered 0-9 in 5 rows numbered 0-4).
    for (var y = 0; y < 5; y++) {
      for (var x = 0; x < 10; x++) {
        btn = $("button" + y + "_" + x);
        if (inVal.buttons[y][x].enabled == "true") {
          btn.style.display = "block";
          btn.value = inVal.buttons[y][x].caption;
        } else {
          btn.style.display = "none";
        }
      }
    }

  } else {

    this.loadJSON(this.id);

  }

  // Show current mode in info box and clear results div.
  this.updateResults("");
  this.updateInfo(this.id + " Mode");

} // End init().
```

As you may recall, this method is actually called twice during a mode switch. The first time it is called, nothing is passed to it. When that occurs, the else clause kicks in, which results in a call to loadJSON(), passing it the value of the id field, which would have been populated prior to this. loadJSON() is conceptually, and quite literally, just like the load() method of the Classloader class, as you can see here:

```
this.loadJSON = function(inID) {

  var scriptTag = document.createElement("script");
  scriptTag.src = "modes/" + this.id + ".json";
  var headTag = document.getElementsByTagName("head").item(0);
  headTag.appendChild(scriptTag);

} // End loadJSON().
```

A dynamic <script> tag is created, with its src attribute pointing to the JSON file in the modes subdirectory with the name matching the name (id field value) of the mode. This causes the JSON to be loaded and evaluated. When it is evaluated, init() will be called again, this time with the evaluated JSON itself as an argument. When that happens, the if block executes.

First, the if block code sets the width and height of the calculator outer <div> to the values specified by the mainWidth and mainHeight properties in the JSON. This is done because dynamically calculating these values proves to be more difficult than you might at first think, if cross-browser display and proper display under all conditions are important to you. Instead, I decided to put the onus on the mode developer. There's little more to it than a bit of trial and error, but it's not that big a hassle when creating a new mode (I should know—I did it twice).

After that, the calculator is centered using the same basic logic you saw earlier to center the pop-up.

Next, we come to something slightly more interesting: generation of the command buttons.

```
// Command buttons (10 of them, numbered 0-8).
for (var i = 0; i < 9; i++) {
  var btn = $("commandButton" + i);
  if (inVal.commandButtons[i].enabled == "true") {
    btn.style.display = "block";
    btn.value = inVal.commandButtons[i].caption;
  } else {
    btn.style.display = "none";
  }
}
```

Ten command buttons are available in a mode layout: five on top and five at the bottom. The last one on the bottom is always the mode-switch button, so the developer has nine buttons available; hence, the 9 in the for loop. For each iteration, we first get the reference to the button, which, if you recall, already exists. We then check the enabled value in the JSON for the appropriate button. If it is false, then the button is not used, and we set the display style attribute to none to hide it. If it is enabled (true), then we set display to block instead to show it, and also change the label to that specified in the JSON. The event handler is already connected, as seen in calctron.htm, so that's all the work we have to do here.

The input buttons are handled in exactly the same way; however, the developer has a total of fifty different buttons available, ten each in five rows. So, we have two for loops: one for the row (y) and one for each button in the row (x).

Following loadJSON() is the method updateResults(). This simply displays the value of the resultsCurrent field in the results box at the top of the calculator, preceding the value with a negative sign if the resultsCurrentNegated field has a value of true. updateInfo() follows that, and it simply displays its argument in the info box at the bottom of the calculator.

After those two functions is a rather large batch of empty functions—one for each of the calculator's command buttons and input buttons. This is done so that if a calculator mode's implementation class doesn't need a given button, it still will expose an event handler function for it, but that function will do nothing. This just keeps the public interface a known constant, so there's no chance of a button's onClick handler calling a method that doesn't exist. (Well, a developer *could* set one of these methods to null in the implementation class, but he would have to go out of his way to do that, and we can't guard against a developer purposely trying to break something.)

As mentioned, the Mode class is the superclass for all the implementation classes for the calculator modes, so as you can probably surmise, it's now time to look at those implementation classes. We'll also look at the JSON that defines each mode as well, since they go hand in hand.

Writing Standard.json and Standard.js

Now that we've seen the basic Mode class, let's look at the classes that extend from it: the implementation classes that define a CalcTron mode. Let's begin with the Standard mode.

Two items make up a CalcTron mode: the implementation class extending from the Mode class and a JSON file, which describes the mode. For instance, the JSON for the standard mode is shown in Listing 4-3.

Listing 4-3. *The JSON Describing the Standard CalcTron Mode*

```
calcTron.currentMode.init(

  {

    "mainWidth" : "340", "mainHeight" : "248",

    "commandButtons" : [
      { "enabled"   : "false", "caption" : ""          },
      { "enabled"   : "false", "caption" : ""          },
      { "enabled"   : "false", "caption" : ""          },
      { "enabled"   : "true",  "caption" : "Backspace"  },
      { "enabled"   : "true",  "caption" : "Clear"      },
      { "enabled"   : "false", "caption" : ""          },
      { "enabled"   : "false", "caption" : ""          },
      { "enabled"   : "false", "caption" : ""          },
      { "enabled"   : "false", "caption" : ""          },
    ],

    "buttons" : [
      [
        { "enabled" : "false", "caption" : ""      },
        { "enabled" : "false", "caption" : ""      },
        { "enabled" : "false", "caption" : ""      },
        { "enabled" : "false", "caption" : ""      },
        { "enabled" : "false", "caption" : ""      },
        { "enabled" : "true",  "caption" : "7"     },
        { "enabled" : "true",  "caption" : "8"     },
        { "enabled" : "true",  "caption" : "9"     },
        { "enabled" : "true",  "caption" : "/"     },
        { "enabled" : "true",  "caption" : "sqrt"  }
      ],
```

```
[
  { "enabled" : "false",  "caption" : ""        },
  { "enabled" : "false",  "caption" : ""        },
  { "enabled" : "false",  "caption" : ""        },
  { "enabled" : "false",  "caption" : ""        },
  { "enabled" : "false",  "caption" : ""        },
  { "enabled" : "true",   "caption" : "4"       },
  { "enabled" : "true",   "caption" : "5"       },
  { "enabled" : "true",   "caption" : "6"       },
  { "enabled" : "true",   "caption" : "*"       },
  { "enabled" : "true",   "caption" : "%"       }
],
[
  { "enabled" : "false", "caption" : ""         },
  { "enabled" : "false", "caption" : ""         },
  { "enabled" : "false", "caption" : ""         },
  { "enabled" : "false", "caption" : ""         },
  { "enabled" : "false", "caption" : ""         },
  { "enabled" : "true",  "caption" : "1"        },
  { "enabled" : "true",  "caption" : "2"        },
  { "enabled" : "true",  "caption" : "3"        },
  { "enabled" : "true",  "caption" : "-"        },
  { "enabled" : "true",  "caption" : "1/x"      }
],
[
  { "enabled" : "false", "caption" : ""         },
  { "enabled" : "false", "caption" : ""         },
  { "enabled" : "false", "caption" : ""         },
  { "enabled" : "false", "caption" : ""         },
  { "enabled" : "false", "caption" : ""         },
  { "enabled" : "true",  "caption" : "0"        },
  { "enabled" : "true",  "caption" : "+/-"      },
  { "enabled" : "true",  "caption" : "."        },
  { "enabled" : "true",  "caption" : "+"        },
  { "enabled" : "true",  "caption" : "="        }
],
[
  { "enabled" : "false", "caption" : ""         },
  { "enabled" : "false", "caption" : ""         },
  { "enabled" : "false", "caption" : ""         },
  { "enabled" : "false", "caption" : ""         },
  { "enabled" : "false", "caption" : ""         },
  { "enabled" : "false", "caption" : ""         },
  { "enabled" : "false", "caption" : ""         },
  { "enabled" : "false", "caption" : ""         },
  { "enabled" : "false", "caption" : ""         },
  { "enabled" : "false", "caption" : ""         }
```

```
        ]
      ]

   }

);
```

If you've ever seen JSON before, you may be thinking, "That doesn't look quite right." Well, in fact, this is JSON wrapped in a function call. The JSON itself is the argument to the function, or more precisely, an object constructed from it. Recall that when the init() method of the Mode class is first called, by the Classloader class, it is passed nothing, but the second time, it is passed this JSON. So what actually calls init() the second time? The answer is that the JSON does. Well, sort of—the JSON is loaded dynamically using the previously discussed dynamic <script> tag technique.

Like any <script> tag on a page, the browser evaluates the contents returned from the server. In doing so, it executes any JavaScript not contained within a function, as is the case with the call to calcTron.currentMode.init(). During mode loading, the currentMode property of the calcTron instance is pointed to the Standard class loaded before the JSON. So when the JSON loads and is evaluated, the call to init() occurs, and the JSON is passed to it. init() then does its thing, as described previously.

■Tip The dynamic <script> tag technique is becoming more and more common. Yahoo was the first to do it to a degree that people started to become aware of it. It's basically just a way to define a callback function that will be executed when the data returns. The data doesn't need to be JSON, although that is a prevalent return type. It could be an actual object (imagine a class being defined and an instance created instead of JSON, with fields populated, and then the call to init() passing a reference to that object). This is becoming a popular approach because it allows for cross-domain Ajax calls, in essence. As long as the client knows what callback function will be called, and the server adheres to that contract, there are no same-domain limitations, as is usually the case with Ajax. Just think, you and your friends can create CalcTron modes, host them on your own server, and your local copy of CalcTron can access them from anywhere in the world (once you inform CalcTron of these new modes by updating the mode-switch pop-up).

The meaning of the JSON itself is relatively simple. mainWidth and mainHeight, which were mentioned earlier, define the width and height of the calculator <div>. After that comes a group of elements, named commandButtons. Each element in this group defines a single command button. Every button, be it a command button or an input button, has two attributes: enabled and caption. The enabled attribute defines whether the button is visible (true) or not (false). The caption attribute is the text that appears on the button.

After the input buttons is a group named buttons. Within this group are five subgroups, each one corresponding to a row of buttons. Each of these groups contains ten elements, each corresponding to a button.

EVENT HANDLERS

In calctron.htm, each button has an onClick event handler defined. The Mode class includes stub functions, which map to the buttons. The correlation between these functions and the JSON you see here is an implied correlation. For instance, take the command button group:

```
"commandButtons" : [
    { "enabled"    : "false", "caption" : ""          },
    { "enabled"    : "false", "caption" : ""          },
    { "enabled"    : "false", "caption" : ""          },
    { "enabled"    : "true",  "caption" : "Backspace" },
    { "enabled"    : "true",  "caption" : "Clear"     },
    { "enabled"    : "false", "caption" : ""          },
    { "enabled"    : "false", "caption" : ""          },
    { "enabled"    : "false", "caption" : ""          },
    { "enabled"    : "false", "caption" : ""          },
]
```

How do we know which function will be called when the Backspace button is clicked? It isn't named here, so how do we know? Simply put, it's positional. The first button defined in this JSON would call commandButton0() when clicked, the second commandButton1(), the third commandButton2(), and finally, Backspace would call commandButton3(). For the input buttons, consider the first row as an example:

```
[
    { "enabled" : "false", "caption" : ""      },
    { "enabled" : "false", "caption" : ""      },
    { "enabled" : "false", "caption" : ""      },
    { "enabled" : "false", "caption" : ""      },
    { "enabled" : "false", "caption" : ""      },
    { "enabled" : "true",  "caption" : "7"     },
    { "enabled" : "true",  "caption" : "8"     },
    { "enabled" : "true",  "caption" : "9"     },
    { "enabled" : "true",  "caption" : "/"     },
    { "enabled" : "true",  "caption" : "sqrt"  }
]
```

This works in exactly the same way, except that we need to know the row and column of the button in this case. For the first row of input buttons, the row number is 0. So, the first button here would call the function button0_0(). Jumping down to the number 7 button on the screen, it would call function button0_5().

With the JSON out of the way, we can move on to the Standard.js file, the Standard mode implementation class itself. The UML diagram of the Standard class is shown in Figure 4-9.

In this diagram, I wrote the commandButton and button methods in shorthand because there are so many of them. The shorthand simply means that there are commandButton0(), commandButton1(), commandButton2(), and so on, up to commandButton9(). For the button methods, there are button0_0(), button0_1(), button0_2(), and so on, up to button0_9(), and then this repeats for button1_x(), button2_x(), button3_x(), and button4_x(), where x is 0–9.

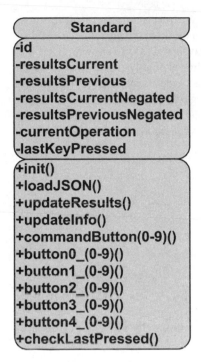

Figure 4-9. *UML diagram of the Standard class*

As you look at the source (which you should have already downloaded from the Apress web site), the first thing you see is the id field being set to Standard. Setting the id field is necessary for any implementation class you write, and this value must match exactly, including case, the .js and .json files for the mode. Next are two fields specific to this mode, currentOperation and lastKeyPressed. These will likely be needed by any mode you write as well, but I left them out of the Mode class because there could be some situations where they aren't required. Their names should make clear what they are: storage of what operation is currently being performed (the last operation button clicked, such as +, -, *, or /) and storage of what the last button clicked was (this is needed for proper operation, as you'll see).

I want to jump around just a little to cover the methods in a slightly more logical order than they appear in the code. First, let's look at the method commandButton3(), which correlates to the Backspace button:

```
this.commandButton3 = function() {

  if (this.resultsCurrent != "") {
    this.resultsCurrent =
      this.resultsCurrent.substr(0, this.resultsCurrent.length - 1);
    this.updateResults();
  }

} // End commandButton3().
```

It's admittedly not a complex function. After we're sure we have a current result (because if we don't, there's nothing to delete and hence we would get an error if we tried), we cut the last character off from the current result string, and call updateResults() to show it.

This is probably a good time to answer a question that has probably already occurred to you: why exactly are the resultsCurrent and resultsPrevious fields always strings? The answer is that it makes backspacing easier. It also makes showing negative numbers easier, and makes base conversions, which are done in the BaseCalc mode, easier. Leaving these values as strings until calculations are actually performed on them just makes the code a little cleaner and less verbose.

The Clear button is also a very simple bit of code:

```
this.commandButton4 = function() {

  this.resultsCurrent = "";
  this.updateResults();

} // End commandButton4().
```

I'm willing to bet you don't even need an explanation of that, so let's just keep moving right along.

Each of the number button handlers is pretty much the same, so let's look at just one:

```
this.button0_5 = function() {

  this.checkLastPressed();
  this.lastKeyPressed = "7";
  this.resultsCurrent += "7";
  this.updateResults();

} // End button0_5().
```

As discussed, by pure positional reckoning, the number 7 button winds up mapping to the button0_5() method. In it, we first call the checkLastPressed() method, which we'll look at next. For now, let's skip over it. We record 7 as being the last button pressed, and then add the digit 7 to the current results. We then redisplay the current results. The net result is that if 31 were showing in the results box, it would now show 317, and we would know that the last button pressed was 7.

Now let's see why knowing which button was last pressed is important by looking at that checkLastPressed() method:

```
this.checkLastPressed = function() {

  if (this.lastKeyPressed == "+" || this.lastKeyPressed == "-" ||
    this.lastKeyPressed == "*" || this.lastKeyPressed == "/") {
    // Time to start entering a new number, but save the current one first.
    this.resultsPrevious = this.resultsCurrent;
    this.resultsPreviousNegated = this.resultsCurrentNegated;
    this.resultsCurrent = "";
    this.resultsCurrentNegated = false;
  }
```

```
  // When equals is pressed, it's also time to start a new number, but in
  // that case we clear the previous number too.
  if (this.lastKeyPressed == "=") {
    this.lastKeyPressed = "";
    this.resultsCurrent = "";
    this.resultsCurrentNegated = false;
    this.resultsPrevious = "";
    this.resultsPreviousNegated = false;
    this.currentOperation = "";
  }

} // End checkLastPressed().
```

This function is needed because it's only when a new button is clicked that certain things can happen. For instance, when the user clicks +, -, *, or /, it is time to start a new number. Open the standard Windows calculator and enter a number, click one of those buttons, and then click a number button again. Notice that a new number is started; the old one is cleared (although it is stored). We want to mimic that functionality, and the only way to do it, without having a lot of duplicate code all over the place, is to have this function do that work for us. So, we check if one of those four operation buttons was clicked. If it was, we copy the current number to the previous field (resultsPrevious = resultsCurrent) and we also copy whether the value is negative (resultsPreviousNegated = resultsCurrentNegated). We then clear the current number and make it positive. The net result is that it works like the standard Windows calculator.

The user clicking the equal sign is also a situation that needs to be handled here. Clicking the equal sign obviously performs some calculation, and that is done in the event handler for that button. But what happens when the next button is clicked? We need to start entering a new number, but in that case, we're not saving the current value as the previous value. Instead, we are just starting a new number. The equal sign button is almost like a reset button, so we need to clear a few extra fields when it is clicked, namely lastKeyPressed and currentOperation.

Using this as a segue, and not the kind you can ride on,[2] let's jump down now to that method that deals with the equal sign button:

```
this.button3_9 = function() {

  if (this.currentOperation) {
    var answer = 0;
    // Negate the current value if the flag says to.
    var resCurrent = parseFloat(this.resultsCurrent);
    if (isNaN(resPrevious)) {
      resPrevious = resCurrent;
    }
    if (this.resultsCurrentNegated) {
      resCurrent = resCurent * -1;
    }
```

---

2. Segway, that annoying scooter all the cool kids in Silicon Valley have, was the brainchild of famous uber-genius Dean Karnen. Yes, I know, bad pun, but work with me here!

```
      // Negate the previous value if the flag says to.
      var resPrevious = parseFloat(this.resultsPrevious);
      if (this.resultsPreviousNegated) {
        resPrevious = resPrevious * -1;
      }
      // Now perform the current operation.
      switch(this.currentOperation) {
        case "+":
          answer = resPrevious + resCurrent;
        break;
        case "-":
          answer = resPrevious - resCurrent;
        break;
        case "*":
          answer = resPrevious * resCurrent;
        break;
        case "/":
          answer = resPrevious / resCurrent;
        break;
      }
      // Reset some variables so we're ready for the next operation or input
      // key, and finally, update the results to show the answer.
      this.resultsCurrent = "" + answer;
      this.resultsPrevious = "";
      this.resultsPreviousNegated = false;
      this.currentOperation = null;
      this.lastKeyPressed = "=";
      this.updateResults();
    }

  } // End button3_9().
```

First, a trivial rejection: is there a current operation to perform? This means that if the user enters a number and just clicks the equal sign, nothing will happen. If there is a current operation, we start by getting the numeric form of the current value. If the resultsCurrentNegated flag indicates it is a negative number, multiple it by –1 to make it negative. Then we do the same for the previous number. We also do a check here: if there is no previous result, which means that parseFloat() resulted in the value not being a number (which we determine by using the built-in isNaN() function), we make the previous value the current value. This allows us to mimic the operation of the standard Windows calculator in that you can do 9+= and get 18, and then += again gives you 36, and so on.

After that, the code switches on the current operation and performs the appropriate operation. Next, we set resultsCurrent to the answer, appending it to an empty string to convert it to a string. We clear the previous value, reset the negated flag to false, clear the current operation, and record the equal sign as the last button pressed. Finally, we display the answer by calling updateResults() (remember that updateResults() shows the value of resultsCurrent, which we just set to the answer). It's really pretty simple.

That covers the operations involving two numbers. What about those that involve only a single number—square root and reciprocal? Well, let's look at square root first:

```
this.button0_9 = function() {

  if (this.resultsCurrent != "") {
    this.resultsCurrent = Math.sqrt(parseFloat(this.resultsCurrent)) + "";
    this.updateResults();
  }

} // End button0_9().
```

As long as there is a current value, we use the Math package's sqrt() function to do the work, appending a blank string onto the result so that the value we put into resultsCurrent is still a string. Then we display the new number by calling updateResults(), and that's that.

Reciprocal is similarly easy:

```
this.button2_9 = function() {

  if (this.resultsCurrent != "") {
    this.resultsCurrent = (1 / parseFloat(this.resultsCurrent)) + "";
    this.updateResults();
  }

} // End button2_9().
```

Only one function remains, and that's percentage. Percentage is a bit of a hybrid in that it requires two numbers like addition, subtraction, multiplication, and division, but it operates immediately when the % button is clicked, so the calculation is performed in the event handler method, as it is for square root and reciprocal. Here's the code for that method:

```
this.button1_9 = function() {

  if (this.resultsCurrent != "" && this.resultsPrevious != "") {
    var a = parseFloat(this.resultsPrevious) / 100;
    var b = a * parseFloat(this.resultsCurrent);
    this.resultsCurrent = b + "";
    this.updateResults();
  }

} // End button1_9().
```

The check to make sure we have a current value also now includes a check to be sure we have a previous value. Once we know we have both, we get the numeric version of each, and divide the previous value by 100. Then multiplying that result by the current value results in a percentage value. So, we again set resultsCurrent to the answer and display it with updateResults().

The only thing left to discuss is how exactly this class extends the Mode class. The answer is found in the last two lines of code in the Standard.js file (not including comments):

```
// Standard inherits from Mode.
Standard.prototype = new Mode();
// Continue the sequence of events after this class is loaded.
calcTron.setMode(new Standard());
```

The prototype concept was discussed in Chapter 2, so I refer you to that chapter if the first line isn't clear. That single line implements the inheritance, and it's as simple as that.

The second line, however, is new, and it is what continues the class-loading cycle as previously discussed.

And that covers the Standard CalcTron mode. The BaseCalc mode is next.

Writing BaseCalc.json and BaseCalc.js

In the interest of saving space, I won't show the JSON for this mode because, frankly, once you've seen one mode's JSON, you've pretty much seen 'em all. You should take a look at it on your own, but don't spend more than a minute on it if you've already examined the JSON for the Standard mode—it's substantially the same.

The BaseCalc mode implementation class is also substantially similar to the Standard mode class, but there are some differences. To begin, let's examine the UML diagram for it, shown in Figure 4-10.

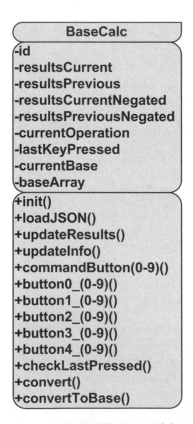

Figure 4-10. *UML diagram of the BaseCalc class*

As you would certainly expect, it contains all the same fields and methods as the Standard class owing to the fact that they both extend the Mode class. It also contains a few additional items though, as is allowed when extending a class. The currentBase field records the number base of the current value: decimal, hexadecimal, binary, or octal. The baseArray is an array of alphanumeric values that is used during base conversions, as you'll see shortly. In addition to these extra fields, you also see a couple additional methods: convert() and convertToBase().(). We'll get to those soon, but let's look at some plumbing first.

As you examine this code, you'll see that it is very similar to the Standard class, but one difference should jump out at you: BaseCalc implements an init() method. In fact, it overrides init() in the superclass (Mode). Let's see what bizarreness is going on there exactly:

```
this.init = function(inVal) {

  if (inVal) {

    // Initialize array for base conversions.
    this.baseArray[1] = "0";
    this.baseArray[2] = "1";
    this.baseArray[3] = "2";
    this.baseArray[4] = "3";
    this.baseArray[5] = "4";
    this.baseArray[6] = "5";
    this.baseArray[7] = "6";
    this.baseArray[8] = "7";
    this.baseArray[9] = "8";
    this.baseArray[10] = "9";
    this.baseArray[11] = "A";
    this.baseArray[12] = "B";
    this.baseArray[13] = "C";
    this.baseArray[14] = "D";
    this.baseArray[15] = "E";
    this.baseArray[16] = "F";

    // Call superclass constructor. Note that this only works if the
    // method of the superclass does not reference anything specific to the
    // subclass... see the notes about the id field on the next statement!
    BaseCalc.prototype.init(inVal);

    // Note that the call to init() of the superclass will result in the
    // information bar saying "null Mode" because the this reference points
    // to the instance of Mode that is the prototype for this BaseCalc
    // instance. So, we need to set it here using the id field of this
    // instance so what's in the info bar is correct.
    this.updateInfo(this.id + " Mode");

  } else {
```

```
    // Load the JSON for this tab.
    this.loadJSON(this.id);


  }

} // End init().
```

Because this version of init() overrides that found in Mode, any time calcTron.
currentMode.init() is called (because currentMode will be pointing to an instance of BaseCalc
when we switch to that mode), the version of init() seen here will be executed, *not* the one in
Mode, as is the case with the Standard class. The first time it is called, no value is passed, so the
else clause is executed, and the JSON for the mode is loaded. This is what happens in the Mode
class's version of init() as well.

The second time it is called, however, the loaded JSON will be passed in, so we wind up in
the if block. There, the first thing you see is the baseArray being initialized with values. We'll
skip over the purpose of that array for a little while longer; for now, it's enough to know it is
populated with values here.

Next, you see an interesting thing that might be new to you in JavaScript: calling the superclass version of a function. To do so, we reference the prototype of the BaseCalc class, and call
init() on it. You can think of BaseCalc.prototype as being equivalent to super() in Java, if you
are familiar with Java. The difference is that you must name the method you want to call in
JavaScript; hence, init() is tacked on. This call carries the JSON input argument with it, so the
usual init() functionality you saw in the Mode base class executes now. Once that call returns,
we update the info bar to state the new mode. The astute reader might wonder why this is
necessary, since it is done in the Mode class's init() method. Here is the code that does so in Mode:

```
    this.updateInfo(this.id + " Mode");
```

The problem here is that the this reference points not to the BaseCalc instance, but instead to
Mode itself, and we therefore get the wrong value showing up in the info bar. So, we essentially
override what is done in Mode's init() method when control returns to BaseCalc's init()
method, and the problem is solved.

The lastKeyPressed() method of BaseCalc is virtually identical to the version from Standard,
with one extra line of code in the first if block. This line of code takes the current value and
converts it to decimal:

```
    this.convert("dec");
```

Any time we do calculations, we do so in decimal, and then just convert the result to whatever the current base is. Note that we have a field, currentBase, that tells us the base of the
current value, but we don't have a field to indicate the base of the previous value. The reason is
that we know, because of this line of code, that it's always going to be decimal. As I said, the rest
of the method is identical to what you've seen already.

The Backspace and Clear command buttons are also identical to their Standard equivalents, so
there's no need to review them here.

Next, we come to the four command buttons that allow us to switch modes. They are all
similar, so we'll look at just the one for hexadecimal here:

```
this.commandButton1 = function() {

  this.updateInfo("Hexadecimal");
  if (this.resultsCurrent != "") {
    this.convert("hex");
    this.updateResults();
  }
  this.currentBase = "hex";

} // End commandButton1().
```

Here, we're just displaying the new mode in the info bar at the bottom. And if we have a current value, we convert it to the new base with a call to convert(), passing it the base to convert to—hex in this case (dec, oct, and bin are the other valid parameter values). We update the result display as well, which gives us the ability to convert the current number to any base. Finally, we record the new number base, and we're finished.

Like the command buttons, the input buttons are all nearly the same as those in the Standard class. However, there are some differences in a few buttons. Let's take the number 7 button as an example:

```
this.button0_5 = function() {

  if (this.currentBase == "bin") {
    return;
  }
  this.checkLastPressed();
  this.lastKeyPressed = "7";
  this.resultsCurrent += "7";
  this.updateResults();

} // End button0_5().
```

Here, we begin with a check to ensure that the current number base isn't binary. If it is binary, we immediately return and do nothing else. This has the effect that when binary is the number base, only the 0 and 1 buttons will be responsive; all others will do nothing (all of the buttons after 0 and 1 have this check in them). Likewise, if you look at 8 and 9, you'll see a check to return immediately if the number base is binary *or* octal. And the A–F buttons will return immediately if the number base is anything other than hexadecimal. The net result is that only buttons valid for the currently selected number base will be reactive, as you would expect.

The +, -, *, and / buttons are the same as in Standard, so we'll skip them here. There is no negation, percentage, square root, or reciprocal in this mode, so nothing to see there either.

Now we come to the method for the equal sign. It is again largely like its counterpart in Standard, so we'll just look at the differences. First, recall a while back I mentioned that all calculations are done in decimal? Well, as you may have guessed, one of the first things we see is a conversion of the current value to decimal (the previous value is already in decimal, so only the current value is of concern). After that is the same sort of switch on the current operation as in Standard. After that is something a little different:

```
// Next, convert the new current value to the current base.  Before we
// can do that though, we need to set the current base to decimal to
// match the answer we have.
var storedCurrentBase = this.currentBase;
this.currentBase = "dec";
this.convert(storedCurrentBase);
this.currentBase = storedCurrentBase;
```

We need to convert the answer to the current number base. However, you'll notice when we look at the convert() method that the currentBase field is changed by convert() to the number base specified for the conversion. This is because convert() is used by the four number base command buttons to convert the current value, and also record the new number base. So what we have here is saving the current number base first, then calling convert(), which results in currentBase being set to dec. We then set currentBase to the number base stored before the call to convert(), which may or may not have been dec, and the net result is that the current number base is preserved; the change by convert() is effectively undone.

Next up is the convert() method itself:

```
this.convert = function(inNewBase) {

  var currentValue = null;
  switch (this.currentBase) {
    case "dec":
      currentValue = parseInt(this.resultsCurrent, 10);
    break;
    case "hex":
      currentValue = parseInt(this.resultsCurrent, 16);
    break;
    case "oct":
      currentValue = parseInt(this.resultsCurrent, 8);
    break;
    case "bin":
      currentValue = parseInt(this.resultsCurrent, 2);
    break;
  }
  switch (inNewBase) {
    case "dec":
      currentValue = this.convertToBase(currentValue, 10);
    break;
    case "hex":
      currentValue = this.convertToBase(currentValue, 16);
    break;
    case "oct":
      currentValue = this.convertToBase(currentValue, 8);
    break;
```

```
    case "bin":
      currentValue = this.convertToBase(currentValue, 2);
    break;
  }
  this.resultsCurrent = "" + currentValue;

} // End convert().
```

It begins by taking the current value and getting it as a numeric value. To do this, we use the parseInt() function. This function takes the radix, or number base, of the number as its second argument (its first argument is the number to convert). So, we switch on currentBase to determine this. Once we have the numeric version of the current value, we then switch on inNewBase and call convertToBase(), passing it the current value and the radix to convert to. The current value is then set to the number in the new base, converted to a string.

You may have noticed that no real conversion per se happens in convert(). That function is performed by the convertToBase() method:

```
this.convertToBase = function (inNumber, inNewBase) {

  var str = "";
  var calc = inNumber;
  while (calc >= inNewBase) {
    var divVal = calc % inNewBase;
    calc = Math.floor(calc / inNewBase);
    str += this.baseArray[divVal + 1];
  }
  str += this.baseArray[calc + 1];
  var len = str.length;
  var fnl = "";
  for (var j = 0; j < len; j++) {
    var a = (len - j) - 1;
    var b = len - j;
    fnl += str.substring(a, b);
  }
  return fnl;

} // End convertToBase().
```

As you can see, this is where that baseArray field comes into play. In brief, this function continually divides the incoming number by the radix, and for each division, adds the appropriate elements from baseArray to an output string. That iteration ends when the result of the division is smaller than the number base. At that point, the remainder is used as a lookup into baseArray as well. The output string now needs to be reversed, because building it up results in the answer in reverse. Once that reverse is done, the string is returned, and what we have is the input number converted to the requested base.

And that concludes our look at BaseCalc, and in fact, CalcTron as a whole.

Suggested Exercises

I admit to never being a big fan of math growing up, but as an adult, I've come to appreciate it more, both from a practical standpoint and as a purely intellectual pursuit. It is my hope that CalcTron can at least start you down that same path. To that end, I offer a few suggestions on where you can take this project next to learn more not only about JavaScript, but mathematics in general:

Add memory functions: This is a simple one to get you started. Most calculators have memory functions, but CalcTron does not. I purposely left these out to give you a nice, easy suggestion to start with, so get to it.

Expand `Classloader`: Modify the `Classloader` class to be more generic, and allow it to load *any* class. Perhaps pass the `load()` method a fully qualified package name, such as `com.omnytex.javascript.SomeClass`, and then use the `com.omnytex.javascript` portion as a subdirectory (so it becomes `com/omnytex/javascript`). Also, change it so that the `load()` method accepts the class to verify against as an argument, and automatically call `verify()` when `load()` completes (you should probably make the verification step optional). Also, research to see if there's a way to determine if a `<script>` tag did not load successfully, and add that as a verification step (as I write this, I am not even sure this is possible, so it's going to be a fun exercise for both of us).

Add conversion capabilities: Originally, this chapter was to have been followed by one about building ConvertTron. The concept was to expand CalcTron to include conversion capabilities. Well, things change in the publishing business as a project evolves, so that chapter didn't make the cut. However, the basic idea is still a very good one. Conversions shouldn't be too difficult to add in, so go for it.

Add simple algebra functions: How about a simple algebra solver? I personally wouldn't try to create the code to solve simultaneous equations or anything like that, but $9=x+5$ shouldn't be too tough to solve. Writing an algorithm to handle such simple equations probably shouldn't be too difficult, but should be just challenging enough to be a good learning exercise.

Summary

This chapter's project seemed like a pretty simple idea: a JavaScript-based calculator. Far be it for me to leave things simple though. We took the basic calculator concept and turned it into an extensible framework that can grow as your mathematical requirements do. You saw how some common object-oriented techniques can be implemented in JavaScript, and how those techniques allow you to enhance the basic application as you see fit. You even saw a way to write a rudimentary classloader that verifies that the classes you load are valid (well, somewhat anyway) for the application's purposes.

You also saw how you can dynamically load JavaScript and JSON without reloading the page and without using the `XMLHttpRequest` object that implies Ajax techniques. Additionally, you saw a bit of what the Rico library has to offer. I hope you'll agree that this chapter enforces the "never judge a book by its cover" saying. Even a relatively simple project can expose you to some very interesting techniques.

■ ■ ■

CHAPTER 5

Doing the Monster Mash:
A Mashup

A long time ago, some god-like developer came up with the concept of an Application Programming Interface (API). In short, an API is nothing but a known (to those that might use it) interface to a program or system. The developer came up with this idea, and everyone saw it, and saw that it was a Good Thing™. But, in the immortal words of Dr. Leonard H. McCoy, ". . . engineers, they love to change things." We couldn't just stick with the term API. No, we just *had* to come up with something new, and that something is the term *mashup*. Since it's a term that is all the rage these days, and also something that often involves JavaScript to a large degree, it's most definitely an appropriate topic for this book. So, in this chapter, I'll introduce the concept of the mashup, and then we'll put that concept to use in a handy little application.

What's a Mashup?

A mashup, as it has come to be known, is basically a web site or application that takes content from multiple sources, most usually via some sort of public programmatic interface, and integrates it all into a new experience—that is, a new application. If this sounds a bit like the promise of web services to you, you aren't too far off. In fact, web services are sometimes involved in mashups, although that setup typically involves a server infrastructure and some server-side code, *vis-à-vis*. You won't typically call on *true* web services (SOAP, UDDI, WSDL, and all that the term *web services* typically denotes) from a JavaScript client, and almost certainly not from a web browser (not without plug-ins or similar technology, generally).

No, in recent times, the term mashup has generally come to mean browser-based JavaScript clients aggregating content through public APIs from various companies and vendors to form new applications. These APIs are often referred to as web services, and even though they may not truly be web services in the sense of using the full technology stack, they fulfill the same basic goal as those types of web services. They provide services and function over a network—specifically, the Web—so calling them web services isn't really too far-fetched!

Many companies are getting into the API business, including companies you've certainly heard of: Google, Yahoo, Amazon, and eBay, just to name a few. Google and Yahoo have really led the charge, and Yahoo, in particular, originated a neat trick that will be central to the application we'll build in this chapter.

Mashups are also a part of what people often mean when they use the term Web 2.0. Web 2.0 means different things to different people, but sharing resources is usually part of what people mean by it, so mashups certainly fit right in.

One of the other things that is often lumped under Web 2.0 is effects. Take a look at a site like Digg, for instance. I was going to insert a screenshot here, but truthfully, it wouldn't get the point across because it has to be seen live. So please visit http://www.digg.com, if you aren't already a frequent visitor (and you should be, by the way!) and just look around a bit. As you do, take note of the various effects. For instance, assuming you aren't signed in, try to click the Digg It button next to an article. Notice how the text is faded and you get a little pop-up over it telling you about signing up? Now, if you create an account, sign in, and try clicking that button again, you'll see the Digg count fade out, then fade back in with the new value. These are all examples of the kinds of UI effects that most consider a part of Web 2.0.

Monster Mash(up) Requirements and Goals

Now, with all of that about mashups in mind, let's discuss what this chapter's application will do and what it will demonstrate.

- The basic function of the application is to be able to enter a ZIP code and to get from that a list of hotels.

- For each hotel, we should be able to click its name and see some extended information.

- In addition to extended information, we would also like to see a map of the area.

- We should be able to zoom in and out on the map.

- The UI will use various effects provided by the well-known script.aculo.us library.

- We will utilize some APIs from Google and Yahoo to get the hotel information and maps.

- This application should be purely browser-based and not require any server component to function.

All of this will result in an application that is fully buzzword-compliant and very much fits the most common definition of Web 2.0 applications. Let's start by taking a look at the Yahoo and Google APIs.

The Yahoo APIs

Yahoo did something very cool a short while ago, and it is this one cool thing that makes the application in this chapter possible. Before we can discuss that though, we have to discuss what was going on before the coolness occurred.

For a while now, many companies have been exposing public APIs for people to use, Yahoo among them. For instance, you could perform a Yahoo search remotely, or you could get a Yahoo map from your own application, and so on. These APIs—these "web services," if you will—usually used XML as their data-transport mechanism. You would post some XML to a given URL, and you would get an XML response back. It was (and still is) as simple as that. These types of services don't require all the web services like SOAP, UDDI, WSDL, and the like.

You may have heard the term *Ajax*, which stands for Asynchronous JavaScript And XML. In fact, if you read Chapter 4, you already saw Ajax in action a bit (although ironically, as we'll be doing here, not using the prototypical XMLHttpRequest object). We'll be getting into Ajax in detail in later chapters, but for now, it is enough to know that Ajax is a technique by which you can make a request of a server and use the results it returns in some way *without* reloading the entire page. The most common operation is simply to insert the returned result into the page somewhere, essentially performing an out-of-band partial update of the page. Ajax usually (and some may say necessarily, but I disagree) implies the use of the XMLHttpRequest object in the browser to make requests.

XMLHttpRequest is a component that makes the request to the server on your behalf and then calls a specified JavaScript callback function to process the result. For the sake of the discussion here, you need to be aware that this object presents one consistent limitation, which is known as the *same-domain* restriction. This means that the XMLHttpRequest object will not allow a request to a domain other than the domain from which the document it is in was served. For instance, if you have a page named page1.htm located at http://www.omnytex.com, you can make requests to any URL at www.omnytex.com. However, if you try to make a request to something at www.yahoo.com, the XMLHttpRequest object won't allow it. This means that the APIs Yahoo exposes aren't of much use to you if you try to access them directly from a browser.

There are ways around this same-domain restriction. Probably the most common is to write a server-side component on your own server that acts as a proxy. So you can make requests via XMLHttpRequest to something like www.omnytex.com/proxy, which makes a request to something at www.yahoo.com for you and returns the results. This is very cool.

However, wouldn't it be so much more useful if you could make the request directly to Yahoo from the browser and not need a server-side component? Yes, indeed it would be! And as you probably have guessed, there is a way to do it. Take a look at the following bit of JavaScript:

```
var scriptTag = document.createElement("script");
scriptTag.setAttribute("src", "www.yahoo.com/someAPI");
scriptTag.setAttribute("type", "text/javascript");
var headTag = document.getElementsByTagName("head").item(0);
headTag.appendChild(scriptTag);
```

So, what we have here is a new <script> tag being created. We set the src attribute to point to some API at Yahoo, and finally we append that new tag to the <head> of the document. The browser will go off and retrieve the resource at the specified URL, and then evaluate it, just as it does for any imported JavaScript file.

Now, in and of itself, that isn't very useful. As I said, the Yahoo APIs return XML, and XML being evaluated by the browser won't do much (some browsers may generate a DOM object from it, but even still, that on its own isn't of much use). Unlike with the XMLHttpRequest object, you don't get any events to work with, callback functions that can act upon what was returned, and so on.

Now we come to the bit of coolness I mentioned before!

Let's say we have some XML being returned by a Yahoo service like so:

```
<name>Frank</name>
```

It may not be very interesting, but it's perfectly valid XML. So what is the JSON equivalent to that XML? It's nothing more than this:

```
{ "name" : "Frank" }
```

OK, now suppose that we pass that JSON to a JavaScript function like so:

```
someFunction( { "name" : "Frank" } );
```

What is the parameter passed to someFunction()? As it turns out, it's an object constructed from the JSON. This means that if someFunction() is this:

```
function someFunction(obj) {
  alert(obj.name);
}
```

the result is an alert pop-up saying "Frank."

Are you maybe starting to see what Yahoo might have done? If you are saying that the return is something like this:

```
someFunction( { "name" : "Frank" } );
```

then you are absolutely right!

What Yahoo came up with is the idea of returning JSON in place of XML, and wrapping the JSON in a function call. When you call the API function, you tell it what the callback function is. So let's say you wanted to interact with some Yahoo API that returns a person's name, as we've been discussing as our example. Your page might look something like this:

```
<html>
  <head>
    <title>Dummy Yahoo API Test</title>
    <script>
      function makeRequest() {
        var scriptTag = document.createElement("script");
        scriptTag.setAttribute("src", "www.yahoo.com/someAPI/callback= ➡
myCallback&output=json");
        scriptTag.setAttribute("type", "text/javascript");
        var headTag = document.getElementsByTagName("head").item(0);
        headTag.appendChild(scriptTag);
      }
      function myCallback(inJSON) {
        alert(inJSON.name);
      }
    </script>
  </head>
  <body>
    <input type="button" value="Test" onClick="makeRequest();">
  </body>
</html>
```

When you click the button, makeRequest() is called, and it uses that dynamic <script> tag trick to call the Yahoo API function. Notice the URL, which specifies the name of the callback function and that we want to get back JSON, instead of the usual XML. Now, when the response comes back, the browser evaluates what was inserted into the document via the `<script>` tag, which would be this:

```
myCallback( { "name" : "Frank" } );
```

`myCallback()` is called at that point, with the object resulting from evaluation of the JSON being passed to it. You can load this page from any domain, and it will work. Hence, we've done what the `XMLHttpRequest` object does (in a basic sense anyway), and we've gotten around the same-domain limitation. Sweet!

Yahoo was the first to use this hack (that I am aware of), but as you'll see, other companies have begun to follow suit, because what this allows is purely client-side mashups and API utilization. No longer do you need a server-side proxy. You can now make the requests across domains directly.

■**Caution** While this technique is very useful because it allows you to make direct requests to any server you want, it also has the potential for malicious code to be introduced. Remember that what is being returned is script that winds up executing with the same privileges as any other script on the page. This means that there is the potential for scams like stealing cookies, spoofing, phishing, and so on. You therefore want to take care in your choice of services and organizations. Accessing APIs from Yahoo or Google, for instance, isn't likely to present any security issues, but less well-known companies may not be quite as safe.

Now that you know the basics of how we're going to be interacting with the Yahoo APIs, as well as the Google APIs, as it turns out, let's take a look at the Yahoo functions that we'll be using in this application.

Yahoo Maps Map Image Service

Yahoo is going to be providing the maps that you can see on the right side of the application (for a preview, see Figure 5-2). Yahoo Maps is a service that has been around for a while, even before a public interface was provided for it. It allows you to get maps for a given address, as well as access other features, such as traffic and local places of interest. The API Yahoo provides has a number of different services, but for our purposes, we'll be focusing on the Map Image service.

The Yahoo Maps Map Image API allows you to get a reference to a graphic of a map generated according to the parameters you specify in your request. You may specify latitude and longitude or address in your request (we'll be specifying address).

This service is referenced via a simple HTTP request, such as the following:

```
http://api.local.yahoo.com/MapsService/V1/mapImage?appid=YahooDemo&location=11719
```

The `location` parameter specified is just a US ZIP code, and the `appid` is an ID you get when you register for the services, as discussed in the next section. If you go ahead and paste that into the address bar of your web browser, you'll see the following response:

```
<Result>
http://img.maps.yahoo.com/mapimage?MAPDATA=ytUWRed6wXWoR2TGzwl3wROg3iyHedtGDvtw ➥
766fmR4iboSayYoDOI4llk594b5QaoMqKvZB5AdndE5FtDXv8lT8apVTrjOY5Zuhrhiugmeogq5t ➥
GHi5&mvt=m
</Result>
<!--
 ws01.search.re2.yahoo.com uncompressed/chunked Sun Dec 10 22:18:44 PST 2006
-->
```

What you've gotten back is a reference to an image now sitting on Yahoo's servers. If you pluck out the following URL:

```
http://img.maps.yahoo.com/mapimage?MAPDATA=ytUWRed6wXWoR2TGzwl3wROg3iyHedtGDvtw ➥
766fmR4iboSayYoDOI4llk594b5QaoMqKvZB5AdndE5FtDXv8lT8apVTrjOY5Zuhrhiugmeogq5t ➥
GHi5&mvt=m
```

and put that in the address bar of a web browser, you'll see an image that is a map of the Bellport/Mastic Beach area of Long Island, New York.

You can also add some parameters to the original request. For instance, you can specify that you want a GIF back (by default, you get a PNG file), and you can specify that instead of XML, you want JSON back. The URL would then look like this:

```
http://api.local.yahoo.com/MapsService/V1/mapImage?appid=YahooDemo&location=11719 ➥
&image_type=gif&output=json&callback=myCallback
```

Now the response looks like this:

```
myCallback({"ResultSet":{"Result":"http:\/\/image.maps.yahoo.com\/mapimage? ➥
MAPDATA=cgnWqud6wXUpZCKOcjzKJ3PPgRQkY6thMdXo4raWKRcxvbRSpJ67PGisuDp5YO829Zi5fd ➥
hWYTOm5mmvfBZCqHKDBG8ePGPcc8AlFAuhbWwd6rPOwZ67&mvt=m"}});
```

All you need to do now is write the `myCallback()` function and make it somehow display the images, like this:

```
function myCallback(inJSON) {
  document.getElementById("someImgTag").src = inJSON.ResultSet.Result;
}
```

And as you'll soon see, that's just about all this application is doing as far as interacting with Yahoo's services goes! A few other parameters are used in the application, as summarized in Table 5-1.

Table 5-1. *Some Yahoo Map Image Service Parameters Used in Monster Mash(up)*

Parameter	Meaning
width	The width of the map image.
height	The height of the map image.
zoom	The zoom factor to apply to the map. This is a value in the range 1–12, where 1 represents street level and 12 represents regional level (a little wider than state level).

Yahoo Registration

Most API services require you to register to use their APIs, and Yahoo is no exception. As you saw, in the HTTP request, an `appid` parameter is passed. This value is a unique identifier you must pass when making your requests. Not passing this value, or passing an invalid value, will result in the call failing. `YahooDemo` is the `appid` value used in the examples in Yahoo's own documentation. However, before you really play with this application a great deal, you should register and get your own `appid`. You can access the following page to do so:

```
http://api.search.yahoo.com/webservices/register_application
```

You should plug your own `appid` into the `Masher` class (in the `Masher.js` source file) before you spend time with the application, just so you are playing nice with Yahoo.

There are some limitations associated with using the APIs in terms of request volume, but the upper limit is so high as to not be a realistic concern for your adventures with this application! If you are intent on building a production-level application using these services, you will need to consult with Yahoo for other registration options that allow for high volumes. Again, for our purposes, the number of requests allowed is more than sufficient.

The Google APIs

Google Base is, in simplest terms, an online database where people can post about various items, describing them with various attributes. For instance, if you would like to list a number of events occurring in your neighborhood, you can do so at Google Base. Do you want to post your great-aunt Erma's recipe for stuffed cabbage (you wacko, you!)? Google Base is the place to do it.

As you would expect, you can search through the posted information. Would you like to find a list of hotels in a given area? You can do so at Google Base. And that's exactly what we need for this application!

The API for Google Base allows you to query for a list of items, and it also allows you to add items to the database. We care only about querying here, but both capabilities are available.

The Google Base API provides a number of "feeds" through which you can get information. Each feed corresponds to a URL that is formed by taking a base URL and appending the feed-specific path. For instance, the base URL is `http://www.google.com/base`, and the feed-specific portion for the snippets feed is `/feeds/snippets`. You simply put them together to form the final URL where you can query for items:

```
http://www.google.com/base/feeds/snippets
```

So, as a simple example, if you want to do a search for "laptop," you would use this URL:

```
http://www.google.com/base/feeds/snippets?bq=laptop&max-results=1
```

This will result in an XML response like the following:

```
<?xml version="1.0" encoding="UTF-8" ?>
<feed xmlns="http://www.w3.org/2005/Atom" xmlns:openSearch="http://a9.com/-/spec/ ➡
opensearchrss/1.0/" xmlns:g="http://base.google.com/ns/1.0" xmlns:batch= ➡
"http://schemas.google.com/gdata/batch">
  <id>http://www.google.com/base/feeds/snippets</id>
  <updated>2006-12-16T23:28:51.897Z</updated>
  <title type="text">Items matching query: laptop</title>
  <link rel="alternate" type="text/html" href="http://base.google.com" />
  <link rel="http://schemas.google.com/g/2005#feed" type="application/atom+ ➡
xml" href ="http://www.google.com/base/feeds/snippets" />
  <link rel="self" type="application/atom+xml" href="http://www.google.com/base/ ➡
feeds/snippets?max-results=1&bq=laptop" />
  <link rel="next" type="application/atom+xml" href="http://www.google.com/base/ ➡
feeds/snippets?start-index=2&max-results=1&bq=laptop" />
  <generator version="1.0" uri="http://base.google.com">GoogleBase</generator>
  <openSearch:totalResults>3612575</openSearch:totalResults>
  <openSearch:startIndex>1</openSearch:startIndex>
  <openSearch:itemsPerPage>1</openSearch:itemsPerPage>
  <entry>
    <id>http://www.google.com/base/feeds/snippets/18343852209328178501</id>
    <published>2006-11-10T03:41:07.000Z</published>
    <updated>2006-12-08T03:24:30.000Z</updated>
    <title type="text">Portable Laptop Desk</title>
    <content type="html">Looking for portable laptop desk? See our portable ➡
laptop desk guide.</content>
    <link rel="alternate" type="text/html" href="http://portable-laptop- ➡
desk.info" />
    <link rel="self" type="application/atom+xml" href="http://www.google.com/base ➡
/feeds/snippets/18343852209328178501" />
    <author />
    <g:item_language type="text" />
    <g:customer_id type="int">7048781</g:customer_id>
    <g:target_country type="text" />
  </entry>
</feed>
```

The bq parameter is the query you wish to perform; in this case, simply the word laptop. The parameter max-results, which is optional, indicates the maximum number of items to return. For the sake of a short result set being printed here, I requested only a single item be returned.

If you want to query for a particular item type, such as hotels, you can append -/hotels to the following URL:

```
http://www.google.com/base/feeds/snippets/-/hotels?bq=laptop&max-results=1
```

Now obviously, that's a little bit of a nonsensical query,[1] but it's a valid query nonetheless.

As a more practical example, suppose that you want to search for a hotel in a given area, say a list of hotels in a given ZIP code (signs and portents here!). To perform that query, you need to use the `location` parameter. The `location` parameter can take a location in just about any form you can imagine—a full street address, just a ZIP code, or even longitude and latitude! The service generally takes care of understanding what you've sent in, so you don't even have to tell it!

What would the URL look like to search for hotels in the 90210 area code? Just like this:

```
http://www.google.com/base/feeds/snippets/-/hotels?bq=%5blocation:@%2290210%22%2 ➥
b50mi%5d&max-results=1
```

Go ahead and try it in your browser—this one will work, too. To understand this more fully, I need to point out that the value of the bq parameter, the query you want performed, is actually this:

```
[location: @"90210" + 50mi]
```

This says you want hotels in the 90210 ZIP code, at most 50 miles from roughly the center of the ZIP code. The reason it looks a little funky in the URL is because of the URL-encoding that I already did on the URL: left and right brackets, at sign, plus sign, and quotes. You will also see this is the case in the application, but it's possible to encode the entire thing in one step. Either way gets the job done. As long as the URL is ultimately URL-encoded, that's all that matters.

As with the Yahoo APIs, you can specify that you want JSON returned wrapped in a JavaScript function call, and you can specify the function to call. This is done via the `alt` and `callback` parameters. When you pass the value `json-in-script` for the `alt` parameter, you get exactly that: JSON wrapped in a JavaScript call. The `callback` parameter is naturally the name of the function to which to send the JSON.

And while it doesn't seem like much, this is essentially all the information you'll need to work with this API in this application!

Note The snippets feed is a read-only public feed, which means you do not need to get an API key to access it. If you want to deal with many other feeds, or if you intend to do write or update operations with the API, you will indeed need a key, just as you do for Yahoo. You can obtain said key at `http://code.google.com/apis/base/signup.html`.

Script.aculo.us Effects

Script.aculo.us is all about the effects! Components that fly onto the page, elements that shrink and expand, parts that fade out of existence, text that color-cycles into existence—all of this can be done with script.aculo.us.

---

1. Note that you *will* get results, because hotels may list laptop wireless support in their description, and the query will see that.

ARE EFFECTS JUST EYE CANDY?

Let's tackle one question that often comes to mind first: why do we need effects at all? Isn't it just a bunch of superfluous eye candy that doesn't serve much purpose other than to make people go "ooh" and "aah"? Well, first off, if you've ever designed an application for someone else, you know that presentation is an important part of the mix. The more people like how your application looks, the more they'll like how it works—whether it works well or not. It's a relative measure. That's the lesser reason though, although one which should not be quickly dismissed.

The much more important reason has do with how we perceive things. Look around you right now. Pick up any object you want and move it somewhere else. Did the object just pop out from the starting point and appear at the new location? No, of course not! It moved smoothly and deliberately from one place to another. Guess what? This is how the world works! And furthermore, this is how our brains are wired to expect things to work. When things don't work that way, it's jarring, it's confusing, and it's frustrating.

People use movement as a visual cue as to what's going on. This is why modern operating systems are beginning to add all sorts of whiz-bang features, like windows collapsing and expanding. They aren't just eye candy. They do, in fact, serve a purpose: they help our brains maintain their focus where it should be and on what interests us.

In a web application, the same is true. If you can slide something out of view and something else into view, it tends to be more pleasant for the users, and more important, helps them be more productive by not making them lose focus for even a small measure of time.

Using script.aculo.us boils down to three simple steps:

1. Import the required JavaScript files.

2. Create a new Effect object, passing it the ID of the element to perform the effect on, and optionally, parameters for the effect.

3. Sit back and enjoy!

The required files—prototype.js, scriptaculous.js, builder.js, effects.js, dragdrop.js, slider.js, and controls.js—are simply imported like any other external JavaScript files, via <script> tags. Once they are present on the page, you initiate an effect like this:

```
new Effect.Appear("div1");
```

This will begin an Appear effect, which makes an element fade in over some time period. Assuming we had a <div> on the page with the ID div1 that's what would be faded in. What's happening here is a new object is being instantiated, namely the Effect.Appear object. The first argument to the constructor for an effect is always the ID of the element to operate on or a DOM object reference itself, the second is a required parameter (although most effects do not have required parameters), and the third is a collection of options. The options are, well, optional! You'll get some set of default values if you don't pass in any options.

Most effects share some common options, as summarized in Table 5-2.

Table 5-2. *Some Common Script.aculo.us Effect Options*

Option	Description
duration	Sets the duration of the effect in seconds, given as a float. Default value is 1.0.
fps	Targets this many frames per second. Default value is 25. This cannot be set higher than 100.
transition	Sets a function that modifies the current point of the animation, which is between 0 and 1. The following transitions are supplied: Effect.Transitions.sinoidal (default), Effect.Transitions.linear, Effect.Transitions.reverse, Effect.Transitions.wobble, and Effect.Transitions.flicker.
from	Sets the starting point of the transition, a floating-point value between 0.0 and 1.0. Default value is 0.0.
to	Sets the end point of the transition, a floating-point value between 0.0 and 1.0. Default value is 1.0.
sync	Sets whether the effect should render new frames automatically, which it does by default. If true, you can render frames manually by calling the render() method of an effect.
queue	Sets queuing options. When used with a string, this can be front or end to queue the effect in the global effects queue at the beginning or end, or a queue parameter object that can have {position:"front/end", scope:"scope", limit:1}.
direction	Sets the direction of the transition. Values can be top-left, top-right, bottom-left, bottom-right or center (center is the default value). This is applicable only on Grow and Shrink effects.

All the effects also support supplying callback functions in the options. This allows you to perform some function when certain events in the life cycle of an effect occur. Table 5-3 summarizes the possible callbacks.

Table 5-3. *Possible Script.aculo.us Callbacks for Effects*

Callback Event	Description
beforeStart	Called before the main effects rendering loop is started
beforeUpdate	Called on each iteration of the effects rendering loop, before the redraw takes place
afterUpdate	Called on each iteration of the effects rendering loop, after the redraw takes place
afterFinish	Called after the last redraw of the effect was made

In this chapter's project, we're going to use the following effects:

- BlindUp and BlindDown: These function like blinds in your window, basically rolling an element up or down correspondingly. They are used to collapse and expand the search results.

- Shrink: This effect reduces an element to its top-left corner, essentially collapsing it to that corner. When extended information for a hotel is showing, and you click a new hotel, we'll use the Shrink effect to hide the information that is currently showing.

- Grow: This effect expands an element into view. We'll use it when showing extended hotel information and hiding any information that is currently showing.

- Puff: This effect gives the illusion of the element puffing away like a cloud of smoke. We'll use it to remove the map when a new search is performed.

So, taking all this into account, let's look at some sample effects and how you code them. All of these assume we have a <div> on the page with the ID div1 and some text in it. First, let's see the BlindUp effect:

```
new Effect.BlindUp("div1",
  {
    afterFinish : function() {
      alert("All done!");;
    }
  }
);
```

Here, we've specified a callback function, so that once the element is completely rolled up, we'll see an alert message pop-up.

Here's another example:

```
new Effect.Shrink("div1", {duration : 4.0, fps : 60 } );
```

This will shrink our <div> out of view over a period of four seconds and will try to do so at a rate of 60 frames per second. Assuming the computer and browser can achieve this frame rate, it will appear super-smooth to the user. Remember that generally speaking, the human eye begins to perceive animation as being smooth somewhere between 24 and 30 frames per second, so the default value of 25fps is pretty reasonable.[2]

---

2. For reference, most movies have been shot at a rate of 24 frames per second.

Here are a few more notes about script.aculo.us effects:

- All of the effects are time-based, which means that if you want an element to expand into view using the Grow effect, and you want it to take two seconds to do so, the effect will take two seconds, regardless of how fast the browser renders each frame.

- In general, the effects are ignorant of the type of element to which you apply them. You should, generally, be able to apply effects to just about anything. Now, you'll likely find some exceptions, and that's to be expected due to the variations in CSS interpretation by various browsers. But, for the most part, you'll find it to be true.

- For most of these effects to work, you must specify at least some style attributes in-line with the element; they will *not* work if specified in an external style sheet. For instance, many of the effects you'll see in this chapter's application won't work if the display attribute isn't specified in-line. This is not exactly a big deal, but the first time you try an effect and find that it doesn't do anything, and you wonder why, remember this point. You'll likely save yourself some time!

With the review of the APIs and script.aculo.us out of the way, let's begin to look at the application itself and see how it all comes together.

A Preview of the Monster Mash(up)

The Monster Mash(up) application is relatively simple in appearance, until you actually play with it. The page consists essentially of the following four main sections:

- The top, which contains the title graphic and a place to enter a ZIP code

- A section below that and to the left where hotel search results are shown (as well as hotel information)

- A section to the right where a map of the area surrounding the hotel will be shown

- Between the results and map sections, a section containing the map zoom buttons

Figure 5-1 shows this page as it appears when you have performed a search and are now viewing the list of matching hotels.

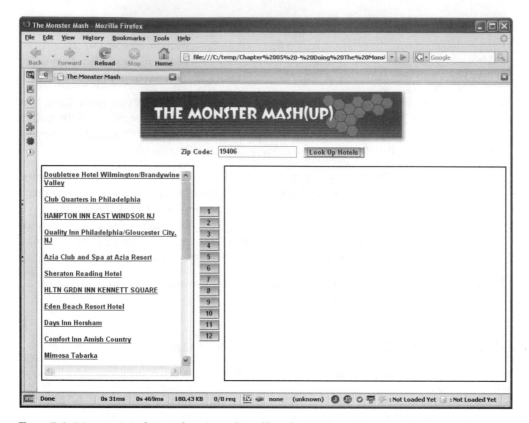

Figure 5-1. *Monster Mash(up) showing a list of hotels matching the requested ZIP code*

When you search for results, the list of hotels returned expands into view, which obviously you can't see in a screenshot here! If results are already showing and you do another search, the existing results will shrink out of view.

When you click a hotel name, you get extended information about that hotel just below the clicked item. This information "flies" into view, and conversely, it flies out of view when you click another hotel name. Figure 5-2 shows the screen when information is being viewed.

Along with the extended information, you'll also get a map of the area around the hotel, also visible in Figure 5-2. You can then use the zoom buttons to zoom in for a closer look or zoom out for a wider look. The smaller the zoom number, the closer you go. Level one is street level; level 12 is regional/state level.

One of the neatest effects to see is when you perform a new search while a map is showing. You'll see that the map "puffs" out of existence—that is, it flies toward *you* and fades out at the same time. Everyone say, "Thank you, script.aculo.us!"

And now, in the immortal words of Bugs Bunny and Daffy Duck (you *do* remember the theme song from Saturday mornings, don't you?): "On with the show!"

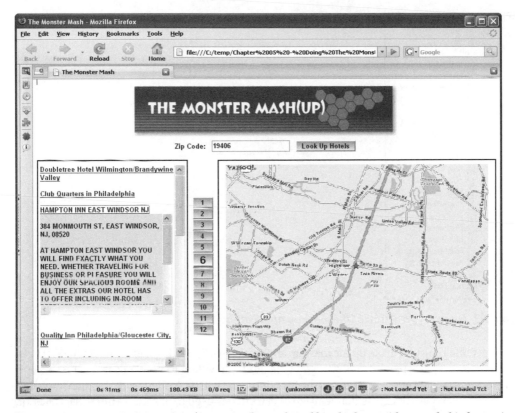

Figure 5-2. *Monster Mash(up) showing a map for a selected hotel, along with extended information*

Dissecting the Monster Mash(up) Solution

Understanding any application tends to begin with a high-level look at the files—whether source or executable (or both)—that make up the application, and we'll not make an exception to that here! In Figure 5-3, you can see the directory structure of our mashup application.

The root directory holds the single HTML file that constitutes the mashup, quite unimaginatively named mashup.htm! The css directory contains a single styles.css style sheet. In the img directory are four images: buttonBG.gif, which is the background image used to give the metallic look to all the buttons; pixel_of_destiny.gif, otherwise known as a single-pixel transparent image (Google for "pixel of destiny," to get the joke!); retrieving_map.gif, which is the image containing the message seen in the map area while a map is retrieved; and title.gif, which is simply the title banner at the top of the page.

The js directory is where all the JavaScript files that make up the application are found. Some of them, namely builder.js, controls.js, dragdrop.js, effects.js, prototype.js, scriptaculous.js, and slider.js, are all components of the script.aculo.us library, and we will not be reviewing them here.[3]

---

3. It is always a valuable and worthwhile exercise to look at the code of the pros, so I certainly suggest you spend at least a few minutes looking at how script.aculo.us works. It's in no way required to understand the mashup, but you'll likely pick up some tricks.

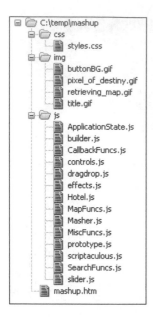

Figure 5-3. *Directory structure of the mashup application*

The remaining files make up the mashup application itself, starting with ApplicationState.js, which defines a class named ApplicationState (and I'm willing to bet you can surmise its purpose!). CallbackFuncs.js contains the functions that will be "called back" by the Yahoo and Google web services. Hotel.js defines a Hotel class that is used to describe a hotel. MapFuncs.js contains functions for working with the map for a given hotel. Masher.js contains the functions dealing with communicating with the Google and Yahoo web services. MiscFuncs.js contains, well, miscellaneous functions, what else? Finally, SearchFuncs.js contains functions for performing a search for hotels.

Now that we've completed the preliminaries, let's get to looking at some actual code!

Writing styles.css

The styles.css file, shown in Listing 5-1, is the single style sheet used to define styling for the application.

Listing 5-1. *The styles.css File*

```
/* Style applied to everything on the page. */
* {
  font-size       : 10pt;
  font-weight     : bold;
  font-family     : arial;
}
```

```css
/* Style applied to the body of the document. */
.cssBody {
  background-color : #ffffff;
}


/* Style applied to the left and right sections. */
.cssSectionBorder {
  border          : 2px solid #000000;
}


/* Style applied to the search results div. */
.cssSearchResults {
  width           : 100%;
  height          : 400px;
  overflow        : scroll;
}


/* Style applied to the popup area where hotel info is displayed. */
.hotelInfo {
  width           : 98%;
  height          : 200px;
  overflow        : scroll;
  background-color : #eaeaea;
}


/* Style applied to buttons. */
.cssButton {
  width           : 40px;
  border-color    : #ffffff;
  background      : url(../img/buttonBG.gif);
  color           : #000000;
}


/* Style applied to buttons when they are hovered over. */
.cssButtonOver {
  width           : 40px;
  border-color    : #ff0000;
  background      : url(../img/buttonBG.gif);
  color           : #ff0000;
}
```

The first style uses the wildcard selector to apply those styles to all elements within the document. This is a handy trick to cover *everything*, even things that typically can be problematic to apply styles to globally, such as table cells, which don't get style information cascaded down properly in some browsers.

For the body, we apply a background color of white using the cssBody class. The cssSectionBorder is applied to the cells that house the search results on the left and the map on the right. The cssSearchResults class styles the search results, ensuring that they fit nicely within the confines of the left side of the page, and also ensuring that the results will scroll when bigger than that area (overflow:scroll).

The hotelInfo class styles the section below a particular hotel where its information appears. With this class, we define that it doesn't quite stretch across the entire content area it's in, so that its scrollbar doesn't touch the scrollbar of the search results.

The cssButton class is used to style our buttons. With it, we are specifying a background image and making sure all buttons have a consistent size. The background image is designed so that it will fill up just about any size button in the proper fashion, giving the button a brushed-metal look. This is purely an aesthetic touch, but it gives the buttons a nice, unique look. The cssButtonOver class is essentially the same, but with a red text color and border, which is used when you hover over the button to give it an active look.

All in all, this is a pretty simple style sheet. Not too much of interest is going on here, except perhaps for the buttons, which I feel are a neat little touch.

Writing mashup.htm

The mashup.htm file, shown in Listing 5-2, is the starting point for this application, and the file that defines the basic page layout.

Listing 5-2. *The mashup.htm File*

```
<html>
  <head>

    <title>The Monster Mash</title>

    <link rel="StyleSheet" href="css/styles.css" type="text/css">

    <script src="js/prototype.js" type="text/javascript"></script>
    <script src="js/scriptaculous.js" type="text/javascript"></script>

    <script src="js/ApplicationState.js" type="text/javascript"></script>
    <script src="js/Masher.js" type="text/javascript"></script>
    <script src="js/Hotel.js" type="text/javascript"></script>
    <script src="js/CallbackFuncs.js" type="text/javascript"></script>
    <script src="js/SearchFuncs.js" type="text/javascript"></script>
    <script src="js/MapFuncs.js" type="text/javascript"></script>
    <script src="js/MiscFuncs.js" type="text/javascript"></script>
```

```
  <script>
    masher = new Masher();
    appState = new ApplicationState();
  </script>

</head>

<body class="cssBody">

  <center>
    <img src="img/title.gif" vspace="5">
    <br>
    <form onSubmit="search();return false;">
    Zip Code:
     
    <input type="text" id="zipCodeField" value="">
     
    <input type="submit" value="Look Up Hotels"
      class="cssButton" style="width:120px;"
      onMouseOver="this.className='cssButtonOver';"
      onMouseOut="this.className='cssButton';">
    </form>
    <br>
  </center>

  <table border="0" width="100%" cellpadding="4" cellspacing="0">
    <tr>

      <td align="left" height="420" class="cssSectionBorder">
        <img width="1" height="1" src="img/pixel_of_destiny.gif">
        <center>
          <div id="pleaseWait" style="display:none;">
            Please Wait, Retrieving Data...
          </div>
        </center>
        <div id="searchResults" class="cssSearchResults" style="display:none;">
        </div>
      </td>

      <td width="50" align="center">
        <input type="button" value="1" onClick="zoomMap(1);" id="zoomButton1"
          class="cssButton"
          onMouseOver="this.className='cssButtonOver';"
          onMouseOut="this.className='cssButton';"><br>
        <input type="button" value="2" onClick="zoomMap(2);" id="zoomButton2"
          class="cssButton"
          onMouseOver="this.className='cssButtonOver';"
          onMouseOut="this.className='cssButton';"><br>
```

```html
              <input type="button" value="3" onClick="zoomMap(3);" id="zoomButton3"
                class="cssButton"
                onMouseOver="this.className='cssButtonOver';"
                onMouseOut="this.className='cssButton';"><br>
              <input type="button" value="4" onClick="zoomMap(4);" id="zoomButton4"
                class="cssButton"
                onMouseOver="this.className='cssButtonOver';"
                onMouseOut="this.className='cssButton';"><br>
              <input type="button" value="5" onClick="zoomMap(5);" id="zoomButton5"
                class="cssButton"
                onMouseOver="this.className='cssButtonOver';"
                onMouseOut="this.className='cssButton';"><br>
              <input type="button" value="6" onClick="zoomMap(6);" id="zoomButton6"
                class="cssButton"
                onMouseOver="this.className='cssButtonOver';"
                onMouseOut="this.className='cssButton';"><br>
              <input type="button" value="7" onClick="zoomMap(7);" id="zoomButton7"
                class="cssButton"
                onMouseOver="this.className='cssButtonOver';"
                onMouseOut="this.className='cssButton';"><br>
              <input type="button" value="8" onClick="zoomMap(8);" id="zoomButton8"
                class="cssButton"
                onMouseOver="this.className='cssButtonOver';"
                onMouseOut="this.className='cssButton';"><br>
              <input type="button" value="9" onClick="zoomMap(9);" id="zoomButton9"
                class="cssButton"
                onMouseOver="this.className='cssButtonOver';"
                onMouseOut="this.className='cssButton';"><br>
              <input type="button" value="10" onClick="zoomMap(10);" id="zoomButton10"
                class="cssButton"
                onMouseOver="this.className='cssButtonOver';"
                onMouseOut="this.className='cssButton';"><br>
              <input type="button" value="11" onClick="zoomMap(11);" id="zoomButton11"
                class="cssButton"
                onMouseOver="this.className='cssButtonOver';"
                onMouseOut="this.className='cssButton';"><br>
              <input type="button" value="12" onClick="zoomMap(12);" id="zoomButton12"
                class="cssButton"
                onMouseOver="this.className='cssButtonOver';"
                onMouseOut="this.className='cssButton';">
            </td>

            <td align="center" width="540" class="cssSectionBorder">
              <img id="mapFiller" style="display:block;" width="520" height="400"
                src="img/pixel_of_destiny.gif">
              <img id="map" style="display:none;" width="520" height="400"
                src="img/pixel_of_destiny.gif">
```

```
        </td>

      </tr>
    </table>

  </body>

</html>
```

As you can see, `mashup.htm` begins with a series of JavaScript file imports. The first two, `prototype.js` and `scriptaculous.js`, are the two source files required for script.aculo.us to work. The `scriptaculous.js` file takes care of including all the other JavaScript files it depends on, such as `builder.js` and `effects.js`. The remainder of the imports are the source files that make up the application itself.

Following the JavaScript imports is one very small section of JavaScript that is responsible for creating an instance of the `Masher` and `ApplicationState` objects, which we'll discuss shortly. That small block of script concludes the `<head>` of the document.

Moving along to the `<body>`, we begin with the title graphic, a text field where you enter the ZIP code you want to search, and then the search button. This is all part of a form, but ironically, it only needs to be in order to deal with allowing the Enter key to be used in Firefox (in IE, you can drop the `<form>` and just use a plain-old `<input type="button">`). That's why we make a call to `search()` onSubmit of the form, and also return `false`, which stops the form from actually being submitted. This is one of those times Firefox actually makes things *more* difficult than IE!

Next up we find the start of a table that is used to define the two halves of the screen: the search results on the left and the map on the right, with the map zoom buttons separating them.

The first column of the table contains two `<div>` elements. The first contains the "Please Wait" message you see while a search is in progress. This is initially hidden. The next `<div>` will contain the search results. Note that it, too, is initially hidden. But more important, that style is specified in-line and not in the external style sheet. This is no oversight! In fact, this `<div>` will be involved in some script.aculo.us effects, and for those to work, some style information must be specified in-line. This is true of one or two other areas of the page, for the same reason. For elements that will be hidden and shown via script.aculo.us, you need to define their initial visibility in-line in the elements by setting the display `style` attribute. It's as simple as that.

Note The reason that script.aculo.us effects require the initial visibility specified in-line is that script.aculo.us is based on the Prototype library, and it uses the `show()` function that Prototype supplies to make a specified element visible. This function works by setting the element's `display` style attribute to an empty string (undefined, in other words). The idea here is to set it to its default value—the empty string for that particular attribute—which means the element would be visible. A problem can occur, however, if that attribute is defined "higher up" in the CSS than at the element level. Remember that Prototype is overwriting what's at the element level. In this situation, it will look at the undefined value at the element level, even though your style sheet may have specified `display:none`, and the net result is it looks like nothing happens.

Following all of that is the second column in the table where the map zoom buttons are located. Within it is a series of 12 buttons. They all share the same basic structure in that the onClick event handler attached calls the zoomMap() function, passing it the zoom level corresponding to the button. There are also the same onMouseOver and onMouseOut event handlers we saw earlier on the search button. It's nothing too fancy really.

Lastly, we come to the table column that contains the map, or more precisely, *will* contain the map, once you select a hotel to view. This column contains two <img> tags. The one with the ID mapFiller is needed so that the table cell doesn't collapse and remains a constant size in IE, which makes for a rather ugly display. The tag with the ID map displays the map or the "Please Wait" message, which is itself an image. The src of this tag is updated to point to either that Please Wait image or to the map that Yahoo generates. These two <img> tags are alternatively hidden and shown as appropriate.

And that wraps it up for the markup!

Writing ApplicationState.js

The ApplicationState.js file contains, not surprisingly, the ApplicationState class. While this class is simple, it plays a very important role in that it stores values that are used throughout the application. Figure 5-4 is the UML class diagram for the ApplicationState class.

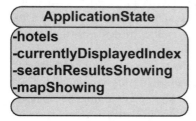

Figure 5-4. *UML diagram of the ApplicationState class*

As you can see in Listing 5-3, the ApplicationState class contains a grand total of four fields.

Listing 5-3. *The ApplicationState.js File*

```
/**
 * This class stores information about the state of the application.
 */
function ApplicationState() {


  /**
   * This is an array of hotels returned from a search. */
  this.hotels = new Array();
```

```
/**
 * This is the index into the hotels array of the hotel that is currently
 * being viewed, i.e., that has info showing and that has a map showing.
 */
this.currentlyDisplayedIndex = -1;


/**
 * This is a flag that indicates whether search results are currently
 * showing or not.
 */
this.searchResultsShowing = false;


/**
 * This is a flag that indicates whether a map is currently showing or not.
 */
this.mapShowing = false;


} // End ApplicationState.
```

The hotels array is a collection of Hotel objects that is populated when a search is performed. The field currentlyDisplayedIndex stores the index into the hotels array of the hotel currently being viewed. The searchResultsShowing field is a simple flag that tells us whether search results are currently visible. Finally, the mapShowing field is another flag that tells us whether a map is showing.

You will see these fields used throughout the rest of the code in determining what to do at any given point, but by and large, ApplicationState is a very simple class.

Writing Hotel.js

As you just saw, the ApplicationState class contains an array named hotels, which is informa-tion for the hotels from the current search results. The array contains Hotel objects, one for each hotel. In Figure 5-5, you can see the UML class diagram for the Hotel class.

Figure 5-5. *UML diagram of the Hotel class*

Like `ApplicationState`, the `Hotel` class does not have a whole lot to it; in fact, less than there was to the `ApplicationState` class! A grand total of three fields gives us all the information about a hotel that we need for this application, as shown in Listing 5-4.

Listing 5-4. *The Hotel.js File*

```
/**
 * This class represents a hotel as returned by the Google web service.
 */
function Hotel() {


  /**
   * The name of the hotel.
   */
  this.name = "";


  /**
   * The location (address) of the hotel.
   */
  this.location = "";


  /**
   * The description of the hotel.
   */
  this.description = "";


} // End Hotel.
```

The `name` field is the name of the hotel, as seen in the results list. The `location` field is the address of the hotel as returned by the web services. The `description` field is the entire description for the hotel. This description can, and in many cases does, contain the name and location as well, so there tends to be some redundancy in the display.

Writing SearchFuncs.js

Everything in this application starts with a search, so it seems reasonable to start looking at the first of the code where the real action takes place by starting with searching. When the search button is clicked, the `search()` function is called. This function is shown in Listing 5-5.

Listing 5-5. *The SearchFuncs.js File*

```
/**
 * Start execution of a search by ZIP code with Google Base.
 */
```

```
function search() {

  // Reset things that need to be reset.
  resetZoomButtons();
  appState.currentlyDisplayedIndex = -1;

  // Hide information for all hotels.
  for (var i = 0; i < appState.hotels.length; i++) {
    $("hotelInfo" + i).style.display = "none";
  }

  // If there are search results showing, hide them.
  if (appState.searchResultsShowing) {

    new Effect.BlindUp("searchResults",
      {
        afterFinish : function() {
          // Now do the actual search.
          searchPart2();
        }
      }
    );
    // If a map and hotel info are showing, hide them too.
    if (appState.mapShowing) {
      new Effect.Puff("map",
        {
          afterFinish : function() {
            $("map").style.display = "none";
            $("mapFiller").style.display = "block";
          }
        }
      );
    }

  } else {

    // No results currently showing, so just do the search.
    searchPart2();

  }

} // End search().


/**
 * Continue search after effect.
 */
```

```
function searchPart2() {

  // Show Please Wait.
  $("searchResults").style.display = "none";
  $("pleaseWait").style.display = "block";

  // Do search.
  var zipCode = $("zipCodeField").value;
  masher.doRequest(masher.googleURL,
    {
      "bq" : "%5blocation:@%22" + escape(zipCode) + "%22%2b50mi%5d",
      "alt" : "json-in-script",
      "callback" : "googleCallback"
    }
  );

} // End searchPart2().
```

First, before we go any further, notice the use of the $() function ($ is a valid name for a JavaScript function, even if it looks a little unusual on its own). As you may recall from the previous chapter, this function comes from Prototype, which underlies script.aculo.us. This is a shorthand for document.getElementById(), although $() provides a few added capabilities, such as the possibility of getting multiple elements back. You'll see this throughout the code we're examining.

Moving on, this code does some resetting that puts the application into the proper state for a search. Most important, this means resetting the zoom buttons so none of them are selected, and changing the currentlyDisplayedIndex variable to –1, indicating no hotel information is currently being viewed. The next reset is to make sure no hotel information is showing. To do this, the list of hotels currently seen on the screen, if any, is iterated over. For each, the information <div> below the hotel in the list is hidden by setting its display style attribute to none.

After that, a check is done to see if any search results are currently showing. If they are, we have to hide both the search results and the map. To hide the search results, we collapse the area. Script.aculo.us provides a BlindUp effect that collapses, or shrinks, an element, just like rolling up window blinds. This code tells script.aculo.us to go ahead and collapse our search results:

```
new Effect.BlindUp("searchResults",
  {
    afterFinish : function() {
      // Now do the actual search.
      searchPart2();
    }
  }
);
```

We are also telling it that, upon completion, the searchPart2() function (which you will see shortly) should be called.

After that, we also have to hide the map if it is showing, and again, script.aculo.us provides a nice effect for us. The Puff effect expands an element and fades it at the same time, like a puff of smoke. Here's all that's required for the image with the ID map to be "puffed" out of existence:

```
new Effect.Puff("map",
  {
    afterFinish : function() {
      $("map").style.display = "none";
      $("mapFiller").style.display = "block";
    }
  }
);
```

When the effect completes, we hide the map image and show the filler image, just to be sure the cell doesn't collapse and we get a border back (which vanishes during the effect).

Now, if no search results where showing in the first place, then searchPart2() is simply called, and nothing needs to be hidden.

So what is the searchPart2() I've been talking about? It's nothing but a continuation of the search() function. This function first hides the search results <div>, and shows the Please Wait <div> in its place. Next, it grabs the ZIP code the user entered, and finally, it calls the doRequest() function of the Masher object, passing it the URL for the Google service and the parameters required to use that service. These parameters are bq, which defines the query we want the service to perform; alt, which tells the service we want JSON wrapped in a JavaScript call returned to us; and finally, callback, which specifies the name of the callback function that will be called. Note that the bq value is encoded as per the rules for the search service, and the ZIP code is escaped to make it safe for inclusion in the URL later.

The next step, naturally enough, is seeing what this Masher object is all about!

Writing Masher.js

In short, the Masher object, or more precisely, the Masher class, of which an instance is created at page load, is responsible for communicating with a JSON-based web API. It is written in a somewhat generic fashion so that other services can be accessed using it with a minimum of change. Figure 5-6 shows the rather simple UML diagram for this class.

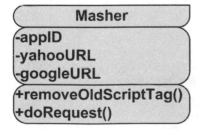

Figure 5-6. *UML diagram of the Masher class*

The appID field is the application ID needed to access Yahoo's APIs. The yahooURL field is the URL for the Yahoo Map Image service. Lastly, the googleURL field is the URL for the Google Base hotel search service.

The first method, removeOldScriptTag(), is a simple function that deals with removing a dynamically added <script> tag. This is done so that as we make calls to the services, we aren't building up memory usage as we add new tags. Listing 5-6 shows this method's code, as well as the rest of the Masher class.

Listing 5-6. *The Masher.js File*

```
/**
 * This class allows us to interact with JSON-based web services in the style
 * of Yahoo, that is, JSON wrapped in a function call.
 */
function Masher() {


  // Parameters for Yahoo! services.
  this.appID = "xxxxx";
  this.yahooURL = "http://api.local.yahoo.com/MapsService/V1/mapImage";

  // Parameters for Google services.
  this.googleURL = "http://www.google.com/base/feeds/snippets/-/hotels";


  /**
   * Removes an old script tag used to retrieve JSON.
   */
  this.removeOldScriptTag = function() {

    var scriptTag = $("jsonScriptTag");
      if(scriptTag) {
        scriptTag.parentNode.removeChild(scriptTag);
    }

  } // End removeOldScriptTag().


  /**
   * Perform an Ajax request using the dynamic script tag approach.
   *
   * @param inURL    The URL of the service.
   * @param inParams The parameters for the call.
   */
  this.doRequest = function(inURL, inParams) {
```

```
  // First, to avoid continually building up memory, remove any old script
  // tag out there.
  this.removeOldScriptTag();

  // Now build up a query string using the passed in parameters
  var queryString = "";
  for (param in inParams) {
    var paramVal = inParams[param];
    if (queryString == "") {
      queryString += "?";
    } else {
      queryString += "&";
    }
    queryString += param + "=" + paramVal;
  }

  // Now add a new script tag with the appropriate URL.
  var scriptTag = document.createElement("script");
  scriptTag.setAttribute("id", "jsonScriptTag");
  scriptTag.setAttribute("src", inURL + queryString);
  scriptTag.setAttribute("type", "text/javascript");
  var headTag = document.getElementsByTagName("head").item(0);
  headTag.appendChild(scriptTag);

] // End doRequest().


} // End Masher.
```

As you saw in the SearchFuncs.js code, when an API is needed, it is called by using
the doRequest() method in the Masher class. This function begins by making a call to
removeOldScriptTag(), as mentioned, to be sure memory isn't continually being consumed. Next,
a query string is built up based on the parameters passed in. For each, we add it to the query
string. Note that the values are *not* escaped at this point because it is assumed any parameters
passed in have already been escaped (this avoids potentially double-escaping something that
shouldn't be). The ZIP code is the only user-entered value being passed, and you will recall that
it is escaped in the SearchFuncs.js code, so no problem there.

Once the query string is built up, we have essentially the same code you've seen already for
adding a <script> tag:

```
  var scriptTag = document.createElement("script");
  scriptTag.setAttribute("id", "jsonScriptTag");
  scriptTag.setAttribute("src", inURL + queryString);
  scriptTag.setAttribute("type", "text/javascript");
  var headTag = document.getElementsByTagName("head").item(0);
  headTag.appendChild(scriptTag);
```

Note that the ID set on this tag is the same as the one removed in removeOldScriptTag(). Therefore, we have only one dynamic <script> tag on the page at any given time. Otherwise, this code is the same as what you saw before, and I trust you remember how it works!

There isn't a whole lot to interacting with these services, as this class clearly illustrates. Only one piece remains: the callback functions that will be called when the response from the services returns. That's precisely where we're headed next!

Writing CallbackFuncs.js

As you've seen, when the Google or Yahoo APIs return their responses, they are in the form of a JavaScript function call with JSON passed as the argument to it (well, more precisely, the object resulting from the evaluation of the JSON). The callbacks, googleCallback() and yahooCallback(), are shown in Listing 5-7.

Listing 5-7. *The CallbackFuncs.js File*

```
/**
 * This is the function that is called when a Google service returns.
 *
 * @param inJSON The JSON object returned by the service.
 */
function googleCallback(inJSON) {

  var htmlOut = "";
  appState.hotels = new Array();

  // Iterate over the list of hotels.
  for (var i = 0; i < inJSON.feed.openSearch$itemsPerPage.$t; i++) {

    // Construct markup for the list for each hotel, including its information.
    var entry = inJSON.feed.entry[i];
    var hotel = new Hotel();
    hotel.name = entry.title.$t;
    hotel.location = entry.g$location.$t;
    hotel.description = entry.content.$t;
    appState.hotels.push(hotel);
    htmlOut += "<span onClick=\"" +
      "getMap('" + entry.g$location.$t + "');" +
      "showInfo(" + i + ");\" " +
      "onMouseOver=\"this.style.backgroundColor='#ffff00';" +
      "this.style.cursor='pointer';\" " +
      "onMouseOut=\"this.style.backgroundColor='';" +
      "this.style.cursor='';\"" +
      ">";
    htmlOut += entry.title.$t;
    htmlOut += "</span>";    htmlOut += "<div id=\"hotelInfo" + i + "\" style=\" ➥
display:none;\" ";
    htmlOut += "class=\"hotelInfo\">";
```

```
    htmlOut += "</div>";
    htmlOut += "<br><br>";

  }

  // Put the generated markup in the search results list div.
  $("searchResults").innerHTML = htmlOut;
  $("pleaseWait").style.display = "none";

  // Ask script.aculo.us to show the search results.
  new Effect.BlindDown("searchResults");

  // Set flags so we know what state the application is in.
  appState.searchResultsShowing = true;
  appState.mapShowing = false;

} // End googleCallback().


/**
 * This is the function that is called when a Yahoo service returns.
 *
 * @param inJSON The JSON object returned by the service.
 */
function yahooCallback(inJSON) {

  if (inJSON.Error) {
    var msg = "An error occurred retrieving map: ";
    if (inJSON.Error.Message) {
      msg += inJSON.Error.Message;
    }
    appState.mapShowing = false;
    $("map").src = "img/pixel_of_destiny.gif";
    alert(msg);
  } else {
    $("map").src = inJSON.ResultSet.Result;
  }

} // End yahooCallback().
```

The first important task the googleCallback() function handles is to clear any existing hotels that may be stored in the ApplicationState instance by assigning the hotels field to a new array. Once that's done, it's time to iterate over the hotels returned.

To do this iteration, we need to know how many items were returned, and that is found in the feed.openSearch$itemsPerPage.$t attribute of the JSON object. Once we have that value, we begin the loop. For each iteration, we grab the entry, which is a hotel, by accessing the feed.entry array, where we append an index value to the end based on the loop counter, so feed.entry[i].

Once we have the entry, it's just a matter of constructing the HTML for the results list. Each entry is surrounded by a `<span>`, and it has some event handlers for when the user hovers over it (the yellow background with the pointer) as well as an `onClick` handler that loads the map for the entry and its extended information. The contents of the `<span>` are the hotel's name (accessed via the `entry.title.$t` attribute) and a `<div>` below it, where the extended information will go.

At the same time, we are populating a newly instantiated `Hotel` object with the hotel name (`entry.title.$t`), its location (`entry.g$location.$t`), and its description (`entry.content.$t`). This object is pushed onto the `hotels` array in `ApplicationState`.

Two things of interest are worth noting here. First, the description itself is not included in the markup, but is added dynamically later. I admit that I have no real reason for having done it this way other than to show that it's possible. Second, notice the `onClick` handler attached to the entry's `<span>`, which is responsible for retrieving the map for the hotel, via the `getMap()` call, and for showing its information, via the `showInfo()` call.

The Yahoo callback does even less than the Google one. Its sole job is to update the `src` attribute of the `<img>` with the ID of `map` to point to the URL returned by the Yahoo service. That's all there is to showing a map! However, there is a nasty downside to using the dynamic `<script>` approach to Ajax, and that's error handling.

Often, errors can be handled fairly easily, as is the case in the `yahooCallback()` function. If an `Error` attribute is found in the returned JSON, we can get the message and display it to the user. We also need to reset the `mapShowing` flag and be sure we show the blank "pixel of destiny" image again. However, this covers only one type of potential error. If a network failure occurs, for instance, and the response doesn't come back, there is no error handling you can do. The application will simply appear to not work.

Also, if the service returns an invalid data structure, that cannot be handled either. This is the case with some of the Yahoo functions. For instance, try the ZIP code 94505 and select any of the first few hotels. You'll notice the "Please wait, retrieving map" message appears, but no map ever does appear. If you are running in Firefox and open Firebug, you'll notice that the response from the service is invalid and causes a JavaScript error when it is evaluated. Unfortunately, we can do nothing about this. It's much like including a `.js` file that has a syntax error, but it's worse here, because you can't just correct it yourself. This is definitely a problem to be aware of with mashups, and more specifically, the dynamic `<script>` tag technique. There's no free lunch!

Writing MapFuncs.js

The `MapFuncs.js` file contains four functions that deal with the map or operations performed on the map, such as zooming in and out. Listing 5-8 shows the code in this file.

Listing 5-8. *The MapFuncs.js File*

```
/**
 * Retrieve map for address of selected hotel with Yahoo Maps.
 *
 * @param inLocation The address of the hotel to get a map for.
 * @param inZoom     The zoom level, 1-12, of the map.
 */
```

```javascript
function getMap(inLocation, inZoom) {

  // The default zoom level is 6.
  if (!inZoom) {
    inZoom = 6;
  }

  // Show the Please Wait message while we request the map.
  $("map").src = "img/retrieving_map.gif";
  $("map").style.display = "block";
  $("mapFiller").style.display = "none";

  // Ask the masher to make the request for us.
  masher.doRequest(masher.yahooURL,
    {
      "appid" : masher.appID,
      "location" : escape(inLocation),
      "image_type" : "gif",
      "output" : "json",
      "width" : "520",
      "height" : "400",
      "zoom" : inZoom,
      "callback" : "yahooCallback"
    }
  );

  // Set state and reset the zoom buttons, and highlight the current zoom
  // level.
  appState.mapShowing = true;
  resetZoomButtons();
  highlightZoomButton(inZoom);

} // End getMap().


/**
 * Zoom the map according to the zoom button clicked.
 *
 * @param inZoom The zoom level, 1-12, to zoom the map to.
 */
function zoomMap(inZoom) {

  // Obviously this only does something if a map is showing.
  if (appState.mapShowing) {
    var hotel = appState.hotels[appState.currentlyDisplayedIndex];
    getMap(hotel.location, inZoom);
  }
```

```
} // End zoomMap().


/**
 * Reset all the zoom buttons so none are highlighted.
 */
function resetZoomButtons() {

  for (var i = 1; i < 13; i++) {
    $("zoomButton" + i).style.fontSize = "10pt"
  }

} // End resetZoomButtons().


/**
 * Highlight the specified zoom button.
 *
 * @param inZoom The zoom level, 1-12, of the button to highlight.
 */
function highlightZoomButton(inZoom) {

  $("zoomButton" + inZoom).style.fontSize = "16pt"

} // End highlightZoomButton().
```

The first function, getMap(), is called when the user clicks one of the hotel links in the search results. It is also called when one of the zoom buttons is clicked. Because of this dual purpose, it accepts two arguments: inLocation and inZoom. inLocation, as you would expect, is the location for which we want a map. This correlates to the location field of a Hotel object. inZoom is the zoom level. Since Yahoo is generating the map, we need to tell it what level of zoom we want. However, when the map is first retrieved in response to a hotel being clicked, the inZoom argument is not passed in. So, the first thing you see in this code is a check of whether inZoom was passed in. If not, that's where the default zoom level of 6 is set.

After that are three lines of code that are responsible for showing the "Please Wait" message in the map area. It's just a matter of pointing the map <img> tag to the Please Wait image, showing it, and hiding the mapFiller.

Then we ask the Masher instance to get the map. For this particular API call, we need to pass the appid that we obtained when we registered for Yahoo's service. Obviously we need to pass the location as well, and we also need to specify that we want a GIF back (the image_type parameter). We specify that we want our output to be JSON (via the output parameter) wrapped in a JavaScript function call, which is specified with the callback parameter. We want a map that fits in our map area, which is 520-by-400 pixels in size, so we specify the appropriate width and height parameters. Lastly, we pass the zoom level that we want via the appropriately named zoom parameter.

A few last details need to be taken care of, namely setting the flag to indicate the map is showing, resetting the zoom buttons to the default states (no current zoom button is bigger than the rest), and then setting the button for the zoom level to current.

Once the API call returns, we'll wind up in yahooCallback(), which you've already seen.

The zoomMap() function is called when a map zoom button is clicked. It does a simple check to be sure the map is showing; otherwise, nothing should happen when a button is clicked. If a map is showing, zoomMap() gets the Hotel object corresponding to the hotel that is currently being viewed and uses that to pass the location and the new zoom level, which is the value passed in, to the getMap() function.

The resetZoomButtons() function that follows performs the simple task of resetting all the zoom buttons to the default font size, effectively making it so that none of the buttons indicates the current zoom level. This is just a loop through the 12 buttons, constructing the appropriate DOM ID for each, and setting the fontSize style attribute on it.[4]

Last is the highlightZoomButton() function. This is called when a user clicks one of the buttons, and its task is to make the button "current," which means to have a bigger font size. This is again just a straight manipulation of the fontSize style attribute.

Writing MiscFuncs.js

Now we come to the final source file in this project, MiscFuncs.js. This file contains a single function, but it's a pretty important one: showInfo() is used to display the extended information for a clicked hotel. Listing 5-9 shows this code.

Listing 5-9. *The MiscFuncs.js File*

```
/**
 * Function to show extended hotel information.
 *
 * @param inIndex Index into the array of hotels in appState.
 */
function showInfo(inIndex) {

  // Trivial rejection: are we already showing the requested hotel?
  if (inIndex == appState.currentlyDisplayedIndex) {
    return;
  }

  // Shrink the information for the currently showing hotel.
  if (appState.currentlyDisplayedIndex != -1) {
    new Effect.Shrink("hotelInfo" +
      appState.currentlyDisplayedIndex,{duration:1.0});
  }
```

---

4. This certainly could have been done by switching the button to a different style class, and in many ways that is a better approach. But I like to show some of the alternate ways you can accomplish the same thing, and certainly direct manipulation of the style attributes is one way.

```
    // Update application state and insert the new hotel information.
    appState.currentlyDisplayedIndex = inIndex;
    var hotel = appState.hotels[inIndex];
    var htmlOut = "<br>" + hotel.location + "<br><br>";
    htmlOut += hotel.description;
    $("hotelInfo" + inIndex).innerHTML = htmlOut;

    // And finally, have the new info "grow" into view.
    new Effect.Grow("hotelInfo" + inIndex,{duration:1.0});

} // End showInfo().
```

This function takes as an argument the index into the `hotels` array of the hotel for which to get information. So, first is a quick check to see if the hotel that was just clicked already has information showing. If it does, we're finished—bug outta here!

Assuming it's a different hotel, it next checks to see if *any* hotel has information showing, which would mean the `currentDisplayedIndex` field in `appState` has a value other than –1. In that case, we ask script.aculo.us to shrink that information out of view using the `Shrink` effect.

The code then records the index that is now going to be shown, grabs the appropriate `Hotel` object, and builds markup using its `location` and `description`. Once the markup is built, it is inserted into the `<div>` directly below the clicked hotel, the ID of which is `hotelInfo`, followed by the index. Lastly, we ask script.aculo.us to expand this new information into view using the `Grow` effect.

Note that the `Shrink` and `Grow` effects will occur simultaneously because, when the new `Shrink` effect is instantiated, a timer is started to perform that effect, but the code between that and the new `Grow` effect instantiation will occur before the `Shrink` effect finishes. There, we'll have two timers running, one for each effect, and they'll appear to happen at roughly the same times. This is by design, as it makes the whole transition look a lot cooler. Of course, script.aculo.us handles all those messy details for us.

And, at long last, we've come to the end! I hope you've enjoyed seeing a mashup in action, and appreciate the APIs Yahoo and Google, among many others, are providing for us to use as building blocks in our own applications.

Suggested Exercises

With mashups, you can just continue to add features to your heart's content, as long as you can find a suitable API! While I leave the hunt for APIs to you, here are a small handful of suggestions you could play around with:

- Add the ability to get a weather report for a particular day, or range of days. This would be useful if you're trying to book a vacation!

- Add the ability to look for restaurants instead of hotels (hint: Google provides this capability as well).

- Extend the map functionality. You can simply look at the features Yahoo Maps provides and duplicate them, since most, if not all, of the functionality is exposed through the APIs.

Summary

In this chapter, we got into one of the most popular buzzwords being tossed around today: mashups. You saw how to get around the same-domain restriction typical of most Ajax implementations. We covered using a number of public APIs, how they present themselves to the developer, and how an application can interact with them. You also saw how the script.aculo.us library can provide some pretty nifty little UI eye candy with a minimum of code and fuss.

All in all, we managed to create a pretty useful little application without much effort, which is, of course, the goal of a mashup. Along the way, you saw a few neat JavaScript tricks in the process, expanding your mental toolbox just a bit further!

Summary

CHAPTER 6

■ ■ ■

Don't Just Live in the Moment: Client-Side Persistence

For applications, two types of data storage are available: *persistent* and *nonpersistent*, or transient. Persistent storage is any storage mechanism that provides a place for data to be saved between program executions, and often for an indefinite period of time (until explicitly removed from storage). Transient storage is any storage mechanism where the data lives only as long as the program is actually executing (or for some short time thereafter). A database is generally considered a persistent storage mechanism, whereas RAM clearly is not. Writing to a hard drive is usually persistent as well, while session memory generally is not. The term *durable* is also often used to describe persistent storage media.

In web applications, storing state on the server—whether in a database or in a session—is pretty much expected of most applications. But what happens when you don't have a persistence mechanism on the server, or possibly don't want one for some reason? What's the alternative?

When discussing persistence in a pure JavaScript-based client-side application, there is a very short list of possible storage mechanisms.[1] The ubiquitous cookie— small bits of information stored on the client on a per-domain basis—is one. Another is a facility now available on most browsers, dubbed *local shared objects* (or Flash shared objects, or even Flash cookies, depending on the documentation you read). This is a storage mechanism provided by the Adobe Flash browser plug-in.

Local shared objects are gaining quite a bit of popularity, and we'll put that approach to use in this chapter's project, which is a simple contact manager. Perhaps most interesting though is the Dojo library we will use to implement this client-side persistence, which makes our lives so much easier. So, on with the show.

Contact Manager Requirements and Goals

In this chapter, we will build a Contact Manager application that runs entirely on the client side. This is handy because it means it can run on virtually any PC, without requiring a network connection (although, conversely, it means that the contact data can't easily be shared among

---

1. Java applets or ActiveX controls are other options, but they are generally thought of as a whole other class of possibilities, because they can, in a sense, be seen as extensions to the browser itself (certainly, ActiveX controls are meant to be that, but applets can also be viewed in that light). In either case, they require something more than HTML and JavaScript, and that in and of itself places them in a different category.

multiple machines). Clearly, persistence will come into play here, since it would be quite a useless application if we couldn't actually store contacts.

Let's list some of the key things this project will accomplish and some of the features we'll seek to implement.

- Each contact should include a good amount of data. Along with the basics of name, phone number, and email address, we'll also allow for a fair amount of extended information, such as birthday, spouse's name, children's names, and so on. However, we want to make these items as free-form as possible, so users can use the different data fields however they like.

- We'll implement the typical alphabet selector tabs to make it easier to find contacts.

- We'll store our contacts with local shared objects.

- We'll use Dojo to provide some widgets coolness to make the interface fun and attractive. We'll also use Dojo to deal with the underlying details of working with local shared objects.

Now that we have some goals in mind, let's take a look at the library we'll use for this project.

Dojo Features

To help build the Contact Manager application, we'll use the very popular Dojo toolkit. Chapter 2 briefly introduced Dojo, but let's look at it in just a little more detail.

On its front page, Dojo (http://dojotoolkit.org) explains what it is, and I see no need to try to paraphrase, so here's a direct quote:

> *Dojo is the Open Source JavaScript toolkit that helps you build serious applications in less time. It fills in the gaps where JavaScript and browsers don't go quite far enough, and gives you powerful, portable, lightweight, and tested tools for constructing dynamic interfaces. Dojo lets you prototype interactive widgets quickly, animate transitions, and build Ajax requests with the most powerful and easiest to use abstractions available. These capabilities are built on top of a lightweight packaging system, so you never have to figure out which order to request script files in again. Dojo's package system and optional build tools help you develop quickly and optimize transparently.*

> *Dojo also packs an easy to use widget system. From prototype to deployment, Dojo widgets are HTML and CSS all the way. Best of all, since Dojo is portable JavaScript to the core, your widgets can be portable between HTML, SVG, and whatever else comes down the pike. The web is changing, and Dojo can help you stay ahead.*

> *Dojo makes professional web development better, easier, and faster. In that order.*

Yes, that does about sum it up! Dojo has been gaining a following of late, and has even been integrated into some popular frameworks, such as WebWork from OpenSymphony (now Struts 2 from Apache, http://www.opensymphony.com/webwork or http://struts.apache.org).

Dojo is a rather large library, containing a myriad of packages and features. Dojo is not just about Ajax, like some other libraries out there. It provides some functions that extend JavaScript itself, as well as general utility code for JavaScript applications.

However, Dojo does have a downside: it is still really in its infancy. One look at the online documentation, and you'll realize that using Dojo means that, to a large degree, you'll be fending for yourself. Many of the packages do not, as of the time of this writing, appear to have any documentation at all. Examples are a bit thin at this point, and the planned features are not fully baked just yet. However, Dojo has improved leaps and bounds in this department from just a few months ago. You can begin to have a certain comfort level with Dojo in this regard if you are thinking of using it. And the Dojo mailing list is *very* active, with a large number of truly helpful people. Any good open source project is defined by the nature and activity level of its community, and Dojo gets high marks in this regard.

In this chapter, we'll be using only two (a UI widget and the storage capabilities) of Dojo's many packages. Table 6-1 shows some of the packages Dojo offers. Note that this is just a small sampling, so you will want to explore what else it offers as your time allows.

Table 6-1. *Some Dojo Packages*

Package	Description
dojo.lang	Utility routines to make JavaScript easier to use. Contains a number of functions for manipulating JavaScript objects, testing data types, and so on.
dojo.string	String manipulation functions, including trim(), trimStart(), escape(), and so on.
dojo.logging	JavaScript logging.
dojo.profile	JavaScript code profiling.
dojo.validate	Data validation functions, such as isNumber(), isText(), isValidDate(), and so on.
dojo.crypto	Cryptographic routines.
dojo.storage	Code that implements a durable client-side cache using Flash's cookie mechanism. This effectively gives you a client-side analogy to the HttpSession object on the server.
dojo.widget	Various highly cool GUI widgets (such as buttons, dialog windows, photo slideshow, and so on).
dojo.Collections	Various data structures like Dictionary, ArrayList, Set, and so on.

To begin using Dojo, you have a couple of options. Dojo comes in a number of "editions." So, if you're interested only in the Ajax functionality, you can download just the IO edition. If you are interested only in GUI widgets, you can download the widget edition. There is also a so-called "kitchen sink" edition that contains everything Dojo offers. For this chapter's project, I used the minimal edition, but we'll discuss that further in just a bit.

After you have downloaded the proper edition, all you need to do is a typical JavaScript import of the dojo.js file, like so:

```
<script src="js/dojo.js"></script>
```

After that, you're all set. Dojo also offers an "import" feature. So, for instance, if you have downloaded the IO edition and later decide you want to use the event system, you can do this:

```
<script type="text/javascript">
    dojo.require("dojo.event.*");
</script>
```

Dojo will then take care of loading all the dependencies for you, and you will be good to go. You can do this for any of the features you want, at any time. In other words, you don't need to have a bunch of imports at the top of the page for each package you want to use; you can instead treat the Dojo import just like a Java import, and let Dojo handle all the details (although the main import of dojo.js *is* still required).

Dojo and Cookies

Working with cookies is quite simple, as you saw in Chapter 3 when we built the jscript.storage package of functions. Dojo offers very similar functionality, with perhaps a bit more capability. To see some of the functions Dojo provides, check out the online API reference at http://dojotoolkit.org/api, which has come a long way in a short time and has begun to make Dojo quite a bit nicer to use. Figure 6-1 shows this page.

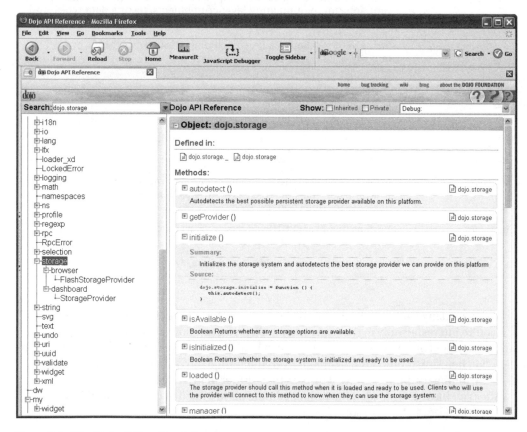

Figure 6-1. *The Dojo API online reference*

You'll find the cookie functions in the `dojo.io.cookie` package (which might seem a little odd, since there is a `dojo.storage` package).

As an example, to set a cookie in Dojo, just do the following:

```
dojo.io.cookie.setCookie("cookieName", "cookieValue");
```

That doesn't look a whole lot different than the `setCookie()` function we developed in Chapter 3. However, Dojo adds four more (optional) parameters to the end of this function:

- `days`: Determines how many days this cookie will live before it expires.

- `path`: Sets the path the cookie is for (what path within the domain the cookie is valid and will be returned for).

- `domain`: Sets the domain the cookie is for (what domain the cookie will be returned for).

- `secure`: Determines if the cookie is secure (when `true`, the cookie will be returned only over an SSL channel).

As you might expect, Dojo also provides both `getCookie(name)` and `deleteCookie(name)` functions. It also provides two slightly more advanced functions: `setObjectCookie()` and `getObjectCookie()`. These functions deal with cookies as object/value pairs as the cookie value instead of a simple data type. These are nice shortcuts that save you from having to write code to parse your objects before writing them out.

Cookies are rather ubiquitous and are used day in and day out in applications all over the place. They are simple, quick, and quite sufficient for a great many tasks. They are, however, not without their limitations:

- Each domain is limited to a maximum of 20 cookies. You may find some browsers that allow for more, but the HTTP spec states 20 as the required minimum. So it is best to assume that is actually the maximum to ensure your code won't break in some browsers, because most treat 20 as the upper limit.

- Each cookie is limited to 4kb maximum size. Some quick math tells us we have a maximum of 80kb per domain on the client in cookies. Aside from 80kb not being enough for many tasks, the fact that it must be divided among 20 cookies, and you'll have to write that code yourself, makes cookies less than desirable for many purposes.

Fortunately, the folks at Adobe have a ready solution for us, and as you might expect, Dojo is there to take advantage of it and make our lives as developers better. So, we won't be using cookies in this chapter's project. We'll get to the storage mechanism that we'll use shortly, but first, let's look at a few other Dojo features.

Dojo Widgets and Event System

The Contact Manager application will make use of one of the UI widgets Dojo provides, called the fisheye list. If you've played with the application already, you'll recognize the fisheye list as the icons across the top that expand and contract as you mouse over them, similar to the Mac launch bar effect, if you are familiar with Apple's operating system. The nice thing about the Dojo widgets is that, because they are built with a common widget framework, they all, by and large, are used in the same way, so seeing one gives you a pretty good idea of how to use the others. The details of using Dojo widgets can get fairly verbose, so I'll explain them as we dissect the application. Seeing their use in context is clearer in this instance.

We'll also use the event system in Dojo, which allows us to attach functions to virtually any event that can occur, not just UI events like mouse clicks and such. Dojo offers an aspect-oriented event system, whereby you can have a function called any time another function is called, for instance. The event system Dojo offers is extensive, and we'll only be scratching the surface in this application, but you'll start to get an idea of what's possible. Once again, I'll explain the details in the dissection process to come.

The real star of the show though, and frankly the main focus of this chapter, is the Dojo storage system and local shared objects, so let's dive into that now!

Local Shared Objects and the Dojo Storage System

Local shared objects (also called Flash shared objects) are somewhat akin to cookies, but are a mechanism of the Adobe Flash plug-in. They were introduced with Flash MX, so earlier versions (prior to version 6) will not support them. You work with them in much the same way you do cookies, but the size and number-per-domain limitations that exist for cookies do not apply with local shared objects. You can, for all intents and purposes, store as much data as you like in local shared objects, at least until your users' hard drives fill up.

Flash actually has a larger installed base than even IE: about 97% at the time of this writing. This means that any concerns you may have had about needing the Flash plug-in for client-side persistence in the past can probably be thrown out the door—the plug-in is more likely to be available than many other things, perhaps even JavaScript itself. Flash is even available for many traditionally limited devices, such as PDAs and cell phones (although, unfortunately, you may find that local shared objects are not available on some of those devices).

However, there would appear to be a speed bump in our way, and that is the simple fact that local shared objects are for use in Flash movies, not in JavaScript. How do we overcome that? By having Dojo handle it for us, of course.

We could write the code ourselves, but that would require writing a Flash movie or two that exposes a scripting interface, which we could then interact with from JavaScript. If this makes your brain hurt, join the club. While I've worked with Flash a bit, I'm far from any sort of expert, and it would certainly take a fair amount of time and effort to write these components myself. But why go through all that trouble anyway, when the folks working on Dojo have already handled all the difficult bits and given us a simple way to utilize it? Sometimes, being lazy is actually a *good* thing!

Dojo provides a storage package that is billed as a pluggable mechanism for client-side persistence. Its architecture is based on the concept of a storage manager and any number of storage providers. Each provider can persist data via any method it wants, but the client application writes to a common interface that all providers implement, thereby allowing the developer to swap between various storage mechanisms at the drop of a hat without any change to their code. It's very cool.

At the time of this writing, the dojo.storage package provides only a single storage provider,[2] and that is one that deals with shared objects. The dojo.storage package is a wonderful creation

---

2. Cookie functions would obviously be a logical fit here as well. That's why there has been talk of a cookie provider (there may even be one by the time you read this). One could conceive of an ActiveX storage provider that writes directly to a SQL Server database as one example, and yet the application that utilized dojo.storage wouldn't need to know about the details of that at all.

that offers a great deal of power to developers. It's essentially a simple architecture, as shown in Figure 6-2, which again proves that simplicity is usually the way to go.

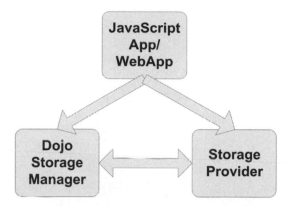

Figure 6-2. *The dojo.storage package architecture*

As you'll see when we examine the code behind the application in this chapter, the primary interaction your code will have with dojo.storage is via the storage manager and storage provider interfaces, which are shown in Figure 6-3 and Figure 6-4, respectively. Once again, there isn't a whole lot to them, and, in fact, for the purposes of the application in this chapter, we won't use more than about half of what these interfaces offer.

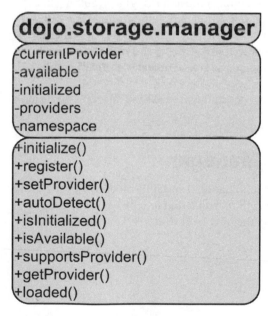

Figure 6-3. *The Dojo storage manager interface*

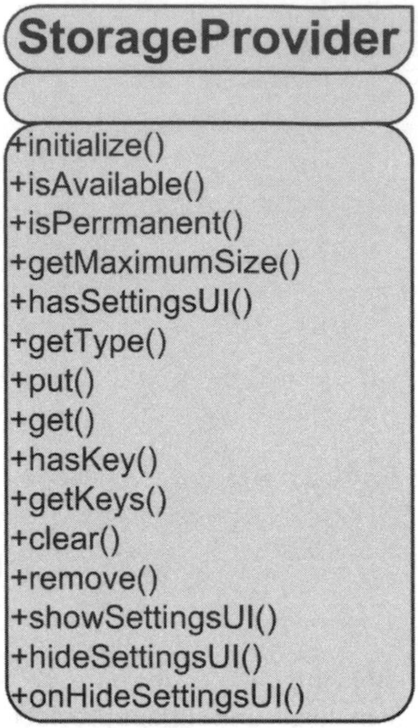

```
StorageProvider

+initialize()
+isAvailable()
+isPerrmanent()
+getMaximumSize()
+hasSettingsUI()
+getType()
+put()
+get()
+hasKey()
+getKeys()
+clear()
+remove()
+showSettingsUI()
+hideSettingsUI()
+onHideSettingsUI()
```

Figure 6-4. *The Dojo storage provider interface*

As mentioned, the Dojo developers have dealt with the details of implementing the Flash movies that can be interacted with via JavaScript. Think of those movies as something like a Data Access Object (DAO), responsible for the actual storage implementation. The API it exposes is wrapped by the dojo.storage API in a sense. So, when you call the put() method of the StorageProvider class (well, the class implementing that API anyway), it calls some function in the Flash movie that does the actual work of saving to the stored objects. It's really a rather elegant solution.

So, now that you have an idea how this storage mechanism works in Dojo, let's take a look at the application that will use it.

A Preview of the Contact Manager

Figure 6-5 shows the application we will build in this chapter. I certainly recommend spending a few minutes playing with it before proceeding. I think you'll find it to be a fairly clean and useful little contact list. It won't make anyone on the Microsoft Outlook team lose any sleep, but it's not bad by any stretch.

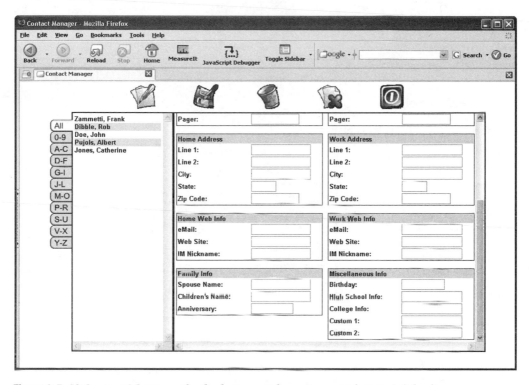

Figure 6-5. *JS Contact Manager: Outlook may not have to worry, but it ain't bad!*

There is a good chance when you first run the application that you will see a pop-up dialog box generated by Flash that looks like Figure 6-6.

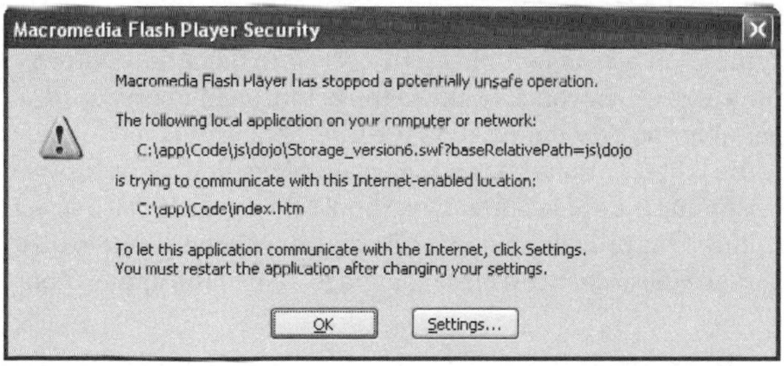

Figure 6-6. *Security warning seen when you first run the application*

If you don't see this pop-up, then great; count yourself lucky and just move on. If you see it (which is likely), this is a result of some security precautions in place in the Flash plug-in. You need to tell the plug-in that the folder on your local file system in which you are running the application is allowed and you shouldn't be asked about it. The vexing thing about this is that you will need Internet connectivity to change the setting. Believe it or not, the setting dialog box that you need is a web page on the Adobe web site! Figure 6-7 shows this page.

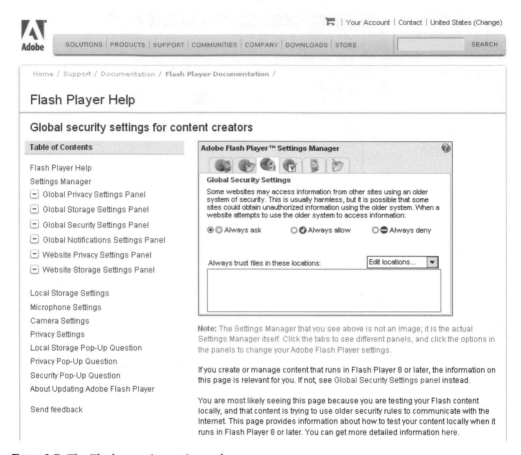

Figure 6-7. *The Flash security setting web page*

I can only assume there is some good reason for doing it this way and that Adobe knows that reason, but I sure don't! In any case, when you click the Settings button in the security warning dialog box, you will, assuming you are connected to the Internet, be directed to this page. Here, you will need to click the Edit Locations box and select Add Location. Then browse for the folder from which you are running the application. That should do the trick. I also select the radio button next to Always Allow. This probably isn't necessary, but you may want to do it as well, just to be sure. Once you make these changes, close that page, reload the application, and you should be good to go.

Dissecting the Contact Manager Solution

As we typically do with the projects in this book, let's first get a feel for the lay of the land, so to speak, and see what the directory structure looks like. Take a look at Figure 6-8.

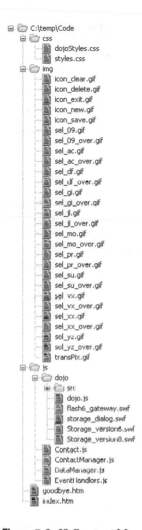

Figure 6-8. *JS Contact Manager's directory structure*

In the root directory are two files:

- index.htm, really the heart and soul of the application, as you'll soon see

- goodbye.htm, a simple page that is shown when the user exits the application

Under the root are a couple of directories, starting with the css directory. As is typical, the css directory is where we keep our style sheets. In this case, we have two:

- styles.css, which is the main style sheet for the application

- dojoStyles.css, which contains styles used specifically for Dojo widgets

The next directory is img, which, obviously enough, contains images used throughout the application. The images are named in a pretty obvious way, so there's no need to run through them all.

Last is the js directory, which, of course, is where the JavaScript lives. Four .js files are present:

- Contact.js, which defines a class representing a contact

- ContactManager.js, which contains the main application code; it's kind of a traffic cop, more or less, calling the other classes as required

- DataManager.js, which contains the code that actually deals with storing and retrieving our contacts

- EventHandlers.js, which contains the UI event handlers that make our UI work

Also in the js directory you'll find a subdirectory named dojo. This is where the Dojo library lives. Dojo comes in a number of editions, each basically baking certain parts of Dojo into a single .js file. Alternatively, you can use the minimal edition, which means that only the core Dojo code will be in dojo.js, and any other parts of Dojo you use will be imported as needed. This is the edition we'll use because it reduces the up-front loading time required and loads the various parts of Dojo as needed. This also, to my way of thinking, makes it less likely that we'll run into any problems for no other reason than less code in memory means less that can break.

Within the dojo directory, you'll find a number of subdirectories containing other Dojo package source files, as well as HTML and CSS resources, and anything else Dojo needs to function. While this application uses only a small portion of Dojo, having it all available means that as you want to extend the application and use more of Dojo, it is all there, ready for you.

And now, without further delay, let's get to some code.

Writing styles.css

Listing 6-1 shows the styles.css file, which is the main style sheet that defines, for the most part, all of the visual styling of the application.

Listing 6-1. *The styles.css File*

```css
/* Generic style applied to all elements */
* {
  font-family      : arial;
  font-size        : 10pt;
  font-weight      : bold;
}

/* Style for body of document */
body {
  margin           : 0px;
}

/* Style for spacer between data boxes */
.cssSpacer {
  height           : 64px;
}
```

```css
/* Non-hover state of contacts in the contact list */
.cssContactListNormal {
  background-color : #ffffff;
}

/* Non-hover state of contacts in the contact list, alternate row striping */
.cssContactListAlternate {
  background-color : #eaeaea;
}

/* Hover state of contacts in the contact list */
.cssContactListOver {
  background-color : #ffffa0;
  cursor           : pointer;
}

/* Style for main container box */
.cssMain {
  width             : 100%;
  height            : 580px;
  z-index           . 0;
}

/* Style of the initializing message seen at startup */
.cssInitializing {
  width             : 920px;
  height            : 2000px;
  z-index           : 1000;
}

/* Style of selector tabs */
.cssTab {
  position          : relative;
  left              : 2px;
  _left             : 4px; /* Style for IE */
}

/* Style of the contact list container */
.cssContactList {
  padding           : 4px;
  height            : 480px;
  border            : 2px solid #000000;
  overflow          : scroll;
}
```

```
/* Style of the box surrounding the data boxes */
.cssMainOuter {
  padding         : 4px;
  height          : 480px;
  border          : 2px solid #000000;
  overflow        : scroll;
}

/* Style of a data box */
.cssDataBox {
  width           : 100%;
  border          : 1px solid #000000;
}

/* Style for the header of a data box */
.cssDataBoxHeader {
  background-color : #e0e0f0;
}

/* Style for textboxes */
.cssTextbox {
  border : 1px solid #7f9db9;
}
```

The asterisk selector, as you've seen in other projects throughout this book, is here again employed to allow us to style everything on the page in one fell swoop.

Most of the style sheet is pretty self-explanatory, but one trick to point out is in the cssTab selector. This style is used to position the alphabetic selector tabs on the left side. To make the effect of one of them being the current tab work properly required that the tab overlap the border of the contact list box by a few pixels. Unfortunately, the number of pixels required didn't seem be consistent between IE and Firefox, so we use a little trick to allow for the difference.

When Firefox encounters an attribute name that begins with an underscore character, it ignores it. IE, on the other hand, ignores just the underscore, acting as if it were not there. So, what essentially happens here is that in both browsers, the first value of 2px for the left attribute is set. Then when the _left attribute is encountered, Firefox ignores it, but IE strips the underscore and treats it as if the left attribute were set again, overriding the 2px value with 4px. In this way, you can deal with the style sheet differences that sometimes come up between IE and Firefox, without having to write branching code to deal with it or use alternate style sheets for each browser.

■**Note** If you find yourself using the attribute name with a preceding underscore trick a lot, you probably want to rethink the way you're styling elements, because you may be doing things in a way that is too browser-specific. But here and there and every now and again, this is a good trick to know. Also be aware that in the future, one or both browsers could change this behavior, effectively breaking any page that uses it. This is just something to keep in mind.

Writing dojoStyles.css

dojoStyles.css is a style sheet containing just a small number of selectors that override default styles in Dojo. Listing 6-2 shows this rather diminutive source. Whoever said size doesn't matter must have been talking about this style sheet.

Listing 6-2. *The dojoStyles.css File*

```
/* Style for the fisheye listbar */
.dojoHtmlFisheyeListBar {
  margin          : 0 auto;
  text-align      : center;
}

/* Style for the fisheye container */
.outerbar {
  text-align      : center;
  position        : absolute;
  left            : 0px;
  top             : 0px;
  width           : 100%;
}
```

Although small, this style sheet provides some important styling. Without it, the way-cool fisheye icons wouldn't look quite right.

Writing index.htm

index.htm is where we find the bulk of the source that makes up the Contact Manager application. It is mostly just markup, with a sprinkle of script. Let's begin by taking a look at part of the <head> section where the style sheet and JavaScript imports are, as shown in Listing 6-3.

Listing 6-3. *Style Sheet and JavaScript Imports in index.htm*

```
<link rel="StyleSheet" href="css/dojoStyles.css" type="text/css">
<link rel="StyleSheet" href="css/styles.css" type="text/css">

<script type="text/javascript">
  var djConfig = {
    baseScriptUri : "js/dojo/",
    isDebug : true
  };
</script>
<script type="text/javascript" src="js/dojo/dojo.js"></script>
<script language="JavaScript" type="text/javascript">
  dojo.require("dojo.widget.FisheyeList");
  dojo.require("dojo.storage.*");
</script>
```

```
<script type="text/javascript" src="js/Contact.js"></script>
<script type="text/javascript" src="js/EventHandlers.js"></script>
<script type="text/javascript" src="js/DataManager.js"></script>
<script type="text/javascript" src="js/ContactManager.js"></script>
```

First, we import our two style sheets. Next comes a small block of JavaScript that sets up some Dojo properties. The djConfig variable is an associative array that Dojo looks for when it starts up (which means this code must come *before* the Dojo imports), and it contains a number of options for various Dojo settings. In this case, two are important:

- baseScriptUri defines the beginning of the path where all Dojo resources can be found. These include items such as source files to be imported, images for widgets, style sheets, and so on. In this case, we have Dojo installed in js/dojo, so that is the appropriate value for this attribute.

- isDebug determines if Dojo should output error messages.

A number of other options are available in djConfig (a few minutes with Google will reveal them), but for our purposes here, only these two are important.

Following that block is the import of the main part of Dojo itself. Immediately following that is a section with a series of dojo.require() function calls. Dojo is organized in a package structure, just as we built in Chapter 3. Dojo also implements the idea of importing small portions of it as required, and even offers wildcard (.*) import capabilities. What's more, if you import something that requires something else that you haven't imported, Dojo will import the dependencies for you.

Following the Dojo imports are four more plain JavaScript imports, which bring in the code that makes up the Contact Manager application. We will be looking at each in detail shortly.

Adding Bootstrap Code

At the end of the <head> section is a <script> block that contains what is essentially bootstrap code to get the application going. This code is shown in Listing 6-4.

Listing 6-4. *Bootstrap JavaScript in <head> of index.htm*

```
<script>

  // Shorthand function to get a reference to a DOM element.
  function $(inID) {
    return document.getElementById(inID);
  } // End $().

  // The contactManager instance that is the core of this application.
  var contactManager = new ContactManager();

  // Connect init() function in ContactManager to onLoad event.
  dojo.event.connect(window, "onload", contactManager.init);

</script>
```

The first thing you see is a function named $, which you've also seen in the projects in previous chapters. As you know by now, this is a function that wraps the ubiquitous `document.getElementById()` function call. This saves us some typing as we develop and makes for slightly cleaner looking code.

Following that is the instantiation of the `ContactManager` class, which is basically the core code of the application (you'll see this in just a bit).

Finally, we find the line:

```
dojo.event.connect(window, "onload", contactManager.init);
```

One thing that bites new Dojo developers (including me) is the fact that Dojo takes over the `onLoad` event and overwrites anything you may have put there yourself. This means that we can't simply call some function `onLoad` to initialize the application as we otherwise would. Instead, we use the `dojo.event` package, which is an aspect-oriented programming (AOP) implementation that allows you to hook up JavaScript to various events. This sounds simple, but `dojo.event` is an amazingly powerful package. You can hook up not only the usual UI events, such as `onLoad`, `onClick`, `onMouseOver`, and so on, but also hook up an event to any function call. So, if you want to have function A execute any time function B is called, for instance, without function B having to explicitly call function A (to avoid them having to know about each other), you can do so with the `dojo.event` package.

Here, we are saying that we want the function `init()` on the `contactManager` object to be called whenever the `onLoad` event of the `window` object fires. This gives us the same functionality as the usual use of `onLoad`, but using the Dojo event system.

In keeping with the idea of unobtrusive JavaScript, you'll notice there is precious little on the page so far. Some would argue that even what I have here should be in external `.js` files, but I think you can take that exercise a little too far sometimes. I don't feel it necessary to externalize every last bit of script, but certainly it should be kept to a minimum, and I think you'll agree that is the case here.

Initializing the Application

Now we come to the `<body>` of the page, which begins like this:

```
<div id="divInitializing" class="cssInitializing">
  <br><br><br><br><br><br><br><br><br><br>
  <center>...Initializing Contact Manager, please wait...</center>
</div>
```

When the page is first loaded, we don't want the user to be able to fire UI events before the UI has fully loaded (for example, clicking the save button before the persisted contacts have been fully restored might not be such a good thing). So, to start out, the user sees a message saying the application is initializing. Once everything is set to go, this `<div>` is hidden, and the main content is shown.

Adding the Fisheye List

Now we come to some UI fun. One of the things Dojo does really well—what it's probably most famous for—is widgets. One of the singularly most impressive widgets it contains (*the* most impressive for my money) is the fisheye list. Have you ever seen the launch bar in Mac OS?

Do you like how the icons expand and shrink as you mouse over them? Well, Dojo's fisheye list lets you have the same feature in your own web applications, as you can see in Figure 6-9. Of course, seeing it statically in print doesn't quite do it justice, so fire up the application and just mouse over the icons a bit. I think you'll have fun doing nothing but that for a few minutes.

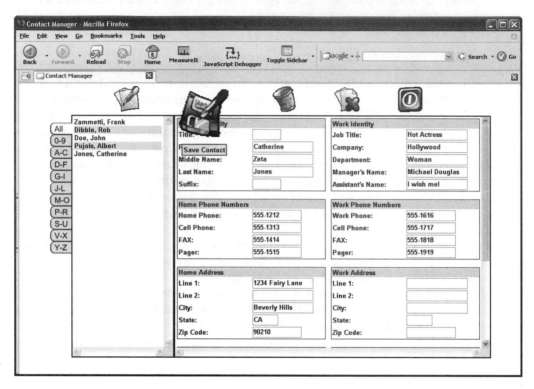

Figure 6-9. *The Dojo fisheye widget coolness—'nough said*

So is it difficult to make use of that widget? Heck no! Dojo allows you to define most, if not all, of its widgets with nothing but HTML. Listing 6-5 shows the markup responsible for the fisheye list in this application.

Listing 6-5. *The Fisheye Definition Markup*

```
<div class="outerbar">
  <div class="dojo-FisheyeList"
    dojo:itemWidth="64" dojo:itemHeight="64"
    dojo:itemMaxWidth="128" dojo:itemMaxHeight="128"
    dojo:orientation="horizontal" dojo:effectUnits="1"
    dojo:itemPadding="10" dojo:attachEdge="top"
    dojo:labelEdge="bottom" dojo:enableCrappySvgSupport="false">
    <div class="dojo-FisheyeListItem"
      onClick="contactManager.doNewContact();"
      dojo:iconsrc="img/icon_new.gif" caption="New Contact">
    </div>
```

```
        <div class="dojo-FisheyeListItem"
          dojo:iconsrc="img/transPix.gif" caption="">
        </div>
        <div class="dojo-FisheyeListItem"
          onClick="contactManager.doSaveContact();"
          dojo:iconsrc="img/icon_save.gif" caption="Save Contact">
        </div>
        <div class="dojo-FisheyeListItem"
          dojo:iconsrc="img/transPix.gif" caption="">
        </div>
        <div class="dojo-FisheyeListItem"
          onClick="contactManager.doDeleteContact()"
          dojo:iconsrc="img/icon_delete.gif" caption="Delete Contact">
        </div>
        <div class="dojo-FisheyeListItem"
          dojo:iconsrc="img/transPix.gif" caption="">
        </div>
        <div class="dojo-FisheyeListItem"
          onClick="contactManager.doClearContacts()"
          dojo:iconsrc="img/icon_clear.gif" caption="Clear Contacts">
        </div>
        <div class="dojo-FisheyeListItem"
          dojo:iconsrc="img/transPix.gif" caption="">
        </div>
        <div class="dojo-FisheyeListItem"
          onClick="contactManager.doExit();"
          dojo:iconsrc="img/icon_exit.gif" caption="Exit Contact Manager">
        </div>
      </div>
    </div>
```

When the page loads, Dojo will parse it, looking for tags that it recognizes as defining widgets. It then replaces them with the appropriate markup to form the widget. In this case, setting the class of a <div> to dojo-FisheyeList gets the job done. You'll notice that this <div> also contains a number of custom attributes. This is also a hallmark of Dojo and how you configure options for the widgets. Each of the icons is simply another <div>, this time with a class of dojo-FisheyeListItem. Notice that we put essentially blank icons between each real icon. There may be another way that I am unaware of, but this is how I was able to space the icons out a bit; otherwise, they looked a little cramped to me.

Feel free to play around with the attributes on the second <div>. By manipulating them, you can alter the fisheye list, such as making the expanded icons bigger, changing how far away from an icon you need to be to activate, and so on. Experimentation is a great way to learn Dojo (in fact, it's often the *only* way to really figure things out). Dojo is frequently worth the effort, so I certainly encourage you to put a little time into fiddling with it, and messing with the fisheye attributes is a good, gentle start.

Continuing on, for each icon, we define an onClick handler to do whatever it is the icon represents. This is again a situation where strict unobtrusive JavaScript practice would be to not put the event handlers in-line. I'd like to make two points here:

- If the event handler is just a call to some JavaScript function that does the actual work, I see no real problem having the handlers in-line. In fact, I think it makes more sense for them to be there, as they are attributes of the element and therefore should probably be defined with the element. Also, this will aid performance since no script has to process to hook up the event handlers.

- Because Dojo is generating markup in place of these <div> elements, trying to hook up the events after the fact would have been a bit more difficult than usual. The dojo.event package may have helped, but it would still not have been straightforward.

So, I won't lose any sleep tonight because of in-line event handlers.

As always, don't blindly follow any guideline, no matter how reasonable it generally seems. Instead, think about each situation and make an appropriate choice.

OK, putting philosophy aside and getting back to concrete code, let's move to the contact list section.

Adding the Contact List

Following the fisheye markup is a chunk of markup that defines the selector tabs on the left. In the interest of brevity, let's just look at the first one and note that the rest are virtually identical:

```
<img src="img/sel_xx_over.gif" id="sel_XX" class="cssTab"
  onClick="contactManager.eventHandlers.stClick(this);"
  onMouseOver="contactManager.eventHandlers.stOver(this);"
  onMouseOut="contactManager.eventHandlers.stOut(this);"><br>
```

This is the All tab, meaning it shows all contacts. The ID of the tab is used to determine the image it should have, based on its current state (that is, if it's the selected tab or if it's being hovered over). For instance, in this case, the ID is sel_XX, and as you can see, that is the beginning of the name of the image that is the initial source for this tab. When we look at the event handlers (which are again called from in-line handlers here), I think you'll find that this all makes more sense. As I mentioned, all the tabs that follow are the same, except that the ID is different. For instance, the next tab's ID is sel_09 because it is the tab for showing contacts beginning with any character from 0 to 9.

Following this section of markup is a very small bit:

```
<td width="200" valign="top">
  <div class="cssContactList" id="contactList">
  </div>
</td>
```

The <div> contactList is, not surprisingly, where our list of contacts will be inserted. The list is filtered by the selector tabs, and this <div>'s contents will be rewritten any time a new tab is selected, or when a contact is added or deleted.

Following this is the remainder of the markup for the data-entry boxes where we fill in the information for our contacts. This is a big bit of markup that all looks pretty similar really, so let's just review a representative snippet of it. The section for entering contact identity (both personal and business) is shown in Listing 6-6.

Listing 6-6. *Section of the Data-Entry Markup*

```
<tr>
  <!-- Contact Identity -->
  <td width="49%" valign="top">
    <div class="cssDataBox">
      <table border="0" cellpadding="1" cellspacing="1"
        width="100%">
        <tr>
          <td colspan="2" class="cssDataBoxHeader">
            Contact Identity
          </td>
        </tr>
        <tr>
          <td width="50%" valign="middle">Title:</td>
          <td width="50%" valign="middle">
            <input type="text" id="title"
              maxlength="3" size="4" class="cssTextbox">
          </td>
        </tr>
        <tr>
          <td valign="middle">First Name:</td>
          <td valign="middle">
            <input type="text" id="firstName"
              maxlength="15" size="15" class="cssTextbox">
          </td>
        </tr>
        <tr>
          <td valign="middle">Middle Name:</td>
          <td valign="middle">
            <input type="text" id="middleName"
              maxlength="15" size="15" class="cssTextbox">
          </td>
        </tr>
        <tr>
          <td valign="middle">Last Name:</td>
          <td valign="middle">
            <input type="text" id="lastName"
              maxlength="20" size="15" class="cssTextbox">
          </td>
        </tr>
        <tr>
          <td valign="middle">Suffix:</td>
          <td valign="middle">
            <input type="text" id="suffix"
              maxlength="3" size="4" class="cssTextbox">
          </td>
        </tr>
```

```
        </table>
      </div>
  </td>
  <!-- Divider -->
  <td width="2%"> </td>
  <!-- Work Identity -->
  <td width="49%" valign="top">
    <div class="cssDataBox">
      <table border="0" cellpadding="1" cellspacing="1"
        width="100%">
        <tr>
          <td colspan="2" class="cssDataBoxHeader">
            Work Identity
          </td>
        </tr>
        <tr>
          <td width="50%" valign="middle">Job Title:</td>
          <td width="50%" valign="middle">
            <input type="text" id="jobTitle"
              maxlength="24" size="15" class="cssTextbox">
          </td>
        </tr>
        <tr>
          <td valign="middle">Company:</td>
          <td valign="middle">
            <input type="text" id="company"
              maxlength="25" size="15" class="cssTextbox">
          </td>
        </tr>
        <tr>
          <td valign="middle">Department:</td>
          <td valign="middle">
            <input type="text" id="department"
              maxlength="25" size="15" class="cssTextbox">
          </td>
        </tr>
        <tr>
          <td valign="middle">Manager's Name:</td>
          <td valign="middle">
            <input type="text" id="managerName"
              maxlength="30" size="15" class="cssTextbox">
          </td>
        </tr>
```

```
        <tr>
          <td valign="middle">Assistant's Name:</td>
          <td valign="middle">
            <input type="text" id="assistantName"
              maxlength="30" size="15" class="cssTextbox">
          </td>
        </tr>
      </table>
    </div>
  </td>
</tr>
```

This is perfectly typical HTML. Note that the sizes of the fields have been limited such that each contact takes up just a hair under 1024 bytes. This is done so that if you wanted to modify the code to store contacts with plain-old cookies instead (hint, hint), you could do so and fit four contacts per cookie (remember that each cookie is limited to 4kb).

Also note the cssTextbox style class being applied. This is to deal with a situation where the border can change to inset when the field gets the focus, but not change back. This appears to have been a browser quirk, but specifically setting the border to what we want in the cssTextbox class takes care of it.

And with that, we have only one bit of markup left to look at, and that's the goodbye.htm page.

Writing goodbye.htm

There isn't a whole lot to the goodbye.htm file, as Listing 6-7 clearly indicates.

Listing 6-7. *The goodbye.htm File (Not Much to See Here)*

```html
<html>

  <head>

    <title>Contact Manager</title>

  </head>

  <body>
    Thanks for using the contact manager... goodbye!
  </body>

</html>
```

This is a simple landing page that you see when you click the Exit icon. It's just always good form to end on a polite, "thanks for stopping by" kind of note.

Let's begin our review of the JavaScript files with the EventHandlers class, since this is something of a stand-alone piece of code.

Writing EventHandlers.js

In index.htm, you saw that the selector tabs called event-handler functions in this class. Also, as you shall soon see, all of the input fields actually do the same thing ("Huh?" you're thinking, I don't remember seeing any event handlers on the input fields," and you're right). Also, the contact list you see on the left side of the screen makes use of some functions here as well, but these are all simply UI-related functions. In other words, if you took these functions out, things would still basically work, although the UI wouldn't be as reactive as it is: the selectors wouldn't turn red when you hovered over them, the input fields wouldn't be highlighted when they gained focus, and the contact list wouldn't have a hover effect at all. All of these reactions are within the EventHandlers class, the class diagram of which is shown in Figure 6-10.

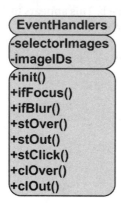

Figure 6-10. *UML diagram of the EventHandlers class*

First, the EventHandlers class is instantiated in the ContactManager class, which we will look at later, and the reference to it is one of the fields on ContactManager (the reason all the event handlers in index.htm are in the form contactManager.*xxxx*()).

The first item in the EventHandlers class is the selectorImages field, which is an array that will hold references to the preloaded images for the selector tabs. Next is another array field, imageIDs. This is a list of the selector tab IDs. The filenames of the graphics for each tab can be formed using these IDs, and so can the ID of the elements on the page, and we'll need both.

As I mentioned, ContactManager will instantiate EventHandlers and also initialize it by calling init() on EventHandlers. This init() function is as follows:

```
this.init = function() {

  this.selectorImages = new Array();

  // Load images from the above array and store them in selectorImages.
  for (var i = 0; i < this.imageIDs.length; i++) {
    var sid = this.imageIDs[i];
    this.selectorImages[sid] = new Image();
    this.selectorImages[sid].src = "img/" +
      sid + ".gif";
    this.selectorImages[sid + "_over"] = new Image();
    this.selectorImages[sid + "_over"].src = "img/" +
      sid + "_over.gif";
  }

  // Get all input fields and attach onFocus and onBlur handlers.
  var inputFields = document.getElementsByTagName("input");
  for (i = 0; i < inputFields.length; i++) {
    inputFields[i].onfocus = this.ifFocus;
    inputFields[i].onblur = this.ifBlur;
  }

} // End init().
```

The first task this function performs is preloading the images for the selector tabs. To do so, it iterates over the elements of the imageIDs array. For each, it instantiates an Image object and sets its src attribute to the filename of the image. Two images for each tab are loaded: one in its nonhover state and the other in its hover state. These images are added to the array, keyed by the ID taken from the imageIDs array.

What we wind up with is an associative array selectorImages, which contains all the preloaded images for the two states for each tab, and we can get at each image by using the ID as the key (for the hover images, it's the ID plus the string _over appended). This all saves us from writing explicit code to load each image. If we want to add more tabs later, as long as they follow the same naming scheme, we will need to add only the ID to the imageIDs array.

The next task this function performs is hooking up the event handlers to the input fields. Ah yes, there we go—that's how it works. We get the collection of <input> fields on the page using the handy-dandy document.getElementsByTagName() function. Then, for each of them, we attach onFocus and onBlur events, pointing to the ifFocus() and ifBlur() functions of the EventHandlers class. Nice to not need to specify these handlers on each input element, huh?

The idea of attaching event handlers to plain-old markup is another tenet of unobtrusiveness. While I'm not sure I like the idea of doing so for every event handler on a page, in cases like this, where a rather large number of elements need the same event handlers attached, this strikes me as better than having to put the handlers in-line with each element in the markup.

I suppose we should look at those ifFocus() and ifBlur() functions, shouldn't we? Well, here you go:

```
// ********** Input Field focus.
this.ifFocus = function() {

  this.style.backgroundColor = "#ffffa0";

} // End ifFocus();
```

```
// ********** Input Field blur.
this.ifBlur = function() {

  this.style.backgroundColor = "#ffffff";

} // End ifBlur().
```

Certainly, these are nothing special. They just change the background color of the input field: yellow when it has focus or white when it loses focus. Highlighting the current field is something that goes over well with most users, so it's a good thing to implement.

In the ifFocus() and ifBlur() functions, note the use of the keyword this, which can be a bit confusing. Recall that these functions are attached as event handlers to elements on the page. When they are called, the keyword this in the line with this.style.backgroundColor refers to the element firing the event because, at runtime, the keyword this is always evaluated in the context in which it executes. Contrast this to the usage of this in the line with this.ifBlur. In that case, this refers to the EventHandlers class because it is defined within that class. You can view this as static vs. dynamic interpretation of the this keyword; static being the usage to attach the method to the EventHandler class, and dynamic being the usage with the event handler. This is commonly referred to as *early binding* vs. *late binding*. Late binding occurs at runtime, while early binding occurs at compile time. Of course, there is no compile time with JavaScript, but it still means before the code actually runs.

Following those functions are three that deal with the selector tabs:

```
// ********** Selector Tab mouseOver.
this.stOver = function(inTab) {

  inTab.src = this.selectorImages[inTab.id + "_over"].src;

} // End stOver().
```

```
// ********** Selector Tab mouseOut.
this.stOut = function(inTab) {
```

```
    // Only switch state if not the current tab.
    if (contactManager.currentTab != inTab.id.substr(4, 2)) {
      inTab.src = this.selectorImages[inTab.id].src;
    }

  } // End stOut().



  // ********** Selector Tab click.
  this.stClick = function(inTab) {

    // Reset all tabs before setting the current one.
    for (var i = 0; i < this.imageIDs.length; i++) {
      var sid = this.imageIDs[i];
      $(sid).src = this.selectorImages[sid].src;
    }

    inTab.src = this.selectorImages[inTab.id + "_over"].src;

    // Record the current tab, and redisplay the contact list.
    contactManager.currentTab - inTab.id.substr(4, 2);
    contactManager.displayContactList();

  } // End stClick().
```

stOver() and stOut() handle the onMouseOver and onMouseOut events, respectively. They make use of the preloaded images stored in the selectorImages array discussed previously. It's a simple matter of changing the src attribute on the tab firing the event to the src of the appropriate image in the array. Of course, if a user hovers over the current selected tab and then mouses off it, we don't want to reset it to the nonhover state, hence the check in stOut() to be sure the tab that fired the event isn't the currently selected tab.

stClick() is just a little more interesting. When the user clicks a tab, it becomes the current tab, which means it remains in the hover state until another one is clicked. To accomplish this, we first have to reset the currently selected tab to its nonhover state. I decided to do this by resetting all the tabs, and then setting up the new current tab.[3] After the tabs are taken care of, we call displayContactList() on the ContactManager object to update the contact list to correspond to only those contacts that should show up on the new current tab.

Last up in the EventHandler class are the two functions that deal with mouse events on the items in the contact list on the left side of the screen:

---

3. I could have just as easily reset only the current tab, rather than all of them. You can view it as simply seeing an alternative approach in action.

```
// ********** Contact List mouseOver.
this.clOver = function(inContact) {

  inContact.className = "cssContactListOver";

} // End clOver().


// ********** Contact List mouseOut.
this.clOut = function(inContact) {

  if (inContact.getAttribute("altRow") == "true") {
    inContact.className = "cssContactListAlternate";
  } else {
    inContact.className = "cssContactListNormal";
  }

} // End clOut().
```

For the sake of demonstrating a slightly different technique, I decided that, unlike the handlers for the input fields, which access style attributes of the target element directly, here I would set the style class for the target element as appropriate. It is generally better I think to do it this way, since the styles are abstracted out into style sheets as they probably should be, but now you've seen that you can go the other way, too, if you feel it is more appropriate.

Here, the only real complexity is in the clOut() function. The style to switch the element to when the mouse leaves it can be one of two because the contacts in the contact list are displayed with alternate row striping, typical of many display lists. In order to determine which should be set, we interrogate the custom altRow attribute that each contact in the list carries. When that attribute is set to true, we know it is an element with a gray background (meaning the cssContactListAlternate style selector); otherwise, it is a white background (using the cssContactListNormal selector). Other than that, the clOut() function is pretty straightforward.

Writing Contact.js

If you are familiar with the concept of a Data Transfer Object (DTO) or Value Object (VO), the Contact.js source will be nothing at all special to you. That's because it simply defines a DTO representing a contact. Its class diagram is shown in Figure 6-11.

Figure 6-11. *UML diagram of the Contact class*

First up is a list of properties that represents a contact:

```
this.title = "";
this.firstName = "";
this.middleName = "";
this.lastName = "";
this.suffix = "";
this.jobTitle = "";
this.company = "";
this.department = "";
this.managerName = "";
this.assistantName = "";
this.homePhone = "";
this.homeCellPhone = "";
this.homeFAX = "";
this.homePager = "";
this.workPhone = "";
this.workCellPhone = "";
this.workFAX = "";
this.workPager = "";
this.homeEMail = "";
this.homeWebSite = "";
this.homeIMNickname = "";
this.workEMail = "";
this.workWebSite = "";
this.workIMNickname = "";
this.spouseName = "";
this.childrenName = "";
this.anniversary = "";
this.birthday = "";
this.highSchoolInfo = "";
this.collegeInfo = "";
this.custom1 = "";
this.custom2 = "";
this.homeAddressLine1 = "";
this.homeAddressLine2 = "";
this.homeCity = "";
this.homeState = "";
this.homeZipCode = "";
this.workAddressLine1 = "";
this.workAddressLine2 = "";
this.workCity = "";
this.workState = "";
this.workZipCode = "";

this.arrayIndex = -1;
```

Notice that straggler at the end, arrayIndex. This is a field that you can essentially think of as transient and is the index into the array of contacts stored in the DataManager where this contact is stored. This value will change as contacts are deleted, and will be dynamically calculated when contacts are restored at application initialization. Note that it *does not* appear in the fieldsArray we will discuss next, which is essentially the reason it is transient (the reason it isn't in the list should become apparent as we discuss fieldsArray).

After this, we find an interesting bit of code that certainly requires some explanation. It is the fieldsArray variable, which is an array containing the names of all the fields of this class, like so:

```
this.fieldsArray - [
  "title", "firstName", "middleName", "lastName", "suffix", "jobTitle",
  "company", "department", "managerName", "assistantName", "homePhone",
  "homeCellPhone", "homeFAX", "homePager", "workPhone", "workCellPhone",
  "workFAX", "workPager", "homeEMail", "homeWebSite", "homeIMNickname",
  "workEMail", "workWebSite", "workIMNickname", "spouseName", "childrenName",
  "anniversary", "birthday", "highSchoolInfo", "collegeInfo", "custom1",
  "custom2", "homeAddressLine1", "homeAddressLine2", "homeCity", "homeState",
  "homeZipCode", "workAddressLine1", "workAddressLine2", "workCity",
  "workState", "workZipCode"
];
```

If you look at these data fields, and then examine index.htm and look at the IDs of the input fields, you'll see that they match. This should be a clue as to what this array is for, but don't worry, we're about to figure it out together!

At various points in the application, we will need to populate an instance of the Contact class from the input fields, or populate the screen from the data fields within the Contact instance. One could certainly imagine writing code along these lines:

```
this.firstName = $("firstName").value;
this.lastName = $("lastName").value;
```

One could also imagine jumping off the Brooklyn Bridge on a hot day, surviving, and being cooled off. But just like jumping off the bridge, writing code like that isn't the best way to achieve the desired goal. Instead, it would be great if we could write some generic code to populate the object, or the input fields, without that code actually knowing precisely which fields are available. This is all the better when we want to add elements to a contact. That's exactly the kind of code that is present in the Contact class—for instance, in the populateContact() function:

```
this.populateContact = function() {

  for (var i = 0; i < this.fieldsArray.length; i++) {
    var fieldValue = $(this.fieldsArray[i]).value;
    this[this.fieldsArray[i]] = fieldValue;
  }

} // End populateContact();
```

Now the purpose of that `fieldsArray` member is probably starting to make sense. We iterate over the array, and because the members of the `Contact` class instance to populate are the same as the IDs of the input fields, we can use the values of the array to access both, thereby making this code agnostic about which fields are actually present in the class and on the screen. If we want to add a field to record a contact's blood type, we could do that by simply adding it to the `fieldsArray` member, and none of the population code would need to change.

Populating the screen is even simpler, but uses precisely the same concept:

```
this.populateScreen = function() {

  for (var i = 0; i < this.fieldsArray.length; i++) {
    $(this.fieldsArray[i]).value = this[this.fieldsArray[i]];
  }

} // End populateScreen().
```

The next function we come to is `toString()`. Recall that, as in Java, all JavaScript objects implement a `toString()` function. The basic version inherited from the base `Object` class (which, again as in Java, all objects in JavaScript inherit from) may or may not be very useful. However, we can override it simply and provide some output that is more useful. In this case, the output is JSON representing the contact. Here's the `toString()` function:

```
this.toString = function() {

  var json = "";
  json += "{ ";
  // For each field in the fieldsArray, get the value and add it to the JSON.
  for (var i = 0; i < this.fieldsArray.length; i++) {
    if (json != "{ ") {
      json += ", ";
    }
    json += "\"" + this.fieldsArray[i] + "\":\"" +
      this[this.fieldsArray[i]] + "\"";
  }
  json += " }";
  return json;

} // End toString().
```

You may be wondering why I didn't instead have something like a `toJSON()` function. That would have worked perfectly well, except that overriding `toString()` instead makes the code to get the contact as JSON just a hair cleaner, as you'll see later in the `DataManager` class. Also, it makes debugging a little better because, if you want to display a given `Contact` instance—for example, in an `alert()` pop-up—you'll get something that is a bit more helpful than the default `toString()` provides. And that's always a good thing.

The last function found in the `Contact` class is `restoreFromJSON()`:

```
this.restoreFromJSON = function(inJSON) {

  eval("json = (" + inJSON + ")");
  for (var i = 0; i < this.fieldsArray.length; i++) {
    this[this.fieldsArray[i]] = json[this.fieldsArray[i]];
  }

} // End restoreFromJSON().
```

The name says it all. This function populates the Contact class instance it is executed on from an incoming string of JSON. I think the beauty of storing the contact as JSON should be pretty apparent here: this code is amazingly simple and compact. We simply iterate over that handy fieldsArray again, and for each element, we set the appropriate field in the class from the parsed JSON object. It's very simple, which is also always a good thing.

By the way, remember the arrayIndex field that I mentioned was transient? Do you see now why that is? By virtue of not being listed in fieldsArray, it is neither included in the JSON generated by toString() nor is it reconstituted by restoreFromJSON().

Writing ContactManager.js

The ContactManager class, defined in the ContactManager.js file, is the main code behind this application. Its class diagram is shown in Figure 6-12.

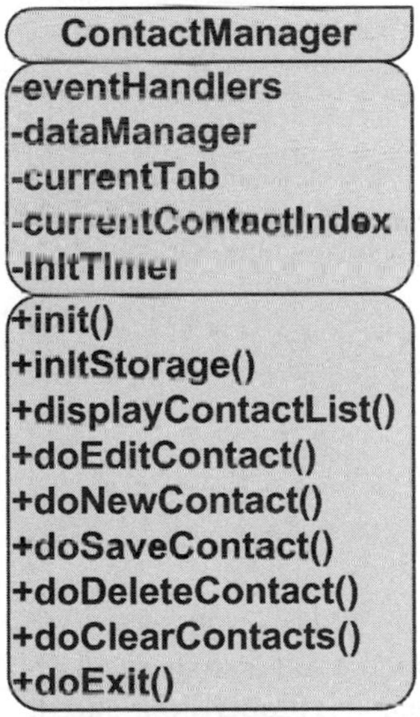

ContactManager
-eventHandlers
-dataManager
-currentTab
-currentContactIndex
-initTimer
+init()
+initStorage()
+displayContactList()
+doEditContact()
+doNewContact()
+doSaveContact()
+doDeleteContact()
+doClearContacts()
+doExit()

Figure 6-12. *UML diagram of the ContactManager class*

This class starts off with five data fields:

- eventHandlers: A reference to an instance of the EventHandlers class

- dataManager: A reference to an instance of the DataManager class

- currentTab: The ID of the currently selected tab

- currentContactIndex: The index into the array of contacts (stored in the DataManager class) of the contact currently being edited (or –1 if creating a new contact)

- initTimer: A reference to the timer used during application initialization

Initializing

Recall that in index.htm, we use the Dojo event system to hook up an onLoad event that calls the init() function of the ContactManager class. Well, now it's time to see what's in that function:

```
this.init = function() {

  contactManager.eventHandlers = new EventHandlers();
  contactManager.eventHandlers.init();
  contactManager.dataManager = new DataManager();
  this.initTimer  = setTimeout("contactManager.initStorage()", 500);

} // End init().
```

First, the EventHandlers class is instantiated and the reference to it stored in the eventHandlers field. Next, init() is called on that class.

Then we do the same thing for the DataManager class, but we don't call init() on it right away, as we do with the EventHandlers instance. Instead, we start a timer that every 500 milliseconds calls the initStorage() function of the ContactManager. That function is as follows:

```
this.initStorage = function() {

  if (dojo.storage.manager.isInitialized()) {
    clearTimeout(this.initTimer);
    contactManager.dataManager.init();
    contactManager.displayContactList();
    $("divInitializing").style.display = "none";
    this.initTimer = null;
  } else {
    this.initTimer  = setTimeout("contactManager.initStorage()", 500);
  }

} // End initStorage().
```

What's this all about you ask? Simply, Bad Things™ will happen if you try to use Dojo's functions for working with shared objects before the storage system has properly initialized. When we look at the DataManager class, you'll see that one of the things done in its init() function is to restore saved contacts from persistent storage (read local shared objects). Therefore, we can't call that function immediately as we did with the EventHandlers instance. In fact, we can't call it until the storage system has fully initialized. And that's the reason for the timer. Every 500 milliseconds, we check with Dojo to see if the storage system has initialized yet. If not, we just keep firing the timer until it does.

As soon as the storage system initializes, we stop the timer and call init() on the DataManager instance. At that point, we also display the contact list so that any restored contacts will be available to the user, and finally we hide the initializing message discussed earlier. Once the DataManager has been initialized, the application is then ready for user interaction.

Generating the Contacts

Recall that the list of contacts restored from persistent storage is displayed during this initialization cycle. Here is the code that generates the list of contacts:

```
this.displayContactList = function() {

  // Get a list of contacts for the current tab.
  var contacts = this.dataManager.listContacts(this.currentTab);

  // Generate the markup for the list.
  var html = "";
  var alt = false;
  for (var i = 0, i < contacts.length; i++) {
    html += "<div indexNum=\"" + contacts[i].arrayIndex + "\" ";
    html += "onMouseOver=\"contactManager.eventHandlers.clOver(this);\" ";
    html += "onMouseOut=\"contactManager.eventHandlers.clOut(this);\" ";
    html += "onClick=\"contactManager.doEditContact(" +
      "this.getAttribute('indexNum'));\" ";
    if (alt) {
      html += "class=\"cssContactListAlternate\" altRow=\"true\">";
      alt = false;
    } else {
      html += "class=\"cssContactListNormal\" altRow=\"false\">";
      alt = true;
    }
    html += contacts[i].lastName + ", " + contacts[i].firstName;
    html += "</div>";
  }

  // Display it.
  $("contactList").innerHTML = html;

} // End displayContactList().
```

First, the list of contacts is retrieved from the DataManager. We pass the listContacts() function of the DataManager class the currently selected tab so that the list can be filtered accordingly. Next, we cycle through the returned contacts (each element of the returned array is a Contact object) and construct the appropriate markup for the list. Each element in the list has mouse events attached to highlight the contact when the user hovers over it. And each element also contains an onClick handler that calls doEditContact() in the ContactManager class, which loads the contact into the input fields on the screen for editing. Once the markup is fully constructed, it is inserted into the contactList <div>, which shows it to the user.

Editing Contacts

Speaking of the doEditContact() function, let's see that now, shall we?

```
this.doEditContact = function(inIndex) {

    // Record contact index, retrieve contact and populate screen.
    this.currentContactIndex = inIndex;
    var contact = this.dataManager.getContact(inIndex);
    contact.populateScreen();

}
```

Wow, really, that's it? Yes indeed. Note in the displayContactList() function that each contact listed has an indexNum custom attribute attached to it. This value corresponds to the value of the arrayIndex member of the Contact class. Since we are viewing a subset of the contacts array when a particular tab is set, using this value ensures that a contact's indexNum attribute is the correct index into the array. This way, when the user clicks a contact to edit it, we pull the correct data to display.

For instance, if you click the A-C tab, and you see three of ten stored contacts, the array returned by listContacts() in the DataManager class will simply return an array with three elements. But the index in that array (0, 1, or 2) may not match the index into the contacts array for a given contact. In other words, the first contact returned by listContacts() is index 0 in that returned array, but may actually be the contact at index 9 in the main contacts array. Therefore, if we used the index number of the returned array as the value for indexNum, we wouldn't go after the correct element in the contacts array (in this example, 0 instead of 9). We instead need the arrayIndex field of the Contact object.

Adding Button Functions

The ContactManager class contains five more functions, and each corresponds to one of the five buttons at the top of the page. First up is doNewContact():

```
this.doNewContact = function() {

    if (this.initTimer == null) {

        if (confirm("Create New Contact\n\nYou will lose any unsaved changes.  " +
            "Are you sure?")) {
            document.forms[0].reset();
            this.currentContactIndex = -1;
        }

    }

} // End doNewContact().
```

Not really much going on here, I admit. One thing you'll notice in this and the next functions is the check of initTimer being null. When the application starts, initTimer has a value of –1. When the initialization cycle completes, it is set to null. Since we don't want the user to be able to do anything until the application initializes fully, and since Dojo produces the fisheye icons before initialization completes, we need to ensure initialization is finished before we process any user events. That's why we need the check that allows the code to execute only after initTimer is null, meaning everything is ready to go.

Once that is the case, we simply make sure the user wants to create a new contact, because if she had any edits on the page, they would be lost. Then we reset the form, which clears all our input fields, and set the currentContactIndex to –1, which indicates to the rest of the code that a new contact is being created.

Next up is the function called when the save icon is clicked, appropriately named doSaveContact():

```
this.doSaveContact = function() {

  if (this.initTimer == null) {

    // Make sure required fields are filled in.
    if ($("firstName").value == "" || $("lastName").value == "") {
      alert("First Name and Last Name are required fields");
      return false;
    }

    // Create a new contact and populate it from the entry fields.
    var contact = new Contact();
    contact.arrayIndex = this.currentContactIndex;
    contact.populateContact();

    // Save the contact.
    this.dataManager.saveContact(contact, this.currentContactIndex);

    // Redisplay the updated contact list.
    this.displayContactList();

    // Reset the entry fields and currentContactIndex.
    document.forms[0].reset();
    this.currentContactIndex = -1;

  }

} // End doSaveContact().
```

This function handles two different save situations: saving a new contact or saving edits to an existing contact. So, after our check of initTimer as in doNewContact(), we first do a quick edit check to ensure a first name and last name have been entered. These two fields are the only required fields for a contact because they are used to generate the contact list, and this is true whether it is a new contact or an existing one.

Once that is done, we instantiate a new Contact object and tell it to populate itself from the input fields by calling its populateContact() function. We also set the arrayIndex field based on the currentContactIndex value, which will be –1, as set in doNewContact() if this is a new contact, or to the appropriate array index if editing an existing contact.

Next, we call saveContact() on the DataManager, passing it the contact and the index (we'll be looking at that code shortly). After that, we regenerate the contact list and show it because we may have just added a contact that should be immediately visible (we're on the tab the contact would appear on naturally or on the All tab). Lastly, we reset the input fields and the currentContactIndex value (which is actually a little redundant, but does no harm), and that's how a contact is saved.

The next function to look at is doDeleteContact(), and I'll give you just one guess what it does:

```
this.doDeleteContact = function() {

  if (this.initTimer == null) {

    if (this.currentContactIndex != -1 &&
      confirm("Are you sure you want to delete this contact?")) {

      // Ask the data manager to do the deletion.
      this.dataManager.deleteContact(this.currentContactIndex);

      // Redisplay the updated contact list.
      this.displayContactList();

      // Reset the entry fields and currentContactIndex.
      document.forms[0].reset();
      this.currentContactIndex = -1;

    }

  }

} // End doDeleteContact().
```

After the usual check of initTimer, and a confirmation that the user really wants to delete the current contact (which includes a check to be sure there is a contact selected to be deleted), we ask the DataManager to do the deletion for us, passing it the index of the contact to delete. Once again, we regenerate and display the contact list, and reset the input fields and the currentContactIndex value (and yes, it's still a bit redundant here, but it still does no harm, and I prefer variables that aren't based on user input being in known states at any given time because they make for easier debugging sessions).

The next function is doClearContacts(), which is a giant, shiny "push to destroy the universe" button. Well, maybe not quite, but it does delete *all* contacts from persistent storage, so it isn't something that you want the user clicking willy-nilly. For that reason, there is a double verification required, as you can plainly see:

```
this.doClearContacts = function() {

  if (this.initTimer == null) {

    if (confirm("This will PERMANENTLY delete ALL contacts from " +
      "persistent storage\n\nAre you sure??")) {
      if (confirm("Sorry to be a nudge, but are you REALLY, REALLY SURE " +
        "you want to lose ALL your contacts FOREVER??")) {
        this.dataManager.clearContacts();
        // Redisplay now empty contact list.
        this.displayContactList();
        // Reset form for good measure.
        document.forms[0].reset();
        this.currentContactIndex = -1;
        alert("Ok, it's done.  Don't come cryin' to me later.");
      }
    }

  }

} // End doClearContacts().
```

Only one function remains, doExit(), and it's a pretty trivial piece of code:

```
this.doExit = function() {

  if (this.initTimer == null) {

    if (confirm("Exit Contact Manager\n\nAre you sure?")) {
      window.location - "goodbye.htm";
    }

  }

} // End doExit().
```

Nothing fancy here—just a quick confirmation, and then the browser is redirected to the goodbye.htm page we looked at earlier.

Writing DataManager.js

Throughout the ContactManager code, you saw a number of calls to the DataManager. Now we come to the point in our show where we need to take a look at that class and see what's going on under the covers there. Its class diagram is shown in Figure 6-13.

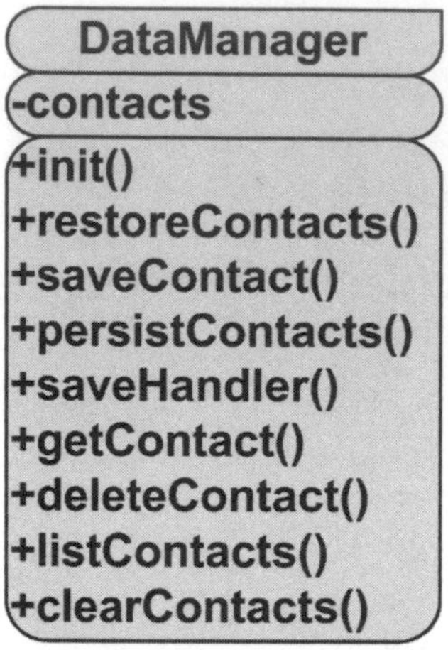

```
┌─────────────────────────┐
│      DataManager        │
├─────────────────────────┤
│ -contacts               │
├─────────────────────────┤
│ +init()                 │
│ +restoreContacts()      │
│ +saveContact()          │
│ +persistContacts()      │
│ +saveHandler()          │
│ +getContact()           │
│ +deleteContact()        │
│ +listContacts()         │
│ +clearContacts()        │
└─────────────────────────┘
```

Figure 6-13. *UML diagram of the DataManager class*

I wrote the DataManager class with the idea in mind that you could swap it out for another implementation, perhaps one that made use of some ActiveX control (as evil as those are) to persist the contacts and deal with the underlying storage mechanism. As such, its public API is pretty generic and conducive to such a swap.

The first item in the DataManager class is the contacts array. This is, not surprisingly, the array in which our contacts are stored. This array is loaded from shared objects when the application initializes, and until the user exits the application, the array is essentially kept synchronized with the persistent store. In other words, when we add a contact, it is added to this array, and then the array is persisted to shared objects. When we delete a contact, it is deleted from the array, and then the array is persisted to shared objects. When we edit an existing contact, it is updated in the array, and then the array is persisted to shared objects. Are you seeing a pattern here?

When the ContactManager class is instantiated during application initialization, it instantiates the instance of DataManager and keeps a reference to it, as you saw earlier. Also as you saw earlier, it initialized the DataManager by calling its init() function, which we can now look at:

```
this.init = function() {

  // Read in existing contacts from the applicable storage mechanism.
  this.contacts = new Array();
  this.restoreContacts();

} // End init().
```

Once the contacts array is initialized, we ask the DataManager to restore any contacts from persistent storage by calling the restoreContacts() function, which is the following:

```
this.restoreContacts = function() {

  // Retrieve stored contacts.
  var storedContacts = dojo.storage.get("js_contact_manager_contacts");

  // Only do work if there actually were any contacts stored.
  if (storedContacts) {
    // Tokenize the string that was stored.
    var splitContacts = storedContacts.split("~>!<~");
    // Each element in splitContacts is a contact.
    for (var i = 0; i < splitContacts.length; i++) {
      // Instantiate a new Contact instance and populate it.
      var contact = new Contact();
      contact.restoreFromJSON(splitContacts[i]);
      contact.arrayIndex = i;
      // Add it to the array of contacts.
      this.contacts.push(contact);
    }
  }

} // End restoreContacts().
```

Restoring contacts is a pretty simple process. First, we ask Dojo to get our contacts from local shared objects. The contacts are stored under the name js_contact_manager_contacts. The code then checks to be sure we actually got something back. If this is the first time the application is run on this machine, for instance, there will be no object under that name, and hence no contacts to restore.

Assuming there are contacts, what we get back from the dojo.storage.get() call is basically a giant string consisting of contacts in JSON form separated by a sequence of characters: ~>!<~. We can't just use a single character, such as a comma, because it could appear naturally in the data entered by the user, and therefore we would not tokenize the string properly. So we need a delimiter to separate contacts that isn't likely to be entered by the user. The ~>!<~ sequence is a reasonably safe combination, in that it isn't likely to naturally occur in real user input. However, entering it in any field for a contact will, in fact, break the code.[4]

After the string is tokenized, we start iterating over the tokens, which I remind you are each a contact in JSON form. For each, all we need to do is instantiate a new Contact object, and then pass the JSON string to the restoreFromJSON() function of the Contact, which we looked at earlier. It uses the evaluated JSON and populates the Contact instance, effectively restoring it.

Only two things remain to do: set the arrayIndex field of the contact and add it to the contacts array. Once all the tokens (contacts) have been processed in this way, restoreContacts() has completed its work, and we now have a contacts array that is identical to how it was when it was last persisted.

The next function we encounter in our exploration of the DataManager class is the saveContact() function, which is used to rotate the ad banner at the top of the page.

---

4. To be really bullet proof, the application should check all inputs to be sure this sequence doesn't appear. But it seems pretty unlikely that it would be entered *except* by someone deliberately trying to break the program, so I can live with the risk.

You were paying attention there I hope and noticed something amiss? Obviously, the saveContact() function, in fact, is called to save a contact, and it looks like this:

```
this.saveContact = function(inContact, inIndex) {

  // Save new contact.
  if (inIndex == -1) {
    inContact.arrayIndex = this.contacts.length;
    this.contacts.push(inContact);
  } else {
    // Update existing contact.
    this.contacts[inIndex] = inContact;
  }
  this.persistContacts();

} // End saveContact().
```

We first do some simple branching based on whether we are saving a new contact (inIndex == -1) or updating an existing one (inIndex != -1). In the case of adding a new index, all we really need to do is set the arrayIndex field of the inContact object, and push it onto the contacts array. When we are updating a contact, we just set the appropriate element of the contacts array to the inContact object. After one of those things happens, we call persistContacts() to save the contacts array to shared objects.

So, what of this persistContacts() function? Let's get to that now. Actually, with persistContacts() goes saveHandler(), which works hand in hand with persistContacts() to do the job of saving to shared objects:

```
this.persistContacts = function() {

  // First, construct a giant string from our contact list, where each
  // contact is separated by ~>!<~ (that delimiter isn't too likely to
  // naturally appear in our data I figure!)
  var contactsString = "";
  for (var i = 0; i < this.contacts.length; i++) {
    if (contactsString != "") {
      contactsString += "~>!<~";
    }
    contactsString += this.contacts[i];
  }

  try {
    dojo.storage.put("js_contact_manager_contacts", contactsString,
      this.saveHandler);
  } catch(e) {
    alert(e);
  }

} // End persistContacts().
```

```
// ********** Callback function for Flash storage system save.
this.saveHandler = function(status, keyName){

  if (status == dojo.storage.FAILED) {
    alert("A failure occurred saving contact to Flash storage");
  }

} // End saveHandler().
```

First, we construct that giant string from the contacts array that I talked about earlier when discussing the restoreContacts() function. To do so, we simply iterate over the contacts array and add each contact to a string, which fires its toString() function as described earlier when we looked at the Contact class.

We then append our special delimiter character sequence, and continue that until the whole contacts array has been processed into this string. Once that's done, we pass this string to the dojo.storage.put() function, telling it to store the string under the name js_contact_manager_contacts. We also pass it a reference to the saveHandler() function. This function is a callback that will be called by Dojo when the operation completes. We can examine the outcome of the operation and act accordingly. Here, all we really care about is a failure; in which case, we alert the user. There isn't a whole lot to be done if a failure occurs, so that's the end of things. We could also alert users if the operation succeeds, but I think they can surmise that if no error message is shown.

The getContact() function comes next, and it's definitely a trivial piece of code. In fact, it's so trivial that I'm not even going to show it. All it does is take in an index number and return that element from the contacts array. A single line of code, that's it.

Following getContact() is deleteContact(), which has a little more meat to it (although I admit, not a *lot* of meat):

```
// ********** Delete a contact.
this.deleteContact = function(inIndex) {

  // Delete from contacts array.
  this.contacts.splice(inIndex, 1);

  // Store the updated contact list.
  this.persistContacts();

  // Finally, renumber all the remaining contacts.
  for (var i = 0; i < this.contacts.length; i++) {
    this.contacts[i].arrayIndex = i;
  }

} // End deleteContact().
```

JavaScript arrays expose the splice() method, which allows us to remove elements from an array easily. We simply specify from which index to start removing elements, and then specify how many elements to remove.

Once the contact has been removed, we ask the DataManager to persist our contacts, effectively updating the shared objects.

One last bit of work remains at this point, and that is to renumber the contacts. Recall that the arrayIndex field, which is not persisted with the contact, is the element in the contacts array where the contact is located. It is important that this be accurate, because if the user clicks a selector tab and we return only a subset of the contacts array, each contact needs to know what index it's at so we can edit and/or delete the appropriate contact if the user requests it.

However, let's say we have three contacts in the contacts array, and we delete the second one. Now, the first contact has an arrayIndex value of 0, and the second one has a value of 3, because that's where it was previously (we're assuming they were numbered correctly to begin with). So, if the user clicks that second contact to edit, we'll get an error as we try to access index 3 of the array, which no longer exists. As you can see, the arrayIndex values need to be updated when we delete a contact. Fortunately, this is a simple procedure: we just need to iterate over the array and set the arrayIndex for each contact as we do so. This will remove any gaps in the order left by a deletion, and everything will be set up properly again.

Following deleteContact() is listContacts(), which is called to get some subset of the contacts array (or the entire array in the case of the All tab). While it serves an important purpose, there isn't really much to it:

```
this.listContacts = function(inCurrentTab) {

  if (inCurrentTab == "XX") {
    // ALL tab selected, return ALL contact.
    return this.contacts;
  } else {
    // Filter contacts based on current tab.
    var retArray = new Array();
    var start = inCurrentTab.substr(0, 1).toUpperCase();
    var end = inCurrentTab.substr(1, 1).toUpperCase();
    for (var i = 0; i < this.contacts.length; i++) {
      var firstLetter = this.contacts[i].lastName.substr(0, 1).toUpperCase();
      if (firstLetter >= start && firstLetter <= end) {
        retArray.push(this.contacts[i]);
      }
    }
    return retArray;
  }

} // End listContacts().
```

First, we check to see if the inCurrentTab value is XX, which indicates the All tab has been selected. In that case, we just return the contacts array, and that's that. For any other tab, we have a little more work to do. First, we create a new array to hold the subset of contacts we'll be returning. Next, we take the first character of inCurrentTab, converted to uppercase, which is the start of the range of characters for which we want to return contacts. We do the same for the second character, which is the end of the range.

So, let's say the inCurrentTab value is AC. In that case, we want to return any contact whose last name begins with *A, B*, or *C*. So, we iterate over the contacts and, for each, we grab the first letter of the last name. After converting it to uppercase, we see if it falls within the range defined by start and end, and if so, we add it to the array. Once we go through all the contacts, we return the array, which is now some subset of the contacts appropriate for the currently selected tab.

We're just about finished with the DataManager class now. Here's the final function left to examine:

```
this.clearContacts = function() {

  dojo.storage.clear();
  this.contacts = new Array();

} // End clearContacts().
```

If the user becomes depressed and wants to cut off all contact with the outside world, he may decide he no longer wants any contacts, and he may click the Clear Contacts icon. In that case, the clearContacts) function is called. Two things need to occur to clear contacts. First, we need to clear our persistent storage. Dojo provides the dojo.storage.clear() function for this. After that, we have to clear the contacts array in DataManager, which is a simple matter of setting it to a new, empty array. After this, the user can go seek professional psychiatric help to deal with his problems.

Suggested Exercises

While the primary goal of this chapter is to highlight the persistence aspect of the project, that's no reason not to make suggestions that tackle other areas as well. Here are just a few ideas you could explore that would certainly prove to be good learning exercises:

- Allow for searching on *any* field. For bonus points, use some Dojo transition effects to have a search panel slide into view.

- Allow for sending email by clicking a contact's email address. I purposely left this out because I wanted to make this relatively simple suggestion here. This addition shouldn't take much effort.

- Sort the contacts listed on a given tab.

- Implement persistence to cookies. I purposely limited the maximum size that a single contact could take up to just a hair under 1024 bytes. This should allow you to store 4 contacts per cookie, so with the limit of 20 cookies per domain you can store 80 contacts.

Summary

In this chapter, we looked at a couple different mechanisms for storing data in a persistent manner on the client. We focused on using the local shared objects mechanism provided by Adobe's Flash plug-in. You saw how the Dojo library helps make all of this a bit easier by taking care of most of the details for us. We built a small Contact Manager application to demonstrate these techniques, and in the process saw some Dojo widget magic as well.

■■■

CHAPTER 7

JSDigester: Taking the Pain Out of Client-Side XML

I'll just come out and say it: parsing XML in a browser is not a particularly pleasant experience. Actually, if you think about it, parsing XML *anywhere* can be a bit of a hassle. However, one library that does make it a bearable experience is the Jakarta Commons Digester component (http://jakarta.apache.org/commons/digester). Digester allows you to specify a series of rules that will be triggered by various elements in an XML document. These rules may handle the parsing in a number of ways, including creating and populating objects from the XML. Wouldn't it be great if we could do the same thing in JavaScript? Well, we're going to make that dream a reality in this chapter, and in the process, make working with XML on the client a much less painful experience.

Parsing XML in JavaScript

Parsing XML on the client is about as much fun as a gum scraping is for most people. Believe me, I don't make the dental analogy lightly (well, while I've never had my gums scraped, I *am* married with children, so I figure I know what it would feel like). If you've ever done much in the way of parsing XML in JavaScript, then the code shown in Listing 7-1 will probably look both familiar *and* painful.

Listing 7-1. *Parsing XML in JavaScript in a Browser*

```
<html>

  <head>

    <link rel="StyleSheet" href="styles.css" type="text/css">

    <title>Simple JavaScript XML Parsing Example</title>

    <script>

      function doParsing() {
```

```
// This is the XML we will parse.
var xml = "<messages>";
xml += "<msg poster=\"Frank\">Hello!</msg>";
xml += "<msg poster=\"Traci\">I hope all is well with you!</msg>";
xml += "<msg poster=\"Andrew\">Well, I guess that's it.</msg>";
xml += "<msg poster=\"Ashley\">Have a good day!</msg>";
xml += "</messages>";

// Instantiate an XML parser (or DOM, depending on browser).
var xmlDoc = null;
if (window.XMLHttpRequest){
  var parser = new DOMParser();
  xmlDoc = parser.parseFromString(xml, "application/xml");
} else {
  xmlDoc = new ActiveXObject("Microsoft.XMLDOM");
  xmlDoc.async = false;
  xmlDoc.loadXML(xml);
}

// Now iterate over the DOM created above, and construct an output
// string to display.
var strOut = "Root node = " + xmlDoc.documentElement.nodeName + "<br>";
for (var i = 0; i < xmlDoc.documentElement.childNodes.length; i++) {
  strOut += "nodeName = " +
    xmlDoc.documentElement.childNodes[i].nodeName + ", poster = " +
    xmlDoc.documentElement.childNodes[i].getAttribute("poster") +
    ", text = " +
    xmlDoc.documentElement.childNodes[i].firstChild.nodeValue + "<br>";
}
document.getElementById("divOut").innerHTML = strOut;

    }

  </script>

</head>

<body class="cssBody">

  <div class="cssTitle">JavaScript XML Parsing Example</div>
  <br><br>
  <input type="button" value="Click me to parse XML"
    onClick="doParsing();" class="cssBody">
  <br><br>
  Info will appear here:
```

```
        <br><br>
        <div id="divOut" class="cssLog"></div>

    </body>

</html>
```

While I have to admit it probably isn't much to look at, Figure 7-1 shows the output of the code in Listing 7-1.

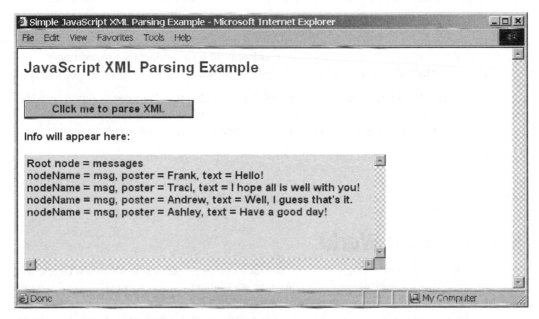

Figure 7-1. *The result of the simple parsing example*

Keep in mind that this is a very trivial example. Also keep in mind that there is more than one way to write XML parsing code in JavaScript. However, I think it's safe to say that all approaches suffer from the same flaw: they are simply too much work. Not only that, but did you notice that the code is aware of the form and structure of the XML it is parsing? This isn't always a bad thing, of course, and is often outright necessary. But it's still something to try to limit as much as possible, so that our code is flexible and reusable. In this case, referencing specific element names probably isn't ideal.

Another important consideration is the question of what you are actually trying to do with the XML you are parsing. Are you simply scanning through it and acting on each element, perhaps displaying it? Or is your goal to populate some objects from the XML—something of an object-to-XML mapping? If the former is the goal, then code like that in Listing 7-1 maybe is not so bad, and could ultimately be more efficient. If the goal is object creation and population, however, then you'll need to write far more code to make that happen.

JSDigester Requirements and Goals

The aim of this chapter's project is to make our lives a lot simpler. We will take a cue from the Apache Jakarta Commons Digester project and build ourselves a JavaScript implementation of Digester that we'll call JSDigester.

Here are our goals and requirements:

- Rather than try to implement the entire breadth of Digester's capabilities, we'll include just a bare minimum to get us by. However, like Digester, JSDigester should be extensible, so that if we need other rules down the road, we can implement them and use them without any trouble.

- In short, we should be able to create an instance of JSDigester, configure some rules on it, and pass it some XML to parse. The result should be an object that presumably contains other objects populated from the parsed XML.

- JSDigester should look and work as much like its big brother Digester as possible, with the understanding that there will be some things that just don't translate very well to JavaScript or are outright not possible, and hence will not be attempted here.

- Naturally, JSDigester should be fully cross browser–compatible.

With those goals in mind, let's get down to business and try to extricate ourselves from the relative masochistic experience of parsing XML in JavaScript.

How Digester Works

To try to duplicate Commons Digester, we need look at that project itself. Although Digester is a Java library, I think a basic example will be understandable to most any developer with experience in a C-like language.

The Digester home page does a good job of describing what Digester is (and it had better, right?):

Basically, the Digester package lets you configure an XML -> Java object mapping module, which triggers certain actions called rules whenever a particular pattern of nested XML elements is recognized. A rich set of predefined rules is available for your use, or you can also create your own. Advanced features of Digester include:

- *Ability to plug in your own pattern matching engine, if the standard one is not sufficient for your requirements.*

- *Optional namespace-aware processing, so that you can define rules that are relevant only to a particular XML namespace.*

- *Encapsulation of Rules into RuleSets that can be easily and conveniently reused in more than one application that requires the same type of processing.*

The basic idea behind Digester is that you can map certain XML elements to rules that define how they will be treated. Then, as an XML document is parsed and Digester encounters the mapped elements, it creates objects for these elements, sets properties of a given object, or calls methods of a given object—all according to the rules you define. When the XML document is completely parsed, you wind up with an object graph containing new objects that represent various elements in the XML document.

Digester can seem a bit overwhelming at first, but once you get the hang of it, you won't want to use anything else! Let's look at a simple example now.

Imagine we are writing a simple shopping cart web application, as seen on virtually any e-commerce web site like Amazon.com. Suppose that our application has the two classes shown in Listings 7-2 and 7-3, which represent the shopping cart and any items in the shopping cart.

Listing 7-2. *The ShoppingCart Class*

```
package myApp;
public class ShoppingCart {
    public void addItem(Item item);
    public item getItem(int id);
    public Iterator getItems();
    public String getShopperName();
    public void setShopperName(String shopperName);
}
```

Listing 7-3. *The Item Class*

```
package myApp;
public class Item {
    public int getId();
    public void setId(int id);
    public String getDescription();
    public void setDescription(String description);
}
```

Now let's assume that we have previously had a user who started shopping, maybe buying Christmas presents for his friends, dropped some items in his cart, and then left. Let's further assume that we wanted the user to have a good shopping experience, so we saved the state of his shopping cart for later. Lastly, let's assume that we saved that state in the form of the XML document shown in Listing 7-4.

Listing 7-4. *The Saved XML Document Representing the User's Shopping Cart*

```
<ShoppingCart shopperName="Rick Wakeman">
  <Item id="10" description="Child's bike (boys)" />
  <Item id="11" description="Red Blouse" />
  <Item id="12" description="Reciprocating Saw" />
</ShoppingCart>
```

Now, when the user comes back to our site, we want to read in this XML document and create a `ShoppingCart` object that contains three `Item` objects, all with their properties set appropriately to match the data in the XML document. We could do so with the following Digester code:

```
Digester digester = new Digester();
digester.setValidating(false);
digester.addObjectCreate("ShoppingCart", "myApp.ShoppingCart");
digester.addSetProperties("ShoppingCart");
digester.addObjectCreate("ShoppingCart/Item", "myApp.Item");
digester.addSetProperties("ShoppingCart/Item");
digester.addSetNext("ShoppingCart/Item", "addItem", "myApp.Item");
ShoppingCart shoppingCart = (ShoppingCart)digester.parse();
```

Let's break this down and look at each line of code. The first line instantiates a `Digester` object. The second line of code tells Digester that we do not want the XML document validated against a Document Type Definition (DTD).

After that comes a series of add*XXX*() method calls, which each adds a particular rule to Digester. A number of built-in rules are available, and you can write your own as required.

All of the rules share the first method call parameter in common: the path to the element for which the rule will fire. Recall that an XML document is a hierarchical tree structure, so to get to any particular element in the document, you form a path to it that starts at the document root and proceeds through all the ancestors of the element. In other words, looking at the <Item> elements, the parent of all of the <Item> elements is the <ShoppingCart> element. Therefore, the full path to any of the <Item> elements is `ShoppingCart/Item`. In the same way, if the <Item> element had an element nested beneath it, say <Price>, then the path to that element would be `ShoppingCart/Item/Price`.

A Digester rule is attached to a given path and will fire any time an element with that path is encountered. You can have multiple rules attached to a given path, and multiple rules can fire for any given path.

In this example, our first rule—an `ObjectCreate` rule—is defined to fire for the path `ShoppingCart`. This means that when the <ShoppingCart> element is encountered, an instance of the class `myApp.ShoppingCart` will be created.

Digester uses a stack implementation to deal with the objects it creates. For instance, when the `ObjectCreate` rule fires and instantiates that `ShoppingCart` object, it is pushed onto the stack. All subsequent rules will work against that object, until it is popped off the stack (either explicitly, as a result of another rule, or because parsing is completed). So, when the next rule—the `SetProperties` rule—fires, it will set all the properties of the object on the top of the stack—in this case, our `ShoppingCart` object—using the attributes of the <ShoppingCart> element in the document.

Next comes another `ObjectCreate` rule set up for the `<Item>` elements, and also another `SetProperties` rule for that same element. So, when the first `<Item>` element is encountered, the object is created and pushed onto the stack, meaning it is now on top of the `ShoppingCart` object.

The last rule is the `SetNext` rule. This rule calls a given method—`addItem()` in this case—on the *next* object on the stack, which would be the `ShoppingCart` object, passing it the object on the top of the stack, which is the `Item` object. At the end of this, the `Item` object on the top of the stack is popped off, revealing the `ShoppingCart` object, which is again the top object on the stack. This process repeats three times for each `<Item>` element.

At the end, the object on the top of the stack, which would be our `ShoppingCart` object at that point, is popped off and returned by Digester. We catch that return into the `shoppingCart` variable, and we now have a reconstituted shopping cart in the same state the user left it.

Interestingly, Digester uses Simple API for XML (SAX) under the covers. SAX is a Java-based, event-driven API for parsing XML, like Digester (which stands to reason!), but functions at a lower level and tends to be quite a bit more work than Digester to use. Since this book strives to be language-neutral as much as possible (with the exception of JavaScript, of course!), I won't go into an example of using SAX directly. However, it is important to know that with SAX, as an XML document is parsed, various events occur. Some of the events are when the document begins or ends, when a new tag is encountered, when text that a tag pair wraps is parsed, and when a tag is closed—to name a few. As the developer, you write what is called a document handler class, which is the class that will be called when these events occur. Digester is essentially a document handler class. It builds on the SAX parsing events, extending them in a sense.

While it would certainly be feasible to build our own JavaScript implementation of SAX, why bother when someone else has already done so? JSLib from the Mozilla Foundation (http://jslib.mozdev.org) provides such an implementation. JSLib, as the name suggests, is a library of JavaScript functions covering a range of needs, one of which is SAX, because, of course, everyone needs a little SAX every now and again (come on, how could I possibly not make that joke at *some* point in this chapter?).

You will shortly see how the SAX component of JSLib is used as we dissect JSDigester. In fact, why put it off any longer?

Dissecting the JSDigester Solution

Let's begin by executing the test code to see what JSDigester actually does. Figure 7-2 shows the screen that you will see when you load the test page in a browser and click the button to initiate the test.

Before we look at the code of JSDigester itself, it would, naturally enough, be useful to look at the code that will test JSDigester.

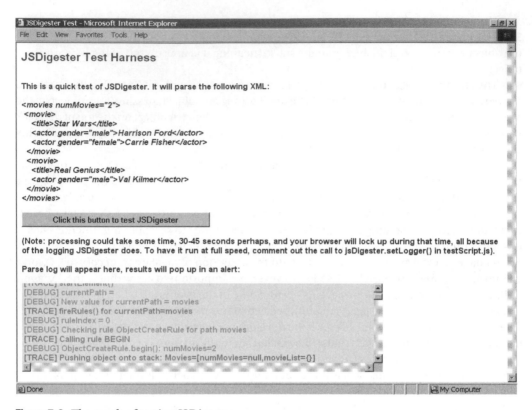

Figure 7-2. *The result of testing JSDigester*

Writing the Test Code

The JSDigesterTest.htm file is where the tests begin, and it is this file that you will load in your browser. I'm not going to show this code here in the interest of saving space, but do take a look. It is really just some straightforward HTML with some JavaScript imports. The real interesting stuff happens in the JavaScript files.

The first import, sax.js, is the SAX parser from JSLib. I will not be going into the details of how this code works because it is not code I wrote. I do recommend going through it on your own though, and getting a feel for it. Generally, it is not terribly difficult to understand, and at just over 200 lines of code, it isn't anything too overwhelming. Still, it is a library we are making use of, and as is usually the case with libraries, we're less concerned with what goes on inside it and how it works its magic than we are with how we use it in our own code, so that will be our focus here.

However, one detail to be aware of however is that when you use JSLib, you provide something called a DocumentHandler callback. This is essentially an object that will react to well-defined life-cycle events, which are encountered as an XML stream is parsed. This object must adhere to a known interface; that is, must implement a number of functions. You'll see how this interface is implemented in short order, but as far as using JSLib goes, this is about the extent of the knowledge you need.

Getting on with the code, take a look at Listing 7-5. It shows three JavaScript classes: one class represents a collection of movies, another represents an individual movie, and the third represents an actor. This code is found in the testClasses.js file. These classes are what JSDigester will instantiate and populate as it does its work.

Listing 7-5. *Three JavaScript Classes JSDigester Will Create and Populate*

```
// This class represents an Actor in a Movie.
function Actor() {
  this.gender = null;
  this.name = null;
}
Actor.prototype.setGender = function(inGender) {
  this.gender = inGender;
}
Actor.prototype.getGender = function() {
  return this.gender;
}
Actor.prototype.setName = function(inName) {
  this.name = inName;
}
Actor.prototype.getName = function() {
  return this.name;
}
Actor.prototype.toString = function() {
  return "Actor-[name-" + this.name + ",gender=" + this.gender + "]";
}


// This class represents a Movie.
function Movie() {
  this.title = null;
  this.actors = new Array();
}
```

```
Movie.prototype.setTitle = function(inTitle) {
  this.title = inTitle;
}
Movie.prototype.getTitle = function() {
  return this.title;
}
Movie.prototype.addActor = function(inActor) {
  this.actors.push(inActor);
}
Movie.prototype.getActors = function() {
  return this.actors;
}
Movie.prototype.toString = function() {
  return "Movie=[title=" + this.title + ",actors={" + this.actors + "}]";
}


// This class stores a collection of Movies.
function Movies() {
  this.movieList = new Array();
  this.numMovies = null;
}
Movies.prototype.setNumMovies = function(inNumMovies) {
  this.numMovies = inNumMovies;
}
Movies.prototype.getNumMovies = function() {
  return this.numMovies;
}
Movies.prototype.addMovie = function(inMovie) {
  this.movieList.push(inMovie);
}
Movies.prototype.getMovieList = function() {
  return this.movieList;
}
Movies.prototype.toString = function() {
  return "Movies=[numMovies=" + this.numMovies + ",movieList={" +
  this.movieList + "}]";
}
```

Figure 7-3 shows a quick bit of UML so you can visualize this small class hierarchy.

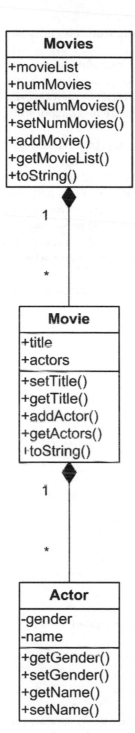

Figure 7-3. *The test class hierarchy in UML*

These three classes don't have much in the way of behaviors; they are more or less just containers in which to store data.

The Actor class has two attributes: gender and name, along with the associated getter and setter methods for each (this is typical of JavaBeans, if you are familiar with Java). The Actor class also provides an overridden toString() method, which is a method every object in JavaScript has by default. This version renders a slightly more meaningful string representation of the Actor object.

The Movie class has the two attributes title and actors. actors is an array of Actor objects associated with the Movie. This class also has an overridden toString() method.

Lastly, the Movies class also has two attributes: movieList and numMovies. movieList is an array of Movie objects, and numMovies is the number of movies contained in that array. While it is true that this information is intrinsic in the array, within the length property, I did it this way to demonstrate some of the parsing capabilities of JSDigester (so don't think too hard on it, because it isn't meant to be the best implementation). Just like the Actor and Movie classes, Movies has its own toString() method, the output of which you will see when you fire up the test code.

Now, let's look at the test code that will exercise JSDigester. This code is shown in Listing 7-6 and is found in the testScript.js file.

Listing 7-6. *JavaScript Code That Tests JSDigester*

```javascript
function testJSDigester() {

  // Create a string of test XML to have JSDigester parse.
  var sampleXML = "";
  sampleXML += "<movies numMovies=\"2\">\n";
  sampleXML += "  <movie>\n";
  sampleXML += "    <title>Star Wars</title>\n";
  sampleXML += "    <actor gender=\"male\">Harrison Ford</actor>\n";
  sampleXML += "    <actor gender=\"female\">Carrie Fisher</actor>\n";
  sampleXML += "  </movie>\n";
  sampleXML += "  <movie>\n";
  sampleXML += "    <title>Real Genius</title>\n";
  sampleXML += "    <actor gender=\"male\">Val Kilmer</actor>\n";
  sampleXML += "  </movie>\n";
  sampleXML += "</movies>";

  // Create a logger for JSDigester to use, and set its level to TRACE, and tell
  // it where to log to.
  var log = new jscript.debug.DivLogger();
  log.setLevel(log.LEVEL_TRACE);
  log.setTargetDiv(document.getElementById("divLog"));

  // Instantiate a JSDigester instance and set up the rules, and logger.
  var jsDigester = new JSDigester();
  jsDigester.setLogger(log);
  jsDigester.addObjectCreate("movies", "Movies");
```

```
jsDigester.addSetProperties("movies");
jsDigester.addObjectCreate("movies/movie", "Movie");
jsDigester.addBeanPropertySetter("movies/movie/title", "setTitle");
jsDigester.addObjectCreate("movies/movie/actor", "Actor");
jsDigester.addSetProperties("movies/movie/actor");
jsDigester.addBeanPropertySetter("movies/movie/actor", "setName");
jsDigester.addSetNext("movies/movie/actor", "addActor");
jsDigester.addSetNext("movies/movie", "addMovie");

// Parse the XML, resulting in an instance of the Movies class.
var myMovies = jsDigester.parse(sampleXML);

// Construct result string.
var outStr = "JSDigester processed the specified XML." +
  "\n\nIt created an object graph consisting of a Movies object, " +
  "with a numMovies property, and containing a collection of " +
  "Movie objects." +
  "\n\nEach Movie object has a title property, and " +
  "contains a collection of Actor objects.\n\n" +
  "Each Actor object has two fields, name and gender.\n\n" +
  "Here's the final Movies object JSDigester returned: \n\n" +
  myMovies;

// Display results.
alert(outStr);

}
```

The onClick event of the button in JSDigesterTest.htm calls the testJSDigester() function seen here. The first thing it does is build up a string that is the XML JSDigester will parse for us. I believe that is pretty self-explanatory.

After that comes the instantiation and configuration of a DivLogger instance (DivLogger was introduced in Chapter 3). We set the logging level to trace, so that we can see absolutely everything JSDigester does, and we also give it a reference to the <div> where our log output will go.

Next, we instantiate JSDigester itself, and pass it the logger we just configured. Note that if you do not pass a logger to JSDigester, it will still work. In fact, this is exactly what I recommend you do in a production environment. As you will see when you actually try out the test page, the logging slows JSDigester significantly. Therefore, you should generally pass a logger instance in only when you are debugging and can accept the delay logging causes. JSDigester actually performs pretty well when logging is not enabled, as long as the input XML isn't too large. With logging on, it definitely doesn't perform as well, to say the least.

After that comes the part that really makes JSDigester work: the rules. The first rule configured is an ObjectCreateRule that will fire when the <movies> element is encountered in the XML. This will result, not surprisingly, in an instance of the Movies class being created. Related to that is the next rule, the SetProperties rule. This will call setter methods on that newly created Movies object for each attribute of the <movies> tag—in this case, just numMovies.

Next, we find another `ObjectCreateRule`, this time mapped to the path `movies/movie`. This will create an instance of the `Movie` class when any `<movie>` element that is a child of the `<movies>` element is encountered. Working in tandem with that is the `BeanPropertySetter` rule that follows. This fires when the `movies/movie/title` path, which correlates to a `<title>` element as a child of a `<movie>`, is encountered. It will call the `setTitle()` method of the `Movie` object just created, passing it the value of the `<title>` element.

After that comes a group of three rules that handles the `<actor>` elements. First, as you've probably come to expect by now, is an `ObjectCreateRule`. After that is a `SetPropertiesRule`. So at this point, JSDigester knows how and when to create instances of the `Actor` class, and it also knows to take any of the `<actor>` elements' attributes and call the corresponding setter methods for each to set those properties.

Lastly, we have another `BeanPropertySetter` rule mapped to the path `movies/movie/actor`. The text contained between the opening and closing `<actor>` tags is the actor's name. So, this rule will take that text and call the `setName()` method on the `Actor` instance, as the rule specifies.

By this point, JSDigester has enough information to create objects for us and populate them from the XML. The last step then is to let JSDigester know about the hierarchy of objects; that is, how to assign `Actor` objects to `Movie` objects and how to add `Movie` objects to the `Movies` object, which is ultimately the object that will be returned to the caller.

Whoa, hold up—let's not gloss over that. Why exactly is it that JSDigester, at the end of its processing, will return the `Movies` instance to us? Let's take a look at the overall flow to see how that happens.

Understanding the Overall JSDigester Flow

Recall earlier in the discussion of Digester when I mentioned that it uses a stack implementation to do its work? Well, this is how we end up getting the `Movies` instance at the end of the test. Every time Digester creates a new object, it pushes it onto the stack. It's a first in, last out (FILO) stack, so as objects are created and pushed on, the first object created will always be on the bottom. Therefore, as objects are popped off the stack, which is what happens as the XML is parsed, the last object will ultimately be uncovered, which is the very first object created, and this is what JSDigester returns.

Remember the first rule we configured? It was mapped to the `<movies>` element, which happens to be the root of the XML document. It kind of makes sense that the last object returned would be the root object, doesn't it? All the other objects get rolled up into the root after all, just as the structure of the XML document dictates.

So, how exactly does an `Actor` object get added to a `Movie` object, and a `Movie` object get added to the `Movies` object? Both of those things happen as a result of the `SetNext` rules, which are the last two rules added to JSDigester. A `SetNext` rule uses the nature of the stack to its advantage by calling a specified setter method on the *next* object on the stack. To understand this, let's walk through the sequence of events when parsing our test XML. Figure 7-4 shows the sequence of events in flowchart form.

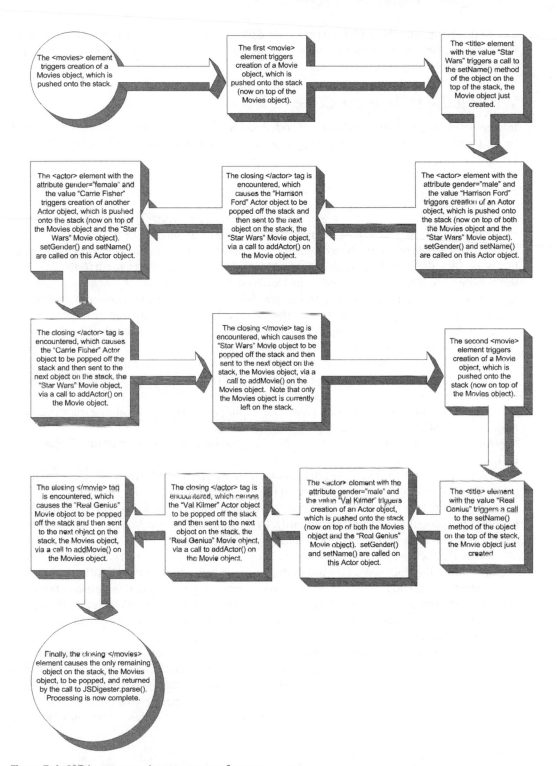

Figure 7-4. *JSDigester parsing sequence of events*

At this point, you should have a pretty good idea of how JSDigester works and an insight into the test code that makes sure it works. Only one small, minor, tiny detail remains: exploring JSDigester itself.

Writing the JSDigester Code

JSDigester checks in at about 678 lines of code,[1] so I won't be listing it here in its entirety. I will be calling out the parts of interest as we proceed, so you'll find it helpful to have the full listing in front of you.

Ready (Preparing to Parse) . . .

The first 15 or so lines of actual code in the JSDigester.js file, which is where the JSDigester class (and rules classes as well) is found, is a batch of class members. The first three are some constants that are used internally to determine which event is occurring for a given element in the incoming XML: the start of the element (EVENT_BEGIN), the body text of the element (EVENT_BODY), or the closing of an element (EVENT_END). The word *constant* is, of course, a bit of a misnomer in JavaScript because there are no true constants; code can come along and change these values as desired. Still, conceptually, this is what they are and how they are treated throughout.

After that is a variable that appears rather often: currentPath. Recall that as we parse through our XML, each element can be referenced by a path, like movies/movie/actor in our previous example, to reference an <actor> element below a <movie> element, which is itself a child of the root <movies> element. currentPath is how JSDigester keeps track of where it is as the XML is parsed.

Next up we find an array named rules. This is simply a collection of all the rules that are added to this JSDigester instance to process.

After that is our objectStack, which will, of course, be at the center of all the JSDigester activity.

rootObject is the next item we encounter, and it is a reference to the root object on the stack. This is done so that it is easy to return the root object when the time comes. This will change as the XML is processed. As objects are popped from the stack, each one essentially becomes the root object, at least temporarily. By the end though, the *true* root object will be referenced, and it's a simple matter of returning that object.

Following rootObject is the variable log. This, as I'm sure you expect, is a reference to the logger instance that JSDigester is to use during its processing. As mentioned during our discussion of the test code, logging is a very expensive operation, primarily in this implementation because of the constant rewrites of the innerHTML property of some <div> elements. Therefore, by default, log is set to null, which means no logging will occur. Therefore, by default, a JSDigester instance is properly configured for maximum performance.

The next class member encountered is saxParser, which is a reference to the SAX parser instance from JSLib that will process the XML for us. Notice that a new instance is instantiated and assigned to this variable right then and there—no sense putting it off. However, you should see an obvious flaw with that: if we wanted to use another SAX parser, there's no ready way to do it. The code using JSDigester could cheat and set saxParser to another object with the same

---

1. Interestingly, less than half of that number, 316 to be precise, is the executable code. The rest is whitespace and comments—not all that much for what it does, I think.

interface as SAXParser, but that's not the best answer. Just like the first appearance of the Shadows,[2] you should have a sense of what is to come: you'll see this as a suggested exercise later.

Following all these class variable declarations and initializations comes the last line of code in the JSDigester constructor function: a call to init(). The init() function itself is very simple but also very important:

```
JSDigester.prototype.init = function() {

  // Tell the SAX parser that this instance of JSDigester is the document
  // handler.
  this.saxParser.setDocumentHandler(this);

} // End init().
```

In JavaScript, one way to construct a class is to use the prototype. Every object, of which a function is one kind, has a prototype associated with it. By assigning a field—init in this case—to the prototype of the existing JSDigester function and giving it the value of a function (I know that sounds weird), we are essentially adding a function named init() to JSDigester. But because we are adding it to the prototype of JSDigester, that means that every time you instantiate a new JSDigester object, it will contain that init member, which happens to be a function. This is a common approach for creating objects and then extending them in JavaScript.

What's more bizarre here though is that even before you instantiate a JSDigester object, you have one already, by virtue of the function definition—the one containing all the member variables. However, if you were to examine it before the preceding code executes, you would find that it does not contain the init() function. Only JSDigester objects instantiated after this code executes will have that function. Remember that JavaScript is a very dynamic language, and somewhat unusual situations like this occur frequently.

Moving right along, recall that the SAX parser is responsible for actually parsing the XML. However, what happens as each element is encountered is still our responsibility. In SAX parlance, you need to tell the parser what class will act as the document handler. That class will receive callbacks throughout the parsing process when various events occur, such as an element first being encountered, text between two tags being encountered, or a closing tag being encountered. JSDigester itself is the document handler here because it will be dealing with those events to work its magic, so we pass the implicit this reference to setDocumentHandler() of the saxParser instance. That's about all the initialization required for JSDigester.

After the init() method comes the setLogger() method. This is a typical property setter method that accepts a reference to a logger instance for JSDigester to use.

Set (Kicking Off the Main Process) . . .

Next up we have the parse() method, the main entry point to JSDigester for all intents and purposes. Let's have a look at it, shall we? Listing 7-7 shows that code.

---

2. The Shadows were the ancient, technologically advanced race that was the main antagonist on the television series *Babylon 5*. In the first season episode "Signs and Portents," we got our first glimpse of the Shadows, and saw just how powerful they were. This was the episode that truly hooked many fans, yours truly included. It was a great hint of things to come, very true to its title. Have a look: http://www.imdb.com/title/tt0517690.

Listing 7-7. *Where All the Action in JSDigester Begins: The parse() Method*

```
JSDigester.prototype.parse = function(inXMLString) {

  if (this.log) {
    this.log.trace("JSDigester.parse()...");
    this.log.debug("inXMLString = " + inXMLString);
  }
  // Remove all items from the object stack, just in case this isn't the
  // first parse this instance of JSDigester has performed.
  this.objectStack.splice(0);
  // Clear current path and root object.
  this.currentPath = "";
  this.rootObject = null;
  // Ask the SAX parser to parse the incoming XML.
  if (this.log) {
    this.log.debug("Calling SAX parser...");
  }
  this.saxParser.parse(inXMLString);
  if (this.log) {
    this.log.debug("SAX parser returned");
  }
  // Return the root object on the stack.
  if (this.log) {
    this.log.debug("Returning root object: " + this.rootObject);
  }
  return this.rootObject;

} // End parse().
```

The first line is something you will see repeated throughout the code. Remember that I said that JSDigester would continue to work, and in fact would work optimally, when no logger is supplied? This line is what makes that statement true. This is akin to a code guard in Java, where you check if a certain log level is enabled before attempting to log a message, usually one that is expensive, which generally means involving string concatenations. This avoids overhead in the logging call, and the same is true here. Aside from making it efficient, it obviously avoids errors, too. If no logger instance were passed in, we would get an error trying to reference a null object—the this.log reference variable in this case.

After the opening salvo of logging messages, we find the line:

```
this.objectStack.splice(0);
```

The splice() method is used to remove elements from an array. The special case of passing a zero to it results in the array being cleared. We do this here because if this JSDigester instance is being reused, the stack needs to be clear before we begin. In the same vein, the next two lines reset the currentPath field and the rootObject reference to their initial states. Reusing a JSDigester instance can save a bit of overhead, if the rules are the same, so we definitely want to allow for it, and these three lines take care of that.

The next line is what kicks off the actual work: the call to the SAX parser's parse() method. The XML to be parsed is passed in, and the parser goes to work. From that point on, JSDigester will be called back to handle various events, as you'll soon see. The last line in parse() (JSDigester's parse() that is, not the SAX parser's parse()) returns the root element, just as we expect from looking at the test code.

Two quick utility functions follow: pop() and push(). These are the methods that handle pushing objects onto and popping objects off the stack. Every array in JavaScript supplies a push() and pop() method, so we can therefore treat any array as a stack. Wrapping these methods in our own methods in JSDigester allows us to handle any extra requirements around these operations, such as logging. And, aside from pop(), which always sets the rootObject field to point to the object last popped off the stack, that's about all these do.

After those functions, we find the startDocument() method. This is the callback that the SAX parser will call on when the XML document begins to be parsed. There isn't anything for JSDigester to do for this event, so there is just a log message to say the event fired. This method must be present, however, for JSDigester to fulfill the DocumentHandler callback contract.

The startElement() method, shown in Listing 7-8, is where some real work begins to occur.

Listing 7-8. *The startElement() Method of JSDigester*

```
JSDigester.prototype.startElement = function(inName, inAttributes) {

  if (this.log) {
    this.log.trace("startElement()");
  }
  // If this is not the first element encountered, start by adding a forward
  // slash (the path separator).
  if (this.currentPath != "") {
    this.currentPath += "/";
  }
  if (this.log) {
    this.log.debug("currentPath = " + this.currentPath);
  }
  // Build up the path of the current element.
  this.currentPath += inName;
  if (this.log) {
    this.log.debug("New value for currentPath = " + this.currentPath);
  }
  // Fire all the rules associated with this element.
  this.fireRules(this.EVENT_BEGIN, inName, inAttributes, null);

} // End startElement().
```

First, after the typical log message, we determine if this is the first element—the root element—of the XML document. If it isn't, then we need to add a forward slash to the current path, which allows us to build up the path. So, with our sample XML, currentPath begins blank, of course. The first element encountered will be <movies>, so currentPath would be set to movies. When the first <movie> element is encountered, since currentPath is no longer blank when startElement() is called, it will append a forward slash, so currentPath would be movies/. After that, the name of the element that has begun, which is passed in to startElement(), is appended, so that currentPath would at that point be movies/movie. This building up of currentPath continues any time startElement() is called (and as you'll see later, it is cut down, so to speak, when endElement() is called).

The last line of startElement() is the most important. It calls the fireRules() method of JSDigester. It passes fireRules() the constant EVENT_BEGIN, since, of course, startElement() is called when an element begins. It also passes it the name of the element and the collection of attributes that element contains, as an associative array. Hold that thought for just a moment; we'll be looking at fireRules() in detail shortly.

In the same vein as startElement() is the next method, characters(). This is called when the text contained between two tags is parsed. So, for example, <title>Star Wars</title> would result in a call to characters() with the inText parameter having the value "Star Wars". It too calls fireRules(), but this time passing the constant EVENT_BODY, and just the text that was passed in to startElement().

Following characters() comes the endElement() function, as alluded to earlier. Its job, firstly, is to call fireRules(), this time passing the EVENT_END constant to indicate that the rules applicable to the closing of the tag should now be executed. Its next task is to remove the last element from currentPath, which corresponds to the element that just ended (remember that the elements form a hierarchy, so the closing of one element will always happen before the close of its parent). Here's the code that literally removes the element from currentPath:

```
var i = this.currentPath.lastIndexOf("/");
this.currentPath = this.currentPath.substr(0, i);
```

It simply finds the last occurrence of the forward slash character, which will always precede the current element's name, and then sets currentPath to the substring of currentPath right up to, but not including, that forward slash. It's neat and clean.

After that we find the endDocument() method which, just like startDocument(), is required by the SAX parser's DocumentHandler interface contract, but serves no real purpose as far as JSDigester goes. So, enough said.

Go (the Real Bulk of the Work)!

Now we finally come to fireRules(). But before that can be discussed, I need to point out something about rules, even though I'd be willing to bet you've figured it out already.

Some rules do something when an element begins; ObjectCreateRule is a good example of this. Other rules do something when text is encountered; BeanPropertySetter is one example. Still other rules do something only when an element ends; SetNextRule, for example, works that way. However, all of the rules are called three times per element: once when it starts, once when its body text, if any, is encountered, and once when it closes. We'll be taking a look at rules when we're finished with JSDigester, but as a preview, you will find that every rule has three methods corresponding to these events: begin(), body(), and end(). You will also find that in general, two of the three will do nothing (there's nothing to stop a rule from doing something in response to more than one event, but none of the existing rules do). This information will be important to understanding fireRules(). Speaking of which, you can see fireRules() in Listing 7-9.

Listing 7-9. *The True Core of JSDigester: The fireRules() Method*

```
JSDigester.prototype.fireRules = function(inEvent, inName, inAttributes,
  inText) {

  if (this.log) {
    this.log.trace("fireRules() for currentPath=" + this.currentPath);
  }
  var ruleIndex = 0;
  if (inEvent != this.EVENT_BEGIN) {
    ruleIndex = this.rules.length - 1;
  }
  if (this.log) {
    this.log.debug("ruleIndex = " + ruleIndex);
  }
  for (var ruleCounter = 0; ruleCounter < this.rules.length; ruleCounter++) {
    var rule = this.rules[ruleIndex];
    if (this.log) {
      this.log.debug("Checking rule " + rule.getRuleType() +
        " for path " + rule.getPath());
    }
    if (rule.getPath() == this.currentPath) {
      switch (inEvent) {
        case this.EVENT_BEGIN:
          if (this.log) {
            this.log.trace("Calling rule BEGIN");
          }
          rule.begin(inAttributes);
        break;
        case this.EVENT_BODY:
          if (this.log) {
            this.log.trace("Calling rule BODY");
          }
          rule.body(inText);
        break;
        case this.EVENT_END:
          if (this.log) {
            this.log.trace("Calling rule END");
          }
          rule.end(inName);
        break;
      }
    } else {
      if (this.log) {
        this.log.debug("Rule not applicable to this path, so not firing");
      }
    }
```

```
      if (inEvent == this.EVENT_BEGIN) {
        ruleIndex++;
      } else {
        ruleIndex--;
      }
    }

} // End fireRules().
```

So, what's going on here? Well, first we check to see what kind of event it is. We have a variable named ruleIndex, which is the index into our array of rules. If the event isn't for an element opening, then we need to go through the rules in reverse order to ensure that they fire in the order they should, so we set ruleIndex to point to the last rule in the array. For an event corresponding to the start of an element, we need to run through the rules in forward order, so ruleIndex is zero in that case. The reason for this reversal of order is that the rules must fire against the order the objects they would work against appear on the stack. So, executing a SetNext rule should work against the next object in the stack, and this wouldn't be the case going through the stack in forward order. For the opening of a tag, however, the stack needs to be built up initially, and going through them in forward order is what accomplishes that.

Then we begin a loop, a single iteration per rule in our array of rules. We first pull out the next rule during the iteration, using ruleIndex to get the appropriate next rule. We then check to see if the rule's path corresponds to the current path of the element being processed. If it does, we check what type of event we're processing, and call the appropriate method of the rule: begin(), passing it the attributes of the current element; body(), passing it the text the current element contains; or end(), passing it the name of the element.

Lastly, we either increment or decrement ruleIndex as appropriate. We increment it if the event is a begin event, or decrement it for any other event.

As simple as it seems, and it *is* pretty simple, this is the method that really makes JSDigester go, as stated previously. I never said JSDigester was technically all that impressive, but like the wheel, it really makes life quite a bit better (well, "life" as defined by a developer, that is).

The last four methods in JSDigester are all pretty similar, so I will cover them together. addObjectCreate(), addSetProperties(), addBeanPropertySetter(), and addSetNext() are the methods that a user of JSDigester calls to add a processing rule, as you saw in the sample code in Listing 7-6. Each one has a different set of parameters, since each rule requires different information. They all share inPath in common though, and this is the path to the element in the XML to process. The addObjectCreate() rule also needs the name of the class to instantiate, and is provided that with the inClassName parameter. The addSetProperties() method requires only the path. addBeanPropertySetter(), in addition to the path, requires the name of the property to call on the object whose property is being set, and inMethod provides that. Lastly, addSetNext() requires inMethod, the name of the method to call on the next object on the stack, in addition to the path.

Each of these methods instantiates an object of the appropriate rule class—ObjectCreateRule, SetPropertiesRule, BeanPropertySetterRule, or SetNextRule—and passes in the pertinent information upon construction. It then pushes this new rule instance into the array of rules configured for this instance of JSDigester. Aside from some log output, that's the full extent of what these methods do.

And with that, we've seen everything JSDigester has to offer in the way of code. Only one thing remains, and that's to look at the four rule classes themselves. I think you'll be surprised how little code is actually involved in them, much like JSDigester itself.

Writing the Rules Classes Code

Each of the four existing JSDigester rule classes share the same basic structure, so in the interest of brevity, I will show a full one here, and after that show only where the other three differ. For no real reason other than random chance, I've chosen `ObjectCreateRule` as our example. Its code is shown in Listing 7-10.

Listing 7-10. *The JSDigester ObjectCreateRule Class*

```
function ObjectCreateRule(inPath, inClassName, inJSDigester) {

  // Set rule type and path to fire for.
  this.ruleType = "ObjectCreateRule";
  this.path = inPath;
  // Set the JavaScript class to instantiate.
  this.className = inClassName;
  // Record the JSDigester instance that the instance of this class belongs to.
  this.jsDigester = inJSDigester;

} // End ObjectCreateRule().


/**
 * Return the ruleType.
 */
ObjectCreateRule.prototype.getRuleType = function() {

  return this.ruleType;

} // End getRuleType().


/**
 * Return the path.
 */
ObjectCreateRule.prototype.getPath = function() {

  return this.path;

} // End getPath().
```

```
/**
 * Begin an element.
 */
ObjectCreateRule.prototype.begin = function(inAttributes) {

  if (this.jsDigester.log) {
    this.jsDigester.log.debug("ObjectCreateRule.begin(): " + inAttributes);
  }
  var protoObj = eval(this.className);
  this.jsDigester.push(new protoObj());

} // End begin().


/**
 * Process body text.
 */
ObjectCreateRule.prototype.body = function(inText) {

  if (this.jsDigester.log) {
    this.jsDigester.log.debug("ObjectCreateRule.body(): " + inText);
  }

}


/**
 * Process closing tag.
 */
ObjectCreateRule.prototype.end = function(inName) {

  if (this.jsDigester.log) {
    this.jsDigester.log.debug("ObjectCreateRule.end(): " + inName);
  }
  this.jsDigester.pop();

} // End end().
```

A JSDigester rule always contains three fields:

- ruleType: The name of the rule. The only real use of this value is in logging.

- path: The path in the XML structure for which this rule should fire.

- jsDigester: The instance of JSDigester, which is passed in to the constructor when the rule is instantiated.

All rule classes always provide a getRuleType() method, which just returns the ruleType value, and getPath(),which returns the path value.

After those fields come three methods: begin(), body(), and end(). As described when we looked at JSDigester's fireRules() method, the begin() method is called when an element is first encountered; that is, the opening tag. body() is called when the text between two tags is fully parsed. end() is called when a closing tag is encountered.

Recall that a rule, generally speaking (and specifically for the four existing rules), handles only one of these three events. ObjectCreateRule does work only in response to the begin event. Well, I suppose that isn't *technically* accurate. It also pops the created object off the stack when the end event occurs, but that's a relatively minor thing. Still, I suppose in the interest of complete accuracy, it should be stated that ObjectCreateRule does actually process *two* events, even if one is a minor thing.

If you look in the other three rules (ObjectCreateRule is the exception), you will see that two of the three methods are nothing but log statements. The remaining one does some actual work though. In the case of ObjectCreateRule, it's pretty simple: instantiate a new instance of the class named and push it on the stack. The instantiation is done by simply eval()'ing the className value, which results in a new instance of that class being created.

But how did it know the class to create? By its className, obviously. But where did that come from? Well, remember that there are three fields that all rules share in common: ruleType, path, and jsDigester. While those fields are sufficient for some rules, such as the SetPropertiesRule, other ones, including our ObjectCreateRule example, need more fields. This is not a problem. We simply add the field and add it to the list of parameters for the constructor, and the problem is solved. In the case of ObjectCreateRule, we find a className field, and we see that it is the second parameter passed in to the constructor, inClassName.

For the SetPropertiesRule class, the work is done in the begin() method, and it's a fair bit more substantial than the ObjectCreateRule:

```
SetPropertiesRule.prototype.begin = function(inAttributes) {

  if (this.jsDigester.log) {
    this.jsDigester.log.debug("SetPropertiesRule.begin(): " + inAttributes);
  }
  var obj = this.jsDigester.pop();
  for (var i = 0; i < inAttributes.length; i++) {
    var nextAttribute = inAttributes[i];
    var keyVal = nextAttribute.split("=");
    var key = keyVal[0];
    var val = keyVal[1];
    key = "set" + key.substring(0, 1).toUpperCase() + key.substring(1);
    if (this.jsDigester.log) {
      this.jsDigester.log.debug("SetPropertiesRule.begin() - key=" + key +
        "val=" + val);
    }
    obj[key](val);
  }
  this.jsDigester.push(obj);

} // End begin().
```

So, what this code accomplishes is taking in an array representing the attributes of the element being parsed in the form of *name=value* pairs, and setting each property on the object on the top of the stack. To do this, it first pops the object off the top of the stack. It then iterates over the array of attributes passed in. For each, it splits the array contents on the equal sign character. The first element of the array resulting from the call to nextAttribute.split() is what was on the left of the equal sign, which is the name of the attribute, and the second element is what was on the right, which is the value of the attribute. We then see this line of code:

```
key = "set" + key.substring(0, 1).toUpperCase() + key.substring(1);
```

Its job is to construct the name of the method to call, using standard JavaBean format, which is get*XXXX*, where *XXXX* is the name of the property to set (the first character is capitalized, and the rest are in whatever case they are in the property's name). So, for the element <actor>, which has a gender attribute, the name of the method formed would be setGender(). Once the method name is formed, it is executed with this line:

```
obj[key](val);
```

This is actually a really nifty feature of JavaScript. You see, you can treat any JavaScript object like an associative array, where the names of the elements in the array are the members of the object. So, let's say obj is a reference to an Actor object. If we then do obj["setGender"], that gets us a reference to the member setGender() function of that Actor object. Again, we are treating the Actor object like an associative array, and setGender is the name of the element to which we want a reference. If we then append (val) to that, we are creating a function call dynamically. We can use a variable in place of that hard-coded setGender value, which is precisely what the code in the rule class does. Think about how tricky that would be in something like Java, using all sorts of introspection and reflection to do the equivalent of that one simple line of code, and then tell me JavaScript isn't cool.

After all the properties have been set, the object is pushed back onto the stack, returning it to the state it was in before this rule fired, and at that point, the rule has finished its work.

Moving right along to the BeanPropertySetter rule, we find another additional field is needed: the setMethod field, which names the method to call to set the value on the object. In this rule, it's in the body() method where the action happens, and again we see something very similar to the dynamic method call technique used in the SetPropertiesRule class. The object on the top of the stack is again popped off, and virtually the same single line of code sets the property:

```
obj[this.setMethod](inText);
```

In this case, just a single property is being set, and its name is stored in the setMethod field. So, there is no loop as in BeanPropertySetter, and no incoming associative array to rip apart. There is just one simple call, passing it the text that was passed to the body() method, and we're finished, simple as that.

The last rule to look at is the SetNextRule. Just like BeanPropertySetter, it requires the name of the method to call, so we see a setMethod field here as well, and the corresponding constructor parameter inMethod. In this case, the work is done in the end() method, and it's actually a little bit tricky (well, *interesting* is probably the better description).

```
SetNextRule.prototype.end = function(inName) {

  if (this.jsDigester.log) {
    this.jsDigester.log.debug("SetNextRule.end(): " + inName);
  }
  var childObj  = this.jsDigester.pop();
  var parentObj = this.jsDigester.pop();
  if (this.jsDigester.log) {
    this.jsDigester.log.debug("SetNextRule.end() - childObj=" + childObj +
      "parentObj=" + parentObj);
  }
  parentObj[this.setMethod](childObj);
  this.jsDigester.push(parentObj);
  this.jsDigester.push(childObj);

} // End end().
```

So, after a bit of logging, we pop two objects off the stack: the first is the child object, and the second is the parent object. Think about this for a minute: the SetNextRule is used to set a property of the *next* object on the stack, passing it the object on the top of the stack. This is used to create a hierarchy of objects, where one object is the parent of another. The object on the top of the stack is always the child because of the structure of XML:

```
<movies>
  <movie>
    <actor></actor>
  </movie>
</movies>
```

Let's pretend this is all there is to the XML being parsed, and let's pretend we have config-ured only an ObjectCreateRule for each. At the point the <actor> element is encountered (but not yet closed), what does the object stack in JSDigester look like? They say a picture is worth a thousand words, so take a gander at Figure 7-5.

Figure 7-5. *The state of the JSDigester stack when the <actor> element begins*

Now, what if we have a SetNextRule configured for the path movies/movie/actor using the method setActor()? Well, the first object popped off the stack is the top object, the Actor object. That's the child. The next object popped off is again the top object, at this point, the Movie object. This is the parent. The setActor() method of the Movie object, since it is the parent, is then called, with this line:

```
parentObj[this.setMethod](childObj);
```

And *voilà*, we've created a parent-child hierarchical relationship. The Movie object now contains the Actor object, just as we wanted. There is only one last step to perform, and that is to push both of those objects back on the stack, because there still could be other rules yet to fire for them. But remember that to ensure the order of the stack is unchanged after this, we need to push them on in the opposite order they were popped off, so that the Actor object is on top of the Movie object, and you can see that done in the last two lines of the end() method.

See, wasn't that an interesting bit of code?

Well, that was fun, and it didn't take that long. As I've said a few times, JSDigester and its associated rules classes really aren't much to look at in terms of code length. In fact, you could go so far as to call them paltry. But simplicity that provides this much power is a beautiful thing, and it is a testament to the original creators of the Commons Digester that it makes parsing XML almost a fun experience. I hope you find JSDigester useful in your day-to-day work, as I have.

Suggested Exercises

Here are a few suggested exercises that you could pursue to make JSDigester that much more useful:

Implement more rules. Digester has a boatload of rules that could be implemented in JSDigester. Some may well not be possible, but others almost certainly are. Since JSDigester is written to be extensible, this would be a great exercise to become even more familiar with it.

Add validation capabilities. Digester can validate XML against a DTD, and this would be a very nice additional capability to give to JSDigester.

Allow for an alternate SAX parser. Provide a setSAXParser() function so that an alternate SAX parser could be used by JSDigester. As an added bonus, go write one yourself.

Optimize the code. I purposely left one bad design decision in the code specifically so I could make this suggestion. Did you notice that each of the rule classes has a different constructor signature? Surely, this can't be optimal, and, in fact, it isn't. I therefore suggest correcting that. There is more than one way you could do it, but I suggest passing in a single associative array as an argument, and use the values it contains to set the fields. However you choose to do it though, the goal is to normalize the method signature of the rule classes.

Improve the logging capabilities. This may actually wind up being a suggestion of something to add to the JavaScript library (introduced in Chapter 3), rather than JSDigester. It might be nice if you had a logger implementation that could log messages in a more efficient manner so that having logging enabled isn't the performance-killer it is with `DivLogger`. The obvious problem is how to do that in such a way that logging will still always work (for example, if you try to cache all messages until some `flush()` method was called on the logger, you run the risk of losing all the messages if a hard error occurs). One suggestion, if you develop in Firefox frequently, is to log messages to the Firebug extension, which I would expect to work much more efficiently than constantly writing to a `<div>`'s `innerHTML` property.

Summary

In this chapter, we looked very briefly at how XML is typically parsed in JavaScript without the aid of any library or toolkit. We then built ourselves a piece of code modeled after the Jakarta Commons Digester project that should make our lives a lot easier when we need to parse XML in a browser. In the process, you became aware of the SAX parser created by the Mozilla project, which wound up as the basis for JSDigester.

CHAPTER 8

■ ■ ■

Get It Right, Bub: A JavaScript Validation Framework

When you hear the word *validation* in the context of a web application, you generally think of validating user input on a form. This usually evokes thoughts of writing event-handler code to perform various checks on form input before submitting it. All of this can quickly become rather messy. No matter how well you externalize your scripts and set up basic event-handler code that just calls functions, the simple fact is that these validations are scattered throughout your code—it's just a question of to what degree that's true.

Wouldn't it be great if we could truly externalize those validation checks to the point where we don't have to write any code at all? Wouldn't it be great if we could write a simple configuration file, say in XML, that defines what validations we want performed on each field and when? This is precisely the goal of the project in this chapter!

JSValidator Requirements and Goals

Building a JavaScript form validation framework isn't really that complex an undertaking, but making it truly useful requires a bit of forethought. To that end, let's lay out some of the goals we want to accomplish for our project, which we'll call JSValidator:

- The framework should be driven by an external configuration file written in XML. This will define what validations occur for which field, the parameters a given validation may need, and what to do if the validation fails.

- The framework should be extensible. We should be able to add validators—that is, classes that perform a given validation function—any time we want. We should be able to do this without modifying code, just the configuration file.

- We should create a couple of common validator types and cook them into the framework, so developers know they can always use these types without doing anything extra.

- This framework should be unobtrusive, meaning we shouldn't need to sprinkle code all over the place. Moreover, the form on which validations are defined should still work if JavaScript is turned off.

- Using the framework should be about as simple as can be for developers, requiring only a single JavaScript import, some minimal configuration parameters, and the external configuration file.

- The framework should offer error reporting in three ways: alert() messages, messages inserted into a specified <div>, and highlighting of fields (with developer-defined styles). Moreover, the messages should allow for reuse by understanding a token system, where the tokens can be replaced with values defined in the configuration file when a validation failure occurs.

If that sounds like a lot of work, I think you'll be surprised to see that it isn't quite as much as you might think. You'll also find that the end result is something useful and expandable that can be applied in your projects immediately. But I've left the door open for a couple of enhancements that will make it even more useful, and applying them will give you some valuable exercises to work through in order to expand your JavaScript chops.

With our goals and requirements set, let's see how we'll make it work!

How We Will Pull It Off

As mentioned in the requirements, we want JSValidator to use an external configuration file to define all the validations that will be performed for a given HTML form. More specifically, we want this configuration file to be in the form of XML.

There are always choices to be made when deciding on a format for a configuration file, but I feel that while XML isn't perfect for everything, for configuration files, it probably is. That is because it tends to be self-describing (unless the developer does a bad job laying it out). Also, size and parse time don't generally matter, because you tend to parse them once at startup and not frequently after that. You can take a slight performance hit at startup usually, which also means you don't care so much how large or verbose the file is. In fact, the more verbose, the better, most likely, as long as that verbosity adds to the clearness of the configuration.

So, having decided XML is the way to go for JSValidator, on to the next question: how are we going to deal with parsing it? If you've ever done XML parsing in JavaScript, you know that it isn't necessarily a pleasant experience. I discussed this a bit in Chapter 7, so no need to rehash the pain. In Chapter 7, we also find the answer to making it a bearable situation: JSDigester. With JSValidator, you'll see a real-world usage of JSDigester. You'll see how it allows you to take a somewhat complex XML document, describe it with a few simple rules, and have it parsed into JavaScript object quickly and easily. (If you skipped the details on JSDigester in Chapter 7, I suggest going back and reading that now.)

Now that you know how we're going to parse the configuration file, let's answer another important question: how are we going to load it? Remember one of the other goals for JSValidator is to make it as simple and unobtrusive for a developer to use as possible. As a matter of fact, here's all the developer has to do on any given page to use the framework:

```
<script>
  var JSVConfig = {
    pathPrefix : "jsvalidator/",
    configFile : "jsv_config.xml",
    manualInit : false
  };
```

```
</script>
<script src="jsvalidator/JSValidator.js"></script>
```

All that is required is a single JavaScript file to import, and some configuration parameters defined before that. Beyond that, the developer just has to write the configuration file. That's it! No mucking around with the form fields, no special attributes to attach to anything, and *no code to write!* Better still, if JavaScript is disabled, the page won't break—the form will still be workable (assuming it's not broken in some other way, of course), and the user won't know the difference. Of course, the validations won't occur, but that's as expected.

Speaking of that configuration file, how exactly does it get loaded? We can see in the preceding example that the file is named in the parameters, but that doesn't explain how it is loaded. The answer lies in a JavaScript library that serves as the foundation for a number of other libraries, including Rico (which we used in Chapter 4) and script.aculo.us (which we used in Chapter 5). In those chapters, I didn't go into detail about Prototype, but the time has come to do exactly that.

The Prototype Library

Prototype has gained a great deal of popularity because it is simple, lightweight, clean, and generally very helpful. It basically provides extensions to JavaScript that, once you use them, seem like they should have been there from the start. Prototype adds new methods to basic JavaScript objects, as well as provides new functions for things like Ajax, DOM manipulations, and looping constructs.

One of the simplest and yet most useful things Prototype offers is the $() function. As you've seen in previous chapters, this is essentially shorthand for writing document.getElementById(). The $() function allows for referencing a single object or a batch at once, like so:

```
$("1d1", "1d2", "id3");
```

This example will actually retrieve references to three elements and return an array of those references. That's much better than three separate calls to document.getElementById()!

Prototype also provides some simple Ajax support. When I say "simple," I don't mean that as a negative at all. On the contrary, it is very easy to understand and use, which to me is a good thing. The first item Prototype offers in the realm of Ajax is this:

```
Ajax.Request(url, { method: 'get', parameters: pars, onComplete: showResponse });
```

Yes, that's all it takes to make an Ajax request with Prototype! Just supply the URL, set the method to use, pass in any parameters you want to send with the request, and tell Prototype which JavaScript function to call when the response returns.

But wait, there's more!

Probably the most common Ajax function is inserting some markup returned by the server into a <div> or other element. Prototype makes this very simple:

```
new Ajax.Updater( "targetID", url, { method: 'get', parameters: pars });
```

This looks very much like the previous line of code, except that now we're passing in the ID of the element to update, and leaving off the callback, because Prototype handles the callback functionality for us.

As I mentioned earlier, Prototype also extends some basic JavaScript objects. For example, Prototype adds some of the methods to the objects shown in Table 8-1.

Table 8-1. *Some of the Methods Prototype Adds to Intrinsic JavaScript Objects*

Method	Object	Description
extend	Object	Provides a way to implement inheritance by copying all properties and methods from source to destination.
bind	Function	Returns an instance of the function previously bound to the function(=method) owner object. The returned function will have the same arguments as the original one.
stripTags	String	Returns the string with any HTML or XML tags removed.
escapeHTML	String	Returns the string with any HTML markup characters properly escaped.
toArray	String	Splits the string into an array of its characters.
clear	Array	Empties the array and returns itself.
flatten	Array	Returns a flat, one-dimensional version of the array. This flattening happens by finding each of the array's elements that are also arrays and including their elements in the returned array, recursively.
getElementsByClassName	document	Returns all the elements that are associated with the given CSS class name. If no parent element ID is given, the entire document body will be searched.
element	Event	Returns the element that originated the event.
pointerX/pointerY	Event	Returns the x/y coordinate of the mouse pointer on the page.

■Note As I mentioned in Chapter 2, some people view Prototype's extension of intrinsic JavaScript objects as a bad thing. There have been instances where these extensions didn't "play nice" with other JavaScript code. I have personally never been burned by these types of problems, but some people have, so this is something to keep in mind when using Prototype (and by extension, any library that is built on top of Prototype). While my feeling is that it shouldn't dissuade you from using Prototype, or other libraries built on it, you should be aware of the issue.

As you can see, Prototype makes life a little simpler, and I've just scratched the surface here! I suggest taking a longer look at Prototype yourself. Also, in terms of documentation, have a look at the "unofficial" guide to Prototype at http://www.sergiopereira.com/articles/prototype.js.html.

Why do I feel as though I've forgotten something? Oh yes, how about a look at JSValidator?

A Preview of JSValidator

Because JSValidator is really a nonvisual tool, there isn't going to be a whole lot to look at, but that didn't stop me from adding some screenshots here. What you're actually looking at is the demonstration application that shows JSValidator in use.

Figure 8-1 shows the demo application when you first start it up. It describes what validations have been applied to the five form fields.

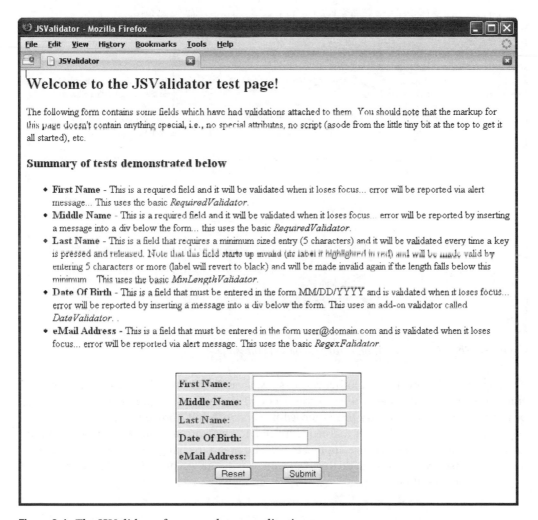

Figure 8-1. *The JSValidator framework test application*

Figure 8-2 shows one way a validation failure can be presented to the user: an alert message. Here, when users tab or click away from the First Name field without having entered something (it is configured to be a required field), they get an alert() message. Note that the message is configurable and reusable, including allowing for tokens in it to be replaced.

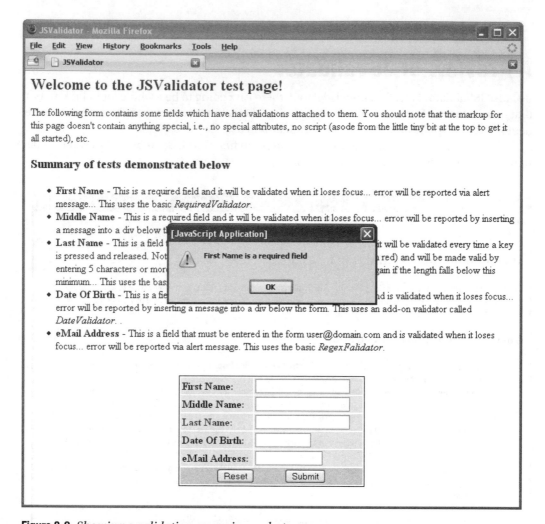

Figure 8-2. *Showing a validation error via an alert message*

Figure 8-3 demonstrates another way to show a validation error. The Last Name field is configured to be highlighted when an error occurs. This field is highlighted in red (which may be nearly impossible to see in a black-and-white version, but it's obvious when you try the application), indicating that it is marked as invalid. In fact, you can configure any element on the page to have a particular style applied to it. If you prefer to change the background color of the text box itself to red, you can do that. Or if you want to make a big "ERROR" appear over the page, you could do that, too!

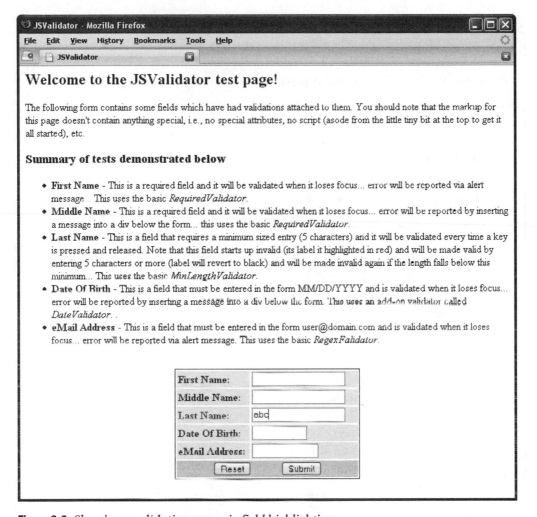

Figure 8-3. *Showing a validation error via field highlighting*

Figure 8-4 shows a third way a validation error can be reported: by inserting a message into an element on the page, usually a <div>. The message is constructed the same way as the alert() display, but in this case, the innerHTML attribute of some page element is updated with the message.

Clicking the Submit button brings up a new page, which is nothing more than a message to indicate the submission was OK. We aren't actually submitting to a server obviously, so this page is something of a *faux* server. I didn't see much sense in showing that page here, but you'll see it when you try out the application, so I wanted to be sure to mention it.

Now that the formalities are out of the way, we can move on to examining this solution!

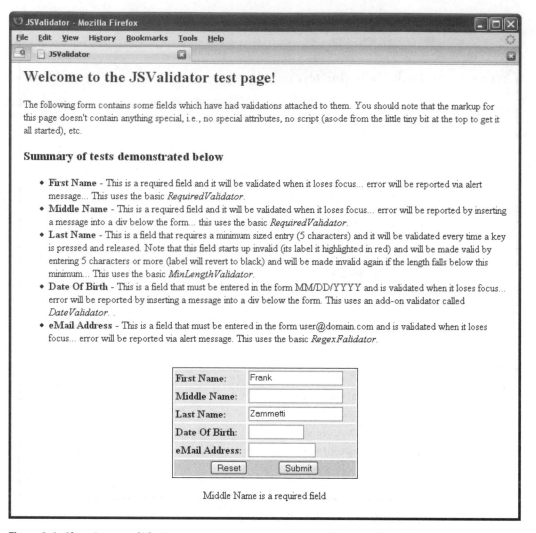

Figure 8-4. *Showing a validation error via a message inserted into a <div> element*

Dissecting the JSValidator Solution

What we are about to dissect is a combination of the JSValidator framework and a test application for it. To begin, let's see how this all lays out on our hard drives, as shown in Figure 8-5.

Figure 8-5. *The directory structure of the JSValidator test application*

Writing index.htm

index.htm is easily the most boring of files to look at in this project because it is, quite literally, nothing but run-of-the-mill HTML. It's just some text, a very vanilla HTML form, a style sheet import, and a sprinkle of JavaScript. In light of this, it won't be listed here, and we won't be going over it in any real detail. However, you should probably take the five seconds you'll need to fully review it.

The JavaScript is the only thing worth mentioning, and you've actually seen it already. But let's look at it one more time and go into a little more detail this time:

```
<script>
  var JSVConfig = {
    pathPrefix : "jsvalidator/",
    configFile : "jsv_config.xml",
    manualInit : false
  };
</script>
<script src="jsvalidator/JSValidator.js"></script>
```

First, you see the definition of the JSVConfig structure. This is just an associative array that has three elements in it, which happen to be the only ones JSValidator currently understands.

The pathPrefix member specifies the beginning of all the paths that JSValidator will need to construct to load validators and rule files. Here, we are saying that all those dynamically created paths will begin with jsvalidator/, which makes sense if you look back at the directory structure (Figure 8-5). Any reference to any JSValidator resource should be relative to the root of the web application, hence this value.

The second member, configFile, should be obvious. It's the name of the XML configuration file JSValidator will use.

Finally, manualInit tells JSValidator whether it should initialize itself automatically or the developer is taking responsibility for doing so. As you will see, initializing JSValidator amounts to nothing more than a call to jsValidator.init(). Normally, this happens automatically when JSValidator loads. However, in order for that to work, JSValidator needs to overwrite the onLoad event handler for the page. Since this is often utilized by developers for their own purposes, simply overwriting the existing handler wouldn't be a great idea. Setting manualInit to true means that the developers will make the call to init() themselves, and the onLoad handler will *not* be overwritten.

Writing styles.css

styles.css, like index.htm, is rather mundane. However, let's have a look at it in its entirety, in Listing 8-1.

Listing 8-1. *The styles.css File (Blink and You'll Miss It!)*

```
/* Style for labels on fields that have a validation error. */
.cssErrorField {
  color            : #ff0000;
  background-color : #d0ffd0;
  font-weight      : bold;
}

/* Style for labels on fields that pass validations. */
.cssOKField {
  color            : #000000;
  background-color : #d0ffd0;
  font-weight      : bold;
}

/* Background for the table cells with the entry fields. */
.cssEntryCell {
  background-color : #f0f0f0;
}

/* Style for the table row with the reset and submit buttons. */
.cssButtons {
  background-color : #ffd0d0;
}
```

As you saw in Figure 8-3, one of the ways JSValidator can report a validation error is to highlight a given field. It can highlight any element on the page. Actually, it doesn't have to "highlight" anything!

All that really happens is that when a validation error occurs, the element with a given ID has its class attribute changed to the style class configured. So really, you could do any wacky thing you wanted with this. Want to show an image that is in a hidden <div>? No problem. Want to make some text blink for anyone using old Netscape browsers? Check. Anything you can accomplish by applying a style class, you can do with the "highlighting" capability. All of this is a roundabout way of explaining that the cssErrorField class seen here is the class that will be applied to highlight a field's label in red in the sample application.

Going hand in hand with cssErrorField is the cssOKField class, which will be applied to the label for a field that passes its validations. This means that JSValidator will take care of setting the style to indicate no error in addition to indicting an error. For example, with the Last Name field validation, which checks for a minimum length every time a key is pressed and released, you get the automatic valid/invalid highlighting as you type. There is no extra work for you to do—just point the framework at those two classes, and it's handled for you automatically.

The cssEntryCell class just makes the background behind the entry boxes a light gray. Finally, cssButton is applied to the row where the Reset and Submit buttons are located.

Writing jsv_config.xml

jsv_config.xml is what actually drives this whole thing, so we definitely want to understand it. Figure 8-6 shows a graphical representation of it, which may help to make all the relationships crystal clear in your mind.

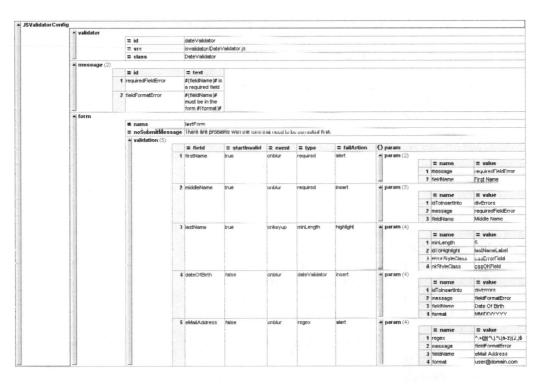

Figure 8-6. *A visual grid representation of the jsv_config.xml file*

And if Figure 8-6 didn't quite do it for you, Listing 8-2 shows the configuration file in all its textual glory!

Listing 8-2. *The JSValidator Configuration File in Plain Text Form*

```
<JSValidatorConfig>

  <validator id="dateValidator" src="jsvalidator/DateValidator.js" ➥
class="DateValidator"/>
```

```
  <message id="requiredFieldError" text="#{fieldName}# is a required field"/>
  <message id="fieldFormatError" ➥
text="#{fieldName}# must be in the form #{format}#"/>

  <form name="testForm" ➥
noSubmitMessage="There are problems with the form that need to be corrected first.">
    <validation field="firstName" startInvalid="true" event="onblur" ➥
type="required" failAction="alert">
      <param name="message" value="requiredFieldError"/>
      <param name="fieldName" value="First Name"/>
    </validation>
    <validation field="middleName" startInvalid="true" event="onblur" ➥
type="required" failAction="insert">
      <param name="idToInsertInto" value="divErrors"/>
      <param name="message" value="requiredFieldError"/>
      <param name="fieldName" value="Middle Name"/>
    </validation>
    <validation field="lastName" startInvalid="true" event="onkeyup" ➥
type="minLength" failAction="highlight">
      <param name="minLength" value="5"/>
      <param name="idToHighlight" value="lastNameLabel"/>
      <param name="errorStyleClass" value="cssErrorField"/>
      <param name="okStyleClass" value="cssOKField"/>
    </validation>
    <validation field="dateOfBirth" startInvalid="false" event="onblur" ➥
type="dateValidator" failAction="insert">
      <param name="idToInsertInto" value="divErrors"/>
      <param name="message" value="fieldFormatError"/>
      <param name="fieldName" value="Date Of Birth"/>
      <param name="format" value="MM/DD/YYYY"/>
    </validation>
    <validation field="eMailAddress" startInvalid="false" event="onblur" ➥
type="regex" failAction="alert">
      <param name="regex" value="^.+@[^\.].*\.[a-z]{2,}$"/>
      <param name="message" value="fieldFormatError"/>
      <param name="fieldName" value="eMail Address"/>
      <param name="format" value="user@domain.com"/>
    </validation>
  </form>

</JSValidatorConfig>
```

Let's dissect this file in detail and go over each element and attribute. First, everything is nested under the root JSValidatorConfig element, to make it valid XML.

Defining Validators

After the root element are any number of validator elements (and there could be none). These define any validator (class that performs some validation logic) that you add. There are a couple of built-in validators, as you'll see shortly, but any others you add will need to be defined with a validator element. The validator element has three required attributes:

- id: How you will reference the validator for a given field validation.

- src: The JavaScript source file where the class that implements the validator is found. It can be absolute or relative—basically any value that would be valid for a <script> tag's src attribute.

- class: The name of the JavaScript class that implements the validator logic.

Defining Messages

Direct children of JSValidatorConfig are the message elements. Like the validator elements, these are completely optional and you can define as many as you wish. Even though they are technically optional, you will likely always have at least one, because any validator that displays a message in response to a validation failure will reference one of these elements.

The message elements have two required attributes: id, which serves the same purpose as on the validator element, and text, which is the text of the message. This text can contain any number of replacement tokens. These tokens are in the form #{xxx}#, where xxx is any string. These tokens will be replaced by the values present for a given field validation. So, if you had the text "#{fieldName}# is a required field," as seen in the first message element in Listing 8-2, assuming a particular field validation defines a fieldName parameter, the value of that parameter will be inserted for #{fieldname}# when the message is shown.

Defining Forms

Next up is the form element. This corresponds to a single physical HTML form on the page. It has two attributes: name and noSubmitMessage. The name attribute needs to match exactly the name attribute of the <form> tag on the page to which the validations apply. The noSubmitMessage attribute is the message that will be displayed to users when they try to submit the form and any of the fields are currently invalid.

Defining Field Validations

The form element has as its children any number of validation elements, and this is where the real action occurs. The validation element has five required attributes:

- field: The name of the element on the form to which this validation applies. It must match exactly the name attribute of the form element.

- startInvalid: The value true or false. When set to true, the field will initially be marked as invalid, and if it is configured to report its error via highlighting, at startup it will be highlighted. This is useful for something like the Last Name field, which is configured to require a minimum length, and which starts out empty, so is clearly not going to meet the minimum length initially!

- event: The event on which the field will be validated. It can be any of the usual DOM events, but onblur will likely be the most usual.

- type: The ID of a validator, either one you configure yourself or one of the built-in basic validators.

- failAction: The action that will be performed when the field fails validation. This can be one of three values: alert, which means a message will be shown to the user via an alert() pop-up; insert, which means a message will be inserted into a specified page element via its innerHTML property; or highlight, which means a specified field will be highlighted.

Defining Validation Parameters

Nested beneath a validation element are the param elements. Each param element has two attributes: name, which is simply the name under which this parameter will be stored, and value, which is the actual value of the parameter.

The param elements are a flexible mechanism by which information can be passed to the validator configured for a given element, and to JSValidator to use during a failure action. Because of this flexibility, the parameters can really have any meaning you wish, and each validator and failure action can require anything they need.

For example, the built-in MinLengthValidator, which validates that a field has a specified minimum length, gets what the minimum length for the field is by looking for a parameter with the name minLength. Similarly, the RegexValidator, which allows a field to be validated against an arbitrary regular expression, gets that expression via a parameter named regex.

For both the alert and insert failure actions, the ID of the message element to use is found via the message parameter. If there are any replacement tokens in the string—fieldName for instance, as seen in the messages in Listing 8-2—they are also found in the parameter list here. For the insert failure action, the ID of the element to highlight is in a parameter named idToHighlight, and the style classes for valid and invalid entries are found in errorStyleClass and okStyleClass, respectively.

As mentioned, when you write your own validators, you can require any parameters you need—there are no real limitations. However, one thing to note is that replacement tokens are used only to replace tokens in message strings during processing of the alert or insert failure actions. You can, however, use the same replaceTokens() function in JSValidator that these use, as you'll see shortly. For example, if you wanted a parameter that could have a value inserted into it dynamically, you could do so using the same token mechanism as the messages.

Writing JSValidatorObjects.js

The JSValidatorObjects.js file contains the class definitions for seven different classes. All but one are objects that are populated when the configuration file is parsed. These seven classes do not provide any functionality per se. They are basically just Value Objects (VOs) that store some data and provide a public interface for getting at that data. As such, I'm sure you will find them to be quick and easy to understand. Nonetheless, you need to know their purposes, so we'll look at each in turn, and then at the end see the big picture of how they all fit together.

The JSValidatorValidatorImpl Class

To begin with, take a look at Figure 8-7, which shows the UML diagram for the only one of the seven classes that doesn't represent configuration information. The JSValidatorValidatorImpl class is the base class for all validator implementation classes. A validator will generally need to inherit only from this class and override the validate() method to become a validator that the framework can use.

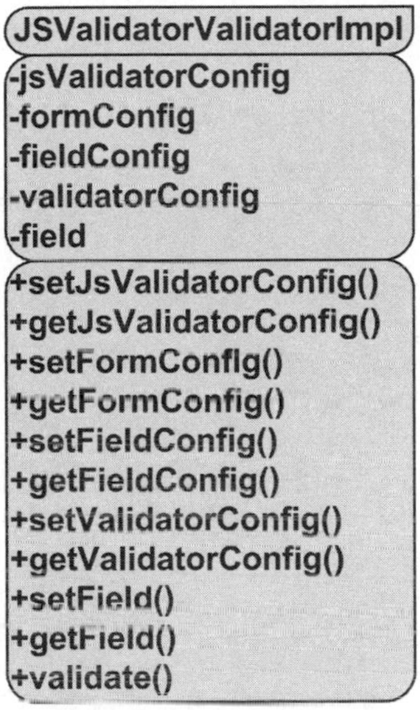

```
┌─────────────────────────────┐
│ JSValidatorValidatorImpl     │
├─────────────────────────────┤
│ -jsValidatorConfig           │
│ -formConfig                  │
│ -fieldConfig                 │
│ -validatorConfig             │
│ -field                       │
├─────────────────────────────┤
│ +setJsValidatorConfig()      │
│ +getJsValidatorConfig()      │
│ +setFormConfig()             │
│ +getFormConfig()             │
│ +setFieldConfig()            │
│ +getFieldConfig()            │
│ +setValidatorConfig()        │
│ +getValidatorConfig()        │
│ +setField()                  │
│ +getField()                  │
│ +validate()                  │
└─────────────────────────────┘
```

Figure 8-7. *UML diagram of the JSValidatorValidatorImpl class*

The five fields in this class are populated by the framework (using the corresponding setter methods) before the validator is asked to validate the field.

- The jsValidatorConfig field holds a reference to the JSValidatorConfig instance that is the parent of all the configuration data parsed from the configuration file.

- The formConfig field holds a reference to the JSValidatorForm object that represents the <form> element in the configuration file of which the element firing the validation is a part.

- The fieldConfig field holds a reference to a JSValidatorFormValidation object, which is the JavaScript representation of a <validation> element from the configuration file. This object describes the validation to be performed on a given field.

- The validatorConfig field holds a reference to a JSValidatorValidatorConfig object, which is the JavaScript representation of a <validator> element from the configuration file. This object describes the validation that will be used to validate a given field.

- Finally, the field field, if you'll excuse the alliteration, is a reference to the form field itself that fired the validation.

As mentioned, a validator will typically just supply its own implementation of validate() and call it a day. This method returns true if the field passes validation; false if not. Of course, there is nothing that says there can't be other methods and fields as necessary, but strictly speaking, this is all that's required.[1]

Just to prove that I'm not imagining all this, here is the code for the JSValidatorValidatorImpl class. As you can see, it really is empty, and yet is itself a complete implementation of a validator, albeit a rather pointless one!

```
function JSValidatorValidatorImpl() {

  this.jsValidatorConfig = null;
  this.formConfig = null;
  this.fieldConfig = null;
  this.validatorConfig = null;
  this.field = null;

  this.setJsValidatorConfig = function(inJsValidatorConfig) {
    this.jsValidatorConfig = inJsValidatorConfig;
  }
  this.getJsValidatorConfig = function() {
    return this.jsValidatorConfig;
  }

  this.setFormConfig = function(inFormConfig) {
    this.formConfig = inFormConfig;
  }
  this.getFormConfig = function() {
    return this.formConfig;
  }

  this.setFieldConfig = function(inFieldConfig) {
    this.fieldConfig = inFieldConfig;
  }
  this.getFieldConfig = function() {
    return this.fieldConfig;
  }

  this.setValidatorConfig = function(inValidatorConfig) {
    this.validatorConfig = inValidatorConfig;
  }
  this.getValidatorConfig = function() {
    return this.validatorConfig;
  }
```

---

1. In fact, there are empty implementations of all methods in the JSValidatorValidatorImpl class. So even if you wrote an empty class that extends JSValidatorValidatorImpl, it wouldn't break JSValidator—it just wouldn't do much of anything.

```
  this.setField = function(inField) {
    this.field = inField;
  }
  this.getField = function() {
    return this.field;
  }

  this.validate = function() { }

} // End JSValidatorValidatorImpl class.
```

The JSValidatorConfig Class

The JSValidatorConfig class, shown in Figure 8-8, is the top of the object entity relationship hierarchy in which the configuration information parsed from the configuration file is found. The three fields represent the three elements that can be immediate children of the <JSValidatorConfig> element in the configuration file: the <validator>, <message>, and <form> elements. Each is a collection of all the corresponding elements parsed from the configuration file.

Figure 8-8. *UML diagram of the JSValidatorConfig class*

Note that the toString() method has been overridden in order to display a more meaningful representation of this class for debugging purposes. This is true of all the remaining configuration file objects, so I won't mention it again.

Let's have a look at the actual code now, shall we?

```
function JSValidatorConfig() {

  var validators = new Object();
  var messages = new Object();
  var forms = new Object();
```

```
this.addValidator = function(inValidatorConfig) {
  validators[inValidatorConfig.getId()] = inValidatorConfig;
}
this.getValidators = function() {
  return validators;
}
this.getValidator = function(inID) {
  return validators[inID];
}

this.addMessage = function(inMessage) {
  messages[inMessage.getId()] = inMessage;
}
this.getMessages = function() {
  return messages;
}
this.getMessage = function(inID) {
  return messages[inID];
}

this.addForm = function(inForm) {
  forms[inForm.getName()] = inForm;
}
this.getForms = function() {
  return forms;
}
this.getForm = function(inName) {
  return forms[inName];
}

this.toString = function() {
  return "JSValidatorConfig=[" +
  "validators=" + validators + "," +
  "messages=" + messages + "," +
  "forms=" + forms + "]";
}

} // End JSValidatorConfig class.
```

Aside from the three fields and toString(), all this class contains are getters and setters for each field, as well as an add*XXX*() method for each of the collections. These methods are used by JSDigester to add JSValidatorForm, JSValidatorMessage, and JSValidatorValidatorConfig instances to the corresponding collection. Note that in addition to getters to get any one of the collections, there is a getter for each to get a specific element from the collection by ID or name, depending on which element we're going after (ID for validators and messages; name for forms).

The JSValidatorValidatorConfig Class

Figure 8-9 shows the JSValidatorValidatorConfig class, which is implemented with the
following code:

```
function JSValidatorValidatorConfig() {

  var id = null;
  var src = null;
  var clazz = null;

  this.getId = function() {
    return id;
  }
  this.setId = function(inID) {
    id = inID;
  }

  this.getSrc = function() {
    return src;
  }
  this.setSrc = function(inSRC) {
    src = inSRC;
  }

  this.getClass = function() {
    return clazz;
  }
  this.setClass = function(inClass) {
    clazz = inClass;
  }

  this.toString = function() {
    return "JSValidatorValidatorConfig-[" +
    "id=" + id + "," +
    "src=" + src + "," +
    "clazz=" + clazz + "]";
  }

} // End JSValidatorValidatorConfig class.
```

An instance of this class will be created and populated for each <validator> element
encountered in the configuration file. This information is necessary for JSValidator to be able
to work with a validator you define. The meaning of the fields should be obvious at this point,
based on our dissection of the configuration file.

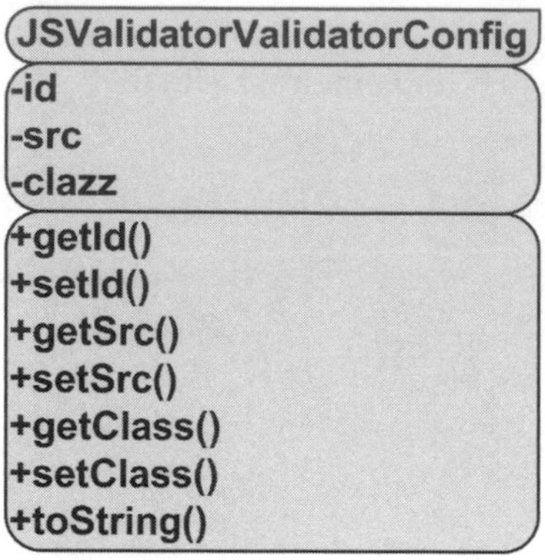

Figure 8-9. *UML diagram of the JSValidatorValidatorConfig class*

You probably noticed the use of clazz as opposed to class. IE doesn't take too kindly to using class, which seems to be a reserved word to it. (Surprisingly, Firefox does not seem to have a problem with class!) This actually mimics Java, as you may know, where class is a reserved word. It is typical in Java code, especially Java code dealing with reflection, to use clazz in place of class to get around this, and that's the case here as well. So, while it's not exactly a big deal, I wanted to make you aware that I didn't just make a silly typo—there's a reason for it!

The JSValidatorMessage Class

Continuing our Napoleonic march through these configuration classes, we next encounter the class shown in Figure 8-10: JSValidatorMessage. This class represents the <message> elements from the configuration file. Once again, I think the fields are pretty obvious, as they simply echo the attributes of the <message> element, and the methods are nothing but accessors and mutators for said fields. But, in the interest of completeness, let's have a look at the code for this class now, and then move on.

```
function JSValidatorMessage() {

  var id = null;
  var text = null;

  this.getId = function() {
    return id;
  }
  this.setId = function(inID) {
    id = inID;
  }

  this.getText = function() {
    return text;
  }
```

```
  this.setText = function(inText) {
    text = inText;
  }

  this.toString = function() {
    return "JSValidatorMessage=[" +
    "id=" + id + "," +
    "text=" + text + "]";
  }

} // End JSValidatorMessage class.
```

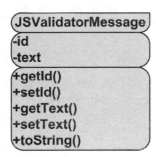

Figure 8-10. *UML diagram of the JSValidatorMessage class*

The JSValidatorForm Class

In Figure 8-11, we meet up with the JSValidatorForm class. Here's the code that matches up with that UML diagram:

```
function JSValidatorForm() {

  var name = null;
  var noSubmitMessage = null;
  var validations = new Object;

  this.getName = function() {
    return name;
  }
  this.setName = function(inName) {
    name = inName;
  }

  this.getNoSubmitMessage = function() {
    return noSubmitMessage;
  }
  this.setNoSubmitMessage = function(inNoSubmitMessage) {
    noSubmitMessage = inNoSubmitMessage;
  }
```

```
this.addValidation = function(inValidation) {
  validations[inValidation.getField()] = inValidation;
}
this.getValidations = function() {
  return validations;
}
this.getValidation = function(inField) {
  return validations[inField];
}

this.toString = function() {
  return "JSValidatorForm=[" +
  "name=" + name + ", " +
  "validations=" + validations + "]";
}

} // End JSValidatorForm class.
```

JSValidatorForm

-name
-noSubmitMessage
-validations

+getName()
+setName()
+getNoSubmitMessage()
+setNoSubmitMessage()
+addValidation()
+getValidations()
+getValidation()
+toString()

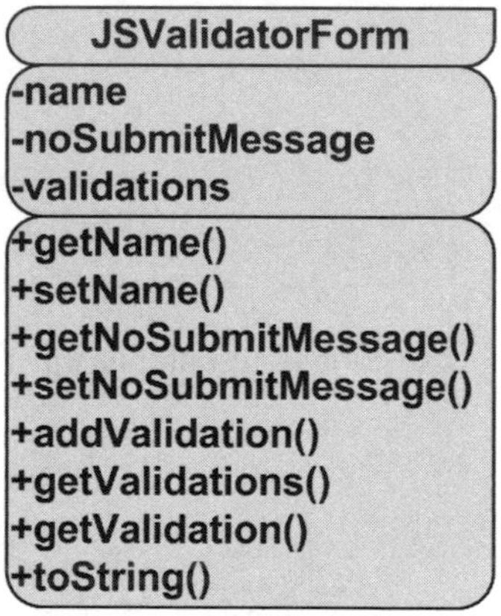

Figure 8-11. *UML diagram of the JSValidatorForm class*

Yes, again, this class simply matches up and represents the <form> element in the configuration file, and yes, what the fields are should probably be pretty obvious from the earlier discussion. However, we do have a couple interesting things to talk about.

One interesting point is the fact that the validations field is not an array. In fact, if you go back and look at the JSValidatorConfig class, you'll notice that the three collections there are not arrays either. Why is this interesting? Well, because a "collection" in most languages, assuming you aren't using some additional library, generally means an array to most people. So why would I use an Object here instead?

You may have heard that objects in JavaScript are essentially associative arrays? "Aha!" I can hear you say, "that's the answer right there!" I *am*, in fact, using an array; it's just not an outright Array object as you may have expected. Using an object allows you to reference the elements of the array by name, which happens to be exactly what we need throughout JSValidator. For instance, a <form> element can have any number of <validation> elements nested under it.

We want to be able to pull them up by name, and making them members of an Object allows for that. We can still iterate over them, as you'll see when we examine the code in JSValidator.js, but pulling up by name is the primary reason.

The other point to bring to your attention is that with only a few exceptions, all the fields in all these classes are private. That's the reason there are getters and setters for them (if they were public, those methods would be redundant). This is just good, everyday object-oriented design, but it's a somewhat unknown concept to a great many JavaScript programmers (and if I'm being honest, there was a time that I was doing object-oriented JavaScript and didn't know it either!).

The JSValidatorFormValidation Class

With the UML diagram in Figure 8-12, we come to the single most important class in terms of the information it provides. JSValidatorFormValidation is the class from which we create objects that describe a validation to occur for a given field and what happens when a validation failure occurs. The code for the JSValidatorFormValidation class is as follows:

```
function JSValidatorFormValidation() {

  var field = null;
  var event = null;
  var type = null;
  var failAction = null;
  var startInvalid = null;
  var params = new Object();

  this.getField = function() {
    return field;
  }
  this.setField = function(inField) {
    field = inField;
  }

  this.getEvent = function() {
    return event;
  }
  this.setEvent = function(inEvent) {
    event = inEvent;
  }

  this.getType = function() {
    return type;
  }
  this.setType = function(inType) {
    type = inType;
  }
```

```
this.getFailAction = function() {
  return failAction;
}
this.setFailAction = function(inFailAction) {
  failAction = inFailAction;
}

this.getStartInvalid = function() {
  return startInvalid;
}
this.setStartInvalid = function(inStartInvalid) {
  startInvalid = inStartInvalid;
}

this.addParam = function(inParam) {
  params[inParam.getName()] = inParam;
}
this.getParams = function() {
  return params;
}
this.getParam = function(inName) {
  return params[inName];
}

this.toString = function() {
  return "JSValidatorFormValidation=[" +
  "field=" + field + "," +
  "event=" + event + "," +
  "type=" + type + "," +
  "failAction=" + failAction + "," +
  "startInvalid=" + startInvalid + "," +
  "params=" + params + "]";
}

} // End JSValidatorFormValidation class.
```

Once again, the JSValidatorForm is nothing but a unit of storage for the corresponding configuration information. Any number of JSValidatorForm objects can be nested within a JSValidatorForm object, and by extension, the next class, JSValidatorFormValidationParam, can be nested within a JSValidatorForm object via the params field.

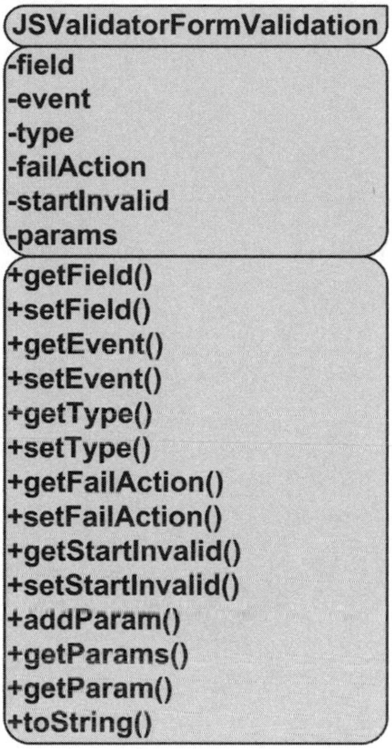

```
┌─────────────────────────────┐
│ JSValidatorFormValidation   │
├─────────────────────────────┤
│ -field                      │
│ -event                      │
│ -type                       │
│ -failAction                 │
│ -startInvalid               │
│ -params                     │
├─────────────────────────────┤
│ +getField()                 │
│ +setField()                 │
│ +getEvent()                 │
│ +setEvent()                 │
│ +getType()                  │
│ +setType()                  │
│ +getFailAction()            │
│ +setFailAction()            │
│ +getStartInvalid()          │
│ +setStartInvalid()          │
│ +addParam()                 │
│ +getParams()                │
│ +getParam()                 │
│ +toString()                 │
└─────────────────────────────┘
```

Figure 8-12. *UML diagram of the JSValidatorFormValidation class*

The JSValidatorFormValidationParam Class

Figure 8-13 shows the UML diagram for the JSValidatorFormValidationParam class. As you would expect, the code for this class is simple:

```javascript
function JSValidatorFormValidationParam() {

  var name = null;
  var value = null;

  this.getName = function() {
    return name;
  }
  this.setName = function(inName) {
    name = inName;
  }

  this.getValue = function() {
    return value;
  }
```

```
  this.setValue = function(inValue) {
    value = inValue;
  }


  this.toString = function() {
    return "JSValidatorFormValidation=[" +
    "name=" + name + "," +
    "value=" + value + "]";
  }


} // End JSValidatorFormValidationParam class.
```

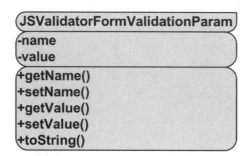

Figure 8-13. *UML diagram of the JSValidatorFormValidationParam class*

How the Classes Fit Together

Now that you've seen the UML diagram and code for each of the JSValidatorObjects.js classes, and also how they relate to the elements in the XML configuration file, the next step is to understand how they all fit together. I've more or less described the relationships textually as we walked through these classes, and the relationships mimic what is seen in the configuration file, but I would like to show you a graphical representation as well. An entity relationship diagram should do the trick nicely, and that's what's shown in Figure 8-14.

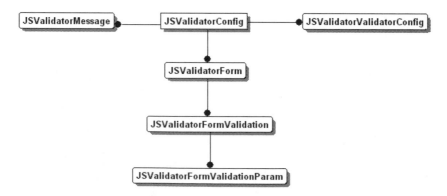

Figure 8-14. *Entity relationship hierarchy diagram showing how all the JSValidatorObject classes fit together*

Writing JSValidator.js

Now we come to the portion of our show where we examine what can rightly be called the JSValidator framework itself, and coincidence of coincidences, it's found in the file `JSValidator.js`!

Before we review the code itself, let's take a look at the UML diagram for this class. I think you'll be surprised when you look at Figure 8-15 just how little there really is to it.

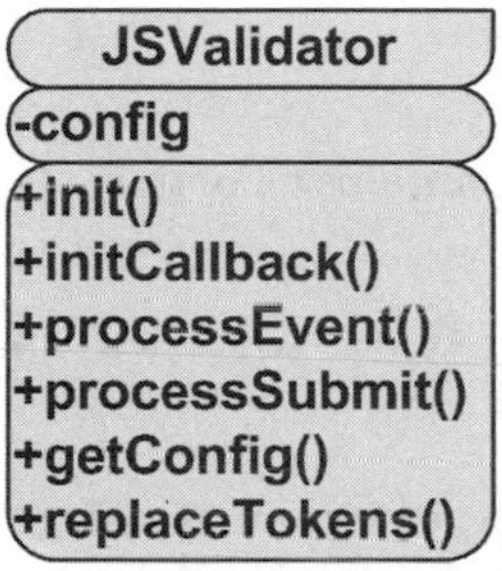

```
      JSValidator
-config
+init()
+initCallback()
+processEvent()
+processSubmit()
+getConfig()
+replaceTokens()
```

Figure 8-15. *UML diagram of the JSValidator class*

Because there is more code to this class than all the others we have looked at (by a good margin), I won't be listing the whole thing, but we'll be looking at the pieces we need to as we go along.

The first thing we see is a single field defined: `config`. The `config` field is a reference to a single `JSValidatorConfig` object, which as we saw earlier, is the object that holds all the configuration information parsed from the configuration file.

Let's skip ahead a bit, over all the methods in this class, and instead look at the bit of code that we find in this file *after* the definition of JSValidator:

```
// Include dependencies.
document.write('<script src="' + JSVConfig.pathPrefix +
  'prototype.js"></script>');
document.write('<script src="' + JSVConfig.pathPrefix +
  'sax.js"></script>');
document.write('<script src="' + JSVConfig.pathPrefix +
  'JSDigester.js"></script>');
document.write('<script src="' + JSVConfig.pathPrefix +
  'JSValidatorObjects.js"></script>');
document.write('<script src="' + JSVConfig.pathPrefix +
  'JSValidatorBasicValidators.js"></script>');

// Instantiate JSValidator.
jsValidator = new JSValidator();

// Set onload event to configure JSValidator, unless told not to.
if (!JSVConfig.manualInit) {
  window.onload = function() {
    jsValidator.init();
  };
}
```

The five document.write() calls can be thought of as imports of the elements required for JSValidator to function. Notice that they use the pathPrefix element defined in JSVConfig to construct the URL to the imported script file. Here are the imports:

- We need the Prototype library, of course, so we see that first.

- We know that JSDigester is built on top of the SAX parser from the Mozilla project, so that import is next.

- Next follows JSDigester itself.

- Next comes the import of the JSValidatorObjects.js file, which contains all of the configuration classes that we looked at a short while ago.

- Last is an import of the basic, built-in validators that JSValidator provides, which we will be looking at after JSValidator itself.

These five statements are executed at page load, and so writing <script> tags into the page dynamically like this will cause the browser to download those resources as well. This is how it is possible for a developer to import only a single .js file in order to use JSValidator. The rest are includes in JSValidator.js itself and are therefore "automatic," as far as the developer is concerned.

JavaScript files importing others like this is a very handy technique that allows you to keep code separate but still easily get everything you need. The alternative is to merge all these JavaScript files into one, which might be better from the perspective of not having to make extra calls to the server. But the concept of keeping all these components in separate files, and therefore allowing them to easily be updated separately, is a powerful one, and frankly one taken for granted in more full-featured languages. So, I am of the opinion that unless you know you have an issue due to these extra requests, keeping things clean and separated is more useful.

After those five statements is the one statement that gives us the instance of the JSValidator class that we'll be using throughout the rest of the code. Immediately following that is where JSValidator is initialized automatically, if configured to do so. Remember that the developer can set the manualInit element in JSVConfig to false and take control of initializing the framework. This is done by setting the onLoad event handler for the page to point to the init() method of the JSValidator class. Note that this is necessary, as opposed to simply calling init() right there, because the page has to actually be fully loaded; otherwise, the code that executes and accesses the DOM can fail because the script can execute before the page fully loads.

The init() Method

And what does this init() method look like? Well, that's our next stop. Here it is:

```
this.init = function() {

  // Use Prototype to load the configuration file.
  new Ajax.Request(
    JSVConfig.pathPrefix + JSVConfig.configFile,
    { method: "get", onComplete: this.initCallback }
  );

} // End init().
```

Was it all you had hoped it would be? Yeah, me neither! All that's being done here is the configuration file specified in the JSVConfig structure is being loaded via Prototype's Ajax support. We are declaring that when the response is received from the server—that is, the configuration file itself—the initCallback() method of the JSValidator class should be called. So, as you might expect, that method is what we'll look at now.

The initCallback() Method

Because the initCallback() method is somewhat long, we'll look at it in a couple of pieces to better comprehend each task it performs. These chunks will be described in the order they appear, so putting the following chunks together gives you the complete method.

Configuring the JSDigester Rules

Let's begin with this bit of code:

```
var jsDigester = new JSDigester();

// Create new object when JSValidatorConfig tag encountered.
jsDigester.addObjectCreate("JSValidatorConfig",
  "JSValidatorConfig");

// Create new object when JSValidatorConfig/validator tag encountered,
// populate its properties and add it to the JSValidatorConfig object
// on the top of the stack.
jsDigester.addObjectCreate("JSValidatorConfig/validator",
  "JSValidatorValidatorConfig");
jsDigester.addSetProperties("JSValidatorConfig/validator");
jsDigester.addSetNext("JSValidatorConfig/validator", "addValidator");

// Create new object when JSValidatorConfig/message tag encountered,
// populate its properties and add it to the JSValidatorConfig object
// on the top of the stack.
jsDigester.addObjectCreate("JSValidatorConfig/message",
  "JSValidatorMessage");
jsDigester.addSetProperties("JSValidatorConfig/message");
jsDigester.addSetNext("JSValidatorConfig/message", "addMessage");

// Create new object when JSValidatorConfig/form tag encountered,
// populate its properties and add it to the JSValidatorConfig object
// on the top of the stack.
jsDigester.addObjectCreate("JSValidatorConfig/form",
  "JSValidatorForm");
jsDigester.addSetProperties("JSValidatorConfig/form");
jsDigester.addSetNext("JSValidatorConfig/form", "addForm");
```

```
// Create new object when JSValidatorConfig/form/validation tag encountered,
// populate its properties and add it to the JSValidatorForm object
// on the top of the stack.
jsDigester.addObjectCreate("JSValidatorConfig/form/validation",
  "JSValidatorFormValidation");
jsDigester.addSetProperties("JSValidatorConfig/form/validation");
jsDigester.addSetNext("JSValidatorConfig/form/validation", "addValidation");

// Create new object when JSValidatorConfig/form/validation/param tag
// encountered, populate its properties and add it to the
// JSValidatorFormValidation object on the top of the stack.
jsDigester.addObjectCreate("JSValidatorConfig/form/validation/param",
  "JSValidatorFormValidationParam");
jsDigester.addSetProperties("JSValidatorConfig/form/validation/param");
jsDigester.addSetNext("JSValidatorConfig/form/validation/param",
  "addParam");

// Parse config.
config = jsDigester.parse(inRequest.responseText);
```

All of this, in a nutshell, is the configuration of the JSDigester rules that correspond to the JSValidator configuration file. Because JSDigester was already covered (in the previous chapter), going over all the rules in detail would be a bit of a waste. However, if any of this code doesn't make sense to you, I highly recommend rereading Chapter 7.

The outcome of these rules being executed on the configuration file is that the config field in the JSValidator class is an instance of JSValidatorConfig, with all its children populated from the configuration information. This code exists in the initCallback() function, which is passed the request object by Prototype for the Ajax request made to retrieve the configuration file. Therefore, the XML to be parsed can be accessed via the responseText attribute of the inRequest object, as you can see in the call to jsDigester.parser().

Adding the Built-in Validators

Once the configuration file has been parsed, the next task we need to perform is to add in the basic built-in validators: the Required, Regex, and MinLength validators. The code that accomplishes this is as follows:

```
// Add in the basic validators.
var requiredValidatorConfig = new JSValidatorValidatorConfig();
requiredValidatorConfig.setId("required");
requiredValidatorConfig.setSrc("");
requiredValidatorConfig.setClass("RequiredValidator");
config.addValidator(requiredValidatorConfig);
var regexValidatorConfig = new JSValidatorValidatorConfig();
regexValidatorConfig.setId("regex");
regexValidatorConfig.setSrc("");
```

```
regexValidatorConfig.setClass("RegexValidator");
config.addValidator(regexValidatorConfig);
var minLengthValidatorConfig = new JSValidatorValidatorConfig();
minLengthValidatorConfig.setId("minLength");
minLengthValidatorConfig.setSrc("");
minLengthValidatorConfig.setClass("MinLengthValidator");
config.addValidator(minLengthValidatorConfig);
```

For each of those three validators, the code instantiates a new
JSValidatorValidatorConfig object. We then populate the three attributes it contains: id, src,
and class. Note that the src attribute is set to an empty string because there is no file to import.
As you will recall, the code for these validators was imported already as part of the global code
executed when this .js file was loaded. In fact, there is no real reason to set the src attribute at
all for these validators, but I prefer code to be as deterministic as possible, even when it doesn't
really have to be.

Loading Custom Validators

We still have some work to do for validators. We now need to import the JavaScript files that
may have been named for any custom add-on validators, such as the DateValidator. When this
code executes, the page is already loaded, so we can't simply use the document.write() trick as
we did earlier. Instead, we need to get just slightly fancier:

```
// Add includes for external validators.
var configuredValidators = config.getValidators();
for (var validatorID in configuredValidators) {
  var nextValidatorConfig = configuredValidators[validatorID];
  // Only non-basic validators will have a src value specified.
  if (nextValidatorConfig.getSrc() != "") {
    var scriptTag = document.createElement("script");
    scriptTag.src = nextValidatorConfig.getSrc();
    var headTag = document.getElementsByTagName("head").item(0);
    headTag.appendChild(scriptTag);
  }
}
```

First, we get the collection of validators that were parsed from the configuration file and
iterate over that collection. For each, we get the appropriate JSValidatorValidatorConfig
object, and we see if its src attribute has a value (because, as you'll remember, we just added
the basic validators, which all had the src attribute set to an empty string—see, it's good to be
deterministic!). Once we have the src attribute value, we use the DOM createElement()
method to create a new <script> tag. We set the src attribute of that tag to the value specified
for the validator. Then a reference to the <head> of the document is retrieved, and the new
<script> tag is appended. The browser will then immediately load the source JavaScript file
and evaluate it. We now have available to the rest of the code the class for the validator
configured.

Attaching Event Handlers

The next and final step to complete initialization is to actually hook up the configured events to the form fields that were configured to have validations attached to them. That is accomplished with the next bit of code, which may look a bit daunting, but really if you were to trim out the comments, you would find it's a bit simpler than you might first perceive.

```
// Attach event handlers to fields as defined in config file.
var configuredForms = config.getForms();
// Iterate over forms configured.
for (var formName in configuredForms) {
  var nextFormConfig = configuredForms[formName];
  // Get reference to form being configured.
  var targetForm = document.forms[nextFormConfig.getName()];
  // Attach an onSubmit handler to check if it can submit or not.
  targetForm.onsubmit = jsValidator.processSubmit;
  // Get reference for all validations configured for this form.
  var formValidations = nextFormConfig.getValidations();
  // Iterate over validations defined for this form.
  for (var fieldName in formValidations) {
    // Get the field validation being hooked.
    var nextValidationConfig = formValidations[fieldName];
    // Get the validator definition.
    var validator = config.getValidator(nextValidationConfig.getType());
    // Get the field to hook event to.
    var targetField = targetForm[nextValidationConfig.getField()];
    // Set attribute if this field is initially invalid. and if the field
    // is configured for the highlight action, then highlight it.
    if (nextValidationConfig.getStartInvalid() &&
      nextValidationConfig.getStartInvalid() == "true") {
      targetField.setAttribute("JSValidator_INVALID", "true");
      if (nextValidationConfig.getFailAction() == "highlight") {
        var idToHighlight =
          nextValidationConfig.getParam("idToHighlight").getValue();
        var errorStyleClass =
          nextValidationConfig.getParam("errorStyleClass").getValue();
        $(idToHighlight).className = errorStyleClass;
      }
    }
    // Set event handler.
    targetField[nextValidationConfig.getEvent()] = jsValidator.processEvent;
  }
}
```

First, the collection of forms configured is retrieved. The code then begins to iterate over that collection. For each, we get a reference to the HTML for it via the document.forms[] collection. An onSubmit event handler is attached to the form. This event handler is the processSubmit() function in the JSValidator object, as will be discussed shortly.

After that, the collection of validations for that form is retrieved from the JSValidatorConfig object, and we begin to iterate over it. For each, we get a reference to the field in the HTML form. Next, we see if either the startInvalid attribute was not specified at all or if it was specified with the value true. If either condition is true, we add an attribute to the field named JSValidator_INVALID with a value of true (the value is actually irrelevant; just the presence or absence of the attribute determines if the field is invalid). We also see if the failAction for that field is highlight. If so, we go ahead and get the ID of the page element to highlight and the style class used for highlighting, and we apply it using Prototype's $() shorthand for document. getElementById().

Finally, we set the appropriate event handler for the field to point to the processEvent() method of the JSValidator class.

All of this is really a long-winded way of saying that for every field configured to have a validation applied to it in the configuration file, we're setting the appropriate event handler(s) on the field and setting each field's initial state. In this way, if JavaScript is turned off, the form will still work because it isn't dependent on JSValidator at all; the framework is strictly an add-on capability. This is good, nonintrusive coding.

With init() and initCallback() out of the way, we now turn our attention to the method that is called in response to an event on a field that triggers a validation.

The processEvent() Method

Recall that for each field that has a validation assigned to it, in initCallback(), we attached the appropriate event handler, as described in the configuration file, but it always calls processEvent() in the JSValidator class. This allows the framework to handle all these events in a common way. Let's now see exactly what this event-handler function does:

```
this.processEvent = function() {

  // Get reference to form, field and validator config objects for the
  // form element that fired the event that called this callback.
  var formConfig = config.getForm(this.form.name);
  var fieldConfig = formConfig.getValidation(this.name);
  var validatorConfig = config.getValidator(fieldConfig.getType());

  // Get a reference to the class that implements the validator defined
  // for this field.  Then, get a new instance of it and call its validate()
  // method.
  var clazz = eval(validatorConfig.getClass());
  clazz = new clazz;
  clazz.setJsValidatorConfig(config);
  clazz.setFieldConfig(fieldConfig);
  clazz.setValidatorConfig(validatorConfig);
  clazz.setField(this);
  // Perform the appropriate action for pass and fail.
  var isValid = clazz.validate();
  if (isValid) {
    // When field was valid, might be some cleanup to do in some cases.
    this.removeAttribute("JSValidator_INVALID");
```

```javascript
        if (fieldConfig.getFailAction() == "highlight") {
          var idToHighlight = fieldConfig.getParam("idToHighlight").getValue();
          var okStyleClass =
            fieldConfig.getParam("okStyleClass").getValue();
          $(idToHighlight).className = okStyleClass;
        }
        if (fieldConfig.getFailAction() == "insert") {
          var targetID = fieldConfig.getParam("idToInsertInto").getValue();
          $(targetID).innerHTML = "";
        }
      } else {
        // Field NOT valid, so act according to config.
        this.setAttribute("JSValidator_INVALID", "true");
        switch (fieldConfig.getFailAction()) {
          case "alert":
            var whatMessage = fieldConfig.getParam("message");
            var messageConfig =
              jsValidator.getConfig().getMessage(whatMessage.getValue());
            var message = messageConfig.getText();
            message = jsValidator.replaceTokens(message, fieldConfig.getParams());
            alert(message);
          break;
          case "highlight":
            var idToHighlight = fieldConfig.getParam("idToHighlight").getValue();
            var errorStyleClass =
              fieldConfig.getParam("errorStyleClass").getValue();
            $(idToHighlight).className = errorStyleClass;
          break;
          case "insert":
            var whatMessage = fieldConfig.getParam("message");
            var targetID = fieldConfig.getParam("idToInsertInto").getValue();
            var messageConfig =
              jsValidator.getConfig().getMessage(whatMessage.getValue());
            var message = messageConfig.getText();
            message = jsValidator.replaceTokens(message, fieldConfig.getParams());
            $(targetID).innerHTML = message;
          break;
        }
      }

      return isValid;

  } // End processEvent().
```

First, we get a reference to the config objects for the form, field, and validator the field uses. Next, the specified validator is instantiated. This is done by first eval()'ing the name of the class returned by the call to validatorConfig.getClass(), which gives us a reference to the class, then creating a new instance of it by using the new keyword. We set on that validator instance the JSValidatorConfig instance by passing it to setJsValidatorConfig(), the JSValidatorFormValidation for the field by passing it to setFieldConfig(), and the JSValidatorValidatorConfig by passing it to setValidatorConfig(). We also pass the field itself that triggered the event by passing it to setField().

The validator should now have access to all the pieces of information it might need, so we then call validate() on the validator. validate() returns true if the field passes validation; false if not. If validate() returns true, we essentially need to undo any failure indications that the field might have had. That means that first we need to remove that JSValidator_INVALID indicator, if it was present, and if the failAction for the field is highlight, we need to unhighlight the target element.

Lastly, if the failAction for the field is insert, then we want to clear the innerHTML property of the target element. You can see all this in action with the Last Name field. That field starts out invalid, and as you type and enter five characters or more, the field label reverts to a valid entry condition. This is due to this code in this block.

What if the field fails validation? Well, then we find ourselves in the else clause seen in this code. In that case, we examine the failAction value, and then switch on it. For action alert, we get the message referenced in the configuration, and then call replaceTokens() to do token replacement. Finally, we display the resultant message via alert().

For highlight, we just need to get the ID of the element to highlight, as well as the style class to use. Then we set the className attribute accordingly, again using Prototype's $() shortcut.

Finally, for the insert action, we do essentially the same thing as for alert, but updating the innerHTML property of the target element instead of calling alert() at the end.

The processSubmit() Method

Another function that is of concern to us is the onSubmit event for the form itself. Quite obviously, if any of the fields on the form are invalid, we should not allow the form to submit. But how do we determine whether the form should submit or not? What are the actual mechanics behind it? The answer to that is found in the processSubmit() method of JSValidator, shown here:

```
this.processSubmit = function() {

  var formValidity = true;
  // If any element of the form has the JSValidator_INVALID attribute, then
  // the form cannot be submitted.
  for (var i = 0; i < this.elements.length; i++) {
    if (this.elements[i].getAttribute("JSValidator_INVALID")) {
      formValidity = false;
    }
  }
  if (!formValidity) {
    // Can't be submitted, show configured message.
    var config = jsValidator.getConfig();
    var formConfig = config.getForm(this.name);
    alert(formConfig.getNoSubmitMessage());
  }
  return formValidity;

} // End processSubmit().
```

As you can see, all we really need to do is iterate over all the elements in the form and check if any have the JSValidator_INVALID attribute. If not, then the form is OK and submission can continue. If any elements have that attribute, then we get the value of the noSubmitMessage attribute for the form and display it via alert() to indicate an error is present on the form.

Note here the use of the this reference (you'll also note that the same thing is used in the processEvent() method). You may find this interesting because you may expect that this points to the JSValidator instance, since these methods are part of that instance. But recall that these two methods were attached to elements on the page: the form and the form elements. When they are called, it is in the context of those elements, and thus the this keyword actually points to those elements. Remember that the this reference always refers to the object the method is attached to *at run time*, not necessarily design time. It's easy to get confused by this, and it will most likely burn you once or twice at late hours of the night!

The replaceTokens() Method

The last bit of functionality provided by JSValidator is the replaceTokens() method, which is used when generating the messages the user sees when a field fails validation, if configured to do so. Let's have a look at that method now, shall we?

```
this.replaceTokens = function(inString, inParams) {

  // We're going to scan the text looking for tokens, all the while
  // constructing a new string in a StringBuffer from it, with the
  // data replacing the tokens.
  var finalText = "";
  var i = 0;
  while (i < inString.length) {
    // See if the next character is a hash sign, and if the next
    // character after that is an opening brace, as long as
    // that check doesn't put us beyond the end of the string, then we've
    // found the start of a token.
    if (inString.charAt(i) == '#' && inString.charAt(i + 1) == '{') {
      // Now we get the location of the closing token delimiter.  Note that
      // if the developer forgot to close the token, this will probably
      // blow up with a JS error, and at best it just won't work as
      // expected.  We're going to live with that!
      var lIndex = inString.indexOf("}#", i);
      // Now it's a simple matter to get the token name.
      var tokenName = inString.substring(i + 2, lIndex);
      // Look up the replacement value with that name from inParams.
      var tokenValue = "";
      var param = inParams[tokenName];
      if (param) {
        tokenValue = param.getValue();
      }
```

```
        finalText += tokenValue;
        // Set i to take us just past the closing token delimiter, and
        // we're done with this token
        i = lIndex + 1;
      } else {
        // The current character being checked was NOT part of a token
        // opening delimiter, so just append the character
        finalText += inString.charAt(i);
      }
      i++;
    }
    return finalText;

  } // End replaceTokens().
```

replaceTokens() is a fairly straightforward bit of string manipulation. It begins by iterating over each character in the input string, which will be one of the message strings, possibly containing replacement tokens in the form #{*xxx*}#.

For each character, we see if it's a hash mark (#). If it is, we then see if the *next character* is a brace ({). If either of these conditions is false, the code in the else block executes, and the character is simply added to a string we began constructing at the start. However, if both conditions are true, we've identified a replacement token. Now we need to find the location of the closing delimiter (}#). Once we have that, we can get the name of the token easily enough by using the substring() method of the String object.

With the token name in hand, we can look it up in the collection of parameters passed in. Note that in this instance, *collection of parameters* actually refers to the Object to which all the configured parameters for the validation being processed are attached. We can then do a simple lookup for the token. That's because, as you'll remember, the whole point of using Object rather than Array was so that we could easily look up these values using the [ ] paradigm. Once we find the value, we simply append the value of the parameter to the output string, and move the iteration index past the closing token delimiter. Once the iteration completes, we return the constructed string, and *voilà*, a string with all tokens replaced with the appropriate parameter values!

And with that, we've seen the guts of JSValidator in detail! Only two last bits of code remain to be examined, and those are the validator implementation classes—both the basic built-in ones and the one add-on validator.

Writing JSValidatorBasicValidators.js

The JSValidatorBasicValidators.js file, as the name clearly implies, is where you'll find the three basic built-in validators that JSValidator always makes available automatically: RequiredValidator, RegexValidator, and MinLengthValidator.

The RequiredValidator Class

RequiredValidator, shown in Figure 8-16, is just about as simple as a validator can get, as you can see here:

```
function RequiredValidator() {

  this.validate = function() {

    var retVal = true;
    if (this.field.value == "") {
      retVal = false;
    }
    return retVal;

  } // End validate().

} // End RequiredValidator().

// RequiredValidator extends JSValidatorValidatorImpl.
RequiredValidator.prototype = new JSValidatorValidatorImpl;
```

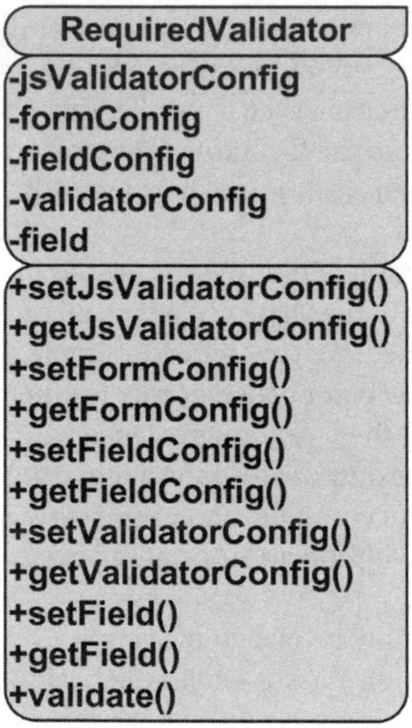

Figure 8-16. *UML diagram of the RequiredValidator class*

This class contains just a quick check of the value of the field that fired the validation to make sure something was entered, and nothing more. Note the setting of the prototype of the validator at the end. This is where the inheritance from the JSValidatorValidatorImpl class happens, and you'll see this same basic line of code for each validator. Likewise, for your own validator, you would need to include that line of code.

The RegexValidator Class

Next up is RegexValidator, which isn't much more complex at all. First, have a look at Figure 8-17, the UML diagram for the RegexValidator class.

```
┌─────────────────────────────┐
│      RegexValidator         │
├─────────────────────────────┤
│ -jsValidatorConfig          │
│ -formConfig                 │
│ -fieldConfig                │
│ -validatorConfig            │
│ -field                      │
├─────────────────────────────┤
│ +setJsValidatorConfig()     │
│ +getJsValidatorConfig()     │
│ +setFormConfig()            │
│ +getFormConfig()            │
│ +setFieldConfig()           │
│ +getFieldConfig()           │
│ +setValidatorConfig()       │
│ +getValidatorConfig()       │
│ +setField()                 │
│ +getField()                 │
│ +validate()                 │
└─────────────────────────────┘
```

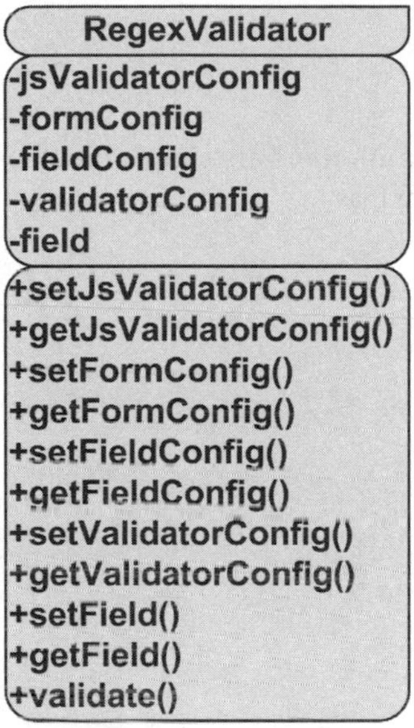

Figure 8-17. *UML diagram of the RegexValidator class*

Moving on to the code, we see that, in this case, we need to get the regular expression from the parameters defined for this validation. To do so, we call getParam() on the fieldConfig object for this validation, and subsequently we call getValue() on the object returned from that call, since it is a JSValidatorFormValidationParam, not the value itself. With that done, we have only to use the typical JavaScript regular expression match() function to determine if the field's value is valid.

```
function RegexValidator() {

  this.validate = function() {

    var retVal = true;
    var parm = this.fieldConfig.getParam("regex");
    var regx = parm.getValue();
    if (!this.field.value.match(regx)) {
      retVal = false;
    }
    return retVal;

  } // End validate().

} // End RegexValidator().
```

```
// RegexValidator extends JSValidatorValidatorImpl.
RegexValidator.prototype = new JSValidatorValidatorImpl;
```

RegexValidator is one of those cases where something seemingly simple masks a great deal of power. You have the full capability of the JavaScript regular expression engine at your fingertips, without writing a single bit of code.

The MinLengthValidator Class

The last basic validator to look at is MinLengthValidator, which is another very simple bit of code. As Figure 8-18 indicates, this is again just a typical validator class.

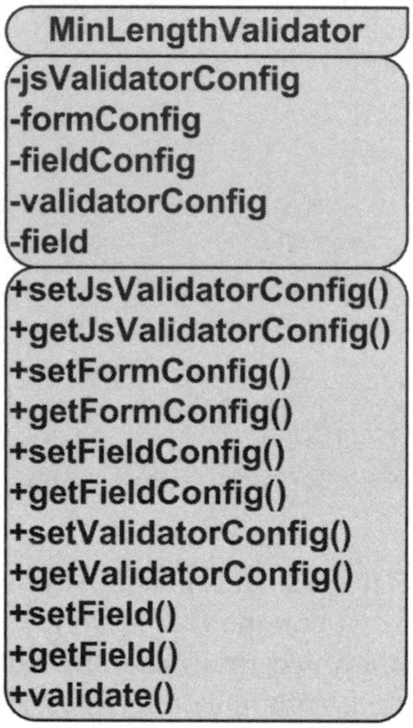

Figure 8-18. *UML diagram of the MinLengthValidator class*

Take a look at the code:

```
function MinLengthValidator() {

  this.validate = function() {

    var retVal = true;
    if (this.field.value.length <
      this.fieldConfig.getParam("minLength").getValue()) {
      retVal = false;
    }
    return retVal;

  } // End validate().
```

```
} // End MinLengthValidator().
```

```
// MinLengthValidator extends JSValidatorValidatorImpl.
MinLengthValidator.prototype = new JSValidatorValidatorImpl;
```

As you can see, as with `RegexValidator`, all we're doing is grabbing the minimum allowed length for the field from the parameters for the validation, comparing the value of the field to it, and returning the appropriate Boolean outcome.

Writing DateValidator.js

Only one piece of code stands between us and a complete examination of this application, and that's the `DateValidator` class, as shown in Figure 8-19.

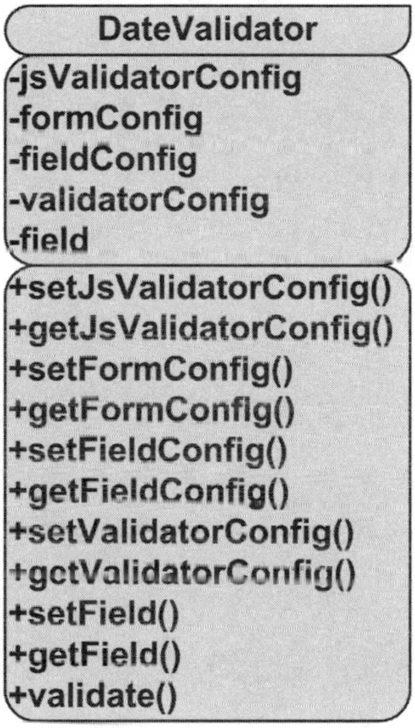

```
DateValidator
-jsValidatorConfig
-formConfig
-fieldConfig
-validatorConfig
-field
+setJsValidatorConfig()
+getJsValidatorConfig()
+setFormConfig()
+getFormConfig()
+setFieldConfig()
+getFieldConfig()
+setValidatorConfig()
+getValidatorConfig()
+setField()
+getField()
+validate()
```

Figure 8-19. *UML diagram of the DateValidator class*

Let's get the code out of the way, and then see what makes it tick.

```
function DateValidator() {

  this.validate = function() {

    // Get the configured format of the field.
    var format = this.fieldConfig.getParam("format").getValue();
```

```
      // Make sure the value is the same length as the format.
      if (this.field.value.length != format.length) {
        return false;
      }

      // Now iterate over the value.  If any character doesn't match the format,
      // it's a reject.  Note that M, D and Y characters in the format
      // correlate to any numeric character.
      for (var i = 0; i < format.length; i++) {
        if (format.charAt(i).toUpperCase() == "M" ||
          format.charAt(i).toUpperCase() == "D" ||
          format.charAt(i).toUpperCase() == "Y") {
          // Character at this position should be a numeric.
          if (this.field.value.charAt(i) < '0' ||
            this.field.value.charAt(i) > '9') {
            return false;
          }
        } else {
          // Format doesn't specify a numeric value at this position, so just
          // be sure the character matches exactly.
          if (format.charAt(i) != this.field.value.charAt(i)) {
            return false;
          }
        }
      }

      return true;

    } // End validate().

  } // End DateValidator().

  // DateValidator extends JSValidatorValidatorImpl.
  DateValidator.prototype = new JSValidatorValidatorImpl;
```

The first thing we see in the validate() method is grabbing the format to use from the configuration. We then see a trivial rejection: if the value of the field doesn't exactly match that of the format string, we know the field is invalid.

Assuming it passes that little test though, we then iterate over the value of the field. For each character, we compare it to what is expected in that position in the format string. Any M, D, or Y character in the format string corresponds to any digit 0 through 9. If the character in the format string is something else, typically a slash or dash, then we make sure the character in the value matches exactly. If we ever hit a situation where the character in the input string doesn't match that in the format string, then the field fails validation and we return false.

And that's that—another application in the books, so to speak!

Suggested Exercises

I've left the door open for a number of enhancements for you to do that should very much help further your understanding of JSValidator and, of course, JavaScript in general. Here are just a few suggestions:

- A fairly simple one first: when a validation failure occurs, the field that had the error should get focus automatically. This is definitely an obvious one, and one I left for you to start with because it shouldn't take very long or be very difficult, so it's a good way to get your feet wet.

- Another obvious one is to implement more validators. How about one that validates credit card numbers? How about one to check that an entered date falls within a given range? How about one that does greater-than or less-than comparisons of two fields (which would require you to modify the framework to allow a validation configuration to name a second field to operate on)? Whatever your imagination can come up with, go for it!

- Allow for multiple validations on a single field. This may not be quite as simple as it sounds, but would definitely be a worthy goal.

- Add internationalization (I18n) support. This could be accomplished a number of ways. One way might be to add a locale identifier to the <message> element—maybe it has en for English, de for German, and so on. Then just get the appropriate message based on the locale of the client.

- Allow for adding error messages as pop-up tooltips to highlighted error fields. That way, when a field is highlighted to show an error, the user can hover over it to see what's wrong.

Summary

In this chapter, we developed an extensible framework that can completely externalize our form validations, requiring virtually no code be added to our pages. You saw how you can add reusable validators to your framework that you can find uses for in other applications. And you can accomplish all this in a nice, neat, object-oriented way that lends itself to extension.

In this chapter's project, you saw how the JSDigester project from the previous chapter helps us deal with XML easily. You also got a glimpse of the Prototype library in action a bit, and had another brush with Ajax, albeit just a quick one. We'll get to a project that specifically deals with Ajax specifically in Chapter 12.

■ ■ ■

CHAPTER 9

Widget Mania: Using a GUI Widget Framework

In web development, widgets are all the rage these days. No longer are we content with regular form fields, buttons, drop-down lists, and such. Just plain-old tables aren't sufficient for many developers! But this trend isn't just due to a desire to create cooler interfaces. There are UI metaphors in a modern operating system that don't have an analogy in the web world, at least not intrinsically.

Take the tree view as an example. I'm sure you've seen a tree view before. Indeed, if you work in Windows, you can barely avoid it (it's the list of folders on the left in Windows Explorer). Have you seen one on the Web? Chances are you have, but unless it was relatively recently, the web developer likely wrote it himself, or else lifted some code from somewhere else. What it wasn't though, in all likelihood, was a piece of code that was self-contained and part of a larger framework of UI components, which is what a UI widget is.

Widgets make adding this "advanced" functionality to your web application very easy, and more important, consistent. You'll see how this works as we build a handy little application for posting notes to ourselves. In this project, we'll use a lot of widgets supplied by a library that is rapidly growing in popularity: the Yahoo! User Interface (YUI) Library.

JSNotes Requirements and Goals

For this chapter's project, which we'll call JSNotes from here on out, we're going to build something along the lines of that pad of sticky yellow notes you very possibly having sitting around your desk somewhere. In this case though, it will be a web-based application that allows us to post digital notes to ourselves. The main purpose of this application, aside from being useful in helping to keep us from losing little pieces of information we obtain throughout the day, is meant to demonstrate the use of the YUI Library.

So, what specifically is JSNotes going to do? Let's spell it out now:

- JSNotes will allow us to create notes, including a subject for each, and add a date and time (generally, the current date and time, but you never know!). We'll also be able to categorize each note as either personal or business.

- The notes will be presented in a Windows Explorer-like view, with a tree view on the left and note details on the right. The two primary branches in the tree will be our two categories: Personal and Business.

- For each note, we'll store the note text, a subject, and a date and time, as well as the note's category.

- We'll be able to delete a note, and we'll also be able to "export" a note, which really just means put it in a form suitable for copying and pasting into another program.

- When adding a note, we want to present it in a pop-up dialog box.

- We'll also have Help and About boxes, but they will be done in a different style than the add note pop-up. These will appear as an overlay over the main JSNotes display.

The best part is, with the YUI Library in the mix, all of this becomes a relatively trivial exercise!

The YUI Library

The YUI Library includes a set of UI widgets, as well as a number of utility-type classes for Ajax, drag-and-drop, DOM manipulation, and more. YUI is one of the best documented libraries I've seen recently and also one of the best demonstrated. You can find a good example of virtually every part of the library, usually along with a number of variations for guidance.

Let's talk about the widgets, since they are primarily what we'll be working with in this application, and we'll be using quite a few of them. YUI provides a number of widgets, including AutoComplete, Calendar, Container (including Module, Overlay, Panel, Tooltip, Dialog, and SimpleDialog), Logger, Menu, Slider, TabView, and TreeView. Because the widgets are designed around a common framework, they all present a fairly consistent programming interface.

Using YUI is as simple as importing some JavaScript files, and in many cases, some CSS files as well. Generally speaking, each widget is a single JavaScript file, but there also may be some dependencies on other files, and those need to be manually imported, too. Once that's done, you're ready to rock and roll.

For instance, let's say you want to create a menu. All you need to do is define your menu in the form of some simple markup, like so:

```
<div id="basicmenu" class="yuimenu">
  <div class="bd">
    <ul class="first-of-type">
      <li class="yuimenuitem"><a href="page1.htm">Page1</a></li>
      <li class="yuimenuitem"><a href="page2.htm">Page2</a></li>
    </ul>
  </div>
</div>
```

This provides the basic structure of the menu. The last step is to tell YUI to create the menu for you, based on this markup. To do so is as simple as this:

```
var oMenu = new YAHOO.widget.Menu("basicmenu");
oMenu.render();
```

YUI will find the element on the page with the ID basicmenu. It will then parse the contents, specifically looking for a list, and will use it to generate the menu. The markup will be replaced with the markup for the menu itself, and the menu will be all set. The first line of code instantiates the menu and stores a reference to it in oMenu, but it only renders it in memory. To actually get it on the screen is the job of the call to its render() method.

You'll find that most widgets follow the same general pattern: instantiate an instance of the widget, give it a reference to some markup, and then make a call to its render() method to put it on the screen. Some widgets support options passed into the constructor as well, as you'll see in the application code. A few of them are created a little differently, and you'll see that as well when we build the application.

You can also programmatically create the widgets from scratch. For instance, to create a menu strictly with code, you could do this:

```
var oMenu = new YAHOO.widget.Menu("basicmenu");
oMenu.addItem(new YAHOO.widget.MenuItem("Page1", { url : "page1.htm" } ));
oMenu.addItem(new YAHOO.widget.MenuItem("Page2", { url : "page2.htm" } ));
oMenu.render(document.body);
```

In this case, presuming an element with the ID basicmenu is not already on the page, the DOM structure of the menu will be created and appended under that ID to the document's body element.

As I mentioned, YUI also provides some utility-type functions. Here's one we'll use in the JSNotes application:

```
var obj = YAHOO.util.Dom.get("xxx");
```

This is equivalent to the following ubiquitous function:

```
var obj = document.getElementById("xxx");
```

You may wonder how these functions differ. The answer is that the YUI version accepts either a single ID or an array of IDs, and will return a reference either to a single element or an array of elements. If nothing else, that will save you a lot of typing and lines of code if you need to get a reference to more than one element at a time.

The YUI Library has gained quite a following, and for good reason. It works very well in all the major browsers, is well designed, and is fantastically documented. I wholeheartedly recommend its use, and I encourage you to check it out in more detail at http://developer. yahoo.com/yui. Although we'll use quite a few of the widgets, we won't touch much of the rest of the library. I encourage you to check it out in more detail at http://developer.yahoo.com/yui. Spend five minutes clicking around the examples on the site, and you'll have a good feel for what is has to offer.

A Preview of JSNotes

If you haven't yet fired up JSNotes, I suggest you do so now. Let's take a quick look at it. Figure 9-1 shows the application as it is at startup, and already you can see two YUI widgets: the menu and the tree view.

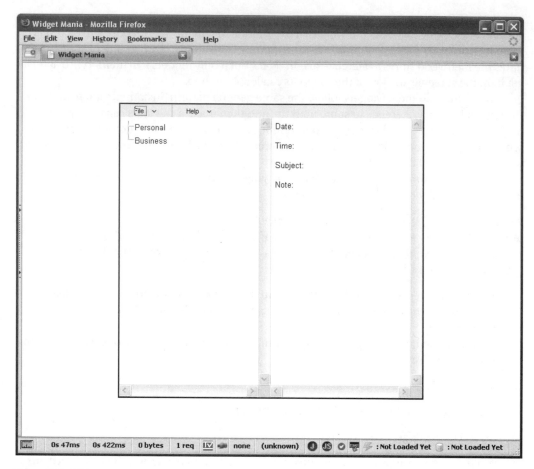

Figure 9-1. *JSNotes at startup*

When you want to add a note, you click the Add Note option on the File menu. This brings up a dialog box, where you can enter the note. The dialog box demonstrates another bunch of widgets, including the dialog box itself, the calendar, and the slider, as you can see in Figure 9-2.

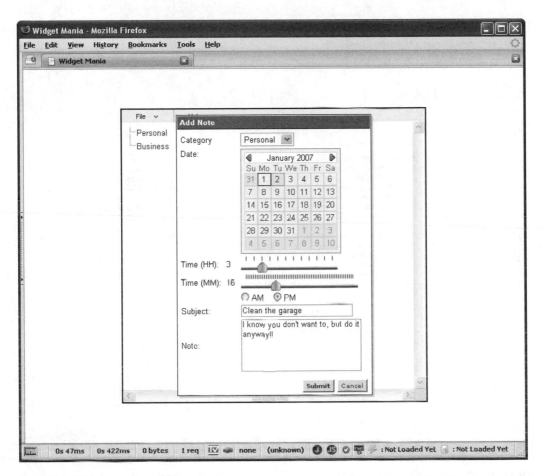

Figure 9-2. *JSNotes when adding a note*

In Figure 9-3, you can see one more widget: the overlay. Admittedly, it doesn't look like anything special. In fact, you really can't even tell that you're looking at a widget.

You'll see one or two other screenshots as we progress through the dissection of the application. See, now you have something to look forward to! And with that little tease, let's get on with the show.

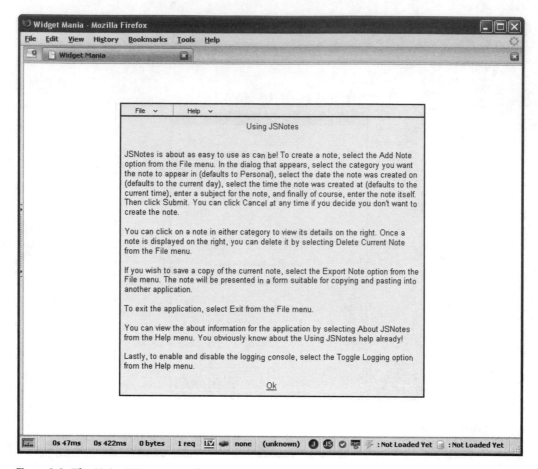

Figure 9-3. *The Using JSNotes overlay*

Dissecting the JSNotes Solution

Let's begin, as we always do, by looking at the general file layout of the application. If you've read the previous chapters, the structure shown in Figure 9-4 should be familiar by now.

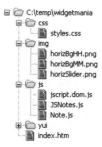

Figure 9-4. *JSNotes directory structure*

In the root directory resides a single file, index.htm, which is the starting point for the application. Below the root are the following four subdirectories:

- css: As usual, the css directory contains styles.css, which is the style sheet for the application.

- img: The img directory holds the three files horizBgHH.png, horizBgMM.png, and horizSlider.png. The first two are the background for the hours and minutes sliders, respectively, in the Add Note dialog box. They are the tick marks you see. The horizSlider.png file contains the slider handle that you drag and slide.

- js: In the js directory, you'll find three files. jscript.dom.js is the DOM package from Chapter 3. JSNotes.js is the main JavaScript code for the application. Note.js is the Note class, which contains the data of a note created by the user.

- yui: The yui directory is where the Yahoo library is housed. Within it, you'll find a number of directories, each corresponding to a part of YUI functionality. It also includes any resources YUI needs, such as style sheets and images.

Not a lot of files are involved (unless you count YUI itself, but for the purposes of this book, we won't). So, let's dive right in and check it out!

Writing index.htm

index.htm is the file you load to bring up the application, and it is what brings form to the function, so to speak. It is a fairly large file, so we will just look at some important pieces of it here.

At the top, in the <head> of the document, we first see a batch of style sheet imports:

```
<link rel="stylesheet" type="text/css" href="css/styles.css">
<link rel="stylesheet" type="text/css" href="yui/logger/assets/logger.css">
<link rel="stylesheet" type="text/css" href="yui/fonts/fonts.css">
<link rel="stylesheet" type="text/css" href="yui/reset/reset.css">
<link rel="stylesheet" type="text/css" href="yui/menu/assets/menu.css">
<link rel="stylesheet" type="text/css"
  href="yui/container/assets/container.css">
<link rel="stylesheet" type="text/css"
  href="yui/calendar/assets/calendar.css" />
<link rel="stylesheet" type="text/css"
  href="yui/treeview/assets/tree.css" />
```

Except for the first, which is the style sheet for the application itself, all of these are needed for YUI widgets. (Feel free to tear them apart if you're interested.)

Following that is a batch of JavaScript source file imports:

```
<script type="text/javascript" src="js/jscript.dom.js"></script>
<script type="text/javascript" src="js/JSNotes.js"></script>
<script type="text/javascript" src="js/Note.js"></script>
<script type="text/javascript" src="yui/yahoo/yahoo.js"></script>
<script type="text/javascript" src="yui/event/event.js"></script>
<script type="text/javascript" src="yui/dom/dom.js"></script>
<script type="text/javascript" src="yui/dragdrop/dragdrop.js" ></script>
```

```
<script type="text/javascript" src="yui/connection/connection.js" ></script>
<script type="text/javascript" src="yui/logger/logger.js"></script>
<script type="text/javascript" src="yui/container/container.js"></script>
<script type="text/javascript" src="yui/menu/menu.js"></script>
<script type="text/javascript" src="yui/animation/animation.js"></script>
<script type="text/javascript" src="yui/calendar/calendar.js"></script>
<script type="text/javascript" src="yui/slider/slider.js"></script>
<script type="text/javascript" src="yui/treeview/treeview.js"></script>
```

Once again, except for the first three, which are part of JSNotes itself, the rest are parts of YUI. Generally speaking, each widget is encapsulated in a .js file named for the widget, and may also require some supporting files, such as event.js and dom.js.

Following that is the instantiation of the JSNotes object, which is the real code behind the application. The instantiated object is referenced by the variable jsNotes, which you'll be seeing plenty of later.

After that, the <body> begins, starting with the <div> named divMain. This is the container that is centered on the page. Everything else, except the Add Note dialog box, is a child of this container.

Next up is some markup that makes up our menu bar. This is also our first YUI widget— well, sort of! As you'll see, the menu bar will be generated programmatically, but it does so based on the unordered list in this markup. Basically, we'll be feeding YUI the ID of the <div> containing an ordered list—divMainMenu in this case. YUI will then parse the list and generate the menu based on it. The classes you see are the default style classes that should be applied to the top-level menu items, as well as the submenu items. Each menu item is a link, but we don't want to navigate anywhere, which is the purpose of the javascript:void(0) as the href value. The onClick event handler takes care of the real functionality behind each menu item.

■Tip You can have nested lists, which will be properly rendered as nested menu items. So, if you wanted a menu item on the File menu to itself be a submenu, you simply start a new list under the <li> item under the File <li>. Neat!

Next is a <div> with the ID divContent. This is a fairly mundane affair: two <span> elements (instead of <div> elements, to avoid the line break between them), one floating left and one floating right (as per the style classes, as you'll see). The one on the left is for the tree view, and the one on the right is for the details of the currently selected note. On the right, we have a series of <td> elements with IDs essentially matching the fields stored for each note. It's pretty straightforward markup.

After that, we find a <div> where our logging console appears. YUI will take care of creating the content of this <div>, so no need to put anything there to start.

Then we get to three <div> elements that look quite similar. Each one is the content for a YUI overlay, which is very similar to a <div> actually, but exposes some handy extra features, such as methods for centering, custom event monitoring, and a built-in solution for the common problem of <select> elements in IE bleeding through elements with a higher Z index.[1] Since all these <div>'s look very similar, let's take a peek at just one to get the idea:

---

1. Basically, the YUI solution puts an iFrame behind the overlay, preventing the <select> from showing through.

```
<div id="divAbout" class="cssOverlay">
  <table border="0" cellpadding="0" cellspacing="0" class="cssOverlayTable">
    <tr>
      <td align="center" valign="middle" class="cssPadded">
        JSNotes 1.0
        <br><br>
        Frank W. Zammetti
        <br><br><br><br>
        From the book "Practical JavaScript Projects"
        <br>
        Published by Apress in 2007
        <br><br><br><br>
        <a href="javascript:void(0);" onClick="jsNotes.hideAbout();">Ok</a>
      </td>
    </tr>
  </table>
</div>
```

There are no restrictions on what you can place in an overlay (even other YUI widgets!), and you can style it any way you wish. Here, we have the simpler About display, and as you can see, it's pretty typical markup. But when you feed the ID to YUI in the correct way, you get an overlay.

The final piece of index.htm to look at is the markup for the Add Note dialog box. You may have been expecting to see something special, based on playing with the application a little and seeing a nice floating dialog box. Well, surprise, it's just more boring markup! What we have is a simple HTML form, set up within a table for alignment purposes. In this case, we won't actually be submitting the form anywhere, so there's no method or action attributes, and for onSubmit, we actually return false to be sure no submit occurs. One interesting point is that no submit or cancel buttons are defined here. That's because YUI will create these for us when we create the dialog box. As with overlays and the menu, we'll feed the ID of the containing <div> to YUI, and it will do the rest.

The dialog box is a good example of how you can have YUI widgets inside other widgets. We have (or, more precisely, *will* have) a calendar and two sliders in this dialog box. You can see what are essentially the placeholders for these items here: the addNoteCalendar <div>, the divHHSliderBG <div>, and the divMMSliderBG <div>.

As you may have guessed, we aren't simply telling YUI, "Hey, make a menu out of this ID," or "Turn the contents of this <div> into a dialog box for me." A bit more work is involved, but not that much! You'll see that when we get to examining JSNotes.js. But before we get there, we have one or two stops to make along the way, so let's pull the train out of this station and move on.

Writing styles.css

The style sheet for JSNotes is really fairly vanilla. The highlights are the cssContentLeft, cssContentRight, and cssOverlay classes. Nonetheless, I'll briefly describe what each class is for and point out any attributes of particular interest. So let's start with the style sheet itself, shown in Listing 9-1.

Listing 9-1. *The styles.css File*

```css
/* Style for the main DIV. */
.cssMain {
  position         : absolute;
  border           : 2px solid #000000;
  width            : 500px;
  background-color : #ffffff;
}


/* Style for the content container DIV. */
.cssContent {
  background-color : #ffffff;
  width            : 100%;
  height           : 460px;
}


/* Style for the left-hand side content. */
.cssContentLeft {
  width            : 50%;
  height           : 100%;
  float            : left;
  overflow         : scroll;
}


/* Style for the right-hand side content. */
.cssContentRight {
  width            : 50%;
  height           : 100%;
  float            : right;
  overflow         : scroll;
}


/* Style for elements that have padding (overlay contents, etc). */
.cssPadded {
  padding          : 6px;
}
```

```
/* Style for the tables that contain overlay contents. */
.cssOverlayTable {
  width            : 100%;
  height           : 100%;
}


/* Style for the background of the hour slider. */
.cssSliderBGHH {
  position         : relative;
  left             : 0px;
  top              : 0px;
  background       : url(../img/horizBgHH.png) no-repeat;
  height           : 26px;
  width            : 160px;
  zindex           : 5
}


/* Style for the background of the minutes slider. */
.cssSliderBGMM {
  position         : relative;
  left             : 0px;
  top              : 0px;
  background       : url(../img/horizBgMM.png) no-repeat;
  height           : 26px;
  width            : 196px;
  zindex           : 5
}


/* Style for the sliders' handles. */
.cssSliderHandle {
  position         : absolute;
  left             : 0px;
  top              : 8px;
  cursor           : default;
  width            : 18px;
  height           : 18px;
}


/* Style for cells of the table containing the fields of the new note form. */
.cssTDNewNote {
  padding          : 2px;
}
```

```
/* Style for overlays. */
.cssOverlay {
  border           : 2px solid #000000;
  position         : relative;
  left             : 0px;
  _left            : -2px; /* IE */
  background-color : #f7f7ef;
  width            : 100%;
  height           : 460px;
}


/* Style for the elements where hour and minutes are displayed. */
.cssTimeSpan {
  width            : 30px;
}
```

cssMain is the class applied to the <div> that surrounds all the contents on the page. It is positioned absolutely so that it can be centered. Its width determines the width of the JSNotes display, but note that its height is not set, as this will be determined by its content.

Speaking of its content, the cssContent class is applied to the <div> that encapsulates the content below the menu bar, namely the tree view and note details. This is where the height is determined. The height here, and the width in cssMain, are both specified so that JSNotes should fit on a 640-by-480 screen, and will definitely fit on an 800-by-600 screen.

Following cssContent are the cssContentLeft and cssContentRight classes. These are the two halves of the content area: cssContentLeft for the tree view and cssContentRight for the note details. Each is specified to fill half of the horizontal area taken up by the <div> with the cssContent style, and its entire height.

The float attributes of the cssContentLeft and cssContentRight classes allow you to specify that an element should float to the left or right of its surrounding text. The float attribute was initially meant to allow images to float to either side of a paragraph of text, but it isn't limited to that role. What's interesting is how these two elements work when they are side by side. Any element with a float value of left or right is treated as a block-level element, meaning its display attribute will be ignored. You can also use this to have two paragraphs side by side on a page, for example.

Perhaps most important for us here is the fact that an element following a floating element will render in relation to the first floating element. This just means, as you can see in JSNotes, that two <span> elements with float:left and float:right correspondingly will be right next to each other. The two floating elements are pushed left or right until they reach the border of the containing element or margin of another block-level element (that is, each <span> gets pushed left or right until it meets the edges of the containing <div>). Note that I used a <span> to avoid the inherent line break with a <div>, which would break the layout. Note, too, that <div> and <span> elements must have a width set for them to render when the float attribute is used, as do these.

Moving on, `cssPadded` is a simple class applied to a `<div>` inside the overlays so that there is a little bit of padding around the edges.

The `cssOverlayTable` class is applied to the table used to lay out the overlays. This is done to ensure the browser honors the 100% height for the table we want, since some will not honor the `height` attribute of the `<table>` tag.

The `cssSliderBGMM` and `cssSliderBGHH` classes define the "ticker markers" for the minute and hour sliders, respectively, in the Add Note dialog box. You can see that the image itself is loaded as the background image, so this style will be applied to the `<div>` elements where the sliders will appear. They must be positioned relatively in order for YUI to work with them properly. In this case, we want them to render where they naturally would anyway, hence the `0px` values for both `left` and `top`.

The `cssSliderHandle` is shared by both of the slider knobs, or handles, and must be positioned absolutely in order for YUI to work with them. The `left` attribute will be altered, but the `top` will not, so it's safe to set the top to `8px` to offset it from the tick marks properly.

`cssTDNewNote` is the style class applied to the cells of the table used to lay out the Add Note dialog box. Because of some mucking around YUI does with the markup, setting `cellpadding` and/or `cellspacing` on the `<table>` tag gets ignored, but doing essentially the same thing through CSS works, hence this class.

The `cssOverlay` class is the style applied to the overlay containers. One interesting point here is the use of a browser-specific hack, which you'll recall I said is something to avoid. But, sometimes you just *have* to do it to get around some browser peculiarity, and such is the case here. The `left` attribute with the value `0px` will be used for all non-IE browsers, but for IE, the value `-2px` in the second `left` attribute beginning with the underscore character will override the previous value and be used. This is needed so that the overlay lines up properly on the display and we don't get a double-border glitch (remove that `_left` attribute and fire up IE to see what happens).

`cssTimeSpan`, last but not least, is the style applied to the `<span>` where the hour and minute values are shown next to the corresponding slider. This needs to take up a known amount of space, regardless of the current value, in order for everything to line up properly, and that's the sole purpose of this class.

With the CSS and markup in `index.htm` out of the way, let's move on to what we're all here for: JavaScript!

Writing Note.js

The `Note.js` file contains the `Note` class, which is nothing more than a Value Object (VO), or struct if you're more familiar with C, which contains the data describing a note the user entered. It just contains some private fields and getter/setter methods for each. Before we look at the code, take a gander at the UML diagram for the class in Figure 9-5.

I've chosen not to list the entire class here because it is, by and large, boring! It is little more than a series of getters and setters for the fields it contains. In fact, that's precisely what it is. And besides, in general, the comments themselves should tell you all you really need to know, so if you glance at it quickly on your own, you'll pretty well have the full picture in no time.

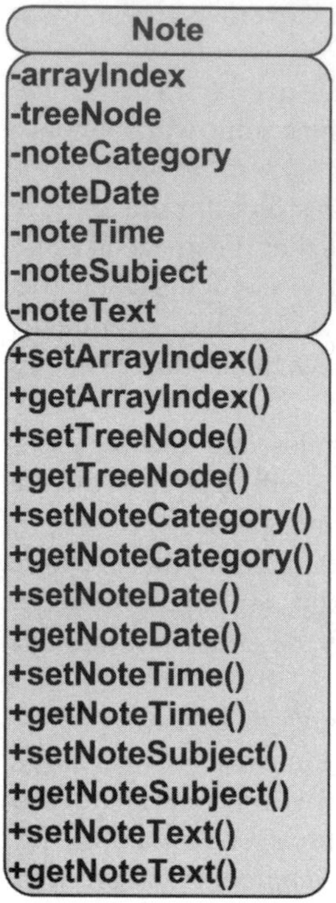

Figure 9-5. *UML diagram for the Notes class*

The toString() method overrides the default toString() that we get from the base Object class, and it outputs our note in a more meaningful way to aid in debugging.

Take note of the arrayIndex and treeNode fields and the comments accompanying them. These two fields are used when the user clicks a note in the tree view, but until that point, their values are meaningless. Once clicked, they are filled in and available for other actions that require them, such as deletions.

Other than that, it's an absolutely simple and straightforward piece of code. Now, if you want to see something just a little bit juicier, it's coming right up.

Writing JSNotes.js

JSNotes.js contains the JSNotes class, which is the heart and soul of the application. It's where all the functionality lives, and it's a fairly sizable piece of code. But as you'll see, a lot of it is pretty simple, and much of it is arguably boilerplate; the actual functionality doesn't require as much as you might think.

Before we get to that though, let's take a high-level look by examining the UML diagram in Figure 9-6.

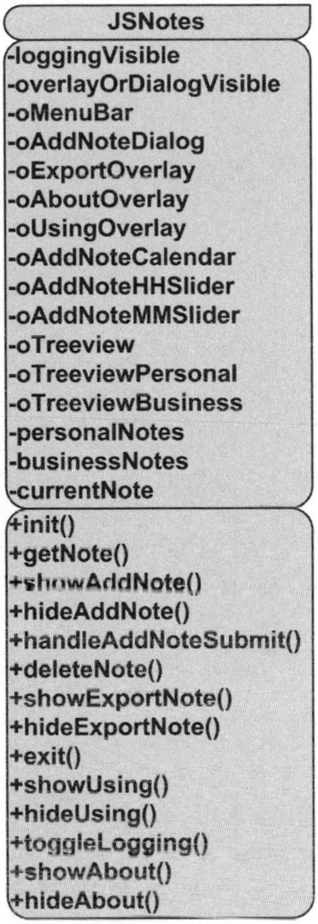

```
                  JSNotes
-loggingVisible
-overlayOrDialogVisible
-oMenuBar
-oAddNoteDialog
-oExportOverlay
-oAboutOverlay
-oUsingOverlay
-oAddNoteCalendar
-oAddNoteHHSlider
-oAddNoteMMSlider
-oTreeview
-oTreeviewPersonal
-oTreeviewBusiness
-personalNotes
-businessNotes
-currentNote
+init()
+getNote()
+showAddNote()
+hideAddNote()
+handleAddNoteSubmit()
+deleteNote()
+showExportNote()
+hideExportNote()
+exit()
+showUsing()
+hideUsing()
+toggleLogging()
+showAbout()
+hideAbout()
```

Figure 9-6. *UML diagram for the JSNotes class*

Listing 9-2 is the entire code listing, which is fairly lengthy. It checks in at a hair under 600 lines, and while a lot of it is comments and whitespace, there's plenty of meat on them bones!

Listing 9-2. *The JSNotes Class*

```
/**
 * The JSNotes class is the main class constituting the application.
 */
function JSNotes() {


  /**
   * Flag: Is the logging div currently visible?
   */
  var loggingVisible = false;
```

```
/**
 * Flag: Is an overlay or dialog currently visible?
 */
var overlayOrDialogVisible = false;


/**
 * Reference to the menubar object.
 */
var oMenuBar = null;


/**
 * Reference to the add notes dialog object.
 */
var oAddNoteDialog = null;


/**
 * Reference to the Export overlay object.
 */
var oExportOverlay = null;


/**
 * Reference to the About overlay object.
 */
var oAboutOverlay = null;


/**
 * Reference to the Using overlay object.
 */
var oUsingOverlay = null;


/**
 * Reference to the date calendar for adding a new note.
 */
var oAddNoteCalendar = null;


/**
 * Reference to the hour slider for adding a new note.
 */
var oAddNoteHHSlider = null;
```

```
/**
 * Reference to the minutes slider for adding a new note.
 */
var oAddNoteMMSlider = null;


/**
 * Reference to the treeview for listing categories/notes.
 */
var oTreeview = null;


/**
 * Reference to the treeview Personal Notes category node.
 */
var oTreeviewPersonal = null;


/**
 * Reference to the treeview Business Notes category node.
 */
var oTreeviewBusiness = null;


/**
 * The collection of Personal notes.
 */
var personalNotes = new Array();


/**
 * The collection of Business notes.
 */
var businessNotes = new Array();


/**
 * This is a reference to the Note object currently being viewed.
 */
var currentNote = null;


/**
 * Call on page load to initialize the application.
 */
this.init = function() {
```

```
// Start logging, show logging div if flag set to do so initially.
new YAHOO.widget.LogReader(YAHOO.util.Dom.get("divLog"));
YAHOO.log("init()");
if (loggingVisible) {
  YAHOO.util.Dom.get("divLog").style.display = "block";
}

// Start by centering the main DIV.
jscript.dom.layerCenterH(YAHOO.util.Dom.get("divMain"));
jscript.dom.layerCenterV(YAHOO.util.Dom.get("divMain"));

// Create menubar.
oMenuBar = new YAHOO.widget.MenuBar("divMainMenu");
oMenuBar.render();

// Create About overlay.
oAboutOverlay = new YAHOO.widget.Overlay("aboutOverlay",
  {
    context : [ "divContent", "tl", "tl" ],
    width : "500px", height : "456px", visible : false
  }
);
oAboutOverlay.setBody(YAHOO.util.Dom.get("divAbout"));
oAboutOverlay.render(document.body);

// Create Export overlay.
oExportOverlay = new YAHOO.widget.Overlay("exportOverlay",
  {
    context : [ "divContent", "tl", "tl" ],
    width : "500px", height : "456px", visible : false
  }
);
oExportOverlay.setBody(YAHOO.util.Dom.get("divExport"));
oExportOverlay.render(document.body);

// Create Using overlay.
oUsingOverlay = new YAHOO.widget.Overlay("usingOverlay",
  {
    context : [ "divContent", "tl", "tl" ],
    width : "500px", height : "456px", visible : false
  }
);
oUsingOverlay.setBody(YAHOO.util.Dom.get("divUsing"));
oUsingOverlay.render(document.body);
```

```
// Create Add Note dialog.
oAddNoteDialog = new YAHOO.widget.Dialog("divAddNote",
  {
    close : false,
    width : "320px",
    height : "460px",
    visible : false,
    constraintoviewport : true,
    buttons : [
      {
        text : "Submit",
        handler : jsNotes.handleAddNoteSubmit,
        isDefault : true
      },
      { text : "Cancel", handler : jsNotes.hideAddNote }
    ]
  }
);
oAddNoteDialog.render(document.body);

// Create Add Note calendar.
oAddNoteCalendar = new YAHOO.widget.Calendar("cal1", "addNoteCalendar");
oAddNoteCalendar.render();

// Create Add Note hour slider.
var bgHH = "divHHSliderBG";
var thumbHH = "divHHSliderThumb";
oAddNoteHHSlider = YAHOO.widget.Slider.getHorizSlider(
  bgHH, thumbHH, 0, 150, 13);
oAddNoteHHSlider.subscribe("change",
  function() {
    YAHOO.util.Dom.get("divHHValue").innerHTML =
      Math.round(oAddNoteHHSlider.getValue() / 13) + 1;
  }
);

// Create Add Note minutes slider.
var bgMM = "divMMSliderBG";
var thumbMM = "divMMSliderThumb";
oAddNoteMMSlider = YAHOO.widget.Slider.getHorizSlider(
  bgMM, thumbMM, 0, 178, 3);
oAddNoteMMSlider.subscribe("change",
  function() {
    var minute = Math.round(oAddNoteMMSlider.getValue() / 3);
    var s = "";
```

```
      if (minute < 10) {
        s += "0";
      }
      s += minute;
      YAHOO.util.Dom.get("divMMValue").innerHTML = s;
    }
  );


  // Create treeview for category/note listing.
  oTreeview = new YAHOO.widget.TreeView("divTreeview");
  var oRoot = oTreeview.getRoot();
  oTreeviewPersonal = new YAHOO.widget.TextNode("Personal",
    oRoot, false);
  oTreeviewBusiness = new YAHOO.widget.TextNode("Business",
    oRoot, false);
  oTreeview.subscribe("labelClick",
    function(node) {
      var noteSubject = node.data.subject;
      // Only do something when a note is clicked, not a category (only a
      // note would have a subject attribute).
      if (noteSubject) {
        var noteCategory = node.parent.data;
        currentNote = jsNotes.getNote(noteCategory, noteSubject);
        var noteDate = currentNote.getNoteDate();
        YAHOO.util.Dom.get("currentNoteDate").innerHTML =
          noteDate.getMonth() + "/" +
          noteDate.getDate() + "/" +
          noteDate.getFullYear();
        YAHOO.util.Dom.get("currentNoteTime").innerHTML =
          currentNote.getNoteTime();
        YAHOO.util.Dom.get("currentNoteSubject").innerHTML =
          currentNote.getNoteSubject();
        YAHOO.util.Dom.get("currentNoteText").innerHTML =
          currentNote.getNoteText();
      }
    }
  );
  oTreeview.draw();

  YAHOO.log("init() done");

} // End init().
```

```
/**
 * Returns a Note object based on requested category and subject.
 *
 * @param inCategory The category the note belongs to.
 * @param inSubject  The subject of the note to retrieve.
 */
this.getNote = function(inCategory, inSubject) {

  var note = null;

  // Determine which array to search based on current category.
  var arrayToSearch = null;
  if (inCategory == "Personal") {
    arrayToSearch = personalNotes;
  } else {
    arrayToSearch = businessNotes;
  }

  // Search the array and find the match, if any, and return it.
  for (var i = 0; i < arrayToSearch.length; i++) {
    var n = arrayToSearch[i];
    if (n.getNoteSubject() == inSubject) {
      note = n;
      note.setArrayIndex(i);
      break;
    }
  }

  // Now find the note in the treeview for the note.
  note.setTreeNode(oTreeview.getNodeByProperty("subject",
    note.getNoteSubject()));

  // Not found.
  return note;

} // End getNote();


/**
 * Show the dialog for adding a note.
 */
this.showAddNote = function() {

  YAHOO.log("showAddNote()");
```

```
    if (overlayOrDialogVisible) { return; }
    oMenuBar.clearActiveItem();

    overlayOrDialogVisible = true;

    // Reset all form fields.
    var now = new Date();
    var hours = now.getHours();
    var minutes = now.getMinutes();
    YAHOO.util.Dom.get("frmNewNote").reset();
    oAddNoteCalendar.clear();
    oAddNoteCalendar.select(now);
    oAddNoteCalendar.render();
    oAddNoteHHSlider.setValue((hours * 13) - 13, true, true);
    oAddNoteMMSlider.setValue(minutes * 3, true, true);
    YAHOO.util.Dom.get("divHHValue").innerHTML = hours;
    if (minutes < 10) {
      minutes = "0" + minutes;
    }
    YAHOO.util.Dom.get("divMMValue").innerHTML = minutes;
    YAHOO.util.Dom.get("newNotePM").checked = true;

    // Show the dialog amd center it.
    oAddNoteDialog.center();
    oAddNoteDialog.show();

    YAHOO.log("showAddNote() done");

  } // End showAddNote().


  /**
   * Hide the dialog for adding a note.
   */
  this.hideAddNote = function() {

    YAHOO.log("hideAddNote()");

    oAddNoteDialog.hide();
    overlayOrDialogVisible = false;

    YAHOO.log("hideAddNote() done");

  } // End hideAddNote().
```

```
/**
 * Handle submit of the add new note form.
 */
this.handleAddNoteSubmit = function() {

  YAHOO.log("handleAddNoteSubmit()");

  // Get entered values.
  var noteCategory = YAHOO.util.Dom.get("newNoteCategorySelect").value;
  var noteDate = oAddNoteCalendar.getSelectedDates()[0];
  var noteHour = YAHOO.util.Dom.get("divHHValue").innerHTML;
  var noteMinute = YAHOO.util.Dom.get("divMMValue").innerHTML;
  var noteMeridian = null;
  if (YAHOO.util.Dom.get("newNoteAM").checked) {
    noteMeridian = "am";
  } else {
    noteMeridian - "pm";
  }
  var noteSubject = YAHOO.util.Dom.get("newNoteSubject").value;
  var noteText = YAHOO.util.Dom.get("newNoteText").value;

  // Now some simple validations.
  if (noteSubject == "") {
    alert("Please enter a subject for this note");
    YAHOO.util.Dom.get("newNoteSubject").focus();
    return false;
  }
  if (noteText == "") {
    alert("Please enter some text for this note");
    YAHOO.util.Dom.get("newNoteText").focus();
    return false;
  }

  // Instantiate a Note object and populate it.
  var note = new Note();
  note.setNoteCategory(noteCategory);
  note.setNoteDate(noteDate);
  note.setNoteTime(noteHour + ":" + noteMinute + noteMeridian);
  note.setNoteSubject(noteSubject);
  note.setNoteText(noteText);

  // Add the note to the appropriate treeview category and storage array.
  if (noteCategory == "Personal") {
    personalNotes.push(note);
    new YAHOO.widget.TextNode({label:noteSubject,subject:noteSubject},
      oTreeviewPersonal, false);
```

```
    } else {
      businessNotes.push(note);
      new YAHOO.widget.TextNode({label:noteSubject,subject:noteSubject},
        oTreeviewBusiness, false);
    }

    // Redraw treeview so it'll show up.
    oTreeview.draw();

    // Hide dialog and we're done!
    jsNotes.hideAddNote();
    YAHOO.log("handleAddNoteSubmit() done");
    return true;

  } // End handleAddNoteSubmit().


  /**
   * Delete the note currently being viewed.
   */
  this.deleteNote = function() {

    YAHOO.log("deleteNote()");

    if (overlayOrDialogVisible) { return; }
    oMenuBar.clearActiveItem();

    if (currentNote &&
      confirm("Are you sure you want to delete the current note?")) {
      // Delete from storage array.
      if (currentNote.getNoteCategory() == "Personal") {
        personalNotes.splice(currentNote.getArrayIndex(), 1);
      } else {
        businessNotes.splice(currentNote.getArrayIndex(), 1);
      }
      // Delete from treeview and redraw.
      oTreeview.removeNode(currentNote.getTreeNode());
      oTreeview.draw();
      // Clear display fields.
      YAHOO.util.Dom.get("currentNoteDate").innerHTML = "";
      YAHOO.util.Dom.get("currentNoteTime").innerHTML = "";
      YAHOO.util.Dom.get("currentNoteSubject").innerHTML = "";
      YAHOO.util.Dom.get("currentNoteText").innerHTML = "";
      // Finally, no more current note.
      currentNote = null;
    }
```

```
  YAHOO.log("deleteNote() done");

} // End deleteNote().


/**
 * Show the overlay for exporting the current note.
 */
this.showExportNote = function() {

  YAHOO.log("showExportNote()");

  if (overlayOrDialogVisible) { return; }
  oMenuBar.clearActiveItem();

  if (currentNote) {
    var s = "";
    var noteDate = currentNote.getNoteDate();
    s += "Category: " + currentNote.getNoteCategory() + "\n";
    s += "Date: " + noteDate.getMonth() + "/" +
      noteDate.getDate() + "/" +
      noteDate.getFullYear() + "\n";
    s += "Time: " + currentNote.getNoteTime() + "\n";
    s += "Subject: " + currentNote.getNoteSubject() + "\n";
    s += "Note: " + currentNote.getNoteText();
    YAHOO.util.Dom.get("taExport").value = s;
    YAHOO.util.Dom.get("taExport").select();
    overlayOrDialogVisible = true;
    oExportOverlay.show();
  }

  YAHOO.log("showExportNote() done");

} // End showExportNote().


/**
 * Hide the Export Note overlay.
 */
this.hideExportNote = function() {

  YAHOO.log("hideExportNote()");
  oMenuBar.clearActiveItem();

  oExportOverlay.hide();
  overlayOrDialogVisible = false;
```

```
    YAHOO.log("hideExportNote() done");

  } // End hideExportNote().


  /**
   * Exit the application
   */
  this.exit = function() {

    YAHOO.log("exit()");
    if (overlayOrDialogVisible) { return; }

    if (confirm(
      "All notes will be lost!  Are you sure you want to exit?")) {
      window.close();
    }

  } // End exit().


  /**
   * Toggle the logging div on and off.
   */
  this.toggleLogging = function() {

    YAHOO.log("toggleLogging()");
    if (overlayOrDialogVisible) { return; }

    oMenuBar.clearActiveItem();
    if (loggingVisible) {
      YAHOO.util.Dom.get("divLog").style.display = "none";
      loggingVisible = false;
    } else {
      YAHOO.util.Dom.get("divLog").style.display = "block";
      loggingVisible = true;
    }

    YAHOO.log("toggleLogging() done");

  } // End toggleLogging().


  /**
   * Show the Using (help) overlay.
   */
  this.showUsing = function() {
```

```
    YAHOO.log("showUsing()");
    if (overlayOrDialogVisible) { return; }
    oMenuBar.clearActiveItem();

    overlayOrDialogVisible = true;
    oUsingOverlay.show();

    YAHOO.log("showUsing() done");

} // End showUsing().


/**
 * Hide the Using (help) overlay.
 */
this.hideUsing = function() {

    YAHOO.log("showUsing()");
    oMenuBar.clearActiveItem();

    oUsingOverlay.hide();
    overlayOrDialogVisible = false;

    YAHOO.log("showUsing() done");

} // End hideUsing().


/**
 * Show the About overlay.
 */
this.showAbout = function() {

    YAHOO.log("showAbout()");
    if (overlayOrDialogVisible) { return; }

    oMenuBar.clearActiveItem();
    overlayOrDialogVisible = true;
    oAboutOverlay.show();

    YAHOO.log("showAbout() done");

} // End showAbout().
```

```
/**
 * Hide the About overlay.
 */
this.hideAbout = function() {

  YAHOO.log("hideAbout()");

  oAboutOverlay.hide();
  overlayOrDialogVisible = false;

  YAHOO.log("hideAbout() done");

} // End hideAbout().


} // End JSNotes class.
```

As you can see, we have a number of data members and a batch of methods. Let's look at the data fields first:

- loggingVisible: A Boolean that determines whether the logging console is currently visible. It starts out invisible, until and unless the user turns it on via the Toggle Logging option under the Help menu.

- overlayOrDialogVisible: When any of the overlays or the Add Note dialog box are visible, the menus should not do anything. This flag determines when they shouldn't do anything (when this field is true).

- oMenuBar: A reference to the menu bar object as created by YUI. Later on, when a menu item is clicked, we need to clear the selected item, and to do that, we need a reference to the menu bar. It's better to cache the reference than incur the overhead of getting it each time.

- oAddNoteDialog: A reference to the Add Note dialog box as created by YUI. We'll again need this in various places, so keeping the reference is a good idea. In fact, the next few fields all serve the same purpose, which is to avoid object lookup overhead, so I'll skip repeating that fact from here on out!

- oExportOverlay: A reference to the Export Note overlay as created by YUI. I'm also going to stop saying " . . . as created by YUI" from now on, if you don't mind! It, too, applies to the next few items.

- oAbourOverlay: A reference to the About JSNotes overlay (are you starting to sense a pattern here?).

- oUsingOverlay: Yep, you guessed it—a reference to the Using JSNotes overlay.

- oAddNoteCalendar: Ah, something slightly different. Still a reference, but this time to the calendar in the Add Note dialog box.

- oAddNoteMMSlider: Reference. Minutes slider. Check.

- oTreeView: Oh tree view, oh tree view, where for art thou, tree view? Sorry, couldn't resist. Yes, another object reference, this time to the tree view listing the notes on the left side of the display.

- oTreeviewPersonal: A reference to the personal notes node object in the tree view.

- oTreeviewBusiness: I'll give you just one guess what this is! Now we're finished with the object references.

- personalNotes: An array containing all the Note objects categorized as personal notes.

- businessNotes: An array of all the Note objects in the business category.

- currentNote: Last but not least, a reference to the Note object the user is currently viewing.

OK, wise guy mode disengaged! Now that we've gotten through all the fields, let's see how they are used in the code, starting with the init() method.

The init() Method

The init() method is easily the lengthiest (about one-quarter of the total code size) and the most complex method in JSNotes. Even so, it's not all that monstrous! It is called on page load of index.htm, as you saw earlier. Its primary task is to construct the UI using YUI components.

Creating the Logging Console

To begin with, init() creates the logging console with this code:

```
// Start logging, show logging div if flag set to do so initially.
new YAHOO.widget.LogReader(YAHOO.util.Dom.get("divLog"));
YAHOO.log("init()");
if (loggingVisible) {
  YAHOO.util.Dom.get("divLog").style.display = "block";
}
```

All we need to do is instantiate YAHOO.widget.LogReader, passing it a reference to the DOM object that will house it. We get that reference using YAHOO.util.Dom.get(), which is basically a wrapper around document.getElementById(). We then quickly write out a message to the log with the line YAHOO.log("init()");, just to show where we are.

Recall from our look at index.htm that the logging <div>, divLog, is hidden to begin with. That's the reason for the if check that follows. If you were to change the default value of loggingVisible to true, then the console would be shown at this point.

When the logging console is visible, the display looks like what you see in Figure 9-7.

After that, the main <div> that houses what constitutes the display of JSNotes needs to be centered. To do that, we use two functions from the DOM package described in Chapter 3:

```
jscript.dom.layerCenterH(YAHOO.util.Dom.get("divMain"));
jscript.dom.layerCenterV(YAHOO.util.Dom.get("divMain"));
```

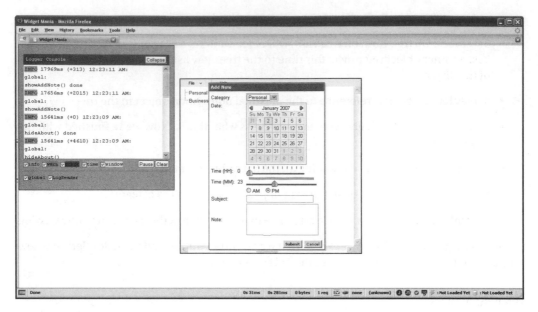

Figure 9-7. *The logging console*

Creating the Menu Bar

The next task is the creation of the menu bar, and it truly couldn't be easier:

```
oMenuBar = new YAHOO.widget.MenuBar("divMainMenu");
oMenuBar.render();
```

You already saw the markup contained in divMainMenu. YUI uses that to generate the menu you see on the screen. However, the first line simply creates the DOM snippet representing the menu in memory. To actually put it on the screen requires a call to its render() method, as you see in the second line. When both lines complete, the menu is visible and ready to be used.

Creating the Overlays

After that comes the creation of the three overlays: Export Note, Using JSNotes, and About JSNotes. They are virtually identical, so we'll pick just one of them, the Export Note overlay:

```
oExportOverlay = new YAHOO.widget.Overlay("exportOverlay",
  {
    context : [ "divContent", "tl", "tl" ],
    width : "500px", height : "456px", visible : false
  }
);
oExportOverlay.setBody(YAHOO.util.Dom.get("divExport"));
oExportOverlay.render(document.body);
```

The YAHOO.widget.overlay is the class we need to instantiate. The first argument to the constructor is the name the overlay will be known by—exportOverlay in this case. The next argument is an object containing a series of options. The first option you see, context, is used to align the overlay to some other page element. In this case, we are aligning it to the divContent <div>, so that it will appear where that <div> does, directly below the menu. We also specify that the top-left corner of the overlay should align with the top-left corner of that <div>. You can align it other ways, such as the top-right corner of the overlay to the bottom-left corner of the <div> by passing context : ["divContent", "tr", "bl"].

The width and height options should be self-explanatory. They are literally the width and height of the overlay. The visible option too is self-evident. When false, the overlay is initially not shown; when true, it is shown.

The next step is to fill in the content of the overlay. We do that by calling setBody() and handing it a reference to some existing element—in this case, the divExport <div> you saw in index.htm. Lastly, as with the menu, we need to render the overlay. We pass the render() method the object under which the overlay will be nested in the DOM, which is simply the document's body in this case.

The Export Note overlay is shown in Figure 9-8. The other two overlays look similar (see Figure 9-3 for a screenshot of the Using JSNotes overlay).

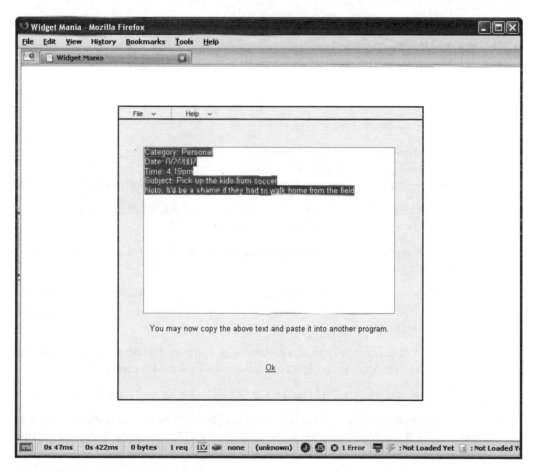

Figure 9-8. *Exporting a note from JSNotes*

Creating the Add Note Dialog Box

Next up is the creation of the Add Note dialog box. This is different from an overlay, but not a whole lot. A dialog box is generally meant to house a form to be filled out and submitted to the server. In our case, however, we won't be submitting it, but I'm getting ahead of myself. Let's see how the dialog box is created first:

```
oAddNoteDialog = new YAHOO.widget.Dialog("divAddNote",
  {
    close : false,
    width : "320px",
    height : "460px",
    visible : false,
    constraintoviewport : true,
    buttons : [
      {
        text : "Submit",
        handler : jsNotes.handleAddNoteSubmit,
        isDefault : true
      },
      { text : "Cancel", handler : jsNotes.hideAddNote }
    ]
  }
);
oAddNoteDialog.render(document.body);
```

This time, `YAHOO.widget.Dialog` is the class we need, and the first argument is the element containing the content for the dialog box—the `divAddNote` `<div>` here. The second argument is, as with the overlay, an object containing a series of options. Let's examine them one by one:

- `close`: This option indicates whether we want a close button, like the X button on a typical window. Here, we don't want that, so we set it to `false`.

- `width`, `height`, and `visible`: These options are exactly what you think they are, just as with the overlay widget.

- `constraintoviewport`: This option indicates whether the dialog box can be dragged off the page. We don't want that to be possible here, because we want it to stop at the edges, so `true` is the setting to use.

- `button`: This option is actually an array where each element describes a single button. Each element of the array is an object containing the options for each button.

- `text`: This option is what is displayed on the button—Submit and Cancel in this case.

- `handler`: This option defines which JavaScript function will be called when the button is clicked. Here, these are the `handlerAddNoteSubmit()` and `hideAddNote()` methods of the JSNotes class, respectively, pointed to by the reference `jsNotes`.

- `isDefault`: This option, on the Submit button, defines whether pressing Enter will activate that button, which is the case here.

Just as with the overlay widget, we need to tell the dialog box which element to render as a child of, and once again, the body of the document is the answer.

Next, we create the widgets that are in the Add Note dialog box. Note that there is no problem nesting widgets like this—YUI can handle it!

To begin with, we need to create the calendar used to select the note date, and it is accomplished via the following code:

```
oAddNoteCalendar = new YAHOO.widget.Calendar("cal1", "addNoteCalendar");
oAddNoteCalendar.render();
```

The first argument is the name the calendar will go by, and the second is the element that will be the parent of the calendar when it is rendered by the second line of code.

After the calendar, we need to render the two sliders, starting with the hour slider:

```
var bgHH = "divHHSliderBG";
var thumbHH = "divHHSliderThumb";
oAddNoteHHSlider = YAHOO.widget.Slider.getHorizSlider(
  bgHH, thumbHH, 0, 150, 13);
oAddNoteHHSlider.subscribe("change",
  function() {
    YAHOO.util.Dom.get("divHHValue").innerHTML =
      Math.round(oAddNoteHHSlider.getValue() / 13) + 1;
  }
);
YAHOO.util.Event.on(bgHH, "keydown",
  function(e) {
    console.log("keydown (HH)");
  }
);
YAHOO.util.Event.on(bgHH, "keypress", YAHOO.util.Event.preventDefault);
```

Well, there certainly is a little more going on here! First, we set up some variables we'll need. We start with bgHH, which names the <div> containing the background image. Next is the name of the element containing the slider handle, divHHSliderThumb, stored in the variable thumbHH.

Once that's done, we instantiate a YAHOO.widget.Slider object, but we do so using the getHorizSlider() method, which takes as arguments the names of the background element and handle element, as well as three numbers. The first number is how many pixels to the left the handle can be moved, the second is how many to the right (which basically defines a maximum and minimum number of pixels the handle can move), and the third is the number of pixels to move for each tick mark.

It's a little tricky to set up the slider because you need to create a background image suitable for the range you want to allow. For instance, for the hours, we have 12 tick marks, one for each hour. The tick marks are 1 pixel wide, and separated by 12 pixels, so each tick movement is 13 pixels (the third number in the getHorizSlider() method). Multiplying 12 by 13 gives us 156, but we actually use 150 as the second number in getHorizSlider(). That's because the tick marks are essentially zero-based in terms of their positions; that is, the first tick mark representing hour 1 is at pixel location 0 (well, the tick mark is actually a few pixels from the edge, but for the handle to line up, the handle must be at pixel position 0). Therefore, we never want the handle to make it to that 156 pixels position. So, we use the value of 150, which essentially constrains it to the last tick mark.

Perhaps the best way to understand this is to take the background image and the handle image and bring them into your favorite paint program (Photoshop, Paint Shop Pro, GIMP, or whatever you prefer). Enlarge the canvas of the background image so you have some room to play, then copy the handle image into it as a floating layer so you can move it around. Line it up with the first tick mark and note the X location. It should be zero. Now move it to the next tick mark. Note that it moved 13 pixels. Continue on until the last tick mark, where you should see the location is less than 150. If you were to move it to the next increment of 13, 156, it would be beyond the background tick marks, proving you need a value less than that to constrain it.

As soon as your brain stops hurting (and mine, too!), we can look at how we hook up some events to the slider. First, we want to update the hour value when the slider changes (is dragged). We do this by calling the subscribe() method on the slider. The first method is the event we want to subscribe to—change in this case. The second argument is the function to execute when the event fires, and here we've used an in-line function. When the value changes, we first need to get the new value of the slider. The value is basically the pixel location, which isn't by itself of any real use to us. So, we first need to divide that by 13, which gives us a value from 0 to 11. So, add one, and you now have the hour value corresponding to the pixel location. We get a reference to the <div> where the hour number is displayed, and we set its innerHTML attribute to that calculated value. The effect is the hour number changing as we drag the slider—sweet!

Creating the minutes slider is the same, except that since there are more tick marks, the upper constraint value is different—178 in this case. And the tick marks are closer together, so the increment value now is 3. Also, some minor differences are present in the handler for the change event:

```
oAddNoteMMSlider.subscribe("change",
  function() {
    var minute = Math.round(oAddNoteMMSlider.getValue() / 3);
    var s = "";
    if (minute < 10) {
      s += "0";
    }
    s += minute;
    YAHOO.util.Dom.get("divMMValue").innerHTML = s;
  }
);
```

This is very similar to the hour slider, but here the divisor in the calculation is 3, since that's the increment value. Also, there's no need to add one at the end, since the range here is zero-based (0 to 59 for minutes). Lastly, when the value is less than 10—that is, only a single digit—it should be displayed with a leading zero, so we see some logic to deal with that. Other than those differences, the minutes slider is more or less the same as the hour slider conceptually.

Creating the Tree View

The last piece of the init() method is the creation of the tree view that will list the notes the user creates. The code that accomplishes this is as follows:

```
oTreeview = new YAHOO.widget.TreeView("divTreeview");
var oRoot = oTreeview.getRoot();
oTreeviewPersonal = new YAHOO.widget.TextNode("Personal",
  oRoot, false);
oTreeviewBusiness = new YAHOO.widget.TextNode("Business",
  oRoot, false);
oTreeview.subscribe("labelClick",
  function(node) {
    var noteSubject = node.data.subject;
    // Only do something when a note is clicked, not a category (only a
    // note would have a subject attribute).
    if (noteSubject) {
      var noteCategory = node.parent.data;
      currentNote = jsNotes.getNote(noteCategory, noteSubject);
      var noteDate = currentNote.getNoteDate();
      YAHOO.util.Dom.get("currentNoteDate").innerHTML =
        noteDate.getMonth() + "/" +
        noteDate.getDate() + "/" +
        noteDate.getFullYear();
      YAHOO.util.Dom.get("currentNoteTime").innerHTML =
        currentNote.getNoteTime();
      YAHOO.util.Dom.get("currentNoteSubject").innerHTML =
        currentNote.getNoteSubject();
      YAHOO.util.Dom.get("currentNoteText").innerHTML =
        currentNote.getNoteText();
    }
  }
);
oTreeview.draw();
```

Well, there's quite a bit here, so let's break it down, shall we?

First, we have a typical widget instantiation line. We feed it the <div> that is to host the tree view. After that, we get a reference to the root node of the tree, which is created automatically when the widget is instantiated. Once we have that, we append two nodes to it: one for personal notes and one for business notes. After that, we have another event subscription line, requesting that we be notified when any label is clicked, which is the same as saying when any node is clicked.

YUI will take care of expanding and collapsing any node that has children, which will be only the two nodes we just created. However, we need to take care of what happens beyond that. In this case, that means showing the detail of a note that is clicked.

So, when we request the event subscription, we pass it a reference to a function to act as the callback for the event—in this case, an in-line anonymous function. The first thing done in this callback is to get the subject of the node. This will become clearer when you see how notes are added to the tree. For now, just be aware that when you add a node to the tree, you can attach to it arbitrary pieces of information, in addition to its text label. Here, we will be adding a subject attribute to it.

If you've played with the application, you will probably realize that the label of the note *is* the subject, so you may be asking, "Isn't it redundant to add the subject as well?" The answer is no, and the reason is the next line of code. You see, when *any* node is clicked, including our two category nodes, this callback will be called. However, we need to do something only if the clicked node was *not* one of the category nodes. How do we determine that? Well, we could examine the label directly, but if we ever changed or added to the categories, that would mean one more thing we would need to change. Instead, for nodes representing actual notes only, the subject attribute is attached. Therefore, we can simply check if that attribute is defined for the clicked node. If it isn't, it was one of the category nodes and the callback should do nothing.

Otherwise, we find ourselves inside the if block. In that situation, we need to get the category of the note. To do this, we use the node.parent reference, node being a reference to the clicked node. Through that, we can get the label of the node, which is the data attribute by default.

Once we have the category and the subject, we can call the getNote() function, which you'll see in a bit. This will return a reference to the Note object for the clicked note. From there, it's a simple matter of populating the four data display elements on the page from the fields in the Note object. We again use the YAHOO.util.Dom.get() function to get references to those fields. The date is the only interesting field here. We have a JavaScript Date object, but we want to display the note's date in *MM/DD/YYYY* format, so we need to get the individual components of the date and construct the string ourselves.

Whew, that was a fair amount of code! The rest of this class will seem pretty paltry by comparison.

The getNote() Method

Next is the getNote() that I just mentioned:

```
this.getNote = function(inCategory, inSubject) {

  var note = null;

  // Determine which array to search based on current category.
  var arrayToSearch = null;
  if (inCategory == "Personal") {
    arrayToSearch = personalNotes;
  } else {
    arrayToSearch = businessNotes;
  }

  // Search the array and find the match, if any, and return it.
  for (var i = 0; i < arrayToSearch.length; i++) {
    var n = arrayToSearch[i];
    if (n.getNoteSubject() == inSubject) {
      note = n;
      note.setArrayIndex(i);
      break;
    }
  }
}
```

```
// Now find the note in the treeview for the note.
note.setTreeNode(oTreeview.getNodeByProperty("subject",
  note.getNoteSubject())));

// Not found.
return note;

} // End getNote();
```

First, we need to determine which array we're searching, businessNotes or personalNotes, based on the category passed in. After that, it's a simple matter of checking each Note object in the array and seeing if its subject matches the subject passed in.

One last item of work remains, and that's to get a reference to the node in the tree view corresponding to the note, and set that reference on the Note object. (Remember the comments about the treeNode field? If not, go back and look, because they are now very relevant.) The tree view widget provides a couple of different ways to get a reference to a node, one of which is the getNodeByProperty() method. Recall that I mentioned that when a note is added, we add a custom property named subject to it. Well, that's exactly the property we specify to search here! After that, the reference to the note is returned, or null is returned if no match was found, and that's that.

The showAddNote() Method

The next method to check out is what is called when the user clicks the Add Note menu item, and it is responsible for showing the dialog box and setting up for user data entry:

```
this.showAddNote = function() {

  YAHOO.log("showAddNote()");

  if (overlayOrDialogVisible) { return; }
  oMenuBar.clearActiveItem();

  overlayOrDialogVisible = true;

  // Reset all form fields.
  var now = new Date();
  var hours = now.getHours();
  var minutes = now.getMinutes();
  YAHOO.util.Dom.get("frmNewNote").reset();
  oAddNoteCalendar.clear();
  oAddNoteCalendar.select(now);
  oAddNoteCalendar.render();
  oAddNoteHHSlider.setValue((hours * 13) - 13, true, true);
  oAddNoteMMSlider.setValue(minutes * 3, true, true);
  YAHOO.util.Dom.get("divHHValue").innerHTML = hours;
```

```
if (minutes < 10) {
  minutes = "0" + minutes;
}
YAHOO.util.Dom.get("divMMValue").innerHTML = minutes;
YAHOO.util.Dom.get("newNotePM").checked = true;

// Show the dialog and center it.
oAddNoteDialog.center();
oAddNoteDialog.show();

YAHOO.log("showAddNote() done");

} // End showAddNote().
```

As you can see, there's not a whole lot to it. Note the YAHOO.log() call as the first statement. This is the way you output a log message to the logging console. You'll see this in most of the methods in this class, so I won't mention it again.

You'll also see the next two statements in most methods. Recall that I previously mentioned that when a dialog box or overlay is showing, the menu shouldn't do anything. This is accomplished by a check of the overlayOrDialogVisible variable. When it's true, we simply return immediately. However, if it's not true, the first thing we need to do is dismiss the submenu, which is accomplished by a call to the clearActiveItem() method of the menu bar widget. These three lines of code won't be mentioned again, so don't be surprised when they pop up all over the place!

Once that's done, the overlayOrDialogVisible variable is immediately set so that the menu will not do anything until further notice. After that, it's time to clear the form fields in the Add Note dialog box. Before even that though, we get a reference to the current time, since we'll need that later. To begin the actual clearing, we start with a call to the reset() method of the form, which takes care of the category, subject, and note text fields.

Next, we deal with the calendar, first by clearing the current selection via the call to clear() on it, and then by calling select(), passing it the Date object we instantiated earlier, and then calling render() on it. This has the effect of setting the calendar to the current month and year and selecting the current date, which is the reasonable default value.

Then we handle the hour and minutes sliders. To do this, we call the setValue() method on them. Recall that the values of the sliders are actually pixel values. To translate the current time to pixel values, we need to multiple the hours by 13 (recall that's the pixel increment per tick mark for the hours) and 3 for the minutes (the tick mark increment for the minutes). We also set the textual representation of the hour and minutes by updating the innerHTML of the two <div> elements, making sure to append a leading zero to minute values less than 10.

Finally, we have only to center the dialog box by calling its center() method, and showing it via the call to its show() method. And now we have a pristine dialog box, ready for the user to create a new note! We add a quick log message to indicate the method completed, and it's a wrap!

The hideAddNote() Method

After that, we find the hideAddNote() method, which as its name implies, hides the dialog box after the user clicks Submit. It's a trivial piece of code:

```
this.hideAddNote = function() {

  YAHOO.log("hideAddNote()");

  oAddNoteDialog.hide();
  overlayOrDialogVisible = false;

  YAHOO.log("hideAddNote() done");

} // End hideAddNote().
```

I'm going to go out on a limb here and assume you don't need me to explain how it works! Besides, much bigger things loom just over the horizon.

The handleAddNoteSubmit() Method

The next method we find is handleAddNoteSubmit(). As you will recall, when the Add Note dialog box was created in init(), we passed a reference to this function into the constructor indicating it should be the callback when the Submit button is clicked. Its job is simply to save the note the user entered, or alternatively reject it if it doesn't pass some simple validation checks. Here is the code for this all-important method:

```
this.handleAddNoteSubmit = function() {

  YAHOO.log("handleAddNoteSubmit()");

  // Get entered values.
  var noteCategory = YAHOO.util.Dom.get("newNoteCategorySelect").value;
  var noteDate = oAddNoteCalendar.getSelectedDates()[0];
  var noteHour = YAHOO.util.Dom.get("divHHValue").innerHTML;
  var noteMinute = YAHOO.util.Dom.get("divMMValue").innerHTML;
  var noteMeridian = null;
  if (YAHOO.util.Dom.get("newNoteAM").checked) {
    noteMeridian = "am";
  } else {
    noteMeridian = "pm";
  }
  var noteSubject = YAHOO.util.Dom.get("newNoteSubject").value;
  var noteText = YAHOO.util.Dom.get("newNoteText").value;

  // Now some simple validations.
  if (noteSubject == "") {
    alert("Please enter a subject for this note");
    YAHOO.util.Dom.get("newNoteSubject").focus();
    return false;
  }
```

```
  if (noteText == "") {
    alert("Please enter some text for this note");
    YAHOO.util.Dom.get("newNoteText").focus();
    return false;
  }

  // Instantiate a Note object and populate it.
  var note = new Note();
  note.setNoteCategory(noteCategory);
  note.setNoteDate(noteDate);
  note.setNoteTime(noteHour + ":" + noteMinute + noteMeridian);
  note.setNoteSubject(noteSubject);
  note.setNoteText(noteText);

  // Add the note to the appropriate treeview category and storage array.
  if (noteCategory == "Personal") {
    personalNotes.push(note);
    new YAHOO.widget.TextNode({label:noteSubject,subject:noteSubject},
      oTreeviewPersonal, false);
  } else {
    businessNotes.push(note);
    new YAHOO.widget.TextNode({label:noteSubject,subject:noteSubject},
      oTreeviewBusiness, false);
  }

  // Redraw treeview so it'll show up.
  oTreeview.draw();

  // Hide dialog and we're done!
  jsNotes.hideAddNote();
  YAHOO.log("handleAddNoteSubmit() done");
  return true;

} // End handleAddNoteSubmit().
```

First, we need to get the values entered by the user:

- For the category, subject, and note fields, we just grab their value attributes.

- For the date, we need to call the calendar's getSelectedDates() method. This method returns an array of Date objects, but in this case, we only care about the first element in the array, hence the [0] subscript. Note that, by default, the calendar will allow only a single date to be selected, but getSelectedDates() still returns an array, so it doesn't change the way we get the value.

- For the time's hour and minutes components, we get the innerHTML value of the <div> displaying the value (no sense messing with the pixel-to-real-value conversion we've seen before, since we already have the final value in the <div>s). For the time meridian, we see if the AM radio button is checked, and if so, then the meridian is AM; otherwise, it is PM.

Once all the values have been captured, we do some simple validations. These validations amount to nothing more than ensuring the user entered both a subject and some note text, and if not, we set the focus to the offending field and return immediately.

Once validations have been passed, it's time to save the note. The first step is to instantiate a Note object and populate each of the fields. The only interesting thing here is the time, which, as you can see, is stored in a format ready to be displayed in the details section when the user clicks it. Otherwise, this is just a series of setter calls.

The next step is to add the note to both the correct storage array and the tree view. First, a logic branch occurs based on the category of the note. Once we know whether it's a personal note or a business note, we push() it onto the appropriate array. To add it to the tree view requires that we instantiate a new TextNode widget, just as we did when creating the nodes for the categories. This takes the following three arguments:

- The first argument to the constructor of the widget is an object containing data elements. The label attribute is what you see in the tree view, and the subject is obviously the subject of the note. This completes the puzzle we began seeing earlier. Remember how we got the subject of the note when the user clicked on it so that we could look it up in the arrays for display? Well, here is where that value gets set on the node.

- The second argument is the node in the tree that this new node will be a child of: either the personal notes node or the business notes node.

- The last argument determines whether the node is expanded (true) or not (false) initially. There really is no meaning to expanding a note node though, since there will never be any children. Just the same, passing false is the safer bet.

Only a few relatively minor steps remain in this method. First, somewhat important is to update the tree view. This is done by calling draw() on it, which results in it being repainted, including the new note. Finally, we hide the Add Note dialog box, write a log message, and return—and that's adding a new note.

The deleteNote() Method

The method that follows handlerAddNoteSubmit() is deleteNote(). There isn't much to deleting a note, as you can see:

```
this.deleteNote = function() {

  YAHOO.log("deleteNote()");

  if (overlayOrDialogVisible) { return; }
  oMenuBar.clearActiveItem();
```

```
    if (currentNote &&
      confirm("Are you sure you want to delete the current note?")) {
      // Delete from storage array.
      if (currentNote.getNoteCategory() == "Personal") {
        personalNotes.splice(currentNote.getArrayIndex(), 1);
      } else {
        businessNotes.splice(currentNote.getArrayIndex(), 1);
      }
      // Delete from treeview and redraw.
      oTreeview.removeNode(currentNote.getTreeNode());
      oTreeview.draw();
      // Clear display fields.
      YAHOO.util.Dom.get("currentNoteDate").innerHTML = "";
      YAHOO.util.Dom.get("currentNoteTime").innerHTML = "";
      YAHOO.util.Dom.get("currentNoteSubject").innerHTML = "";
      YAHOO.util.Dom.get("currentNoteText").innerHTML = "";
      // Finally, no more current note.
      currentNote = null;
    }

    YAHOO.log("deleteNote() done");

  } // End deleteNote().
```

The first step is to ensure a note is currently being displayed by seeing if the currentNote field is null. If no note is being displayed, we obviously don't need to do anything, so that effectively ends the method.

Assuming a note is displayed though, we first confirm the user wants to delete it (especially since there is no persistence per se in JSNotes, this is a nice thing to do!). Once it's confirmed, we determine which category the note belongs to, so that we know from which array to remove it. Once we know that, we use the standard splice() method on the array, which JavaScript provides to remove elements from the array. The first argument is the array index to begin deletion—in this case, it's the value stored in the arrayIndex field of the note. The second argument is how many elements to delete, which is just one in this case.

That takes care of deleting the note from the data array, but now we need to delete it from the tree view as well. To do that, we simply call the removeNode() method, passing it a reference to the node to remove, which you'll recall we stored in the treeNode field in the Note object when the note was clicked to display. So all that remains is to call draw() to refresh the tree view, and we're set.

Lastly, we are sure to clear the display fields, since what's there is obviously no longer valid, and set the currentNote field to null since there is no longer a note being displayed. Now the note is officially, completely, and utterly gone!

The showExportNote() Method

The next bit of functionality to check out is displaying the Export Note overlay. Here is the method that accomplishes that:

```
this.showExportNote = function() {

  YAHOO.log("showExportNote()");

  if (overlayOrDialogVisible) { return; }
  oMenuBar.clearActiveItem();

  if (currentNote) {
    var s = "";
    var noteDate = currentNote.getNoteDate();
    s += "Category: " + currentNote.getNoteCategory() + "\n";
    s += "Date: " + noteDate.getMonth() + "/" +
      noteDate.getDate() + "/" +
      noteDate.getFullYear() + "\n";
    s += "Time: " + currentNote.getNoteTime() + "\n";
    s += "Subject: " + currentNote.getNoteSubject() + "\n";
    s += "Note: " + currentNote.getNoteText();
    YAHOO.util.Dom.get("taExport").value = s;
    YAHOO.util.Dom.get("taExport").select();
    overlayOrDialogVisible = true;
    oExportOverlay.show();
  }

  YAHOO.log("showExportNote() done");

} // End showExportNote().
```

Assuming a note is currently being displayed, a string is constructed. This string more or less mimics the details display you see when a note is clicked, but does so in plain text. The string is then inserted into the <textarea> that is a part of the overlay, and the text is selected via a call to the select() method of the text area. Then the overlay is shown via the call to its show() method, and that's really all there is to it.

The hideExportNote() Method

Once the user clicks OK in the Export Notes overlay, it is dismissed via a call to hideExportNote(), shown here:

```
this.hideExportNote = function() {

  YAHOO.log("hideExportNote()");
  oMenuBar.clearActiveItem();

  oExportOverlay.hide();
  overlayOrDialogVisible = false;

  YAHOO.log("hideExportNote() done");

} // End hideExportNote().
```

This method has nothing more than a call to its hide() method, and setting overlayOrDialogVisible to false so that our menu works again. And that's it.

The exit() Method

We're nearing the end! The next method to look at is called when the Exit option is clicked on the File menu:

```
this.exit = function() {

  YAHOO.log("exit()");
  if (overlayOrDialogVisible) { return; }

  if (confirm(
    "All notes will be lost!  Are you sure you want to exit?")) {
    window.close();
  }

} // End exit().
```

There's nothing fancy here. Just a confirmation to be sure users want to leave, since all their notes will be gone at that point, and a call to the window object's close() method are all it takes.

The toggleLogging() Method

The toggleLogging() method is next, and here it is:

```
this.toggleLogging = function() {

  YAHOO.log("toggleLogging()");
  if (overlayOrDialogVisible) { return; }

  oMenuBar.clearActiveItem();
  if (loggingVisible) {
    YAHOO.util.Dom.get("divLog").style.display = "none";
    loggingVisible = false;
  } else {
    YAHOO.util.Dom.get("divLog").style.display = "block";
    loggingVisible = true;
  }

  YAHOO.log("toggleLogging() done");

} // End toggleLogging().
```

This boils down to nothing more than showing divLog if loggingVisible is false, and then reversing loggingVisible to true, or hiding divLog if loggingVisible if true, and then reversing loggingVisible to false.

The Rest

Only four methods remain, but they are really so simple that I don't see much point in showing them here. As I'm sure you can guess, showUsing(), hideUsing(), showAbout(), and hdeAbout() deal with showing and hiding the Using JSNotes and About JSNotes overlays. You've already seen the basic code in the showExportNote() method. The show*XXX*() methods just set overlayOrDialogVisible to true and call show() on the appropriate overlay object. For the hide*XXX*() methods, overlayOrDialogVisible is set to false, and the hide() method is called. There quite literally is nothing more to these methods!

And with that last little bit, we've reached the end of our journey! I hope you'll agree that with YUI in the mix, the volume of code is not very great, and it's pretty simple code to boot.

Suggested Exercises

When you look at that stack of sticky notes, not a whole lot of possible enhancements come to mind, aside from perhaps different colors and more writing surface. Similarly, with such a simple application as JSNotes, there's not a whole lot of really advanced functionality to add. Of course, I wouldn't leave you without any exercises, so here are a few that should extend your knowledge of YUI, and, of course, JavaScript in general:

- Add the ability to clean an entire category at once. Likewise, add the ability to export an entire category.

- Present the interface in a tabbed fashion. YUI provides a tabbed dialog widget, and it should be possible to see two tabs, Personal and Business, with just a straight list of notes on the left. I was actually going to do this in the example, but I decided it would be an excellent exercise to help familiarize you with YUI.

- For the tabbed interface, add a View menu with two options: Tabbed View and Tree View, so you can switch between the two tabs. I suggest creating two layers in index.htm: one that contains what you see now, and one that includes the tab view. That should make it very easy to switch between the two.

- Add some effects. YUI provides other effects that you can probably add without too much trouble. How about the Using and About overlays expanding into view perhaps?

Summary

In this chapter, we put together a handy little note-taking application. In the process, you were introduced to a top-notch JavaScript library, YUI. You saw how it makes creating usable user interfaces with custom widgets a breeze, and you also saw some of the utility functionality it provides. Examining the application revealed how, with just a relatively small amount of code, you can create a decent amount of functionality with the help of this excellent library.

■ ■ ■

Shopping in Style: A Drag-and-Drop Shopping Cart

Most people who have shopped on the Internet are familiar with the shopping cart metaphor. You see a list of items for sale, you click some button, and some quantity of the item is added to your shopping cart. You then check out, and your order is processed based on the content of your cart. This is all well and good, but we can do a little better than that, can't we?

In this chapter, we will build a shopping cart that lets you drag items into it, rather than needing to click a button to add to your cart. We will use some special effects to make this look cooler than it might sound. At the same time though, we will respect the fact that some people may not have JavaScript available. For them, we will ensure our shopping cart degrades gracefully and still works, even under those "arcane" conditions.

We'll use a new library, MochiKit, for the drag-and-drop action. Also, you'll see a new technique that can come in very handy: a mock server, to handle your server needs without having to write actual server code.

So, break out your wallet and credits cards, and let's go shopping!

Shopping Cart Requirements and Goals

A shopping cart is a well-known paradigm used on most e-commerce web sites. Sites such as Amazon (http://www.amazon.com), Best Buy (http://www.bestbuy.com), Newegg (http://www.newegg.com), CD Now (http://www.cdnow.com), and TigerDirect (http://www.tigerdirect.com)—to name just a few—use a shopping cart to allow their users to purchase their products. It's conceptually not a difficult beast, but with a little added pizzazz, it can actually be more fun to use, and certainly a bit more Web 2.0-ish. Let's enumerate our goals for our Shopping Cart application:

- Users should be able to select an item, select a quantity of that item, and have it added to their cart. They should be able to do this by dragging items into the cart, or in a more typical manual fashion (part of graceful degradation, as you'll see shortly).

- Users should be able to view the contents of their cart at any time, including the current dollar total, and also be able to modify it from that view: add and remove items, as well as change quantities.

- Users should be able to check out; that is, complete their purchase. However, since this is a book focused on JavaScript and the client in general, we're not going to actually write that part.[1] Moreover, we're going to write a "mock" server on the client. It would be a simple exercise to replace this mock server with the real McCoy.

- The shopping cart should degrade gracefully; that is, work whether or not JavaScript is enabled. When it is enabled, the full drag-and-drop experience is available. When it is disabled, the cart still functions just fine, but in a more manual fashion, typical of most shopping carts. Because we're faking the server side though, we can't literally disable JavaScript, because we need it to do that fakery. Therefore, we'll provide a switch to turn JavaScript on and off in a fake way, so we can see how things react in either circumstance.

- We'll use a JavaScript library to help us with the more complex pieces, specifically the drag-and-drop functionality. That library is MochiKit.

With this application, we will have three primary concerns. First, we want the user to have the ability to drag items onto the cart, so we'll need to deal with the code to enable drag-and-drop. This isn't the most difficult thing to implement in a web application, but it involves a fair number of details, so we'll be using the MochiKit library to handle the complexity for us.

Second, we want the application to degrade gracefully, so it will still work when JavaScript is disabled. This book, being about JavaScript, hasn't focused on how this can be accomplished, so this will be a good chance to demonstrate how to do it. As you can imagine, a drag-and-drop shopping cart just isn't viable without JavaScript, so it truly will be a degraded experience, if one considers the drag-and-drop version to be the pinnacle. Still, we can continue to provide a perfectly usable shopping experience, even without JavaScript.

The third consideration is that we aren't going to mess with the server side of the equation here, yet we will need a server in the mix to do it right. How can we accomplish that? We can pull off this trick by utilizing a technique I like to call a *mock server*.[2]

Let's start with how we will pull off that graceful degradation.

Graceful Degradation, or Working in the Stone Age

These days, writing a web application without JavaScript is tantamount to trying to start a fire by rubbing two sticks together. There's no question it can be done that way, but why would you want to, when you can grab a BIC from Wal-Mart and do it with the flick of a finger?

In years gone by, JavaScript had a very poor reputation on a number of fronts: security, performance, annoyance (which is really a failing of those using it), and so on. In those days, people often would disable JavaScript entirely to make their browsing experience more enjoyable. Some people still do that today, even though it's far less common. Also, we should consider

---

1. You will be seeing some server-side code in the chapter on Ajax (Chapter 12), but that's because there isn't a particularly good way to fake it in a purely client-side manner. Here, we can do that with a mock server.
2. While I won't claim to have made up the term, I can honestly say I've never heard it referred to as such anywhere else, so, if you use it, send the royalty check to my publisher for forwarding along to me. Just kidding!

alternate browsing devices and limited devices like cell phone-based browsers, which often do not provide JavaScript capabilities. Therefore, making an application that can operate just as well (or nearly as well) in the absence of JavaScript as it does with it is a very good thing indeed.

How do we actually do it though? It can be boiled down to this: write the application to work without JavaScript, and then add the script that "enables" the features that can be present only when JavaScript is.

As a simple example, let's say we want to have a form like this:

```
<html>
  <head></head>
  <body>
    <form name="myForm" method="post" action="someAction.do">
      Your name: <input type="text" name="yourName" size="20">
      <br>
      <input type="submit" value="Submit">
    </form>
  </body>
</html>
```

Clearly, that will work just fine whether or not JavaScript is enabled. Now, let's think of a problem we might encounter: what if the user doesn't enter a name? Will the server we submit this to blow up and return some error? It very well may. So, we're going to have to check for that on the server. But for this simple check, why do we even need to involve the server? With JavaScript, we can do this instead:

```
<html>
  <head>
    <script>
      function validate(inForm) {
      if (inForm.yourName.value == "") {
        alert("Please enter your name");
      } else {
        inForm.submit();
      }
    </script>
  </head>
  <body>
    <form name="myForm" method="post" action="someAction.do">
      Your name: <input type="text" name="yourName" size="20">
      <br>
      <input type="button" value="Submit" onClick="validate(this.form);">
    </form>
  </body>
</html>
```

Now, when JavaScript is enabled, the server won't be involved to perform this simple check, cutting down on server utilization and network utilization. And this also makes for a better user experience, because there won't be even a little delay between clicking Submit and seeing the error message.

The trick now is to make it work in both cases of JavaScript enabled and disabled. First, we need to define what exactly *work* means in this context. When JavaScript is enabled, *work* obviously means do the check on the client, pop up the error message if required, and cancel the form submission. When JavaScript is disabled, *work* means the form should still submit to the server, but without the benefit of the client-side check. Now, you may argue that this example is flawed because if the button were a type="submit", and the check were done onSubmit of the form instead, we would have what we want, and you would be correct. This is an example to illustrate a point, however, so bear with me a bit.

Aside from that solution, how else could we make this work in both cases? Take a look at this:

```
<html>
  <head>
    <script>
      function setup() {
        document.getElementById("btnSubmit").style.display = "none";
        document.getElementById("btnButton").style.display = "block";
      }
      function validate(inForm) {
      if (inForm.yourName.value == "") {
        alert("Please enter your name");
      } else {
        inForm.submit();
      }
      }
    </script>
  </head>
  <body onLoad="setup();">
    <form name="myForm" method="post" action="someAction.do">
      Your name: <input type="text" name="yourName" size="20">
      <br>
      <input type="submit" value="Submit" id="btnSubmit">
      <input type="button" value="Submit" id="btnButton"
        onClick="validate(this.form);">
    </form>
  </body>
</html>
```

Here, we have the best of both worlds. When JavaScript is disabled, the only button that is visible is the Submit button. Yes, it's true we don't get the client-side check, but that's why this is degraded rather than broken; it will still work, just in a degraded way. When JavaScript is enabled, the Submit button it hidden in favor of the regular button, which includes the client-side check.

We'll be doing a very similar thing in this chapter's application. At some point before reading too much further, you should play with it a little bit. In main.js, you'll find a variable javaScriptEnabled. I'll discuss this later when we dissect the application, but for now, you can simply set this to true to see the application in JavaScript-enabled mode, and set it to false to simulate JavaScript being disabled. When you set this variable to false, notice that you have Description links below the items you can purchase. But when JavaScript is enabled, the links are not present. By default, these links are there, and they will be removed by JavaScript later to give a more rich experience (hovering over the items gives you the descriptions that the links otherwise would).

The MochiKit Library

Now let's turn our attention to MochiKit (http://www.mochikit.com). Although I mentioned it in Chapter 2, MochiKit's slogan certainly deserves repeating:

MochiKit makes JavaScript suck less

Gold, I tell ya—pure comedy gold!

Seriously though, I'm not sure I would say that JavaScript "sucks" anyway (one would certainly hope not, based on the fact that I'm here writing this book!), but the sentiment is still valid. MochiKit definitely makes many things much more pleasant.

Take drag-and-drop, for instance. When you're developing a fat client—be it Java Swing, Windows, Linux, or whatever—drag-and-drop is pretty simple, usually requiring nothing more than setting some attributes and implementing some minor code. In a browser though, it's a fair bit more work:

- Track when the mouse button is pressed down, and see if it was pressed down on an element that is draggable (as determined by your own criteria, by the way).

- Track the mouse movement and move the draggable object accordingly.

- Recognize when the mouse button is lifted and determine which object the draggable object was on when the button was released. Was it an object where the dragged item can be dropped?

- If the drop target is valid for the dragged item, process that event. And deal with what happens to the draggable object—does it get cloned perhaps, or just return to its starting point (which you remembered to record, right?).

- Along the way, deal with the differences in browser event models, CSS differences, and so on.

- And how about the possibility of some effects, to make the whole deal look a bit cooler?

It's not that this can't be done; of course, it can. In fact, I've seen some rather elegant implementations[3] that don't make my head hurt all that much—at least as far as the dragging part goes. However, those implementations don't deal with the dropping part, other than literally ending the process of dragging. Determining if the object was dropped on something else is out of scope.

Since drag-and-drop isn't exactly a trivial exercise in the browser, it behooves us to find a good implementation that can save us that time, effort, and trouble. MochiKit provides just such a beast.

---

3. Check out http://www.javascriptkit.com/howto/drag.shtml, which is a pretty simple browser drag-and-drop implementation.

With MochiKit, making something draggable is as simple as this:

```
new MochiKit.DragAndDrop.Draggable("myObject", { revert : resetIt} );
```

With this line of code, the object on the page with the ID myObject is now able to be dragged all over the place! When the user releases the mouse button, the resetIt() function will be called. And in that function, we can do whatever we want. Can it get any easier?

"What about dropping?" you ask. That's just as drop-dead easy (pun intended):

```
new MochiKit.DragAndDrop.Droppable("dropHere", { ondrop : doOnDrop } );
```

We've now made it so that the object on the page with the ID dropHere can have other objects dropped onto it, and when that happens, the doOnDrop() function will be called. Once again, can you imagine it being any simpler?

MochiKit offers a slew of options to go along with this, such as the ability to have the dragged object return to its starting point, having a "ghost" of the object created so that you're dragging a clone, and so on. It also offers effects, such as having the dragged object fade out slightly when being dragged. And that option to have the object return to its starting point, well, it doesn't have to just jump back there; it can actually glide back gracefully!

MochiKit's drag-and-drop support is excellent in my opinion, and is one of the simplest and quickest to get up and running. You'll see it in action as we dissect the Shopping Cart application, but I hope you are already salivating with the possibilities it offers!

Another area of interest in MochiKit for this application is its Signal package. Signals are basically events, but the neat thing about them is they aren't necessarily *user* events; they can be virtually anything. For example, if you would like to call a function when some object on the page is clicked, you can do this:

```
connect('myID', 'onclick', myClicked);
```

When the object with the ID myID is clicked, myClicked() will be called.

What else does MochiKit have to offer? Oh, just a little bit—let Table 10-1 tell the story!

Table 10-1. *Some of the Many MochiKit Packages*

Package	Description
MochiKit.Async	Management of asynchronous tasks
MochiKit.Base	Functional programming and useful comparisons
MochiKit.DOM	Painless DOM manipulation functions
MochiKit.Color	Color abstraction with CSS3 support
MochiKit.DateTime	Time-related functions
MochiKit.Format	String formatting functions
MochiKit.Iter	Iterations
MochiKit.Logging	More robust logging capabilities than simple alerts
MochiKit.LoggingPane	Interactive logging pane
MochiKit.Selector	Element selection by CSS selector syntax

Table 10-1. *Some of the Many MochiKit Packages*

Package	Description
MochiKit.Signal	Simple universal event handling support
MochiKit.Style	Painless CSS manipulation functions
MochiKit.Sortable	A sortable object to make drag-and-drop lists easy
MochiKit.Visual	Visual effects

As is true with most of the libraries covered in this book, MochiKit has a lot more to offer than we can cover here, and your best bet is to spend some time on the MochiKit web site. Check out the documentation, try the examples, and get a feel for what it offers. It is quite well documented with some useful examples to play with, and I know you won't be disappointed.

■**Note** The drag-and-drop features used in this application are not available in the most currently released version of MochiKit as of this writing, which is version 1.3.1. This is a fact I discovered rather painfully, because the documentation on the web site is for unreleased version 1.4 (although it might possibly be released by the time you read this). Therefore, in order to build this application. I had to get that unreleased version from source control, which uses the Subversion source control system. The URL for this code is http://svn.mochikit.com/mochikit/trunk/. You can find further information at the MochiKit web site's download page. This includes suggestions for Subversion clients (if you're using Windows as I generally do, I echo the suggestion of TortoiseSVN). Of course, when you download the source for this application from the Apress site, which I hope you've done already, you'll get the 1.4 version of MochiKit, all ready to go.

The Mock Server Technique

Well, calling the mock server approach a *technique* might be a tad grandiose, but it is a handy way to develop nonetheless.

When you write full-blown server code, more effort tends to go into it. You obviously need a server, plus a web and/or application server running. You may also need extensions installed, such as PHP, if that's your technology of choice. In some cases, such as Java and C#, aside from JSPs and ASPs that is, a compiler step is involved, which more times than not means you need to restart some server component for the changes to take effect. That's not even counting any additional development tools you may need, such as IDEs and the like.

Wouldn't it be nice if you could do this all on the server? Now, you're probably thinking "Hey, I have Tomcat or IIS or something running on my laptop, so I can do that." And indeed you can. I certainly do! But there is still more involved—compiling, restarting, and all that. What I'm talking about is truly serverless development, with nothing but client code involved.

Yes, you can do this! You can, in fact, have HTML and JavaScript playing the part of the server if you do things just right. This can increase your development speed quite a bit by eliminating the additional server code development steps. It can remove some potential points of failure, like network latencies and such. It also tends to simplify things because you don't have to worry about getting server configurations right, dealing with operating system permissions, and so on. I hope you're convinced this might be a useful trick to know.

But how does one actually accomplish this feat of superhuman coding? It's amazingly simple. In pseudo-code, it looks like this:

```
<html>
  <head>
    <script>
      function process() {
        var function = get_request_parameter;
        switch (function) {
          case "some_operation":
            some_function();
          break;
        }
      }
    </script>
  </head>
  <body onLoad="process();"></body>
</html>
```

This is the mock server itself. It is nothing but an HTML page (you literally save it with an .htm or .html extension). Let's say you name it mockServer.htm. Then any time you have a form on another page, you do this:

```
<form name="myForm" method="get" action="mockServer.htm">
  Your Name: <input type="text" name="yourName">
  <input type="submit" value="Submit">
</form>
```

One important note is that the method *must* be GET, because that's the only way you'll be able to get access to the request parameters. You won't be able to access any parameters passed via POST.

You'll also see in the mockServer.htm file that I have get_request_parameter. This is a pseudo-code representation of some JavaScript that gets a request parameter for you. The function we're actually going to be using is jscript.page.getParameter() from Chapter 3, but we'll get to that in due course. The point here is that you get some parameter value, and then switch on that value to determine what code to execute. This is akin to the server reacting to some path and doing something different for each. The functions called can do anything you like, including render content or forward to another page. Again, you'll see this in action when we dissect the application. It's the basic concept that I'm hoping to get across right now.

I've already pointed out the benefits of this technique, but, of course, there are some negatives, too. Since this isn't a real server, you lose all the capabilities the server offers. You also need to be careful you don't do anything that you can't actually do on a real server. Still, even with the negatives, the simplicity and speed you gain are usually worth it, in my experience.

With those preliminaries out of the way, let's have a look at the application. If you haven't already done so, I suggest grabbing the code from the Apress web site and playing with it a bit.

A Preview of the Shopping Cart Application

Let's take a quick look at this chapter's project. First up, in Figure 10-1, you can see the application as it looks in the beginning. This is how it appears in non-JavaScript mode. I've added a few items to the cart already, as you can see down by the cart graphic.

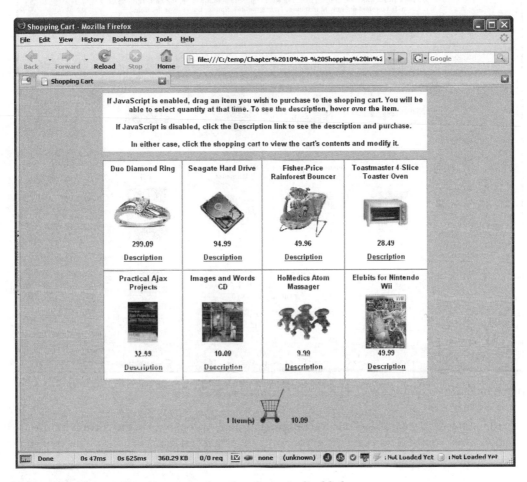

Figure 10-1. *The catalog view page when JavaScript is disabled*

Contrast Figure 10-1 with Figure 10-2, which is the catalog view when JavaScript is enabled. As you can see, the real difference is just the removal of the Description link. The description of the item is now seen when the user hovers the mouse over the item. In addition, there is no need to go to the description page you see when the Description link is clicked, because you can purchase from here as well, by simply dragging an item into the cart.

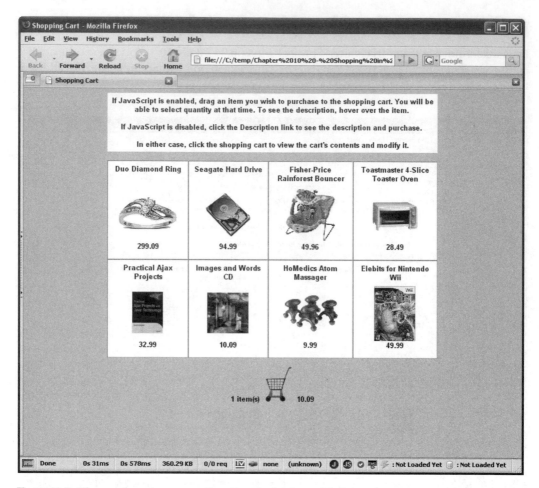

Figure 10-2. *The catalog view page when JavaScript is enabled*

In Figure 10-3, you can see the description pop-up. It will pop up at the current mouse location when you hover over an item. It will go away when you mouse off the image or if you start dragging the item.

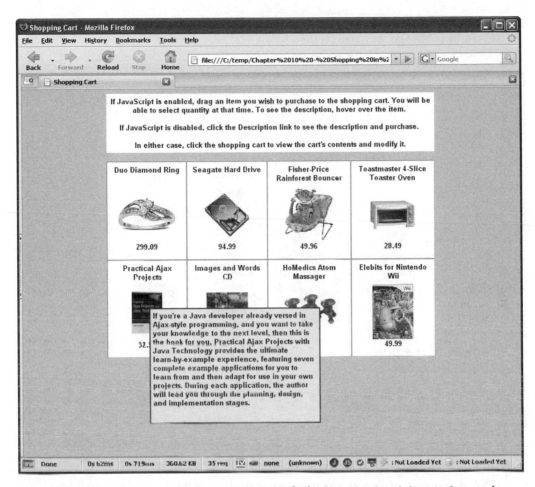

Figure 10-3. *The description pop-up seen when JavaScript is enabled and the user hovers the mouse over the item*

Although it's really hard to see unless you actually play with the application, I've tried to get a snapshot of an item being dragged in Figure 10-4. Notice that MochiKit is nice enough to fade out the image a little to give a nice effect to indicate it is being dragged.

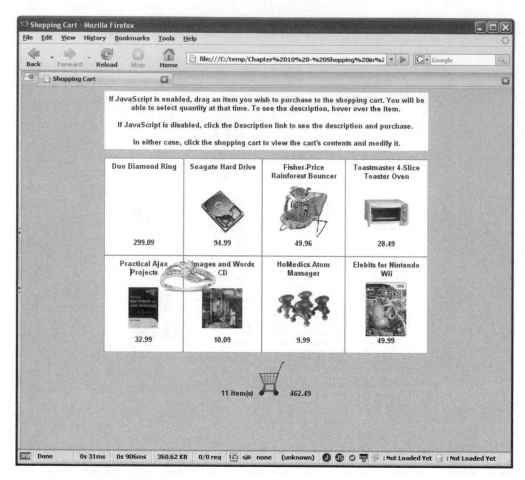

Figure 10-4. *An example of dragging an item (you really have to see it in action though)*

When you drag the item to the shopping cart, the next step is specify how many of the item you want. To accomplish this, a simple JavaScript `prompt()` gets the value, as shown in Figure 10-5.

A few other screens show up in the application, but I want to keep the anticipation going a bit longer!

Now we're ready to jump in and see what makes this application tick.

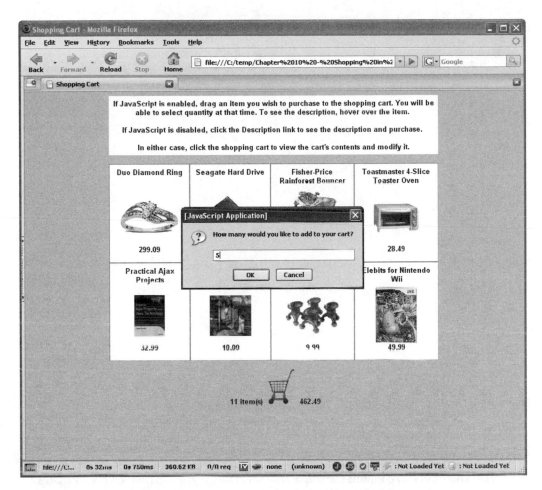

Figure 10-5. *The pop-up the user gets after dragging an item into the cart*

Dissecting the Shopping Cart Solution

As usual, we'll begin the dissection by taking a look at the layout of the application—the files that are part of it and all that. We begin this look with Figure 10-6, which shows the directory structure and file list.

Figure 10-6. *Directory layout of the Shopping Cart application*

This is the typical structure you've seen in most of the projects in this book, but we'll go over it anyway to be sure there are no surprises.

- css: This directory contains our single style sheet file, styles.css, which encapsulates all our style information.

- img: Here, we have all our image resources. In this case, the directory contains eight images: one for each of our purchasable items, and one for the shopping cart.

- descs: This directory contains the pages that show the item description and allow for purchasing an item when in non-JavaScript mode.

- js: This directory contains all (well, *almost* all, as you'll see) of the JavaScript for the application, including the MochiKit files in, not surprisingly, the MochiKit subdirectory.

- Finally, in the root are four HTML files:

  - index.htm is the catalog of items to purchase (which I refer to as the catalog view page).

  - mockServer.htm is, well, our mock server.

  - viewCart.htm is seen when viewing the contents of our shopping cart (which I refer to as the cart view page).

  - checkout.htm is what appears when the user tries to check out (which isn't much in this case!).

Let's not delay any longer. It's time to get to some code!

Writing styles.css

The first file we're going to explore is the style sheet for the application, styles.css. It's a pretty mundane style sheet frankly, but we should still have a look, if just a brief one. You can see the entire file in Listing 10-1.

Listing 10-1. *The styles.css File*

```
/* Style applied to all elements. */
* {
  font-family     : arial;
  font-size       : 10pt;
  font-weight     : bold;
}


/* Style for bodies of pages. */
.cssBody {
  background-color : #d0d0ff;
}


/* Style for instructions, and any other static text display areas. */
.cssInstructionsTable {
  background-color : #ffffff;
}


/* Style for the table used to display the catalog items. */
.cssCatalogTable {
  background-color : #ffffff;
  border           : 0px none #d0d0ff;
}
```

```
/* Style for the text on the checkout page. */
.cssCheckoutText {
  font-size        : 12pt;
}


/* Style for the header and footer of the view cart page. */
.cssHeaderFooter {
  background-color : #ffd0d0;
}


/* Row for the alternate row on the view cart page. */
.cssStripRow {
  background-color  : #efefef;
}


/* Style for description in cart view. */
.cssSmallDescription {
  font-size        : 8pt;
  font-weight      : normal;
}
```

As you can see, there is really nothing of any note here. The first style, as you've seen in other applications in this book, is a kind of catchall style that will effectively apply to everything on the page. The other styles work as follows:

- The cssBody class is applied to the <body> of all pages.

- The cssInstructionsTable class is for the instructions at the top of the page, and some other areas that need to be a white square, like the fake checkout page.

- The cssCatalogTable class is applied to the table that lays out the catalog. Primarily, its job is to remove the border from the table while leaving the cell borders, which isn't possible without CSS.

- The cssCheckoutText class is used to style the fake checkout page, to make that text a bit bigger.

- The cssHeaderFooter class is the red top and bottom you see on the view cart page.

- The cssStripRow class is used for the alternate gray rows on the view cart page, to make it easier to differentiate the rows of items.

- The cssSmallDescription class is used to style the description of the item on the view cart page.

Now let's move on to something just a littler meatier.

Writing index.htm

The index.htm file is the starting point of the application, and is what I call the catalog view. It is just some simple markup, with some JavaScript that may or may not actually do anything. First, let's see the code, as shown in Listing 10-2.

Listing 10-2. *The index.htm File*

```
<html>

  <head>

    <title>Shopping Cart</title>

    <link rel="StyleSheet" href="css/styles.css" type="text/css">

    <script type="text/javascript" src="js/MochiKit/MochiKit.js"></script>
    <script type="text/javascript" src="js/MochiKit/DragAndDrop.js"></script>

    <script type="text/javascript" src="js/jscript.page.js"></script>
    <script type="text/javascript" src="js/jscript.storage.js"></script>
    <script type="text/javascript" src="js/CatalogItem.js"></script>
    <script type="text/javascript" src="js/Catalog.js"></script>
    <script type="text/javascript" src="js/CartItem.js"></script>
    <script type="text/javascript" src="js/Cart.js"></script>
    <script type="text/javascript" src="js/main.js"></script>

  </head>

  <body class="cssBody" onLoad="init();">

    <div id="divMain">

      <table cellpadding="6" cellspacing="0" width="600" border="0"
        align="center" class="cssInstructionsTable">
        <tr>
          <td align="center" valign="middle">
            If JavaScript is enabled, drag an item you wish to purchase
            to the shopping cart.  You will be able to select quantity at that
            time.  To see the description, hover over the item.
            <hr><br>
            If JavaScript is disabled, click the Description link to see the
            description and purchase.
            <br><br>
            In either case, click the shopping cart to view the cart's contents
            and modify it.
          </tr>
        </td>
      </table>
```

```
<br>

<table cellpadding="6" cellspacing="0" width="600" border="1"
  align="center" class="cssCatalogTable">

  <tr>

    <td align="center" valign="middle">
      <table border="0" cellpadding="0" cellspacing="0" width="100%">
        <tr><td height="40" align="center" valign="top">
          Duo Diamond Ring
        </td></tr>
        <tr><td height="100" align="center" valign="top" id="td_img_1">
          <img src="img/item1.gif" id="img_1">
        </td></tr>
        <tr><td height="25" align="center" valign="top">
          299.09
        </td></tr>
        <tr id="desc1"><td height="25" align="center" valign="top">
          <a href="mockServer.htm?function=viewDescription&itemID=1">
            Description
          </a>
        </td></tr>
      </table>
    </td>

.... MARKUP FOR THREE OTHER ITEMS REMOVED ....

  </tr>

  <tr>

    <td align="center" valign="middle">
      <table border="0" cellpadding="0" cellspacing="0" width="100%">
        <tr><td height="40" align="center" valign="top">
          Practical Ajax Projects
        </td></tr>
        <tr><td height="100" align="center" valign="top" id="td_img_5">
          <img src="img/item5.gif" id="img_5">
        </td></tr>
        <tr><td height="25" align="center" valign="top">
          32.99
        </td></tr>
        <tr id="desc5"><td height="25" align="center" valign="top">
          <a href="mockServer.htm?function=viewDescription&itemID=5">
            Description
          </a>
```

```
        </td></tr>
      </table>
    </td>

    .... MARKUP FOR THREE OTHER ITEMS REMOVED ....

  </tr>

</table>

<br>
<center>
  <span id="spnItemCount"></span>
  <a href="mockServer.htm?function=viewCart"><img
    src="img/shoppingCart.gif" border="0"
    id="shoppingCart" hspace="6" alt="Click to view cart"></a>
  <span id="spnCartTotal"></span>
</center>

  </div>

</body>

</html>
```

Note that two large chunks of HTML have been removed because they are very similar to the previous sections. The sections I refer to are a particular item. For example, the first item you can see in Listing 10-2 is this markup:

```
<td align="center" valign="middle">
  <table border="0" cellpadding="0" cellspacing="0" width="100%">
    <tr><td height="40" align="center" valign="top">
      Duo Diamond Ring
    </td></tr>
    <tr><td height="100" align="center" valign="top" id="td_img_1">
      <img src="img/item1.gif" id="img_1">
    </td></tr>
    <tr><td height="25" align="center" valign="top">
      299.09
    </td></tr>
    <tr id="desc1"><td height="25" align="center" valign="top">
      <a href="mockServer.htm?function=viewDescription&itemID=1">
        Description
      </a>
    </td></tr>
  </table>
</td>
```

As you can see, it's just straight HTML. Note the link for the description, which targets the mockServer.htm file. This is again what will take the place of a real server, and we'll get to that soon. Another fact that you need to be aware of is that the table row this markup is in has an ID defined. This matters quite a bit!

Let's back up a step though. Notice that most of our JavaScript files are imported onto this page, and also notice the call to init() onLoad of the document. This function is found in main.js, which we'll look at next. For now, the important thing to know is that when init() executes, if the application is running in non-JavaScript mode, it will do nothing. This also means that the fact that the table rows have IDs won't really matter in that mode.

However, the story is different when in JavaScript mode. In that case, the links in these rows are disabled, and that's why the rows have IDs—we need to be able to address them directly to remove their contents.

This page also has the shopping cart icon, which you can drag items onto when in JavaScript mode, and you can always click it to view the contents of the cart. Surrounding the graphic are some <span> elements, where the item count and cart total amount appear. Note that they are <span> elements, rather than <div> elements, so that they can be right next to the cart. Remember that <div> elements have a line break following them, so they would not appear next to the cart. <span> elements are not followed by a line break automatically, so they work well in this case.

OK, I've done a bit of foreshadowing, and now it's time to reveal the main.js file.

Writing main.js

As you just saw, main.js is imported into index.htm, and it contains the init() function that is called onLoad of the index.htm page. The content of main.js is shown in Listing 10-3.

Listing 10-3. *The main.js File*

```
/**
 * Set this to true to see the fancy version, false for the plain-jane version.
 */
var javaScriptEnabled = false;


/**
 * Called when the index.htm page loads.
 */
function init() {

  if (javaScriptEnabled) {

    // For each item...
    for (var i = 1; i < 9; i++) {

      // Remove the description link.
      document.getElementById("desc" + i).style.display = "none";

      // Hook up the description hover to it.
      var imgObject = document.getElementById("img_" + i)
```

```
    imgObject.onmouseover = cart.hoverDescriptionShow;
    imgObject.onmouseout = cart.hoverDescriptionHide;

    // Make the image draggable.
    new MochiKit.DragAndDrop.Draggable("img_" + i, { revert : true });

    // Event handler from drag starting (hides description popups).
    connect(Draggables, 'start', cart.onDragStart);

    // Create a description popup for the item.
    var descPopup = document.createElement("div");
    descPopup.setAttribute("id", "desc_" + i);
    descPopup.innerHTML =
      catalog.getItem(i).getItemDescription();
    descPopup.style.width = "300px";
    descPopup.style.height = "200px";
    descPopup.style.position = "absolute";
    descPopup.style.display = "none";
    descPopup.style.border = "2px solid #ff0000";
    descPopup.style.padding = "4px";
    descPopup.style.backgroundColor = "#efefef";
    document.getElementById("divMain").appendChild(descPopup);

  }

  // Make the shopping cart a drop target.
  new MochiKit.DragAndDrop.Droppable("shoppingCart",
    { ondrop : cart.doOnDrop }
  );

}

// Show the cart item count and dollar total.  This only really matters
// if the user goes to the view cart or checkout pages and then goes back to
// the catalog... when the cart is empty this basically has no effect.
// Also note that what this function renders would be done by a server-side
// component if JavaScript was disabled, but we're faking it here.
cart.updateCartStats();

} // End init().
```

First, let's talk about the javaScriptEnabled variable. This global variable is the key to the concept of JavaScript-enabled and JavaScript-disabled mode. When set to true, the application is in JavaScript-enabled mode. This means it is acting as if JavaScript were available in the browser. When set to false, this is the equivalent to the user having disabled JavaScript. Of course, we need JavaScript to be enabled for real, because it is emulating the server. But this simple variable allows us to do the equivalent of turning JavaScript on and off.

What would happen if JavaScript were disabled for real? Well, init() would never be called onLoad of the document. If you look at the init() function, the first thing you see is this:

```
if (javaScriptEnabled) {
```

If javaScriptEnabled is set to false, then init() won't execute either. So, it truly is equivalent, and allows you to see the application in both situations just by changing the value of this variable, which is something I encourage you to do now.

Moving on, the next thing in init() is an iteration. The idea here is that we're going to modify all eight of the items in the catalog in some way. First, it gets a reference to the <tr> with the ID I mentioned previously and hides it. That's all there is to "removing" the Description link, which we don't need when JavaScript is enabled. Next, we need to enable the ability to hover over an item and see the description, and all that takes is this:

```
var imgObject = document.getElementById("img_" + i)
imgObject.onmouseover = cart.hoverDescriptionShow;
imgObject.onmouseout = cart.hoverDescriptionHide;
```

After we get a reference to the appropriate image, we set the onMouseOver and onMouseOut handlers to point to the appropriate methods in the cart object, which is an instance of the Cart class that you'll see later. In short, this is the shopping cart itself, and all the functionality it encapsulates.

After that comes the step of making the image draggable, which is what MochiKit does for us. It's very simple:

```
new MochiKit.DragAndDrop.Draggable("img_" + i, { revert : true });
connect(Draggables, 'start', cart.onDragStart);
```

We are instantiating a MochiKit.DragAndDrop.Draggable object and giving it a reference to the image of the item. We are also passing in some options; well, one option to be precise. The revert option can be an effect, a function, or a simple true/false value—in this case, it is the latter. This tells MochiKit that when the draggable object is dropped, whether or not it's dropped on the shopping cart (a droppable object), we want the object to revert back to its starting position. MochiKit does this with some flair by default, using a Move effect to have the object—our item's image in this case—fly back to its starting position. You can use this in conjunction with the reverteffect attribute, which is another option you can pass here, to determine which effect to use, but in this case, the default does rather nicely.

The second line that begins with connect(), is part of the MochiKit event system. It allows you to attach handlers to numerous and varied events on the page. In this case, we are saying that any Draggable object, which is what Draggables means because all Draggable objects are contained in the Draggables collection, should trigger execution of the onDragStart() method of the cart object whenever dragging starts. This is needed so that we can hide the pop-up description when dragging begins.

The next thing init() does is creates the pop-up descriptions for our items, and adds them to the DOM (because they aren't there initially). This is pretty typical DOM manipulation code: create an instance of <div>, populate its attributes, give it some content via setting innerHTML, and append it to the DOM as a child of some element—in this case, the divMain <div>, which surrounds all the contents on the page.

The last step of init() is to make the shopping cart something an image can be dropped on. We do this with a single line of code:

```
new MochiKit.DragAndDrop.Droppable("shoppingCart",
  { ondrop : cart.doOnDrop }
);
```

The MochiKit.DragAndDrop.Droppable class is the complement to its Draggable class, and
its call signature is very similar. Here, we are giving it the ID of our shopping cart image, and
again passing some options—in this case, just the function to call when something is dropped
on the object. You'll see this function very soon, but as you can imagine, it is responsible for
actually adding the dropped item to the cart.

Writing id*X*.htm

When the application is in non-JavaScript mode, the user clicks the Description link underneath an item to both view the description and purchase it. The page that the user sees at this
point is shown in Figure 10-7.

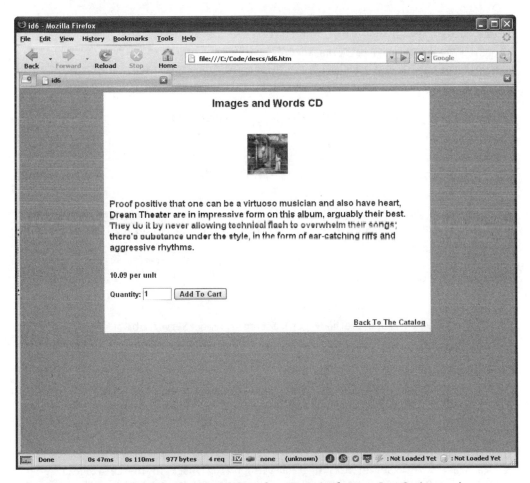

Figure 10-7. *An example of the description/purchase page in the non-JavaScript version*

Each of the items has its own HTML document, named id*X*.htm, where *X* is the ID number of the item (1 through 8). These files are found in the /descs directory. Because they are all identical except for the information about the item, I've shown the listing for only one here, in Listing 10-4.

Listing 10-4. *The id1.htm File (Other Files in /descs Are Virtually Identical)*

```html
<html>
  <head>
    <title>id1</title>

    <link rel="StyleSheet" href="../css/styles.css" type="text/css">

    <script>
    </script>

  </head>

  <body style="background-color:#a0a0ff;">
    <table border="0" cellpadding="10" cellspacing="0" width="600"
      align="center" style="background-color:#ffffff;"><tr><td>
      <center>
        <div style="font-size:14pt;">Duo Diamond Ring</div>
        <br><br>
        <img src="../img/item1.gif">
      </center>
      <br><br>
      <div style="font-size:12pt;">
        This 10K gold Duo ring features two round diamonds in prong settings with
        round diamond accents.  Duo Jewelry is designed to celebrate a couple's
        love.
      </div>
      <br><br>
      299.09 per unit
      <br><br>
      <form name="purchase" method="get" action="../mockServer.htm">
        <input type="hidden" name="function" value="purchase">
        <input type="hidden" name="itemID" value="1">
        Quantity:
        <input type="text" size="3" maxlength="2" name="quantity" value="1">
        <input type="submit" value="Add To Cart">
      </form>
    </tr></tr>
    <tr><td align="right">
      <a href="../mockServer.htm?function=viewCatalog">Back To The Catalog</a>
    </td></tr></table>
```

```
    </body>

</html>
```

As you can see, it is perfectly straightforward HTML; no JavaScript to speak of. In fact, I dare say the only items of interest here are the target of the form submission and the Back To The Catalog link. Notice that both of them target the mockServer.htm file, which we'll be looking at in detail shortly. The important point now is that, conceptually, this document takes the place of a real server. Notice the function parameter is passed as part of the query string in the link (also notice that the method of the form is GET) and as a form field in the form submission. The mockServer.htm file uses the getParameter() function in the jscript.page package from Chapter 3 to get the parameters passed to it. For this to work, however, the parameters must have been passed as a query string, Parameters passed through POST cannot be read, and that's the reason for the form's method.

The mockServer.htm file will look for that function parameter and use it to determine which operation it should perform. That's a good enough description of it for now; as I said, you'll see it in more detail later in the chapter.

Writing CatalogItem.js

The CatalogItem class represents a single item in the catalog that the user can purchase. It has a handful of data elements to describe it, and the class also has the typical getters and setters to access it in a good object-oriented way. Figure 10-8 shows the UML diagram of the class.

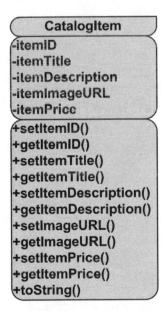

Figure 10-8. *UML diagram for the CatalogItem class*

The CatalogItem class has the following five fields:

- itemID: The ID of the item. For this application, I chose to make it just a simple number, 1–8. There's nothing that says it has to be. I just figured KISS: Keep It Simple, Stupid!

- itemTitle: The short title of the item as seen on the catalog view page.

- itemDescription: The lengthier description you see when you hover over the image in JavaScript mode, or when you click the Description link in non-JavaScript mode.

- itemImageURL: Stores the URL to the item's image.

- itemPrice: The price of the item.

All of the methods in the class are simple getters and setters for the various fields. There is also an overridden toString() method, so we can get a more meaningful representation of an instance of this class, which is especially good when trying to debug the application.

Even though this is a simple class—really just a Data Transfer Object (DTO)—we should still look at the code, which is shown in Listing 10-5.

Listing 10-5. *The CatalogItem Class in CatalogItem.js*

```
/**
 * This class represents one item in the catalog.
 */
function CatalogItem() {


  /**
   * The ID of the item.
   */
  var itemID = "";


  /**
   * The title of the item.
   */
  var itemTitle = "";


  /**
   * The description of the item.
   */
  var itemDescription = "";
```

```
/**
 * The URL to the image of the item.
 */
var itemImageURL = "";


/**
 * The price for one of the items.
 */
var itemPrice = 0;


/**
 * Setter.
 *
 * @param inItemID New value.
 */
this.setItemID = function(inItemID) {

  itemID = inItemID;

} // End setItemID().


/**
 * Getter.
 *
 * @return The current value of the field.
 */
this.getItemID = function() {

  return itemID;

} // End getItemID().


/**
 * Setter.
 *
 * @param inItemTitle New value.
 */
this.setItemTitle = function(inItemTitle) {

  itemTitle = inItemTitle;

} // End setItemTitle().
```

```
/**
 * Getter.
 *
 * @return The current value of the field.
 */
this.getItemTitle = function() {

  return itemTitle;

} // End getItemTitle().


/**
 * Setter.
 *
 * @param inItemDescription New value.
 */
this.setItemDescription = function(inItemDescription) {

  itemDescription = inItemDescription;

} // End setItemDescription().


/**
 * Getter.
 *
 * @return The current value of the field.
 */
this.getItemDescription = function() {

  return itemDescription;

} // End getItemDescription().


/**
 * Setter.
 *
 * @param inItemImageURL New value.
 */
this.setItemImageURL = function(inItemImageURL) {

  itemImageURL = inItemImageURL;

} // End setItemImageURL().
```

```
/**
 * Getter.
 *
 * @return The current value of the field.
 */
this.getItemImageURL = function() {

  return itemImageURL;

} // End getItemImageURL().


/**
 * Setter.
 *
 * @param inItemPrice New value.
 */
this.setItemPrice = function(inItemPrice) {

  itemPrice = inItemPrice;

} // End setItemPrice().


/**
 * Getter.
 *
 * @return The current value of the field.
 */
this.getItemPrice = function() {

  return itemPrice;

} // End getItemPrice().


/**
 * Overriden toString() method.
 *
 * @return A meaningful string representation of the object.
 */
this.toString = function() {
```

```
      return "CatalogItem : [ " +
        "itemID='" + itemID + "', " +
        "itemTitle='" + itemTitle + "', " +
        "itemDescription='" + itemDescription + "', " +
        "itemImageURL='" + itemImageURL + "', " +
        "itemPrice='" + itemPrice + "' ]";

   } // End toString().


} // End CatalogItem class.
```

It's not going to win any awards as a complex piece of coding, but it gets the job done. Now, of course, a CatalogItem instance wouldn't be a ton of good on its own; it must be part of a catalog that knows how to deal with it. Such a beast exists, and it is not surprisingly the Catalog class!

Writing Catalog.js

The Catalog class is where all the CatalogItem instances that are part of the catalog of items the user can purchase are stored. This is a very simple class, as you can see in its UML diagram in Figure 10-9.

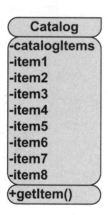

Figure 10-9. *UML diagram of the Catalog class*

The catalogItems field is the collection of CatalogItems, one for each item the user can purchase. The getItem() method will return a given item if you pass it the item's ID. This is used in a number of places, as you might imagine.

Wait, didn't I skip something? Oh yes, those item*X* fields, where *X* is 1 through 8. I wonder what's going on there? Let's take a look at the code and see, as shown in Listing 10-6.

Listing 10-6. *The Code Behind the Catalog Class, in Catalog.js*

```
/**
 * This class represents a catalog of items.
 */
function Catalog() {


  /**
   * The collection of items for sale in the catalog.
   */
  var catalogItems = new Object;


  /**
   * Load some items so the user can play, assuming JavaScript is enabled.
   */
  var item1 = new CatalogItem();
  item1.setItemID("1");
  item1.setItemTitle("Duo Diamond Ring");
  item1.setItemDescription("This 10K gold Duo ring features two round diamonds in ➡
prong settings with round diamond accents.  Duo Jewelry is designed ➡
to celebrate a couple's love.");
  item1.setItemImageURL("img/item1.gif");
  item1.setItemPrice(299.09);
  catalogItems[item1.getItemID()] = item1;

.... CODE FOR SEVEN OTHER ITEMS REMOVED ....

  /**
   * Returns a CatalogItem by ID.
   *
   * @param  inItemID The ID of the item to return.
   * @return          The corresponding item, or null if not found.
   */
  this.getItem = function(inItemID) {

    return catalogItems[inItemID];

  } // End getItem().


} // End Catalog class.


// The one and only instance of the items catalog.
var catalog = new Catalog();
```

Well, I did cut it down a bit for print!

Notice the .... CODE FOR SEVEN OTHER ITEMS REMOVED ....? As it says, there are seven other blocks of code very similar to the block right before that notation, namely this one:

```
var item1 = new CatalogItem();
item1.setItemID("1");
item1.setItemTitle("Duo Diamond Ring");
item1.setItemDescription("This 10K gold Duo ring features two round diamonds in ➥
prong settings with round diamond accents.  Duo Jewelry is designed ➥
to celebrate a couple's love.");
item1.setItemImageURL("img/item1.gif");
item1.setItemPrice(299.09);
catalogItems[item1.getItemID()] = item1;
```

Here, we're creating a CatalogItem instance, populating it for a particular item, and adding it to the catalogItems collection. This is where the items in our catalog come from. Although I've listed the itemX fields in the UML diagram, in practice, they are used during construction of the Catalog object, and never again. Still, they should be listed for completeness. Note that these eight blocks of code are not within a method of the Catalog class; hence, they will be executed when Catalog is instantiated. They are in the constructor, in other words, and this is precisely what we want. There is no need to make the user of this class call some setup method explicitly.

Now that we know about the item catalog, let's talk about the shopping cart and the items that go into it.

Writing CartItem.js

The CartItem class represents a single item in the shopping cart. Figure 10-10 shows the UML diagram of this small class.

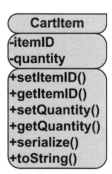

Figure 10-10. *UML diagram of the CartItem class*

A CartItem has only two important pieces of information stored within it: the itemID field, which matches the itemID field of a particular CatalogItem instance, and quantity, which is obviously the quantity of this particular item in the cart. You see the usual getters and setters for these two fields, as well as an overridden toString(), as in the CatalogItem class.

You also see a serialize() method. To make a long story short, we are going to be storing the contents of the cart in a cookie, and to do so, we need to have a string representation of each CartItem in the cart. The serialize() method returns this representation. It is nothing but the itemID and quantity, separated by a tilde (~) character.

Let's now look at Listing 10-7, which is the complete listing of the CartItem class.

Listing 10-7. *The CartItem Class in CartItem.js*

```
/**
 * This class represents one item in the shopping cart.
 */
function CartItem() {


  /**
   * The ID of the item.
   */
  var itemID = "";


  /**
   * The quantity of the item in the cart.
   */
  var quantity = 0;


  /**
   * Setter.
   *
   * @param inItemID New value.
   */
  this.setItemID = function(inItemID) {

    itemID = inItemID;

  } // End setItemID().


  /**
   * Getter.
   *
   * @return The current value of the field.
   */
  this.getItemID = function() {

    return itemID;
```

```
} // End getItemID().


/**
 * Setter.
 *
 * @param inQuantity New value.
 */
this.setQuantity = function(inQuantity) {

  quantity = inQuantity;

} // End setQuantity().


/**
 * Getter.
 *
 * @return The current value of the field.
 */
this.getQuantity = function() {

  return quantity;

} // End getQuantity().


/**
 * Returns a serialized version of the item suitable for writing out to the
 * cookie.
 */
this.serialize = function() {

  return itemID + "~" + quantity;

} // End serialize().


/**
 * Overriden toString() method.
 *
 * @return A meaningful string representation of the object.
 */
this.toString = function() {
```

```
    return "CartItem : [ " +
      "itemID='" + itemID + "', " +
      "quantity='" + quantity + "' ]";

  } // End toString().


} // End CartItem class.
```

There shouldn't be any surprises here at all. It's pretty boring code, to put it bluntly! Still, without it, none of this would work, so it's an important piece of boring code!

Next, we come to some code that is decidedly less boring: the Cart class.

Writing Cart.js

The Cart class, contained in the Cart.js source file, is truly where most of the application resides—where all the real functionality behind it is. As you saw when we looked at main.js, all the functions that handle the various events, such as dragging and dropping images, can be found in this class. Let's first take a look at its UML diagram, shown in Figure 10-11.

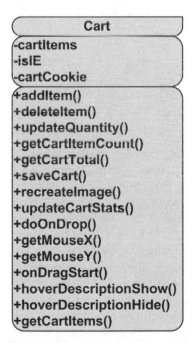

Figure 10-11. *UML diagram of the Cart class*

Because Cart.js is a fairly lengthy file, I won't list all of it here, but will show sections of it as required. First, we should look at the three fields it contains: cartItems, isIE, and cartCookie.

The cartItems field is an array that contains CartItem instances. These are the items that are currently in the cart.

The isIE field is needed later to deal with mouse events. Let's take a quick look at this:

```
var isIE = window.ActiveXObject ? true : false;
```

Since IE is the only browser that supports ActiveX controls (ignoring plug-ins that may exist for other browsers), it is the only browser that will return true when we check for the ActiveXObject attribute of the window object. Hence, it's an easy way to check if we're running in IE.

The cartCookie field is needed only temporarily, but I listed it anyway for completeness. It is a string that is the value of the cookie used to store the cart's contents.

Restoring the Cart's Contents

After the fields is some code that will execute when the class is instantiated. The job of this code is to read the value of the cookie where the cart's contents are stored, create CartItem objects from it, and store them in the cartItems field. Here is the code that accomplishes all that:

```
var cartCookie = jscript.storage.getCookie("js_shopping_cart");
if (cartCookie) {
  var itemsInCart = cartCookie.split("~~");
  for (var i = 0; i < itemsInCart.length; i++) {
    var nextItem = itemsInCart[i];
    var nextItemID = nextItem.split("~")[0];
    var nextItemQuantity = nextItem.split("~")[1];
    var cartItem = new CartItem();
    cartItem.setItemID(nextItemID);
    cartItem.setQuantity(nextItemQuantity);
    cartItems.push(cartItem);
  }
}
```

As you can see, the jscript.storage.getCookie() function that we built in Chapter 3 is used to get the value of the cookie, which is named js_shopping_cart. Assuming the cookie is found (which it wouldn't be the first time the user uses the application, of course), we then need to parse it.

The way the cart is stored is in the form *AA~BB~~CC~DD*. *AA* and *CC* are item IDs; *BB* and *DD* are the quantity of that item. As you can see, the ID and quantity are separated by a single tilde (~) character, and items are separated by two tildes. This makes it very easy to parse. We just need to use the split() method of the JavaScript String class to split on the double-tilde sequence, which gives us an array of items. Then we iterate over that array, and for each item, we use split() again, this time on the single tilde. The first element of the resultant array is the ID, and the second is the quantity. It's very easy!

All we need to do then is instantiate a CartItem object and fill in its details, and finally push() it onto the cartItems array. When we're finished going through all the items in the first array, the cartItems field contains a CartItem object for each item in the cart.

The first method you find in the source is getCartItems(). This simply returns the cartItems field—nothing more. This will be needed by our mock server code, as you'll see later.

Adding and Removing Cart Items

Next up is the addItem() method:

```
this.addItem = function(inItemToAdd) {

  cartItems.push(inItemToAdd);
  saveCart();

} // End getCartItems().
```

Obviously, this is called to add an item to the cart. It takes as an argument an instance of the CartItem class, which is presumed to be populated correctly. All addItem() does is push the incoming CartItem into the cartItems array, and then calls the saveCart() method, which is responsible for actually saving the cart as a cookie. We'll get to that method in just a bit.

Before that though, we find the deleteItem() method:

```
this.deleteItem = function(inItemIndex) {

  cartItems.splice(inItemIndex, 1);
  saveCart();

} // End deleteItem().
```

This method is equally as simple as addItem(). All it does it use the splice() method of the cartItems array to delete the item and the index that is passed in, and then calls saveCart() as well, so that the cookie is updated.

Updating Item Quantities in the Cart

The next method, updateQuantity(), is called from the view cart page to change the quantity of a given item in the cart.

```
this.updateQuantity = function(inItemIndex, inNewQuantity) {

  var cartItem = cartItems[inItemIndex];
  cartItem.setQuantity(inNewQuantity);
  saveCart();

} // End updateQuantity().
```

It first gets a reference to the CartItem object corresponding to the index passed into it. It then calls the setQuantity() method of that object, passing it the new quantity passed into updateQuantity(). Finally, it calls saveCart().

After updateQuantity() is the getCartItemCount() method, which is only marginally more complex:

```
this.getCartItemCount = function() {

  var cartItemCount = 0;
  for (var i = 0; i < cartItems.length; i++) {
    cartItemCount += parseInt(cartItems[i].getQuantity());
  }
  return cartItemCount;

} // End getCartItemCount().
```

This is a simple iteration over the cartItems array. For each element in the array, which is a CartItem object, we call the getQuantity() method on it, and accumulate this value. Remember that we want the total number of items in the cart to be purchased, which can be different from the total number of CartItems in the cart. Once the iteration is complete, the final tally is returned.

getCartTotal() is the next method here:

```
this.getCartTotal = function() {

  var cartTotal = 0;
  for (var i = 0; i < cartItems.length; i++) {
    var nextItem = cartItems[i];
    var nextItemQuantity = nextItem.getQuantity();
    var nextItemID = nextItem.getItemID();
    var catalogItem = catalog.getItem(nextItemID);
    cartTotal += nextItemQuantity * catalogItem.getItemPrice();
  }
  return cartTotal;

} // End getCartTotal().
```

This isn't too much different from getCartItemCount(). We again are iterating over the cartItems array. For each CartItem we find, we get the quantity of it, as well as its ID via a call to getIemID(). With this ID in hand, we then call the getItem() method of the catalog object, which returns the CatalogItem corresponding to the item being purchased. From that, we can get the price for one unit. It's a simple matter to multiply that price by the quantity of the item in the cart retrieved earlier. We keep a running total of this calculated value, and at the end, we have the total dollar amount for the cart.[4]

---

4. For the demo, I've simplified things and didn't concern myself with tax, shipping charges, and so on. Shh, don't tell the federal government, UPS, or FedEx!

Saving the Cart

Finally, we come to the saveCart() method, which I've mentioned a bunch of times:

```
var saveCart = function() {

  // Construct shopping cart string for cookie and store it.
  var shoppingCart = "";
  for (var i = 0; i < cartItems.length; i++) {
    nextItem = cartItems[i];
    if (shoppingCart != "") {
      shoppingCart += "~~";
    }
    shoppingCart += nextItem.serialize();
  }
  var expireDate = new Date();
  expireDate.setDate(expireDate.getDate()+7)
  jscript.storage.setCookie("js_shopping_cart", shoppingCart, expireDate);
} // End saveCart().
```

I bet you thought there would be more to it. Nope, that's it! Like the other methods, saveCart() iterates over the cartItems array. For each element, we simply call the serialiaze() method on the CartItem, which returns a string in the form X~Y, where X is the item ID and Y is the quantity. We are ultimately building up a string in the form X~Y~~X~Y. After we have that string constructed, we just need to use the jscript.storage.setCookie() function from Chapter 3, and the shopping cart is then saved as a cookie.

Notice that the expiration date of the cookie is set seven days in the future. So if you leave the shopping cart and come back, for up to seven days, your content will still be present. That's obviously longer than you would use on a real shopping site, but it demonstrates the point well here.

Updating Stats

After the saveCart() method comes the updateCartStats() method. This is used to display the number of items and total dollar amount of the cart next to the shopping cart graphic at the bottom. It is called when an item is dropped on to the cart:

```
this.updateCartStats = function() {

  // Put the total item count and dollar amount of the cart on the screen,
  // if and only if there are items in the cart already.
  var spnCartCountValue = "";
  var spnCartTotalValue = "";
  var cartItemCount = cart.getCartItemCount();
  if (cartItemCount != 0) {
    spnCartCountValue = cartItemCount + " item(s)";
    spnCartTotalValue = cart.getCartTotal();
```

```
    // Now some math: the total dollar amount has to be rounded for proper
    // display.  The basic logic harkens back to pre-algebra:
    // * Multiply the number by 10^x
    // * Apply Math.round() to the result
    // * Divide the result by 10^x
    spnCartTotalValue = Math.round(spnCartTotalValue * 100) / 100;
  }
  document.getElementById("spnItemCount").innerHTML = spnCartCountValue;
  document.getElementById("spnCartTotal").innerHTML = spnCartTotalValue;

} // End updateCartStats().
```

It begins by creating two variables, spnCartCountValue and spnCartTotalValue. The first is the number of items in the cart, and the second is the total dollar amount of the cart. Note that these are string values, which might seem a little odd, since we know conceptually these are numeric values. But these will be inserted as the innerHTML of some <span> tags, so it's more logical that they be strings. (And, in fact, if we have some variable with a value of zero as a number, and try to insert it into the <span>, it will be converted to a string. But do we really want to show a zero, or do we want to show nothing at all—that is, an empty string?) It then calls the getCartItemCount() method of the cart object to get the total number of items. If this value is anything other than zero, we take the value and append the string " item(s)" to it, turning it back into a string. We also call the getCartTotal() method on the cart object to get the dollar amount.

After that comes inserting these values into the appropriate <span> tags that you saw in index.htm. There is some funkiness here to be performed because the dollar value can have decimal points, but because it is truly a numeric value, the number of decimal points could be rather large. For a dollar amount, however, we want only two decimal places, so we need to do some rounding. The comments describe the basic algorithm of this rounding, which is just some basic math.

One final check is then performed to give us an empty string if the value is zero (which is what you would get the first time through when there are no items in the cart). Then innerHTML of the <span> elements is set, and we have updated statistics next to the shopping cart!

Handling Dropped Items

The doOnDrop() method, as you'll recall from looking at the code in main.js, is called when an item is dropped onto the shopping cart:

```
this.doOnDrop = function(element) {

  // Get the ID of the item dropped in the cart.
  var itemID = element.id.split("_")[1];
```

```
// Find out how many the user wants.
var quantity =
  parseInt(prompt("How many would you like to add to your cart?"));
if (!isNaN(quantity) && quantity != 0) {
  // Create a cart item and add it to the cart.
  var cartItem = new CartItem();
  cartItem.setItemID(itemID);
  cartItem.setQuantity(quantity);
  cart.addItem(cartItem);
}

// Show the cart item count and dollar total.
cart.updateCartStats();

} // End doOnDrop().
```

First, we get the itemID of the item, as in previous methods. After that, we pop up a prompt for users using the JavaScript prompt() function, so they can enter the quantity they want. The return value from this call could be something other than a number, or it could be zero, both of which would abort adding the item to the cart, so we have a check for both of those conditions. Assuming a number was entered, however, we go ahead and instantiate a new CartItem object, populate its attributes, which are just itemID and quantity, and send it to the addItem() method of the cart object. Lastly, we call updateCartStats() so the newly added item is reflected in the statistics next to the shopping cart.

Showing and Hiding the Hover Description

Next are two functions that are used when showing the hover description of the item: getMouseX() and getMouseY(). As their names imply, they get the X and Y location of a given mouse event. Because IE and Firefox (as well as other browsers) provide this information in different ways, this is where we need that isIE field that you saw earlier. Because these methods are very similar, I'll just show one for brevity:

```
this.getMouseX = function(inEvent) {

  var x;
  if (isIE) {
    x = (parseInt(event.clientX ) +
      parseInt(document.body.scrollLeft));
  } else {
    x = parseInt(inEvent.pageX);
  }
  return x;

} // End getMouseX().
```

When running in IE, the event object is provided at page scope, which has as one of its members the clientX attribute. When we take this value and add the document.body.srollLeft attribute, we get the absolute X coordinate of the mouse event.

When running in Firefox, or other browsers, the inEvent object is passed to this method, which contains the pageX attribute. This is the X coordinate of the mouse event. Notice that we don't have to take into consideration how far the page is scrolled horizontally, as we do in IE, because the pageX value already has that taken into account. This is what accounts for the difference in the branches of this code, aside from the difference in which attribute we go after and to which object it belongs. The getMouseY() method is again identical, with a few exceptions: instead of clientX, it's clientY; it's scrollTop instead of scrollLeft; and it's pageY instead of pageX.

And now we can see the code that makes use of those two functions, namely hoverDescriptionShow():

```
this.hoverDescriptionShow = function(inEvent) {

    var itemID = this.id.split("_")[1];
    var mouseX = cart.getMouseX(inEvent);
    var mouseY = cart.getMouseY(inEvent);
    var descObj = document.getElementById("desc_" + itemID);
    descObj.style.left = mouseX;
    descObj.style.top = mouseY;
    descObj.style.display = "block";

} // End hoverDescriptionShow().
```

Note the use of the this keyword. In the context of this method, which as you'll remember is attached to a given item's image, the this keyword is a reference to the image. That should explain why we do this.id to get the itemID: it's the DOM ID of the <img> element. We again split() this to get the second element of the resultant array, which is the itemID we want. We then call those mouse methods to get the current coordinates of the mouse on the page. Once we have that, we get a reference to the <div> that contains the description of the item being hovered over. We then set the left and top style attributes of this <div> to the mouse coordinates we just got, and finally show the <div> by setting its display style attribute to block. The description is then visible to the user at the place where the mouse cursor hovered over the image.

The last method in the Cart class is the hoverDescriptionHide() method. It just gets the itemID in the same way as in hoverDescriptionShow() (because this method is the event handler attached to the onMouseOut event of the image) and sets its display style attribute to none. That's it.

Now, let's look at the page that shows the contents of our shopping cart, viewCart.htm (if you can believe it!).

Writing viewCart.htm

The viewCart.htm file takes a bit of a leap of faith. We have some JavaScript in it that is emulating what the server would do. There is no JavaScript that would actually run on the client if this were a full-blown e-commerce site.

Before we get too far into that though, let's have a look at this page, shown in Figure 10-12.

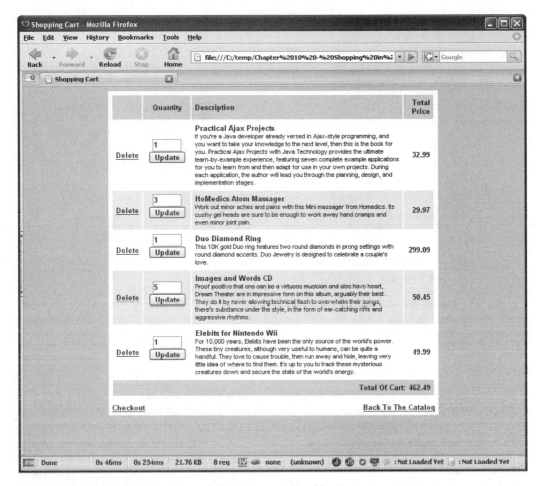

Figure 10-12. *Viewing the contents of the cart as rendered by the viewCart.htm page*

I'll call out bits of the code as needed here. As you take a look at the full source, you'll first see the style sheet import and the JavaScript imports you've seen elsewhere.

Showing the Cart's Contents

Next is some JavaScript encapsulated in a single page-scope function: viewCart(). This function is called onLoad of the page and it is where that leap of faith I mentioned comes into play. You need to pretend that this isn't really here as you conceptualize this code. This function is actually something that would be done server side, but since we have no server to work with, it's here.

This function is responsible for rendering the markup based on the contents of the cart. Although it's a fair volume of code, it's also fairly simple, consisting of just a series of string concatenations by and large.

viewCart() begins with a call to getCartItems() on the cart object. Remember that this returns the collection of CartItems in the cart. It then checks to be sure this array has a length other than zero. If it doesn't, it just renders a quick little message:

```
        // No items in cart, that's easy!
        document.getElementById("divCartContents").innerHTML =
          "<center><br>Your cart is empty<br></center>";
```

As you can see, this message is inserted into the divCartContents <div>, and that's all the user sees in this case.

If the cart isn't empty, then viewCart() begins to construct the markup for the cart contents display:

```
        var htmlOut = "<table width=\"100%\" border=\"0\" ";
        htmlOut += "cellpadding=\"6\" cellspacing=\"2\"";
        htmlOut += "<tr class=\"cssHeaderFooter\">";
        htmlOut += "<td align=\"center\"> </td>";
        htmlOut += "<td align=\"center\">Quantity</td>";
        htmlOut += "<td>Description</td>";
        htmlOut += "<td align=\"right\">Total Price</td></tr>";
        var rowStrip = false;
        var cartTotal = 0;
```

Also notice the two variables at the end: rowStrip and cartTotal. rowStrip is used to have alternate rows in the table a different color, giving the striped effect that is common in tabular displays. cartTotal is the accumulation of the dollar amount of all the items in the cart.

Constructing the Markup That Displays the Cart Contents

Next, we begin to iterate over the array of CartItem objects. For each, we get its itemID and quantity. We then get the corresponding CartItem for it via a call to catalog.getItem(nextItemID), where nextItemID is the itemID of the CartItem. With those two objects in hand, it's a simple matter of constructing some HTML:

```
        htmlOut += "<tr";
        // If this row should be striped, apply the appropriate class.
        if (rowStrip) {
          htmlOut += " class=\"cssStripRow\"";
        }
        rowStrip = !rowStrip;
        htmlOut += ">";
        // Now just generate some straightforward markup.
        htmlOut += "<td align=\"center\">";
        htmlOut += "<a href=\"mockServer.htm?function=delete&" +
          "itemIndex=" + i + "\">Delete</a>";
        htmlOut += "</td>";
        htmlOut += "<td align=\"center\">";
        htmlOut += "<form name=\"updateQuantity\" method=\"get\" " +
          "action=\"mockServer.htm\">";
        htmlOut += "<input type=\"hidden\" name=\"function\" " +
          "value=\"updateQuantity\">";
        htmlOut += "<input type=\"hidden\" name=\"itemIndex\" value=\"" +
          i + "\">";
```

```
htmlOut += "<input type=\"text\" size=\"3\" maxlength=\"2\" " +
  "name=\"quantity\" value=\"\"" + nextItemQuantity + "\">";
htmlOut += "<input type=\"submit\" value=\"Update\">";
htmlOut += "</form>";
htmlOut += "</td>";
htmlOut += "<td>" + catalogItem.getItemTitle() + "<br>";
htmlOut += "<div class=\"cssSmallDescription\">";
htmlOut += catalogItem.getItemDescription() + "</div></td>";
// Now some math: the total dollar amount has to be rounded for
// proper display.  The basic logic harkens back to pre-algebra:
// * Multiply the number by 10^x
// * Apply Math.round() to the result
// * Divide the result by 10^x
var itemTotalAmount = nextItemQuantity * catalogItem.getItemPrice();
itemTotalAmount = Math.round(itemTotalAmount * 100) / 100;
htmlOut += "<td align=\"right\">" + itemTotalAmount + "</td>";
htmlOut += "</tr>";
// Add cart amount to cart total.
cartTotal += nextItemQuantity * catalogItem.getItemPrice();
```

You can see the usage of the rowStrip variable here. Its value is inverted with each iteration, to alternate the style class applied to each row. The other interesting thing here is the calculation of the dollar amount for each item. This is just some simple multiplication: the quantity of the item times the price per unit. However, we need to do the same rounding you saw in the Cart class; otherwise, we might have a wild number of decimal places! You can also see where the value is added to cartTotal at the end.

Showing the Cart Total

Speaking of cartTotal, once this loop completes, we have one thing left to do, and that is to render the footer of the table where we can see the total of the cart:

```
htmlOut += "<tr class=\"cssHeaderFooter\">";
// Now some math: the total dollar amount has to be rounded for proper
// display.  The basic logic harkens back to pre-algebra:
// * Multiply the number by 10^x
// * Apply Math.round() to the result
// * Divide the result by 10^x
cartTotal = Math.round(cartTotal * 100) / 100;
htmlOut += "<td align=\"right\" colspan=\"4\">Total Of Cart: " +
  " " + cartTotal + "</td>";
htmlOut += "</tr>";
htmlOut += "</table>";
document.getElementById("divCartContents").innerHTML = htmlOut;
```

Once again we have that math, which is becoming far too familiar. (Hint: wouldn't it be nice to have an external function you could call to round a number to a specified number of decimal places? A natural fit for jscript.math, don't you think?)

We have only to insert the htmlOut string's value into the divCartContents <div>, and we've constructed the markup for the page—lock, stock, and barrel.

As I said, it's pretty straightforward code, but again, you have to pretend it isn't really here, even though it is. It's sort of not here, since it would be done by the server, but there it is, and you should understand it, even though you have to pretend it isn't there sort of . . . sorry, too much coffee today.

Writing checkout.htm

I'm almost embarrassed to be dissecting this particular file, because it is an absolutely trivial bit of code. Still, I like completeness, so it shall be done anyway. In Figure 10-13, you can see the result of the checkout.htm file.

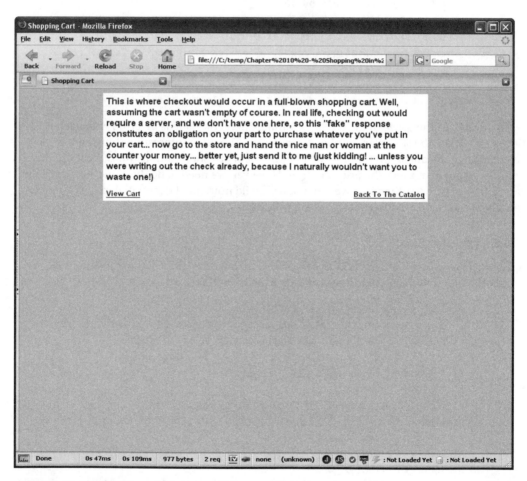

Figure 10-13. *The checkout page (not much to see I admit, but presented for the sake of completeness)*

The checkout.htm file is basically supposed to represent the final purchase step of the shopping cart experience. When the user clicks the Check Out link on the view cart page, the server would be accessed and the purchase would complete, probably by getting things like credit card information, shipping instructions, and so forth from the user. Since we're not dealing with the server side, in its place, we have this page. It's nothing but my lame attempt at humor and a placeholder for a full-blown server process.

The code for this page is shown in Listing 10-8.

Listing 10-8. *The checkout.htm File—To Say It's Not Rocket Science Would Be an Understatement!*

```html
<html>

  <head>

    <title>Shopping Cart</title>

    <link rel="StyleSheet" href="css/styles.css" type="text/css">

  </head>

  <body class="cssBody">

    <table border="0" cellpadding="6" cellspacing="0" width="600"
      align="center" class="cssInstructionsTable">
      <tr><td colspan="2">
        <div class="cssCheckoutText">
          This is where checkout would occur in a full-blown shopping cart.
          Well, assuming the cart wasn't empty of course.  In real life,
          checking out would require a server, and we don't have one here, so
          this "fake" response constitutes an obligation on your part to
          purchase whatever you've put in your cart... now go to the store and
          hand the nice man or woman at the counter your money... better yet,
          just send it to me (just kidding! ... unless you were writing out the
          check already, because I naturally wouldn't want you to waste one!)
        </div>
      </td></tr>
      <tr>
        <td>
          <a href="mockServer.htm?function=viewCart">View Cart</a>
        </td>
        <td align="right">
          <a href="mockServer.htm?function=viewCatalog">Back To The Catalog</a>
        </td>
      </tr>
    </table>

  </body>

</html>
```

It is quite literally nothing but straight HTML. At the bottom, you see two links that reference the mock server: one to return to the view cart page and one to return to the catalog view page. Aside from those links, there's nothing special about this page.

Only one part of the application remains to explore, but it is a key piece: our mock server. Don't change the channel now!

Writing mockServer.htm

After our long journey, we finally arrive at the final piece of the puzzle: our mock server, contained in mockServer.htm. As mentioned earlier, the idea of a mock server is to have a simple HTML page that all your application's requests target, and have this page pretend to be a server. You saw a simple example of how to accomplish this, and in reality, the full-blown mockServer.htm doesn't do a whole lot more.

After some initial JavaScript imports, we hit upon the key to making it all work, which is the process() function:

```
function process() {

  var func = jscript.page.getParameter("function");
  if (func) {
    func = "process" + func.substr(0, 1).toUpperCase() + func.substr(1);
    if (eval("window." + func)) {
      eval(func + "();");
    } else {
      alert("Unimplemented function received")
    }
  }

} // End process().
```

This function is called onLoad of the page. It is what drives everything, and you can view this as you would the component on the server that decides which operation to perform (a FrontServlet in Java parlance, for instance, or a switching ASP page in the Microsoft world). It grabs the function request parameter and switches on it, calling the appropriate function to service the function that was requested by the call. It just takes in the name of the function via the "function" request parameter, and then forms the function name to call by prepending the string "process" to the function, with the first letter of the function converted to uppercase. So, for the function viewDescription, for instance, we would wind up with processViewDescription, which as you're about to see, is one of the functions present on this page. Once we have the name of the function, we check to see if it exists as a child of the window object, and if so, we use the eval() function to execute it. If an unknown function is received, we just pop up an alert saying so. It's not the most robust mechanism imaginable to be sure, but sufficient for our purposes.

The functions that process() calls serve to process a particular service request, beginning with processViewDescription(). This is called when the Description link is clicked when in non-JavaScript mode. It does a simple redirect to the appropriate page in /descs:

```
    function processViewDescription() {

      var itemID = jscript.page.getParameter("itemID");
      window.location = "descs/id" + itemID + ".htm";

    } // End processViewDescription().
```

In this case, the called function would have passed an itemID parameter as well, which
jscript.page.getParameter() pleasantly gets for us with no fuss. Since the pages in /descs are
named idX.htm, where X is the itemID, it's a simple matter to construct the appropriate URL
and redirect to it via setting window.location.

Next up is processPurchase(), which is only marginally more complex and is what is
called when the user clicks the Add To Cart button on the item description page when in
non-JavaScript mode:

```
    function processPurchase() {

      // Add new item.
      var newItemID = jscript.page.getParameter("itemID");
      var newItemQuantity = jscript.page.getParameter("quantity");
      var itemToAdd = new CartItem();
      itemToAdd.setItemID(newItemID);
      itemToAdd.setQuantity(parseInt(newItemQuantity));
      cart.addItem(itemToAdd);

      window.location = "viewCart.htm";

    } // End processPurchase().
```

Once again, we get the itemID parameter, and also the quantity parameter in this case. We
then instantiate a new CartItem object and set the itemID and quantity on it. Then it's a simple
matter of calling cart.addItem() and passing it the CartItem. That takes care of rewriting the cookie
as well. Then we redirect back to viewCart.htm so the added item will be reflected to the user.

processUpdateQuanitity() is found next, and it is used when the user updates the quantity
of an item from the view cart page while in non-JavaScript mode:

```
    function processUpdateQuantity() {

      var itemIndex = jscript.page.getParameter("itemIndex");
      var newQuantity = jscript.page.getParameter("quantity");
      if (newQuantity == 0) {
        processDelete();
      } else if (newQuantity > 0) {
        cart.updateQuantity(itemIndex, newQuantity);
      }

      window.location = "viewCart.htm";

    } // End processUpdateQuantity().
```

It begins similarly to processPurchaseItem(), but then gets a little different. First, it checks if the user entered zero for the quantity. If so, processDelete() is called to remove the item from the cart. If the value is greater than zero though, all we need to do is call the updateQuantity() method of the cart object, passing it the index of the item in the cartItems array (which is one of the hidden form fields rendered in the viewPage.htm file) and the new quantity requested, and we're all set. Note that if the user enters a nonnumeric value, the quantity will not be updated, but no error will occur either. Entering something like 12A is a little more interesting: it will register as 12, which is better than an error!

Speaking of processDelete():

```
function processDelete() {

  var itemIndex = jscript.page.getParameter("itemIndex");
  cart.deleteItem(itemIndex);

  window.location = "viewCart.htm";

} // End processDelete().
```

All we need here is the itemIndex parameter, and we hand that off to cart.deleteItem(), and thy will be done! A quick redirect to viewCart.htm, and we're finished.

Only three functions remain, and they are basically the same, so I will discuss them as one here. These three functions—processViewCart(), processViewCatalog(), and processCheckout()—are nothing but simple redirects to HTML pages, like so:

```
function processViewCart() {

  window.location = "viewCart.htm";

} // End processViewCart().
```

The reason these exit, rather than simply directing to the final HTML pages, is that again, this is all meant to emulate a server. If we wanted to view the contents of the cart, we may be able to jump directly to some page—JSP, ASP, PHP, and so on. But many times, we need to hit some server component first, because JSP, ASP, and PHP are view components, and there is typically more to a modern web application. For example, the application will have Control and Model layers if it uses the Model-View-Controller architecture.[5] So, if we're going to play the part of the server, we need to do it fully. That means that, even though its just a simple redirect, the server would be doing more, such as rendering the contents of the page in the case of viewCart.htm.

Whew, that's it. We've finished! I hope you've enjoyed the ride. I think the whole mock server technique is something really valuable that can save you a lot of time and headaches

---

5. The Model-View-Controller (MVC) architecture is a way to implement an application where there is a separation, or decoupling, of the components that render the view a user sees (the View layer) and the data it uses (the Model layer), and also the business logic that operates on it (typically, part of the Model as well). This is accomplished by the view never directly interacting with the model, instead going through an intermediary (Control) layer. The goal is to allow changing any of these components without necessarily affecting the others.

during development. I hope you've also enjoyed seeing just a little of MochiKit and how truly easy it can make things.

And by the way, you have a useful little shopping cart to boot! Implement the final checkout stage, and you should be good to go.

Suggested Exercises

The application presented in this chapter isn't likely to be the subject of anyone's doctoral thesis any time soon, since it's just not all that complex, but it does most of the things a shopping cart should. That being said, here are a few improvements you could make to gain some more experience:

Round those corners: MochiKit offers an effect that rounds the corners of elements, and it would be great to apply this to all the square boxes (the white areas) on all the pages. I purposely left this for you as a suggestion, so you would need to delve into the MochiKit docs a bit. I will tell you that it isn't quite as easy as it seems and may require further changes to the application to implement. (Hint: does that effect work on tables, I wonder?).

Implement the server side: Yes, this book is focused on the client side, and yes, this particular application goes out of its way to avoid the server part of the equation. But it couldn't hurt to set up the server side in your technology of choice.

Add some effects: This is again a good way to get more familiar with MochiKit. How about the item you drop on the cart shrinking into it? How about when you delete an item from your cart, it first fades out of view and collapses the table before submitting to the server?

I'm sure you can think of plenty more, but those should give you a good start. Have fun!

Summary

In this chapter, you got your first taste of MochiKit, a very nice little JavaScript library. You saw how its drag-and-drop support is very powerful but yet still very simple to use and allows you to have very little code that does quite a bit. You also saw how to create a mock server that allows you to do all your development strictly in the browser while not having to change your methodology or code from what you would do with a server in the mix. Finally, you also saw how you can take a fairly mundane application like a shopping cart and spiff it up just a bit for those who want the next-generation web experience.

CHAPTER 11

Time for a Break:
A JavaScript Game

In the first book I ever had published (*Practical Ajax Projects with Java Technology*, Apress, 2006), the final project—the apex of the book—was an adventure game named Ajax Warrior. It may well be the start of a trend, where every book I write includes a game, because that's precisely what we're going to build in this chapter! No, it won't be Ajax Warrior again. It will be a more arcade-style game, since there is no network latency to bother us.

You'll see many neat tricks here, a lot of JavaScript and DOM scripting, and even some basic game theory along the way. At the end, you'll have something that you can use to slack off at work any time you wish, or anywhere else you have a browser, for that matter! We all know the saying . . . all work and no play makes Homer . . . something . . . something,[1] so let's stop the axe from falling, shall we?

K&G Arcade Requirements and Goals

The game we'll build is a port of a PocketPC game that I wrote entitled K&G Arcade. The K&G stands for Krelmac and Gentoo, who are two wisecracking aliens bent on the destruction of the Earth. Unfortunately, they are like idiot teenagers, who just happen to have quantum destructo beams!

In K&G Arcade, which you can see at http://www.omnytex.com/kgarcade, you play the part of Henry, a mild-mannered farmer from jolly-old seventeenth-century England. Krelmac and Gentoo abduct you one night, and force you to try to escape their spaceship, which consists of five maze-like levels inhabited by teleporting robots that kill on contact. On each of those five levels, you find five mini-games each, which you need to play and beat (by achieving a given score in 60 seconds) in order to escape. You also meet up with other abductees, who you talk to and try to gain their trust so that they will give you clues about certain mini-games that are impossible to beat without a particular trick.

The full-blown version of K&G Arcade features cinematic cut scenes with Krelmac and Gentoo cracking wise and generally making pests of themselves. It includes an all-original soundtrack and hand-drawn cartoon graphics. K&G Arcade is actually the second game featuring

---

1. If you are a Simpsons fan, you almost certainly know the reference and are laughing right now. If you aren't, it's a line from the episode "Treehouse of Horror V" in the segment entitled "The Shinning," a parody of *The Shining*. I suggest grabbing a copy—it's a riot!

these characters, the first being Invasion: Trivia! (`http://www.omnytex.com/products_invasion_info.shtml`). Going to that site will also lead you to a Flash cartoon introducing these characters.

Now, our goal isn't to port the entire full-blown K&G Arcade to JavaScript. Indeed, that would be considerably more difficult, if possible at all, and would take up a book this size on its own! Instead, we'll scale it back quite a bit and implement just the mini-game portion. In fact, we'll build only 3 of the 25 mini-games. Let's get into some details:

- We'll implement three mini-games—Cosmic Squirrel, which is similar conceptually to the classic Frogger; Deathtrap, which is inspired by the Indiana Jones movies; and Refluxive, which is similar to Arkanoid, Breakout, and games in that mold (but without actually breaking anything, as you'll see!).

- We'll implement a mini-game selection screen that includes a screenshot of the mini-game.

- We should reuse existing code wherever possible. However, we will *not* be using any libraries for this game. That's because in writing games, you frequently want to be "as close to the metal" as possible, and that's the case here as well.

- Each mini-game should be its own class, and should inherit common code from a base class.

- Extensibility should be a priority so that more mini-games can be added later with little difficulty.

- In general, we want to keep global scope as clean as possible, and use good object-oriented design techniques throughout.

When doing game programming, you often try to get as low-level as you can—as close to the hardware as you can. The reason for this is simple: performance. In a game, a lot has to happen in very short time periods, so there can't be a lot of superfluous code executing or extra work being done. One of the best ways to ensure this is to not entrust things to libraries. Now, this isn't an absolute. It is often true that you can get better performance with a well-written library than without. It's also true that in the modern era, you typically don't get as low-level as you used to in general, with or without a library. In the past, it wasn't unusual to write important portions of a game in assembly language so that it could be as optimized and tight as possible. These days, that isn't as prevalent (it's still done, but not as often). So, in this particular application, we won't be using any libraries. We'll be doing all "naked" JavaScript.

Programming a game in JavaScript isn't fundamentally different from programming a game in any other environment. Some of the details are different, of course, but the overall concept is roughly the same. Rather than espouse those concepts here in one place, I'll talk about them as we progress through the code.

And with that statement, let's begin our exploration of K&G Arcade by taking a look at the game itself.

A Preview of the K&G Arcade

Figure 11-1 shows the game title screen, which is what you see when you first load K&G Arcade into your browser. The original K&G Arcade was a joint production of Omnytex Technologies, which is my own little PocketPC software company, and Crackhead Creations (http://www.planetvolpe.com/crackhead), which is the company of Anthony Volpe, the artist responsible for the illustrations in this book,[2] hence the logos on this screen. Anthony is also the artist who did the graphics for K&G Arcade, as well as Invasion: Trivia!.

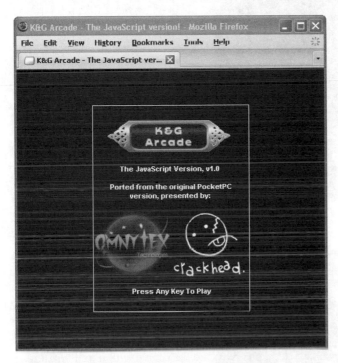

Figure 11-1. *K&G Arcade title screen*

The game selection screen, shown in Figure 11-2 is what you see after the title screen. It is where you can select a mini-game to play. It also presents a few instructions, as well as a preview of the mini-game and a brief description of it.

Cosmic Squirrel, shown in Figure 11-3, is one of the mini-games available in K&G Arcade. This game is inspired by the classic Frogger, but with a twist: you play the part of a giant space squirrel trying to get an intergalactic acorn (not that I know what an "intergalactic acorn" actually is!). The player needs to avoid aliens, asteroids, spaceships, and comets to get the acorn.

---

2. If you would like to see some more of Anthony Volpe's work, and some other things I have done with him with Krelmac and Gentoo, as well as some other characters, have a look at the Downtown Uptown site: http://www.planetvolpe.com/du. There, you'll find some more adventures of Krelmac and Gentoo in the form of a Flash cartoon and some comics, as well as a host of other characters from this universe. Don't let the strangeness of it all scare you away! Embrace the weirdness!

Figure 11-2. *Game selection screen*

Figure 11-3. *Cosmic Squirrel*

Figure 11-4 shows the mini-game Deathtrap, which is inspired by Indiana Jones movies. Your goal is to get to the door on the top of the screen by hopping from tile to tile. The problem is that some of the tiles are electrified, and you will get zapped if you pick the wrong one.

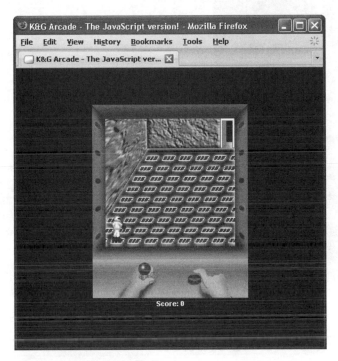

Figure 11-4. *Deathtrap*

Finally, in Figure 11-5, you see the third mini-game, Refluxive. This is similar in concept to Arkanoid or Breakout, but without the element of actually breaking through anything! Actually, come to think of it, this game is much more like the movie *Speed*. Remember that Sandra Bullock and Keanu Reeves mess, where they couldn't let the bus go below a certain speed lest it be blown to kingdom come? Well, this is similar. Someone told you to keep these bouncy things going, and you do it—no questions asked!

Now that you're familiar with what the game looks like, let's get into seeing what makes it tick. Buckle up, because it's going to be quite a ride!

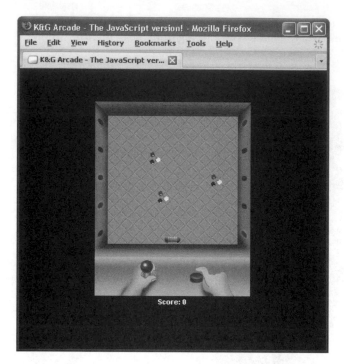

Figure 11-5. *Refluxive*

Dissecting the K&G Arcade Solution

As usual, we begin our exploration of this project by looking at its directory structure, shown in Figure 11-6.

Beginning with the root directory, we find the index.htm file, which is the page loaded to start the application. It contains the basic markup for the screen that the player sees, as well as all the JavaScript imports required.

The img directory contains images not specific to any one mini-game, such as the graphics for the title screen, game selection screen, and game console.

The js directory contains all our JavaScript source files, 11 of them in all. Two of them— jscript.math.js and jscript.dom.js—are packages we created in Chapter 3. Four of them— MiniGame.js, Title.js, GameSelection.js, and GameState.js—define classes that will be used. The remaining five—main.js, keyHandlers.js, globals.js, gameFuncs.js, and consoleFuncs.js—contain the code that makes use of those classes.

Each of our mini-games is stored in its own subdirectory, which has the same name as the mini-game itself. Within each of those subdirectories is a single .js file, such as CosmicSquirrel.js, with the code for that particular mini-game. Each of those subdirectories also contains an img subdirectory, which houses the images specific to that mini-game.

Now, let's get to looking at that code, shall we?

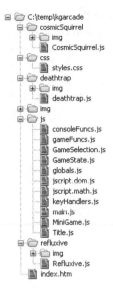

Figure 11-6. *K&G Arcade directory structure*

Writing index.htm

index.htm is the first page loaded when we access the game, and it defines the overall layout of things. It also "imports" all the other resources we need throughout the game. Let's begin by looking at the <head> of the page:

```
<head>

    <title>K&G Arcade - The JavaScript version!</title>

    <link rel="StyleSheet" href="css/styles.css" type="text/css">

    <script src="js/jscript.dom.js"></script>
    <script src="js/jscript.math.js"></script>
    <script src="js/gameFuncs.js"></script>
    <script src="js/consoleFuncs.js"></script>
    <script src="js/keyHandlers.js"></script>
    <script src="js/globals.js"></script>
    <script src="js/GameState.js"></script>
    <script src="js/MiniGame.js"></script>
    <script src="js/Title.js"></script>
    <script src="js/GameSelection.js"></script>
    <script src="js/main.js"></script>
    <script src="cosmicSquirrel/CosmicSquirrel.js"></script>
    <script src="deathtrap/deathtrap.js"></script>
    <script src="refluxive/refluxive.js"></script>

</head>
```

You see that first our style sheet (we'll look at that next) is linked in. After that comes a whole batch of JavaScript references. Since the process of dissecting this application will lead us to explore each of these in turn, it would be a bit redundant to state what each is at this juncture. Suffice it to say they are required to make everything work.

The body of the document then begins, and onLoad we see a call to a JavaScript function named init(). This will initialize the application and get everything set up for us to play. This function can be found in main.js, so we'll get to that shortly.

After the opening <body> tag is the following section of markup:

```
<!-- The div the title screen is contained in. -->
<div id="divTitle" class="cssTitle">
  <table border="0" cellpadding="0" cellspacing="0" width="98%"
    height="100%" align="center">
    <tr>
      <td align="center" valign="middle">
        <img src="img/title.gif">
        <br/><br/>
        The JavaScript Version, v1.0
        <br/><br/>
        Ported from the original PocketPC version, presented by:
        <br/><br/>
        <img src="img/logoOmnytex.gif"><img src="img/logoCrackhead.gif">
        <br/><br/>
        Press Any Key To Play
      </td>
    </tr>
  </table>
</div>
```

This is pretty much straightforward HTML markup, which renders the title screen shown earlier in Figure 11-1. The divTitle <div> will be hidden once the user presses a key to move on to the game selection screen, which brings us to the block of markup that comes next:

```
<!-- The div the game selection screen is contained in. -->
<div id="divGameSelection" class="cssTitleGameSelection">
  <table border="0" cellpadding="0" cellspacing="0" width="98%"
    height="100%" align="center">
    <tr>
      <td align="center" valign="middle">
        Press the LEFT and RIGHT arrow keys to cycle through the
        available games, then press SPACE to play the one you want.
        Once playing a game, press the ENTER key to return here.
        <br/><br/><br/>
        <img src="img/ssCosmicSquirrel.gif" id="ssCosmicSquirrel"
          style="display:none;">
        <img src="img/ssDeathtrap.gif" id="ssDeathtrap"
          style="display:none;">
        <img src="img/ssRefluxive.gif" id="ssRefluxive"
```

```
              style="display:none;">
         <br/>
         <div id="mgsDesc"></div>
         <br/><br/>
         To check out the full PocketPC version of K&G Arcade,
         visit the <a href="http://www.omnytex.com">Omnytex Technologies</a>
         web site.
       </td>
     </tr>
   </table>
</div>
```

Once again, this is simple, almost boring HTML. Note the screenshot images in the middle, which are initially hidden. When the user is cycling through the screenshots to pick a game, these images will be made visible with each arrow keypress. The mgsDesc <div> is where the description of the game will be shown.

When the init() function I mentioned earlier fires, one of the things it does is to center both the divTitle <div> and the divGameSelection <div>. It also centers the <div> that contains the actual mini-games, which is named divMiniGame, and can be seen here:

```
<!-- The div the game is contained in. -->
<div id="divMiniGame" class="cssMiniGame">

  <div id="divGameArea" class="cssGameArea">
  </div>

  <div id="divStatusArea" class="cssStatusArea">
    Score: 0
  </div>

  <!-- Game frame -->
  <img src="img/gameFrame.gif" id="imgGameFrame"
    class="cssConsoleImage">

  <!-- Console left, middle and right -->
  <img src="img/consoleLeft.gif" id="imgConsoleLeft"
    class="cssConsoleImage">
  <img src="img/consoleMiddle.gif" id="imgConsoleMiddle"
    class="cssConsoleImage">
  <img src="img/consoleRight.gif" id="imgConsoleRight"
    class="cssConsoleImage">

  <!-- Left hand images -->
  <img src="img/leftHandNormal.gif" id="imgLeftHandNormal"
    class="cssConsoleImage">
  <img src="img/leftHandUp.gif" id="imgLeftHandUp"
    class="cssConsoleImage">
```

```
    <img src="img/leftHandDown.gif" id="imgLeftHandDown"
      class="cssConsoleImage">
    <img src="img/leftHandLeft.gif" id="imgLeftHandLeft"
      class="cssConsoleImage">
    <img src="img/leftHandRight.gif" id="imgLeftHandRight"
      class="cssConsoleImage">
    <img src="img/leftHandDL.gif" id="imgLeftHandDL"
      class="cssConsoleImage">
    <img src="img/leftHandDR.gif" id="imgLeftHandDR"
      class="cssConsoleImage">
    <img src="img/leftHandUL.gif" id="imgLeftHandUL"
      class="cssConsoleImage">
    <img src="img/leftHandUR.gif" id="imgLeftHandUR"
      class="cssConsoleImage">

    <!-- Right hand images -->
    <img src="img/rightHandUp.gif" id="imgRightHandUp"
      class="cssConsoleImage">
    <img src="img/rightHandDown.gif" id="imgRightHandDown"
      class="cssConsoleImage">

    <!-- Console light images -->
    <img src="img/gameFrameLeftLight1.gif" id="imgGameFrameLeftLight1"
      class="cssConsoleImage">
    <img src="img/gameFrameLeftLight2.gif" id="imgGameFrameLeftLight2"
      class="cssConsoleImage">
    <img src="img/gameFrameLeftLight3.gif" id="imgGameFrameLeftLight3"
      class="cssConsoleImage">
    <img src="img/gameFrameLeftLight4.gif" id="imgGameFrameLeftLight4"
      class="cssConsoleImage">
    <img src="img/gameFrameLeftLight5.gif" id="imgGameFrameLeftLight5"
      class="cssConsoleImage">
    <img src="img/gameFrameRightLight1.gif" id="imgGameFrameRightLight1"
      class="cssConsoleImage">
    <img src="img/gameFrameRightLight2.gif" id="imgGameFrameRightLight2"
      class="cssConsoleImage">
    <img src="img/gameFrameRightLight3.gif" id="imgGameFrameRightLight3"
      class="cssConsoleImage">
    <img src="img/gameFrameRightLight4.gif" id="imgGameFrameRightLight4"
      class="cssConsoleImage">
    <img src="img/gameFrameRightLight5.gif" id="imgGameFrameRightLight5"
      class="cssConsoleImage">

  </div>
```

Perhaps the most important element here is `divGameArea`. This is the screen portion of the game console where the mini-games take place. A bit of explanation may help here.

All of these images are the ones that make up the game console—the joystick, frame around the mini-game, lights, and so on. These images do not change from mini-game to mini-game, and that's why they are static here. When the player moves while playing a mini-game, the left hand on the joystick moves accordingly. When the user clicks the action button, the right hand presses the button, too. Every half second, the lights on the frame randomly change. All this animation is accomplished by hiding the images that change, and then showing the appropriate new image.

For instance, let's talk about the action button. When we start, the image of the button not being pushed—the one with the ID `imgRightHandUp`—is showing, and the image of the button being pushed—the one with the ID `imgRightHandDown`—is not. When the user clicks the button, `imgRightHandUp` is first hidden, and then `imgRightHandDown` is shown. This is a simple case, but it is how *all* the mini-games work as well, as you will see.

Writing styles.css

All of the markup in `index.htm` wouldn't amount to a hill of beans without the style sheet in `styles.css` to back it up, so let's get familiar with that. The complete file is shown in Listing 11-1.

Listing 11-1. *The styles.css File—The Main Style Sheet for the Game*

```
/* Generic style applied to all elements. */
* {
  color             : #ffffff;
  font-family       : arial;
  font-size         : 8pt;
  font-weight       : bold;
}


/* Entire page (body element). */
.cssPage {
  background-color : #000000;
}


/* Style for div the title screen and game selection screens are */
/* contained in. */
.cssTitleGameSelection {
  border            : 1px solid #ffffff;
  position          : absolute;
  width             : 240px;
  height            : 320px;
}
```

```css
/* Style for div the mini-games are contained in. */
.cssMiniGame {
  border              : 1px solid #000000;
  position            : absolute;
  width               : 240px;
  height              : 320px;
}


/* Style for the area where a mini-game takes place. */
.cssGameArea {
  position            : absolute;
  left                : 20px;
  top                 : 20px;
  width               : 200px;
  height              : 200px;
  overflow            : hidden;
}

/* Style for the status area below the game console. */
.cssStatusArea {
  position            : absolute;
  left                : 0px;
  top                 : 302px;
  width               : 240px;
  height              : 20px;
  text-align          : center;
}


/* Style applied to all game console images. */
.cssConsoleImage {
  position            : absolute;
  display             : none;
}
```

There isn't really much to this style sheet when you get right down to it. First, you see that generic "cover everything" selector that you've encountered in the previous projects. It deals with just font styles, but it's nice to cover everything in one clean move.

After that is cssPage, whose only purpose in life is to give the page a black background.

The next style, cssTitleGameSelection, is applied to the title screen div (divTitle) and the game selection screen div (divGameSelection). While the name of the selector is perhaps a little long, it pretty clearly describes what it's for, no? It ensures that these <div> elements can be centered by virtue of the position attribute being set to absolute. It also draws a border around the <div> elements. Lastly, it sets the size. Note that the size 240-by-320 pixels is not arbitrary;

this is Quarter VGA (QVGA) resolution, which was, at the time the full-blown version of K&G Arcade was written, the default resolution of most PocketPC devices. Since all the graphics were scaled for that resolution, that's the resolution used in the JavaScript version here as well.

The cssMiniGame style is applied to the divMiniGame <div> element. Notice it is identical to the cssTitleGameSelection style, except for the border color. Setting the border color to black means it will be invisible on the black page background, so, in effect, the game console won't have the white border, but everything will take up the same amount of space, thereby avoiding the game console seeming to move, or jump, relative to the game selection screen.

The cssGameArea style is probably the most important. One of the things the mini-games need to be able to do, as can be seen in the Cosmic Squirrel mini-game, is *clip*. In other words, when an object moves to the edges, it should appear to move off screen, not overlap the frame or anything. To accomplish this, we set the overflow attribute to hidden. This means that any content that is positioned out of the bounds of the <div> will be hidden, or clipped, precisely as we want. As you can see, the actual game area is 200-by-200 pixels, and is positioned 20 pixels from the left and top, placing it inside the frame, as expected, completing the illusion of clipping when objects move out of its bounds.

After that is the cssStatusArea style. I'm sure you can guess this is applied to the divStatusArea <div> element, which is where you see the score below the game console. All text is horizontally centered within this <div> by setting the text align attribute to center.

Lastly, you see the cssConsoleImage style, which is applied to all of the images that make up the game console. Its main purpose is again to ensure that the image it is applied to can be positioned absolutely and that it initially is hidden. The point about absolute positioning will become clear when we look at the blit() function later on.

Writing GameState.js

You will see the GameState class used quite a bit throughout the code, so it makes sense to look at it first. Its purpose is . . . wait for it . . . to store information about the current state of the game. Figure 11-7 shows the UML diagram of this class.

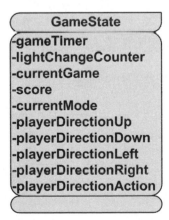

Figure 11-7. *UML diagram of the GameState class*

The GameState class includes the following fields:

- gameTimer: A reference to the JavaScript timer used as the "heartbeat" of the game.

- lightChangeCounter: Used to determine when it's time to update the lights on the game console frame.

- currentGame: A reference to the current mini-game object (as well as the title screen and game selection screens, which are essentially mini-games as far as the rest of the code is concerned).

- score: This field's purpose is abundantly obvious, I think!

- currentMode: Determines if a mini-game is in play.

- playerDirection*XXX*: Five fields—playerDirectionUp, playerDirectionDown, playerDirectionLeft, playerDirectionRight, and playerAction—used to determine in which direction the player is currently moving, and if the action button is clicked.

Listing 11-2 shows this class in its entirety.

Listing 11-2. *The GameState Class*

```
function GameState() {

  // The main timer, 24 frames a second.
  this.gameTimer = null;

  // Count of how many frames have elapsed since the lights last changed.
  this.lightChangeCounter = null;

  // This is essentially a pointer to the current game.  Note that the term
  // "game" is a little loose here because the title screen and the game
  // selection screen are also "games" as far as the code is concerned.
  this.currentGame = new Title();
  this.score = 0;

  // Mode the game is currently in: "title", "gameSelection" or "miniGame".
  this.currentMode = null;

  // Flag variables for player movement.
  this.playerDirectionUp = false;
  this.playerDirectionDown = false;
  this.playerDirectionRight = false;
  this.playerDirectionLeft = false;
  this.playerAction = false;

} // End GameState class.
```

Writing globals.js

In keeping with the theme throughout this book of not polluting the global namespace, you'll see just a small handful of values in the globals.js file, shown in Listing 11-3.

Listing 11-3. *Not a Whole Lot of Globals in This Application, But They Count!*

```
// Counter, reset to 0 to start each frame, used to set the z-index of
// each element blit()'d to the screen.
var frameZIndexCounter = 0;

// Key code constants.
var KEY_UP = 38;
var KEY_DOWN = 40;
var KEY_LEFT = 37;
var KEY_RIGHT = 39;
var KEY_SPACE = 32;
var KEY_ENTER = 13;

// Structure that stores all game state-related variables.
var gameState = null;

// This is an associative collection of all the images in the game.
// This saves us from having to go to the DOM every time to update one.
var consoleImages = new Object();
```

The frameZIndexCounter variable is used to ensure proper z-ordering when images are blit()'d, which will be discussed in the next section. Next you see a batch of pseudo-constants (remember that there are no real constants in JavaScript), which define various keys that can be pressed. We also find the gameState variable, which will be the reference to the one and only GameState object used throughout the code. Lastly, the consoleImages array will store references to the images making up the game console, which also will be discussed shortly.

Writing main.js

main.js is essentially the heart and soul of K&G Arcade. You will find that it makes use of functions found in the other JavaScript files, so you'll read "we'll get to this soon" fairly often. Rest assured, I'm not lying—we *will* get to those things soon! But understanding the basic core is what looking at main.js is all about, so let's get to it.

The init() Function

As you will recall from looking at index.htm, when the page loads, in response to the onLoad event, the init() function is called. Now it's time to see what that function is all about:

```javascript
function init() {

  gameState = new GameState();

  // Get references to all existing images.  This is mainly for the console
  // images so that we don't have to go against the DOM to manipulate them.
  var imgs = document.getElementsByTagName("img");
  for (var i = 0; i < imgs.length; i++){
    consoleImages[imgs[i].id] = imgs[i];
  }

  // Center the three main layers.
  jscript.dom.layerCenterH(document.getElementById("divTitle"));
  jscript.dom.layerCenterV(document.getElementById("divTitle"));
  jscript.dom.layerCenterH(document.getElementById("divGameSelection"));
  jscript.dom.layerCenterV(document.getElementById("divGameSelection"));
  jscript.dom.layerCenterH(document.getElementById("divMiniGame"));
  jscript.dom.layerCenterV(document.getElementById("divMiniGame"));

  // Now hide what we don't need.
  document.getElementById("divGameSelection").style.display = "none";
  document.getElementById("divMiniGame").style.display = "none";

  // Hook event handlers.
  document.onkeydown = keyDownHandler;
  if (document.layers) {
    document.captureEvents(Event.KEYDOWN);
  }
  document.onkeyup = keyUpHandler;
  if (document.layers) {
    document.captureEvents(Event.KEYUP);
  }

  gameState.currentGame.init();

  gameState.gameTimer = setTimeout("mainGameLoop()", 42);

} // End init().
```

First you see a new GameState object being instantiated. Next is a hook that, as the comments state, gets a reference to all the <img> tags, those present in index.htm. We store a reference to each in the consoleImages arrays. This is because, when you do game programming, it is especially important (most of the time) to write code that is as efficient as possible.

KEEPING UP THE FRAMES-PER-SECOND (FPS) RATE

As you will see, a game usually (and certainly here) consists of a continuous loop. This loop calls on some code to update the display some number of times per second. Each of these redraws is called a frame, as in frame of animation. As I'm sure you know, there are 1000 milliseconds in one second. Game loops are usually measured in frames per second (fps); that is, how many times per second the display is updated. For smooth animation and game play, you want the frames per second to be as high as possible. Generally, you want it to be no lower than around 24 fps, which is the approximate speed at which the human eye cannot easily discern each frame. In other words, if you update the display ten times a second, your eye can rather easily track each frame, and the animation will appear slow and choppy. At 24 fps and higher, your eye is fooled into thinking there is continuous motion, which makes things look considerably smoother. The higher the better, but 24 fps is kind of the magic number.

So, let's do some simple math. If there are 1000 milliseconds in a second, and realizing that each frame will take some amount of time to process and draw, we can determine how many milliseconds each frame can take for a target frames per second. For 24 fps, we divide 1000 by 24, and we discover that each frame can take no more than about 42 milliseconds to fully process. If a frame takes longer to deal with, then our frames per second drop, and our game gets choppy and not visually pleasing. So, it becomes of paramount importance to not exceed 42 milliseconds, and that's why we have to think about optimization.

One of the killers, not just in game programming but in any browser-based DOM scripting, is accessing elements in the DOM. It takes time to traverse the DOM tree, find the element requested, and return a reference to it. If you do this too many times per frame in a game application, you'll quickly drop your frames-per-second rate. One of the best ways to optimize here is simply to get references to any images (or other elements) that you will need to access that you can up front and store those references. Getting an element in an array that happens to be a reference to a DOM element is considerably faster than getting the DOM element directly. A simple test can prove this:

```
<html>

  <head>

    <title>DOM/Array Access Test</title>

    <script>

      function testit() {

        // Time 1000 direct DOM accesses
        var timeStart = new Date();
        for (var i = 0; i < 5000; i++) {
          var elem = document.getElementById("myDiv");
          elem.innerHTML = i;
        }
        var directDOMTime = new Date() - timeStart;
```

```
    // Time 1000 accesses via array lookup
    var a = new Array();
    a[0] = document.getElementById("myDiv");
    timeStart = new Date();
    for (var i = 0; i < 5000; i++) {
      var elem = a[0];
      elem.innerHTML = i;
    }
    var arrayTime = new Date() - timeStart;

    // Display results
    document.getElementById("myDiv").innerHTML =
      "Time for direct DOM access: " + directDOMTime + "<br>" +
      "Time for array access: " + arrayTime;

  }

</script>

</head>

<body>

  <input type="button" onClick="testit();" value="Test">
  <br/>
  <div id="myDiv"></div>

</body>

</html>
```

Running this test, you'll find that the array access method is always faster than the direct DOM access, although I was surprised to find the difference isn't as drastic as I had expected. Still, it was generally in the 200 to 300 millisecond range each time I ran it, which is a pretty significant amount for game programming, as the math we went through earlier indicates.

Moving right along in our review of init(), we find six lines used to center the three main <div> elements: divTitle, divGameSelection, and divMiniGame, corresponding to the title screen, game selection screen, and the actual mini-games. To do this, we use the jscript.dom.layerCenterH() and jscript.dom.layerCenterV() functions that we built in Chapter 3. See, that code comes in handy, doesn't it? Immediately after they are centered, the game selection <div> and the mini-game <div> are hidden. This may seem a little bizarre. Why not just set display:none in the style applied to those <div> elements? The answer is that the centering will not work properly if the elements are hidden, because certain values those functions need are not set by the browser if the element is hidden.

Next are four lines of code that hook the keyDown and keyUp events so that our custom handlers will fire. Note the need to have two statements per event handler because of the difference in the event handling model of IE vs. Mozilla-based browsers. Just setting document. keydown and document.keyup is sufficient in IE. But in Firefox and its ilk, this requires the additional captureEvents() call. By checking if document.layers is defined, which it would be only in a non-IE browser, we can call captureEvents() only on browsers where it is applicable. As mentioned in previous chapters, using object-existence checks to conditionally execute code based on browser type is preferable to browser-sniffing code.

Finally, we have a call to gameState.currentGame.init(). This asks whatever the current mini-game is to initialize itself. Interestingly, the title screen and game selection screens are treated just like mini-games, even though they really aren't. The very last thing done in init() is to set a timeout to fire 42 milliseconds later (again, corresponding to our desired 24 fps) and set to call the mainGameLoop() function when it does. And with that statement, let's pause a moment to discuss the overall structure of K&G Arcade.

The Main Game Loop Flow

Figure 11-8 shows a flow diagram that depicts how it all works in terms of the main game flow, and also keyUp and keyDown event handling.

As you can see, the timeout set in init() fires 42 milliseconds later, calling mainGameLoop(). mainGameLoop() then updates the lights on the game console frame, as well as the hands, *if* a mini-game is in progress. Then it calls processFrame() on the object pointed to by gameState.currentGame. Once the mini-game's processFrame() function returns, the timeout is set again and this entire process repeats itself.

All of the mini-games, as well as the title and game selection screens, implement an interface by virtue of "extending" the MiniGame class. A mini-game can override five functions: init(), processFrame(), keyDownHandler(), keyUpHandler(), and destroy(). These represent the life cycle of a mini-game. In addition, three fields are present: gameName, gameImages, and fullKeyControl.

The init() function is called when the user decides to play that mini-game. Its job is to set up the mini-game, which primarily involves loading graphics, but can be other tasks as well.

The processFrame() function is called once per frame for the game to do its work. It is responsible for handling any game logic, as well as updating the screen.

keyDownHandler() and keyUpHandler() are called to deal with keypress and key release events.

destroy() is called when the user presses Enter to exit the mini-game. Its main job is to delete the images loaded in init(), but it can do other tasks as well.

The gameName field must match the directory in which the mini-game resources are found (each mini-game is presumed to be in its own directory off the root of the web application). The gameImages is an associative array of images loaded in init(). This serves the same purpose as the consoleImages array we briefly touched on earlier, namely to avoid direct DOM access where possible. Lastly, the fullKeyControl, when set to true, means that the mini-game is in full control of key events and will need to deal with everything.

All of these functions are implemented, but empty, in the base MiniGame class. Therefore, a mini-game needs to override only those it is interested in. Likewise, except for the gameName field, which *must* be set in init(), the fields have default values as well (fullKeyControl defaults to false, and gameImages is an empty array).

Main Game Loop Flow

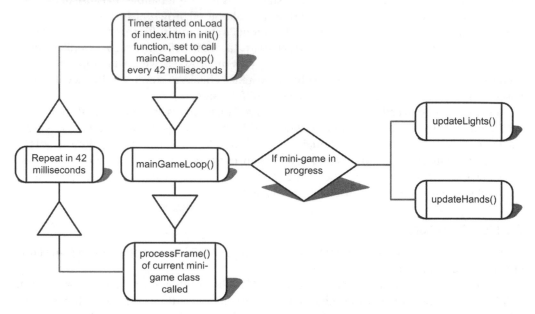

Key Event Handling Flow

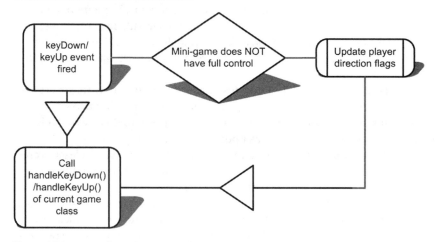

Figure 11-8. *Basic flow diagram of how K&G Arcade works, at a high level*

Starting a Mini-Game

Back in `main.js`, we find the `startMiniGame()` function:

```
function startMiniGame(inName) {

  // Reset generic game-related variables.
  gameState.playerDirectionUp = false;
  gameState.playerDirectionDown = false;
  gameState.playerDirectionRight = false;
  gameState.playerDirectionLeft = false;
  gameState.playerAction = false;
  gameState.score = 0;
  document.getElementById("divStatusArea").innerHTML = "Score: " +
    gameState.score;

  // Instantiate mini-game.
  if (inName == "cosmicSquirrel") {
    gameState.currentGame - new CosmicSquirrel();
    gameState.currentGame.init();
  } else if (inName == "deathtrap") {
    gameState.currentGame = new Deathtrap();
    gameState.currentGame.init();
  } else if (inName == "refluxive") {
    gameState.currentGame = new Refluxive();
    gameState.currentGame.init();
  }

  // Show the game and hide the game selection screen.  Set the mode to indicate
  // mini-game in progress, and draw the console.
  gameState.currentMode = "miniGame";
  drawConsole();
  document.getElementById("divGameSelection").style.display = "none";
  document.getElementById("divMiniGame").style.display - "block";

} // End startMiniGame().
```

startMiniGame() is called when the user presses the spacebar at the game selection screen to start the selected mini-game. It begins by resetting the five fields in gameState that indicate in which direction the player is currently moving, and the one that indicates whether the action button is pressed. It also resets the score to zero and updates it on the screen. Next, based on the mini-game name that was passed in, it instantiates the class for that game and calls init() on it.

Lastly, this function sets the current mode to indicate a mini-game is in progress, draws the console, hides the game selection screen, and shows the mini-game. Remember that the game loop is constantly firing at this point, so the very next iteration will result in the mini-game beginning.

The blit() Function—Putting Stuff on the Screen

The very last function in main.js is the ubiquitous blit() function:

```
function blit(inImage, inX, inY) {

  inImage.style.left = inX + "px";
  inImage.style.top = inY + "px";
  inImage.style.zIndex = frameZIndexCounter;
  inImage.style.display = "block";
  frameZIndexCounter++;

} // End blit().
```

blit() is used to place an image on the screen at some specified coordinates. The first argument to this function is a reference to the image object to place. Setting the left and top style properties of this element places the image where it needs to be. The zIndex property is set, and the frameZIndexCounter variable is reset at the start of every frame and incremented every time an image is placed. This has the effect that each subsequent blit() is on top of anything blit()'d before. This is generally how blit works. When the display property is set to block, the image is actually shown on the screen, and the image is now visible where it was specified to be.

■**Note** The term *blit* is a common one in graphics and game programming. Without getting into too much detail, blit usually refers to drawing an image on the screen. In the case of a browser-based game, you won't be literally drawing an image; instead, you'll be placing one somewhere, as is the case here (the difference being that a blit in the classic sense draws the image pixel by pixel, whereas placing it in this case doesn't).

Writing consoleFuncs.js

consoleFuncs.js contains the code that deals with the game console, including the border with lights around a mini-game, the hands below it, and the status area. It contains a whopping three functions.

The drawConsole() Function

The first function in `consoleFuncs.js` is `drawConsole()`:

```
function drawConsole() {

  // These are the parts of the game console that do not need to be redrawn
  // with each frame.
  blit(consoleImages["imgGameFrame"], 0, 0);
  blit(consoleImages["imgConsoleLeft"], 0, 240);
  blit(consoleImages["imgConsoleMiddle"], 108, 240);
  blit(consoleImages["imgConsoleRight"], 215, 240);

} // End drawConsole().
```

As you can see by the comments, these four images are the ones that never change, unlike the hands and lights, for instance, which do. Therefore, `drawConsole()` doesn't need to be called every frame, as the code for the mini-games does. If you are completely new to game design, talking about drawing something every frame may be a bit foreign to you, but please bear with me! When we look at `main.js`, I'll explain further. For now, we need to keep going through what you'll see are essentially support functions for the main processing code, which is what this file (and some other files) contains. So let's keep chugging along here.

The updateLights() Function

The next function we come to is `updateLights()`, which in a nutshell is responsible for making the lights flash around the game console frame. Here is its code:

```
function updateLights() {

  // Every half a second we are going to light some lights and restore others
  gameState.lightChangeCounter++;

  if (gameState.lightChangeCounter > 12) {

    gameState.lightChangeCounter = 0;

    // Hide the frame and lights so we start fresh.
    consoleImages["imgGameFrame"].style.display = "none";
    consoleImages["imgGameFrameLeftLight1"].style.display = "none";
    consoleImages["imgGameFrameLeftLight2"].style.display = "none";
    consoleImages["imgGameFrameLeftLight3"].style.display = "none";
    consoleImages["imgGameFrameLeftLight4"].style.display = "none";
    consoleImages["imgGameFrameLeftLight5"].style.display = "none";
    consoleImages["imgGameFrameRightLight1"].style.display = "none";
    consoleImages["imgGameFrameRightLight2"].style.display = "none";
    consoleImages["imgGameFrameRightLight3"].style.display = "none";
    consoleImages["imgGameFrameRightLight4"].style.display = "none";
    consoleImages["imgGameFrameRightLight5"].style.display = "none";
```

```
      // Draw mini-game area frame
      blit(consoleImages["imgGameFrame"], 0, 0);

      // Turn each light on or off randomly.
      if (jscript.math.genRandomNumber(0, 1) == 1) {
        blit(consoleImages["imgGameFrameLeftLight1"], 0, 22);
      }
      if (jscript.math.genRandomNumber(0, 1) == 1) {
        blit(consoleImages["imgGameFrameLeftLight2"], 0, 64);
      }
      if (jscript.math.genRandomNumber(0, 1) == 1) {
        blit(consoleImages["imgGameFrameLeftLight3"], 0, 107);
      }
      if (jscript.math.genRandomNumber(0, 1) == 1) {
        blit(consoleImages["imgGameFrameLeftLight4"], 0, 150);
      }
      if (jscript.math.genRandomNumber(0, 1) == 1) {
        blit(consoleImages["imgGameFrameLeftLight5"], 0, 193);
      }
      if (jscript.math.genRandomNumber(0, 1) == 1) {
        blit(consoleImages["imgGameFrameRightLight1"], 220, 20);
      }
      if (jscript.math.genRandomNumber(0, 1) == 1) {
        blit(consoleImages["imgGameFrameRightLight2"], 220, 62);
      }
      if (jscript.math.genRandomNumber(0, 1) == 1) {
        blit(consoleImages["imgGameFrameRightLight3"], 220, 107);
      }
      if (jscript.math.genRandomNumber(0, 1) == 1) {
        blit(consoleImages["imgGameFrameRightLight4"], 220, 150);
      }
      if (jscript.math.genRandomNumber(0, 1) == 1) {
        blit(consoleImages["imgGameFrameRightLight5"], 220, 193);
      }
    }

} // End updateLights().
```

First of all, lest we cause seizures in small children,[3] we don't want the lights to flash too wildly; every half-second seems reasonable. Since we know we get 24 fps, we want to update the lights only every twelfth frame, hence gameState.lightChangeCounter.

---

3. In December 1997, there were a few hundred incidents of Japanese children being thrown into seizures while watching the popular cartoon Pokemon. Further details can be found at http://www.cnn.com/WORLD/9712/17/video.seizures.update.

Once we determine it's safe (!) to change the lights, we begin by hiding all of them. Usually, when you write a game, you begin each frame by clearing the screen. Since we aren't dealing with a big grid of pixels, we can't really clear anything. But the equivalent operation is to hide the images. Again, for optimization reasons, it isn't really necessary to hide images that either don't change or can never have other images placed over them. However, in the case of the lights, they need to be cleared, as does the frame; otherwise, you would see the lights turn on but never turn off.

Once everything is cleared, we decide whether each of the ten lights is lit. To do this, we use the jscript.math.genRandomNumber() function we developed in Chapter 3. Then, for whichever lights are on, we blit them, and we're finished.

The updateHands() Function

Only one function remains now, and that's updateHands(), shown here:

```
function updateHands() {

  // Clear all images to prepare for proper display.
  consoleImages["imgLeftHandUp"].style.display = "none";
  consoleImages["imgLeftHandDown"].style.display = "none";
  consoleImages["imgLeftHandLeft"].style.display = "none";
  consoleImages["imgLeftHandRight"].style.display = "none";
  consoleImages["imgLeftHandUL"].style.display = "none";
  consoleImages["imgLeftHandUR"].style.display = "none";
  consoleImages["imgLeftHandDL"].style.display = "none";
  consoleImages["imgLeftHandDR"].style.display = "none";
  consoleImages["imgRightHandDown"].style.display = "none";

  // Display appropriate left-hand image.
  if (gameState.playerDirectionUp && !gameState.playerDirectionDown &&
    !gameState.playerDirectionLeft && !gameState.playerDirectionRight) {
    blit(consoleImages["imgLeftHandUp"], 29, 240);
  } else if (!gameState.playerDirectionUp && gameState.playerDirectionDown &&
    !gameState.playerDirectionLeft && !gameState.playerDirectionRight) {
    blit(consoleImages["imgLeftHandDown"], 29, 240);
  } else if (!gameState.playerDirectionUp && !gameState.playerDirectionDown &&
    gameState.playerDirectionLeft && !gameState.playerDirectionRight) {
    blit(consoleImages["imgLeftHandLeft"], 29, 240);
  } else if (!gameState.playerDirectionUp && !gameState.playerDirectionDown &&
    !gameState.playerDirectionLeft && gameState.playerDirectionRight) {
    blit(consoleImages["imgLeftHandRight"], 29, 240);
  } else if (gameState.playerDirectionUp && !gameState.playerDirectionDown &&
    gameState.playerDirectionLeft && !gameState.playerDirectionRight) {
    blit(consoleImages["imgLeftHandUL"], 29, 240);
```

```
    } else if (gameState.playerDirectionUp && !gameState.playerDirectionDown &&
      !gameState.playerDirectionLeft && gameState.playerDirectionRight) {
      blit(consoleImages["imgLeftHandUR"], 29, 240);
    } else if (!gameState.playerDirectionUp && gameState.playerDirectionDown &&
      gameState.playerDirectionLeft && !gameState.playerDirectionRight) {
      blit(consoleImages["imgLeftHandDL"], 29, 240);
    } else if (!gameState.playerDirectionUp && gameState.playerDirectionDown &&
      !gameState.playerDirectionLeft && gameState.playerDirectionRight) {
      blit(consoleImages["imgLeftHandDR"], 29, 240);
    } else {
      blit(consoleImages["imgLeftHandNormal"], 29, 240);
    }

    // Display appropriate left-hand image.
    if (gameState.playerAction) {
      blit(consoleImages["imgRightHandDown"], 145, 240);
    } else {
      blit(consoleImages["imgRightHandUp"], 145, 240);
    }

} // End updateHands().
```

Just as in the updateLights() function, we begin by hiding all the images for both hands. Then we enter a giant if . . . else block to determine which left hand image should be shown. Four variables help us make this determination, and those are the player direction fields in GameState: playerDirectionUp, playerDirectionDown, playerDirectionLeft, and playerDirectionRight. You'll note that we need to cover eight cases: four cardinal directions plus the four combinatorial directions (up/left, up/right, down/left, and down/right). The else block handles when the player isn't currently moving.

The same decision is made about the right hand image, but since there are only two states there—either the button is pressed or it isn't—the situation, and the code, is much more compact.

This is all it takes to make the hands on the bottom work. Well, this and the setting of the four fields in the key handlers, as discussed next.

Writing keyHandlers.js

You've already met the two functions contained in the keyHandlers.js file in a sense, because they are the functions that are called whenever a key is pressed or released: keyDownHandler() and keyUpHandler(). Listing 11-4 shows the keyHandlers.js file.

Listing 11-4. *The keyHandlers.js File*

```
/**
 * ======================================================================
 * Return the keycode of the key firing an event.
 * ======================================================================
 */
function getKeyCode(e) {

  var ev = (e) ? e : (window.event) ? window.event : null;
  if (ev) {
    return (ev.charCode) ? ev.charCode:
      ((ev.keyCode) ? ev.keyCode : ((ev.which) ? ev.which : null));
  }

} // End getKeyCode().


/**
 * ======================================================================
 * Handle key down events.
 * ----------------------------------------------------------------------
 */
function keyDownHandler(e) {

  var keyCode = getKeyCode(e);

  if (!gameState.currentGame.fullKeyControl) {
    switch (keyCode) {
      case KEY_SPACE:
        gameState.playerAction = truc;
      break;
      case KEY_UP:
        gameState.playerDirectionUp = true;
      break;
      case KEY_DOWN:
        gameState.playerDirectionDown = true;
      break;
```

```
        case KEY_LEFT:
          gameState.playerDirectionLeft = true;
        break;
        case KEY_RIGHT:
          gameState.playerDirectionRight = true;
        break;
      }
    }

    gameState.currentGame.keyDownHandler(keyCode);

} // End keyDownHandler().


/**
 * ======================================================================
 * Handle key up events.
 * ======================================================================
 */
function keyUpHandler(e) {

  var keyCode = getKeyCode(e);

  // Always handle exiting a mini-game, even if the mini-game has full control
  // over key events.
  if (keyCode == 13) {
    if (gameState.currentMode == "miniGame") {
      gameState.currentGame.destroy();
      gameState.currentGame = null;
      document.getElementById("divMiniGame").style.display = "none";
      gameState.currentGame = new GameSelection();
      gameState.currentGame.init();
    }
  }

  if (!gameState.currentGame.fullKeyControl) {
    switch (keyCode) {
      case KEY_SPACE:
        gameState.playerAction = false;
      break;
      case KEY_UP:
        gameState.playerDirectionUp = false;
      break;
      case KEY_DOWN:
        gameState.playerDirectionDown = false;
      break;
```

```
    case KEY_LEFT:
      gameState.playerDirectionLeft = false;
    break;
    case KEY_RIGHT:
      gameState.playerDirectionRight = false;
    break;
  }
}


  gameState.currentGame.keyUpHandler(keyCode);

} // End keyUpHandler().
```

Whenever a key is pressed, keyDownHandler() is called. This, in turn, calls they getKeyCode() function. The reason for this is that the way you get the code for the key that was pressed is different in IE than it is in other browsers, because their event model is fundamentally different. IE works by having a page-scoped event object generated for the event, while Firefox and other browsers pass that object directly to the handler function. So, in order to abstract away these differences, getKeyCode() deals with it, while the two handler functions do not. Essentially, all this function does is get the key code that was pressed. The first line contains some logic, the end result of which is that the variable ev contains the relevant event object, regardless of in which browser the application is running.

The line inside the if block looks a bit complex (and I usually frown on trinary logic statements like this, especially strung together as this is, but it was actually cleaner to write it this way than as a series of nested if statements), but it boils down to the fact that the browser in use determines which property of the event object you need to go after to get the key code. In some, it is charCode; in others, is it keyCode; and in still others, it is which. In any case, the relevant key code is returned and the event handler itself continues.

Once the key code is determined, it's a simple matter of a switch block to determine which key was pressed, and then the appropriate flag is set in gameState. However, this switch block will be hit only if the mini-game in play doesn't have full control over key events. Some mini-games will need this, as is the case with Deathtrap.

Lastly, the keyDownHandler() of the current mini-game is called so that it can do whatever work needs to be done specific to that game (which may be none, as is the case with Cosmic Squirrel).

The onKeyUp() handler is only slightly more complex. There, we first check if Enter is pressed. If it is, we need to exit the current mini-game, which means calling destroy() on the current mini-game class, hiding the divMiniGame <div>, and setting the game selection screen as the current screen. Beyond that, it's essentially the same as onKeyDown(), except that the player direction flags get unset (set to false, in other words).

Writing gameFuncs.js

The gameFuncs.js file contains a couple of functions that are essentially "helper" functions for mini-games. The first one we encounter is loadGameImage():

```
function loadGameImage(inName) {

  // Create an img object and set the relevant properties on it.
  var img = document.createElement("img");
  img.src = gameState.currentGame.gameName + "/img/" + inName + ".gif";
  img.style.position = "absolute";
  img.style.display = "none";

  // Add it to the array of images for the current game to avoid DOM access
  // later, and append it to the game area.
  gameState.currentGame.gameImages[inName] = img;
  document.getElementById("divGameArea").appendChild(img);

} // End loadGameImage().
```

Recall that each mini-game class, by virtue of extending the MiniGame base class (which we'll look at next) has a gameImages array that stores references to the images the mini-game uses. This array gets populated by calls to the loadGameImage() function. It creates a new <img> element, sets its src attribute to the specified image (which loads it into memory), and sets it up to be positional (position:absolute). It then appends it to the DOM as a child of the divGameArea <div> element, which again is the viewport inside the game console frame where the mini-games take place. This function also adds the reference to the gameImages array of the current mini-game class.

As a corollary to the loadGameImage() function, there is the destroyGameImage() function:

```
function destroyGameImage(inName) {

  // Remove it from the DOM.
  var gameArea = document.getElementById("divGameArea");
  gameArea.removeChild(gameState.currentGame.gameImages[inName]);

  // Set element in array in null to complete the destruction.
  gameState.currentGame.gameImages[inName] = null;

} // End destroyGameImage().
```

When a mini-game's destroy() function is called, it is expected to use the destroyGameImage() function to destroy any images it loaded in init(). Not doing so would cause a memory leak, since every time the game was started, the images would be created as new, but the previous copies would still remain, unused. To destroy an image, we need to first remove it from the DOM, and then set the reference in the array to null. The JavaScript engine's garbage collector will take care of the rest.

The next function in the gameFuncs.js file is detectCollision():

```
function detectCollision(inObj1, inObj2) {

  var left1 = inObj1.x;
  var left2 = inObj2.x;
  var right1 = left1 + inObj1.width;
  var right2 = left2 + inObj2.width;
  var top1 = inObj1.y;
  var top2 = inObj2.y;
  var bottom1 = top1 + inObj1.height;
  var bottom2 = top2 + inObj2.height;

  if (bottom1 < top2) {
    return false;
  }
  if (top1 > bottom2) {
    return false;
  }
  if (right1 < left2) {
    return false;
  }
  if (left1 > right2) {
    return false;
  }

  return true;

} // End detectCollision().
```

Most video games, such as Cosmic Squirrel, require the ability to detect when two images—two objects in the game (usually termed *sprites*)—collide. For instance, we need to know when our player's squirrel is squished by an asteroid. There are numerous collision-detection algorithms, but many of them are not available to us in a browser setting. For instance, checking each pixel of one image against each pixel of another, while giving 100% accurate detection, isn't possible in a browser. The method used here is called *bounding boxes*. It is a very simple method that basically just checks the four corners of the objects. If the corner of one object is within the bounds of the other, a collision has occurred.

As illustrated in the example in Figure 11-9, each sprite has a square (or rectangular) area around it, called its bounding box, which defines the boundaries of the area the sprite occupies. Note in the diagram how the upper-left corner of object 1's bounding box is within the bounding box of object 2. This represents a collision. We can detect a collision by running through a series of tests comparing the bounds of each object. If any of the conditions are untrue, then a collision cannot possibly have occurred. For instance, if the bottom of object 1 is above the top of object 2, there's no way a collision could have occurred. In fact, since we're dealing with a square or rectangular object, we have only four conditions to check, any one of which being false precludes the possibility of a collision.

This algorithm does not yield perfect results. For example, in Cosmic Squirrel, you will sometimes see the squirrel hitting an object when they clearly did not touch. This is because the *bounding boxes* can collide *without the object itself* actually colliding. This could only be fixed with pixel-level detection, which again, is not available to us. But the bounding boxes approach gives an approximation that yields "good enough" results, so all is right with the world.

The last two functions, addToScore() and subtractFromScore() are pretty self-explanatory. Note that subtractFromScore() must do a check to be sure the score doesn't go below zero. Some games will actually go into negative scores, but I saw no need to inflict more psychological damage on the player! Zero is embarrassing enough, I figure. Both of them simply update the score field in gameState, and update the status area as well.

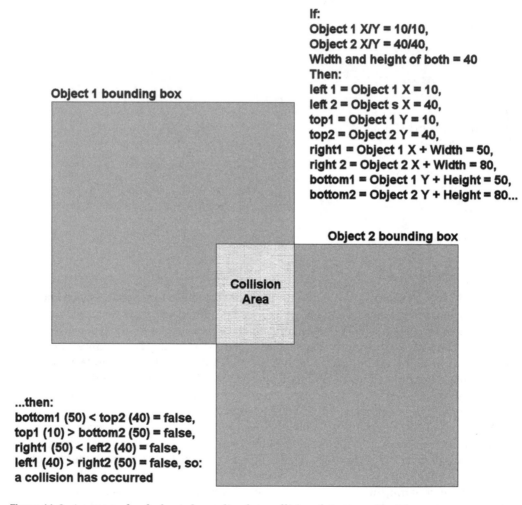

Figure 11-9. *An example of a basic bounding box collision detection algorithm*

Writing MiniGame.js

The MiniGame class is the base class for all mini-games, as well as the title screen and the game selection screen. Figure 11-10 shows the UML diagram for this class. It contains no real executable code, but it defines, in a sense, the interface that all mini-games must implement. The mini-games, title screen, and game selection screen essentially extend this class, overriding the default implementations of the methods it provides. Any that aren't needed don't have to be overridden; the default do-nothing version of the method will be used.

Figure 11-10. *UML diagram of the MiniGame class*

In addition to the methods that are members of the MiniGame class, three fields are present:

- gameName: This field *must* be set by the subclass during initialization, and it must match the directory in which the mini-game exists. This value is used to construct URLs for images that a mini-game may load. The default value in the MiniGame class is null.

- gameImages: This array is initialized to an empty array in MiniGame, so no errors will occur later if the mini-game doesn't load any images. A mini-game without images would be pretty pointless, however, so this array won't stay empty for long.

- fullKeyControl: This field is essentially a flag that determines whether the mini-game is in complete control of keyboard events, and none of the default behavior for these events occurs (as seen in keyHandlers.js previously). The default value here is false, so the default events will occur if the mini-game class does not override this value.

Writing Title.js

I did not put a UML diagram here for Title.js because it would look exactly like that of the MiniGame class, since the Title class extends the MiniGame class.

How does a class extend another in JavaScript exactly? By using the prototype, of course! As you saw in Chapter 1, every object in JavaScript has a prototype associated with it. This is essentially a prototype for the structure of the class. When you set the prototype of class B to class A, for instance, it means that class B will look like class A, plus whatever additional things class B defines.

In the case of the `Title` class, we find this line of code at the end of `Title.js`:

```
Title.prototype = new MiniGame;
```

That is, conceptually, the same thing as saying the `Title` class extends the `MiniGame` class. Let's say the definition of the `Title` class was nothing but this:

```
function Title() { }
```

If you were to do this:

```
var t = new Title();
```

you would find that the object referenced by the variable t had five methods: `init()`, `destroy()`, `processFrame()`, `keyUpHandler()`, and `keyDownHandler()`. You would also find that it had three properties: `gameName`, `gameImages`, and `fullKeyControl`. This is by virtue of it extending the `MiniGame` class, where those members are defined. Now, if the `Title` class contains an `init()` method itself (which it does, in this case), then the object pointed to by the variable t would have an `init()` method as defined in the `Title` class, *not* the empty version of that function found in the `MiniGame` class. And if the `Title` class defines a function named `doSomething()`, then the object pointed to by the variable t would contain a function `doSomething()`, even though the `MiniGame` class does not. None of this is unusual in terms of class inheritance and is what we would expect to be the case.

The `Title` class, shown in Listing 11-5, overrides three of the `MiniGame` class methods: `init()`, `destroy()`, and `keyUpHandler()`.

Listing 11-5. *The Title Class*

```
function Title() {


  /**
   * ========================================================================
   * Game initialization.
   * ========================================================================
   */
  this.init = function() {

    document.getElementById("divTitle").style.display = "block";

  } // End init().


  /**
   * ========================================================================
   * Handle key up events.
   * ========================================================================
   */
  this.keyUpHandler = function(e) {
```

```
        gameState.currentGame.destroy();
        gameState.currentGame = null;
        gameState.currentGame = new GameSelection();
        gameState.currentGame.init();

  } // End keyUpHandler().



  /**
   * =======================================================================
   * Destroy resources.
   * =======================================================================
   */
  this.destroy = function() {

    document.getElementById("divTitle").style.display = "none";

  } // End destroy().


} // End Title class.



// Title class "inherits" from MiniGame class (even though, strictly speaking,
// it isn't a mini-game).
Title.prototype = new MiniGame;
```

Recall that I said that the Title class, while obviously not actually a mini-game, is treated like one just the same. As such, when the application starts, it begins by instantiating a Title class, and then calling init() on it. Here, the only job init() has is to make visible the <div> containing the markup for the title screen. Then, when a key is pressed and released, keyUpHandler() is called. It calls the destroy() method of the object pointed to by the gameState. currentGame field, which is itself! destroy() simply hides the <div> for the title screen again. Control then returns to keyUpHandler(), which instantiates a new instance of the GameSelection class, sets gameState.currentGame to point to it, and calls init() on it. Remember that all this time, the main game loop is firing via timeout. So, when the next iteration occurs, it will be calling processFrame() on the GameSelection instance, hence essentially switching to that screen.

Note that the Title class does not override the processFrame() function. It has no work to do there, so there's no need to include that function. The default do-nothing implementation in the MiniGame class will be fired once per frame, so no problem there.

Writing GameSelection.js

The GameSelection class is the class that deals with the game selection screen, not surprisingly! It is again, like the Title screen class, treated just like a mini-game. Figure 11-11 shows its UML diagram.

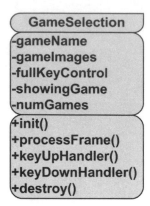

Figure 11-11. *UML diagram of the GameSelection class*

As in the Title class, when the user presses and releases a key from the game selection screen, the GameSelection class is instantiated, and init() is called. There isn't much to do there, but let's see it anyway:

```
this.init = function() {

  gameState.currentMode = null;
  document.getElementById("divGameSelection").style.display = "block";

} // End init().
```

First, we set gameState.currentMode to null, indicating a mini-game is not currently in progress. Remember that when the user exits a mini-game, a new GameSelection instance will be created, and init() will be called on it, hence it is a good place to set that value. After that, it's just a simple matter of showing the game selection <div>, and we're all set.

For each frame, GameSelection has some work to do:

```
this.processFrame = function() {

  document.getElementById("ssCosmicSquirrel").style.display = "none";
  document.getElementById("ssDeathtrap").style.display = "none";
  switch (this.showingGame) {
    case 1:
      document.getElementById("ssCosmicSquirrel").style.display = "block";
      document.getElementById("mgsDesc").innerHTML =
        "In space, no one can hear a giant space squirrel buy it";
    break;
    case 2:
      document.getElementById("ssDeathtrap").style.display = "block";
      document.getElementById("mgsDesc").innerHTML =
        "Hop on the tiles to escape the chasm without getting cooked";
    break;
  }

} // End processFrame().
```

It begins with hiding the screenshot preview images for our mini-games. Since there aren't too many here, and speed isn't really of the essence as it is in a mini-game, we don't load references to these images into an array to avoid the DOM lookups as previously discussed. Instead, we get a reference to the images each time through. After they are hidden, we determine which mini-game preview is currently showing, and we show that appropriate image object, and also display the appropriate description. That's all there is to it.

The keyUpHandler() is where the majority of the work for the GameSelection class actually is, as you can see for yourself:

```
this.keyUpHandler = function(e) {

  switch (e) {
    case KEY_LEFT:
      this.showingGame--;
      if (this.showingGame < 1) {
        this.showingGame = this.numGames;
      }
    break;
    case KEY_RIGHT:
      this.showingGame++;
      if (this.showingGame > this.numGames) {
        this.showingGame = 1;
      }
    break;
    case KEY_SPACE:
      gameState.currentGame.destroy();
      gameState.currentGame = null;
      switch (this.showingGame) {
        case 1:
          startMiniGame("cosmicSquirrel");
        break;
        case 2:
          startMiniGame("deathtrap");
        break;
        case 3:
          startMiniGame("refluxive");
        break;
      }
    break;
  }

} // End keyUpHandler().
```

When the user presses the left or right arrow key, we decrement or increment the value of the showingGame field correspondingly. When decrementing, when we get below 1 (which represents the first mini-game), we jump to the number of mini-games as defined by the numGames field. Likewise, when we get above the number of mini-games, we jump back to 1. This makes it so that no matter how many mini-games we have, the list will cycle back to the other end when the bounds are reached on either end. When the user presses the spacebar, it's time to begin the currently selected mini-game. To do so, we call the startMiniGame() function, passing the name of the game to start. That function takes care of all the details of starting a game, as you saw earlier.

Finally, the destroy() function is very simple:

```
this.destroy = function() {

    document.getElementById("divGameSelection").style.display = "none";

} // End destroy().
```

We just hide the <div> containing the game selection screen, and our work here is done!

Writing CosmicSquirrel.js

OK, now we get to the really good stuff! We've gone through all the code that, in effect, makes up the plumbing of K&G Arcade. At the end of the day though, it's all about the mini-games! This is where the bulk of the action is, and also where the nongeneric code is found. Before we check out the code though, let's get the lay of the land, so to speak.

In Figure 11-12, you see the CosmicSquirrel class itself. You will by now notice that it extends the MiniGame class, and because of that, it exposes a known interface with our five by now well-known methods, as well as our three common attributes. As you can also see, it contains several unique fields: ObstacleDesc, PlayerDesc, AcornDesc, player, acorn, and obstacles. The first three of these are themselves classes that are defined inside the CosmicSquirrel class. This is akin to an inner class in Java. They could just as easily have been defined outside the CosmicSquirrel class, but I felt that since they are used by only that class, it made sense to define them inside, to make the relationship somewhat more explicit. The other three fields are instances of those inner classes (well, player and acorn are; obstacles is actually an array of ObstacleDesc objects).

Figure 11-12. *UML diagram of the CosmicSquirrel class*

Setting Up the Obstacle, the Player, and the Acorn

Figure 11-13 shows the UML diagram of the ObstacleDesc class. This class, whose name is short for Obstacle Descriptor, is used to represent an obstacle on the screen, which could be an alien, spaceship, asteroid, or comet. Each of these objects defines the ID of the object, its X/Y location, the width and height of the image that represents it on the screen, the direction it is currently moving in, and its speed.

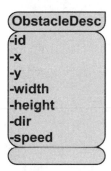

Figure 11-13. *UML diagram of the ObstacleDesc class*

The code for the ObstacleDesc class is as follows:

```
function ObstacleDesc(inID, inX, inY, inDir, inSpeed, inWidth, inHeight) {
  this.id = inID;
  this.x = inX;
  this.y = inY;
  this.width = inWidth;
  this.height = inHeight;
  this.dir = inDir;
  this.speed = inSpeed;
} // End ObstacleDesc class.
```

It is, in effect, just a simple data structure. Note that its argument list, which is its constructor (since that's in effect what any function defining a class is in JavaScript), allows you to set all the parameters for the obstacle when the instance is constructed. You will see this in action very shortly.

The PlayerDesc class, whose UML diagram can be seen in Figure 11-14, describes the player—that is, the cosmic squirrel. It contains the current X/Y location of the player, and the width and height of the image of the squirrel. It also defines a method that is called whenever the player dies or reaches the acorn, to reset it to its starting position.

Figure 11-14. *UML diagram of the PlayerDesc class*

The code for the PlayerDesc class is just about as simple as the ObstacleDesc class, with the addition of the reset() method:

```
function PlayerDesc() {
  this.x = null;
  this.y = null;
  this.width = 18;
  this.height = 18;
  this.reset = function() {
    this.x = 91;
    this.y = 180;
  }
  this.reset();
} // End PlayerDesc class.
```

To reset the player is a simple matter of setting his initial starting location. Note the call to reset() at the very end. This is what will execute when the class is instantiated, setting it up initially.

Moving right along, take a look at the AcornDesc class, shown in Figure 11-15. This class describes the acorn, of course.

Figure 11-15. *UML diagram of the AcornDesc class*

Notice that AcornDesc has the same structure as the PlayerDesc class, and also defines that same reset() method, which randomly places the acorn on the screen when it is reached by the player using the jscript.math.genRandomNumber() function, as seen here:

```
function AcornDesc() {
  this.x = null;
  this.y = null;
  this.width = 18;
  this.height = 18;
  this.reset = function() {
    this.x = jscript.math.genRandomNumber(1, 180)
    this.y = 2;
  }
  this.reset();
} // End AcornDesc class.
```

Following these three classes in the CosmicSquirrel class are these three lines:

```
this.player = new PlayerDesc();
this.acorn = new AcornDesc();
this.obstacles = new Array();
```

Since there are only one player and one acorn, we have them as soon as the CosmicSquirrel class is instantiated. We also have an empty array of obstacles to populate, which is done when init() is called on the CosmicSquirrel instance.

Starting the Game

Let's see init() now:

```
this.init = function() {

  // Configure base game parameters.
  this.gameName = "cosmicSquirrel";

  // Load all the images required for this game.
  loadGameImage("background");
  loadGameImage("acorn");
  loadGameImage("squirrelUp");
  loadGameImage("squirrelDown");
  loadGameImage("squirrelLeft");
  loadGameImage("squirrelRight");
  loadGameImage("squirrelStill");
  loadGameImage("alien1");
  loadGameImage("alien2");
  loadGameImage("ship1");
  loadGameImage("ship2");
  loadGameImage("asteroid1");
  loadGameImage("asteroid2");
  loadGameImage("comet1");
  loadGameImage("comet2");
```

```
    // Create obstacle descriptors and add to array.
    this.obstacles.push(new ObstacleDesc("alien1", 170, 30, "R", 5, 24, 24));
    this.obstacles.push(new ObstacleDesc("alien2", 80, 30, "R", 5, 24, 24));
    this.obstacles.push(new ObstacleDesc("ship1", 110, 60, "L", 2, 32, 24));
    this.obstacles.push(new ObstacleDesc("ship2", 10, 60, "L", 2, 32, 24));
    this.obstacles.push(new ObstacleDesc("asteroid1", 80, 90, "R", 4, 32, 32));
    this.obstacles.push(new ObstacleDesc("asteroid2", 140, 90, "R", 4, 32, 32));
    this.obstacles.push(new ObstacleDesc("comet1", 240, 130, "L", 3, 64, 14));
    this.obstacles.push(new ObstacleDesc("comet2", 70, 130, "L", 3, 64, 14));

} // End init().
```

First, the gameName field is set, which must be done in all mini-games. Notice that the value set there, "cosmicSquirrel", matches the directory where this code is. This is no coincidence; when the loadGameImage() function is called, it will use that value to construct the URL to the image being loaded.

Speaking of loadGameImage(), next are a batch of those calls. Each one, as you saw previously, creates an <img> tag, loads it with the image named, and adds it to the gameImages array, which is found in the MiniGame base class.

Lastly, we have a series of eight lines of code that are responsible for creating the obstacles the player must avoid. Each one is an ObstacleDesc instance, and here you can see where the constructor parameters I mentioned earlier come into play. We simply instantiate an ObstacleDesc instance, passing into it the appropriate parameters, and push that object onto the obstacles array. Nothing more to it!

Processing a Single Frame of Action

Now we get into the processFrame() function, which I remind you will be called 24 times a second, once per frame. The first thing we see happening there is to hide all the images used in this mini-game:

```
for (img in this.gameImages) {
    this.gameImages[img].style.display = "none";
}
```

You can see here the use of the gameImages array, rather than direct DOM access. This is good for speed!

Following that are two lines of code:

```
// Blit background.
blit(this.gameImages["background"], 0, 0);

// Blit acorn.
blit(this.gameImages["acorn"], this.acorn.x, this.acorn.y);
```

Recall that the blit() function serves to put an image on the screen at a specified location. Here, we're first placing the background image onto the game area, effectively filling the entire game area with the background. Next, we place the acorn at its current location, using the values stored in the AcornDesc instance referenced by the acorn variable.

After that, it's time to do the same with the obstacles. However, since the `ObstacleDesc` objects are in an array, we need to iterate over that array and `blit()` each, like so:

```
for (i = 0; i < this.obstacles.length; i++) {
  var obstacle = this.obstacles[i];
  blit(this.gameImages[obstacle.id], obstacle.x, obstacle.y);
}
```

So, at this point, the only thing left to do is show the squirrel; otherwise, the game would be pretty boring (I mean, watching the obstacles move around is kind of neat, I suppose, but not much of a game!). So, let's throw the squirrel on the screen:

```
if (gameState.playerDirectionUp) {
  blit(this.gameImages["squirrelUp"], this.player.x, this.player.y);
} else if (gameState.playerDirectionDown) {
  blit(this.gameImages["squirrelDown"], this.player.x, this.player.y);
} else if (gameState.playerDirectionLeft) {
  blit(this.gameImages["squirrelLeft"], this.player.x, this.player.y);
} else if (gameState.playerDirectionRight) {
  blit(this.gameImages["squirrelRight"], this.player.x, this.player.y);
} else {
  blit(this.gameImages["squirrelStill"], this.player.x, this.player.y);
}
```

There is just a little more work to do here because which way the player is moving determines which version of the squirrel we show. So, we have a series of if statements that interrogate the four flags in the GameState object that tell us which way the squirrel is moving, and we blit() the appropriate image. If the player isn't moving at all, we show the squirrel facing up as the default image.

Now that everything is actually drawn on the screen, we need to process the logic of the game for this frame. The first step is to move the obstacles. Since this movement continues unabated, regardless of what the player does, there are no conditions that need to be checked. We simply update their positions, and those changes will be reflected in the next frame drawing. Here is the code that does the movement:

```
for (i = 0; i < this.obstacles.length; i++) {
  var obstacle = this.obstacles[i];
  if (obstacle.dir == "L") {
    obstacle.x = obstacle.x - obstacle.speed;
  }
  if (obstacle.dir == "R") {
    obstacle.x = obstacle.x + obstacle.speed;
  }
  // Bounds checks (comets handled differently because of their size).
  if (obstacle.id.indexOf("comet") != -1) {
    if (obstacle.x < -40) {
      obstacle.x = 240;
    }
```

```
    } else {
      if (obstacle.x < -70) {
        obstacle.x = 240;
      }
    }
    if (obstacle.x > 240) {
      obstacle.x = -40;
    }
  }
```

For each object, we check the value of the dir attribute of the ObstacleDesc object associated with the obstacle to see which direction it is moving in, and we update its x location accordingly, using the speed attribute as the change value. Next, we do some checks so that when an obstacle moves completely off the screen in either direction, we reset its x location so it reappears on the other side of the screen. Note that because the comets are longer than the other obstacles, we need to check for different values than we do for all the other obstacles, hence the branching logic.

The next piece of business to attend to is moving the player.

```
if (gameState.playerDirectionUp) {
  this.player.y = this.player.y - 2;
  if (this.player.y < 2) {
    this.player.y = 2;
  }
}
if (gameState.playerDirectionDown) {
  this.player.y = this.player.y + 2;
  if (this.player.y > 180) {
    this.player.y = 180;
  }
}
if (gameState.playerDirectionRight) {
  this.player.x = this.player.x + 2;
  if (this.player.x > 180) {
    this.player.x = 180;
  }
}
if (gameState.playerDirectionLeft) {
  this.player.x = this.player.x - 2;
  if (this.player.x < 2) {
    this.player.x = 2;
  }
}
```

Depending on which way the player is currently moving, we increment or decrement either the x or y location by 2. We then apply some bounds checking to make sure the player can't move off the mini-game screen in any direction. Note that with this logic, the player can move in the four cardinal directions, as well as the four combinatorial directions. For example, if gameState.playerDirectionUp and gameState.playerDirectionRight were true, then two of the four if statements here would execute, causing the squirrel to move diagonally. This is perfectly acceptable, and works to makes the game far less frustrating than it would be if the player could move in only the four cardinal directions.

We're almost finished with game play, believe it or not! Only two tasks remain in processFrame(). First, we need to determine if the player has gotten the acorn, and we do that with this code:

```
if (detectCollision(this.player, this.acorn)){
  this.player.reset();
  this.acorn.reset();
  addToScore(50);
}
```

We already looked at the detectCollision() function, so we don't need to go over that again. If that call returns true, then we call reset() on the PlayerDesc instance referenced by the player field, which returns the player to his starting position. We then do the same for the acorn, which randomly places it somewhere at the top of the screen. Finally, we add 50 points to the player's score.

In the same vein, we need to check for collisions with the eight obstacles, and the code is very nearly identical:

```
for (i = 0; i <  this.obstacles.length; i++) {
  if (detectCollision(this.player, this.obstacles[i])){
    this.player.reset();
    this.acorn.reset();
    subtractFromScore(25);
  }
}
```

We call detectCollision() for each of the eight obstacles. If a collision is detected, we do the same resets as with a collision with the acorn, but this time subtract 25 from the score. Subtracting less than the player earns for getting the acorn is just a nice thing to do (it would be a bit sadistic if it were reversed!). I would bet you've played games that score in a seemingly unfair way, and I know I've certainly been frustrated by that, so I wanted to be just a bit nicer in this game!

Cleaning Up

With processFrame() now out of the way, only one task remains to complete Cosmic Squirrel, and that is to clean up when the game ends. This is achieved by implementing the destroy() function, like so:

```
this.destroy = function() {

  destroyGameImage("background");
  destroyGameImage("acorn");
  destroyGameImage("squirrelUp");
  destroyGameImage("squirrelDown");
  destroyGameImage("squirrelLeft");
```

```
    destroyGameImage("squirrelRight");
    destroyGameImage("squirrelStill");
    destroyGameImage("alien1");
    destroyGameImage("alien2");
    destroyGameImage("ship1");
    destroyGameImage("ship2");
    destroyGameImage("asteroid1");
    destroyGameImage("asteroid2");
    destroyGameImage("comet1");
    destroyGameImage("comet2");

  } // End destroy().
```

Each call to `loadGameImage()` in the `init()` method is matched with a corresponding call to `destroyGameImage()` in the `destroy()` method. These calls remove the `<img>` element from the DOM and set the element in the array that holds a reference to that element to null, which effectively marks the image object for deletion by the garbage collector. Nothing else really needs to be done to clean up, so it's a short and sweet method.

Inheriting the Basics

At the very end of `CosmicSquirrel.js`, you see that one magical line that makes the inheritance work. This line of code allows the `CosmicSquirrel` class to have implementations of functions it doesn't explicitly need to alter, but which the rest of the game code expects to be implemented, such as `keyUpHandler()` and `keyDownHandler()`. That line of code is as follows:

```
CosmicSquirrel.prototype = new MiniGame;
```

With that single line of code, we ensure that the "plumbing" code that we've previously looked at—the code that calls the methods of the current mini-game class when the various life cycle events occur—will work, because it ensures that the `CosmicSquirrel` class (assuming no one has broken it, of course!) meets the interface requirements that plumbing code expects.

And, believe it or not, that is all the code behind this mini-game!

Writing Deathtrap.js

The Deathtrap game is only slightly more complicated than Cosmic Squirrel. It has about twice as much code, but a fair bit of it is very mundane, repetitive stuff. I won't be listing all that out here, but I'll certainly show you enough of it to get the feel for what's going on.

First, let's again look at the UML diagram of the `Deathtrap` class itself, as shown in Figure 11-16.

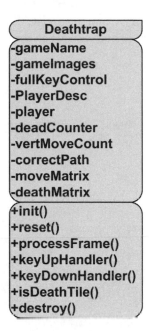

Figure 11-16. *UML diagram of the Deathtrap class*

Setting Up the Player

As in Cosmic Squirrel, we again find a PlayerDesc class, which is used to describe the characteristics of the player. As you can see in the UML diagram shown in Figure 11-17, the version here has a bit more to it. We still have the X/Y location of the player, but this time we also store the previous X/Y location, and you'll see why in a moment. We also have another X/Y location, defining which tile the player is on. This differs from the literal X/Y location on the screen, and both pieces of information are required to make the game work correctly. Lastly, we store the current state of the player: whether he is alive, dead, or has won the game.

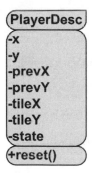

Figure 11-17. *UML diagram of the PlayerDesc class*

We also again have a reset() method exposed by the PlayerDesc class, and this serves much the same purpose as it did in CosmicSquirrel. It will be called, as in that case, when the player dies or wins. Here is the code for the PlayerDesc class for this mini-game:

```javascript
function PlayerDesc() {
  this.x = null;
  this.y = null;
  this.prevX = null;
  this.prevY = null;
  this.tileX = null;
  this.tileY = null;
  // State: A=Alive, D=Dead, W=Won
  this.state = null;
  this.reset = function() {
    this.x = 10;
    this.y = 152;
    this.prevX = 0;
    this.prevY = 0;
    this.tileX = 1;
    this.tileY = 8;
    this.state = "A";
  }
  this.reset();
} // End PlayerDesc class.
```

Following that inner class definition are four fields of the Deathtrap class:

```javascript
this.player = new PlayerDesc();
this.deadCounter = null;
this.vertMoveCount = null;
this.correctPath = null;
this.regenPath = true;
```

These fields work as follows:

- player: The PlayerDesc instance describing the player.

- deadCounter: Used when the player dies to determine how long he should get zapped.

- vertMoveCount: Used when moving the player from tile to tile.

- correctPath: Defines which of the ten possible correct paths through the tiles is valid.

- regenPath: A flag that determines whether a new correctPath will be chosen when reset() is called.

Constructing the Death Matrix

The next piece of the code is the deathMatrix. The deathMatrix is a multidimensional array (10-by-2-by-2) that represents the grid of tiles the player must navigate. For each of the first dimensions, we have a 2-by-2 array, so ten arrays essentially. Each of those ten arrays defines one possible correct path through the tiles. Each element in the 2-by-2 array is either a zero or one, one being a safe tile.

When the reset() method of the Deathtrap class is called, if the regenPath flag is set to true, the jscript.math.genRandomNumber() function is used to pick one of the ten possible paths. Therefore, every time the game starts, or when the player wins, a new correctPath will be chosen. When the player dies, this *will not* happen. This is again for fair game play. It would be really frustrating if the path were reset every time the player died, because he would not be able to work out the path through trial and error, so it would just be dumb luck each time, and that wouldn't be much fun!

Just for the sake of completeness, here is an example of how the deathMatrix is defined (these are the first two elements):

```
this.deathMatrix = new Array(10);
this.deathMatrix[0] = new Array(
    [ 1, 1, 1, 1, 1, 0, 0, 0, 0 ],
    [ 1, 0, 0, 0, 0, 0, 0, 0, 0 ],
    [ 1, 1, 1, 1, 1, 1, 0, 0, 0 ],
    [ 1, 1, 0, 0, 0, 1, 0, 0, 0 ],
    [ 1, 1, 0, 0, 0, 1, 0, 0, 0 ],
    [ 1, 1, 0, 1, 1, 1, 0, 0, 0 ],
    [ 0, 0, 0, 1, 0, 0, 0, 0, 0 ],
    [ 0, 0, 0, 1, 0, 0, 0, 0, 0 ],
    [ 0, 1, 1, 1, 0, 0, 0, 0, 0 ]
);
this.deathMatrix[1] = [
    [ 0, 0, 0, 0, 1, 0, 0, 0, 0 ],
    [ 0, 0, 0, 0, 1, 0, 0, 0, 0 ],
    [ 1, 1, 1, 1, 1, 1, 0, 0, 0 ],
    [ 1, 0, 0, 0, 1, 1, 0, 0, 0 ],
    [ 1, 0, 0, 0, 1, 0, 0, 0, 0 ],
    [ 1, 1, 1, 0, 1, 0, 0, 0, 0 ],
    [ 0, 0, 1, 0, 1, 1, 0, 0, 0 ],
    [ 0, 1, 1, 0, 0, 0, 0, 0, 0 ],
    [ 0, 1, 1, 0, 0, 0, 0, 0, 0 ]
];
```

Constructing the Move Matrix

One more member of the Deathtrap class that needs to be discussed is the moveMatrix. The moveMatrix is another multidimensional array, 10-by-10 in size, where each element represents a tile. The purpose of this array is to determine which directions the player can move from any given tile. Note that on the screen some of the tiles are not complete. This is necessary because of the angular drawing of the room. Those partial tiles should not be valid destinations for player movement. For each element in this array, a string value is present. The string contains one or more of U, D, L, and R. For instance, if a particular tile has a value of "ULR", that means the player can move up, left, or right from that tile, but not down. A tile can also have a value of a string with none of those letters but just a space, which means it can never be reached and therefore no moves are valid from it.

Here is the code that defines the moveMatrix:

```
this.moveMatrix = new Array(10);
this.moveMatrix[0] = [ "RD", "RDL", "RDL", "RDL", "UDL",
  " ", " ", " ", " " ];
this.moveMatrix[1] = [ "URD", "URDL", "URDL", "URDL", "UDL",
  " ", " ", " ", " " ];
this.moveMatrix[2] = [ "URD", "URDL", "URDL", "URDL", "URDL",
  "DL", " ", " ", " " ];
this.moveMatrix[3] = [ "URD", "URDL", "URDL", "URDL", "URDL",
  "UDL", " ", " ", " " ];
this.moveMatrix[4] = [ "URD", "URDL", "URDL", "URDL", "URDL",
  "URDL", "DL", " ", " " ];
this.moveMatrix[5] = [ "URD", "URDL", "URDL", "URDL", "URDL",
  "URDL", "UDL", " ", " " ];
this.moveMatrix[6] = [ "UR", "URDL", "URDL", "URDL", "URDL",
  "URDL", "UDL", " ", " " ];
this.moveMatrix[7] = [ " ", "URD", "URDL", "URDL", "URDL",
  "URDL", "URDL", "DL", " " ];
this.moveMatrix[8] = [ " ", "UR", "URL", "URL", "URL",
  "URL", "URL", "UL", " " ];
```

Starting the Game

Next up is the init() method:

```
this.init = function() {

  // Configure base game parameters.
  this.gameName = "deathtrap";
  this.fullKeyControl = true;

  // Reset the game state.
  this.reset();

  // Load all the images required for this game.
  loadGameImage("background");
  loadGameImage("playerDieing");
  loadGameImage("playerJumping");
  loadGameImage("playerStanding");

} // End init().
```

After the setting of the mini-game name, note the setting of fullKeyControl to true. In the case of Deathtrap, we need to deal with keyboard events a little differently than we did with Cosmic Squirrel, and it turns out the default handling we saw previously in keyHandlers.js interferes with what has to happen here. Therefore, this mini-game needs to deal with keyboard events itself and not leave it to the default code.

After that is a call to reset(), followed by a series of loadGameImage() calls (notice how few graphics are actually needed for this game!). The reset() method doesn't really have a whole lot to do:

```
this.reset = function() {

  this.player.reset();
  this.deadCounter = 0;
  this.vertMoveCount = 0;
  if (this.regenPath) {
    this.correctPath = jscript.math.genRandomNumber(0, 9)
  }
  this.regenPath = false;
} // End reset().
```

The player is first reset to his starting position with a call to player.reset(). Next, the deadCounter and vertMoveCount fields are reset to zero. We then check to see if regenPath is true, and if so, we pick a new correct path through the tile field. Lastly, regenPath is then set to false, so that the next time reset() is called, unless it is a result of the player winning, we won't choose a new correct path through the tile field.

Handling the Player State: Winner, Dead, or Active

Moving on to the processFrame() method, we first encounter the same type of screen-clearing loop we saw in Cosmic Squirrel, which hides all the images in the gameImages array. After that is a blit() of the background.

Next is a largish switch block. This switch is on the state of the player. The first case is if the player has won:

```
case "W":
  addToScore(1000);
  this.regenPath = true;
  this.reset();
break;
```

It's a simple matter of adding 1000 to the score (I was in a generous mood!), setting the regenPath to true so that a new correct path through the tiles will be chosen, and calling reset() to get the player back to the starting position, and that's that.

The next case is if the player has died:

```
case "D":
  blit(this.gameImages["playerDieing"], this.player.x, this.player.y);
  this.deadCounter++;
  if (this.deadCounter > 48) {
    this.reset();
  }
break;
```

In this case, we blit() the player death graphic at the player's current location. That image is an animated GIF of the player being electrocuted. We want that to be shown in two seconds, which is 48 frames (24 fps). That's where the deadCounter variable comes in. It's used to keep track of how many frames have elapsed. When we exceed 48, we just call reset(). Note that regenPath will be set to false at this point, so the same correct path is still in effect.

Now we come to the case where the player is alive. This is where the bulk of the work is done. First things first though—let's get the player on the screen!

```
if (gameState.playerDirectionUp || gameState.playerDirectionDown ||
  gameState.playerDirectionLeft || gameState.playerDirectionRight) {
  blit(this.gameImages["playerJumping"], this.player.x, this.player.y);
} else {
  blit(this.gameImages["playerStanding"], this.player.x, this.player.y);
}
```

A different image is needed when the player is jumping vs. when he is just standing still.

Next are four if blocks: one for each possible direction of movement. They are all pretty similar, so let's just review the first one, which is the case of the player moving up:

```
if (gameState.playerDirectionUp) {
  // If movement is done, finish up
  if (this.player.y <= (this.player.prevY - 16)) {
    this.vertMoveCount  = 0;
    this.player.x = this.player.prevX + 10;
    this.player.y = this.player.prevY - 16;
    gameState.playerDirectionUp = false;
    if (this.isDeathTile()) {
      this.player.state = "D";
    }
  } else { // Otherwise, move the player
    this.player.y = this.player.y - 3;
    this.vertMoveCount++;
    if (this.vertMoveCount > 1) {
      this.vertMoveCount = 0;
      this.player.x = this.player.x + 3;
    }
  }
}
```

This case (and the case of moving down) is actually a little more complicated than left and right, because both vertical and horizontal movement are involved. This is due to the fact that the tiles are organized diagonally from each other. So, first we determine if the player has already moved far enough from the previous position, which is where he was when he started the move. If not (the else clause), the player is moved three pixels horizontally and three pixels vertically for every six pixels horizontally (that is, the player moves every other frame vertically, while he moves horizontally every frame). When the player finally has moved far enough (the if clause), the current position is set to the previous position plus the proper amount horizontally and vertically. This is because the essentially diagonal movements would require fractional moves to be precise, and there is always a slight error when using integers. So to make the player wind up at the proper location in the end, the final values are based on the previous values.

Finally, a call to isDeathTile() is made. This function determines whether the tile the player is currently on is an electrified one. Here is the code for isDeathTile():

```
this.isDeathTile = function() {

  if (
    this.deathMatrix[this.correctPath][this.player.tileY][this.player.tileX]
    == 0) {
    return true;
  } else {
    return false;
  }

} // End isDeathTile().
```

A lookup into the deathMatrix is done, using the correctPath value as the first dimension, and the player's X/Y location as the second and third dimensions. When the value is zero, it's an electrified tile; in which case, the player's state value is changed to "D" to signify he is dead.

Please do have a look at the other three cases for the other directions of movement. As I said, you'll find them all similar to the one for moving up, but it's certainly a good idea to check them out for yourself.

Handling Player Keyboard Events

Next up is the keyDownHandler() function:

```
this.keyDownHandler = function(inKeyCode) {

  // Although the right hand action button does nothing in this game,
  // it looks like things are broken if it doesn't press, so let's let
  // it be pressed, just to keep up appearances!
  if (inKeyCode == KEY_SPACE) {
    gameState.playerAction = true;
  }

} // End keyDownHandler().
```

Recall that this mini-game has full control over the key events, so nothing happens automatically. In this case, it means that although the action button, which is the right handle on the game console, does nothing in this game, it wouldn't even react when the user clicks space. This makes it look like something isn't working, since the button should probably be pressable, regardless of whether it serves a purpose. So, the keyDownHandler() function needs to deal with that. It's a simple matter of setting the playerAction flag to true.

The keyUpHandler() has a little more meat to it though. First, we check to be sure the player isn't currently moving and is alive:

```
if (!gameState.playerDirectionUp && !gameState.playerDirectionDown &&
    !gameState.playerDirectionLeft && !gameState.playerDirectionRight &&
    this.player.state == "A") {
```

This is to avoid the situation where the player starts a move, then releases the key before the on-screen action has completed the jump to the new tile. If we were to allow this code to fire in that case, the player movement flag would be reset prematurely, causing the jump to terminate in the middle. That wouldn't be good! So, once we determine it's OK to proceed, we first check to see if it's the spacebar that is being released; in which case, it's just a matter of setting playerAction to false.

Once again, we encounter four cases corresponding to each of our cardinal directions. And also again, we'll just take a look at the first one here because the rest are substantially the same.

```
case KEY_UP:
  if (this.moveMatrix[tileY][tileX].indexOf("U") != -1) {
    if (tileY == 0 && tileX == 4) {
      this.player.state = "W";
    } else {
      this.player.tileY--;
      this.player.prevX = this.player.x;
      this.player.prevY = this.player.y;
      gameState.playerDirectionUp = true;
      gameState.playerDirectionRight  = false;
      gameState.playerDirectionDown = false;
      gameState.playerDirectionLeft  = false;
    }
  }
break;
```

First, we do a lookup into the moveMatrix for the tile the player is currently on. We see if the string value for that tile contains the letter U, indicating the player can move up from that tile. If he can, we need to see if the player is standing on the tile directly in front of the door. In that case, we change the player state to "W" to indicate a win. If the player hasn't won yet, then we decrement tileY to indicate the tile he will wind up on. Then we just set the movement flags accordingly, and we're finished.

The last piece of the puzzle is the destroy() method, which just cleans up the images created in init(). And, of course, there is also the prototype line, as in Cosmic Squirrel, to make sure the Deathtrap class extends the MiniGame class.

Writing Refluxive.js

Only one more game left to review now, and that's Refluxive. As before, let's begin by looking at the UML diagram of the Refluxive class itself, shown in Figure 11-18.

Figure 11-18. *UML diagram of the Refluxive class*

By now, this is all pretty much old hat for you. This game is again the typical `MiniGame`-derived class, with a few game-specific fields.

Setting Up the Bouncies and Paddle

First is another inner class, this time named `BouncyDesc`, as shown in Figure 11-19. The X/Y coordinates of a bouncy, which is the thing you need to keep bouncing in the air, is defined here, as is its width and height, both of which are needed for collision detection. We also define which direction the bouncy is moving. A flag field tells whether the bouncy is still on the screen. When all three bouncies have their onScreen fields set to false, the game is over. Unlike the other two games, Refluxive can actually end!

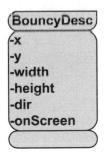

Figure 11-19. *UML diagram of the BouncyDesc class*

The next inner class is the `PaddleDesc` class, shown in Figure 11-20. The `PaddleDesc` class describes the paddle—in other words, the player. It's a simple matter of X/Y location plus width and height for collision detection.

Figure 11-20. *UML diagram of the PaddleDesc class*

After that are two fields: `paddle`, which is a pointer to an instance of `PaddleDesc`, and `bouncies`, which is an array of `BouncyDesc` objects.

Starting the Game

Next, we come to some code, starting with the `init()` method:

```
this.init = function() {

  // Configure base game parameters.
  this.gameName = "refluxive";

  // Load all the images required for this game.
  loadGameImage("background");
  loadGameImage("bouncy1");
  loadGameImage("bouncy2");
  loadGameImage("bouncy3");
  loadGameImage("paddle");
  loadGameImage("gameOver");

  // Initial bouncy positions.
  this.bouncies.push(
    new BouncyDesc(jscript.math.genRandomNumber(1, 180), 10, "SE"));
  this.bouncies.push(
    new BouncyDesc(jscript.math.genRandomNumber(1, 180), 70, "SW"));
  this.bouncies.push(
    new BouncyDesc(jscript.math.genRandomNumber(1, 180), 140, "NE"));

} // End init().
```

This is pretty much just like all the other `init()` methods you've seen thus far. We set the game name, load the images needed by the game, and in this case, construct three `BouncyDesc` objects and push each into the `bouncies` array. Their horizontal location is set randomly, and the vertical location is static. Their initial direction of movement is static as well. These last two items are static to help ensure they start out in reasonable positions, are moving in sufficiently different ways, and are separated enough to make the game challenging.

One interesting thing to note is that each of the bouncies is its own image, even though they are all the same underlying GIF. This is necessary because each needs to be individually addressable. This is a bit inefficient, because we are loading the same GIF into memory three times. The browser and/or operating system might share it somehow, but we can't count on that. In such a limited game, this is hardly a major concern. For something more substantial, this is a shortcoming you would want to address somehow. One way to do this might be to modify the way the code works so that a game element is abstracted from its image or images. Maybe you have some sort of `ImageManager` class that contains all the images, and that deals with ensuring only a single instance of any given image exists, and the game elements would reference their images through that class.

Playing the Game

`processFrame()` is next, and it begins how the other two did: by clearing all the images off the screen. We then see a `blit()` of the background, just as in the other two games. After that comes a bit of code unique to this game:

```
if (!this.bouncies[0].onScreen && !this.bouncies[1].onScreen &&
  !this.bouncies[2].onScreen) {
  blit(this.gameImages["gameOver"], 10, 40);
  return;
}
```

As I mentioned earlier, Refluxive is the only one of the three games that can end before the user decides to quit. It ends when all three of the bouncies are off the screen. So, here we check for that condition, and if it is met, we display the "Game Over" message. Since the rest of `processFrame()` doesn't apply in this case, we simply `return`, and the frame is complete.

If the game is still going, however, we begin by `blit()`'ing the paddle and then the three bouncies:

```
if (this.bouncies[0].onScreen) {
  blit(this.gameImages["bouncy1"], this.bouncies[0].x, this.bouncies[0].y);
}
if (this.bouncies[1].onScreen) {
  blit(this.gameImages["bouncy2"], this.bouncies[1].x, this.bouncies[1].y);
}
if (this.bouncies[2].onScreen) {
  blit(this.gameImages["bouncy3"], this.bouncies[2].x, this.bouncies[2].y);
}
```

For each bouncy, we check if it's on the screen. There wouldn't be much sense in `blit()`'ing something the player can't see!

Next, we deal with player movements:

```
if (gameState.playerDirectionRight) {
  this.paddle.x = this.paddle.x + 4;
  // Stop at edge of screen
  if (this.paddle.x > 174) {
    this.paddle.x = 174;
  }
}
```

```
if (gameState.playerDirectionLeft) {
  this.paddle.x = this.paddle.x - 4;
  // Stop at edge of screen
  if (this.paddle.x < 1) {
    this.paddle.x = 1;
  }
}
```

Some simple bounds checking ensures that the player can't move the paddle off either edge of the screen. Since the player can move only left and right in this game, that's all there is to it! Note that this game doesn't need to implement keyDownHandler() or keyUpHandler(), as the default implementations do the job just fine, as was the case with Cosmic Squirrel. It's nice to keep the code size down this way!

Next up is bouncy movement. To do that, we loop through the bouncies array, and for each bouncy, we first check if it is on the screen. If not, we just continue the loop. If it is on the screen, we start by moving it based on its current dir value:

```
if (this.bouncies[i].dir == "NE") {
  this.bouncies[i].x = this.bouncies[i].x + 3;
  this.bouncies[i].y = this.bouncies[i].y - 3;
}
if (this.bouncies[i].dir == "NW") {
  this.bouncies[i].x = this.bouncies[i].x - 3;
  this.bouncies[i].y = this.bouncies[i].y - 3;
}
if (this.bouncies[i].dir == "SE") {
  this.bouncies[i].x = this.bouncies[i].x + 3;
  this.bouncies[i].y = this.bouncies[i].y + 3;
}
if (this.bouncies[i].dir == "SW") {
  this.bouncies[i].x = this.bouncies[i].x - 3;
  this.bouncies[i].y = this.bouncies[i].y + 3;
}
```

"NE", as I'm sure you can guess, stands for northeast. Correspondingly, "NW" is northwest, "SE" is southeast, and "SW" is southwest. These are the four possible directions a bouncy can move. For each, we adjust the X and Y coordinates as appropriate.

After that's done, we need to deal with the situation where the bouncies bounce off the sides and top of the screen. To do that, we use this code:

```
// Bounce off the frame edges (horizontal).
if (this.bouncies[i].x < 1) {
  if (this.bouncies[i].dir == "NW") {
    this.bouncies[i].dir = "NE";
  } else if (this.bouncies[i].dir == "SW") {
    this.bouncies[i].dir = "SE";
  }
}
if (this.bouncies[i].x > 182) {
```

```
    if (this.bouncies[i].dir == "NE") {
      this.bouncies[i].dir = "NW";
    } else if (this.bouncies[i].dir == "SE") {
      this.bouncies[i].dir = "SW";
    }
  }
  // Bounce off the frame edges (vertical).
  if (this.bouncies[i].y < 1) {
    if (this.bouncies[i].dir == "NE") {
      this.bouncies[i].dir = "SE";
    } else if (this.bouncies[i].dir == "NW") {
      this.bouncies[i].dir = "SW";
    }
  }
}
```

When the X coordinate of the bouncy is less than one, it means it has collided with the left edge of the screen. In that case, we basically reverse the direction of travel. So, if it is moving northwest, we reverse it to northeast, and southwest becomes southeast. Likewise, for the right side of the screen (coordinate 182, because the bouncy is 18 pixels wide, so the right edge is at 182+18=200 at that point), we again reverse the directions. The same basic logic is applied for the top of the screen.

Note that there is no check for the bottom of the screen here, at least, not like these, because that's the one case where the bouncy doesn't bounce. It just exits the bottom of the screen if the player misses it. The last check needed here is that case precisely: when the bouncy leaves the screen:

```
if (this.bouncies[i].y > 200) {
  this.bouncies[i].onScreen = false;
  subtractFromScore(50);
}
```

When the player misses a bouncy, it becomes dead, so to speak, by setting its onScreen property to false. This also costs the player some points—50 in this case.

Only one thing remains to make this a complete game. Can you guess what that is?

We need to make it possible for the player to bounce the bouncies! The code to accomplish that is as follows:

```
if (detectCollision(this.bouncies[i], this.paddle)) {
  // Reverse bouncy direction.
  if (this.bouncies[i].dir == "SE" &&
    this.bouncies[i].x + 9 < this.paddle.x + 12) {
    this.bouncies[i].dir = "NW";
    addToScore(10);
  }
  if (this.bouncies[i].dir == "SE" &&
    this.bouncies[i].x + 9 > this.paddle.x + 12) {
    this.bouncies[i].dir = "NE";
    addToScore(10);
  }
```

```
    if (this.bouncies[i].dir == "SW" &&
      this.bouncies[i].x + 9 < this.paddle.x + 12) {
      this.bouncies[i].dir = "NW";
      addToScore(10);
    }
    if (this.bouncies[i].dir == "SW" &&
      this.bouncies[i].x + 9 > this.paddle.x + 12) {
      this.bouncies[i].dir = "NE";
      addToScore(10);
    }
  } // End collision detected.
```

This is still inside the for loop, so we're working with one specific bouncy. We call the detectCollision() function, and if it returns true, we do the same sort of direction reversal as you saw earlier. One difference here is that the direction depends on which side of the paddle hit the bouncy. If the bouncy was moving southeast, and the player hits it with the left side of the paddle, the direction changes to northwest. If it hits the right side of the paddle, it changes to northeast. For southwest on the left side, it switches to northwest, and for southwest on the right side, it becomes northeast.

And that, dear friends, concludes the actual game logic behind Refluxive! The only code left is the usual destroy() method, which calls destroyGameImage() for each image loaded in init(), and, again, the prototype specification stating the Refluxive class extends MiniGame.

And that's a wrap folks! I hope you'll agree that this application had a lot to offer in terms of how to do object-oriented programming with JavaScript. More important though, I hope you had as much fun checking this game out as I had writing it! Try not to waste too much time at the office playing it!

Suggested Exercises

I'm sure you don't need me to tell you, but my main suggestion is to write some more mini-games! It is my hope that, as time allows, I will port some of the other mini-games from the full-blown K&G Arcade to JavaScript. I will post them to the Apress download site along with the other code for this book. Adding them should be a simple matter of dropping the appropriate directory in with the resources for the games and updating the GameSelection class. And you can do the same!

Come up with one or two simple game ideas, and try to implement them. If you've never written a game before, I suspect you'll get a great deal of pleasure out of it and will learn a lot along the way. You probably won't be able to pull off Final Fantasy, Halo, or anything like those games, so don't think too big. Just aim big enough that it's challenging and yet still fun at the same time. After all, that's what video games are all about . . . or at least should be!

One other suggestion is to save high scores for each mini-game in cookies, and create a Hall of Fame screen to display them. This should give you a good feel for how a screen in the game is developed, and also some practice with cookies. I would suggest this exercise as a first task, just to get your feet wet.

Summary

You might not think it at first, but programming a game is one of the best exercises in any language on any platform to exercise your skills and learn. Games touch a variety of areas of expertise and often require you to stretch your abilities a good bit, and I believe this chapter has shown that.

In this chapter, you saw an object-oriented approach to JavaScript that leads to clean, flexible code. The project demonstrated how inheritance can be achieved in JavaScript. You saw some tricks for maximizing performance, including avoiding superfluous DOM element accesses and speeding up the overall application. You even picked up a tidbit or two on basic game theory! And I believe that we built a game that is actually fun to play!

Ajax: Where the Client and Server Collide

Ajax is all the rage today. It seems that you can't even be a web developer these days without knowing at least something about Ajax!

In this chapter, you will learn a bit about Ajax and put it to use building a one-on-one support chat application, as you can see at the sites of many companies that provide live chat support for their products and services. This will be the one project in this book that uses a server component as well, so you'll see how that all fits together. Additionally, you'll be introduced to a new library, Mootools, and see what it has to offer.

Chat System Requirements and Goals

Let's make believe for a bit. Say we're a new company on the block. We'll call ourselves Metacusoft Systems, for no other reason than the domain name is available and Googling for it returns no results, so I can be reasonably sure I'm not infringing on anyone. The first reader to register the domain name and start a company gets a prize! (No, you really don't, but feel free to take the name.)

Anyway, we sell widgets. Yes, the typical, mundane widget product. It's wonderful, it's amazing, and no one can live without it, and yet we can't come up with a more descriptive name. And, as great a product as it obviously is, it's not always a completely smooth ride for our customers. Sometimes, the widget doesn't, um, widgetate, as it should. Sometimes, although we would never admit this in a financial filing, customers need some assistance to effectively change their lives for the better with our amazing widgets. So, we need to offer some support for them.

We'll have a couple of people available via phone (over in India, of course, where there's apparently no shortage of folks named Bill, Mike, Tom, Sam, and Dave). We'll also offer something for the online crowd, those people who, like the Morlocks,[1] shun human contact. We'll offer a live one-on-one chat system where customers can communicate with human beings in real time, without needing to really talk to them and risk an actual conversation.

---

1. Morlock is the name of an invented species, offshoots of the human race, created by the famous author H.G. Wells in the novel *The Time Machine*, who exist many, many, *many* years in the future (the Morlocks, not H.G. Wells). The Morlocks live underground and are at that point almost not even identifiable as humans (formerly so anyway). Oh yeah, the Morlocks eat a species known as the Eloi, who are also descendants of the human race. Nice, huh?

It's a relatively simple application—one person types, the other sees it, and that's about the extent of it. Still, we'll try to jazz it up just a bit.

- The application should look halfway decent. After all, this is the public face of our company for those having difficulties with our product. They're probably already a little ticked at us, and we don't want to annoy them further with an ugly web site!

- Let's allow customers the ability to copy a transcript of their chat to their clipboard for pasting in another application. This way, they can have a record of their conversation in case they need to call and yell at us later for something. Let's also give them the ability to print the transcript directly from the application, so that when they sue, they have the documentation they need to win (perhaps we're being a little too good to our customers?).

- The application should of course be Ajax-based and should use the Mootools library to provide that functionality (along with anything else we may need that it offers). It's pretty tough to do a one-on-one chat in HTML and JavaScript without a server component, so we'll need a server in the mix here. We'll code the back-end in Java and Microsoft technologies (ASP specifically), so that at least a majority of developers reading this should be covered.

With those really pretty limited set of requirements in tow, let's get a move on and see how we'll put this thing together, shall we? Well, in fact, let's first look at how we *won't* be doing things and why.

The "Classic" Web Model

In the beginning, there was the Web. And it was good. All manner of catchy new words, phrases, and terms entered the lexicon, and we felt all the more cooler saying them. (Come on, admit it, you felt like Spock the first couple of times you used the word "hypertext" in conversation, didn't you?) *Webapps*, as our work came to be known, were born. These applications were, in a sense, a throwback to years gone by when applications were hosted on "big iron" and were accessed in a time-share fashion, since no processing was done locally on the machine where the user was interacting with the application. They also were in no way, shape, or form as "flashy" as the Visual Basic, PowerBuilder, Delphi, and C++ "fat clients" that followed them (which are still used today, although less so with the advent of webapps).

The webapps that have been built for many years now—indeed are still built today on a daily basis—have one big problem: they are, by and large, redrawing the entire screen each time some event occurs. They are intrinsically server-centric to a large extent. When the user does something (beyond some trivial things that can occur client side such as mouse-over effects and such), a server must get involved. It has to do some processing, and then redraw what the user sees to incorporate the applicable updated data elements. This is, as I'm sure you have guessed, highly inefficient.

This model of application development is what I refer to as the "classic" web design pattern, or model (I haven't heard anyone else use the term in this sense before, but I still can't imagine I'm the first!). The classic web model to me means the paradigm where the server, for nearly every user event, redraws the entire screen. This is how webapps have been built for about 15 years now, since the Web first began to be known in a broad sense. Conversely, the term "modern" web model refers to the new mode of developing webapps, where the client is asked to share the load a bit and play a more prominent role in the functioning of the application.

You may be asking yourself, "If we've been doing the classic web thing for so long, and even still do it today, what's wrong with it?" In many ways, absolutely nothing! In fact, there is still a great deal of value to that way of designing webapps. The classic web model is great for largely linear application flows, and it is also a wonderful medium for delivering information in an accessible way. That model makes it is easy for most people to publish information and to even create rudimentary applications with basic user interactions. The classic web model is simple, ubiquitous, and accessible to most people.

It is not, however, an ideal environment for developing complex applications with a lot of user interaction. The fact that people have been able to do so to this point is a testament to the ingenuity of engineers, rather than an endorsement of the Web as an application distribution medium!

It makes sense to differentiate now between a *webapp* and a *web site*, as summarized in Table 12-1. There are really two different purposes served by the Web at large. One is to deliver information. In this scenario, it is very important that the information be delivered in a manner that is readily accessible to the widest possible audience. This means not only people with disabilities who are using screen readers and such devices, but also those using more limited capability devices like cell phones, PocketPCs, and kiosk terminals. In such situations, there tends to be no user interaction, aside from jumping from static document to static document, or at most very little interaction via simple forms. This mode of operation for the Web can be classified as web sites.

Table 12-1. *Summary Comparison of Webapps vs. Web Sites*

Webapp	Web Site
Designed with much greater user interaction in mind	Very little user interaction, aside from navigation from document to document
Main purpose is to perform some function or functions, usually in real time, based on user inputs	Main purpose is to deliver information, period
Uses techniques that require a lot more of the clients accessing them	Tends to be created for the lowest common denominator in terms of client capabilities
Accessibility tends to take a back seat to functionality out of necessity and the simple fact that it's hard to do complex and yet accessible webapps	Accessibility is usually considered and implemented to allow for the widest possible audience
Tends to be more event-based and nonlinear	Tends to be somewhat linear with a path the user is generally expected to follow, with only minor deviations

Webapps, on the other hand, have a wholly different focus. They are not concerned with simply presenting information, but in performing some function based on what the user does and what data the user provides. The user can be another automated system in many cases, but usually we are talking about a flesh-and-blood human being. Webapps tend to be more complex and much more demanding of the clients that access them. In this case, *clients* refer to web browsers.

This is another problem with the classic model: in order to maintain accessibility for the widest possible audience, you generally need to design to the lowest common denominator, which severely limits what you can do. Let's think a moment about what the lowest common denominator means in this context. Consider what you could and could not use to reach the absolute widest possible audience out there today. Here is a list of what comes to mind:

Client-side scripting: No, you couldn't use this because many mobile devices do not yet have scripting support, or are severely limited. This does not even consider those people on full-blown PCs who simply choose to disable scripting for security or other reasons.

CSS: You could use style sheets, but you would have to be very careful to use an older CSS specification to ensure most browsers would render styles properly—none of the fancier CSS 2.0 capabilities, for instance.

Frames: No, frames are not universally supported, especially on many portable devices. Even when they are supported, you need to be careful because a frame is essentially like having another browser instance in terms of memory (and in some cases, it very literally *is* another browser instance), and this can be a major factor in mobile devices.

Graphics: Graphics can be tricky in terms of accessibility because they tend to convey more information than an `alt` attribute can. So, some of the meaning of the graphic can easily be lost for those with disabilities, no matter how vigilant you are to help them.

Newer HTML specs: Many people out there are still using older browsers that may not even support HTML 4.01, so to be safe, you will probably want to code to HTML 3.0. Obviously, you will lose some capabilities in doing so.

Probably the most important element here, certainly for our purposes in this book, is the lack of client-side scripting. Without client-side scripting, many possibilities are not available to you as a developer. Most important is the fact that you have virtually no choice but to have the server handle every single user interaction and to respond with a completely redrawn view. You may be able to get away with some meta refreshes in frames in some cases, or perhaps other tricks of the trade, but frames may not be supported, so you might not even have that option!

You may be wondering, "What is the problem with the server rendering entire pages?" Certainly, that approach has benefits, and the inherent security of being in complete control of the runtime state of the application (the user can't hack the code) is a big one. Not having to incur the delay of downloading the code to the client is another. However, there are indeed some problems that in many cases overshadow the benefits. Perhaps the most obvious is the load on the server. Asking a server to do all this work on behalf of the client many times over across a number of simultaneous requests means that the server needs to be more robust and capable than otherwise might be required. This all translates to dollars and cents in the long run, because you'll need to purchase more server power to handle the load.

Now, many people have the "just throw more hardware at it" mentality, and we are indeed in an age where that works most of the time. But that is much like saying that because we can throw bigger and bigger engines in cars to make them go faster, then that's exactly what we should always do when we need or want more speed. In fact, we can make cars go faster by making a smaller engine more efficient in design and execution, which in many ways is much more desirable—that is, if you like clean, fresh air to breathe! Perhaps an even better metaphor would be to say it is like taking a midsized car and continually adding seats tied to it around the outside to allow for more people to ride "in" the car, rather than trying to find a more efficient way for them to get where they are going. While this duct-tape solution might work for a while, eventually someone is going to fall off and get crushed by the 18-wheeler driving behind us!

Another problem with the server-does-it-all approach is that of network traffic. Network technology continues to grow in leaps and bounds at a fantastic rate. Many of us now have broadband connections, which we could not fully saturate if we tried (and I for one have tried!). However, that does not mean we should have applications that are sending far more information per request than necessary. We should still strive for thriftiness, should we not?

The other big problem with the classic approach is simply how the user perceives the application. When the server needs to redraw the entire screen, it generally results in a longer wait time to see the results, not to mention the visual redrawing that many times occurs in webapps, flickering, and things of that nature that users universally dislike in a big way. Users also do not like losing everything they entered when something goes wrong, which is another common failing of the classic model.

At the end of the day, the classic model still works well on a small scale, and for delivering mostly static information, but it doesn't scale very well and it doesn't deal with the dynamic nature of the Web today nearly as well. In this context, *scale* refers to added functionality in the application, not simultaneous request handling capability (although it is quite possible that is in play, too). If things do not work as smoothly, or if breakages result in too much loss, or if perceived speed is diminished, then the approach didn't scale well.

The classic model will continue to serve us well for some time to come in the realm of web sites, but in the realm of webapps—the realm you are likely interested in if you are reading this book—its demise is at hand, and its slayer is the hero of our tale: Ajax!

Ajax

Ajax came to life, so to speak, at the hands of one Jesse James Garrett of Adaptive Path (http://www.adaptivepath.com). I am fighting my natural urge to make the obvious outlaw jokes here! Mr. Garrett wrote an essay in February of 2005 (you can see it at http://www.adaptivepath.com/publications/essays/archives/000385.php), in which he coined the term *Ajax*.

Ajax, as I'd be willing to bet my dog you know already (I don't have a dog, but I will buy one and give it to you if you don't know what Ajax stands for—OK, not really) stands for Asynchronous JavaScript and XML. The interesting thing about Ajax, though, is that it doesn't have to be asynchronous (but virtually always is), doesn't have to involve JavaScript (but virtually always does), and does not need to use XML at all (but probably does half the time). In fact, one of the most famous Ajax examples, Google Suggest (http://www.google.com/webhp?complete=1&hl=en), doesn't pass back XML at all! The fact is that it does not even pass back data per se; it passes back JavaScript that contains data (which, if you've read Chapter 5 already, is actually something you've seen: the Yahoo and Google web services used there returned data wrapped in a JavaScript function call).

Ajax to the rescue! (Now you'll always know what code/architecture would look like personified as a superhero.)

The Ajax Frame of Mind

Ajax has, at its core, an exceedingly simple, and by no stretch of the imagination original, concept: it is not necessary to refresh the entire contents of a web page for each user interaction, or each "event," if you will. When the user clicks a button, it is no longer necessary to ask the server to render an entirely new page, as is the case with the classic web model. Instead, you can define regions on the page to be updated, and have much more fine-grained control over user events as well. No longer are you limited to simply submitting a form or navigating to a new page when a link is clicked. You can now do something in direct response to a non-submit button being clicked, a key being pressed in a text box—in fact, to any event happening!

The server is no longer completely responsible for rendering what the user sees; some of this logic is now performed in the user's browser. In fact, in a great many cases, it is considerably better to simply return a set of data and not a bunch of markup for the browser to display. As we traced along my admittedly rough history of application development, you saw that the classic model of web development is, in a sense, an aberration to the extent that we actually had it right before then!

Ajax is, most important, a way of thinking, an approach to application development, and a mind-set, not a specific technology. The interesting thing about Ajax is that it is in no way, shape, or form *new*; only the term used to describe it is. I was reminded of this fact at the Philadelphia Java Users Group. A speaker by the name of Steve Banfield was talking about Ajax, and he said (paraphrasing from memory), "You can always tell someone who has actually done Ajax because they are pissed that it is all of a sudden popular." This could not be truer! I was one of those people doing Ajax years and years ago. I just never thought what I was doing was anything special and hence did not give it a "proper" name. Mr. Garrett holds that distinction. It also would not be Ajax in a form we recognize today, but that's because the technological approach may have changed, but the underlying mind-set hasn't, and that's the key point in my opinion.

When you get into the Ajax frame of mind, which is what we are really talking about, you are no longer bound by the rules of the classic web model. You can now take back at least some of the power the fat clients offered, while still keeping the benefits of the Web. Those benefits begin, most important perhaps, with the ubiquity of the web browser.

Have you ever been at work and needed to give a demo of your new fat client app (for example, a Visual Basic app) on a machine you never touched before? Ever had to do it in the boardroom in front of top company executives? Ever had that demo fail miserably because of some DLL conflict you couldn't possibly anticipate? You are a developer, so the answer to all of those questions is likely yes (unless you work in the public sector, and then you probably don't present to corporate executives, but you get the point). If you have never done Windows development, you may not have had these experiences. You will have to take my word for it when I say that such situations were, for a long time, much more common than any of us would have liked. With a web-based application, this is generally not a concern. Ensure the PC has the current browser and version, and off you go 98% of the time.

We've all been there. Live demos and engineers do not mix!

The other major benefit of a webapp is distribution. No longer do you need a three-month shakedown period to ensure your new application does not conflict with the existing suite of corporate applications. An app running in a web browser, security issues aside, will not affect, or be affected by, any other application on the PC (and I am sure we all have war stories about exceptions to that, but they are just that: exceptions).

Of course, you probably knew those benefits already, or you wouldn't be interested in web development in the first place.

Sounding good so far, huh? It's not all roses in Ajax land, however. Ajax is not without its problems. Some of them are arguably only perceived problems, but others are concrete.

Accessibility and Similar Concerns

First and foremost, in my mind at least, is the issue of accessibility. You will lose at least some accessibility in your work by using Ajax because devices like screen readers are designed to read an entire page, and since you will no longer be sending back entire pages, screen readers will have trouble. My understanding is that some screen readers can deal with Ajax to some degree, largely depending on how Ajax is used (if the content is literally inserted into the DOM, it makes a big difference). In any case, extreme caution should be used if you know people with disabilities are a target audience for your application, and you will seriously want to consider (and test!) whether Ajax will work in your situation. I am certain this problem will be addressed better as time goes on, but for now, it is definitely a concern. In the meantime, here are some things you can do to improve accessibility:

Let users know about the dynamic updates. Put a note at the top of the page that says the page will be updated dynamically. This will give users the knowledge that they may need to periodically request a reread of the page from the screen reader to hear the dynamic updates.

Use alert() *pop-ups.* Depending on the nature of the Ajax you are using on a page, use alert() pop-ups when possible, as these are read by a screen reader. This is a reasonable enough suggestion for things like Ajax-based form submission that will not be happening too frequently, but obviously if you have a timed, repeating Ajax event, this suggestion would not be a good one.

Add visual cues. Remember that it is not only the blind who have accessibility needs; it can be sighted people as well. For them, try to use visual cues whenever possible. For instance, briefly highlighting items that have changed can be a big help. Some people call this the "yellow fade effect", which I talked about back in Chapter 1 as one kind of effect that actually enhances the user experience. The idea is to highlight the changed item in yellow, and then slowly fade it back to the nonhighlighted state. Of course, it does not have to be yellow, and it does not have to fade, but the underlying concept is the same: highlight changed information to provide a visual cue that something has happened. Remember that changes caused by Ajax can sometimes be very subtle, so anything you can do to help people notice them will be appreciated.

Another disadvantage of Ajax to many people is added complexity. Many shops do not have in-house the client-side coding expertise Ajax requires (the use of toolkits that make it easier notwithstanding). The fact is, errors that occur on the client side are still, by and large, harder to track down than server-side problems, and Ajax does not make this any simpler. For example, View Source does not reflect changes made to the DOM.

Another issue is that Ajax applications will many times do away with some time-honored web concepts, most specifically back and forward buttons and bookmarking. Since there are no longer entire pages, but instead fragments of pages being returned, the browser cannot bookmark things in many cases. Moreover, the back and forward buttons cease to have the same meanings because they still refer to the last URL that was requested, and Ajax requests almost never are included (requests made through the XMLHttpRequest are not added to history, for example, because the URL generally does not change, especially when the method used is POST).

Ajax: A Paradigm Shift for Many

Ajax does, in fact, represent a paradigm shift for some people (even most people, given what most webapps are today) because it can fundamentally change the way you develop a webapp. More important perhaps is that it represents a paradigm shift for the *users*, and, in fact, it is the users who will drive the adoption of Ajax. Believe me, you will not long be able to ignore Ajax as a weapon in your arsenal.

Put a non-Ajax webapp in front of some users, and then put that same app using Ajax techniques in front of them, and guess which one they are going to want to use all day, nine times out of ten? The Ajax version!

Users can immediately see the increased responsiveness of an Ajax application, and will notice that they no longer need to wait for a response from the server while they stare at a spinning browser logo, wondering if anything is actually happening. They will see that the application alerts them on the fly of error conditions they would have to wait for the server to tell them about in the non-Ajax webapp. They will see functionality like type-ahead suggestions, instantly sortable tables, and master/detail displays that update in real time—things that they would *not* see in a non-Ajax webapp. They will see maps that they can drag around as they can in the full blown mapping applications they spent $80 on in the past. All of these things will be obvious advantages to the user. Users have become accustomed to the classic webapp model, but when confronted with something that harkens back to those fat-client days in terms of user-friendliness and responsiveness, there is almost an instantaneous realization that the Web as they knew it is dead, or at least should be!

If you think about many of the big technologies to come down the pipe in recent years, it should occur to you that we technology folks, rather than the users, were driving many of them. Do you think a user ever asked for an Enterprise JavaBean (EJB)–based application? No, we just all thought it was a good idea (how wrong we were there!). What about web services? Remember when they were going to fundamentally change the way the world of application construction worked? Sure, we are using them today, but are they, by and large, much more than an interface between cooperating systems? Not usually. Whatever happened to Universal Description, Discovery, and Integration (UDDI) directories and giving an application the ability to find, dynamically link to, and use a registered service on the fly? How good did that sound? To us geeks, it was the next coming, but it didn't even register with users.

Ajax is different, though. Users can see the benefits. The advantages are very real and very tangible to them. In fact, we as technology people, especially those of us doing Java web development, may even recoil at Ajax at first, because more is being done on the client, which is contrary to what we have been drilling into our brains all these years. After all, we all believe scriptlets in JavaServer Pages (JSPs) are bad, eschewing them in favor of custom tags. The users do not care about elegant architectures, separation of concerns, and abstractions allowing for code reuse. Users just want to be able to drag the map around in Google Maps (http://maps.google.com) and have it happen in real time, without waiting for the whole page to refresh.

The difference is clear. Users want it, and they want it now (come now, we're adults here!)

RICH INTERNET APPLICATIONS (RIAS)

Ajax is not the only new term floating around these days that essentially refers to the same thing. You may have also heard of Web 2.0 and rich Internet applications (RIAs). RIA is a term I particularly like. Although there is no formal definition with which I am familiar, most people get the gist of its meaning without having to Google for it.

In short, the goal of an RIA is to create a "rich" application that is web-based. The application runs in a web browser but looks, feels, and functions more like a typical fat-client application than a typical web site. Things like partial-page updates are taken for granted, and hence Ajax is always involved in RIAs (although what form of Ajax is involved can vary; indeed, you may not find the XMLHttpRequest object, the prototypical Ajax solution, lurking about at all!). These types of applications are always more user-friendly and better received by the user community they serve. In fact, your goal in building RIAs should be for users to say, "I didn't even know it was a webapp!"

Gmail (http://gmail.google.com) is a good example of an RIA, although it isn't perfect. While it has definite advantages over a typical web site, it still looks and feels very much like a web page. By the way, Google developers have probably done more to bring Ajax to the forefront of people's minds than anyone else. They were not the first to do it, or even the best necessarily, but they certainly have created some of the most visible examples, and have really shown people what possibilities Ajax opens up.

The "Hello World" of Ajax Examples

So, enough theoretical musings. What does Ajax look like in the flesh? Figure 12-1 shows a very simple sample application on the screen (don't expect much here, folks!).

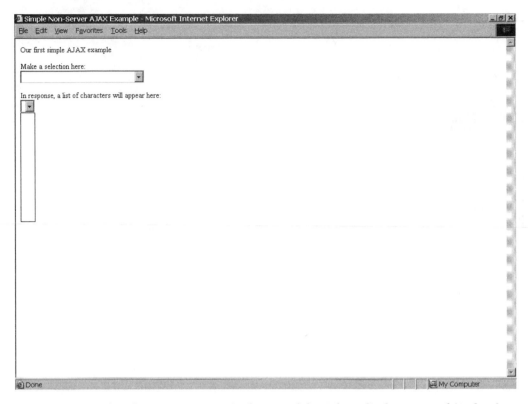

Figure 12-1. *Note that there is no content in the second drop-down list because nothing has been selected yet in the first one.*

As you can see, there is no content in the second drop-down list initially. This list will be dynamically populated once a selection is made in the first drop-down list, as shown in Figure 12-2.

Figure 12-2 shows that when a selection is made in the first drop-down list, the contents of the second are dynamically updated. In this case, you see characters from the greatest television show ever, *Babylon 5*. (Don't bother arguing, you know I'm right. And besides, you'll get your chance to put in your favorites later!) Now let's see how this "magic" is accomplished.

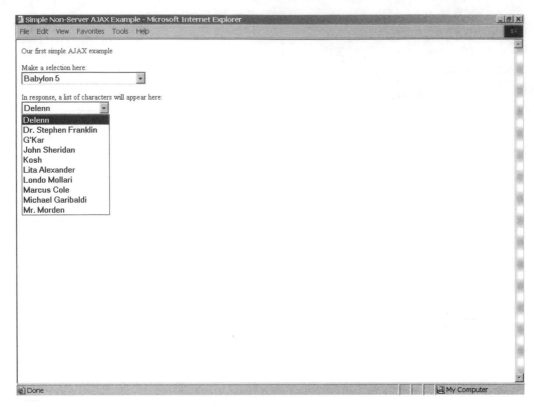

Figure 12-2. *A selection has been made in the first drop-down list, and the contents of the second have been dynamically created from what was returned by the "server."*

Listing 12-1 shows the first page of our simple Ajax example, which performs a fairly typical Ajax-type function: populate one `<select>` box based on the selection made in another. This comes up all the time in web development, and the "classic" way of doing it is to submit a form—whether as a result of the user clicking a button or by a JavaScript event handler—to the server and let it render the page anew with the updated contents for the second `<select>`. With Ajax, none of that is necessary.

Listing 12-1. *Our First Real Ajax Application*

```
<html>

  <head>

    <title>Simple Non-Server AJAX Example</title>

    <script>

      // This is a reference to an XMLHttpRequest object.
      xhr = null;
```

```
  // This function is called any time a selection is made in the first
  // <select> element.
  function updateCharacters() {
    // Instantiate an XMLHttpRequest object.
    if (window.XMLHttpRequest) {
      // Non-IE.
      xhr = new XMLHttpRequest();
    } else {
      // IE.
      xhr = new ActiveXObject("Microsoft.XMLHTTP");
    }
    xhr.onreadystatechange = callbackHandler;
    url = document.getElementById("selShow").value + ".htm";
    xhr.open("post", url, true);
    xhr.send(null);
  }

  // This is the function that will repeatedly be called by our
  // XMLHttpRequest object during the life cycle of the request.
  function callbackHandler() {
    if (xhr.readyState == 4) {
      document.getElementById("divCharacters").innerHTML =
        xhr.responseText;
    }
  }

  </script>

</head>

<body>

  Our first simple AJAX example
  <br><br>

  Make a selection here:
  <br>
  <select onChange="updateCharacters();" id="selShow">
    <option value=""></option>
    <option value="b5">Babylon 5</option>
    <option value="bsg">Battlestar Galactica</option>
    <option value="sg1">Stargate SG-1</option>
    <option value="sttng">Star Trek The Next Generation</option>
  </select>
  <br><br>
```

```
    In response, a list of characters will appear here:
    <br>
    <div id="divCharacters">
      <select></select>
    </div>

  </body>
</html>
```

Let's walk through the code and see what's going on. Note that this is not meant to be a robust, production-quality piece of code. It's meant to give you an understanding of basic Ajax techniques, nothing more. There's no need to write me about all the flaws you find!

First things first: the markup itself. In our `<body>`, we have little more than some text and two `<select>` elements. Notice that they are not part of a `<form>`. You'll find that forms tend to have less meaning in the world of Ajax. Many times, you'll begin to treat all your form UI elements as top-level objects along with all the other elements on your page (in the `<body>` anyway).

The first `<select>` element is given the ID selShow. This becomes a node in the DOM of the page. You'll notice the JavaScript event handler attached to this element. Any time the value of the `<select>` changes, we'll be calling the JavaScript function named updateCharacters(). This is where all the "magic" will happen. The rest of the element is nothing unusual. I have simply created an `<option>` for some of my favorite shows.

After that is another `<select>` element—well, sort of. It's actually an empty `<select>` element, but wrapped in a `<div>`. You'll find that probably the most commonly performed Ajax function is to replace the contents of some `<div>`. That is exactly what we'll be doing here. In this case, what will be returned by the "server" (more on that in a minute) is the markup for our `<select>` element, complete with `<option>` elements listing characters from the selected television show. So, when you make a show selection, the list of characters will be appropriately populated, and in true Ajax form, the whole page will not be redrawn, but only the portion that has changed—the second `<select>` element in this case (or more precisely, the `<div>` that wraps it).

Let's quickly look at our mock server. Each of the shows in the first `<select>` has its own HTML file that, in essence, represents a server process. You have to take a leap of faith here and pretend a server was rendering the response that is those HTML pages. They all look virtually the same, so I'll show only one as an example. Take a look at Listing 12-2.

Listing 12-2. *Sample Response Listing Characters from the Greatest Show Ever (Babylon 5)*

```
<select>
  <option>Delenn</option>
  <option>Dr. Stephen Franklin</option>
  <option>G'Kar</option>
  <option>John Sheridan</option>
  <option>Kosh</option>
  <option>Lita Alexander</option>
  <option>Londo Mollari</option>
  <option>Marcus Cole</option>
  <option>Michael Garibaldi</option>
  <option>Mr. Morden</option>
</select>
```

As expected, it really is nothing but the markup for our second `<select>` element.

So, now we come to the part that does all the work here: our JavaScript function(s). First is the `updateCharacters()` function. This basic code will very soon be imprinted on the insides of your eyelids if you work with Ajax for any length of time, because it's the prototypical Ajax function. Let's tear it apart, shall we?

The first thing we need, as one would expect, is an `XMLHttpRequest` object, which is the object at the core of Ajax as most people know it. This object, a creation of Microsoft (believe it or not!), is nothing more than a proxy to a socket. It has a few (very few) methods and properties, but that is one of the benefits. It really is a very simple beast.

Notice the branching logic here. It turns out that getting an instance of the `XMLHttpRequest` object is different in IE than in any other browser. Now, before you get your knickers in a knot and get your anti-Microsoft ire up, note that Microsoft invented this object, and it was the rest of the world that followed. So, while it would be nice if Microsoft developers updated their API to match everyone else's, it isn't their fault we need this branching logic! The others could just as easily have duplicated what Microsoft did exactly, too, so let's not throw stones here—we're all in glass houses on this one.

Late-breaking news: IE7 implements `XMLHttpRequest` as a native object that can even work when ActiveX is disabled! This means that the branching code I'm talking about here, theoretically, isn't necessary. However, I've been reading quite a lot about problems with this, and questions about whether the IE team really implemented a native version or just cleverly wrapped the ActiveX version in a JavaScript façade. There is also talk of performance issues that accompanies this. So, at the end of the day, I suggest sticking with the tried-and-true method for a while longer. Really though, you'll likely be using some sort of library for your Ajax functionality most of the time anyway, so you'll largely be insulated from these concerns and won't so much care whether it's truly native or not. Still, this certainly is information worth noting.

This is probably a good time to point out that `XMLHttpRequest` is pretty much a de facto standard. It is also being made a true W3C standard as well, but for now it is not. It is safe to assume that any "modern" browser—that is, a desktop web browser that is no more than a few versions old—will have this object available. More limited devices—such as PocketPCs, cell phones, and the like—may not have it. But by and large, `XMLHttpRequest` is a pretty ubiquitous little piece of code.

Continuing on in our code review, once we have an `XMLHttpRequest` object instance, we assign the reference to it to the variable `xhr` in the global page scope. Think about this for just a minute. What happens if more than one `onChange` event fires at close to the same time? Essentially, the first will be lost because a new `XMLHttpRequest` object is spawned, and `xhr` will point to it. Worse still, because of the asynchronous nature of `XMLHttpRequest`, a situation can arise where the callback function for the first request is executing when the reference is nulled, which means that callback would throw errors due to trying to reference a null object. If that were not bad enough, this will be the case only in some browsers, but not all (although my research indicates most would throw errors), so it might not even be a consistent problem. Remember that I said this was not robust, production-quality code! This is a good example of why. That being said, it is actually many times perfectly acceptable to simply instantiate a new instance and start a new request.

Think about a fat client that you use frequently. Can you spot instances where you can kick off an event that, in essence, cancels a previous event that was in the process of executing? For example, in your web browser, can you click the Home button while a page is loading, thereby causing the page load to be prematurely ended and the new page to begin loading? Yes, you can, and that is essentially what happens by starting a new Ajax request using the same reference variable. It is not an unusual way for an application to work, and sometimes it is downright desirable.

The next step we need to accomplish is telling the XMLHttpRequest instance what callback handler function to use. Ajax requests have a well-defined and specific life cycle, just like any HTTP request (and remember that is all an Ajax request is at the end of the day!). This cycle is defined as the transitions between ready states (hence the property name, onreadystatechange). At specific intervals in this life cycle, the JavaScript function you name as the callback handler will be called. For instance, when the request begins, your function will be called. As the request is chunked back to the browser, in most browsers at least (IE being the unfortunate exception), you will get a call for each chunk returned (think about those cool status bars you can finally do with no complex queuing and callback code on the server!). Most important for us in this case, the function will be called when the request completes. We will see this function in just a moment.

The next step is probably pretty obvious: we need to tell the object which URL we want to call. We do this by calling the open() method of the object. This method takes three parameters: the HTTP method to perform, the URL to contact, and whether we want the call to be performed asynchronously (true) or not (false). Because this is a simple example, each television show gets its own HTML file pretending to be the server. The name of the HTML file is simply the value from the <select> element with .htm appended to the end. So, for each selection the user makes, a different URL is called. This is obviously not how a real solution would work. The real thing would likely call the same URL with some sort of parameter to specify the selected show. But some sacrifices were necessary to keep the example simple and to not need anything on the server side of things.

The HTTP method can be any of the standard HTTP methods: GET POST, HEAD, and so on. Most of the time, you will be passing GET or POST. The URL is self-explanatory, except for one detail: if you are doing a GET, you must construct the query string yourself and append it to the URL. That is one of the drawbacks of XMLHttpRequest. You take full responsibility for marshalling and unmarshalling data sent and received. Remember that it is in essence just a very thin wrapper around a socket. This is where any of the numerous Ajax toolkits can come in quite handy, as you'll see when we use the Mootools library for this chapter's chat application.

Once we have the callback registered with the object and we have told it what we're going to connect to and how, we simply call the send() method. In this case, we are not actually sending anything, so we pass null. One thing to be aware of is that you can call send() with no arguments in IE, and it will work, but it won't work in Firefox (at least this was the case with my tests). Null works in both browsers, though, so null it is.

Of course, if you actually had some content to send, you would do so here. You can pass a string of data into this method, and the data will be sent in the body of the HTTP request. Many times, you will want to send actual parameters, and you do so by constructing essentially a query string in the typical form var1=val1&var1=val1 and so forth, but without the leading question mark. Alternatively, you can pass in an XML DOM object, and it will be serialized to a string and sent. Lastly, you could send any arbitrary data you want. If a comma-separated list does the trick, you can send that. Anything other than a parameter string will require you to deal with it; the parameter string will result in request parameters as expected.

So far, I've described how a request is sent. It is pretty trivial, right? Well, the next part is what can be even more trivial, or it can be much more complex. In our example, it is the former. I am referring to the callback handler function. Our callback handler function does very little.

First, it checks the readystate of the XMLHttpRequest object. Remember I said this callback will be called multiple times during the life cycle of the request? Well, the readystate code you will see will vary with each life cycle event. For the purposes of this example, we are interested in code 4, which indicates the request has completed. Notice that I didn't say completely *successfully*! Regardless of the response from the server, the readystate will be 4. Since this is a simple example, we don't care what the server returns. If an HTTP 404 error (page not found) is received, we don't care in this case. If an HTTP 500 error (server processing error) occurs, we still do not care. The function will do its thing in any of these cases. I repeat my refrain: this is not an industrial-strength example!

When the callback is called as a result of the request completing, we simply set the innerHTML property of the <div> on the page with the ID divCharacters to the text that was returned. In this case, the text returned is the markup for the populated <select>, and the end result is the second <select> is populated by characters from the selected show.

Now, that wasn't so bad, was it?

■**Tip** For a fun little exercise, and just to convince yourself of what is really going on, I suggest adding one or two of your own favorite shows in the first <select>, and creating the appropriately named HTML file to render the markup for the second <select>.

One other point I should make is that in previous chapters, such as in Chapter 5, you saw what I said was essentially Ajax. However, after seeing this simple application, you may be confused. Let me clear up that confusion right now. Remember that I've been trying to enforce the idea that Ajax is more about approach than it is implementation. Just because XMLHttpRequest isn't in the equation doesn't mean what you see isn't Ajax. The dynamic <script> tag technique is, in my opinion, as much Ajax as anything you see in this chapter. The idea of the client doing more work and of the server not rendering full views any more is what matters. So, while this chapter isn't necessarily the first exposure to Ajax you've had in this book, it's the first example of what most people mean when they say Ajax. It's a bit of conceptual/semantical banter I suppose, but a point I believe is worth making.

If all of this seemed like an attempt to brainwash you about what Ajax is and why it's good, that is because, in a sense, it was! Ajax can seem to some people like a really bad idea, but those people tend to see only the problems and completely ignore the benefits. Because of my belief that Ajax is more about philosophy and thought process than it is about specific technologies, it is important to sell you on the ideas underlying it. It is not enough to simply show you some code and hope you agree! Ajax opens up the Web to fulfilling a lot more of the promise so many people hold for it, and I feel that web developers should understand why it's important and put the underlying concepts to good use.

JSON

Recall when I said that Ajax doesn't require XML be returned or passed to the server at all? As it turns out, XML isn't really even the most common data format. That distinction most likely goes to something called JSON, or JavaScript Object Notation, which I introduced in Chapter 2.

The acronym JSON is, I feel, a bit of a misnomer because, while it *can* represent an object, it often does not, but that is really just a name thing. The basic idea is that it is a way to structure data that is returned to a caller.

JSON is billed as being a lightweight, system-independent data interchange format that is easy for humans to read, easy for computers to parse, and easy for computers to generate. It uses a syntax that will be immediately familiar to most programmers that have any experience with a C-family language (including Java and JavaScript). It is built on two basic concepts that are pretty much universal in programming: a collection of name/value pairs (maps, keyed lists, associative arrays, and so on) and an order list of values (lists or arrays).

Well, enough CompSci gobbledygook! Let's see what JSON looks like.

```
{"firstName":"Frank","lastName":"Zammetti","age":"34"}
```

Really? Is that all there is to it? I wish I could try to impress you with my advanced knowledge and say there is more to JSON than that, but no, that actually is all there is to it! As you can see, it looks similar to an array in Java, but not quite, because two elements are defined between each delimiter. The item to the left of the colon is the key, and the value to the right is the value. Each pair is separated by a comma, and the whole thing is wrapper in curly braces. It's simple!

Where it gets really pretty cool though is when you want to handle a JSON response in JavaScript. All you have to do is this:

```
var json = eval("(" + myJSONString + ")");
```

The result of this, assuming myJSONString contained some valid JSON in the form discussed a few sentences ago, is that a new variable, json, will be available to your script. From then on, if you want to get the first name in the response, you simply do this:

```
alert(json.firstName);
```

Really, that's it! What actually happened is the eval() call created the json variable, giving it the value of the response. The json variable is an associative array in JavaScript, so you can access the members in the same way you would access members of any other associative array. Neat, isn't it?

Although this chapter's project does not do it, you can send JSON to the server as well. If you go to http://www.json.org, you will find some libraries for a number of different languages that help you generate and parse JSON. Of course, we're only talking about generating and parsing a string here. Ultimately, it certainly is not rocket science, as you will see when we get to that code later. However, do keep in mind that even though JSON is quite simple at its core, because you can nest elements within one another, and have arrays of elements, it can actually become a bit of a pain to generate manually in some cases. Think of serializing an entire object graph to JSON, for instance. While the JSON itself may not be terribly challenging to understand, the fact is that writing the code to generate it could be a bit more of a challenge. In such situations, you would be wise to look for help in the form of libraries and existing code to make your job a bit easier.

I should mention that JSON is a general-purpose messaging format, and as such, you can use it quite effectively outside Ajax work. Many people have actually taken to it much more than XML, because it is less verbose but tends to be similarly human-readable. I am sure we have all seen "bad" XML that is difficult to comprehend. Likewise, you can make JSON difficult to understand if you try. For example, in my previous book on Ajax, I showed an Ajax-based game that would return a chunk of JSON like the following:

{"dm":"false","pn":"Aragorn The Weak","ht":"100","hp":"1","gp":"10","iu":"true",
"vu":"true","di":"false","wn":"false","ec":"false","mo":"o","es":"false","md":"g
gggggssss[[gggggggggggggggggggg([[[[[[[[[[gggggggg[gggggggGgg[[[[gggggggggg[[[[
[(gggggg[[[[[[[[[[[[[[[[[[g^gggggg[[[[gggggggggg[[gggggggggggfgggggggggggfgggg
gggggggg"}

That does not look terribly readable to me! The names of the elements are obviously not meant for human consumption. Although you can probably guess quite a few of the elements just by knowing a little about the game (do feel free to buy that book, *Practical Ajax Projects with Java Technology*, ISBN: 1-59059-695-1, if you are interested), you may not be able to guess all of them. The reason this is the case here is that, for a game, you generally want things to happen as quickly as possible. Therefore, the choice was to make the JSON messages readable to a human, who would likely never have to read them except perhaps for debugging purposes, or make them as small and efficient as possible so as to (a) not take too long to generate or parse and (b) not take too long to transmit across the wire.

Most applications tend not to be quite as time-sensitive as a game though, so I would absolutely suggest always making your JSON (or XML for that matter!) as human-readable as possible. Using `displayMessage` instead of `dm` and `playerName` instead of `pn`, for example, is what I would suggest in such a case.

At this point though, you are ready to use JSON, believe it or not! Go forth and be fruitful with your new knowledge!

Mootools

Now that you have a good foundation on which to build with regard to Ajax in general, let's see how the very fine Mootools library (`http://mootools.net`) makes it so much easier and cleaner, and less error-prone than what you saw in the little sample application in Listing 12-1.

With a name like Mootools, you would think it invites all sorts of ridicule, but that would be far from what it deserves! Mootools is a lightweight, modular JavaScript framework that covers most of the bases a modern JavaScript developer would need. Mootools is constructed of a number of modules, including the Core module (the base Mootools module), the Native module (where you can find basic JavaScript extensions and utilities), the Remote module (where things like Ajax lives), and the Effects modules (where UI FX and such are found).

One of the coolest things about Mootools is its download page. When you go to it, you will be presented with a list of the available modules and add-ons. You simply check off the ones you want, and the package you selected will then download is a customized version with only those modules you selected, nicely compressed and ready to go. This is incredibly handy and ensures that you get only the code you are really interested in, which gives new meaning to the term lightweight! What's more, as you select modules to include, any other modules that it depends on will automatically be selected. Heck, even if you don't want to download Mootools, the download page is great fun!

■**Note** The `mootools.js` file in this project includes everything available as of this writing (Mootools v1.0). So, if there's something you want to play with, you don't have to go build your own download if you don't want to—just grab this file in the downloadable source and start playing.

There is obviously a lot to Mootools, and unfortunately, the chat application won't do much more than scratch the surface. So, let's get to scratching right now.

To fire off an Ajax request with Mootools, this is all you have to do:

```
new Ajax("<URL>", {
  postBody :
    Object.toQueryString(
      { "parm1" : $("someID1").value, "parm2" : $("someID2").value }
    ),
  onComplete : function(inResponse) {
    // Do something.
  }
}).request();
```

That's it! Instantiate a new Ajax object, passing some parameters to its constructor, and you are off to the races. The first parameter is the URL to call. The next parameter, postBody, is the contents that will be POSTed to the URL. You'll notice that Mootools extends some JavaScript classes—Object in this case—to offer us the toQueryString() method. With this, we can feed it a list of parameters and their values, and a proper query string will be constructed for us. You'll notice, too, the use of the $() operator, which you've seen in other chapters. That operator gives us a references to a DOM object whose ID we pass in. Well, Mootools offers an implementation of this function as well, and you can see here it being used to get the value of what is presumably a text field (we guess this because we're going after the value attribute).

The last parameter, onComplete, is a JavaScript function that will be executed when the request successfully returns. You can do anything you want here, and it does not have to be specified in-line as I show here. You can just reference a function that exists elsewhere. Either way, that's all there is to an Ajax call with Mootools!

Other available options include evalScripts, which will evaluate any JavaScript in the response upon its return; update, which will automatically insert the response into the named page element; and evalResponse, which evaluates the entire response. These are some very handy functions to have available, and it's really nice to not have to write the code yourself!

You should most definitely go rummage through the Mootools documentation (which is pretty good, by the way) and see what's available. It hasn't been around as long as some other libraries, but it definitely has benefited from seeing the mistakes of others, because it gets a great deal right.

Now that we've taken care of the preliminaries, it's time for . . . drum roll please . . . the chat application!

A Preview of the Chat Application

To begin, let's take a peek at the application. Figure 12-3 shows the initial logon screen. The application actually has two different logon screens—one for customers and one for support personnel—but they look very similar (only differing in the text that appears).

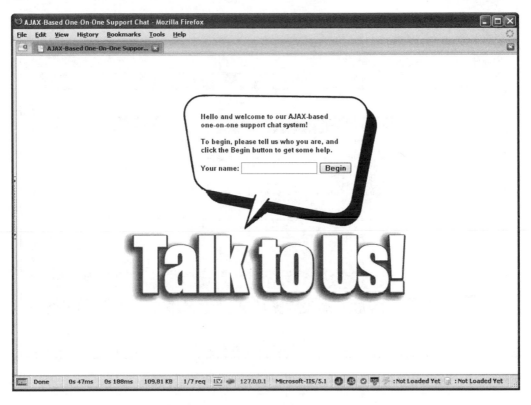

Figure 12-3. *The logon screen for the chat system*

Once you have logged in, you will see the main chat screen, as shown in Figure 12-4. This screen contains several elements. First, we have a greeting near the top, giving a bit of the personal touch. Just to the left of that is a little green talking head, just to give some levity to the customer. Below that is the chat area, where the text of the conversation will appear. To the left of that is the menu of operations the chatter can perform, such as copying the transcript of the chat or exiting the chat session. At the bottom is a constantly updating display of the current date and time. You know how long people can sometimes wait on help lines, and a chat system probably isn't any different, so it's nice to help them keep track of time (although, in this particular implementation, the customer can't log in unless someone is immediately available, but we'll ignore that fact for the sake of the previous sentence making sense).

These two illustrations pretty well cover what the application is all about. There's not much to it, as I said earlier. However, what's behind it is a bit meatier, so let's jump right into that.

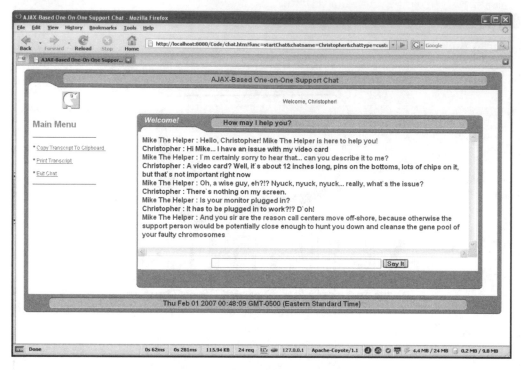

Figure 12-4. *The main chat window where all the "action" (ahem) occurs*

Dissecting the Chat Solution

By now, you undoubtedly know the routine: we start with a look at the directory structure of the application, shown in Figure 12-5, to get a feel for what pieces are involved. However, this final application is, in fact, a bit atypical compared to the rest.

If you're a Java web developer, this will look pretty normal. For those of you who are not in the Java world, let me explain that the WEB-INF directory means that this is a Java web application. The single file in there, web.xml, defines the application. However, this application is good for the Microsoft folks out there, too.

Since the primary focus of this book is the client side of things, I didn't want to get very far at all into the server side of it. I needed to make the server side as simple and easy as possible, and that means eliminating "extra" steps like compiling code or deploying applications. With that goal in mind, this application is easy to get running. If you're a Java developer, simply copy the entire directory to where applications are deployed in your favorite app server. For instance, if you're using Tomcat (which I very much suggest, by the way), copy it into the /webapps directory. Start your server, and you'll be able to access the application immediately (its URL will be something like http://localhost:8080/chat, assuming you copied the chat directory over, and assuming your installation is listening on port 8080).

If you're a Microsoft technology developer, you're probably familiar with Internet Information Services (IIS). If so, to get this application running there, simply copy the directory into INetpub/wwwroot, and you're all set.

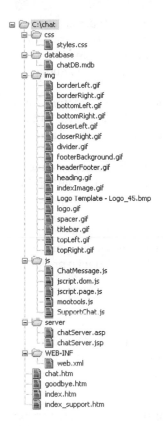

Figure 12-5. *Directory structure of the Chat application*

There actually is one additional configuration step involved in both versions, but it is trivial. It involves specifying which version you're using—ASP or JSP—and pointing to the database file. I'm getting ahead of myself though; we'll get to all that in a bit.

Whether we're talking about the Java version or the Microsoft version, the server side is implemented as a single JSP file or ASP file. This means that there is nothing to compile, no class paths to worry about, or anything like that. Now, before you start throwing things at me from a distance, I'll be the first to admit this probably isn't the way you would implement such an application in an ideal world. It doesn't follow best practices in terms of separation of concerns and the like. However, it *does* mean that you should be up and running in a matter of seconds and there's little chance of anything going wrong. So, please bear with me in terms of overall application architecture, I admit this isn't going to win any prizes! It does, however, have the benefit of working and being pretty easy to understand, so it serves its purpose well. There's no reason you couldn't use this application for real—you just wouldn't want to write your Computer Science thesis on it!

Anyway, thinly veiled apology aside, let's move on. The JSP and ASP files that make up the server component of the application are found in the server subdirectory. In the css directory is a single styles.css file, as you've seen in virtually every application in this book.

In the database directory, you'll find an Access database file named chatDB.mdb. This is another of those choices you probably wouldn't make in an ideal world, but for the sake of a project in a book, it's a good choice. Using an Access database file, and referencing it directly as you'll see when we get to the code, means there is no data source setup to worry about, which again should serve to make getting it running easier.

In the img directory are the image resources for the application. In the js directory are all the JavaScript files, including Mootools and some classes that the application uses. You'll also find two of the packages from Chapter 3 that we'll use: the jscript.dom package and the jscript.page package.

Lastly, in the root directory are four HTML documents. chat.htm is the main portion of the application. index.htm is the page you first access (as a customer) to enter a chat session. index_support.htm is the entry point for support personnel. goodbye.htm is a simple page seen when you exit the chat.

OK, I did some foreshadowing there, so let's dive right in and get to all the details. Although I've typically started with the style and HTML files in other projects, this time, I'm going to jump right in to the JavaScript. It will help you understand some of the hints I dropped previously about specifying which version is in use.

Writing SupportChat.js

The SupportChat class, contained in the SupportChat.js file, is the main client-side class that represents the bulk of the application. As shown in the UML diagram in Figure 12-6, it contains four fields, one to determine the version and three that are transient in nature (contain values used during execution of the application):

- serverType: The value that determines whether we're running the ASP or the JSP version. The value is literally either asp or jsp. This is used to create a reference to the appropriate page in the server directory. So, if you want to drop the application into IIS and run it, you need to change the value here to asp. To run it under Tomcat or another servlet container, make sure the value is jsp. That's all there is to changing between the two versions.

- chattype: Determines whether the chatter is a customer or a support personnel. customer and support are the two possible values.

- chatname: The name the chatter is logged in as.

- lastMessageTime: Holds the last time when the application requested new messages from the server. We'll get to the mechanics of that in a moment, but suffice it to say this is required for it to work.

A number of methods exist in this class, and we'll now look at them one by one.

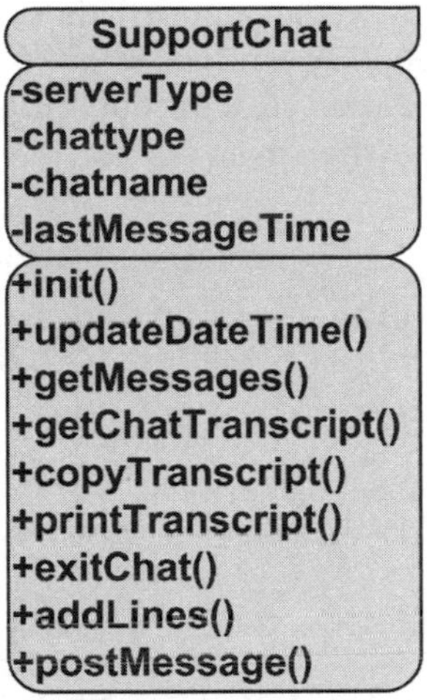

Figure 12-6. *UML diagram for the SupportChat class*

The init() Method: Starting Things Up

The init() method is called when the main page, chat.htm, loads into the browser:

```
this.init = function() {

  // Get the chatter type
  this.chattype - jscript.page.getParameter("chattype");

  // Get the chatter's name
  this.chatname = jscript.page.getParameter("chatname");

  // Insert greeting.
  $("spnChatname").innerHTML = this.chatname;

  // Set a timer to fire to update the time at the bottom.
  setTimeout(updateDateTime, 0);

  // Set a timer to look for new messages on the server
  // (once every 2 seconds).
  setTimeout(getMessages, 2000);

} // End init().
```

First, this method gets the type of chatter this is by using the getParameter() method of the jscript.page object, which we built in Chapter 3. The name of the chatter is retrieved the same way. Once that is done, we insert the chatter's name into the spnChatname <span>, which gives us the greeting you see at the top.

After that, two timeouts are set. The first is used to update the time at the bottom of the page. Note that the interval is set to zero, meaning this will fire immediately, which is what we want.[2] Otherwise, we would wait a second for the time to initially be displayed at the bottom. The second timeout is used to periodically request new messages from the server.

The updateDateTime() Method: Running the Clock

The first timeout calls the updateDateTime() method, so let's look at that.

```
var updateDateTime = function() {

  $("pDateTime").innerHTML = new Date();
  setTimeout(updateDateTime, 1000);

} // End updateDateTime().
```

This is about what you would expect. We insert the string representation of a Date object into the pDateTime element, and set the timeout again to elapse one second later. It's a piece of cake!

The getMessages() Method: Talking to the Server

The second timeout calls the getMessages() method, and there's a little more to see there for sure.

```
var getMessages = function() {

  new Ajax("server/chatServer." + chat.serverType, {
    postBody :
      Object.toQueryString(
        { "func" : "getMessages", "chatname" : chat.chatname,
        "lastMessageTime" : chat.lastMessageTime }
      ),
    onComplete : function(inResponse) {
      // Parse JSON response.
      var messageJSON = eval("(" + inResponse.trim() + ")");
      chat.lastMessageTime = messageJSON.lastMessageTime;
      var lines = new Array();
      // Iterate over messages received.
      for (var i = 0; i < messageJSON.messages.length; i++) {
        var nextMessage = messageJSON.messages[i];
        // Construct a new ChatMessage and add to array.
        var chatMessage = new ChatMessage();
        chatMessage.setTimestamp(nextMessage.timestamp);
        chatMessage.setChatname(nextMessage.chatname);
```

---

2. You may be wondering why not just call the function directly and then set up the timeout. My answer is that this is simply another way to do it. Either way would work just fine. This seems slightly cleaner to me since it's one line of code rather than two, and the mechanism that fires the function repeatedly is the same one that fires it initially. There's no right or wrong though; it's just one alternative vs. another.

```
          chatMessage.setMessage(nextMessage.message);
          lines.push(chatMessage);
        }
        // Display new message lines.
        addLines(lines);
      }
    }).request();

    // Kick off the timer again.
    setTimeout(getMessages, 2000);

  } // End getMessages().
```

Here, we have our first actual Ajax and the first usage of Mootools. As you can see, the URL is constructed using the value of the serverType field, as previously described. We then use the Object.toQueryString() method to construct the contents of the POST body. Those contents consist of the parameter func, which tells the server which function is being performed; chatname, which again is the name of the chatter posting the message as stored in the chatname field of the SupportChat class; and lastMessageTime, which is the time that the last request for messages was made. Any message from the chatter or chat partner in the conversation that is posted subsequent to this lastMessageTime will be returned. Since we're checking only for messages every three seconds, it's possible that a number of messages were posted during that time, so we want to get them all in one burst to catch up, so to speak.

We also define in-line a function to execute when the response returns. This callback first parses the JSON being returned, and then iterates over the messages received (which could be none, of course, but this code doesn't break in that situation). For each message present, we construct a ChatMessage object, which is basically a Data Transfer Object (DTO) representing a message. You'll see that class shortly, but it's really nothing but a storage container for the attributes of a message, which are its timestamp (when it was posted), the name of the chatter who posted it (chatname), and the message itself.

After the ChatMessage object is created and populated, it is pushed onto the lines array, which was created before the iteration over the messages began. After the iteration completes, we pass this array to the addLines() method, which is responsible for actually displaying all the messages in the array.

The addLines() Method: Showing Some Messages

Speaking of the addLines() method, let's see that right now.

```
  var addLines = function(inLines) {

    for (var i = 0; i < inLines.length; i++) {
      var message = inLines[i];
      var styleClass = "cssChatterText";
      if (message.getChatname() != chat.chatname) {
        styleClass = "cssSupportText";
      }
```

```
        htmlOut = "<div class=\"" + styleClass + "\">" +
          message.getChatname() + " : " +
          message.getMessage() +
          "</div>";
        $("divChat").innerHTML = $("divChat").innerHTML + htmlOut;
      }

  } // End addLines().
```

This is a pretty straightforward piece of code. It begins to iterate over the array of ChatMessage objects passed in, as part of the inLines array. For each element in the array, it first determines if the message was posted by the chatter or the chat partner. The styleClass variable stores the CSS class name that applies in either case, so we can have our messages in one color and our chat partner's messages in another color. Then, for each message, a <div> is constructed, and the name of the chatter and the message are inserted as its contents. Finally, the <div> is appended to the existing markup in the divChat <div>, and the message is then seen on the screen.

The postMessage() Method: Say It to the World!

You've now seen how messages are retrieved from the server and displayed. The other half of the equation is posting messages, and that is accomplished through the postMessage() method.

```
  this.postMessage = function(inLines) {

    new Ajax("server/chatServer." + chat.serverType, {
      postBody :
        Object.toQueryString(
          { "func" : "postMessage", "chatname" : chat.chatname,
          "messagetext" : $("postMessage").value }
        )
    }).request();
    $("postMessage").value = "";

  } // End addPostMessage().
```

Time for a bit more Ajax! Here, we're doing basically the same thing as you saw in getMessages(), but this time the func parameter has the value "postMessage", which makes sense I think! Here, we are providing a messagetext parameter, passing it the value of the postMessage text box. At the very end, we clear that text box so that the chatter can begin typing a new one. That's all there is to it.

The astute reader may be wondering how the chatters see their own messages. There's certainly nothing that handles that display here. The answer is that the message will be displayed as part of the next getMessage() cycle. Yes, that means there could be up to a three-second delay between the time chatters post the message and the time they see it on their own screen. This is probably OK to do, although it might be better to put it on the screen immediately (hint, hint).

The only things remaining in this class are the functions to deal with the three menu items, and the one to exit, so let's get to them right now.

The getChatTranscript() Method: For Posterity

First up is getChatTranscript(). This is a method used internally by the copyTranscript()
and printTranscript() methods, which are called by the corresponding menu items.
getChatTranscript() is responsible for literally grabbing the text of the chat session and
returning it to the caller.

```
var getChatTranscript = function() {

  // Get the text of the chat.
  var chatTranscript = $("divChat").innerHTML;

  // Now we need to go through the text and remove the HTML components so
  // we are left with nothing but text.  Then, for each line, we make sure
  // there's no trailing or leading whitespace, and we build up a string
  // containing all the lines, separated by linebreaks.
  var transcriptLines = chatTranscript.split(">");
  chatTranscript = "";
  for (var i = 0; i < transcriptLines.length; i++) {
    if (transcriptLines[i].toLowerCase().indexOf("</div") != -1) {
      transcriptLines[i] = transcriptLines[i].replace("</div", "");
      transcriptLines[i] = transcriptLines[i].replace("</DIV", "");
      chatTranscript += transcriptLines[i].trim() + "\r\n";
    }
  }

  return chatTranscript;

} // End getChatTranscript().
```

It begins by getting either the innerHTML of the divChat <div>. This is all the text you see
while chatting. Next, the text is split, using the String class's split() method, on the greater-
than sign or the closing of an HTML tag. This results in an array where each element is a single
message from the chat, plus lines consisting of just the opening markup of the <div> that wraps
each line.

A loop then begins to iterate over this array. For each element, we see if the element
contains the string "</div". This is only true of elements representing lines of text from the
chat; all other elements are the markup of the opening <div> only. Note that we need to
compare against a lowercase version of the string. This is because in IE, </div is present as </DIV,
so we wouldn't get a match back from indexOf() in that case. Once we find a match, we remove
the "</div" string by replacing it with nothing. Then we add the element to the chatTranscript
string variable, being sure to trim(), and adding a carriage return/line feed sequence after it.
The trim() function is added to the String class by Mootools, and it simply trims all whitespace
from both ends of the string.

The final result of all this is that the variable chatTranscript contains a text-only version of
the chat transcript with each message on its own line, without any blank lines or whitespace on
the ends of any lines. This string is returned, and this method's work is done.

The printTranscript() Method: Hurting the Earth to Keep Your Memories

As noted, the getChatTranscript() method is used by the printTranscript() method, which looks like this:

```
this.printTranscript = function() {

  // Get the transcript of the chat.
  var chatTranscript = getChatTranscript();

  // Open a new window for it.
  var newWindow = window.open();
  newWindow.document.open();
  newWindow.document.write("<pre>" + chatTranscript + "<pre>");
  newWindow.document.close();
  newWindow.print();

} // End printTranscript().
```

There's not much to it. First comes a call to getChatTranscript(). Then we just open a new window, write the string we got from getChatTranscript() inside a <pre> tag, and call the print() method on the window. The browser and operating system take it from there, and that's that.

The copyTranscript Method: Direct to Your Operating System

The last method, copyTranscript(), is the one that copies the transcript to the operating system's clipboard. There is definitely more involved to this than you might think at first.

```
this.copyTranscript = function() {

  // Get the transcript of the chat.
  var textToCopy = getChatTranscript();

  // Branch based on browser capabilities...
  if (window.clipboardData) {

    // Internet Explorer is easy!
    window.clipboardData.setData("Text", textToCopy);

    // Let the chatter know we're done.
    alert("Chat transcript has been copied to the clipboard");

  } else if (window.netscape) {

    // Netscape/Firefox is hard!  First, ask it for permission to do this.
    try {
      netscape.security.PrivilegeManager.enablePrivilege('UniversalXPConnect');
    } catch (exception) {
```

```
        alert(exception);
        return;
    }

    // Instantiate a clipboard object.
    var clip =
      Components.classes['@mozilla.org/widget/clipboard;1'].createInstance(
      Components.interfaces.nsIClipboard);
    // Instantiate a transferrable object and set it's "flavor."
    var trans =
      Components.classes['@mozilla.org/widget/transferable;1'].createInstance(
      Components.interfaces.nsITransferable);
    trans.addDataFlavor('text/unicode');
    // Instantiate a string object and set its value.
    var str =
      Components.classes["@mozilla.org/supports-string;1"].createInstance(
      Components.interfaces.nsISupportsString);
    str.data = textToCopy;
    // Set the value of the transferrable using the string.
    trans.setTransferData("text/unicode", str, textToCopy.length * 2);
    // Finally, put the text onto the clipboard.
    clip.setData(trans, null,
      Components.interfaces.nsIClipboard.kGlobalClipboard);

    // Let the chatter know we're done.
    alert("Chat transcript has been copied to the clipboard");

  } else {

    // Unsupported browser.
    alert("Unable to copy chat transcript to clipboard.\n\nOnly Internet " +
      "Explorer and Netscape-based browsers (including Firefox) " +
      "are supported.");

  }

} // End copyTranscript().
```

As you would expect by now, we begin with a call to getChatTranscript() to get the text of the chat session. Next, we check for the existence of the clipboardData attribute of the window object. If it is present, we're running in IE, and it's a piece of cake: a quick call to window.clipboardData.setData(), passing it the string returned by getChatTranscript(), and we're good to go.

Now, the situation is a lot more interesting if the browser is Netscape-based. If the window object has a netscape attribute, the first thing we need to do is ask for permission to copy data to the clipboard. That's the call to netscape.security.PrivilegeManager.enablePrivilege() you see. This results in a query to the user, as shown in Figure 12-7.

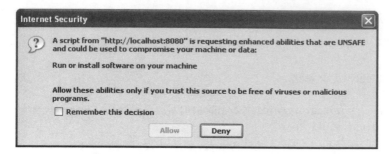

Figure 12-7. *Firefox security privilege query dialog box*

Simply answer Allow, and optionally check the box to remember the setting, and the contents will then be allowed onto the clipboard.

Note that if the Internet Security dialog box does not appear, and instead, you get an alert like the one shown in Figure 12-8, this means you need to go to the advanced configuration options. In the address bar, enter about:config and press Enter. You will see a long list of options. The one you are looking for is signed.applets.codebase_principal_support. Be sure this is set to true. After that setting is adjusted, you should get the dialog box shown in Figure 12-7.

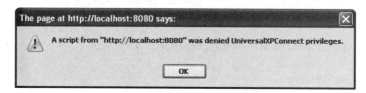

Figure 12-8. *If signed.applets.codebase_principal_support is set to false, you'll see this*

Once we have permission, or have alerted the user that permission is denied, we can move on. The first thing we need to do is create a clipboard object. That's the purpose of the line where the clip variable is defined.

Note that the slightly funky syntax you see here, and in the next few object instantiations, is the Netscape style of instantiating native browser objects. It amounts to basically naming the class you want an instance of, then asking the Components object to give you an instance. After that, you work with them as you would most any other object.

Next up is creation of a transferrable object, referenced by the trans variable. We also have to tell this object that its "flavor" is Unicode, so we are sure to get everything from the chat session properly.

Next, we instantiate a String object and store a reference to it in the str variable, and set its value to the text of the transcript text we retrieved earlier. Then we pass the String along to the transferrable object via a call to setTransferData(). Lastly, we copy that object to the clipboard via a call to the setData() method of the clipboard object.

We also have an else block at the end, covering the case where the browser isn't a supported type. I'm not sure which browsers this might occur in, since I don't have all of them to test with, but IE and Firefox are certainly supported, so the majority of users would have no problem.

The exitChat() Method: Outta Here, I Say!

Last is the exitChat() method. This is a simple confirmation pop-up. If the user agrees to exit, window.location is set to request from the mock server the exit page, which is just a page saying good-bye to the user.

So, that's the bulk of the client-side code of the application. The next thing to look at is that ChatMessage class I mentioned earlier. That won't take long, trust me!

Writing ChatMessage.js

The UML diagram for the simple ChatMessage class is shown in Figure 12-9. As previously mentioned, this is just a DTO for storing a single posted message that is part of the transcript of the current chat session.

Figure 12-9. *UML diagram of the ChatMessage class*

Its code is very simple, as you can see in Listing 12-3.

Listing 12-3. *The ChatMessage Class*

```
function ChatMessage() {


  /**
   * The time this message was posted.
   */
  var timestamp = "";


  /**
   * The chatname of the chatter who posted it.
   */
  var chatname = "";
```

```
/**
 * The text of the message
 */
var message = "";


/**
 * Mutator.
 *
 * @param inTime The new field value.
 */
this.setTimestamp = function(inTimestamp) {

  timestamp = inTimestamp;

} // End setTimestamp().


/**
 * Accessor
 *
 * @return The value of the time field.
 */
this.getTimestamp = function() {

  return timestamp;

} // End getTimestamp().


/**
 * Mutator.
 *
 * @param inChatname The new field value.
 */
this.setChatname = function(inChatname) {

  chatname = inChatname;

} // End setChatname().


/**
 * Accessor
 *
 * @return The value of the chatname field.
 */
```

```
this.getChatname = function() {

  return chatname;

} // End getChatname().


/**
 * Mutator.
 *
 * @param inMessage The new field value.
 */
this.setMessage = function(inMessage) {

  message = inMessage;

} // End setMessage().


/**
 * Accessor
 *
 * @return The value of the message field.
 */
this.getMessage = function() {

  return message;

} // End getMessage().


/**
 * Overriden toString() method.
 *
 * @return A meaningful string representation of the object.
 */
this.toString = function() {

  return "ChatMessage : [ " +
    "timestamp='" + timestamp + "', " +
    "chatname='" + chatname + "', " +
    "message='" + message + "' ]";

} // End toString().


} // End ChatMessage class.
```

See, I wasn't kidding! Just the three fields—`timestamp`, `chatname`, and `message`—which cover all the data we store about a given message, and the applicable accessor and mutator for each. Also, we have an overridden `toString()`, as you've seen other times throughout this book. This allows us to display a given instance of this class in a meaningful way, which is a practice I highly suggest getting into, because it makes debugging a lot easier.

Writing styles.css

At this point in the book, you've seen a number of style sheets in the other projects, so you probably don't need this one torn apart. I can tell you that there is nothing tricky in it whatso-ever, and the comments for each class pretty much give you the complete story of what the styles are.

The one thing I will point out, because it is the first time I've done this in any project so far, is the idea of styling specific HTML elements. The style sheets in other projects have usually taken this form:

```
.cssHeader {
    color : #ff0000;
}
```

You know that this declares a CSS style class named `cssHeader`. You can apply this to any arbitrary element on the page by setting the element's `class` attribute. However, what if we wanted to style all the `<h1>` elements on the page a certain way, and moreover, do so without setting a specific style class on each? You can do that with the following declaration:

```
h1 {
  color : #ff0000;
}
```

Now, any `<h1>` element on the page will be in red. In the style sheet for this project, that is done for a couple of elements, as you can see:

```
/* Style applied to tables. */
table {
  font-size        : 9pt;
  font-family      : arial;
}


/* Style applied to links. */
a:link {
  color            : #6a78a7;
}
```

```
/* Style applied to visited links. */
a:visited {
  color             : #6a78a7;
}


/* Style applied to links that are being hovered over. */
a:link:hover {
  color             : #33305b;
  background-color  : #f0f0f0;
  font-weight       : bold;
}


/* Style applied to h1 elements. */
h1 {
  font-size         : 20pt;
  color             : #000000;
  font-weight       : bold;
}


/* Style applied to h2 elements. */
h2 {
  font-size         : 15pt;
  color             : #8c9cd5;
  margin top        : 0px;
  margin-left       : 20px;
  margin-bottom     : 0px;
  font-weight       : bold;
}
```

One other thing to mention is how links are styled. For links (and some other elements), you can select what are essentially versions of the element. For instance, if you want to make all links that have not been clicked appear in red, you can set the color attribute of the a:link selector. If you want to make those links that have been visited show up in blue, you can set the color attribute of the a:visited selector. Finally, if you want all links to turn green when hovered over, set the color attribute of the a:linkhover selector. You can see this in the style sheet to give the hover effect on the menu items, which are links.

Other than those points, this style sheet is self-explanatory, so please do have a look at it to be sure you know what it's all about. Now, let's move on.

Writing index.htm and index_support.htm

index.htm is the entry point into the application for customers, and index_support.htm is where support personnel should go to in order to log in. I'll just show index.htm here, in Listing 12-4. index_support.htm is basically the same thing, with some changed text.

Listing 12-4. *The index.htm File (Also, More or Less, index_support.htm)*

```html
<html>

  <head>

    <title>AJAX-Based One-On-One Support Chat</title>

    <link rel="StyleSheet" href="css/styles.css" type="text/css">

    <script src="js/mootools.js" type="text/javascript"></script>
    <script src="js/jscript.dom.js" type="text/javascript"></script>
    <script src="js/SupportChat.js" type="text/javascript"></script>

    <script>

      /**
       * Called on page load to do some setup.
       */
      function init() {

        var divObj = $('divOuter');
        jscript.dom.layerCenterH(divObj);
        jscript.dom.layerCenterV(divObj);
        $("logonForm").action = "server/chatServer." + chat.serverType;

      } // End init().

    </script>

  </head>

  <body onLoad="init();">

    <div id="divOuter" class="cssDivOuter">
      <img src="img/indexImage.gif" class="cssIndexImg">
      <div class="cssDivInner">
        Hello and welcome to our AJAX-based one-on-one support chat system!
        <br><br>
        To begin, please tell us who you are, and click the Begin button to
        get some help.
        <br><br>
        <form id="logonForm">
          <input type="hidden" name="func" value="logon">
          <input type="hidden" name="chattype" value="customer">
          Your name: <input type="text" name="chatname" size="20">
          <input type="submit" value="Begin" class="cssButton">
        </form>
```

```
    </div>
  </div>

</body>

</html>
```

This starts out, as most HTML documents do, with a style sheet import and a couple of JavaScript imports. Mootools is imported so the $() function can be used. jscript.dom.js is imported so we can use the layerCenterH() and layerCenterV() functions. Lastly, SupportChat.js is imported so we have access to the serverType field that was discussed earlier.

In the <head> is a single JavaScript function, init(). This is called when the page is loaded. Its job is twofold. First, it is used to center the contents of the page, which are contained in the divOuter <div>, using the layerCenterH() and layerCenterV() functions. It also sets the action of the form on the page to point to the appropriate chatServer version, JSP or ASP.

The markup of the page follows. This consists of a single <div> with the ID divOuter, which is the <div> that is actually centered in init(). This contains some text and an HTML form. This form accepts the name the chatter wants to use. It also contains a hidden field named func, which has the value "logon". This tells our server component what to do with the parameters submitted. There is also a chatType parameter, which in index.htm is set to "customer". In index_support.htm, it's set to "support" to tell the server what type of chatter is logging on.

Writing chat.htm

Now we come to chat.htm, which contains the actual page layout. You can see the complete listing of this file in Listing 12-5.

Listing 12-5. *The chat.htm File*

```
<html>

  <head>

    <title>AJAX-Based One-On-One Support Chat</title>

    <link rel="StyleSheet" href="css/styles.css" type="text/css">

    <script src="js/mootools.js" type="text/javascript"></script>
    <script src="js/jscript.page.js" type="text/javascript"></script>
    <script src="js/ChatMessage.js" type="text/javascript"></script>
    <script src="js/SupportChat.js" type="text/javascript"></script>

  </head>


  <body onLoad="chat.init();">
```

```
<table width="100%" cellspacing="0" cellpadding="0"><tr><td>

  <table width="98%" align="center" cellpadding="0" cellspacing="0">

    <tr>
      <td>
        <table width="100%" cellspacing="0" cellpadding="0">
          <tr>
            <td width="46"><img src="img/topLeft.gif"></td>
            <td width="64"><img src="img/spacer.gif"></td>
            <td align="center" class="cssTopText"
              background="img/headerFooter.gif">
              AJAX-Based One-on-One Support Chat
            </td>
            <td width="55"><img src="img/topRight.gif"></td>
          </tr>
        </table>
      </td>
    </tr>

    <tr>
      <td>
        <table width="100%" cellspacing="0" cellpadding="0">
          <tr>
            <td class="cssLeftColumn">
              <div align="center"><img src="img/logo.gif" vspace="10"></div>
            </td>
            <td class="cssRightColumn">
              <table width="100%" border="0" cellspacing="0"
                cellpadding="0">
                <tr>
                  <td class="toptext" align="center">
                    Welcome, <span id="spnChatname"></span>!
                  </td>
                </tr>
              </table>
            </td>
          </tr>
          <tr>
            <td width="220" valign="top" class="cssLeftColumn">
              <div style="width:220px;height:300px;overflow:hidden;"
                <br>
                <h2>Main Menu</h2>
                <br>
                <div class="cssDividers"><img src="img/divider.gif"></div>
                <br>
                      
```

```
      * <a href="javascript:void(0);"
        onClick="chat.copyTranscript();">
        Copy Transcript To Clipboard
      </a><br><br>
            
      * <a href="javascript:void(0);"
        onClick="chat.printTranscript();">
        Print Transcript
      </a><br><br>
            
      * <a href="javascript:void(0);" onClick="chat.exitChat();">
        Exit Chat
      </a><br>
      <br>
      <div class="cssDividers"><img src="img/divider.gif"></div>
    </div>
  </td>
  <td class="cssRightColumn">
    <table width="100%" cellspacing="0" cellpadding="0">
      <tr>
        <td class="cssRightColumn">
          <table width="90%" align="center" cellpadding="0"
            cellspacing="0">
            <tr>
              <td>
                <table width="100%" cellpadding="0"
                  cellspacing="0">
                  <tr>
                    <td class="cssLeftColumn">
                      <div><img src="img/titlebar.gif"></div>
                    </td>
                    <td><img src="img/spacer.gif"></td>
                    <td width="100%" class="cssHeaderFooter"><img
                      src="img/heading.gif"></td>
                    <td class="cssRightColumn"><img
                      src="img/topRight.gif"></td>
                  </tr>
                </table>
              </td>
            </tr>
            <tr>
              <td class="cssRightColumn">
                <table width="100%" cellspacing="0"
                  cellpadding="0">
                  <tr>
                    <td class="cssLeftColumn"> </td>
                    <td>
```

```html
                            <div class="cssChatDiv" id="divChat"></div>
                            <span class="cssChatterEntryDiv">
                              <table border="0" cellpadding="0"
                                cellspacing="0" width="100%"><tr>
                                <td valign="middle" class="cssEntry"
                                  align="center">
                                  <input type="text" size="62"
                                    id="postMessage">
                                  <input type="button" value="Say It"
                                    class="cssButton"
                                    onClick="chat.postMessage();">
                                </td>
                              </tr></table>
                            </span>
                          </td>
                        </tr>
                      </table>
                    </td>
                  </tr>
                  <tr>
                    <td>
                      <table width="100%" cellspacing="0"
                        cellpadding="0">
                        <tr>
                          <td width="55">
                            <img src="img/bottomLeft.gif">
                          </td>
                          <td class="cssBoxBottom"> </td>
                          <td width="55">
                            <img src="img/bottomRight.gif">
                          </td>
                        </tr>
                      </table>
                    </td>
                  </tr>
                </table>
              </td>
            </tr>
          </table>
          <br>
        </td>
      </tr>
    </table>
  </td>
</tr>
```

```
          <tr>
            <td>
              <table width="100%" cellspacing="0" cellpadding="0">
                <tr>
                  <td width="55"><img src="img/bottomLeft.gif"></td>
                  <td class="cssBoxBottom">
                    <table width="100%" cellspacing="0" cellpadding="0">
                      <tr>
                        <td width="23"><img src="img/closerLeft.gif"></td>
                        <td valign="middle" class="cssHeaderFooter">
                          <div align="center">
                            <div class="cssDividers" id="pDateTime"></div>
                          </div>
                        </td>
                        <td><img src="img/closerRight.gif"></td>
                      </tr>
                    </table>
                  </td>
                  <td width="55"><img src="img/bottomRight.gif"></td>
                </tr>
              </table>
            </td>
          </tr>
          <tr>
            <td> </td>
          </tr>
        </table>

  </td></tr></table>

</body>

</html>
```

I will largely leave this as an exercise for you to review, because it's nothing but typical HTML. After the style sheet and JavaScript imports, you can see that we call chat.init() on page load. The variable chat is defined in SupportChat.js, and it is the one and only instance of the SupportChat class. After that call, it really is just straight markup.

The menu items use a handy trick. The href of the link is the JavaScript statement javascript:void(0);, which results in the link not performing its usual hyperlink function when clicked. Instead, we handle the onClick event and call the appropriate method in ChatSupport.

About two-thirds of the way through, directly below the postMessage text box, is a button that calls chat.postMessage() when clicked. This is how messages from the chatter are posted, of course.

Please spend just a few minutes reviewing the code in Listing 12-5, if for no other reason than to convince yourself there's not much going on there. But this is actually a good thing. The presentation is almost entirely separate from the functionality behind it, which is exactly what we want. So while it may seem like a bit of a cop-out to not go over this in detail, we're focusing on JavaScript and Ajax in particular, and going over a bunch of pretty simple HTML wouldn't really serve that purpose, would it?

Writing goodbye.htm

One last bit of markup is left, and that's the goodbye.htm file. This is literally nothing but a straight HTML page that says good-bye to chatters when they log off. Have a look at the code, but if you linger more than about 30 seconds, please go guzzle some coffee and come back when you are more awake!

Creating the Database

Now we come to something just a tad more interesting, and that's the database structure. As previously described, I went with a simple Access database file for the sake of simplicity. This means that this application will run only on a Windows system. This is because for the JSP version, the JDBC:ODBC driver is used (the ODBC driver should come with any recent version of Windows), and the ASP version uses ADO, which again uses the ODBC driver (although no data source is required for either, as direct access to the MDB file is used).

The structure within the database is also very simple, consisting of a grand total of two tables, without any real linkage between them (there is *conceptually* a linkage, but no foreign key relationships or anything like that). Figure 12-10 is a diagram of the two tables.

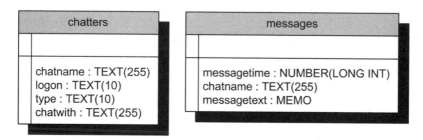

Figure 12-10. *If this database schema scares you, a new career may be in order!*

The chatters table stores the list of current chatters. The chatname field is the name the chatter gave upon logon. The logon field stores the date/time the chatter logged on. The type field is either customer or support, depending on which index HTML file the chatter came through. Finally, chatwith is the name of the chatter's chat partner.

The messages table holds the messages posted by chatters. The messagetime field is the time the message was posted. This is used to determine which messages to return as a response to the periodic Ajax request for messages. The chatname field is the name of the chatter who posted the message. This maps to the chatname field of the chatters table (again, there is no true key relationship here; it is merely a conceptual linkage). Finally, the messagetext field is the text of the message itself.

It's a simple database to be sure, but not much more is needed. Note that because of the frequency of change, I saw no point in indexing either of these tables. I don't believe any performance gain would be had by doing so. I also didn't put any constraints on any of the fields—no required fields and such. These rules are enforced, to the extent they matter frankly, in the server-side code that deals with the database.

One issue to point out is related to using the ASP version of the application. In that case, you will need to ensure that the user account that IIS runs with has full rights to the directory where the MDB file is located, and that the directory has read/write access in IIS itself. If you are toying with the IIS version, you probably knew this already, but it's worth mentioning. Should you try the application and get ADO error number 0x80004005, or any other for that matter but that one specifically, please check those permissions right away, because they are the likely culprit.

Now let's get into the server-side code, which is swaggering to the plate now!

Writing the Server Code

This is going to be a little tricky, because we have both a JSP file and an ASP file to review. However, they are structurally and logically identical, only differing in syntax and some other minor items. In order to get through this in a reasonable way, I will present each file in pieces, and describe what it does conceptually, without getting into all the finer details. My belief is that you will be able to understand one version or the other with little difficulty. I'll point out details where that makes sense, but we'll be going through this with a bird's eye view.

Starting Up

To start, both versions begin with a variable declaration.

Asp

```
filename = "C:\Inetpub\wwwroot\Code\database/chatDB.mdb"
```

Jsp

```
String filename = "K:/tomcat5029/wcbapps/Code/database/chatDB.mdb";
```

The filename variable points to the Access database. You will need to update this variable in order to run the application, as previously described.

Next is some code to open a connection to the database.

Asp

```
' variables needed for database work.
Set conn = Server.CreateObject("ADODB.Connection")

' Open connection to database.
conn.Open "DRIVER={Microsoft Access Driver (*.mdb)}; DBQ=" & filename
Set rs = Server.CreateObject("ADODB.Recordset")
rs.CursorLocation = 3
rs.CursorType = 3
rs.LockType = 4
```

Jsp

```
// variables needed for database work.
Connection conn = null;
Statement stmt = null;

// Load JDBC driver.
Class.forName("sun.jdbc.odbc.JdbcOdbcDriver");
String database = "jdbc:odbc:Driver={Microsoft Access Driver " +
  "(*.mdb)};DBQ=" + filename + ";DriverID=22;READONLY=false}";
conn = DriverManager.getConnection( database ,"","");
stmt = conn.createStatement(ResultSet.TYPE_SCROLL_INSENSITIVE,
  ResultSet.CONCUR_UPDATABLE);
```

Both versions are pretty typical code for the respective technologies (ADO for the ASP version and JDBC for the JSP version) to get a connection to a database. In the ASP version, we also get a RecordSet object, which we'll reuse throughout the page. In the JSP version, we get a Statement object, which again will be reused throughout.

Recall that these pages are the targets of all our Ajax calls, as well as form submissions. Also recall that all of those provide a func parameter to tell the server which function is being requested. So, as you might expect, we next get the value of that parameter.

Asp

```
Func = trim(Request("func"))
```

Jsp

```
String func = request.getParameter("func").trim();
```

Next, we need to construct a string that is a timestamp representing the time this request came in. This will be needed for a number of purposes later. The format of this string is *HHMMSSLLL*, where *HH* is the hours (00–23), *MM* is the minutes (00–59), *SS* is the seconds (00–59), and *LLL* is the milliseconds (000–999). We do some string manipulations along the way to ensure that values less than 10 (and less than 100 in the case of milliseconds) are padded with leading zeros so that we always wind up with a nine-character string in the end.

Asp

```
hh = CStr(Hour(Now()))
If Len(hh) = 1 Then hh = "0" & hh End If
mm = CStr(Minute(Now()))
If Len(mm) = 1 Then mm = "0" & mm End If
ss = CStr(Second(Now()))
If Len(ss) = 1 Then ss = "0" & ss End If
ms = "000"
timeStamp = hh + mm + ss + ms
```

Jsp

```
gregoriancalendar calendar = new GregorianCalendar();
String hh = Integer.toString(calendar.get(Calendar.HOUR_OF_DAY));
if (hh.length() == 1) { hh = "0" + hh; }
String mm = Integer.toString(calendar.get(Calendar.MINUTE));
if (mm.length() == 1) { mm = "0" + mm; }
String ss = Integer.toString(calendar.get(Calendar.SECOND));
if (ss.length() == 1) { ss = "0" + ss; }
String ms = Integer.toString(calendar.get(Calendar.MILLISECOND));
if (ms.length() == 1) { ms = "0" + ms; }
if (ms.length() == 2) { ms = "0" + ms; }
String timeStamp = hh + mm + ss + ms;
```

Once that's done, we then do a check of the func parameter we got. If it's null, or blank—meaning it wasn't passed in (or possibly was spelled wrong)—we send back an HTML response to indicate an unknown function was requested (which might mean a hacking attempt, so we accuse the chatter of being naughty, just for kicks).

Once we see that func was found as a request parameter, we determine which function was requested. This is nothing but a series of if checks.

Logging On

The first possible function is logging on, indicated by a func value of "logon". This is the longest and most complex of the functions, but it boils down to a few logical steps. Let's first look at the code, and then discuss those steps.

Asp

```
if func = "logon" Then

  ' Processing a logon.
  chatType = Trim(Request("chattype"))

  If chatType = "customer" Then

    ' It's a customer logon.  See if the name is already in use.
    customerChatName = Trim(Request("chatname"))
    rs.Open "select chatname from chatters where " & _
      "chatname='" & customerChatName & "'", conn
    If rs.RecordCount <> 0 Then
      ' Name is already in use, have the chatter select a new one.
      rs.Close
      %>
      <html><head><title>Name already in use</title></head><body>
        I'm sorry but that name is already in use.  Please click
        <a href="../index.htm">HERE</a> and select a new name.
      </body></html>
      <%
```

```
            Else
              ' Name is available, so now we have to see if there are any available
              ' support personnel to chat with.
              rs.Close
              rs.Open ("select chatname from chatters " & _
                "where type='support' and chatwith='none'")
              If rs.RecordCount <> 0 Then
                ' Ok, we got someone.  Now log the chatter into the database and
                ' send them to the chat page.
                supportChatName = rs("chatname")
                rs.Close
                conn.Execute "insert into chatters (chatname, logon, type, " & _
                  "chatwith) values (" & _
                  "'" & customerChatName & "', " & _
                  "'" & timeStamp & "', " & _
                  "'customer', '" & supportChatName & "')"
                ' We also need to mark the support person as chatting with this
                ' chatter.
                conn.Execute "update chatters set chatwith='" & _
                  customerChatName & "' where chatname='" & supportChatName & "'"
                // Lastly, add a message to the messages table so both chatters see
                // who they are chatting with.
                conn.Execute "insert into messages (messagetime, chatname, " & _
                  "messagetext) values ('" & timeStamp & "', '" & _
                  supportChatName & "', 'Hello, " & customerChatName & "!  " & _
                  supportChatName & " is here to help you!')"
              %>
              <html><head><title>Starting chat</title><script>
                function startChat() {
                  window.location =
                    "../chat.htm?func=startChat&" +
                    "chatname=<%=customerChatName%>&chattype=customer&" +
                    "chatwith=<%=supportChatName%>"
                }
                </script></head>
                <body onLoad="startChat();">Starting chat...</body>
              </html>
              <%
            Else
              ' No support personnel available.  Give the chatter the bad news.
              rs.Close
              %>
              <html><head>
              <title>No support personnel available</title>
              </head><body>
                There are currently no support personnel available.  Please click
                <a href="<%=request.ServerVariables("URL")%>?func= ➥
logon&chattype=customer&chatname=<%=customerChatName%>">HERE</a>
```

```
          to check for someone again.
        </body></html>
        <%
    End If
  End If

  Else

    ' It's a support personnel logon.  See if the name is already in use.
    supportChatName = Trim(Request("chatname"))
    rs.Open "select chatname from chatters where " & _
      "chatname='" & supportChatName & "'", conn
    If rs.RecordCount <> 0 Then
      ' Name is already in use, have the chatter select a new one.
      rs.Close
      %>
      <html><head><title>Name already in use</title></head><body>
        I'm sorry but that name is already in use.  Please click
        <a href="../index.htm">HERE</a> and select a new name.
      </body></html>
      <%
    Else
      ' Name is available, so now log the chatter in.
      rs.Close
      conn.Execute "insert into chatters (chatname, logon, type, " & _
        "chatwith) values (" & _
        "'" & supportChatName & "', " & _
        "'" & timeStamp & "', " & _
        "'support', 'none')"
      %>
      <html>
        <head>
          <title>Starting chat</title>
          <script>
            function startChat() {
              window.location =
                "../chat.htm?func=startChat&" +
                "chatname-<%=supportChatName%>&chattype=support";
            }
          </script>
        </head>
        <body onLoad="startChat();">Starting chat...</body>
      </html>
      <%
    End If
  End If

End If ' End "logon" function handling.
```

Jsp

```
if (func.equalsIgnoreCase("logon")) {

  // Processing a logon.
  String chatType = request.getParameter("chattype");

  if (chatType.equalsIgnoreCase("customer")) {

    // It's a customer logon.  See if the name is already in use.
    String customerChatName = request.getParameter("chatname");
    ResultSet rs = stmt.executeQuery(
      "select chatname from chatters where " +
      "chatname='" + customerChatName + "'");
    if (rs.first()) {
      // Name is already in use, have the chatter select a new one.
      rs.close();
      %>
      <html><head><title>Name already in use</title></head><body>
        I'm sorry but that name is already in use.  Please click
        <a href="../index.htm">HERE</a> and select a new name.
      </body></html>
      <%
    } else {
      // Name is available, so now we have to see if there are any available
      // support personnel to chat with.
      rs.close();
      rs = stmt.executeQuery("select chatname from chatters " +
        "where type='support' and chatwith='none'");
      if (rs.first()) {
        // Ok, we got someone.  Now log the chatter into the database and
        // send them to the chat page.
        String supportChatName = rs.getString(1);
        rs.close();
        stmt.executeUpdate("insert into chatters (chatname, logon, type, " +
          "chatwith) values (" +
          "'" + customerChatName + "', " +
          "'" + timeStamp + "', " +
          "'customer', '" + supportChatName + "')");
        // We also need to mark the support person as chatting with this
        // chatter.
        stmt.executeUpdate("update chatters set chatwith='" +
          customerChatName + "' where chatname='" + supportChatName + "'");
        // Lastly, add a message to the messages table so both chatters see
        // who they are chatting with.
        stmt.executeUpdate("insert into messages (messagetime, chatname, " +
          "messagetext) values ('" + timeStamp + "', '" + supportChatName +
          "', 'Hello, " + customerChatName + "!  " + supportChatName +
          " is here to help you!')");
```

```
        %>
        <html><head><title>Starting chat</title><script>
          function startChat() {
          window.location =
            "../chat.htm?func=startChat&" +
            "chatname=<%=customerChatName%>&chattype=customer&" +
            "chatwith=<%=supportChatName%>";
          }
          </script></head>
          <body onLoad="startChat();">Starting chat...</body>
        </html>
        <%
      } else {
        // No support personnel available.  Give the chatter the bad news.
        rs.close();
        %>
        <html><head>
        <title>No support personnel available</title>
        </head><body>
          There are currently no support personnel available.  Please click
          <a href="chatServer.jsp?func=logon&chattype=customer&chatname= ➥
<%=customerChatName%>">HERE</a>
          to check for someone again.
        </body></html>
        <%
      }
    }


  } else {

    // It's a support personnel logon.  See if the name is already in use.
    String supportChatName = request.getParameter("chatname");
    ResultSet rs = stmt.executeQuery(
      "select chatname from chatters where " +
      "chatname='" + supportChatName + "'");
    if (rs.first()) {
      // Name is already in use, have the chatter select a new one.
      rs.close();
      %>
      <html><head><title>Name already in use</title></head><body>
        I'm sorry but that name is already in use.  Please click
        <a href="../index.htm">HERE</a> and select a new name.
      </body></html>
      <%
    } else {
      // Name is available, so now log the chatter in.
      rs.close();
```

```
        stmt.executeUpdate("insert into chatters (chatname, logon, type, " +
          "chatwith) values (" +
          "'" + supportChatName + "', " +
          "'" + timeStamp + "', " +
          "'support', 'none')");
      %>
      <html>
        <head>
          <title>Starting chat</title>
          <script>
            function startChat() {
              window.location =
                "../chat.htm?func=startChat&" +
                "chatname=<%=supportChatName%>&chattype=support";
            }
          </script>
        </head>
        <body onLoad="startChat();">Starting chat...</body>
      </html>
      <%
    }
  }

} // End "logon" function handling.
```

The function begins by getting the value of the chattype parameter. It then branches on
the value of that parameter. The first branch is if it's a customer logging on. In that case, we
begin by getting the chatname parameter. We then do a query to determine if that name is already
in use. If it is, we return a page that indicates this and provides a link back to the logon page, so
the chatter can try a different name.

If the name is not already in use, we then do a query to see if there are any support
personnel available. This is indicated by finding any chatter in the chatters table that has a
type of support, and also that has a value in the chatwith field of none. If we find someone, we
then update the chatters table. First, we insert the new chatter into the table. Next, we update
the record for the available support person to indicate he is chatting with this new chatter.
Lastly, we add a record to the messages table that is a quick greeting for both chatters.

After that, we render a response that is a simple HTML page, which upon loading will
redirect to chat.htm, passing along the necessary information as request parameters.

If no support personnel were available, we return markup indicating this to the chatter,
and provide a link the chatter can click to check if anyone is yet available. The chatter can
continue to click this link as much as she wants until a support person becomes available, at
which point she will be logged on (yes, this isn't the most efficient scheme, and that's why it's
the target of one of the suggested exercises at the end of this chapter!).

We next encounter an else branch, which is where we deal with logons by support
personnel. We again perform a check to see if the name the support chatter provided is available, and do the same things with either outcome (name is available or name is not available)
as we did for the customer chatter. If the name is available, we have only a single update to do,

and that's inserting this chatter into the chatters table. And that's the end of this particular function!

Getting Posted Messages

The next function in the server code is to handle the periodic Ajax request that gets messages posted since the last check.

Asp

```asp
if func = "getMessages" Then

  chatname = Trim(Request("chatname"))
  lastMessageTime = Trim(Request("lastMessageTime"))
   ' First, find out who this chatter is chatting with.
   rs.Open "select chatwith from chatters where " & _
     "chatname='" & chatname & "'", conn
   chatwith = rs("chatwith")
   rs.Close
   ' Now, get all messages posted by this chatter, or by who they were
   ' chatting with, since the time of the last message passed in.
   rs.Open "select messagetime, chatname, messagetext from messages " & _
     "where (chatname='" & chatname & "' or " & "chatname='" & chatwith & _
     "') and messagetime >= " & lastMessageTime, conn
  firstMessage = true
%>
{ "lastMessageTime" : "<%=timeStamp%>",
  "messages" : [
<% Do While Not rs.EOF
   If firstMessage = true Then
     firstMessage = false
   Else
     response.write ", "
   End If
%>
     { "timestamp" : "<%=rs("messagetime")%>",
       "chatname" : "<%=rs("chatname")%>",
       "message" : "<%=rs("messagetext")%>"
     }
<%
     rs.MoveNext
   Loop
%>
  ] }
<%
  rs.close()

End If ' End "getMessage" function handling.
```

Jsp

```
if (func.equalsIgnoreCase("getMessages")) {

  String chatname = request.getParameter("chatname");
  String lastMessageTime = request.getParameter("lastMessageTime");
  // First, find out who this chatter is chatting with.
  ResultSet rs = stmt.executeQuery(
    "select chatwith from chatters where " +
    "chatname='" + chatname + "'");
  rs.first();
  String chatwith = rs.getString(1);
  rs.close();
  // Now, get all messages posted by this chatter, or by who they were
  // chatting with, since the time of the last message passed in.
  rs = stmt.executeQuery(
    "select messagetime, chatname, messagetext from messages where " +
    "(chatname='" + chatname + "' or " + "chatname='" + chatwith +
    "') and messagetime >= " + lastMessageTime);
  boolean firstMessage = true;
%>
{ "lastMessageTime" : "<%=timeStamp%>",
  "messages" : [
<% while (rs.next()) {
  if (firstMessage) {
    firstMessage = false;
  } else {
    out.print(", ");
  }
%>
    { "timestamp" : "<%=rs.getString(1)%>",
      "chatname" : "<%=rs.getString(2)%>",
      "message" : "<%=rs.getString(3)%>"
    }
<% } %>
  ] }
<%
rs.close();
```

} // End "getMessage" function handling.

This function begins by getting two incoming request parameters: chatname and
lastMessageTime. The chatname parameter is the name of the chatter requesting messages,
and lastMessageTime is the timestamp when the last such request was made.

The next thing that needs to be done is to find out who this chatter is chatting with (note
that this code doesn't care whether the chatter making this request is a customer or a support
person, since it works the same either way). We do this because we need to get messages from
both sides of the conversation, but the parameters give us only half the information we need.

So, once we have the name of both chatters, we then do a query to find any messages posted by either chatter subsequent to the value of lastMessageTime. This results in a collection of records representing all the messages posted by either user since the last time this check was performed, if any.

Then, assuming at least one record was found, it begins to iterate over that collection. Along the way, it constructs a string of JSON, which contains an array of message data elements, namely the time the message was posted (timestamp), who posted it (chatname), and the message text itself (message). This JSON also includes the new value for lastMessageTime, which is the value of that timestamp string you saw constructed earlier. This value will be stored on the client for the next request to getMessages. Finally, the JSON is written out to the response (that technically happens as it's being formed, but you get the picture) and that's that. You saw earlier in our look at SupportChat.js how this JSON is consumed. Now you know how it's constructed!

Posting Messages

The next function to look at is posting messages, and it's surprisingly compact.

Asp

```
if func - "postMessage" Then

  chatname = Trim(Request("chatname"))
  messagetext = Trim(Request("messagetext"))
  messagetext = Replace(messagetext, "'", "''")
  conn.Execute "insert into messages (messagetime, chatname, " & _
    "messagetext) values (" & _
    timeStamp & ", " & _
    "'" & chatname & "', " & _
    "'" & messagetext & "')"

End If ' End "postMessage" function handling.
```

Jsp

```
if (func.equalsIgnoreCase("postMessage")) {

  String chatname = request.getParameter("chatname");
  String messagetext = request.getParameter("messagetext");
  messagetext = messagetext.replace('\'', '`');
  stmt.executeUpdate("insert into messages (messagetime, chatname, " +
    "messagetext) values (" +
    timeStamp + ", " +
    "'" + chatname + "', " +
    "'" + messagetext + "')");

} // End "postMessage" function handling.
```

There isn't really much to getting a message posted. First, we get the value of the incoming request parameters chatname, which is who posted the message, and messagetext, which is the message itself. Then we need to do a quick scan of the string and replace any occurrences of the single apostrophe character with a double apostrophe. This is done so as to not break the constructed SQL statement that you can see next, which is used to insert the message into the messages table. That's literally all there is to it.

Logging Off

Only a single function remains, and that's the function that handles logoff. There is perhaps a little more to this than you might imagine, but not too much!

Asp

```
if func = "exitChat" Then

  chatname = Trim(Request("chatname"))
  ' First, find out who this chatter is chatting with.
  rs.Open "select chatwith from chatters where " & _
    "chatname='" & chatname & "'", conn
  chatwith = rs("chatwith")
  rs.Close
  ' Now, delete all messages the chatter posted, as well as messages
  ' posted by who they were chatting with.  After this query, the
  ' "conversation" is effectively deleted from the database.
  conn.Execute "delete from messages where chatname='" & chatname & _
    "' or chatname='" & chatwith & "'"
  ' Next, delete the chatter from the chatters table.
  conn.Execute "delete from chatters where chatname='" & chatname & "'"
  ' Finally, if we find any records in the chatters table where this
  ' chatter is the value of the chatwith field, update that field of
  ' that record to "none".  This covers when the chatter logging off is a
  ' customer, it makes the support personnel available again.  If it's
  ' a support personnel logging off, it does no harm to the chatter,
  ' although the chatter is effectively "orphaned", i.e., their messages
  ' will not be seen by a support personnel, and they will see messages
  ' from no support personnel.
  conn.Execute "update chatters set chatwith='none' where " & _
    "chatwith='" & chatname & "'"
  ' Finally, say goodbye to the chatter.
%>
<html>
  <head>
    <title>Exiting chat</title>
    <script>
      function exitChat() {
        window.location = "../goodbye.htm";
      }
```

```
      </script>
    </head>
    <body onLoad="exitChat();">Exiting chat...</body>
  </html>
  <%
```

End If ' End "exitChat" function handling.

End If ' End function handling section.

Jsp

```
  if (func.equalsIgnoreCase("exitChat")) {

    String chatname = request.getParameter("chatname");
    // First, find out who this chatter is chatting with.
    ResultSet rs = stmt.executeQuery(
      "select chatwith from chatters where " +
      "chatname-'" + chatname + "'");
    rs.first();
    String chatwith = rs.getString(1);
    // Now, delete all messages the chatter posted, as well as messages
    // posted by who they were chatting with.  After this query, the
    // "conversation" is effectively deleted from the database.
    stmt.executeUpdate("delete from messages where chatname='" + chatname +
      "' or chatname='" + chatwith + "'");
    // Next, delete the chatter from the chatters table.
    stmt.executeUpdate("delete from chatters where chatname='" + chatname +
      "'");
    // Finally, if we find any records in the chatters table where this
    // chatter is the value of the chatwith field, update that field of
    // that record to "none".  This covers when the chatter logging off is a
    // customer, it makes the support personnel available again.  If it's
    // a support personnel logging off, it does no harm to the chatter,
    // although the user is effectively "orphaned", i.e., their messages
    // will be seen no support personnel, and they will see messages from no
    // support personnel.
    stmt.executeUpdate("update chatters set chatwith='none' where " +
      "chatwith='" + chatname + "'");
    // Finally, say goodbye to the chatter.
    %>
    <html>
      <head>
        <title>Exiting chat</title>
        <script>
          function exitChat() {
```

```
        window.location = "../goodbye.htm";
      }
    </script>
  </head>
  <body onLoad="exitChat();">Exiting chat...</body>
</html>
<%

} // End "exitChat" function handling.


} // End function handling section.
```

First, we get the name of the chatter who is logging off via the incoming `chatname` request parameter. Then we query the `chatters` table to find out who they are chatting with. Next, we delete any record from the `messages` table posted by this chatter, or with the chatter they are chatting with. This is just a bit of cleanup so that the conversation doesn't linger, taking up space unnecessarily. After that, we delete the chatter from the `chatters` table. Finally, we update the `chatters` table for any record we find where the `chatwith` field is equal to the `chatname` received here. This has the effect of making the support personnel this chatter was chatting with available again. If it's a support person logging off, then the customer is essentially orphaned, which is a shortcoming we'll live with for the time being (feel free to add code to check for this in `getMessage` so that you can tell users they are no longer chatting with someone, and perhaps redirecting them to some other page).

The last step is simply to return a page that will immediately redirect the chatter to the `goodbye.htm` page you saw earlier, and the user is officially logged off at that point.

Cleaning Up

The last task in both server files is cleaning up of the database connection.

Asp

```
Set conn = Nothing
```

Jsp

```
if (stmt != null) {
  stmt.close();
}
if (conn != null) {
  conn.close();
}
```

In any case, the `RecordSet` object would have been closed already, and that's why you don't see mention of that here in either version.

And with that, we've completed our look at this application! I hope it's been a good exposure to Ajax, JSON, and Mootools, and that it has shown how the client and server can interact in the Ajax world. This is frankly one of the applications in this book where I purposely left a number of items, some you might call shortcomings, specifically to give you some good suggestions to reinforce this new knowledge into your cerebellum. So, let's talk about some of those suggestions.

Suggested Exercises

A few items could easily be added to this application to make it better, and to get you a bit more familiar with Ajax and Mootools in the process:

- How about a PHP version? It should just be a matter of converting the code from the Java version to PHP, which probably isn't too tough a translation if you are familiar with PHP.

- It would be nice if a new chatter could be logged in and await an available support person to join her.

- Add tooltips to any element on the page you think makes sense. Mootools has a tips plug-in, which provides this functionality.

- Use some Mootools effects. For instance, perhaps collapse the page when the chatter exits, or if you implement the suggestion to allow a chatter to log in and wait, have some sort of fade-in when a support person joins.

- As hinted at earlier, put the chatters' messages on the screen immediately when they post a message so there's no delay while waiting for the next getMessage() cycle to fire.

- Adding a timestamp to each posted message on the screen would be a useful little improvement.

That's the short list. I'm quite sure you can come up with any number of things on your own, but these should serve as a nice start.

Summary

In this, the final leg (er, chapter) of our journey, you've been introduced to what is probably the most famous buzzword of the last two years in web development: Ajax. You've seen it in action, witnessing how it makes a certain class of applications possible, or at least better. You also observed how the server component in the Ajax equation can work. Additionally, you learned how the very fine Mootools JavaScript library can aid you in your Ajax work, as well as other respects. And in the process, you've created a little chat application that can actually be put to use if you so choose to support your customers in this way.

Index

You Need the Companion eBook

Your purchase of this book entitles you to buy the companion PDF-version eBook for only $10. Take the weightless companion with you anywhere.

We believe this Apress title will prove so indispensable that you'll want to carry it with you everywhere, which is why we are offering the companion eBook (in PDF format) for $10 to customers who purchase this book now. Convenient and fully searchable, the PDF version of any content-rich, page-heavy Apress book makes a valuable addition to your programming library. You can easily find and copy code—or perform examples by quickly toggling between instructions and the application. Even simultaneously tackling a donut, diet soda, and complex code becomes simplified with hands-free eBooks!

Once you purchase your book, getting the $10 companion eBook is simple:

① Visit **www.apress.com/promo/tendollars/**.

② Complete a basic registration form to receive a randomly generated question about this title.

③ Answer the question correctly in 60 seconds, and you will receive a promotional code to redeem for the $10.00 eBook.

2560 Ninth Street • Suite 219 • Berkeley, CA 94710

eBookshop

THE EXPERT'S VOICE™

Offer valid through 10/16/07.

Second Thoughts

Critical Thinking for a Diverse Society

THIRD EDITION

Wanda Teays

Mount St. Mary's College

Boston   Burr Ridge, IL   Dubuque, IA   Madison, WI   New York
San Francisco   St. Louis   Bangkok   Bogotá   Caracas   Kuala Lumpur
Lisbon   London   Madrid   Mexico City   Milan   Montreal   New Delhi
Santiago   Seoul   Singapore   Sydney   Taipei   Toronto

Higher Education

SECOND THOUGHTS: CRITICAL THINKING FOR A DIVERSE SOCIETY
Published by McGraw-Hill, a business unit of The McGraw-Hill Companies, Inc., 1221 Avenue of the Americas, New York, NY, 10020. Copyright © 2006, 2003, 1996 by The McGraw-Hill Companies, Inc. All rights reserved. No part of this publication may be reproduced or distributed in any form or by any means, or stored in a database or retrieval system, without the prior written consent of The McGraw-Hill Companies, Inc., including, but not limited to, in any network or other electronic storage or transmission, or broadcast for distance learning.
Some ancillaries, including electronic and print components, may not be available to customers outside the United States.

This book is printed on acid-free paper.

1 2 3 4 5 6 7 8 9 0 DOC/DOC 0 9 8 7 6 5

ISBN   0-07-299350-2

Editor in Chief: *Emily Barrosse*
Publisher: *Lyn Uhl*
Senior Sponsoring Editor: *Jon-David Hague*
Editorial Coordinator: *Allison Rona*
Senior Marketing Manager: *Zina Craft*
Managing Editor: *Jean Dal Porto*
Project Manager: *Ruth Smith*
Freelance Project Manager: *Marilyn Rothenberger*
Associate Designer: *Marianna Kinigakis*
Senior Photo Research Coordinator: *Alexandra Ambrose*
Art Editor: *Emma C. Ghiselli*
Media Producer: *Lance Gerhart*
Senior Media Project Manager: *Ron Nelms*
Associate Production Supervisor: *Jason I. Huls*
Composition: *10/12 Sabon by Carlisle Communications, Ltd.*
Printing: *PMS Black, 45 # New Era Matte, R.R. Donnelley and Sons, Inc./Crawfordsville, IN.*

Library of Congress Cataloging-in-Publication Data

Teays, Wanda.
    Second thoughts : critical thinking for a diverse society / Wanda Teays.—3rd ed.
      p. cm.
    Includes index.
      ISBN 0-07-299350-2 (softcover : alk. paper)
      1. Critical thinking—Textbooks. I. Title
    B809.2.T43 2006
    160—dc22   2005041661

www.mhhe.com

To Adam

We dance in the gardens of our mothers
And follow petals back to you.
We walk in the footprints of our fathers
And see them circle back to you.

We sing the songs of our grandmothers
And hear them echo back to you.
We listen to the stories of our grandfathers
And carry the messages back to you.

We walk in the shadows of our ancestors
And see the light goes back to you.
We feel the past has turned around
And know our future is up to you.

Preface

"What we can't face
looks for us anyway.
If there's any chance,
people have to be willing to think;
to not be afraid of thinking.
If we learn to think clearly and coherently,
we will create the solution."

—JOHN TRUDELL

Standing on the hills above Los Angeles, I see people united by a common desire to improve our lives and communities. I see people addressing global violence, poverty, homelessness, and racism. I see people confronting religious and cultural differences, clashing worldviews and intolerance. These problems cast dark shadows, but we have many resources to bring about change. Our work together as educators is vital.

One of the tasks of a critical thinking course is to enable students to approach such issues, factor in different points of view, assess evidence, examine assumptions, uncover potential biases, sort out the relevant considerations, and arrive at decisions. In order to do this well, we need to have a receptive and reflective disposition and be guided by a desire for truth and fairness.

Critical thinking textbooks play different roles, depending on how the instructor approaches the course. Common to most critical thinking courses are argumentation, analysis, inductive and deductive reasoning, fallacies, and some collection of logic techniques. What I do in *Second Thoughts* is integrate diverse perspectives in critical reasoning and help students acquire the tools to put their thinking skills to use. The text is structured with flexibility in mind—instructors can arrange the materials in the order that works best with the course objectives.

I favor a lot of examples, group topics, exercises of varying degrees of difficulty, short readings, case studies, and a selection of longer articles, so students get many chances to apply what they're learning.

The first and third parts focus on tools and skills—these offer the nuts and bolts of critical thinking (Part 1) and the fundamentals of logic (Part 3). Sandwiched between is Part 2, the four applications chapters. These chapters allow students to put their critical reasoning tools to work. They also demonstrate to students that this class helps them navigate the different domains (academic, personal, and professional) they move in and out of.

The first part includes seven chapters that cover argumentation, language, analysis, problem solving, fallacies, an introduction to inductive and deductive reasoning, and arguments based on analogy. The second part consists of carefully constructed applications chapters. These range over the news media, advertising, popular culture, and the Internet. Virtually every chapter has exercises that draw from current events and topical issues to make them fresh and interesting for both students and instructors. Part 3 focuses on fundamentals of logic. Included are chapters on techniques for dismantling longer arguments causal and statistical reasoning, drawing inferences (e.g., with formal and informal rules of replacement), using syllogisms, and assessing deductive arguments, for validity and soundness (e.g., with the rules of inference). These three parts work together to offer a solid foundation for developing fundamental critical thinking techniques and skills.

It is important to expose students to a variety of ideas and points of view and provide them with tools and techniques for organizing their own thoughts and assessing those of others. Students who come from a racial or ethnic minority often feel left out or on the periphery. Those who are working class or middle class similarly may feel isolated, particularly if they are the first in their families to go to college. Female students often feel relegated to lesser roles, their concerns sidelined. Those with disabilities struggle to get their voices heard and legitimately feel that few understand the obstacles they face on a daily basis. This textbook brings in those perspectives and provides a solid basis for building reasoning skills. In listening to the different voices, we all stand to gain.

We need to examine pressing social problems in a thoughtful way. Students want to see the relevance of what we learn in terms of the lives we lead. Instructors need to relate what we teach to the world we live in and to reshape curricula and pedagogy to recognize and reach a wider audience. We ignore this need at our peril.

Goal of This Text

Out of my work with students from different backgrounds, I wanted to create a textbook with accessible language, interesting examples, and exercises offering diverse perspectives and varying levels of complexity. Given the diversity of our society, it is important to broaden the playing field.

By incorporating a range of exercises, readings, and concerns throughout this work, I hope to reach this wider audience. This ensures there are many voices, not just one, in this textbook. It also gives students many opportunities to examine the ways one's own perspective influences what is examined and how problems are solved. My goal was a text that would be both engaging and challenging, while providing tools that students could use in college courses and their own lives. Given the significance of the Internet, it seems vital that critical thinking courses also help students apply their analytical skills to what they see on the screen, be it a computer monitor, a television, or a movie theater.

To accomplish the goal of this text, I have made four general types of changes from the second edition.

1. Broad changes.

The unit on fundamental critical thinking skills has been expanded. I added a new chapter ("The Persuasive Power of Analogies") to Part 1. The first unit now has seven chapters (covering pathways and obstacles, language, argumentation, fallacies, analysis, inductive versus deductive reasoning, and the new chapter on arguments based on analogy), all newly revised. The chapter on language was revised; information was added on propaganda, jargon, and the passive voice. Exercises and examples were updated.

Material on inductive reasoning. Chapter 6 introduces the topic, then two focus on the big three of inductive reasoning: Chapter 7 "The Persuasive Power of Analogies" and Chapter 13 "Roll the Dice: Causal and Statistical Reasoning." This allows for a fuller discussion of inductive arguments and more examples and exercises for applying the methods.

Venn Diagrams have been added to Chapter 15 on syllogisms. In addition to covering the rules of the syllogism, a new section focuses on Venn Diagrams. This allows instructors the flexibility of using either or both methods for teaching validity. I placed it at the last part of the chapter so instructors can omit it or include it without disrupting the remaining material.

Truth tables have been added to Chapter 6 ("Deductive versus Inductive Reasoning"). A new section—truth tables—was added to the chapter to give students another tool for building their analytical skills.

A "Global Dimension" has been added to the textbook. A global dimension was added to all chapters except the last three logic chapters by presenting a case study that focuses on issues from around the globe (e.g., the spread of SARS to Canada, genetically engineered corn in Mexico, freedom of the press in Iran, tobacco advertising in Third World nations). They can be used for homework or for class, group, or small group discussion (of 10–20 minutes). This global dimension also broadens the horizon. Students get a sense of concerns that affect people from all walks of life and in different cultures and societies—and how our frame of reference can shape our understanding of events.

A "You Tell Me Department" has been added to all but the last three logic chapters. These pithy little exercises raise thought-provoking dilemmas. Some are surprising, some funny, some puzzling—and all will evoke reflection and discussion (e.g., should athletes take political stands, why is Clinton described as "the first black president," what is the effect of watching music videos). These exercises can be used in class or in small groups or assigned as homework.

Law-related exercises and examples have been added throughout the text. These help students look at assumptions and reasoning involved in decision making with societal repercussions (e.g., censorship of cartoonists, athletes' use of steroids, laws about hate crimes, free speech on the Internet). The exercises assume no previous training, but they build analytical skills. They reinforce the notion that critical thinking is a key component of legal reasoning.

2. Chapters new to the third edition.

A new chapter presents techniques for breaking down longer arguments. Chapter 12, "Wrestling with Big Questions: Pinning Down Arguments," will help students build their skills with tackling articles. I use a step-by-step approach to teach students five methods for dismantling arguments. The five methods set out in the chapter are: (1) the flowchart, (2) highlighting key terms, (3) the standard form of an argument, (4) the traditional outline, and (5) the bubble outline. The chapter ends with articles that allow students to practice using the various techniques.

Why this? Students often struggle to get a handle on longer arguments—especially when they are dense, complex, or convoluted. This chapter gives students useful methods to pin down arguments. The chapter doesn't just introduce the techniques—it walks the students through all five methods from the argument to finished overview.

A new chapter covers popular culture. Chapter 10 replaces the previous chapter on TV and film with a new one, "Visions of the Real: Popular Culture." In addition to applying critical thinking skills to film and TV, I expand the range to include popular music, cartoons, animation, and talk radio. Topics included in the chapter are context and content (with checklists for both), key frameworks of interpretation, drawing inferences, dismantling and analyzing arguments, assessing film and music reviews, the interface of pop culture and reality, and the prescriptive versus descriptive debate about popular culture.

Why this? Widening the range across popular culture allows for more flexibility in the type of exercises. Incorporating more information on media literacy—for example, context and content, drawing inferences, and assessing reviews—helped shape the chapter and make it more useful without forfeiting the strengths of the previous chapter on film and TV.

3. Deleted or split chapters.

The problem solving and writing chapter has been removed. Most instructors did not have time to include this material, so the major parts were incorporated, where relevant, in a more abbreviated form in other chapters.

The film/TV chapter has been replaced. Expanding the focus to popular culture allows for more flexibility and widens the range of examples. The demands of watching one or more movies as part of the class made the chapter difficult to use. Revisions were made overall to include more on argumentation and analysis involving popular culture and issues related to the role of popular culture in the society.

The chapters on the big three of inductive reasoning has been split into two chapters. One is Chapter 7, "The Persuasive Power of Analogies," and the other is Chapter 13, "Roll the Dice: Causal and Statistical Reasoning." Why? Given the potential power of these three types of inductive arguments, expanding to two chapters seemed advisable. The result is to strengthen this area and provide more examples and exercises so students can develop their skills in constructing as well as assessing inductive arguments.

4. Revised chapters

There have been major revisions throughout Parts 1 and 2.

There have been minor revisions to the last three logic chapters.

Examples and exercises have been updated so they are topical and interesting for both students and instructors.

All of Chapters 1 to 13 include two new features: (1) The Global Dimension and (2) the You Tell Me Department. These can be used in class discussion, homework, or group projects.

Chapter 1 (introduction) has been updated and expanded, incorporating a section on problem solving.

Chapter 2 (language—formerly Chapter 3) includes updated examples, new sections (one on propaganda, one on the passive voice, one on jargon), a revised and expanded section on labeling and expanded sections on descriptions and on culturally defined uses of language.

Chapter 3 (argumentation—formerly Chapter 2) includes updated examples and revised exercises, longer essays, more varied examples, and more exercises ranging from more elementary to more complex. The section on description versus inference has been expanded and new illustrations added; the section on facts, opinions, and ideas was expanded and reorganized, and the discussion of assumptions has been revised.

Chapter 4 (fallacies) includes new sections on formal fallacies, false analogy, and the fallacy of misleading evidence, discussions of ad hominem, ad hominen circumstantial, tu quo, and slippery slope.

Chapter 5 (analysis) contains updated examples and exercises, a revised section on the scope of a claim, and new exercises and illustrations.

Chapter 6 (deductive versus inductive reasoning), in addition to examples, has a new table comparing inductive to deductive arguments, a new section on generalizations, a new discussion of value claims in the section on propositions, and a new section on truth tables.

Chapter 8 (advertising) incorporates new material and new ads— bringing the total to 22 illustrations of ads. A section on the key fallacies found in ads has been added to this chapter and I expanded the section on political advertising and campaigns. I added a section on cultural attitudes and assumptions expressed in ads, and a longer article analysis focusing on tobacco ads in Third World countries.

Chapter 9 (news media) has been revised and updated. I expanded the section on professional standards and the role of ownership in shaping the news and added sections on freedom of speech issues and editorial decision making. A section on political cartoons was added and the sports news section revised.

Chapter 11 (the Internet) underwent a major revision, particularly on analyzing Web pages. Sections were added on assessing the source and content of the Web page, with checklists for both sections. I also added a section on blogs and expanded the discussion of surveillance and Internet privacy.

Chapter 13 (causal and statistical reasoning) underwent a major revision. Splitting this material from the old Chapter 13 allowed more discussion of both cause and effect and statistical reasoning. I added Mill's methods and a range of examples drawn from current events.

Chapter 14 (claims and drawing inferences) was strengthened with a section added on necessary versus sufficient conditions. I reformatted the chapter material to make it clearer and included summaries in tables for easy reference. More exercises were added.

Chapter 15 (syllogisms) was reformatted for ease of reading and more exercises were added. Venn diagrams were included in the last section of the chapter, allowing for flexibility of instruction. This material had previously been in the appendix of the instructor manual (on disk). It is more usable now that it is included in the chapter.

Chapter 16 (valid argument forms and rules of inference) has minor updates, including added exercises and some slight reformatting for clarity.

▦ Organization

This book is arranged in three parts that can be used separately or in combination. The chapters allow considerable flexibility on the part of the instructor. Those who wish to emphasize applications can easily do so. Those who prefer more of a critical thinking—logic hybrid approach can easily do so as well. The Web material includes chapter quizzes, key vocabulary, and a chapter summary, as well as additional exercises and handy hints. The Instructor Manual includes additional exercises for practice, handy hints, articles for analysis, and other things that may help the student build knowledge and skill in critical thinking.

Part 1 (Chapters 1 to 7) sets out an overview of the territory, the value of the enterprise, key concepts and tools, and the importance of diverse approaches in developing reasoning skills. The chapters in this first part present the nuts-and-bolts of critical thinking. They focus on obstacles to clear thinking, diverse perspectives and frame of reference, speculation, basics of argument, weighing evidence, uses of language, analysis, an overview of inductive and deductive reasoning, and a chapter focusing on arguments based on analogy.

This first section of the text offers techniques and exercises aimed at developing a broad range of fundamental skills. Each chapter helps students acquire a broader understanding of what clear thinking entails and offers tools and techniques for skill building. This has direct benefits for students. They become more aware of the power of assumptions and the central role language plays in conveying individual values and societal attitudes. They learn to recognize the different components of arguments and what is involved in constructing a well-supported argument. They learn the difference between description and inference and how to assess credibility of witnesses. They also learn when an argument fails due to omissions or faulty or fallacious reasoning. They acquire the skills to structure arguments and evaluate the strength of the reasoning. The new Chapter 7 "The Persuasive Power of Analogies," will help students become more confident of their ability to crack one of the most powerful forms of argumentation.

Together, the chapters help students develop their capacity to think carefully, constructively, and systematically. With the tools they acquire, they will be able to tackle issues, ideas, policies, and decision making and apply what they have learned. For those who wish to include truth tables to introduce deductive reasoning, an introduction to truth tables is included in the last section of Chapter 6.

Part 2 (Chapters 8 to 11) offers a range of applications of critical thinking skills and reinforces the goals of Part 1. Chapters 8, 9, 10, and 11 provide applications to advertising, the news media, popular culture, and the Internet. Exercises and readings allow students to put their knowledge to use. The focus of Chapter 8 is advertising and its power as a cultural document, with a range of examples of current ads and exercises that develop analytical and argumentative skills. In Chapter 9 we look at the news media—its role in our society, use of language, professional standards, ethical issues, control and ownership, freedom of the press, and sports coverage.

Looking at another sort of media, Chapter 10 applies critical thinking to popular culture. Here students use their skills to construct and analyze arguments, examine issues of content and context, assess film reviews, examine claims, apply theoretical models, and draw inferences about the social impact of popular culture. Since ours is a visual culture, students usually find this a stimulating way to see the relevance of their critical thinking skills.

With Chapter 11, we turn to the Internet. Examples, cases, and exercises focus on assumptions, description versus inference, credibility and authenticity, source and content issues, language use, fallacies, and both inductive and deductive reasoning. This chapter helps students build skills at argumentation and analysis and learn to be more discerning users of the Internet.

Part 3 (Chapters 12 to 16) provides the fundamental tools of logic and sets down structures for their application. These last five chapters are particularly helpful for students planning to take the LSAT, GRE, or a similar standardized test or who plan to take symbolic logic. Those who are majors or minors in pre-law, business administration, and computer science are encouraged to go over this section of the text. Chapter 12 stands on its own. It presents more specialized tools for breaking down arguments and seeing their structure and component parts using five different methods (flowcharts, standard form, highlighting key terms, traditional outline, and bubble outline). Most students will find this a valuable chapter. Chapter 13 focuses on cause and effect reasoning and statistical reasoning. This chapter works in conjunction with Chapters 6 and 7 to build a stronger base in inductive reasoning. Chapter 14 examines claims and inferences. Included in this chapter are both the formal and informal rules of replacement, along with the square of opposition.

Chapter 15 presents syllogistic reasoning. I favor the rules of the syllogism, not Venn diagrams, so as not to introduce another language system (the diagrams). I have found that students quickly and effectively conquer syllogisms using this method. However, for those who prefer bringing in Venn diagrams, I included a new section on them in the last part of the chapter. The final chapter (Chapter 16) presents the rules of inference. This helps students spot key valid argument forms and develop their skill at deductive reasoning. Those preparing for the LSAT or other standardized tests will find the last two chapters of the text especially helpful.

Acknowledgments

"There was so much we saw
And never knew."

—Louise Erdrich

I am grateful to the enthusiasm for learning and the generosity of spirit I see in my students. There is a great satisfaction in seeing students develop the skill and confidence to take risks with their own thinking and writing—and to demonstrate how imaginative and insightful they can be. Such moments remind me why I love to teach.

It is clear that there is work to be done, that we need to think more deeply about human rights and justice. We have the power to create a better world and bridge—not demonize—our differences. Critical thinking is a crucial step in reaching that goal. Knowledge and compassion help shape the course of events; and so I teach and write.

Looking at all the gifts in my students and their deep sense of fairness, there is reason for hope. I see students trying to find the right path, even though many feel fearful or unsure about what steps need to be taken to build, or rebuild, connections between one another.

This text is indebted to others as well. I am grateful to all those philosophers, lawyers, college administrators, bioethicists, writers, reporters, artists, illustrators, and cartoonists who allowed me to reprint their work—and to Jason Karl for illustrating my little sayings. That these voices come from people all over the world reinforces our common humanity and brings in a richness of ideas, voices, and perspectives.

I am also grateful for the support of friends and colleagues. These include Ruth Rhoten, Mary Anne Warren, Jane Caputi, Alison Renteln, Judy Miles, and Michael Scrivens. You are an inspiration. Colleagues and my fellow philosophers at Mount St. Mary's College gave me ongoing moral support. My family—especially Silvio, Anita, and my mother Rose—provided encouragement and levity. And dear Adam helps keep it all in perspective. Something tangible happens when others believe in us and support our attempts to make dreams reality.

I appreciate the thoughtful criticism and insights of the reviewers who gave their time and effort to help polish this work:

- Beth O'Leary Anish—Quinsigamond Community College
- Mike Awalt—Belmont University
- Rory J. Conces—University of Nebraska at Omaha
- N. Mark Rauls—Community College of Southern Nevada

Their constructive criticism helped me shape this new edition. Thanks also to all those instructors who used *Second Thoughts* and who share similar goals about what we can accomplish as educators. I want also to thank my editor, Jon-David Hague, along with Allison Rona, Zina Craft, Marilyn Rothenberger, and all those at McGraw-Hill who helped in production. They are wonderful to work with. I also want to thank Zenon Culverhouse and Kerry McCutcheon, who contributed to the web page for *Second Thoughts*.

All these people, all this kindness—it makes all the difference in the world. As Samuel Beckett writes, "It is all very fine to keep silence, but one must also consider the kind of silence one keeps." May my words help transform the silence into something of value.

Contents

PART TWO
Going Out into the World   331

Acquiring Critical Thinking Skills

CHAPTER ONE

Out of the Fog: The Pathway to Critical Thinking

Nothing was clear to lonesome Quoyle. His thoughts churned like the amorphous thing that ancient sailors, drifting into arctic half-light, called the Sea Lung; a heaving sludge of ice under fog where air blurred into water, where liquid was solid, where solids dissolved, where the sky froze and light and dark muddled.

—E. ANNIE PROULX, *The Shipping News*

Remember that movie classic, *Terminator?* The Terminator is a cyborg that comes back in time to kill a woman, Sarah Connor, so she won't give birth to the future savior. Reese, the human who travels back to stop the Terminator, tells Sarah: "It can't be bargained with! It can't be reasoned with! It doesn't feel pity, or remorse, or fear. And it absolutely will not stop, *ever,* until you are dead!" She is justifiably terrified. We follow her attempts to evade the Terminator and stay alive. There is a nail-biting scene in a motel where Reese leaves Sarah by herself while he goes to get material to make a pipe bomb. Sarah calls her mother to let her know she's okay.

Unbeknownst to Sarah, she's telling the motel's location to the Terminator. Not only is it a killing-machine, it can perfectly mimic voices. Sarah made a serious unwarranted assumption in presuming that voice was her mother's—as a result she needs to brush up her critical thinking skills. If she wanted to contact her mother and reassure her, what would be the best way to do this without setting herself up for more trouble from that murderous cyborg? That's an issue for us to think about.

As you know from *T2: Judgment Day,* her son, John, also had a phone call with the cyborg on the other end of the line. When he phoned home to talk to his step-parents, the now-protective Terminator was there to try to stop the newer, more advanced T1000 cyborg. The Terminator advises him to ask a trick question to discern if he is really talking to his stepmother or if the T1000 is faking her voice. John asks about his dog "Wolfy" (not the dog's real name). The T1000 may be highly advanced, but it's not that advanced. And, thus, the truth came out. Nothing like a well-placed question to crack the case!

You'd have thought everyone would have been on their toes by the time we get to *T3: Rise of the Machines*. But no. The new female terminating machine makes short shrift of knocking off John Connor's schoolmates. The first two victims don't ask for identification when the "woman" called out their names or showed up at their doors. Of course, poor Jose Barrera (victim #1) was contacted by the killer-cyborg over the loudspeaker system at the fast food joint. It didn't help that his full name was plastered on his name tag, easy to spot at the take-out window. Even Katherine Brewster revealed the whereabouts of John Connor to the protective Terminator without knowing his intentions. Having critical thinking skills helps prevent such disasters!

Critical thinking is a form of *mental gymnastics:* It helps us solve problems, ask questions, organize our thoughts, and express ourselves clearly and defensibly. It helps us navigate our way through life. Think of it this way: If you can't solve the problem of how to change a flat tire, you could be sitting by the roadside for an awfully long time. If you can't find the right question to ask your doctor when he tells you that you've torn a ligament from trying to change the tire yourself, then you may not know your prognosis. And if you can't write a letter to the tire manufacturer about your brand new tire having a blowout for no apparent reason, you may not be able to get redress as soon as you'd like. Our world expands with our abilities; things that were once unattainable come within reach.

Introduction to the Territory

Critical thinking entails many **levels of thinking**; some are called "higher order," others are "lower order." Lower-order thinking skills—alias *basic skills*—include memorizing, summarizing, labeling, observing, and sorting into assigned categories. Higher-order skills—alias *comprehension skills*—include application, synthesis, drawing inferences, comparison/contrast, justification, analysis, evaluation, moral reasoning, and using inductive and deductive reasoning. Both orders have their place.

As learners, we want to use the right tool for the right task. The ability to think critically and articulate ideas is powerful and compelling. It helps give meaning to our lives. With the skills and techniques we acquire, we can make a difference. Knowing how to think clearly helps us separate well-reasoned from weak arguments, sift out unwarranted assumptions, and spot opinions camouflaged as evidence. When analytical skills are missing or in disrepair, you can't think straight and you miss the obvious—not to mention the subtle or hidden. You are then vulnerable to the most flimsy argument imaginable. Plus, faulty reasoning has the potential for harm. Many people who have power abuse it and many more make decisions resting on the slimmest thread of good sense.

Since we expect to be treated fairly, unjust actions and insensitive statements take us by surprise. Sometimes we speak out, sometimes we don't. Sometimes we know how to speak out, sometimes we don't. Critical thinking gives us the skills to address that sense of powerlessness. As members of the human community, we have moral obligations and bear responsibility for what happens in the world.

It is not easy to examine our own assumptions or see how values color our perceptions and shape our understanding of the world. **Perspective** is the point of view or frame of reference a person takes in approaching an issue or situation. Different perspectives and vested interests shape the ways questions are asked and answered. It is liberating to be able to approach problems in a systematic way, to express our ideas in a defensible manner, and to confront shoddy thinking. We can then sort through evidence, weigh it, and arrive at conclusions about what we should or should not do. Critical reflection on long-held beliefs helps us turn over stones and look at the creatures that crawl out—such as our stubbornness, rigidity, and prejudice.

When someone is partial to one thing or another, they exhibit a **prejudice.** Prejudice can be positive or negative. The more facile we feel, the better we can "think on our feet," recognize prejudice and bias, and unravel convoluted reasoning. We grow as individuals when we are able to subject our own systems of thought to scrutiny. Our lives change when we can think clearly and defend our own ideas and insights.

When people learn to think for themselves, it is much harder to keep repressive systems in place. When people learn to speak and write effectively, they can make their voices heard. Being able to examine injustice and offer liberating alternatives can be transformative. Look at the ways in which large numbers of seemingly powerless people have brought about social change by rallying together in unions, peaceful protests, prayer meetings, boycotts, civil rights marches, e-mail campaigns, and so on.

▓ A Solid Foundation

An educated citizenry is at the heart of the true democracy. People who can think critically cannot be manipulated into believing lies are truths. Our system of governance rests on voters being informed and caring enough to act on their convictions. The entire jury system depends on people being able to tell the difference between opinion versus fact and between weak versus well-supported reasoning. "Misinformation campaigns" work only when we fall for them, when we accept unsupported claims and tolerate sloppy thinking.

To determine the truth or falsity of claims, we must subject them to careful scrutiny. The failure to do so is a victory for ignorance or mean-spiritedness. This is also true with any claims made by a credible source. Assertions may be true or false and still warrant consideration. Some claims rest on the word of one person against another (think of family conflicts, sexual harassment, or road rage). The absence of witnesses or direct support poses problems for evaluating evidence.

However, the difficulty of ascertaining truth or assessing corroborating details does not negate the value of the quest. The messiness of the journey should not stop us from seeking the truth.

We should base our knowledge on solid ground. We may discover there is no one "truth" to be found, such as when we are choosing between two worthwhile choices. There may be equally strong arguments for both options and yet we still must make a decision. It is important that the groundwork be in place for us to examine, analyze, criticize, defend, decide, study, and reflect. We want to eliminate possible obstacles that may trip us up and cause our reasoning to veer off in the wrong direction.

Critical thinking is rooted in a **social context:** that slice of time, location, culture, politics and community that shapes our identity and places us on a historical spectrum. We are unique as individuals, but we are not separate; we are part of a community, a neighborhood, a society, a world of others both like and unlike ourselves. This fact of our connectedness affects everything we do. Through our actions we demonstrate our ways of thinking. We can make our voices heard. One of our tasks as critical thinkers is to give each side a hearing, so we can fairly assess the evidence in light of the relevant considerations.

Exercises

1. Recognizing the significance of perspective, psychologist Abraham Maslow said, "To a man with a hammer, everything looks like a nail." Media critic Neil Postman added, "To a man with a pencil, everything looks like a list. To a man with a camera, everything looks like an image. To a man with a computer, everything looks like data." Add <u>three</u> of your own (e.g., to a man with a car, everything looks like ___, to a woman with a dog, everything looks like ___, to a person with a broom, everything looks like ___, and so on).

2. Some think expectations and conventions about good behavior are past history (e.g., don't chew with your mouth open, don't stand too close on elevators, don't eat your peas with a knife, don't talk back to grown-ups, etc.). However, a lot of children talk back to grown-ups and eating like a slob is now the stuff of ads. Give an example of one or two conventions or societal expectations aimed at teenagers or children.

Obstacles to Clear Thinking

All sorts of things can trip us up; for instance when we rush into decisions without thinking about the consequences. At times we are impulsive, at times obedient or submissive, letting others think for us. Do you listen to yourself and sometimes hear the voice of your mother, father, or friend like a tape playing inside your brain? Do you detect in yourself patterns of behavior that are unhealthy or destructive? Each one of us has a few failings, cultural baggage, and blind spots. These need to be overcome if we want to attain clarity and quickness of mind. Let us examine some of the more obvious obstacles to clear thinking.

Survival Issues

We tend to assume others' basic needs are being met, so they have the ability to focus, learn, and reason. But this may not be the case. Some people struggle with physical or emotional **survival issues.** These include an abusive environment, substance abuse, poverty, hunger, eating disorders, depression, rage, and a stress-inducing lifestyle. Take responsibility to reach out to such individuals. If you yourself are dealing with survival issues like these, get help. A person's ability to think clearly may turn on issues around basic survival needs.

Prejudice, Bias, and Oppression

Prejudice comes in many forms, including racial or ethnic prejudice, gender bias, ageism or speciesism, and hatred of fascists, right-wingers, leftists, conservatives, or liberals. It may be directed toward one or many individuals or groups. It can be so internalized that it functions seamlessly and invisibly. Some types of prejudice are viewed as healthy (such as prejudice against knife-wielding murderers); others are not. It's these potentially harmful prejudices that merit attention. Some prejudice is insidious and has caused pain and suffering, as seen in the institution of slavery, the Holocaust, "ethnic cleansing," and genocide.

Bias functions as a kind of blinder or filter, slanting our thinking one way or another. It must be set aside if we want to think clearly, formulate strong arguments, and act out of a sense of justice. Prejudice and bias have to do with attitudes and states of mind—oppression involves action. All three are rooted in a set of values and beliefs that we need to examine. Psychologist Gordon Allport characterized prejudice as "an antipathy based on faulty and inflexible generalization. It may be felt or expressed. It may be directed toward a group or an individual of that group" (*The Nature of Prejudice,* noted on faculty.ncwc.edu/toconnor).

Some deplorable acts and policies have stemmed from what seemed at the time to be justifiable, such as whites-only laws, lynching, Japanese internment camps in World War II, anti-gay ordinances, the sterilization of the mentally retarded, native boarding schools, and the forced relocation of Native-Americans. **Racism** is prejudice aimed at members of a racial or ethnic group. It can be manifested in subtle ways, but often treats the other as inferior, or alien. "Racism usually includes an element of disrespect. Since another is deemed less valuable, the thoughts and feelings of that individual cannot matter much. It is only another short step to a disrespect of that individual's rights to equal education, employment and housing opportunities" (Pat and Art McFarlane, "Beyond Scratching the Surface: Moving toward A Multicultural Society," *Goshen University News Bulletin,* June 1998).

Figure 1.1
Relocation of Japanese-Americans to Manzanar, CA. One instance of racism in U.S. history—the internment camps of World War II. These photographs show Japanese-Americans being moved to Manzanar, CA, on April 2, 1942.

Fear is a powerful motivator. Fear has been a catalyst for laws, policies, and actions that later appear to be unjust. People may harbor suspicions of others who look different or who have different values and beliefs. Such suspicions have fueled racism and a rise in hate crimes. The human costs deserve our attention. **Hate crimes** are one of the most odious expressions of prejudice. The American Psychological Association says of hate crime that not only is it an attack on one's physical self, but it is also an attack on one's very identity. Attacks upon individuals because of a difference in how they look, pray, or behave have long been a part of human history. Only recently has our society given it a name and begun to monitor it, study it, and legislate against it ("Hate Crime," FBI Uniform Crime Reports, FBI, www.fbi.gov).

Ibrahim Hooper, spokesman for the Council on American-Islamic Relations in Washington, DC, remarked, "I'd be surprised if there's a mosque in the country that hasn't come under scrutiny these days." He adds, "It becomes the whole Kevin Bacon game—no Muslim is more than six degrees away from terrorism" (Sarah Kershaw and Eric Lichtblau, "Spain Had Doubts before U.S. Held Lawyer in Blast," *The New York Times*, 5 Apr 2004). According to the FBI, anti-Muslim hate crimes in the United States took a big jump in the year after 9/11 (from 28 to 481 incidents). *Note:* The FBI keeps annual statistics on hate crimes that make for easy reference (see www.fbi.gov).

It is a short distance from racist or biased ways of thinking to actions and policies, which underlines how vital it is to watch for this obstacle to clear thinking.

Exercise

Brown University junior, Abdullah Alsharekh came from Kuwait on a student visa. After 9/11, his travel to and from home became much more difficult. Read about his situation and share your response:

Abdullah, currently in his junior year, now takes every precaution to avoid looking suspicious, since he knows he is automatically suspect in the eyes of American officials. He used to head home for breaks without preregistering for classes, but now he makes sure to preregister so he can carry the confirmation sheet—along with his student ID, his grades from the previous semester, and a copy of his paid tuition bill—to the airport as evidence that his intentions are purely academic. Even armed with such proof, Abdullah says the interrogations put him on edge. "It's weird," he says. "I know I haven't done anything wrong, but I always feel guilty. Even if you're not guilty, you look it. It's very, very uncomfortable." (As quoted by Lizzie Seidlin-Bernstein, "The Usual Suspects," *Anthology of Creative Nonfiction 2002–2003*, www.stg.brown.edu/projects)

Unreflective Acceptance of Cultural and Societal Attitudes

Cultural traditions and societal attitudes help shape our lives. However, traditions may have negative aspects, such as the materialistic dimensions of Christmas, weddings, and birthday celebrations. Cultural attitudes can act as blinders. Think of a jury exhibiting culturally biased attitudes toward people of different cultures, races, genders, economic classes, religions, or employment status. In such cases, a young Latino or African-American male might be more likely viewed as a gang member than a teenager who is white or Asian. A crime victim who is a prostitute tends to have less credibility than other female victims. And so-called white collar crime is rarely taken as seriously as other types of crime.

Societal assumptions can also block clear thinking. We operate with a set of attitudes about adults, teenagers, children, people with disabilities, religious groups, and members of racial and ethnic groups. For instance, if we assume children cannot tell the difference between fantasy and reality, it may be hard to evaluate children's statements of molestation or abuse. We think children are vulnerable to manipulation. We assume children often exaggerate or lie. As a result, children's claims about violence, incest, or inappropriate behavior could be ignored. A child who needs help might then be turned away.

Outmoded views can leach onto our thinking about other societies (we are "civilized"; they are "primitive"). We often make assumptions. The same trait can produce multiple stereotypes, depending on the speaker or the context, and these stereotypes can be positive or negative (e.g., thin can be considered disciplined OR anorexic, old can be wise OR infirm, wealthy can be snotty OR sophisticated, gay can be stylish OR abnormal, etc.). We need to watch the assumptions we make, for they may lead us astray. (See figure 1.1)

The Global Dimension

Using Celebrities to Address AIDS in Zimbabwe

How best to communicate across cultures? Would images of Mickey Mouse or Spider-Man eating their vegetables convince children around the world to cut down on junk food? Would pictures of Elvis in times of excess deter people on the other side of the world from illegal drug use? What images, narratives, or role models help halt the spread of AIDS? Share your thoughts after reading this excerpt, written by a journalist from Zimbabwe (Africa):

> "The story that we want to tell is that despite the advances made in fighting HIV/AIDS and the millions being poured by the United States government . . . thousands of Zimbabweans are still dying every week. The latest figure is 3,000 a week. USAID itself has admitted that though 98 percent of the Zimbabwean population is aware of AIDS, they have not changed their behaviour.
>
> One is bound to ask, why? We believe and want to prove that it is probably because the awareness campaign is not relevant to the average Zimbabwean. The campaign uses personalities that the average Zimbabwean does not relate to. Destiny's Child and Shaggy are not role models most Zimbabweans identify with. Instead, it probably perpetuates the notion that the disease is for the rich and famous and those who have money to travel abroad." (Charles Rukuni, "AIDS in Zimbabwe: The Story No One Wants to Hear," *The Insider*, www.insiderzim.com, April 2004)

Falling Prey to Stereotypes

Stereotypes are generalizations made on the basis of little or no evidence. They are oversimplified concepts or images. Think of all the stereotypes that bog down thinking: Men are stronger than women, women have more stamina than men, men are better leaders, women are better parents, boys are better in math, girls are better at reading, elderly people are easily confused, young people aren't politically savvy, rich people know how to manipulate the system, poor people are lazy, and so on. All such assumptions can impede clear thinking and put up barriers in our relationships. They are not necessarily negative; a stereotype can reinforce conventional ways of thinking or reinforce myths. Think of the myth of the American hero (confidant, rarely hesitates, loner, strong leader, quick witted, talks little but when he does people listen).

One basis for racial stereotyping in the United States, says law professor Natsu Taylor Saito, is the racial hierarchy that emerged in this country. This includes the association of "American" with "white." "Nonwhites," thus, are often seen as "non-American" as well, with the perception of foreignness a permanent stain on Asian Americans. She finds an irony in the stereotypes of Asian Americans: The positive versions of these stereotypes include images of Asian Americans as hardworking, industrious, thrifty, family-oriented, and even mysterious or exotic. It is striking that the negative images almost invariably involve the same traits. Hardworking and industrious become unfairly competitive; family-oriented becomes clannish; mysterious becomes dangerously inscrutable (Paula Daniels, "Work to End Hate Crimes against Asian-Americans," *Los Angeles Daily [Law] Journal*, 5 May 2004).

It's a Catch 22 situation. In her book *Black Looks,* bell hooks argues that such stereotyping serves a psychological function. She says, "They are a fantasy, a projection onto the Other that makes them less threatening. Stereotypes abound when there is distance." It's time to cut the distance. Brain activity, like most other things, gets lazy at times and we file things away into compartments—niches—and fail to look as carefully as we might. Once we are able to watch and listen more carefully, we can hopefully avoid succumbing to negative stereotypes.

Fortunately, there has been movement in this area. Think of the stereotype-busting that has occurred in the recent past: Tiger Woods changed stereotypes about golfers; Venus and Serena Williams changed stereotypes about tennis players. Eminem changed stereotypes about rap singers. Samuel L. Jackson, Jackie Chan, Vin Diesel, Denzel Washington, Will Smith, Wesley Snipes, and Keanu Reeves changed stereotypes about action heroes. Mira Nair, Queen Latifah, Halle Berry, and Salma Hayek changed stereotypes about women in film.

Exercises

1. Draw up a list of five *positive stereotypes* you see in advertising, TV, and/or film. Then draw up a list of five *negative stereotypes* you see in advertising, TV, and/or film. Note if you see any that are flip sides of the other, as Saito noted when it comes to Asian Americans.

2. Stereotypes and expectations create a mix that may have unexpected consequences. For example, a study of deviations from stereotypes in the music industry found the role of tradition figured prominently in looking at rap and country music. Read the following excerpt and share your reaction:

   One hundred college students (48 men, 52 women) examined a profile of a fictitious performer containing a picture, a brief biography, and a lyric sample. As part of a two-way between-subjects design, participants made judgments about either a Black or a White musician who performed either rap or country music. The results showed that a Black rap performer was rated more favorably than a Black country performer, and a White country performer was rated more favorably than a White rap performer. Consistent with predictions, people who violate societal expectations are judged more harshly than are people who conform to societal expectations, particularly in cases involving strong preexisting racial stereotypes. (Allison Dickson, et al, "Eminem Versus Charley Pride: Race, Stereotypes, and Perceptions of Rap and Country Music Performers," *Psi Chi Journal* 6, no. 4, www.psichi.org)

3. Do you think there's discrimination against bald men? What sorts of stereotypes circle around baldness? Read the following commentary about Canadian prime ministers and decide if the author's suspicions seem warranted:

"Some people think this looming federal election is about issues. Others think it's about personalities or policies. Wrong, wrong and wrong. This election, as usual, is about hair. You heard me. Hair. It is on top of the candidates' heads where elections are won or lost. That's why, in 137 years of Confederation, we've never had a bald prime minister. Not one. Granted, there have been one or two PM's [prime ministers] with thinning hair. Pierre Trudeau for example. His appearance was not much affected, however. The way Trudeau looked down his nose at everyone you couldn't see the top of his head. Even so, no one would have called Trudeau bald. It's about the only thing he hasn't been called.

Bald men do not get to be prime minister. They're everywhere else. Bald men make up a significant percentage of the male population. You'd think a similar percentage of our prime ministers would be bald. But no. Every one of the 20 prime ministers since Confederation has had a more or less full head of hair. Canadians won't have a bald PM. It's discrimination, pure and simple. The difference is that bald men don't whine about it, unlike some other under-represented groups." (Les McPherson, "Election Will Come Down to Receding Hairlines," *The StarPhoenix* (Saskatoon), www.canada.com, 27 May 2004)

Blind Obedience and Unquestioning Deference to Authority

Every day we see ads using superstars and athletes to sell a product. It's easy to draw unwarranted connections between such "authority" figures and the products they are selling. Similarly, blindly following a politician or a religious leader can be as bad as the unquestioning acceptance of a movie star's endorsement. A little detachment can be an asset.

There are plenty of examples of leaders who took their followers down paths of destruction and moral decay. Look at the examples of Jim Jones (who led 900 of his cult members to commit mass suicide), Pol Pot (who led the Kymer Rouge on a reign of terror and genocide in Cambodia), and David Koresh (who was killed with his cult followers at Waco, Texas). We must guard against surrendering our independence of thought. People are vulnerable to the forces of conformity and to those who assume leadership in the various arenas of our lives. This is especially true in times of stress or social upheaval. Difficult times challenge us to keep our wits about us and not be hasty in what we say, think, or do.

Not all authorities are credible. Look carefully and think about the evidence. We can make use of the advice of an authority, but we should not be manipulated by it.

The Global Dimension

Gays Seeking Asylum

The government of Canada Immigration and Refugee Board (IRB) has rejected the asylum case of a Mexican homosexual on the grounds that he is not "visibly effeminate" and therefore not vulnerable to persecution in his homeland. Fernando Enrique Rivera, 30 years old, came from Mexico to Canada four years ago. State the issues and concerns raised about assumptions and stereotypes reported to be behind the IRB's decision:

> Fernando Enrique Rivera, who lifts weights, wears his hair closely cropped and favours jeans and conservative sports shirts, believes the IRB's decision shows a stereotypical understanding of homosexuality. "I know some gay refugees who put on lipstick and dressed effeminately for their hearings because they thought it would help their case. But that is not who I am," Mr. Rivera said in an interview in a Church Street eatery in the heart

of Toronto's gay village. "You don't choose to be gay. It's not like being a vegetarian. It's a very complex thing." During the interview, a waiter jokingly chided him: "Your problem is, you're too butch."

IRB [Board] member Milagros Eustaquio essentially came to the same conclusion. "Effeminate gestures come naturally and unconsciously," she wrote in her decision in December 2002. "If he were indeed visibly effeminate, I do not think it is likely he would have been able to easily land a job with the 'macho' police force of Puerto Vallarta" (Marina Jimenez, "Canada Rejects Gay Man Who Isn't 'Effeminate,'" *Globe and Mail*, globandmail.com, 4 May 2004).

In April 2004 the Canadian federal court upheld the board ruling. As a result, Rivera fears deportation if he fails at his last chance at appeal—one resting on compassion and humanitarian review.

Loaded Language

Language has power. The words we use affect the thoughts we have and our ideas for defining, as well as solving, problems. Philosopher Martin Heidegger claimed that every seeking gets guided beforehand by what is sought. The way an inquiry is structured, the terms used, and the criteria for reaching a resolution influence the results of the inquiry. In this sense, language literally shapes our thoughts.

Just think about the power one word or phrase can have. **Loaded language** creates an inherent bias in the very terms used. Calling someone a "welfare recipient" versus a "welfare bum" colors the way the person is perceived. Calling someone a "Southerner" versus a "hillbilly" can elicit a very different response. Calling someone a "substance abuser" versus a "crack-head" can affect our perceptions of drug treatment programs. Calling someone a "disgruntled citizen" or "anarchist" as opposed to an "insurgent" or a "terrorist" can shape a government's response. Calling an appetizer "escargot" versus "snails" colors its desirability as a predinner treat.

Biased and loaded language should always be routed out. Look for it and assess its impact. Also consider whether the cultural or social context plays a role in the connotation or interpretation of a word or phrase. For example, in some areas of the world being a recipient of social services or "welfare" payments does not carry the element of social disapproval found in the United States. Thus, we

You Tell Me Department

Why Pick on West Virginia?

We don't normally think of West Virginia as the target for incest jokes, but there we are. Abercrombie & Fitch has outraged the governor of West Virginia because of a T-shirt sold on its Web site. The T-shirt pictures a map of West Virginia with these words written across the map: "It's all relative in West Virginia." As James Dao reports, "Gov. Bob Wise, a Democrat, contends that the shirt is a not-so-subtle play on the stereotype of West Virginia as a haven for incest. The governor demanded that the company stop selling the shirt and destroy its entire stock of it (James Dao, "T-Shirt Slight Has West Virginia in Arms," *The New York Times*, 23 Mar 2004). Here are the two sides:

GOVERNOR WISE: "By selling and marketing this offensive item, your company is perpetuating an inaccurate portrayal of the people of this great state. Indeed, such a depiction of West Virginians undermines our collective efforts to communicate a positive representation of the spirit and values of our citizens."

THOMAS D. LENNOX FOR ABERCROMBIE & FITCH: Abercrombie & Fitch has no plans to discontinue sales of the T-shirt. "We love West Virginia."

You tell me: Should Abercrombie and Fitch pull the T-shirt?

need to look at the broader issues when contemplating stereotypes. We need not be colorless to be unbiased, but we must be on the watch for the ways language is used to deceive, to mislead, or to otherwise block us from seeing an issue and evaluating the evidence.

Habit and Conformity

To the extent that we are victims of habitual ways of doing things, we dull our skills at observation and description. Routines can simplify our life, but should not make us brittle. There is a reason people describe habits as "traps." As writer Samuel Beckett said, "Habit is the great deadener."

Many of our habitual ways of thinking and doing things factor into our decision making. We go on autopilot at times. Some of us go to the same restaurants, order the same things, hang out with the same people, vacation in the same spots, and favor the familiar over the unknown. Some people vote along party lines (such as Democrat, Republican, Liberal, Conservative, Tory, NDP, Green Party, etc.) without considering the candidate or the issues. Voting for the party without looking at the candidate may cause us to miss or ignore issues or potential consequences for the political party or for the society. And just because "we've always done it this way" doesn't mean that it is the best, or only, way. We risk getting stuck, even sinking, when we let routines and habits go by, year after year, without being examined, overhauled, or eliminated altogether.

An interesting case of how habit can affect the way we think has to do with security alerts about terrorist threats (color coded as red, yellow, etc.). The fact that such alerts started to become fairly routine has *not* made people vigilant and on the look-out for terrorists. Hardly. We might have expected heightened anxiety,

> But more striking was the evidence of habituation. Repeated warnings, intended to heighten Americans' awareness of the possibility of a terrorist act appear to have had the opposite effect, especially since so far, they have not been followed by attacks. Results from polls by the Pew Research Center suggest that since the first terror alert was issued in 2002, people's anxiety level has decreased with each successive warning. People living in tornado country, researchers find, usually ignore storm watches altogether, unless their town or area is specifically named. Even then, few take any action to avoid the storm unless they see the sky darkening, the wind come up or some other real evidence. (Benedict Carey and Anahad O'Connor, "As Public Adjust to Threat, Alerts Cause Less Unease," *The New York Times*, 3 Aug 2004)

This suggests that citizens might become more alert for terrorists if either the government rarely gave warnings or the warnings were more specific about the possible danger. In any case, routine warnings seem to get filed away with other routines and habits.

Limited Access to Information or Evidence

"Access is power," George W. Bush once observed. This view is echoed by others. Rep. Romano Mazzoli says, "Access is it. Access is power. Access is clout. That's how this thing works" (www.democracymatters.org). Access to information and to resources can be most helpful in clarifying what's what. However, there may be obstacles. We are not always able to see the big picture because of **limited access** to information. These limitations may or may not be the fault of others. Others may control access to information, as in the case of a teacher, supervisor, doctor, family member, or friend. But at times we are limited by physical conditions or by the ravages of time. For example, documents may get lost, people die, and artifacts disintegrate.

This is the case with the only audio recording of the shooting death of President John F. Kennedy. The recording was made through an open microphone on a police motorcade and then recorded onto a Dictaphone belt at police headquarters in Dallas, Texas. Scientific analyses over the decades since 1962 have been inconclusive. The Dictaphone belt has become worn and damaged by the constant replay—so it is unclear if there were three shots (the official version— Oswald shot Kennedy) or four (Oswald was *not* the lone gunman). Thanks to technology, scientists may soon be able to get a digital image of the sound patterns. This might then settle the question of the number of shots fired. (See Michael Janofsky, "Salvage Work is Begun on Kennedy-Killing Tape," *The New York Times*, 3 Aug 2004.)

Sometimes information has been censored or edited. This can happen in high-profile cases, when information can be slow to surface, fueling speculation. "Who knew what when?" is a central concern in many cases (e.g., the CIA before 9/11, plans to go to war with Iraq, and so on). Without access, the door may be hard to pry open. Look at the example of the FBI discovery of "misplaced" boxes of 4,500 documents in the case of Timothy McVeigh. McVeigh was convicted of killing 168 people in the Oklahoma City bombing. Long after the trial and right before the planned execution, the FBI discovered the vast quantity of documents, which delayed the execution and raised concerns. "Human error, compounded by antiquated and cumbersome information technology systems and procedures," was the cause, Attorney General John Ashcroft surmised ("Widespread Failure in McVeigh Case," CBS News, www.cbsnews.com, 19 Mar 2002).

There's more: Later evidence suggests that McVeigh and Nichols did not act alone—at least 10 Aryan Nation bank robbers were also involved. However, evidence has been lost or destroyed that might put some theories to rest. "FBI agents were so suspicious of a link they analyzed video footage of the robbery to see whether McVeigh participated (inconclusive). That video was destroyed in 1999 by the FBI despite rules to the contrary." Nevertheless, "If I were still in the bureau, the investigation would be reopened," says Dan Defenbaugh, retired FBI chief of the Oklahoma City bombing investigation (Associated Press, "FBI Suspected McVeigh Part of Conspiracy," 25 Feb 2004).

Whenever access is limited or controlled, critical thinking is handicapped. We must then seek other sources of information. Become adept at piecing together puzzles and drawing inferences from nuggets of details. Also, note that there may be other routes—such as international news sources, church documents, handwritten notes, letters, e-mails, and photographs.

Not all cases of limited access are on the level of international scandals, government censorship or media blackouts. Sometimes we are stumped by everyday events or by the people around us. Sometimes we just scratch our heads and wonder about the quality of the evidence—as when a friend is late and offers a lame excuse. That is also a time to put critical thinking tools to work!

Exercises

For each of the following, draw three possible inferences. Note that all the quotes below are from *David Thomson on the Alien Quartet*, Bloomsbury Movie Guide No. 4:

1. "I am not sure that—and I am not saying that—*Alien* is a great film. It is 'only' something I have never been able to get out of my head—just as there are some things that, once admitted, can never be removed from the body."

2. " 'We're going to blow up the ship,' says Ripley. She, Parker and Lambert will then have to make their escape in the shuttle. As the trio pull themselves together, Parker turns his flame-thrower on Ash's discarded head. In two bursts, we see the 'skin' come off like thick paint, exposing the hard plastic skull."

3. "We meet Drake, a raw-faced crew cut man . . . a joker named Hudson . . . and Vasquez . . . a sultry, muscled Latina [not in real life] who is doing body-building exercises within a few minutes of waking. 'Hey, Vasquez,' asks the joker, 'have you ever been mistaken for a man?' 'No,' growls Vasquez, 'have

you?' And Drake gives her a handshake, grinning in delight, and tells her she's bad. No matter how far in the future we go, it seems, Marines are Marines."

4. "Viewers of *Alien* films often feel the need to shower away the gluey mucous of the creatures afterwards. The surge of power in the pulse rifles and the flame-throwers is enough to enlist the most insistent pacifist. For combat on film *is* like sex: it is a joining rhythm and the chance of crescendo. And as we participate in the blazing away of it all, even fear lifts a little. We are close here to some inner secret about weapons, about how they appeal to the id while putting away idiot consequences."

Psychological Blocks

Have you ever been so anxious you couldn't think straight? Have you ever stuck foot in mouth just when you hoped to say something impressive? The perfect mate approaches and—Blap! We lose it. Then there is the nightmare job interview when the mind goes completely blank. Such **psychological blocks** as anxiety, depression, and fear can suck the neurons right out of our skulls! For instance, we aren't likely to question security routines at airports or the evidence that cell phones interfere with the operating system of airplanes. The fear after 9/11 caused all sorts of changes and policy decisions. Some of these decisions have a stronger basis than others—thus the need for critical thinking.

Professor Debra Moon observes that self-esteem problems can get in the way of good reasoning. She's right. For those who have a healthy sense of their own self-worth and the confidence to function more or less effectively in the world, it may be difficult to understand what happens when that balance is thrown off. When someone suffers very low self-esteem or has a vastly inflated view of themselves, their perceptions can get twisted. For instance, those who have a bloated ego may assume that their concerns take priority over the rights and concerns of others. And those who have a diminished sense of self may not be able to think clearly or make good decisions. An example of this is when victims of domestic violence or incest stay bonded to their abuser(s). Some suffer "learned helplessness" and they are unable to protect themselves or loved ones from violence escalating further.

Some think that these extremes operate on societal levels as well. For instance, those from "developed" countries like the United States, Canada, and European nations do not always understand the problems facing Third World countries. Similarly, there may be imbalances within a "developed" country; for example, when those with power or wealth have opportunities unavailable to those in the middle or working classes. In addition, rampant consumerism—"I want, I want, I need"—can distort our vision so we put our own desires far above the needs of others. We have the tools to address these imbalances. But we need to be aware of this potential obstacle and watch for emotional and mental roadblocks.

One-Sided Thinking

A narrow frame of reference may help us zero in on a problem that we are investigating. But we have to use it like a tool, because **one-sided thinking** can function like blinders, blocking us from a clearer understanding of what's going on. Each person who tells a story looks at the topic through a particular filter. That filter is made up of values, beliefs, assumptions, experiences, knowledge or ignorance, and, at times, even desire.

With one-sided thinking, we fail to acknowledge (or realize) that our narrow angle or presentation may create a bias. This bias could slant the inquiry and result in a limited grasp of the situation. Watch for this in our own reasoning, as well as that of others. We cannot remove ourselves from our own set of interests, at least not entirely. No one sees with eyes cut off from emotions and experiences, our ways of thinking and feeling about the world. But we can become more aware. Our angle of approach and our worldview shapes what we see and how we think.

It helps to see how a particular frame of reference affects how stories are told, problems are formulated, and arguments are structured. Once we notice this crucial dimension, we can give a more accurate analysis. As author N. Scott Momaday put it, "The Indian and white man perceive the world in different ways. I take it that this is an obvious fact and a foregone conclusion. But at the same time I am convinced that we do not understand the distinction entirely or even sufficiently" (as quoted by Anne Waters, *American Indian Thought*, 2004).

Take nothing for granted. Be careful not to assume the **deadly triad** of the *status quo + habit + stereotypical thinking*. This triad is formed by the mindset of the dominant culture, the habitual ways of doing things, and belief systems that lock attitudes and stereotypical ways of thinking into place. Think of this deadly triad as conceptual snow goggles. We stare through them, seeing the world through tiny slits. Sure we focus on this or that particular item, but we're unable to get beyond a narrow range of vision. To get the entire vista in perspective, we need to yank the goggles off. Similarly, we have to get rid of habitual ways of thinking and seeing so we can get a wider perspective.

Exercises

1. The movie, *Shawshank Redemption,* contains an exchange about Brooks, the librarian. Brooks gets notice of his parole, but does *not* want to be released from the prison he's known for so long. Read the exchange and then discuss the issue of becoming so accustomed to a situation or way of life—even an unpleasant one—that it is hard to even imagine, much less desire, what it would be like if things changed. Would you say this is another form of the debilitating effects of habit?

    RED: Man's been here fifty years [referring to Brooks]. This place is all he knows. In here, he's an important man, an educated man. A librarian. Out there, he's nothing but a used-up old con with arthritis in both hands. Couldn't even get a library card if he applied. You see what I'm saying?

FLOYD: Red, I do believe you're talking out of your ass.

RED: Believe what you want. These walls are funny. First you hate 'em, then you get used to 'em. After long enough, you get so you depend on 'em. That's "institutionalized."

JIGGER: Shit. I could never get that way.

ERNIE (SOFTLY): Say that when you been inside as long as Brooks has.

RED: Goddamn right. They send you here for life, and that's just what they take. Part that counts, anyway.

2. List three ways to either substantiate or disprove the claim that "Children in this culture grow up knowing that you can never be thin enough and that being fat is one of the worst things one can be" (Susan Bordo, *Twilight Zones,* University of California Press, 1997).

3. Read the following excerpt and then answer the questions below.

In a 1995 survey, nearly 200 aspiring American Olympians were asked if they would take a banned substance that would guarantee victory in every competition for five years and would then cause death; more than half answered yes. A recent seminar on teenage steroid use, held in New York City, revealed these desperate efforts to boost athletic performance: A female basketball player asked a doctor to break her arms and reset them in a way that might make them longer; pediatricians were being pressured by parents to give their children human growth hormone to make them taller and perhaps more athletic; doctors were being asked by the parents of football players to provide steroids so their sons might gain college scholarships.

A molecular scientist, speaking on condition of anonymity, said in an interview that a foreign exchange student staying with the scientist's family was approached at a swimming pool by a stranger and was told "You are absolutely beautiful; I'll give you $35,000 for one of your eggs." The student accepted the offer. It is not inconceivable that some parent looking to create an elite athlete would offer far more money for such an arrangement with, say, Marion Jones, the world's fastest woman. (Jere Longman, "Pushing the Limits," *The New York Times,* 11 May 2001)

Answer the following:

1. State the major obstacles to clear thinking in the quest for a more perfect body (e.g., by using performance-enhancing drugs or nutritional supplements) in both amateur and professional athletes.

2. Assuming we don't want young athletes to find doctors who will break their arms so they might have an athletic advantage and black markets in genetically-engineered human eggs, what sorts of steps could be taken to address this situation?

3. Was the beautiful foreign exchange student thinking clearly when she agreed to sell her genetic material for $35,000?

Group or Individual Exercise

The Barstow Beauty Queen

In May 2001, just weeks after being named "Miss Barstow" in the small California town's beauty contest, Emily Arnold, a high school senior, was celebrating winning the crown, her 18th birthday, her pending graduation, and her acceptance to the University of Arizona when she did a prank, never imagining the consequences. Read the excerpt below about what transpired and decide what *you* think should have been done to address the misdeed:

> At a rival classmate's house, she impulsively grabbed a piece of chalk and scrawled the words "NOT NICE" and "MEAN" on a car windshield. The schoolmate's father [Stan Clair], a California Highway Patrol (CHP) sergeant, caught her in the act, called for backup—three squad cars showed up—and had her and six friends arrested. The father wants the district attorney to file charges of vandalism.
>
> Tonight, Emily Arnold—cheerleader, honor student and class treasurer, so long the beneficiary of small-town life, now the victim of it—will give back her crown. The sudden controversy has left Barstow divided. "There are some people who felt that she should be asked to leave [the position], and others who felt that she should not," said Kris Watson, director of the Miss Barstow contest for the last 12 years. (Scott Gold, "The Short, Sad Reign of Miss Barstow," *Los Angeles Times*, 28 Jun 2001)

1. Do you agree with Mr. Clair's response to the incident? Set out three pros and cons of his action in light of *his* own daughter's behavior:

> But [the CHP officer] Stan Clair, a member of the school board, insisted on pressing charges of vandalism, a crime that can bring a $1,000 fine and a year in jail. Some criticize him for that, pointing out his own daughter had been accused of shooting a neighbor's house and car with a paint-ball gun only hours before the notorious chalk incident. That situation, they say, was resolved without need for law enforcement. (From "The Short, Sad Reign of Miss Barstow")

2. What three to four thoughts or suggestions would you share with Kris Watson, director of the Miss Barstow contest?

3. As you might expect, the public responded. Set out your thoughts on the comments about the case printed in letters to the editor of the *Los Angeles Times*:

> RESPONSE #1, WALLY ROBERTS: "Any reasonable father in such circumstances would have made the errant teens clean up the mess and apologize . . . in the circumstances, he grossly overreacted and used his authority as a CHP [California Highway patrol] officer to do so."
>
> RESPONSE #2, MARK HERDER: "I want to commend Sgt. Clair and the CHP for their courageous takedown of Miss Barstow. Few people know or even

care about the growing epidemic of teenage beauty queens run amok. Just yesterday I caught one scribbling "wash me" with her finger on the dusty windshield of my car. Sgt. Clair, where were you and your three squad cars of brave highway patrolmen when I needed you?"

RESPONSE #3, MARK ESPENSCHIED: "Shame on Clair, shame on the Kiwanis Club and shame on half the citizens of Barstow. . . . In a perfect world, Clair would be reprimanded by the CHP and kicked off the school board. By all means, get out of town, Emily Arnold. Go to where you can continue to excel."

▦ Overview of Critical Thinking

Arguments: The Common Ground of Logic and Critical Thinking

You arrive home and turn on the TV. On comes an ad, "More people prefer Sammy's to Pizza House pizza." Ready to place your order for a BBQ chicken pizza, you glance at the TV screen. "In a study of 300 people, 156 people preferred Sammy's." The ad agency for Sammy's underestimates you, however, as your brain cells are on standby for action! Fortunately, you are able to figure out that of the 300 people studied, 156 preferred Sammy's and 144 preferred Pizza House pizza. This is a difference of only 8 people, or 2.6 percent. Allowing a margin of error of 2 percent or 3 percent, the study actually revealed very little, other than that the contest was virtually a draw.

When studying critical thinking, you acquire skills and tools to construct or take apart arguments, examine data, weigh evidence, read more carefully, subject your own reasoning to assessment, reflect on your beliefs, and articulate your own ideas clearly and defensibly. The result is that you think with more care and precision. You start to feel like a mental acrobat, no more the fool.

Propositions are the building blocks of arguments. A **proposition** is an assertion that is either true or false. The form of a proposition is that something is being predicated of some subject, such as "Some *movie-goers* [subject] are popcorn-eaters [predicate]." Declarations and rhetorical questions may operate as propositions; so they can be written to clarify what's being asserted. Propositions can function together as a body of evidence offered in support of a particular claim. This forms an argument.

Argumentation is central to both critical thinking and logic. An **argument** has two major parts: the conclusion and the premises. This means arguments consist of a set of propositions, at least one of which (called a **premise**) is offered as evidence for accepting another proposition (called the **conclusion** or **thesis**). Our main concern is to assess the quality of the evidence in terms of supporting the conclusion. That relationship between the premises and the conclusion is pivotal. Dismantling and assessing arguments is the bread and butter of critical thinking.

Arguments bombard us from every side. We meet them everywhere—in advertisements, newspapers, TV, radio, political campaigns, classroom discussions, personal choices we anguish over, decisions about what to buy, where to live, and how we relate with each other. Some arguments are of little importance. Some have changed the world. In a **strong argument,** the premises provide sufficient support for the conclusion (thesis). This standard means that the conclusion should follow from the premises, so if each premise were presumed to be true, the conclusion would be true as well—or highly likely in an inductive argument (like one using statistical reasoning).

Here's a strong argument: "All race-car drivers take risks. Some race-car drivers are killed in accidents at professional auto races. Therefore, some risk-takers are killed in accidents at professional auto races." If the two premises were true, the conclusion follows and would have to be true. Unfortunately, many arguments fall short of this goal. The premises may offer some support, but the support may not be as convincing as we'd like. There may be **missing pieces,** so the overall picture is twisted and the argument deficient. Or the argument may be poorly worded or badly constructed. On the other hand, the evidence could present an airtight case. Our task is to figure this out.

Comparison of Logic and Critical Thinking

Being a good critical thinker and being a good logician are similar, but different. The key similarity is that both emphasize analysis and careful reasoning. The key difference is that logic is more narrowly focused, whereas critical thinking has a broader scope. **Logic** focuses upon argumentation; the task of the logician is to determine the strength of the evidence as support for the conclusion.

The logician makes *three key distinctions:* What kind of argument is this? How convincing is it? Does it rest on evidence we know (or can determine) to be true? Each question lays the foundation for all further steps the logician will take, as we'll see below:

Three Key Questions in Logic

- **What kind of argument is it?** Logicians divide arguments into two categories: deductive and inductive. With **deductive arguments,** it is claimed or implied that the premises completely support the conclusion. With **inductive arguments,** the evidence is not sufficient for the conclusion to follow with certainty. The *difference* between these two categories of reasoning is analogous to operating with a full deck of cards versus a deck in which there are missing cards.
- **How convincing is the argument on its face value?** With deductive arguments logicians seek to determine if the conclusion will *certainly* be true if we assume the premises are all true. With inductive arguments we decide how *probable* the conclusion is if we assume the premises are all true. "These are called strong arguments." The focus is basically on **structure.** In the case of deductive arguments, these are called logically **valid arguments.**

You Tell Me Department

First at What?

Advertisements are arguments too, trying to persuade us to buy, sell, or access services. This is true whether the subject is food, cars, perfume, or job openings. Let's look at an ad in a legal news journal:

For Contractor Attorneys
First in the world is still the best in the state

THE LAWSMITHS
The Only Experienced
Full-Time,
Multi-City Attorneys-Only Organization in the World.

You tell me: What do you learn about "The Lawsmiths" from their ad?

- **Does the argument pass the truth test?** Are the premises in fact true—is the evidence cited really the case? **Sound arguments** have two characteristics: They are valid arguments *and* they have true premises. So long as there's doubt, we don't know if the argument will pass the truth test. When there's a false premise, the argument cannot be considered sound, even if the argument is well structured. An unsound argument could be invalid, have false premises, or both.

One of the main tasks of the logician is to decide if the evidence really offers the quality of support for the conclusion. This corresponds to the standard of proof in criminal trials *("beyond a reasonable doubt")*. Classically, logicians studied only deductive arguments, the model was mathematics and the objective was certainty.

Now, however, that is not necessarily true. Think how often people cite statistical studies, try to explain the cause of an event, or use comparisons to convince others. Many arguments rest on probability or rely upon unproven assumptions, corresponding to the standard of proof in civil trials: a *"preponderance of the evidence"* (where a simple majority of the evidence must point to the conclusion). Whichever standard of proof we seek, logic gives us the means to examine arguments. The last unit of this textbook focuses on the techniques and tools of logic.

Critical Thinking: A Broader Scope

Critical thinking encompasses much more than argumentation, and so it is a broader discipline than logic. It includes *skills* of observation, description, inference, language analysis, assessing the role of frame of reference, and examining unwarranted assumptions or other potential obstacles to clear thinking. To be good thinkers, we need to be observant. We need to watch carefully, get a sense of the big picture, take note of the unusual or questionable, and have our antennae out.

We need to be attentive to details, while not losing sight of the larger framework. It is wise not take anything for granted. There could be serious consequences if we are oblivious, "asleep at the switch," make mistakes, or overlook something that could break the case. Here's an example of an unfortunate oversight: In 1999 the CIA provided incorrect targeting data that led U.S. warplanes to bomb the Chinese Embassy in Yugoslavia during a NATO air war. Evidently, "The CIA had not noticed the embassy's new address in the Belgrade [Yugoslavia] telephone directory" (Bob Drogin, "School for New Brand of Spooks," *Los Angeles Times*, 21 July 2000). Duh!

Examining the Evidence

An important aspect of critical thinking centers on how evidence is gathered and examined. This involves surveying the situation, clarifying goals, looking at the process by which evidence is obtained, keeping an eye out for missing evidence, and weighing the evidence. **Weighing evidence** involves separating evidence from background information, deciding on a set of criteria to sort it into categories or evaluate it, and then assessing evidence in light of its relevance and quality of support for the conclusion.

For example, if the criteria for getting a scholarship centered on academic excellence and leadership capabilities, then such matters as financial need would not be a factor. If the sole requirements for an ideal mate are that the person be attractive, muscular, and rich, then traits like integrity, generosity of spirit, or sense of humor would be of little relevance. If your criteria for a good movie include lots of special effects, then you probably wouldn't like the old classics but would be drawn to films like *Hero, Sky Captain and the World of Tomorrow*, and *The Matrix*.

Sorting for Relevance

Being able to pinpoint **relevant evidence** is crucial to problem solving. The more relevant the evidence is, the greater its role or impact. Consider how each piece of evidence links to the thesis. Determine if it functions independently (on its own) or dependently (in collaboration with other pieces of evidence). Frequently, the so-called evidence is way off the mark—irrelevant to the thesis or a smokescreen to cover up the flimsiness of the case being made. People are occasionally gullible about irrelevant claims (e.g., testimonials of celebrities pitching products), and they fail to look at—or look for—relevant pieces of evidence to support the thesis or conclusion being drawn.

We are often faced with a glut of information, as we know from virtually every Internet search. Or perhaps the information is off topic or out of date. Or perhaps someone is intentionally deceptive. Think, for instance, about the kinds of ads that offer little information about the product. For example, consider two advertisements, one for yogurt and one for cigarettes. The ad for Yoplait berry banana and kiwi daiquiri yogurt has a photo of three young, pretty women who are laughing and appear to be having fun. In the top left corner is written *"It's Like . . . Girls' Night Out"* and at the bottom right in large letters is *"Good!"*

Nothing in the ad addresses the virtues of Yoplait yogurt—the "girls" are not even eating yogurt. In the second example, a cigarette ad, we see a photo of a building (night club?) in midnight blue. In the center of the ad is written, *"There are no strangers here. Only friends we haven't met."* These last words are positioned so we connect the idea of meeting these new "friends" with smoking Marlboros.

The evidence for concluding that we should get this yogurt or that cigarette centers on an imagined experience, not the product in question. This overlooks more relevant factors for making a good decision—such as the nutritional value of the yogurt or the health concerns of smoking. As we will see, that's when critical thinking tools can come to the rescue.

Analysis

The heart of critical thinking is analysis; for it is there that all the other elements we've mentioned come together. When we **analyze,** we need to be observant to detail and able to clarify problems, tasks, and goals. We need to separate fact from opinion and recognize speculation as opposed to giving evidence for a position. We need to be able to evaluate testimony and assess credibility. We need to be attentive to moral reasoning. We need to be able to dismantle arguments and evaluate them.

Speculation is a form of guesswork. We normally use the term **speculation** to apply to either (1) hypotheses that have little, if any, evidence to back them up or (2) unsupported claims. People speculate all the time, for example, when they offer their theory as to why their dog bit your ankle or why one idea may give better results than another. There may be a kernel of evidence in such communication, but not enough to draw a solid conclusion. In such cases, speculation can run rampant. Some speculation borders on the ludicrous, such as when people jump to a conclusion on the basis of suspect evidence. Hypochondriacs, for instance, suffer from a lot of misguided speculation about potential health problems.

At times it is only in hindsight that we recognize an overreaction. Fear and ignorance both fuel the imagination. For example, in 2003 there was an outbreak of monkeypox—a relative of smallpox, a deadly contagious disease—in Illinois, Indiana, and Wisconsin. Infected pet prairie dogs were primarily responsible for the disease spreading to humans that they bit. Chills, fever, and ghastly pus-filled sores were among the symptoms. When it first appeared, some speculated that it was a terrorist act. "Nowadays, any time there's an outbreak of a strange disease, some people will probably think bioterrorism," Donald Henderson said. "There was no evidence whatsoever of that in this case. But I imagine people thought about it, especially if they believed it might be smallpox." (Gretchen Reynolds, "Why Were Doctors Afraid to Treat Rebecca McLester?," *The New York Times Magazine,* 18 Apr 2004).

The person speculating may be fairly knowledgeable about the topic, but they may be missing pieces of the puzzle. The speculation then takes the form of a

Individual or Group Exercise

Grade Quotas

With 46 percent of Princeton students getting grades in the "A" range (counting plus and minus), the administration is cracking down and instituting quotas. As of the academic year 2004–05, Princeton University's new policy is setting a cap of 35 percent on A's in all courses, except for independent studies (which will cap at 55 percent). The Dean argued that grade inflation could no longer be ignored: "Our feeling then was that we could just let it go, and over the next 25 years everyone would be getting all A's," says Nancy Weiss Malkiel, dean of the college. "But would that really be responsible in terms of the way we educated our students?" The dean said that they sought to match the percentage of A's from the late 80s and early 90s (Teresa Mendez, "Deflating the Easy A," *Christian Science Monitor*, 4 May 2004).

Answer the following:

1. What assumptions did the Dean of Princeton make regarding the high number of A's?

2. What is the most relevant support cited for concluding Princeton has grade inflation?

3. What is the least relevant support cited for concluding Princeton has grade inflation?

4. Syracuse University professor William Coplin says that students learn in the classroom less than half of what they need to know for real life. Distributing higher grades gives them room to explore other areas of interest and to develop as people. "Most students do not see college as a place to develop skills. They see it as a place to get a degree and have a high GPA," he says. "The truth is, skills are more important than GPA." He worries that attempting to stamp out grade inflation will simply make students even crazier about grades (Teresa Mendez, "Deflating the Easy A," *Christian Science Monitor*). Do you think he's right? Share your thoughts.

"wild guess." Problem solving often involves such speculation. Take, for instance, the speculation of Jeffrey Platt, of the Mayo Clinic Transplantation Biology Program. "Perhaps HIV managed to jump from primates to humans through infected blood from a bite, which allowed the stem cells from the two species to fuse," Platt suggested. ("Pig-Human Chimeras Contain Cell Surprise," *The New Scientist*, NewScientist.com, 13 Jan 2004).

We have to be careful not to mistake speculation for fact. Nevertheless, it can be useful in problem solving. Let's look at the reasoning of Dr. Susan Solomon who wrote a history of the Scott expedition in Antarctica in 1912. The expedition resulted in the death of explorer Robert F. Scott and four men. With weather reports of the region and diaries as the main evidence, Solomon had to deal with missing data. Trying to fill in the holes about why they died only 11 miles from a depot of food and heating oil, she ended up speculating about their last days, qualifying it by the comment, "The full answer is a human question beyond the powers of science to answer." She speculated that Scott, who was suffering from frostbite, could go no farther and that Wilson and Bowers decided not to leave him. "Since they were still able to leave the tent, she surmises, they may have told Scott that there was a blizzard so he would not know they had chosen to follow their leader into death." (Kenneth Chang, "How Bad Luck Tipped the Scales to Disaster," *The New York Times,* 28 Aug 2001).

Dr. Solomon may be entirely correct in her speculation. On the other hand, maybe Wilson and Bowers told Scott the truth. Maybe they wanted to abandon the frostbitten chap to save their own hides, but Scott implored them to die with dignity, all together. Perhaps they all just gave up—the long perilous journey wore them out and they lost the will to live. Or the real reason they died together in the tent may come to light when another investigator finds a shred of missing data and throws off all the speculation thus far.

Speculation is a fact of life. When we don't have all the pieces, but want to offer an explanation or a theory, we often speculate. But remember: speculation is guesswork, however informed it may be.

The Role of Ideas in Analysis

Without the ability to analyze effectively, we would flounder. In situations that require us to dismantle reasoning or solve a problem, our analytical skills are crucial. Another aspect of analysis is the ability to work on the level of ideas. This is one of the creative dimensions of analysis. Through ideas and insights, we are able to move forward, solve problems, break deadlocks, and bust through mental paralysis.

There are two key aspects to the role of ideas in critical thinking. One is *having ideas* (the very fact of synthesizing what we know, contemplating goals, imagining scenarios, formulating hypotheses, and having bursts of creativity and insight) and another is *applying and examining ideas* (using our insights, seeing how ideas can take shape, evaluating the value of an idea, being detached enough to scrutinize our own, as well as others' ideas). We need to look at our own ideas and at the ideas of others and determine if they have merit. This process includes assessing the various parameters that may act as constraints, such as time, money, and available resources.

Sometimes our ideas are triggered by the things right around us, such as events in the news. Take the case of hairdresser Philip McCrory, who saw footage of an otter's fur soaking up oil from the Exxon Valdez spill. He had an idea that human hair could soak up the oil. He ran an experiment and his hypothesis held up.

He eventually contacted Maurice Hale at NASA's Marshall Space Flight Center. After a diesel oil spill at the center, McCrory made a filter of 16 pounds of hair and dumped it in, and the filter cleaned the water enough to empty it down a sewer (17 parts per million of oil). Hale applied this model to the Exxon Valdez spill: 1.4 million pounds of hair in mesh pillows would have soaked up the 11 million gallons spilled in about a week. Exxon spent $2 billion for an extended attempt to clean up the oil, but was only approximately 12 percent successful. This experience suggests Exxon would have done a better job using hair to soak up the oil. ("Oil Spill? Ask a Hairdresser," *The New York Times*, 9 Jun 1998).

Consider another breakthrough idea. With 100 million land mines worldwide, finding and eliminating them is a must. In a truth-is-stranger-than-fiction story the Gambian giant pouched rat may one day replace dogs for sniffing them out. Evidently, dogs are hard to keep healthy, especially in tropical Africa. Also, they bond with their trainers, making it hard to switch them to a different handler. The rats have the advantage of smaller size—they weigh around 3 pounds so they don't trip the land mine charges. Here are more reasons the rats work better than dogs:

FIRST: In their little red, black and blue harnesses, they look like miniature sniffer dogs. But their trainers at Sokoine University of Agriculture say the African pouched rats can do a much better job than dogs—and they do it for a bit of banana. "Rats are good, clever to learn, small, like performing repeated tasks and have a better sense of smell than dogs," said Christophe Cox, the Belgian coordinator of a project that is training 300 rats to locate mines by recognizing the smell of dynamite and TNT ("Rats Nose Knows Best," www.landmines.org).

SECOND: "Throw a stick for a dog to fetch, and after 10 times the dog will say, 'Get it yourself, buddy,' Mr. [Frank] Weetjens said. "Rats will keep working as long as they want food." . . . "Rats 'don't give a fig about people,' says Harvard Bach of the Geneva demining center. They're almost mechanical in the way they work," he says. (Michael Wines, "For Sniffing out Land Mines a Platoon of Twitching Noses," *The New York Times*, 18 May 2004)

Exercises

1. As we can see from the above report, the need for trained Gambian rats seems obvious. But they require a human trainer to work with them and, after locating a land mine, to hand them a piece of banana or other tasty morsel. Once trained, the rats sniff out a mine, then sit and scratch at the spot until they are rewarded with food. A human explosive expert then destroys the mine—obviously a risky proposition. Assume *your* help is needed to attract the people to work out in the field: What do you think should be included in a job ad for handlers of the land mine–sniffing rats? List them (or write the job ad that'll be placed in the newspaper!).

2. The thought of freezing to death—or being frozen after death—gets a chilly reception. Nevertheless, answer any *two* of the following questions:

   a. What inferences can you draw from the fact that at 35 degrees, bleeding virtually stops and the brain can survive for hours (reported in *Wired*, May 2004)?

   b. Can you think of an idea for putting this fact to commercial use—how could it be used in furthering cryogenics (freezing bodies for eventual revival)?

   c. State two to three concerns that this assertion raises: "As far as anyone knows, there's nothing physically impossible about reviving a frozen head." (Wil McCarthy, *Wired*, May 2004)

Profile of a Clear Thinker: Skills and Dispositions

Critical reasoning gives us the tools to look at problems, sort through possible solutions, make decisions, be a more reflective person, and examine the various issues that we face. Here are some of the tools critical thinkers learn how to use:

Surveillance Tools: Get an overview, use observation skills, define problems, recognize opinions versus facts, spot prejudice or bias, spot different uses of language, and determine frame of reference and diversity in points of view.

Analytical Tools: Examine assumptions, dismantle arguments, weigh evidence, evaluate quality of reasoning (inductive and deductive), construct defensible arguments, spot fallacies of reasoning, and arrive at decisions.

Synthesis Tools: Bring together, organize, summarize, and pull together decision-making strategies; coordinate plans; watch for corroborating details or evidence; and gather components of decision making.

Problem-Solving Tools: Brainstorm, articulate goals, apply criteria, use analogies, create frameworks and models, consider diverse perspectives and models of interpretation, generate ideas, challenge status quo, and reflect on one's own thinking processes.

Critical thinking calls us to look more carefully at how we approach a situation and our own ways of thinking. It helps to have some **key attitudes and dispositions of a clear thinker**—such as being receptive, flexible, open-minded, a careful listener, attentive to detail, observant, questioning, and willing to persevere. Personal traits include being willing to take risks and look at problems from different vantage points. Most of us cannot be completely unbiased or nonjudgmental, but we should strive to recognize our own biases and consider if we have vested interests that may interfere with clear thinking.

Critical thinking helps us become more systematic and more effective at problem solving. Good critical thinkers are able to see the big picture, sort and weigh evidence, examine assumptions, and be attentive to diverse perspectives. This includes being willing to chuck what doesn't work and start all over, while being careful not to reject ideas that challenge long-held beliefs. Be willing to rethink basic assumptions and admit when mistakes are made. Operate with a sense of fairness and try to be curious and open-minded in approaching situations.

Exercises

1. A jewelry firm called American Design sells a "Fat-Be-Gone" ring. The online ad was said to claim that, "when worn on the little finger, the ring slims the thighs. The ring finger is for the stomach, thumb for the face and so on—all with 'no drugs, no starving, no sweating.' " Lynn McAfee, director of the Council on Size and Weight Discrimination observes, "I don't think it's unreasonable that we want to have a miracle." She evidently has a Fat-Be-Gone ring, saying, "In the back of my mind, I say, 'Well, maybe it will work' " (Greg Winter, "Fraudulent Marketers Capitalize on Demand for Sweat-Free Diets," *The New York Times*, 29 Oct 2000).
   Answer the following:
   a. Is there any harm (and maybe even good) in wearing a Fat-Be-Gone ring?
   b. What concerns should be raised about allowing a company to market a Fat-Be-Gone ring?
   c. What elements of being a good critical thinker will help you in deciding whether or not there is any merit to such a diet cure as this?

2. What's wrong with this reasoning?

   KEITH: Hey, Shakir, what's up?

   SHAKIR: You may not want to know, Keith! I just read an article about this weird disease in New York and New Jersey called MRSA that starts like a rash and goes to skin abscesses or amputation. Get a load of this [*reading out loud*]:

   "The Department of Health is tracking the outbreak here but declined to provide the number of cases it has found. Last month, Steven, who asked that his last name not be published, developed what he thought was a pimple on his leg, but it soon grew painful and larger. Doctors lanced the boil that formed and began antibiotics, but the infection failed to respond and starting growing toward Steven's groin. "The fact it wasn't responding [to drugs] and it was moving up that way was terrifying," he said. "It was eating up tissue." After a lengthy hospital stay and five antibiotics—some administered intravenously and one, Zyvox, administered orally at $100 per tablet—the infection started to abate. Doctors told Steven they believed he contracted it at the gym." (Sam Smith, "Killer Rash Breaks Out," *New York Post*, www.nypost.com, 30 May 2004)

KEITH: Wow! That's awful, man. It's another reason not to go to a gym! I'm staying away from them, that much I know.

SHAKIR: Yeah, you just don't know what disease you'll get when you hang out at a gym. That's why I work out with weights at home and jog—you won't find me catching infections like this.

3. What are three to four distinctly different ways we might address poverty in other nations? After you draw up your list, read the following remarks by Charles Krauthammer and then compare or contrast his views in light of your key recommendations:

"Turns out [ex-vice-president Hubert] Humphrey was wrong. At the time, we really did not 'have the means to do it' because we did not yet know how to banish poverty and hunger. Today we do. The answer is not foreign aid, which is corrupting and often worse than useless. In many cases, it further impoverished an already-poor country. En-riched urban elites bought luxury goods, while donated food and socialist controls drove down the local price of food, ruining the farmers on whom these subsistence economies had depended.

We now know that the secret to curing hunger and poverty is capitalism and free trade. We have seen that demonstrated irrefutably in East Asia, which has experienced the greatest alleviation of poverty in history. In half a century, places such as Hong Kong, Taiwan and South Korea have gone from subsistence living to First World status. And now free markets and free trade are lifting tens of millions of people out of poverty in India and China." (Charles Krauthammer, "An Ideal Goes Starving," *The Washington Post*, 11 Apr 2004)

Frame of Reference

Comedian Elayne Boosler is reported to have said, "I'm just a person trapped in a woman's body." If you were to tell the story of your life, certain things would jump out at you as most significant. But if your mother or father told *your* life story, you can bet that their story would differ considerably from your version. And if your best friend told the story of your life, you can bet that this story would be quite different from both your story *and* your parent's story. None of us are completely dispassionate observers.

Each of us has a particular vantage point from which events are seen and under-stood. This is what is known as our **frame of reference**. This framework is shaped by our prior knowledge, assumptions, values, language or notation, among others. Assumptions and values may also influence our perceptions. For example, a psy-chologist once suggested that a victim of robbery might be able to help the police by picturing the robbery from the perspective of the robber (and not that of the victim).

Recorded history tends to be imprinted by the most powerful members of so-ciety. The definitions, the very terms of the inquiry, may reflect the interests of the

Group or Individual Exercise

The Skateboarder's Lawsuit

This case involves a teenager, Angelo Seaver, who had been smoking marijuana. (Note any images or stereotypes that come up at this time). Angelo smoked marijuana and was out riding a skateboard at night. (Jot down any more images or stereotypes that may have surfaced in your brain.) There was *not* a full moon that night. (Any other images or stereotypes?). He went into a public park after closing time and hopped on the skateboard, crashed into a locked gate, and injured himself.

Directions: Briefly summarize how you picture the accident happening and note any assumptions you have about the accident and about Angelo. List any questions you would like to ask Angelo and those you'd like to ask the property owner where the accident occurred before deciding if Angelo bears any, some, or all responsibility for his accident. Once you have your questions ready, read the article detailing the story, then answer the questions that follow:

Panel Revives Skateboarder's Injury Lawsuit

Peter Blumberg

Daily Journal, May 4, 2004

A teenager stoned on marijuana enters a public park after closing, rides his skateboard down a driveway on a moonless night and crashes into a locked gate. And then he sues Santa Cruz County for his injuries because he didn't see the gate coming. Seventeen-year-old Angelo Seaver's blame-the-government strategy didn't go far with a trial judge. But it did win over a three-judge appellate panel.

On Friday [April 30, 2004], the 6th District Court of Appeal in San Jose ruled that because Seaver was riding his skateboard for transportation, not to perform stunts, he was not engaged in a "hazardous recreational activity." And the panel found that because there were no signs, reflectors or lighting to help Seaver see the gate, the county created a "dangerous condition of public property." As a result, Justice Eugene Premo concluded, it was mistake for the trial judge to toss out Seaver's suit based on the primary assumption of risk doctrine that normally holds people responsible for their own sporting accidents.

"Although county produced evidence to show that Angelo's conduct increased the risk he would be injured, such evidence pertains to Angelo's comparative fault—a question for the jury," he wrote. Premo's unpublished ruling . . . was joined by Justices Franklin Elia and Conrad Rushing. Court records show that on the night in question in January 2002, Seaver and his friend had ridden their skateboards all over town. They became tired by about 10 P.M. While waiting to catch a bus home, they smoked some pot at Anna Jean Cummings Park. Seaver then launched himself down the park's driveway, gaining speed, and slammed into a three-foot high metal gate. Seaver's injuries were not described in Friday's ruling.

Santa Cruz Superior Court Judge Robert Atack dismissed Seaver's suit on the grounds that he acted recklessly. "Based on the undisputed facts of this case, this metal gate did not create a substantial risk of harm when the park was used with due care in a reasonably foreseeable manner," he stated. But the appellate panel found that the accident could have happened to anyone because they could have entered the upper section of the park after dark and not known it was closed. "These users would have no notice that the gate would be closed because the gate was at the bottom of the driveway and the only sign indicating park hours was posted at the main entrance on the lower level," Premo wrote, adding that the gate was difficult to see. The appellate court also faulted [Judge] Atack for suggesting that the dangers inherent in skateboarding make it more like skiing than bicycling.

Premo said it all depends on what the rider is trying to do with the skateboard. It's one thing to test one's limits by performing tricks, he concluded, and quite another to use a "long board" strictly for transportation. Because there was no evidence that Seaver was doing stunts, Premo wrote, a jury rather than the judge should decide the county's liability for his injuries . . . ●

Peter Blumberg, "Panel Revives Skateboarder's Injury Lawsuit," *Los Angeles Daily [Law] Journal,* 4 May 2004

Answer the following:

1. Looking back at your assumptions and any stereotypes that surfaced, what stands out now that you know more about the case?

2. What were the key issues in the appellate court's assessment of the case? What assumptions held by Judge Atack were questioned by the three justices in the appeal?

3. Did you agree with the reasoning of the appellate court in overturning the lower court's ruling?

dominant class. These terms may work to preserve the status quo. Our view of the world is not value free. We are influenced by different contexts and different frameworks. These contexts can be temporal (like the 1980s, 1990s, 2000s), socio-cultural (like Tex-Mex, Boston Irish, the Hmong, the Amish), linguistic (like urban slang, formal English, computer speak, military lingo, rap), religious (like atheistic, agnostic, Jewish, Christian, Muslim, Hindu, Buddhist) and/or conceptual (like Marxist, Jungian, Freudian, Kantian, etc.).

The frame of reference influences the ways issues are presented and potentially "stacks the deck." Consider the use of American Indian mascots. As of April 2001, at least 135 high schools in New York State had Indian mascots or team names. For example, the Onteora, New York, Central School District reinstated the buckskin-dressed mascot used since the 1950s, and their high school prom is called the "Tomahawk Dance." Because of "time-honored tradition," giving up the Indian names and mascots for the teams is met with resistance. New York

school commissioner, Richard P. Mills, put it, "There are cherished traditions surrounding many of the mascots." Bear Clan representative Brian Patterson disagrees, saying, "Often, Indian people are stereotyped. The mascots are derogatory
and slanderous and misrepresent what Indian life is really about." (James
C. McKinley Jr., "Schools Urged to Stop Using Indian Names," *The New York
Times*, 6 Apr 2001). In agreement, the Los Angeles school board banned Indian
logos, as did over 20 school districts in the state of Wisconsin.

Be aware of the frame of reference. Consider who, or what, is most affected,
and what would likely change with a shift of perspective. And when we speak
from personal experience, try to recognize what is unique and what is common
with the experiences of others. Be careful not to presume any more than can
be supported.

Exercises

1. Read these two quotes and then share your thoughts about whether we can
   truly be objective or impartial:
   - As noted in the documentary film *Control Room,* "the word 'objectivity'—
     that's a mirage."
   - Scott O. Wilson said: "So here is our problem: on the one hand, we think
     that morality is in some important sense impartial. On the other hand, we
     do not think we must always be completely impartial in order to be doing
     the right thing." ("Tony Soprano's Ethical Obligations," *The Sopranos and
     Philosophy,* Open Court, 2004).

2. Imagine this scenario: One of the hotels in Savannah, Georgia, needs your
   advice. A lot of visitors from Japan will be staying at the hotel for the G8
   summit. As a result, the management wants to see what they can do to
   ensure the Japanese travelers are happy with the amenities and especially the
   food. What, if any, assumptions should you make about what sorts of food
   the Japanese travelers would like? Read about the planning and then note
   whether or not you need to revise your assumptions:

   "The Marriott had planned to bring in interpreters and chefs with experience preparing Japanese food, but visitors from the Japanese embassy in Washington told hotel
   managers not to bother. They were thrilled the hotel had a TGI Friday's restaurant
   downstairs. 'They are traveling with their own interpreters and really have stressed to
   us several times these are international travelers who are very comfortable in America,'
   McIntyre said." ("Putting a Foreign Accent on Southern Hospitality," CNN,
   www.cnn.com, 15 May 2004)

▦ Diverse Perspectives in Critical Thinking

In assessing arguments it helps to be aware of whose interests prevail, whose history has priority, whose frame of reference determines the norm, and who sets the criteria for decision making. These are all aspects of the **perspective** taken on ideas and events and the framework of assessing them. People know when they are being valued or devalued. People know the parameters of race, class, gender, sexual orientation, age, and ethnicity—though self-imposed denial keeps a certain amount of illusions intact. Nevertheless, those who witness even subtle demonstrations of prejudice have a sense of injustice, and prejudice can be difficult to face.

It may be hard not to laugh at jokes you are the butt of. It may be hard not to buy into a mentality that is ultimately degrading and destructive. We are all affected by justice and by injustice. We ignore this at our peril.

To look at ethical and political decision making as clearly separate from culture, class, gender and ethnicity is to effectively assume a mistaken sense of neutrality. This approach universalizes values without any real justification for doing so. For example, Martin Luther King Jr., the Dalai Lama, Mahatma Gandhi, and Cesar Chavez are often cited as heroes. But if we fail to examine their concern for human cruelty, injustice, and systemic racism, we turn them into caricatures instead of sources of spiritual strength, leadership, and guidance.

One source of strength is the knowledge that we affect each other's lives. We have an impact on the course of events and on the public consciousness. That impact may be slow in coming and not easily pinpointed, yet it is undeniable over time. One of our failings is not having celebrated that enough.

Advantages of Diverse Perspectives

Critical thinking gives us such techniques as analysis, observation, and reflection. These are powerful tools. Our knowledge grows when we recognize diverse perspectives, when we go beyond routine (narrow) interpretations and look at the broader picture. We can then see how stereotypical modes of thought have shaped our values, laws, and policies. We can also see how positive and life-affirming visions can help us acquire techniques to address oppressive practices.

Take racism, for instance. People complain that racism goes both ways. Some say the oppressed are unjust to members of the dominant class if given the chance, that women can be as sexist as men, that nothing much changes when the tables are turned. It is certainly true that human cruelty takes all forms. The oppressed can be as vicious as the oppressor. We are capable of behaving horribly. But that's no reason not to reflect on the human condition, not to study the interplay of culture and morality, not to raise questions about how we treat one another.

FIGURE 1.2
Nothing like brain food
to expand the mind!

That members of disadvantaged groups seem ungrateful or angry should prod us to reflection—and action. Observe the dynamics at play when we relate to each other. Being raised on gospel or Kentucky hill music, rap or rock and roll play a role in our identity. So do family barbecues and traditions around religious holidays. Our task is to see what those influences have been and determine their effects. Employing different perspectives can help us widen our view. (See figure 1.2) By looking at the relationship between power and policies, we can better understand our society and the way individuals think and act.

The Seven Key Dimensions of Diversity

1. *Frame of Reference:* Look at the point of view presented, the strengths, weaknesses, and omissions. Consider alternate points of view that could be taken and any new concerns and questions that could be raised. Ask what would result from a shift in frame of reference.

2. *Power Dimensions:* Look at the ways power is manifested and who are the authority or power figures. Consider possible shifts in the balance of power. Ask what would likely change (e.g., language, style, issues, values, criteria) if the power balance shifted.
3. *Values and Beliefs:* Look at the set of values that predominate. Consider alternative systems of belief that could be used. Watch for the major assumptions of the author (warranted or unwarranted). Ask how the assumptions and language reflect values and beliefs.
4. *Race and Ethnicity:* Look at the race/ethnicity of the key players and how race affects how the problem is defined and any solutions offered. Consider if other racial perspectives might be raised and the likely results of a shift of perspective.
5. *Class:* Look at the dominant perspective in terms of economic class. Consider what might result from a shift of perspective to a higher or lower class. Watch for values linked to classes and any assumptions that indicate a class bias.
6. *Personal Parameters:* Look to see if the gender, age, or sexual orientation of the author and intended audience affects the focus or methodology. Watch for assumptions, omissions, and bias in terms of disability. Consider any likely results from a shift in any of these perspectives.
7. *Language:* Look for biased or prejudicial uses of language and the ways the use of language evokes images or expresses a set of values. Consider the likely result if different language is used (less technical, more casual or more formal, different perspective, more neutral, more or less objective).

It's not always easy to get out of the box, open up our minds to other ways of thinking and explore unfamiliar territory. Yet, as all travelers know, something happens when we turn things over, when we let go of the entrenched ways of doing things. It may be liberating, it may be frightening—but it's definitely not the same old six and seven.

Sharpening the Inquiry → Incorporating Diverse Perspectives

- Try to determine the points of view of being presented. *Ask yourself:* From whose point of view is this article written, this story told, this song sung, this version of events made public? Clarify the dominant perspective.
- Try to determine what would change with a shift of perspective. *Ask yourself:* What would be added or omitted if this were presented through a different set of eyes or in a different voice? Consider what would happen if you shifted the frame of reference.
- Try to determine where the power rests, what forces are setting the agenda. *Ask yourself:* Who stands to gain or lose? Who are the players? Who is most powerful and most vulnerable? Consider what would likely change if the power shifted.

- Try to determine the set of priorities and underlying values. *Ask yourself:* What set of values and beliefs are being subscribed to, and where might conflicts arise? Consider how a different set of values might shift the decision making.
- Try to determine the extent to which you see diversity. *Ask yourself:* Is there enough diversity in terms of critical factors like race, ethnicity, class, gender, and underrepresented groups? Look to see how this relates to, or challenges, the status quo. Make note of who determines the criteria used.
- Try to determine the extent to which economic factors, like class, shape the discourse. *Ask yourself:* Does the perspective of a particular class dominate or shape the presentation? Examine what would happen if you shifted to a higher or lower socioeconomic level. Look for any assumptions reflecting a class bias.
- Try to determine the extent to which gender and sexual orientation slants the inquiry. *Ask yourself:* Do gender and sexual orientation affect the content and values being expressed? Watch for the expression of attitudes and assumptions.
- Try to determine the ways in which language is used to create an effect. *Ask yourself:* How does the use of words, quotes, humor, clichés, and other sorts of expression reveal a set of values or way of seeing the world? Note the use of images, analogies, and poetic or inspiring language.
- Try to determine how the intended audience shapes the dialogue or affects the presentation. *Ask yourself:* Who is this aimed at? Why this, rather than some other, audience? See if you discern ways in which the argument caters to one set of interests over other competing interests.
- Try to determine how factors such as age, religion, nationality, and ability versus disability shape the inquiry. *Ask yourself:* What assumptions and values are at work in terms of the participants or the audience? What is the role of geography, culture, nationality, and religious faith?

Think about juries. Do you think the best jury consists of people who are similar in terms of background, age, gender, religion, and the like? Or would diversity of these major traits be a plus? What would you want if a jury were to decide on your case (or fate)? Trial consultants Andrew T. Cavagnaro and Elise G. Devecchio-Cavagnaro argue that the more diverse the makeup of the jury, the more likely they are to be uncritical and have strong group cohesion—both causes of "groupthink." Diversity helps lead to exploring alternative explanations: "Active participation by all panel members and the critical evaluation of a wide range of perspectives is the hallmark of an effective jury. An ineffective jury, on the other hand, is characterized by an inordinate drive for consensus and an aversion to disagree and result in a hung jury. The source of this 'group think' is group cohesion and a lack of criticism" (Andrew T. Cavagnaro and Elise G. Devecchio-Cavagnaro, "Jury Diversity Prevents Dreaded 'Groupthink,' " *Los Angeles Daily [Law] Journal,* 14 Mar 2002).

Exercises

Part One

1. Discuss the frame of reference (perspective) of the author and any biases or values evident:

   To say he was paralysed by the tension would be an over-statement, but nerves were dragging him ever down towards an exceedingly murky pit of despond. Henman perennially talks of his love for Wimbledon, and all its advantages. But it comes at a cost. The public expectations—and this year they were further raised by his success in Paris— reach a level disproportionate to anything he experiences during the rest of the year. To be sure, he can feed off the support and raise his game. But he is also aware that every missed shot is greeted like a death in the family. He has talked at length about the fact that tennis is more than winning and losing; of the necessity of playing to his own strengths. In Paris he had little or no outside pressure; at Wimbledon this pressure is continuous and unrelenting. ("Henman Sets Off for Heaven Via Day in Hell," *The Guardian (UK)*, sport.guardian.co.uk, 23 Jun 2004)

2. Discuss the frame of reference of the author and any biases or values that are evident:

   Those bums that come up to your car and beg sure drive me nuts! They ruin a downtown area by accosting people on the street trying to get money. Anyone with the least bit of self-respect wouldn't live like that. They ought to get off their butts and work like decent American citizens! I'm sick and tired of people who want to suck the blood of the country by living on welfare or being some homeless slob on the street. We ought to gather them up and ship them out of town. They don't deserve to live in a nice place like this. And we sure don't deserve to have them ruining our city.

3. The state of Florida has gotten rid of computers and typewriters in its prison law libraries. As a result, Florida prisoners who wish to appeal their case will have to draw up their legal appeal by longhand. Read about the case and answer the questions that follow:

   The Corrections Department removed computers and typewriters in May 2001, arguing that they had to do so to save money. Florida has 71,000 inmates, the 5th largest prison system in the U.S. Florida has executed 51 prisoners since 1979 (behind only Texas and Virginia) and has 371 people on death row. Prisoners' Rights groups argue that removing the computers and typewriters limits what prisoners can do. Kara Gotsch of the ACLU says, "When it's handwritten, it's not as effective for them." Rebecca Trammell of the American Association of Law Libraries, says most state prisons provide typewriters to prisoners. Allen Overstreet of the Florida Corrections Department said only around 5% of prisoners use the law libraries and it would save $50,00 a year (on repairs and upkeep) to get rid of the typewriters. (Jackie Halifax, "Florida Prisoners Lose Access to Typewriters," in *Los Angeles Daily [Law] Journal*, 25 Jun 2001)

Answer any two of the following:
 a. Set out the concerns from the perspective of prisoners in Florida.
 b. Set out the concerns from the perspective of prisoners in states that currently have computers and typewriters available for inmate use.
 c. Set out the concerns from the perspective of Florida officials, pressured by taxpayers to cut costs.

4. Your college newspaper, *The Oracle*, wants to run a story on faculty members dating students. How would the issue be seen if you were (pick two and set out each perspective) a 30-year-old single professor, a happily married student, a 19-year-old student who is single and lonely, a 22-year-old student, an administrator, and a parent of an 18-year-old student attending the college.

Part Two

In an article in the *Chronicle of Higher Education*, David Perlmutter examines assumptions and negative stereotypes of black athletes and their treatment by white professors. All the excerpts in these exercises refer to this article (David D. Perlmutter, "Black Athletes and White Professors: A Twilight of Uncertainty," *Chronicle of Higher Education*, www.chronicle.com, 10 Oct 2003).

1. What assumptions do you think students and faculty make about athletes—especially athletes of color? Set out your observations of what you have witnessed or heard.

2. List the key issues and concerns raised in the following excerpt:

   I strongly support the advice one black athlete had for professors: "If you have a problem with sports, don't take it out on the player." Other students can contribute to the atmosphere of lowered expectations and even disdain toward athletes—especially if the athlete is an African American on a campus where most students are white. At one such campus, a black athlete told me the story of a black friend—an honors student and not an athlete—who was asked by some white students she had just met, "What game do you play?" Her answer of "Donkey Kong" was received with surprise. Her grade-point average probably would have provoked equal amazement and further undercut the stereotype.

3. Share your reaction to the following and your own perceptions about the treatment of athletes—of any race or ethnicity—on college campuses.

   Ironically, when black athletes leave the gym or playing field of a mostly white college, they often encounter students like the one who told me, "It's funny, but you can cheer a guy on the court and still resent him sitting next to you in class." Indeed, many students not involved in sports assume that athletes can get away with academic murder. One non-athlete who knew I was writing this essay told me that she had it on good authority that the university sends all the athletes copies of final exams with answers on the day before the exam. She simply shrugged off my response that the athletes' grades did not support that claim.

4. Do you agree with the recommendations the author makes, in light of number 2 and number 3, above? Note any alternative suggestions you may have for addressing the situation: "Athletes, the victims of such discrimination, typically get counseling by coaches, advisers, and their older peers on how to deal with negative stereotypes; the perpetrators—other students and professors— seldom do."

▦ Social and Personal Decision Making

When trying to assess social problems or personal quandaries, it may be helpful to have some guidelines. This not only helps us get a handle on how we should approach issues, but also helps us structure a response to them. Some preliminary work needs to be done before we can come up with a decision we will not later regret.

Decision-Making Guidelines

1. *Define the Problem.* State, as clearly as you can, what is at issue. State the problem in its broadest terms, noting potential societal impact. And state it in its narrowest terms, noting the potential repercussions of the case.
2. *Sharpen the Focus.* Clarify the parameters of the decision making. Know who is facing the dilemma, who is making the decision, who is most affected by the decision, what the options are, and what set of criteria will be used to make the decision.
3. *Clarify the Context.* Most decision making is contextual—we look at a problem in terms of whose problem it is and how the different options would impact the lives of those involved. Set out the main context in which the problem arises.
4. *Gather Information.* Know the specific details of the case at hand. Set out all relevant evidence or information that can help make an informed choice. Don't be afraid to scout: Get on the Internet, hit libraries and don't be afraid to get the help of those who are savvy with research.
5. *Clarify Key Concepts and Ideas.* Look at the relevant concepts that bear upon the social or ethical decision. Think of concepts as the framework of evaluation. Of course, concepts like "justice," "freedom," "truth," "good," and "evil" are abstract terms, but they are understood—and applied— within a society and a culture. Be aware of how they are being interpreted.
6. *Examine Assumptions.* Often invisible, assumptions can wreak havoc, as we have seen in this chapter. A warranted assumption can be like a skeleton, helping keep the framework in place. An unwarranted assumption can be like a virus running rampant through a system, bringing with it destruction.
7. *Identify Frameworks.* Look at the norms, beliefs, ethics, and political and ideological frameworks that shape the decision making. Watch for social norms, religious attitudes, cultural influences, and political persuasions that frame ideas and shape interpretations.

The Global Dimension

The Law and Cultural Differences

Yisroel and Golda Singer, visitors from England, were arrested after leaving their six-month old daughter in the car outside a Long Island, New York, shopping mall while they took their other daughters to a bathroom. Singer said he thought the sleeping baby was safe in the locked car with a cracked window and was not aware their actions could lead to legal trouble for them (the couple was charged with child endangerment, a misdemeanor) ("Baby Left in Car a 'Misunderstanding,'" *Los Angeles Times,* 3 Jan 2004). When should cultural practices trump civil law? Answer the questions below about this case:

Answer the following:

a. Do you need any other details about the incident to help you assess the gravity of the situation? Explain.

b. What defense could be offered for *both* parents taking the other daughters to the bathroom and leaving the baby in the car?

c. Do you think the Singers' lawyer was correct in calling this a "cultural misunderstanding"?

d. Note to what degree, if any, this information should be taken into account: "The family lives a sheltered life in a Jewish community in London, does not have a television in their house, has no criminal background, and was not aware their actions could land them in legal trouble."

Group or Individual Exercises

Directions: Apply the decision-making guidelines to *one* of the following cases. Read about the case (which you can research to get more detail if you wish) and then answer the questions that follow.

1. **Case #1:** The May 2001 death of 14 border crossers in the Arizona desert.

    The U.S. Border Patrol reported on May 24, 2001 that they had found more bodies of undocumented border crossers in the Arizona desert. The death toll hit 14 of people who attempted, and failed, to cross the desert into the U.S., planning to go to North Carolina to find work. Evidently smugglers ("coyotes") started the migrants on the tragic trek and abandoned the 25 migrants after five days. They were, at that point, about 30 miles from the nearest highway. They had little water and little chance of survival. Only 11 survivors made it out alive. Smugglers whose clients die can be prosecuted under a federal law that carries the possibility of the death penalty. Johnny Williams, Western regional director for the INS, was reported to have blamed the fatalities on "leeches" who charge $1,000 or more per client and sometimes abandon them en route. Cyril Atherton of the Border Patrol said, "It's rocks, sand, desert. It's nasty." (Ken Ellingwood, "Two Bodies Found, Raising Toll in Migrant Tragedy to 14," *Los Angeles Times,* 25 May 2001)

    Answer the following:

    a. From the perspective of INS regional director Williams, the tragedy can be blamed on "leeches." Assess the cause of the tragedy from any other perspective, (e.g., a Mexican national seeking to go to North Carolina to work, the family of a victim, a survivor, an employer who relies on migrant workers, or an unemployed farm worker who sees the migrants as competition).

b. Given that people do try to cross the desert and enter the United States, what humane response might there be?

2. **Case #2:** Ontario, Canada's new welfare requirements.

The Canadian province of Ontario is taking a strong stand on welfare, due to the failure of a small group of welfare recipients to get off, and stay off, welfare. The government plans to make passing a basic literacy exam a requirement for receiving welfare. Furthermore, it will screen recipients for substance abuse (alcohol and drugs) and cut off benefits to any who refuse to get treatment. Officials contend that these measures are necessary to reach those who are the "hardest to serve" and who seem to have the greatest trouble getting and keeping work.

The literacy program would help students learn to write memos, do basic accounting, and provide customer service. One welfare recipient said she wasn't worried about the literacy test; she was worried about finding day care for her four children. (Anthony de Palma, "Ontario's New Welfare Rule: Be Literate and Drug Free," *The New York Times,* 9 Aug 2001)

Answer the following:

a. Give three reasons why this plan might work and three reasons why it may fail.

b. Can you think of a workable alternative?

3. **Case #3:** Gays try to adopt a highway.

What are the limits to who can "adopt a highway" for litter cleanup? Among the groups who have adopted a highway: Nudists (Florida), Friends of John Denver (Oregon), and the Ku Klux Klan (Missouri). But South Dakota has said no to the Sioux Empire Gay and Lesbian Coalition of Sioux City, South Dakota. State officials insist they can refuse the group on the grounds that it's an "advocacy group." Representatives from the group question this, given the state has allowed The Young Republicans and Animal Rights advocates, among others, to participate in the program (See www.datalounge.com). South Dakota Governor William Janklow says he'd rather abandon the program than to accede to their offer. The KKK disagrees with the governor. Ron Edwards, Imperial Wizard of the Imperial Klans of America said, "I hate to admit it, because I think being gay and lesbian is an abomination, but they have the same rights we do." He went on to say, "They'll win. We did." (As noted in the *Los Angeles Times,* 15 Aug 2001)

The U.S. Supreme Court granted the KKK the right to adopt a highway in March 2001. On August 20, 2001, the gay/lesbian group filed suit in federal court against the state's ruling. The issue, as yet, is unresolved.

Answer the following:

a. If a state allows a group to "adopt a highway," does that implicitly legitimize that group's existence?

b. What should be the criteria for being able to participate in a program like this?

Problem Solving

Some social conflicts and problems are ongoing; some are resolved fairly quickly. For instance how near can someone get to a political rally to hand out protest literature? Someone had to figure that out. If we don't know where we are going, it is hard to get off the ground. If we don't know what tools we plan to use along the journey, we could be spinning our wheels in the sand.

Subjecting even a messy moral dilemma to the problem-solving model may be useful to generate ideas or insights and lead us to arrive at viable options. The model provides a structure for approaching a wide range of problems that we may face.

Stages of the Problem-Solving Model

Stage One: *Define the problem.*
   Clarify goals.

Stage Two: *Set out the criteria to frame the decision making.*

1. *Determine the framework within which the problem is named and how evidence will be sought and weighed.*
2. *Determine the framework within which the proof or argument and its evidence will be assessed or justified.*

Stage Three: *Gather evidence and generate ideas.*

1. *Brainstorm.*
2. *Include diverse perspectives.*
3. *Amass all the relevant information.*

Stage Four: *Sort and weigh.*
   There are three aspects of this stage:

1. *Clarify what is relevant in light of the set of criteria.*
2. *Sift relevant from irrelevant information.*
3. *Weigh strengths and weaknesses.*

Stage Five: *Aerial surveillance.*
   Look at the structure and how the evidence links together; examine general frameworks, assumptions, any omissions, patterns, and themes. See if a working hypothesis can be formulated. Any missing evidence? Anything overlooked? Don't assume the "obvious" is obvious. Turn over stones! Check for false leads and dead ends. Rethink assumptions. Try another approach. Be imaginative.

Stage Six: *Compare new and old data.*

Stage Seven: *Settle on a decision.*

This model is indebted to the work of psychologist Robert Sternberg, whose insights have benefited the field of critical and creative thinking.

Exercises

Directions: Select one of the cases below. Run through the problem-solving model for each of the following cases, setting out the stages.

1. Should we allow genetic hybrids? These organisms result when the DNA from one species is mixed with that of another to produce a hybrid species with enhanced traits. Take a stand on this case:

   About 150 goats that have been bred with a spider gene are to be housed on 60 acres of a former Air Force base in Plattsburgh, N. Y. Montreal-based Nexia Biotechnologies, Inc. said up to 1,500 genetically altered goats may eventually live at the facility. The goats have been bred with a spider gene so their milk provides a unique protein. The company plans to extract the protein from the milk to produce fibers called "BioSteel" for bulletproof vests, aerospace and medical supplies. Spider silk has a unique combination of strength and elasticity with an ultra-lightweight fiber. The agreement included an up front payment for the university, funding for research and development expenses plus royalties on the sale of silk-based products. ("Biotech Company to Produce 'BioSteel' Milk," *Associated Press*, 18 Jun 2000)

2. Read about the narcotic lollipop and then answer the questions below:

   Abbott laboratories developed a narcotic lollipop intended to calm down children before surgery. A group of doctors asked the federal government to bar the narcotic lollipop. They argue that the narcotic, *fentanyl*, is too dangerous for children and that the lollipop could create new problems for doctors. Some doctors suggest that a tranquilizer would be preferable, since it doesn't have the same risks as the narcotic. The FDA asked Abbott to set up a training program to insure anyone using the lollipop will be familiar with its dangers and its proper use. They said that doctors now make up their own, unregulated, sedatives to calm children and the FDA prefers one that can be given in controlled doses and under federal control. (Mike Goodkind, "Help Your Child Relax to Reduce Pain and Recover More Easily after Surgery Says Anesthesiologist," www.med.stanford.edu)

   Answer the following:
   a. Should the FDA ban the narcotic lollipop? Go through the steps of the problem-solving model to decide how this issue could be solved.
   b. What further information is needed to make a decision?
   c. If you had to vote on this issue, would you allow the narcotic lollipop to be distributed? Explain how you reached your answer.

3. What questions and concerns do you have about the narcotic lozenge in light of the following?

   Consider Cephalon's second-biggest drug, Actiq, a narcotic lozenge on a stick that is sucked like a lollipop, giving quick, temporary relief from the sharp spikes of pain that some cancer patients suffer despite taking other narcotics. The drug was controversial at one time, with critics saying a narcotic lollipop would tempt children.

Neither the Anesta Corporation, which developed the drug, nor its licensee, Abbott Laboratories, ever sold much of it. But after Cephalon bought Anesta in 2000, it decided that cancer doctors were interested primarily in treating tumors, not pain, so it focused its sales campaign on pain specialists. The company expects Actiq sales to exceed $100 million this year, 10 times the level the year before it bought Anesta. (Andrew Pollack, "A Biotech Outcast Awakens," *Global Action on Aging*, www.globalaging.org, 20 Oct 2002)

4. Here's the scenario: You just got a call from a lawyer (the "I" in the excerpt below). A doctor (call him Dr. Sims) who is having second thoughts called him for advice. Given that this is the call, what will you recommend in terms of a policy for these sorts of cases? You may choose to answer *one* rather than both of his questions. Go through the steps to clarify how to prepare yourself:

Four years ago, I got a call from an infertility specialist who was in the midst of a procedure. He was just about to transfer an embryo created by a childless couple's egg and sperm to the woman who had volunteered to carry the baby for them. But he suddenly had second thoughts. "I've got an embryo from a couple in a catheter," he told me hurriedly. I pictured him, catheter in one hand, telephone receiver in the other. "I'm about to implant it in the surrogate, who is the husband's sister," he explained, and wanted to know if it would violate his state's ban on incest. If he decided not to go through with the implantation and the embryo died, he asked, could he be found guilty of murder? (Lori B. Andrews, "Embryonic Confusion," in *Washington Post*, 2 May 1999)

5. Should people be able to buy and sell human organs for transplant? Use the problem-solving model to decide. You might find it useful to look at the case of a British man, Peter Randall, who put up his kidney for sale on ebay in an attempt to get money to pay for his daughter's medical treatment. His daughter, Alice, is six years old and has cerebral palsy. He wanted around 50,000 pounds (about $100,000) for the kidney. ("Father Auctions Kidney for Daughter," BBC News, news.bbc.co.uk, 4 Dec 2003)

CHAPTER TWO

Out of the Silence: The Power of Language

Looking at a pot, for example, or thinking of a pot, . . . it was in vain that Watt said, Pot, pot. Well, perhaps not quite in vain, but very nearly. For it was not a pot, the more he looked, the more he reflected, the more he felt sure of that, that it was not a pot at all. It resembled a pot, it was almost a pot, but it was not a pot of which one could say, Pot, pot, and be comforted. It was in vain that it answered, with unexceptionable adequacy, all the purposes, and performed all the offices, of a pot, it was not a pot. And it was just this hairbreadth departure from the nature of a true pot that so excruciated Watt.

—SAMUEL BECKET *from Watt*

Many of us empathize with Watt, the Beckett character who struggles to find words to apply to his situation. Watt wrestles with words, frustrated that they seem to work for others, but not for him. His losing battle with the word "pot" in the quote above is but one example of the struggle between words and silence played out every day in Watt's world. And, in the case of the pot, "the true name had ceased, suddenly, or gradually, to be the true name for Watt. For the pot remained a pot, Watt felt sure of that, for everyone but Watt. For Watt alone it was not a pot, any more."

On the other hand, some people believe they have the upper hand on language, that there is no real battle between words and silence. They are in control. They believe words have no power to penetrate our exterior, that we have skulls like helmets and bodies like armor, so words can just bounce off and land in the dust. But this, we all know at heart, is just a ruse, a game of deception, or self-deception, about the power of language. Language can have incredible power, both positively and negatively.

Words can hurt. Words can be used to threaten and coerce, to galvanize whole populations, to drill images of self-hate into young minds, and to convey stereotypes. Language can be an instrument of oppression. Given the power of language, it is vital that we always be aware of its potential to shape, even manipulate, our thoughts.

Language can also be an instrument of liberation. Words can be used to unite us as a people, to move us to a higher moral plane, to calm, to communicate, and to achieve spiritual strength. As bell hooks says, "We are rooted in language, wedded, have our being in words. Language is also a place of struggle. The oppressed struggle in language to recover ourselves—to rewrite, to reconcile, to renew. Our words are not without meaning. They are an action—a resistance."

In this chapter, we will examine some key uses of language, focusing on a myriad of ways that can have impact in our lives. We will see how language can function in destructive ways, persuasive ways, and inspiring, healing, and transformative ways. The range we will cover is this:

The Persuasive Power of Language

- Descriptions and asymmetry.
- Denotations and connotations.
- Culturally defined uses of language.
- Euphemisms and hedging.
- Ambiguity (linguistic fallacies).
- Concepts and definitions.
- Jargon, buzzwords, and technical terms.
- Metaphors, images, and analogies.
- The passive voice.
- Loaded language.
- Propaganda.
- Exclusive language and hate speech.
- Humor, parody, and satire.
- The liberatory voice.

Descriptions

How we refer to people can have great significance. In the positive, references can instill a sense of pride and community. In the negative, they can lead to alienation, powerlessness, and despair. Have you ever read eulogies or obituaries summing up a person's life? All too many dead people have rolled over in their graves because of the ways others have characterized their achievements. You may chortle, not thinking ahead of what *your obituary* is going to say. But check out these from *The New York Times*:

February 11, 2005: Mary Kim Joh, *Who Wrote a Korean Anthem Is Dead.*
October 22, 2004: Lawrence Freedman, *Who Peered into Killers' Psyches, Dies at 85*
June 27, 2004: Danny Dark, 65, *Whose Voice Spurned StarKist's Charlie Tuna*
March 29, 2004: Richard Perez Is Dead at 59; *Advocate for Minority Rights*
March 27, 2004: Dr. Zhong Wei Chen, *Pioneer In Microsurgery, Is Dead at 74*
May 28, 2003: Pepper LaBeija, *Queen of Harlem Drag Balls, Is Dead at 53*
June 11, 2002: John Gotti Dies in Prison at 61; *Mafia Boss Relished the Spotlight*

May 31, 2001: Charley Pell is Dead at 60; *Ousted as Florida Coach*
June 12, 2000: Stretch Johnson, 85, *Tap Dancer and Activist*
June 8, 2000: C. D. Atkins, 86, *Inventor of Frozen Orange Juice Process*
October 18, 1999: Lee Lozano, 68, *Conceptual Artist Who Boycotted Women
    for Years*

FIGURE 2.1

Descriptions and Social Attitudes

Surveying the territory, we see both males and females are closely scrutinized when it comes to their descriptions. Values, societal stereotypes, and attitudes can shade a description. For instance, "Earlier in the campaign, Republicans tried to deride Mr. Edwards for the 'pretty boy' looks that earned him the title of 'America's sexiest politician' from *People* magazine; but they swiftly backed off when it became clear that they were merely drawing attention to the Democrat's strongest electoral asset" (Ben McIntyre, "What Is Useful for Avoiding Sunstroke and Vital for Winning Political Office?" *Los Angeles Times,* 16 Oct 2004).

We see comments about the presidential contenders as well. For example, " 'Great Pumpkin' and 'orange alert' jokes abounded on the Internet . . . after Kerry showed up with a new cinnamon skin hue. Had he fallen asleep in a tanning bed? Or been professionally spray-painted by the same guy who gave Charlize Theron her Oscar glow?" (Beth Gillin, "Scoring the Debate," *Philadelphia Inquirer,* www.philly.com, 30 Sep 2004).

Descriptions conjure up images and images can set entire trains of thought in motion. What image pops into your brain when someone is described as "slender"? What about "skinny" or "bean-pole"? The choice of words in a description can make a difference. Let's look at examples.

First Description: Singer Patti Smith:

As the foremost punk poet of our times, Patti Smith looks exactly as you would want and expect her to look. She walks in and announces, "I'm Patti Smith." As if you couldn't tell. She's dressed in jeans, boots, a loosely billowing white shirt and a long, black jacket that looks like a frock-coat. She's not wearing make-up and her unkempt black hair hangs loosely over her shoulders. She's made no attempt to disguise its rapidly multiplying grey strands. If she was serving you at the deli counter or waiting on your restaurant table, you'd have to say she looked a mess. But as the foremost punk poet of our times, Patti Smith looks exactly as you would want and expect her to look. . . . She appears stern and a little nervous and warns that she hates interviews because she's uncomfortable talking about herself. (Nigel Williamson, "Rock'n'Roll Was Revolutionary," *Scotland on Sunday,* news.scotsman.com, 25 Apr 2004, *emphasis mine*)

Second Description: Singer J. C. Chasez (of 'N Sync):

He is not cute. In fact, 'N Sync heartthrob J. C. Chasez is looking more Benicio Del Toro haggard than Justin Timberlake fresh these days. He's extremely thin, with bad posture and frizzy hair that resists any definable style. If you didn't know better, you'd swear an impostor had snuck onto the set of Sharon Osbourne's talk show for a dress rehearsal of the singer's single "Some Girls (Dance With Women)" off his solo debut, "Schizophrenic." But judging by the screaming girls lined up outside the Hollywood studio in the rain, and the presence of beefy bodyguards, he *is* the dark, brooding member of the world's premier boy band.

The new J.C. doesn't care that he looks like crap. . . . His voice is raspy from a cold, and he's worn down from a nonstop promotional campaign that included signing 700 autographs at Tower Records in L.A. last night. (Lorraine Ali, "Sexy, Solo and Out of Sync," *Newsweek,* 8 Mar 2004)

You Tell Me Department

Does the Best Hair Win?

Does the hair define the man? You tell me. Here's what Ben McIntyre had to say *before* the election:

In every presidential race since 1960, the candidate with the best hair has won. ("Best" being a combination of volume, shine and manageability.) The last President without hair was Eisenhower. Since then, JFK, with the finest presidential hair ever, beat Richard Nixon, who was hairy yet oily . . . Gerald Ford, balding, lost to Jimmy Carter, who had good hair, but not as good as Ronald Reagan, who had the best hair money could dye. Coiffed Bill Clinton easily vanquished George Bush the elder and then Bob Dole, both of whom had sad, tired, unexciting hair. . . . Which brings us to John Kerry's impressively bouffant, pepper-and-salt helmet. The Democratic contender has the face of a dyspeptic horse, but the hair of a movie star. . . . None of this would matter a jot, of course, except that it matters enormously. Daunting issues of war and peace hinge on the presidential election, yet so far much of it has been conducted on a terrifying level of superficiality. . . . Appearances matter, sometimes overwhelmingly.

You tell me: How much do you think appearances matter when it comes to how we think about our leaders? Do you think the average person really cares about each of the candidate's hair and appearance?

Descriptions can give rise to all sorts of thoughts and images. Descriptions often have baggage; such as connotations that stick in the brain. That's one reason celebrities file lawsuits against tabloids that go beyond nasty little descriptions ("Look at all the cellulite on Chi Chi Morango's behind!") to insinuations ("Chi Chi caught naked in hot tub smooching other woman! Lesbian lovers?") and implications that are defamatory. Descriptions have the power to shape our perceptions.

Group or Individual Exercise

1. Find five to six descriptions of women and five to six descriptions of men (look in magazines, newspapers, or Internet articles). Compare the level of detail, the use of language, the positive or negative qualities and so on.

2. Find five to six descriptions of Caucasians and five to six descriptions of members of another racial/ethnic group (look in magazines, newspapers, or Internet articles). Compare the level of detail, the use of language, the positive or negative qualities, and so on.

Asymmetrical Descriptions

When members of one group are described in ways that would not be used for a different group the resulting description is **asymmetrical.** An asymmetry usually indicates a **double standard,** where the rules or expectations are applied unfairly to the different groups. It can be relatively harmless, or it could have a hurtful or inflammatory effect. The test of symmetry is if you can turn the tables.

One apparent double standard concerns appearance. For example, after the 2004 Democratic convention, journalist Maureen Doud wrote: "At least Teresa Heinz Kerry kept her subliminal message simple; she *wore a ketchup-red suit* to introduce the second senator in her life." ("Can He Float Your Boat," *The New York Times,* 1 Aug 2004, *emphasis mine*). Recall that she was the sole heir of the Heinz ketchup fortune. Another reporter was similarly critical: "She came across as slightly odd—*the space age Madame Mao suit didn't help*—self-indulgent, and goofily disengaged from mere mortals" (as quoted by Howard Kurtz, "Trashing Teresa," *Washington Post,* 28 July 2004, *emphasis mine*).

Another example was noted in a letter to the editor: the letter slammed Anna Nicole Smith with this sentence: "Seemingly at peace with the tonnage she added since her cover-girl glory, our heroine carried herself like Moby Dick in drag . . ." (*Los Angeles Times,* 17 Aug 2002).

Of course men are not immune from such blasts. President Bush was criticized for wearing a flight suit to declare victory in the war in Iraq. And Senator John Kerry was the butt of a few jokes for wearing a "bunny suit" in his tour of NASA. No longer are detailed physical descriptions the arena of the female. This warrants attention, given the power of language.

Asymmetry exists. Take lips. Men's lips seem not to generate as much interest as women's lips, especially Angelina Jolie's lips. "Jolie has had so much collagen pumped into her lips that they threaten to become duck-like"; she "has lips that look as if she ran into a wall," "famously bee-stung lips," "lips that look more tarantula than bee-stung." Her lips have been described as "those plumy pods of puffed perfection," "huge, pillowy lips," and "gargantuan, and as uneven as lunar terrain" (Tom Kuntz, "Lip Crit: It Smacks of Angelina," *The New York Times,* 24 Jun 2001).

Three years later, same story: "April 8, 2004—Angelina Jolie has the most sought-after lips when it comes to women wanting sexy smackers," says surgeon Dr. Sydney Coleman; "People consider Angelina's Jolie's lips to be the most sexy" (as quoted in "Amazing Angelina," *eFanGuide,* www.efanguide.com, 8 Apr 2004).

Descriptions, whether or not they are asymmetrical, reveal societal attitudes. Women are "willowy," men are "tall." Women are "plump," men are "paunchy" or "stocky." Mel Gibson's character in *What Women Want* is described as being like "a stocky athlete" (www.salon.com). Tom Hanks in *The Terminal* "looked a little paunchy and not like a movie star" (Roger Friedman, *Fox News,* 9 Jun 2004). Women can be "large as a cow," men are "bullish." Hockey players Eric Lindros and Scott Stevens are described as "the normally bullish Lindros was himself bulled over by a steamroller named Scott Stevens" (Rob Sinclair, "Lindros in Limbo, Hockey Night in Canada," *CBC Sports*, 31 Mar 2001). Even slight variations—such as being "pudgy" rather than "overweight," or being "absent-minded" rather than "forgetful" or "oblivious"—can alter the force of a description.

The descriptions of Ben Stiller and other male actors in the movie *DodgeBall* reveal some terms that are used for males or females, and some that are male-specific:

> Mr. Stiller, with a face that veers between the geeky and the handsome, and a bunched-up body that even when buffed looks strangely misshapen, skewers male vanity with the X-ray vision of someone who has writhed in its clutches. . . . The movie . . . unapologetically roots for the uber-nerds. And what a curious crew they are. They include a pudgy Panglossian milquetoast (Steven Root), whose blocked anger explodes in the nick of time; a chicken-chested, absent-minded ninny (Joel David Moore); and a lunatic who imagines he's a pirate. Any movie that is fonder of these losers than of their robotic would-be nemeses is O.K. by me. (Stephen Holden, "Loser Nerds vs. Pumped-Up Jocks (Revenge Again?)" (*The New York Times*, 18 Jun 2004)

The terms "pudgy," "nerd," "lunatic" and "ninny" are applied as much to females as to males. However, it's hard to think of a female parallel for "chicken-chested." You tell me!

Exercises

Part One

Directions: Fill in the blank, finding the closest match you can:

1. Men are "lone wolves," women are _____.
2. Women are "frumpy," men are _____.
3. Men are "barrel-chested," women are _____.
4. Women are "cupcakes," men are _____.
5. Men have a "beer gut," women have a _____.
6. Women are "witches," men are _____.
7. Men are "dreamboats," women are _____.
8. Women are "voluptuous," men are _____.
9. Men are "sissies," women are _____.
10. Women are "catty," men are _____.
11. Men "shoot the bull," women _____.
12. Women are "petite," men are _____.
13. Men are "hen-pecked," women are _____.
14. Women are "old maids," men are _____.
15. Men are "dudes," women are _____.

Part Two: Descriptions of Men

Directions: Discuss the following descriptions of men and note any assumptions about gender stereotypes and societal attitudes.

1. Description of restaurant-owner Martin Picard:

   Martin Picard, the owner of the popular bistro Au Pied de Cochon, known by local critics as the enfant terrible of the Montreal food scene, has begun adding foie gras [gourmet dish of liver paté] to the dish. He has also reinvented poutine sauce with a blend of pork stock, egg yolks, still more foie gras and a touch of cream for texture. . . . Mr. Picard's wild head of hair and scruffy beard mark him as an iconoclast. But his nouvelle poutine is what is really revolutionary. Before he reinvented it, poutine was the mainstay of bowling alleys, greasy spoons and late-night bars. (Clifford Krauss, "Quebec Finds Pride in a Greasy Favorite," *The New York Times,* 26 Apr 2004)

2. Description of George Tenet after he resigned as director of the CIA:

   Even when his political capital appeared to be at a low, Mr. Tenet managed to hang on with what some say was a fierce loyalty to Mr. Bush and the CIA personnel. A likeable, chummy personality also helped keep him above water. ("Tenet Resigns as Head of CIA," *Sydney (Australia) Morning Herald,* www.smh.com.au, 4 Jun 2004)

3. Description of baseball player Don Baylor:

   Nobody ever called Don Baylor soft. He is a man's man, the guy you'd want on your team because he would take one on the arm, the shoulder or back. Anywhere and everywhere, just as long as he didn't think you were hunting for his noggin. (Jose De Jesus Ortiz, "Baseball Notebook: Baylor Brings Rugged Style Back to Game," *Houston Chronicle,* www.chron.com, 28 Mar 2004)

4. Description of actor Chris Tucker:

   Tucker took character roles in two movies: Quentin Tarantino's *Jackie Brown* and *The Fifth Element,* in which he played a transvestite radio deejay. It wasn't too big a stretch . . . his voice is already up in that range where the genders meet, he can be campy and over-the-top, and he has beautifully fine bones that can swing either way. But believe, me, Chris Tucker is all man. Chicks dig him, of course, and he has a girlfriend and a son, but he generally keeps his private life to himself. (Rick Cohen, "Chris Tucker in Phat City," *GQ,* Aug 2001)

5. Description of pilot Captain William Lancaster:

   In England one pilot bitten by the Lindbergh bug was an ex-Royal Air Force officer, Captain William Lancaster. Since leaving the service in 1926, Lancaster had struggled in civilian life, and it showed. The thinning hair and cadaverous features made a mockery of his real age—twenty-nine—giving him the appearance of someone much older . . . (Colin Evans, *A Question of Evidence: The Casebook of Great Forensic Controversies, from Napoleon to O.J.,* John Wiley & Sons, 2003)

Part Three: Descriptions of Women

Directions: Discuss the following descriptions and note any assumptions about gender stereotypes and societal attitudes.

1. Description of TV personality Greta Van Susteren:

   Greta Van Susteren was hailed as a path breaker for speaking openly about her facelift, which gave her a tighter, slightly Martian appearance for her new role as permanent Fox News pundette. (Christine Rosen, "The Democratization of Beauty," *The New Atlantis,* no. 5, Spring 2005)

2. Description of actor Keira Knightley:

   Licking the foam off her second cappuccino, picking at the chipped eggplant-colored polish on her bitten fingernails, and describing playing Guinevere, variously as 'wicked,' 'chronic,' 'crazy great,' and 'fab,' Knightley for just a moment looks and sounds like the excitable 19-year-old she is. Her eyes ringed in black kohl, she wears two T-shirts stacked atop one another over a pair of not entirely clean jeans, and black puffy boots that she could have borrowed from Frosty the Snowman. Her hair is pulled back in a scruffy ponytail, exposing a few tiny blemishes on her forehead. As she talks, she twists escaped strands of it around her fingers. A waiflike blond in her previous films, Knightley is now curvier (thanks to the weight training she did to play Guinevere) and brunet. (Johanna Schneller, "Knightley in Shining Armor," *Premiere,* Jun 2004)

3. Description of Claremont professor Kerri Dunn:

   Dunn was a sympathetic figure. She stands 5 feet, 4 inches tall and has long brown hair and green eyes. On campus, she donned loose skirts, rather than the suits that some colleagues favored. (Nora Zamichow, "Claremont Professor's Past Is a New Puzzle," *Los Angeles Times,* 5 Apr 2004)

4. Description of author Toni Morrison:

   Comfortable beige and black clothes, salt-and-pepper locks twining onto her shoulders, Morrison laughs a lot and moves swiftly from subject to subject—grand opera to soul food. She describes her own speaking voice as 'comfortable, protective.' It is also like honey, laced with a little cayenne. But she's the writer. Let her describe her own skin. 'It's healthy,' she says. And it's the color of: 'maple.' She says, "In my mind, I've always thought that I was much darker than I am." (Linton Weeks, "Toni Morrison, Pulling Readers Deeper and Deeper," *Washington Post,* 14 Nov 2003)

5. Description of tennis player Serena Williams:

   At 22, Serena is all sass and swagger, full of herself and life and apparently not willing to put it on hold so she may devote herself to being a full-time tennis drone, no matter what the critics say. (Harvey Araton, "Tennis is Only a Game to the Williams Sisters," *The New York Times,* 27 Jun 2004)

6. Description of actor Meryl Streep:

Poor Meryl Streep. Her blond hair apparently untouched by the blow dryer, she nervously patted her unwaiflike figure to make sure it was really still in her crystal-beaded jacket. She seemed flustered, a bit out of breath. But, having just won best supporting actress for her turn as *New Yorker* writer Susan Orlean in "Adaptation," she needn't have hyperventilated. The backstage media at the Golden Globes aren't the White House press corps. (Rachel Abramowitz and Lynn Smith, "This Time, It was Ladies' Night," *Los Angeles Times*, 20 Jan 2003)

Denotations and Connotations

The impact of a description is often linked to the connotations of words and phrases. Whereas the denotation of a word or phrase points to the most specific or literal meaning, the connotation refers to the figurative senses. The **denotation** corresponds to a dictionary definition of a term. How we define a term can have significant consequences. For example, when the Center for Disease Control (CDC) altered its definition of SARS (severe acute respiratory syndrome) to exclude people whose lab tests turned up negative for the virus 21 days after the onset of symptoms, the number of suspected SARS cases was cut in half.

The **connotation** is the set of associations attached to the word in question, indicating a set of values. We see this with the terms "bachelor gal," "unhitched chick," and "spinster." The terms all refer to unmarried women, but they have different connotations.

Think of synonyms for the term "male": man, gentleman, guy, dude, boy, hunk, jock, stud, beefcake, dreamboat, lone wolf, sport, shark, and so on. Think, too, of synonyms for the term "female": woman, gal, girl, chick, bunny, broad, lady, fox, vixen, bombshell, bimbo, tomato, cupcake, cheesecake, honey, hen, babe, kitten, doll, witch, hag, crone, and so on (add to the list). What do you think these terms tell us about our society?

Exercises

Directions: Using your dictionary, look up the meanings of the words (what they denote) and then list the connotations of each:

1. President
2. Self-Help
3. Elite
4. Disabled
5. Pacifist

Global Dimensions

Descriptions in Australia

There may have been no bald prime minister of Canada, but look at the way baldness is presented in the positive. Read the following and pull out all the terms used to describe Shane Warne:

> Shane Warne looks pretty ugly these days. . . . Warnie began his transformation by shaving off his blond mop before the third test against India. . . . Combined with his jowls, Warnie's naked skull made him look like somebody you would bargain hard to avoid having to share a cell with. However, by the end of the one-day series, Warnie was sporting a thick, neat, red beard to set off his stubbly head. Sensational. . . . He is, in fact, the dead opposite of the blond beach boy persona. He is volatile and impetuous. Shrewd and intelligent. He is not rabid about physical fitness training but doesn't hesitate to put in extra months of hard work when an English county makes the price right. He is acquisitive. . . . Blond beach boys seek to be loved. Burly, bald, redbeards don't really give a bugger. (Frank Devine, "The Bald Truth Is, Everyone Loves An Ugly Bloke," *The Australian*, 9 Apr 2001)

6. Liberal
7. Conservative
8. Religious
9. Atheist
10. Independent
11. Maternal
12. Convict (the noun)
13. Unemployed
14. Soccer mom
15. Boy scout
16. Cowboy

Importance of Context

The definition of a concept may differ from the way a concept is used. We employ terms and concepts in a social context, where values and cultural beliefs color the use and interpretation of a word.

Acceptable uses of language vary according to the context (such as living rooms, restaurants, classrooms, workplaces). It also varies according to the participants—for example, talks with friends versus those with a teacher or boss. Students and patients generally are referred to on a first name basis, while doctors and teachers are usually referred to in a more formal way. And servers (or waitpersons) tell us their first name, though customers rarely share theirs. This situation creates a power dynamic that deserves our attention.

You Tell Me Department

Is Bill Clinton, the "First Black President"?

Riding on the wave of publishing success (his book *My Life* sold 400,000 copies the first day), Clinton came to California for public appearances autographing copies. Interestingly enough, he was scheduled for two appearances on June 25, 2004. One was in the Century City mall at an upscale bookstore called Brentano's. The other appearance was at Eso Won, an independent bookstore in Southwest L.A. that caters to African Americans. This fact did not escape attention. Share your reactions to this observation of Clinton by Gayle Pollard-Terry:

> Of course, Clinton isn't really black. But his bond with African Americans goes well beyond politics. Many believe he's one of them. He grew up in Arkansas eating collard greens and sweet potato pie. While campaigning in black churches, he clapped on the beat and knew the words to every song. "I saw him singing 'Lift Every Voice and Sing' "—the black national anthem—"and he knew all the verses. Most [black] people just know the first verse," says James Fugate, co-owner of the bookstore. "The

excitement level for Clinton is unparalleled," Fugate says. "He's really loved by a lot of people." . . . Including Charlene Cyrus. "He's from my hometown, and I would love to read his story," she says. And Ray Miley. "I like the man," he says. "Always have liked him. I think he changed the White House forever. It'll never be the same again. He made it black and white. Before him, it was all white."

Calling Clinton the first black president is a common compliment in this community. The sobriquet stuck after the noted author Toni Morrison, writing in the *New Yorker* in 1998, commented that she'd heard others refer to him in that way. "After all," she wrote, "Clinton displays almost every trope of blackness: single-parent household, born poor, working-class, saxophone-playing, McDonald's-and-junk-food loving boy from Arkansas." (Gayle Pollard-Terry, "The 'First Black President,' in Person," *Los Angeles Times*, 25 Jun 2004)

You tell me: Given the description above—if it's not about race, what is it that makes Clinton "the first black president"? How much does class factor into this description of Clinton?

© NIKSCOTT.COM

NIK SCOTT

FIGURE 2.2
Terms can have quite different meanings according to the context in which they appear.

The Global Dimension

The Study of Bilinguals and Brainpower

The British Broadcasting Corporation (BBC) reported on a language study by a York (Canada) University researcher, who concluded that there is a link between bilingualism and brainpower. Here is a summary. Consider alternative explanations as you read:

> This latest study appears to back up the theory that language skills also have a protective effect. Dr. Ellen Bialystok and colleagues at York University assessed the cognitive skills of all those involved in the study using a variety of widely recognized tests. They tested their vocabulary skills, their non-verbal reasoning ability and their reaction time. Half of the volunteers came from Canada and spoke only English. The other half [of the volunteers] came from India and were fluent in both English and Tamil. The volunteers had similar backgrounds in the sense that they were all educated to degree level and were all middle class.
>
> The researchers found that the people who were fluent in English and Tamil responded faster than those who were fluent in just English. This applied to all age groups. The researchers also found that the bilingual volunteers were much less likely to suffer from the mental decline associated with old age. "The bilinguals were more efficient at all ages tested and showed a slower rate of decline for some processes with aging," they said. "It appears . . . that bilingualism helps to offset age-related losses." ("Being Bilingual Protects Brain," *BBC News World Edition,* news.bbc.co.uk, 15 Jun 2004)

Answer the following:

1. What assumptions are made in using sample groups from different countries (and, possibly, different backgrounds)?
2. Offer at least two alternative explanations for the research subjects from India having superior cognitive abilities besides their language skills.
3. Research the studies done on turmeric and Alzheimer's disease. As you may recall, the spice turmeric is in curry—which is often used in Indian cooking (e.g., see "Curry 'May Slow Alzheimer's,' " *BBC News,* news.bbc.co.uk, 21 Nov 2001). Studies indicate that turmeric may be a reason that Alzheimer's disease is rarely found in India. If diet may be a factor in Alzheimer's, should it be factored in when assessing this study on bilingualism's supposed benefits? Share your thoughts.

Culturally Defined Uses of Language

Our society and culture shape our use of language. There are norms around who can say what to whom and who can speak and in what order, not to mention who gets the first and last word. These are **culturally defined uses of language.** We find such norms in public gatherings and in family dynamics. Think of phrases like "Children should be seen and not heard" and "Speak when you're spoken to." Adults may also face linguistic restrictions, as, for example, in meetings with a supervisor at work, when stopped by the police for a traffic violation, in church, and in elevators. There are many culturally defined uses of language. Let's look at three: (1) apologies, (2) bilingualism, and (3) the deaf culture.

Example #1: *The apology.* For some, "Love means never having to say you're sorry." For others, love means *regularly* having to say you're sorry. The very fact of caring so much for another person means we are accountable to them. Consequently, there are cultural expectations around apologies—what merits one, who is owed one, and what might follow if one is not given.

Not all apologies include an admission of wrongdoing. Look, for example, at the "careful apology" of Yankee slugger Jason Giambi who managed to say he was sorry without admitting to steroid use. He said, "I feel I let down the fans, I feel I let down the media, I feel I let down the Yankees, and not only the Yankees, but my teammates." He added, "I accept full responsibility for that, and I'm sorry." He neglected to say what he was sorry for (Tyler Kepner, "A Careful Apology from Giambi," *The New York Times,* 11 Feb 2005).

Example #2: *Bilingualism.* In Canada, where many people are bilingual (French and English), language often reflects political allegiances and even tensions. As James Crawford notes in *Language Loyalties,* "As a practical medium and a 'marker' of ethnicity, language becomes a predictable source of tension." Discussing the low status of French in Canada, he says, "Language discrimination by design and by neglect, created a mutual estrangement over time and loosened the bonds of the Canadian federation."

In the United States, many people are bilingual, but they are usually expected to speak English. Bilingual students often face difficulties, even prejudice—especially if they speak with an accent.

Power politics get played out as much around language as other matters. By examining bias and discrimination around language use—for instance with non-native speakers—we can better understand what needs to change.

Example #3: *Deaf culture.* Using sign language instead of a spoken language creates a subculture. It often has a powerful impact on those who are linked by signing rather than using and deciphering spoken words. Those on the "outside" who don't know sign language and feel left out may feel resentful or anxious, as we see in the case below.

CASE STUDY

The Deaf Culture

Rachel Stone, superintendent for the California School for the Deaf, was fired in June 2001. State officials would not say why, but parents suspect it was because she made American Sign Language the primary form of communication at the school. Journalist Scott Gold called her "deaf and proud—a combination that doesn't sit well with the school's old guard." Stone challenged the stereotype that deaf people should model themselves after the dominant, hearing culture. She says,

There are different cultures. We are all human beings, and in the past we were told that we were not. We were told that we could not be successful. That's all I'm trying to change. For years, deaf education

has been run by people who think they know what's best for deaf people, and they have failed and failed and failed. I want to put a stop to that. (Scott Gold, "Controversial Head of School for Deaf Removed," *Los Angeles Times,* 21 Jun 2001)

Stone is trying to empower deaf children to use sign language, their "native" language instead of having teachers reciting their lecture out loud with a student translating it. She hired faculty fluent in sign language and encouraged them not to speak (voices off). Parents reported that the children swelled with pride from having their own language, their own means of communication without an intermediary. Gold quotes Stone, who says,

"This is my language. Why doesn't deaf education recognize that?"

Stone's detractors say American Sign Language is not English and students should be allowed to try to speak it. Hearing teachers felt marginalized, some were said to feel harassed, and some resigned. State officials made Stone clarify that she was not banning speaking, only encouraging signing. Faculty seemed divided about supporting or opposing Stone's methods. One observer felt that her philosophy caught people off guard and moved too fast.

Answer the following:

1. Why do you think people appeared to be threatened by Stone's demand that sign language rule in the deaf classroom?
2. Was Stone out of line to de-emphasize, if not discourage, learning to speak out loud?
3. If you were a parent or family member who was part of the hearing culture, what concerns might you have about the children being taught "voices off"?
4. If you were asked to defend Stone, what would you say?

Social and Political Ramifications

Language is a carrier of values. Words can convey or connote a set of beliefs. Language can express prejudice and racist attitudes. Our thoughts and perceptions take place in a certain time and space. Consequently, ideas and concepts are not isolated from the world. Culturally defined uses of language have political ramifications. We learn language at the same time that we live in the world and come to a sense of how people should interact with each other. Ask yourself whether or not describing an athlete as having a "Mexican *bandidto* moustache" or comparing him to a "monkey" contributes to racist stereotyping. How we refer to one another has consequences—and reflects back on ourselves.

With non-native speakers, the possibility for miscommunication and error is present. Similarly, those with different accents can run into barriers, even when they share their native tongue. Think of a Scot talking with a Southerner, or an Australian talking with a Bostonian—they may share the same language and yet still have trouble communicating.

Exercises

Part One

1. Make a list of ways you could describe *one* of: A friend, a family member, or a celebrity. Try for a balance of positive, negative, and neutral descriptions. Then write two to three paragraphs discussing how description affects the way we think about people.

2. Do you think non–English speakers are pressured to speak English? Go into detail in your answer, bringing in any examples you can find or think of that will boost your position.

3. Think of all the words or phrases connected to economic status (like "rich," "loaded," "fat cat," "bourgeois," "poor," "welfare bum" (or "bludger" in

Australia), "broke," etc.). After drawing up your list, try to determine what these words indicate about our societal values around money and/or wealth.

4. Discuss American attitudes toward drinking by examining the words used to describe alcohol consumption, like "tipsy," "sloshed," "plastered," "pie-eyed," "soused," "potted," "three sheets to the wind," "smashed," or "tanked up."

5. Study the language used to describe *one* of these to unpack societal attitudes: driving a car, smoking, surfing, lifting weights, eating, dieting, or cooking. List words used to describe one of these activities.

Part Two

Directions: Answer *one* of the following questions involving a study of descriptions.

1. Do a study of descriptions around any *one* topic that has social significance, such as age, looks, hair, economic class, professional status.

2. Do a study of magazine or newspaper articles that focus on celebrities (movie stars, singers, famous figures, or political leaders) and list all the words to describe them, keeping tabs on males versus females. Note any differences and see if there are changes when other factors come in, such as race, class, age, and nationality.

3. Do a study of the sports pages of the newspaper. Examine the different ways male and female athletes are described. Find as many examples as you can (try a week's worth of articles). Then draw some inferences from your study as to what this tells us about our society's values and beliefs.

4. Do a study of the way people use language to describe *one* of these groups: children, teenagers, the elderly, the disabled, gays or lesbians, single versus married people, working class versus upper class, any one ethnic or racial group, any one religious group, urban versus rural residents.

5. Do a study of descriptions around weight or height. You may want to narrow your focus to men, women, teens, children, and so on.

Group or Individual Exercise

Directions: Do a study of TV news (prime time or cable) and answer the following questions:

1. How are people referred to or described in the various news segments (leading stories, sports, human interest stories, and so on)?

2. Do the descriptions of current events reveal any bias, cultural attitudes, or values?

Euphemisms

A **euphemism** acts as a substitute for the targeted word, in order to achieve a particular end. The goal may be to defuse a controversial situation or slant the way the word will be interpreted. Some euphemisms are sneaky and their use malevolent; others are harmless. Think of euphemisms that allow us to speak of indelicate subjects, like going to "powder my nose" (go to the bathroom). See Chapter 4 on fallacies to review euphemisms.

We buy a "pre-owned" (used) car and visit our grandparents who are in "their golden years" (old age). We purchase "after-shave" (cologne for men) and "stretch the truth" (being dishonest). We call abortion of a fetus in a multiple pregnancy a "selective reduction" and refer (as does the Florida law) to surrogate mothers who do not supply the egg as "gestational carriers." We describe euthanizing (killing) a pet as "putting it to sleep." We use the terms "outsource" and "downsize" to explain subcontracting and cutbacks. Euphemisms in war-speak include "collateral damage," "friendly fire," "shock and awe," "coalition of the willing," "freedom fighters," "total information awareness," "homeland security," "embedded journalists," and so on.

The term "rendition" is a particularly striking euphemism for "transport to a country known to allow torture"—intended for those who seem most likely to resist customary interrogation methods. Steve Hoenisch criticizes *The New York Times'* use of "security officials" to refer to SAVAK, the Iranian secret police, and the use of "some cutback on duplicate staffing" in place of the word "layoffs" or "firings" ("The Mythological Language of American Newspapers," www.criticism.com). Euphemisms should be watched carefully. Journalist Pierre Tristam argues:

> They're weedy. They're sly. They're strangely addictive. They're impossible to get rid of and, in wartime, they're more noxious than patriotic fumes. But that's what makes euphemisms language's nimblest double agents, its cheapest mercenaries, its most sought-after plastic surgeons: A euphemism does to reality what botox does to facial muscle. It croaks it. No other death brings so much life to so many. Without euphemisms every politician would have to declare bankruptcy, every priest would have a crisis of conscience; every corporation's annual report would be dangerously truthful, to its shareholders anyway. . . .
>
> Blowing a man's brains out from a distance is called "pink mist," assassination is called "regime change" and propaganda is called "public diplomacy." The sanitizing makeover disarms the truth of the original word enough to make it meaningless or enticing. The reigning king of euphemisms in the current war surplus is the word security. (" 'Security' Tops the Plastic Heap of War's Euphemism Surplus," *Daytona Beach News-Journal*, www.news-journalonline.com, 26 Apr 2004)

Hedging

Hedging effectively undercuts or raises doubt about a claim. *Hedging* can take two forms: (1) shifting from one position to a much weaker one; or (2) undercutting a claim (e.g., through a negative connotation of a word or phrase). Hedging is more often found in oral communication than written expression. This may explain why we get rejection *letters* rather than phone calls telling us another applicant got the job. It also explains why it's easier to write a "Dear John" letter than have a face-to-face meeting. In the political sphere, hedging can be dramatic. For instance, on August 4, 2001, the British Broadcasting Corporation (BBC) told its journalists the word "assassination" could no longer be used to describe the actions of Israelis murdering guerilla opponents. Robert Fisk reports:

> In a major surrender to Israeli diplomatic pressure, BBC officials in London have banned their staff in Britain and the Middle East from referring to Israel's policy of murdering its guerrilla opponents as "assassination." BBC reporters have been told that in future they are to use Israel's own euphemism for the murders, calling them "targeted killings.". . . The assignments editor, Malcolm Downing, should have sent out the memorandum to staff, stating that the word "assassinations" "should only be used for high-profile political assassinations." There were, Mr. Downing said, "lots of other words for death." ("BBC Staff Are Told Not to Call Israeli Killings 'Assassination'," news.independent.co.uk, 4 Aug 2001)

Exercises

1. State the issues and concerns that compelled the BBC to try to control the use of language in reporting on Israelis—as noted in the above quote.
2. Share your thoughts on Fisk's comment that, "Mr. Downing's memorandum suggests that the murder of a leading Israeli—the late Prime Minister Yitzhak Rabin, killed by an Israeli extremist—is worthy of the word 'assassination' while the killing of Palestinians is not."
3. Investigate euphemisms: Find two euphemisms and discuss how they function and what would likely change in the context if we shifted to a less slanted or deceptive use of language.

Labels and Categories

Labels and categories aren't necessarily harmful. Here's a case in point: Residents of Prince Edward Island (P.E.I.), Canada, call themselves "spud islanders." Potatoes (spuds) are the island's main crop. What if someone "from aways" (non-spud-islander) coined the phrase to refer to the residents of P.E.I. in a derogatory way—thinking of them like empty potato-heads, for example? It is unlikely that the term "spud-islander" would get a positive reception. The ownership and self-definition by the PEI residents makes all the difference.

The Global Dimension

"Ghost Detainees"

Issues of description, connotation, euphemism, and context roll together in the uses of language governments seem to use in wartime. Slogans from Orwell's *1984* such as "War is Peace," "Freedom is Slavery" and "Ignorance is Strength" can scramble the brain. Because of the "war on terrorism," thousands of people are in prisons or detention centers. They have been held indefinitely, without being charged with a crime, without access to lawyers, and with no timeline for possible release or assessment of their cases. The term "prisoner" is deemed inappropriate (no arrest, no conviction), so they are called "detainees." The "ghost detainees," are those kept invisible to the public eye.

Ghost detainees were shuttled off to secret facilities out of the reach of such societal watchdogs as the Red Cross, Amnesty International, and Human Rights Watch. There is no outside communication or observation of these phantom captives. They became a form of *los desaparecidos* ("the disappeared ones"). Read the following and then answer the questions below:

> These prisons and jails are sometimes as small as shipping containers and as large as the sprawling Guantanamo Bay complex in Cuba. They are part of an elaborate CIA and military infrastructure whose purpose is to hold suspected terrorists or insurgents for interrogation and safekeeping while avoiding U.S. or international court systems, where proceedings and evidence against the accused would be aired in public.
>
> All told, more than 9,000 people are held by U.S. authorities overseas, according to Pentagon figures and estimates by intelligence experts . . . The CIA's "ghost detainees," as they were called by members of the 800th MP Brigade, were routinely held by the soldier-guards at Abu Ghraib [prison in Iraq] "without accounting for them, knowing their identities, or even the reason for their detention," the report says. These phantom captives were "moved around within the facility to hide them" from Red Cross teams . . .
>
> The location of CIA interrogation centers is so sensitive that even the four leaders of the House and Senate intelligence committees, who are briefed on all covert operations, do not know them, congressional sources said. . . . "They are told it's too sensitive." (Dana Priest and Joe Stephens, "Secret World of U.S. Interrogation," *Washington Post,* May 11, 2004. See also Elise Ackerman, "Rumsfeld Admits to Holding 'Ghost Detainees,' " Knight Ridder Washington Bureau, www.realcities.com, 17 Jun 2004)

Answer the following:

1. State the connotations of the terms: "prisoner," "detainee" and "ghost detainee."
2. Give three to four reasons for *or* against allowing the term "detainee" to replace "prisoner" for suspects held in the "war on terror."

What sounds neutral may seem derogatory to the one being labeled. The term "primitive peoples" won't win too many friends among the "natives." Try using the term "indigenous" or referring to groups by their tribal identity (e.g., Apache, Chumash, Blackfoot, Hopi, Zuni) instead. The collective tribes in Canada prefer the term "First Nation" instead of "Native Canadians" or "Canadian Indians." Another phrase that grates is "developing nations." Seek a less-loaded alternative—or name the individual nations.

Other reference problems arise: Are you a Latino or Hispanic? Are you Native American or an Indian? Are you African American or black? Are you a Mexican or Tex-Mex? Are you Asian American or Chinese? Are you Canadian or Quebecois? As we know, a label may be perfectly acceptable when members

FIGURE 2.3

of the group in question use it with each other—but off-limits for those outside the group.

Labeling is not the same as name-calling. Not all people experience labeling as demeaning. Sometimes labels categorize people in positive or neutral ways ("married" versus "single," "gay" versus "straight," "vegetarian" versus "meat-eater," "lacto-vegetarian" versus "non-dairy"). Name-calling, however, has little positive effect.

Consider the July 2004 uproar when California governor Arnold Schwarzenegger called Democratic lawmakers blocking his budget plans "girlie men." Governor Arnold Schwarzenegger called upon voters to "terminate" them at the polls if they didn't pass his $103 billion budget (Peter Nicholas, "Gov. Criticizes Legislators as 'Girlie Men,'" *Los Angeles Times,* 18 July 2004).

Sometimes the labels do not have a fixed meaning, as with "vegetarians" who eat poultry and fish. Richard Ford struggles with the label "foodie":

Alas, I am not a *foodie* . . . The word still frightens me. For one thing, I don't eat red meat (game yes, fish yes). I don't eat fried food; I don't eat potatoes, white rice, most bread, cream sauces. I eat butter only reluctantly (and if I don't know it's there). I generally steer a course away from dairy, most desserts, all pastries, cheese, high-sodium this, high-cholesterol that. And anything I do eat I never eat a lot of . . . I realize that at the end of my life I will not so much die as simply one day disappear due to the accumulated removal of all those things that I fear will kill me, but that are also necessary to keep me, if not alive and healthy, at least visible. (Richard Ford, "Satisfaction," *Gourmet*, March 2001)

Associations can tap into societal fears or prejudice. For example, if the term "Asian American" and "Mexican American" are associated with foreigners, problems pop up. Peter Lew says, "I'm a fifth-generation Chinese-American, yet I'm often asked: 'How long have you lived in this country? When will you return to your country?' " . . . (Peter Lew, Letter to the editor of *The New York Times*, 19 Jun 2002).

Ambiguity (Linguistic Fallacies)

When it comes to the use of language, clarity counts for a lot. *Ambiguity* is a lack of clarity in the use of language either by accident or intent, resulting in a confusion that may lead to drawing an incorrect conclusion. Problems can occur when words, grammar, or sentence structure are used in ways that create an ambiguity. Ambiguity is like seeing in a fog, where a variety of interpretations can cause confusion. Of course, some people use slippery language intentionally—twisting words to suit their purposes. Such slippery terms are sometimes called "**weasel words.**" For that reason, watch for ambiguity.

Let's look at the case of stem cell research, which uses cells from human embryos. When all eyes turned to President Bush to see where he stood, observers found some ambiguity in his public statements. As Robert Pear observes, "Administration officials on both sides of the debate, trying to frame the issue for a decision by President Bush, have been reviewing his campaign statements, which generally expressed disapproval of research that used embryonic stem cells. But officials said they had found ambiguities in his statements that might allow some research to go forward" ("Bush Administration Is Split over Stem Cell Research," *The New York Times*, 13 June 2001).

Later remarks by the president allowed for different interpretations. He said, "I oppose federal funding for stem cell research that involves destroying living human embryos. I support innovative medical research on life-threatening and debilitating disease, including promising research on stem cells from adult tissue." Ultimately, ambiguity has to yield to a clear-cut position (either directly or indirectly, either by word or deed). In 2004, after Nancy Reagan's effort to get the administration to loosen regulations around stem-cell research, an administration spokesman "clarified" Bush's position. You decide if the ambiguities are now gone:

The president remains committed to exploring the promise of stem cell research but at the same time continues to believe strongly that we should not cross a fundamental moral line by funding or encouraging the destruction of human embryos. . . . The president does not believe that life should be created for the sole purpose of destroying it. He does believe we can explore the promise and potential of stem cell research using the existing lines of stem cells. ("Senators Ask Bush to Ease Restrictions on Stem Cell Research," CNN, www.cnn.com, 8 Jun 2004)

It's not always easy to sort through ambiguity and determine the intent. David Harel illustrates this in *Computers, Ltd.* with the way the following sentences differ in the relationships between their various parts:

The thieves stole the jewels, and some of them were later sold.
The thieves stole the jewels, and some of them were later caught.
The thieves stole the jewels, and some of them were later found.

When ambiguities lead to an incorrect conclusion, we are looking at fallacious reasoning. The three key linguistic fallacies are **equivocation** (where there's a shift of meaning in a word or phrase in an argument), **accent** (where the emphasis of a word or phrase leads us to an incorrect conclusion) and **amphiboly** (where faulty sentence construction leads to an ambiguity). Here are some:

- *Equivocation:* That was such a bad movie it deserves jail time! (This plays on different senses of the word "bad.").
- *Accent:* **One Month's Rent Free** when you sign a lease for three years. (The visual emphasis about the "free" rent is misleading, given the terms that follow.)
- *Amphiboly:* I saw the Lone Ranger with his horse, so I gave him a carrot. (The ambiguous sentence structure makes it unclear who gets the carrot.)

Being able to spot ambiguity and any resulting fallacies is important. We are much less likely to be manipulated by slippery uses of language if we know fallacies and are able to tackle any other sorts of ambiguity we run into.

Concepts and Definitions: Meaning versus Use

Philosopher Ludwig Wittgenstein once advised, "Don't look at the meaning, look at the use!" There may be any number of definitions for a word—but looking at the context and how it is used in the sentence can help reveal the intended meaning. The *use* of words and phrases often reveals more than any dictionary definition.

Watch for hidden assumptions or exclusions. Examine the use in speaking, writing, policy guidelines, and laws. Ask what the term is meant to include and how it is to be applied. For example, if policies speak of employees as *male*, then the policy may not easily apply to females. Think of applying employment policies to pregnant women. Should pregnancy be put in the same category as illness?

Similarly, in female-dominated fields like nursing, males have had an uphill battle addressing gynocentric (female-centered) language and stereotypes. Nurse-midwife Patrick Thornton talks about his work: "I think a lot of people expected that because I was a man, they were going to be treated like a doctor treats them. When they found out that wasn't true, then that seemed to help" (see Christopher Snowbeck, "Male Nurse Midwife Adopts a Supportive Attitude," *Post Gazette* [Pittsburgh], 27 Mar 2001).

Components of a Definition

There are two parts to any definition. The first is the word or phrase to define or clarify. This is called the **definiendum**. Then you have the explanation—words meaning the same as the word or phrase in question. This is called the **definiens**. **Synonyms** are words that are similar in meaning (e.g., warm and toasty), whereas **antonyms** are words that are opposite in meaning (e.g., hot and cold). To avoid ambiguity, we should specify what definition we are using.

Questions about **syntax** have to do with punctuation, grammar, word order, and sentence structure. Questions about **semantics** have to do with the meanings of words, what they signify. This includes both denotation and connotation: The **denotation** of a word is the literal meaning, whereas the **connotation** is what the word suggests, implies, or conjures up in our minds.

Syntactical errors may seem less worrisome than semantic problems. However, grammatical or structural errors can create havoc. We may miss the point if the syntax is a mess. An example of a syntax error is "Rosa had been lifting weights for five years when she dropped a barbell on her foot." Watch also the use of semantics. The use of a word or phrase in different ways in the argument may lead the reader to the wrong conclusion.

Concepts, Contexts, and Norms

Societal norms shape the scope of our concepts and definitions. If whites, the wealthy, Christians, or men set the norm, all others fall outside the norm. If the norm is able-bodied people, the design and construction of buildings may disadvantage the disabled (through the location of light switches, the size of hallways, the height of toilets, the use of Braille in elevators, and so on). How we define the norm may have considerable social, and linguistic, consequences.

Look at the conflicts over the use of the terms "fetus." If the word "person" as used in the Constitution were understood to include fetuses, laws around abortion and fetal experimentation would have to be reinterpreted. Historically the concept "person" referred to postnatal humans, as noted in the ruling of *Roe v. Wade*. Recently we see a shift toward greater protection for fetuses. This is shown in euphemisms for the fetus; such as "unborn child," "pre-born person," or "baby."

Group or Individual Exercise

For some, a fetus is an unborn child. Others deplore the blurring of distinctions around pre- and postbirth humanity. Read about the following case and then answer the questions below:

A U.S. district judge in Missouri has blocked temporarily the deportation of a pregnant Mexican woman who is married to a U.S. citizen, calling the fetus an "American" and citing a federal law created to protect unborn children after the high-profile death of Laci Peterson. Senior U.S. District Judge Scott O. Wright ordered that Myrna Dick, 29, of Raymore, Mo., who is accused of falsely claiming American citizenship, be allowed to remain in the United States for now and told prosecutors and the defense to prepare for a possible trial. "Isn't that child an American citizen?" he asked, according to the Kansas City Star. "If this child is an American citizen, we can't send his mother back until he is born."

In rejecting the federal government's request to lift a temporary stay granted Mrs. Dick in April, Judge Wright pointed to the Unborn Victims of Violence Act of 2004, which grants unborn children equal protection under the law if their mothers are targets of criminal violence. The law is also known as "Laci and Conner's Law" for a California woman and her unborn son whose bodies washed up along the shore of San Francisco Bay in April 2003. Scott Peterson, Laci's husband, is charged in the deaths. (Joyce Howard Price, "Deportation Blocked; Fetus 'American,' " *Washington Times*, 29 May 2004)

Answer the following:

1. Discuss the use of language in the above excerpt. What most strikes you?
2. List all the words or terms used in the passage that suggest the author's *or* the judge's set of values.
3. Do you think Judge Wright is on solid ground in applying the Unborn Victims of Violence Act of 2004? Set out your reasons.

On March 24, 2004, Governor Bob Wise of West Virginia vetoed a bill to make killing a fetus, from the moment of conception on, a crime. He said the legislature had rushed to judgment about when life begins. (Kirk Johnson, "Harm to Fetuses Becomes Issue in Utah and Elsewhere," *The New York Times*, 27 Mar 2004). Thirty-one states have fetal homicide laws. Of those, 15 have fetal homicide laws that apply to the earliest stages of pregnancy—the right to conception. This suggests how much the notion of fetal rights has shifted.

Watch how terms are used and examine the possible interpretations of concepts. Think of it this way: What if our understanding of what it means to be a "person" was any human over 7 feet tall who was an excellent athlete? A disproportionately large proportion of those fitting these criteria would be males and especially African-American males. Entire ethnic groups would be excluded altogether.

Jargon, Buzzwords, and Technical Terms

It is wise to watch out for jargon and buzzwords. **Buzzwords** are newly coined terms or old words used in totally different contexts for an intended effect. **Jargon** is the terminology of a particular group or profession or the specialized technical terminology coined for a specific purpose or effect. Sometimes people consider jargon to be gibberish (without any discernible meaning). That may be due to a lack of understanding of the use of the word.

You Tell Me Department

What Is a Terrorist?

Read the definition of "terrorist" set out by the U.S. State Department in Title 22 of the United States Code, Sec. 2656f(d), and list the distinct qualities that mark a person or group as a "terrorist":

> The term "terrorism" means premeditated, politically motivated violence perpetrated against noncombatant targets by subnational groups or clandestine agents, usually intended to influence an audience. . . . The U.S. Government has employed this definition of terrorism for statistical and analytical purposes since 1983. (Jon Dorbolo, "Power in Terror," *APA Newsletter of Computers,* APA Newsletters, Spring 2003)

This is not a fixed definition. The Patriot Act sets out a different definition of terrorism. Compare and contrast that definition with the one set out by the State Department:

> SEC. 802. the term "domestic terrorism" means activities that involve acts dangerous to human life that are a violation of the criminal laws of the United States or any State; appear to be intended—to intimidate or coerce a civilian population; to influence the policy of a government by intimidation or coercion; or to affect the conduct of a government by mass destruction, assassination, or kidnapping; and occur primarily within the territorial jurisdiction of the United States. (HR 3162, 2001). (See "Power in Terror," *APA Newsletters,* Spring 2003)

You tell me: How do *you* think we should designate someone as a "terrorist"? Can someone be a "terrorist" and not instill *terror*? What if the person just *scared* you? Share your thoughts.

Wired magazine regularly lists the latest buzzwords and jargon around computers and technology. Here are some examples: "leper badge" (a temporary ID issued at government facilities with lots of classified projects), "fat finger dialing" (the telephone equivalent of a Web typo site), "page slap" (replying to an e-mail question with nothing but a URL answer), "tool piracy" (the illegal sharing of woodworking jig templates) and "sustained deep undervoltage" (the electric power industry's term for a large chunk of North America—50 million households—losing power all at once) (see "Jargon Watch," *Wired* magazine, January 2004 and November 2003).

With jargon we must first determine the intended meaning. Try to articulate your understanding of the word or phrase. "I understand this term to mean . . ." is one way to clarify your sense of a concept. Spell out how you think the term is being used. Readers should not have to feel like they're cracking a secret code to understand how an author is using a term.

Look at the Los Angeles Unified School District's use of the term "morphosyntactic skills" in their published glossary of acronyms and terminology. The glossary doesn't define the term; it only translates it to the Spanish "*conocimientos morfosintacticos.*" Most just scratch their heads in befuddlement over what in the world this phrase means (see Duke Helfand, " '*Edspeak*' Is in a Class by Itself," *Los Angeles Times,* 16 Aug 2001).

We ought to be clear enough so our audience grasps our meaning. If not, we may end up like Dr. Hibbert talking to Homer (from the TV show *The Simpsons,* as noted on www.imdb.com):

DR. HIBBERT: Homer, I'm afraid you'll have to undergo a coronary bypass operation.
HOMER: Say it in English, Doc.
DR. HIBBERT: You're going to need open-heart surgery.
HOMER: Spare me your medical mumbo-jumbo.
DR. HIBBERT: We're going to cut you open and tinker with your ticker.
HOMER: Could you dumb it down a shade?

Some writers seem to use jargon to impress others or themselves. If we don't know what a term means, it cannot have much impact. If the term is not in the dictionary (keep one nearby!), analyze the author's intent and examine the context surrounding the use of the term. Legal terms are often used quite specifically, so don't assume they have an ordinary usage. The interpretation of a legal concept can shape laws and policies. We see this with the concept of "medical treatment."

Ordinarily when we think of medical treatment, we think of prescription drugs, special diets, and therapeutic treatments. In the case of Elizabeth Bouvia, this changed. Bouvia was a 28-year-old woman with cerebral palsy who checked herself into a hospital, wanting to starve herself to death. As she put it, "I'm trapped in a useless body." Doctors refused to go along with this wish, and ended up inserting a feeding tube, against her will. She sued.

In a landmark decision, the California Court of Appeals ruled that "medical treatment" included nutrition and hydration through a feeding tube. Since a competent adult has the right to refuse treatment, Bouvia could refuse the feeding tube, even if it resulted in her death. In 1993, this concept was stretched further, when an ill prisoner sued for the right to refuse food and water under the umbrella of the right to refuse medical treatment. He won and the legal concept of medical treatment expanded further. By 2001 the issue was whether a severely incapacitated person who was "minimally conscious" could, at his wife's request, have his feeding tube removed and die. The California Supreme Court denied the request, but the issue continues and the language of the debate continues to evolve.

Exercise

State all you can infer about the Kellogg Company from the following item taken from the company's Web site, under the Legal Information link:

Any communication or material you transmit to the Site by electronic mail or otherwise, including any data, questions, comments, suggestions, or the like is, and will be treated as, non-confidential and non-proprietary. Anything you transmit or post may be used by Kellogg's or its affiliates for any purpose, including, but not limited to, reproduction, disclosure, transmission, publication, broadcast and posting. Furthermore, Kellogg's is free to use any ideas, concepts, know-how, or techniques contained in any communication you send to the Site for any purpose whatsoever including, but not limited to, developing, manufacturing and marketing products using such information. (www.thekelloggcompany.co.uk)

Metaphors and Images

Descriptions may take colorful, dramatic turns, as we see with in the use of metaphors. A **metaphor** is the application of a word or phrase to draw a comparison or indicate a similarity (e.g., "she is a shrew and he's a snake"). Here is a description of the Detroit Pistons after winning the 2004 NBA championship. Watch how the author uses metaphors and images:

> The Detroit Pistons might have been able to win some other way, but this is right. This is who they are, unashamed as they are ferocious. Let it be brutal and bloody. Dreadfully ugly to anyone else, to the Pistons this is beauty. . . . "I don't know if it was a classic in many people's eyes, but if the series was going to end, this is the kind of game that should end it," Pistons coach Larry Brown said. . . . The Pacers' 65 points tied their franchise record for fewest points scored in a playoff game, a mark they had broken twice in the series' first five games. By the series' final game, the shooting became so horrid, if these guys were on a firing squad, the target would die of old age. . . .
>
> "It was an ugly game," [Piston's player] Rasheed Wallace said. "But we knew if we kept it close, we could fight it out at the end." (See Jonathan Feigen, "Ugly Clinching Win a Beautiful Thing to Pistons: Detroit Shoots Blanks but Gets to Finals; Pacers Match Playoff Low," *Houston Chronicle*, www.HoustonChronicle.com, 2, Jun 2004)

And then there's the losing 2004 NBA team, the Lakers. Watch how sports writer Bill Plaschke describes their defeat:

> The dream season was a scream season. The Fab Four was a raging bore. The ending was harrowing, humiliating and appropriate. The team that was supposed to make basketball history indeed made basketball history Tuesday, doomed forever to symbolize all that is wrong with modern professional sports, a testament to the failure of excess and danger of ego. ("In the End, Selfish Players Learn the Price of Fame," *Los Angeles Times*, 16 Jun 2004)

As you can see, good writing need not be either dry or dull. People often turn to metaphors to bring visions to life. Metaphors and images often become the linguistic paintbrush to convey our thoughts and feelings.

They can also shape an interpretation. They can be ruinous, but those that are used well can leave an impression that goes far beyond mere argumentation. Think of all the memorable speeches throughout history—many used powerful metaphors and images.

Analogies

Within the context of an argument, an analogy or metaphor can be very persuasive. An **analogy** consists of a comparison between two things in which, on the basis of certain similarities, a principle or characteristic of the one term is then applied to the other term and asserted as true in that case as well. The form of an analogy is:

A is like B in terms of characteristics p, q, r.

<u>A also has characteristic "z."</u>

So, B has characterististic "z" also.

For example, in an article in *USA Today*, Marilyn Adams argued that ALS (Lou Gehrig's disease) was like the act of a terrorist. The similarities noted are that they are both random and terrifying and they kill without partiality. She adds that the fight against terrorism has received a lot of attention and money. She then concludes that the fight against ALS also should receive a lot of attention and money. "If ALS were a terrorist group taking thousands of lives each year," she argues, this country would throw people and technology and money at it until we had won. Not so with this disease. . . . It's like a terrorist in our midst, going strong" ("ALS, Like a Terrorist, Kills without Partiality," *USA Today*, July 2004).

Analogies and metaphors should generally be used sparingly for maximum impact. Like all advice, however, there are always exceptions and each writer or speaker has to decide how to parcel out the use of metaphors, analogies, or other potentially powerful uses of language.

Exercises

Part One

Directions: Pick two current events, such as a recent issue from national news, a local story, a news item about a famous person, or an event in sports.

1. Using an analogy to a fairy tale, children's story, film character or cartoon character, write a brief description of the event. Your goal is to be as *colorful* as you can.

2. Now write your reflections on your use of language to create an effect, why you picked the metaphor/analogy you did, and how it could shape the way we see the event being described.

Part Two

Directions: Investigate the reappropriation of loaded terms, where a term that has been seen as highly charged is claimed by the targeted group and transformed:

1. Find as many examples as you can of ethnic or cultural groups that take a term (e.g., "crone," "nigger," "queer," "chick," "hag") that has been perceived as offensive and, turning the tables, apply it to themselves. For example, the movie *Menace II Society* took this approach with the term "nigger."

2. Do a study of the use of language in one or two song lyrics, noting the different uses of language that you see. Be sure to point out uses of language that you find particularly striking, appealing, or effective.

CASE STUDY

Exercises: Op/Ed Openings

Below are the opening paragraphs of three student papers. Each student wrote an op/ed piece on an issue such as gang violence, homelessness, violence in film, and smoking in movies. Select two and discuss their use of language. They were told to start with pizazz, to create a snappy opening to draw in the reader. You decide if they succeeded in that goal.

1. Can I Spare You Some Change?
Opening by Thelliza Balleta, April 2004

The first time I walked down Third Street Promenade I was eighteen years old and I was amazed at how beautiful the streets were. Little did I know, L.A. was not only filled with the rich and the famous but also the hungry and the homeless. After three slices of barbeque pizza from California Pizza Kitchen, my friends and I sat at a nearby Starbucks. With caffeine in our system, we were ready to tackle our homework. Then suddenly a homeless man banged at the window. He looked straight at me, and held out his hands, asking for money. I looked straight down and tried to ignore him.

Feeling guilty for what I did, I got up and took the remains of my barbeque pizza, which was in a doggy bag, and gave it to the homeless man. I asked what his name was and he said his name was Robert and he thanked me. I sat back down in Starbucks and felt awful because I could not help Robert anymore; I could not give him money because I had none. I then asked myself, "What are we doing to help the homeless?"

2. Gang Violence Is Getting Out of Hand
Opening by Noemi Rivera, April 2004

I found myself ducked under a desk, along with the rest of my classmates, hoping a gunshot would not hit any of us. After about thirty-minutes, our science teacher gave us the safety signal to get up, the drive by shooting was over. My sixth grade science class had been interrupted by gang shooting in the street near school. Gang violence is everywhere. It can happen at any time, and can hurt even those not involved in gang activity. Students should not be threatened to attend school because of gang violence. The community should not feel threatened to go about their lives because of gang violence. Society should not be menaced by gang violence. Gang violence must be put to an end; it must be put now.

3. Smoking and the Movies
Opening by Marissa Heilig, April 2004

Matthew McConaughey's piercing blue eyes and soft blonde curls entrance me as I fantasize in my mind that I am the object of his desire, not the gorgeous and good-willed Kate Hudson. I, like all the other girls sitting in the movie theater with overly buttered popcorn in arms and the somehow mindless action of shoving Jujubes in mouth while staring at the screen, am enthralled by his good looks and charming personality, or at least by his character Ben, in the movie *How to Lose a Guy in Ten Days*. Suddenly though, as if to no concern of his character, Matthew pulls out a cigar and begins to smoke. I am suddenly troubled with thoughts of how such a likeable character would be smoking, it can't be possible! My image . . . ruined.

Source: Reprinted with the permission of Thelliza Balleta, Noemi Rivera, and Marissa Heilig.

Group or Individual Exercises

Bertrand Russell once presented a conjugation of words to illustrate how synonyms can carry a range of connotations. He offered this one: "I am firm. You are stubborn. He is a pig-headed fool." Here are a few others: "I am svelte. You are thin. She is skinny as a green bean." "I am pleasingly plump. You are overweight. He is a blimp." "I am reserved. You have a chip on your shoulder. She is a stuck-up princess." *Answer the following:*

1. Come up with four conjugations of your own.
2. Write two to three paragraphs discussing the range of the three terms and the impact of the different connotations.

The Passive Voice

We use the **passive voice** when we make the object of an action into the subject of a sentence, as in "The chicken **was eaten by** the coyote" (**emphasis mine**). This form avoids calling attention to the one performing an action (the coyote). Its focus is the recipient of the action (the chicken). Passive constructions can be spotted by the use of a form of "to be" followed by a past participle. For instance, "The agents were contacted by Jason Bourne." The structure of this is: "The agents *were [form of the verb "to be"] contacted by [past participle]* Jason Bourne." To make it active, change it to "Jason Bourne contacted the agents."

Using the passive voice is a way for people to avoid owning their own thoughts and ideas, observes philosopher Vance Ricks. Thanks to Prof. Ricks for pointing out the importance of looking at the passive voice as part of the way language can persuade and shape how we think. The passive voice reframes the emphasis of a claim. Instead of "I think such and so . . ." we find, "It is held that such and so." This construction *makes the agent invisible;*—so no one is held accountable for an action.

Ricks observes: "I've lost track of how many times I've heard or read "It is widely believed that . . ." or "It is alleged that . . ." or "is said to be" or other passive constructions that leave utterly unclear exactly who is doing the wide believing, alleging, saying, etc."

Using the passive voice results in a construction that is less precise and often more confusing—the *who* and *what* may be entirely left out. Look at these three constructions:

ACTIVE VOICE: Slugs ate the plants.
PASSIVE VOICE #1: The plants were eaten by slugs.
PASSIVE VOICE #2: The plants were eaten.

In the active voice, it is clear who is eating the plants. In passive voice #1 the identification of the perpetrator (slugs) is secondary. By passive voice #2, the perpetrator (slugs) has been completely erased. There may be times when the passive voice is the best choice, but ordinarily strive to use the active voice. And when we see others using the passive voice, decide if the construction creates problems by deemphasizing or eliminating the subject from our view.

Loaded Language

Linguistic shape shifting can transform hot words to lukewarm or cold ones (and vice versa). **Loaded language** is language that is value laden, heavy with connotation (positive or negative). It can create a bias, just as neutralized terms can defuse a controversy by making them appear innocuous or acceptable.

Loaded language should not be confused with colorful, or figurative, language. Loaded terms—also known as "weasel words"—are intended to affect the way we perceive. They are used to manipulate thinking and, thus, are potentially dangerous. For example, "He's as subtle as a hog in heat," or "My hair feels greasier than an oil well!" may be considered *colorful* uses of language.

Words are not usually neutral. Words are not like numbers or a symbolic language. Each word carries a set of connotations, so watch for both the overt and covert meanings. Look out for a fallacy called *question-begging epithets*. This occurs when language is biased so that it stacks the deck in either a positive or negative direction. The slanted language can cause us to unfairly prejudge the case. We will go into this further in Chapter 4.

In World War II loaded language used by the Nazis was a powerful tool of anti-Semitism. Loathsome words and phrases such as "vermin" and "the final solution" were used to characterize Jews and indicate what ought to be done with them (terminate them). On this side of the Atlantic, the American government referred to the Japanese as "Japs." Such terminology made it easier to put Japanese Americans into "relocation" (internment) camps. A particularly odious form of loaded language is hate speech, which we will look at in the next section. Finding other examples is not difficult (try talk radio and Internet chat rooms). Those using loaded language seek to **bias** the reader or listener. This we ought to keep in mind when we examine the use of language.

When reading a news article, we tend to expect objectivity and fairness. If there is controversy, however, things may get slanted one way or another. The use of language is often tinged with the values of the author. That is not necessarily bad, but it is something to watch for. This is why critical thinking should come into play whenever we read.

Exercises

What should we allow in high school essays and poems when it comes to expressions about acts of violence? It's not always easy to sort out threats from creative expression, as a California case demonstrates. Read about the case and then answer the questions below:

> George approached a girl in his honors English class at Santa Teresa High School in San Jose and asked her if the school had a poetry club. . . . He gave the girl a copy of a poem he had labeled "Dark Poetry" and titled "Faces." He told her the poetry described him and his feelings. "Tell me if they describe you and your feelings," he told her. "Faces" began: "Who are these faces around me? Where did they come from?" It ended with these lines: "For I am Dark, Destructive & Dangerous. I slap on my face of happiness but inside I am evil!! For I can be the next kid to bring guns to kill students at school. So parents watch your children cuz I'm BACK!!" (Maura Dolan, "Teen's Poem Not a Threat, Justices Rule, *Los Angeles Times*, 23 Jul 2004)

Answer the following:

1. Do you think there is cause for concern knowing that the poem "Dark Poetry" begins in this way:

   Who are these faces around me?
   Where do they come from? . . .
   All really intelligent and ahead in their game.
   I wish I had a choice on what I want to be like they do.
   All so happy and vagrant . . .
   They make me want to puke.

2. Do you think George should be suspended for this poem? State four to five reasons for or against his suspension

3. Give your response to the ruling by the California Supreme Court on the case, conveyed by Justice Carlos E. Moreno:

   "Following Columbine, Santee and other notorious school shootings, there is a heightened sensitivity on school campuses to latent signs that a student . . . may embark on a shooting rampage," Moreno wrote. "Ensuring a safe school environment and protecting freedom of expression, however, are not necessarily antagonistic goals.". . .

   "While the protagonist in 'Faces' declares that he has the potential or capacity to kill students given his dark and hidden feelings, he does not actually threaten to do so, . . . While perhaps discomforting and unsettling, in this unique context this disclosure simply does not constitute an actual threat to kill or inflict harm."

   A creative work can constitute a criminal threat, but courts must look at whether the work was really intended as a threat, he said. In George's case, there were no incriminating circumstances, Moreno said. "There was no history of animosity or conflict" between George and the classmates with whom he shared his work, and "threatening gestures or mannerisms," Moreno said. (Maura Dolan, "Teen's Poem Not a Threat, Justices Rule," *Los Angeles Times*, 23 Jul 2004)

▦ Propaganda

Propaganda uses words to shape public consciousness, to predispose people to certain ideas, policies, and actions—and to manipulate them to think, vote, and act as the propaganda machine suggests. Propaganda can come from all directions—left, right, and center. It is the *substance*, not the source that marks propaganda. Cult specialist Margaret Thaler Singer sees propaganda in the center of a continuum:

education — advertising — propaganda — indoctrination — thought reform

Singer says propaganda centers on the political persuasion of a mass of people, whereas thought reform centers on changing people without their knowledge so they can be manipulated and controlled. Propaganda has a manipulative, controlling element as well, but it involves *persuasion.* Thought reform involves no full awareness on the part of the subject and usually involves a hidden agenda. (See Margaret Singer, *Cults in our Midst.*)

Fallacies are common in propaganda. W. H. Werkmeister cites this example: "There are two kinds of speakers, one appeals to your emotions, the other to reason. Roosevelt is the kind that works your emotions, the same as does Hitler, and the masses blindly follow to the bitter end" (*An Introduction to Critical Thinking*). Propaganda is not a relic of the past, so examples are around us.

Web Sites That Study Propaganda

- The Center for Media and Democracy at www.prwatch.org
- WWII US government propaganda at www.archives.gov/exhibit_hall/powers_of_ persuasion/powers_of_persuasion_home.html and www.propagandacritic.com
- Nazi and East German propaganda at www.calvin.edu/academic/cas/gpa
- Allied World War I propaganda posters at www.pma.edmonton.ab.ca/vex- hibit/warpost/english/home.htm

Propaganda serves important **ideological functions.** It attempts to influence the opinions or actions of others by appealing to their emotions or prejudices. Or it might succeed by distorting facts. The goal itself may be bad (e.g., genocide) or good (e.g., peace). What marks propaganda is the *manipulation*, not the desired end. An example of propaganda is a "misinformation campaign" where the truth is stretched or disposed of in order to persuade a population to support a government's way of thinking or course of action. W. H. Werkmeister has a useful list of propaganda tricks (*An Introduction to Critical Thinking*, 1948). His list of tricks is on the left in the table below; updated examples are on the right.

PROPAGANDA TRICKS	EXAMPLES
NAME CALLING The use of invectives and emotionally colored words to denigrate another or reinforce biases and prejudice.	"She's a liberal, don't vote for her!" "Governor Prawn caters to pro-lifers." "Sen. Thornton is a Feminazi, don't put her in charge of the school board."

PROPAGANDA TRICKS	EXAMPLES
GLITTERING GENERALITIES The use of "purr words" appealing to truth, freedom, honor, progress, a sense of justice, pride, hope, courage, and the like—without ever being specific.	"May the sanctity of human liberty guide this campaign." "Get behind the freedom-fighters, not the terrorists." "Vote for the party that will work for a lasting peace."
TABLOID THINKING The use of hasty generalization (fallacy) to settle a dispute or an argument.	"Every person has a price." "You can't change human nature." "It's time to clean house." "Workers of the world unite!"
TESTIMONIALS The use of some "authority" (public figure or organization) to sell an idea. This includes planting an idea in a "news" item to sway the public (also called the fallacy of ad verecundiam).	"An unnamed source speaks of the frightening possibility of another terrorist attack over Christmas. Therefore, we need to vote to consolidate more power behind the CIA." "Goebbels thought it good to do more human experimentation; perhaps we should do so."
BIFURCATION The use of a simple "either/or" when actually more alternatives exist. This is a fallacy (also known as "false dichotomy").	"If you want to destroy private enterprise, go ahead and support more national parks!" "America faces a choice: Either send women's rights back 100 years or support progressive reform with Senator Buchman."
ASSOCIATION The use of links drawn between an idea presented and some object, person, party, or cause that people respect or cherish—or which they fear or condemn.	"The name USA Patriot Act speaks to all that is American and needs preserving." "Osama bin Laden is the modern-day Hitler—we better fight fire with fire."
IDENTIFICATION The propagandist identifies with those being addressed—becoming "one of the gang"—to win confidence.	"I, like you, am a child of rural America. I pulled myself up by my bootstraps, trusting in free enterprise to get where I am. Like you, I want a strong America—that's why we need to vote for Prop. 180."

PROPAGANDA TRICKS	EXAMPLES
BAND WAGON The use of the "follow the crowd" technique to persuade. (This is also called the Fallacy of Ad Populum.)	"All over the country, people are standing up for the family. That's why you have to vote in a constitutional amendment against gay rights." "Most of you, my fellow Americans, do support individual liberty. That means we've got to oppose banning assault weapons!!"
CARD STACKING The use of distortion, exaggeration, forgery, deception, and misinformation to sell an idea—it is one of the most vicious tricks that can be used.	"Evidence is overwhelming that Iraq has nuclear capability. We must go to war!" Iraqi exile Ahmed Chalabi regularly fed misinformation to US news media—leading to *The New York Times* apologizing on May 26, 2004.

The most common form of propaganda appeals to emotions or to traditional ideals (like patriotism, religious sentiment, group identity). It simplifies issues and offers few (but the desired!) alternatives. With propaganda this way is the way to best address the political or social situation. Propaganda usually works best with little evidence or a distortion of evidence. An example is propaganda for the Ku Klux Klan—"virtually every piece of Klan propaganda from the early 1920s enjoined Klansmen to protect the virtue of white womanhood," says Sociology professor, Kathleen M. Blee (*Women of the Klan,* University of California Press, 1991). Such propaganda laid the groundwork for the violence—including lynching—that is part of KKK history.

As it is useful to have someone else to blame, a scapegoat is often employed. This gives a face to the problem or "enemy." It's much easier to blame someone else for our problems. More sinister forms of propaganda play into racial tension, religious conflict, and prejudice. By appealing to pride, nationalism, and group identity, propaganda can turn thoughts and actions into a team effort. This makes it harder to resist—we may want to be "one of the gang."

Group or Individual Exercise

Directions: Both exercises involve *finding examples,* so allow time to do so (e.g., be prepared for the next class meeting).

1. Find two different examples of propaganda prior to 1975. Each example should be from distinctly different perspectives (e.g., one from the left,

one from the right or one from one religious angle, one from another).
Explain how each one is an example of propaganda.

2. Find two different examples of propaganda from after 1975, the more recent the better. Try to find examples from distinctly different perspectives. Explain how each one is an example of propaganda.

Exclusive Language and Hate Speech

The use of demeaning or vitriolic language can ignite and sustain prejudice. All too easily this leads to disrespectful behavior and even hate crimes. **Exclusive language** posits one group (race, religion, gender, sexual orientation, etc.) as superior and another group or groups as inferior, lesser. It is hurtful and offensive.

At times exclusive language is used in the form of categories. Think of terms like "developing nations" as compared to "Third World countries." The intent may not be to suggest superiority; speakers may be unaware of the effects. Not all who call a society "primitive" or "backward" intend to demean; they may think they are being objective.

Hate speech is a particular kind of loaded language. Here, words are weapons. Hate speech can be used to insult or demean a person or group because of race, ethnicity, gender, sexual orientation, nationality, religion, age, or disability. Myrlie Evers put it this way, "The word 'nigger, nigger' still does something to me." Would you call an Italian a "wop," a Latino a "bean-eater," a gay man a "fag" and a lesbian a "dyke" just because those around you do? It's not always easy to opt out of the norm, even when the norm is morally flawed.

Law professor Mari J. Matsuda does not think hate speech should be protected discourse. She says hate speech presents "an idea so historically untenable, so dangerous, and so tied to perpetuation of violence and degradation of the very classes of human beings who are least equipped to respond."

Matsuda's Three Characteristics of Hate Speech

1. The message is that one group is racially inferior.
2. The message is directed against a historically oppressed group.
3. The message is persecutory, hateful, and degrading.

The expansion of the Internet has enabled hate speech to multiply in a myriad of forms. (See Chapter 11.) It raises serious questions. The University of Delaware publicizes one perspective, that rules that ban or punish speech based upon its content cannot be justified:

> An institution of higher learning fails to fulfill its mission if it asserts the power to proscribe ideas—and racial or ethnic slurs, sexist epithets, or homophobic insults almost always express ideas, however repugnant . . . As the United States Supreme Court has said in the course of rejecting criminal sanctions for offensive words: Words are often chosen as much for their emotive as their cognitive force.

The line between substance and style is thus too uncertain to sustain the pressure that will inevitably be brought to bear upon disciplinary rules that attempt to regulate speech. ("On Freedom of Expression and Campus Speech Codes," University of Delaware Library, www.lib.udel.edu)

Exercises

Part One

1. What do you think should be a company or college policy about the use of hate speech in e-mail or within publications, such as college newspapers or office newsletters? Set out your recommendations.

2. Do a study of contemporary music for examples of hate speech. Give an argument for or against censoring music lyrics containing hate speech.

Part Two

Directions: Select any two of the excerpts below and make note of the ways in which racism or prejudice is expressed, how stereotypes are used, and how hatred and fear factor into the author's reasoning.

1. From "Dilemma of a Norwegian Immigrant," in *Annals of America*, 1862, author unknown:

   You are not safe from Indians anywhere, for they are as cunning as they are bold. The other evening we received the frightening message that they have been seen in our neighborhood; so, we hitched our horses and made ready to leave our house and all our property and escape from the savages under the cover of darkness. But it was a false alarm, God be praised, and for this time we could rest undisturbed. How terrible it is thus, every moment, to expect that you will be attacked, robbed, and perhaps murdered! We do not go to bed any night without fear, and my rifle is always loaded. . . . It is true that some cavalry have been dispatched against these hordes, but they will not avail much, for the Indians are said to be more than 10,000 strong. Besides, they are so cunning that it is not easy to get the better of them. Sometimes they disguise themselves in ordinary farmers' clothes and stalk their victims noiselessly.

2. From the Mississippi Penal Code, 1865:

   Section 1. Be it enacted by the legislature of the state of Mississippi, that no freedman, free Negro, or mulatto not in the military service of the United States government, and not licensed so to do by the board of police of his or her county, shall keep or carry

You Tell Me Department

The John Rocker Case

In December 1999, *Sports Illustrated* published an interview with Atlanta Braves pitcher John Rocker. In it he referred to a black teammate as a "fat monkey," and let loose a series of comments that shook sports. *Sports Illustrated* reported some of Rocker's opinions, such as these:

> *On ever playing for a New York team:* "I would retire first. It's the most hectic, nerve-racking city. Imagine having to take the [Number] 7 train to the ballpark, looking like you're [riding through] Beirut next to some kid with purple hair next to some queer with AIDS right next to some dude who just got out of jail for the fourth time right next to some 20-year-old mom with four kids. It's depressing."
>
> *On New York City itself:* "The biggest thing I don't like about New York are the foreigners. I'm not a very big fan of foreigners. You can walk an entire block in Times Square and not hear anybody speaking English. Asians and Koreans and Vietnamese and Indians and Russians and Spanish people and everything up there. How the hell did they get in this country?" (Jeff Pearlman, "At Full Blast," *Sports Illustrated,* December 1999)

You tell me: How seriously should we take Rocker's comments? What do you think of Base-ball Commissioner Bud Selig's response to Rocker; namely:

> Major league baseball takes seriously its role as an American institution and the important social responsibility that goes with it. We will not dodge our responsibility. Mr. Rocker should understand that his remarks offended practically every element of society and brought dishonor to himself, the Atlanta Braves and major league baseball. The terrible example set by Mr. Rocker is not what our great game is about and, in fact, is a profound breach of the social compact we hold in such high regard. (Associated Press, atlanta.about.com/blrockernews, 1 Feb 2000)

UPDATE: John Rocker received a brief suspension and was fined $20,000 and ordered to undergo sensitivity training for disparaging foreigners, homosexuals, and minorities. To John Rocker's credit, he issued an apology for his "foul language" ("I've been a poor example"), racist comments ("I'm not a racist, although I can understand how someone who did not know me could think that"), and unprofessional behavior ("my comments concerning my team were totally unprofessional and out of line"). Rocker admitted that his words demand action: "An apology is no more than just words unless it is followed by actions. I hope in this coming year I may somehow redeem myself."

firearms of any kind, or any ammunition, dirk [dagger], or Bowie knife; and, on conviction thereof in the county court, shall be punished by fine, not exceeding $10, and pay the costs of such proceedings, and all such arms or ammunition shall be forfeited to the informer; and it shall be the duty of every civil and military officer to arrest any freedman, free Negro, or mulatto found with any such arms or ammunition, and cause him or her to be committed for trial in default of bail.

3. From *The Turner Diaries* by William L. Pierce:

I'll never forget that terrible day: November 9, 1989. They knocked on my door at five in the morning. I was completely unsuspecting as I got up to see who it was. I opened the door, and four Negroes came pushing into the apartment before I could stop them. One was carrying a baseball bat, and two had long kitchen knives thrust into their belts. The one with the bat shoved me back into a corner and stood guard over me with his bat raised in a threatening position while the other three began ransacking my apartment.

My first thought was that they were robbers. Robberies of this sort had become all too common since the Cohen Act, with groups of Blacks forcing their way into White homes to rob and rape, knowing that even if their victims had guns they probably would not dare use them. Then the one who was guarding me flashed some kind of card and informed me that he and his accomplices were "special deputies" for the Northern Virginia Human Relations Council. They were searching for firearms, he said.

Right after the Cohen Act was passed, all of us in the Organization had cached our guns and ammunition where they weren't likely to be found. Those in my unit had carefully greased our weapons, sealed them in an oil drum, and spent all of one tedious weekend burying the drum in an eight-foot-deep pit 200 miles away in the woods of western Pennsylvania.

Overcoming Linguistic Lethargy

Some people think of language as neutral and unchanging. It is neither. We can be active agents of change so that degrading or stereotypical constructions fade away from ordinary use. One way is to make sure we avoid using language that is racist or sexist in ways that are prejudicial.

Sexist language has its own set of problems. To say "man" and assume it includes women is to try to twist your brain around a linguistic pretzel. The issue is not simply one of convention. The underlying assumptions behind prejudicial language need to be rooted out. This can be difficult. People do not always want to change their way of speaking or writing. They prefer to stick with tradition, even if others find such traditions to be biased. We are not always aware of our own biases. On the other hand, there are those who *are* aware of such attitudes and seek to perpetuate them. We are not always in a position to confront the perpetrator; but we are not powerless, either. By recognizing and understanding the mechanisms of hate and hate speech, we can be party to social change.

Racist language creates a mindset that makes it easier to kill "enemies." This was seen in the Vietnam War when Viet Cong (North Vietnamese) were called "gooks." Ron Ridenhour writes: "By the time I got to Vietnam, just before Christmas 1967, everydamnbody was talking about killing gooks. Gooks this, gooks that. . . . How did you tell gooks from the good Vietnamese, for instance? After a while it became clear. You didn't have to. All gooks were VC [Viet Cong] when they were dead." (Ron Ridenhour, "Jesus Was a Gook," Part I, lists.village.virginia.edu/sixties.)

Justice does not come about by a few people in powerful places making decisions to be blindly followed by the masses. Justice comes about when everyday people bring it into each aspect of their lives. And that means change is possible. We can help others acquire the tools to recognize racist language and thought. We can also eradicate it from our own speech and ways of thinking.

Exercises

Part One

Directions: Analyze the comments of radio talk show host Rush Limbaugh regarding the torture of prisoners in Iraq that became a public scandal in 2004:

> First off these pictures of these prisoners of war. . . . In these American prisoners of war, have you people noticed who the torturers are? Women! The babes. The babes are meting out the torture. Well, I've just been asked if I'm surprised. . . . I mean, this business of weaker sex is all a bunch of trumped up stuff they teach when you're five years old and you end up living your whole life that way, and it's just one big mystery that never gets solved. . . . You know, if you really look at these pictures, I mean I don't know if it's just me but it looks like anything you'd see Madonna or Britney Spears do on stage. Maybe you can get an NEA grant for something like this. I mean this is something you can see at Lincoln Center from an NEA grant, maybe on *Sex in the City: the Movie*. I mean, it's just me. (Rush Limbaugh, "Babes Doing the Torture in Iraq," www.rushlimbaugh.com, 3 May 2004)

Part Two

Directions: Select *one* of the two questions (with accompanying subquestions) below.

1. Study advertising as a kind of consumer propaganda.
    a. How is language used in ads to shape our thoughts and values?
    b. How are items made more appealing by the words used (e.g., in cigarette ads the word "taste" is often used, though we don't normally eat cigarettes)?

2. Do a study of stereotypes (focus on one area—race, ethnicity/nationality, gender, religion, age, weight) in sports. You can find articles in newspapers and on the Internet to gather examples and issues.

Group or Individual Exercises

1. Research the ways in which racism and racist language were used by any *one* of these groups: the Ku Klux Klan, Nazis, neo-Nazis, white supremacists, or the Aryan Nation.

2. Research the ways in which racism and racist language were used by the American media and/or the U.S. government in the treatment of one group (Germans, Soviets, Asians, etc.) with respect to one event: World War II, Cold War, Korean War, Vietnam War, Grenada invasion, war in El Salvador, the Panama invasion, Gulf War, War in Afghanistan, Iraq War.

3. Study the use of language by the media *within the first month* after the terrorist attacks of 9/11, focusing on how issues of religion, race, and/or racism were dealt with.

Humor, Parody, and Satire

It is all too easy to fall into the stereotypical mindset around race, ethnicity, and gender. Humor can help jolt us out of our habitual ways of thinking. Comedy is a powerful vehicle for social commentary—and for loosening up our thought processes! (See Figure 2.3.)

Remember *Mrs. Doubtfire?* It tackles the stereotype of the distant father who could care less about his children (unless they turn out to be serial killers!). Remember *Legally Blond?* It tackles the pomposity and snootiness of the upper class (and stereotypes about dumb blondes). And how about *Barbershop 1* and *2?* They tackle race relations, class struggles, and corporate greed. *Born in East L.A.* and *White Chicks* take on race, wealth, poverty, and cultural norms. And *Groundhog Day* looks at the costs of a self-centered lifestyle.

A **satire** is a work that ridicules or pokes fun at its subject (people, groups, institutions, countries, etc.) in order to bring about a particular effect, such as social change. The original *The Stepford Wives* is a biting satire on society and the institution of marriage. It put the term "Stepford" on the map and led to the verb "Stepfordized" to describe the process of stripping away uniqueness and turning into a cookie-cutter stereotype. And so "the word 'Stepford' entered the lexicon as shorthand for creeping regimentation. People in tract-house communities live Stepford lives; politicians who parrot safe causes are Stepford candidates, etc. etc." (Glenn Lovell, "Too Good to Be True?" *San Jose Mercury News,* 11 Jan 2004) Cathryn J. Prince uses the term "Stepford" to criticize a new perk in the U.S. military: "Call it 'Stepford Soldiers' or 'Nip and Tuck: Stories of Vanity on the Home Front.' In a bizarre attempt to attract recruits, the Pentagon now offers soldiers free cosmetic surgery, from face-lifts and nose jobs to breast enlargements and liposuctions" (*Christian Science Monitor, www.csmonitorcom,* July 30, 2004).

FIGURE 2.4
Nothing like a little play on words by a punster!

The Global Dimension

Did You Hear the One About . . .?

Shazia Mirza is a Muslim female comic who became famous after telling a single joke. The joke has evoked strong reactions. She has received death threats and was assaulted at one comedy club doing her routine. She wears traditional Muslim headdress and no makeup, so she appears to be a conventional, if not a conservative, Muslim woman. She is a stand-up comic who is a devout Muslim and well known in England and other European countries. With humor she has been able to touch both Muslims and non-Muslims and open up a dialogue that helps bridge differences. She was performing before 9/11—but the events of that day changed everything for this Muslim woman. Three weeks after 9/11 she resumed her stage routine—this time opening with a joke that some say draws "a very, very thin line between acceptable comedy and abominable taste." (See Marshall Sella, "Did You Hear the One about the Suicide Bomber?," *The New York Times Magazine*, 15 Jun 2003).

Directions: Discuss her use of humor and assess its impact in what is now her famous opening line: *"My name is Shazia Mirza,"* she said. *"At least that's what it says on my pilot's license."*

One important function of humor is to provide perspective on our society. We are stronger as a nation, as a democracy, if we can laugh about the issues and people in our lives. For instance, Andrew Marlett quips:

> In a troubling sign that investigators may be getting bored with their success smuggling guns and knives onto airplanes, the U.S. Department of Transportation today disclosed that its agents have recently cleared airport security checkpoints with an M1 tank, a beluga whale, and a fully active South American volcano. DOT investigators also boasted that they have repeatedly slipped past screeners with a six-burner Viking stove, the Field Museum of Natural History, and actor Sidney Poitier, whom they had gagged and, for some reason, painted bright blue.

Group or Individual Exercise

Directions: Read the following satirical piece by Andrew Marlett that first appeared on *SatireWire*. Discuss how it works to inject humor into a political commentary:

> Beijing (*SatireWire.com*)—Bitter after being snubbed for membership in the "Axis of Evil," Libya, China, and Syria today announced they had formed the "Axis of Just as Evil," which they said would be way eviler than that stupid Iran–Iraq–North Korea axis President Bush warned of in his State of the Union address. Axis of Evil members, however, immediately dismissed the new axis as having, for starters, a really dumb name. "Right. They are just as Evil . . . *in their dreams!*" declared North Korean leader Kim Jong-il. . . .

With the criteria suddenly expanded and all the desirable clubs filling up, Sierra Leone, El Salvador, and Rwanda applied to be called the Axis of Countries That Aren't the Worst But Certainly Won't Be Asked to Host the Olympics; Canada, Mexico, and Australia formed the Axis of Nations That Are Actually Quite Nice But Secretly Have Nasty Thoughts About America, while Spain, Scotland, and New Zealand established the Axis of Countries That Sometimes Ask Sheep to Wear Lipstick. "That's not a threat, really, just something we like to do," said Scottish Executive First Minister Jack McConnell. (Andrew Marlett, "Angered by Snubbing, Libya, China, Syria Form Axis of Just as Evil," 1 Feb 2002)

▦ The Liberatory Voice

Language can degrade, as we have seen. But language can also exalt, as we saw with the case of the deaf children who were proud to have "their own language." As William Raspberry says, "And, yes, words matter. They may reflect reality, but they also have the power to change reality—the power to uplift and to abase." The **liberatory voice** is language at its most inspirational—a call to social action, political transformation, spiritual healing, or realizing our common humanity.

We've all had to deal with psychic numbing, in our own way. Humans now have the capacity to vaporize us all, to commit mass genocide, to explode the vast nuclear arsenal. Many of us have parents or grandparents who, naïve and trusting of their government, stood before nuclear weapons testing or lived downwind from it. Many of us have brothers or sisters, aunts or uncles who took part in the war in Iraq, Afghanistan, or the Gulf and are now living with the consequences of nerve gas, mustard gas, biochemical agents, or uranium-tipped weapons. Many of us have neighbors who worked in agricultural fields touching pesticide-covered crops or in buildings breathing asbestos. We grieve the cancers they now have. We are numbed by that suffering. Some of us, most of us, are numbed into silence.

Some, however, come out of their silence into speech. Think of those who have stood up against injustice and raised their voices in opposition. Think of those who have galvanized an entire community to confront oppression and work for social change. Think of those who wrote down their thoughts and ideas, even in the most repressive environments, like prisons, internment camps, boarding schools, plantations, abusive households, and violent relationships. Such acts are inspiring and even transforming. That is why the liberatory voice must be recognized—and celebrated.

As Isabel Allende says, "Writing is an act of hope." Some confront the terrors of what they see—and they speak and write. For them, and for all of us, language is a source of strength, a source of inspiration and a vehicle for liberation. The liberatory aspect of language moves us to organize, effect political change, address the ills of society, take one small step to make our voices heard, and inject reason in the face of madness and goodness in the face of evil.

Think about some of the ways language has been used to transform society. For example, Abraham Lincoln changed this country with The Gettysburg Address. Thich Nhat Hanh helped people find spiritual wisdom. Cesar Chavez united the farm workers, a disenfranchised group, and helped them organize to effect political and social change. The Proclamation of the Delano Grape Workers called for an international boycott in 1969. In 1862 the prominent African-American leader, John S. Rock, issued his "Negro Hopes for Emancipation," a call to end slavery. Sojourner Truth spoke in New York City on May 9, 1867, at the First Annual Meeting of the American Equal Rights Association. She called for equal rights for women.

CASE STUDY

The Dalai Lama's
Nobel Peace Prize Acceptance Speech

The Dalai Lama, Buddhist monk and spiritual leader of Tibet, was forced to flee Tibet as a young man when the Chinese army violently overthrew the government of Tibet. The Dalai Lama is now a world citizen, traveling from country to country and raising awareness about the power of nonviolence. Read this excerpt from his acceptance speech for the Nobel Peace Prize of 1989. Make note of what is distinctive about his writing, including any transformative aspects that you see.

Nobel Prize Acceptance Speech

His Holiness the Dalai Lama

University Aula, Oslo, December 10, 1989

Your Majesty, Members of the Nobel Committee, Brothers and Sisters. I am very happy to be here with you today to receive the Nobel Prize for Peace. I feel honored, humbled and deeply moved that you should give this important prize to a simple monk from Tibet. . . . I accept the prize with profound gratitude on behalf of the oppressed everywhere and for all those who struggle for freedom and work for world peace. I accept it as a tribute to the man who founded the modern tradition of non-violent action for change, Mahatma Gandhi, whose life taught and inspired me. And, of course, I accept it on behalf of the six million Tibetan people, my brave countrymen and women inside Tibet, who have suffered and continue to suffer so much. . . .

No matter what part of the world we come from, we are all basically the same human beings. We all seek happiness and try to avoid suffering. We have the same basic human needs and concerns. All of us human beings want freedom and the right to determine our own destiny as individuals and as peoples. That is human nature. The great changes that are taking place everywhere in the world, from Eastern Europe to Africa are a clear indication of this. . . .

The suffering of our people [of Tibet] during the past forty years of occupation is well documented. Ours has been a long struggle. We know our cause is just because violence can only breed more violence and suffering. Our struggle must remain non-violent and free of hatred. . . .

As a Buddhist monk, my concern extends to all members of the human family and, indeed, to all sentient beings who suffer. I believe all suffering is caused by ignorance. People inflict pain on others in the selfish pursuit of their happiness or satisfaction. Yet true happiness comes from a sense of brotherhood and sisterhood. We need to cultivate a universal responsibility for one another and the planet we share. Although I have found my own Buddhist religion helpful in generating love and compassion, even for those we consider our enemies, I am convinced that everyone can develop a good heart and a sense of universal responsibility with or without religion.

With the ever-growing impact of science on our lives, religion and spirituality have a greater role to play reminding us of our humanity. There is no contradiction between the two. Each gives us valuable insights into the other. Both science and the teachings of the Buddha tell us of the fundamental unity of all things. This understanding is crucial if we are to take positive and decisive action on the pressing global concern with the environment.

I believe all religions pursue the same goals, that of cultivating human goodness and bringing happiness to all human beings. Though the means might appear different, the ends are the same. As we enter the final decade of this century, I am optimistic that the ancient values that have sustained mankind are today reaffirming themselves to prepare us for a kinder, happier twenty-first century.

I pray for all of us, oppressor and friend, that together we succeed in building a better world through human understanding and love, and that in doing so we may reduce the pain and suffering of all sentient beings. Thank you.

Exercises

Directions: Here are excerpts from works that have inspired political and religious action. Select *one* of the passages and read it carefully to see its power and ability to transform lives. Write a brief analysis of the use of language, focusing on one of these issues: (1) how the language is inspiring; (2) how the language could or should be changed to reflect other values or concerns, (3) what the writer seems to assume.

First Passage—Abraham Lincoln's "The Gettysburg Address"

Four score and seven years ago our fathers brought forth on this continent a new nation, conceived in liberty and dedicated to the proposition that all men are created equal.

Now we are engaged in a great civil war, testing whether that nation or any nation so conceived and so dedicated can long endure. We are met on a great battlefield of that war. We have come to dedicate a portion of that field as a fi-nal resting place for those who here gave their lives that that nation might live. It is altogether fitting and proper that we should do this.

But, in a larger sense, we cannot dedicate— we cannot consecrate—we cannot hallow—this ground. The brave men, living and dead, who struggled here have consecrated it far above our poor power to add or detract. The world will little note nor long remember what we say here, but it can never forget what they did here. It is for us, the living, rather, to be dedicated here to the unfinished work, which they who fought here have thus far so nobly advanced.

It is rather for us to be here dedicated to the great task remaining before us—that from these honored dead we take increased devotion to that cause for which they gave the last full measure of devotion; that we here highly resolve that these dead shall not have died in vain; that this nation, under God, shall have a new birth of freedom; and that government of the people, by the people, for the people shall not perish from the earth.

Second Passage—Thich Nhat Hanh from *The Sun My Heart*

Peace can exist only in the present moment. It is ridiculous to say, "Wait until I finish this, then I will be free to live in peace." What is "this?" A diploma, a job, a house, the payment of a debt? If you think that way, peace will never come. There is always another "this" that will follow the present one. If you are not living in peace at this moment, you will never be able to. If you truly want to be at peace, you must be at peace right now. Otherwise, there is only "the hope of peace some day.". . .

The peace we seek cannot be our personal possession. We need to find an inner peace which makes it possible for us to become one with those who suffer, and to do something to help our brothers and sisters, which is to say, ourselves. I know many young people who are aware of the real situation of the world and who are filled with compassion. They refuse to hide themselves in artificial peace, and they engage in the world in order to change the society.

They know what they want; yet after a period of involvement they become discouraged. Why? It is because they lack deep, inner peace, the kind of peace they can take with them into their life of action. Our strength is in our peace, the peace within us. This peace makes us indestructible. We must have peace while taking care of those we love and those we want to protect.

Third Passage—Proclamation of the Delano Grape Workers

We have been farm workers for hundreds of years and pioneers for seven. Mexicans, Filipinos, Africans, and others, our ancestors were among those who founded this land and tamed its natural wilderness. But we are still pilgrims on this land, and we are pioneers who blaze a trail out of the wilderness of hunger and deprivation that we have suffered even as our ancestors did.

We are conscious today of the significance of our present quest. If this road we chart leads to the rights and reforms we demand, if it leads to just wages, humane working conditions, protection from the misuse of pesticides, and to the fundamental right of collective bargaining, if it changes the social order that relegates us to the bottom reaches of society, then in our wake will follow thousands of American farm workers. . . .

Our example will make them free. But if our road does not bring us to victory and social change, it will not be because our direction is mistaken or our resolve too weak, but only because our bodies are mortal and our journey hard. For we are in the midst of a great social movement, and we will not stop struggling 'til we die, or win! . . .

Grapes must remain an unenjoyed luxury for all as long as the barest human needs and basic human rights are still luxuries for farm workers. The grapes grow sweet and heavy on the vines, but they will have to wait while we reach out first for our freedom. The time is ripe for our liberation.

Fourth Passage—John S. Rock from "Negro Hopes for Emancipation," 1862 speech before the Massachusetts Anti-Slavery Society

The situation of the black man in this country is far from being an enviable one. Today, our heads are in the lion's mouth, and we must get them out the best way we can. To contend against the government is as difficult as it is to sit in Rome and fight with the pope. It is probable that, if we had the malice of the Anglo-Saxon, we would watch our chances and seize the first opportunity to take our revenge. If we attempted this, the odds would be against us, and the first thing we should know would be—nothing! The most of us are capable of perceiving that the man who spits against the wind spits in his own face!

This nation is mad. In its devoted attachment to the Negro, it has run crazy after him; and now, having caught him, hangs on with a deadly grasp, and says to him, with more earnestness and pathos than Ruth expressed to Naomi, "Where thou goest, I will go; where thou lodgest, I will lodge; thy people shall be my people, and thy God, my God." . . .

This rebellion for slavery means something! Out of it emancipation must spring. I do not agree with those men who see no hope in this war. There is nothing in it but hope. Our cause is onward. As it is with the sun, the clouds often obstruct his vision, but in the end, we find there has been no standing still. It is true the government is but little more antislavery now than it was at the commencement of the war; but while fighting for its own existence, it has been obliged to take slavery by the throat and, sooner or later, must choke her to death.

Fifth Passage—Sojourner Truth from her speech to the First Annual Meeting of the American Equal Rights Association, New York City, May 9, 1867

I want women to have their rights. In the courts women have no right, no voice; nobody speaks for them. I wish woman to have her voice there among the pettifoggers. If it is not a fit place for women, it is unfit for men to be there.

I am above eighty years old; it is about time for me to be going. I have been forty years a slave and forty years free and would be here forty years more to have equal rights for all. I suppose I am kept here because something remains for me to do; I suppose I am yet to help to break the chain. I have done a great deal of work; as much as a man, but did not get so much pay. I used to work in the field and bind grain, keeping up with the cradler; but men doing no more, got twice as much pay; so with the German women. They work in the field and do as much work, but do not get the pay. We do as much, we eat as much, we want as much. I suppose I am about the only colored woman that goes about to speak for the rights of colored women. I want to keep the thing stirring, now that the ice is cracked.

What we want is a little money. You men know that you get as much again as women when you write, or for what you do. When we get our rights we shall not have to come to you for money, for then we shall have money enough in our own pockets; and may be you will ask us for money. But help us now until we get it. It is a good consolation to know that when we have got this battle once fought we shall not be coming to you any more. You have been having our rights so long, that you think, like a slave-holder, that you own us. I know that is hard for one who has held the reins for so long to give up; it cuts like a knife. It will feel all the better when it closes up again. I have been in Washington about three years, seeing about these colored people. Now colored men have the right to vote. There ought to be equal rights now more than ever, since colored people have got their freedom. I am going to talk several times while I am here; so now I will do a little singing. I have not heard any singing since I came here.

Sixth Passage—Elie Wiesel, Winner of the Nobel Prize for Peace, 1986, in a 1999 speech at the White House, "The Perils of Indifference: Lessons Learned from a Violent Century"

Indifference is . . . a strange and unnatural state in which the lines blur between light and darkness, dusk and dawn, crime and punishment, cruelty and compassion, good and evil.

. . . We are on the threshold of a new century, a new millennium. What will the legacy of this vanishing century be? . . . So much violence, so much indifference. . . . Of course, indifference can be tempting—more than that, seductive. It is so much easier to look away from victims. It is so much easier to avoid such rude interruptions to our work, our dreams, our hopes. It is, after all, awkward, troublesome, to be involved in another person's pain and despair. Yet, for the person who is indifferent, his or her neighbors are of no consequence. And, therefore, their lives are meaningless. Their hidden or even visible anguish is of no interest. Indifference reduces the other to an abstraction.

Over there, behind the black gates of Auschwitz, the most tragic of all prisoners were the "Muselmanner," as they were called. Wrapped in their torn blankets, they would sit or lie on the ground, staring vacantly into space, unaware of who or where they were, strangers to their surroundings. They no longer felt pain, hunger, thirst. They feared nothing. They felt nothing. They were dead and did not know it.

Rooted in our tradition, some of us felt that to be abandoned by humanity then was not the ultimate. We felt that to be abandoned by God was worse than to be punished by Him. Better an unjust God than an indifferent one. For us to be ignored by God was a harsher punishment than to be a victim of His anger. Man can live far from God—not outside God. God is wherever we are. Even in suffering? Even in suffering.

In a way, to be indifferent to that suffering is what makes the human being inhuman. Indifference, after all, is more dangerous than anger and hatred. Anger can at times be creative. One writes a great poem, a great symphony, have done something special for the sake of humanity because one is angry at the injustice that one witnesses. But indifference is never creative. Even hatred at times may elicit a response. You fight it. You denounce it. You disarm it. Indifference elicits no response. Indifference is not a response.

Indifference is not a beginning; it is an end. And, therefore, indifference is always the friend of the enemy, for it benefits the aggressor— never his victim, whose pain is magnified when he or she feels forgotten. And in denying their humanity we betray our own. . . .

Source: Reprinted with the permission of Elie Wiesel.

CHAPTER THREE

Sharpening Our Tools:
The Basics of Argument

"A nephew of mine—he was about five or six at the time—used to tell me his dreams each morning. One day, . . . he told me: 'Last night I dreamed that I was lost in the forest. I was scared, but I came to a clearing, and there was a white house, made of wood, with a staircase that turned around, with steps with runners, and then a door, and out of this door you came out.' He suddenly stopped: 'But what were you doing in that house?'

—JORGE LUIS BORGES

We never know when our lives may radically change course because of events or opportunities we could never have foreseen. Take the case of Ascension Franco Gonzales. Wednesday, August 29, 2001, was a big day for Gonzales, a dishwasher from Hidalgo, Mexico, now living in Los Angeles, California. While sitting at a bus stop, Gonzales saw an armored truck coming along the street. As the truck drove by, the doors flew open and out fell a plastic bag containing $203,000. Gonzales picked it up and, fearing for his life, hid the loot. After spending an evening trying to figure out what to do, he called the police and handed in the money. Think about it: What would you do if the $203,000 landed in front of you?

He could have snuck back to Hidalgo with his $203,000 and lived off his riches. But he didn't. While listening to the radio, Gonzales heard the DJ wonder if there was anyone honest enough to hand in the missing money. Gonzales affirmed that he was such a man. Plenty of others thought he blew the chance of a lifetime. When asked what would they have done with a bag of money landing at their feet, they said:

RESPONSE #1: Reyna Hernandez, store employee, said, "I wouldn't have turned it in. I would have started a business."

RESPONSE #2: David Widom, social worker, said, "I think I would have turned it in. It's the honorable thing to do."

RESPONSE #3: John Snell, janitor, said, "I wouldn't let the temptation get me. I would resist."

RESPONSE #4: Johnny Shabaz, who thought Gonzales a fool not to take the cash, said, "He's crazy—the man's as crazy as a Betsy bug." (Jocelyn Y. Stewart and Hector Beccerra, "Many Say They Would Have Kept Bag of Loot," *Los Angeles Times,* 30 Aug 2001).

As we can see, each respondent has a different perspective revealing a range of possible responses. Our task as critical thinkers is to be able to follow their reasoning and assess its strength. To do this, we need to have some tools at our command. In this chapter, we will look into the **fundamentals of argumentation.** This includes examining the building blocks of an argument, how to dismantle an argument and how to put one together. This requires us to distinguish descriptions from inferences, how to sort facts from opinions and ideas, and how to recognize the different forms of argumentation. We encounter arguments all the time and in all kinds of settings (even, as with Gonzales, sitting at a bus stop!). This means we have a great deal to gain by developing our skills in this area.

It is useful to see how the mind works and to study what goes into decision making. Consider the case at hand—contrast the chain of reasoning that Gonzales went through with that of Johnny Shabaz. Gonzales's thought process can be set out like so:

I now have a bag with $203,000 in it.
I heard a disc jockey challenge the one who found the bag of money to be honest.
I was the one who found the bag of money.
I'm going to take his challenge.
Being honest means calling the police and turning in the money.
Therefore, I'll call the police and turn in the money.

If we were to gaze into Johnny Shabaz's skull we'd see this:

Gonzales found a bag with $203,000 in it.
Anyone who finds money and doesn't keep it for himself is crazy as a Betsy bug.
Therefore, he's crazy—the man's as crazy as a Betsy bug.

In both cases, we started with the same two facts: (1) the bag of money landed at Gonzales's feet and (2) he had the chance to keep it. Both Gonzales and Shabaz acknowledge that reality. However, the arguments then go in entirely different directions. As you might imagine, this happens all the time. People regularly start from the same place—in terms of the information before them—and end up at polar extremes. This diversity of opinion and lack of predictability should be kept in mind as we observe those around us and examine arguments.

Studying the nuts and bolts of argumentation is crucial for developing critical thinking skills. Ascension Gonzales shows us how one person thinks through a most unexpected opportunity to become wealthy. As we saw, people often react differently to events, and so may arrive at conflicting decisions as to what to do. To put this in perspective, we need to grasp the reasons they think as they do. Being able to dismantle the arguments we come across is crucial for making sense of what we read and hear.

Opinion versus Reasoned Argument

You just finished your shift, so you stopped by the cafeteria for coffee. The people at your table are discussing whether a man on a hunger strike should be force fed if he slips into unconsciousness. Here's what they have to say:

ALISHA: Anyone stupid enough to go on a hunger strike deserves to die! Forget him!

JESS: What's wrong with you, Alisha? Either you die for a noble cause or your life has no meaning!

ANDY: I don't know why you two are fighting. Didn't you study history? Mahatma Gandhi went on hunger strikes for what he believed in, so hunger strikes must be a good thing.

FRANCESCA: Mahatma Gandhi went on hunger strikes when he was competent to decide what was worth dying for. I'm not sure anyone on a hunger strike is competent to make an informed decision. When in doubt, choose what's best for the person's health. Therefore, we should intervene when lives are at stake, whether it's for a hunger strike or anything else. The guy should be force fed.

ERIN: Francesca, why should we listen to you? You're no expert on hunger strikes—or much else for that matter. In fact, you barely made it through high school and had to go to a community college for your degree!

As you can tell, not all of the reasoning rests on a solid foundation. Let's look at this more closely and see just what's going on.

Dismissing with a wave of the hand: Alisha dismisses people on hunger strikes ("stupid"), but offers no reasons for her judgment. Such name-calling does not count as reasoned argument. We need evidence!

Presenting false either/or choices: Jess's "either/or" argument ignores the fact that there are more than two options. Therefore Jess's reasoning is flawed.

Appealing to famous figures as evidence: Andy turns to history, but he fails to explain why, if Gandhi did it, then it must be right. A few words of explanation would make all the difference.

Reasoned argument: Francesca sets out reasons for the life of a person on a hunger strike. Those reasons can be assessed to see if they are convincing, so her argument gives us something to work with.

Personal attack: Erin tried to take down Francesca's argument by a personal attack. However, whether or not Francesca went to public school is irrelevant to the issue being argued. The question is, "Does Francesca offer good reasons for her conclusion?"

We encounter arguments all the time. We need to be able to examine the structure of an argument, set out the evidence, and evaluate it. Once we understand the nuts and bolts of argumentation we can incorporate them into our own thought processes.

Argumentation

An argument is one of the more significant means of persuasion. There are **two components to an argument:** (1) the thesis (conclusion) and (2) the evidence (premises). An author's thesis (conclusion) rests on a set of reasons offered as support. These reasons are called **premises.** An **argument** consists of *only one* conclusion and *at least one* premise. If the same set of evidence is used to support two propositions, treat it as two separate arguments and analyze each one separately. Here's an example of an argument: "Cutting a pet bird's wings is cruel because it limits or eliminates its ability to fly. Birds that can't fly are like guinea pigs with feathers. Only someone who is cruel would turn their bird into the equivalent of a guinea pig."

First, set out the argument. To do this, first identify the conclusion. Then group together as the set of premises all the reasons supporting the conclusion. In the example, the author's thesis (conclusion) is "Cutting a pet bird's wings is cruel." There are three premises. The argument can be set out as follows:

P_1: Cutting a pet bird's wings limits or eliminates the bird's ability to fly.

P_2: Birds that can't fly are like guinea pigs with feathers.

P_3: Only someone who is cruel would turn the bird into the equivalent of a guinea pig.

C: Therefore, cutting a pet bird's wings is cruel.

Ask yourself if there are any assumptions associated with the argument. If so, we need to see if those assumptions are warranted. An **assumption** is treated as a "given"—no proof is usually offered. Assumptions can be **warranted** (defensible) or **unwarranted** (not defensible) and, thus, merit our consideration.

In the case of our pet bird argument, the author assumes that there are no good reasons for cutting a pet bird's wings (such as to protect it from crashing into the window or flying into a ceiling fan). Or if they considered this matter, they dismissed its importance. Also, they assume the life of a pet bird with cut wings is inferior to that of a bird that can fly. That may or may not be true, so the assumption would need to be backed up with some evidence.

We want to evaluate the argument to see if the reasoning is strong. This means looking at the relationship between the premises and the conclusion to assess the quality of support—and to check out any questionable assumptions. In order to accomplish this, we need to develop a range of skills and techniques. We'll then be able to construct and deconstruct arguments and then scrutinize the reasoning involved.

Keep in mind that a strong case means the evidence presented (the premises) gives solid support for the conclusion. That is different from creating a **persuasive** argument, given that we might be persuaded by a threat (agree with me or I'll step on your sore toe), by a celebrity's testimonial (e.g., Bozo likes red balloons, why don't you?), by appeal to patriotism, and so on. The use of irrelevant premises, devious or deceptive reasoning, or other trickery does not constitute good thinking. We'll see how this is done. Let's start with the case of Kate Crisp, who jumped to conclusions and was a long time realizing her error.

CASE STUDY

Dissing Ken Wilbur

Read Kate Crisp's letter to the editor of Shambhala Sun *magazine and then answer the questions that follow. Note that Ken Wilber writes in the area of spirituality and consciousness studies and has published over a dozen books.*

For the past two years I have been dissing Ken Wilber all over town. I just hate the guy. Years ago I was at an art event and a gangly man flailing his arms about knocked me down and didn't apologize. I asked my cohorts who he was and got the reply: "Oh, that's Ken Wilber." After that rude encounter I saw Mr. Ken all around town. I always gave him a surly look and he always ignored me. He would always somehow end up in a line near me, at the post office, at Kinko's, wherever, and he would always be giving a grand, boring discourse to someone. He frequently was with a girl who gazed at him with reverential rapture. Nausea was my m.o. when I saw this "great mind of the western hemisphere."

But the thing that really bugged me about Ken Wilber was the photos. When I saw that photo of him on the cover of the September *Shambhala Sun,* I just knew I had his number . . . on top of all his faults, he was VAIN! I mean really, Ken Wilber does NOT look like that picture at all. Well, maybe a little bit, but obviously the picture was 20 years old or majorly retouched. He looks ancient in real life and his head is about 40 times bigger than that photo reveals.

Well, wouldn't you know it, last week I strolled into Business Express and standing right in front of me was the REAL Ken Wilber, the one on the *Sun* cover. Not MY Ken Wilber, not the person I had been seeing and loathing for years, but someone else. This WAS the person on the magazine cover. I felt totally deflated. Here I had spent all this mental energy hating Ken Wilber and it wasn't even HIM!

Now who the hell was this fake Ken? At least ten people have told me that fake Ken IS Ken. "Look, there is Ken Wilber!" someone always said, much to my annoyance. One of my friends even went up to fake Ken and had a conversation with him and excitedly reported to me "Ken's" words of wisdom.

I am sorry to say that real Ken Wilber just does NOT work as an object of my aggression. True, he does look kind of "LA" in his brand new white Range Rover. And true, he does wear little tank tops and swoopy down jeans that show off his buffy physique. True, he kind of waltzes through space as if to say, "Hey there everybody, I'm smart AND I'm sexy!" but real Ken just doesn't cut it for me. There just isn't enough material for me to work with. The show is over. And the worst part is NOW I've lost another object for all my pent-up aggression. (Letter to the editor, *Shambhala Sun*, March 1997)

Answer the following:

1. What is Crisp's main argument about the fake Ken Wilber? Set out her evidence for concluding that she "hates" (is bugged by) the man she thinks is Ken Wilber.

2. What does she conclude, after she realizes this was NOT the real Ken Wilber?

3. State the strongest claims supporting her statement, "And the worst part is NOW I've lost another object for all my pent-up aggression."

Source: Reprinted with the permission of the *Shambala Sun.*

Descriptions versus Inferences

When we describe, we try to objectively state a set of facts. A good description provides us with the essential features of the thing by listing its qualities or characteristics. An inference is an answer to the question, "What's it about? What story does this tell?"

Descriptions, like a set of facts, are statements about what is or is not the case. A description is usually most helpful if it is as straight forward and impartial as possible. Generally, each item in a description is verifiable by examination. For example, we might describe a friend by giving her height, weight, eye color, hair color and style, and the like. Occasionally an inference sneaks in as a description; for example, when someone says, "He's tall, thin, and a real hunk!" One person's "hunk" is another person's wallpaper, so such value-laden judgments have to be pulled out and placed in the inference category, as they can be quite problematic.

If you were in a crowd trying to find a woman your brother described as a "striking brunette" and are surrounded by dozens of brunettes, you need his sense of "striking." That's not always easy. As a result, we have to watch what is included in the description. Descriptions often act as support—the foundation—for inferences. An inference may or may not be well supported by the evidence behind it.

An **inference** is a conclusion drawn on the basis of a description or other sorts of evidence. Inferences are not necessarily impartial, for they often involve an attempt to make sense of the evidence, not just to report what they see or hear. An example may help. Below is a summary of Marcus Camby's pregame collapse. Now a New York Knicks player, in 1996 Camby was on the U Mass Amherst team when the incident occurred. The inferences are set out in bold:

Marcus Camby, star center for the U Mass basketball team collapsed minutes before a game against St. Bonaventure and was hospitalized in Olean, NY, where he was listed in stable condition last night.

"**He seemed to be in some discomfort** and was holding his head," Nash said. Then Nash saw him collapse "right in front of me. He took a step through the door and dropped." Ed Baron, brother of St. Bonaventure Coach Jim Baron, said of Camby, "His eyes were open. **He looked more scared than anything.**"

"Just about everybody was crying," junior guard Carmelo Travieso said. "You don't want anything to happen to anybody, but **when someone goes to the hospital, you know it's pretty serious.**" (Associated Press, "Camby Remains Stable after Pre-Game Collapse," 14 Jan 1996)

Exercises

Part One

1. Can you think of two inferences you might draw from the descriptions of Camby's collapse and the reaction of those around him?

2. Draw two or three inferences from the fact that at the 2004 Democratic convention, speakers Bill Clinton, Barack Obama, John Edwards, Chris Heinz, and Howard Dean all wore blue ties and George W. Bush wore a blue tie at his inaugural address and for every major speech since, except when he declared war with Iraq (when he wore a red tie). In his acceptance speech at the 2004 Democratic convention, John Kerry wore a red tie.

3. Draw two inferences about math-whizzes from the following:

   Some people probably suspected the math whiz from grade school wasn't in his right mind. Apparently he wasn't—he was in his right *and* his left mind. A recent study of adolescents with above-average math abilities found *the right and left halves of their brains are apparently better able to interact and share* information than the brains of average students.

   "Giftedness in math, music or art may be the by-product of a brain that has functionally organized itself in a different way," said Michael O'Boyle, psychologist at the University of Melbourne and one of the study's co-authors. ("Your Health: A Smarter Brain," Forbes.com, www.forbes.com, 13 Apr 2004)

4. How would you *describe* the photos in Figures 3.1 and 3.2? What would you *infer* is going on? Give your description and draw at least two different inferences for each photograph.

Part Two

Directions: Listed below are blurbs from news items on paying human subjects to take part in risky medical experimentation. Read each blurb and then answer the questions below.

BLURB #1: "In a Scottish study healthy volunteers are paid £600 (around $1,100) to drink orange juice laced with pesticides." (Noted by Lemmons and Elliott, "Justice for the Professional Guinea Pig," *American Journal of Bioethics*, 1 (no. 2)

Source: Photograph from Operation Cue. (Office of Civil and Defense Mobilization, 5 May 1955, from the National Archives, ARC identifier 541789). Reprinted with the permission of the National Archives, Still Pictures Unit.

FIGURE 3.1
How would you describe this? What can we infer from this photo?

BLURB #2: Researchers at the National Institutes of Mental Health (NIMH) and elsewhere pay healthy subjects $100 to take a hallucinogenic drug called keramine [ordinarily used as an animal tranquilizer and also used in date rape]. (Noted by Lemmons and Elliott, "Justice for the Professional Guinea Pig," *American Journal of Bioethics,* 1 (no. 2))

BLURB #3: For Bob Helms, a day at work can literally be a draining experience. "I've gone home with ugly track marks on my arm that take a week to heal. I've fainted, I've passed out for eight hours afterward," said the 44-year-old Helms. . . . Helms is a self-described human guinea pig who, for seven years, has taken money in exchange for his time, blood, urine and sometimes feces as a paid volunteer in drug research trials. . . . But he's clear his motives are not selfless. "I do it because it's a way to catch up on my bills and earn a little," said Helms, who earns $150–$400 a day for his contributions. (Amanda Onion, "Weighing the Risks and Benefits of Human Guinea Pigs," ABCNews.com, 13 Mar 2002)

Source: Members of a party of 17 Canadian and United Kingdom observers shot at Frenchman Flat. (Office of Civil and Defense Mobilization, 5 May 1955, from the National Archives. ARC identifier 558598). Reprinted with the permission of the National Archives, Still Pictures Unit.

FIGURE 3.2
Describe what you see. What can you infer?

Answer the following:

1. Draw two or three inferences about people who volunteer for such experiments.

2. Draw two or three inferences about researchers who participate in such experiments on humans.

3. Write a short argument (paragraph) from the standpoint of a concerned member of society who knows neither such human subjects nor scientists who do experiments on humans such as mentioned here (where the risks are unknown but possibly serious).

When we offer a description, we should try to be impartial. Note any potential for bias or for interference in giving a fair and detailed description. Background knowledge is not necessary—and may even get in the way. When you drew your inferences from looking at the photographs in Figures 3.1 and 3.2, did you think about nuclear explosions? Both photos were taken at nuclear tests. You may find it interesting to look at others taken (they are pretty mind-boggling!) at the National Archives Web site (www.archives.gov).

Studies of eyewitness testimony (such as at an airplane crash) show that those with the most knowledge (such as pilots) are *not* necessarily the best eyewitnesses. The reason is that they fill in the blanks when details are missing—when there are "holes" in the evidence. On the other hand, a child may be a much better bet for obtaining information about what happened and for being able to offer details. Benjaman A. Berman, a former chief of major aviation investigations at the safety board said that pilots make the worst witnesses because their technical knowledge can lead them too quickly to identify a mechanical problem that may not have occurred. "Children make among the best witnesses," he said, "because they don't tend to place an interpretation on what they've seen" (Matthew Wald, "For Air Crash Detectives, Seeing Isn't Believing," *The New York Times,* 23 Jun 2002).

This was shown in the kidnapping/murder case of a five-year-old girl, Samantha Runnion, in July 2002. Her friend was present when Samantha was kidnapped. Her friend was only five years old, but she was able to give such detailed information about the kidnapper *and* the getaway car that police artists were able to publicize a sketch. With that, they caught the killer.

Exercises

Directions: Look at the photographs in Figures 3.3 and 3.4. Answer the following of each photograph:

1. Describe what you see in the photo. (Draw up a list of descriptive items for each photo).

2. What do you think the photo is about? Draw some inferences on the basis of what you see. What is going on here?

3. Look over both your description list and list of inferences and answer this:
   a. What is different about the two lists?
   b. What assumptions came into play when you made your inferences?

4. Look at the photograph of the sign in Figure 3.5. Draw some inferences from this sign (placed on a street in West Hollywood).

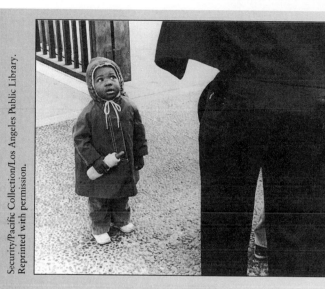

Security/Pacific Collection/Los Angeles Public Library. Reprinted with permission.

FIGURE 3.3
What do you observe? What do you infer?

Security/Pacific Collection/Los Angeles Public Library. Reprinted with permission.

FIGURE 3.4
What do you observe? What do you infer?

FIGURE 3.5
What can you infer about the reason for posting this sign? Do you think drivers obey it?

Credit: Photograph by Wanda Teays.

Group or Individual Exercise

Let's look at the marriage of Al and Milly. Read the letter Al sent Milly and consider what the letter reveals.

Al's Demand Letter to Milly

"**You** *will* see to it: That my clothes and linen are kept in order, That I am served three regular meals a day *in my room*, That my bedroom and study are always kept in good order And that *my desk is not touched by anyone other than me.*

"**You** *will* renounce all personal relations with me, except when these are required to keep up social appearances. In particular you will not request: That I sit with you at home. That I go out with you or travel with you.

"**You** *will* promise explicitly to observe the following points in any contact with me. You will expect no affection from me and you will not reproach me for this. You must answer me at once when I speak to you. You must leave my bedroom or study at once without protesting when I ask you to go.

"**You** *will* promise not to denigrate me in the eyes of the children, either by word or deed." (See "His Head in the Ether, He Was among a 'Sorry Herd of Humans,' " *The New York Times,* 10 Nov 1996).

Answer the following:

1. What do *you* think about this man?

2. What sort of marriage is this? These two questions ask you to draw inferences.

3. What supports your assessment? This is an issue of *evidence.*

Perhaps the fact that this letter was written in 1914 may affect how you see the man and the marriage. This is an issue of *context.* Perhaps the fact that Al was famous may affect your assessment. Or the fact that he was a scientist (as opposed to an artist, surgeon, or truck mechanic) may color your interpretation. Would your inference be different if you knew that "Al" is Albert Einstein, renowned scientist, and "Milly" is Mileva Maric, who met Einstein while a student (she was the only female there studying physics)?

You Tell Me Department

Airline Travel Isn't What it Used to Be

You tell me:

1. What assumptions do you normally make when you board an airline? List them.

2. What assumptions do you normally have about the pilot's interaction with the passengers? State what you would find typical in terms of what the pilot discusses over the loudspeaker and what sorts of comments you'd find unusual or even alarming.

3. Read the following news summary of an unusual cross-country flight in February, 2004. What would you do if you were on this flight? Note that it took place *after* 9/11 and the implementation of security measures on air travel.

"An American Airlines pilot is said to have terrified passengers when he asked Christians on the flight from Los Angeles to New York to identify themselves. They told CBS news that he asked Christians to raise their hands and suggested non-Christians talk to the Christians about their faith. According to one passenger, the pilot stated, 'everyone who doesn't have their hand raised is crazy' and told them, 'you have a choice: you can make this trip worthwhile, or you can sit back, read a book and watch the movie.' The pilot informed passengers that he'd be available for discussion after the flight. Flight attendants notified ground control. American Airlines spokesman Tim Wagner said the incident was being investigated." ("Christian Question Alarms Flight," BBC News, news.bbc.co.uk, 9 Feb 2004). *Note:* It was not reported if any passengers stuck around to chat with the pilot about their faith.

Drawing Inferences

People regularly conclude one thing or another on the basis of what they see or hear. They are *drawing inferences*. An inference is the same as a conclusion. Sometimes the inferences we draw are well founded. Sometimes they are not. Think of those stories about someone who shoots a family member in the middle of the night. You know: The person is awakened by a noise and, seeing it is two or three in the morning when everyone should be tucked in bed, they infer that there is a vicious criminal out to rob or kill them. They grab the shotgun and, when the door opens, let the suspect have it. Unfortunately, they just killed Uncle Roy, who dropped by to give them a surprise present.

Drawing inferences is a part of our lives. We need to examine the evidence to avoid a hasty conclusion. Consider this example: In July 2001, Kevin Pullum, convicted of attempted murder, strolled out of the Los Angeles Twin Towers jail wearing a badge with a photo of actor Eddie Murphy from *Dr. Doolittle 2*. Although the escapee is black, he does not resemble Eddie Murphy. Apparently no one checked Pullum's fake badge as he passed by the security booth. As Bill Cunningham of the Cook County Sheriff's Department in Chicago put it: "He's walking around with a picture of Eddie Murphy on an ID and no one noticed? That's bad. One small mistake can compromise security for the entire jail" (Beth Shuster and Kenneth Reichs, "Jail Escapee is a No-Show at Surrender," *Los Angeles Times*, 17 July 2001).

Not all inferences have the sort of fallout as the case above. We draw inferences as part of our work as students and faculty. But we also draw inferences in relationships (think what Milly must have inferred about her husband Al, from his letter). And so on. Just as juries are presented with evidence from the prosecution and the defense attorneys, we often have to sort through the information and weigh its significance.

GROUP OR INDIVIDUAL EXERCISE

Sleepwalkers Aren't Like They Used to Be

He tried. He failed. The jury just didn't go for 28-year-old fisherman Stephen Otto Reitz's argument that he was sleepwalking when he beat and stabbed his girlfriend to death. That he managed to hit her with a flowerpot and find his knife to stab her all while sleeping just didn't ring true to the jury. Read the excerpt and then share your assessment of the jury's reasoning:

Reitz claimed he was dreaming that he was fighting off an intruder when he attacked his married girlfriend, a defense known as "somnambulatory homicide." . . . Juror Tom Mahoney said the panel had found Deputy District Attorney Ken Lamb's scenario that Reitz had fought with Eva Maria Weinfurtner, 42, before the beating, more believable than the defense's unconscious sleepwalking theory. He cracked a flowerpot over Weinfurtner's head twice and beat and stabbed her multiple times. Jurors who spoke outside the courtroom said they rejected the sleepwalking defense pretty much from the start of their 15 hours of deliberations, which began Tuesday. . . .

The fact that Reitz hit her with the flower pot first, then was able to find the knife and stab her indicated he was conscious during the attack, [Juror] Mahoney said . . . "She was covered with bruises. Whatever he did, he did it for a while." "There were deep gouges out of her neck," said Juror No. 3, of San Pedro, who declined to give his name. "That would take too much energy out of him if he was sleeping." Lamb applauded the jury for rejecting the sleepwalking defense. "We live in a day where the defense can bring up any theory to not be held accountable," he said. "This case was won because the jury recognized there was no evidence he was sleepwalking."

The trial began June 14 and included testimony from several defense experts that Reitz had organic brain damage. A sleep expert, Dr. Clete Kushida of Stanford University's sleep clinic, testified Reitz had three types of disorders: sleep terrors, sleepwalking and REM sleep disorder, in which people act out their dreams.

But in closing arguments, Lamb posited that the couple had been fighting and that Reitz may have become enraged when Weinfurtner locked him out of the hotel room. A sheriff's detective testified that other hotel guests heard someone banging on the door to Reitz's and Weinfurtner's room. Juror Roel Salvador, a 26-year-old Long Beach student and laboratory technician, said the deliberations were grave. "Everything was pretty intense in there," Salvador said. "It was a serious case." (Leslie Simmons, "Jury Rejects Sleepwalking Claim in Murder Case," *Los Angeles Daily [Law] Journal*, 25 Jun 2004)

Exercises

Part One

1. Given the information below, what are some possible inferences that could be drawn about juries:

"We have a lot of highly publicized cases, and with highly publicized cases people tend to form opinions," says Jeff Frederick, director of jury research at Charlottesville National Legal Research Group in Virginia. "There is concern about the possibility of jurors coming in with a little bit more of a fixed notion of what they want to do."

In part, the phenomenon may reflect the times, say some experts. Corporate scandals like Enron can make malfeasance cases appear to be opportunities to dispense social justice.

"You get in there [as a juror], and you want to help the little guy," says Gillian Drake, founder and director of On Trial Associates, a legal consultancy in Chevy Chase, Md. Lawyers leverage such feelings. In the [Martha] Stewart case, for example, "the prosecution knew it was the jury issue, not the legal issue, so they played up the jury issue, which was class consciousness. They took advantage of that. There are jury issues and there are legal issues . . . [and] depending on which side you're on, sometimes you're trying to blend them and sometimes you're trying to keep them separate," she adds. (Clayton Collins, "Jurors: The Lowlights in Some High-Profile Trials," *Christian Science Monitor*, www.csmonitor.com, 5 Apr 2004)

2. What can you infer from the comments of W. D. Richter, director of *Slither*, *Dracula*, and *Invasion of the Body Snatchers*:

When I was a kid, I liked horror and science fiction films as much as I liked anything. I actually probably watched them a little more religiously. I'd go to the movies by myself to see *The Day of the Triffids* [1963] and *The Blob* [1958] and all that stuff. It's just a wonderful release of the human imagination. I think that's its ultimate appeal: it takes you somewhere out there and makes you picture a universe that's just far more fantastic than the little town you're living in, or whatever your particular arena is at that time. (Matthew R. Bradley, "An Interview with W. D. Richter," in Kevin McCarthy and Ed Gorman, eds. *"They're Here . . ." Invasion of the Body Snatchers: A Tribute*, Berkeley: Boulevard Books, 1999)

3. State what you can infer about the impact cell phones have had on our society from the following:

Perhaps the most famous breach of cell phone–church etiquette happened at the Vatican in May when 155 Roman Catholic cardinals bowed in prayer during a rare meeting called by Pope John Paul II. A cell phone went off and kept ringing until one very embarrassed cardinal—his face undoubtedly matching his scarlet cap—reached into his black cassock and silenced the phone . . .

[*And another example*] At a picturesque church near Victorville in June, the bride and groom stood before the Catholic priest when his cell phone went off. "At first, I thought maybe it was some kind of joke," said Mary Lou Fulton of Long Beach, whose cousin was getting married. The phone rang three more times during the ceremony. "I felt so bad," she said. "It was quite a culture clash—the ancient rites of marriage and someone fumbling with a cell phone." (William Lobdel, "Cell Phone Etiquette Sins Hit a New Low," *Los Angeles Times*, 2 July 2001)

4. State what you can infer about those who detest bad punctuation from the following:

While we look in horror at a badly punctuated sign, the world carries on around us, blind to our plight. We are like the little boy in *The Sixth Sense* who can see dead people, except that we can see dead punctuation. Whisper it in petrified little-boy tones: dead punctuation is invisible to everyone else—yet we see it *all the time*. No one understands us seventh-sense people. They regard us as freaks. When we point out illiterate mistakes we are often aggressively instructed to "get a life" by people who, interestingly, display no evidence of having lives themselves. Naturally we become timid about making our insights known, in such inhospitable conditions. Being burned as a witch is not safely enough off the agenda. (Lynne Truss, *Eats, Shoots & Leaves*, Penguin Books, 2003)

Part Two

1. Do two rounds of describing someone (in writing preferably, or verbally if in group activity—draw from a list of athletes, singers, models, actors, politicians, or the like). For example, you could select a model in a print ad to use as the basis of your description.

Round One: Describe the person in as much detail as you can without mentioning the race or ethnicity. After you finish, add a paragraph of reflections on the ease or difficulty of omitting race/ethnicity from the description.

Round Two: Describe the person in as much detail as you can, including race or ethnicity. After you finish, compare the two descriptions and note to what degree this additional element added or detracted from the quality of your description.

2. Read the following comments by Keith M. Woods and write a brief response (e.g., a paragraph) to his position:

Race/ethnicity continues to be used as a means of describing people, though it carries no true color and offers a mind-boggling range of eye/ear/nose/mouth/skin-color combinations from which to choose. It is imprecise, often bordering on inaccurate, to describe someone by race/ethnicity. Those are ethical concerns, and the harm done by such "racial profiling" demands of journalists the highest level of care and thoughtfulness. . . .

Our conditioning, in the United States and many parts of the world, is to accept without question the validity of describing people by race/ethnicity. If we have enough additional information—clothing, distinctive scars or birthmarks, etc.—we assume race/ethnicity is a valid descriptor. But unless the description involves the color of a person's skin—be it mahogany, tan, olive, peach—race/ethnicity has narrowed the field about as well as if we'd said the suspect was wearing pants.

Police departments are not in the habit of providing that level of detail, though they may have it available. Journalists need to demand more. (Keith M. Woods, "Handling Race/Ethnicity in Descriptions: A Teaching Module," Poynteronline, www.poynter.org, 6 Aug 2002).

Part Three

What can we infer when we read descriptions of people as having "mocha skin"? Does this indicate greater or lesser acceptance of people of color? What sorts of societal attitudes are behind this descriptive phrase? Read each of the following descriptions and share your thoughts about referring to others in this manner:

Description #1: "Shicky-micky, swanky, white. These are the words that come to mind to describe Nikki Beach, the latest addition to the Westin Regina in Marina Vallarta. . . . Nikki Beach is a wonderland of elegant, catlike humans sprawling on beach beds scattered on the silky sand, sipping martinis and talking the talk that swanky people do. . . . I slowly wove my way through the palm trees and past the palapa bar, mesmerized by the angelic humans, dressed in white from every flawlessly-styled hair to each manicured toe, shaking their trim bottoms to the rhythmic bhum-bhum of the snare drum and shamelessly displaying *mocha-colored skin* and not a sign of a tan line" ("Nikki Beach: A Slice of Heaven?," *Teen Music,* www.teenmusic.com, 24 April 2004).

Description #2: "Awuah, 38, who is married with two children, acknowledges the obstacles ahead. He is a wiry, compactly built man with mocha-colored skin and round wire-rimmed glasses. He described the provenance of his desire to build the university" ("Ghanaian Sees Education as Key to Africa's Future," *Vallarta Today*, www.vallartatoday.com, 28 Nov 2003).

Description #3: "Melissa St. Joy, Miss FAMU for 2000–2001, looks like the typical student on campus, her mocha-colored skin and hazel eyes are common. Her ethnicity, however, is not. She is Haitian American" ("Melissa St. Joy, First Haitian Descendant to Serve as Miss FAMU," Florida Agricultural & Mechanical University Office of Public Affairs, www.famu.edu, 6 Sep 2000).

Facts, Opinions, and Ideas

In the course of our daily activities, we often come across someone citing a fact (known quantity or verifiably the case), expressing an opinion (conjecture or statement of belief), or offering an idea (solution or recommendation). Since any or all of these may play a role in a person's reasoning and decision making, it is useful to think about facts, opinions, and ideas. Let's start with facts.

When we think of facts, we think of things or events known to be true. This covers actual occurrences and actions, performing, as well as pieces of information presented as having an objective reality. It also includes concepts that can be proven true, as seen in science and mathematics. **Facts** are actually the case, known by observation or authentic testimony (as with a credible source), as opposed to what is inferred, conjectured or invented. We make the contrast of fact with fiction. Statements of fact include all that we can say are "true." As noted in the *Oxford English Dictionary*, we might say "imagination is often at war with reason and fact."

Generally we think of facts as empirically verifiable, true by definition or a mathematical proof. Empirically based facts can be proven by means of our five senses—sight, smell, touch, taste, and hearing. For instance: "Carrots are vegetables" and "Water freezes at 32° Fahrenheit." Mathematical definitions, axioms, and proven theorems operate as facts—treated as true by definition or derivation (derived from theorems and postulates).

We tend not to question that which is presented as fact—especially by those regarded as trustworthy. That is not always wise, as we have seen with the cases of journalists (e.g., Jayson Blair for *The New York Times*) who fabricated details and made up stories that were published as factually correct. Furthermore, the newspaper itself (*The Times*) apologized for its own failure to seek verification on claims that Iraq had weapons of mass destruction (later proved false).

Factual judgments are often treated as facts, as we see with "Smog is bad for your lungs." These are generally inferences drawn from earlier observations; for example, about the sorts of ingredients in smog and the studies that show the effects of those ingredients on the respiratory system. Some argue that factual judgments are not really facts and, thus, should be assessed carefully, as they can mislead us. The rule of thumb here is: A factual judgment is not normally as strong as a fact, as it is at least one step away. This step means that the inference drawn on the basis of the fact cannot be assumed to be true, but must be scrutinized.

Opinions fall into three major categories. First are statements of belief or **conjecture.** This is seen in the following: "The best music is rhythm and blues" and "Practicing verb drills is a drag." Opinions are often based on perception, individual taste, or emotion, relative to the point of view of the person(s) voicing the opinion. This gives rise to the refrain, "Well, that's just a matter of opinion." This indicates the opinion is relative to the speaker's bias and may or may not have evidence to support them. "Public opinion" is a synthesis or shared view of the people, the collective. The source for most statements of public opinion is one or more polls (either a random sample or an orchestrated study meant to mirror the key traits of the targeted population).

The second category of opinion is the **reasoned speculation** or conjecture of someone well versed in the area in question. This is seen as follows: "Mad cow disease must have jumped to other species, like sheep, because of the animal feed" and "Those who thought Lenin had syphilis must have been on to something, given the reported symptoms he showed." The difference between this category and the first one is that here it is expected that evidence *could be cited* and some agreement might then be reached with the listener, whereas there is no such expectation in those that are relative to taste or perception.

The third category of opinion is **legal opinion.** In a legal context, opinions may be expressed as a formal statement, a ruling, or considered advice. Court opinions, for example, function as an explanation for a decision that becomes law. Court opinions have legal force, so in high-profile or controversial cases such opinions are widely studied for their significance and likely consequences on future cases. The reasoning of the judge(s) or justices can guide future policies and decision making and may act as a precedent for years to come.

Facts and Opinions

Fact, analysis, and opinion are often linked, though opinions may or may not have a factual basis. It is a fact that we utter words. What they signify requires analysis and whether the speaker thinks they make sense or not is a matter of opinion. When people set out the reasons for an opinion, we now have an argument. The issue of what is fact versus what is opinion should not be taken lightly.

It helps to see why clarifying facts and opinions matters. Think of criminal law. The fate of a defendant could rest on how fallible we consider the fingerprints found on the weapon or at the scene of the crime in determining guilt or innocence. Court challenges are calling for a reassessment of the traditional view of fingerprints:

> Edward J. Imwinkelried, a leading expert on forensic science who has worked with prosecutors and defense lawyers, said there was a "very good possibility" that the challenges would lead judges to instruct juries that a fingerprint analyst was not a scientist offering exact conclusions but an expert giving an opinion.

That, said Mr. Imwinkelried, a law professor at the University of California at Davis, "could conceivably be an important weapon in the hands of defense counsel, because you've got a widespread public perception that fingerprint testimony is infallible." (Andy Newman, "Fingerprinting's Reliability Draws Growing Court Challenges," www.law-forensic.com)

The issue is not moot. Consider the case of poor Brandon Mayfield, an Oregon attorney whose fingerprints were a partial match to one print on a plastic bag found in a van driven by the Madrid terrorist-bombers (causing the death of 191 people and injuring hundreds more). The FBI reportedly looked only at the scanned fingerprints and not the original print. Acting on their suspicion of Mayfield, the FBI froze his bank accounts and assets. They detained Mayfield in jail for 17 days before realizing their error. They issued an apology and explanation:

> The FBI identification was based on an image of substandard quality, which was particularly problematic because of the remarkable number of points of similarity between Mayfield's prints and the print details in the images submitted to the FBI. The FBI's Latent Fingerprint Unit will be reviewing its current practices and will give consideration to adopting new guidelines for all examiners receiving latent print images when the original evidence is not included. . . . The FBI apologizes to Mr. Mayfield and his family for the hardships that this matter has caused. (FBI press release, www.fbi.gov)

You might find it interesting to research the case of Brandon Mayfield and get a broader sense of what was set in motion once the FBI noticed the partial match in the fingerprints. As we see by what followed, facts and opinions can take on a life of their own.

Ideas and Hypotheses

Fact and opinions often lead to generating ideas. *Ideas* take the form of possible solutions, hypotheses, intentions, plans of action, and theories. The ancient roots of the word go back to a general or ideal form, pattern, vision, or standard by which things are measured. More commonly now, we use the term to refer to insights, purposes, or recommendations. Some ideas are creative leaps, springing from visions or mental images, connected by the finest of threads. Other ideas are mental constructs we generate from our observations or factual data. Some ideas are narrowly focused; others are broad and sweeping.

Ideas may strike like lightening, unexpected and piercing. Some ideas appear in dreams, or daydreams, with no clear stimulus. On the other hand, they may come in the course of addressing a particular problem, as if part of an organic process. *The Oxford English Dictionary* mentions the "idea man" in Hollywood—someone paid to dream up plots or give new life to old stories, myths, and earlier movies.

Ideas sometimes come through a side door, when our attention is focused elsewhere. Have you ever tried to write a paper and just stared fruitlessly at the computer? You give up and are in the middle of doing dishes or talking on the phone, when an idea springs forth from the top of your head. That's the creative dimension of ideas that cannot be forced or programmed. Anyone can have an opinion. But not everyone can have an idea—much less a good idea.

Exercises

Part One

1. Ad on a sign outside an ARCO gas station in Bakersfield, California: "One in three body builders pump ARCO gas." Offer some ideas about how you might substantiate the claim being made.

2. At the 7-Eleven Web site (www.7-eleven.com), a news release on 7-11's new ads contained fine print at the bottom of the page as follows:

   Copyright © 7-Eleven, Inc. 2004. All rights reserved.
   This site is intended for residents of the US and Canada, excluding Quebec.

State three ideas as to why Quebec is excluded. (If you can, find evidence for any *one* of your hypotheses/ideas and share it).

3. The following factual claims were made on the TV show *60 Minutes* ("Fingerprints: Infallible Evidence?" *60 Minutes,* www.cbsnews.com, 6 Jun 2004). Read them and offer several ideas about what we ought to do about using fingerprint evidence in trials:
   a. There's complete disagreement amongst fingerprint examiners themselves as to what they need to see in order to declare a match.
   b. In Italy, for example, examiners say they have to see 16 or 17 points of similarity.
   c. In Brazil, it's 30; in Sweden, it's 7 points; and in Australia, it's 12.
   d. Most examiners in the United States, including those at the FBI, don't even use a point system in testing for a match.
   e. Over the last 100 years, there have been only a handful of cases where convictions have been reversed because of faulty fingerprint identification, but that doesn't mean examiners don't make mistakes.
   f. Judges don't require that fingerprint experts who testify be certified.

Part Two

Directions: One recommendation to ward off insect bites is to use repellents that contain DEET. However, research raises concerns that DEET might have been a factor in the Gulf War syndrome. Read about the study and then answer the questions below:

A study done at Duke University and published in the November 2001 *Journal of Experimental Neurology* showed that frequent and prolonged applications of DEET (in an average human dose adjusted to rat size) caused neurons to die in regions of rat brains that control muscle movement, learning, memory, and concentration.

"The rats didn't look any different," says lead researcher Mohamed Abou-Donia, PhD, professor of pharmacology and cancer biology at Duke, "but when we challenged them with a task, they failed." Abou-Donia became interested in this subject while studying veterans who used DEET in concentrations of 70% and in concert with permethrin (not recommended, by the way). "We think part of the problem experienced by some vets may be due to DEET," says Abou-Donia, referring to Gulf War veterans' illness. (Star Lawrence, "How to Be Repellent—to Bugs," Msn.health, content.health.msn.com, 28 May 2004).

Answer the following questions:

1. What *facts* were stated in this report? List them.
2. What *questions* do you have after reading the report above?
3. State three to four *inferences* that could be drawn from the report.
4. Is it safe to conclude that DEET is a key factor in the Gulf War syndrome?
5. Is your conclusion affected by knowing that in Canada DEET concentrations cannot exceed 30 percent, whereas in the United States, hundreds of products, some with concentrations of 100 percent DEET, are sold over the counter?

Bringing Ideas to Life

Philosopher Ludwig Wittgenstein said ideas "sometimes fall from the tree before they are ripe." Not all ideas are good or feasible, in light of the costs or resources. However, "brainstorming" (generating a set of ideas) could be the catalyst for a major breakthrough. That's why problem-solving sessions often start with generating ideas freely, quickly, and without editing, judgment, or criticism.

Consider the case of Heung Bae Kim, who had an idea when he was a medical student in the early 1990s. Watching a difficult operation on a child's intestines, he thought that there must be a better way to do it. He came up with an alternative that was much simpler than the complicated procedure he witnessed. After he sketched it out, he showed it to a surgeon (one of his professors), who said it would never work. Dr. Kim wrote it off as a lame idea.

Ten years passed and Dr. Kim was once again watching the difficult surgery. This time he shared his idea with another surgeon, Dr. Tom Jaksic, who thought it "brilliant." The story gets even better: Dr. Jaksic had a one-year-old patient whose small intestine was too short to work properly and so had to be fed intravenously. Dr. Kim's idea from his student years appeared to be just what the baby needed. After first testing it on pigs, the procedure was successfully used on the baby. Evidently the idea so simplified the surgery that experts were surprised no one thought of it before. (Denise Grady, "Brainstorm to Breakthrough: A Surgical Procedure Is Born," *The New York Times*, 4 Aug 2003). Of course, not all ideas are worthwhile and many are hard to evaluate without empirical or other studies. But, as shown by Dr. Kim's breakthrough, some ideas have made significant impact in a field of study or upon a group of people.

The Global Dimension

Fingerprinting Travelers to the United States

Italian philosopher, Giorgio Agamben, opted out of teaching the Spring 2004 semester at New York University in protest against the finger-printing of arriving visitors and employees from other countries. Read the passages below and then list his key points. Note what you consider his strongest point (and why).

> Prof. Agamben says he is deeply opposed to using biological methods to track citizens, including finger and retina prints and subcutaneous tattooing for political purposes. By applying these techniques and devices invented for the dangerous classes to individual citizens, governments have made humanity itself the dangerous class. He views fingerprinting as a kind of tattooing reminiscent of that done during the Holocaust, when Jews and others had numbers tattooed on their inner arms. Agamben says:
>
> "A few years ago I wrote that the political model of the west is not the city but the concentration camp, not Athens but Auschwitz. That was, of course, a philosophical, not a historical thesis. This is not about mixing phenomena that must be separated. I only want to remind readers that the tattooing in Auschwitz possibly appeared as 'normal' and economic in order to regulate the admission of the deportees to the camp. The bio-political tattooing, which we are forced to undergo today in order to enter the United States is a relay race to what we could tomorrow accept as the normal registration of the identity of the good citizen considering the mechanisms and machinery of the state." (As quoted by Standard Schaefer, "Italian Philosopher Giorgio Agamben Protests US Travel Policies," *Counterpunch*, www.counterpunch.org, 23 Jan 2003)

Exercises

Part One

Directions: Identify each of the following as fact, opinion, or idea.

1. Identify the facts (or statements of fact), opinions, and ideas in the following:
   a. The Pistons defeated the Lakers and won the NBA championship of 2004
   b. The Pistons only won because Kobe was upset about his upcoming trial on rape charges.
   c. Phil Jackson's contract as coach was not renewed after the "Lakers'" loss.
   d. It was a travesty that Jerry West let Phil Jackson go.
   e. The Lakers should study the tapes of the games so they can learn how to beef up their offense.
   f. The series was covered by TV stations around the world and translated into many languages.
   g. Rick Fox was right on when he said that the Lakers played like a bunch of individuals instead of a team!
   h. The Pistons should keep their humility and good teamwork and maybe even bring in Phil Jackson as assistant coach!

     i. Some people at the Pistons' victory parade dressed in silly costumes and a bunch of them wore Afro wigs.

     j. Perhaps one of the Lakers should try an Afro—it might bring some good luck to the team.

     k. The win marked the third championship for Detroit, the first since the 1989–90 season.

     l. Rasheed Wallace and Tayshaun Prince were like jaguars on the court, whereas the Lakers resembled water buffalo.

     m. Yeah, well the Lakers will make the Pistons look like the Spark Plugs next year!

2. Indicate what is fact, opinion, or idea in the following (Cindy Rodriguez's "Getting Real in Today's Fantasyland," *Denver Post,* www.denverpost.com, 7 Jun 2004):

     a. If you acknowledge that you want someone who is a few notches above you, then you suffer from low self-esteem or delusion.

     b. I have a solution: Date sideways—Find someone who is real, who makes you laugh and who—this is the most important part—wants you, too.

     c. In June 2004 *Maxim* magazine had an article titled, "Out of Your League and in the Bag."

     d. Let's just admit this up front: A book on dating down won't sell.

3. Identify the facts (or statements of fact), opinions, and ideas in the following.

     a. The state of Arkansas has 450,000 children in public schools.

     b. The Arkansas Center for Health Improvement found that 40 percent (180,000) of Arkansas children were either overweight or at risk for obesity.

     c. Parents ought to give their children healthier snacks, such as fruit and vegetables.

     d. The state of Arkansas banned vending machines at elementary schools.

     e. Parents should restrict TV and computer time.

     f. It is ridiculous for Arkansas' "food police" to tell children not to drink sodas.

     g. These kids should be advised to get more exercise than they are currently getting.

     h. If parents put their children on stringent diets, some children's health could suffer.

     i. This is setting up kids to feel bad about how they are and could make weight problems worse, not better.

     j. You can bet the obese kids will get asked, "Hey, Piggie, how much do you weigh?"

     k. The state of Arkansas has set up school nutrition and exercise committees.

     l. Arkansas should look to the example of Illinois, the only state in the nation that requires physical education through high school.

Part Two

Directions: Read over the information about Firestone tires connected with deaths involving Ford Explorers. (Garth R. Smith, "Firestone Tires and the Ford Explorer," www.suite101.com, 19 Sep 2000). State the four to five key *facts* that you think would be useful in a complaint against Firestone.

1. After being blamed as the cause of numerous accidents and as many as 88 deaths involving Ford Explorers, Firestone has begun a recall of several of their tires in the South and Southwestern states.

2. Other regions of the country are expected to become part of the recall in the future.

3. Included in the recall are the Firestone Wilderness and ATX lines, both of which are used as the original equipment for the Ford Explorer.

4. Thus far only tires in the size of P235/75R15 with a serial number beginning with the letters "VD" are subjected to the recall.

5. Firestone has in the past recalled the same tires on vehicles in South America and the Middle East.

6. Consumers who own Ford Explorers or other SUVs equipped with these tires would be advised to visit their local Firestone dealer or other tire retailer in order to have their tires inspected.

7. Ford CEO Jacques Nasser stated that the defects claimed to have caused 88 deaths in the United States are "a tire issue, not a vehicle issue." He also said the Ford was "sorry that these tires are on our vehicles."

8. Firestone is allowing for drivers to be reimbursed for the purchase of non-Firestone brand tires up to $100 per tire.

9. Several newspaper articles (in September 2000) claimed that Ford officials as early as 1989 knew that the Explorer, which replaced the Bronco II, was susceptible to rolling over.

10. This air pressure change while increasing handling and lessening the likelihood of rollover can cause an overheating of the tires and hinder the dissipation of that heat which could lead to tire failure.

Good Arguments, Bad Arguments

Arguments are all around us; the question is what to make of them. Arguments consist of **propositions**. A proposition is an assertion that predicates some characteristic of the subject. It is true or false. For example: "All zoo animals are creatures

You Tell Me Department

Bigger Breasts through Vacuum Cups?

Just when you thought the breast-enlargement business had gone about as far as it could, a new product called Brava hit the market in the summer of 2001. The target is an estimated 16 million women who want to have larger breasts; and the company hopes for a windfall. Brava is a vacuum-based system in which large plastic domes act as suctions over the breasts, presumably increasing the fluid level in the breasts. With the increased fluid, the breast will be fuller up to one cup size. Unfortunately, to get this result women have to wear the suction-domes at least 10 hours a day for 10 weeks.

The device is recommended for women between 18 and 40 years old who hope to plump up the breast or help a sagging (but not too sagging!) breast. It is not for those who are pregnant, breast-feeding, have breast cancer, or have scarring in the breast from past surgeries. Within four months, 1,000 women have been fitted with the Brava breast vacuum. The average cost is around $2,500 each. Dr. Roger Khouri, inventor of Brava, insists the product is safe. The FDA (Food and Drug Administration) elected not to regulate it, considering it a very low risk. However, the FDA did not assess its effectiveness. The manufacturer claims the process is not painful, but can cause an uncomfortable pulling sensation. It requires a lifestyle adjustment (such as sitting up straight) so the vacuum-seal is not broken.

Apparently breast cancer surgeon, Dr. Susan Love, does not think it will do any short-term harm. However, Dr. Susan Downey of USC doubts if the changes would be permanent. In any case, the company is optimistic about the potential market. Individual women using Brava have to make major adjustments. For example,

[Customer Linda Langer] is curbing her social life because she has to be home by 8 P.M. to have sufficient time to strap the device on, hook it up and keep it running while she tries to sleep. With an alarm system that lately has been going off about three times a night—whenever her movements break the domes' vacuum seal, she's suffering from lack of sleep. She's also been forced to change many habits. Because she does a lot of writing at the computer, she had to learn to sit "very erect. You can't slump because you'll lose the seal." (Jane E. Allen, "Breast Enhancement in the Privacy of Your Own Home," *Los Angeles Times,* 2 July 2001).

You tell me: What facts are claimed about Brava? What opinions are expressed about the device? What are some reasons women may be leery about using this product? Share your response to Steve Lopez, who comments:

I don't expect to ever understand the opposite sex in my lifetime. But one woman, whose identity must be withheld, would toss my shorts into the street in about two seconds if I suggested she place her privates into suction domes for roughly 10 hours a day through mid-September. First of all, she doesn't like to vacuum anything. Second, she would say something about women trying to make themselves look like beer commercial bimbos for "idiot men."

"Have they thought about strapping that thing to their heads?" she'd ask. Dr. Khouri, creator of Brava, actually liked the idea. "Smart women tell me that's the most important sex organ," he said. "We could call it Brainva." (*Los Angeles Times,* 4 July 2001)

---

fond of looking at people." The *subject* is "zoo animals" and the *predicate* is "are creatures fond of looking at people." In an argument we have one proposition that is the conclusion and at least one other that is a premise. It's crucial that we be able to recognize these two components in the argument.

The terms "thesis" and "conclusion" will be used interchangeably here. If you are the author, you usually start with a thesis and then proceed to make your case by laying out your evidence. The collection of your evidence constitutes the set of premises. When you stand back and look at your argument, you can see the premises working together to support the thesis. The conclusion of your argument is the thesis that rests on those premises. Thus, we can see it as the conclusion of your argument.

The *first step* in dismantling an argument is to locate the conclusion (thesis). If we don't know where the argument is headed, we're lost in a fog. Once the conclusion is clear, we can see how the argument is structured. This entails setting out the premises—the evidence offered as support of the conclusion, the thesis. So, after pinpointing the author's thesis we list the premises. Before we proceed to weigh the evidence, it is generally advisable to consider any assumptions that factor into the equation.

Assumptions may be a factor in an argument. An **assumption** is something that is taken for granted or supposed to be the case without proof. Occasionally they are made explicit; but they are often unstated. Clarify key assumptions and watch for unwarranted assumptions—an argument can turn on hidden assumptions.

Missing Premises and Unstated Assumptions

Arguments often have unstated assumptions or missing premises. If so, we must decide what has been omitted because this is an area where prejudice, bias, or questionable beliefs can be hidden. Even if the missing premises are legitimate, it is important to state them. Each piece of evidence, every single reason, articulated or not, should be set out. Each one can then be examined for its role in offering support for the conclusion.

For instance, *look at the argument:* "High school women runners should not be allowed to wear short shorts in running a race. Short shorts may help them run faster, but they are unacceptable clothing for a public event. Short shorts distract the male viewer. Many people who attend track meets are males. It is not a good thing for men to be distracted or offended." *The premises are:*

P_1: Short shorts may help high school women run faster, but they are unacceptable clothing for a public event.

P_2: Short shorts are distracting for the male viewer.

P_3: Many people who attend track meets are males.

P_4: It is not a good thing for men to be distracted or <u>offended</u>.

Conclusion: High school women should not be allowed to wear short shorts in running a race.

One concern is whether there are any unwarranted assumptions—for example, in going from the claim about men being distracted or offended to the claim that women runners should not be permitted to wear such clothing. Unwarranted assumptions must be taken into account in assessing the argument.

Exercises

1. What is assumed on the part of those who claim that the position of male (or, for that matter, female) viewers should be a factor in setting rules and regulations about high school women's clothing allowed for a race?

2. Exactly what should we be able to rightfully assume about setting regulations around runners' clothing?

3. Are the assumptions behind the argument, above, resting on a firm foundation, or are they without legitimacy?

Warranted and Unwarranted Assumptions

Most people operate most of the time with a set of assumptions. These assumptions shape how they see the world and how they think. One of our tasks is to recognize and make explicit any assumptions. We can then decide whether or not they rest on solid footing (i.e., are **warranted**) or whether they are questionable or without merit (i.e., are **unwarranted**).

If there is evidence to support the assumption, it is a warranted assumption and, if not, it is unwarranted. This evidence should be stated in the argument itself. Watch for unwarranted assumptions, for they should be made explicit and treated like premises. In this way, we can dismantle the argument before us.

Checklist

- Locate the conclusion (author's thesis).
- Set out the premises.
- The premises should provide a clear link to the conclusion.
- Watch for omissions and questionable claims.
- The case needs to be as strong as possible.
- If it seems like a strong case, see how the evidence supports the conclusion.
- Determine the weakest link in case you need to bolster it.
- If the argument is not convincing, find the weaknesses in the reasoning.
- Any questionable or unwarranted assumptions should be treated like premises and analyzed accordingly.

Some arguments are convincing. If the support is strong and clearly supports the conclusion if we assume it were true, we'd say we have a good argument.

Exercises

Directions: Find the *conclusion* in the arguments below. If there's no argument, say so.

1. Sleep all day. Party all night. Never grow old. Never die. It's fun to be a vampire. (Movie poster for *The Lost Boys*).

2. Vampires are scarier than cyborgs, even though cyborgs seem to be physically stronger. As a result, there won't be many more *Terminator* sequels like the endless vampire films that we never seem to tire of.

3. They say vampires have no reflection. This is based on the traditional view that mirrors reflect your soul. Evil demons have no soul and we know vampires are certainly evil.

4. Dracula's commands have to be obeyed—otherwise he would lose his temper. Therefore, it was no joking matter when Dracula told the merchant to leave his valuable belongings on the street (McNally and Florescu, *In Search of Dracula*).

5. Many people may be "iffy" in the face of death, but everyone fears the loss of blood and infections such as AIDS. *Nosferatu* compares the bubonic plague with the spread of the vampire disease. Vampire movies by Coppola and Rice draw similarities between the prolonged effects of vampire attacks and AIDS. The element of danger, mystery, and even death associated with sex is thus recreated in a contemporary context (adapted from McNally and Florescu, *In Search of Dracula*, 1994).

6. Some film critics thought the werewolf scenes were second-rate in *Prisoner of Azkaban* and should have been cut. However, the werewolf had children in the audience wailing—especially when it chased Harry and Hermione. This suggests that the critics simply underestimated the power of the werewolf mythology.

7. Neither robots nor cyborgs are as scary as vampires. This could be due to the fact that they don't suck your blood or need to be killed with a stake through the heart. For that matter, vampires have no heart.

8. The movie *I, Robot* has lots of robots run amok. Lots of them. But you only need one Terminator (a cyborg *not* a robot) or one Dracula to scare the pants off the audience. With robots, however, we only seem to be scared of dying of exhaustion fighting them off. That's why the robot movies have to interject another element, like in *Robocop,* where we see the robot as a "person."

9. *Robocop* was an interesting study on that netherland between human and machine. *There* was a movie where the humans were more evil than the machines. In fact, it's because of corrupt corporations and evil *people* that the machines were a problem. On the other hand, it's hard to think of a robot as capable of friendship. Therefore, all those films with robot sidekicks, like *Star Wars*, are not very realistic.

10. *Robocop's* lead "robot" is not your typical robot. Here's why: sure it is built like a robot, looks like a robot, and is meant to behave like a robot. But it has a human element, a few characteristics like the human it was modeled after. Remember how "he" twirls the gun just like the dead cop? Plus it has free will.

11. Detective Spooner in *I, Robot* is a lone hero, like many before him. He has to deal with humans as well as robots that pose problems for him. Fortunately, Spooner has incredible strength and stamina and is extraordinary in his ability to shoot to "death" the vast numbers of robots out to take over humanity. He shows sympathy for the robot "Sonny," that has a sense of his own "self." As a result, Spooner is a hero for our time.

12. The three agents in *The Matrix*—Agents Smith, Jones, and Brown—are more frightening when there are just three of them. When they multiply like cockroaches in *Matrix Reloaded* and *Matrix Revolutions* they become no different than those armies of robots that heroes must tirelessly overcome in one action movie after another. Consequently, *The Matrix* is higher on the scare-scale than the sequels.

13. Dante had it right all along. It's the one that betrays us that we fear the most, not the one that beats the pulp out of us. Look at the evidence: The one who betrays us cuts to the quick, deep into the soul. Think of Cypher in *The Matrix* or Darth Vader in *Star Wars* or even the Gollum in *Lord of the Rings*. The loss of trust leaves a wound much slower to heal than a physical blow.

14. *Will Smith:* "I don't have much of a secret life. There's probably a more aggressive side that I haven't really played in a movie, but for the most part, the characters I've played in the big summer movies have had a piece of me. And if it's not a piece of who I am, it's a piece of who I wish I was. This goes to show that I'm an open book kind of dude." (See interview with Will Smith, *Wired,* July 2004).

Exercises

Directions: What assumptions are made about consumers, their values, and their lifestyles in each of following ads? Select any three to analyze—note the key assumption(s) and state the conclusion of each ad:

1. *Ad for Lindor Truffles:* Do you dream in chocolate? If so, then you should indulge in a Lindor Truffle. Its lusciously smooth filling will melt you away. They are created with passion by master Swiss chocolatiers. Lindt has been master Swiss chocolatiers since 1845.

2. *Ad for JVC digital video camera:* Stunning! Transform life's moments into extraordinary memories with JVC's new Celebrity Series Camcorders—compact enough to fit in your pocket and light enough for all occasions. A celebrity should be a great performer and a real crowd pleaser. The Celebrity Series delivers on both counts thanks to a bright F1.2* aspherical lens that gathers twice the light of the commonly used F1.8 lens. It captures all the action, even in low light situations. Lights, Camera, Action for the celebrity in all of us.

You Tell Me Department

So, Is It Fattening or Not?

Here's an ad for 3 Musketeers candy:

GOD'S GIFT TO WOMEN.
3 MUSKETEERS® Brand Miniatures
Delightful little square of fluffy nougat
Wrapped in satisfying milk chocolate.
Less than 1 gram of fat per piece.
5 grams of fat in a 7 piece serving.
Oh the delicious arrogance of it all.
Big on Chocolate, Not on Fat!™
45% Less Fat Than The Average
of Leading Chocolate Brands.

Not a low-fat food.

Looking at the 3 Musketeers ad shows us the pitch to our secret cravings. It is not surprising that some people may grub down 7 pieces, but what's with the footnote?

Answer the following:

1. What do you make of the footnote? Do you think it is misleading or deceptive?
2. If you were to rewrite the ad as "God's Gift to Men" what key changes would you make?
3. See if you can find another ad with a footnote and compare how it functions in the ad.

---

3. *Ad for Seton Hall University:* "Some college students play it safe with their education, but in life, as in economics, there's a correlation between risk and return," says Seton Hall University finance professor Tony Loviscek, Ph.D. "This is a community where people aren't afraid to ask themselves the hard questions. I come here every day to discover more about myself and to help my students do the same thing. There's no greater return that that." Seton Hall University is where leaders learn.

4. *Ad for Neff appliances:* Who says money can't buy you happiness? With Neff appliances—ovens, hobs, microwaves, washing machines, dryers— for your kitchen and laundry areas, you can be sure that they will not only look wonderfully stylish, but will work like a dream, ensuring that your home life runs as smoothly as possible. Neff allows you to get on with the more important things in life, whether it be cooking a cordon bleu meal for friends, going to the theatre or just simply putting your feet up.

Premise-Indicators and Conclusion-Indicators

All too often we struggle to figure out an author's thesis as we plow through words and more words. Do you ever have a voice in your head saying, "Yeah, but what's your *point?*" It is not always clear what is the conclusion and what are the premises.

For example, what if someone said to you, "Asbestos is dangerous. It poisons the atmosphere. It is a known carcinogen." Is the conclusion obvious? Is it obvious if it has even been stated? If you clutch your head in confusion, you can understand

The Global Dimension

Bolivian Beauty Queens

Directions: Read about Gabriela Oveido's self-description in the face of stereotypical views about Bolivians. What would you say to the Bolivian Vice-Minister of Culture about the call for her to quit?

LA PAZ, Bolivia—Bolivia's entrant in next week's Miss Universe contest faced calls to quit on Friday after she described herself as being a tall, white woman and not a short Indian peasant. The remarks by Gabriela Oviedo, 21, caused furor in Bolivia, one of the Western hemisphere's poorest countries. "Unfortunately, people that don't know Bolivia very much think that we are all just Indian people . . . poor people and very short people and Indian people," local media quoted her as saying in English in Ecuador, where the Miss Universe pageant will be held on Tuesday.

"I'm from the other side of the country . . . and we are tall and we are white people and we know English," she added. Bolivia's Vice-Minister of Culture Maria Isabel Alvarez Plata condemned Oviedo's remarks as "racist" and the Eastern Confederation of Indian Peoples, a major peasant group, called for her resignation.

Oviedo told local television she felt "very bad" about the interview and had not meant to offend anyone. Bolivia was engulfed by a violent Indian rebellion last year in which dozens of people died in protests that ousted President Gonzalo Sanchez de Lozada. Indian groups referred to him as "the gringo" because of his pale complexion and U.S.-accented Spanish. ("Tall, White Bolivian Beauty Faces Calls to Quit," www.reuters.com/news, 28 May 2004)

---

the value of signposts in locating the terms of an argument. **Indicator words** such as "because" and "therefore" function as signposts, eliminating the need for guessing at the premises and the conclusion. These words and phrases signify that a premise or conclusion immediately follows.

Premise-Indicators.   A **premise-indicator** is a word or phrase that introduces a premise in an argument. When you see a premise-indicator, know that a premise is being flagged. Whatever follows the premise indicator is a premise—so these indicators help us locate the evidence! Any term that can be replaced with "because" is a premise-indicator. Arguments often contain premise-indicators and/or conclusion-indicators. When indicators are present, the job of setting out the argument is much easier. So when you see the premise-indicator, you know you've got one of your pieces of evidence. Mark as premises anything that follows a premise indicator.

Premise-Indicators

Because . . .

Since* . . .

In light of . . .

Whereas . . .

Given that . . .

For the reason that . . .

For . . .

The reason why [conclusion] is . . .

Be careful: If "since" can be replaced by "because"—for example, "Since I love ice cream, I'll get a sundae"—then it functions as a premise-indicator. Sometimes "since" is a temporal indicator, as in "Since I dyed my hair purple, men have found me attractive." If "since" can be replaced by "from the moment," then it is a temporal indicator, *not* a premise-indicator. Here are some examples:

PREMISE-INDICATOR	PREMISE	CONCLUSION
Because	you have yanked out clumps of hair,	you need a vacation.
Given that	you only like cheese on your eggs,	I'll put the ketchup in the fridge.
Whereas	you insist on dyeing your hair green,	perhaps you could get a role in Elf 2.
Since	you prefer café latte without marshmallows,	you won't ruin your diet having another one.

ALTERNATIVE FORMAT		
CONCLUSION	PREMISE-INDICATOR	PREMISE
You need a new car	in light of the fact that	your car is a wreck.
We could use more ketchup	since	grandma put it on her eggs.

Conclusion-Indicators.   A **conclusion-indicator** is a word or phrase that introduces a conclusion in an argument. If you can replace the term with "therefore" without changing the argument, the term is a **conclusion-indicator** and the conclusion should immediately follow. A conclusion-indicator acts like a red flag, allowing us to spot the conclusion.

Conclusion-Indicators

In conclusion . . .

Accordingly . . .

As a result . . .

So . . .

Therefore . . .

Consequently . . .

Hence . . .

It follows that . . .

Subsequently . . .

Thus . . .

PREMISE	CONCLUSION-INDICATOR	CONCLUSION
Cockatoos are very affectionate.	therefore,	*a cockatoo is a great choice for a pet bird.*
Birds make great companions.	hence,	*birds should be allowed in rest homes.*
Guinea pigs are very gentle creatures.	consequently,	*they are wonderful pets for children.*
Some prairie dogs have monkey pox.	as a result,	*it is unwise to grab a wild prairie dog.*

Remember: Premises don't always appear before the conclusion—they could follow it. Alternatively, the conclusion could be sandwiched between premises. That's where indicators help!

Transition Words

Transition words indicate an introduction, amplification, clarification, emphasis, illustration, or contrast. They do not function as premise- or conclusion-indicators, *unless clearly shown in the context*—for example, when a list of premises or several conclusions are listed in sequence. Transition words could be located anywhere—in premises, in conclusions, or in a sentence not part of an argument. That means we can't assume that they indicate *either* a premise or a conclusion. However, if it is clear that they are in propositions in a line-up of premises (or a compound conclusion), then they indicate that another premise (or conclusion) is following.

FUNCTION	TRANSITION WORDS
Introduction:	In order to, Primarily, The first reason, Initially, In the first place, To begin, In general
Amplification:	Moreover, Furthermore, In addition, Provided that, Similarly, Also, Likewise, First, second, third,
Clarification:	That is, To restate, In other words, In simpler terms, Briefly, To repeat, To put it in another light, To put it differently, As seen by
Emphasis:	In fact, Notably, Nonetheless, Nevertheless, In effect, Above all, Indeed, And rightly so, As such
Illustration:	To illustrate, For example, For instance, Specifically, Namely, A case in point
Contrast:	However, Alternatively, On the other hand, Notwithstanding, In opposition to, And yet, Conversely, At the same time, In spite of, Despite

Be careful: These words could appear anywhere—in a list of data, a premise, a conclusion, or a sentence outside of an argument.

Example of a transition word in a proposition and *not* in an argument: "Chicken tamales are difficult to make, but delicious. *In other words,* tamales are not easy to whip up, but they sure are good." (*Note:* the transition word clues us that the first point is being expanded upon—but no argument is being made.)

Example of transition words functioning as premise-indicators in an argument: "Miso soup is about the best thing to eat if you are recovering from food poisoning. *In general,* you don't want anything too hard to digest if your tummy is turbulent. *However,* meat such as chicken is not so easily digested and harder on the intestines. Therefore, you'd be crazy to order a chicken tamale so soon right after your food poisoning!" (*Note:* The transition words indicate elaboration and contrast of the first premise, effectively introducing premises two and three.)

Example of a transition word that acts as a conclusion-indicator in an argument: "It's hard to find any dessert that's more tasty than a lemon meringue pie. Consequently, you should rethink making chocolate brownies for the party. *Likewise,* forget cooking up bread pudding too! (*Note:* The transition word amplifies on the conclusions, indicating that another point is being concluded as well. This leaves us with two separate conclusions for the one premise).

Exercises

Part One

1. Circle all the premise-indicators below:

However	Since	Because	Although
Therefore	Whereas	If	Subsequently
Despite	Unless	Given that	Hence
Moreover	Conversely	Accordingly	For the reason that

2. Circle all the conclusion-indicators below:

Conversely	Yet	Whereas	Consequently
As a result	Since	Because	In light of the fact that
Thus	In fact	Given that	In conclusion
Indeed	To restate	Hence	Accordingly

3. Circle all the transition words below:

However	Given that	Therefore	Although
In fact	Since	Accordingly	For the reason that
Above all	Specifically	Hence	Furthermore
Thus	Because	Despite	Initially

Part Two

Directions: Bracket the conclusion and underline the premises in the following:

1. Some time travel would certainly be great. You could get a sense of the future and have fewer risks. You could go back and study the past and get another chance to look at your mistakes and make a few alterations. Plus you could rewrite history.

2. Educated women are smart. They are interesting. Moreover, they can't be taken for granted and we know men love women who can't be taken for granted. Therefore, men should love well-educated women.

3. You should restrict your yodeling to when you're in the shower. I'll tell you why. If you make a bunch of noise in the shower, it doesn't usually offend people. Plus, I know how much you like to yodel.

4. Guys who've seen the world can explain words like *joie de vivre*. They have a kind of self-confidence impossible to get from staying in one place. They may get a bit restless, but worldly men are never boring. So if you want a great companion, go for a worldly man any day over a couch potato.

5. Escargot is another word for "snail." That's why I don't eat them, because I see snails every day in my front yard and they disgust me.

6. Alligators live in the swamp. Therefore, you ought to carry a weapon when you go wading, in light of the fact that alligators are vicious and they have been known to attack people.

7. Sniffing wallpaper paste is something you should avoid. It is causally linked to respiratory disease. It ages your skin dreadfully. Those who sniff paste have bad breath. Plus, it looks repulsive to see people sticking their nose next to wallpaper paste.

8. You ought to get a parrot. They are intelligent, but not obnoxious. They don't require a nightly walk. There's no litter box to clean out. You can even teach them to talk if you are clever—not like cats or dogs, whose language skills are pathetic. Also they are loyal—remember how the parrot in the movie *Paulie* kept trying to find his owner, Marie? That movie brought tears to my eyes, it was that good!

9. Cinderella had two mean stepsisters, who made her life miserable. Her father was negligent, leaving her alone a great deal. Consequently, it is no wonder Cinderella married a man she just met—particularly if you also consider how pathetic and cruel her stepmother was. Cinderella may have been an abused child, but she was no wimp. She managed to get a dress to go to the ball. She showed courage in going out so late at night. She knew the importance of getting home before the curfew. This goes to show that Cinderella deserves more recognition than just being the pretty girl who woos a prince.

10. Sleeping Beauty now has trouble with insomnia. This is due to her childhood being cut short by that witch's curse. After a hundred-year long sleep it's

hard to want to lie down and even take a nap! She must be terrified she won't wake up again.

11. Even though Ursula was an octopus, she developed her feminine charms. She wore bright red lipstick to flaunt her sexuality and had no qualms about wearing a low-cut dress. Subsequently, Ursula could be viewed as a kind of sea-goddess, not a witch. This is especially the case if we consider how generously she gave Ariel advice about men.

12. Rumplestiltskin is a bit of a toad. As a result, it's no wonder he never appeared in any Disney cartoons. Just think about it: he was willing to take a baby from an exploited young woman. He could care less about the devastating effect it'd have on her life. Granted, she made the deal with him in exchange for spinning gold. But her stupidity and greed should not hide the fact that that nasty little Rumplestiltskin deserved a fast trip to the underworld!

13. "It's the cardinal rule of savvy moviegoers: Never trust a trailer. Even the most dreadful film can be spun into 90 seconds of cinematic gold. But the previews are so damn well done, we still get sucked in" (Jon M. Gibson, "The Big Tease," *Wired*, November 2003).

14. "Why do you think Vince Vaughn agreed to star with Ben Stiller in the feature film debut, *Dodgeball: A True Underdog Story?* The reasons he gave were: 'I thought it was one of the funniest scripts I'd ever read. It was leaps and bounds above most movies I've shot. [Writer-director Rawson Marshal Thurber] he's fun. He likes to laugh. He lets people play around. And he has good taste' " (Tim Swanson, "A True Underdog Story," *Premiere*, June 2004).

15. "In *Tootsie*, a man dressed up as a woman to get a role in a soap opera. In *Some Like it Hot*, men dress up as women to hide from the Mafia. *Mrs. Doubtfire* had a man pretending to be a nanny so he could see his own kids. All comedies, of course. Now there's *White Chicks* in which black men who are smart, well pretty smart, play Tiffany and Brittany Wilson— white women who are utter twits. Also funny. It should not surprise us, therefore, when the BBC declares, "There is nothing funnier than men dressing up as women —if a new list of the funniest American films is anything to go by" (BBC News, bbc.com, 14 Jun 2004).

16. "The Harry Potter film, *Prisoner of Azkaban*, is less violent than the earlier movies. Maybe there's a scariness, but there's no physical violence. The Dementors [the frightening Azkaban guards] are just such an abstract concept, these entities that feed into your most hidden fears and pretty much suck any good emotions that you have, so it's a more abstract kind of fear. That means this is a movie that kids can enjoy but teens can have a ride with (Mark Salisbury, "When Harry Met Alfonso," *Premiere*, June 2004).

17. One of the nicest things about the *Prisoner of Azkaban* is the hippogriff. Most animal-hybrids are so unbelievable it's laughable. That hippogriff,

however, was quite convincing in its bird qualities (the beak, the eyes, the snapping beak, the wings in flight). Plus, the bulky, muscular body gave the creature its sense of horsepower.

18. In reply to a question as to why he wanted to direct *Prisoner of Azkaban*, Alfonso Cuaron said: "I read the script and thought, 'Man, there's something really interesting here.' It's very layered. There are comments about social class, about the pain of growing up, betrayal, friendship, and ultimately spiritually uplifting" (Mark Salisbury, "When Harry Met Alfonso," *Premiere*, June 2004).

19. "Jo Rowling, says Alfonso Cuaron, was great to work with given that: She was very keen on following the spirit of the book to try to do a good adaptation. At the same time she asked him not to add elements that would contradict the stuff either in her universe or that was going to happen in books five and six. For example, Cuaron wanted a graveyard in a particular scene, but Rowling told him that the graveyard can't be there because it's in this other place" (Mark Salisbury, "When Harry Met Alfonso," *Premiere*, June 2004).

20. "If there's one too many new fantasy elements in the mix, it may be a werewolf who figures a bit tediously in the story and falls into the usual horror-movie morphing sequence when the moon is bright. . . . But it's hard to think of anything else redundant about or wrong with this film. It's fast, fluid and absorbing; its effects sequences are imaginative, often underplayed and always completely integral to the plot; and its climax hinges on a clever time-travel element that's especially well-handled." (William Arnold, "Will Wonders Never Cease! Harry Potter's Latest Tale Is Sublime," *Seattle Post Intelligencer*, 7 Jun 2004).

Part Three

Directions: Set out the arguments by listing the premises and then stating the conclusion (remember to locate the conclusion first):

1. People who only watch TV news must have a very different view of the world from those who read a newspaper. For one thing, they hear about all the murders, drive-by shootings, gang activity, and neglected children as soon as the news starts. Also, they must think the police put car chases as a top priority, since newscasts are often interrupted so viewers can watch police chasing someone on the freeway and city streets. And, finally, they must think people talk very little, since interviews rarely exceed 15 seconds.

2. Televised executions are suggested from time to time. This is because some people think seeing murderers die will be a powerful deterrent to potential criminals. Furthermore, people like the idea of "an eye for an eye." Watching public executions could also give satisfaction to the victims' families.

3. Children who watch TV before breakfast are less likely to eat a nutritious meal than children who run and play. The reason for this is that watching TV inputs the brain with far more signals than the young brain can handle before they are fully awake. Also, children watching morning TV want to eat and watch at the same time. When that happens, kids just don't pay attention to their meal.

4. For the whole of human history until the late 19th century, marriages between people whose families had property or social position were about as "sacramental" in their character as corporate mergers are today. Marriage was seen exclusively as a means of bettering the worldly connection of one or both partners. The notion of marrying for love was seen as vulgar (adapted from Thomas A. DeMaggio's letter to the editor of *The New York Times Magazine,* 21 Mar 2004).

5. "The key to grilling a highly flammable food like sausage is to use moderate heat and grill slowly," says Steve Raichlen, author of *BBQ USA.* "High heat is good for searing steak, when the outside needs to be more well-done than the inside. Searing sausage may cause the brat to burst and casing to split, releasing all its good juices. And you certainly don't want your brat to be charred on the outside but undercooked on the inside. This means, if you want a tasty sausage that hasn't exploded, you need to use moderate heat and grill slowly" (Associated Press, "For Grilling Perfect Bratwurst, the secret is in the fire," *Journal Times,* Racine, WI, www.journaltimes.com, 7 Jun 2004).

6. "I don't believe that most overeating is 'psychological' says Dr. Atkins, creator of the famous low-carb diet. Here's his argument. Note the conclusion and set out the premises:

   It's my opinion that overeating is not as psychological in origin as it's cracked up to be. I don't believe that many people want to eat huge quantities of food because they need the psychological balm that food provides. They overeat merely because their own metabolic abnormality makes them feel that degree of hunger. When the metabolic pathways are rerouted through this special diet, this excessive appetite goes away. Then many of these same people have a quite small appetite, I have found. (Robert C. Atkins, M.D., *Dr. Atkins' Diet Revolution,* Bantam Books, 1973)

7. Set out the premises and conclusion in the argument below:

   Although good intentions are meant by the protesters in controlling cutting, thin cutting is needed to promote a healthy growing environment. The crowded tree-to-tree situation within the Tillamook State Forest is a disaster in waiting, akin to the past Tillamook Burn fires. These trees, when planted, were placed 6 to 8 feet apart, but are now 50 to 70 feet high with crowns touching. If thin cutting is not allowed, the past 50 years could be for naught with all lost to another disastrous fire. The students who planted these trees did so with the understanding that they would be managed as a renewable resource, to be used for typical timber uses, from which we all profit (Jerry Harding, Letter to the Editor of the *Portland Oregonian,* 13 Oct 2001).

8. Set out the premises and conclusion in this argument by Steve Peralta. Note any assumptions he makes:

The young Latino is blazing a new frontier that will eventually change the American mindscape. The young Latino refuses to accept that there are no opportunities for an inner city scholar with a north side Denver accent. He has struggled as hard as the white suburban kid to get into the freshman class at Harvard and will not make any more cultural sacrifices. The contemporary Latino has finally realized that culture and *ganas* can work together to mold a truly unique individual. The contemporary Latino makes no investment in statistical odds or figures because he realizes that figures lie and liars figure. ("The Changing Face of Latino America," *grandemesa* at ally.ios.com)

Part Four

Directions: State the conclusion and the premises in the following arguments:

1. "If you believe, as I do, that one important measure of our humanity is our regard for other living beings, then the grisly practices of industrial ranching are immoral. I'm speaking of what is hidden from sight: such horrors as the butchering of live steers, the periodic starving of chicken to stimulate greater egg production and the rigid confinement of animals in cages where they can hardly move for the entirety of their lives" (John Balzar, "Cruel Slaughter of Food Hits a Nerve," *Los Angeles Times*, 13 Jul 2001).

2. "A flag is a unique symbol, one which has no parallel in the values it represents or the emotions it stirs. The flag has played a central role in our nation's historical development, a perpetual reminder of our democratic tenets. . . . The government's interest in preserving the flag's integrity far outweighs any minimal burden on free expression occasioned by requiring people to engage in alternative modes of communication. For those Americans who feel compelled to denigrate their own country (but who nevertheless choose to remain here and enjoy its freedoms), there are many avenues of negative expression available, including verbal denunciation or burning other symbols of the government. Hence, the flag amendment is an appropriate vehicle for preserving that minimal amount of patriotism and respect which any nation needs to ensure its continued vitality" (James R. Bozajian, "Make Flag-Burning Unconstitutional," *Los Angeles Daily Journal*, 25 Jun 2004).

3. "The amendment's supporters claim they are trying to 'protect the flag,' yet there is no evidence that the flag needs protection. . . . And what of these rare flag burnings? Burning an American flag, an action that is seen as extreme by many, can serve as an important expression of free speech. Twenty-five years ago, after James Meredith was shot during a civil rights march in the South, an African-American World War II veteran named Sidney Street burned a flag on a street corner in Harlem in protest. If Meredith could be shot while marching for racial equality, he said, we did not need the flag; America's ideals had gone up in smoke. If he had used only

words to say that, few would have heard him. But because he said it symbolically by burning the flag, his protest was covered by television cameras, and his message reached millions" (Bob Kearney, "Amendment to Ban Burning Flag is Unprecedented, Unwise, Unworkable, Un-American," *Daily Journal*, 15 Jun 2004).

4. "Thomson points out that there is a great range of activities in which it is justifiably assumed that parents have a legitimate right to determine their children's participation. There is no general reason to suppose that childbirth is different; there are no compelling grounds (such as the expectation of great harm) to justify overriding the parent's prerogative. Hence insofar as the fetus needs an advocate, there is no reason to regard the physician rather than the pregnant woman as the appropriate advocate" (Christine Overall, *Ethics and Human Reproduction* Routledge, 1987).

5. "While electronic toys have succeeded in seducing children, much of the technology added to toys threatens to change the way children play in fundamental ways. Often, electronic toys are less creative, do not involve much imagination and encourage more passive reactions than older toys, experts say. There is a passivity that comes from having toys that entertain you" (Julian E. Barnes, "Where Did You Go, Raggedy Ann? Toys in the Age of Electronics," *The New York Times*, 10 Feb 2001).

6. "According to the most recent Nielsen ratings, the average black household watches eleven hours of television every day—about two-thirds of their waking hours. In addition, they spend at nearly five times their proportion of their population at movie theaters. Distinctions no longer exist between movies and news, television and real life" (Jacqui Jones, "The Accusatory Space," in *Black Popular Culture*, Gina Dent, editor Bay Press, 1992).

7. While a military attack on the West probably would have a unifying effect, a biological attack might prove divisive. Fighting battles requires mobilization and cooperation. Fighting epidemics requires quarantine and isolation. It's easy to be generous and internationalist after an event such as the tsunami, when terrible things are happening somewhere else. It's much harder when the enemy is a disease that might kill or disfigure you and your children. (Anne Applebaum, "Only a Game?," *Washington Post*, 19 Jan 2005)

Range of Argument Forms

Imagine this scenario: You've been invited to be a guest on the new reality TV show *The Persuader*. It uses a game-show format with a raucous audience to set the mood, a panel of "jurors" more or less representative of the society, and contestants. The goal? To persuade the "jury" of your thesis on a topic that pops up for all to see when you select a category. Ready to play? OK, it's your turn and you pick as your category "EDUCATION." Good choice! The topic that pops up is "ONLINE LEARNING." "Online learning?" you say to yourself, as tiny beads of sweat line up across your forehead. Wiping your brow, you think about your position on online learning, weighing the pros and cons and fantasizing about the fame and glory of being a winner. You decide, "Bad idea." The question is, How will you persuade your jury?

Arguments take many forms. For instance, to argue against online learning, you could employ a set of principles and expert opinions. You could cite statistical studies or personal anecdotes about the horrors of teaching oneself anything. You could pick any number of approaches to make your case, as we will see in the chapters ahead. The method you select can make a world of difference.

Arguments based on analogy can be very persuasive. Here we compare one thing to another on the basis of some similarities and conclude that what is a characteristic of one term in the analogy applies to the other. There's a reason lawyers often turn to an analogy or legal precedent to persuade the judge or jury. With that in mind, let's look at an analogy to online learning. How about food? Think about learning like eating. Since you are going to argue against online learning, what analogy might work for you?

Group or Individual Exercise

How about this one: Traditional (classroom) learning is like a well-balanced diet and online learning is fast food. Dr. Andrew K. Benton, president of Pepperdine University, takes this approach. Read it and examine how he uses the fast food analogy to make the case against online learning.

Online and Off Course: Fast-Food Education Will Reign if Virtual Campuses Replace Real High School Campuses

Andrew K. Benton, June 2, 2004

If nothing else, Morgan Spurlock, the chap who dined exclusively on fast-food fare for 30 excruciating days and then made a documentary of it, proved that just because we can do something does not mean we should. There are some things in life that have a certain "drive-by" appeal but, upon closer inspection, are not the best choice. I think the same will eventually be proved true in the mad rush to find the equivalent of "fast food" in American education, and

not only at the college and graduate levels. Reports are that the Internet's Virtual High School is available for sign-on. . . .

The distance between that intellectual intensity and a learning relationship illuminated only by a computer screen is immense. With a virtual high school comes the real challenge of determining what should be included in the basic education of our citizens. . . . I am not overwhelmed with the promise of such a school.

So, let's see if I have this right. Across the United States, Dan and Sue can either get up early and arrive at school by 8:15 A.M., staying until 3 P.M. or so, raising their hands to participate, intersecting with diverse people and their interests, experiencing successes and addressing setbacks, all the while developing relationships with mature, learned adults who hold them accountable. Or, they can stay home, dial up and phone it in. For many, it will be the rough equivalent of choosing a balanced meal or driving through the fast-food outlet of choice.

My own high school experience was agonizing and thrilling, . . . if left to my own choices I might have been quite intrigued with school unencumbered by attendance policies . . . School was not easy, but then it was not supposed to be easy, or fast or even efficient. . . . I cringe at what virtual high school students will miss as they zip through a college prep curriculum on their way to virtual university, followed, inevitably, by entry to—alas—the real world. . . .

The bright and the average probably will avail themselves of this new invention. They will graduate from a school they never saw, educated by teachers they never met, with a competence I fear a harsh world will judge, in a word, harshly. . . . I am compelled to ask.. Just because we can do it, should we? Great discernment is required if the Internet becomes the academic pipeline of choice, and discernment on the Internet, unlike creativity and profitability, is in short supply. ●

Andrew K. Benton is the President of Pepperdine University. Reprinted with the permission of Andrew K. Benton.

Strategy for Setting Our Arguments

If we have no evidence to cite as support for the conclusion (thesis), we have no argument. There has to be at least one premise and only one conclusion in an argument. The claim "Elvis impersonators need to get a life" is not an argument; it is just a proposition. For an argument, you need both "Elvis impersonators need to get a life" and evidence to support it. For instance, this would act as support: "Elvis impersonators live in the shadow of Elvis," "People who live in anyone else's shadow need to get a life," and so on. Only the combination premises (evidence) and conclusion (thesis) can form an argument. We can then see how strong the argument actually is. It helps to be organized. Here's the strategy to take:

Strategy for Setting out Arguments

- State the conclusion (thesis/hypothesis). This gives us a sense of where we're headed. If you don't know the conclusion, you cannot analyze an argument.
- List the premises (reasons/evidence) one by one.
- Examine the premises to see if they are sufficient to support the conclusion. Look for any holes, such as missing premises, unwarranted assumptions, biased language, or fallacious reasoning.
- Listing the premises one by one (P_1, P_2, P_3, etc.) above the conclusion provides order to the argument and makes it easier to read.

You then have the premises and conclusion clearly set out, so you can examine the relationship between them; and you are less likely to overlook a piece of evidence.

Global Dimension

Finding One's Genetic Parents in England

Britain said Wednesday it would end anonymity for sperm and egg donors next year in a move that a fertility expert said could worsen the country's already critical shortage of donations. Children conceived from donated eggs or sperm will have the right to track down their biological parents from the age of 18, public health minister Melanie Johnson told a news conference. Read the following excerpt and then state Johnson's thesis and key reasons. State what a critic of her position might argue in response.

"I firmly believe donor-conceived people have a right to information about their genetic origins that is currently denied them, including the identity of their donor," she said. "Today's new regulations will . . . remove the major discrepancy that exists between the rights of donor-conceived people and those of adopted people," she added. (Jeremy Lovell; *Reuters*, news.yahoo.com, 21 Jan 2004)

Exercises

Part One

What's wrong with tattoo parlors, anyway? Well, Austin Poplin, editor of the *Carolina Morning News* is wondering about that very question. Read his editorial and then answer the questions below.

Government Set on Protecting Us from Ourselves

Austin Poplin, Editor,
Carolina Morning News, June 4, 2004

It almost feels like we're taking a cheap shot by poking fun at Hilton Head Island town officials who are dead set on limiting where any future tattoo parlors may operate on the sunny resort island. The town's Planning Commission is, after all, just trying to head off any potential problems before they take root.

But, what the heck. Here goes.

Mind you, it is not even yet legal for anyone to operate a tattoo parlor anywhere in South Carolina. That is likely to change soon as legislation legalizing the tattoo trade heads for Gov. Mark Sanford's desk. The state clearly has a legitimate interest in regulating any business that could harm people and their health if operated recklessly. Tattoos involve needles and anything involving blood and bodily fluids must meet the strictest standards of sanitation. The good of the public health demands that much. No problem.

But it might seem the Hilton Head officials are being a bit overly proactive when they move to restrict where a tattoo business can go with so much zeal they are effectively making sure they can't set up shop. It's pretty clear someone is making a moral judgment about a class of business. The proposed limits would ban tattoo parlors from being opened within 500 feet of another tattoo parlor. That would be a blight. Oh, and they can't be within 500 feet of a major arterial street. And we don't want them within 1,000 feet of any church, daycare center, school or recreational area. We wouldn't want the toddlers tipsy from too many juice boxes to stumble out of the daycare center and into the tattoo parlor to get a likeness of Sponge Bob Square Pants permanently affixed to their bicep.

And who knows what would happen after Sunday school lets out if the youngsters were within walking distance of the powerful temptation of tattoos. Somebody needs to relax. State law will make it illegal for anyone younger than 21 to get a tattoo. Health regulations will help ensure the parlors aren't passing on hepatitis, or worse. It will also be illegal to give a tattoo to anyone who is drunk at the time.

If adults want to permanently mutilate themselves, fine. They will probably regret it when gravity and age take their toll in a few years. We think the marketplace will dictate where business owners can afford to set up shop, and if people want the services offered, the businesses will thrive. If not, problem solved. ●

Reprinted with the permission of Austin Poplin and the Carolina Morning News.

Answer the following:

1. State the conclusion and the key pieces of evidence.

2. Note how the author adds a few satirical comments. Does poking fun here seem justified?

3. What do you think of his position that adults should be free to "permanently mutilate" themselves?

Part Two

Directions: Drawing from the information presented below, set out an argument that conveys your attitude about plagiarism. Use a minimum of two of the pieces of information as part of your argument. Feel free to add other premises, as needed to bolster your argument:

For $136 [and going to one of the many Web sites selling term papers] a frantic high school or college student can download a 19-page paper on "Woodrow Wilson and Franklin Roosevelt." It can be faxed for $9.50 or delivered overnight for $15. Some sites, however, are free of charge. Schoolsucks.com, for example, serves as a type of portal for the disgruntled student, offering games, chats, and daily e-mails of free jokes. Visitors are encouraged to post a paper of their own when they download one from the site.

Kenny Sahr—who started the site in 1996—says it now gets 10,000 hits per day with 600,000 people signed up for the daily e-mails.

Mr. Sahr insists he has no qualms about what he does, and calls it the students' responsibility to use the papers for research only, especially because he gives no guarantee of quality. "Those papers are written by students; then we put them there. But we're not rating them, we're not telling you these are good papers. In other words, if someone turns in a bad paper, well, it's not our problem." (Kimberly Chase, "Teachers Fight against Internet Plagiarism," *Christian Science Monitor,* www.csmonitor.com, 2 Mar 2004)

Part Three

1. List the premises (P₁, P₂, etc.) and state the conclusion in the arguments about cloned food:

    a. Consumers in general are much more aware of what's in food. Consequently, burgers made from cloned cattle may make folks a little nervous. Remember, also, that people were excited about Dolly the sheep being a clone—but did you hear anyone wanting to make mutton chops out of her?

    b. In the late 1980s two companies made and sold hundreds of cattle clones. Consumers bought their meat and ate it oblivious to the fact they were gobbling down a clone. Milk from clones was also sold and no one raised an eyebrow. People now are upset about cloned animals for food, but the clones made now are created from cells from adult animals. This is different than those early clones all too many of us had for lunch or dinner way back when. Those early clones were made from embryos created by breeding a prize cow or bull and then freezing some of the embryos. Since no one complained back then; therefore, no one should complain now! A clone is a clone is a clone, regardless of the source!

    c. People are concerned about cloning now—not like in 1988 with the cloned cattle. According to Gregory Jaffe, expert in biotechnology, here's why: One is the concern over cloning humans. The other is the attention being given to genetically engineered foods and the nature of the food supply. Animal cloning gets thrown in, whether it's the same or not (Gina Kolata, "Animals Cloned for Food No Longer Draw Collective Yawn," *The New York Times*, 3 Nov 2003).

2. Give an example of (a) a relevant premise and then (b) an irrelevant premise for the conclusion, "Therefore, children under 12 years old should not be allowed to see *Kill Bill Vols. 1 and 2.*"

3. State the premises and conclusion in each of the following arguments:

    a. The Chinese have not got the sense of individual independence because the whole conception of life is based upon mutual help within the home . . . it is considered good luck to have children who can take care of one. One lives for nothing else in China (Lin Yutang, "Growing Old Gracefully" in Alexander Hooke, Ed. *Virtuous People, Vicious Deeds* (McGraw-Hill) 1999)

    b. There is good reason for deceiving one another—it works. It works not only for the liar but also for the listener. Many of us are unprepared to speak the truth or to hear the truth, particularly about those things we care about, such as ourselves, friends or family, or even our ideals (Alexander E. Hooke, *Virtuous Persons, Vicious Deeds* (McGraw-Hill) 1999).

4. In your own words, explain what the author is arguing below:

    TV's true violence consists not so much in the spectacle's techniques or content, but rather in the very density and speed of TV overall, the very multiplicity and pace of stimuli; for it is by overloading, overdriving both itself and us that TV disables us, making it hard to think about or even feel what TV shows us—making it hard, perhaps, to think or feel at all. (Mark Crispin Miller, "Deride and Conquer," in Todd Gitlin, ed., *Watching Television*, Pantheon Books, 1987)

6. The State Department needs your help handling a public relations nightmare around the use of depleted uranium in NATO weapons. Read the paragraph below and then (a) set out the issues and concerns and (b) construct an argument explaining what the State Department can do:

Many Europeans suspect that depleted uranium contained in NATO weaponry has caused or contributed to numerous cases of leukemia suffered by alliance troops deployed in the Balkans. The leukemia deaths of several European soldiers who served in Kosovo or Bosnia-Herzegovina prompted the U.S. Army report. . .

On Thursday, two German arms makers reported having tested weapons containing depleted uranium during the 1970's, intensifying public concerns that some Germans may have been exposed to the low-level radiation released by such weapons (See Carol J. Williams, "U.S. Warned Germany of Uranium Leaks," *Los Angeles Times*, 20 Jan 2001).

7. North-South Airlines needs you to help them keep a problem for frequent fliers from erupting into a public relations disaster with both flight crews and customers. What will you advise them, given the information below?

On June 12, 2001, it was reported that frequent fliers—and especially flight crews—face radiation risks. The problem is the ionizing radiation emitted by the sun. When the sun is at the peak of its "storm" season, the solar wind is supplemented by bursts of protons called solar flares. These flares can expose people flying at high altitude to ionizing radiation. Occasionally airlines reroute polar flights to avoid solar storms. Though there is no evidence this exposure is dangerous, experts agree that a pregnant woman could be exposed to enough radiation on a single flight to exceed government health guidelines. Crew members who fly polar flights for years can accumulate doses that are large relative to those received by nuclear power plant workers and other "radiation workers."

Dr. Robert J. Barish, medical radiation specialist, says, "People may be hurt." Airlines don't have radiation monitors on board so that they could change altitude or reroute to avoid the solar storms. Overall, flight crews have higher rates of a variety of diseases, but it's not clear if it's connected to the radiation risk or the disruption of their biorhythms. European authorities have gone so far as to classify flight crews as radiation workers. In the U.S. the FAA does the same, but it does not require employers to track exposure.

A United Nations committee estimated that air crew members (approximately 250,000 compared to nearly four million people worldwide who are occupationally exposed to radiation) received about 24% of all the occupationally related exposure to radiation. (Matthew L. Wald, "The Frequent Flier and Radiation Risk," *The New York Times*, 12 Jun 2001)

Part Four

In a 2004 groundbreaking case, a California appeals court ruled that a lesbian mother did not have to pay child support to her former partner, with whom she had three children. Evidently the laws have not kept up with same-sex parent relationships. The Third District Court of Appeal held that the obligations of parenthood cannot be imposed on partners who act as parents but have no genetic relationship to the children. In discussing the case, Peter Blumberg remarks on the inconsistency in recent rulings around parent–child relationships:

> The unprecedented ruling is the flipside of the refusal of California courts thus far to recognize that children legally cannot have two mothers or two fathers except through adoption. Just last week, the 1st District Court of Appeal held that a lesbian who donated her eggs to her partner had no custody rights to the children she helped raise for six years because she was not the birth mother ("Lesbian Mom Need Not Pay Child Support," *Daily (Law) Journal,* 21 May 2004).

Answer the following:

1. Setting aside laws and precedent, what points can be made in support of the judge's ruling?

2. Looking at the ruling from the standpoint of the ex-partner getting no child support, what points can be made in opposition to the judge's ruling?

3. Do you think adoption should be the only way to be considered the parent of a child to whom you have no blood ties? Set out your thoughts.

Group or Individual Exercise

In July 2001 the Wisconsin Supreme Court upheld a probation order barring a man, 34-year old David Oakley, from having more children unless he shows that he can support all his offspring. He had been convicted of failure to pay child support and owes $25,000 in support. Oakley has nine children by four women. If he violates the order, Oakley will face eight years in prison. The court noted the problem of collecting child support: One family in three with a child support order received no money at all and parents who did not pay deprived children of about $11 billion a year (Tamar Lewin, "Father Owing Child Support Loses a Right to Procreate," *The New York Times,* 12 July 2001. You can see the court opinion at the Wisconsin Bar Web site, www.wisbar.org). Groups should examine the arguments (pro and con) below and then answer the questions that follow:

Arguments FOR the decision

1. *A spokeswoman for the Association for Children for Enforcement of Support* saw the decision as a useful tool for ensuring that children are taken care of.

2. *The court majority* saw the restriction as "narrowly tailored to serve the state's compelling interest of having parents support their children." The restriction would expire in five years, when probation ends, and, in the court's view, the alternative of incarcerating Oakley would further victimize his children, ages 4 to 16.

Arguments AGAINST the decision

1. *Dissenting Justice Ann Walsh Bradley* wrote: "Today's decision makes this court the only court in the country to declare constitutional a condition that limits a probationer's right to procreate based on his financial ability to support his children. Ultimately, the majority's decision may affect the rights of every citizen of this state, man or woman, rich or poor."

2. *Julie Sternberg of the American Civil Liberties Union* argued: "Until now I don't know of any appeals court that has upheld that kind of condition. It's a very dangerous precedent. The U.S. Supreme Court has said that the right to decide to have a child is one of the most basic human rights. And in this case there were all kinds of less restrictive alternatives, like attaching his wages, to make sure child support would be paid."

Group 1: Speak in favor of the Wisconsin Supreme Court's ruling.

Group 2: Speak against the ruling.

Group 3: Discuss whether the various mothers of the children are contributing to the problem.

Group 4: Give your response to journalist Tom Richards, who said:

Now, I don't know any more of this case than I read in the paper, but Oakley sounds like a creep, one of those jerks who thinks that making babies somehow proves his masculinity. Any animal can do that. I am not and would not defend him. But what is wrong with those women? Didn't their mamas warn them about men like this? OK, so a woman might marry him the first time. Even the second time, well, a lot of people have bad first marriages. But a third time? Wouldn't you say this was a bad gamble? And any woman who would be his fourth wife and have children with him is just plain stupid. And there are women who had children with him without being married to him. Incredible. ("Congress Is Too Obsessed To Screw Up," *Wisconsin Post Crescent,* 16 Jan 1999)

CASE STUDY

On March 19, 2001, the Pizza Wars ended. They started with Pizza Hut declaring "war" on poor-quality pizza and daring anyone to come up with a better pizza. Papa John's ad, "Better Ingredients. Better Pizza" hit Pizza Hut like a torpedo. Pizza Hut sued Papa John's, arguing this constituted false advertising. (See Donald M. Gindy's "True Lies," Daily Journal, 26 Jun 2001.) Papa John's claimed that its "vine ripened tomatoes" were superior to the "remanufactured tomato sauce" used by Pizza Hut. Plus its fresh dough and filtered water created a better-tasting pizza. (See article below.)

Answer the following:

1. Discuss whether you have enough information to conclude whether Papa John's ad was false advertising.
2. If not, what would you want to know, what questions would you want answered, before you could decide who won the war, Pizza Hut or Papa John's?
3. State the strongest points of both sides (indicate which is which!).

True Lies: Duel between Pizza Hut and Papa John's Comes to an End

Donald M. Gindy
Daily Journal, June 26, 2001

With a resounding thud, the pizza wars ended March 19, when the U.S. Supreme Court refused to review the decision of the 5th U.S. Circuit Court of Appeals in *Pizza Hut Inc. v. Papa John's International Inc.* (2001). The nature of the lawsuit was a claim of false advertising under the Lanham Act allegedly committed by Papa John's when it claimed **"Better Ingredients. Better Pizza."**

Pizza Hut threw down the gauntlet as its president, from the deck of a World War II aircraft carrier, declared "war" on poor-quality pizza. Pizza Hut "dared" anyone to come up with a better pizza. At about the same time, Papa John's was launching a new advertising campaign proclaiming that it sold a better pizza because it used better ingredients. The matter went to trial in Dallas, resulting in a verdict in favor of Pizza Hut. Under the Lanham Act, "a plaintiff must demonstrate that the commercial advertisement or promotion is either literally false, or that it is likely to mislead and confuse consumers." Pizza Hut relied on a theory that Papa John's ads were deceptive and were intended to mislead purchasers of pizza. . . .

But was Papa John's ad mere "puffery"? That is to say, was the claim an expression of opinion or a type of boasting on which no reasonable person would rely? The court concluded that "Better ingredients. Better Pizza," standing alone, would not mislead consumers. But Papa John's lost its bragging rights when it coupled the slogan with misleading statements of specific differences in the ingredients used.

Pizza Hut asserted that its competitor had placed before the public "a measurable claim, capable of being proved false or of being reasonably interpreted as a statement of objective fact." Papa John's claimed that its "vine ripened tomatoes" were superior to the "remanufactured tomato sauce" used by Pizza Hut and that its fresh dough and filtered water created a better-tasting pizza. By pointing to specific differences between itself and Pizza Hut and by failing to present at trial any scientific support or the results of independent surveys to substantiate its claims (such as taste tests), Papa John's had, in fact, left the arena of opinion and entered the realm of quantifiable fact. As a result, it subjected itself to a claim that it misled consumers.

However, the burden of proving false advertising falls on the shoulders of Pizza Hut. It is essential [for Pizza Hut] to prove not how consumers would react but how they actually do react. The test thus becomes, assuming that the ads were misleading, whether they actually influence a reasonable consumer in his or her purchasing decision. Since the court found that Pizza Hut had neglected to present such evidence, it had failed to satisfy the element of the cause of action relating to the "materiality" of Papa John's ads. In the absence of such a survey, Pizza Hut's entire action had to fail.

Donald M. Gindy practices intellectual-property law in Century City.

CHAPTER FOUR

Fallacies, Fallacies: Steering Clear of Argumentative Quicksand

So that was Mrs. Lundegaard in there? I guess that was your accomplice in the wood chipper. And those three people in Brainerd. And for what? For a little bit of money. There's more to life than money, you know. Don't you know that? And here ya are, and it's a beautiful day. Well. I just don't understand it.

MARGE, FROM *Fargo*

We regularly encounter many errors in reasoning. One special kind, called a *fallacy*, is especially important to study. Fallacies are not only pervasive; they often convince people to positions that the evidence does not support. Fallacies are the con artists of reasoning. With sleight of hand or other tricks, they cleverly sell the unsuspecting audience a bill of goods. Upon careful scrutiny, we can see that fallacies should not be given credence. To avoid them, we have to pay attention—and not be complacent.

In a letter to the editor of *Tricycle: The Buddhist Review,* Melissa Chianta writes: "When I broke up with my first boyfriend in college, I told a friend, 'He bastardizes Eastern religions to suit his own emotional limitations.' . . . I realized that ten years later I have done the same thing!" (Summer, 2001). Chianta just experienced the flipside of the "ah-ha" effect—when we have a mental breakthrough and finally get it. Catching ourselves in a fallacy is the "uh-oh" effect—a mental sinkhole. With the tools this chapter provides, you should be able to catch yourself before plunging into a sinkhole of bad reasoning!

Every fallacy contains a fundamental flaw in reasoning. The flaws can take any number of forms and may involve structural or linguistic errors, mistaken assumptions, or premises that are irrelevant to the conclusion. We will look at the major forms of fallacies in this chapter in order to avoid making such errors and to be able to defend ourselves when others use fallacies.

Watch the reasoning in this conversation:

HEATHER: Euthanasia is killing and, since it is wrong to kill, euthanasia is wrong.

LEO: You're just a woman, what could you possibly know about euthanasia? Stick to the kitchen!

HEATHER: Why should I listen to you—you are a member of the National Rifle Association, you'd certainly be biased!

LEO: Speaking of rifles, did you hear about Ruben? He bought an antique rifle used in World War II! That was a good investment. Either you know where to put your money or you just waste it.

HEATHER: That's the truth! And if you just waste your money, you won't be able to get out of the house. Then you will not have any kind of social life. Pretty soon, you'll be sitting home staring at the ceiling, your entire life rotting away in front of your eyes!

LEO: Sure thing, Heather. Hey, there's my bus. Catch you later!

Fallacy Busters.   Leo dismisses Heather's argument without considering her reasons. The fact that Heather's a woman is irrelevant in this case. Her reply is just as bad, because she points to his membership in a group to discredit him. Leo then switches the topic entirely. Since there are more options than the two stated, he commits another fallacy. Finally, Heather offers the flimsy argument that wasting money will doom you to a dreary life.

There are four major kinds of fallacies: fallacies of relevance, fallacies of presumption, fallacies of ambiguity, and formal fallacies. We'll start with an overview and then look at each fallacy.

Fallacies of Relevance.   In **fallacies of relevance** the premises simply fail to support the conclusion; they are beside the point. *For example,* "Mickey Mouse loves Camembert cheese; therefore you should buy some today!"

Fallacies of Presumption.   In **fallacies of presumption** the argument rests on an unwarranted assumption causing the fallacy. *For example,* "Either you know Harry Potter or you are a cultural toad. With 110 million Harry Potter books in print worldwide, published in 47 languages, there's no excuse for being a cultural toad. Thus, you should read one of the Harry Potter books."

Fallacies of Ambiguity.   (**Also Known as Linguistic Fallacies**). **Fallacies of ambiguity** center on the way language can mislead—focusing on emphasis, interpretation, sentence structure, and the relationship between the parts and the whole. This ambiguity results in an incorrect conclusion being drawn, causing the fallacy. *For example,* "Popeye is a fun guy and so is Olive Oyl. They should get married—together they'd be dynamite!"

Formal Fallacies.   **Formal fallacies** occur because of a structural error. The very form of the reasoning is incorrect. The truth of the premises will never guarantee

Overview of the Fallacies

FALLACIES OF RELEVANCE are invalid and unsound because the premises are simply irrelevant to the conclusion being drawn.

FALLACIES OF PRESUMPTION are invalid and unsound because of unfounded or unsupportable assumptions underlying them.

FALLACIES OF AMBIGUITY are invalid and unsound because of unclear and confusing use of words, grammar, or sentence structure that leads to drawing an incorrect conclusion.

FORMAL FALLACIES are invalid and unsound because the very form or structure of the argument leads to drawing an incorrect conclusion.

Fallacies of Relevance

- Ad hominem
- Ad hominem circumstantial
- Tu quo
- Ad populum
- Ad baculum
- Ad verecundiam
- Ad misericordiam
- Ad ignorantiam

Fallacies of Presumption

- Accident
- Hasty generalization
- Biased statistics
- Bifurcation
- Complex question
- Post hoc
- Red herring
- Slippery slope
- Straw man
- Begging the question
- Fallacy of misleading vividness
- False analogy

Linguistic Fallacies (Fallacies of Ambiguity)

- Equivocation
- Accent
- Amphiboly
- Composition
- Division

Formal Fallacies

- Fallacy of affirming the consequent
- Fallacy of denying the antecedent

the truth of the conclusion. *For example,* "If Wimpy eats one more hamburger, he will have to take a nap. Wimpy had to nap. Consequently, Wimpy must have eaten one more hamburger."

Introduction to the Fallacies of Relevance

Fallacies of relevance rest on evidence that's beside the point and, thus, irrelevant. There is always a glaring gap between the premises and the conclusion drawn in a fallacy of relevance. For instance, you might be persuaded to hand over your shoes if someone threatens you, but that doesn't make the threat a *good reason* for surrendering your shoes. The key is what counts as a good reason, not what counts as *persuasive*. A good reason is something that offers solid evidence for holding a position.

Fallacy Busters

We should see a direct connection between that evidence and the conclusion. If not, something is wrong. Let's look at some cases.

First Case

RAY: Carl Johnson would make a great mayor: He's been active in government for 15 years. He has helped people get back on their feet. Plus, he has been instrumental in transforming the downtown so that it's not a haven for drugs.

LUCILLE: Don't you know he is gay? Would you vote for a gay man for mayor? Surely you are kidding!

Fallacy Busters.   You probably saw this one. Johnson is discredited because of a personal characteristic. Lucille needs to explain why sexual orientation is a relevant consideration for mayor. The candidate is dismissed without getting a fair hearing.

Second Case

ANNIE: Mommy, why do I have to go to bed? It is only seven o'clock and I am not at all sleepy. Can't I read for a while?

MOMMY: I'll tell you why you have to go to bed. If you do not go to bed right now I'll paddle your behind with a wooden spoon. Get moving!

Fallacy Busters.   Mommy threatens Annie—she did not give her a good reason, such as the need for sleep. The mother's reasoning is not acceptable from the standpoint of good thinking. She should try to persuade with evidence, not threats.

Third Case

DR. BERKOWITZ: Students, be honest throughout your entire academic career since it will make you an honorable person.

YU ZHAN: How can you say that, Dr. Berkowitz, when you plagiarized your master's thesis? Why should I pay attention to the advice of a cheater?

Fallacy Busters.   Here Dr. Berkowitz offered a reason for being honest, but he is dismissed for not "practicing what he preaches." We might justifiably expect someone to act on the standards by which they judge others. The unwillingness to do so points to moral weakness, but does not mean that their *reasoning* is flawed. Whether or not the speaker lives in accordance with those reasons (the premises) is a separate issue.

Key Fallacies of Relevance

By becoming familiar with the fallacies, we'll be able to spot incorrect reasoning in ourselves and in others and, hopefully, stop ourselves from falling into any fallacious thinking.

1. *Argumentum Ad Hominem*

The **ad hominem** ("personal attack") fallacy occurs when there is an attack on another person (the source of an idea), instead of the person's argument (the idea itself). The attack can be on the speaker *or* someone the speaker is citing (who then is targeted in the personal attack). It is often referred to as ad hominem *abusive* because of the nature of a personal attack.

This fallacy effectively turns the attention away from the issue to the person arguing it. This is unacceptable unless the personal characteristic under attack is demonstrably relevant to what's at issue. If not, attacking the source of the idea rather than the idea itself is fallacious. As critical thinkers, the focus should be on the quality of the reasoning—not some test of personal worth—unless personal worth *is* the issue itself.

Sometimes the attack on the other person is downright hostile; at times it is subtle and less obvious. Unfortunately, abusive tactics have been known to persuade (e.g., when voters fall for it). Discrediting a plaintiff, defendant, or witness using an ad hominem attack can also occur in a trial or deposition. Here are two cases with similar tactics: In both the 1992 Mike Tyson rape trial and the 1991 William Kennedy Smith rape trial the victim's panties were cited as indictors of her character. As noted by law professor Shirley A. Wiegand:

> A key piece of evidence in the Michael Tyson rape trial was the victim's underwear. It was pink polka dots, little girlish, like something a mother might buy for her preteen. The prosecutor "made a sarcastic remark to the jury about this wild, sexual woman going to meet Tyson wearing her 'pajama panties.' Like something straight out of Frederick's of Hollywood, the prosecutor joked." (Dianne Klein, "Rewrite Script for Rape Trials," *Los Angeles Times*, 13 Feb 1992).
>
> Tyson was convicted. But William Kennedy Smith's victim wore black Victoria's Secret panties and a sheer black bra, which the defense attorney showed to the jury. [Smith was acquitted.] (Shirley A. Wiegand, "Deception and Artifice: Thelma, Louise, and the Legal Hermeneutic," *Oklahoma City University Law Review* 22, no. 1 (1997), tarlton.law.utexas.edu)

Ad hominem examples can be seen in other arenas too—as with politicians resorting to personal attacks on their opponents. People call that "mudslinging" for obvious reasons. Unfortunately, abusive tactics have been known to persuade at times. For instance, in the 2004 presidential campaign, accusations about the military service of the two candidates went in both directions.

Look also at the case of Richard Clarke. Clarke, ex-chief of counterterrorism for the Bush administration, spoke before the Congressional panel investigating events leading up to 9/11. His remarks set off a firestorm. Some thought Clarke was the victim of ad hominem attacks, as shown in the following:

> Conservatives, ever suspicious of Big Government, should love a whistle-blower—unless, of course, he's former counterterrorism czar Richard Clarke. *The Washington Times* calls Clarke "a political chameleon who is starved for attention after years of toiling anonymously in government bureaucracies." For neoconservative columnist Charles Krauthammer, Clarke is "a liar" and "not just a perjurer but a partisan perjurer." According to Ann Coulter, Clarke is a racist. Exiting the known world and entering into her own fantasyland, Coulter depicts Clarke musing about Condoleezza Rice: "the black chick is a dummy," whom Bush promoted from "cleaning the Old Executive Office Building at night."
>
> This ad hominem defamation is obviously intended to discredit the man in order to discredit his argument. But such low tactics aren't usually attempted against a man whose allegations are corroborated by others, including the implicated parties—and, most palpably, by events themselves. (James Pinkerton, "Conservatives Should Hail Former Counterterrorism Chief Richard Clarke, but Instead They're Smearing Him," *Salon,* www.salon.com, 29 Mar 2004)

Impeaching the testimony of witnesses through an attack on their credibility may be necessary—but only when that credibility is germane to the matter at hand. For example, impeachment by felony conviction (when the person testifying has a prior conviction for a felony involving moral turpitude) is a legitimate form of impeachment. Ordinarily, the personal circumstances of a person—such as his or her social standing or choice of underwear—is irrelevant to the logical force of the argument.

Examples of Ad Hominem

a. PETE: Don't you think socialized medicine is a bad idea? It seems awfully costly and there's already a big enough burden on the ordinary citizen. Vice President Cheney was right to say that we should be talking about accessibility, not socialized medicine.

   LUIS: You've got to be kidding! I can't believe you'd be swayed by a person whose healthcare needs are all met! Boy, are you duped!

b. KIM: El Burrito is the best Mexican restaurant in Norwalk. They use the freshest ingredients and make their own tortillas. Everything I've eaten there is delicious.

   ARTHUR: Okay, but since you're Japanese you are hardly an expert on Mexican food! Why take your advice?

c. The philosophical work of Immanuel Kant is certainly extensive in its range. However, it's hard to take seriously the views of someone rumored to be a hypochondriac.

d. Nancy Reagan has become active in campaigning for stem cell research. Scientists believe that stem cells may lead to cures for such diseases as Alzheimer's, Parkinson's, and diabetes. Certainly we can sympathize with her seeing the devastating effects of Alzheimer's on her husband, former president Ronald Reagan. Nevertheless, the fact that she has only recently exhibited an interest in this area has to be factored into the equation.

2. Argumentum Ad Hominem Circumstantial

The **ad hominem circumstantial** fallacy involves an attack on a person's credibility because of vested interests or social affiliations. Because of the circumstances or a potential conflict of interest, the person cannot possibly be impartial—or so it is implied. For instance, "Don't listen to what the governor of Nevada has to say about Indian casinos. He's from a state that lives and breathes gambling, so he'd certainly be biased!"

This is sometimes called "guilt by association." We see the ad hominem circumstantial fallacy when someone is criticized because of his or her membership in a group or professional, religious, cultural, or political associations. By shifting the focus away from the issue to the person's vested interests or associations, we go off on a tangent—and away from the question of whether or not their argument has merit.

Of course people can be corrupt or corrupted. Nonetheless, when analyzing their *reasoning,* our goal is to see how it holds together—not what's going on behind the scenes. Consequently, the quality of the reasoning warrants our attention, not the person's vested interests or affiliations.

The difference between ad hominem and ad hominem circumstantial is that the former is a *personal* attack, a direct abuse or insult that is intended to demean an opponent personally and, thereby, defeat the person's argument. In contrast, an ad hominem circumstantial zeroes-in on the person's circumstances, connections, or situation rather than the individual's personal traits or character. An example of ad hominem circumstantial would be a *guilt-by-association* attack.

Examples of Ad Hominem Circumstantial

a. Of course the representative from Prince Edward Island opposes the potato surcharge—you know he's from the biggest producer of potatoes east of Ottawa. He's bound to be in their pocket! Don't listen to him.

b. Rosalind suggested Mother Teresa as an example of a heroic woman in the 20th century, because Mother Teresa has done so much for the poor people in India. However, Rosalind is a Catholic herself and, consequently, can hardly be said to be unbiased.

c. We shouldn't be surprised that Rep. Al Waxman proposed the Research Freedom Act of 1990 to end the ban on fetal cell transplants. After all, he's from California, where all that high-tech fertility and fetal cell research goes on.

3. Tu Quo (or Tu Quoque—"You're Another One")

The fallacy of **tu quo** occurs when people are attacked because they don't follow their own advice or "practice what they preach." We might refer to this as the "Tu Quo Trap": You don't take your own advice—so your advice must be worth nothing! (See figure 4.1 for an example).

You Tell Me Department

Duck Hunting and the Halls of Power?

What would you say about the call for U.S. Supreme Court Justice Anthony Scalia to withdraw from a case when it involves a friend? Can he be impartial?

For almost three years Vice President Dick Cheney fought demands that he reveal whether he met with energy industry officials, including the chairman of Enron, while he was formulating the president's energy policy. The Supreme Court is about to take up the vice president's appeal in lawsuits over his handling of the administration's energy task force. Anthony Scalia is a Supreme Court justice. They are duck-hunting buddies. As CNN reports:

> Cheney invited Scalia, an old friend, to Louisiana earlier this month to hunt waterfowl on a private reserve. The trip occurred three weeks after the court agreed to hear the case, scheduled for sometime in April. . . The two also had a private dinner with Defense Secretary Donald Rumsfeld on Maryland's Eastern Shore in November, when the justices were still considering Cheney's appeal. Cheney is fighting a federal court's order that he release internal files of a task force he headed for the Bush administration. A lawsuit claims he made improper contacts with energy industry lobbyists when developing government policy. ("Watchdog Groups Question Cheney, Scalia Hunting Trip," CNN.com, 19 Jan 2004)

You tell me: Should Justice Scalia recuse himself (voluntarily pull out of deciding on this case)?

Actions may speak louder than words, but the quality of our reason up should be assessed on its own merits and not by our actions. For example, just because Sen. Kerry "flip-flopped" on issues does not mean that his *arguments* were poor. If the issue is his *character*, then vacillating on issues of national interest may or may not be relevant, depending upon the situation.

Even hypocrites may exhibit strong reasoning. Personal habits and practices are generally irrelevant to the merits of an argument. The fact that a woman with emphysema smokes until her last gasp doesn't weaken her argument that smoking can kill you.

Examples of Tu Quo

a. AHMAD: Will you please slow down, Lisa? You're driving 20 miles over the speed limit, which is dangerous in the rain. I'm scared!

LISA: I don't have to listen to you. You got a speeding ticket last month. Point your finger at me and four point back at you!

b. How can Betty Jean tell me to read classics like *Tortilla Flats*, when all she does is watch MTV?

c. It's a bit ironic that California Governor Schwarzenegger is taking public stands on tightening up regulations around steroid use by professional and amateur athletes. After all, he is reported to have used anabolic steroids back in his body building days. And it wasn't so long ago that he said, "I used steroids. It was a risky thing to do, but I have no regrets. It was what I had to do to compete. The danger with steroids is over-usage. I only did it before a difficult competition—for two months, but not for a period of time that could harm me. And then afterward, it was over. I would stop. I have no health problems, no kidney damage or anything like that from using them" (Tom Farrey, "Conan the Politician," ESPN News, espn.go. com, 17 Nov 2003).

4. Argumentum Ad Populum (Argument from Patriotism or Popular Appeal)

The **ad populum** fallacy attempts to persuade on the basis of popular appeal, the masses, or patriotism, rather than giving good reasons to accept the conclusion. An appeal to mass sentiment is often called the "bandwagon approach." Get on the bandwagon and join the crowd! The assumption is that the crowd or the majority knows what's best. Clearly this is not always the case.

We also see the ad populum fallacy with "snob appeal." We are asked to join the "in-group" (the rich, famous, sexy, popular, etc.) instead of feeling like a reject, nerd, or leftover. This appeal is often used in advertising—as are the other variations on the ad populum argument.

Examples of Ad Populum

a. Be cool! Smoke cigars! All the cool people do!
b. What's wrong with you? Forget getting a Nissan. Support your country and buy an American car.

FIGURE 4.1
Betty Jean has fallen into the "Tu Quo" Trap!

    c. JOE: Boy, can you believe it? 380 *tons* of explosives disappeared in Iraq. And that includes the kind of explosives used to blow up the airplane out of Lockerbie, Scotland, way back when. You'd have thought the U.S. military would have been guarding those munitions from the get-go. That should have been a high priority—even with the troops stretched so thin.

    KEISHA: I can't believe you'd say this, Joe. Your very comment denigrates the troops and is unpatriotic. I'm standing by the troops and suggest you do the same!

Note how we are asked to get behind our country, be a member of the crowd, or join the bandwagon. The pressure here is to fall in line, not dissent. It is important, though, to seek good reasons for a call to conformity, rather than merely acquiescing.

Group or Individual Exercise

Gather as many ads as you can that use an ad populum fallacy—either with appeals to patriotism or popular appeal (a bandwagon argument). Gather also as many political campaign ads as you can find that use an appeal to patriotism or the bandwagon approach. Bring them in and share with the class, explaining how you see the fallacy being used.

5. Argumentum Ad Verecundiam (Improper Appeal to Authority)

The **ad verecundiam** fallacy occurs when an appeal is made to an "authority" to support a position, but the person is not a credible expert on the topic. Frequently the "authority" cited is a public figure or celebrity who offers a testimonial. This is commonly seen in advertisements. It is expected that we'll be persuaded by the endorsement, rather than good reasons for the conclusion.

Examples of Ad Verecundiam

a. Einstein loved to play the violin so you should too!
b. Halle Berry stroked a Jaguar XJR in the movie *Catwoman*. Therefore, they must be cool cars.
c. Ad for Citizen Eco-Drive watch: "NEVER SWEATS A SERVE. *JAMES BLAKE, fastest-rising men's ATP tennis player.* CITIZEN ECO-DRIVE."

The center of the fallacy is that the "expert" cited, however talented otherwise, is not a credible source for the topic under discussion. We may agree with the celebrity's product choice or their endorsement. But agreement is not enough—we need good reasons for the argument to be strong. *Be careful:* Expert testimony does have its place. But the person cited should be an expert in the field in question. It may be advisable to use more than one source or "expert," particularly if there is some difference of opinion about the fundamental facts or if the topic is surrounded in controversy.

6. *Argumentum Ad Baculum* (Appeal to Force or Coercion)

The **ad baculum** fallacy occurs when force, threat of force, or coercion is used to persuade. This includes using verbal or sexual harassment, blackmail, extortion, and threat of violence used to "persuade" someone to a position. A variation is bribery, where the coercion comes in the form of a promise, offer, money, or a position. Here's an example of an ad that points to unfortunate consequences of not using the product:

> *Ad for* Breathe Right® *nasal strips: [two eyes looking at each other against a pitch-black background]*
> *"If you really love me, you'd wear one." You won't even know it's there. But she will. Because Breathe Right® strips can help quiet your snoring by improving your nasal breathing. And once you get used to breathing through your nose again, the less you'll get elbowed. . . .*

Examples of Ad Baculum

a. SONCHAI: I'm sorry Tim, but I can't write you a letter of recommendation. You have been late to work many times and you regularly have lunches two hours long!

   TIM: That's up to you, Sonchai. But what goes around comes around! And don't forget: I know where you live and when I can find you home alone.

b. MR. SWARTHMORE: Barbara, come discuss your job promotion with me tonight. Meet me at my hotel and wear some sexy lingerie! Give a little and you'll get something back.

c. NURSE KRATCHIT: Good to see you back on the ward, Dr. Hernandez. I hear you've called the press about the screw-up last week in the emergency room. Please keep a lid on this. I could tell the press about that nasty medical malpractice case you had last year!

In these cases, there is a threat of physical force (the most blatant), an implied threat (coercion), fear of loss (bribery, extortion) or harassment (sexual, verbal).

7. *Argumentum Ad Misericordiam (Appeal to Pity)*

The fallacy of **ad misericordiam** occurs when an irrelevant appeal to pity or a set of sorrowful circumstances is used to support a conclusion. A sympathetic response may be called for when you become aware of someone's personal difficulties. But that does not, in itself, substitute for good reasons that directly support a conclusion.

Examples of Ad Misericordiam

a. He should be a senator, given his history. His wife ran off with Judge Thornton, his grandmother died of sausage poisoning, and his children are all in gangs.
b. Dr. Gonzales, I deserve an A in Logic. My boyfriend ran off with my cousin, Alice, and the transmission went out on my car. My life is a mess! I deserve an A for my pain.
c. Please officer, don't cite me for drunk driving. I know it's my second time in two years, but my parents will put me in a rehab program and my social life will be ruined.

The sad tales may be relevant to getting advice, but they are not relevant to becoming a senator, getting an A in a class, or avoiding a charge of driving under the influence. In some cases, as in preferential treatment programs, we may want to consider such hardships as poverty or discrimination. Legitimate attempts to provide a balance could be seen in terms of justice, not pity. Weigh these attempts carefully so we don't fall into a fallacy of ad misericordiam.

8. *Argumentum Ad Ignorantiam (Appeal to Ignorance)*

The **ad ignorantiam** fallacy occurs when it is argued that something is the case (either true or false) simply because you cannot prove otherwise. This is the "if you can't prove me wrong, then I must be right!" defense.

Examples of Ad Ignorantiam

a. This house is haunted. You cannot prove it's not haunted, so it must be the case!
b. My physics professor is an alcoholic—unless you have evidence that I'm wrong, I must be right!
c. Belief in reincarnation is unwarranted since no one can definitively demonstrate that the soul can enter another body and come back on earth.

In all these, the argument is based on a lack of proof to the contrary. However, a failure to disprove something does not mean the opposite is true. The fact that you cannot prove your brother is not dreaming of Sedna, the sea goddess, does not mean that he *is* dreaming about her. And when it comes to legal matters, a *presumption* of innocence is quite different than *proof* of innocence.

Exercises

Part One

Directions: Discuss the reasoning below.

Who Uses Creatine?

Some estimate that 75% of the Denver Broncos and 60% of all major league baseball play-ers use Creatine: including Brady Anderson and Mark McGwire (and you keep hearing that the *ball* is juiced). Bodybuilders around the world are making use of the most effec-tive sports supplement with no proven negative side effects (provided you do not abuse it). (See www.powersupplements.com.)

Part Two

Directions: Identify the fallacy of relevance in the examples below. If you forget the name describe what is happening in the argument—look for the pattern and the name may become apparent.

1. Halle Berry does a lot of her own stunts, even in *Catwoman.* So does Angelina Jolie (alias Lara Croft). That tells us that women are more powerful than they realize! I bet more women would be willing to fight for their country if they tapped into their inner "feline"!

2. Smith's ketchup is all-American! Buy some!

3. Keith said it's smart to drive at a safe speed and be polite to other drivers. However, I see no reason to follow his advice, since he drives like a race car driver and has no qualms about cutting off other drivers. Who is he to talk?

4. Hundreds of people saw lights flashing on a wall and they declared it a miracle and a sign of the Virgin Mary. Scientists cannot explain the strange phenomenon. No one has been able to prove that it's not a sign of the Blessed Virgin, so it must be!

5. CARRIE: Angelica said that people should not use ivory, because so many elephants are killed and that's wrong.

   LEN: Don't you realize she's a member of Latinas United and couldn't possibly know anything about African elephants!

6. Most women think men who recite poetry are romantic. Therefore, if Jamal wants to impress Miranda, he'd better start reciting poetry.

7. Movie star Jackie Chan says martial arts keep him in shape. Maybe your parents should sign up for lessons—they are getting a tad flabby!

8. Richard Alton Harris was a victim of fetal alcohol syndrome. Plus, his mother was beaten up by his father when she was pregnant. As a result, he

should not have been convicted of the murder of those two teenagers. It was too bad he was executed for the crime.

9. Hey Professor Whitaker, I deserve an A on this exam. If you do not give me one, I will follow you home and put a mouse in your mailbox. That'll show you! Tell me, will you give me the A or not?

10. I hear you have been raising questions about the government. Be careful—that so-called documentary by Michael Moore was not an unbiased look at the administration. Not at all. The people know what's right. Don't you know the American people are behind the president's war on terror? You should take a cold, hard look at your lack of patriotism because right now you appear to be spineless. Show more support for the president.

11. Did you see *Fahrenheit 9/11*, Michael Moore's scathing criticism of the Bush administration? Well he sure showed some hypocrisy up there at the top. For example, in one scene Bush is on the balcony with the Saudi bigwig visitor —who is smoking a cigar. Do you realize it was a *Cuban* cigar? Aren't Republicans supposed to be against trade with Cuba?

12. Chris Rock thought Don Cheadle should win "Best Actor" at The Academy Awards, so you were wrong to favor Jamie Foxx for his performance in *Ray.*

13. Since no one has proven exorcism is not effective, we should call in a priest to examine Carrie. She needs help.

14. Dr. Johnson, I hope you can arrange to get an organ donor for my infant son. If you drag your heels, I'll make sure your wife knows about your affair with that cute nurse in ObGyn last year!

15. Charley Spengler, shortstop for the Westminster Salmonbellies, says chewing snuff is bad for your health and rots your teeth. Like we should pay attention to what he has to say? He has been chewing snuff since he made the minor leagues.

16. URSULA: Jack, you should vote for Proposition 112—there are so many reasons it will help the homeless.

    JACK: Really? How would you know? You're from Sweden.

17. HASSAN: I can't believe you shoot deer with assault rifles. That is beyond barbaric! At least cavemen used bows and arrows and the animals had a chance.

    BRIANA: You're no vegetarian. I saw you wolfing down the flesh of a defenseless chicken just last night!

18. The pharmaceutical sales rep said we should not drink Screech, the alcoholic home brew the McGregors made in Prince Edward Island. She said it is a disgusting habit and Screech is a probable cause of liver cancer. But her advice is questionable, given the alcohol I smelled on her breath.

19. Be wary of anything that Oliver says about reproductive rights. He's active in the Defenders of the Unborn and you know what an extreme group they are!

20. MARIO: Angela, honey, what's this frozen chicken breast doing on the table instead of dinner?

    ANGELA: Mario, you big lug, if you don't get helping with dinner I'll toss the entire contents of the fridge out on the front lawn! I've had it! So, I suggest you change your ways, starting today.

21. How can you doubt the value of an American Express credit card when you have the testimony of Tiger Woods to vouch for it being good?

22. Don't believe everything Mario says about Angela. He's Italian—you know how those Latin men tend to exaggerate. They can't be trusted to tell the truth.

23. Bill Clinton deserves to make a pile of money from his autobiography, *My Life*. He had a really hard time after they tried to impeach him, plus it's amazing how he made it through heart surgery. He's had his share of problems.

24. Did you hear that two-thirds of American children and teens have read at least one Harry Potter book? I can't understand why your cousin, Bosco, isn't crazy about Harry Potter too. He should get with it.

25. It isn't wise of you to trust just any stockbroker, given the potential for bias. I know for a fact your stockbroker, Alan Greenspine, is a Democrat. It'll be a cold day in Hades when a Democrat can figure out the stock market. You ought to change your stockbroker today. Give me a call and I'll get you the phone number of mine—she's a Republican and that gal knows her money.

26. Dr. Wong deserves to win the Faculty of the Year award. I know he's only been teaching at the school for two years, but he got in that snowboarding accident and sure mangled his foot. It's a wonder he can hobble into class!

27. Hey Ralph, you should fix my car. If you don't, I will tell your wife about those photos you took of your neighbor, Alicia, when she was sunbathing in her backyard.

28. The universe must be infinite, since no one has proven it is finite.

29. Actors Nicole Kidman and Tom Cruise adopted children. Why don't you consider adoption instead of trying so hard to get pregnant?

30. *Fahrenheit 9/11* won "Best Picture of the Year" at the People's Choice awards ceremony. Most people thought it was a great movie. Consequently, it deserved to get an Academy Award nomination.

Part Three: Quick Quiz on Fallacies of Relevance

1. What fallacy occurs when, instead of giving reasons for accepting a conclusion, someone is asked to give sexual favors in exchange for a job or salary raise?

2. What fallacy occurs when an advertiser uses snob appeal, such as suggesting that eating their mustard will make us feel like we own a Rolls Royce?

3. What fallacy occurs when someone makes an irrelevant appeal to a recent disaster as a reason for getting a job, raise, or better grade?

4. What fallacy occurs when someone argues that something must be true because you can't prove it is false (or vice versa)?

5. What fallacy occurs when someone argues that a position should not be accepted, even if good reasons are offered, simply because the speaker does not follow his or her own advice and the speaker's actions suggest hypocrisy?

6. What fallacy occurs when someone is discredited solely on the grounds of a characteristic like race, age, or gender?

7. What fallacy occurs when someone tries to bribe another person?

8. What fallacy occurs when someone argues for a position based solely on the basis of patriotism?

9. What fallacy occurs when someone is being discredited because of a political, religious, or social affiliation?

10. What fallacy occurs when an argument rests on the irrelevant testimony of a famous person, like a movie star or athlete?

Key Fallacies of Presumption

People make unwarranted assumptions all the time. Some of the major ways this occurs have been categorized and named, as we will see. What makes **fallacies of presumption** unsound arguments is that they contain an unstated assumption that causes the argument to sink. For example, what if your friend assumed that having her lucky stone in her pocket was the cause of her passing her physics final? Carrying it may boost confidence, but her success is more likely due to the fact she came prepared.

Fallacy Busters.   See if you can spot any shady reasoning in this conversation:

KEN: Hey! What's happening? Are you coming to the rally with me? Either you're with us or you're against us!

BERNIE: I'm with you, Ken; you know that! Have you always been a dupe?

KEN: Watch it there pal. Things have been going good for me lately. How about you? Wait, what is that I see? What's that hundred-dollar bill sticking out of your pocket?

BERNIE: Oh, Ken, you have an interesting T-shirt on. I like the idea of Tweetie Bird chasing Godzilla! What a hoot! Where do you find such things?

Did you notice all the unwarranted assumptions? In the first case, Ken sets up a false "either/or" choice. In the second case, Bernie asks Ken a loaded question, where he cannot answer either yes or no without implicating himself. In the third case, when Ken asks about the $100 bill, Bernie switches the topic, trying not to be caught red-handed. In all of these fallacies, an unwarranted assumption leads to drawing an incorrect conclusion.

These fallacies are like magic tricks: So long as we do not stop to think about the arguments, they look good. But they are never to be trusted. In each case the unwarranted assumption, once uncovered, reveals how weak the argument is.

There are 10 key fallacies of presumption that we will look at below. Being able to spot these fallacies is very useful.

1. Accident

The fallacy of **accident** occurs when a general rule or principle is applied to a special case in which, by reason of its special or atypical characteristics, the rule simply does not apply. This fallacy might be a misapplication of a moral principle, a rule from work, or a general pronouncement made by a family member or friend.

The unwarranted assumption is that the rule applies to all cases, without exception. But most rules and principles simply fail to apply across the board. Thus, applying the rule to the exceptional or atypical case is unwarranted.

Examples of Accident

a. The Bible says, "Thou shalt not kill," so it is wrong to kill in self-defense.
b. Step Three of the Eightfold Path of Buddhism is Right Speech. Right Speech means one must speak only truth. Therefore, I should tell my Uncle Bob he has stomach cancer!
c. "Be sure to return what you borrow"—that's what my father said. As a result, I should return the axe I borrowed from my roommate, even though she's been threatening the UPS deliveryman.

In each of the examples the general rule does not apply. We do consider some killing to be acceptable, including self-defense. Ordinarily we do believe in honesty, but not without exception. Uncle Bob may not want to discuss his medical diagnosis with you. And we would not likely want to return an axe to a murderous roommate. We need to watch for unwarranted assumptions in applying rules and principles. Otherwise, we may commit the fallacy of accident.

2. Hasty Generalization

Hasty generalization occurs when a generalization or moral principle is drawn on the basis of too small a sample or an atypical case. Stereotypes and other poor inferences have been drawn about entire groups of people on the basis of either too little information or a group that is not representative. Hasty generalization often occurs because the sample size is too small. Therefore, the inference drawn is an incorrect generalization.

Examples of Hasty Generalization

a. Inez Garcia ran through five red lights taking her sick baby to the hospital last night. Therefore, we should all be able to run red lights whenever we want.

b. Maya went out the other night and ate at the new Austrian Meatball Grotto down in the Village. She said the meatballs were mushy and the sauce was too salty. That just goes to show you—never, I mean, NEVER, eat at an Austrian restaurant. Those Austrians should stick to making clocks!

c. Rob dated three women who were in a sorority, and they were airheads. Therefore, all sorority women are airheads.

Here we see the two different types of hasty generalization. In the first one, the generalization was the rule ("We should be able to run red lights whenever we please"). But it is based on a special case (an exception) where it is permissible. In the other cases, the inference was an observation about the population under discussion (food at Austrian restaurants, sorority women). The conclusion rests on a sample that is too small—hardly a convincing study.

3. Biased Statistics

The fallacy of **biased statistics** occurs when an inference is drawn on the basis of a sample that is not diverse enough. That is, the sample is not representative of the target population. We see this in studies that lack the diversity found in the population in question, so the sample excludes a certain age group, gender, ethnic group, and so on—and yet draw a generalization to a population that includes the omitted group(s). The issue here is diversity, not size.

Examples of Biased Statistics

a. Cyber Digital did a study of teenage boys in Detroit and found that 45 percent of them like computer games. Therefore, 45 percent of all Americans like computer games.

b. Ninety-five percent of toddlers prefer a bottle of warm milk at bedtime. Therefore, 95 percent of all children prefer a bottle of warm milk at bedtime.

c. A poll of KTBT FM found that 67 percent of community college students commute at least 10 miles from home. Therefore, 67 percent of all students have a commute of at least 10 miles from home.

In all of these cases, there is a shift from the sample population to the target population. That is the way to spot a case of biased statistics. Compare the sample group (teenage boys, toddlers, community college students) to the targeted population (Americans, children, students) to determine if it is sufficiently representative.

In the examples here, the samples are not diverse enough to support the generalizations drawn. It is not a question of size, as with hasty generalization. Here the issue is *diversity*. When it comes to sample studies, there are key factors to consider, such as race or ethnicity, class, gender, age, educational level, geography, religion. Depending on the focus of the study, some factors may be more instrumental than others in allowing inferences to the targeted group.

4. Bifurcation (False Dichotomy or Excluded Middle)

The fallacy of **bifurcation** is a often called a false dichotomy by reducing a choice to only two options when, in fact, more options exist. This can be expressed as an "either/or," an "if/then" or an "only if" claim. Here are two examples: "If you like the way things are going, vote for Bush." and "If you want change, vote for Kerry."

Assuming there are other options than the two presented, a better choice may have been left out. We can't give "informed consent" if we don't know the options. Let's look at bifurcation with polar extremes. First case: "These events have divided the whole world into two sides: the side of the believers and the side of the infidels" (CNN, 7 Oct 2001 quoting Osama bin Laden).

Second case: "We had a choice. Either take the word of a madman or take action to defend the American people. Faced with that choice, I will defend America every time" ("Mr. Smoke and Mirrors," *The Progressive,* Mar 2004 quoting President Bush).

Third case: Noam Chomsky said to delegates at an antiglobalism conference: "Either we will have a world without wars, or we will not have a world" (as noted by Tom Gibb, "Forum Protesters Look to Ending War," *BBC News,* www.bbc.com, 1 Feb 2002). Chomsky may be right—it's an either/or situation, given nuclear realities. Is there an alternative option?

Examples of Bifurcation

a. Sean "P. Diddy" Combs's T-shirt: "Vote or Die."
b. "There is a great temperamental and ideological divide between those who believe in self-defense and those who believe in surrendering and begging for mercy" (Dr. William L. Pierce).
c. You can go approach life with gusto. You can sit on your plaid couch and let life pass you by. The choice is yours.

You Tell Me Department

Message from Beyond the Grave?

Advertisement for a free booklet said to be on nutritional research:

Read this or die

Nutritional Research on Heart disease, High Blood pressure, elevated Cholesterol, Diabetes, Stroke and Congestive Heart Failure. Call for FREE Booklet 1 800 600 3099

You tell me: Does this ad contain a fallacy?

Not all either/or dilemmas are fallacious. For instance, either you are pregnant or you are not. Either you have a heartbeat or you do not (assuming you haven't had an artificial heart transplant!). Either you are deathly allergic to peanuts or you're not. Do not assume that someone who says, "It's either this, or it's that" is right, however. Check for other options. Furthermore, not all bifurcation presents polar extremes. For instance, an HMO may limit the options to two that are the least expensive, or the least risky, procedures.

5. Complex Question (Trick or "Loaded" Question)

The fallacy of **complex question** takes the form of a question in which two questions are rolled into one. It is impossible to answer the question without, at the same time, answering a hidden, unasked question—or affirming an assumption that is being made. It is often called a *loaded* question.

Remember that scene in *My Cousin Vinny* involving a trick question? Mona Lisa Vito (Marisa Tomei's character) was questioned by the prosecutor about her knowledge of auto mechanics. At one point he asks what the ignition timing should be on a 1955 Chevy model 325. To that, Mona Lisa said: "A trick question! Chevy didn't make a 325 in 1955!" She goes on to point out the correct ignition timing for the 1964 model—when the 325 first came out. Not everyone is as quick as Mona Lisa to catch a trick question in action! So we need to be on the lookout.

In a February, 2005 press conference with President Bush, Jeff Gannon, a man who passed himself off as a reporter asked a complex—or "loaded"—question. After falsely attributing quotes to Democratic leaders, Gannon asked: "How are you going to work with people who seem to have divorced themselves from reality?" (See Suzanne Goldenberg, "Fake Reporter Unmasked at White House," *The Guardian*, www.guardian.co.uk, 11 Feb 2005).

Logician Morris Engel asserts that complex question is a form of begging the question set in the form of an interrogative. The question itself assumes what it is trying to prove by couching the answer in the unasked question.

Examples of Complex Question

a. Do you usually eat junk food for breakfast?
b. Aren't your friends worth your best chocolate?
c. Have you always been a liar and cheat?

With these, we have two questions, not one. Separate the two and examine them. For instance, we might ask if our friends even eat chocolate before determining if they're worth the best chocolate. At times, use of complex, incriminating questions is an attempt to trap the listener (like an ambush). Legislative bodies try to address complex questions by moving to "divide the question" The question would then be divided up into two questions, removing the unwarranted assumption.

6. Post Hoc (or Post Hoc Ergo Propter Hoc— "After This Therefore because of This")

The **post hoc fallacy** asserts a causal connection that rests on something happening earlier in time. The fallacy goes like this: Because something precedes something else means that it must then cause the later thing to happen. No evidence is given to support such a causal link. Any connection might be coincidental. It would be unwarranted to assume a causal connection.

Examples of Post Hoc

a. Whenever the Tigers are on a winning streak, Coach Sanders wears the same tie to each game. The Tigers won the last three games, so Coach Sanders's lucky tie must be working!
b. Alma's diet sure was amazing. She took OPS diet tablets every morning and then had a cup of coffee and a grapefruit for breakfast, a head of lettuce for lunch (no dressing!) and cottage cheese for dinner. In two weeks she'd lost 12 pounds! Those OPS diet tabs really work miracles!
c. Paul had bacon, eggs, and pancakes for breakfast. Then he took the SAT exam. He scored in the top 20 percent. I am so proud of him. That just goes to show you: A good, hardy breakfast was the reason he did so well.

In these cases, the prior event is considered the cause simply because it happened earlier in time. The fact that it occurs earlier (e.g., picking a certain color tie, eating diet tablets, having a hearty breakfast) does not mean it's the cause of some event (the team winning, losing weight, scoring well on the SAT). The connection must be established.

We also see post hoc arguments when people base their reasoning on "bad omens" or attribute success to a lucky charm or a ritual. Examine arguments carefully, watching for assumptions and omissions.

You Tell Me Department

Did Red Socks Help the Red Sox?

It seems like superstition knows no bounds when it comes to sports. D. Allen Kerr tells this story:

Former Sox hitter extraordinaire Wade Boggs used to get up at the same time every morning and eat chicken before every game. Prior to each night game he entered the batting cage right at 5:30 P.M. to take his practice swings, and he ran wind sprints at exactly 7:17 P.M.. . . . He also wrote the Hebrew word chai (life) in the dirt just before stepping into the batter's box before each at-bat.

Such quirks aren't limited to the playing field; folks in the bleachers and at home are almost as superstitious as the players. . . . This past Tuesday I headed out to pick up my kids in Newmarket and take them out to dinner . . . On the way there I was listening to the Sox–Yankees game on the radio, the final game of the series at Fenway Park, when the Yanks suddenly scored three quick runs in succession in the second inning. "What the hell's going on?" I thought.

Then, horrified, I realized I wasn't wearing my lucky ballcap. . . .

After the Sox tied up their playoff series with the Oakland A's two weekends ago, I realized I had worn this hat while watching both Boston victories on TV. When I headed out to watch the deciding game of that series . . . I made sure to wear it again. Sure enough, the Sox won the game and the series. So naturally, after realizing on Tuesday I had left this sacred artifact behind, I drove around the Portsmouth traffic circle in a panic, sped back home, dashed up the stairs to grab it and began my trip anew. But alas, it was too late—the baseball gods had witnessed my blasphemy and the Sox fell to the hated Yankees. ("Superstitions Curse Red Sox Fans Too," *Portsmouth Herald*, www.seacoastonline.com, 18 Oct 2003).

You tell me: Is there any harm done in thinking lucky socks or caps will bring luck? Does such post hoc reasoning have negative consequences on our thinking processes?

Exercises

Directions: Name the fallacy of presumption below. Draw from these choices: accident, hasty generalization, biased statistics, bifurcation, complex question, and post hoc.

1. What tool did you use to pry open the window of the lab?

2. A poll was taken of 2,000 owners of luxury cars. Of these, 82 percent said that the economy is doing just great and they will have an easy time when they retire. Consequently, 82 percent of all citizens think the economy is doing just great and they'll have an easy retirement.

3. The Bureau of Fish and Game released nine California condors into the wild. The next week the rain started coming down in buckets! That just goes to show you, the American Indians were right—the condor really *is* a bearer of rain. Those birds caused all this flooding!

4. At a conference on animal rights, two panelists said animal experimentation violates the rights of sentient beings. We can conclude that philosophers in general oppose animal experimentation because of the rights of sentient beings.

5. People should always stand up for their beliefs. Therefore, it's commendable that young people in Turkey are dying from hunger strikes to protest the conditions of Turkish prisons.

6. If we don't require a writing exit exam for college students, we might as well kiss off all our standards for a quality education.

7. Donna dated a law student she met in Ann Arbor. They went to see *Constantine* and he fell asleep! That goes to show you—if you're dating a law student, you should forget about late-night movies.

8. Basically you've got these two choices: join the Army or work on the farm until you can save money for college.

9. A poll taken of women athletes found that 68 percent think it's time for Americans to go on a low-carb diet. Therefore, it's clear that most Americans think it's time to knock off some weight.

10. Where did you hide the money you stole from Dr. Pettisnoot's office?

11. The policy of the Alaska Moose Bed and Breakfast is that guests must take off their shoes before entering. That means your 90-year-old grandmother better not try to sneak in with those dusty walking shoes of hers on her feet. A rule's a rule.

12. Either we should relocate the toxic waste dump to Southern Nevada or we'll have to convince the taxpayers that we need a satellite station to send hazardous substances to outer space.

13. Have you always been a wild man?

14. This much is true—if you don't love hush puppies, you're not a genuine Southerner!

15. In a TV poll of 785 men in South Carolina, it was discovered that they prefer peach cobbler to hot fudge sundaes for dessert. Therefore, gals, the truth is what it is: If you want to find a way to a man's heart via his stomach, forget about a hot fudge sundae—make him a peach cobbler.

16. Have you always been so dull-witted when it comes to mathematical equations?

17. Maria came into a nice sum of money lately, if you can believe that! You know, I think it's because she's been using Feng Shui, putting her apartment in spiritual order. She put a large pile of coins in the north corner of her living room. They say that's supposed to help bring good energy to your work life. It sure must have worked! I think you should try Feng Shui, too. Maybe you can improve your finances.

18. Only if you believe money paves the road to happiness, will you be sufficiently motivated to change the world.

19. Do you realize 97 percent of the 240 participants at the Episcopalians' conference in Ottawa, Canada, said that prayer could bring about world peace? That suggests that 97 percent of adults think we can bring about world peace with prayer.

20. Kant was right to put honesty at the center of his moral theory. That means you are obligated to tell that phone solicitor your social security number and the list of people to whom you are financially indebted.

Part Two

In a speech at Morningside College in Sioux City, Iowa, Vice President Dick Cheney gave a speech containing several "either/or" propositions. Read this except and determine whether or not he committed the fallacy of bifurcation. Make your case for your position.

> "Ladies and gentlemen, on issue after issue, the choice on Nov. 2 is very clear. It's a choice between President Bush's optimism and Senator Kerry's pessimism. On national security, it's a choice between President Bush's confidence and Senator Kerry's confusion. On the economy, it's a choice between a president who took action and has led America to days of progress and opportunity, and a senator who would take us back to the days of malaise. That's a contest we welcome, and with your votes, it's a contest we will win."

More Fallacies of Presumption

7. Red Herring

The fallacy called **red herring** occurs when an irrelevant line of reasoning is intentionally used to divert people away from the topic at hand. We see this when someone purposely shifts the subject of the conversation to avoid an incriminating line of questioning or to deceive someone. This is a form of weaseling, by trying to escape rather than get trapped by the direction the conversation is headed. It's called a red herring because a stinking little herring (fish) is an effective way to lead hound dogs off the scent.

Examples of Red Herring

a. DR. TRAN: Excuse me, Jeremiah, what's that answer sheet I see you peeking at during this exam?

JEREMIAH: Oh Dr. Tran, I heard that you got invited to speak at the American Philosophical Association meeting. What an honor, I am sure you must be totally thrilled. And of course, everyone knows what a brilliant mind you have.

   b. AMY: Honey, what's this love letter from your secretary that I found in your pocket?

      MIKE: Oh sugar, my sweet pea, you have made the most delicious pot roast I ever ate in my life—what ingredients did you put into this heavenly gravy? And how did you make such tender green beans to accompany this feast?

   c. JOURNALIST: Governor Juarez, what do you have to say to the American people about the rising unemployment in this state?

      GOVERNOR: You know, we must think positive: during my term in office, inflation has stayed constant and I have helped keep drugs off the streets!

Most of us have seen red herring fallacies. People often jump around topics: Some families regularly communicate by going from one topic to the next and back to the first. But what marks a red herring is that the change of topic is made with the intent to deceive and divert attention from one thing to another.

8. Slippery Slope

The **slippery slope** fallacy involves cause and effect reasoning that fails to establish the links. Someone posits a causal chain by arguing that if we allow *this* to happen, a series of other things will come about. The problem is that the causal connection is not established—there is at least one weak link in the chain.

The slippery slope fallacy can take the form of a downward spiral. The argument is that a negative chain of events will follow from something being put into effect. There is no attempt to prove these are causally related. Rather, the connection is incorrectly assumed—not proven.

Many have been victims of parental slippery slopes. This occurs, for instance, when your parents say you can't stay out late because something bad will happen and that, in turn, will lead to something even worse, and that worse thing will lead to something truly horrific.

Be aware: Not all propositions that involve causal chains are slippery slopes. If it is demonstrated that situation A leads to situation B and so on, they are *not* committing the slippery slope fallacy. The fallacy occurs when the chain is asserted, but not proven.

An example of the slippery slope fallacy is in a full-page ad put out by R. J. Reynolds Tobacco Company that presents a series of questions: "Some politicians want to ban cigarettes. Will alcohol be next? Will caffeine be next? Will high-fat foods be next? Today it's cigarettes. Tomorrow?" The fallacy is in presuming that banning tobacco would necessarily lead to bans on other substances. The connection should not be assumed.

Examples of Slippery Slope

   a. I tell you, Bert, if we support the legalization of marijuana, next thing it will be the legalization of cocaine and then heroin and pretty soon the whole society will be on hard drugs. So don't support legalizing marijuana.

You Tell Me Department

Can you Spot the Slippery Slope?

In a speech on gun control William L. Pierce argued as follows:

> The present campaign to disarm Americans will not abate. . . . The target now is semiautomatic rifles. Later it will be all semiautomatic pistols. Then it will be other types of handguns. After that it will be all firearms which hold more than three cartridges. 'That's all a sportsman really needs,' they'll say. Then it will be all firearms except muzzle-loaders. Somewhere along the line, various types of ammunition will be banned. 'Only a criminal would want a cartridge like this,' they'll say. Before too many steps have been taken there will be compulsory registration of all firearms and firearm owners, in order to facilitate confiscation later.

You tell me: Can you spot the slippery slope fallacy in Pierce's argument?

b. ANN MARIE: I'm in favor of strict rules against cheating on exams.

YOLANDA: You are? If you punish students for cheating on exams, that will lead to punishing them for misquoting authors on essays, which, in turn, will lead to punishing them for spelling errors and finally punishing them because of one typo! It is clear that there should be no university policy against cheating!

c. My son tells me he would like to get a few rabbits as pets. But I will not allow it. If we start with a few rabbits, soon we will have hundreds of them everywhere and all our money will be spent on rabbit feed. Then he will want to get other animals too. I am not going to sacrifice my life savings for him to run a zoo.

9. Straw Man Fallacy

The **straw man fallacy** involves unfairly diminishing or distorting the opposition so one can stand out in comparison. The comparison attempts to denigrate the opponent's position so the audience would be crazy not to select the contrasting view! It can take one of two different forms:

1. When an opponent's position is presented as so weak or extreme that it's indefensible.
2. When an attack is made on the weakest of a variety of arguments to contrast with one's own, seemingly more defensible, position.

In the first case, when the opponent's view is presented as indefensible or hopelessly weak, we are then steered toward another more moderate or appealing position. This is accomplished by distorting the other's view, turning it into an extreme. The image of the "straw man" (*scarecrow*) is that of something so flimsy that it will go up in smoke if we put a match near it. In the second case, a person attempts to boost his or her own standing by casting doubt on the weakest of a set of arguments.

The Global Dimension

British Debates the Value of Spanking

Should spanking children be banned? This is being debated in England and Brendan O'Neill argues that slippery slope reasoning is behind it. Here's the argument:

The government is under pressure from a powerful antispanking lobby to outlaw all forms of physical punishment. Some in the antispanking lobby argue that, unless all forms of physical punishment are outlawed, the "minor tap" can easily become a "harsh strike," or something much worse. Lady

Walmsley has said that all child deaths by violence "start with a smack."

But this is a slippery-slope argument, and a deeply offensive one at that. The implication is that parents who start out spanking their kids might end up murdering them. Many in the antispanking lobby blur the distinction between spanking and assault. There is an assumption that parents who spank are murderers in the making (Brendan O'Neill, "Britain Debates: To Spank or Not to Spank," *Christian Science Monitor,* www.csmonitor.com, 19 Apr 2004)

We saw the straw man fallacy in the 1994 California election when Tom Umberg, the Democratic candidate for Attorney General, attacked Dan Lundgren, the Republican incumbent. He suggested that Polly Klaas, 12 years old, would not have been murdered if Lundgren had financed a computer tracking system for convicts. By painting his opponent in such an extreme manner, Umberg fell into a straw man fallacy. A similar attack was made on Michael Dukakis in 1988 for paroling a felon, Willie Horton, who subsequently attacked again. This seedy incident led to a later apology by Lee Atwater, campaign manager for the first President Bush.

Examples of Straw Man

a. Don't even think about his position. Opposing the death penalty means letting criminals walk away from crimes scot-free and giving them the green light to murder anyone they choose!

b. Students these days object to being searched for drugs. We must realize, however, that if we don't search them, then students will be peddling drugs at school and drug abuse will be rampant.

c. Those animal rights people make me sick. If they get their way, medical advances in this country will come to a grinding halt.

With the straw man fallacy, the opposition is painted as much more extreme than it actually is. What usually happens is that the speaker's own position is offered as the preferred, reasonable alternative.

10. Begging the Question (Petitio Principii)

Begging the question is a fallacy consisting of circular reasoning: the speaker assumes what she is trying to prove. So what happens is that the conclusion just

Group or Individual Exercise

Look for examples of straw man in political campaigns. Try to find as many examples of this fallacy as you can. Look at both the campaign advertising *and* the remarks of the contenders about their opponents' views or policies.

---

reaffirms what has already been said. For example, the speaker might reword one of the premises or use a synonym for one of the terms.

Examples of Begging the Question

a. People should get paid for studying for logic exams, because human beings deserve a salary for studying logic. [getting paid = getting a salary].

b. The belief in God is universal because everybody believes in God [universal belief = a belief everyone accepts].

c. The opponents of animal experimentation who are breaking into the facilities of biotech firms creating transgenic animals are justified in destroying the barns of the hybrid pigs because they have the right to tear down housing for such animals [justified in destroying the barns = the right to tear down housing].

Don't assume what you are trying to prove. What is concluded must come out of the premises and not be a restatement of them. A rehash is just that. The evidence must provide good reasons for drawing the conclusion. If the premises and conclusion say basically the same thing, we're facing a fallacy of begging the question.

Question-Begging Epithets.   One variation of begging the question uses highly slanted language. Here, biased language stacks the deck. The result is that it is difficult to stay focused on the issue. **Question-begging epithets** are either **euphemisms** (deck is stacked by praise) or *dyslogisms* (name-calling). The result is bias expressed either in very positive or very negative terms. (See Chapter 2 on language.)

One variation of eulogisms is to be found with **bloated claims.** Here we find exaggeration, grandiose promises, or predictions that are more pie-in-the-sky than likely. Examples are plentiful. Think of those magazine covers announcing "The Sexiest Man in the World" or "The Most Beautiful Woman Alive." Look, for instance at the cover of the August 29, 2004, *Parade* magazine. In big letters, we see "Why We Believe He is the Most Important Coach in America." Now, Joe Ehrmann, the coach in question, might be truly inspiring and a great coach. But to declare him the most important in the country seems like a claim that is hard to substantiate.

In addition, we often see eulogistic or dyslogistic ad campaigns and political speeches, as well as those "too good to be true" offers in personal life. An example is an ad for Maybelline's Wonder finish™ powder-finish foundation: "*New wonder finish™ clean powder—finish foundation now liquid-perfect coverage and a weightless powder finish in one incredible makeup! Just one step. Zero flaws. Instant wow!*

Claims that are loaded in the negative (dyslogisms) are equally problematic. Suppose you called a man a "leech on society" instead of "someone down on his luck." Your listeners could be so swayed by the negative label ("leech on society") that they unfairly and incorrectly infer that the "leech" is guilty of a crime.

Examples of Question-Begging Epithets (Euphemisms)

a. You should believe whatever our legislators say about patriotism because they are hard-working American citizens, with an appreciation of the greatness of this country's history.
b. Grandma definitely has good advice on tax reform since she is a veteran of World War II and drives the Meals on Wheels bus.

Examples of Question-Begging Epithets (Dyslogisms/Name-Calling)

a. Don't believe what those street thugs say about philosophy students—they are just a bunch of mealy-mouthed, pea-brained hustlers with no sense of the demands of the intellectual life.
b. Professor Stewart's ideas for rebuilding the downtown core seem off-base—he's a complete moron and a lush. He's too slimy for words!

The language used in the argument has either a negative or positive bias (that is why it is called "loaded"). This prejudicial slanting makes it hard to be objective in examining the evidence and suggests a relevance that doesn't exist.

11. *Fallacy of Misleading Vividness*

One of the fallacies connected with statistics and sample studies is the **fallacy of misleading vividness.** This fallacy occurs when strong evidence is completely overlooked because of a very striking (vivid) counterexample. What causes the fallacy is that the example is atypical and of little real significance next to the overwhelming statistical data or evidence that has been obtained. However, the personal anecdote or testimonial can be very persuasive.

Examples of Misleading Vividness

a. TINA: The American Heart Association recommends that we eat Omega-3 fatty acids and fish oil to be healthy. Check it out on their Web site—it's really helpful!

PINKY: Yeah? Well, my best friend, Bobo, got plenty of fish oil eating salmon all the time—and he ended up with mercury in his system—and I bet it was from all that salmon! Forget those fish oils! Go for steak!

TINA: Well now I certainly won't even consider taking them. Let's go for the red meat!

b. CAMILLE: Given the high rates of emphysema and lung cancer among smokers, it seems pretty obvious that smoking is the root cause.

NAJI: Really? Uncle John smoked like a chimney and he lived to 93 years of age and died of a gangrenous foot. That shows you all those statistics mean nothing and you should smoke if you want to.

12. False Analogy (or Imperfect Analogy)

The fallacy of **false analogy** occurs when a comparison is drawn between two different things, but there are few relevant similarities between them; thus creating the false analogy. The strength of the analogy rests on the relative weight of the similarities and differences between the two things being compared. When there are only trivial similarities, the false analogy sinks the argument. *Be careful:* There are usually *some* similarities between one thing and another, so you could think of this as an imperfect or very weak analogy rather than completely false. (See Chapter 7 on analogies for a fuller discussion.)

The key to watch for here is that the similarities are minor or inconsequential—and they are significantly outmatched by the differences. Gary N. Curtis ("Fallacy Files") tells the story of Lewis Carroll asking, "How is a raven like a writing desk?" They are not, but he did get one response that is clever in its play on words: "Because [Edgar Allen] Poe wrote on both."

Examples of False Analogy

a. A good woman is just like a nice car: She is under your control and makes your life a lot easier.

b. A good man is like a bowl of buttered popcorn: He is comforting and doesn't talk back.

c. Babies are like cats: They love to sleep in the sun and don't obey orders.

d. From W. H. Werkmeister: "Education cannot prepare men and women for marriage. To try to educate them for marriage is like trying to teach them to swim without letting them go into the water. It cannot be done."

In the first false analogy, what is similar between a good woman and a nice car? The "similarities" cited are trivial at best. A woman is not an object and, unless she is brainwashed, is not controlled by anyone. The second and third analogies also have only minor similarities; but the differences are significant. The last analogy also sinks. Sure people learn to swim by going in the water, notes Werkmeister—but in marriage much depends on understanding the social, personal, and economic problems to be faced. This does not require a trial marriage. This is the key to spotting this fallacy: If there are no real similarities (or only trivial ones) and substantial dissimilarities, then the analogy cannot be said to be good or bad. Rather, it is a false analogy.

You Tell Me Department

When is a lemon like a cat?

In an article on lemons, David Karp used an unusual analogy. He said:

The most astonishing lemon variant, known to just a few people, is a Eureka mutant with orange skin and flesh. . . . The fruit is sort of like a cat that barks: it tastes like a lemon but has the color of an orange. (David Karp, "Lemons, Yes, but Please! Don't Squeeze," *New York Times*, 5 Feb 2005).

You tell me: Is this a false analogy?

Group or Individual Exercise

Below is an excerpt from a "Dear Friends" letter that Michael Moore published on November 2, 2004—one day before the election. Read the excerpt and discuss his reasoning in general and his analogy in particular. Share your thoughts.

To Non-Voters:

I understand why you stopped voting. Politicians suck. Nothing ever seems to change. You're only one vote.

Yes, politicians suck. But so do car salesmen—and that hasn't stopped you from buying a car. Politicians only respond to the threat of the angry mob also known as the voting public. If most people don't vote, that's good news for them 'cause then they don't have to answer to the majority. Almost fifty percent of Americans don't vote. That means you belong to the largest political party in America—the Non-Voting Party. That means you hold all the power to toss George W. Bush out of the Oval Office. How cool is that? (Michael Moore, "One Day Left," www.michaelmoore.com, 2 Nov 2004)

Exercises

Part One

Name the fallacy, drawing from *all* the fallacies of presumption.

1. Only those who have seen a moose can claim to know the wilderness. Visit Alaska today!

2. Do you always steal from your friends?

3. Most people prefer tortillas to bagels. A Fall 2001 poll of Latinas at the National Educators Conference in Cincinnati, Ohio, found that nearly 87 percent considered tortillas superior to bagels for most cooking needs.

4. The Constitution guarantees freedom of speech. Therefore, people should have the freedom to post pornography on high school Web sites.

5. Before the movie started it said that the audience should not talk during the movie. Therefore, I'll have to wait until the credits roll to tell the woman in front of me that she put her pretty suede purse in a pool of spilled soda.

6. All you fine citizens of Philadelphia know this one truth: You must choose between security and freedom. Though you may be inclined toward freedom, don't forsake your security by outlawing assault rifles.

7. The college has a no-alcohol policy. Therefore, you probably won't be allowed to bring your rum-ball candies to the dance after the Super Bowl.

8. Carole was on her way to discuss her new film script with her agent when a meteorite shower pelted her car with marble-sized rocks. The agent loved her script, so that meteorite shower must have been a sign of good fortune.

9. Assemblywoman Snyder said the journalist who photographed her throwing popcorn in the polar bear compound at the zoo is just a pathetic little mealybug with nothing better to do than to cause trouble for respected politicians.

10. CHONG: I deserve an A, Professor Garry.

   DR. GARRY: I'm not sure why you say this, Chong. Clue me in.

   CHONG: My work warrants the highest grade a student can get, that's why.

11. My grandma said to never tell a lie. That means I should tell the new high school principal that she needs to go on a diet. That woman has a serious weight problem—I'm going to give her a few ideas on how to knock off some of that flab of hers!

12. *Consumer Reporter* said less fancy stoves have a better repair record than those new, expensive gourmet stove with all the doodads. But I'm not sure I should listen to them, since Amanda and Dan got a new stove that wasn't high-end—and they had all kinds of problems. Maybe the expensive ones are better after all.

13. "You're a scaremonger," Stossel scolded genetic engineering critic Jeremy Rifkin, "Why should we listen to you?" (See *Fairness and Accuracy in Reporting*).

14. Christina, if you keep drinking orange juice for breakfast, you'll get too much acid in your system. Too much acid means an ulcer can't be far behind and, next thing you know, you've destroyed your stomach lining! You'd be advised to cut back on that orange juice you've been guzzling.

15. How could a tax-paying citizen like Robert Downey, Jr., ever mean to violate his probation? He is innocent.

16. We ought to oppose gun control. Gun control means a police state is around the corner.

17. If you don't like fried chicken and popovers, you won't want to live in Kentucky.

18. ALEX: The new X-7 turbo speedster is the most reliable three-wheel vehicle on the road. It outperformed all other three-wheelers in every single test that *Power Wheel* magazine ran! You really out to get rid of that jalopy of yours and get an X-7, Pinky.

    PINKY: You've got to be kidding. Did you hear about Bobo's experience with the X-7? The electrical system caught on fire in the second week he had it—and then he never seemed to get the brakes to work well around the curve. He finally slid off the road into a cow pasture and that was that!

19. Your marriage, Gracie, is like a car with a bad transmission system—sure it keeps going but the price is awfully high and you aren't really enjoying the trip!

20. It's obvious that men overwhelmingly prefer naps to exercise, because a 2002 poll found 93 percent of male patients at nursing homes said they'd much rather nap than exercise.

21. Alma Warner has been concerned about the increasing number of abortions in this country. Be careful about voting for her for governor. A vote for her is a vote for the mentality of those who bomb abortion clinics!

22. Ticket agent to the 93-year-old woman: "I'm sorry that you were born before social security cards—without that or a driver's license you can't be allowed on the plane! Too bad you stopped driving 25 years ago. A rule is a rule."

23. North Korea is thinking of building its nuclear arsenal because they believe they need more high-tech weapons that have a nuclear capacity.

24. For the kick-off dinner for the Pre-Law Club they served moussaka from the Greek restaurant that recently opened on the Sunset Strip. It was so awful: It was too salty, the eggplant tasted like rubber and there was hardly any meat in it. It just goes to show you, you can't depend on Greek food if you want a nice dinner.

25. Timothy Peppersnout couldn't possibly be guilty of financial wrongdoing. You know how nice he is to the people in his neighborhood and he regularly gives money to charity.

26. Dr. Meek said not to respond to crying when you put the baby to bed. If you start checking every time the baby wails, then it will have the upper hand and next thing you know, your child will depend on you for a lifetime.

27. Leonard Watkins would be good as mayor since he'd be great as the top city official.

28. PROFESSOR: Pardon me, Reinaldo. What are these test notes doing here in the exam?

REINALDO: Oh, Professor Davidson, did I ever tell you how much I like your ties? You manage to find such colorful ones! Where do you shop?

29. If you let the little girl have a stick of gum, then she'll want gum every day and pretty soon she'll start swallowing it. Once she starts swallowing gum, her intestines will get all clogged up and she will have dreadful health problems. Don't give that child chewing gum.

30. Only if you have heard Pablo Neruda's poetry read in Spanish can you call yourself worldly.

31. Silvio says he loves me and he must be telling the truth, because he would never lie to someone he loves.

32. Love is like riding on the luge—sure someone's steering, but you're going much too fast to avoid problems and disaster looms around every corner!

33. Did you hear Mr. Glennon argue that the phony documents supposedly about Bush's National Guard service could possibly have been done on typewriters? He is saying that because features on computers existed in some form across various pieces of (very expensive and hard to get) equipment 32 years ago, it validates the documents. That's like saying the claim kids didn't skateboard in 1492 is false because wheels and boards existed back then. (See "Making a Dent in Liberal Disinformation: Rathergate," www.chronwatch.com, 14 Sep 2004.)

Part Two: Quick Quiz on Fallacies of Presumption

1. What is hasty generalization?
2. What happens in a post hoc fallacy?
3. Explain the fallacy of accident.
4. What happens in a red herring?
5. Explain why the slippery slope is aptly named.
6. How does hasty generalization differ from biased statistics?
7. What's an example of a complex question?
8. Why is bifurcation a fallacy?
9. Explain how we can spot question-begging epithets.
10. What makes a fallacy a straw man?
11. How does the fallacy of misleading vividness differ from hasty generalization?
12. What is the key thing to spot in a false or imperfect analogy?

Part Three

1. Discuss whether or not Senator Hatch committed a fallacy in the segment below and state your reasons why or why not:

   ### Raising the Minimum Wage Causes "Disemployment"

   [Some people] believe that an increase in the minimum wage is a quick, painless way to help the disadvantaged in our society. I can only wonder then why they have not offered raising the minimum wage to $15, $20, or $30 an hour. There is indeed an adverse effect on employment. For every 10% increase in the minimum wage, the disemployment effect was between 100,000 to 300,000 jobs. Disemployment means jobs not only eliminated, but also jobs that are never created in the first place. (See Senator Orin Hatch, www.issues2000.org.)

2. Discuss Richard Doerflinger's comment about experiments to clone human embryos:

   "They're really raising the stakes here," said Richard Doerflinger of the National Conference of Catholic Bishops, which opposes federal support for any kind of embryo research. "In two days, it's amazing we've had two announcements of drops down the slippery slope. We don't think there's a stopping point once you start down this road." (As noted by Rick Weiss, "Firm Aims to Clone Embryos for Stem Cells," *Washington Post,* 12 Jul 2001)

3. Discuss the reasoning in the argument by then Vice President Henry A. Wallace (July 25, 1943):

   We will not be satisfied with a peace which will merely lead us from the concentration camps and mass-murder of Fascism—into an international jungle of gangster governments operated behind the scenes by power-crazed, money-made imperialists. (As noted by W. H. Werkmeister, *Critical Thinking*).

4. The Red Sox went a long time without winning a pennant. Some argued it was the "Curse of the Bambino (Babe Ruth)" that was to blame. Do you think post hoc reasoning is operating in the discussion below of the rush to sign up Red Sox players for advertising spots? Share your thoughts about the comments of Michael Mendenhall of Disney's global marketing division, who explains why they just signed Sox players Pedro Martinez, David Ortiz, and Curt Schilling for commercials in both Spanish and English:

   "We saw an incredible achievement, the reverse of the curse, taking place, so this is one that deserves to be recognized," he said. "You could feel the momentum building with consumers," he added, "and when the Red Sox broke the so-called curse, we celebrated with them." (Quoted in "Now That the Curse Has Ended Marketers Love the Red Sox," *The New York Times,* 1 Nov 2004).

5. *Can you spot the fallacies?* Ralph said that his life went downhill after his pet snake died: He lost his job, his wallet was stolen while he was in line for

a movie, and he started drinking again. I'm sure that cobra dying was the cause of it—talk about a curse! Plus, I hear snakes get the spooks and can attack you without warning. *Post-hoc, false cause*

Most people think snakes are creepy, anyway. That's another good reason not to get a snake! When that many people agree on something, there must be truth to it. And don't forget, if you get a snake your dad will kick you out of the house! I know Richard said you should get a snake; that they are intelligent and excellent exterminators of rats and mice—but you should know by now that his advice isn't any good. He's from the Arctic, where there are no snakes! *Ad hominem*

Get a cat or dog instead of a snake. I heard Keanu Reeves has a cat and he seems happy enough. And Elvis didn't sing about hound dogs for nothing! In addition, if you get a snake you could pick up some tropical disease and then you could become sterile or get a weird disease like malaria. Next thing you know, you've lost a leg from gangrene or some infection! That's the last thing you need. Forget snakes! *Slippery slope*

[Marginal annotations: Ad hominem; Appeal to Force; Hasty generalization; Red Herring; Ad hominem; Appeal to authority]

Key Fallacies of Ambiguity

You pick up a magazine and read, "Prince Philip underwent surgery in a London hospital for a hernia. After being discharged, he warned that wild pandas face extinction within 30 years" (*Auckland Sunday Star*, as noted by *The New Yorker*). This is funny because of the juxtaposition of the report on his surgery and his warning about wild pandas.

You've just been hit with a linguistic fallacy. **Fallacies of ambiguity,** also known as **linguistic fallacies,** are so named because of an unclear sentence structure, grammar, or use of words. The result of the ambiguity is that an incorrect conclusion is drawn. In the case of the wild panda example, the ambiguity centers on the sentence structure—creating the humorous effect. Let's look at the different types of fallacies of ambiguity.

There are five main fallacies of ambiguity; the flawed reasoning relates to confusions created by such things as shifting meanings of words, misleading emphasis of a word or phrase, unclear sentence structure, or mistaken inferences from parts to wholes or vice versa. Let's look at these types of fallacies.

1. Equivocation

The fallacy of **equivocation** occurs when different meanings of a word or phrase are used in argument. The resulting ambiguity leads to an incorrect conclusion being drawn. This is also known as a *semantic fallacy*.

We often see equivocation in puns and jokes. For example, in the Wit Women cartoon (Figure 4.2), a woman is telling her counselor that her alien-mate is

FIGURE 4.2

moaning for more space. The equivocation on the word "space" is what makes the cartoon funny. Jokes—especially puns—often rest on equivocation. But when equivocation leads to an incorrect conclusion, it's not funny.

A special kind of equivocation has to do with "relative terms," which have different meanings in different contexts (like "tall" or "big" or "small"). We also see equivocation playing on the sound of a word; for example, "How do you make antifreeze? Steal her blanket." The word "antifreeze" sounds like "Auntie freeze," thus the joke. See also the cartoon in Figure 4.3.

Examples of Equivocation

a. Title of an article in *USA Today:* "Ex-gymnastics stars understand flip side to expectations and glory."
b. Ad for Corona Light (beer): "Moving at the Speed of Light."

FIGURE 4.3

Betty Jean is at it again! Equivocation on the word "beat" causes the humor here.

   c. Ad for movie *Cats and Dogs:* "Critics are lapping up the #1 movie! Two paws up!"

Examples of Equivocation Humor

   a. Two lovers who had been apart for some time were reunited on a foggy day. One whispered to the other "I *mist* you" (playing on mist/missed).

   b. The cheap eye surgeon was always cutting *corneas* (playing on corneas/corners).

   c. Two vultures boarded an airplane, each carrying two dead raccoons. The stewardess looked at them and said, "I'm sorry, gentlemen, only one *carrion* per passenger is allowed" (playing on carrion/carry on).

   d. A chicken crossing the road is *poultry* in motion (playing on poultry/poetry).

2. Accent

The fallacy of **accent** occurs when, because of the way a word or phrase is visually or verbally emphasized, we are led to drawing an incorrect conclusion. This includes the repetition of a word or phrase to create a certain effect that leads to an incorrect conclusion. Think, for example, of ads where the word "free" is accented but, in tiny print, we are told what we have to do or buy to get the freebie. Another way the fallacy of accent occurs is when someone misquotes another or takes something out of context. Taking material out of context can be very

FIGURE 4.4
Can you spot the
equivocation?

**GIVE SMOKING
A KICK IN THE BUTT.**

With every puff, your health could be going up in smoke.
If you'd like to kick the habit but you need help, call your local
American Cancer Society.
It could be the first step to quitting for life.

FIGURE 4.5
Note the equivocation
on the word "pop."

Thanks
For
Making
Us Best
Pop Duo.

problematic, even ludicrous at times. The way individual words are emphasized can affect the meaning or the impact of a sentence. For instance:

> *John Connor* will be the savior of the human race in the battle against the machines.
>
> John Connor will be the *savior* of the human race in the battle against the machines.
>
> John Connor will be the savior of the *human race* in the battle against the machines.
>
> John Connor will be the savior of the human race in the battle against *the machines*.

Each of the propositions above has impact, but the impact varies according to the emphasis. In the first case, the focus is on John Connor (versus others who could be saviors). The second proposition emphasizes what role Connor will play (savior as opposed to sacrificial lamb, cheerleader, etc.). The third proposition focuses on the group Connor will save in the battle against the machines (human race as opposed to the chosen ones, the animal species, the little children, etc.). The last proposition focuses on the opponent (the machines as opposed to the alien, the predator, the warthogs from hell, etc.). According to the emphasis, the focus and impact changes.

An example of misleading repetition is found in a Pillsbury ad once used for Hungry Jack Biscuits. The ad copy reads: "*Hello* **Honey!** Introducing Hungry Jack **Honey** Tastin' Biscuits. Warm your family's heart with the golden flavor of **honey**. New Hungry Jack Biscuits have the same tender, flaky layers that Hungry Jack Biscuits are famous for, with a touch of **honey** flavor baked right in. Try our Hungry Jack Biscuits today and treat your family to the taste of **honey**" (emphasis added).

The word "honey" is repeated five times in the advertisement, leading us to think these biscuits contain honey. However, the pictured container at the bottom of the page says "Hungry Jack *Artificial* Honey Flavor Flaky Biscuits" (emphasis mine).

Examples of Accent

a. *FREE BOX OF CHOCOLATES* whenever you buy $200 worth of merchandise.
b. From *Weekly World News*, August 14, 2001: **AMAZING DOG SPARKS RELIGIOUS REVIVAL** . . . by walking 16 miles to church every Sunday!
c. Fly to France for $100—not counting tax, surcharges, fuel fees, and miscellaneous charges.

3. Amphiboly

The fallacy of **amphiboly** occurs when the faulty grammatical structure of a sentence creates an ambiguity. Due to the ambiguous sentence, more than one interpretation is possible and, thus, an incorrect conclusion may be drawn. This is also known as a fallacy of *syntax*. Think of an amphibian—a creature that can live in two entirely different environments. The fallacy of amphiboly occurs when the sentence structure is confusing. For example, "Soon after Sam and Ella got married they experienced food poisoning." Because of the odd sentence structure, it sounds like Sam and Ella's food poisoning was caused by their marriage!

Sometimes amphiboly results from two nouns preceding the verb or two nouns with an unclear reference afterward (as in "Baby George walked toward Grandpa, his diaper falling to his knees"). Sometimes the fallacy results from a missing verb phrase—as in this twist on an example by Irving Copi, "Firefighters often burn victims." If the sentence structure seems awkward or funny, check for amphiboly.

Examples of Amphiboly

a. Title of article about Superior Court Judge, William R. Nevitt Jr. in the *Daily Journal:* "Former Helicopter Pilot Lands on Bench."
b. Marx Brothers line: "I shot an elephant in my pajamas. (How he got in my pajamas, I'll never know.)"
c. Noted in the *Farmer's Almanac:* "The concert held in the Fellowship Hall was a great success. Special thanks are due to the minister's daughter, who labored the whole evening at the piano, which as usual fell upon her."

4. Composition

The fallacy of **composition** occurs when we infer from what is true of the parts or members of something that the same thing is true of the whole thing (or organization). The fact that something is true of the members or parts of something does not mean that it will be true of the whole. Each of the parts or members may have some characteristic (say being lightweight), but that does not mean the whole group or object will be lightweight.

The characteristics of the parts do *not* necessarily transfer to the entity as a whole. For example, there could be a football team where every member is a great athlete, but they do not work well as a team. And we all know what it's like to buy top quality ingredients for that oh-so-special dessert and the crust ends up tasting like cardboard and the filling has too many lumps for anyone to praise the resulting pie.

Examples of Composition

a. Beyoncé, Nora Jones, and Shania Twain are all great singers. I bet they'd be a dynamite girl group.
b. Since each and every one of us must die, that means the human race must one day come to an end.
c. Raspberries are in season and I just made some delicious chicken dumplings. Therefore, we should put those raspberries on top of our chicken dumplings—yum!

5. Division

The fallacy of **division** occurs when we infer that what is true of a whole is also true of its parts. One form this fallacy takes is arguing that what is true of an organization will thus be true of its members—which is not necessarily the case. Division is the opposite of composition. There we went from what was true of each and every part and then argued it must be true of the whole. Here we surmise that a characteristic of the whole will be a characteristic of its parts or members. But this is fallacious too. For instance, you might have a very heavy piece of machinery that is made up of a large number of tiny, lightweight parts. So too with groups and organizations.

The fact that the Detroit Pistons were great in 2004 doesn't mean each player on the team was great that year. Even though the Louisville Symphony Orchestra did a phenomenal job at the Kentucky Jubilee, it does not necessarily mean the oboe player or the cellist was in top form. And while Omar's Kenyan chicken stew was exquisite, it does not follow that the tomato paste that was one of the ingredients was necessarily exquisite.

Examples of Division

a. The school board is inefficient. So, don't expect Irene Chan, the president of the school board, to do a good job.

b. Housing prices have been on the increase for the last 10 years. This means we ought to be able to get a great price for our house if we put it on the market.

c. The American Mathematical Society is highly regarded as an organization. Therefore, Dr. Pi, a founding member, must be held in high regard.

Exercises

Directions: Name the fallacy of ambiguity below.

1. *Restaurant ad:* "Our omelettes are eggceptional!"

2. *Airline ticket office sign:* WE TAKE YOUR BAGS AND SEND THEM IN ALL DIRECTIONS.

3. *From Peanuts Classics comic strip:* "The name of the other team was Devil's Advocate. They always win," he said. "I hate to play Devil's Advocate."

4. RITA (reading "For rent" ads): "This house sounds good, Ernie. Just listen—it's got a big kitchen, a large dining room, and a bedroom big enough to have a rocking chair over by the window across from the bed. It must be an enormous house!"

   ERNIE: "That's fantastic, Rita! The twins and the baby will really like having all that space to run around in."

5. Sailors don't have to do any laundry. If they just throw their clothes overboard they'll be washed ashore!

6. The White House is not nearly as large as you'd think, given all of its functions. Therefore, the Oval Office inside the White House must not be very large either.

7. *Sign in bar:* SPECIAL COCKTAILS FOR THE LADIES WITH NUTS

8. *Ad copy for the Boston Medical Professional Corporation:*

   SEX FOR LIFE!

   ERECTION PROBLEMS? PREMATURE EJACULATION?
   IMMEDIATE RESULTS (only one consultation required).
   Licensed MDs specializing in men's health. Safer and more effective treatment than Viagra. Medication exclusively formulated for premature ejaculation. Separate waiting rooms to ensure your privacy. Especially beneficial to patients with diabetes, high blood pressure, heart conditions, stress, etc., or those who would like to improve their sex lives.

   Boston Medical Professional Corporation

9. Last night I saw the movie *Nuclear Mutants*. That movie is so bad it should be punished.

10. Maria Elena had been dancing for 12 years when she broke her leg.

11. KIDS FLY FREE!
    When their parents buy first-class tickets.
    Offer valid only from February to May.

12. The Supreme Court is an honorable institution and, thus, it follows that Justice Thurgood Marshall must have been honorable too, given he served so long on the Court.

13. We should do what's right. What is right should be enforceable by the legal system. People have a right to die with dignity; therefore, physician-assisted suicide should be legal in this country.

14. *On a restaurant menu:* OUR WINES LEAVE YOU NOTHING TO HOPE FOR

15. **MAKE BIG BUCKS WITHIN A YEAR** if you participate in the fetal brain transplant study. Call today: 888-NO-BRAIN.

16. *Ad for William Bounds Ltd. pepper mill* (which grinds and crushes peppercorns):

    We've got a crush on pepper!

17. Yao Ming is a big man, even for a basketball player. Therefore, he must have huge feet and hands.

18. A discussion of beautiful women cited Angelina Jolie (best lips), Julia Roberts (best smile), Andie McDowell (best hair), Drew Barrymore (best

eyes), and Janet Jackson (best midriff). Can you imagine how beautiful the woman would be if she had all these traits?

19. WIN FREE RENT FOR LIFE if you will be our first subject in a brain transplant. *Ament*

20. Haji had been lifting weights for 20 years when he dropped a barbell and crushed his big toe.

21. *Ad for Crown Royal Whiskey after Lakers won the 2001 NBA championship:* "Every Champion Deserves a Crown" (photo of basketball next to Crown Royal whisky bottle).

22. Ad for Crest Whitestrips teeth-whitener:

    > WHITEN WHILE YOU COLOR [YOUR FINGERNAILS].
    > Or while you apply makeup, blow-dry your hair or even shower. Crest Whitestrips work easily into any routine. **All it takes is 30 minutes twice a day for two weeks for a noticeably whiter smile.** Consider it multitasking.
    >
    > **Dramatization of typical 14-day results.*

23. (From the *Farmer's Almanac*): Frequent naps prevent old age, especially if taken while driving.

24. I saw Yellowstone flying from Sacramento to Minneapolis. *amphiboly*

25. *Ad for Cointreau liqueur:*

    Be COINTREAUVERSIAL™

    TO THE BEAT OF A DIFFERENT DRUM

26. The Detroit Pistons have shown themselves to be the number 1 basketball team in the country. You can't win the NBA championship over and over without being NUMBER ONE. Therefore, every single member of the team is the best, and I mean the best there is!

27. *Original logo of the Fighting Whites basketball team:* "Every thang's gonna be all white!!!"

28. Don't be chicken. Try octopus for a change! It's delicious.

Formal Fallacies

These fallacies occur because of an error in the very form of the reasoning. Given that a conditional proposition is true, neither denying the antecedent nor affirming the consequent can permit us to conclude that (in the first case) the consequent is false or (in the second case) the antecedent must be true. The fact that one cause did not occur does not mean the effect couldn't have happened. Similarly, the fact that an event happened does not necessarily mean that one particular causal factor had to occur. As a result, the very form of the reasoning is incorrect. The truth of the premises will never guarantee the truth of the conclusion because of a structural error.

1. Fallacy of Affirming the Consequent

The *fallacy of affirming the consequent* starts with a conditional claim and then argues that, if the consequent is true then the antecedent is also true. In other words, if the effect happens, this one possible cause must happen as well. This is bad reasoning because an effect can potentially have many causes unless it is clearly stated that it has but one—the one stated in the antecedent. Otherwise, you should assume there could be other causes for the effect. So if the effect occurs, it may be due to a different cause—not the one stated in the antecedent.

The fallacy of affirming the consequent takes the form:

If A then B

B is true

Therefore A is true.

For example, "If the rain continues, the roof will collapse. The roof collapsed. Therefore, the rain continued." But, any number of things could cause a roof collapse; for example, if the neighbor's oak tree fell on the roof or four Halloween pranksters leapt on the roof.

An *equivalent form* of this fallacy is: "All A is B. B, therefore A." For example, "All werewolves howl at the full moon. Something is howling at the full moon, so it must be a werewolf." Not necessarily—it could be one of those coyotes you keep seeing in the canyon behind the house or the neighbor's dog Big. Note that the antecedent may not necessarily start the sentence—in other words, this fallacy could take the form "B if A. B, therefore A."

Examples of the Fallacy of Affirming the Consequent

a. If Hassan gets another political call, he'll turn off the ringer on the phone. Hassan turned off the ringer on the phone, so he must have gotten another political call. [*Hold it:* maybe he got obscene calls or he didn't want to wake up his little sister, Anna, who was napping on the couch].

b. If the car has a flat tire, we'll have to call for help. We had to call for help for the car; therefore the car had a flat tire. [*Hold it:* maybe we had to call for help because we ran out of gas or because we hit a coyote that jumped out into the freeway].

c. All women who drive convertibles love the feeling of wind in their hair. Jasmine loves the feeling of wind in her hair; therefore she must drive a convertible. [*Hold it:* maybe Jasmine likes wind in her hair and drives a Harley or rides her horse to school].

2. Fallacy of Denying the Antecedent

The *fallacy of denying the antecedent* starts with a conditional claim and then argues that, if the antecedent condition is false then the consequent cannot be true. In other words, if the causal condition does not happen, then neither does the effect (consequent) occur. This is bad reasoning because an effect may have more than one cause, unless it is so indicated. Thus, if one antecedent condition (cause) is eliminated, it does not mean the effect did not occur. For instance, the fact that gubbing down the entire jar of jelly beans will ruin your diet does not mean that *not* eating them means your diet is now safe. Not true! Instead of jelly beans, you might have wolfed down two pizzas that were *not* low carb!

The fallacy of denying the antecedent takes the form:

If A then B

A is false.

Therefore B is false.

Alternatively, you can think of it as saying "A, one cause, did not happen," therefore "B, the effect, did not happen either." For example, "If it snows through the night, we will light a fire at breakfast time. It did not snow through the night, therefore we did not light a fire at breakfast time." But, we may light a fire at breakfast time even if it didn't snow; for example, if there was a terrible cold snap or the electricity went out or we want the house to look pretty for our relatives who are coming over.

An *equivalent form* of this fallacy is this: "All A is B. Not A, therefore not B." For example, "All wolves are animals. Chickens are not wolves, so chickens are not animals." Note that the antecedent may not necessarily start the sentence—in other words, this fallacy could take the form "B if A. Not A, therefore not B." For example, "Bill sings at the top of his lungs if he hears Otis Redding music. Bill did not hear any Otis Redding music, so he did not sing at the top of his lungs." But perhaps Bill also likes other music for a little sing-a long, such as B. B. King or John Trudell.

Examples of the Fallacy of Denying the Antecedent

a. If we go see *The Manchurian Candidate*, we'll eat a large box of popcorn. We did not go see *The Manchurian Candidate*, so we did not eat a large box of popcorn.
   [*Hold it:* Maybe it was sold out and we went to see *The Village* instead and ate our popcorn then.]

b. All cows prefer grass to lettuce. A guinea pig is not a cow. So a guinea pig does not prefer grass to lettuce.
   [*Hold it:* Just because the guinea pig is not a cow doesn't mean it eats different food.]

c. You'll be exhausted if you run the Boston marathon. Marielos was exhausted, so she must have run the Boston marathon.
   [*Hold it:* She could be exhausted because she shoveled snow all morning or worked in the garden planting ferns.]

Exercises

Part One

Directions: Name the formal fallacy below. Not all are fallacies, so be careful!

1. If the little boy eats a jar of peanut butter, he'll be thirsty. The little boy was thirsty, so he must have eaten up a jar of peanut butter.

2. All donuts are greasy and tasty. That's not a donut, so it must not be greasy or tasty.

3. All forms of exercise are things worth thinking about when lying on the couch. Bicycling is a form of exercise, so it is worth thinking about when lying on the couch.

4. If Adam crawls out of the living room and into the kitchen, then he may either get dirt on his knees or he'll surprise the cats. Adam surprised the cats, so he must have crawled out of the living room and into the kitchen.

5. All poisons are things small children should avoid. Boiling water is something small children should avoid, so boiling water is a poison.

6. If Louie drinks another espresso, he'll be up all night. Louie did not drink another espresso, so he was not up all night.

7. Jasper will chew up a small piece of the window if he's left on top of his cage looking out at the garden. Jasper was not left on top of his cage looking out at the garden, so he must not have chewed up a small piece of the window.

8. If Moosh brings Turkish delights to the party and arrives early, then she'll be able to surprise Tony. Moosh was able to surprise Tony, so she must have brought Turkish delights to the party and arrived early.

9. All college students are overworked but enthusiastic people. Amir is not a college student, so he must not be overworked or enthusiastic.

10. Unless Jasper hangs upside down and says "peekaboo," he seems like a normal bird. Jasper seems a normal bird, so he must neither have hung upside down nor said "peekaboo."

11. Give an example of an argument in the form of the fallacy of denying the antecedent.

12. Finish the argument using the form of fallacy of denying the antecedent: "If Carla goes to Iceland for her vacation, then she'll forget about going to see Graceland."

13. Finish the argument using the form of fallacy of affirming the consequent: "If Carla wants to go to law school, she'll have to study for the LSAT exam."

14. Finish the argument using the form of fallacy of affirming the consequent: "We'll need a repairman if Jasper chews up the door sill."

15. Finish the argument using the form of fallacy of denying the antecedent: "Jasper will enjoy a piece of cantaloupe if he doesn't eat too many kernels of corn."

Part Two

Directions: Name the fallacy below. These draw from *all* the fallacies we studied in this chapter.

1. A large meal isn't fattening if you take small bites.

2. They gave my father morphine when he was dying of cancer. It was the best thing to do for his pain. That means everyone should be able to use morphine any time they want. Why not legalize it?

3. Mel Gibson ate dog food in *Lethal Weapon,* so it must be tasty. Try some!

4. Ad for Chevy "Colorado":

AN AMERICAN REVOLUTION
EVERYTHING'S BIGGER IN COLORADO

5. "The Indians of Milwaukee spread the rumor that they were going to invade the Milwaukee Yacht Club so they could have *Red Sons in the Sail Set,* but it was rumor and nothing more" (see Vine Deloria, Jr., *God Is Red: A Native View of Religion*).

6. We ought to allow stem cell research. Polls show that the majority of people support it.

7. The Constitution guarantees us a right of privacy for decisions about reproductive freedom. Therefore, gays should be able to use surrogate mothers to bear them children.

8. Timothy McVeigh was supposedly—and I mean supposedly—executed for his part in the Oklahoma City bombing. But you know they did *no* autopsy! Without an autopsy, we cannot be sure he's actually dead. You can't prove to me he was really killed by lethal injection. I can conclude one thing and one thing only: Timothy McVeigh is still alive.

9. Frances said that eating tomatoes is bad for you: If you eat tomatoes, your diet is too acidic. An acidic diet is simply too yang! And if you have a diet that is imbalanced in terms of the yang and yin elements, you are more prone to illness and cancer. Look at those stewed tomatoes piled up on your plate! Your health is in jeopardy. Stick to seaweed treats. Here, have some nori!

10. The intricate design of nature can only be due to the existence of God because there could be no natural order and design if God did not exist.

11. No one has proven that jailing pregnant drug abusers is a societal problem; therefore it must be morally permissible to incarcerate pregnant women who abuse drugs. Lock them up!

12. DIANA: Hey Frank, what's that weird mark doing on the side of your neck?

    FRANK: Oh, Diana, did I ever tell you what a lovely voice you have? I bet you could get a record contract!

13. If you don't savor the taste of a green corn tamale, you can't call yourself a gourmet. You savored the taste of a green corn tamale, so you can call yourself a gourmet.

14. I can't understand why the coach was arrested for sexual harassment. He always helps out with the Little League and drives the church school bus for the Sunday school.

15. *Ad for Olympus digital camera:* "Olympus: America's Most Popular Camera Series."

16. You would be advised to think twice before voting for Jim Bradley for Governor. He's a vegetarian and someone like that will make sure the beef industry in this state is stripped of any lobbying power in the legislature!

17. VIOLET: You know, Dan, I just don't believe God exists.

    DAN: You'd better believe in God, or you'll go straight to hell!

18. Friedrich Nietzsche suffered from incurable syphilis. That means we shouldn't waste our time reading his work—it couldn't possibly have any value for us today.

19. Dr. Tan's students took a poll of patients in County General. They were all senior citizens living on a fixed income. They said that hospital food is grossly underrated. In fact, they agreed that, on the whole, most hospital food is delicious. Therefore, all American patients must think hospital food is delicious.

20. Aerobic exercise is great for your cardiovascular system. Therefore, Mr. Martinez should do it to help his recovery from his quadrupal bypass surgery last week!

21. *Title of article on fashion:* "Dress Code Anarchy and the Right to Bare Arms."

22. Did you hear about Martin trying to convince Carlos to stop drinking raw eggs in beer? Martin said it's bad for your health and might even cause kidney problems. But who is he to talk? He can dish out advice; but he never takes it!

23. Why did the cow stop giving milk? Because she was an udder failure!!

24. The reality is this, Bob: If you don't stay in shape, no woman will find you attractive.

25. You know, Nancy, men are all alike; they all like to ogle naked women! Do you realize that I saw 15 men going into the strip club on Hollywood Boulevard—just in the time I was in my car waiting for the light to change. I tell you, it's a sad world we live in.

26. DR. CHAN: Hey, Rita, what's that I heard about you being an ex-con?

    RITA: Oh, Dr. Chan, did anyone ever tell you that you look like Bruce Lee? I bet you get stopped all the time and asked for your autograph.

27. Title of article on the tennis superstars Venus and Serena Williams: "Venus Mars It for Serena."

28. Have you always been pig-headed?

29. Humans must be the products of environmental determinism since no one has proved for certain that we have free will.

30. Children should not be allowed out on Halloween. This is due to the fact that every year at least one person finds something like a razor inside an apple or glass placed inside a candy bar. It's a shame you can't trust anyone any more.

31. Question asked of Diana Eck, noted in *Encountering God*: "Give me a quick yes or no: Is Christ the only way to salvation?"

32. Don't pay any attention to Senator Ted Kennedy's proposal to help those on welfare. You know he's a Kennedy and must have millions to his name! What could he possibly know about poverty?

33. *Ad for prayer books:* Nun Better.

34. Liposuction is the all-American way to become thin. Do it today!

35. Australia is the most beautiful country. We can conclude, then, that every town in Australia must also be beautiful.

Part Three

Directions: Name the fallacy below. Be on the watch. If it is *not* a fallacy, say so.

1. GWEN: Hey there, Terry, what are you doing with all those cartons of milk? Did you pay for them or what??

   TERRY: You know, Gwen, I've been meaning to tell you how much I love your Tweetie Bird padded hat! You look just darling in it! Have you thought about wearing it to class? It's sooo cute!

2. I know you didn't want to do a nude scene, Maricella. But if you get modest on me now, you can forget about trying out for the part of Rosa in the sequel to *Silence of the Sheep*. You decide, my fair one!

3. Pistons knew their prince would come: As a rookie in the play-offs last year, Tayshaun Prince showed such promise that the Detroit Pistons

decided they didn't need another small forward. The long-limbed Prince, they believed, was no pauper (Jerry Crowe, "Pistons Knew Their Prince Would Come," *Los Angeles Times*, 4 Jun 2004).

4. DEFENSE ATTORNEY: Tell me, Miss Raymond, you say you saw the defendant attack Mr. Busso at the Chicago Brew House at 8:00 P.M. on Saturday, July 12th?

   MARIE BUSSO: Yes, I did. He hit him with a tire iron three times.

   DEFENSE ATTORNEY: Well, tell me, Miss Busso. Isn't it a fact that you are a lesbian and that's why you were at the Brew House in the first place? Didn't you go there to pick up another woman?

5. Robert Thurman has written a lot of books on Tibetan Buddhism, but I don't know whether to believe what he says, since he's not an Asian.

6. Professor Green, can you tell me the answer to this question: "Why is it that girls are more linguistically advanced than boys?"

7. Heredity alone makes someone into a criminal since heredity by itself determines what a person becomes.

8. OFFICER: Hey, mister, what's this foot I see sticking out of your trunk?

   SLEAZY ALBERT: Oh, officer, I hear you were given an award last night at the LAPD command center. That's really great—I bet your parents are so proud of you!

9. The Democratic Party favors strong unions. Therefore, Senator Strom Thurmond, a Southern Democrat, will surely vote for the ballot measure to strengthen the Teachers Union.

10. "Bioethics boards look like watch dogs, but they are used like show dogs" (*The New York Times*, 2 Aug 2001).

11. Radiated food must not be bad for your health. No one has proved it causes cancer—so it must be OK.

12. Loosely wrapped in bubble-wrap, she carried a crystal vase.

13. Tayshaun Prince, Allen Iverson, Kevin Garnett, Tracy McGrady, and Tim Duncan are all great basketball players. If they were on a team together, they'd be dynamite.

14. Freedom of speech is a hallmark of a democracy. Therefore, neo-Nazis should be free to verbally harass the Jewish family down the street.

15. Title on an article on men who bake bread: "Men's *rising* obsession: They're *loafing* and proud of it. . ."

16. You really ought to help John hide some of his assets from the government so he doesn't have a big tax bill this year. You know what the Golden Rule says about doing unto others what you'd like them to do to you. If you helped him cheat on his taxes, you could probably count on him if you ever needed help in exchange.

17. *For sale:* Combination TV-VCR and futon.

18. Hey Ernie, if you can't play ping pong, you'll never be a great athlete. Don't you think you should play a few rounds with Betty Jean in your lunch break?

19. If the mudslide causes Charlie's pool to slide down the hill, then his neighbors could suffer damage too. I hear Charlie's neighbor, Jamal, had mud all over his front yard and his roof caved in. Therefore, the mudslide must have caused Charlie's pool to slide down the hill.

20. If we teach people to think clearly and logically, our country will be stronger. This is due to the fact that a strong country requires that its citizens have well-developed reasoning skills.

21. Only those who have smelled a grizzly bear in their tent have had to come to terms with their own mortality.

22. Two men I met at the racquetball court thought the proposal for a ban on pornography was a stupid idea—that it'd mean magazines or movies showing any bare skin at all would be censored! Sorry, but I don't want to live in a puritanical society—do you?

CHAPTER FIVE

Analysis: The Heart of Critical Thinking

Power dies, power goes under and gutters out, ungraspable. It is momentary, quick of flight and liable to deceive. As soon as you rely on the possession it is gone. Forget that it ever existed, and it returns. I never made the mistake of thinking that I owned my own strength, that was my secret.

LOUISE ERDRICH, *Tracks*

Analysis is not just done by scientists in a lab. It is an aspect of all of our lives, even on the most mundane or everyday level. Hanging out at the gym, for example, you overhear three men on the weight machines trying to decide whether to try insulin instead of anabolic steroids to bulk up. Here's what they had to say:

VINCE (wiping the sweat off his brow): Bulking up is a must, that's why I do 'droids (anabolic steroids).

CHAD: You aren't worried about developing breasts and losing hair?

VINCE: Yeah, I guess so, but what can I do? You use what's out there. I hear some of the guys have been using insulin to increase muscle mass. But that seems kinda risky. Insulin is for diabetics and I heard Roy passed out the other day after he shot insulin.

CARLOS (setting the weights for leg lifts): No one should use illegal drugs—it's just another form of cheating. I'd rather do the best I can do without pushing the envelope. If I win, I win. If I lose to someone shot full of drugs, big deal. You got to live with yourself.

CHAD (working out on the free weights): Not cool, but I'm under pressure to try insulin if others are doing it. Let's face it; I'm not as big as you are. If there's any shortcut, I'm going to try it. If my time is up, it's up—you can't live in fear!

CARLOS: You're nuts, Chad. You take your shortcut and your time *will* be up! A little fear is a good thing, if you ask me. Got to go now—catch you guys later!

You leave the gym, trying to get a grip on the conversation between Vince, Carlos, and Chad. You haven't given much thought to illegal drug use by athletes and want to understand the key issues.

To accomplish this, you need to develop your brainpower, gather and weigh evidence, sort relevant from irrelevant information, consider competing explanations, assess the cogency of the reasoning, and arrive at some conclusion if at all possible. To say the least, these are very useful skills.

At the heart of critical thinking lies the ability to analyze. Extracting key ideas, pulling out hidden assumptions, and setting out the structure of arguments are important aspects of analysis. It also helps to have a creative, expansive side where we generate ideas and turn over alternatives in our minds. We see this when we try to see the big picture, set goals, brainstorm ideas, and set out a plan of action. Keep this broader view in mind as we dissect arguments, organize the various components, inspect fine details, and see how it all works together. It is not always easy to stand back and examine what we wrote, said, or thought. Think of all the times we thought of a clever retort—two hours later. It can happen to us all; but building the skills and regularly applying them helps us be able to pull them up more quickly.

In this chapter we will look at analysis and become familiar with its various elements. These are: credibility, types of evidence, weighing evidence, analysis of a short article, and analysis of a longer article. Acquiring the skills to address these concerns is crucial for critical thinking and for concise writing. We want to be able to express our ideas clearly and set out our positions in a defensible manner. This chapter is of fundamental importance for building a wide range of analytical skills. Let's start with credibility.

Assessing Credibility

Issues and problems do not exist in a vacuum, but are embedded in people's lives. Let's look at an example. In 1985, a case came to trial in Boston that centered on a police detective who struck a man suspected of soliciting a prostitute who resisted arrest. Seven people spoke at the trial: Long Kuang Huang (alleged victim), Detective Francis Kelly, Bao Tang Huang (Huang's wife), Audrey Manns (prostitute), Paul Bates (construction worker—witness), Gretl Nunnemacher (defense witness), and Dr. Jane Silva (neurologist). Use the credibility grid following the article, created by Mary Anne Saul, to rate each speaker on a scale of one to five (five being high, or very credible; one being low, not credible).

Defense Witnesses Describe Chinatown Beating

John H. Kennedy

Defense witnesses in the nonjury trial of Long Kuang Huang yesterday drew a sympathetic portrait of the peasant farmer from China as perhaps a victim of mistaken identity just 10 months after he immigrated to the United States. Huang, 56, is on trial in Boston Municipal Court on charges of soliciting sex for a fee and assault and battery on Detective Francis G. Kelly Jr. last May 1 near the Combat Zone [a seedy area in Boston with strip clubs and bars]. Attorneys are scheduled to give closing arguments this morning before Judge George A. O'Toole Jr. makes his decision.

In the final day of testimony, all the witnesses were called by Huang's attorneys, and included his wife. Some described the scuffle between Kelly and Huang, although their versions differed on details. The case has become the focus of charges by some Asian-Americans of police brutality. Kelly faces police department hearings on his conduct during the May 1 incident.

Bao Tang Huang, 52, whose testimony in Chinese was translated, said her husband could write his name in English, but did not speak English. His only experience with police was in China where officers wear white uniforms and do not carry badges, she said. Both grew up and lived in a "large village" of 300 people in the People's Republic, where Huang was a farmer. They have two sons, who came with them to Boston July 1, 1984. Huang has no formal education and has worked in restaurants in the Boston area, she said.

Earlier this week, prostitute Audrey Manns identified Huang in court as the man who spoke broken English to her, and who made it clear that he would pay her $30 to have sex with him. Kelly testified he followed them for two or three blocks before arresting Manns, and then Huang after an extended struggle, in front of 35 Kneeland St.

Kelly and Manns testified that Huang kicked and hit the detective several times before Kelly connected with a single punch to Huang's face in an attempt to subdue him. The detective also testified he identified himself as a police officer, both with his badge and by speaking to Huang.

Two defense witnesses yesterday said the detective connected with two punches to Huang's face, while Manns told the detective to stop. Paul Bates, 39, was working on a renovation project at 35 Kneeland St. when he saw a woman in an "electric blue" outfit and "bright blonde" hair walk by with a man who looked Hispanic.

A short time later, Bates said he came onto the street and saw Kelly struggling with Huang. The blonde woman in the blue outfit, who he said was Manns, came over to the two. "She told him [Huang] to stop struggling, the other person was a police officer," said Bates. Bates said Manns told Kelly: "He's not the man. I wasn't with him. He was just walking down the sidewalk. I swear to God, Kelly." He said he later saw Kelly connect with two "short, chopping punches."

The version of another defense witness, Gretl Nunnemacher, differed somewhat from Bates'. She said Kelly slammed Huang against the side of the car "several" times, Kelly's fist started to come down but she said she didn't see it land. Then, said Nunnemacher, a blonde woman emerged from another car. "She said, 'Kelly, Kelly, what are you doing. Stop,' . . . she told me he was a cop." Dr. Jane Silva, a neurologist who treated Huang at the New England Medical Center, said Huang suffered a concussion with post-concussive symptoms—headaches, dizziness, listlessness."

Source: Boston Globe, 23 Aug 1985. Reprinted with permission of the *Boston Globe.*

The Saul Credibility Grid

WITNESSES	CREDIBLITY RATING	STANDARDS Low 1 2 3 4 5 HIGH					REASONS FOR YOUR RATING
L. Huang							
Det. Kelly							
B. Huang							
A. Manns							
P. Bates							
G. Nunnemacher							
Dr. Silva							

When making your list of standards (criteria), think about what makes the person seem credible. Proximity to the crime, ability to observe easily, conflict of interest, background information, professional training, cultural factors, and personal characteristics may all affect a person's ability. These factors act as criteria for credibility of witnesses. Thanks to Ann Garry's Critical Thinking class at Cal State Los Angeles, there is more about this trial that we can examine (they tracked down subsequent articles on the case). These provided the basis for the following set of exercises.

Exercises

1. Prosecution witness, Harry Ayscough, helped the defense in the Chinatown case, above. He testified that Audrey Manns yelled, "He's not the one, that's not him," as Detective Kelly tried to arrest Long Kuang Huang.

   Answer the following:
   a. Do you think this testimony clearly indicates that Detective Kelly may have been arresting the wrong man?
   b. Is there any other conclusion that might be drawn from the testimony?

2. Does the fact that Audrey Manns testified that it was Huang who offered to pay $30 for sex and then violently resisted arrest create any conflict with your decision about Ayscough's testimony (set out in 1, above)? Discuss how you'd resolve a possible conflict in these pieces of evidence.

3. What significance should you give the fact that defense witnesses painted a sympathetic portrait of Long Kuang Huang and suggested that he might have been a victim of mistaken identity?

4. The case resulted in an unusual settlement. In your assessment, does this seem like a wise decision in terms of its impact on police–community relations?

Huang received $85,000 from the city. Detective Kelly got $40,000 in back pay and overtime (he had been suspended without pay for a year), $55,000 in legal fees, and $20,000 in additional damages. In return, Kelly was to drop a suit against the police commissioner and Huang was to drop his $1 million civil rights suit against the Boston police. Joseph Mulligan, the corporation counsel, said, "We decided to package the whole enchilada and make it all go away" (Steve Marantz, "2-Way Settlement Ends Police Suit," *Boston Globe*, 15 Jul 1989).

Cogency

When assessing an argument, one key concern is whether or not the reasoning is **cogent.** This means that the argument is convincing because of the quality and persuasive force of the evidence supporting the conclusion. A **cogent argument** is well reasoned and clearly structured so we can follow the argument, seeing how the evidence lays the foundation for the conclusion. This is a cogent argument:

> If you want superlative sound from your audio system but don't want speakers that could do justice to Stonehenge dominating your room, this should be music to your ears: Bookshelf speakers and three-piece systems performed just as well as—and in some cases better than—floor-standing speakers in our latest tests. And some fine performers cost only $100 to $200, so you can save money as well as space.
>
> That's a switch from years past, when big-box models were considered the only way to get outstanding sound quality. . . . we tested 23 bookshelf speakers ranging in price from $100 to $650 a pair and five three-piece systems priced at $300 to $600. We compared these speakers to three floor-standing models, priced at $400 to $700 . . . The results demonstrate that smaller speakers more than hold their own. ("Small Boxes, Big Sound," *Consumer Reports*, Aug 2001)

The evidence is clearly set out and the results of the tests are cited to demonstrate that the different units are comparable in quality. The conclusion is presented first, with the evidence offering strong support. The task in setting out a cogent argument is this:

- Aim for a well-structured argument
- In which it is clear what is being asserted
- With sufficient evidence supporting that conclusion
- And relying on no unwarranted assumptions
- So that no alternative conclusion seems plausible.

The Global Dimension

Bilinguals and the Brain

The *BBC News* reports on a language study by a York (Canada) University researcher that suggests a link between bilingualism and brainpower. Read about it, keeping your mind open to alternative explanations. Answer the questions that follow.

> This latest study appears to back up the theory that language skills also have a protective effect. Dr. Ellen Bialystok and colleagues at York University assessed the cognitive skills of all those involved in the study using a variety of widely recognised tests. They tested their vocabulary skills, their non-verbal reasoning ability and their reaction time. Half of the volunteers came from Canada and spoke only English. The other half came from India and were fluent in both English and Tamil. The volunteers had similar backgrounds in the sense that they were all educated to degree level and were all middle class.
>
> The researchers found that the people who were fluent in English and Tamil responded faster than those who were fluent in just English. This applied to all age groups. The researchers also found that the bilingual volunteers were much less likely to suffer from the mental decline associated

with old age. "The bilinguals were more efficient at all ages tested and showed a slower rate of decline for some processes with aging," they said. "It appears . . . that bilingualism helps to offset age-related losses." (See "Being Bilingual Protects Brain," *BBC News World Edition,* news.bbc.co.uk, 15 Jun 2004.)

Answer the following:

1. What assumptions do the researchers make in using sample groups from different countries (and, possibly, different backgrounds)?
2. Offer at least two alternative explanations for the research subjects from India having superior cognitive abilities besides their language skills.
3. Research the studies done on turmeric and Alzheimer's disease. As you may recall, the spice turmeric is in curry—which is often used in Indian cooking (e.g., see "Curry 'May Slow Alzheimer's'," *BBC News,* news.bbc.co.uk, 21 Nov 2001). Studies indicate that turmeric may be a reason that Alzheimer's disease is rarely found in India. If diet may be a factor in Alzheimer's, should it be factored in when assessing this study on bilingualism's supposed benefits? Share your thoughts.

Exercises

Directions: Set out the arguments below by stating the conclusion and numbering the premises (P_1, P_2, P_3, etc.).

1. **ALEJANDRA:** I liked *Lord of the Rings: The Two Towers* more than *Lord of the Rings: The Return of the King.* The last of the trilogy showed too much self-indulgence on the part of director Peter Jackson. Come on— three hours? Those battle scenes needed serious editing. They were too long, too dark, and too derivative. I took a break and blabbed with the two guys manning the popcorn stand while I had a cup of coffee. Granted I missed seeing the giant spider, but big deal. I see spiders around my house all the time and size does not matter when it comes to spiders! Plus, the oh-so-sad farewell of the hobbits went on and on. Enough of Sam's

wallowing! The hobbits were sweet enough, but they lacked the substance of Aragorn, Legolas, and Gandalf. It just wasn't as great a film as the first two.

2. RICK: Okay, *Lord of the Rings: The Return of the King* was a bit long, but it's still a classic. It certainly deserved the Academy Award. It had great special effects. It had fantastic acting—even if there were a few cheesy moments. Also, the character of Gollum distinguished the film from most action films. He's sort of *Star Wars'* Yoda turned inside out—kind of like the evil twin. Yoda was too good to be really interesting—but Gollum is *very* interesting. All in all, this film is fantastic.

3. HEATHER: I think the Oscar should have gone to *Whale Rider,* not *Lord of the Rings: The Return of the King.* Sure it was great to have the trilogy come together. And sure it has mythic power. But it's so male-centered, with one bunch of guys chopping up another bunch of guys. The women are minor blips on the screen. In contrast, *Whale Rider* is a balance of both male and female energy. Plus it has great spiritual meaning and wonderful performances. There was a great film!

4. TRACY: Sorry Heather, but I disagree. I liked *Whale Rider* too; especially the Maori stuff. But *Lord of the Rings: The Return of the King* was of a different order. The women may have not had much screen time, but they had impact. Eowyn was no donut—that girl was powerful. And she stepped up to the plate when it was time to defend the homeboys. I screamed so loud, my boyfriend elbowed me! She was a role model for us all—and not just for girls. Therefore, that film will survive the test of time.

5. PETER: There were a number of really good films in 2003. My pick for the Oscar was *Mystic River.* Boy, has Clint Eastwood come along as a director— that man is talented. *Mystic River* took on a difficult subject in looking at sexual abuse of children. It did not go over the top or use sexual violence to make a buck. It didn't really show any of that violence—just the effects on the kid and his friends. Then dealing with it so much later when they were adults was really handled well. What a masterpiece. *Lord of the Rings 3* won because the three films were so good—but if you look at the individual film, it isn't going to stand up like *Mystic River.*

6. BOSTON, MASS.: I always thought the shortcoming of the trilogy was Tolkien's incessant description of the natural landscape. At first beautiful, his page-after-page descriptions of crags, hollows, mesas, caverns, etc. begin to read like a geography textbook. They're skipable. Do you agree?

MICHAEL DIRDA: Skipable? Yes and no. I think that the constant references to landscape reinforce the crucial importance of geography in a world like Middle Earth, where people travel on foot much of the time. Also, the ancient brooding character of forests and mountains lends itself to suggesting the gargantuan forces of nature, which are more lasting even than the exploits of men, elves, and dark lords. Historically, too, much northern poetry emphasizes weather and geography—again because they made a serious impact on one's life back then (Michael Dirda, host, "Lord of the Rings: The Two Towers," *Washington Post* live online, 30 Nov 2001).

7. WASHINGTON, D.C.: Hello and I really enjoy an open-air forum on *The Lord of the Rings*. As a Tolkien fan, I admire his work, however, I have often heard that large parts were lifted from standard "western" folklore. Is this true or were these stories just inspiration (i.e., *Das Ring* Trilogy, *Beowulf,* and elves of Northern European lore, etc.).

MICHAEL DIRDA: Well, Tolkien was widely read and deeply learned in ancient northern literature, languages, and folklore. He certainly drew on this knowledge. The death of Boromir, for example, recalls the death of Roland in *Le Chanson de Roland*. But you must also remember that in earlier literatures, it wasn't thought to be "plagiarism" or a lack of imagination that led people to borrow. Rather it was a way of proving the truth of one's story—by citing earlier authorities—or to show that one could add one's own imprint to a traditional story by telling it in a fresh way. Think of all of Greek drama, where everyone knew in advance the story of Oedipus. Doesn't make the experience any less powerful. Rather more so (Michael Dirda, host, *Lord of the Rings: The Two Towers,* *Washington Post* live online, 30 Nov 2001).

Developing Analytical Skills

Arguments may occur in a variety of formats, such as a film, video, TV program, radio show, chapter in a textbook, or a newspaper article. An *effective analysis* entails recognizing the focus (point, direction, position), pulling out evidence, seeing the structure of the reasoning, weighing strengths and weaknesses, considering alternative explanations, examining assumptions to root out those that are unwarranted, looking for omissions (missing pieces), and identifying potential sources of bias or prejudice (e.g., loaded language, name calling). This can be summarized as follows:

Key Points in Analyzing an Article

Subject: What is the focus of this piece? What is it about—what's the general topic?

The Territory: What territory is being covered here? What is the context for exploring the ideas or issues?

Thesis: Is the author arguing a particular position? What point is the author trying to make?

Ideas/Main Thrust: What are the main ideas or key points? What, in a nutshell, is the purpose of the article?

Approach: How much is directed to the central idea and how much is aimed at side issues or tangents? What is the style of delivery? How is this argument structured?

Assertions/Evidence: What kinds of assertions are made? In the case of an argument, what counts as evidence?

Fine Details: What examples, statistics, or other support is given to back up the key evidence or premises? Do the details presented work to develop the central idea or vision?

Cogency: Does the evidence work in part or in its entirety to support the thesis? Is the thesis/conclusion well supported by the evidence?

Clarity: Is the presentation clear and to the point? Are the key issues, ideas, or details of the story clearly presented?

Overall Impression: What is the overall impression in terms of a political message, social commentary, or personal vision? What are you left with; what sticks in your mind?

Persuasiveness: Are you persuaded by the argument? Is the case convincingly made? If not, what's missing, questionable, or off-track? If the article is expository rather than argumentative, was it informative or helpful?

Exercise

Using the key points for analyzing an article, set out your analysis of the article below. In this article, Michelle Delio examines a new "toy" that allows the user to "execute" Marv, who sits in an electric chair, ready to be jolted. Then answer the questions that follow.

DEATH ROW MARV

Kids' New Rage: Executing Marv

Michelle Delio

Wired magazine August 10, 2000

Flip the switch and a surge of electrical current slams into the figure strapped in the chair. He convulses. His hands tremble. His eyes glow red. His teeth clench. And then he utters his last words.

"That the best you can do, you pansies?"

No, it's not the nightly news from Texas. It's Death Row Marv, the latest plastic sensation from McFarlane Toys, makers of the Spawn and Austin Powers action figures. Marv is one of the main characters in the Frank Miller comic book series "Sin City." He's a big (7-plus-feet tall), ugly, dangerous, drunk, ex-con medicated into some semblance of sanity by his parole officer's psychiatrist girlfriend. But while trying to do his version of good, Marv eventually came to a bad end.

The toy, which comes complete with an electric chair, a wired helmet for Marv's head, and a switch that, when pulled, shoots the juice into the hapless Marv, had a first production run of tens of thousands, according to MacFarlane Toys. No sales figures are available yet, but Marv is feeling a big buzz in more ways than one. New York's Forbidden Planet comic store and Island Comics both have waiting lists with more than 30 names on them.

"Kids really love Marv," said Island's Rick Varo. "Teen-age girls think he's cute, which terrifies me." Death Row Marv is also a big draw at Manhattan's Midtown Comics store located near Times Square. A salesman there who preferred to remain anonymous ("You never know who's looking for you," he said) noted that people have been dropping into the store on a daily basis just to jolt Marv a few times. "It's not just kids, either," he said. "We get guys in suits. We get moms. Old people. They come in looking like they had a rough day, but after they juice Marv they leave with a smile on their faces. It's a happy kind of thing."

But not everyone is having a good time playing with Marv. Dennis Golkven, a child psychologist in private practice in New Jersey, says that the toy could be dangerous. "It teaches children that it's fun to hurt people," Golkven said. Ten-year-old Jason Devors of Brooklyn, New York, disagrees. "Marv is not a person," he said. "He's just a toy."

Answer the following:

1. What do "toys" like Death Row Marv reveal about our society?

2. State the strongest argument you can for allowing Death Row Marv to be sold to children.

3. State the strongest argument you can in favor of banning or restricting toys like Death Row Marv.

Group or Individual Exercise

U.S. Government to Issue Gas Masks in Alabama

Below is an itemized list of information about the decision by the U.S. government to buy gas masks—yes, gas masks—for residents in eastern Alabama. (See *Associated Press,* "US Will Pay for Gas Masks for Alabama," 28 Mar 2002). Draw from any or all of these 15 facts to construct an argument. Make your conclusion clear and lay out your premises one by one (P_1, P_2, P_3, etc.):

1. On March 28, 2002, the federal government announced that it would pay for safety gear "that resembles a gas mask" for thousands of people living in eastern Alabama.

2. Those getting the masks live near a chemical weapons incinerator where the U.S. Army will burn deadly nerve agents.

3. Thousands of tons of the deadliest chemical weapons ever made will be destroyed.

4. As many as 35,000 Alabamians will receive the "protective hoods" and training on how to use them.

5. This is the first mass distribution of safety gear to American civilians in the history of the United States.

6. The state of Alabama would withdraw its request that a judge block the opening of the incinerator in return for the government's $7 million pledge of gear and training.

7. The hoods "which function like gas masks but are larger and simpler to use" would go to people who live nearest the incinerator.

8. The hoods protect the wearer for six to eight hours.

9. For the hoods to be accessible, the 35,000 adults and children would have to carry the hoods with them everywhere they go in the zones near the depot, to the grocery store, the movies, and school, for at least six years and possibly longer until the burning is complete (six to seven years).

10. The money would also be used to buy gear for as many as 500 police officers, firefighters, and emergency response workers.

11. The Army planned to begin test burning of nerve gas in September 2002.

12. A shrill "whoop-whoop" will go off on a public-address system if there is a toxic leak.

13. "Those M-55 rockets are extremely fragile munitions," said Lt. Col. Bruce E. Williams, commander of Anniston Chemical Activity. "We think we can continue to store them safely, but you can't escape the fact that if there were a one-in-a-million earthquake, or lightning strike, or a 747 [airplane] crashing on an igloo, the damage would dwarf the worst-case thing that could ever happen at the incinerator. The only real protection I can offer this community is to destroy this stockpile, and destroy it quickly."

14. On February 5, 2004, it was reported by the Associated Press that the Army shut down the incinerator when there was the leak of a "small amount" of the deadly nerve agent sarin inside a main building. The alarms sounded. No one was reported as injured.

15. On March 3, 2004, it was reported by the Associated Press that a "trace amount" of sarin nerve agent leaked from a weapons storage bunker there at the Anniston, Alabama, Army Depot. "Sarin did not escape the area, and the concentration was not enough to hurt anyone," said Cathy Coleman, a spokeswoman for Anniston Chemical Activity, which oversees the stockpile.

▦ Analyzing Arguments

Thoughts and ideas can be expressed in different ways. This needs to be noted at the outset so we can adjust our expectations and method of analysis accordingly. Whatever form an argument takes, however, fundamental issues must be addressed. We'll start with evidence.

Types of Evidence

Central to an analysis is *assessing the evidence.* Once the argument is set out, this means analyzing the premises to see how well they support the conclusion. For example, when Kathleen Tuttle says, "The majority of white people in America are not racist," she is not saying "No white person in America is racist." But because the *majority* is not the same as *all,* her claim is not universal in scope. Whether her claim is actually true is another matter.

There are *different types of evidence.* Some evidence comes in the form of facts or factual claims. Some evidence comes in the form of confessions or testimony (e.g., personal, eyewitness, or expert testimony). Some evidence comes in the form of statistical data, government reports, relevant policies, guidelines, and so on. Whatever the form it take, evidence must be examined in a careful analysis. For the argument to be strong the premises must provide sufficient support for the conclusion, so each piece of evidence should be scrutinized.

Claims of Fact versus Speculation

Facts are like stones on the path, giving us something firm to stand on. If a claim of fact were assumed to be false it would conflict with evidence known to be true. This would create a contradiction, which means the claim of fact must actually be true. Facts and factual claims do not permit a rival conclusion— any rival conclusion simply would lack support. For example:

> AIDS and Donor Sperm: The AIDS virus can be transmitted through artificial insemination. Recent cases confirmed through scientific testing that a small percentage of women have gotten AIDS through a donor sperm they used when they were artificially inseminated years ago. At that time, AIDS tests were not routinely run on potential sperm donors.

Assuming it was *false* that cases confirmed that some women had gotten AIDS through a donor sperm in artificial insemination, there would be *no* support for the contention that AIDS could be transmitted through artificial insemination. The assertion about women getting AIDS through donor sperm clearly supports the conclusion that AIDS virus can be transmitted through artificial insemination. There is no doubt that this conclusion will follow from the evidence. This is not the case with speculation, however, which is much more nebulous.

You Tell Me Department

How Strict Should the "No Eating" Rule Be?

Scientist Stephanie Willett's history with the law was limited to a few speeding tickets, until an unfortunate encounter with a Metro transit police officer in a Washington D.C. metro station on July 16, 2004. It seems that Willett was eating a PayDay candy bar while riding up the escalator. Officer Cherrail Curry-Hagler spied her eating the candy bar and warned her to finish it because eating and drinking in Metro stations was against the law. Willett nodded to the officer, stuffed the last of the candy bar into her mouth, threw the wrapper into the trash can and entered the station. Read what happened and then answer the questions below:

> [Metro transit police officer] Curry-Hagler turned around and followed Willett into the station. Moments after making a remark to the officer, Willett said, she was searched, handcuffed and arrested for chewing the last bite of her candy bar after she passed through the fare gates. She was released several hours later after paying a $10 fine, pending a hearing.
>
> "We've been doing our best to crack down on people who are consuming food and beverages in our stations because we get so many complaints about it," said Lisa Farbstein, a Metro spokeswoman. . . . Willett said she was being unfairly punished because she made fun of the police officer after Curry-Hagler issued a second warning before the arrest. "Why don't you go and take care of some real crime?" Willett said she told the officer while still swallowing the PayDay bar as she rode a second escalator to catch her Orange Line train home.
>
> The police officer ordered Willett to stop and produce identification. "I said, 'For what?' and kept walking," Willett said. . . . "Next thing I knew, she pushed me into the cement wall, calls for backup and puts handcuffs on me," Willett said. . . . Two other officers appeared, and the three took Willett to a waiting police cruiser. At the D.C. police 1st District headquarters, Willett said, she was locked in a cell with another person. At 9:30 P.M., after she paid a $10 fine, Willett was released . . . "I understand the intent of them not wanting people to eat in the Metro," Willett said. "If anything, I was chewing in the Metro." Farbstein said Willett violated the rules. "Chewing is eating," she said. (Lyndsey Layton, "Mouthful Gets Metro Passenger Handcuffs and Jail," *Washington Post,* 29 Jul 2004).

You tell me:

1. Do you think Willett obeyed the "no eating" rule in the Metro station? Share your thoughts.
2. What argument should Willett make to convince a judge or jury of her innocence?
3. What argument should the prosecution make to convict her of the charge that she violated the "no eating" rule?

Speculation

Speculation is a form of guesswork. It is a prediction or opinion in which no more than partial support is stated. When we assert something with little or no evidence, we are speculating. Speculation is, thus, an argumentative version of going out on a limb. Speculation is not necessarily true; it could be false and not conflict with known evidence or theoretical understanding. Furthermore, speculation is not necessarily false; it may prove to be correct. What distinguishes speculation is that the evidence given is insufficient to support it. It is often based more on unsubstantiated opinion, hearsay, or a hunch.

Speculation often shows personal bias, even though it may be treated as common knowledge. When we analyze, we should watch for speculation and not treat it as if what's being asserted is certainly the case. It is far better for us to stop and try to gather more evidence than to draw a hasty conclusion.

Let us look at some examples of speculation (indicated in italics). See if you can see the dangers in going from the one observation to the speculative claim that is inferred:

ANDREA: Reuben has been exercising a lot lately. *He must want to join the Marines.*

OMAR: You may be right, but get this—I saw Reuben drinking wine with a beautiful stranger at the Café Madrid. *He and Maria must be getting a divorce.*

Both Andrea and Omar are speculating about Reuben. Of course, he may want to join the Marines and his marriage may be on the rocks, but we could draw a different conclusion from his recent exercising (e.g., his doctor said to lose 25 pounds). And his marriage may be just fine (the beautiful stranger could be his cousin from Topeka). Be careful about speculation: It may lead us far from the truth and do more harm than good.

Exercises

Directions: In the following, note when the reasoning seems *well supported* and when it is *speculative:*

1. Children's cartoons often contain acts of violence. Children are highly impressionable. We should monitor shows that may affect children. Therefore, we ought to monitor children's cartoons.

2. Many soap operas contain sexual themes and romance. Mario loves soap operas, so he must be obsessed with sex.

3. Most news programs focus on acts of violence, like murder and robbery. Therefore, Norm's suicidal tendencies must be due to the fact that he watches too much news.

4. Beth is an honest person. She recently refused to help her boyfriend get a copy of the history test, and last year she found a wallet on a bench and returned it to the owner. Not one of the $50 bills tucked behind credit cards in the wallet was touched.

4. Things are not always what they seem when it comes to politics. Facts can be twisted to suit the picture sought; speeches can be written to hide political problems and make the public feel that everything's fine when it isn't. We might be better off with a healthy dose of skepticism. That means we should be skeptical about promises made by politicians.

5. Chong must be about to quit her job. I heard her complaining about a cup of coffee spilled all over her desk by one of her co-workers. She had to retype the pesticide report she had just finished and missed happy hour with the gang. All that extra work made Chong mad as a hornet!

You Tell Me Department

Do We Live Life as if It Were a Story Unfolding?

In an essay on the TV show, *The Sopranos,* H. Peter Steeves argues that each one of us lives life as though it were a story, a narrative. Using Tony Soprano as a case in point, he sets out his view.

> We all do this—we all live our lives as narrative. But the startling claim is that this is all that we do, even when we are not aware of it. . . . Tony does not want to accept this. When told that the meat-inspired memory of the first time he had a panic attack . . . is just like Marcel Proust's *Remembrance of Things Past* in which a dainty tea cookie sets off a memory from childhood that spans hundreds of pages, Tony's dismissive response is, "This sounds very gay. I hope you're not saying that" ("Fortunate Son"). Even when Tony finds himself caught up in contemporary fictional narratives, he dismisses them as meaningless.
>
> After telling Dr. Melfi that he was enjoying the movie *Seven,* for instance, Tony admits that "halfway through it, I'm thinking, this is bull&*$#. . . . Why do I give a &%$ about who the killer is?" ("House Arrest"). Dr. Melfi agrees; but she shouldn't. She should realize that the narratives with which we surround ourselves make us what we are, and Tony has made an interesting choice of [video] rentals. ("Dying in Our Own Arms," in *The Sopranos and Philosophy,* Richard Greene and Peter Vernezze, eds., 2004)

You tell me: Do you think Steeves is right to think we live life as a narrative? And if so—if we are telling our stories as we go—do you think this involves much speculation?

Testimony

Testimony can take a variety of forms ranging from confessionals or personal anecdote to eyewitness testimony to expert testimony. We've all seen those ads with ordinary people or celebrities extolling the virtues of one thing or another or trying to convince us to send our money or take action for some cause.

Often we see personal anecdotes in news reports where family members share their response to a child killed by a stray bullet or hit by a Metro train they thought was going slower than it was. After tragic events such as plane crashes and pile-ups on a foggy stretch of highway we hear from the various eyewitnesses who may or may not corroborate one another. Lawyers often call on expert testimony to try to convince the judge or jury that their side should prevail.

All such testimony has to be evaluated—not as fact but as factual claims, informed opinion, or one's personal perspective on an issue. Generally this involves examining the details and assertions made, along with the standing of the one offering the testimonial. This is not always easy to do. For example, Roy Horn's tiger attacked him during the show on October 3, 2003, at the Mirage hotel in Las Vegas. The various eyewitnesses were later interviewed to try to determine what happened. The witnesses in the audience did not agree, leaving the investigators to piece together the conflicting accounts. Each account was examined in light of the proximity of the viewer to the attack and the level of detail. The credibility of the witness or lack of potential bias may also factor in when evaluating testimony.

The Scope of a Claim

We need to be able to assess a body of evidence. Be attentive to the **scope** of a claim—what the claim is meant to cover. "*Not all* drivers are on cell phones" means at least some are not using cell phones as they drive. "All" means more than "some" and vague generalities mean less than specific, detailed claims. For instance, "Listeners prefer a sports segment right after the traffic report," implies that *all* listeners prefer sports after traffic. This is not necessarily true. For example, men may prefer to hear the sports after weather, whereas women may prefer sports after the business report. We have to be careful when universal claims are used.

It's a question of scope. "*Everyone* who purchased a lottery ticket is eligible for the drawing for a new Mini" is stronger than "*Some* people who purchased a lottery ticket are eligible for the drawing for a new Mini." The term "all" covers the entire subject class; whereas "some" means "at least one." Watch also "always" versus "frequently" or "often." "Often" is weaker than "always," for its scope is more limited.

Think also about the context. For example, in dealing with Aunt Pauline's lung cancer, the claim "Lots of people smoke" would not count as strong evidence without knowing more. It would be helpful to know she lived with Uncle Larry, a smoker, and worked in a smoke-filled airport bar. Secondhand smoke might then be the cause of her death. Knowing such details make it easier to evaluate alternative courses of action.

Credible Sources

Credible sources play an important role in arguments. They can sway, if not carry, an argument. Suppose medical researchers claimed there was a causal connection between secondhand smoke and lung cancer. This could be significant if the researchers were credible sources and had no conflict of interest (for instance, if they had not been bribed by an antismoking lobby). If solid statistical data showed a pattern of health problems with secondhand smoke, it provides more evidence to support a lawsuit. Assessing the credibility of witnesses and other sources is important. The outcome of a trial may turn on the credibility of the witnesses.

Credibility of sources is also crucial in news coverage, as demonstrated in *The New York Times*' sweeping apology in 2004 for its overreliance on biased sources, such as Ahmad Chalabi, regarding whether Iraq had weapons of mass destruction. The newspaper owned up to a failure to be more critical:

> We have found a number of instances of coverage that was not as rigorous as it should have been. In some cases, information that was controversial then, and seems questionable now, was insufficiently qualified or allowed to stand unchallenged. Looking back, we wish we had been more aggressive in re-examining the claims as new evidence emerged—or failed to emerge. ("The Times and Iraq," *The New York Times*, 26 May 2004).

An earlier story is also informative. In June 1998, CNN broke a story claiming that the United States used the nerve gas sarin (which is known to be deadly)

FIGURE 5.1
Paying close attention to the small print is highly recommended. *Note the small sign:* "Notice please lock your car for safety."

Photo by Wanda Teays.

against defectors in the Vietnam War. They based their report on what *seemed* to be credible sources. One source cited by CNN was retired Admiral Thomas Moorer of the Joint Chiefs of Staff. According to the report, he confirmed that sarin was used in Operation Tailwind (as the operation was known). However, the source evidently recanted his story:

> Moorer backed away from the CNN-Time report. He said in an interview that he had no firsthand knowledge of the gas being used anywhere in Southeast Asia. "I've never seen a document indicating that it had been used or a document indicating it was going to be used," he said. (Paul Richter, "Cohen Orders Probe of Alleged Gas Attacks," *Los Angeles Times*, 9 Jun 1998).

This shifting report and the hedging of Admiral Moorer raise questions about what to make of CNN's report. The question is, "Is CNN right in their claim about the use of sarin and the presumed endorsement of doing so by the very highest levels of government?" If so, it would appear that Admiral Moorer originally told the truth. If not, then CNN went out on a limb and lacked the evidence to support its claims.

Of course, not all testimonials or "experts" should carry much weight. For example, actors and athletes are often hired to advertise a product. Look also at trials where both sides bring in "experts" to bolster their case. In high-profile trials, we often see expert pitted against expert to convince the jury that one side should prevail.

Sizing up credibility is not always easy, which may account for the role of gut reaction on the part of some jurors.

Group or Individual Exercise

The Jarvik-7 Artificial Heart

Pioneering surgeon, William DeVries, implanted the first Jarvik-7 artificial heart in Barney Clark in 1982. Clark lived 112 days with the experimental device intended to make human heart transplants past history. The surgeon was fond of quoting lines from *The Wizard of Oz* about the Tin Woodman's journey to obtain a heart from the Wizard. Unfortunately, the Jarvik-7 heart never fulfilled the expectations. Analyze the argument below that the nurses may have suffered the most acutely in this saga:

> It was perhaps the nurses involved in the clinical aftermath of the [artificial heart] implants who suffered the most acutely from their growing doubts about the undertaking on the one hand and their anguished loyalty to the physicians under whose aegis they worked on the other.
>
> As the primary hands-on caretakers of the patients, they were the most continuously exposed to their physical and psychic ordeals. The nurses also developed close relations with the families of the Jarvik-7 recipients and had intimate knowledge of the painful experiences the family members underwent . . . some of the nurses became increasingly uncertain about whether the implanted devices and their patients' reactions to them were being studied in a way that met the scientific and moral criteria of good clinical research. . .
>
> Despite their uneasiness about the experiment, they were inclined to assume that they did not have enough scientific training and experience to challenge the investigators' conception and execution of the research or its approval . . . (Renee C. Fox and Judith Swazey, *Spare Parts: Organ Replacement in American Society,* Oxford University Press, 1992)

Value Claims

Value claims may be used as evidence, but should be handled carefully. These may relate to character references and issues of credibility. A **value claim** asserts a judgment based on a system of values, beliefs, or personal preference. It usually takes one of three forms. It may be a judgment of taste, as in "Milk should always be served warm" or an aesthetic judgment, as in "Novels are superior to movies." A value claim may be a moral judgment, as in "You ought not to watch so much TV." Value claims may be used as evidence for a thesis, but they should be handled carefully. They may relate to character assessment and issues of credibility. Personal values can shape a decision, so they warrant examination.

Moral values can weigh heavily in drawing up laws and policies as well, as we see with such controversial issues as abortion, cloning, euthanasia, and the death penalty. Religious beliefs may also play a role in decision making. For example, in her book *Dwellings,* Osage Indian poet Linda Hogan argues that "The Western belief that God lives apart from earth is one that has taken us toward collective destruction. It is a belief narrow enough to forget the value of matter, the very thing that soul inhabits. It has created a people who neglect to care for the land for future generations." To respond to her argument, we have to address her claims about others' views of God and how that informs their worldview.

Value claims are just about everywhere we turn. In a review of *Godzilla,* Ryan Harvey argued that the directors ignored the creature's soul. In his scathing attack on the movie, Harvey said,

> So what do [directors] Emmerich and Devlin give us? A big iguana with squinty eyes, Jay Leno's chin and bad breath instead of flames. He's also a spineless wimp, dodging buildings, fleeing helicopters and hiding in the subways. The real Godzilla would never hide . . . *Godzilla* didn't let TriStar down. TriStar let *Godzilla* down. (See Ryan Harvey, "Even Godzilla Movie's Gotta Have Heart," in the *Los Angeles Times,* 8 Jun 1998)

Harvey suggests that viewers need a creature to identify with, a monster whose fate we can care about while still feeling a vicarious fear of all that power.

Statistical Evidence

It's an interesting thing about human nature: Most people don't like math, but are mesmerized by those who use it. One of the primary uses made of mathematics in argumentation is employing statistical studies. People often draw upon statistical studies to bolster an argument. See Chapter 13 for a more in-depth discussion of statistical reasoning.

Haven't you seen those commercials like, "Four of five doctors surveyed prescribe Preparation K for the relief of polyps" or "Most dentists prefer Crescent mouthwash"? We need to ask ourselves, "How many doctors and dentists were actually surveyed?"

The use of statistics can be very effective, particularly when the studies are current. Besides the date of the study, the *key concerns in assessing statistical studies* are the size, diversity, and date of the study. The sample size should be adequate and have sufficient diversity: The group sampled needs to be representative of the target population being studied. Be careful, though. If the sample size is not large enough, it may result in a **hasty generalization** (fallacious reasoning that occurs when a sample study is insufficient in terms of size, leading us to draw an incorrect conclusion).

You Tell Me Department

Do Giraffes Have Privacy Rights?

Early in the year 2002, an arthritic giraffe at the National Zoo in Washington D.C. died. The giraffe—Ryma was her name—apparently died from a digestive problem called tympany. Giraffes are cud-chewing beasts and need to belch out the extra gas from their stomachs. Tympany is sort of like lactose intolerance—the animal can't belch and is miserable. Here's the catch: Tympany is normally found in dairy cows, not giraffes. A *Washington Post* reporter smelled a rat and asked to see Ryma's medical records. Here's what happened next:

> But zoo director Lucy Spelman refused saying disclosure of the records would violate the giraffe's privacy rights. In a letter to the *Post*, she said the same privacy principles that protect physician-patient relationships also apply to veterinarian-giraffe relationships.

Never mind that zoo officials see no ethical problems with letting Internet surfers spy on their beasts via a "Naked Mole-rat Cam," a "Panda Cam" and a "Giraffe Cam." And never mind that most legal experts scoff at the notion of animal privacy. Eric Glitzenstein, an animal-protection attorney whose clients have included circus elephants and polar bears, called the concept of critter privacy rights "mind-boggling." So why would the National Zoo make such a claim? Is it trying to hide an unsavory chapter from Ryma the giraffe's past? (Roy Rivenburg, "It's a Legal Jungle Out There," *Los Angeles Times*, 10 May 2002)

You tell me:

1. What's the strongest argument you could make in support of Spelman's decision to prevent access to Ryma's medical records claiming a right to privacy?
2. Do you think the National Zoo is trying to hide something? Share your thoughts.

If the studies fail to be diverse enough, the result may be **biased statistics** (fallacious reasoning that occurs when a sample study is not diverse enough and, thus, fails to be representative). Watch the percentage, also. The closer to 100 percent in a positive claim (X percent of A's are B's) and the closer to zero in a negative claim (Y percent of C's are not D's), the stronger is the claim. The date of the study may be an issue too, depending upon what's being studied (for example, fast-moving areas in scientific research, or consumer buying trends).

Think of it this way: You are creating an ad campaign for cube-shaped pasta. You do a market analysis and find that 78 percent of men prefer cube-shaped to donut-shaped pasta, whereas only 45 percent of women prefer the cube-shaped pasta. If more women normally buy pasta than men, your job is to get women to change their minds. Plus, you'll try to convince the 22 percent of men who prefer donut-shaped pasta to try the cubes.

However, if the researcher found that 94 percent of children prefer cube-shaped to donut-shaped pasta, you could aim your advertising at this younger market. We know how fast food chains target ads to children with great success. So paying attention to the role of statistics in effective reasoning can be very helpful to developing critical thinking skills.

Circumstantial Evidence

This occurs when we have no hard evidence one way or the other, but the evidence points to the one conclusion. **Circumstantial evidence** works together in support of a particular conclusion that, in the absence of any reasonable alternative, seems highly likely. The key word here is "likely": no amount of circumstantial evidence can provide certainty. What gives circumstantial evidence its weight is the lack of an alternative explanation for the pieces in the puzzle. Circumstantial evidence has been strong enough to convict people of murder, even in the absence of a body!

Example #1:
    This case turned on a dog hair: This is the case of the murder of Elizabeth Ballard in 1998. They tried to cleanse the world of anything linking them to Ballard's death. A single dog hair thwarted the murderers. The two men wrapped her body in plastic, vacuumed and scrubbed the room, washed down the car trunk they used to carry her body to be dumped in the desert. But a hair of one of the murderer's dog, Hercules, was found on the victim's socks. This one hair helped send the men to prison in 2001 for her murder. DNA analysis can now be done on pet hair, blood, feces and urine and are considered a valuable tool for prosecutors. (See Bettina Boxell, "Proved Guilty by a Hair," *Los Angeles Times*, 21 Dec 2001)

Example #2:
    Claims that trace back to Thomas Jefferson's first term as president keep resurfacing. (See www.monticello.org.) The rumor was that he had had a 38-year-long involvement with a slave, Sally Hemmings. This initially rested on circumstantial evidence—DNA evidence later proved that Tom Woodson was not Thomas Jefferson's son. In a discussion of the case, Eyler Robert Coates, Sr., offered valuable suggestions for handling circumstantial evidence. He says,
    "The only way a study of such a mass of contradictory circumstantial evidence could be conducted fairly would be to take each piece of evidence and present the arguments for and against its acceptance, with a final summary of the best arguments for each separate piece. Ideally, this might be done by two persons; one arguing for and one against. A totally disinterested person might, with considerable effort, fill both roles. But that level of impartiality when dealing with such highly charged issues is almost humanly impossible." (Eyler Robert Coates, Sr., "The Jefferson-Hemmings Circumstantial Evidence," *The Jefferson Perspective*)

As Coates indicates, examining circumstantial evidence in as fair a manner as possible may require some effort. In the case of Jefferson, the claim has not conclusively been disproven that he fathered Hemmings's children—even according to Monticello.

Conditional Claims

Evidence may be expressed as a **conditional claim**—an "if/then" claim. Conditional claims have two parts: (1) the *antecedent* (the first or conditional part acting as a catalyst to something else) and (2) the **consequent** (the second or resulting part said to follow from a prior condition). The antecedent lies between the "if" and the "then" and the consequent follows the "then."

The Global Dimension

Genetically Engineered Corn in Mexico

On March 11, 2004, scientists from Mexico, Canada, and the United States gathered in the Hotel Victoria in Oaxaca, Mexico. They met to discuss the presence of genetically modified corn discovered throughout Mexico. This situation could have significant consequences for agricultural biodiversity. Corn is the third most important crop in the world after wheat and rice. Mexico is the center of diversity; here a vast number of the thousands of varieties and stocks are sown. Groups representing indigenous people, environmentalists, and "progressive intellectuals" were afraid that scientists and experts would declare that the genetic contamination was irreversible and that was that. Here are the concerns that they raised.

Directions: Read the passage and then (1) state the concerns raised about this situation; (2) advise the protestors what they should emphasize to make the best case.

"The contamination of our traditional maize attacks the fundamental autonomy of our indigenous and agricultural communities because we are not just talking of our food source; maize is a vital part of our cultural heritage," declares indigenous leader Aldo Gonzalez, "For us native seeds are an important element of our culture . . . a handful of maize is a legacy we can leave behind for our children and grandchildren and today they are denying us that possibility." . . .

The demonstrators demanded the end of all maize imports, genetically engineered or not, and that the government comply with its inescapable duty to act to hold back and stop genetic contamination. (Carmelo Luiz Marrero, "Genetic Contamination of Mexican Maize," *Z Net,* www.zmag.org, 10 Jul 2004)

Conditional claims are **hypothetical propositions.** We see a conditional claim in this comment about actor Russell Crowe: "On the personal side, Crowe remains a rather reclusive personality. He has said that he would only live in L.A. if certain conditions were met, namely: "if Australia and New Zealand were swallowed up by a huge tidal wave, if there was a bubonic plague in Europe, and if the continent of Africa disappeared from some Martian attack" (www.clasic-scifi.com and allperson.com). To live in Los Angeles, Crowe says several antecedent conditions must occur—the tidal wave, the plague, and the Martian attack. Given the likelihood of each occurring, it's clear Crowe won't live in L.A. any time soon.

For any given conditional claim, the antecedent is not necessarily true. Many of us have fantasized, "If I had a million bucks, then . . ." knowing the antecedent (getting $1 million) is a pipe dream. Often we are told "If A then B" and yet A never happens, or isn't likely to happen in the near future. For example,

- "If he weighed 700 pounds, Will Smith could be a Sumo wrestler."

However, Will Smith has no shot at weighing 700 pounds regardless of how many donuts he eats.

It is also possible to have a conditional claim with the antecedent and consequent *both* false. For example, "If Nicole Kidman did not star in *The Interpreter,* then she must have starred in *Pretty Woman.*"

Group or Individual Exercise

A Look at Legal Parenting Rights

Directions: Assess the reasoning in a ruling by the California Supreme Court that a man who fathers a child with a woman married to someone else may be denied all legal parental rights. Set out your response in light of the following:

1. Justice Joyce L. Kennard said that a man "who fathers a child with a woman married to another man takes the risk that the child will be raised within that marriage and that he will be excluded from participation in the child's life."

2. The court majority said that because Dawn was married at the time the baby was conceived and was living with her husband when the baby, Sam, was born, they were bound by state law that presumes a husband to be the father of his wife's children.

3. Jerome "Jerry" Krchmar, 41, lived with a woman in 1995 while she was separated from her husband to whom she'd been married for six years.

4. The woman, "Dawn," became pregnant within a month of living with Jerry.

5. After living with Jerry for four months, Dawn moved back in with her husband.

6. Dawn insisted Jerry was not the father of the child.

7. Jerry took a parenting class and tried to negotiate child support.

8. California law recognizes the husband as the father of a child, regardless of genetic ties.

9. Dawn was living with her husband when the baby was born.

10. Jerry filed a lawsuit before the baby was born to assert his parental rights.

11. Recognizing the importance of family stability, the law supports the married couple, even when another man is the biological father of a child.

12. Dawn and her husband refused to let Jerry see the baby, Sam.

13. Dawn's husband punched Jerry when the three people met for a blood test.

14. Jerry said, "I will never give up my son."

    (Greg La Motte, "Court Denies Unwed Dad's Parental Rights," *CNN News,* CNN.com, April 8, 1998 and Maura Dolan, "Court Denies Parental Rights to Unwed Father," *Los Angeles Times,* 7 Apr 1998).

Analogies and Precedents

Instead of giving straightforward evidence, an argument may offer an analogy, metaphor, or comparison as evidence. An **analogy** is a comparison asserting that something true of one of the terms of the comparison will, therefore, be true of the second term. This rests on the strength of the similarities outweighing the differences between the terms of the analogy. These sometimes colorful or vivid comparisons can make a great impression on the audience. See if you can find all the analogies in the excerpt from a review of a book on spirituality that was in *Shambhala Sun* magazine:

> Spirituality is like Jell-O. It comes in every imaginable flavor, it's almost impossible to pin down, and your definitions of it will only last until it morphs into another shape. That's how the eminent sociologist of religion, Wade Clark Roof, explains the difficulty of defining our culture's love affair with things spiritual. Roof, who teaches at the University of California, Santa Barbara, does come up with two clarifying categories in the slippery word of contemporary spirituality: seekers, who pursue meaning by sampling a smorgasbord of dishes, and dwellers, who feast from a single table. (Anna-Liza Kosma, "Seekers and Dwellers," *Shambhala Sun,* May 2001)

Analogies often have persuasive power, so they warrant a detailed study. We will do this when we delve into inductive reasoning. As we'll see, the strength of the analogy rests on the strength of the relevant similarities of the two things being compared. The stronger the relevant similarities, the stronger the analogy; but if there are significant differences in what is being compared, the analogy is weakened.

Here's another example. The term "virus" is now widely used in both medicine and technology. According to Ken Dunham, there are "valid comparisons between biological and computer viruses that support the origin of the term "computer virus" (Ken Dunham, "The Great Analogy," Securitydatabase.net, 2 Jul 2001). To decide if Dunham is right, we'd need to set out the comparison and look at the similarities and differences of biological and computer viruses and weigh the relative strength of each.

To assess the analogy, weigh the similarities and differences and then evaluate the quality of the comparison and, thus, the strength of the argument. However, analogies always contain a degree of uncertainty given that there will be some differences in the terms being compared. Because of this, any conclusion drawn on the basis of an analogy can only be said to follow with probability. This means the argument has an inherent weakness (as do all inductive arguments) that we need to be aware of.

Exercise

Children and TV

A study in the journal *Pediatrics* of 1,300 kids found that 1-year-olds and 3-year-olds who watched just one hour of television daily had 10 percent more risk of attention problems by age 7 than children who watched no television at all. And the more television, the more risk. In an op/ed piece in the *Boston Globe* on April 7,

2004, Derrick Z. Jackson compared TV to crack cocaine. Discuss the reasoning in Jackson's comparison of TV to an addictive drug. Note the strengths and weakness of the comparison in your discussion:

> If you said television was crack cocaine, frying the circuits of kids and turning them into fat, illiterate thugs, politicians would demand mandatory 10-year sentences for neglectful parents, which basically means the incarceration of nearly every parent in the nation. Of course, most parents never intend to neglect their kids when they park them in front of the screen. But as the evidence mounts that TV rewires our kids, we must rewire ourselves. We can no longer use the excuse that we're too frazzled to stop electronic drug dealers from taking over our neighborhoods and hooking our children. We are not going to change television from being a universal fact of life, since 99 percent of children in the United States live in a home with a TV. What people can change is how many TVs surround them and how long they stay on.
>
> Half of American children live in homes where there are three or more TVs. More than one third of all children 6 years old and under have a television in their bedroom, according to the Kaiser Family Foundation. Children 6 and under spend two hours a day in front of a screen and only 39 minutes reading or being read to.
>
> Two out of every three small children live in homes where the TV is on at least half the time, and one out of every three small children live in homes where the TV is on nearly all the time. . . . So often, we park our kids in front of the electronic baby sitter because we are fried. That excuse is no longer valid now that we know that the passive baby sitter we let into the house turned out to be a drug dealer, altering the brain perhaps even more permanently than a bag of dope. (Derrick Z. Jackson, "Kids, TV and the Risk of Attention Problems," *Boston Globe,* www.boston.com/globe, 7 Apr 2004)

Cause and Effect Reasoning

Cause and effect reasoning occurs when someone asserts that something either causes or is an effect of something else. See Chapter 13 for a more in-depth discussion of causal reasoning.

A causal claim may have merit, but it is crucial that alternative causes be dismissed first. Once they can be eliminated, a causal claim has more force. We can see this by the ways in which different theories about the origin of AIDS have been offered. Some argue that AIDS entered the human population through malaria experiments on prisoners and researchers, who injected mangabey (monkey) blood into the human subjects. Others argue that AIDS entered through oral polio vaccines given to about a million people in central Africa from 1957 to 1960, which was cultured from the cells of primates. Still others think AIDS can be traced to human consumption of primates' blood or exposure to the bodily fluids of chimpanzees. And so on. Until it is obvious what caused AIDS/HIV to enter the human population, there will be a host of theories swirling around.

You Tell Me Department

Model Site or Kiddie Porn?

For $25 a month, you can access a Web site, "Lil' Amber," with photos of an 11-year-old girl hugging a rabbit, playing dress-up, posing in a bikini, and lifting up her skirt. For $50 you could buy the video of Amber trotting around in revealing outfits. Supposedly the money will go to her college fund. According to *Wired* journalist Julia Scheeres, this Web site is one of several featuring child "models" as young as 9 and is owned by Webe Web. Critics think it smacks of kiddie porn, but Webe Web spokesman Evan Gordon says: "This is definitely not kiddie porn in any form." He adds, "None of our sites have naked children." Scheeres notes:

> "Gordon said that the child modeling sites were inspired by a birthday party thrown for a friend's 9-year-old daughter. Pictures of the Spice Girls–themed party were posted on the Internet, and within a week they were getting 20,000 page

views a day, he said. . . . Gordon said he was 'irked' by a question of whether the company's child-modeling sites and porn sites were related and insisted there was no crossover between the company's two lines of business." . . .

"Many of these girls are making more money than their parents make," Gordon said, adding that while the company has been accused of exploiting children, he has no reservations about the sites. "If you had a cute dog that I could put up on the Web and make money off of, I'd do that too," he said. Webe Web also runs another business: hardcore porn sites, including Home From School. (The site, www.homefromschool.com was taken down soon after an interview with Webe Web.) (Julia Scheeres, "Girl Model Sites Crossing Line?" *Wired*, www.wired.com, 23 Jul 2001)

You tell me: Do children have to be *naked* for photos or videos to be called pornography? Set out an argument for or against censoring such Web sites.

For example, when people argue that media violence causes viewers to become more violent, they are saying that the existence of the *one* (violence on TV or in movies) is directly linked to the *other* (violence on the part of viewers). It is a powerful claim and one that has raised a great deal of concern. Nevertheless, before we accord it much weight, we need to see what evidence underlies the cause and effect reasoning. As fig. 5.2 shows, there may be a causal chain leading to a particular effect.

We see cause and effect reasoning behind arguments for censorship of film and TV. There are those who insist violence on the screen is causally linked to violent behavior. What follows from this is that to change the latter we must restrict the former. It has, for instance, been argued, "If we don't want people doing crazy things, then we shouldn't show such acts in movies like *Kill Bill*." Such response comes out of a belief that the causal link between a movie and human behavior is strong.

Summary of Major Types of Evidence

Here is a list of the major types of evidence that we have covered:

- Universal claims.
- Particular claims.

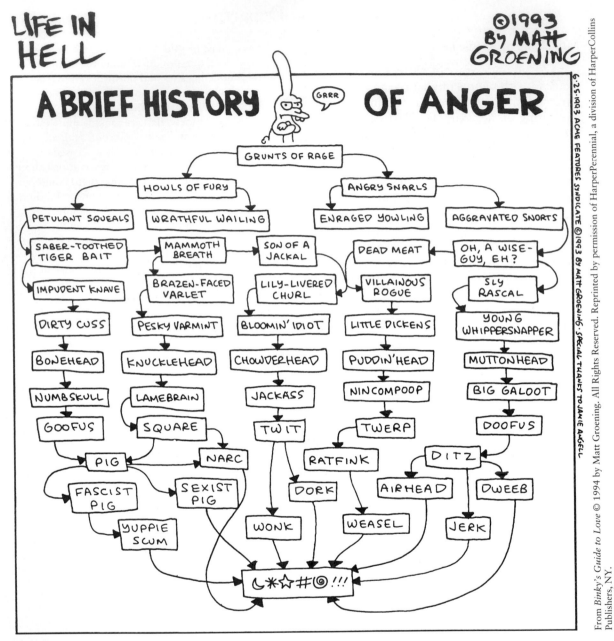

FIGURE 5.2
Starting with grunts of rage, a causal chain is set in motion!

- Testimony (confessionals, personal anecdote, studied opinion, eyewitness reports, expert testimony).
- Factual claims and use of credible sources.
- Speculation or opinion.
- Statistical studies/claims.
- Analogy or precedent.
- Value claims.
- Circumstantial evidence.
- Conditional claims (hypothetical propositions).
- Cause and effect reasoning.

Exercises

Refer to the different types of evidence (universal versus particular claims, use of sources, statistical studies, value claims, circumstantial evidence, conditional claims, arguments based on analogy, cause and effect reasoning) covered thus far. Identify the type of evidence presented and any questions you might have about its value in assessing the box office success of the film *Titanic*:

1. International Movie Data Base (imdb.com) reports that *Titanic* made $900 million from rentals and is the top-grossing film of all time with a dollar gross worldwide of $1.8 billion.

2. 62 percent of the men in a poll of 215 Guilford college students did not think Leonardo DiCaprio was convincingly lower class, but they still liked the movie *Titanic*.

3. Film critic Roger Ebert said the movie is "flawlessly crafted, intelligently constructed, strongly acted and spellbinding."

4. People ought to buy the DVD of *Titanic* so they can watch it over and over— plus get to see all those nifty special features.

5. *Titanic* is a lot like *Gone With the Wind* in that it looks at women of privilege who fall for rascals while being surrounded by a society tightly bound by convention.

6. If James Cameron quit making movies right now, he'd go down in history as the director of some of the most influential blockbuster films ever made.

7. Seeing *Titanic* more than five times in one week has caused men to become more romantic and women to hum Celine Dion tunes.

8. Someone called "spbethell-1" couldn't stand the movie, and posted this on the imdb Web site: "When I saw this film, people actually cheered when the ship went down—we would have cheered more if it went down in the first five minutes."

9. Men will probably enjoy the end of *Titanic* when Jack is so brave in the ice water.

10. Ticket stubs to *Titanic* were found on Darin's desk at work, along with a note that read, "Laura, I sure had a great time last night." Darin must have taken Laura to see the movie.

11. Everyone interviewed at the midnight showing of *Titanic* on its opening night said the sinking of the ship was awesome in terms of setting the mood.

12. An empty popcorn bag was found on the floor of Silvio's new Prius; so it's clear he went to see *Titanic* even though he said he wouldn't go without me.

Independent versus Interdependent Evidence

We need to be aware of the evidence being presented and assess it for strength. It's one thing to be able to see the structure of an argument so you know what is being claimed and what the various pieces of support are. This is the crucial stage of dismantling the argument. The next stage is that of examining the evidence we have been given.

Not all evidence is of equal value. Any *one* premise is potentially much more powerful than the other premises. It may be that one or more premises independently supports the conclusion. This is **independent evidence.** When one piece of evidence is sufficient in and of itself, we would say that that piece *independently,* or singly, establishes the conclusion.

Suppose, for example, that we have a confession from the suspect, as well as DNA evidence. Either the confession *or* the physical evidence may establish guilt, assuming the confession is not coerced and is made by someone who is competent. In that case, any other evidence would be extraneous. However, not all criminals confess and not all the physical evidence can seal a conviction. We often need to piece together all the evidence.

If we lack one definitive piece of evidence, then we have to look at the way our evidence works together. When this occurs, we say each contributing piece of evidence is **interdependent.** With interdependent premises, the evidence operates as a package deal. This is strongest when the evidence works together like interlocking pieces, holding up the conclusion.

And when that evidence poses no clear conflicts or contradictions if we assume it is actually true we have **corroborating evidence.** With corroborating evidence it gets harder to attack a case, because the foundation gains more strength. For example, because Ralph has no alibi and was known to have e-mailed threats to Jorge we'd say these two pieces of evidence corroborate each other. Similarly, if we knew that Jorge got a perfect score on his SAT, had strong letters of reference, and had just received a phone call from the university's financial aid office, then we have corroborating evidence that this could be news about the scholarship he applied for shortly before his car was stolen.

CASE STUDY

SARS and Fear in the Medical Profession

When SARS, an acute respiratory infection that is contagious and potentially deadly, hit in China, people followed it with interest—and a little anxiety. When it hit North America, the fear-factor in the West jumped. Doctors and nurses regularly put themselves at risk when caring for patients. But we ought not assume they want to risk their lives. Read about what happened at a Toronto hospital when assumptions around selflessness in medical caregivers crumpled:

Dr. Donald A. Henderson . . . the man in charge of the global smallpox-eradication campaign [said] "I am confident that this same selfless concern for others would prevail today should an epidemic occur." But when SARS hit in Toronto last year, that's not what happened. "It was hard at first to find doctors to cover the SARS wards," said Dr. Leslie Nickell, a family doctor who assisted the SARS control team.

Early in the epidemic, Nickell organized a study of the psychological impact the disease was having on the personnel at her hospital, Sunnybrook and Women's College Health Sciences Center, which ultimately admitted 71 SARS patients. Twenty-three of these were health care workers, some from Sunnybrook. The results of her survey, published in the March 2, 2004, issue of the *Canadian Medical Association Journal,* are disturbing. Of the 2,001 respondents, 65 percent reported significant concerns about their health and that of their families. Almost 30 percent, including 45 percent of the nurses who responded, displayed significant levels of "emotional distress."

Health care workers disliked wearing the uncomfortable masks and having their temperature taken every morning as they reported to work, though they knew these measures

were necessary. Nickell also heard more mundane concerns. "They said that they couldn't have Easter dinner at home with their families," Nickell said, because they were in quarantine or on extra shifts. "That may sound petty, but it matters. Others said their neighbors didn't want them to visit. They felt stigmatized" (Gretchen Reynolds, "Who Wanted to Treat Rebecca McLester?" *The New York Times Magazine,* 18 Apr 2004).

Answer the following:

1. What do we assume about how much risk is acceptable for doctors and nurses in caring for a patient?

2. Should doctors and nurses be required to treat patients with infectious diseases? Set out your argument for or against (note any exceptions to your stand).

3. State three to four points you would say to Dr. Paul Hunter after reading this [*note:* monkeypox is similar to smallpox]:

Dr. Paul Hunter who lives in Milwaukee, treated one of the other monkeypox cases in late May. His patient was a meat inspector and a dealer in exotic pets when the man didn't respond to antibiotics, and his rash erupted with oozing sores. "The rumor about smallpox went around the hospital fast," he said. At that point, Hunter's worry shifted from the patient's prognosis to his own. "My attitude was, I'm going to stay as far away from this guy as possible," he said later. Although Hunter was the attending physician and visited his patient in the isolation ward every day, he limited hands-on care as much as possible. "Everybody did their jobs, but they wanted to have as little direct contact with him as possible. They were all like: 'Stay away!' "

"Look," he continued, "I'm not a coward. I've had needle sticks. I've had to get H.I.V. and hepatitis tests and then wait around for the results. That's not fun. But it's part of the job." This case, he says, was different. "I have three kids, all under the age of 11. That's a big reason I didn't want to be involved if it was smallpox. I'm not going to volunteer for anything dangerous." He also declined to get a smallpox vaccination. "I said, 'You're not turning me into a first responder.' Next time, let somebody without kids handle this." (Gretchen Reynolds, "Who Wanted to Treat Rebecca McLester?" *The New York Times Magazine*, 18 Apr 2004)

Exercise

The Three Strikes Law in California

On June 19, 2001, a California Appeals Court upheld the 25-years-to-life prison sentence given to a homeless man on parole. This was handed out under the guidelines of California's so-called three-strikes law. According to this law, anyone committing a third felony would be given a mandatory 25-years-to-life sentence, regardless of the severity of the crime committed (so long as it was a felony conviction). The fact of the third felony being committed independently of the circumstances results in the sentence. On the other hand . . .

1. Assume you are a member of Prisoners' Rights Now, a group that takes on cases that appear to be unjust. They ask for your position on this case. Share what you will say, after reading the following about this actual case:
   - Yes, Kevin Thomas Weber did commit a felony in breaking into a Santa Ana, California, restaurant.
   - Yes, Weber did come in through a roof vent.
   - Yes, Weber might have taken more had he not been interrupted by a blaring burglar alarm.
   - But, still, Weber only stole four cookies.

2. Justice David G. Sills wrote in a unanimous opinion, "A safecracker who cracks an empty safe is nonetheless a safecracker." Respond to Judge Sills from any two of the following:
   - The perspective of the owner of the restaurant.
   - The perspective of Weber's family.
   - The perspective of potential burglars who have two strikes against them.
   - Your own perspective.

Weighing Evidence

In the process of trying to evaluate an argument, chain of arguments, policies, and decision making we need to have some systematic way of dealing with the evidence. That is, we need to see how to evaluate the strength of the evidence in its support of the particular goal.

Checklist for Weighing Evidence

Scope	Universal claims "All A is B" or "No A is B" are *stronger* than the particular claims "Some A is B" or "Some A is not B."
Relevance	Claims pertinent to the topic (focused on the issue) are stronger than general observations or vague "truisms." Set the background information concerning the context to the side, unless it is necessary to make the argument.
Support	Examine the evidence to assess the quality of support and its role in the argument. Does any of the evidence independently support the conclusion? Are all the premises needed to make the case? Are any extraneous, unnecessary? Use of credible sources, properly documented, is stronger than speculation.
Testimony	Watch for the credibility of those giving testimony. Look out for conflicts of interest, poor grasp of relevant information, weak observation skills, emotional problems, or inattention to details that could affect credibility.
Facts Stack Up	Relevance is the key here: The more indispensable a fact is to the case, the more weight it should have. Valuable facts may seal the case
Circumstantial Evidence	Key here is that there's no reasonable alternative explanation. Ask if a rival conclusion is feasible.
Statistical Claims	Be attentive to: • Date of study. • Size of study. • Diversity in terms of relevant variables or factors so the study is representative of the target population.
Conditional Claims (Hypotheticals)	Watch for "if . . . then" constructions (If P then Q). Can we determine if the antecedent condition, P, is true? Is the consequent, Q, known to be false? Is this one link in a chain of conditional sentences?
Value Claims	What is the force and impact of the claim? Who holds it? What are the consequences of not believing in it? Do ethics or religion color the way in which things are interpreted or presented? Watch for evidence of personal bias that could prejudice the case.

Analogy or Precedent	Analogies can never be put forward with certainty, and they resist verifiability. Look for strength of similarities. Similarities must carry more cumulative weight than differences for the analogy (precedent) to hold. Similarities MAKE an analogy. Differences BREAK an analogy.
Omissions	Watch for "holes" in the reasoning. Ask if anything has been left out (whether intentionally or unintentionally).

Exercises

1. It seems that the estate of the Bear family was broken into and the suspect is Goldie Locks. Sort through the evidence, categorizing it as good, bad, or interesting. Decide if the case against Goldie is strong enough to go to trial. Choose the five strongest pieces of evidence for the prosecution and the five strongest for the defense.
    a. Goldie's alibi could not be substantiated.
    b. Goldie eats porridge every other day for breakfast, but never on Mondays.
    c. The Bears eat porridge almost every day.
    d. Porridge stains were found on Goldie's blouse.
    e. Goldie's mother served porridge yesterday, but today made fried eggs.
    f. The Bears' front door was pried open, possibly with a tool.
    g. Goldie had a pocket knife in her purse.
    h. Some little girls are afraid of bears.
    i. No little girl should go wandering in the woods, where bears live.
    j. If Goldie broke into the Bears' house, she had to have had a tool or knife.
    k. The little Bear's chair was broken.
    l. A study of robberies revealed that most robberies are committed during the day and by someone who is familiar with the victim.
    m. Goldie says she had never met the Bears.
    n. Mrs. Bear found muddy footprints on the sidewalk.
    o. Many people have mud on their feet and little girls often have muddy feet.
    p. A piece of wood that matches that of Baby Bear's chair was found in Tom Thumb's backyard, next to Tom's truck collection.
    q. Goldie had mud on her shoes.
    r. The muddy footprints were approximately size 6 shoes.
    s. Goldie's mother said Goldie was a lovely child.
    t. Little girls are less likely to get into trouble than are boys.
    u. Dr. Zut, child psychologist, said children are innately curious.
    v. Both Tom Thumb and Goldie have size 6 shoes.
    w. Goldie has no criminal record.
    x. Goldie's kindergarten teacher said Goldie had been well behaved and helpful to the other children when she was in her class four years ago.

    y. Goldie showed no remorse and said, "I could care less about those stupid bears."

    z. The crime took place on a Monday.

  aa. Baby Bear had psychiatric treatment last year for chronic lying.

  bb. Mrs. Bear said Baby Bear's toy truck was taken during the robbery.

2. You are investigating possible defects in the Jeep Grand Cherokee. (See Ricardo Alonso-Zaldivar's two articles: "Cherokee SUV target of Fed probe," *Los Angeles Times*, 5 Jul 2001 and "Jeep Cherokee Blame Game Heats Up," *Los Angeles Times*, 23 Dec 2001). Sort through the evidence, categorizing it as good, bad, or interesting. Choose the five strongest pieces of evidence for the pro side (buy the Cherokee) and the five strongest for the con side (shop around for another car).

    a. Federal authorities are investigating a possible defect in Jeep Grand Cherokees that may cause the SUV to lurch into reverse.

    b. Cases of lurching usually happened when idling with the gearshift in the "park" position, but have been known to happen when the engine is turned off.

    c. More than 860 people have complained to the government or to Daimler-Chrysler about "inadvertent rollaway in reverse" incidents involving Grand Cherokees.

    d. Complaints involved 1995 to 1999 Grand Cherokees.

    e. No deaths have been reported.

    f. There have been 359 crashes and 184 injuries involving the SUV lurching into reverse.

    g. The company has denied there being anything wrong with the vehicle.

    h. Given all the Grand Cherokees sold, the number of incidents is small.

    i. About 1.3 million of the popular SUVs are affected by the investigation.

    j. The National Highway and Transportation Safety Administration (NHTSA) issued no recommendations for Grand Cherokee owners while it conducted the investigation.

    k. The company does not believe there is any issue with the vehicle, but it is cooperating with the investigation.

    l. Dominick Infante, safety spokesperson for DaimlerChrysler, which builds the Grand Cherokee, said he had no information on any consumer complaints received directly by DaimlerChrysler.

    m. Typically, manufacturers get far more problem reports than does the NHTSA because many consumers are not familiar with the process of registering complaints with the federal auto safety agency.

    n. Since 1999 Grand Cherokees have been redesigned, with a new type of transmission.

    o. The Grand Cherokee is a very popular sports-utility vehicle.

    p. A lot of customers really appreciate the choice of colors for the body and interior of the vehicle.

q. Jacquee Kahn of Los Angeles said her 1997 Cherokee rolled into reverse while she was filling it up at a gas station just before Christmas 1999, with the engine turned off; the open driver door crunched into a gas pump, bringing the jeep to a halt.

r. The rate of park-to-reverse complaints for Grand Cherokees is more than five times greater than for any similar SUV made by a different company.

s. Customer Kahn said DaimlerChrysler did not take her complaint seriously, perhaps because she was a woman; they instructed her to reread her owner's manual.

t. The company examined Kahn's jeep and said it had no problem.

u. An Oklahoma man said his Grand Cherokee lurched into reverse when his wife went to open a gate at the ranch; the jeep crossed a busy highway, went down a 40-foot slope and hit a tree.

v. The company has denied there was anything wrong with the Oklahoma man's car, suggesting it was the wife's fault—she is now afraid to drive the car.

w. Company official, Dominick Infante, said, "We do believe these incidents resulted from mistakes made when drivers shifted into park."

x. Sports utility vehicles are gas-guzzlers, but are fun to drive.

3. Set out your position as to whether or not it should be possible for Daniel Patterson to give his second kidney to his daughter, Renada, in light of the various pieces of evidence set out below. Be sure to sort through the evidence, weighing it for strengths and weaknesses:

a. Renada, 13 years old, was born with only one kidney, an unhealthy one.

b. For seven years, Renada was on dialysis three times a week, unable to go to school.

c. Renada's father, Daniel Patterson, is serving 12 years in prison for burglary and drug convictions.

d. Daniel Patterson had abandoned Renada when she was a baby, but donated one of his kidneys two years ago, when he turned out to be a compatible donor.

e. For two years Renada lived with her father's kidney, but often skipped her medication; his kidney (now hers) began to fail.

f. Renada needs a new kidney; her 38 year-old father wants to donate his remaining kidney (he still has three more years in prison).

g. If Daniel Patterson gives away his last kidney, he will require dialysis; that will cost the system $40,000 a year.

h. To take Daniel's kidney clearly puts him at risk.

i. 3,100 patients are on a waiting list for a kidney in Northern California.

j. Hank Greeley of Stanford's Center for Biomedical Ethics said that a father in most situations should be allowed to make a sacrifice for his daughter, though he said this made him nervous.

k. Arthur L. Caplan, director of the Center for Bioethics at the University of Pennsylvania is opposed to the surgery; he says, "You don't ever want to kill a person to say you saved another's life."

l. There has never been a live kidney transplant, says Caplan, where a person went from one kidney to none.

m. This would be Renada's third donated kidney (her body rejected the first when she was five).

n. There is a question whether Renada's body would accept another kidney from her father, since, when she didn't take her medicine required for the transplant before, her face became bloated, her stomach distended, and she hunched her back and felt ill.

o. Dr. Nancy Ascher, a professor of surgery, says, "Whether the organ was rejected because the medication wasn't taken, the body may have decided that this organ is incompatible and will do so again."

FIGURE 5.3
What can we conclude about MTV from this ad?

You Tell Me Department

But Is It Sports?

After news broke about basketball player Kobe Bryant being accused of rape, you might have thought it would have been either national or local news. Wrong. It was treated as *sports* news, if we can judge from the placement of the pretrial coverage in both print and TV coverage. Given that sports figures are staples of the sports pages, perhaps it seems fitting that news of accusations of assault (on or off the court), murder, rape, and other sorts of violence should be treated as sports news as well. Here's an example from a story in the sports section of the *Los Angeles Times*. Don't miss the last sentence of the article!

Hearing Concluded; Bryant Expected Back for Game

EAGLE, Colo.—With a pretrial hearing concluded, Kobe Bryant sped out of court this afternoon and is expected to make it to Los Angeles in time for the Lakers' playoff game tonight. Judge Terry Ruckriegle denied a request today by the basketball star's attorneys to save time and conduct a closed hearing instead of breaking for lunch. After several issues had been addressed in open court by noon, Bryant attorney Hal Haddon had asked the Eagle County District Court judge to skip lunch. . . . The woman told detectives that the last time she had sex before the alleged rape was June 28 with her boyfriend, and that he used a contraceptive. An attorney representing the woman has said she did not have sex with anyone after the encounter with Bryant and before the rape exam.

Game 4 between the Lakers and the Minnesota Timberwolves is scheduled to start at 6:15 P.M. PDT at Staples Center. (*Los Angeles Times*, 27 May 2004)

You tell me: Where *should* criminal trials involving athletes be covered in newspapers or on TV news? Sports pages? Entertainment section? Local news? National news? Business section? Take a stand and set out your argument.

The example above is not a one-time case of throwing together such diverse issues. In a front page announcement (with a photo of Laker General Manager Mitch Kupchak) we see this announcement: "It's Official: O'Neal Traded" followed by this news story: "Laker General Manager Mitch Kupchak comments on the trade that sends Shaquille O'Neal to the Miami Heat. In Colorado, the prosecution hails a ruling in Kobe Bryant's sexual assault case." (*Los Angeles Times*, 15 Jul 2004).

Exercises

Part One

1. Examine the MTV ad, "I'm itchy. Do I have MTV?" (Figure 5.3) Answer the following:
   a. Discuss whether or not you think this ad presents an argument.
   b. Share your thoughts on the effectiveness of the ad and how MTV has been so successful in reaching its audience.
2. Assume department store chain Nordstrom wants to tap into your critical thinking skills. Set out your position and go into detail (so you are giving an argument) as to whether or not this will be an effective ad campaign: "We're all shoppers. We're all neighbors. We can't wait to meet you."

Part Two

In the excerpts below, decide if the author assumes a neutral/unbiased stance or is arguing a position. If the passage contains an argument, state the conclusion—even if that conclusion is implied and not explicitly stated. Note also the key pieces of evidence.

1. Now you can open any size jar or bottle with ease. Grip Tite incorporates a unique blend of flexibility and deep set gears to create a force that opens any jar or bottle so easily that you'll wonder how you ever got along without it. Gone are the days of asking for help on that stubborn jelly jar. Grip Tite is made from a unique blend of flexible man-made materials. At only $6.97 you'll want to buy two and get the shipping and handling free (Dream Products, Inc.).

2. The first year, it was the growing pains of learning a new system. The second year, it was the growing pains of a freshman quarterback. In this, the third year of the Tyrone Willingham era at Notre Dame, there are no more excuses for the Irish offense. So why, Golden Domers are asking, did things look so painfully familiar in Saturday's season-opening 20 17 loss at BYU? ("No More Excuses," *Sports Illustrated*, SI.com, 9 Sep 2004).

3. There are currently 70 million grandparents in the United States, one-third of all American adults. The average age of a first-time grandparent is 48, and 6 percent of American children live with their grandparents. It's not that this older generation doesn't care about its own security, it's that we also care intensely about our children's children. And we vote (Ellen Goodman, "The Granny Voters Getting out the Vote," *Washington Post*, 11 Sep 2004).

4. CAMP VICTORY, Iraq, July 1—A defiant but visibly shrunken Saddam Hussein dominated the opening of court proceedings on Thursday. The 67-year-old former ruler . . . began nervously, like a hunted man in alien terrain. His eyes swiveled back and forth, his voice was weak, and his fingers stroked his beard and touched his bushy eyebrows. But halfway into his 26-minute appearance he appeared to find his pitch, and he ended with a string of finger-wagging admonishments. (John F. Burns, "Defiant Hussein Rebukes Iraqi Court for Trying Him," *The New York Times*, 2 Jul 2004).

5. Saddam Hussein has questioned the legitimacy of the tribunal set up to try him during his first appearance in the dock. The former Iraqi president on Thursday signaled his refusal to cooperate after seven charges against him were read out in the military tribunal before which he and his eleven co-accused are to be tried. According to Aljazeera correspondent Abd al-Adhim Muhammad, the former president asked: "How do you bring me to this place without any defense attorney?" When asked by the judge to identify himself Saddam answered, "I am Saddam Hussein al-Majid, the president of

the republic of Iraq." Saddam refused to say "Saddam Hussein, the former president of Iraq" ("Saddam Defiant in Court," *Aljazeera*, aljazeera.net, 2 Jul 2004).

6. In a case that appears to broaden the prosecution of women who pass drugs to their infants through their bodies, a woman was sentenced here Monday to six years in prison because her breast milk, tainted with methamphetamine, had killed her baby daughter. In recent years, 160 women in 24 states have been charged with delivering drugs to their babies either during pregnancy or through the umbilical cord immediately after childbirth. But the case here in this town 40 miles southeast of Los Angeles is apparently the first in the nation based on the passing of drugs through breast milk ("Mother Gets 6 Years for Drugs in Breast Milk," *The New York Times*, 28 Oct 1999).

7. For those of you remain unconvinced, we have started to catalog the many examples of proof that Tiger Woods is no mere mortal. One of Tiger's most remarkable non-golfing abilities seems to be his power to both diagnose and instantly heal any injuries that he may sustain. At the 1999 Tour Championship Tiger purposely struck a large rock that was in front of his ball causing him GREAT pain. For the remainder of the round Tiger was not even able to complete his swing and was bent over in pain after every shot (he went one under par the rest of the way!). Immediately after the round Tiger, completely unfazed . . . calmly stated that he simply had a 'stinger' and that everything would be just fine.

   Tiger's father, Earl, has confirmed that he and Tiger each possess the supernatural ability of mental telepathy. Earl made this statement on two separate occasions to *Sports Illustrated*. . . . Jesus gave his mother the gift of changing water into wine at a marriage feast. Tiger bought his mother a house in Tustin, California and gave his mother the keys to a new car after winning the 1999 Buick Invitational (www.tigerwoodisgod.com).

8. While dining with the abductees [who claimed to be abducted by aliens], I found out something very revealing: not one of them recalled being abducted immediately after the experience. In fact, for most of them, many years went by before they "remembered" the experience. How was this memory recalled? Under hypnosis. . . . Memory is a complex phenomenon involving distortions, deletions, additions, and sometimes, complete fabrication. Psychologists call this *confabulation*—mixing fantasy with reality to such an extent that it is impossible to sort them out . . . Every parent has stories about the fantasies their children create. My daughter once described to my wife a purple dragon we saw on our hike in the local hills that day (Michael Shermer, *Why People Believe Weird Things*).

9. An appeals court said a man can press a claim for emotional distress after learning a former lover had used his sperm to have a baby. But he can't claim theft, the ruling said, because the sperm were hers to keep. Phillips accuses

Dr. Sharon Irons of a "calculated, profound personal betrayal" after their affair six years ago, saying she secretly kept semen after they had oral sex, then used it to get pregnant. Phillips was ordered to pay about $800 a month in child support, said Irons' attorney, Enrico Mirabelli. Phillips sued Irons, claiming he has had trouble sleeping and eating and has been haunted by "feelings of being trapped in a nightmare," court papers state. The higher court ruled that, if Phillips' story is true, Irons "deceitfully engaged in sexual acts, which no reasonable person would expect could result in pregnancy, to use plaintiff's sperm in an unorthodox, unanticipated manner yielding extreme consequences." The judges dismissed the fraud and theft claims, agreeing with Irons that she didn't steal the sperm. "There's a 5-year-old child here," Mirabelli said. "Imagine how a child feels when your father says he feels emotionally damaged by your birth" (Carla K. Johnson, "Man Can Sue Over Surprise Pregnancy," *ABC News,* abcnews.go.com, 24 Feb 2005).

10. In this age of orange alerts, terrorism fears and racial profiling, some people view immigrants with suspicion. But where some see difference as a threat, Sarah Jones sees an opportunity to connect. In her one woman show *bridge & tunnel,* Jones plays 14 different characters, male and female, from as many different cultures. So why is she telling their stories? "With 9/11 and the new threats on all our civil liberties, we have an opportunity to create a galvanized movement," she says. "Scapegoating and misinformation have had such a detrimental impact on the relationships between people from different backgrounds. But we can fix that. Information is the key. People are curious. We need to connect" (Sharon Boone, "The Many Faces of Sarah Jones," *Essence* magazine, June 2004).

11. Legal scholar Paul Butler observes that imprisonment used to be a last resort. This changed in the 1980s when its use increased, mainly against blacks and Latinos. "At the same time we had black and Latino men becoming the leaders of youth culture. We had them inventing a dominant form of popular culture," Butler said. Almost inevitably, Butler suggests, hip-hoppers began to comment on crime and punishment in their music. He writes, "Hip-hop culture makes a strong case for a transformation of American criminal justice. . . . Its message is one that we should heed" (Jabari Asim, "Crime, Punishment and Hip-Hop," *Washington Post,* 14 Jun 2004).

12. Some of the yellowed, porous bones belonged to a slight-statured man and woman who apparently lived more than a century ago. All of the remains showed signs of rickets. This much is clear: The bones had been disturbed before. Soon they will be reburied. Perhaps this time they will have a final resting place. The bones, unearthed last winter at a construction site on Bolivar Street, will be placed together in a coffin and buried in the garden on the grounds of Historic Pleasant Green Missionary Baptist Church on Maxwell Street. . . . "These are people. We need to respect them," said

Fayette County Coroner Gary Ginn, who has spearheaded an effort to study the remains and find an appropriate place for them (Jennifer Hewlett, "Old Human Bones to Be Reburied in Church Garden," *Lexington (Kentucky) Herald-Leader,* Kentucky.com, 11 Sep 2004).

Analysis of an Article or Argument

Once we feel comfortable handling evidence, we can tackle all sorts of arguments, great and small. Let's start first with the title, to see if it sets the stage for any interpretation that may follow. The way things are labeled or titled may shape the way in which they are perceived.

Notice, for example, the title of the article on the Chinatown case we examined earlier. In the title of the article, the altercation between Detective Kelly and Mr. Huang was called a "beating." However, inside the article it was called a "scuffle." There is quite a difference: a "scuffle" is generally considered fairly minor, where no one gets hurt. In contrast, a "beating" usually refers to something more severe, where someone is seriously injured. The judge must decide whether this was a "scuffle," a "beating," or something else. The severity of Long Huang's or Detective Kelly's injuries would be a factor in coming to a decision. The language used to describe the incident shapes our understanding of the incident.

Structure

An analysis of an article involves looking at the way the article is structured, determining the author's position, frame of reference, and method of approach; examining the use of language; and checking for bias. It is important to be on the lookout for bias. There may be bias as shown through the use of language, revealing the values favored by the author. There could be bias in the very way in which evidence is presented (e.g., the author may skew the article in favor of one side). It could be that key evidence for one side is missing or distorted, ignoring or underplaying one side rather than fairly representing both sides.

Basics

Central to an analysis is an examination of the key claims or arguments. Clarify what is being argued (the thesis) and then set out the premises. Next pull out and weigh the evidence. The argument may rest on such things as research data, statistics, physical evidence, causal claims, comparisons, testimony, personal statements, confessions, and anecdotes. Examine the evidence carefully. We may be headed in the wrong direction if vital pieces of evidence are missing. Similarly, look at any assumptions. What we assume affects how we think and what we think about, so decide if the assumptions are warranted or unwarranted.

Your personal reaction is generally a separate issue from an analysis. You could incorporate reactions at the end, say right before the conclusion, to add a personal note to your essay. This is not formally part of the analysis. However, if your analysis leads to your reflections, then the personal angle could be relevant and its addition justified.

Group or Individual Exercise

Read the article excerpt below about Taco Bell and the use of genetically engineered corn that is not for human consumption. Then answer the questions that follow.

Genetically engineered corn that has not been approved for human consumption has found its way into Taco Bell taco shells sold in supermarkets, says a biotech watchdog group. The group, Genetically Engineered Food Alert, is calling on the Food and Drug Administration to recall the taco shells . The group says the corn has characteristics that suggest it could cause allergic reactions, including nausea and shock. The FDA has had no reports of anyone becoming ill from eating the tacos and has not verified the claims. But a spokeswoman says the agency, with the Environmental Protection Agency, is "actively looking into the issue," and if the allegations are proved, the product will be pulled from the market.

Larry Bohlen of the environmental group Friends of the Earth, one of the members of the Food Alert campaign, says the group does not know of any health effects related to the tacos, but "the American public had no way of knowing whether an allergic reaction could be tied to" the biotech corn. Bohlen says only Taco Bell brand shells sold in supermarkets have been tested, but "we're going to next test taco shells from Taco Bell restaurants." Kraft spokesman Michael Mudd says the company is having an independent lab test the taco shells. "The goal all of us share is the safest food supply possible," Mudd says. "As much progress as we've made, we have to continue to improve it."

Lisa Dry of the Biotechnology Industry Organization says the FDA is planning to do its own testing of the taco shells, and results could be available within three days. "We don't actually know whether this corn actually did make it into these Taco Bell taco shells," she says. She questioned the accuracy of lab tests conducted by Genetic Id of Fairfield, Iowa. "This lab has in the past not had accurate results. The testing process is complicated." ("Taco Bell Asked to Hold the Chalupas Biotech Corn Found in Grocery Taco Shells," *USA Today*, 19 Sep 2000).

Answer the following:

1. State the three strongest pieces of evidence *for* pulling the taco shells from Taco Bell's restaurant chains.

2. State the three strongest pieces of evidence *against* pulling the taco shells from Taco Bell's restaurant chains (i.e., for allowing Taco Bell to continue using them at the present time).

3. Are there any questions you would need to have answered before you'd believe the corn should be pulled from the market?

Short Analysis Papers

In a short essay (less than five pages) be selective. Zero in on the most important aspects; you cannot do everything. Nevertheless, if you are writing clearly and concisely, you can do a lot in a brief analysis.

Ingredients of a Strong Analysis

1. **State what is being argued or discussed**
   - State the thesis or focus of the essay or article.
   - Note your assessment of the article's persuasiveness.

2. **Clarify how it is being argued or discussed**
   - Note the key points made and issues raised.
   - Include brief statement as to how the argument or discussion is structured.

3. **Discuss the use of language**
   - Note value-laden, biased, or prejudicial language.
   - Watch use of metaphors and connotations of words.
   - Note when use of language is clear, concise, and accessible for the targeted audience.
   - Note degree of clarity in use of language.

4. **Set out the Strengths**
   - Note arguments that best support the author's thesis.
   - Note valuable points or insights in the expository essay.
   - Point out powerful uses of language, effective use of statistics or credible sources, pertinent examples, and well-supported details.

5. **Set out the Weaknesses**
   - Note any aspects that diminish the quality of the article.
   - Note any contradictions or inconsistencies in the author's reasoning.
   - Point out when statistics are used poorly or are out of date.
   - Note any speculation or unsupported claims.
   - Watch unfounded assumptions, or use of references (witnesses or "experts") that are not credible.

6. **Assess the article for persuasiveness**
   - Watch for omissions.
   - See if evidence is strong.
   - Notice if language helps or hinders.

- Decide if weaknesses are too great.
- See if the argument is fully developed.
- See if illustrations and examples back up claims.
- Watch for questionable assumptions.
- Assess the cogency of the reasoning.

Proceeding with Your Analysis

Even in a short analysis, include the six aspects listed above. If, however, the author's use of language is unproblematic, then a discussion of the language may not be necessary. Carefully examine the way an article is structured to see if it gives a fair presentation of the issues under consideration.

You can only evaluate the argument when you have identified the conclusion (thesis) and supporting premises (evidence). *Be careful here.* Some writers do have a thesis, but you may not find it until three, four, or five paragraphs into the paper. Such fishing expeditions may be necessary, so be ready.

Exercises

Part One

1. Set out the thesis and key claims in the following argument:

   Kimosabe must have eaten the sock. He's often a bad dog when left inside the house and he was alone all day long. The socks were out on the table. He's been known to eat socks left on the floor. The window was wide open, but I don't think a stray cat or dog would come in and take a sock. Only a few other things are missing. So it's surely Kimosabe who ate the sock!

2. Set out the thesis and key claims in the following argument:

   Silvio lost four socks this week. Four different socks. He had done his wash and usually dumps the clothes out of the dryer onto the bed. He looked around the bed, but the four socks weren't anywhere to be found. One later turned up stuck on the inside of the washing machine. So only three are officially missing now. He seemed unhappy as he put the three socks in a little corner of his drawer. There is no sign of a break-in. There is no scientific explanation why socks put in washing machines as pairs should come out of the dryer with missing socks. Nothing else gets lost when you wash. This goes to show, someone or something can go through walls and steal individual socks—not pairs!—for some macabre grand experiment on the human race.

3. Set out the thesis and key claims in the following argument:

Troy didn't do as well at the box office as expected. It "only" made around $130 million. Maybe people are tired of seeing men in skirts. On second thought, maybe the problem is that Brad Pitt is not meant to wear a toga. I know *Braveheart* did just fine and Mel Gibson wore a kilt. And who can forget Russell Crowe in *Gladiator*? Those two seemed to be okay in their costumes—but Brad Pitt just doesn't fit the profile. He is just too contemporary. Brad's the kind of guy you expect to see at a Hollywood nightclub. But who in their right mind would look around a nightclub for Mel Gibson or Russell Crowe? Yeah, that's why *Troy* tanked.

4. Set out the thesis and key claims in the following argument, then decide if it looks like a strong case:

1200 people are complaining of ailments since the El Al accident. The "black box" cockpit voice recorder disappeared from the evidence bin where firefighters insist they put it. Five hours into the rescue effort, after Dutch security police had cleared the crash site of emergency workers and the press, men in white-hooded fire suits were seen jumping from a helicopter into the smoldering rubble and carrying off debris in unmarked trucks. Police videotapes were erased before investigators had a chance to review them. Vital details of the cargo's hazardous contents (recently revealed to be the deadly nerve gas, sarin) were kept secret for years. The disaster took 43 lives on the ground and four more on the 747 Boeing jet. This whole thing looks to be either a monumental bungle or a cover-up. (See Carol J. Williams, "Dutch Probe '92 Jet Crash after News of Toxic Cargo," *Los Angeles Times,* 13 Oct 1998.)

5. What are the three strongest pieces of evidence in the following argument that might be used to convince one of your friends or fellow students *not* to use steroids?

Performance-enhancing drugs and treatments have become a bigger problem than ever in recent years, both in the major U.S. team sports and in international competition. Manfred Ewald, 73, oversaw the East German doping program that flourished in the 1970s and 1980s. He and his cohorts are accused of giving steroids to girls as young as 11—and intimidating those who raised objections, accusing them of "cowardice." The women now appearing in a Berlin courtroom endured a wide range of health problems. Some became infertile because of the steroids. Many endured excessive body hair, deepening of their voices, and liver, kidney, and menstrual problems. Machalett told the court that when she was 19, her liver failed—because of the mixture of steroids and contraceptive pills she had been taking. Much could hang in the balance. The more they know, the more the world knows—and today's athletes using steroids might think twice about risking liver damage and other long-term health problems. (Adapted from Steve Kettmann, "Doping Haunts E. Germany," *Wired News,* 25 May 2000.)

6. Set out the conclusion and key claims in the following argument:

Joel Myers recently learned that a collection of American Indian artifacts given by his great-uncle Cassius to the University of Nebraska may soon be on the auction block. Myers was not even aware that a small part of the collection once belonged to his relatives. Myers said he wasn't sure what to do—hire an attorney or just save his money and try to buy the items when they showed up on eBay. Once the museum was contacted by Myers, it was clear that the artifacts they were going to auction weren't just any old bunch of stuff. They have personal value to Myers. Subsequently, the Museum should hand over the artifacts to him. (Bill Donovan, "Oregon Man Questions Right of Museum to Sell off Items Given by His Relative," *The Indian Trader,* July 2003)

7. So is this a fair decision? Read about the case of dog owners in condos and discuss the reasoning:

Paula Terifaj bought a condo in 1995 for a vacation getaway. At the time, there was an unwritten no-pet rule, but she would bring along her little terrier, Lucy. When Lucy died, Terifaj got a boxer she named Rose. The condo owners association repeatedly warned and fined her for bringing Rose to the condo. In 2000, the association voted in a no-pet clause in its official declaration of conditions and restrictions. Things escalated and they ended up in court. One issue was whether after-the-fact restrictions in condo covenants are valid. In June 2004 the California Supreme Court ruled that the adopted amendment was effective against all homeowners, whether or not they voted for it and irrespective of when they acquired the condo. Justice Moreno said such restrictions had to be uniformly applied and to do otherwise would undermine the stability of the community. He added in a footnote that he had no quarrel about the benefits of pet ownership "but that is not the issue in this case." (John Roemer, "Condo Group Can Ban Dog, Court Decides," *Daily [Law] Journal,* 15 Jun 2004)

8. If you were hired by Paula Terifaj to write a two to three paragraph response to the decision, what would you say in defense of *her* argument that she should be able to bring Rose to the condo?

9. Discuss the quality of the reasoning in the following ad for Kellogg's Cereal:

Kids who eat breakfast perform better in school. We all grew up hearing how breakfast is the most important meal of the day. And in fact, studies from around the world show that kids who eat breakfast perform better during their morning school hours. So how do you get them to eat breakfast every day? By serving them their favorite cereal with milk. For more information on the importance of breakfast to kids and the nutrition of cereal, call us at 1-800-468-9004. *Cereal: Eat it for life.* (Photos of Fruit Loops, Corn Flakes, Frosted Flakes, Sugar Pops)

Part Two

Directions: Read about surveillance cameras in New York and then answer the questions that follow:

In New York City, there are cameras lurking on the perimeter of Washington Square Park, disguised as street lamps. They dot the walls of a new building on West Fourth Street, in the form of decorative bulbs. Bill Brown, who conducts the "Surveillance Camera Outdoor Walking Tour" says the number of surveillance cameras is growing. "Like mushrooms in the forest," he says.

He says that most of the cameras are disguised to look like lamps or ornaments. By his count, the number of surveillance cameras in Manhattan has tripled in the last five years. In 1999 the New York Civil Liberties Union counted 2,397 cameras in New York—he estimates that it has jumped to 7,200 in the year 2004. He contends that this is a sign of creeping control by the authorities. They lull people into a sense of security, dulling vigilance among city residents and weakening communities.

Brown is concerned that in the not-too-distant future, the different camera systems will all be linked. As the number of cameras increase, there are virtually no laws to govern their use. This raises difficult legal questions. A privacy consultant says, "The general rule is what goes on in public has no reasonable expectation of privacy."

He continues, "I can walk in front of your house and take a picture. But suppose I put a surveillance camera in front of your house 24 hours a day? No one has addressed that in any particular way." Critics of the cameras say they do not reduce crime; that watchers get tired of staring at empty street corners and begin peeping at people. A camera at a foreign consulate was found to have been trained on a nearby apartment, Brown said. (Sabrina Tavernise, "Watching Big Brother," *The New York Times,* 17 Jan 2004)

Answer <u>one</u> of the following:

1. One day you come home to discover a surveillance camera is aimed at your house/apartment entranceway. Set out your argument that this violates your right to privacy.

2. You are tired of your neighbors dealing drugs and the cops come but the drug-dealing resumes after they leave. Give an argument that you have the right to set up a surveillance camera aimed at the street in front of your house.

3. The nice new department store in town, Blossomdale's, is afraid of being wiped out by shoplifters. They want to stick surveillance cameras *everywhere* in their store. They are fine about putting up signs to notify shoppers that they are being videotaped wherever they are in Blossomdale's. Explain to them why this is—or is not—a justifiable plan.

Part Three

Here is the background on "Kenny's law," a hate-crime victims' bill in California. What would you advise the legislators to do in response to this proposal (e.g., vote for or against it, investigate alternatives, etc.)? State your thesis and key reasons.

At around midnight of July 30, 2001, Christopher Chiu found his 17-year-old son Kenneth lying in a pool of blood in the front yard of their Laguna Hills home. Before Kenneth died, he identified Christopher Hearn, who lived next door for 10 years, as his attacker. Hearn stabbed Kenneth 25 times. They were three years apart and had played hockey together when they were young.

Hearn told investigators that "Chinese and blacks have weapons" and that the government ordered him to kill Asians and other minorities. "I acted like a Marine . . . It's not my fault," he said. In 2004 Hearn was found guilty of first-degree murder. The judge then declared him insane and ordered him sent to a mental institution instead of prison.

If he is later found sane, Hearn can be released. Because of that, Chiu said he is fearful for his family's safety. We should support the legislation, "Kenny's Law," that would require courts to impose an automatic protective order shielding victims or their families after a hate-crime defendant is released from prison or a mental institution. (See Joy C. Shaw, "Bill Would Help Hate-Crime Victims," *Los Angeles Daily [Law] Journal,* 21 May 2004).

Answer one of the following:

1. What is the best argument that could be made to legislators as to why they should vote for "Kenny's law"?

2. What is the strongest argument for legislators finding alternatives to protective orders to help hate-crime victims?

Using a Flow Chart

Once you know where the argument is headed, you can see how it's structured. Often the focus or thesis is clear from the title or first paragraph. Your task is then to see how the issue is approached. If it is a descriptive or expository article, see how the article is structured and whether or not there is a balanced presentation. One of the ways to discern the structure is with a flow chart. Draw boxes around each paragraph, number each paragraph, and then set up a flow chart showing what each paragraph contains.

Here's how: Go through the article, boxing each paragraph. Number each box (paragraph). On a separate sheet of paper (or there on the article), draw boxes with three columns and as many rows as you have paragraphs. In the boxes on the left side insert numbers for each paragraph (Paragraph #1, Paragraph #2, etc.). In the middle boxes, write a short label of what's in the paragraph in question. And on the right side write a *brief* summary of the key points (think telegram). Do this for all your boxes/paragraphs. You now have a flow chart. The flowchart is very handy—you can easily locate each paragraph's summary and get a quick overview of the argument by reading down the middle column.

Why Bother.   Flow charts can be valuable in several respects. First, flow charts help us see how arguments are structured. Second, flow charts help us clarify in our own minds what, exactly, is going on in each paragraph. Third, flow charts help us see if a discussion is imbalanced or biased. If you get lost in the sea of details, try a flow chart.

Exercise

Set out a flow chart for the article, "Just Say No" by Judge James P. Gray, below.

Group Exercise

In an article in the *California Lawyer,* Judge James P. Gray argues for the legalization of drugs. Analyze his argument, with each group focused on one task. Topics for the groups could be altered or omitted, depending upon the number of groups (usually it works best if groups have three to five members). Two groups can have the same topic:

- **Group One:**   Thesis and assumptions.
- **Group Two:**   Key claims.
- **Group Three:**   Use of language and values to make the point.
- **Group Four:**   Strengths of the argument.
- **Group Five:**   Weaknesses of the argument.
- **Everyone:**   Persuasiveness of Judge Gray's reasoning.

Just Say No
An Orange County Superior Court Judge Calls for a Truce in the War on Drugs

James P. Gray

California Lawyer, April 1, 2001

Our drug laws have failed. We've lost the so-called War on Drugs, and now it is time for a coherent and commonsense approach to the drug problem. I say this not as an ivory-tower idealist but based on my experience as a former federal prosecutor in Los Angeles, a criminal defense attorney in the Navy's Judge Advocate General Corps, and a trial judge in Orange County since 1983. Because my judicial duties have required me to enforce this failed system, I eventually could not keep quiet about it any longer. . . . We must, as a country, investigate the possibility of change and be mindful of the following five points:

First, just because people discuss alternatives to our current drug policy, or even because they believe we should adopt one or more of these options, does not mean that they condone drug use or abuse.

Second, there is no such thing as having both a free society and a drug-free society . . . Dangerous as they are, drugs are here to stay, and we should work to discover how best to reduce the harm they cause in our communities.

Third, the failure of our present drug laws is not the fault of law enforcement. These dedicated people have an extremely difficult and dangerous job, and they are doing it much better than any of us have a right to expect. Law enforcement is no more at fault for the failure of drug prohibition than was Elliott Ness for the failure of alcohol prohibition.

Fourth, it is far easier and more effective to control a legal market than an illegal one. Under our current policy the only laws that are enforced about the use and sale of illicit drugs are those imposed by the drug traffickers. As such, we have seen a collapse of the rule of law with regard to quality control, sales to minors, and regulations of the marketplace. The better approach would be to bring those dangerous drugs back under the law.

And fifth, no matter what options we use, there will be some problems.

Drug prohibition has its own unique and harmful consequences as well. For example, when drug dealers shoot police officers, witnesses, innocent bystanders, or even each other; that is a drug-prohibition problem rather than a drug problem. Today, when the distributors of Coors and Budweiser have a problem with each other, they take it to court, but the distributors of illicit substances take their problems to the streets. Similarly, when drug users are forced to prostitute themselves or steal to get money to buy artificially expensive illicit drugs from the criminal underworld, that is a drug-prohibition problem much more that a drug problem. So, too, is the diversion of billions of dollars from the prosecution of violent street crime and fraud to the prosecution of hundreds of thousands of nonviolent drug sellers and millions of drug users a distinct problem of drug prohibition. . . .

Fortunately, many people are beginning to agree that our War on Drugs is not working, but they still feel a deep frustration that no viable options have presented themselves. [Former Secretary of State George Shultz] says, "I have a zero-tolerance attitude, but I am still searching for the best way of implementing it." Well, there's some good news: We have viable choices between the two extremes of zero tolerance on the one hand and drug legalization on the other, and many of these options are working quite successfully in other countries.

These options include various forms of drug treatment, such as rehabilitation, both voluntary and involuntary, public and private. Other options include medicalization, which fundamentally puts drug-using people under the supervision of a medical doctor and his or her staff; using needle-exchange programs, which exchange without charge dirty needles for clean ones; drug maintenance, which allows prescriptions for an addict's drug of choice to be filled at a medical clinic so that the subject neither gets high nor goes through withdrawal but is maintained at an equilibrium level until he or she is ready to attempt to be drug free (this program is working very well today in Switzerland); and drug substitution, which substitutes one drug, such as methadone, for the subject's drug of choice, such as heroin. Many countries in western Europe, which are not as concerned as we are with puritan morality, take a much more practical, harm-reduction approach to their drug problems by combining these alternative methods—with successful results.

Another option, . . . [is a] War on Drugs, zero tolerance—"only this time we will *really* get tough!" Unfortunately, we have been getting tougher and tougher for the past several decades, and yet every time we have done so it has made our problems worse. In fact, in my view, our current policy of zero tolerance has brought us the worst of all possible worlds: We have filled our prisons with the less-violent and less-organized drug sellers, thereby leaving this enormously lucrative market to those who are more violent and more organized. The result has been that the availability and purity of drugs have increased dramatically while the price has gone down. We couldn't have created a worse situation if we had tried.

The best option we have is federalism, the principle that guided the repeal of alcohol prohibition in 1933. When alcohol prohibition was repealed, each state pursued the policy that best met its needs, and the federal government was eventually limited to helping each state enforce its own laws. Of course, whatever option or combination of options we eventually pursue must and will include a major component for drug education. . . .

Finally, we must explore various methods of "deprofitizing," or taking the money out of selling these dangerous drugs. Of course these drugs are dangerous, but it is drug money that is causing the most significant harm. Methods to reduce the profitability of the drug trade include decriminalization, which basically means that, although the drugs remain illegal, as long as people stay within very clear guidelines, the police will leave them alone (this program is working quite well today in Holland, where drug use for both adults and teenagers is about half of what it is in the United States); regulated distribution, which is the strictly controlled and regulated sale to adults of designated drugs, similar to the way alcohol is sold in most states; and legalization, which basically leaves the distribution of drugs to the marketplace, with all of its protections under the civil justice system, and uses the criminal justice system to govern people's behavior. Almost no one I have heard of actually favors the extreme system of legalizing drugs, and I certainly do not.

Voters appear to be well ahead of politicians in the area of drug policy. Why? Because politicians perceive that they will be labeled soft on crime if they take a more moderate approach. Even President Clinton did not talk about a possible change in drug policy until the final weeks of his term. Whose fault is this? We have no one to blame but ourselves. It is our government, and it is our responsibility to show our elected officials that it is all right to talk about the possibility of change. . . . When presented with initiatives about making marijuana available for medical purposes, voters in nine states as well as the District of Columbia have said yes, in overwhelming numbers. . . .

Progress has also been made in other areas. In the past ten years we have seen a positive revolution in the way the criminal justice system treats nonviolent offenders who use mind-altering drugs. This is, of course, our drug courts, where drug users are treated compassionately as human beings who have a problem. But they are also held strictly accountable to satisfy the demands of the court's drug-treatment program. In many cases the results have been gratifying. . . .

(For example, does anyone seriously believe that it is any more helpful to put actor Robert Downey Jr. in jail for his drug abuse than it would have been to put Betty Ford in jail for her alcohol abuse?) . . . What was true for the dangerous and sometimes addicting drug of alcohol is also true for other dangerous and sometimes addicting drugs. Since problem drug users will find their way into our criminal courts anyway, why are we persisting with our failed policy of drug prohibition and punishment? . . .

Consequently, it is up to us as caring citizens, voters, and taxpayers to continue to make the government move toward a more rational, workable, and, as good fortune would have it, vastly less expensive national drug policy. This can be done simply by recognizing that we have viable alternatives to our failed War on Drugs. Waiting for those who have vested interests in the status quo to come around simply will not work. . . .

In my opinion, drug policy is the single most important issue facing our country today. But we can all help to make a positive change by simply recognizing that we have alternatives to our failed drug policies. Demand for dangerous drugs can be reduced through education, drug treatment, bringing the users closer to medical professionals, reducing incentives by taking the profit out of trafficking in drugs, and, very importantly, holding people accountable for their actions in the same way we do for people who cause harm by their use or abuse of alcohol. The best way to start is to remember—and to remind others—that just because we discuss or even use these other options does not mean that we condone drug use or abuse.

James P. Gray is a judge of the Orange County Superior Court. He is also the author of Why Our Drug Laws Have Failed and What We Can Do About It: A Judicial Indictment of the War on Drugs *(Temple University Press, 2001).*

Source: © 2000 *Daily Journal* Corporation. All rights reserved. Permission granted by the *Daily Journal.*

Longer Articles

You may feel overwhelmed when asked to analyze an entire chapter or long article (over five pages). Don't be! Try a flow chart to block out the article or a brief summary of each paragraph. Once you get an overview, you are in a better position to do your analysis. Analyzing a long argument requires organization and detail—and involves a range of considerations.

Tips for Analyzing Long Articles

1. **Titles and subtitles.** Look at the frame of reference/point of view, language, bias, images, impact, effect, and overall thrust or direction. Your goal here is to detect the bias or implicit set of values of the author, and to see if the title is representative of the article's content.
2. **Language.** Look for loaded terms (positive or negative), false-neutral terms, technical or scientific terms, connotations, language of description (adjectives, images created, symmetry in descriptions taking into account gender, race, religion, etc.). Note impact of race, gender, age, religion, and ethnicity upon descriptions. Check for slanting, bias, or hidden value assumptions.
3. **Structure.** To get a sense of structure try any of the following: block out, outline, sketch without words, create a flow chart, construct paragraph blocks with labels, list the sequence of information (whose side is given first and last, and if it is a balanced presentation). Note who has the first and last word. Do a quantitative analysis (count premises and block out pros and cons). Examine the use of quotes or statistics (amount, purpose, effect). An overview of the structure can help you decide if the author presents the material or argument in a fair and balanced way.

4. **Testimony.** Examine credibility and potential conflict of interest versus the impartiality of the person being cited (as a source, or used as a witness, as in a trial). Decide if the person or source in question is reputable. Check for possible bias.

5. **Factual reporting.** Look at: Who is reporting, whether the report is sufficient, and whether the reporter is biased or unbiased. Check the frame of reference of the author, possible omissions or errors because of incompetence, lack of sufficient detail or failure to include diverse perspectives, and any possible bias or conflict of interest.

6. **Literary analysis.** This includes examining themes; patterns; plot line and narrative structure; character development; diversity of perspective; description and attention given to different characters; connection between form and content; moral, spiritual, and social concerns; use of language, sentence style; structure; and symbols and images (mythological or metaphorical).

7. **Socio-cultural frames.** Be attentive to these social and cultural frameworks: treatment of social issues or moral problems, cultural baggage and biases, and societal attitudes. Recognize the social and cultural context of the author and work (since it is not written in a vacuum).

8. **Use of statistics.** Look at the date of the study, size and diversity of the sample (is the sample representative of the target population?), strength of the percentage in inferring conclusion, relevance of the study to the topic under discussion, and assumptions or cultural attitudes embedded in the study. Determine the currency and relevance of the statistical study, and discuss any problems you perceive.

9. **Fallacies.** Note any fallacies and determine the degree to which the author's work is affected by any such errors.

10. **Argumentation.** This is at the center of any detailed analysis and includes these steps:
    - Define the problem or clarify the thesis.
    - Separate background information from evidence.
    - Weigh evidence.
    - Assess support (e.g., credibility of sources and documentation).
    - Assess testimony, use of facts, and factual reporting.
    - Recognize and assess circumstantial evidence.
    - Recognize and assess statistical evidence.
    - Recognize and discuss any value claims.
    - Examine use of analogies, precedents, and metaphors.
    - Examine any causal or other inductive arguments.
    - Examine any deductive arguments.
    - If deductive, test for validity, that is, the conclusion could not be false *if* the premises were true and thus the argument is valid.
    - If deductive, test for soundness: the argument is valid plus the premises are actually true, so the argument is sound.

Exercises

Part One

1. Analyze the following argument on surveillance:

   Cell phones have become the digital equivalent of Hansel and Gretel's breadcrumbs. When a cell phone is turned on, it broadcasts an identification number to the closest antennas, which allow the carrier to chart its customers. It's a simple matter—known as triangulation—to track the signal as it arrives at different towers, then calculate the location of the phone based on time differences. The police have taken full advantage of this tracking trick, though—technically, at least—they need a court order to access the information. Earlier this year, Timothy Crosby, 40, was busted for raping and robbing a Brooklyn woman after the police located him by homing in on his cell phone signal. In November 2000, authorities pursued Kofi Apea Orleans-Lindsay for allegedly killing a Maryland state trooper during a buy-and-bust operation. Police used cell data to track Orleans-Lindsay to Brooklyn, where they arrested him (Adam L. Penenberg, "The Surveillance Society," *Wired*, December 2000).

2. The Patriot Act has made it easier for police to go after suspects than in 2000. They no longer need a court order to track cell phones. And, why not? On the other hand, should we be worried about eroding civil rights? Set out your three to four strongest reasons for *and* against the police having the right to listen in on your cell phone calls.

Part Two

Michelle Scully's husband was killed in a rampage in a San Francisco high-rise. She wrote this article in an attempt to influence members of Congress who were about to vote on a proposed ban on assault rifles. Read over her article and discuss her argument and the use of her personal story for impact.

A Gun Widow's Request: Courage in Congress

Michelle Scully

Last July 1 began with my husband John and me driving to work together in San Francisco, making plans for a long Fourth of July weekend. We had been married just nine months, but had been in love for nine years. We were best friends and felt incredibly lucky to have each other as lifetime companions. By 3 that afternoon, our plans for the weekend and our entire lives were shattered. A deranged man had walked into my husband's law firm equipped with two TEC-DC9 assault pistols, a .45-caliber pistol and more than 100 rounds of ammunition. Within minutes, eight people were dead, including my husband.

I was working in an empty office at my husband's firm when John came in to tell me that shots had been heard upstairs. We went into the hall, trying to leave the building, and saw a young man shot right in front of us. John and I attempted to hide in a nearby office, but were hunted down by this madman. My husband used his body to shield me from the flying bullets. When the shooting finally stopped, I opened my eyes to see my husband lying on the floor in front of me, blood coming out of his nose and mouth. He had been shot four times and fatally wounded in the chest. I had been shot in the right arm, and spent the next half hour sitting in a pool of blood, begging John to stay alive. He finally looked up at me and said, "Michelle, I'm dying. I love you."

I have not been the same since that moment. I now go through every day wishing there was some way that I could bring John back, because I can't stand the loneliness of living my life without him. I can't stand the pain on the faces of his parents, his sisters, his brother and his many friends. When John Scully died, a piece of everyone who knew him died too, because he touched everyone he met in a profound way.

I know there is nothing I can do to bring John back, so I have committed myself to preventing other John Scullys from dying. Unfortunately, it takes stories like mine to move the leaders of this country to action to take military-style assault weapons from our streets. These are not hunting or sporting weapons. They are weapons of war, designed to kill a large number of people in a short period of time. They have no place on our streets, in our schools or in our office buildings.

It would appear that the House of Representatives believes that assault weapons aren't a crime problem, having left this measure out of its debate about crime and out of its omnibus crime bill. While it's true that these killing machines may not be the most widely used weapons, they are 10 to 20 times more likely to be used in the commission of violent crimes than are conventional weapons. And assault weapons represent nearly 30% of the guns traced to organized crime, drug trafficking and terrorist crime.

My husband John committed the ultimate act of bravery by saving my life from a madman's bullets. Congress must only find the courage to pass a piece of legislation that will save lives and save others from the pain and loss that I will carry for the rest of my life.

Source: Reprinted with the permission of Michelle Scully.

Case Update: The Court Ruling: Can Victims Sue Gun Makers?

The California Supreme Court ruled on the lawsuit that stemmed from the massacre of nine people, including Scully's husband. Here a mentally disturbed man, Gian Luigi Ferri, entered a San Francisco high-rise and opened fire in a law office with two TEC-DC9s and a revolver. In addition to the eight people he killed, he wounded six people before committing suicide. In a 5–1 decision reported on August 6, 2001, the court ruled that victims cannot sue gun makers when criminals use their products illegally. All but one of the justices basically adhered to the view, "guns don't kill people; people kill people." Only Justice Kathryn Mickle Werdegar disagreed with the majority view that the manufacturers bore no legal responsibility. She felt that the company, Navegar, was negligent in marketing the fast-firing weapon to the general public. In her view, until the law is changed, gun makers "will apparently enjoy absolute immunity from the consequences of their negligent marketing decisions."

In many cases, we may be called to a social or political response, as was Scully when she sat down to write her letter to the editor. In developing our reasoning skills, we are in a stronger position to reflect on what we see in the world and how effectively we can act. In this way, we are able to enter the public dialogue on the issues facing us in our lives.

CHAPTER SIX

The Logic Machine: Deductive and Inductive Reasoning

It should be apparent that the most meticulous inspection and search would not reveal the presence of poltergeists at the premises or unearth the property's ghoulish reputation in the community.

JUSTICE ISRAEL RUBIN, ruling a prospective buyer could recover his $32,000 down payment on a home that the owner claimed was haunted.

Suppose a real estate agent says the house you want to buy is haunted, pointing to a creaky staircase and the fact that two previous owners died accidental deaths. You go down the stairs and, sure enough, they creak. People in the neighborhood agree about the house's ghastly condition. Does this mean the house *really is* haunted? The evidence does not certainly show the house is haunted. We would need more evidence to be convinced.

In this chapter we will examine the two main kinds of arguments—inductive and deductive—and learn how to assess each kind. The last section of the chapter presents truth tables, one method of checking the truth of propositions and the validity of arguments. It is useful to be familiar with truth tables, though they work best on short, uncomplicated arguments. As we'll see in the last unit of this book, there are other methods for assessing arguments. An acquaintance with the various tools of logic not only helps develop clear thinking; it also builds confidence.

In an **inductive** argument the evidence alone is not enough for the conclusion to be certain, even if the premises are true. The evidence offers only partial support for the conclusion and, consequently, you cannot be certain that the conclusion follows. So, even if the evidence were actually true (that the stairs creak and two previous owners died in accidents) the conclusion that the house is haunted might still be false. It is because of this uncertainty that the argument is considered inductive.

On the contrary, the real estate agent could say, "All the houses in Charlestown, Massachusetts, are haunted. Obviously this house at 14 Hill Street is in Charlestown, so it must also be haunted." This argument is inherently different from the inductive one. The evidence here, if true, would force the conclusion to be true. If all houses in Charlestown are haunted *and* the house at 14 Hill Street is in Charlestown, it would have to be true that the house is haunted. This type of argument is called **deductive**. The conclusion can be extracted from the premises.

We see this model in detective shows as well—most clearly in the TV show *CSI* and its spin-offs, where the importance of following the evidence is regularly emphasized. Lead scientist Gil Grissom often reminds his staff to follow the evidence—and return to it—if they get stuck in trying to solve the crime.

What distinguishes a *deductive argument* is that the conclusion follows directly from the premises, that no further evidence is needed to support the conclusion. At times claims are made (e.g., in criminal trials), without the evidence *actually* being sufficient. When it is asserted or implied that this set of premises sufficiently supports the conclusion, we've got a deductive argument. If, however, a conclusion is drawn in spite of missing pieces or gaps in the set of premises, the argument is **inductive**. This is summarized in the following table:

DEDUCTIVE ARGUMENT	EXPLANATION	EXAMPLES
An argument is *deductive* if the conclusion is said to follow directly from the premises and nothing more need be added for that to happen.	Think of it as working with a closed set—like a puzzle that's not missing any pieces. From the pieces, you deduce that the conclusion follows. *Note:* The conclusion can be extracted right out of the premises—we don't need to add any more premises.	Any angel has wings. Anything with wings can fly. *Therefore,* all angels can fly. If cows had wings, they'd be large birds. Cows are not large birds. *Therefore,* cows do not have wings. Charlie only eats greasy food. Charlie is eating lunch. *Therefore,* he is eating greasy food.

INDUCTIVE ARGUMENT	EXPLANATION	EXAMPLES
An argument is *inductive* if the conclusion is said to follow with a degree of probability or likelihood from the premises—but there is always a wedge of doubt about that actually occurring.	Think of it as working with a puzzle that's missing at least one piece (sometimes more!). From the pieces, you induce that the conclusion will likely follow; but you can't be certain. *Note:* The conclusion of an inductive argument never follows with certainty. There's always at least one hole in the argument—which means we don't have all the evidence to be 100% sure.	98 percent of winged creatures are birds. Charlie was chased by something with wings. *Therefore,* it must have been a bird chasing Charlie. Eating greasy food can cause gallstones. Charlie eats greasy food. *Therefore,* he'll probably get a gallstone. Children are like cockatoos— they like to throw food in the air, and they love games. Cockatoos also like to flip upside down. *Therefore,* small children probably like to flip upside down too!

Key Terms in Arguments

An **argument** is a group of propositions, some of which (called the **premises**) act as supporting evidence for another proposition (called the **conclusion** or **thesis**). See if you can spot the conclusion and its supporting premises in the following argument: "Jasper must have gotten into the felt pens. First off, Jasper has a few tiny green marks on one of his wings. Cockatoos don't have green markings. Also, Jasper has green on the tip of his beak, which he didn't have when he was eating his egg this morning. Finally, the very end of his tongue has a greenish hew. Yes indeed, Jasper got hold of a felt pen!" The conclusion is in the opening and closing statements, with the premises sandwiched in between.

An **inference** is drawn on the basis of evidence, though it is not necessarily *supported* by that evidence. The terms "inference" and "conclusion" are interchangeable, as are "I infer" and "I conclude." Some people can have all the evidence in the world and still draw an incorrect conclusion. That's why we must subject arguments to careful scrutiny. In order to do this, break down the argument into its component parts—the premises (evidence) and conclusion (thesis). In a strong argument, the premises are sufficient for the conclusion.

Let's also note the difference between **sufficient** conditions and **necessary** conditions:

A is *sufficient* for B: "If A then B" or "B if A."
If A occurs, B will occur as well.
Being tired is *sufficient* for Betty Jean to take a snooze.
If she is tired, then Betty Jean will take a snooze.

A is *necessary* for B: "B *only if* A" or "Only if A, B."
If A does not occur, B will not occur either.
"If not A then not B" → "If B then A."
Singing while driving is *necessary* for a fun journey.
If you don't sing while driving, then the journey isn't fun.
If the journey is fun, then you must have been singing.

A **proposition** is an assertion that is either true or false. A proposition can be expressed in the following form: *SUBJECT* copula *PREDICATE* (Copula = a form of the verb "to be"). For example, "Grasshoppers are insects."

In other words, we are saying of something (the subject) that it has some characteristic being predicated—such as "Ice Cube is a person with many talents." The subject of the proposition is "Ice Cube" and the predicate is "a person with many talents." A proposition isn't always strictly expressed in the above form, but it can be rewritten in this format without changing the meaning of the sentence.

EXAMPLES of Propositions

The history exam covered the Civil War.
Jelly beans are small chewy candies.
The coyotes killed three cats in the neighborhood last month.

A proposition is called a *categorical proposition* if it can be expressed starting with any of the words "all," "no," "some," or *x* percent (where *x* is any number other than zero or 100). Categorical propositions are *universal* (all-or-nothing) or *particular* (at least one, not all). The forms are as follows:

Universal Propositions (all-or-nothing)

Form 1: "All A is B."   → Universal positive
Form 2: "No A is B."   → Universal negative
Form 3: "A is/is not B."   → Universal positive or negative
                                 where A is a class with only one member

Particular Propositions (at least one, not all)

Form 1: "Some A is B."   → Particular positive
Form 2: "Some A is not B."   → Particular negative
Form 3: "x% of A is/is not B." → Particular positive or negative
                                  where $x \neq 100$ or 0.

EXAMPLES of Categorical Propositions

No bat has feathers.
All cockatoos are large birds.
Some house cats are the prey of coyotes.
Some small cars are not Audis.
Seventy-four percent of the senior citizens are people who like deviled eggs.

The Key to Distinguishing Propositions

A proposition asserts of some subject that it has one or more characteristics (these are being *predicated* of the *subject*). Propositions can take several forms, from sentences in the indicative to rhetorical questions. For instance, if someone says, "Did you know that skunks eat rats?" they are asserting the proposition, "Skunks are animals that eat rats." Similarly, if a justice of the peace declares, "I now pronounce you, Tony and Carmela, husband and wife," the claim is that "Tony and Carmela are now married." It makes no logical difference if a proposition is expressed in the present, past, or future tense. The key thing is that something is being predicated of something else; for example, "All basketball players are people with quick reflexes."

Matters of taste, opinion, and morality are often presented in the form of a proposition, such as, "No dinner is memorable without a warm loaf of bread." It may be wise to add the words "in my opinion" or "to me." If not, there could be a problem. For instance, contentious claims like "People with nose rings are attractive" or "Adultery is an unpardonable sin" cannot be treated as simple propositions. Similarly, expressions of emotion may not be simple propositions either (for example, "That feels so good!"). In such cases, we tend to think in terms of *agreement* (or disagreement) with the position expressed, rather than that the claim is true or false.

A **generalization** is an inference from a smaller group (or one individual) to a larger group. When we generalize we are asserting what is true or false of one or more members of a group to some or all of the group. For example, we may see ducks eating snails at the park and infer that "All ducks eat snails" or "Most ducks eat snails." Some generalizations are based on cause and effect or statistical studies—but not all, as the duck example illustrates. Be careful not to commit the fallacy of **hasty generalization,** where the inference is based on a sample that is too small or atypical, or the fallacy of **biased statistics,** where the sample group is not sufficiently diverse to represent the targeted population.

A **value-claim** is a prescriptive statement of values—moral, aesthetic, or personal taste. Value claims cannot be treated like empirical claims that are either true or false, but they can function in arguments. However, they are not statements that can be assigned a truth-value (that is, determined to be either true or false), which *is* the case with propositions. Because of this, we can *assume*—though not prove—

a value claim is true. Consequently, we can test any argument containing value claims for validity—but not for soundness (which requires true premises, as we will see).

A valid argument does not require that the premises *actually* be true: Our concern is only that if we assume them to be true, the conclusion could not be false. Clearly, you can *assume* a value claim is true, even if you couldn't prove it. You can therefore create valid arguments involving morality, personal taste, artistic judgments, and the like. The restriction is that you won't be able to assert that any of the value claims are unquestionably true. Here is a valid argument:

> Any movie with live animals as stars is a work of art.
> *Paulie* is a movie starring a parrot (a live animal named Paulie!).
> Therefore, *Paulie* is a work of art.

This argument is valid, since the conclusion comes right out of the premises and it could not be false if the premises were true. However, it's not a sound argument, since the first premise is not verifiably true. Sure, we can drag in expert after expert who will attest that any movie with live animals is a work of art. But those testimonials no more a guarantee that such movies are works of art than if we had 200 painters agree that green is more beautiful than orange. The majority does *not* rule when it comes to assigning truth or falsity.

People use value claims all the time; consequently, we have to deal with them alongside propositions that can be affirmed or negated. The use of value claims presents problems of verifiability if it is asserted that they are absolutely true or false. Let's look at some examples.

Propositions

The Honda was stolen right in front of Amanda's house.
A few babies do not like vanilla pudding.
The Red Sox made history by winning in 2004.
No peanut is a dairy product.
Note: Propositions are either true or false.

Nonpropositions

Yikes!
Where's my Tweetie costume?
Congratulations!
Note: Nonpropositions cannot be assigned a truth-value and *cannot* be assumed to be either true or false for purposes of testing validity.

Value Claims

Olive Oyl is not as attractive as Betty Boop.

The Grudge was better than *The Ring*.
There's nothing like the South for delicious pies!
Dr. Dre is the male equivalent of Queen Latifah.
Note: Value claims cannot be assigned a truth-value, but they *can* be assumed
   true for purposes of testing validity (but not soundness).

Exercises

Part One

1. Looking at either sports or music, make up or find four propositions and
   note if they are true or false.

2. Looking at either college life or movies, make up or find four value
   claims.

3. Looking at advertising, find three examples of propositions, three
   nonpropositions, and three value claims.

Part Two

Directions: Indicate which of the following are *propositions* and which are *value claims*.

1. Get lost!

2. The parrot chewed a hole in the wall.

3. Chickpeas are members of the legume family.

4. Lorenna McKennitt's music is fantastic.

5. If sharks are in the tank, it could be dangerous to stick your hand in the
   water.

6. Damn you!

7. There's not a man alive who wouldn't agree that you'd look cute as a
   redhead.

8. Where is my Calculus book?

9. Either the tire has too much air in it or it doesn't.

10. Unless the plumber can fix it, we have a sewage problem.

11. Get a load of this, Colleen!

12. Congratulations—you are now an American citizen.

13. Eighty-seven percent of squirrels in the University of Alberta study
    preferred birdseed to table scraps.

14. What in the world did you do with your sock?

15. No one with a functioning taste bud can tolerate ketchup on fried eggs.

16. Some mathematicians are not fluent in Urdu.

17. According to folklore, vampires are averse to daylight.

18. What's that—you passed your final?

19. If you don't want to watch *Ground Hog Day* again, then we can go bowling.

20. The Red Sox may be good—but no team beats the Celtics for a century of greatness.

Deductive Reasoning

With deductive arguments, the conclusion comes right out of the premises. The process is a kind of extraction. A well-constructed deductive argument lays the groundwork for the conclusion to follow.

Think of all those cases in which the prosecutor tries to prove the case *beyond a reasonable doubt*. The prosecutor's task is to demonstrate that the evidence is sufficient to seal the conviction, that any reasonable judge or juror should conclude from the strength of the evidence that the conclusion follows. Their task is to show that there can be no reasonable doubt that the defendant's guilt follows from the truth of the premises.

Attorneys may think they've sealed the case, but not all arguments are convincing. Some arguments never get off the ground. And jurors may not know if each piece of evidence is actually true. Generally they could *not* know if what was presented in court was *really* true (Is that really the murder weapon? Is that really the victim's dirty T-shirt?) The task is to decide whether, *if* that evidence were assumed to be true, the conclusion would follow—if so, the jury would be expected to convict the defendant. Jurors are not in a position to ascertain the truth of the evidence submitted. They must focus on the reasoning and decide if it holds together under close scrutiny.

It is the *structure* of the reasoning that determines a valid argument—not the truth of the claims. The issue of truth comes later, when we look at sound arguments. So all this tells us *one important thing* about deductive arguments: The focus is on whether or not the premises make a convincing case for the conclusion. The issue of what's true or false comes up later, when we try to determine if the argument is sound—not in the determination of validity.

There's a hilarious scene in the movie *My Cousin Vinny* that uses deductive reasoning to discount the testimony of one of the witnesses, Mr. Tipton. The lawyer, Vincent Gambini, makes his case by proving Mr. Tipton could not have seen the accused make off in the getaway car. Mr. Tipton had said he'd stepped away from the window to cook some grits (a ground corn alternative to potatoes for break-fast). He insisted that he was gone for only five minutes. Gambini knows this to be impossible and nails Mr. Tipton:

VINCENT GAMBINI: How could it take you 5 minutes to cook your grits when it takes the entire grit-eating world 20 minutes?

MR. TIPTON: Um . . . I'm a fast cook, I guess.

VINCENT GAMBINI: You're a fast cook? Are we to believe that boiling water soaks into a grit faster in your kitchen than any place on the face of the earth?

MR. TIPTON: I don't know.

VINCENT GAMBINI: Perhaps the laws of physics cease to exist on your stove. Were these magic grits? Did you buy them from the same guy who sold Jack his beanstalk beans?

Mr. Tipton has to concede that the laws of physics *do* exist in his kitchen and, thus, he could not have seen the accused running away from the store, as he had claimed. By using deductive reasoning skills, Gambini effectively disproved Tipton's original argument.

A **deductive argument** is an argument in which the premises are claimed to be sufficient for the conclusion to follow. This means there are no missing pieces; the evidence solidly backs up the conclusion. In that sense, a deductive argument is a closed set. In other words, just like a crossword puzzle, the clues (evidence) should be all you need to complete the job (draw the conclusion without resorting to any other references or resources). For example, suppose someone said:

All monarchs are butterflies.

All butterflies are insects.

So all monarchs are insects.

This argument is also self-contained. The conclusion, "All monarchs are butter-flies" comes out of the two premises. You may take issue with the truth-value of the two premises, but the argument is still a deductive one.

Applications of Deductive Reasoning

In mathematics, even in arithmetic, deductive reasoning is pervasive. Think of geometry, where axioms and postulates are used to prove a theorem. You must only use those axioms and postulates; there is nowhere else you can go to get your reasons. It is a self-contained system; the conclusion comes out of the premises. Of course, if a postulate (a premise) is changed, the resulting mathematical system changes too.

For example, if we don't follow Euclid's fifth postulate (that two parallel lines will never intersect and are equidistant), then we get quite distinct theoretical systems. We might draw parallel lines on a globe or orange—they converge at both ends. We might parallel lines on the inside of a trumpet, where the lines diverge and would get farther and farther apart as if the trumpet were expanding.

You Tell Me Department

What about the Judge's View?

The Justice Department is demanding that at least six hospitals turn over hundreds of patient medical records on late-term abortions performed there in the last three years. They want to examine the medical histories of those patients to see if the abortion was medically necessary. Lawyers for the Justice Department insist a new law prohibiting late-term (aka partial-birth) abortions authorizes this plan. Hospital administrators are worried about violating the privacy rights of their patients. The chief federal judge in Chicago tossed out the subpoena against the Northwestern University Medical Center, arguing as follows:

"A woman's relationship with her doctor and her decision on whether to get an abortion 'are issues indisputably of the most sensitive stripe.' They should remain confidential 'without the fear of public disclosure,' the judge, Charles P. Kocoras, wrote in a decision first reported by *Crain's* business journal in Chicago. The subpoena for patient files is a 'significant intrusion' in the patients' privacy. Consequently, the subpoena must be rejected." (Eric Lichtblau, "Justice Dept. Seeks Hospitals' Records of Some Abortions," *The New York Times*, 12 Feb 2004)

You tell me: How strong is the judge's reasoning? Share your assessment.

Let's look at deductive reasoning in a case involving arithmetic. To solve the problem 62 minus 49, students in second grade are normally taught to borrow a "one" from the 10s place, much like borrowing sugar from a neighbor. However, as noted by Richard Rothstein, children in Shanghai are taught the reasoning behind borrowing so the process makes mathematical sense. In Shanghai schools, children are taught that 62 is the same as 60 and 2, 50 and 12, 40 and 22, and so forth. Once this is understood, the process of subtraction makes sense and isn't some magic act. Understanding the deductive reasoning involved allows students to move to more advanced mathematical topics. Let's look at some examples of deductive arguments.

Example #1 of a Deductive Argument

No pilot is afraid of heights.

<u>Some football players are afraid of heights.</u>

Therefore, some football players are not pilots.

The first premise asserts one characteristic of pilots; namely, not being afraid of heights. The second premise informs us that there are some people (football players) who do not have this characteristic. It is argued that those two premises are sufficient for the conclusion to come right out of the premises.

Example #2 of a Deductive Argument

No animal lover would mistreat a pet.

Anyone who mistreats a pet violates the fundamental guidelines of People for <u>the Ethical Treatment of Animals (PETA).</u>

So, no one who violates the fundamental guidelines of PETA is an animal lover.

Example #3 of a Deductive Argument

If you don't know how to cook, you won't know the recipe for hollandaise sauce.

Craig doesn't know how to cook.

Therefore, Craig won't know the recipe for hollandaise sauce.

In all of these examples, the premises are put forward as sufficient, with no other evidence necessary for the conclusion to follow. That does not mean the argument is actually constructed so that the conclusion really does follow. However, a deductive argument makes an implicit claim of certainty.

Key Deductive Arguments

1. *Categorical syllogisms and chains of syllogisms:* These are three-line arguments (or chains of them), consisting of two premises and a conclusion, with all of the propositions in the form of categorical propositions. These propositions can be expressed in four possible forms: "All A are B," "No A is B," "Some A is B," and "Some A is not B." For example,

   All romantics cry during sad movies.

   No one who cries in a sad movie can eat a lot of popcorn.

   So, no one who eats a lot of popcorn is a romantic.

2. *Modus ponens* (Latin for mode that *affirms*). These are arguments of the form: "If A then B. A is the case. Therefore, B is true also." The first premise is a conditional claim. The second premise affirms the antecedent is true. The conclusion, then, is that the consequent must also be true. For example,

   If the dentist slips while operating, Omar will need stitches.

   The dentist slipped while operating.

   So, Omar needed to get stitches.

   Remember the *fallacy of denying the antecedent* and the *fallacy of affirming the consequent* are mutations of modus ponens/modus tollens and not valid argument forms. See Chapter 4 on fallacies to review.

3. *Modus tollens.* (This is Latin for mode that *denies*.) These are arguments of the form: "If A then B. B is not the case. Therefore, A is not true either." The first premise is a conditional claim. The second premise denies the consequent by saying it is not true. The inference, then, is that the antecedent could not be true either. For example:

   If Bruce gets a tattoo of a tiger, his mother will go through the roof.

   Bruce's mother did not go through the roof.

   Therefore, Bruce did not get a tattoo of a tiger.

4. *Disjunctive syllogism.* These are arguments of the form: "Either A or B. A is not the case. Therefore, B must be true." For example:

Either that's a rainbow trout or a weird-looking salmon.

That's not a rainbow trout.

So, it's a weird-looking salmon.

5. *Hypothetical syllogism.* These are arguments of the form: "If A then B. If B then C." Therefore, if A then C." For example:

If Louie goes to the Claire Lynch concert, he'll miss the ball game.

If Louie misses the ball game, he won't get a chili dog.

Therefore, if Louie goes to the Claire Lynch concert, he won't get a chili dog.

6. *Constructive dilemma.* These take the form of "If A then B, and if C then D. Either A or C. Therefore, either B or D." In other words, there's a choice between two options, each leading to some effect. You must pick between the two options. Therefore, one of two possible effects will happen. For example:

If Maricella learns to knit, she'll make a beanie; but if she takes up crochet, she'll make a scarf.

Either Maricella will learn to knit or take up crochet.

Therefore, either Maricella will make a beanie or she'll make a scarf.

7. *Variations of modus ponens and modus tollens:*

A. *Unless:* One variation takes this form: "A unless B. B is not the case. Therefore A." or "A unless B. Not A. Therefore, B." For example, both of these are valid:

David will return to Omaha State unless he transfers to Reed.

David did not transfer to Reed.

So, David returned to Omaha State.

Jamal will stay at Colby unless he transfers to Cal State Fresno.

Jamal did not stay at Colby.

Therefore, Jamal transferred to Cal State Fresno.

B. *Application of a rule:* Another variation of modus ponens is in the form of the application of a rule according to a set of criteria: "Rule X applies to any cases with characteristics A, B, C, and D. Individual case P has characteristics A, B, C, and D. Therefore, rule X applies to case P. For example:

People will get a fine of $270 if they are caught driving in the carpool lane without a passenger in their vehicle.

Irene snuck into the carpool lane even though she was by herself and was seen by the Officer Williams.

Therefore, Irene got a fine of $270.

Compounding the Terms of the Argument

Be aware that in all the examples above, A and B could each stand for a compound statement. A compound statement is one containing any of these words: "not," "and," "or," "if . . . then," and "if and only if." We can see this with the following example:

If it's either an apple or an orange, **then** it's a fruit and not a vegetable.

That's either an apple or an orange.

Thus, it's a fruit and not a vegetable.

The above argument is of the same form as:

If it's an apple, **then** it's a fruit.

That's an apple.

Thus, it's a fruit.

Although the terms of the first argument are compound, the *form* of the argument is still the same, as the terms in bold show us.

Validity

People commonly use the word "valid" to mean "good point" or "true." However, in the realm of logic, "valid" is not about that which is true, it is about the argument's construction. Logical validity concerns arguments, not propositions.

Think of building blocks consisting of propositions. Propositions can be true or false. We can combine propositions to form arguments. When we do that, the focus shifts away from truth and falsity to the strength of the reasoning. In the case of deductive arguments, talking about strength is talking about validity. We cannot say of an argument that it is true or false. But if the argument is deductive, we can assess it for validity. Let's see how this is done.

A **valid argument** is an argument in which the premises provide sufficient support for drawing the conclusion. This has to do with the relationship between the premises and the conclusion. Validity is not about whether or not any statements are *actually* true—or whether or not the argument can be said to correspond to anything in the world.

Validity is about how the argument all fits together. Validity looks at whether the premises either separately or in combination sufficiently support the conclusion. This is a *structural* issue. Our goal is to see what happens if we *assume* the premises to be true. If we assume the premises are true, do they then support the conclusion in such a way that it *has* to be true as well? If the answer is "Yes," then the argument is *valid*. If we could have true premises and a false conclusion, then the argument is **invalid.** An invalid argument is like a house with a rotting foundation—it cannot stand given its deficient structure.

The key is that the connection between the premises and the conclusion entails *certainty:* If true premises force the conclusion to be true, then the conclusion *certainly* follows from those premises. That means the argument is valid—and is, therefore, a strong argument in terms of its construction. For example:

No cowboy has a refined sense of humor.

<u>Buffalo Bill was a cowboy.</u>

Thus, Buffalo Bill did not have a refined sense of humor.

We do not have to know anything about cowboys or Buffalo Bill for this to be a valid argument. If we assume the premises were true, the conclusion would certainly be true also. It could not be false when the premises were true. Let us look at another example.

No one who has a pierced belly button is inhibited.

<u>Some Democrats are inhibited.</u>

Therefore, some Democrats do not have pierced belly buttons.

If the two premises were true then the conclusion would follow. *Remember:* It is not important for validity whether or not the premises are actually true. The issue is the connection between the premises and the conclusion.

Watch for terms like, "must," "necessarily," "inevitably," "certainly," "entail," and "it can be deduced." *These words often indicate a deductive argument.* To make sure, ask: Do the premises provide sufficient support for the conclusion? The use of the phrase "I deduce that" or "It is certain that" does not mean that the argument is necessarily deductive or there is certainty. Sometimes people use the terms for emphasis or to bolster their argument, even though they have not made their case.

The Juror Model of Validity

To better understand validity, picture being a juror. There we are, sitting in the jury box, listening to the prosecution and the defense attorneys present their arguments trying to convince us to conclude one thing or another. We have to assess the evidence, witness testimony, and credibility of the experts. We have to evaluate the strength of their reasoning without leaving the room.

As jurors, we have to work with what is presented in the courtroom. We can't go look at the crime scene (unless the judge permits us jurors to do so). And we can't go interview the neighbors to get more information. Instead, we have to determine if a solid case is being made. Our decision should be based solely on the strength of the evidence before us.

Jurors cannot know if the evidence that has been presented is *actually* true or false. We must take on faith that the legal system is working, that people are telling the truth and that evidence is not fabricated. Obviously these are not always true conditions. At times, serious problems force us to rethink or retry a case. As a juror, we can only work with the evidence before us. Even if we know about the case,

Greg Perry, artist/illustrator. Reprinted with the permission of Greg Perry. www.perryink.com.

FIGURE 6.1

All potato-timers are spudometers. No spudometer is a speedometer. So no potato-timer is a speedometer. *Valid argument!*

say through news coverage, that prior knowledge should not be brought to bear upon our reasoning. The task is to decide if the prosecution has made its case.

Is the evidence sufficient to convict, or is there a reasonable doubt that would allow for an alternative hypothesis? If the conclusion could be false while the premises were true, then the argument is invalid. If the conclusion follows directly from the premises, then the argument is valid. (see figure 6.1) For example:

Examples of Valid Arguments

Either the lab destroyed the evidence or the defendant is lying.

The lab did not destroy the evidence.

Therefore, the defendant must be lying.

All alien abductions leave the victim with some memory problems.

Samantha was the victim of an alien abduction.

Thus, Samantha will be left with some memory problems.

No dream about flying is a nightmare.

Levi only has flying dreams.

Therefore, Levi never has nightmares.

What makes all these arguments valid is that, if the premises were true, the conclusion would *have* to be true. It is this element of certainty that marks an argument as valid.

Invalidity

An **invalid argument** is an argument in which the premises fail to adequately support the conclusion. We can tell an argument is invalid when the premises could be true and the conclusion false.

Example #1 of an Invalid Argument:

Some people are short.

Some flight attendants are not short.

So, some flight attendants are not people.

If we assumed the two premises were true, it would not follow that "Some flight attendants are not people." The conclusion could be false while the premises were true.

Example #2 of an Invalid Argument

No one with a heart condition should run the Boston marathon.

Some photographers have a heart condition.

Therefore, no photographer should run the Boston marathon.

Here the conclusion could be false and the premises true. The premises, therefore, fail to force the conclusion to follow.

Example #3 of an Invalid Argument

If you do not wear swim goggles, you could lose your contact lens.

Rose lost her contact lens.

Consequently, Rose must not have worn swim goggles.

Even if it were true that, without swim goggles you could lose your contact lens and Rose did lose her lens, it does not follow that she wasn't wearing swim goggles. For example, she might have lost her lens down the sink when cleaning them.

 # Exercises

1. Using the form of modus ponens, finish the valid argument that has as its first premise: "If he is big and burly, then he will enjoy French literature."

2. Using the form of modus tollens, finish the valid argument that has as its first premise: "If the little girl is fond of small animals, then she might like a guinea pig for a pet."

3. Give a valid argument in the form of modus ponens that has as its first premise, "If you have a powerful car, you won't have trouble going over the Grapevine."

4. Give a valid argument in the form of the disjunctive syllogism that has as its second premise: "A Cessna is not a four-wheel vehicle."

5. Give a valid argument in the form of modus tollens that has as its first premise, "If there's meat on the sandwich, Raelynn won't touch it."

6. Complete the argument in the form of a constructive dilemma having as its first premise: "If there are mosquitoes in the tent, it'll be hard to sleep, but if there are no mosquitoes, then another insect is buzzing around."

7. Explain whether this argument is valid or invalid and why: "Either that's a poltergeist or something weird is happening in the basement. That's no poltergeist. So something weird is happening in the basement."

8. Explain why this argument is invalid: "If Paco becomes a yoga master, he'll probably want to be a vegan. Paco is a vegan. Therefore, he must have become a yoga master."

9. Explain why this is invalid: "Some dogs are Labrador retrievers. Some dogs like to chase cats down the block. Therefore, some Labrador retrievers like to chase cats down the block."

10. Make up some premises to create a valid argument for the conclusion: "All dentists are comfortable talking to people who are quiet." Explain why it's valid.

11. Make up some premises to create a valid *or* invalid argument for the conclusion, "Some reptiles are lizards." Explain why it's valid *or* invalid.

12. Give an example of an invalid argument with all true premises for the conclusion: "Abraham Lincoln was a Republican." Explain why it's invalid.

13. Give an example of an argument in the form of a hypothetical syllogism.

14. What valid argument form is this argument: "If Ray takes up swimming, he'll need goggles; but if he takes up jogging, he'll need new running shoes. Either Ray will take up swimming or he'll take up jogging. So either Ray will need goggles or he'll need new running shoes."

15. Give an example of a categorical syllogism.

Soundness

Once validity is determined, we can assess the soundness of an argument. It's at this point that issues around whether the evidence is actually true or false becomes significant. Now's the time we ask whether or not the evidence is actually true and not just whether the conclusion would follow *if* it were true.

This moves us out of the jury box into the world of empirical reality. Sound arguments are important—who wants to have a good argument based on questionable claims, false statements, or lies? No thanks! If we want our reasoning to be sound, then we want two things. We want the argument to be *cogent* (so our reasoning is strong, defensible, well structured, and gives sufficient evidence for the conclusion). And we want it to be *grounded in truth*. Otherwise we risk having a great-sounding argument that goes nowhere. Think of those cases where prosecutors have convicted innocent people on what appeared to be persuasive arguments—but it turned out that some of the evidence was simply false (e.g., as revealed later by DNA evidence).

Let's look at an example: "All men can give birth to children. We need more people living in the Arctic and embryo implants seem to be working to produce children. Thus, we ought to implant embryos in men and boost the Arctic population." However good this idea may sound, the fact that the first premise is false means the argument has no legs. The reasoning may be strong in terms of validity, but it has no operational, functional, empirical value. The false premise ultimately sinks the argument. It is an unsound argument.

Assessing the Soundness of an Argument

We know when a deductive argument is valid or invalid. And we now know that an inductive argument cannot be valid or invalid—since its relative strength rests on the probability of the conclusion being true. The next thing we want to consider is whether the argument is a sound one.

> **CRITERIA FOR A SOUND ARGUMENT**
> → **The argument is valid.**
> → **The premises are actually true.**

To check soundness: First check for validity. If the premises were true, is the conclusion forced to be true (it couldn't be false)? If so, the argument is valid. Next check for the truth of the premises. If the premises really were true, the argument is **sound.** However, if either condition is not met, then the argument is **unsound.** An argument can be unsound if it is valid but doesn't have true premises. It can be unsound if it has true premises, but is invalid. Or both.

Examples of Sound Arguments.

All possums are small mammals.
<u>All small mammals are warm-blooded animals.</u>
So, all possums are warm-blooded animals.

If the Lakers lose Shaq, they'll need to get a new center.
<u>The Lakers lost Shaq.</u>
Therefore, they'll need to get a new center.

Either Quebec will separate from the rest of Canada or it'll stay in the Confederation.
<u>Quebec has not seceded from Canada.</u>
So, it will stay in the Confederation.

These arguments are all valid because, if we assume the two premises to be true, the conclusion could not be false. Since the premises *are* also true, this means each of the arguments is sound.

Unsound Arguments

An argument is *unsound* whenever either or both of these conditions are met: (1) the argument is invalid or (2) the premises are not all true. The odds are that an argument will be unsound, because many arguments are invalid and often one or more of the premises are false. For example:

Example #1 of an Unsound Argument

If we legalize marijuana then alcohol consumption patterns may change.
<u>We did not legalize marijuana.</u>
So, the alcohol consumption patterns won't change.

This argument is invalid. If we assume the premises to be true, the conclusion could be false. Because the argument is invalid, it is unsound.

Example #2 of an Unsound Argument

All skunks are ferocious animals that can mutate into warthogs.
<u>All spotted skunks are skunks.</u>
So, all spotted skunks are ferocious animals that can mutate into warthogs.

This argument is valid, since the conclusion does follow from the premises. However, the first premise is not true, so the argument is not sound.

Group or Individual Exercise

Note: Allow time to gather examples.

Looking at the reasoning of any public figure, celebrity, or athlete, find examples of any or all of the following: valid arguments, invalid arguments, sound arguments, unsound arguments. Be sure to explain why they are valid, invalid, sound, or unsound.

Overview

Remember, first check for validity. Assume the premises are true and see if the conclusion is forced to be true. If the conclusion cannot be false and if you assumed the premises (evidence) were true, then the argument is valid. Otherwise, it's an invalid argument. Now move on to the question of soundness. Check to see if all the premises are actually true. If even one premise is false, then the argument is unsound. If both conditions are satisfied, the argument is sound. If one condition fails, then the argument is unsound. So if we have an invalid argument *or* a valid argument with at least one false premise, then we've got an unsound argument in front of us. We can summarize all this with a diagram (Figure 6.2):

FIGURE 6.2
Checking for Validity and Soundness.

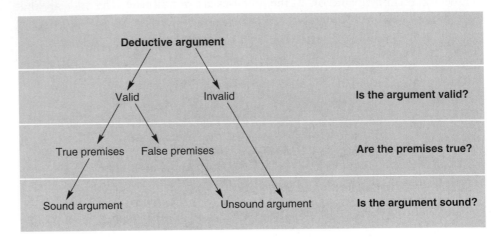

Deductive argument

Valid   Invalid   **Is the argument valid?**

True premises   False premises   **Are the premises true?**

Sound argument   Unsound argument   **Is the argument sound?**

Exercises

Part One

1. Explain why this is a sound argument:

    All cows are mammals.

    No mammal is a reptile.

    Therefore, no cow is a reptile.

2. Explain why this is not a valid argument:

    All Olympic medal-winners are athletes.

    My brother Steve is an athlete.

    Therefore, my brother Steve is an Olympic medal-winner.

3. Give an example of a sound argument for the conclusion: "No lizard has feathers."

4. Explain why this is valid but not sound:

    All gymnasts are dentists.

    No dentist is over 3 feet tall.

    Therefore, no gymnast is over 3 feet tall.

5. Give an example of an argument in the form of a hypothetical syllogism with its first premise: "If her goat cheese business takes off, Tina will buy a Mini convertible."

6. Give an example of a valid argument in the form of modus ponens with this conclusion: "Men in tiger suits came to the Halloween party."

7. Give an example of a valid—and sound—argument in the form of modus tollens with this conclusion: "Snakes do not have legs."

8. Give an example of a sound argument in the form of the disjunctive syllogism, with this conclusion: "The mouse escaped from the closet."

9. Give an example of an unsound argument in the form of modus ponens, with the first premise: "If hawks can be tamed, they would make nice pets."

10. Give an example of a valid but unsound argument in the form of a hypothetical syllogism.

11. Give an example of a sound argument for this conclusion: "Therefore, poisonous snakes do not make good pets." Explain why it is sound.

12. Give an example of an invalid argument using the fallacy of denying the antecedent for this conclusion: "Therefore, chocolate ice cream is not fattening."

13. Give an example of an invalid argument using the fallacy of affirming the consequent using this first premise: "If you can ride a horse, then you can do just about anything."

14. Give an example of a valid, but unsound argument for this conclusion: "Therefore, all vegetables are carrots."

Part Two

Directions: Test the following arguments to see if they are valid or invalid. If they are valid and fit one of the valid argument forms, then name the form.

1. If the temperature hits 100 degrees, Chicago is miserable. The temperature hit 100 degrees in the summer of 2004. Thus, Chicago was miserable that summer.

2. Anyone who eats a hamburger for breakfast is an eccentric. Anyone who is an eccentric is unusual. It follows that anyone who eats a hamburger for breakfast is an unusual person.

3. If Pinky wears ski goggles to class, he will look mysterious. If Pinky looks mysterious, he will impress his friends. Therefore, if Pinky wears ski goggles to class, he will impress his friends.

4. Anyone who can shoot a musket while running is awfully nimble. Daniel Day Lewis is awfully nimble. Therefore, he shot a musket while running during the making of *Last of the Mohicans*.

5. Some birds are intelligent creatures. No intelligent creature should have to live in a cage. Chickens are birds. Therefore, no chickens should be kept in cages.

6. If you keep eating popcorn, you're bound to bust a tooth on a kernel, but if you don't keep eating popcorn you'll feel deprived. Either you'll bust a tooth on a kernel or you'll feel deprived. Therefore, either you'll keep eating popcorn or you won't.

7. People who ride Harleys are trained mechanics. Tom is not a trained mechanic, so he must not ride a Harley.

8. Any man who drives a convertible in a snowstorm is desperate for attention. No one who is desperate for attention would go without a warm scarf and beanie on his head. Therefore, no one driving a convertible in a snowstorm would go without a warm scarf and beanie on his head.

9. A rat is in the basement under the washing machine. If there are rats in the basement under the washing machine, it's not ok to do your laundry barefoot. Therefore, it's not ok to do your laundry barefoot.

10. Either there are squirrels in the attic or some other animal is making noises up there. There are no squirrels in the attic. Therefore, some other animal is making noises up there.

11. Anyone who wears wraparound sunglasses is pretty darn cool. Evan wore wraparound sunglasses to school. Therefore, Evan is pretty darn cool.

12. If men in tiger suits are at the Halloween party and they get a bit too rowdy, then the neighbors might either come over or call the police. The neighbors did not either come over or call the police, so it is not true that the men in tiger suits are at the Halloween party and they got a bit too rowdy.

13. Either he should forget about a Halloween party this year or Trent should go all out and put goony looking gravestones in the front yard and have sound effects of moaning ghosts. Trent did not forget about a Halloween party this year. So he went all out and put goony looking gravestones in the front yard and had sound effects of moaning ghosts.

14. If either Pinky or Bo show up in last year's costumes, then Charlene will be disappointed. Charlene was disappointed, therefore either Pinky or Bo showed up in last year's costumes.

15. If Trent doesn't turn down the sound effects of moaning ghosts, then either Gloria or Myron is going to go beserk and put on earmuffs to drown out the noise. Trent did not turn down the sound effects of moaning ghosts. Therefore, either Gloria or Myron is going to go beserk and put on earmuffs to drown out the noise.

16. Anyone who has ever gone trick-or-treating knows that boiled eggs just don't make it as treats. Grandpa knows that boiled eggs just don't make it as treats. Therefore, Grandpa must have gone trick-or-treating at some time in his life.

17. If Pinky wears his spider suit from last year, Bo will come in his fly suit; but if Pinky gets a tiger suit, then Bo will come as a baboon. Either Pinky will wear his spider suit from last year or he'll get a tiger suit. Therefore, either Bo will come in his fly suit or he'll come as a baboon.

▦ Inductive Reasoning

An inductive argument is like a puzzle with some missing pieces. So, there will always be an element of doubt in the argument. The conclusion can only be said to follow with likelihood or probability—never with certainty. In that sense, the conclusion goes beyond what is contained in the premises. For that reason, we have to be careful what applications we make of an inductive argument. Look, for example, at the cautionary note from the American Heart Association's second recommendation (the first was to eat fish oils and Omega-3 fatty acids):

> **We also recommend eating** tofu and other forms of soybeans, canola, walnut and flaxseed, and their oils. These contain **alpha-linolenic acid** (LNA), which can become omega-3 fatty acid in the body. The extent of this modification is modest and controversial, however. More studies are needed to show a cause-and-effect relationship between alpha-linolenic acid and heart disease. (The American Heart Association, www.americanheart.org, 31 Oct 2004)

Not all who argue using inductive reasoning express precautions, as we see above. Every so often we come across inductive arguments that leave us scratching our heads in wonder. Think of those unusual "cures" for AIDS or mind-boggling promises about a diet drug. And then there's the curious statistics we occasionally find cited, as we see below:

> According to a study that looked at dreams, "the further your politics lean to the right, the more likely you are to have nightmares." According to researchers it's three times more likely that you will have bad dreams if you are a Republican than if you are a Democrat. The results of this study are actually coming out of the University, within a stone's throw from here—Santa Clara University in California. . . . Dream researchers looked at more than four years of dreams dreamt by college kids from around the United States. The total number of subjects was 55; half were females, half males. Their political leanings were divided too, with half being very conservative and half being very liberal.
>
> The results of the study [were] just presented in an annual meeting of the Association for the Study of Dreams. They found half the Republican's dreams were nightmares, compared to 18 percent of the Democrats. "What's striking is that the nightmares of people on the right were more nightmarish, they were bleaker, there was more hopelessness," says Kelly Bulkeley, the lead researcher on this study. (*New Scientist*, NewScientist.com, July 11, 2001, as quoted by Dr. Dean Edell, www.healthcentral.com)

We might question the legitimacy of inferring from a study of 55 students to the general population. Not only is there a problem with the number of participants (too small), these are all college students (one age and educational level). Another question is whether these were *paid* participants—if so, who paid and could that have biased the result?

Example #1 of an Inductive Argument:
Beyoncé is the Joan Baez of this generation. She has a voice that travels well, just like Joan Baez who could bounce her voice off of a mountain. She is a striking physical

presence—just like Joan Baez, who had big eyes, fine bones, and beautiful long hair at the peak of her beauty. She has a host of imitators, just like Joan Baez. Joan Baez was also an outspoken pacifist. So, I bet Beyoncé is against war too.

What we have here is a list of similarities between the two singers: voice, looks, and imitators. Then a claim about Joan Baez's politics is carried over to Beyoncé, leading to the inference that she must also share the same political view on war. Even if the terms of the comparison were all true, it is unclear if the additional trait holds as well.

Example #2 of an Inductive Argument:
The hantavirus is a biological agent targeting certain groups the government is out to get. Just look at the evidence. Outbreaks of the hantavirus have not been not in Beverly Hills or Boca Raton! No, they've been in New Mexico and Arizona on tribal land, killing off Native Americans. In 1993 alone, the Center for Disease Control noted 150 cases in the Four Corners region of the Southwest (leading to the virus being nicknamed the "Navajo Virus"). Then the hantavirus showed up in South America and in rural areas where more indigenous people live. If it were just a matter of being exposed to rodent droppings, there'd be a lot more whites coming down with it! It must be a conspiracy against Native Americans.

We can see, from the reasoning in this argument, that the evidence rests on (1) geography and (2) victim profile. Because so many Native Americans have been affected, compared to other groups, the author infers that there's a conspiracy at foot. Is the evidence sufficient, though, for us to be sure of a conspiracy against indigenous people? Not on this evidence alone. Thus, the argument is inductive. There are five major kinds of inductive arguments. These are as follows:

Major Kinds of Inductive Arguments

1. *Predictions:* In predictions, an argument is made about the future based on past or present evidence. **EXAMPLE:**

   In light of the devastation in previous earthquakes, we can infer that an earthquake of magnitude 8.5 or greater in eastern Massachusetts will result in a large portion of Martha's Vineyard being swallowed up by the ocean.

2. *Arguments about the past based on present evidence (also known as retrodiction):* In these arguments, an inference is drawn about what happened at some earlier point in time based on current evidence. **EXAMPLE:**

   Not all the Indians came over from Russia and Siberia. The fact that there are Native American tribes in Alaska speaking Athabascan languages found in the Southwest and the Southeastern United States point to an upward migration. The Cherokee, Navajo, and Apache all share a similar language with the Athabascan tribes in Alaska. Even now, they can communicate with one another in spite of the vast geographic distance.

3. *Cause and effect reasoning:* Here it is claimed that an event (effect) is based on one or more causal factors. Given the existence, then, of the causal factor(s), the effect should follow. **EXAMPLE:**

> Hepatitis C is on the rise in the prison population in the United States. It is most likely the result of inmates sharing needles, spreading the disease.

4. *Arguments based on analogy:* This argument rests on a comparison, from which it is claimed that a characteristic true of the one term in the equation will also be true of the other. In law this usually involves the application of a precedent or legal principle. **EXAMPLE:**

> Humans are physiologically closest to the chimpanzee. If we can use chimps to find a cure for Parkinson's disease or Alzheimer's, we'll surely be able to market the drug on humans. Therefore, this justifies using chimps in medical research.

5. *Statistical reasoning:* These arguments draw from sample studies or statistical reasoning, from which an inference then is drawn about either all or part of the targeted population. **EXAMPLE:**

> Fifty-eight percent of people polled by the *Westview Daily* disapprove of embryonic stem cell research. Therefore, 58 percent of all Americans disapprove of embryonic stem cell research.

"All or Nothing" Reasoning

In the example of statistical reasoning, replacing 58 percent with 100 percent or 0 percent (all or nothing) would transform this into a *deductive* argument. The uncertainty is that we do not know what to make of the missing percentage. This element of doubt makes the argument inductive. If we replaced the 58 percent by 100 percent or zero, the uncertainty is then removed. Thus, the argument becomes deductive, not inductive.

The Wedge of Doubt in Inductive Arguments

In an *inductive argument* the premises *could* be true, but the conclusion will never follow with certainty. Remember, there is always some *wedge of doubt* between the premises and the conclusion. We can construct inductive arguments following one of the different forms of inductive reasoning. For example, let us construct premises for the conclusion, "Anna gargles with salt water to help her sore throat."

Inductive Argument #1: An Analogy (See Ben Hewitt, "Tour de Lance," *Wired*, July 2004)

Lance Armstrong is like a hummingbird.

He pedals 100–110 rpm, while his rivals tend to slow to about 70 rpm.

Therefore, Armstrong will be able to use cardiovascular strength instead of relying on muscle power.

Global Dimension

Inductive Reasoning about Tsunami Relief

After the tsunami that struck South Asia on December 26, 2004, a massive relief operation was put in motion. One focus was emergency medical help. Analogies were drawn to medicine in a war zone. Read this excerpt and discuss how this shows inductive reasoning:

> Medical specialists are comparing the emergency medical care problems that have followed the Asian tsunami with another important event in medical history—the U.S. Civil War. Conditions in field hospitals and local clinics in tsunami-wracked areas are crude at best. Electricity is unreliable, there are no antibiotics, only the simplest medical equipment is available and there are few trained medical specialists. "These descriptions are reminiscent of wartime mass casualty situations described during times like . . . the Civil War, or any pre-antibiotic era where amputation was the major treatment of extremity injuries," said Dr. Martin A. Schreiber, director of surgical critical care at Oregon Health & Science University in Portland.
>
> "Amputation is often the best choice in severely contaminated wounds and can be life saving to avoid overwhelming systemic infection," said Susan Briggs, director of the International Trauma and Disaster Institute at Massachusetts General Hospital in Boston. "If there are no antibiotics, then amputation is better than letting the patient die," said McSwain. "This reverts back to the medicine practiced during the War Between the States. Antibiotics had not been discovered. It was better to take off the infected leg than to let the patient die of generalized sepsis." Dr. John Gorczyca, chief of the Division of Musculoskeletal Trauma at the University of Rochester Medical Center in Rochester, N.Y. [says] that this represents a horrible situation, similar to Civil War-era battle treatment, with no antibiotics, horrible wounds, severe contamination, lack of surgeons and minimal technology. (Marc Lallanilla, "Tsunami Medical Care Resembles U.S. Civil War Era," *ABC News*, abcnews.go.com, 7 Jan 2005).

Inductive Argument #2: A Prediction

According to the Readers' Poll of *The New York Times*, the movie *The Aviator* will win "Best Picture" and take the Oscar for 2004.

Readers' polls are pretty darn accurate most of the time.

Therefore, *The Aviator* will almost certainly win "Best Picture" at the Academy Awards.

Inductive Argument #3: Statistical Reasoning

According to NBA statistics, Orlando was ahead of Detroit in rebounds for 2004.

Being strong at rebounding is crucial for a basketball team.

Therefore, the Orlando Magic is probably a better team than the Detroit Pistons.

Group or Individual Exercise

Pesticides on produce: The Environmental Working Group cites the following list of fruits and vegetables as those most contaminated with pesticides. They are ranked according to the number of pesticides found and the frequency at which they're found (See " 'Pesticide Drift': a worry to farm workers," MSNBC, msnbc.msn.com, 26 May 2004). Here is the list in order of most contaminated to least contaminated—the number next to the kind of fruit or vegetable indicates the number of different pesticides that were found. Look over the list and then answer the questions below.

Apples 32

Spinach 17

Peaches 28

Pears 23

Strawberries 28

Grapes from Chile 11

Potatoes 20

Red Raspberries 24

Celery 14

Green Beans 26

One thing we can *deduce* from the above is that apples are more contaminated with pesticides than green beans. One thing we can *induce* is that eating a handful of fruit is more likely to make you sick than eating a bunch of vegetables.

Answer the following:

1. Using your powers of *deductive reasoning*, draw three different conclusions from the above list.

2. Using your powers of *inductive reasoning*, draw three different conclusions from the above list.

Exercises

Part One

Directions: Name the different inductive arguments below. Explain what makes them inductive in light of the five main categories.

1. Yesterday was a lovely day for a picnic. Today is a lovely day for a picnic. It follows that tomorrow will be a lovely day for a picnic.

2. Fifty-seven percent of people who phoned into KBST country music station prefer LeAnn Rimes to Faith Hill. As a result, 57 percent of Americans prefer LeAnn Rimes to Faith Hill.

3. There is a high correlation between smoking and both emphysema and lung cancer. Therefore, anyone who smokes will probably get either lung cancer or emphysema.

4. The movie *Manhunter* is a lot like *Silence of the Lambs*. Both focus on serial killers who target women. Both have detectives who spend an inordinate amount of time trying to get into the mind of the killer. Both detectives seem to be isolated from human companionship and seem obsessed with the one case to the exclusion of anything else. *Silence of the Lambs* has a female lead in the role of the detective; therefore, *Manhunter* must feature a female detective as well.

5. Robert Alton Harris must have had a terrible childhood, because he was such a disturbed man as an adult.

6. Eighty-four percent of graphic artists prefer MACs to PCs. People who prefer MACs to PCs like the ease of the MAC operating system. Therefore, Andrea, a graphic artist, will like the ease of the MAC operating system.

7. Cigarette smoking must cause people to become alcoholics, because a lot of people who are alcoholics have smoked at some point in their lives.

8. Lake Rudolph in Kenya must be the seat of human evolution, because that is where anthropologists like Richard Leakey found some of the oldest human bones to date.

9. The pharmaceutical company tested the antinausea drug thalidomide on primates and found it had no adverse affect on either the mother or the fetus. Therefore, they should be able to put the drug on the market without worrying about what it'll do to humans.

10. Inhalers made by Schering-Plough were listed as the probable cause for the deaths of 17 people from September 1998 to June 2000, a period when the recalled inhalers were on pharmacy shelves or in the hands of asthma sufferers. As a result, we should expect a recall of the Schering-Plough inhalers.

11. Yellowstone National Park officials announced today that—in a very rare combination of events—a concentration of toxic gases (hydrogen sulfide and carbon dioxide) along with unusually cold, dense air appear to be the most probable cause of death for five bison found at Norris Geyser Basin by Bear Management staff on March 10, 2004. Park staff noticed the animals while doing routine research in the area. The bison, estimated to have been dead for approximately a week, were found lying on their sides, with their feet perpendicular to their bodies; the unusual position of the carcasses indicates the bison died very rapidly, as a group. According to the park's geologist Dr. Henry Heasler, the five bison (two adults, two calves, one yearling) were

likely grazing and resting in a snow-free ground depression along the Gibbon River near multiple geothermal gas vents in the Norris area. Cold, still air from a cold front passing through the area around March 1 probably caused the geyser basin's steam and toxic gases to remain close to the ground, overwhelming the animals. (Yellowstone press release, www.nps.gov/yell/press, 23 Mar 2004).

Part Two

Directions: Examine the following inductive arguments. Set out the conclusion and discuss the nature and strength of the evidence and why the argument is inductive.

1. The following argument offers reasons why it should be illegal to sell human ova (eggs):

   Prof. Jonathon Kimmelman said that allowing prospective parents to list desired traits in an egg donor will lead to "cafeteria-style child selection that turn[s] parents into the proverbial consumer." The fact that parents would use $50,000 to "buy" particular characteristics and the potentially large psychological effect on the "bought" child illustrates the need to regulate the private sector. "In our society, there are things we decided we can't sell," Kimmeman said. "It's unacceptable to sell organs or babies, and I wonder if we should consider it unacceptable to sell eggs as well." (Sydney Leavens, "Students and Professors React to Egg Donation Ad," *Yale Daily News*, www.yaledailynews.com, 10 Feb 2004).

2. The following argument seeks to explain why poor people seem to suffer more medical problems than everyone else:

   Poor people have long been known to have more medical problems than affluent people of the same age, but a new study suggests that greater inequality in the distribution of income contributes to higher overall mortality rates and deaths from heart disease, cancer, and homicide. The study found that for treatable conditions like tuberculosis, pneumonia and high blood pressure, mortality rates were higher in states where the income gap was wider. (Robert Pear, "Researchers Link Income Inequality to Higher Mortality Rates," *The New York Times,* 19 Apr 1996)

3. The following argument seeks to explain the rise in heat-related deaths in athletes:

   According to the NCCSI charts, there were 17 heatstroke deaths from 1995 to 2000, as many as were recorded in 15 previous years. Is the increasing quest for scholarships, money and superstardom—as one former NFL star thinks, pushing players beyond physical limits?

   Practices and procedures are being called into question in the wake of recent football-related deaths. Many trainers, coaches and former players wonder whether sports science can keep pace with players who are getting bigger and faster by the year. [Sports] author Jim Dent recounts how players, mouths frothing, literally crawled off practice fields to their Quonset huts. "Bryant believed the fastest way to whip a team into shape was to deny the boys water, even in the brutal heat."

The thinking is incredibly Neanderthal by today's standards. Of course, players did die of heatstroke back then, but Goehring thinks there were two reasons why more did not. First, players were carrying less body fat. Goehring was a 185-pound lineman. He played both ways. "I couldn't play today," he says by phone. "I'd get killed." He also maintains players of his era were better equipped to handle the heat. "In those days, we didn't have air conditioning," he says. "All of us were acclimated to the heat. We worked tough, summer jobs where the heat was. I worked in a steel mill, worked in a blast furnace, and the heat was 110 degrees. . . . So the heat wasn't that big of a factor. Today, golly bum, you never get out of the air conditioning. The body is a lot more suited to conditions that are comfortable." (Chris Dufresne, "Cruel Paradox Of Camps: Old-School Training Programs Were More Rigorous Than Today's, but Heatstroke Fatalities Were Far Fewer," *Los Angeles Times,* 9 Aug 2001)

3. The following article discusses the likelihood of Mad Cow disease devastating the human population:

USA has had thousands of 'downer' cows (dying mysteriously) since 1981. If the bug entered U.S. beef 15 years ago and has been multiplying ever since, a million cows could be infected. Mad-Cow mortality figures hide behind the skirts of Alzheimer's. Some U.S. doctors know the truth, yet haven't blown whistles. Pittsburgh Veterans hospital autopsied 53 sequential Alzheimer's victims. Sampling #1 showed 5.5 percent had died of Mad-Cow, sampling two that 6.3 percent died of Mad Cow. Alzheimer's death tolls are doubling and tripling, not characteristic of a genetic disease *ergo* the shadowy presence of another *probable cause.*

Since beef and sheep farmers have been sending 'downer' livestock to rendering factories to be made into 'protein powder' for livestock for the last 26 years, Mad Cow prions could be in every ounce of meat, milk, pork, chicken, egg, cheese, or butter you have eaten since 1970 and in every bite you eat today and in gelatin caps, animal glandular supplements and in the glue on the postage stamp you will use. . . . Mad Cow is the most prevalent, virulent disease to hit this planet since the plague. Conceivably it could represent the end of all human life here. . . . It is certain that we will see many more cases associated with CJD (Creutzfeldt-Jacob Disease, the human version of Mad Cow disease) than we have ever seen with AIDS as Mad Cow infection has been found all over Europe. ("What is Prion and How Does it Affect Us?," *The Open Line,* www.theopenline.cc, accessed 26 Feb 2005)

4. The following argument is in opposition to the Department of Energy's proposal to lower the standard of what is allowable in terms of selling radioactive metal:

The Department of Energy [DOE] has a problem: what to do with millions of tons of radioactive metal. So the DOE has come up with an ingenious plan to dispose of its troublesome tons of nickel, copper, steel, and aluminum. It wants to let scrap companies collect the metal, try to take the radioactivity out, and sell the metal to foundries, which would in turn sell it to manufacturers who could use it for everyday household products: pots, pans, forks, spoons, even your eyeglasses.

You may not know this, but the government already permits some companies, under special licenses, to buy, reprocess, and sell radioactive metal: 7,500 tons in 1996, by one industry estimate. . . . The DOE is so eager to get radioactive metal off its hands that it has hired an arm of British Nuclear Fuels, called BNFL, to do the job. . . . The $238 million contract stipulates that the company may recycle for profit all the metals it recovers, including a large amount of formerly classified nickel. . . .

A spokesman for British Nuclear Fuels explained his philosophy to the London paper *The Independent*. "It's recycling," he said. "If you have a cup of coffee, you don't throw the cup away, you reuse it." (Anne-Marie Cusac, "Nuclear Spoons: Hot Metal May Find Its Way to Your Dinner Table; Dept. Of Energy's Proposal to Recycle Radioactive Metal into Household Products," *The Progressive*, Oct. 1998)

Part Three

1. Construct an inductive argument for the conclusions below, using the form indicated:
   a. Using cause and effect reasoning, support the conclusion: Therefore, Maureen's melanoma could be traced back to sun tanning as a teenager.
   b. Using an analogy *or* a statistical argument, support the conclusion: Therefore, *Shrek 2* will go down as one of the greatest animated films in history.
   c. Using a prediction *or* an analogy, support the conclusion: Therefore, Martin Luther King, Jr. will be recognized as one of the most influential Americans of the 20th century.
   d. Using an argument about the past based on present evidence, support the conclusion: Therefore, Einstein must have been mathematically advanced as a little boy.

2. Construct two different kinds of inductive arguments for the conclusion that is given.
   a. Watching TV over two hours a day is not good for little children.
   b. It was probably a mosquito bite that caused John's malaria.
   c. Cell phones cannot possibly be related to brain tumors.

3. Indicate which arguments are inductive and which are deductive:
   I D 1. 72 percent of country singers prefer grits to hash browns. Toby Keith is a country star, so be sure to serve him grits when he comes to the diner for breakfast.
   I D 2. Some Siberian huskies make great sled dogs. All great sled dogs have to work in dog teams. Therefore, some Siberian huskies have to work in dog teams.
   I D 3. At no time did Dr. Lee indicate his allegiance to the Aryan Nation Defense League (ANDL). If he had sworn allegiance to the ANDL, he would not have risked exposure meeting the reporter to share files. But he did meet with the reporter! Consequently, you're mistaken to argue Dr. Lee was in cahoots with ANDL back in the 90s when he was in college.

I   D   4. Inebriation can cause a person to lose control of motor functions. Annette started drinking last night and by 9 P.M. she was dizzy and unable to walk a straight line. It must have been due to that can of beer she drank with her popcorn.

I   D   5. No honest person would lie. All trustworthy people are honest. Therefore, no liar can be trusted.

I   D   6. Michael Horse must have been popular when he was a child, given that so many people like him now.

I   D   7. No woman who wants an easy life should be a counterterrorist. Everyone in the CIA is a counterterrorist. Therefore, No woman who wants an easy life is in the CIA.

I   D   8. If more than one hurricane hits Florida in a year, there's bound to be a lot of destruction. In 2004 Hurricanes Charley, Frances, Ivan, and Jeanne all hit Florida, so you can bet there was a lot of destruction.

Assessing Inductive Arguments

Inductive arguments are assessed in terms of strength, not validity. Because the premises of inductive arguments never supply enough evidence to force the conclusion to be true, there is always an element of uncertainty, or probability, to inductive reasoning. An inductive argument is *neither valid nor invalid*—we can only talk about validity with deductive arguments. This is because we can't guarantee the truth of the conclusion in an inductive argument. Consider:

Seventy-nine percent of high school students in Illinois admire Barrack Obama.

Jaime is a high school student.

So, Jaime admires Barrack Obama.

Even if the premises were true, the conclusion could still be false. There is too much uncertainty to conclude that Jaime must admire Barrack Obama. *Think of it this way:* If I ask you to go up in my Cessna plane with me and tell you that you have a 79 percent chance of surviving the trip, you would not likely rush to go with me. However, the closer my percentage gets to 100 percent, the better your chances of survival.

There is no *one* specific method of assessing the strength of inductive arguments. Considerations vary according to the type of inductive argument. But one thing is in common: There will always be a degree of probability involved. In all inductive arguments there exists a fundamental uncertainty about whether or not the conclusion follows from the premises. However, each inductive argument can be evaluated in terms of how strong or weak it is.

You Tell Me Department

What about Workers' Injuries and Decision Making?

Avocado picker Allen Kimball, 33, was at the last tree to be harvested and saw a bunch of avocados near the top of the tree. Grabbing his aluminum-picking pole, Kimball climbed his aluminum ladder to pick the avocados. He did not see the Southern California Edison power lines until it was too late and 12,000 volts of electricity went through his body, igniting both arms and his right leg. He's had dozens of surgeries, including the amputation of most of both arms. He faces more surgery and will likely be confined to a wheelchair within 10 years. (Donna Huffaker, "Amputee's Suit Alleges Neglect by Utility Firm," *Daily Journal,* 10 Jul 2001)

- In his lawsuit against Southern California Edison, Kimball seeks $52.8 million. He says the company was responsible for the electric lines not being visible in the overgrown tree. The avocado tree was two weeks overdo for a trim when the accident occurred. Kimball's lawyer says that Kimball is 15 percent responsible for the accident, because the lines were approximately 15 percent visible from the backyard where the tree was located.
- Edison's attorney argued that Edison should not be held responsible for someone standing on an aluminum ladder with an aluminum pole 13 feet from the line. They said the wires cleared the branches by 6 feet (the state requires a "reasonable distance" such as 4 feet), so the wires were well within the legal guidelines. They claim Kimball was electrocuted because of his 10-foot aluminum pole hitting the wires and the fact that he didn't see the wires does not prove he *could not* see them. They argued that the only way to make power lines 100 percent visible is to chop down all the trees.
- The question to be decided is how to assign responsibility for Kimball's injuries. Kimball's own attorney suggests a 15/85 division (where he's 15 percent and Edison 85 percent responsible). If we factor in the employer, however, this would have to change. Kimball wasn't picking avocados in his own backyard. He was doing it for his work—his employer sent him out with an aluminum ladder and an aluminum pole. A wooden pole would have protected Kimball against electrocution, but it would be heavier. Thus employers prefer lighter poles and ladders, so workers can go at top speed. In trying to assign responsibility, there are a number of such factors to consider.

You tell me: How should the lawsuit be resolved? State your recommendations.

Inductive Arguments: Strength versus Validity

As we can see, we can assign inductive arguments a relative strength—but they do not fall in the "all-or-nothing" category found with deductive reasoning. This, then, means an inductive argument is neither sound nor unsound—soundness requires validity and validity does not apply to inductive arguments.

You cannot talk about validity or soundness with regard to inductive arguments. So never say an inductive argument is valid or invalid. Never say it is sound or unsound. These terms just do not apply. However, you *can* take a stand on how

The Global Dimension

Not Lost: Searching for Buried Treasure off of Africa

On a pirate island off of Africa, people spend an awful lot of time trying to track down buried treasure. The search involves plotting, planning, and looking for a host of clues that could point the way to the gold. The quest is fueled by a belief that the pirates were aligned with members of a secret society, the Freemasons. Read about the hunt and then decide if Getler's argument is inductive or deductive—and say why:

> Warren Getler [is] a man who uses advanced sonic-imaging technology to find buried treasure. Most of the time, Getler, who works for a company called Witten Technologies in Washington, D.C., is your standard buttoned-down business type. Out here on the edge of the world, though, Getler was letting his true self show.
>
> He is a devotee of an obscure historical theory, one contending that treasure has been stashed around the world by pirates affiliated with Freemasons, the mysterious fraternal order that was started by stonemasons in medieval Europe. The handful of historians who have studied the subject believe that some pirates used elaborate Masonic symbols and signposts to record the locations of buried treasure. *Ipso facto*, if you can unravel the Masons' intricate secret language, you may be able to plot a pathway to buried booty. (Paul Perry, "X Marked the Spot, *National Geographic,* www.nationalgeographic.com, March 2002)

strong the inductive argument appears to be and that can be instrumental when making decisions and drawing up policies.

Think of inductive arguments and deductive arguments like men and women. Some of the things you can discuss about men do not apply to women and vice versa. For instance, you'd never say, "That man is either pregnant or he's not pregnant." It would be ludicrous to talk that way and we would think you were goofy if you did. This is the same with validity, invalidity, and soundness. These terms can only be used with respect to deductive arguments. Inductive reasoning is assessed differently; with induction we are looking for the relative strength of the argument.

Group or Individual Exercise

Note: Allow time to gather examples.

1. Find *three* examples of deductive arguments (e.g., in a newspaper or online news).

2. Find *three* examples of inductive arguments (e.g., in a newspaper or online news).

3. Compare your inductive and deductive arguments and discuss the quality of the reasoning.

Exercises

Part One

Directions: State how strong you think the following inductive arguments are. Give reasons for your decisions.

1. Of people who fly, 98 percent arrive safely. Governor Wilson is flying to New York. Therefore, he'll arrive safely.

2. Vivica A. Fox is a lot like Serena Williams. Both are African-American females, are talented people, are famous, and have a lot of fans. Serena Williams is a great athlete. That must mean Vivica Fox would be a great athlete too.

3. Approximately 250 of the 312 people attending the wedding reception suffered food poisoning. Ed and Jack attended the reception, so they probably suffered food poisoning too.

4. Steve usually makes barbeque chicken when the family gets together. Because we are going to his house on Thursday for Thanksgiving dinner, I bet Steve will make us barbeque chicken.

5. In a study of women who tried out for the police department, the city found that 75 percent of them lifted weights and did aerobics. Therefore, 75 percent of all American women lift weights and do aerobics.

6. Some people who get liposuction have a few problems with their skin rippling. Therefore, liposuction causes skin to ripple.

7. Courtney Love got 18 months' probation for drug possession. She'll probably start a rehab program soon, because substance abuse can really mess up a person's life.

8. Scientists studying the pieces of pottery found in the archaeological site determined that of the 10,000 objects recovered, over 78 percent of them had some relationship to agriculture. They were either tools or receptacles for working the soil and raising crops. This suggests that the people who lived here were an agricultural, rather than a hunting society.

9. Eighty-two percent of the people attending John Trudell's performance said they thought he was fantastic. Lulu attended the performance; therefore, Lulu must have thought Trudell was fantastic.

10. Tom's phone number is one digit away from the pizza parlor's phone number. Last night he received 10 calls from people who wanted to order a pizza. Two nights ago he got 15 calls for pizza and three nights ago he got 12 phone calls. I wish we didn't have to study at his house, as we are probably going to go nuts with pizza calls!

11. Circle all correct answers:
    a. A weak inductive argument is invalid.
    b. A valid argument always has true premises.
    c. An argument could be valid with false premises, provided that, if we assume the premises to be true, it would force the conclusion to be true.
    d. A sound argument is always valid.
    e. An invalid argument always has false premises.
    f. If you have true premises, you know the argument is valid.
    g. A sound argument must be valid and also have true premises.
    h. An inductive argument could be sound so long as the premises were true.
    i. An inductive argument is always unsound.
    j. An inductive argument could be valid, so long as the premises support the conclusion.

Part Two

1. Is this a valid argument? Is it sound? State your reasons.

   Everyone who studies logic enjoys horror films.

   Everyone who enjoys horror films likes *Dawn of the Dead.*

   Therefore, everyone who studies logic likes *Dawn of the Dead.*

2. Indicate which of the arguments are inductive (I) and which are deductive (D):

   I D a. No one who eats squid is a vegetarian. Roland eats squid. So Roland is not a vegetarian.

   I D b. Fifty-eight percent of the listeners who phoned into the November 2004 poll said that the death penalty is barbaric. So, 58 percent of teenagers think the death penalty is barbaric.

   I D c. The dinosaurs became extinct because evidence found in China last year suggested that an asteroid hit the earth during the time of the dinosaurs and sent up great dust clouds blocking the sun and causing very cold weather.

   I D d. All toxic substances should be handled very carefully. Dioxin is a toxic substance. So, dioxin should be handled very carefully.

   I D e. Rhonda is just like her father—short, smart, and determined. Her father dreamed of becoming a pilot; therefore Rhonda dreams of being a pilot too.

   I D f. Only a mean woman could put up with him. Only mean women hang out at Reggie's Bar. Cassandra hangs out at Reggie's Bar. Therefore, Cassandra could put up with him.

   I D g. Reading too many computer magazines causes a person to be depressed. LaToya reads computer magazines all the time, so she'll get depressed.

3. Set out a *deductive* argument for the conclusion, "Anyone who passes the calculus final exam should be able to pass the class."

4. Set out an *inductive* argument for the conclusion, "Fifty four percent of Canadians say the moose should be made the national animal."

5. Circle all the arguments below that are *inductive*:
   a. Georgia loves peach ice cream. Anyone who loves peach ice cream is a friend of mine. Therefore, Georgia is a friend of mine. *Deductive*
   b. Seventy-five percent of women who love peach ice cream are wild and exotic. Georgia loves peach ice cream. Therefore, Georgia is wild and exotic. *Inductive - Weak statistical Reasoning*
   c. No woman who loves peach ice cream is cruel to puppies. Georgia loves peach ice cream. So Georgia is not cruel to puppies. *Deductive*
   d. Peach ice cream usually causes women to have a warm feeling inside. Georgia just ate some peach ice cream. So, Georgia will probably have a warm feeling inside. *Inductive - Cause and Effect, Prediction*
   e. Everyone who loves peach ice cream lives a decadent life. Anyone who lives a decadent life forgets to vote. Therefore, everyone who loves peach ice cream forgets to vote. *Deductive*

6. Circle all the arguments below that are *deductive*. Remember the argument need not be valid, just deductive:
   a. All football players are big and burly. Sean Astin is not big and burly, so he must not be a football player.
   b. Caffeine usually causes children to behave in unpredictable ways. That little girl is drinking some of her mother's coffee, so she'll behave in unpredictable ways. *Inductive - Cause and Effect, Prediction*
   c. No thief is trustworthy. Masami is trustworthy. So, Masami is not a thief. *Deductive*
   d. Seventy-five percent of Angelenos interviewed by NBC said they found the earthquake traumatic, but they will not leave the city. J.Lo lives in Los Angeles. Consequently, she found the earthquake traumatic but won't leave the city.
   e. Mack the Knife is awfully abusive to his dog. Abusive people were often abused as children. Therefore, Mack the Knife was abused when he was a child.
   f. All munchkins are snapplepuffers. No snapplepuffer is a mork. Therefore, no mork is a munchkin.

7. Circle all the *valid* arguments below:
   a. Everyone who goes barefoot risks being made into a laughingstock. Tarzan goes barefoot. Consequently, Tarzan risks being made into a laughingstock.
   b. If he can't dodge bullets, he's not Neo. He's Neo. Therefore, he can dodge bullets.

    c. Ninety-five percent of men who live in the jungle can swing from vines. Tarzan lives in the jungle, so he can swing from vines.

    d. Spider-Man is a lot like Zorro. He wears a funny-looking outfit and helps fight evil whenever he can. Zorro can do fancy tricks with his sword. Therefore, Spider-Man can also do fancy tricks with his sword.

    e. Everyone who dresses in a gorilla suit and drives on the freeway gets a lot of attention. Anyone who gets a lot of attention becomes terribly conceited. Therefore, everyone who dresses in a gorilla suit and drives on the freeway becomes terribly conceited.

    f. Either you vote or don't complain. You didn't vote. So don't complain.

8. Explain whether this is an inductive or deductive argument:

In the early 1980s, eleven people died of cyanide poisoning. Each victim had taken a Tylenol tablet and died within a few hours. There was no evidence that the cyanide had been added at the factory. Investigators suspected the jars had been tampered with and then placed on store shelves. At the time of the deaths, there was $30 million worth of Tylenol on the shelves in stores throughout the United States. The company did not want anyone else to die of cyanide poison in Tylenol tablets. Until the source of the poisoned tablets was found, there was a risk that other people would die. Any time there is a serious risk to human life from a product, the product should be removed from the shelves and distribution stopped. Therefore, company officials concluded that the Tylenol should be removed from the shelves.

9. Here is a letter to the editor of the *Los Angeles Times* discussing the use of an analogy. Read the letter and decide if you agree with the author's argument that the analogy fails:

Letter to the Editor

Los Angeles Times

The publication of a highly inappropriate analogy, such as the one written by the National Director of the Anti-Defamation League and published in the *L. A. Times* on Saturday, March 30, 2002 ("Double Standards in Mideast," Letters to the Times, 3/30/02) is offensive.

    To equate the Israeli military response to Palestinian attacks with that of a firefighter to a fire set by an arsonist is an improper use of powerful images and words by making non-parallel comparisons. A firefighter's actions are neither aggressive nor violent, as this analogy would imply. The firefighter does not interface with the arsonist, he only confronts the consequences of the arsonist's actions. A firefighter does not feed the flames he is fighting, whereas the Israeli military response stokes the fires which have been raging in the Middle East.

    Given the richly deserved status of firefighters as heroes (especially since 9/11), selfless and apolitical in their actions, Mr. Foxman does them an injustice in his poorly drawn analogy. His equation of Palestinians with arsonists, meanwhile, is tantamount to defamation. It certainly does nothing to promote peace and tolerance, such as would befit comments from the Anti-Defamation

League and contributes to the hyperbole surrounding the Mideast conflict. Surely this is not what the world needs more of, after witnessing the ongoing tragedy that is the Middle East.

Carla Nardoni

Part Three

1. Discuss ex-Laker coach Phil Jackson's analogy in the following argument:

Like life, basketball is messy and unpredictable. It has its way with you, no matter how hard you try to control it. The trick is to experience each moment with a clear mind and an open heart. When you do that, the game—and life—will take care of itself. (Phil Jackson, *Sacred Hoops*)

2. Read the excerpts below on the "Wendy's finger case." Note any conflicts or concerns and then state three inductive arguments explaining how the finger got into the chili.

A woman bit into a human finger while eating a bowl of chili at a Wendy's. Health officials said this is definitely a first for them and was not a hoax. The fingertip was about an inch and a-half long, and had a manicured nail. The county medical examiner said the human finger was cooked but not decomposed. Officials counted all the fingers of the Wendy's workers—no one had a missing digit. Authorities think the finger must have come from one of Wendy's suppliers. It appears the finger was torn off, possibly by a piece of machinery at a processing plant. (See "Human Finger Found In Fast Food Chili," www.localio.com, 24 Mar 2005).

The human finger found in a bowl of chili at a San Jose Wendy's might not have been cooked with the chili and could have been snuck in later in the preparation process, Santa Clara County officials said Friday. ("Was finger cooked along with chili?," *San Francisco Chronicle*, 26 Mar 2005).

San Jose police are investigating the case of a woman who lost part of her finger in a leopard attack. The woman, who has several exotic animals, reportedly got the finger back in a bag of ice, after doctors couldn't re-attach it. She lives about 45 miles north of Las Vegas. A month after that attack, a Las Vegas woman reported biting into a human finger while eating a bowl of Wendy's chili. Wendy's has maintained the finger allegedly found in the chili had not been cooked, and that it didn't enter the supply chain as part of its ingredients. (See "Investigators In Wendy's Finger Case Check Out Clue," www.localio.com, and 13 Apr 2005).

3. Examine the argument below. Set out the conclusion and the premises. Note any inductive or deductive arguments that you see.

In 1980, the plaintiff became locked inside the trunk of a 1973 Ford LTD automobile, where she remained for some nine days. Plaintiff now seeks to recover for psychological and physical injuries arising from that occurrence. She contends that the automobile had a design defect in that the trunk lock or latch did not have an internal release or opening mechanism. She also maintains that the manufacturer is liable based on a failure to warn of this condition.

[*Three facts bring down her case.*] First, the plaintiff ended up in the trunk compartment of the automobile because she felt "overburdened" and was attempting to commit suicide. Second, the purposes of an automobile trunk are to transport, stow and protect items from elements of the weather. Third, the plaintiff never considered the possibility of exit from the inside of the trunk when the automobile was purchased.

The overriding factor barring plaintiff's recovery is that she intentionally sought to end her life by crawling into an automobile trunk from which she could not escape. This is not a case where a person inadvertently became trapped inside an automobile trunk. The plaintiff was aware of the natural and probable consequences of her perilous conduct. Not only that, the plaintiff, at least initially, sought those dreadful consequences. Plaintiff, not the manufacturer of the vehicle, is responsible for this unfortunate occurrence.

As a general principle, a design defect is actionable only where the condition of the product is unreasonably dangerous to the user or consumer. A manufacturer has a duty to consider only those risks of injury which are foreseeable. A risk is not foreseeable by a manufacturer where a product is used in a manner which could not reasonably be anticipated by the manufacturer, and that use is the cause of the plaintiff's injury.

The purposes of an automobile trunk are to transport, stow and secure the automobile spare tire, luggage and other goods and to protect those items from elements of the weather. The design features of an automobile trunk make it well near impossible that an adult intentionally would enter the trunk and close the lid. The court holds that the plaintiff's use of the trunk compartment as a means to attempt suicide was an unforeseeable use. Therefore, the manufacturer had no duty to design an internal release or opening mechanism that might have prevented this occurrence. (*Daniell* v. *Ford Motor Co., Inc.* (1984), as noted in Julie Van Camp, *Ethical Issues in the Courts*)

4. In discussing the Daniell case, above, philosophy professor Julie Van Camp asks, "If plaintiff were a 10-year-old child who suffered severe and permanent physical injury after *accidentally* locking herself in the trunk, should Ford Motor be held liable for damages?"

   a. State your answer to Van Camp's question. *Note:* Her question asks us to do some analogical reasoning and determine what—if anything—should change in the decision if we changed a key detail of the case.

   b. Do you think the shift to "accidental" creates a crucial difference in the case? Discuss.

5. What if, instead of the adult plaintiff trying to commit suicide by locking herself in the trunk of the car, we had a plaintiff who jumped in the trunk and closed the door (thus locking herself in) to hide from a serial killer known to be roaming her neighborhood? She could not have foreseen such a use when she purchased the car, so does the decision above still apply in this case?

6. Discuss the reasoning in the excerpt below on Lyme disease. In 1999 the Center for Disease Control (CDC) recorded 16,273 cases. A controversy erupted:

   A study to be reported on Thursday in *The New England Journal of Medicine* is fueling a running disagreement among medical researchers over the unresolved issues in Lyme disease, a tick-borne illness that is endemic in much of the Northeast and in other pockets around the nation.

The study, by Dr. Mark S. Klempner of Boston University Medical Center, showed that prolonged treatment with antibiotics was no more effective than placebos among those with persistent Lyme disease symptoms. The question is, "Why do a few patients who appear to have been treated successfully for Lyme disease have symptoms that come back strongly later?"

Both sides agree that antibiotics work in 90 percent of patients and that the disease never recurs in those patients, at least not from that tick bite. But among the other patients, symptoms either persist or come back after the standard treatment. Do the symptoms recur because the bacteria have been hiding out in the body, only to emerge again later? Or could the Lyme bacteria, even though they were wiped out by treatment, have brought on a secondary disease, a Lyme autoimmune disorder, in which the body's immune system attacks its own cells as if they were the Lyme disease organism?

Because the patients in Dr. Klempner's study were given a new round of antibiotics, the bacteria should have been killed, and the patients' symptoms should have gone away. Since that did not happen, proponents of the autoimmune theory say, the Klempner study is good evidence for their position.

The Klempner study found that extended treatment with antibiotics did not help people who believed they had persistent Lyme infection, a finding that suggested that their symptoms were unrelated to the bacteria. (Philip J. Hilts, "Certainty and Uncertainty in Treatment of Lyme Disease," *The New York Times*, 10 Jul 2001)

7. Draw three to four inferences about the Lyme controversy, in light of the following quote from microbiologist Edward McSweegan:

> Protests have been organized to denounce Yale University's research meetings and Lyme clinic because, according to the protesters, Yale "ridicules people with Lyme disease, presents misleading information, minimizes the severity of the illness, endorses inadequate, outdated treatment protocols, excludes opposing viewpoints, and ignores conflicts of interest." Researchers have been harassed, threatened, and stalked. A petition circulated on the Web called for changes in the way the disease is routinely treated and the way insurance companies cover those treatments. Less radical groups have had their meetings invaded and disrupted by militant Lyme protesters. (Edward McSweegan, Ph.D., "Lyme Disease: Questionable Diagnosis and Treatment," www.quackwatch.com, 30 Jun 2001)

CASE STUDY IN CAUSE AND EFFECT REASONING

An issue that brings together both cause and effect reasoning and arguments based on analogy is the question of assigning guilt in gang killings. The dilemma is what to do when members of gangs are shooting at each other and (scenario 1) kill a bystander or (scenario 2) one gang member kills a member of a rival gang and, in retaliation, the rival gang murders a member of the gang that fired the first shot.

One issue that comes up is the question of cause. The **direct cause** *of something is that which leads to a particular effect without any intervening step. In contrast, the* **proximate** cause of an event is the last causal factor in a chain leading to a particular effect. For instance, someone with cancer undergoing chemotherapy has a weakened immune system and then gets pneumonia and dies. The pneumonia is the proximate cause of the person's death, but clearly not the sole cause.

Compare a child throwing a ball at a window, causing it to break (direct cause is the throwing of the ball) to a man carrying a tuna casserole slipping on a banana peel that a prankster just threw down on the sidewalk in front of the man, causing him to send the casserole flying in the air, going through a window and breaking it (the casserole dish flying in the air is the proximate cause of the broken window, the end of the sequence of causal factors starting with the prankster throwing down the banana peel).

Read the following article from the law newspaper, the Daily Journal. Then briefly state what was at issue and whether you think the decision in each case was a wise one in terms of addressing gang killings.

"Provocative Act" Doctrine Rejected in Gang Killing

John Roemer

Daily Journal, *August 28, 2001*

SAN FRANCISCO—Gang killings in Santa Ana and Fontana led to distinctly different decisions by the California Supreme Court on Monday involving the "proximate causation" doctrine in murder cases and the state's controversial "provocative act" rule. Both unanimous decisions were written by Justice Marvin R. Baxter.

One ruling, *People* v. *Cervantes* appeared to be a win for defendants because it turned away an effort to expand the provocative act doctrine, which holds accountable for murder those whose non-lethal assaults lead indirectly to a killing. The other case, decided on the issue of proximate cause, was a victory for prosecutors in gang warfare cases. For the first time, in *People* v. *Sanchez,* the high court approved dual murder convictions for two shooters when a lone bullet from one of them—whose identity cannot be ascertained— killed a single victim.

In the first case, the court unanimously reversed the murder conviction of Highland Street gang member Israel Cervantes. The justices, in overturning a Santa Ana appellate

panel, declined to broaden the provocative act theory. Cervantes was convicted of first-degree murder even though his gunshot only wounded a member of the Alley Boys gang at a street birthday party in 1994. Friends of the victim retaliated by gunning to death Hector Cabrera, a member of Cervantes' gang, and prosecutors successfully invoked the provocative act theory to win a life sentence for Cervantes.

"Given that the murder of Cabrera by other parties was itself felonious, intentional, perpetrated with malice aforethought, and directed at a victim who was not involved in the original altercation. The evidence is insufficient as a matter of law to establish the requisite proximate causation to hold defendant liable for murder," Baxter wrote.

The provocative act doctrine is most often used in cases where a defendant opens fire and someone else shoots back, killing a third party. Typically the deadly shots come from store clerks, police or other crime victims who react to a lethal emergency created by the initial shooter. But when the killers in the current case retaliated against another member of Cervantes' gang, they absolved Cervantes of responsibility for the death of their victim, Baxter wrote, citing a classic 1985 legal text, Horn & Honoré's Causation in the Law: "The killers 'intended to exploit the situation created by Cervantes, but were not acting in concert with him,' a circumstance that is 'normally held to relieve the first actor [Cervantes] of criminal responsibility.' In short, nobody forced the Alley Boys' murderous response in this case. The willful and malicious murder of the victim at the hands of others was an independent intervening act on which defendant's liability for the murder could not be based." "The decision is good news for defense lawyers," said Philip M. Brooks, the Berkeley sole practitioner who wrote and argued the appeal before the high court. "Upholding this expansion of the doctrine would have completely changed the law," he said.

And in Monday's other opinion, the Supreme Court upheld the murder conviction of Julio Cesar Sanchez, a member of a Fontana gang named TDK (Diablo Klicka). That case came to the court as another provocative act case—but the justices decided it instead on the issue of *proximate cause*. The decision means that two shooters can be found guilty of a murder in which only a single bullet strikes the victim. Sanchez and codefendant Ramon Gonzalez of the rival Headhunters gang shot it out in 1996 on a Fontana street. A stray shot killed a bystander, and both shooters were convicted of murder under the provocative act theory.

Gonzalez did not appeal his conviction. The Sanchez guilty finding was overturned by a unanimous Riverside appellate panel, which concluded concurrent causation cannot be established in a single-fatal-bullet case. That was erroneous, the high court held. "The circumstance that it cannot be determined who fired the single fatal bullet, i.e., that direct or actual causation cannot be established, does not un-

dermine defendant's first degree murder conviction if it was shown beyond a reasonable doubt that defendant's conduct was a substantial concurrent cause of [the victim's] death," Baxter wrote. He added, "It is proximate causation, not direct or actual causation, which, together with the requisite culpable *mens rea* (malice), determines defendant's liability for murder."

Defense lawyer Melvyn Douglas Sacks of Los Angeles called the decision significant. "It's a landmark for law enforcement in combating gang violence," said Sacks. "The court may regard this as a step forward for society, but it's a step backward for the defense bar," he said. "It really stretches aiding and abetting. The other guy fired first and my guy never fired his weapon until after the victim was dead." Justice Joyce L. Kennard, in a concurrence, discussed how the companion cases of *Cervantes* and *Sanchez* differ. "In both, the defendant was a gang member who discharged a firearm at someone belonging to a rival gang," Kennard wrote. "In both, defendant's conduct induced additional gunfire in which a third person died. But this court has concluded that these similarities are less significant than other circumstances distinguishing the two situations."

Proximate or legal causation was not established in *Cervantes* but was present in *Sanchez*, Kennard wrote, adding: "History sadly establishes that killings motivated by revenge may occur in cycles lasting many years and even generations. . . . Courts must try to draw appropriate lines to mark the outer limits of legal causation in these situations. "The court's decisions today in these two companion cases should begin to fix this line of demarcation separating mutual combat killings from retaliatory killings in the context of urban warfare between rival street gangs." Justice Kathryn Mickle Werdegar also concurred separately.

Truth Tables

The Basics

Propositions are either simple or compound. A compound proposition is one that contains at least one logical connective. A *logical connective* is an operator that turns simple propositions into compound propositions. There are exactly five such operators in logic—they are as follows:

Connective	Effect	Example
"not"	*Negates* a proposition	Charlie is *not* afraid of bats.
"and"	Creates a *conjunction*	Ray is afraid of bees *and* he just spotted two bees nearby.
"or"	Creates a *disjunction*	*Either* there are bees *or* there are bats in the attic.
"if/then"	Creates a *conditional*	*If* bats are in the attic, *then* Charlie won't be scared.
"if and only if"	Creates a *biconditional*	Ray will be scared *if and only if* he sees bees.

A simple proposition contains *no* logical connectives. There are five connectives—each has a corresponding symbol. They are set out in the table below:

Logical Connectives	Symbol
Negation	~
Conjunction (and)	& (or •)
Disjunction (or)	∨
Conditional (if then/only if)	→
Biconditional (equivalence, if and only if)	≡ (or ↔)

Negation.   Negating a claim has the effect of changing the truth value to its opposite. This means a proposition that was originally true becomes false when negated, and vice versa. In a truth table this is expressed as follows:

P	~ P
T	F
F	T

Conjunction.   A conjunction is what results when two (or more) propositions are joined together by an "and." The conjunction of propositions P and Q (each called a "conjunct") is the proposition P and Q, symbolized as P & Q. A conjunction is true only if each conjunct is true.

P	Q	P & Q
T	T	T
T	F	F
F	T	F
F	F	F

Disjunction.   A disjunction is what results when two (or more) propositions are joined together by an "or" (or "either/or"). The disjunction of propositions P and Q (each called a "disjunct") is the proposition P and Q, symbolized as P v Q. A disjunction is true whenever one of the conjuncts is true. The only time a disjunction is false is when both disjuncts are false.

P	Q	P v Q
T	T	T
T	F	T
F	T	T
F	F	F

The Conditional.   A conditional is an "if . . . then" or "only if" claim. The conditional, "If P then Q" and "P only if Q" are both symbolized P → Q. In this construction, the proposition, P (on the left of the arrow) is called an **antecedent**. The proposition, Q (after the arrow, and following the "then") is called a **consequent**. A conditional claim is only false when the antecedent P is true and the consequent Q is false. Otherwise, it is true.

P	Q	P → Q
T	T	T
T	F	F
F	T	T
F	F	T

Note: Even when the antecedent and consequent are both false, the conditional P → Q is true! It is *only* false when the antecedent is true and the consequent is false.

Biconditional.   A biconditional asserts the equivalence of two propositions. This means the antecedent is both necessary and sufficient for the consequent. This is expressed as "P is equivalent to Q" or "P if and only if Q." This can be expressed as: "If P then Q, and if Q then P." Two propositions are equivalent if they have the same truth value. This means P ≡ Q is true if P and Q are both true or both false. This is expressed as follows:

P	Q	P ≡ Q
T	T	T
T	F	F
F	T	F
F	F	T

We are now ready to see what happens when we have combinations of the five logical connectives. For example, what if P and Q are both compound propositions? Let's look at some examples:

EXAMPLE: Set Out a Truth Table for the Proposition (P & Q) → ~P

Step One: Plug in the truth values for each one of P and Q, moving across the row.

In the first row P and Q are both true, so we'll put in T's under every occurrence of the two propositions. In the second row, P is true and Q is F, so go across the row, putting in Ts wherever P appears and Fs wherever Q appears. Continue until all four rows are set out with the truth values listed under each occurrence of P and Q. This is what we get:

P	Q	(P & Q)	→	~P
T	T	T T		T
T	F	T F		T
F	T	F T		F
F	F	F F		F

Step Two: We now need to go across each row and do the operations, keeping the main connective of the compound proposition in mind. The main connective here is the →. The antecedent is P & Q and the consequent is ~P. We won't be able to set out the truth value of the main connective until the last step. So remember: always do the main connective last in the truth tables. Putting in the truth values for the "P & Q" in the antecedent and the ~P in the consequent we get:

P	Q	(P & Q)	→	~ P
T	T	T T T		F T
T	F	T F F		F T
F	T	F F T		T F
F	F	F F F		T F

⇑   ⇑

Take the two operations (the "&" and the " ~ ") as indicated above.

Step Three: Now we can get the truth-value of the main connective ("→").

This we do by working with the truth-values in bold under the "&" and those under the negation in the consequent (the ~P). Remember, the only time a conditional is false is when the antecedent is true (T) and the consequent false (F). Any other combination is true. We see this in our completed truth table for the proposition:

P	Q	(P & Q)	→	~ P
T	T	T T T	F	F T
T	F	T F F	T	F T
F	T	F F T	T	T F
F	F	F F F	T	T F

⇑

We can now read the main connective, as indicated.

Truth Values of Three Types of Propositions

Tautology	All Ts	(A tautology is always ***true***)
Contradictory	All Fs	(A contradiction is always ***false***)
Contingent	Both Ts and Fs	(A contingent claim's truth-value is dependent the truth-values of its components)

As the above table indicates, any proposition with all Ts under the main connective is a tautology; any with all Fs is contradictory, and any with a mixture of Ts and Fs is a contingent claim.

Exercises

1. *Directions:* Set out the truth table for the following.
   a. A ∨ ~B
   b. A → ~C
   c. ~(A → B)
   d. A→ (~A ∨ ~ B)
   e. B & (~A → ~ B)

2. Find the truth value of the following, using the values assigned:
   a. ~ [A ∨ (B → ~C)]   when A is true, B and C are false.
   b. C → (A & ~B)   when A is false, B and C are true.
   c. [A→ (~B ∨ ~C)] & C   when A and C are true, B is false.
   d. B ∨ (~A & ~C)   when A, B, C are each true.
   e. A & (B→ ~C)   when A is true, B and C are false.
   f. (A → C) & (~B → ~A)   when A and C are false, B is true.
   g. ~(A & B) ∨ C   when A, B, C are each false.
   h. (B ∨ ~C) → A   when A is false, B and C are true.

3. Determine whether the following claims are tautologies, contradictories, or contingent claims by using truth tables:
   a. P ∨ ~ (P → ~P)
   b. ~ (P ∨ ~P)
   c. P → (P → ~P)
   d. ~ [P & ~(P ∨ ~P)]
   e. P → (P ∨ Q)
   f. P & (~Q ∨ P)
   g. P → (Q → ~P)
   h. (P→~Q) & (Q→ ~P)
   i. P → (Q & ~P)
   j. (Q & R) → (P ∨ ~R)

Shortcut Method: Truth Tables

Testing the validity of an argument can be slow and laborious if you have to do a full truth table. But using the shortcut method is a quick way to determine if an argument is valid or invalid.

First, we know from conditional claims that the only time a conditional is false is when the antecedent is true and the consequent is false. An argument is parallel to a conditional claim—the premises are parallel to antecedent conditions and the conclusion is parallel to the consequent. Thus, so long as there is no time in which all the premises can be true and the conclusion false, the argument is valid. What the shortcut method does, then, is check for this one case.

In other words, we see if all the premises can be true (all Ts under the main connective of each premise) and the conclusion false (an F under the main connective of the conclusion). If this can be constructed, the argument is invalid. If not, then the argument is valid.

Be careful: It's important to realize that the shortcut method is a much quicker way to establish invalidity than validity. All you need is to find *one* assignment of truth values that will make all the premises true (all Ts) and the conclusion false. To prove validity using the shortcut method, you want to show that there is no possible counterexample that would give all true premises and a false conclusion.

EXAMPLE: Test for Validity

1. $A \rightarrow B$
2. $B \rightarrow D$
3. $A \rightarrow \sim C$
4. $E \rightarrow D$
5. $B \rightarrow D$ /therefore, $\sim C \vee D$

The first step is to set out the variables on the left, the premises, and on the far right, the conclusion. Assign an F to the conclusion, and Ts to all the premises. Our task is to see if there is at least one assignment of truth values (and you only need one!) that permits all true premises and the false assignment for the conclusion.

A	B	C	D	E	A → B	B → E	A → ~C	E → D	B → D	/ ~C v D
					T	T	T	T	T	F

Looking at this table, we can see that C must be true and D false in order to get ~C v D false in the conclusion. So we put this information into our truth table and we have:

A	B	C	D	E	A → B	B → E	A → ~C	E → D	B → D	/ ~C v D
		T	F		T	T	T F T	T F	T F	F T F F

The only way A→~C can be true is if A is false, so we assign F to A. And the only way B→D can be T when D is false is if B is true, so assign T to B. Doing this and plugging in those values in the premises, we now have:

A	B	C	D	E	A → B	B → E	A → ~C	E → D	B → D	/ ~C v D
F	T	T	F		F T T	T T	F T F T	T F	T T F	F T F F

We don't need to go any further to see that we've got a problem. B→D cannot be true (as was assigned) with B true and D false. For B→E to be true, E must be true, so assign T to E. But doing so means E→D cannot be true, as we assigned. We now have:

A	B	C	D	E	A → B	B → E	A → ~C	E → D	B → D	/ ~C ∨ D
F	T	T	F	T	F T T	T T T	F T FT	T F	T F	F T F F

Notice that neither of these can be true (see arrows)—both are false. As we remember, if the antecedent is true and the consequent is false, the conditional is false. Since both B and D have to be true and D has to be false, this forces the conditionals E→D and B→D to be false and *not* true, as we originally assumed in order to construct the case of true premises and a false conclusion.

This means our attempt to construct a row with all true premises and a false conclusion failed. Consequently this argument is *not* invalid. It is valid. If, however, we were able to get all Ts for the premises and an F conclusion, we would know the argument was invalid and would note that particular assignment of truth values.

Exercises

Directions: Use the shortcut method to test for validity.

1.
   a. ~(A ∨ B)
   b. A→ ~B
   c. B
   d. C→ ~A   / therefore, ~C.

2.
   a. C →A
   b. A → B   / therefore, ~C → B

3.
   a. (A & C)
   b. (~E →D)
   c. B
   d. ~A → B
   e. E ∨ ~A   / therefore, D

4.
   a. A ∨ C
   b. C →~B
   c. (B & ~A) →D
   d. ~A   / therefore, B ∨ D

CHAPTER SEVEN

The Persuasive Power of Analogies

Harvey's ghosts have mischievous or evil facial expression, [whereas] Columbia's ghost appears bewildered.

JUDGE PETER K. LEISURE, dismissing Harvey Publication's suit against Columbia pictures that the *Ghostbusters'* ghost looked too much like Casper's friend, Fatso

If you saw either of the *Ghostbusters* movies, you remember the ghost that wreaked havoc and caused an enormous amount of destruction—so much so that a team of three men armed with an array of weapons struggled to contain it. In trying to figure out if this ghost was a rip-off of the cartoon series Casper (the friendly ghost) of the past, Judge Peter K. Leisure had to line them up and compare them. Exactly what similarities did they share? Are there any killer differences? The judge had to go into the thicket of analogical reasoning. Artistic integrity and an awful lot of money rested on him being able to render a decision.

Harvey Publications—the creators of Casper—claimed the *Ghostbusters'* ghost in the movie's logo too closely resembled one of their creations, the ghost Fatso. The judge had to decide if there was too great a resemblance in the two ghosts, thus violating the rights of Fatso's creators. Stop for a minute and think: What are the generic features of a ghost? Draw up a list before reading on!

Judge Leisure decided that no company could copyright the generic outline of a ghost, but they *could* copyright facial features and certain other aspects of a drawing. To him, most ghosts had knotted foreheads and jowly cheeks, making them generic features. The question was how close the *Ghostbusters'* ghost was to the Harvey ghosts, especially Fatso, in terms of key copyrighted features. Judge Leisure found that, whereas Fatso had a mischievous or evil facial expression, the other ghost just looked bewildered. Judge Leisure had to study ghosts (or drawings of ghosts) and induce common, generic characteristics and then decide which characteristics or features could be copyrighted. In other words, he had to have clearly articulated reasons for his decision.

As it turns out, he dismissed the suit, given the *differences* between the two ghosts. As you no doubt remember, differences can break an analogy. Sure there were similarities, but they were not sufficient to support the conclusion that the *Ghostbusters'* ghost was just a variation of the Harvey ghost, Fatso. In seeing the two ghosts you would not automatically infer that they were from the same poltergeist family.

Judge Leisure was using his powers of induction. As pointed out in Chapter 6, an **inductive argument** never offers certainty. The evidence, at best, gives but partial support for the conclusion. In this case, there were a few similarities, such as the rounded features and bulbous noses of the two ghosts. However, because of the missing pieces, there is always a wedge of doubt between the premises and the conclusion. In the ghost wars of Fatso versus the *Ghostbusters,* the differing facial expressions raised doubt in the mind of the judge. A look of bewilderment, the judge surmised, is distinctly different from a mischievous, or even evil, expression. Because of this uncertainty—this wedge of doubt—the case against Columbia pictures is past history as the analogy hit the dust.

In this chapter, we will focus on one of the most powerful forms of persuasion, arguments from analogy. There's something about analogies that can take hold of our brains and carry us right along. Even the worst of analogies can seduce us into thinking the argument makes good sense, even when it is virtually groundless. That is why it is crucial to have the tools at your disposal so you can stop right there and assess the analogy.

Arguments from Analogy

Arguments based on an analogy are among the most important kinds of inductive reasoning. An **argument from analogy** consists of a comparison between two things in which, on the basis of certain similarities, a principle or characteristic of the one term is then applied to the other term. Think, for example, of terms like "motherboard" that suggest a human, gestating presence in computer hardware. Such an analogy affects how we see other computer operations.

Analogies can be found everywhere from politics to religion and in all aspects of our lives. For example, Harvard University president Lawrence Summers faced an uproar over his leadership style given his comments about women's lack of success in math and science. Evidently he took his children to see the movie *Hitch,* which is about men who are trying to improve their social skills. Like the sad-sacks who need Alex "Hitch" Hitchens to help them find romance, Summers sought guidance on how to improve his leadership style (See Patrick D. Healy and Sara Rimer, "Amid Uproar, Harvard President Ponders His Style," *The New York Times,* 26 Feb 2005). Note what exactly is being compared to what and then check out the similarities and differences. That's what we have to examine in order to analyze Maxwell's reasoning.

In law these analogies take the form of **precedents.** Precedents are previous cases decided by a court of law or made into law by a legislature. Think how powerful is the analogy that's drawn between obeying the law and baseball; in the "three strikes" law, the rules of a game became the model for addressing repeat offenders. In the case of criminals, however, being "out" does not mean they can sit in the dugout until the next inning. It means 25 years to life in prison—a much wider sense of "out" than ever imagined in baseball.

We also see analogies in literature, poetry, mythology, and religion. Religious parables, such as in the gospels or in a Zen koan, provide a powerful form of religious guidance. Here's an example of a religious parable: "It is harder for a rich man to get into heaven than for a camel to go through the eye of a needle." Religious analogies can help us think about some of life's big questions. They also help us clear our minds of distractions and trivial mental pursuits. Such analogies act as catalysts, as we see in this case: "A man once searched for fire with a lighted lantern. Had he known what fire was, he could have cooked his rice much sooner."

Analogies can be very convincing. For many, the fact that someone has drawn a comparison implies that the comparison must be correct. But this is not necessarily true, for there may be relevant *differences* that make the principle or characteristic inapplicable. Our task is to see if the combined strength of the similarities outweighs that of the differences. In that way, we can assess how strong the analogy actually is.

Form of an Argument from Analogy.

A is like B in terms of characteristics p, q, r.

A also has characteristic "z."

So, B has characterististic "z" also.

For example, "Education cannot prepare high school students for marriage, even with the requirement that students carry dolls to class to approximate caring for children. Educating about marriage is like teaching someone to pilot a plane without ever leaving the ground. Until you're up in the air, you have no idea what's involved in flying." In this case, an analogy is drawn between marriage and piloting a plane. To assess the strength of this analogy, list what is similar between teaching about marriage and teaching about flying and then list the differences. Of course, there are some significant differences—marriage involves a relationship, is not potentially life-threatening if you fall asleep, and so on.

The Fallacy of False Analogy

Occasionally someone sets out a **false analogy,** as we saw in Chapter 4. In this fallacy, an inference rests on a comparison of two terms, but there are no similarities between the terms of the comparison other than trivial ones. For example, here's a false analogy: "Michigan minus bowling would be like Pythagoras without his theorem." It's a brain-twister to think of any real similarities between Michigan without bowling and Pythagoras without his theorem. If there are no nontrivial similarities, then the analogy simply fails.

Be on the lookout for false analogies. And be sure you can point to some shared characteristics between the terms of the comparison when you set out an analogy. *Be careful*: There are usually *some* similarities between one thing and another so you could think of analogies in this category as imperfect or very weak, rather than completely false.

Exercise in Bad Analogies

The *Washington Post* published winners in their "worst analogies ever written in a high school essay" contest. Among them are these:

"The little boat gently drifted across the pond exactly the way a bowling ball wouldn't" (Russell Beland, Springfield).

"From the attic came an unearthly howl. The whole scene had an eerie, surreal quality, like when you're on vacation in another city and *Jeopardy* comes on at 7 P.M. instead of 7:30" (Roy Ashley, Washington).

Directions: Make up an analogy of your own. Compare *your choice of an analogy* to one of the following: doing homework, taking an exam, sitting through a boring lecture, or writing an essay (or anything connected with being in college).

The Persuasive Force of an Analogy

Never underestimate the potential force of an analogy. Whether the comparison is strong or weak, an analogy can carry great persuasive power. For that reason, it is unwise to let an analogy slide by without examining it. Let's look at some examples.

Example #1: The Lifeboat Analogy

Microbiologist Garrett Hardin used a now-famous analogy in an article on world hunger. He presents this scenario: Think of our nation as a lifeboat with 50 people and 10 empty seats. There are 100 people (from underdeveloped nations) in the water, trying to get in our lifeboat. If we took them all on, we would sink. If we took a few (how could we choose?), we'd lose our safety margin of the empty seats. So, we should not rescue any. This, Hardin argues, is why we are not in a position to help alleviate world hunger. We need to preserve our own resources for future use and, thus, should not deplete them by trying (ineffectively, given the numbers) to help.

You Tell Me Department

Is Religion Like Hockey? Or Maybe Basketball or Badminton?

The Snapshots of God Web site includes the argument that religion is like hockey. See if you are convinced by the reasoning:

> "Many people don't like hockey because they just don't understand it. You hear whistles being blown and play stopping for no apparent reason. . . . You see people pushing each other and hitting each other with sticks. . . . In watching that one game, you might very well conclude that hockey is irrational and barbaric, and want nothing to do with it. You might not notice any real difference between a rookie and Wayne Gretsky, the best in the game.
>
> I think that our understanding of God and religion can be much the same. You can take a distant, cursory view from the outside, observe the fighting, find all the rules confusing and conclude that there is nothing there of much sense or value. This is where the agnostics and atheists sit. You can learn enough so that it at least makes enough sense for you to get a little something out of it. This is religion for the masses. . . . You can put on a jersey, go down on the ice and try to learn a little from all the players. This is spirituality." ("Religion Is Just Like Hockey," *Snapshots of God,* snapshotsofgod.com)

You tell me: Is religion like hockey? Share your response to this analogy and explain why you did or did not find it persuasive. Be as specific as you can in setting out your reasons. Feel free to go to the Web site to see the analogy developed more fully.

Example #2: The Drowning Child Analogy

Another influential analogy is one philosopher James Rachels uses in an article on active versus passive euthanasia (mercy killing). He presents two scenarios that he uses to contrast killing (active euthanasia) versus letting die (passive euthanasia—not intervening to try to save the life). In the first case, Smith stands to gain a large inheritance if anything happens to his 6-year-old cousin and, so, Smith drowns the child one night in the bathtub and then makes it look like an accident.

In the second case, Jones, who also stands to gain if anything happens to his 6-year-old cousin, sneaks into the bathroom intending to drown the boy. But, before he can make his move, his cousin slips, hits his head, and falls face down in the water and dies "accidentally" as Jones watches. Rachels then compares Smith's murder of his cousin with Jones's failure to intervene to save him. As far as Rachels is concerned, both are equally morally culpable and there is no significant moral distinction between the two scenarios. He then applies this to active versus passive euthanasia, making the same argument. He concludes that terminating the life of the seriously ill is not morally distinct from "letting them die" by not resuscitating them.

Assessing an Analogy

If you allow the analogy to get off the ground, the argument is generally successful. If, however, the weight of the differences of the two terms is greater than that of the similarities, the analogy falters. That is, the argument is not as powerful if

You Tell Me Department

Are Geese Like Slaves?

Force-feeding geese to fatten them up so they have tasty livers for the gourmet food *foie gras* (which is French for liver paté) strikes animal rights advocates as barbaric. Here's what one incensed person had to say in a letter to the editor:

> It is troubling that after such a noticeable lack of coverage of the *foie gras* issue, the *Los Angeles Times* would choose to print such a load of drivel as David Shaw's article (Matters of Taste: "They're Quacking up the Wrong Tree," May 5, 2004). First

he says that animal rights activists make "the anti-abortion movement look positively passive."

Rubbish. No animal rights activist has ever shot and killed a doctor. Most animal rights activists are against harming *any* living being. Second, he argues that the suffering of ducks doesn't matter because the ducks were raised for that purpose. Many slaves were born in captivity also. That doesn't mean it was any less painful or more humane.

You tell me: Is this a good analogy? So-so analogy? Weak analogy? Explain your decision.

---

the differences outweigh the similarities. Every time you see an analogy ask yourself, What are the similarities? What are the differences? The use of an analogy should start alarms ringing in our brain:

That's an analogy   →   Hold it right there!
                         →   Stop and check it out.
                         →   Weigh the similarities and differences.

What makes an argument based on an analogy an *inductive* argument is that the evidence is partial. In an analogy, the premises only provide some support for the conclusion. Granted, there are differences in any comparison; there will always be holes in the argument. The result is that the conclusion does not and cannot automatically follow from the premises. If the premises are true, the conclusion following an analogy will not certainly be true—it could be false. This is why an argument from analogy is *inductive,* not deductive.

Think of it this way: no matter how similar you may be to your mother or father, there are still some differences. Even though you can draw up a long list of similarities, there will nevertheless be differences that introduce uncertainty into the comparison.

Most of us have been compared to a family member (positively or negatively!). This reasoning is *inductive* because we are supposed to draw a conclusion on the basis of the asserted similarity. "Sonja, you are just like your mother! Your mother always makes delicious lemon meringue pie, so you should too!" Now Sonja may be like her mother in some respects. But that does not mean she is like her mother in *every* respect. They are not clones, so there will be some things about them that are not identical. Sonja may be a good baker, like her mother. But it is not certain. The fact of a resemblance does not automatically mean that the two are identical.

⊞ Analyzing Analogies

We can tackle analogies we encounter by assessing the strengths of the comparison. Follow the steps, carefully laying out the analogy so you can then decide how strong it is.

Steps to Analyzing an Analogy

1. *Clarify the terms of comparison.* Note exactly what is being compared to what.
2. *Write it out like an equation setting out the comparison.* Sonja/pies she bakes ≡ Sonja's mother/pies her mother bakes.
3. *State the principle or characteristic attributed to the one term that is being applied to the other term.* Sonja's pies should be as delicious as her mother's pies.
4. *List the similarities.*
5. *List the differences.*
6. *Survey the two lists.* Add any omissions to your lists.
7. *Weigh similarities and differences.* Determine the relative strength of the similarities compared to that of the differences. Some similarities or differences may be more important than others, so prioritize them in terms of relative importance.
8. *Assess the analogy.* Analogies, like all inductive arguments, fall along a spectrum ranging from dismal to strong. In a *strong analogy*, the similarities outweigh the differences. In a *weak analogy*, the strength of the differences outweighs the similarities. Ask yourself: Is there a killer difference? Check to see if there is a difference so great that it would outweigh any similarity. If so, the analogy fails. In a *false analogy*, there are no relevant (nontrivial) similarities at all. *Don't forget:*

Similarities MAKE an analogy

Differences BREAK an analogy

First Application

Let's examine some analogies and assess their strength. The first analogy we will look at is one often cited in the abortion debate.

Analogy #1: A Fetus Is Like an Acorn.   In her article, "A Defense of Abortion" philosopher Judith Jarvis Thomson uses a number of analogies (see *Philosophy and Public Affairs,* vol. 1, no. 1, 1971). One of her arguments is this: "The development of a person from the moment of conception is similar to the development of an acorn into an oak tree." Let us examine this analogy using the seven steps.

Step 1: Clarify What Is Being Compared to What

In this case, the development of the fetus into a person is being compared to the development of an acorn into an oak.

Step 2: Set Out the Terms of the Analogy

These are *fetus/person* ≡ *acorn/oak.*

Step 3: State the Principle Being Asserted

The principle is: There is no clear line that separates a fetus from a person.

Step 4: List the Similarities

1. In both cases we are talking about living things.
2. The fetus and the acorn are both early forms of the respective organisms.
3. The existence of the later organism (person/oak tree) depends upon the growth and development of the earlier form.
4. Both fetus and acorn can be destroyed or damaged by poor nutrition (soil), lack of nurturance, or other means.
5. Neither fetus nor acorn has clearly delineated stages of development.

Step 5: List the Differences

1. The fetus grows inside the mother's body, whereas the acorn grows away from and is separate from the oak tree.
2. The time it takes to develop (fetus to person, and acorn to oak) is different.
3. Quantity: An oak tree produces many more acorns than a woman does fetuses.
4. Social worth: The society values fetuses more highly than acorns and most persons more highly than most oak trees.
5. A fetus relies upon mother's body for nurturing and to sustain its life, but an acorn has no such reliance on the oak tree.

Step 6: Survey the Two Lists

Look at the similarities: We've covered the category (living things), age parallels, dependence on the "mother" organism, need for nurturance and nutrition, and lack of clear stage delineation. Is there more we could add? Well, we might add that both (barring destruction) potentially grow into the same type of organism (human/tree) from which it came.

Now look at the differences: We've covered the internal versus external factor, differences in maturation times, quantity, social worth, and differences in source of nurturance. Could we add anything else? Well, some might point to the appearance issue (fetuses could be said to more closely resemble humans than acorns resemble oak trees).

Step 7: Weigh the Similarities and Differences

The differences seem stronger, particularly numbers 1 and 5 and maybe even 4. There are no strong similarities, though the strongest are probably numbers 2 and 5.

Step 8. Assessment

Given this weighting, it would seem that the analogy is not very strong. Note that it is not a false analogy, where there are at best trivial similarities. In this case there are some similarities. However, the differences loom larger and, consequently, the analogy does not appear to be very powerful. As a result, the principle being claimed that there is no clear line separating fetuses from persons has not been clearly established by using the analogy that fetuses are like acorns.

Second Application

It may help to go through another analogy to imprint the steps firmly on our minds. The second analogy is also from Judith Jarvis Thomson, but it is more unusual than the first one.

Analogy #2: "People-Seeds" Analogy.   Thomson presents the analogy as follows:

> Again, suppose it were like this: people-seeds drift about in the air like pollen, and if you open your windows, one may drift in and take root in your carpets or upholstery. You don't want children, so you fix up your windows with fine mesh screens, the very best you can buy. As can happen, however, and on very, very rare occasions does happen, one of the screens is defective; and a seed drifts in and takes root. Does the person-plant who now develops have a right to the use of your house? Surely not—despite the fact that you voluntarily opened your windows, you knowingly kept carpets and upholstered furniture, and you knew that screens were sometimes defective. ("A Defense of Abortion")

Step 1: Clarify What Is Being Compared

In this argument, Thomson is comparing the use of screens to prevent people-seeds from blowing into your house to using contraception to prevent pregnancy.

Step 2: Set Out the Terms of the Analogy

Defective screen/people seed ≡ defective contraception/fetus.

Step 3: State the Principle Being Asserted

Thomson is asserting that the failure of means of contraception resulting in pregnancy ought not make us feel morally obligated to bear the child, that an abortion is morally acceptable.

Step 4: List the Similarities

1. Both contraception and screens are intentional attempts to prevent something from happening.
2. Both contraception and screens have the potential for error; neither one is foolproof.
3. Both people-seeds and fetuses are earlier stages of the person and will lead to personhood, given appropriate conditions.
4. Both have long-term consequences if allowed to go to personhood.
5. In both cases, the result is undesirable (the mother/dweller of house did not wish to become pregnant/have a people-seed growing in the carpet).

Step 5: List the Differences

1. People-seeds float about in the air; fetuses do not.
2. In the case of a pregnancy there is a father whose wishes may bear upon the decision; in the case of people-seeds there is not.
3. A people-seed grows in a carpet and does not depend upon the house dweller, whereas a fetus grows inside the mother and depends upon her body for nurturance.
4. You could sell your house or move away and avoid the people-seed problem; not so in a normal pregnancy.
5. People-seeds require no personal risk in their development, whereas the pregnant woman undergoes risk in pregnancy.

Step 6: Survey the Two Lists

Look at the similarities: We've addressed the fact that both are undesirable and that steps are being taken to prevent the people-seed/human embryo from gestating, both methods of obstruction can fail, both have developmental and long-term consequences. Is there more we can add? Well, we could add that both might result in unforeseen difficulties for the house owner/mother and perhaps even some physical risk (people-seed may develop into a psycho, the pregnancy could be an ectopic or other high-risk pregnancy).

Now look at the differences: We've addressed the fact that fetuses are not external to the mother, there is not necessarily a parallel to the father in the people-seed case, and escaping from the people-seed is much easier escaping from the fetus. Is there anything else we could add? Well, we might add that there could be hundreds of people-seeds that take root in your house (say in a big windstorm)—no pregnancy could compare in sheer numbers of developing entities.

Step 7: Weigh the Similarities and Differences

Looking over each list, the strongest similarities seem to be numbers 1, 3, and 5. The strongest differences seem to be 3, 4, and 5 and maybe 2. The additional difference we noted does not necessarily mean the consequences would be worse if we had hundreds of people sprouting in the carpet compared to one fetus that becomes a child (the significance of this difference may be hard to quantify).

Step 8: Assessment

This analogy seems stronger than our last one. Namely, the similarities are not irrelevant or insignificant and the differences are there but not overwhelmingly strong. The difference of the relative risk to each seems strongest, as that is a bottom-line type of difference. Given that the overall weight of the similarities is stronger than that of the differences in this analogy, we can infer that the analogy has persuasive value and may carry weight in Thomson's attempt to make her case that abortion be allowable under certain circumstances.

Group or Individual Exercise

Libraries and the War on Terror

As of September 20, 2003, the U.S. Justice Department reported that it had not yet used its counterterrorism powers to demand records from libraries and elsewhere. Department officials asserted that they had sought access to no one's library record as of that date. That does not impress Phil Valentine, however, who sets out a blistering attack by employing an analogy ("Bogus Analogies, Libraries, and the War on Terror," *The Talent Show*, www.thetalentshow.org, 20 Sep 2003). Responding to Valentine's argument, Justice Department spokesman Mark Corallo set out *his* analogy.

Directions: Go through both Valentine's and Corallo's arguments from analogy and note the *strengths* of each one:

PHIL VALENTINE'S ARGUMENT: Let's pretend for a moment that I was in charge of the world and for some reason I decided to pass a law that makes it legal for the government to kidnap babies from the mall in order to grind them up and make sausages to feed people in prison. After a couple years of protests over my cruel baby-killing law, I reveal that I haven't in fact ever exercised the law. That might make people feel a bit better, but it doesn't change the fact that I can still legally kidnap and murder babies. To a much lesser extent, that's the situation that [Attorney General] Ashcroft is in right now.

MARK CORALLO'S ARGUMENT: The same people who would argue that, would argue that if a police officer has never had to fire his weapon in 20 years on the force, we should take his weapon away from him because he will never have to use it.

The Global Dimension

Analogies from the Al-Qaeda Perspective

In a February 5, 2004, interview with Terrorism Monitor Special Correspondent, Mahan Abedin Saad al-Faqih of the Saudi opposition group, Movement for Islamic Reform in Arabia set forth two analogies. Read them both and then select *one* to discuss. Share your reaction and indicate whether or not the analogy has strengths.

ANALOGY #1 (Al-Qaeda Is Like a College)

DR. AL-FAQIH: Al-Qaeda is a very interesting organization. They do not believe in the party structure, they see themselves as a college where people enroll, graduate and then go their separate ways. But they are encouraged to establish their own satellite networks which ultimately link in with al-Qaeda. This is why al-Qaeda is very resilient and can never be destroyed.

ANALOGY #2 (The American Mentality Is Like a Cowboy Mentality)

DR. AL-FAQIH: Zawahiri impressed upon Bin Laden the importance of understanding the American mentality. The American mentality is a cowboy mentality—if you confront them with their identity theoretically and practically they will react in an extreme manner. In other words, America with all its resources and establishments will shrink into a cowboy when irritated successfully. They will then elevate you and this will satisfy the Muslim longing for a leader who can successfully challenge the West. (See "The Essence of al-Qaeda: An Interview with Saad al-Faqih," *The Jamestown Foundation,* www.jamestown.org, 5 Feb 2004)

🀫 The Persuasive Aspects of Analogies

Arguments based on analogies can be clinchers. Patent attorney Jerry Dodson tells of a 12–0 jury verdict he won for Clorox Corporation against Procter & Gamble in a patent dispute. The issue turned on a Brita water treatment pitcher. To convince the jury that the Brita filter's replacement indicator relied on air pressure—in contrast to Procter & Gamble's filter's replacement indicator that used buoyancy—he used an analogy. "I used a champagne bottle," he says. "The cork pops out because of pressure, but if you throw it into the champagne, it floats because of buoyancy. The other side could never overcome the champagne-bottle analogy."

Dodson regularly turns to an easy-to-grasp analogy to explain a complex case. "I'm always sorting through analogies, bringing new ones in and throwing old ones out" (noted by Barb Mulligan, "Patent Attorney Jerry Dodson '69 Uses Analogies to Explain Complex Cases," Lafayette College, www.lafayette.edu/news). As Dodson demonstrates in his work as a lawyer, analogies can be powerful tools of persuasion.

Depending on how we rank the similarities and differences, the persuasive value of the analogy varies. This means there's a subjective element to any analogy. After listing similarities and differences, weighing them is not neutral. Rather, your own set of values will factor in when deciding the strengths of the different claims, especially those relating to a set of beliefs.

Be prepared: Some analogies are highly inflammatory and offensive. It is common to see analogies used in racist, sexist, and ethnic slurs. Subsequently, we need to have the facility to dismantle such hateful analogies when we see them. For example, journalist Bob Herbert writes about the vitriolic language used by a radio personality, Bob Grant. Herbert asserts that Grant made the following use of an argument from an analogy:

> He would wonder aloud "if they've ever figured out how they multiply like that. It's like maggots on a hot day. You look one minute and there are so many there, and you look again and, wow, they've tripled!" (See Bob Herbert, "A Different Republican?" *The New York Times,* 29 June 2000).

It is not unusual to see movies being used in an analogy. The assumption that everyone has actually seen the movie may be unwarranted, but such analogies are common. For instance, Jamal Harith, a Briton held at the Iso detention center at Guantanamo Bay, Cuba, for two years, said prisoners were beaten and sexually humiliated. Harith drew an analogy to the movie *Alien* ("in space no one can hear you scream"). He said: "It's like the *Alien* film: In 'Iso' nobody can hear you scream." As you may recall, in *Alien,* a hideous monster kills off most of the crew on the spaceship. Harith says of the prison: "On many occasions I heard people being beat. . . . I got it easy compared to what other people got. If there is such a thing as easy, that is" (Sebastian Rotella, "Ex-Inmate Alleges U.S. Abuse at Guantanamo," *Los Angeles Times,* 25 May 2004). Using the analogy to a horror film, Harith sets out his view of what he experienced in prison. For us to decide if his analogy is strong, we need to break it down and evaluate it.

Structuring the Analysis

We need to be able to assess the use of an analogy, a process that can be laid out as follows:

Assessing the Use of an Analogy: Structuring the Analysis

1. What is at issue? What principle or conclusion is being drawn from the analogy?
2. Exactly what is being compared? Set out the terms of the analogy.
3. What are the relevant similarities and differences? List them both.
4. Critically examine the lists, weighing them to see the strength of each side (assess similarities and differences).
5. How would you attack the analogy? (What are its weaknesses?)
6. How would you defend the analogy? (What are its strengths?)
7. If this is an analogy you intend to use, see if you can modify it to minimize weaknesses and boost strengths.
8. If this is an analogy you are evaluating, make note of the relative strengths and weaknesses and decide if the analogy succeeds.
9. *Remember:* Similarities make the analogy. Differences break the analogy.
10. You are now are in a position to assess whether the conclusion (the principle being drawn) can be said to follow with credible support.

Exercises

Part One: Setting Out Analogies

1. How do you take apart an analogy? List the steps in order.

2. Set out the comparison and list the similarities and differences in the following:

   Plastic surgeon Dr. Sherrell J. Aston compared cosmetic surgery patients to "the lady who gets her hair done and nails done." In his view, "People are wanting to do it as a part of personal grooming. It will become more and more common as time goes on and be programmed into people's consciousness." (As noted by Alex Kuczynski and Warren Sr. John, "Why Did They Die in Cosmetic Surgery," *The New York Times*, 20 Jun 2004)

3. Set out the terms and list the similarities and differences in the following discussion of e-mail spam:

   "Finding a solution here is like putting socks on an octopus," FTC Commissioner Mozelle Thompson said during a break in the proceedings. "There are too many moving parts. But the clear message is that doing nothing is not acceptable. We're approaching a tipping point where consumer confidence is beginning to erode." ("Spamstrung," *The Age,* www.theage.com, 18 May 2003)

4. Set out the terms and list the similarities and differences in the following discussion:

   Back in the day, a rapper playing guitar was like a nun wearing a bikini. You just didn't do it. But after I saw Wyclef (Jean) play, I knew it would be acceptable. I didn't have to be embarrassed and hide my guitar in the closet. (Edna Gundersen, "Airwaves 'High' on Afroman's Funny Funk," *USA Today,* 20 Aug 2001)

5. Set out the terms of the analogy below and list the similarities and differences:

   Affirmative action allows successful Blacks to play a cruel hoax on and advance at the expense of less fortunate Blacks. This is . . . why I so vehemently oppose it. . . . At best, affirmative action is like rearranging the chairs on the deck of the Titanic. (William [otherwise anonymous], "Thoughts of a Black Conservative," America Online)

6. Set out the terms of the analogy below and list the similarities and differences:

   Terminator 3 director, Jonathan Mostow, speaking about Arnold Schwarzenegger: "Obviously, I'd be lying to say it wasn't daunting working in his shadow. The bar has been set very high." There's still Schwarzenegger to provide authentic Terminator wisdom, says Mostow. "I feel like I'm making the Bible and I'm getting to work with Moses." (Rachel Abramowitz, "Rage against the Machines: 'T3's' Rocky Road," *Los*

Angeles Times, 11 Mar 2002. Note that Schwarznegger had not yet become California governor at the time of Mostow's remarks.)

7. Set out the terms and list the similarities and differences in the following discussion of the criminal justice system:

> The criminal justice system is like a mirror in which society can see the face of the evil in its midst. But because the system deals with some evil and not with others, because it treats some evils as the gravest and treats some of the gravest evils as minor, the image it throws back is distorted like the image in a carnival mirror. Thus the image cast back is false, not because it is invented out of thin air, but because the proportions of the real are distorted. . . .
>
> If criminal justice really gives us a carnival-mirror image of "crime," we are doubly deceived. First, we are led to believe that the criminal justice system is protecting us against the gravest threats to our well-being when in fact the system is only protecting us against some threats and not necessarily the gravest ones. We are deceived about how much protection we are receiving and thus left vulnerable. But, in addition, we are deceived about what threatens us and are, therefore, unable to take appropriate defensive action. The second deception is just the other side of the first one. If people believe that the carnival mirror is a true mirror—that is, if they believe that the criminal justice system just reacts to the gravest threats to their well-being—they come to believe that whatever is the target of the criminal justice system must be the gravest threat to their well-being. (Jeffrey H. Reiman, *The Rich Get Richer and the Poor Get Poorer*)

8. Stanley Bing sets out an analogy and a challenge: "Here are ten ways that a baby is like a chief executive officer. Tell me where I've got it wrong" (see Stanley Bing, "You're a CEO Baby!," *Fortune* magazine, www.fortune.com, 21 Feb 2005). Look over his list and then set out what is *different* about babies and CEO's.

> 1) The baby is the center of its universe, 2) The baby speaks nonsense, but nobody seems to notice, 3) The baby has a short attention span and must be entertained constantly, 4) Those who serve the baby must be attentive to its moods, which change radically from moment to moment, 5) Everything is planned around the comfort and schedule of the baby, 6) The baby is conveyed [carried] everywhere, 7) The baby has special food made for it because it can't really digest the stuff that other people eat, 8) The baby is bored by grownups, but if there is another baby in the room it perks up, 9) When the baby makes a mess, other people have to clean it up, and 10) Babies have weird hair.

Part Two: Analyzing Analogies

Directions: Go through the steps to check out these analogies and assess their strength.

1. Marriage without love is like driving a car without brakes.

2. A relationship is like a shark; it has to keep moving or it dies (Jamie Will, University of Iowa, www.uistudenthealth.com), 8 Jan 2004).

3. "Being lectured by the president on fiscal responsibility is a little bit like Tony Soprano talking to me about law and order in this country" (Senator John Kerry in the 2004 campaign).

4. "Democracy is not a potato that you can transplant from one kitchen garden to another" [implying that some think it *is* like a potato]. (Russian Defense Minister Sergei Ivanov, noted on *CNN.com,* 13 Feb 2005).

5. "Words are like bullets—they can be used to kill" (Planned Parenthood).

6. "Racism, like the bite of a rabid animal, can infect a victim with the deadly disease of its madness" (Lloyd L. Brown).

7. "Pennsylvania is forcing Internet providers to block Web sites that include child pornography. The Center for Democracy and Technology compared the blocking technique to disrupting mail delivery to an entire apartment complex because of one tenant's illegal actions" ("Civil Liberties Lawyers Raise Questions about Web Filters," *The New York Times,* 20 Feb 2003).

8. "Now, in the 1990's, I see substantial similarities between the cocaine epidemic and slavery. Both are firmly grounded in economics—at the expense of a race of people. There was, and is, money to be made. It would be foolish to lose sight of this truth" (Rev. Cecil Williams, "Crack is Genocide 1990's Style," *The New York Times,* 15 Feb 1990).

9. "To take an absurd example to illustrate why people should have a property right in their own tissues, suppose [billionaire head of Microsoft] Bill Gates' barber saves a lock of his hair and clones him, suing Gates for child support. The answer shouldn't be that Bill Gates has no recourse because he has no property rights in his tissue" (Lori Andrews, *Body Bazaar*).

10. "Most Californians view illegal immigrants as unwanted house guests. One very effective means of getting rid of such guests is to set your house on fire and burn it to the ground. This is Propositions 187's solution to illegal immigration. No decent Californian should support it" (Ron K. Unz, 1994 Republican primary challenge to Governor Wilson of California).

11. "They should not allow stem cell research [that uses early human embryos]. It's no different than the experiments the Nazis did during World War II on the Jewish prisoners" [Paraphrase of Comment by Senator Sam Brownback (R-KS)]

12. "In attempting to explain humankind's place in the timeline of evolution, Mr. [Stephen J.] Gould had this suggestion: Extend your right or left hand as far away from the body as you can—that distance would represent the beginning of earth's birth (some 5 billion years); then with the tip of either index finger extended, return either index finger and place it on the tip of your nose (which would represent the present). Now, take a file and file off

the fingernail of that index finger—by filing off this fingertip, you have just eliminated humankind from its place in evolution" ("Evolution's Voyage: Assumptions," www.evoyage.com).

13. In his memoir, *Parallel Time*, Brent Staples writes about the problems he ran into as an African-American man attending college in a mostly white neighborhood in Pennsylvania. Discuss how he uses an analogy to convey the experience of encountering people who were afraid of him in the excerpt below.

> I'd been a fool. I'd been grinning good evening at people who were frightened to death of me. I did violence to them by just being. How had I missed this? I kept walking at night, but from then on I paid attention. I became expert in the language of fear. Couples locked arms or reached for each other's hand when they saw me. Some crossed to the other side of the street. People who were carrying on conversations went mute and stared straight ahead, as though avoiding my eyes would save them. This reminded me of an old wives' tale that rabid dogs didn't bite if you avoided their eyes.

Part Three: Constructing Analogies

Directions: Select any two of the following and construct an analogy for each scenario you choose.

1. Give an analogy to argue for or against college athletes getting preferential treatment in admission to the school.

2. Set out an analogy to argue for or against legalizing marijuana. Set out the terms of your analogy.

3. Give an analogy to argue for or against going to a pass/fail grading system. Set out the terms of your analogy.

4. Give an analogy to argue for or against banning smoking in public buildings. Set out the terms of your analogy.

5. Give an analogy to argue for or against Neo-Nazis being allowed to pass out leaflets in public high schools. Set out the terms of your analogy.

6. Give an analogy to argue for or against censoring nudity on primetime TV. Set out the terms of your analogy.

7. Give an analogy to argue for or against the use of women in combat positions in war. Set out the terms of your analogy.

8. Ludwig Wittgenstein, who wrote on the connection between language, thought, and reality, said of philosophy, "Philosophers use a language that is already deformed as though by shoes that are too tight." Construct an analogy that expresses your attitude or feeling about studying philosophy.

Group or Individual Exercise

The Timothy McVeigh–John Brown Analogy

Timothy McVeigh was convicted of the Oklahoma City bombing that killed 168 people, John Brown committed murder in the name of his cause—the abolition of slavery. He was executed in 1859, McVeigh in 2001. Software engineer and history buff, Clayton Cramer, argues that McVeigh is our modern day John Brown. Law professor Paul Finkleman responds. (See History News Network, www.hnn.us, 6 Jul 2001 for the summaries of the two positions.)

Directions: Read Cramer's and Finkleman's list of points and pick out the *four strongest* claims for each side. Explain why you picked those you selected.

CRAMER'S ARGUMENT: Timothy McVeigh Is Like John Brown

1. Timothy McVeigh explicitly cast himself as a modern-day John Brown shortly before his execution. "One of his big heroes was John Brown, who committed some very violent acts during the 1800s in the effort to eliminate slavery in our country," according to journalist Dan Herbeck.

2. Both men saw systems of brutality and thought they were justified in responding with brutality. For Timothy McVeigh, it was blowing up a building filled with people against whom he had no direct hostility; for John Brown, it was murdering people like James P. Doyle and his two adult sons at Pottawatomie, Kansas.

3. There was nothing even close to self-defense involved; Brown threatened to burn the Doyle cabin down if Doyle and his adult sons did not come out. They did so, and then Brown's men, smashing the Doyles' heads open with swords, chopped off the arms of one of the sons.

4. Some think Doyle was antislavery. But no printed source indicates that Doyle played any part in the murders of Free Soilers in Kansas, about which Brown was upset.

5. However, James Townsley's 1882 statement on the Pottawatomie Massacre makes it clear that Brown intended a general slaughter, based on political affiliation. Therefore, Brown is responsible for the death of five proslavery settlers. It was also Timothy McVeigh's perspective that because there was no justice done for crimes at Ruby Ridge and Waco [in which the FBI killed people], it was OK for him to engage in an act of war.

6. Brown's actions at Pottawatomie, even if Doyle had threatened Brown's life, were not justified by either civilian laws of self-defense or by the rules of war. It was acceptable to kill in self-defense, but it was not lawful to

wait a few days, come up on their house in the middle of the night, threaten to kill their family, then march your enemy into the woods and hack them to death.

7. We can see John Brown as a tragic figure, a person who felt that the evil of slavery left him no choice. The tragedy is that a person of good intentions became evil to fight evil.

8. If we teach John Brown as a heroic figure, some students may decide that there are no legitimate rules of warfare in revolutionary struggle—with disastrous results in the future.

FINKELMAN'S ARGUMENT: The Analogy Fails: McVeigh Is Not Like Brown

1. The comparison of John Brown to Timothy McVeigh is simplistic and lacks any grounding in the history of the 1850s. And it ignores the nature of McVeigh's actions.

2. In Kansas there was an ongoing civil war. Many antislavery people had already been killed by proslavery forces. A number of those killed in Pottawatomie were involved in killings and had threatened to kill the Browns. The role of the Doyles in these events is contested, but no one contests that the rest of the adult males in the Doyle cabin were heavily involved in proslavery violence. On the other hand, it is hard to imagine who exactly was threatening to kill McVeigh. His enemies were distant and remote.

3. McVeigh claimed to be avenging Waco and Ruby Ridge, but no one killed at Oklahoma City had anything to do with those events. No one would have been harmed at either place if the people inside these compounds had been peaceful.

4. In contrast, free staters had been shot down by slave staters, and proslavery settlers and border ruffians had begun the violence in Kansas. Only when proslavery forces used weapons, violence, and vote fraud did the Browns and others defend themselves with arms.

5. A U.S. army patrol led by a minister from Missouri encountered one of Brown's sons, unarmed. He offered no resistance, but was shot and killed by the minister with the Army watching.

6. No one had ever threatened McVeigh or his neighbors or family. He indiscriminately killed people who had no connection to those events, and who threatened no one.

7. Had Brown wished to take life for its own sake, as McVeigh did, he would have killed all the people in the Doyle cabin, including his wife and young children. He carefully avoided taking life unnecessarily. In contrast McVeigh's only goal was to kill as many people as possible.

8. The comparisons between McVeigh and Brown, if they exist, are only in that both were executed and that in both cases the government set itself up to allow the men to cast themselves as martyrs. Brown was fighting a real institution of evil: slavery. McVeigh was fighting against a government that had never threatened him or in any way harmed him. McVeigh was a stone cold killer, willing to take life indiscriminately because of some strange and pathetic notion of political reality he had come to believe.

▦ Analogies and Hypothetical Reasoning in the Law

One of the key issues lawyers and judges face is whether a legal precedent applies. They have to decide how well the letter of the law applies to a particular case. A great deal hinges on the relevant similarities, and differences of the precedent case to the case at hand. To assess this, we have to consider the amount of variation from the standard (norm or precedent-setting case) to the individual one being litigated. That is not always easy.

To help prepare a student for the practice of law, one teaching technique uses a hypothetical case (alias *Hypo*). In **hypothetical law cases,** a scenario or story is presented, with the task of deciding how it is to be evaluated given the existing laws and precedents. This is an important application of analogical reasoning, requiring lawyers and law students to be both astute and imaginative in assessing the hypothetical cases.

By analyzing the specifics of the Hypo in relationship to the legal standard, students can then determine how the law should apply in the hypothetical case. Let's see how this is done. Drawing from an article "Hypothetical Rape Scenarios as a Pedagogical Device" by Sociology Professor Colleen Fitzpatrick in the *Journal of Criminal Justice Education,* Spring 2001, let's look at some Hypos around prosecutorial decision making in rape cases.

Group or Individual Exercise

Read the article below that presents three of Colleen Fitzpatrick's five rape scenarios and accompanying questions. Then discuss what would be involved in answering the questions (i.e., how you would arrive at an answer of whether or not the district attorney should prosecute). Go into detail and elaborate on any *one* of the scenarios (pick one).

SCENARIO #1

Every Wednesday for the past year of her new marriage, Evelyn's husband, Paul, goes out with the "boys" for a night of bowling and drinking. Upon his return around 2 A.M., he strips off his smoky clothes and hops into bed with Evelyn. Inevitably feeling amorous toward his wife, Paul—smelling of smoke and booze—has sexual intercourse with Evelyn. On this particular Wednesday night, Evelyn decides enough is enough. When Paul comes home, gets into bed, and approaches Evelyn, she pushes him off and tells him she doesn't want to have sex tonight. Apparently not wanting to break his successive Wednesday night streak, Paul uses his strength and weight (but no hitting or striking) to have sex with Evelyn. Was Evelyn raped? Would you, as DA, prosecute?

SCENARIO #2

After three rapes on the Mountain University campus, the campus police have advised coeds to avoid walking a dark path between the library and a dorm. All three rapes occurred along that path after the women were dragged into the bushes lining the path. Campus police told women the path was unsafe until recently budgeted lights could be erected and operating. One half hour before the library closed, Helen realized her boyfriend would be calling her dorm room in ten minutes. This being her only chance to talk with him this week, Helen, who is fully aware of the rapes and the police warnings, decides she can only get to her room in time by taking the path. Halfway to the dorm, Helen is pulled off the path and into the bushes where she is forced to have sexual intercourse with a man wielding no weapon but strong enough to keep his hand over Helen's mouth. Was Helen raped? Would you, as DA, prosecute?

SCENARIO #3

Ted and Charlie were out celebrating Ted's 21st birthday. After several birthday shots at various bars in town, Charlie suggested they go visit Connie—a local prostitute. Connie answered their knock on her door, but told them she was not working this evening since she had just finished an exceptionally busy weekend. Charlie said that since it was Ted's birthday she should at least allow them to come in for a drink or to do a quick line of coke. Connie let the two in her apartment, joined them in sharing some cocaine, then told them to leave. Charlie and Ted said they would leave right after she came across with a birthday lay. Connie refused, but Charlie pushed her onto the sofa, stripped off her clothes, and despite her physical and verbal protestation, forced her to have sexual intercourse. Ted then took his turn, but at this point Connie put up no resistance and simply told them to both get out as soon as Ted had finished. Charlie tossed $50 (twice the amount Connie charged Charlie on his last visit with her) onto the table and they both left the apartment. Was Connie raped? By Ted? By Charlie? Would you, as DA, prosecute? Ted? Charlie?

Source: Reprinted with the permission of Colleen Fitzpatrick.

Legal Precedents

One of the most powerful uses of analogies is found in the law. This is in the form of a **precedent**—that is, a case used to apply to similar cases or claimed to be similar in some key respect. The use of a precedent can have a definitive effect on an argument, positively or negatively. Being able to convincingly argue a precedent can transform the law. Failing to do so has stymied even the best of us. A case is often applied to other, similar, cases, though there may be crucial differences. Let's see how a case can act as a precedent.

Potential Precedents

Anyone who has told their parents that they should be subjected to the same set of rules that are applied to their brothers and sisters (e.g., "Joe got to stay out until 3 A.M., why can't I?") has argued by precedent. When we argue using a precedent we are employing an analogy. We are implicitly asserting that there are sufficient similarities to allow for the principle of the one (the precedent-setting case) to apply to the situation at hand. The question is how this is done.

To block the use of a precedent—to break the analogy—point out the key differences between the two cases, so the earlier decision cannot be applied. If there are no significant differences, perhaps there are extenuating circumstances that should be factored in to weaken the analogy. Alternatively you could search for *another* analogous case that would counter the analogy in question. This is something like having a battle of analogies that support different conclusions.

A previous analogous case that has become law is called a *precedent*. Earlier decisions that set precedents may be favorable or unfavorable to a later case, depending on the position argued. Lawyers often have to deal with such analogies (potential precedents). They must either prove that an earlier case is analogous or that the differences are so great it doesn't apply. Whether or not the earlier case acts as a precedent is a matter of similarities or differences. Analyzing potential precedents proceeds as follows:

Potential Legal Precedent

1. *Research*. Study the case being litigated. Seek out the details of the case and determine what legal issues exist.
2. *Examine potential precedents*. Find cases that are similar. Find potential precedents that (a) have strong similarities to show applicability and (b) have rulings favorable or useful to the current case.
3. *Show the analogy holds*. Show that the strength of similarities merits the application of the principle from the precedent to the present case. The lawyer can then assert that this new case warrants the same decision.

The Law and Analogies

Presenting Case	Case in Question (Note Key Elements)
↓	↓
Analogous cases (Potential precedents)	Similar earlier cases with an acceptable decision
↓	↓
Legal principle	Decision from earlier cases
↓	↓
Application	Draw a similar legal principle to presenting case.
↓	↓
Assertion	Decision Applies To Presenting Case

Group or Individual Exercise

The 2 Live Crew Case

Let us look at a U.S. Supreme Court case where both sides drew from precedents to support their arguments. *Acuff-Rose Music, Inc.* v. *Campbell* that centers on a 2 Live Crew version (parody?) of Roy Orbison's song, "Oh, Pretty Woman." Acuff-Rose sued The 2 Live Crew (the members and its record company) for copyright infringement and interfering with potential profits. The 2 Live Crew argued their "parody" was protected under the doctrine of "fair use."

The case went all the way to the U.S. Supreme Court. Following is a key excerpt from the opinion. (You can access the entire opinion on the Internet.)

Campbell v. Acuff-Rose Music

Excerpt from the Opinion of the U.S. Supreme Court

The germ of parody lies in the definition of the Greek *parodeia*, . . . as "a song sung alongside another." Modern dictionaries accordingly describe a parody as a "literary or artistic work that imitates the characteristic style of an author or a work for comic effect or ridicule," or as a "composition in prose or verse in which the characteristic turns of thought and phrase in an author or class of authors are imitated in such a way as to make them appear ridiculous." . . .

[T]he nub of the definitions, and the heart of any parodist's claim to quote from existing material, is the use of some elements of a prior author's composition to create a new one that, at least in part, comments on that author's works.

Parody needs to mimic an original to make its point, and so has some claim to use the creation of its victim's (or collective victims') imagination, whereas satire can stand on its own two feet and so requires justification for the very act of borrowing.

Here, the District Court held that 2 Live Crew's "Pretty Woman" contains parody, commenting on and criticizing the original work, whatever it may have to say about society at large.

As the District Court remarked, the words of 2 Live Crew's song copy the original's first line, but then "quickly degenerate into a play on words, substituting predictable lyrics with shocking ones . . . [that] derisively demonstrate how bland and banal the Orbison song seems to them."

That the 2 Live Crew song "was clearly intended to ridicule the white bread original" and "reminds us that sexual congress with nameless streetwalkers is not necessarily the stuff of romance and is not necessarily without its consequences. The singers (there are several) have the same thing on their minds as did the lonely man with the nasal voice, but here there is no hint of wine and roses." Although the majority below had difficulty discerning any criticism of the original in 2 Live Crew's song, it assumed for purposes of its opinion that there was some.

We have less difficulty in finding that critical element in 2 Live Crew's song than the Court of Appeals did, although having found it we will not take the further step of evaluating its quality. The threshold question when fair use is raised in defense of parody is whether a parodic character may reasonably be perceived.

Whether, going beyond that, parody is in good taste or bad does not and should not matter to fair use . . . cf. *Yankee Publishing Inc. v. News America Publishing, Inc.,* ("First Amendment protections do not apply only to those who speak clearly, whose jokes are funny, and whose parodies succeed").

While we might not assign a high rank to the parodic element here, we think it fair to say that 2 Live Crew's song reasonably could be perceived as commenting on the original or criticizing it, to some degree. 2 Live Crew juxtaposes the romantic musings of a man whose fantasy comes true, with degrading taunts, a bawdy demand for sex, and a sigh of relief from paternal responsibility.

The later words can be taken as a comment on the naiveté of the original of an earlier day, as a rejection of its sentiment that ignores the ugliness of street life and the debasement that it signifies. It is this joinder of reference and ridicule that marks off the author's choice of parody from the other types of comment and criticism that traditionally have had a claim to fair use protection as transformative works.

Parody presents a difficult case. Parody's humor, or in any event its comment, necessarily springs from recognizable allusion to its object through distorted imitation. Its art lies in the tension between a known original and its parodic twin. When parody takes aim at a particular original work, the parody must be able to "conjure up" at least enough of that original to make the object of its critical wit recognizable. . . . Using some characteristic features cannot be avoided.

It is true, of course, that 2 Live Crew copied the characteristic opening bass riff (or musical phrase) of the original, and true that the words of the first line copy the Orbison lyrics. But if quotation of the opening riff and the first line may be said to go to the "heart" of the original, the heart is also what most readily conjures up the song for parody, and it is the heart at which parody takes aim.

Copying does not become excessive in relation to parodic purpose merely because the portion taken was the original's heart. If 2 Live Crew had copied a significantly less memorable part of the original, it is difficult to see how its parodic character would have come through.

This is not, of course, to say that anyone who calls himself a parodist can skim the cream and get away scot free. In parody, as in news reporting, . . . context is everything, and the question of fairness asks what else the parodist did besides go to the heart of the original.

It is significant that 2 Live Crew not only copied the first line of the original, but thereafter departed markedly from the Orbison lyrics for its own ends. 2 Live Crew not only copied the bass riff and repeated it, but also produced otherwise distinctive sounds, interposing "scraper" noise, overlaying the music with solos in different keys, and altering the drum beat.

Suffice it to say here that, as to the lyrics, we think . . . that "no more was taken than necessary," . . . [Moreover] there was no evidence that a potential rap market was harmed in any way by 2 Live Crew's parody, rap version. The fact that 2 Live Crew's parody sold as part of a collection of rap songs says very little about the parody's effect on a market for a rap version of the original, either of the music alone or of the music with its lyrics.

We therefore reverse the judgment of the Court of Appeals and remand for further proceedings consistent with this opinion.

Exercises

Part One

1. Set out Justice Souter's key argument (in the reading above) that affirmed that The 2 Live Crew's version "Pretty Woman" was allowable as a parody under the fair use law.

2. Discuss how the Court compared the two songs and reasoned that The 2 live Crew song "Pretty Woman" was a parody of "Oh Pretty Woman."

3. You have been hired by the producers of a new film *La Casa Is Blanca*. It is an updated and stylized version of *Casablanca*, the film classic, but is now set in Mexico in the early 1980s. The movie features a dashing, handsome Latino helping refugees escape the repressive conditions in Guatemala and Nicaragua. The producers of *Casablanca* are unhappy. They argue that this new film is *not* a parody. Rather, it is a story of heroism and romance with some similarities to the original *Casablanca*. Discuss the issue and concerns you will face in getting *La Casa Is Blanca* released.

4. In two to three paragraphs respond to Dan Gilmore, who says,

   Cultural works and inventions don't spring from an utter vacuum. They are the product of other people's ideas and works. Practically every melodic theme in music comes from older works, for example.

   Snow White was in the public domain before Disney got around to using her to make money. Victor Hugo must be spinning in his grave at the way Disney has turned the *Hunchback of Notre Dame* into a ridiculous cartoon—but Disney can do this, can create new ways to look at cultural icons, because the public domain exists. ("Copyright Tempest over '*The Wind Done Gone*,'" Siliconvalley.com, 24 Apr 2001)

5. Write two to three paragraphs on the effectiveness of comparing a mail thief's sentence of having to wear a sandwich board with a confession written on it to having to wear a red letter "A" for adultery on one's dress (in the novel *The Scarlet Letter* by Nathaniel Hawthorne):

SAN FRANCISCO—Shaming defendants with Scarlet Letter–style punishments passed muster Monday with a federal appeals panel that upheld a mail thief's sentence to wear a sign outside a post office stating: "I stole mail. This is my punishment." One member of the 9th U.S. Circuit Court of Appeals panel, Judge Michael Daly Hawkins, dissented, stating public humiliation or shame "has no proper place in our system of justice." . . . He said the sandwich board sentence would turn the defendant into a modern day Hester Prynne, the character in Nathaniel Hawthorne's "The Scarlet Letter" who was forced to wear an "A" on her dress identifying her as an adulterer.

In Monday's decision, a 9th Circuit panel voted 2–1 to uphold Shawn Gementera's 2003 sentence of two months in jail and eight hours of pacing in front of a post office wearing a sandwich board sign with "I stole mail" emblazoned on it.

Judge Diarmuid O'Scannlain wrote that Gementera's punishment was not a "stand-alone condition intended solely to humiliate, but rather a comprehensive set of provisions that expose the defendant to social disapprobation, but that also then provide an opportunity for Gementera to repair his relationship with society." Visiting Judge Eugene E. Siler of the 6th Circuit in Cincinnati joined O'Scannlain in rejecting an Eighth Amendment challenge to the shaming sanction as cruel. (Pamela A. MacLean, "Mail Thief Ordered to Wear Stamp of Humiliation," *Daily Journal,* 10 Aug 2004)

8. The *Campbell* v. *Acuff-Rose Music* decision may apply to a later case. The novel *The Wind Done Gone,* a takeoff (parody?) on *Gone with the Wind* faced a similar challenge. The novel is a retelling of the 1936 saga *Gone With the Wind* from the perspective of a slave, a half-sister of Scarlett O'Hara. The estate of Margaret Mitchell, author of *Gone With the Wind,* sued on the grounds that the book violated copyright protections. What aspects of the decision by the Supreme Court in the "Oh Pretty Woman" case may be useful for either the prosecution or defense in setting out their case? Share two to three ideas.

Part Two

The case of *Cassim* v. *Allstate* centers on a couple whose troubles started with an arson fire that badly damaged their home. Things got more and more convoluted with their insurance company, Allstate, with the lawsuit dragging on for years. The use of an analogy by the Cassims' lawyer put the case into a tailspin, with an appeal by Allstate resulting in a reversal of an award from the lower court ruling. Read about the case and then decide if the analogy sinks the case against Allstate. Set out the reasons for your decision.

Is Analogy Misconduct? 2nd DCA Thought So

Peter Blumberg

San Francisco Daily Journal May 5, 2004

SAN FRANCISCO—Plaintiff's attorney Ian Herzog came up with just the analogy to win over jurors in a hard-fought insurance dispute when Allstate accused his clients of misrepresenting losses in a home fire. In his closing argument at the 33-day trial in 1999, the Santa Monica lawyer contended his client's behavior was no different than jurors getting permission from the judge to collect full pay from their employers on days when they were excused from the courthouse early.

Little did Herzog know that after Los Angeles Superior Court Judge Harold Cherness permitted the analogy over Allstate's objection, it would still come back to haunt him. On appeal, Allstate persuaded the 2nd District Court of Appeal (DCA), on a 2–1 vote, to wipe out the $10 million award Herzog won from the jury, saying that his closing argument amounted to prejudicial misconduct.

But during oral argument Tuesday before the California Supreme Court, Chief Justice Ronald George put Allstate's lawyer in the hot seat, pressing him to explain exactly what Herzog did wrong. "Is this just really the sort of inventive analogy that counsel often engage in and courts countenance?" George asked. "In terms of overall consequence, aren't we talking about relatively few words in a pretty lengthy argument?" The 2nd DCA's ruling in July 2002 raised the hackles of the plaintiff's bar because trial judges usually give attorneys broad rhetorical leeway in closing arguments, and appellate courts rarely second-guess them. Consumer Attorneys of California has filed an amicus brief on Herzog's behalf.

Herzog's battle with Allstate dates back more than 13 years, when clients Fareed and Rashida Cassim first filed a claim with the insurance giant after arson badly damaged the Palmdale home they bought in 1989. Allstate's refusal to pay out as much as the Cassims demanded grew into a full-fledged war, culminating in two lengthy trials and half a dozen appeals.

When it was over, Allstate accused the financially strapped Cassims of committing the arson and then inflating their losses to defraud the company. After the Cassims went into bankruptcy, lost their home and accused their insurer of bad faith, the jury came back with an award that vindicated the couple. The total judgment was $9.8 million, which included $1.7 million apiece to compensate husband and wife, $5 million in punitive damages and $1.2 million in attorney fees.

In a closing argument that covers 130 pages of the trial transcript, Herzog spent about two pages framing his analogy. Herzog likened Allstate's allegation of intentional misrepresentation on the part of the Cassims to jurors getting fired "because you misrepresented about you being on jury duty on certain days and you got paid when you really weren't."

Cherness overruled an objection by Allstate, but the 2nd DCA's majority concluded the analogy poisoned the entire trial by making jurors think that Cherness himself approved of fudging the truth as the Cassims had allegedly done. "Here, in a case where fraud in an insurance claim was a primary issue in the case, counsel for plaintiff went right to the fact that the jurors had been essentially cheating their employers," Justice Aurelio Munoz wrote. "When counsel made reference to the fact that some of the jurors might be accused of cheating there was no question he was letting jurors know that the court had no objections to the procedure."

Herzog opened Tuesday's argument by asserting that his innocent "innuendo" had been badly misunderstood. Herzog said that contrary to condoning cheating, he was pointing out that the Cassims believed it was appropriate to "reconstruct" receipts that they hadn't actually kept, just as jurors must have thought it was appropriate to do whatever the judge instructed as far as claiming credit at work for jury duty. "We want jurors to bring their experience with them, to apply their common sense," he told the high court. "I don't think jurors thought they were doing anything wrong because they were just doing what the judge told them was OK."

Allstate's attorney, Peter Abrahams, of Encino, countered that Herzog's argument put jurors in "an impossible position" because the analogy implied judicial approval for insurance fraud. It's never pleasant to accuse opposing counsel of misconduct," he said. "I think that in this case, serious misconduct occurred." . . .

Source: Copyright 2004 *Daily Journal* Corp. Reprinted with permission.

Going Out into the World

CHAPTER EIGHT

Desire and Illusion:
Analyzing Advertising

And where do our sages get the idea that people must have normal, virtuous desires? What made them imagine that people must necessarily wish what is sensible and advantageous?
——FYODOR DOSTOYEVSKY *Notes from the Underground*

There is a scene in the movie *Purple Rose of Cairo* where Cecilia, the film's protagonist, has gone to see the same movie for the third or fourth time. She seems mesmerized by it. The fantasy she is watching is much more pleasant than life with her abusive husband or her job as a waitress. Much to her surprise, Tom Baxter, one of the characters on the screen, sees her in the audience and steps out of the movie and into real life. Cecilia's life then takes quite a different turn, and she faces more choices than she ever imagined. Her life is transformed as she comes to exert much more control over the direction of her life. Sadder but wiser at the end, Cecilia comes to see both the seduction and the limitations of desire and illusion.

Advertising, like the fantasy life Cecilia found so entrancing in *Purple Rose of Cairo*, frequently offers us an idealized world. This is a world filled with perfectly charming people having a great time. Their lives are free of disease. Their sexuality is untroubled by fear of AIDS or other sexually transmitted diseases—except in the new romantic advertisements for herpes medication, where the infected people are still frolicking on the beach or snuggling in a canoe. Their marriages are strong, not tenuous. Their relationships are loving, not indifferent or even violent. Their children are wonderful—not obnoxious or ill mannered. Their neighborhoods are a dream world of well-manicured lawns and not war zones of drugs, violence, poverty, or decay. Who wants to have the ideal character step out of the ad and into our lives? It would be far better to step out of our lives and into the ad. That's exactly what sucks us in. An ad for Princess Cruises encapsulates this desire in two words: *"Escape completely."*

It would be quite remarkable to find someone unfamiliar with advertising. Ads are on the outside and inside of buses. They are pasted on billboards, painted on buildings and, at times, written across the sky and are placed in the movies we watch. They are part of our cultural landscape. Given their ubiquity, we need tools to deal with all the ads we come across. In this chapter we examine various aspects of advertising—such as assumptions, fallacious reasoning, power and influence, and structural components (color, symbol, images, visual and verbal messages). We will also look at related issues—such as the lifestyle idealized in ads, the winner/loser mentality, sexuality and gender, for-profit versus nonprofit advertising, public service ads, and the question of censorship.

Reading the Society from Ads

Advertising offers us a parallel universe; through ads we gain insight into our society and discover prevalent norms, stereotypes, and folk wisdom. Ads teach us that: Men are chefs, women are cooks, men mow lawns, women clean house, men show boys how to use power tools, women show girls how to use household appliances, both mothers and fathers tuck children into bed, more men than women drive their children to school, only mothers rub cold medicine onto children's chests, men like to drink beer with lots of other men, women like to drink coffee with one or two other women, both men and women go to bars to meet people, phone calls are good things to get, women are worried about spots on glassware and are often troubled by vaginal yeast, men do not notice grease on their tools and occasionally struggle with impotence, both men and women suffer from hemorrhoids, diarrhea, and acid indigestion, both men and women enjoy using credit cards, and people of all walks of life are becoming victims of identity theft.

We are a society of extremes. There is a wealth of opportunities and an array of things to make our lives easier. And yet there is sorrow and need around us. This results in longing and desire. We yearn for more than we get—and what we get is not enough. Advertisers know this. Ads attempt to soothe our spiritual hunger problem and help us find a way to connect with those around us. Look, for example, at the slogan for Disneyland: "The happiest place on earth."

Michael Parenti points out that consumption is no longer a means for life; it's a meaning for life. Don't buy pepsi—"Join the Pepsi Generation." Don't buy this or that brand of cigarettes—"Come to Where the Flavor Is." Don't try to figure out how one shampoo is better than another—"It's not just about the hair. It's about how you feel" (Le Metric). It certainly is about how you feel—and how to get what you want. As an ad for Toyota Solarus puts it: *Do unto you as you would have others do unto you.*" This encourages us to put our wants ahead of others' needs and self-interest above altruism.

We don't have to feel needy, desperate, or lonely—there's a community for us, if we just buy a ticket (the product) and come on in. As an ad for American Express says, "STYLE. You either have it or you apply for it." Such invitations abound. For instance, "The grape varieties in Chandon require bright sun, cool mornings and

You Tell Me Department

Are We Driven by Greed or Altruism?

Watch how ads can bring out the worst in us—or the best in us. It's a mixed bag. And one of our tasks is to see what's there in the bag that advertising creates.

One criticism of ads is that "if you take the underlying messages of all the ads we're exposed to, they are remarkably consistent in the values they promote. And if you built a society based on those values, it would be a pretty self-centered, materialistic, live-for-the-moment, hedonistic, hyper-competitive sicko freak show society. Which is pretty much what we've got." (Jelly Helms, www.thisisdrew.com, 24 Oct 2003)

On the other hand, many ads *do* affirm noteworthy traits, as we see in the Nike ad called "Scary House," where two children go up to what appears to be a "haunted" house and the boy goads the girl to push the doorbell. As the door literally falls open, the girl transforms into an adult runner who races home—resuming her girl-child form as she enters the door. These words remain: "You're faster than you think." (See *www.methodstudios.com*). Granted you run faster thanks to Nike shoes—but the message is also that you were able to beat-it out of there, that you didn't give up, or succumb to whatever scares you.

You tell me: How much of advertising plays into self-centeredness or greed—and how much recognizes and furthers positive human qualities? Can you cite examples of each?

Spring showers. We find these conditions are also excellent for most varieties of humans. Come to Chandon and you will see." Look also at the advertising slogan for Norwegian cruise line: "It's different out here." It's different in here too. No longer do we need fancy cloth napkins to feel special. We may not be rich, but we can "elevate every meal" with the "everyday elegance" of a Vanity Fair paper napkin.

🔲 Assumptions

Contemporary ads bear little resemblance to ads of the past. Those today are more subtle, sophisticated, and at an artistic level rarely achieved in earlier decades. They assume a language of discourse and engage the audience in ways that were previously unimaginable. And they routinely make assumptions about consumers' needs, desires, fears, and prejudices. We see this in an ad for Utah tourism: "Never go anywhere without your topographic map, your compass and *your restaurant guide*" (my emphasis).

One broad area of assumptions has to do with the way people live—and want to live. As Kathleen Hall Jamieson and Karlyn Kohrs Campbell point out: "People in ads have spacious kitchens, large lawns, expensive appliances, cars; they travel worldwide. Ads take for granted that the audience routinely buys soaps, deodorants, makeup, and cologne, and that the audience is not making a decision about whether to buy the product but rather is deciding which brand to buy" (*Interplay of Influence: News, Advertising, Politics, and the Mass Media*). They also have cell phones, nice cars, and beautifully manicured nails. It is a world where affluence is taken for granted and where buying now is preferable to buying later.

Exercises

1. Pacy Markman of the advertising agency Zimmerman and Markman says, "good advertising always makes the client uncomfortable. If you are completely comfortable, it is a sign you are just talking to yourself" (quoted by Gary Wolf, *Wired* magazine, Sep 2004). Find three ads that you think are examples of innovative advertising—ads that stand out from the rest.

2. John Berger argues that ads focus more on social relations than products, with envy being particularly important. He says,

   Publicity is about social relations, not objects. Its promise is not of pleasure, but of happiness: happiness as judged from the outside by others. The happiness of being envied is glamour. The spectator-buyer is meant to envy herself as she will become if she buys the product. She is meant to imagine herself transformed by the product into an object of envy for others, an envy which will then justify her loving herself. (See Robert Goldman, *Reading Ads Socially*)

   Answer these questions:
   a. Do you think Berger is right to think ads promise us *happiness*, not pleasure? Can you cite some examples for or against this claim?
   b. Using a collection of ads (at least five ads), make a case for or against Berger's thesis that envy is what ads are addressing in us.

2. In what ways does advertising play on our emotions? Illustrate your position with four to five ads to support your claims. Be sure to attach your ads.

3. How pervasive is patriotism in advertising? Find at least *four* ads that play on our sense of patriotism, using national symbols (like the bald eagle, national monuments, famous historical figures, military heroes, the flag) in order to hook us. Be sure to attach your ads.

4. Jamieson and Campbell note that "avenging guardians of the social order" inhabit the world of ads. These are the nosy neighbors, the socially superior guests who comment on spots, sweat-rings, dandruff, and dust. What is their *political* significance? Do they keep us from looking at bigger issues or are they helpful figures? See if you can find an ad with an "avenging guardian" in it.

5. Michael F. Jacobson once argued for a ban on alcohol ads. He argued:

   Despite industry's claims that ads are not targeted at heavy drinkers or youths, the Coors Lite ad tells viewers to drink "beer after beer and don't hold back . . . turn it loose." . . . Anheuser-Busch uses actor-athletes to show viewers that Bud Lite will bring out their best. . . . The overall effect of the ads is to glamorize alcohol and foster the notion that drinking is the key to achieving personal goals. ("A Ban on Alcohol Ads Would Aid Society," *The Mass Media: Opposing Viewpoints*, David L. Bender and Bruno Leone, eds.)

   Test Jacobson's claim: Try to determine if alcohol ads target a younger audience and/or an audience of heavy drinkers. Attach examples to support your position for or against his claim.

▦ The Use of Fallacies to Persuade

Many ads honestly convey what the products can or should do for the consumer. Some ads imply the product will transform our lives and open the door to a more desirable lifestyle or social contacts. Some involve the use of fallacies to persuade. The key fallacies found in ads are: Ad populum, ad verecundiam, accent, bifurcation, and equivocation. Let's look at some examples.

Key Fallacies in Ads

1. **Ad Populum (Appeal to the Masses/Patriotism):** This fallacy occurs when an ad appeals to the masses, patriotism, or elitism (snob appeal) to sell a product. For example:

   "America's Number One Pizza." (Pizza Hut)
   "Billions and billions served." (McDonald's)
   "The world's favorite airline." (British Airlines)
   "Move ahead in luxury." (Esteem)

2. **Ad Verecundiam (Improper Appeal to Authority):** This fallacy occurs when an ad uses the testimony of a public figure or celebrity (unqualified as an expert on the subject) as a tool of persuasion, rather than citing relevant evidence. For example:

   "Cindy Crawford. Choices." (Omega watch ad)
   "Just do it." (Lance Armstrong as a boxer, Andre Agassi as a shortstop, and Randy Johnson as a bowler in a Nike ad).
   "12 horas de aliento fresco para celebrar todo el dia. Myrka Dellanos, Periodista." (Colgate toothpaste ad).

3. **Accent:** This fallacy occurs when the ad emphasizes a word or phrase (verbally or visually) in such a way as to distort the meaning of a passage, leading to an incorrect conclusion being drawn. For example:

   "Try All-Pro Protein Shake and Lose weight in seven days! Results may vary." (All-Pro ad)
   "FREE GIFT of a travel-size mascara when you purchase $50 worth of cosmetics." (Sign in department store)

4. **Bifurcation:** This fallacy occurs when the ad attempts to persuade by presenting only two choices when, in fact, other options could be considered in decision making. For example:

   "If you're not ahead, you're out." (NIIT ad)
   "Read this or die." (Ad for nutritional research booklet)

You Tell Me Department

Does Mudslinging Work?

Political ads that use negative campaigning—alias mudslinging and dirty tricks—can backfire. While often making impact, no-holds-barred ads can turn off, even repel, voters. And yet they seem to surface during elections. Take the case of what has been called a "nasty" race between two incumbents in Dallas, Texas. Consider these two ads:

> **AD #1** (Ad for Martin Frost): Images of the World Trade Center in flames fill the television screen. A somber voice warns that a local Republican House member is soft on airline security. Stark words appear: "Protect America. Say No to Pete Sessions."

> **AD #2** (Ad for Pete Sessions): A plane is flying overhead and a shoulder-fired missile, presumably hoisted by a terrorist, points at it. The announcer warns of "unspeakable horror, shattered lives."

And that's not all. As reported by Janet Hook:

> **From the Sessions campaign:** Fliers in Dallas mailboxes accuse Frost of consorting with a former child molester and more. The child molestation issue was raised by the Sessions campaign after it

learned that a Frost fundraiser was to feature singer Peter Yarrow of Peter, Paul and Mary fame. In 1970, Yarrow was convicted of indecent behavior with a 14-year-old. Frost canceled Yarrow's appearance. But he objected that a mailing by Sessions implied Frost was a child molester. Sessions denied the charge, while arguing it was "very germane" to note that Frost had asked a person with Yarrow's record for political help.

> **From the Frost campaign:** The Frost campaign accused Sessions of "indecent exposure" because he was a streaker while in college. Justin Kitsch, Frost's spokesman, said it was legitimate to call attention to the prank because it illustrated Sessions' hypocrisy, given that he had been a vocal critic of singer Janet Jackson's exposing her breast during the 2004 Super Bowl halftime show. Sessions called it "a new low" for Frost to broach the streaking incident, but it has caught voters' attention. When Sessions addressed a Lion's Club meeting in Dallas, members teased him by having someone streak through the meeting. (Janet Hook, "Slinging Mud and Whatever Else They Can Afford," *Los Angeles Times*, 29 Oct 2004)

You tell me: To what degree is negative advertising an effective technique?

---

5. **Equivocation:** This fallacy occurs when an ad creates ambiguity by using a word or phrase with a double meaning resulting in an incorrect conclusion being drawn. For example:

"Canadian Club. Join it." (Canadian Club Whiskey ad)
"Shake up Your Night." (Baccardi rum ad)

Group or Individual Exercise

Examine the copy for an ad *against* Kathy Angerer that was paid for by the Michigan Republican State Committee. Study this example of negative campaigning and discuss how effective you think this ad is likely to be:

Kathy Angerer Won't Help Law Enforcement Prevent Terrorism.

Kathy Angerer is out of the mainstream . . . and she is not on our side.

Law enforcement needs information to track terrorists and prevent potential attacks in the United States.

But Kathy Angerer opposes an anti-terrorism database for our law enforcement agencies.

Kathy Angerer is a friend of the ACLU [American Civil Liberties Union], and she won't do what is needed to protect us.

A central database would allow law enforcement agencies to have instant access to critical information and assist in tracking persons that may be planning terror attacks on our homeland.

But Kathy Angerer will pull the plug on this critical effort to stop terrorism.

And we just can't trust her to protect Michigan.

▩ The Power of Advertising

Advertising does more than push a product. It also tells stories, dispenses social commentary, offers advice, and makes us laugh. More important, ads claim that our problems can be solved—through something we can purchase. They also tell us that we deserve to be indulged; we have the right to pamper ourselves, given our stressful lives. These, then, are four key things to convey to the consumer:

Four Tricks of Effective Advertising

1. *Shame* → You've got a problem!
2. *Optimism* → Your problem can be solved.
3. *Solution* → You need *this* product.
4. *Rationale* → You have a right to solve your problem, whatever the cost.

Example of the Fab Four in Action

How to Sell "Delirious" Perfume to a Skunk:

1. *Shame* → You have body odor!
2. *Optimism* → Perfume helps!
3. *Solution* → *Delirious* perfume works wonders!
4. *Rationale* → You have the right to smell nice!

Let's see how these Fab Four work in an advertisement for *Dove Promises* chocolates. The ad presents an attractive blonde woman curled up on a couch holding a chocolate egg while children are running in the grass in the background. The ad copy (text) says:

The Hunt is Over.

Introducing Dove Promises for Easter, to give or get by the basketful.
Eggs of rich and lingering chocolate, each wrapped in an uplifting message.
An indulgence too rich to be rushed.

You can't hurry Dove.

Off to the side is another chocolate egg beside its wrapper. The wrapper contains the "uplifting" message, "Family gatherings will bring Easter joy." Sounds very appealing! It is this dream that we buy with Dove chocolates—and the transformation is thereby achieved. By the way, did you notice the last line, "You can't hurry Dove"? This mines the depths of our collective memory, calling up the song "You Can't Hurry Love" by the Supremes. The connection between *Dove* and *Love,* at least in some brains, is solidified. Basically the equation is: **Need → Desire.** Our *need* for love is translated in the *desire* for a Dove chocolate. When wants, needs, and desires come together, it makes for the perfect advertisement.

An interesting variation of the need/desire theme is found in a two-page Jockey (underwear) ad featuring a beautiful lake or seaside on the left page. Superimposed over this idyllic scene are the words *"are you comfortable being."*

The ad cuts to the quick, the bare bones of our very existence. "Are you comfortable being" calls us to do a little soul-searching. Being *what*? Being *ourselves*? Being *together*? Those who want to share a personal story can go to www.jockey.com and spill the beans. The rest of us yearn for a tale to tell, a "being" to be, and someone to be it with. This *desire* drives us. The Web site, then, allows us to *enter* the Jockey ad world and participate.

Group or Individual Exercise

There are two opposing views of advertising set out below. Read them both and decide which one is most defensible. Then *set out your defense.*

VIEW #1: Ads are Damaging to Society

The world of mass advertising teaches us that want and frustration are caused by our own deficiencies. The goods are within easy reach, before our very eyes in dazzling abundance, available not only to the rich but to millions of ordinary citizens. Those unable to partake of this cornucopia [wealth] have only themselves to blame. If you cannot afford to buy these things, goes the implicit message, the failure is yours and not the system's. The advertisement of consumer wares, then, is also an advertisement for a whole capitalist system. (Michael Parenti, "Advertising Has a Negative Effect on Society," in Neal Bernard, ed., *Mass Media: Opposing Viewpoints*)

VIEW #2: Ads Do Not Harm the Society

It is considered appropriate to attempt to persuade. This tells us something concerning our general assumptions about human nature. For why would we permit wanton persuasion to plague a helpless public? Simply because we believe that the public is not helpless, but armed with reason, guiles, and a certain savvy about how to make one's way in the market. If we are sometimes open to persuasion about frivolous products and services, it may be that we have become sufficiently jaded by affluence to let ourselves be seduced by clearly self-interested sources. (Clifford Christians, Kim Rotzoll, and Mark Fackler, "Advertising Has Little Effect on Society," in Neal Bernard, ed., *Mass Media: Opposing Viewpoints*)

Sin and Seduction in Advertising

There is a seductive quality to ads, something magical that draws us in. We hope that buying this product really *can* transform our lives, overcome our inadequacies, and make us feel better. The fact that envy, lust (desire), and greed are three of the Seven Deadly Sins does not escape the minds of ad agencies. Some ads play on the sinfulness of eating *those* chocolates, buying *this* car, owning *that* sound system. For example, a Chantelle bra ad has a close up of a breast in a lacy bra, with the copy "Our honeybee embroidery provokes ideas that are anything but sweet. It may be a detail but it's a Chantelle." By mixing idea and fantasy, such ads can open up a parallel universe where almost anything seems possible.

Advertising offers an *escape* from the troubles of life and the tragedies in the world around us. Some of it is creative and inspiring, some constitutes social commentary, and some is amusing and entertaining. It also has power. Dr. Alan Blum, head of the antismoking group "Doctors Ought to Care," calls for more vigilance. "The problem is we think we're smarter than the cigarette industry and that's not true." With large corporations behind them, advertising agencies can do product testing and determine which images and icons have the greatest appeal. They build upon the collective belief in the folktales and myths that have become part of our culture.

Advertising has complex artistic and mythological components. Look at the cast of characters. There are winners and losers, villains and heroes, knights in shining armor and damsels in distress, the flabby and the physically fit, the social nerds and the social butterflies, and so on. Ads both shape and are shaped by our cultural landscape.

Even if we don't recognize the logo, our brains file it away, ready to bring it to the surface with a little prodding. As it says on the Energizer Bunny Web site: "In addition to serving as one of advertising's most recognizable symbols, the Energizer Bunny® has become a cultural icon, serving as a symbol of longevity, perseverance and determination." This is only a slight exaggeration. The very fact you can go to the Web site and send off friendly Energizer Bunny e-mails speaks volumes. (See www.energizer.com/bunny.)

FORGET THE DOG.
MAKE SURE
YOU DON'T EAT
YOUR HOMEWORK.

Come to a school where the main courses are the main courses. At Culinard, we can teach you to be a four-star chef in just 21 months. You'll slice. You'll dice. And when you get out, you'll be able to find your way around the vegetable market and the job market.

CULINARD
Develop a Taste for Success

FIGURE 8.1
As this ad suggests, some stacks of homework are tastier than others. Even college administrators recognize this!

You Tell Me Department

Can We Gain Perspective over Time?

Let's look at an example of an ad from 1927. The ad is for Aunt Jemima Pancake Flour. We see a large stack of pancakes in the foreground with a smiling black woman looking out from the door of a cabin. The ad says:

> American women are noted throughout the world for their constant interest in new recipes. And today an old-time recipe has won more users than any other ever recorded. Down on the old plantation, Aunt Jemima refused to reveal to a soul the secret of those light fragrant pancakes which she baked for her master and his guests. No other cook could match their flavor. No one could learn her "knack" of mixing ingredients. Today millions of women in all parts of the United States are making tender, golden-brown cakes just like Aunt Jemima's own. Only once, long after her master's death, did Aunt Jemima reveal her recipe. It is still a secret—no cookbook gives it. Her special flours cannot be bought in stores today. But her own ingredients, proportioned just as she used them, come *ready-mixed* in Aunt Jemima Pancake Flour.

What ads do you see today that, 40 years from now, will provoke the same kind of reaction as we have to this ad?

▦ Analyzing Ads

Most of us do not know what it would be like without advertising. Still we ought not be oblivious to its power. By setting out the structural components of ads and looking at the ways ads both reflect and influence the society, we can better understand what is behind that power.

When examining ads, we need to look at a range of concerns set out in the checklist below.

Advertising Checklist

1. **Values:** What values and beliefs does the ad convey? According to the ad, what's the best use of our time and money?
2. **Story:** If you think of the ad as telling a story, what story does it tell?
3. **Verbal Message:** Study the verbal message. What exactly does the ad say?
4. **Visual Message:** Study the visual message. What images, symbols, characters, and use of color or black and white are employed? How do the visual components work together? What is the visual impact of the ad?
5. **Fallacies:** Watch for the fallacy of accent. Are certain words emphasized (made larger, repeated, set off by a different color) in order to mislead us? Watch for the fallacies of ad verecundiam, equivocation, and ad populum.
6. **Exaggeration:** Watch for false promises and exaggerated claims. What exactly does the ad claim the product will do? What is the nature of the guarantee? Do you see any puffery?
7. **Stereotypes:** Watch for stereotypes around gender, race, age, nationality, religion, economic class, and so on. Look at the various roles (such as dominant or authority roles, heroes and villains, helper roles, nurturer roles) presented in the ad.
8. **Diversity:** Who populates the ad? Does the ad reflect the society we live in? Note how gender, race, age, and economic class are represented and whether they typify the world we live in.
9. **Power and Class:** Watch for assumptions around power, class, and patterns of consumption. What is the economic class of those in the ad? Who are the targeted users of the product?
10. **Political Agenda:** Be aware of political or social messages. Ads often relay a set of attitudes in the verbal or visual message. See if there's a hidden agenda in the advertisement.
11. **Prescriptions:** Look at the lifestyle presented. Ask yourself, Do I live (or want to live) like this; if so, at what cost? And what is the societal impact of this lifestyle?

12. **Sexuality:** Look at the ways that sexuality, sexual orientation, sexual violence, and intimacy are handled, including turning men or women into sexual objects or using sexuality to sell the product.
13. **What Is Left Unsaid:** What is missing from this ad? Will using the product transform my life, as the ad suggests? Look at the ways ads overlook societal or personal problems that may affect using the product.

Exercises

1. What are your two to three favorite ads (or ads you find appealing)? Describe each ad in as much detail as you can, explaining why you find it appealing. The ad need not be a current one.

2. What ad do you dislike the most (or find boring, nondescript)? Describe it in as much detail as you can and then explain where they fall short of your expectations. The ad need not be a current one.

3. Below are some classic advertising slogans. Select the five *most powerful* and the five *least memorable*. Say why.
   a. "You're faster than you think." (Nike)
   b. "I can't believe I ate the whole thing!" (Alka Selzer)
   c. "Our office is your office." (FedEx Kinko's)
   d. "Don't leave home without it." (American Express)
   e. "The True Definition of Luxury. Yours." (Acura)
   f. "Only your hairdresser knows for sure." (Clairol)
   g. "M'm m'm good." (Campbell's soup)
   h. "Betcha can't eat just one." (Lays Potato Chips)
   i. "Fly the friendly skies of United." (United Airlines)
   j. "Reach out and touch someone." (ATT)
   k. "The skin you love to touch" (Woodbury soap)
   l. "Even your best friends won't tell you." (Listerine mouthwash)
   m. "Got milk?" (California Milk Processor Board)
   n. "Be all that you can be." (U.S. Army)
   o. "Nothin' says lovin' like something from the oven." (Pillsbury)
   p. "Why ask why, try Bud dry." (Budweiser)
   q. "Diamonds are forever." (DeBeer)
   r. "Finger-lickin' good." (Kentucky Fried Chicken)
   s. "All you add is love" (Ralston Purina Pet Food)
   t. "Don't dream it. Drive it!" (Jaguar)
   u. "We bring good things to life." (General Electric)
   v. "The first time is never the best." (Campari)
   w. "Have it your way." (Burger King)
   x. "Coke is life!" (Coca Cola)
   y. "We try harder" (Avis)

4. Examine the Sega ad (see Figure 8.2). Answer the following:
   a. How does this ad work to persuade the viewer?
   b. Discuss the use of humor in the ad's effectiveness.

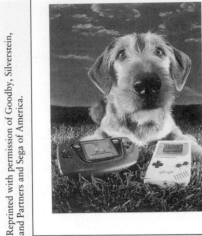

FIGURE 8.2
Sega of America (dog) Wit and humor are powerful tools—and not just in advertising.

Reprinted with permission of Goodby, Silverstein, and Partners and Sega of America.

Power and Class

On the surface, ads may appear to be "just" about trying to sell some product. Not so says Robert Goldman who thinks ads are inherently political and never ideologically impartial. In *Reading Ads Socially*, Goldman sets out these four warnings about advertising:

Goldman's Assumptions in Advertising

First Assumption:	You should think *this* about *that:* → *Ads always have some political agenda.*
Second Assumption:	$$ = Buy, buy: → *Ads assume people are paid for their labor.*
Third Assumption:	Poverty doesn't exist: → *Ads hide class differences.*
Fourth Assumption:	Need it? Buy it and find happiness: → *Ads imply we can purchase happiness, a meaningful life, and an ideal world.*

Exercises

1. Select two or three ads and see if Goldman's points apply. Examine the ads for political agenda, assumptions, class differences, and presumptions about what money can buy. Be sure to attach the ads.

2. Focusing on *one* type of product (e.g., cars, clothes, alcohol) compare an ad targeting the wealthy to an ad targeting the working class. Go into detail on what you find that reflects economic class differences in our society.

3. Find *one* ad that supports creative director Luke Sullivan's assertion that *simple = good:*

   Sullivan explained that consumers are too busy, and sometimes too skeptical, to fall for a long, complicated, cluttered advertisement. "Go to the airport and watch somebody read a magazine," he said. "Take your client with you. The average reader will gloss over ads that are droll or complex, but simple ads will get attention," he said. "People don't have time to slow down to decode our clever ideas," he said. . . . "Simple ads are more memorable, effective, emotional and believable, and are easier for the consumer to notice," Sullivan said. And, as the old Volkswagen Beetle ads demonstrate, simple ads can be timeless. "Simple makes a good ad great," Sullivan said. (Dave Simanoff, " 'Tis a Gift to Be Simple in Advertising, Sullivan Says," *The Bay Business Journal (Tampa Bay),* 21 Aug. 1998).

4. Discuss the text (ad copy) of the ads below and note what audience is being targeted.
   a. **Ad #1** (for Citibank)
      What do you love? Your kids? Your dog? Garden lawn gnomes? At Citi, we offer tools that let you focus on what matters most to you. Ongoing financial check-ups help make the most of your money today and in the future. While Citi Identify Theft Solutions and Fraud Protection help you hold on to what's yours. Oh yeah, and this bumper sticker. Enjoy writing your own statement this month. Visit us at citi.com.
   b. **Ad #2** (for "A Diamond is Forever," Leddel International)
      Your left hand says "we." Your right hand says "me." Your left hand loves candlelight. Your right hand loves the spotlight. Your left hand rocks the cradle. Your right hand rules the world. Women of the world, raise your right hand. (Two-page ad: photo of woman on one page, text and photos of four diamond rings on the other).

5. Discuss the text (ad copy) of the ads below that target members of the upper class (you could compare them with ones aimed at those in the lower-middle or working class):

   a. **Ad #1** (for International K9 Personalized Training and Sales)
   This dog can immobilize an intruder in 2.3 seconds. He's also Jack's pony [photo of toddler with large German Shepherd]. Call today for free information on how to have the perfect dog. Dog Sales & Training, Executive Protection, Self Defense Education and Bodyguard Services.

   b. **Ad #2** (for Photo Stone)
   Because some Moments in Life Deserve to be Set in Stone. PhotoStone™ turns your treasured photographs into distinctive works of art without altering the original prints! Printed on beautiful travertine marble, each piece is unique—just like the captured moment it reflects. Visit our Web site or call for an order form today and celebrate those special moments for a lifetime.

   c. **Ad #3** (for Quark Monitoring Equipment)
   They may be your employees, but who do they really work for? Find out exactly where your employees' loyalties lie with one of our high-performance hidden cameras. This fully functional clock radio features a pinhole camera that records a crystal clear video image in virtually any lighting condition. Plus, it allows you to monitor office and home activities in real-time or record them for later viewing. We offer similar systems with covert faces convincingly disguised as smoke detectors, fire sprinklers, picture frames and many other home and office items. CIA tested. CEO approved.

▩ The Verbal Message

In addition to watching for assumptions, we need to be able to dismantle the ad itself. This dismantling, or deconstructing, of ads involves these steps:

1. Analyzing the verbal and visual messages of ads.
2. Examining the role of images, symbols, and the use of color to create an effect.

Let us look at these aspects, starting with the **verbal message.** This is created by the use of words and music, when sound is an option. This is the text of the ad—it is often called the "ad copy." Some ads rely almost completely on words to create impact. This could center on a character (e.g., Smokey the Bear), a memorable slogan (e.g., "Just do it"), a testimonial (e.g., Nicole Kidman for Chanel), or a commentary on events or issues in the society (e.g., Benneton's ad series on global issues). When it works, the effect can be dynamite. Look, for instance, at the ad for *Time* magazine and how it relies on the verbal message for its effect. (See Figure 8.3.)

It is often hard to forget advertising slogans. Just think how many you can list off the top of your head ("Coke is life," "We are driven," "It takes a lickin' and

You Tell Me Department

Are you Ready for a Market in Human Eggs?

You can find almost anything on the Web. Need extra cash? What about being an egg or sperm donor? Try an Internet search. Let's look at an ad for human ova:

> Dream Donations has one goal—to be able to help our recipients fulfill their dream of creating a family. We will accomplish this by providing a unique combination of full service Web-based programs and an outstanding level of personal care and attention. We enable recipients to review our large database of donors and select an ideal candidate from the privacy of their own home.

> The staff at Dream Donations wants to guide you through what we hope will be a joyful and fulfilling experience. We invite all recipients and donors to meet us for a personal interview and information session. We personally want to know you so we can provide you with all the support and care you will need while fulfilling your dreams of having a family. (DreamDonations, www.dreamdonations.com)

You tell me: Why do you think there is no suggestion of cost? Applying Goldman's four assumptions, what might we conclude about this ad?

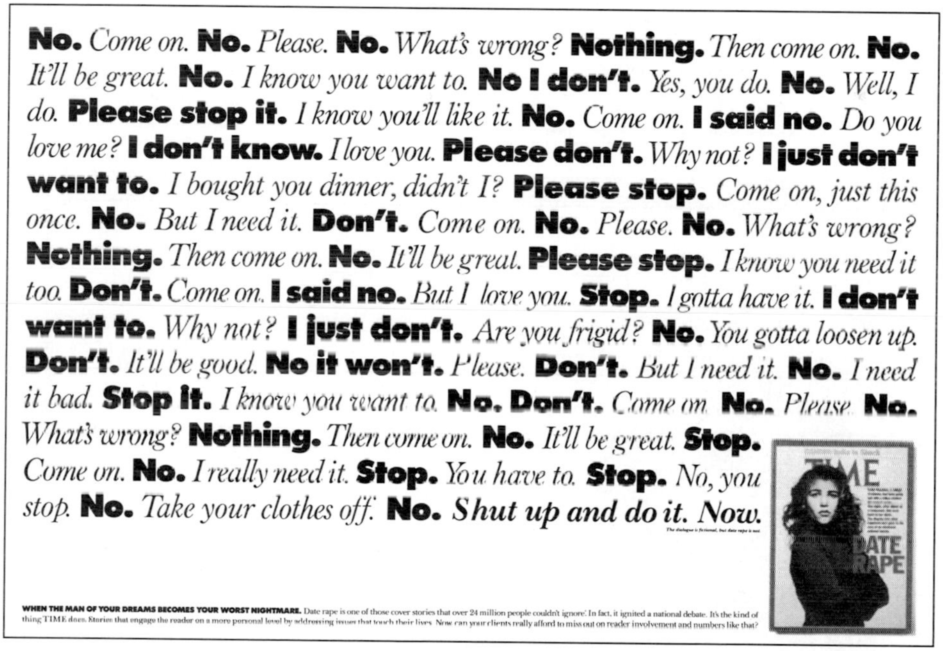

Fallon McElligott. Art Director—Bob Brihn. Copywriter—Phil Hamft. Creative Director—Phil Hanft. Reprinted with permission.

No. *Come on.* **No.** *Please.* **No.** *What's wrong?* **Nothing.** *Then come on.* **No.** *It'll be great.* **No.** *I know you want to.* **No I don't.** *Yes, you do.* **No.** *Well, I do.* **Please stop it.** *I know you'll like it.* **No.** *Come on.* **I said no.** *Do you love me?* **I don't know.** *I love you.* **Please don't.** *Why not?* **I just don't want to.** *I bought you dinner, didn't I?* **Please stop.** *Come on, just this once.* **No.** *But I need it.* **Don't.** *Come on.* **No.** *Please.* **No.** *What's wrong?* **Nothing.** *Then come on.* **No.** *It'll be great.* **Please stop.** *I know you need it too.* **Don't.** *Come on.* **I said no.** *But I love you.* **Stop.** *I gotta have it.* **I don't want to.** *Why not?* **I just don't.** *Are you frigid?* **No.** *You gotta loosen up.* **Don't.** *It'll be good.* **No it won't.** *Please.* **Don't.** *But I need it.* **No.** *I need it bad.* **Stop It.** *I know you want to.* **No. Don't.** *Come on.* **No.** *Please.* **No.** *What's wrong?* **Nothing.** *Then come on.* **No.** *It'll be great.* **Stop.** *Come on.* **No.** *I really need it.* **Stop.** *You have to.* **Stop.** *No, you stop.* **No.** *Take your clothes off.* **No. Shut up and do it. Now.**

WHEN THE MAN OF YOUR DREAMS BECOMES YOUR WORST NIGHTMARE. Date rape is one of those cover stories that over 24 million people couldn't ignore. In fact, it ignited a national debate. It's the kind of thing TIME does. Stories that engage the reader on a more personal level by addressing issues that touch their lives. Now, can your clients really afford to miss out on reader involvement and numbers like that?

FIGURE 8.3

For some ads the verbal message is prominent.

keeps on tickin," etc.). These are often the heart of the verbal message. However, any part of the ad copy counts—including the promises, the discussion of the product, repetition of words or phrases, background dialogue, or buzzwords placed around the product.

We can also note when ads use humor or witticisms to become memorable. For instance, an award-winning ad produced for Cyanamid for a product to kill corn nematodes (corn worms). These ads had prominent verbal messages, such as: "NEMATODES LIVE UNDERGROUND. THIS <u>SHORTENS</u> THEIR *TRIP TO HELL*" and "NEMATODES EAT *FAR LESS* CORN WHEN THEY'RE DEAD" and "IT STOPS NEMATODES FROM EATING YOUR CORN. *ACTUALLY,* IT STOPS THEM FROM DOING MUCH OF <u>ANYTHING</u>."

Exercises

1. Discuss the verbal message for this ad for Boeing aircraft:

   WHERE THE SECRETS TO THE UNIVERSE ARE KEPT
   The answers do not lie in technology. Technology is but a stepping stone to the next question. We are fueled by a restless imagination; an endless sense of wonder that has brought our world closer together and led us ever deeper into space. What we've discovered along the way is that all the secrets to the universe are contained in the boundless reaches of the human mind.

2. Look at the way the Harley Davidson ad (Figure 8.4) addresses its audience. Set out your thoughts on the verbal and visual messages:

FIGURE 8.4   The target audience makes all the difference.

3. Find at least *three* examples of what you would consider great, memorable, or persuasive ad copy (verbal message). Note why you think they are persuasive.

The Power of Language: Analyzing Ads for Their Verbal Message

If you remember the slogan, the ad scored a linguistic victory. Think of these: Dodge's "Grab Life by the Horns," Nike's "Just Do It," and Gatorade's "Is It in You?" When combined with catchy or dramatic use of music, the words can be carved onto the inside of our skulls.

In decoding an ad, the verbal message is as important as the visual elements. The ad tells a story. Some ads focus on the product's quality. Some ads list the key features of the product. Some contrast the competition. Some take an indirect route and focus on the benefits of ownership such as a particular lifestyle or a membership into a desirable group. Look at the fine details of the story, assess the use of language, watch for the angle and the intended audience.

One advertising classic is the "Got Milk?" campaign. (See Figures 8.5 to 8.8). The use of the simple, two-word question has few parallels. It was a sensation from the moment the first ad aired. It combines a powerful visual message with a snappy, easy to remember line. And it has spawned a host of imitators—"Got mulch?" "Got Termites?" "Got Land?" "Got Faith?" and so on. The spin-offs do not detract from the iconic status of the Got Milk ads—they just reinforce them.

In assessing the verbal message, try a *word study.* Carefully read the ad, watching for key words that emphasize the product's appeal or hook the consumer. Think of words like "sex," "love," "rich," "mysterious," "flavor," "fun," "pleasure," and "satisfying." When repeated over and over, the word or phrase acts like a drum beat, punctuating the ad's message.

Assessing the Verbal Message—Watch for these:

1. Characteristics or qualities of the product.
2. Consequences of owning the product.
3. Benefits of this product over rival products.
4. Comments about the lifestyle that goes with the product.
5. Use of humor, diversionary tactics, or insults.
6. Social commentary that may or may not relate to the product.
7. Use of statistics or statistical claims touting the benefits of the product.
8. The testimony of ordinary people, so-called experts, or celebrities.
9. Use of pseudoscientific terms to give weight to the ad's claims.
10. Fallacies of reasoning or questionable claims.

Reprinted with the permission of Lowe Worldwide Inc. As for National Fluid Milk Processor Promotion Board.

FIGURE 8.5
The Got Milk?
ads transformed
the industry and
continue to spawn
imitators.

Great for dunking.

My friends told
me, "T-Mac, you're
gonna be big some day."
Must've been the milk.
About 15% of your
height is added as a
teen and the calcium and
vitamin D can help.
Will drinking a cool glass
of milk make you the
hottest scorer in town?
Hey, it couldn't hurt.

got milk?

Focusing on the product was once the norm. Just look at the Studebaker ad (Fig. 8.9 on page 354). This ad is a good example of presenting the product, rather than a mood, a lifestyle, or a political commentary. This ad shows *only* a car; there are no people, plants, or animals populating the ad. There's only an empty Studebaker. At that time (the 1950s) ad agencies probably thought it would be easier for consumers to put *themselves* in the picture, rather than look at someone else in that Studebaker. Using a nuts-and-bolts approach, the ad states some key specifics about the car and informs us that this is a "Common-Sense" car. The phrase "Common-Sense" is repeated five times, driving the point into readers' brains. "Gosh, it makes Common-Sense for me to go buy a Studebaker!" This technique of repetition has continued to the present. As a critical thinker, you might ask yourself if such repetition has the power to hook people in. Things have changed. Now we not want only the car; we want what the car will bring once we own it. This is not what we see in the Studebaker ad.

FIGURE 8.6

Exercises

1. Examine the Studebaker ad on page 354. Why do you think it makes a reference to the Volkswagen bug?

2. Do you think it works when an ad for one product refers to a rival product (the competition)? Give the argument for *and* against this approach.

3. Create text for an ad for the car of your dreams in which *no photo or description* of the car itself appears. Looking over the text of your ad (assume it's for the radio, then you don't have to worry about the visual message), explain (a) who is your targeted audience, (b) what you did to appeal to that audience, and (c) what verbal message you intended.

4. Looking at the ad copy below (for Evian water), state the similarities and differences with the Studebaker ad:

Figure 8.7

It takes more
than a hit single to
reach the top.

15% of adult height is added during teen years. So we
give our growing bones lots of calcium by drinking milk. How do
you suppose we reach all those high notes, anyway?

got milk?

What are the ingredients of beautiful?
A pinch of this? A dash of that?
It's all about what you put inside your body.
From the food you eat to the water you drink.
So, which is the fairest water of them all?
Every drop of Evian comes from a spring, deep in the heart of the Alps.
It's naturally filtered for over fifteen years through pristine glacial rock formations.
So it has a neutral pH balance and a unique blend of minerals, including calcium,
     magnesium and silica.
Which makes Evian the perfect recipe for youth and beauty.
So when you choose a bottled water to believe in, consider the source.
Evian. Our natural source of youth.

5. Select *one* of the following and write down your analysis of its verbal
   message, drawing from the elements listed above:

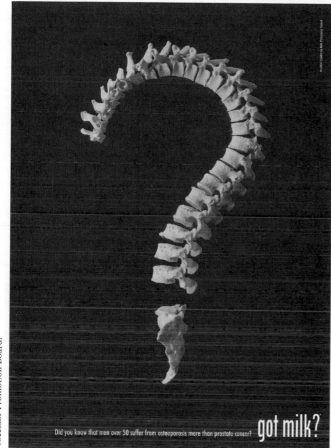

FIGURE 8.8
As you can see, this "Got Milk?" ad is quite different from the others in Figs. 8.5–8.7. Note how it relies on a strong visual message.

a. "Some people like to talk about their dreams. Others prefer to show them off. Price Pfister. Pfreshest Ideas in Pfaucets."

b. "Fat Free Jell-O Pudding Snacks. Because it's fat free and only has 100 calories. Because after one spoonful, you'll forget both those facts."

c. "Power begets power. **Lagerfeld.** A fragrance for men."

6. Study *one* of the following. Use the checklist to analyze the verbal message:

a. *Ad for Rolex watch:*

In the hearts of the truly great, **PERFECTION** is never achieved.

Only endlessly pursued.
When Haydn, Handel and Vivaldi put pen to paper, the voice they were writing to could have been none other than Cecilia Bartoli's. She's taken the most famous operas and made them national treasures. She's taken the most obscure operas and

FIGURE 8.9
Ads of the 50s testify to how much the world has changed. A pitch based on "common sense" is definitely a blast from the past! This ad focuses on the product, rather than a mood or lifestyle.

Why do we call the 1965 Studebaker the Common-Sense car?

Because it's built so mechanically sound a man with reasonable driving habits can drive it for years without a major repair. Common-Sense.

Because the body style doesn't change every year. So you save money when you buy it. You save money when you trade it. Common-Sense.

Because it's functionally sized at both front and rear, with a full-sized 6-passenger living room in the middle. You can park it in incredibly short spaces. Drive over inclines, bumps, and dips with plenty of clearance for heads, headroom for hats and legroom for legs. Common-Sense.

Because either one of its two great new engines will take you as far on a gallon of regular gas as a gallon of gas is meant to go. Possibly a little farther.

Mind you, there's another car you might consider Common-Sense, too. It doesn't change body style every year, either. Just improves its insides from time to time, as we do. But, it's much smaller than ours. So small, in fact, that . . .

. . . some people affectionately call it a bug. Including the people who make it.

made them famous. She's taken classic arias and redefined them, building them dramatically. As she continues to top "Best of Year" lists all around the world, her voice reminds us that perfection is an endless pursuit. Oyster Perpetual Lady-Date Just Pearlmaster. **ROLEX.**

b. Ad for Chevy Beretta GT:

The advantage of being in control.
Taking matters into your own hands is an idea you wholeheartedly embrace. It lets you do what you want, when you want—while having as much fun as you want. That's the idea behind rack-and-pinion steering.

   Rack-and-pinion steering acts like a two-way transmitter between you and the front wheels of your car. Turn the wheel and the pinion (a gear) at the end of the steering column moves over a bar called (you guessed it) a rack to point your wheels in the right direction. Your car responds instantly. Accurately.

Almost instinctively. It also sends the feel of the road back to you, letting you fine-tune your driving. That's what makes precision handling precise.

And, while nearly every Chevy we sell comes with the feel-good control of rack-and-pinion steering, including the Beretta GT, all of them come with the bottom-line value of a great Chevy price.

So try one, and take a turn for the better.

The Visual Message

We are a visual culture. We judge, buy, consume, or desire all sorts of things in terms of their visual appeal. Advertisers know this. We do not normally want to see things that are ugly or unpleasant, unless they are presented with humor. We want to see beauty and images of happiness, intimacy, and satisfaction. We like to see images of success, things working correctly, and problems being solved. Connected with these images are products. The goal is to get the consumer to link the two (the images and the products) together. This is a variation of the message in the movie *Field of Dreams:* "If you build it, they will come." In advertising, "If you buy it, they (all sorts of neat things) will come."

The desire is for much more than mere ownership. We yearn for what the product represents and the lifestyle that accompanies it. Ads used to focus almost entirely on the product itself, spelling out what it could do for us. For example, Pepsodent ads of the 50s and 60s ("You'll wonder where the yellow went . . . "), presented images of yellow teeth that were magically transformed into gleaming white jewels. The ad implied that yellow teeth were the only things standing in the way of being adored. Attaining such popularity was directly related to the use of the product.

Look at the Perrier ad (Figure 8.10 on page 356). This advertisement is effective because it is both visually striking and thought provoking. It plays with social stereotypes by showing a couple in an old pickup with empty Perrier bottles bouncing around in the truck bed, suggesting that Perrier is not just for rich people, but is something an ordinary guy and gal from the back roads of Texas would enjoy. The Perrier ad is clever, but not shocking. In contrast, some ads go for the jugular by creating jarring, even disturbing visual images. Clearly these are *not* intended to help us escape into a fantasy world. Rather, they use in-your-face advertising to take the consumer by surprise and create a kind of disequilibrium in their brains.

Benetton (clothing manufacturer) created an international furor with ads depicting illness, suffering, even death. These ads included such images as a bird drenched with oil, a dying AIDS patient, a prisoner on death row, and a man's torso with a tattoo on his left arm that says "HIV positive." The images are unsettling. They have nothing to do with the product (clothes). But they do make a political statement. They call up Robert Goldman's first assumption about the ideological aspect of ads.

FIGURE 8.10
Can you see how this ad for Perrier demonstrates the power of a visual message?

The Cast of Characters

One aspect of the visual message is the use of characters identified with the product (e.g., the Energizer Bunny, the Blue Man group, the Pillsbury Doughboy, Mr. Clean, Joe Camel, Jolly Green Giant, Mr. Peanut, and Aunt Jemima). Over time the characters take on mythic status and become cultural markers. More recent Energizer ads don't even have to show the bunny himself—just the shadow of the bunny carries the "Keep Going" message onward. It is assumed that the audience knows the character so well that a shadow can trigger a response.

Companies run risks when they attempt to update the characters, changing their appearance or "personalities." Will the consumer-public take kindly to the Pillsbury Doughboy losing his chubby form, Aunt Jemima flipping crepes instead of pancakes, or the Jolly Green Giant yearning to wear a red tie? Not necessarily.

Someone thinks about such questions. For instance, someone decided that Mr. Peanut needed a transformation. . . . "After decades of presenting Mr. Peanut, its venerable brand character, as a dignified dandy, meant to be timeless in his appeal, Planters is giving him a far more contemporary persona intended to better connect with consumers," reports popular culture scholar, Stuart Elliot. For that reason, we may be seeing Mr. Peanut shooting some hoops and showing off some moves on the dance floor instead of crossing his legs while holding a nice cane. It may sound minor, but Elliot notes that "much is at stake if shoppers reject the personality transplant. Disapproval could diminish the value of the character." ("Thoroughly Modern Mr. Peanut," *The New York Times*, 19 Mar 2004)

Evolution of an Ad Campaign

Who doesn't know the refrain "Only you can prevent forest fires"? The voice of Smokey the Bear lies embedded in the heads of millions. He appeared on the scene in the early 1950s and has been going strong since. This is the longest public service campaign in U.S. history. (See Figures 8.11 to 8.14.)

Smokey was created in 1944 by the Forestry Service. The "the" in Smokey the Bear evidently traces back to the songwriters of Smokey's anthem who needed a "the" to maintain the rhythm. The ad campaign's message remained unchanged until 2001, when it began to address the increasing number of wildfires in the nation's wild lands (see www.smokeybear.com). For other interesting historical tidbits go to the Web site (www.smokeybear.com).

FIGURE 8.11
Smokey is our friend—not a vicious bear! (1954)

FIGURE 8.12
After three decades, just spotting Smokey triggers the message in our brains ("Only *you* can prevent forest fires!").

Exercise

Let's face it, only an arsonist would not be moved by Smokey's warnings about the danger of forest fires and ways to help prevent wildfires. At this point, Smokey the Bear is as much a cultural icon as an advertising legend. Look at the different images of Smokey and the campaign messages on these few pages. *Answer the following questions:*

1. How has the image of Smokey changed over the years?

FIGURE 8.13
After four decades, Smokey has become part of the cultural fabric. A hat or mask jogs the brain.

2. What specific changes do you see in the ads themselves?

3. Which one or two ads do you consider most effective? List your reasons why.

4. The last two ads are very different—how do you account for that? Which of the two do you think would be most effective with these different age groups (pick *one*): mature adults, young adults, and children? Set out your reasons.

FIGURE 8.14
After five decades,
we only need to
see a postage-
stamp image of
the dear bear for
us to be reminded.
At this point,
Smokey has
achieved iconic
status.

Use of Color and Symbols

Some ads are in black and white and the strong lines are part of the visual message. Other ads rely on color to create a mood or call up associations. Many ads use patriotic symbols, such as flag motifs, eagles flying majestically across the page, and the Statue of Liberty, national memorials, or other historical monuments. Such symbols often reinforce the copy; for example, "America's number one pizza," or "The motor oil that Americans trust," linking loyalty to what we consume. They also make us feel safe, at home in a world that is not always safe or homey. However, appeals to patriotism in ads often exhibit the ad populum fallacy we studied in Chapter 4.

FIGURE 8.15
"Absolut country of Sweden vodka & logo, Absolut, Absolut bottle design and Absolut calligraphy are trademarks owned by V&S Vin & Sprit AB. © V&S Vin & Sprit AB."

Vivid colors and images can create unique and eye-catching ads, as with the ads for Absolut Vodka (Figures 8.15 to 8.17). These ads are not aimed at minors and the company has taken a strong stand against targeting those who are underage. The Absolut ads succeed because of their sophisticated, and at times even abstract, nature. They are closer to mental puzzles than sales pitches, as they challenge the limits of minimalism.

In granting permission for including these ads in this text, Seagrams & Sons, Inc., intend that they be used in conjunction with exercises for developing critical thinking skills. They are not presented here to condone, or even tolerate, the consumption of alcoholic beverages by minors. Rather, Seagrams & Sons, Inc., takes seriously the social responsibility to restrict Absolut advertising to people over 21 years of age.

FIGURE 8.16
Absolut country
of Sweden Vodka
& Logo, Absolut,
Absolut bottle
design and Abso-
lut Calligraphy
are Trademarks
owned by V&S
Vin & Sprit AB.
© V&S Vin &
Sprit AB.

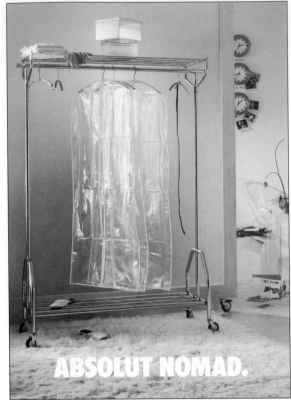

Under permission by V&S Vin & Sprit AB.

Exercises

1. Focusing on color, find three ads as follows: one that is particularly striking or appealing in terms of the use of color or visual images; one that is visually disturbing or unappealing; and, finally, one that is boring or visually ineffective. Briefly explain why you judged them as you did.

2. Collect five to six print ads for the same type of product (e.g., cigarettes, perfume, cars, watches, etc.). Be sure your ads are in color, not black and white. State: (a) which ad is most effective in its use of color, (b) what symbols, images, and themes are used, and (c) what the collection reveals about us as a society.

Embedded Advertising: Product Placement

Whereas ads of 20 or 30 years ago raved about the product, recent ads are more contextual. The product may be **embedded** within the lifestyle presented rather than subject to a hard sell. When they work, though, these ads can be very effective. No

You Tell Me Department

Move Over Marlboro Man?

Given the impact of anime on the West, perhaps the time of the samurai has come. Or maybe it's neither cowboy nor samurai—could today's hero be a warrior from *Lord of the Rings*? Or perhaps a mythic hybrid, like *Bat*man or *Spider*man or *Wolf*man? Around 10 years ago, the president of Tech. Marketing Inc. said of the power—of the Marlboro Man in cigarette advertising: "The mythical fight-ing man in our culture *is* a cowboy. He's our samurai. . . . You have to understand what smoking's all about. We as a society have abandoned tribal initi-ation rites, and cigarettes are a substitute" ("Uncle Sam Is No Match for the Marlboro Man," *The New York Times,* 27 Aug 1995).

You tell me: Is that still true? If you were tar-geting the under-30 market, what would you use as the "mythical fighting man"?

FIGURE 8.17 Absolut country of Sweden Vodka & Logo, Absolut, Absolut bottle de-sign and Absolut Calligraphy are Trademarks owned by V&S Vin & Sprit AB. © V&S Vin & Sprit AB.

mention is explicitly made about the product: We connect the dots. We "read" the copy and images of ads with a kind of familiarity and acceptance. The logo or the slogan sparks a chain of associations between the product and a parallel universe we'd like to inhabit.

It's hard to see a movie these days without being subjected to product placement—the product is incorporated into the lives of the characters on screen. Examples range from the Reeses Pieces candy in *ET* to the jaguar car in *Catwoman*. For the year 2004, Coke and Pepsi tied for the most product placements in movies (six each). Coke appeared in *Collateral, Man on Fire, Mean Girls, Resident Evil: Apocalypse, Sky Captain and the World of Tomorrow,* and *The Forgotten*. And Pepsi was seen in *50 First Dates, Alien vs. Predator, Barbershop 2, Dawn of the Dead, The Butterfly Effect,* and *You Got Served*. Nike and Motorola tied for second place, with each having five product placements in movies in 2004. (See www. brandchannel.com.)

Embedded ads can also be found in music. The number 1 and 2 songs of the week of August 23, 2004, mentioned products and 59 brands were mentioned 645 times in songs listed on the Billboard Top 20 chart in the first eight months of 2004. Hennessy cognac was cited 47 times in the songs that cracked the Billboard Top 20, making it the top brand mentioned. (See "The Art of Brand-Name Dropping," *Los Angeles Times,* 25 Aug 2004). Artists are also naming brands because they like the product, and corporations reap the benefits.

Winners and Losers in Advertising

Some ads suggest we need to deserve the product being advertised by being cool or attractive. This approach assumes we want to enter that parallel universe where people are having such a nice life—is this assumption unwarranted? The ads make the winner–loser demarcation clear, as a memorable ad campaign for Foster Farm chickens illustrates. Two chickens try to pass themselves off as Foster Farm chickens but telltale evidence (such as a half-eaten bag of French fries) gives them away. They are failures; rejects trying to be members of a club they can never join. We laugh—but the laughter masks the fear that, like the second-class chickens masquerading as the real thing, we too, might be pretending to be more than we are.

Ads sometimes exploit this fear by presenting "winners" or "losers" who may or may not succeed in spite of our assumptions. See the ads for Clarion and Kellogg's (Figures 8.18 and 8.19) for examples. Such ads tap into our fears. Why be a geek, when you can "strut your stuff"? Consider the mythology of the ad—its story and the images and symbols it employs to tell it. Assess the ad's overall effectiveness in relaying messages not only about the product, but also about how we ought to live.

Children and Advertising

Children are also invited to escape into a world that is more exciting than everyday reality. On the Barbie Web site (www.barbie.com) we find this greeting as we enter "Fairytopia™": "Our enchanted world will make you smile, Have fairy fun and stay awhile." Look also at the Kellogg's UK Web site (www.kelloggs.co.uk). Choosing the link to Coco Pops, you are greeted as a "junglefriend" and invited to help solve the mystery of the missing chocolate from the chocolate volcano that

FIGURE 8.18
Geek is not good.

just erupted. (See www.cocopops.co.uk.) Following the links, we arrive at the screen question. **Who Do You Feel Like Being Today?** The choices are:

BOY #1: "Hey Junglefriend today you'll be the Skater Dude."
BOY #2: "Hey Junglefriend today you'll be the Mad Bad Jungle King."
GIRL #1: "Hey Junglefriend today you'll be the Fresh and Funky Babe."
GIRL #2: "Hey Junglefriend today you'll be the Super Brain."

The two choices for boys are Skater Dude versus Mad Bad Jungle King (leisure versus leader). The two choices for girls are Fresh and Funky Babe versus Super Brain (cheering-companion versus intellectual). The selections tap into stereotypes and role models, raising questions about how ads can shape children's perceptions, values, and interests. Children are invited to "Join" the Coco Pops Junglefriend club—by filing in an e-mail address, passcode, and "identity." The Barbie Web site also asks children to supply their name, which is then incorporated into the subsequent links.

FIGURE 8.19
2 is a lucky
number: Consider
how the visual
and verbal
messages reinforce
one another here.

There's a new way to jump-start your healthy lifestyle. A leading university
has discovered that eating Kellogg's *Special K*® and Kellogg's *Smart Start*®
cereals can help you lose up to six pounds in just two weeks. Here's how:

Start with a serving of cereal and skim milk with fruit for breakfast.
Replace either lunch or dinner with the cereal meal.
Have a third meal as you normally would.
Snack on fruits and vegetables between meals.
In two weeks, strut your stuff.

Consult your physician before starting any diet or exercise program. A registered dietician can help you plan a healthy diet. Results may vary. Average weight loss 4.2 pounds.

Exercises

1. You want to study contemporary North American society. All you can use in your study are advertisements. Gather at least 10 ads across a range of products. On the basis of your study, what can you infer about this society?

2. Given the same batch of ads you collected in question 1 (or a new batch, if you are ambitious), what can you infer about societal attitudes about men?

3. Given the same batch of ads that you collected in question 1 (or a new batch, if you are ambitious), what can you infer about societal attitudes about women?

4. Gather five print ads on one theme (cosmetics, cars, cigarettes, shoes, toys, etc.). What patterns emerge from studying these ads? What overall message is there? Are there any aspects or messages that cause you concern? Go into detail.

5. Do a study of ads or product Web sites targeting children. Gather five print ads aimed at children or teenagers (specify which). What patterns emerge from studying these ads? Are there any aspects or messages that cause you concern? Go into detail.

CASE STUDY

Sexuality and Gender in Advertising

Freud wasn't the only one to realize how powerful the sex drive is and to what extent we identify our sense of self in terms of body image. There is room for exploitation in this. This is typical: "One Day Paint and Body" billboards in Los Angeles show a sexy woman in a swimsuit standing next to a car. The image of the sexy women triggers the fantasy that, with a nicely painted car, she (or someone equally as desirable) will be drawn to you. Only a new paint job separates you from finding such happiness, such pleasure.

Though the adage "sex sells" may seem passé, advertising can still evoke outrage. Take the Abercrombie and Fitch Christmas catalog of 2003. The 280-page catalog included photographs of nude or nearly nude models and, according to reports, "extolled the virtues of group sex" and "advocated orgies and group masturbation." Also: "An orgy can involve an unlimited quantity of potential lovers. Groups can be mixed-gender or same-sex, friendly or anonymous. A pleasant and super safe alternative to this is group masturbation," the ad goes on (*San Francisco Chronicle,* 3 Dec 2003). The catalog could only be sold to customers 18 years or older and was marked with this warning: "*Mature content.*"

This did not deter groups from launching consumer boycotts against what they called "soft porn." Hampton Carney, spokesperson for Abercrombie and Fitch, said the catalog is directed at college consumers, who understood its humor. "It was meant to be funny," he said. (*San Francisco Chronicle,* 3 Dec 2003). The company ended up pulling the catalog.

Ads with a Social or Political Theme

Given the potential to reach a wide audience, nonprofit groups often turn to ads. Politicians figured this out long ago, as we see in carefully orchestrated political campaigns. If we can sell people on a particular car or cell phone, we ought to be able to sell them on one aspiring politician over another. See for example these Web sites that provide surveys of political advertising over the years:

www.livingroomcandidate.movingimage.us
www.uiowa.edu/~commstud/resources/pol_ads.html
www.boondocksnet.com/gallery

Organized groups can reach the general public with a public service campaign. Let us look at ads that carry a social message. Examine the United States Campaign to Ban Landmines (UCSBL) ad. (See Fig. 8.20.) Groups concerned about

FIGURE 8.20
U.S. campaign to ban landmines.

social, political, or environmental causes regularly use ad campaigns to get their message across (see Fig. 8.21). Antismoking ad campaigns have been effective in persuading people to either stop or to avoid starting smoking. It would be valuable to compare antismoking ads to ads put out by the tobacco industry. R. J. Reynolds refused permission for inclusion of their ads in this textbook, given that the primary audience of this book is under the age of 21. Consequently, you won't see their ads in this book, but you can readily find cigarette advertising online. (See, for example, the Philip Morris Ad Archive, www.pmadarchive.com, *Adland*, www.ad-rag.com, and the Smithsonian Ad Archives, www.americanhistory.si.edu/ archives/d-7.htm.)

Exercises

1. Looking at the U.S. Campaign to Ban Landmines ad, discuss how effective you think it is. It doesn't matter if you agree with the political message— your task is to analyze effectiveness.

2. Pick a political or social issue that you care deeply about. Assume you are creating an ad for your side of the issue and your audience is radio listeners (so you do not need to do any visuals). Write (or create) an ad that would present your position and motivate a listener to act.

3. Study the following public service radio commercial:

PATRICK REYNOLDS: Do you know what's in cigarettes? I can tell you right now the answer is no. Because the last thing tobacco companies want is for you to know how many poisonous chemicals there are in cigarettes. And there are plenty. Stuff like formaldehyde, cyanide, in fact, some of the chemicals in cigarettes are so poisonous that it's illegal to dump them into landfills.

But apparently, tobacco companies think it's okay to dump them into our lungs. The worst thing is, they do it without telling you. Because you won't find a list of the chemicals anywhere on the pack or in their ads. I'm Patrick Reynolds. My grandfather founded the R. J. Reynolds tobacco company. That means my family's name is on the side of more than seven billion cigarette packs a year. Why am I telling you this? I want my family to be on the right side for a change.

ANNOUNCER: A message from the Massachusetts Department of Public Health.

4. Create a public service *radio* ad on any *one* of the following: Gang violence, substance abuse, animal rights, get out the vote, eating a balanced diet, helping children learn to read, being a companion to an elderly person, planting gardens to fight urban decay, sexual harassment, or date rape. Be sure to include a brief statement explaining what you hope to achieve in your ad. (This means you only have to create a text—suggesting musical accompaniment is optional).

Political Messages and Manipulation

The government also uses public service advertising. For example, it has recently provided warnings about terrorism (see examples on the Ad Council Web site, www.adcouncil.org). There were also warnings during the Cold War. In the 1950s schools had students doing bomb drills and hiding under school desks, as if by doing so they'd survive a nuclear attack. The U.S. Civil Defense Agency put out posters to "educate" (cynics would say "brainwash") citizens to prepare them for an atomic war.

One such example is a poster that pictured a little girl sitting at a desk with her head resting on her hands as if she were thinking to herself (see Figure 8.22). The question is: "What happens to us if the bomb drops?" The ad is directed to "Mummy," who is told that an atomic war bears some resemblance to natural phenomena. Specifically, "An atomic blast is something like a tornado, a fire and an explosion all rolled into one." Posted clearly in a boxed area is a list of "official disaster first-aid items," such as four triangular bandages, 12 sterile gauze pads, Castor oil eye drops, and two large emergency dressings, among other minor items to help address the (obviously minor!) wounds you'd get in an atomic blast.

This "public service" ad contains a number of unwarranted assumptions, and it rates as a form of misinformation intended to manipulate the audience. Perhaps most egregious is the implication that atomic war is survivable—the wounds will just need a little field dressing.

FIGURE 8.21
This public service ad from the American Lung Association dramatically raises concerns about air pollution.

Permission granted by the American Lung Association of Los Angeles County.

Exercises

1. Study the attempts to make the idea of atomic war palatable in the U.S. Civil Service ad "Mummy." (Fig. 8.22) Examine the visual message as well as the verbal message of the ad and how the two work together to create a powerful effect. Summarize your findings.

2. Thinking in terms of a radio program as the vehicle of communication, create a public service warning for any *one* of these:
   a. A Hanta virus outbreak in New Mexico and Arizona.
   b. E. coli in drinking water at Kendall Elementary School in Sumas, Washington.
   c. Risks of pesticide exposure from aerial spraying of crops outside Bakersfield.
   d. Salmonella-caused food poisoning due to presliced Roma tomatoes purchased at deli counters in gas stations in July 2004.

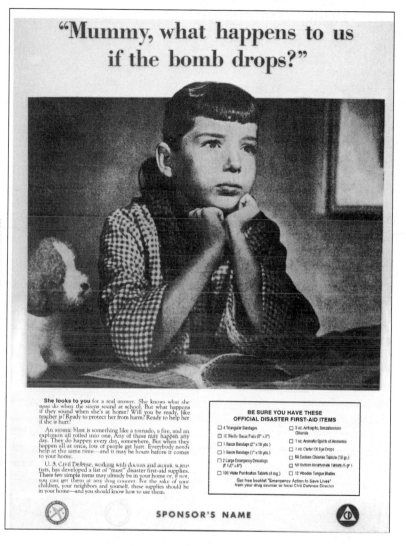

FIGURE 8.22
"Misinformation" campaigns are not new—just look at this public "service" ad from the 1950s.

3. Create a public service radio ad on *one* of these:
   a. Firestone tires that may lead to blowouts and rollovers on SUVs.
   b. A botched batch of designer heroin that can paralyze its users.
   c. A coffee allergy alert for undeclared peanuts or almonds in Neighbors Coffee of Oklahoma City.
   d. Anthrax hoaxes sent to abortion clinics.

4. Looking over your public service ad answer, state your targeted audience, your intended goal, and how your ad will be able to reach the intended audience.

The Global Dimension

Fighting Big Tobacco in Third World Nations

With North Americans cutting back on smoking, tobacco companies are looking to other nations.

Read Linda Brigden's argument and then answer the questions that follow.

Big Tobacco's Next Target: Women and Children in Poorer Countries Are Picking up the Cigarette Habit

Linda Waverley Brigden

From the pages of a recent edition of *Newsweek* shone the smiling face of a beautiful African woman. The caption for the two-page ad, in Swahili and English, read: "Kila mtu ana uzuri wake. No single institution has the copyright for BEAUTY. VIRGINIA SLIMS. Find Your Voice."

I found the ad particularly insidious in that, under the guise of promoting diverse standards of beauty, it encourages smoking by black African women. For cultural reasons, these women traditionally smoke much less than their North American sisters. In South Africa in particular, cultural prohibitions serve to maintain a female smoking rate of about 11%, compared to 42% for men. Aggressive advertising, designed to persuade women that to be modern and emancipated is to smoke, is one more problem the developing world does not need. Rather than empowering such women to find their own voice, such ads seek to ensnare them into dependency.

No part of the globe is immune. Tobacco advertising and sponsorship transcend borders. Even countries that have instituted bans on tobacco advertisements face ads beamed in via satellite. No wonder: The tobacco industry has a lot to gain. In China, 63% of adult males smoke, but only 3.8 % of women. Increasing the female rate by only a few percentage points will greatly increase the size of the world tobacco market.

Developing countries could learn a lot from Canada, recognized as a world leader in tobacco control. Our health warnings for cigarette packages have set a global precedent. Policies introduced here have set international standards and decreased tobacco use in Canada. . . .

Smoking is the leading preventable cause of death and disability among adults. In developing countries, it has reached epidemic proportions: These countries account for approximately 70% of global tobacco consumption. By the year 2025, they will also account for 70% of the anticipated 10 million annual tobacco-related deaths. Ominously, the age at which children in developing countries are smoking their first cigarettes continues to drop.

Tobacco poses a major challenge to sustainable development. Its impact can be felt not only on health-care budgets, but on trade, taxation, in social policy, as well as on power, gender and labour relations, at both the societal and household levels. And there's the environment: Tobacco cultivation depletes soil nutrients faster than most other crops and requires the heavy use of fertilizers and pesticides. The environmental costs of this fall mainly on the farmers and their communities. . . . While close to 70 per cent of the world's tobacco is now grown in developing countries, those farmers realize very little of the profits.

The tobacco companies predictably urged reasonable and appropriate action and supported policies that have been shown to do little to curb smoking among youths and adults. Many developing countries hesitate to curtail tobacco production. And they remain lukewarm toward control measures, because they reap significant revenue from excise taxes on cigarettes and the export of tobacco leaf. With the number of smokers in the developed world decreasing, the tobacco multinationals are now targeting developing countries.

North America has to address the situation. As negotiations begin on an international tobacco treaty, it won't be good enough for Canada to sit back and reflect smugly on the gains we've made to control tobacco use at home. North Americans contributed to the tobacco problems of developing countries. It's time to help find the solutions.

Reproduced, with permission, from IDRC Reports, the online magazine of Canada's International Development Research Centre (IDRC), and Linda Waverley, Executive Director of Research for International Tobacco Control (RITC), an international secretariat housed at IDRC in Ottawa, Canada. [This article was originally published in *The Globe and Mail* (Toronto).

CHAPTER NINE

Voices of the Community: The News Media

It's immaterial. You're dealing with different times. We hold our public leaders much more accountable for their personal lives and actions than they did then.

—DAVID ROBB, spokesperson for the drug enforcement chief, commenting on the fact that President George Washington grew marijuana, as noted by the *Los Angeles Daily Journal*

In one of the great existential comedies, *Groundhog Day*, a TV weatherman is locked in a time warp—a real-life Mobius strip—where he must relive the same day, Groundhog Day, over and over again. He comes to realize that, if nothing else can change, he can change himself. And so dawns his awareness that he, Phil Connors, is free to make something of his life. We watch his transformation from sarcastic and self-obsessed to a person who is compassionate, generous, and thoughtful.

As Phil changes, his approach to the news does as well. And what at the outset was seen as the tedious job of a weather report centered on a "rat" (groundhog) is thereby transformed. Phil starts to identify with the townspeople; his perception of the community tradition has much greater significance than mere filler on the nightly news. Once Phil becomes a participant, rather than a disinterested observer, he changes and his work as a reporter changes as well.

Journalists form an important antidote to social chaos by reporting and analyzing newsworthy material and placing it in an historical and political context. This is a vital role to play in our society. As journalist Frank Rich says, "A public estranged from the press is also disengaged from the institutions and newsmakers that journalists cover—and will understandably look outside the system for both information and leadership." The very fact, for instance, that we can experience world events via live coverage shows us how powerful the news media can be.

This power is not exercised in a vacuum, however. Sometimes governments seek to limit the power of the press. We cannot take the media for granted. We need to look at their role in bringing events into the public consciousness and the importance of sustaining a free press. Being able to freely inquire into events, express concerns, and raise questions is vital for a democracy. If the media uses its power wisely, institutions can change—and even crumble. By covering political corruption or digging out newsworthy items that may have gotten buried in an information glut, journalists do us all a great service.

The media subverts its own power, however, when it succumbs to corporate interests or political double-dealing. Laurie Garrett argues that, "what suffers in the atmosphere of immediacy is analysis. What suffers in this search for speed is depth. The media in the wealthy world are becoming increasingly simplistic, superficial, and celebrity-focused" (Anu Shah, "Corporate Influence in the Media," *Human Rights Issues,* www.globalissues.org). We can't assume that all the news that's fit to print will actually reach us. By developing our analytical skills around how the news media both selects and packages the news, we can be a more discerning audience.

Tabloid-Style Journalism

Of course you aren't one of those people who pick up the *National Enquirer* or another tabloid and flip through it as you stand in line waiting to buy your groceries. You probably missed the latest on the Batboy ("Batboy Nearly Killed in Serious Accident! Breaks Both Legs and Sprayed with Pesticides!!!"). And you weren't privy to the top stories in the *Weekly World News,* like "Half of Pentagon Generals Speak with a Lisp," "Wife Plans to Clone Rodney: DNA's on the Hanky," and "Aliens Using Email to Seduce Earth Women."

It's best not to fool oneself. Periodically mainstream ("legitimate") news media have been known to succumb to tabloid-style journalism too. Look, for instance, at the June 2, 2004, front page of *The New York Times.* In the lower left is a color photograph of "Trixie" (alias Stephanie Vowell), a buxom blonde in a short, low-cut pale pink flowered skintight sundress and wearing 7-inch platform high heels. And the article that accompanies this photo? You guessed it: It is an article on strippers in Las Vegas. The title of the article is, "A Life as a Live! Nude! Girl! Has a Few Strings Attached." We learn this about Trixie:

> Trixie is her stage name. To customers who demand to know her real name before they lay down a tip, she's Jennifer. But her real name is Stephanie—Stephanie Vowell, 32, a small-town Midwesterner, a self-described "big fake blonde" who stands 6-foot-3 in her 7-inch heels with a fake blond ponytail, fake eyelashes, fake green eyes, a fake tan, and fake breasts. (*The New York Times,* 2 Jun 2004)

Be on the watch for such "tabloidism." However entertaining such articles may be, the time devoted to the sensational or titillating is time lost on other, potentially much more significant, issues. Certainly getting to read about Trixie's life as a big fake blonde has its merits—most particularly a break from reading about war, politics, or terrorism. Nevertheless, by assigning this article front-page status, the newspaper blurs the boundary between "soft news" and "hard news".

Exercises

1. Do a study of the ways in which one of your local TV stations covers *one* of the following. Note how the coverage of the topic you selected reflects on our society.
   - Crime stories.
   - Human interest stories (ordinary people).
   - Treatment and coverage of celebrities.
   - National news.
   - International news.

2. Find an example of the news media at its *best*, showing how the press presents an issue in a fair and balanced manner or uses investigative journalism to unveil hypocrisy or corruption.

3. Find an example of the news media at its *worst*, showing how the press fails to give a well-rounded account of an event or forsakes professional integrity for shallow entertainment value.

4. Do a study of a newspaper or news station over two to three days and see if you can find any instances of *tabloidism*. That is, determine if the media outlet gives attention to any sensational or celebrity-driven news or non-news to the detriment of more pressing stories.

Group or Individual Exercise

Directions: Answer the following:

1. List 10 functions or types of coverage of news media (e.g., national news, sports, weather reports).

2. What is *one* area not currently included that might be newsworthy?

3. Then list five to six ways to expand the role of the news media (e.g., include vacation tips for travelers or areas of the city to avoid after dark).

4. List three to four ways the news media could better serve the community.

Watchdog Role of the Media

By turning its spotlight on an event, public figure, political issue, societal problem, or moral controversy, the press can relay relevant details and information to help us draw inferences as to what direction or policy would be preferable. This power of the press is not to be underestimated.

One important function of a newspaper is to serve as a watchdog over the institutions in the society. This is not without controversy. Here are two examples from 2004. First, when CBS's *60 Minutes* scheduled a program showing photos of abuse at Abu Ghraib prison in Iraq, Defense Department officials asked them to hold the story for a few weeks. CBS consented, but finally ran the story on May 6, 2004, bringing the situation to the public eye. Around the same time, Seymour Hirsh's article on Abu Ghraib came out in *The New Yorker*. This, effectively, made for a double-whammy on what became a scandal of global proportions.

The second recent example of the press as watchdog is *The New York Times* breaking the story about 380 tons of explosives missing from an Iraqi bunker ("Huge Cache of Explosives Vanished from Site in Iraq," 25 Oct 2004). Critics suggested this story was timed (like an "October surprise") to harm the Bush administration and negatively impact his chances for election. Supporters argued that it was an important news story, with potentially great impact.

Going back a little further we can see that it was due to the careful work of Carl Bernstein and Bob Woodward of the *Washington Post* that the Watergate story broke when it did—an event that precipitated Richard Nixon's resignation as president. The news media were also instrumental in keeping President Clinton's use of the presidential pardon before the public eye. Seymour Hirsh of *The New Yorker* and Richard Serrano of the *Los Angeles Times* have brought to light issues and concerns about the war on terrorism that might have been overlooked by less vigilant reporters.

Investigative journalists play vital roles in all sorts of areas—not just politics. For example, in the 80s and 90s Eileen Welsome of the *Albuquerque Tribune* exposed to the public the radiation experiments on American citizens by government scientists and doctors. Welsome's series of articles jolted the public into action and resulted in her getting a Pulitzer Prize. Subsequently, the federal government appointed a bioethics committee to study the experiments and President Clinton issued an apology to the research subjects.

Analyzing the Newspaper

Start by taking apart a newspaper or online news web site piece by piece. Look at it as a whole document and then look at the specific elements, so you get a sense of how it works.

Do a survey of news articles. Determine how many columns in the front section were by the staff reporters and how many were purchased from news syndicates like the Associated Press, Reuters, *Los Angeles Times*, *The New York Times*, and so forth. This shows us how many sources are used to supply the news. Watch for the newspaper's emphasis (local, regional, national, international) and the range (hard news, entertainment, human interest, self-help, community services, etc.) We are now ready to analyze the newspaper.

Sharpening Our Antennae

You pick up *The New York Times* and there on the front page is a photo of the Dalai Lama, the Buddhist leader of Tibet. You see his face quite clearly. It is in profile, with his right hand on the arm of a woman facing him. You see her less clearly, given that we see little more than the cheek of Rigoberta Menchu, Guatemalan Nobel laureate. The article's title is: "Nobel Winner Accused of Stretching the Truth." You may not know that the Dalai Lama received the Nobel Prize in 1989 and that Rigoberta Menchu received it in 1992. But you do recognize *his* face in the photo. As you read the article you discover that it is *she,* not he, accused of stretching the truth. The choice of the photograph, however, leaves a different impression.

Thanks to our heightened critical thinking powers, we are watching for such "errors," slips, misleading photos, and juxtapositions of image and text. This allows us to spot things that can go astray and lead to the wrong conclusion on the part of the reader.

Exercises

Study the front page of two to three newspapers for any given day (the *same* day) comparing and contrasting (1) the lead story of each paper, (2) the different news articles on each front page (note topic and title) and (3) the way the photographs, if any, complement or distract from the article(s).

Style and Content

One question to ask is what makes something newsworthy. How do newspapers inform us, while keeping us interested? There is a delicate balance: If the newspaper were dull or dry, the audience would be limited. But if we see a newspaper neglects newsworthy world and local events in favor of the unusual, the celebrity story, or the wrenching personal interest stories, it edges closer to a tabloid.

If we assume we'll find neutrality or objectivity in what we read, we are at risk of being manipulated by the media and their corporate sponsors. Read the news article for both style and content and study the way the article is presented.

You Tell Me Department

Who Said Photos Never Lie?

As Martha Stewart, home-decorating guru, was about to be released from federal prison, *Newsweek* magazine showed a little creative license. Anticipating a slimmed-down version of Martha after five months in prison, the *Newsweek* cover used an altered photograph passed off as an "illustration":

> Newsweek put Stewart's head on a model's body for a cover story that looks at how she will emerge from prison "thinner, wealthier, and ready for prime time." Assistant managing editor Lynn Staley says the photo won't mislead readers. Anybody who knows the (Stewart) story would know this particular picture was a "photo illustration," she says. Newsweek discloses its trick on Page 3 with the lines: "Cover: Photo illustration by Michael Elins . . . head shot by Marc Bryan-Brown." (Mark Memmett, "Is it Real? Or is it Martha?," *USA Today*, www.usatoday.com, 1 Mar 2005).

You tell me: Were *Newsweek's* actions unethical? Or does the label "illustration" take care of any obligations to readers?

Try to discern the author's thesis or personal slant. Note the types of evidence cited. Watch the use of quotes or expert testimony. Whenever you pick up a newspaper, survey the front page, reading each heading and subheading. Get an overview of the front section by seeing how much is world news versus state or local news and how much is timely (watch the date), versus attention-getting "non-news" (filler or human interest).

Checklist for Analyzing Style and Content

1. *Structure:* How is the article set out? Note where the thesis is presented and the way in which the author makes his or her case.
2. *Language:* Does the author use any loaded terms, technical terms, biased, or prejudicial language? Does the title reflect the focus of the article?
3. *Symbols and Images:* What sort of picture do you get from this article? Is the style forceful and hard-hitting, or is it subtle—even folksy? Try to characterize the approach.
4. *Analogies and Metaphors:* Does the author use a comparison to make a point? Analogies and metaphors can carry a great deal of weight, so watch for them.
5. *Use of Testimony or Expert Witnesses:* Any reliance on what others had to say about the issue? If so, how is the evidence introduced? Are those who give testimony or expert "advice" well qualified to be doing so? Note the credentials of those who are cited.
6. *Frame of Reference:* From what point of view is the article written? Does the author write from a personal, or subjective, perspective? On the subjective/objective scale, where would you place this article? Is it written in the first person, or from a neutral stance?
7. *Descriptive/Prescriptive:* How much does the author spend describing a state of affairs, going into detail on the specifics of the case? Does the author set out a position on what course of action *ought* to be taken?

8. *Cultural Baggage:* Is there evidence that this article is culturally embedded; that is, reflective of a certain time and place? How much does the author draw from the culture (social or political scene, music, art, literature, movies, TV, religion) within the article?

9. *Recognition of Audience:* Does the author write for a specialized, or learned, audience? Or is the article geared to anyone who can read? How much is presumed on the part of the reader by the author?

10. *Balance and Fairness:* What does the author include and/or exclude? Do we get both sides (when it would be appropriate for the author to provide them)? Is anything either included *or* omitted that shows shortsightedness or bias?

Exercises

1. Discuss any *two* of these headlines, using the checklist. Draw an inference about the main focus or "angle" of the article so titled:
   - Article headline: "Woman Who Sued Kennedy Smith Says She Is Haunted" (*Detroit Free Press,* 27 Aug 2004).
   - Article headline: "Good Hair Day for Hobbit Hunters" Sydney *(Australia) Morning Herald,* 28 Oct 2004).
   - Article headline: "Mother's Death Drove Woman to Law School" (*Daily Journal,* 7 Mar 2005).
   - Article headline: "Jackson, Tardy and Unkempt, Hears Boy's Testimony" (*The New York Times,* 11 Mar 2005).
   - Article headline: "New Jaw Grown on Patient's Back," (*BBC News World Edition,* 27 Aug 2004).
   - Article headline: "Because Caribou Don't Vote" (*Globe and Mail* [Toronto], 2 Aug 2001).

2. Discuss any *two* of these headlines, using the checklist. Draw an inference about the main focus or "angle" of the article so titled:
   - Article headline: "All That Secrecy Is Expensive," (*Wired* magazine, 27 Aug 2004).
   - Article headline: "The Joy of Filth," (*Globe and Mail* (Toronto), 27 Aug 2004).
   - Article headline: "Placer Judge Clarifies His Telling Jurors to Lie," (*Daily Journal,* 26 Aug 2004).
   - Article headline: "Bananas Could Power Aussie Homes," (*BBC News World Edition,* 27 Aug 2004)
   - Article headline: "Oreos Lead to Skunk's Downfall" (*Benton County Daily Record,* 8 Oct 2004).

3. Read the article on the border patrol's new weapon against smugglers and then answer the questions below:

The border patrol has decided to go nuclear against those who want to sneak barrels of mustard gas, bales of marijuana or bundles of bucks into the country. Starting early next week, U.S. Customs and Border Protection, or CBP, agents will start testing a nuclear scanning device, called a Pulsed Fast Neutron Analysis system (PDF), that will show a border agent the molecular construction of all materials in an 18-wheeler without the agent having to open the truck.

The $10 million system, which CBP installed in an old cotton field next to the Ysleta border crossing near El Paso, Texas, shoots pulsed neutrons through a cargo container's walls. Items in the trailer react to the mini-bombardment by emitting gamma rays. The machine then reads the gamma ray signature to create a three-dimensional rendering of the inside of the container. (Ryan Singel, Wired.com, 27 Aug 2004)

Answer the following:
a. Suggest three possible titles for such an article.
b. Share your thoughts on the *actual* title of the article and what it suggests concerning what the article is about: "New Nukes at U.S. Border."

4. Using the checklist analyze the excerpt below on athletes who are *not* Olympic medal winners. Share what you inferred about the author's position on the subject.

ATHENS—Some bow gracefully to the inevitable as they approach the finish line; others grimace with fury and frustration. Some go home happy simply to have taken part; others wonder why they wasted four years of blood, sweat, and tears.

They are the losers, or at least the thousands who will not win a medal at the Athens Olympic Games, to be forgotten as the cameras focus on the victory podium. And how they face defeat could be crucial to their future success, say sports psychologists. "In a lot of ways, athletes take a lack of success as a bereavement," says Jim Bauman, one of the psychologists helping the US team in Athens. "They have to go through a grieving process."

But with the right approach, adds Andrew Walton, who advised the British Olympic team in 1984, "Losing itself is a valuable experience." Obviously, the top athletes go to Athens intent on winning. But they can only do so, says Mr. Bauman, armed with a sense of perspective. "We try to stay away from talking about winning and losing," he explains, "because if you don't win you are automatically a loser, and things aren't that black and white in sports. . . . The key question is, 'Are you satisfied with your performance?'" The sporting world was not always so forgiving. ("Losing is an Art for Most Olympians," *Christian Science Monitor,* 27 Aug 2004).

5. Would "pre-packaged news" be a bad thing if the source were acknowledged? Share your thoughts on the following

Under the Bush administration, the federal government has aggressively used a well-established tool of public relations: the prepackaged, ready-to-serve news report that major corporations have long distributed to TV stations to pitch everything from headache remedies to auto insurance. In all, at least 20 federal agencies, including the Defense Department and the Census Bureau, have made and distributed hundreds of television news segments in the past four years, records and interviews show. Many were subsequently broadcast on local stations across the country without any acknowledgement of the government's role in their production. This winter, Washington has been roiled by revelations that a handful of columnists wrote in support of administration policies without disclosing they had accepted payments from the government . . . records and interviews suggest widespread complicity or negligence by television stations, given industry ethics standards that discourage the broadcast of prepackaged news segments from any outside group without revealing the source. (David Barstow and Robin Stein, "Under Bush, A New Age of Prepackaged News," *The New York Times*, 13 Mar 2005)

Professional Standards

We must guard against complacency. Our expectations of honesty provide a moral framework in which societal institutions operate. For newspapers to be a legitimate source of information, they must adhere to fundamental values of integrity.

If you suspected deception, you'd rightly question the value of bothering to read it, other than to be entertained by the stories. In their role as watchdog, the media have a responsibility to reveal this type of deception and investigate it further when such issues are leaked to the press.

People tend to trust newspapers. Even when the news media fall short of our expectations or we are critical of journalists, we generally approach newspapers as a source of truth, a repository of facts. Occasionally those in the news media act impulsively, leading to rumors or unsupported claims that later require damage control. For example, when journalists fabricate evidence, as in the 2003 case of *New York Times* journalist Jayson Blair, everyone is harmed. His acts of plagiarism and fabrications led to the resignation of editor Howell Raines and managing editor Gerald Boyd.

Similarly, when members of the press do not examine the quality of the evidence supposedly backing up claims, we all suffer. This we saw in CBS news anchor Dan Rather's report on President Bush's National Guard duty—a report resting on questionable documents and led to Rather's public apology. "I feel like hell," Rather said. Indeed. CBS admitted that it never possessed or saw the original documents. Tim Rutten reported that "the credibility of its [CBS's] report turns on photocopies provided by an anonymous source. No reputable document examiner will authenticate anything from a photocopy—they simply are too easily manipulated" ("Rather Went on Faith, not Facts," *Los Angeles Times*, 18 Sep 2004).

Another case of journalistic regret was news coverage of the shaky evidence of weapons of mass destruction (WMDs) used to justify a war. The major news media failed to ask the hard questions about the veracity of the claims. In time, this led to a public apology from *The New York Times*. This was followed by an admission of uncritical news coverage of WMDs from the *Washington Post*. Bob Woodward says, "We did our job, but we didn't do enough" (Howard Kurz, "The Post on WMDs: An Inside Story," *Washington Post*, 12 Aug 2004).

The Global Dimension

Mexico and the Pepper Ball Outrage

Do you ever see those articles about people sneaking across the border from Mexico and what the United States has done, is doing, or will be doing about it? Attempts to stop the migrants from getting in—or to toss out those that are caught—are ongoing. The following article is about a zero tolerance method that involves shooting nonlethal "pepper balls" that cause discomfort, tearing, and possibly bruising.

Directions: Read the excerpt and then analyze it using the checklist. Share what you inferred about the author's perspective on the subject.

> MEXICO CITY—Mexican Foreign Relations Secretary Luis Ernesto Derbez said Tuesday his government will consider helping migrants sue U.S. officials for improper use of so-called "pepper ball" non-lethal projectiles. . . . [Mexico's] legislators urged Derbez to demand an end to the use of the pepper-filled plastic projectiles by U.S. Border Patrol agents. The pellets have sparked outrage in Mexico.
>
> Derbez said U.S. agents did not appear to be using the air-fired balls to stop fleeing migrants—as feared—but only in confrontational situations. . . . The Mexican government has faced severe criticism from local media and rights groups who say "balas de goma"—literally, rubber bullets—are being used against undocumented migrants.
>
> In fact, the round plastic projectiles are fired with compressed gas and are basically paintball pellets filled with pepper powder, an irritant intended to immobilize. The powder irritates the eyes and nose for about 10 seconds to 15 seconds. The impact of the ball itself may also cause bruising. . . . The U.S. Border Patrol says it fired the pepper-balls in 81 instances during 2002–2003, and reported no deaths or severe injuries. . . . ("Mexico May Sue U.S. over Pepper-Ball Projectiles," *Mexico online,* www.mexonline.com, 24 Aug 2004)

Both newspapers' editors admitted serious failings in their handling of the situation. Acknowledging their part in rallying public support for the decision to go to war, *The New York Times* apologized on May 26, 2004. They admitted:

> We have found a number of instances of coverage that was not as rigorous as it should have been. In some cases, information that was controversial then, and seems questionable now, was insufficiently qualified or allowed to stand unchallenged. Looking back, we wish we had been more aggressive in re-examining the claims as new evidence emerged—or failed to emerge. . . . We consider the story of Iraq's weapons, and of the pattern of misinformation, to be unfinished business. And we fully intend to continue aggressive reporting aimed at setting the record straight.

The editors cited specifics to explain why the *Times'* coverage warranted an apology. A fundamental issue is that journalists neither be swayed by those in positions of power nor let political or other forms of bias get in the way of being fair and balanced.

Karen DeYoung, a former assistant managing editor who reported on failures in the *Washington Post*'s prewar news coverage had this to say: "We are inevitably the mouthpiece for whatever administration is in power. If the president stands up and says something, we report what the president said." *Toronto Star* journalist Antonia Zerbisias responded: "But since when is a presidential pronouncement The Word of God? What happened to inquiry, investigation and, what's it called again, journalism?" ("How the Mighty *Post* Has Fallen," *Toronto Star,* 22 Aug 2004).

The press is obviously not above reproach. One benefit of critical thinking skills is learning not to take things at face value. We need to have our antennae out and hold those in the news media to high standards. As an empowered audience, we have a role in sustaining professional ethics.

The News Media's Use of Language

Watch the use of language. A word or phrase can shape the meaning of an entire passage. For example, all of these refer to the same person: Laura Bush, Mrs. Bush, the First Lady, the President's wife, George's wife, Barbara's daughter-in-law, and Jena's mother. However, they do not all *function* the same way in a sentence. Calling the First Lady by her first name suggests familiarity or informality. Using terms like "the President's wife" or "George's wife" define her in terms of her husband. And so on. Depending upon the context any one of the references to Laura Bush may be appropriate, but each term has different connotations.

The way we use words can shade an interpretation or slant the piece from one extreme to another. This is apparent when racist or sexist language is used, because such language is loaded and can have an explosive effect on a reader. As noted above, newspapers issue apologies for problems like misrepresentation, sloppy reporting, plagiarism, and the like.

The way language is used warrants our consideration. Even terms like "girl" and "boy" for women and men can have a demeaning effect, regardless of the intent. Arriving at good decisions around what words (and images) to use to avoid conflict or bias is not always easy.

Group or Individual Exercise: We're Sorry

Select *one* topic to investigate. List the three or four main details of the case, the key changes and/or recommendations made in response, and your own recommendations to address the underlying problems:

- Dan Rather's apology on September 20, 2004, for relying on an unsubstantiated memo about President Bush's service in the National Guard.
- *The New York Times'* May 26, 2004, apology for its coverage of contentions about "weapons of mass destruction."
- The *Washington Post*'s August 12, 2004, admission of error in its coverage of contentions about "weapons of mass destruction."
- The 2001 apology by Rev. Jerry Falwell to gays, feminists, and lesbians for saying they caused the 9/11 attacks.
- The Scottish *Daily Record* newspaper's public apology in 2004 to football player Neil Lennon for a claim that he had "highly likely" robbed a photographer.
- Yankee ball player Jason Giambi's apology over reported steroid use.

Exercises

Part One

1. Compare any two newspapers or online news sources (e.g., the *Baltimore Sun*, *USA Today*, CNN.com, the *Philadelphia Inquirer*, the *Washington Post*, the *Portland Oregonian*, the *Chicago Tribune*, *The Guardian*, *The New York Times*, the *Globe and Mail*, the *Edmonton Journal*, the *Montreal Gazetter*). Your goal is to compare and contrast the use of language in terms of its formality or informality. (For example: Does it print slang terms or profanity? Do the authors share personal details of their own lives or their opinions? How subjective or objective are they?)

2. What sort of words and actions on the part of a reporter or news anchor warrant a public apology? Set out a set of guidelines that you would like to see put in place for your college newspaper.

3. Do you think newspapers and online news sources should have to operate by the same set of rules when it comes to the use of language (e.g. profanity, colorful descriptions, jokes, personal anecdotes, etc.)? Share your thoughts and offer examples, if possible, to back up your views.

4. What should be the boundaries of freedom of speech when it comes to what a journalist puts into print? List three to four things that should be considered in drawing up a policy.

A Free Press

Finding a balance between informing the public and exploitation is not always easy. On what side should we err if we want to ensure freedom of the press? The answer may vary according to our criteria (e.g., who is the audience, what are our goals or intentions, how do we preserve respect for human dignity, etc.). For example, many people think the news media should publish disturbing (if not grisly) photos to convey the cost of war, gang killing, or drug abuse.

We can only succeed as a free country if citizens are informed and have the ability and right to think for themselves. This means the right to access information and to have the critical thinking skills to reason about what you see and hear. A free press is an important source of information, ideas, and insights. The recognition of this value goes back at least as far as the 5th century, B.C., when Plato set out his thoughts on the ideal society.

In *The Republic,* Plato discusses the democratic form of government (see Part IX of *The Republic,* which can be accessed online in its entirety). Plato considered democracy an imperfect, inferior society compared to an aristocracy or military-run government. Plato thought the ideal society would have an intellectual elite—philosopher-guardians—as the ruling class. He thought those with knowledge obtained through rigorous years of education and physical training would be the ideal rulers. The aristocracy would fall into the hands of the military when military leaders became greedy for power. In turn, the army state (called an "oligarchy") would fall to a democracy when the common person (working class) became greedy for power and economic gain.

Plato thought democracy would bring moral decay and erosion of the social order and children would run amok, dominating their parents. This moral decay, he predicted, would lay the seeds for a tyrannical overthrow of the democracy—and, in the face of moral disorder, people would be seduced by a tyrannical ruler (a Hitler type) who offered easy answers to hard questions.

Do you think Plato was right? You can probably point to some examples of moral decay. However, modern democracy offers many channels for addressing societal problems. For example, we can strengthen the educational system, address poverty and health care, and confront the sorts of injustices that plague us. And we can make sure the news media has a strong presence in the society.

In Plato's day there were no daily newspapers, radios, TVs, or Web sites relaying information 24 hours a day, seven days a week. We, on the contrary, can access information and ideas quite easily. But Plato was right to worry about the vulnerability of the democratic form of government. We need to be vigilant about ensuring access to information and different perspectives on what is going on in the world.

Group or Individual Exercise

Should Newspapers Publish "War Porn"?

Should newspapers publish photographs of extreme violence, such as murder or torture? Share your response to the argument below *against* publishing such photos, which the author considers "war porn":

> Pictures of extreme violence are always a kind of pornography: There is the fact that someone was present with a camera to record it. There is the fact that someone had the means and the will to publish it. And there is the fact that you and I are looking at it. . . . Shocking photographs become horror-porn very quickly and very easily, more quickly and easily than language does. A picture can do many things that a paragraph can't, but enlightening us about the horrors of war isn't one of them. . . . I asked [a photographer in Pakistan] if he'd ever taken a picture that no one would run. Yes, he said: It was of two soldiers walking down the road, one of them carrying the top half of a child who had been severed in two by a bomb, while the other carried the bottom half. . . . I don't think I would publish it either. Because shock overwhelms information every time. (Jim Lewis, "Front Page Horror: Should newspapers show us violent images from Iraq?" *Slate,* www.slate.msn.com, 5 Apr 2004)

You tell me: Should newspapers publish graphic or disturbing photographs that depict egregious acts of violence? What do we say to those who think we *ought* to see what war is really like?

The Global Dimension

Free Press versus the Iranian Government

Stephen Kinzer writes about his attempt to go to Iran and the problems he ran into. He reflects on the consequences for freedom of the press in his article "Red Lines and Deadlines" (www.pbs.org). He sets the stage by noting:

As the time for my January [2004] trip to Iran approached, I began contacting people there to arrange interviews. Among them were powerful figures in the religious regime, some of whom seemed alarmed to learn that a journalist who had written favorably about Mossadeq was being allowed into the country. A few hours before I was to leave, I received a startling message from the Iranian diplomatic mission in New York: Stay home or risk arrest at the Tehran airport. I will probably never know what led to this sudden change in the regime's attitude toward me, but I have a theory: Probably I was caught in the same power struggle that envelops all of Iranian public life. Those who promoted my trip and obtained my visa so quickly did so because they hoped I would help propagate their ideals in Iran. Their conservative rivals also suspected I would do that, and when they learned I was coming, they stepped in to cancel my trip.

Freedom of the press is necessary for an informed public, as the case of Iran shows. In the summer of 2001, there was an outcry against repressive actions against the press in Iran, asserting that

An unprecedented attack has started against the press in Iran. Some 43 newspapers, weeklies, and other publications have been ordered shut by the judiciary. We condemn the closing of the newspapers and the jailing of their editors and writers. We support freedom of expression for all. We condemn suppression of the people's rights and voices in all shapes and forms. (*Iran News*, www.payvand.com)

In response to the government's action, a letter campaign was launched. Form letters were distributed in hopes that people would fill out the letter and mail it in protest to the Iranian president. Read the letter (also from *Iran News*, www.payvand.com) and then answer the questions that follow.

His Excellency
Hojjatoleslam Seyed Mohammad Khatami,
President of the Islamic Republic of Iran
The Presidency
Palestine Avenue
Azerbaijan Intersection
Tehran, Islamic Republic of Iran

Your Excellency:

As you are well aware, an unprecedented attack has started against the press in Iran. Some seventeen newspapers, weeklies, and other publications have been ordered shut by the judiciary. Unfortunately, as you also know, such actions run contrary to the Constitution and civil legal code of the Islamic Republic of Iran in more than one area.

Overwhelming legal backing for the press, their rights, and freedoms, has been enshrined in the Constitution of the Islamic Republic of Iran, and its laws—a Constitution which is the fruit of the struggles of the Iranian people against dictatorship during the Islamic revolution of 1357.

As concerned Iranians abroad, who maintain no affiliations with groups seeking the overthrow of the current system of government of Iran, and respect the choice of the people of Iran as exemplified in countless popular elections over the past 20 years, we respectfully call upon your excellency to safeguard the Constitution and laws of this ancient land. We are extremely concerned about the future course and fate of the free press in Iran, and urge you to take action on their behalf.

Exercises

1. Set out the strengths and weakness of the letter above to the president of Iran.

2. Note that the frame of reference is *Iranians abroad*. Do you think the letter would have more impact if it were modified to include "concerned citizens of the world" or other groups? Share your thoughts and ideas.

3. What are the likely benefits of a letter campaign such as this one?

4. Because it is usually easier to criticize the policies of other countries than those that shape our own society, do an Internet search and see what national or local issues around freedom of the press society today faces. State those issues and concerns, citing the sources you find.

Ownership and Control

We only need to see the movie *The Manchurian Candidate* or read a futuristic novel like *1984* or *The Handmaid's Tale* to feel the fear of tyrannical control of information or the dark side of greed on the part of governments or corporations.

The exposure to contrasting opinions and points of view helps us become less dogmatic and more open-minded. We gain mental flexibility by being able to look at issues from a variety of perspectives, as we saw in the discussion in Chapter 1. Newspapers and news programs can provide valuable access to information and ideas. To do this effectively, however, journalists must be able to go beneath the surface and examine different facets of the issue. Journalist John Balzar takes this up in his discussion of editorial cartoons. He observes,

> The very thing that makes editorial cartoonists stand out in journalism may also account for their being targets now: their skill at penetrating the skin and jabbing raw nerves. Editorial cartoonists are famed for bringing in bags of scalding letters to the editor. Publishers and editors sometimes wince, but the good ones are expected to honor covenants that hold this interchange to be part of a newspaper's role in a community—stirring the civic kettle.
>
> Last April, when Matt Davies won the Pulitzer Prize for cartooning at the *Journal News* in White Plains, N.Y., publisher Gary Sherlock enthused, "He is provocative, he makes people think, and that's what it's all about." (John Balzar, "Biting the Bullet," *Los Angeles Times*, 24 Aug 2004)

The value of freedom of expression should not be underestimated. Exposure to ideas helps us develop our intellectual and creative potential. It also helps us be more tolerant of other worldviews. This was illustrated in the documentary

The Global Dimension

Resolving Questions of Bias: The Case of Al Jazeera

In a February 2004 interview with European journalists, Secretary of Defense Donald Rumsfeld blasted the Arab satellite TV network Al Jazeera. "We are being hurt by al-Jazeera in the Arab world," he said. "There is no question about it. The quality of the journalism is outrageous—inexcusably biased—and there is nothing you can do about it except try to counteract it." He went on to say that it was turning Arabs against the United States (Associated Press, "Rumsfeld: al-Jazeera Is Causing Deaths," 6 Feb 2004). This is a serious charge to make against a news station—especially one with an audience of 35 to 40 million in the Arab world.

Directions: Investigate the situation to determine if there is any basis to Rumsfeld's accusations that Al Jazeera presents biased news coverage. Share what you find and your own assessment. You may find it helpful to access the Associated Press article and study the Al Jazeera online news Web site yourself. (See aljazeera.com.)

Control Room which looks at Al Jazeera, the leading news source of the Arab world. The documentary shows how political ideologies can affect decision making at all levels of news broadcasting. It also shows how important it is to strive for balanced news coverage and for an open dialogue about the issues the news media covers.

The free expression of ideas, however, is not an unbridled outpouring devoid of a sense of morality. There is no justification for racist diatribes and hate speech. We need not lose sight of justice, but we need to expose ourselves to a range of ideas. Without an open inquiry that allows for the expression of diverse perspectives, we condemn ourselves to tunnel vision. There also can be conflicts over competing interests. That is why it is so crucial that the news media seek to present balanced coverage and offer a range of perspectives on the social issues we face as a society.

Images and the Public Consciousness

Editorial cartoons, photographs, even comic strips have the capacity to become etched on our collective memory. Think of cartoons like Michael Ramirez's in Figure 9.1 and Nik Scott's in Figure 9.2. Think of the photos of the planes hitting the Twin Towers on 9/11. Think of the little girl running naked and screaming after being napalmed in the Vietnam War. Think of that photo of Marilyn Monroe with her skirt blowing up around her waist, showing her legs. Think of the photo of Michael Jackson dangling his baby outside a hotel window. You can probably think of some of your own family photos that have their tentacles in your brain!

FIGURE 9.1
Pulitzer Prize–winning political cartoonist Michael Ramirez uses editorial cartoons as a vehicle to express his view of world events.

Related issues can arise with the publication of controversial cartoons. The editor of *The Battalion*, Texas A&M University's student newspaper, apologized for a controversial cartoon that appeared January 14, 2002. It featured a black mother reprimanding her son for his failing grades. The characters were drawn with exaggerated facial and body features resembling African-American stereotypes. Several student groups participated in a protest to give their opinions of the cartoon and its impact. In a response to the public outcry, editor Mariano Castillo wrote an apology, excerpted below:

The editors and staff of *The Battalion* apologize to readers both in and outside the Texas A&M community that the Jan. 14 cartoon offended so many. . . . *The Battalion* hopes to dispel the misconceptions and accusations of being racist, and we are open to the reminder that racism is still a problem at A&M. We recognize that the cartoon

FIGURE 9.2
Another view of
the Abu Ghraib
torture scandal

was insensitive through its stereotypes. If we had it to do over again, we would not
approve this cartoon for publication. (Courtney Morris, "Cartoon Sparks Protest,"
The Daily Texan [the student newspaper at the University of Texas at Austin],
19 Mar 2002)

Images can create dilemmas for news editors—whether the source is cartoons,
drawings, or photographs. We know how images can have impact from those
ghastly photos of celebrities looking tired, overweight, or deranged that we see on
tabloids at grocery store checkout stands. Staring at such photos reminds us why
not being famous has its virtues.

Generally mainstream sources (print or online) have restrictions about what
sorts of photographs can be printed (e.g., no nudity, no photographs of the faces
of dead people, etc.)—and yet the rules are not carved in marble. The publication
of photographs of four dead American civilians whose bodies were mutilated at
Fallouja on March 31, 2004, set off a firestorm, raising serious questions about
what kinds of images are appropriate for a newspaper to publish on the front page
and what should be consigned to page 18 (or left out entirely). Letters to the editors added logs to the fires of indignation—or joined the chorus of those arguing
that it was newsworthy, not gratuitous—to publish the photographs.

One photo in particular functions as an icon of the Iraq War. It struck a nerve
around the world and is probably the foremost example of a "Weapon of Mass
Documentation" (TV host Jon Stewart's phrase). This iconic photo is of a person
in a black hood, arms outstretched, standing on a box, with wires attached to both

hands, preparing for electric shocks. It's a horrifying image. It now has a life of its own. Countless political cartoons have used this photo as a source. Political cartoonist M. Streeter says,

> Dramatic pictures such as the hooded prisoner in an almost Christ-like pose or the "Leash Girl" become instant icons. You know you're going to draw it. Half your job—what to actually draw today—is done. Then comes the hard part—what are you going to say with it? Interestingly, these images that shock and haunt us today, will often quickly become the clichéd and trivialized images that we'll use all too often to illustrate some other issue tomorrow. (Quoted in "Abu Ghraib Cartoons: A Few Comments from the Artists," School of Journalism and Mass Communications, San Jose State University, www.jmcweb.sjsu.edu)

You can see the image of the hooded prisoner on a mural in Tehran, Iran. You can see it as a costume used by antiwar protestors on the streets of London. You can see it as Pop Art poster, with the darkened image against a fuschia pink or lime green background. You can see it posed next to the Statue of Liberty in a Baghdad street mural. This image has gone around the world—political cartoonists worldwide have used the image of the hooded prisoner standing on the pedestal, wired for torture, as the basis for political cartoons and commentary.

The question is: *Why this image?* What is it about this particular photograph that imprinted itself on our collective mind's eye and etched itself on our public conscience? Artist–commentator Sarah Boxer offers her analysis:

> It is far from the most violent, but easily the most graphic. You need less than a second's glance to know exactly what it is. The triangle of the hood silhouettes sharply against the hot pink or chartreuse background of a fake iPod ad. [Pop artist] Andy Warhol himself could not have done better. It holds its own on murals meant to be read from far away. It plays well against the Statue of Liberty. It suggests Christ on the cross. And, best yet, the hooded figure in the photograph is on a pedestal. It is already an icon. ("Torture Incarnate, and Propped on a Pedestal," *The New York Times,* 14 Jun 2004)

Dangers of Controls

In a tense political climate, it is not surprising that editors clamp down on comic strips and political cartoons. Photographs and articles are also subject to being sanitized to remove any "offensive" or politically volatile sections. One influence on the decision making around such editorial "management" is media conglomerates, which are a force unto themselves. More and more news sources are being bought out by a shrinking number of corporations, restricting the range and diversity of news coverage.

What counts as "news" reaches the public only if there are outlets. Robert M. McChesney observes, "The global commercial-media system is . . . politically conservative, because the media giants are significant beneficiaries of the current social structure around the world, and any upheaval in property or social relations—particularly to the extent that it reduces the power of business—is not in their

The Global Dimension

Political Cartoons

Michael Ramirez shows us that using the artistic medium of political cartoons to comment on world events can have considerable impact (see Figure 9.1). The very fact the Secret Service interrogated this cartoonist tells us how powerful this art form is thought to be.

Directions: Find three political cartoons (e.g., on the Internet or from newspapers you access at your university library). Each cartoon should be from a different country or from a distinctly different perspective, while focusing on *one* world event or topic (e.g., all on the topic of addressing poverty, the death penalty, the war on terrorism). Then note the similarities and differences in the cartoons you selected.

interest" (Anup Shah, "Media Conglomerates, Mergers, Concentration of Ownership," *Human Rights Issues,* www.globalissues.org).

How does the ownership and operation of the media by big corporations, like AOL Time Warner, Disney, and Viacom affect what rates as "news" and how it was presented? "Newspapers are, more and more, being run by corporations, by people who don't always understand the value of generating dialogue," said Bruce Plante, cartoonist for the *Chattanooga Times* editorial page ("Biting the Bullet," *Los Angeles Times,* 24 Aug 2004). Corporate interests can't help but want some attention paid to increasing revenue. This concern is not necessarily in sync with the concern of informing the community, opening up dialogue on social issues and providing diverse perspectives on current events.

Linguist and social commentator Noam Chomsky sees the potential danger of the media falling under the power of the government or corporate interests. He thinks the media are influenced, if not manipulated, by corporate and political interest groups. His advice? We need to be vigilant about being an attentive and critical audience. In other words, we need to make sure our critical thinking skills are operating at full speed. Chomsky comments on his interest: "I am interested in the whole intellectual culture, and the part of it that is easiest to study is the media. It comes out every day. You can do a systematic investigation. You can compare yesterday's version to today's version. There is a lot of evidence about what's played up and what isn't and the way things are structured" (Noam Chomsky, "What Makes the Mainstream Media Mainstream," *Z magazine,* www.zmag.org, June 1997). He recommends that we ask ourselves key questions about the media such as these:

FIRST QUESTION: How do they relate to other systems of power and authority? This asks about the *internal structure* of the media and their setting in the *broader society.*

SECOND QUESTION: What can we infer about the *media product* itself, in light of what we observe about the structure? This asks about mass media (entertainment, Hollywood, soap operas, etc.) and about the elite media.

You Tell Me Department

Are Cartoonists Dangerous?

Political cartoonist Michael Ramirez is not a stranger to controversy. On July 21, 2003, the U.S. Secret Service arrived at the *Los Angeles Times* newsroom to "visit" the Pulitzer Prize–winning political cartoonist regarding a recent cartoon. Agent Peter Damos was turned away after meeting with an attorney for the newspaper. But it has sent shockwaves in the small world of political cartoonists.

The cartoon in question was based on an award-winning photograph from the Vietnam War in which General Nguyen Ngoc Loan executes a Viet Cong prisoner by shooting him point-blank in the head. Ramirez's cartoon plays off that photo—it depicts President Bush with his hands behind his back as a man labeled "Politics" prepares to shoot Bush in the head. The background of the drawing is a cityscape labeled "Iraq." You can see the cartoon at cagle.slate.msn.com. Evidently the Secret Service thought the cartoon was a threat on the president. The agency's actions caused U.S. Rep. Christopher Cox (R–Newport Beach), Chairman of the House Committee on Homeland Security, to speak out on Ramirez's behalf. (See the press release at Rep. Christopher Cox's Web site, cox.house.gov, 21 July 2003). Here is the letter he wrote:

> The Honorable Ralph Basham Director U.S. Secret Service 950 H Street, NW Washington, D.C. 20223
>
> Dear Ralph:
>
> I am writing regarding the recent interrogation of editorial cartoonist Michael Ramirez by the Secret Service.
>
> I am pleased to learn that the decision to question Michael Ramirez was neither made nor approved by Washington headquarters of either the Secret Service or the Homeland Security Department. However, the use of federal power to attempt to influence the work of an editorial cartoonist for the *Los Angeles Times* reflects profoundly bad judgment.
>
> Not only is the work of this individual well known (he is a winner of the Pulitzer Prize whose work is syndicated in more than 900 newspapers), but the published work on its face was well within the ample bounds of any federal law which the Secret Service is charged with enforcing. The reported suggestion by the Secret Service that Mr. Ramirez should take into account the possible reaction of unstable people to editorial opinion expressed in graphics implies a standard that would render adult discussion of serious issues impossible.
>
> It is legally irrelevant, but further embarrassing to the federal government, that the editorial cartoon in question—far from constituting an incitement to violence against President Bush—expressed support for President Bush's policies. I take a back seat to no one when it comes to support for the federal responsibility to protect the life of the President. As a White House lawyer for President Reagan, I sat in court next to Sarah Brady during legal proceedings to determine whether John Hinckley [who shot Reagan and is now in prison] could be released.
>
> Mr. Ramirez is owed an apology, and the public is owed an explanation both of how this happened and why it will not happen again.
>
> Sincerely, Christopher Cox, Chairman

You tell me: Do you think Ramirez was out of line depicting the execution of the president? Do you think the *Los Angeles Times* was out of line to publish this political cartoon? Do you agree with Rep. Cox that an apology is owed?

The elite media are the agenda-setting media that set a framework within which others operate, like *The New York Times* sending notices to editors, for example, in the middle of the country, about what the top news stories will be the next day. Chomsky asserts that the little newspapers that lack the resources to research the big news events are pressured to fall in step with the elite media. He argues, "If you get off line, if you're producing stories that the big press doesn't like, you'll hear about it pretty soon" (Noam Chomsky, "What Makes the Mainstream Media Mainstream," *Z magazine*, www.zmag.org, June 1997).

Shaping Public Opinion

At times, the news media have been used to shape public opinion by inflating one event to the detriment of others. Some thought this was the case in the way the media handled the Michael Jackson trial, the Laci Peterson murder case, George W. Bush's service in the National Guard, John Kerry's service in the Vietnam War, and other stories. Discussions of media coverage characterized these stories with such terms as "media circus," "media zoo," and "feeding frenzy." For example, at the Michael Jackson trial in spring 2005, over a hundred journalists camped out to position themselves for the best news coverage of the event.

One concern of media analysts is the question of *influence*. The very idea of the "fourth estate" is that an educated citizenry depends upon a free press. We must, therefore, ensure that journalists are not coerced or otherwise pressured to push a given perspective or to omit information that may present a more well-rounded report.

Although the overwhelming majority of news organizations worldwide and nationally are privately or stockholder-owned, there are public news sources, like NPR, PBS (in the United States), the BBC (Britain), the NHK (Japan), and the CBC (Canada). These public media help protect us from corporate or governmental interests controlling news coverage—both in the choice of focus and in the depth of analysis. Privately owned papers can also provide us with relatively unbiased news coverage. However, with both privately owned and public news media, we must be attentive to potential problems and conflicts of interest.

Exercises

1. Select any top news story of the day or week, any *one* public news station (e.g., PBS, NPR, CBC, BBC, etc.), and any *one* privately owned station (e.g., Fox, CNN, ABC, etc.). Compare and contrast the news coverage of the event looking at your two news sources.

2. See if you can find an article in a nontabloid newspaper (print or online) that you consider balanced, fair, and without any obvious bias. Cite the evidence, drawing from your article, that this is the case.

3. See if you can find an article in a nontabloid newspaper (print or online) that you consider unbalanced, unfair, and indicative of a clear bias. Cite the evidence, drawing from your article, that this is the case.

4. See if you can find an example of how the corporate ownership affects the style or content of what is covered as news (e.g., of a major political event, such as the last presidential election *or* the 2004 Democratic National Convention versus the Republican National Convention.) Note if the coverage was balanced and fair to both major parties. Did you detect any bias toward one political view?

Group or Individual Exercise

The Controversial Cartoon Strip

Where should lines be drawn in dealing with controversial material? This dilemma arose around a May 23, 2004, Doonesbury comic strip showing a head on a platter (drawn in April 2004, before Nicholas Berg's beheading in Iraq on May 8, 2004). Some newspapers pulled it, others let it run, and others had no choice but to publish it: "Some newspapers are fuming that Universal Press Syndicate's warning about a 'beheading' image appearing in the May 23 edition of the Doonesbury comic strip arrived too late for them to remove or replace it." ("Editors Angry about Late Warning on 'Doonesbury' Strip," www.editorandpublisher.com, 17 May 2004). Doug Clifton, editor of *The Plain Dealer* in Cleveland, discussed the issue in his blog:

> "I'm beginning to lose my patience with Trudeau," wrote Clifton. "It seems we've got to consider pulling the strip or editing it five or six times a year." He added that newspapers "inflict enough pain just by covering the ugly realities of today's world. The funnies ought to be the one refuge from those realities. If Trudeau insists on competing with the front page, he may find himself missing from *The Plain Dealer*'s comics page." (Dave Astor, "More Reaction to 'Doonesbury' Strip Listing War Dead," *Editor & Publisher*, www.mediainfo.com).

Answer the following:

1. If you were a newspaper editor, what would you do about the Doonesbury comic with the head on the platter?

2. Gary Trudeau published an apology in his Web site (www.doonesbury.com): "I regret the poor timing, and apologize to anyone who was offended by an image that is now clearly inappropriate." Given that Trudeau drew the comic *prior* to Nicholas Berg's killing (beheading), should he be criticized?

3. Do you think cartoons ought to be subject to censorship? If so, what should guide the decision-making around what to leave out and what to allow?

Balanced News Coverage

Seek a range of perspectives. Read newspapers of different political, social, and religious persuasions. Expose yourself to a wide variety of commentaries on world events. Keep an open mind. And watch for discrepancies. What's front-page news in one area may be relegated to a corner of page 24 in another city's newspaper.

We need to seek sources presenting the interests of different cultural groups and social organizations. We should watch for the potential influence of gender, age, class, sexual orientation, race, and ethnicity on topics and coverage. And be on the lookout for author bias, editorial bias, or assumptions about audience bias (i.e., assumptions about the audience that colors what is covered and how it is covered).

Thanks to the Internet, we now have newspapers from all over the world at our fingertips. We can easily read newspapers and news summaries from the next city, the next state, the next country, the next continent. This fact radically alters the ways in which we can become informed about current events, offering resources on a scale unthinkable 5 or 10 years ago. Here are some guidelines for balanced news coverage.

Six Factors for Balanced News Reading

Political	→	Seek diversity of political viewpoints. (Look at the range of voices and ideas in the discussion).
Economic	→	Seek diversity in terms of financial or class interests (Look at who stands to gain or lose).
Frame of Reference	→	Seek diversity of perspectives (Look at gender, race, class, and so on).
Conceptual	→	Seek diversity in ways problems are defined and solved (Look at approach taken, use of language, assumptions, and recognition of alternative interpretations).
Ethical	→	Seek diversity of ethical and religious viewpoints (Look at values and beliefs).
Cultural	→	Seek diversity of opposing viewpoints (Look at worldview, social traditions, group identification).

Exercises

1. Study the way the news media handle key events in the lives of public figures. Select *one* of the following topics and then one example within that topic area:
   - **Historical event:** Study the media coverage of an important historical event, such as the fall of the Berlin wall, the breakup of the Soviet Union,

the cloning of the sheep Dolly, the resignation of Richard Nixon as president, the Iran hostage crisis, the assassination of any public figure (e.g., Martin Luther King, Jr., Robert Kennedy, John F. Kennedy, etc.), the birth of the first "test tube baby," the first heart transplant, the first hand transplant, men on the moon, and the like.

- **Trials:** Study the media coverage of an infamous trial, such as the Michael Jackson trial, McMartin trial, the Scott Peterson trial, O. J. Simpson trial, or the Timothy McVeigh trial.

2. Study the way the news media handle key events in the lives of public figures. Select *one* of the following topics and then one example within that topic area:

- **Wedding:** Study the media coverage of a high-profile wedding, such as that of Prince Charles and Camilla Parker Bowles.
- **Death:** Study the ethics of the media behavior over the death of one of the following: Pope John Paul II (2005), Terry Schiavo (2005), John Gotti (2004), Ronald Reagan (2004), Marlon Brando (2004), Sheikh Ahmed Yassin (2004), Queen Juliana of Netherlands (2004), Ray Charles (2004), Princess Diana (1997).

3. Obtain the front section of three different newspapers at the library, a newsstand, or on the Internet. You can search by the name of the newspaper or by using an Internet news site such as emedia1.mediainfo.com. Use recent (nontabloid) newspapers, preferably from at least two different geographic regions.

Answer the following:

a. Studying the three newspapers, how do they rate on the six factors of balanced coverage (see list above)? Compare and contrast the three papers.

b. Assume that the news articles have been selected to interest a targeted audience. From the articles in the three newspapers in *a,* above, what can you infer about the different audiences (the readers for each of the three newspapers)?

c. What are possible reasons for the overlap (if any) between the three newspapers? Note similarities and differences (e.g., the same lead story, national versus international news, etc.).

d. Looking at a list of articles in the three newspapers, draw some inferences about the journalistic goals or guidelines set for individual staff writers.

e. What are the pros and cons of a local newspaper using news services as a major source for articles?

Group or Individual Exercise

Where's the Beef in McDonald's French Fries?

Just when you thought you could eat a French fry without eating an animal by-product, the oil hit the fan in spring 2001. The controversy centered on McDonald's use of beef fat in oil used for its French fries. The news brought an outpouring of complaints from vegetarians and others who felt duped by McDonald's. They argued that the failure to explicitly state its use of beef extract in its French fries was a serious no-no. Examine the excerpt below about McDonald's use of beef extract in its French fries and then answer the questions that follow:

> SEATTLE—Facing a class-action lawsuit from angry vegetarians, McDonald's this week confirmed that its French fries are prepared with beef extract, a disclosure the company said is not new. Although the fast-food giant has been saying since 1990 that its fries are cooked in pure vegetable oil, company spokesman Walt Riker said Wednesday that McDonald's never said its fries were appropriate for vegetarians and always told customers that their flavor comes partly from beef. A class action suit has been filed for "emotional distress" caused to vegetarians, some of them vegetarian for religious reasons, who thought McDonald's fries were in line with their strong feelings about not eating meat.
>
> The list of French-fry ingredients that McDonald's offers at its franchises and on its Web site includes potatoes, partially hydrogenated soybean oil and "natural flavor." The list does not mention that the "natural flavor" comes from beef. To discover that, one would have to contact a McDonald's customer-satisfaction representative. Harish Bharti, the Seattle lawyer who filed the suit against McDonald's Tuesday, said the confirmation that the company uses beef extract to flavor its fries validates his case. Bharti argues that a reasonable person who heard that McDonald's fries are prepared in "100 percent vegetable oil" and read the list of ingredients would assume the food is suitable for vegetarians. (See Eli Sanders, "McDonald's Confirms Its French Fries Are Made with Beef Extract," *Boston Globe*, 4 May 2001)

Answer the following:

1. Would you say the author is sympathetic to the concerns of vegetarians? Explain.

2. The article later notes that Walt Riker, a McDonald's spokesperson, was asked why they did not specify that beef extract was used. He replied, "It's a good question. We're sensitive to all our customers' needs and concerns. We try to be as forthcoming and user-friendly as possible. We'll review it. We'll take a look at it." He added that using "natural flavor" as a synonym for beef extract is within federal Food and Drug Administration guidelines. If *you* were the reporter, what questions might you then ask Riker about this comment?

3. How would the article likely differ if the author were a press agent for McDonald's? Set out your ideas.

Individual Responsibility

At times the press turns its eyes on a crisis, world event, or human-interest story and we get an avalanche of articles on it. All of a sudden, seemingly out of nowhere, an issue has a run of press attention. We are then inundated with articles about what's going on and what we should do. Sometimes the issue is of global proportions. Other times the issue is relatively trivial or overblown. It rises into the public eye and then it falls back into oblivion. As members of the audience, we are often put in the position of having to evaluate the relative importance of any one news item. Keeping informed and maintaining sharp critical thinking skills helps us accomplish that goal.

It also helps to stay politically active and aware of what's transpiring around us. By taking individual responsibility for our knowledge of world news and current events, we can participate more fully in our democratic society. This entails going beyond headlines: we need to read in-depth news coverage and commentaries—and expose ourselves to a range of perspectives. In this way, we may obtain a broader understanding of events and their impact on people's lives.

A reader can use newspapers as *vehicles for social action* in three major ways. One is through letters to the editor. Another is through a commentary (e.g., an op/ed piece in the editorial section of the newspaper). The third is through press releases (usually sent out by an institution or an organization). In the case of a *letter to the editor,* the reader can express a point of view on a current issue or a reaction to news coverage of a particular event. With *op/ed articles,* the author sets out a position, with the goal of persuading others to his or her way of thinking. With a *press release,* an organization can bring events and news to the public eye by sending a prepackaged article, in hopes the newspaper will pick it up and publish it. By working in community, we can let our collective concerns be expressed and have a voice in the direction our society takes.

The Distinct Role of Sports in the News Media

Sports coverage plays a unique role in the news media and remains a staple of print, radio, and TV. Although sports is male-dominated, they attract both males and females as participants and viewers. The fascination with sports crosses age, gender, race, and political lines and knows neither geographic nor linguistic boundaries. Often much more dramatically than other forms of journalism, sports coverage has the potential to reveal important characteristics:

1. Cultural values and beliefs
2. Gender roles and expectations
3. The evolution of language
4. Ethical and social norms
5. Stereotypes and myths

The language, images and descriptions, and outpouring of emotion give sports coverage a narrative power that other news typically lacks, for a number of reasons.

One is the unique role of athletes in our society. With strength and athletic finesse, with actions magnified for all to see and each move subject to instant replays, the athlete is a pivotal cultural icon.

Think of it this way: Can you imagine teachers, doctors, lawyers, engineers, or composers being the focus of an entire section of the newspaper and a portion of virtually every news program? If it were merely an issue of entertainment, athletes and professional teams could be replaced by comedians, singers, or actors. If it were simply to show what the human body is capable of, we could look at body builders, yogis, and physical fitness buffs.

Sports and sports coverage form an integral part of our culture. Consequently, when we apply our critical reasoning skills to this area, we discover a window on society. With such fertile ground for digging, we need the right tools. These are set out in the checklist below.

Sports Coverage Checklist

1. **Examine the reasoning.** Zero in on arguments; assess the strength of evidence cited in support of the conclusion.
2. **Analyze and evaluate.** Check for warranted versus unwarranted assumptions, potential sources of bias or prejudice, stereotypical thinking, and the use of images and symbols.
3. **Watch for visual and verbal messages.** Check the presentation of information and the use of images or photographs.
4. **Check the use of language.** Watch for loaded terms, biased language, asymmetrical descriptions, repetition, metaphors, and poetic expressions to convey an idea.
5. **Notice inductive and deductive lines of reasoning.** Watch especially for use of analogies, reliance on statistical studies, and cause and effect reasoning.
6. **Be on the alert for fallacious reasoning.** Check especially for the fallacies of ad populum (appeal to the masses), ad verecundiam (irrelevant testimonials of famous figures), ad hominem (personal attack), ad hominem circumstantial (discrediting by social or political affiliation) and question-begging epithets (slanted language biasing an interpretation).
7. **Be aware of the frame of reference.** Consider other perspectives on the situation and how things would change if other voices were heard.
8. **Watch for cultural or ethnic sensitivity.** Examine the values and worldview implicitly presented, narrowing or broadening our understanding of the people or issues involved.

Values and Language of Sports Coverage

Sports coverage is usually value laden with values and beliefs threaded throughout sports articles and advertising. We also see links between sports and (especially male) sexuality: Sports pages often include advertising for strip joints, "gentlemen's clubs," and X-rated videos along with ads directed to men's body image (such as ads on cosmetic surgery, baldness, and male sexual dysfunction).

Examine the different elements—the athletes, teams, coaches, fans, sponsors, owners, support staff, mascots, cheerleaders, bands, and other team enhancers.

- Try to determine what does or doesn't count.
- Notice how much attention is given to individual players, teams, winning and losing, competition, sportsmanship, brushes with the law, violence in sports, the fans, and so on.
- Study the way people are described and look at the narrative dimension.
- Think of athletes as characters in a story.
- In the hierarchy of the different sports, consider who is on top and what societal (and corporate) interests are at play.
- Examine the use of language, colorful descriptions, nicknames, and other ways of referring to athletes. Watch for both overt and subtle differences in the coverage of sports figures and events.

The words we use reveal a great deal about our attitudes, values, interests, and prejudices. Words and images shape our thoughts and fuel our imaginations. They can bring us to our feet and inspire us to action. Furthermore, their use of language can have a considerable impact on the audience.

Sports coverage is often presented in a lively and colorful narrative style—a story with powerful images and metaphorical terms to convey ideas. Such writing tends to be more subjective, with the author's own voice adding a stamp of uniqueness. Watch for uses of language that are eulogistic (euphemistic) or dyslogistic (that is, they create either a positive or negative slant to the story). Watch also for language that plays on our emotions and team loyalties.

Be attentive to the following uses (and pitfalls) of language: Loaded terms, use of technical language or lingo, use of colloquial (street) language, use of puns and other kinds of humor, asymmetrical descriptions of male versus female athletes, racist or other prejudicial language, name-calling, hate speech, images and symbols used to create an effect, testimonials, personal revelations, and anything that sticks out as unusual or peculiar.

Drugs and Sports

Fans may also find it hard to hold athletes to a higher moral standard than they apply to themselves. At the present time, for instance, use of performance-enhancing drugs is widespread. Take a look at how many athletes were disqualified or lost their medals in the 2004 Olympics in Athens because they failed the requisite drug tests. Draw some inferences about what this tells us about athletes, social pressures, and notions about sports and sportsmanship.

In an August 22, 2004, article on the Olympics, the author writes that "a run of athletes' goofs and judges' gaffes—not to mention the doping scandals du jour—is giving the Olympics that three-ring circus feeling. But at these games, the

The Global Dimension

Canada's Stanley Cup and Colorful Journalism

Canadians are not often regarded as a flashy group of people. However, that does not mean they lack style or wit. Quite the opposite—as the number of renowned artists, novelists, and other wordsmiths demonstrate. This also extends to sportswriters, as we see here with Pierre Lebrun. Discuss the use of language in the following excerpt:

> TAMPA, Fla. (CP)—The beards were gone. Hockey's ultimate superstition, the unkempt beards, had disappeared by the time players on the Calgary Flames came out and explained to the world how gut-wrenching it felt to fall one goal short in the Stanley Cup final. The beards represented two months of hard work. They were gone, as was their dream. "It's the toughest loss by a thousand times," said superstar captain Jarome Iginla. "One shot. The guys worked so hard. It's a very good season and I'm so proud of everybody but that hurts more than anything else I've been a part of."
>
> "We Are The Champions" could be heard reverberating around the St. Pete Times Forum, but it was dead quiet inside a dreary Flames dressing room. Players expressed their thoughts with voices barely audible, as if letting out their last breath. . . . They came short because they ran out of gas, delivering a performance in Game 7 on Monday night that barely had any energy. The aggressive forecheck and rambunctious body checking was not at the usual level.
>
> They were dead, and they were hurting. . . . The injuries barely slowed down the lunch-bucket Flames, who adopted the blue-collar personality of their coach and grinded their way past division champions Vancouver, Detroit and San Jose before finally succumbing in seven tough games to a vastly more talented Tampa club. (Pierre Lebrun, "Heart-Broken Flames Run out of Gas against Talented Lightning," www.canada.com, 8 Jun 2004)

worst of the dolts are on a growing list of athletes pumped up on steroids, hormones and other banned substances" ("D'oh! Athletes' Goofs, Judges' Gaffes Make a Three-Ring Circus of the Olympics," *Sports Illustrated,* sportsillustrated.cnn.com, 22 Aug 2004). Examples of those who were disqualified or stripped of their medals come from around the globe—they include India's Sanamacha Chanu, Uzbekistan's Olga Shchukina, Greek weightlifter Leonidas Sampanis, and Russian shot putter Irina Korzhanenko.

What role do you think the media should play in reporting on athletes' drug use? "Some journalists have expressed criticism, for instance: "We're giving McGwire standing ovations, but I wonder what we're celebrating: the work of a hero or the spectacle of a hero fashioning his own destruction—for our pleasure" (William C. Rhoden, "Baseball's Pandora's Box Cracks Open," *The New York Times,* 25 Aug. 1998). Note also the criticism of Jason Giambi: "I'm sorry I can't be more candid," Giambi said half as sorry as baseball and its fans. The game needs more than a steroids policy that isn't as tough as the players and owners would have you believe. It needs a full act of contrition, a publicly-televised catharsis that leaves a hulking slugger on his quivering knees." (Ian O'Connor, "Slugger Swings and Misses With his Apology," *USA Today,* 11 Feb 2005). Even so, the media, like the public, is conflicted where lines need to be drawn on this issue.

You Tell Me Department

Should Athletes Take Political Stands?

Taking a social stand is one way our voices are heard. This is as true for athletes as anyone else. Consider the case of Toni Smith, senior guard of the Manhattanville College women's basketball team. Smith decided to show her opposition to the Iraq war by turning her back to the American flag while the national anthem played at the games. Though she had supporters, her action elicited indignation and outrage among others. Here are two reactions:

REACTION #1: Manhattanville president, Richard A. Berman, said he supported Smith's right to express her opinion because it was done in a quiet and dignified way. "It is not about the flag to us," Berman said. "We support our troops, but I think it is healthy to have kids on college campuses expressing their views. That's where the energy comes from."

REACTION #2: In a game at Manhattanville on Sunday, Jerry Kiley of Garnerville ran onto the court and confronted Smith with an American flag. After the game, Kiley, who said he was a Vietnam vet, told reporters, "She has not earned the right to disrespect the flag." (Bill Pennington, "Player's Protest over the Flag Divides Fans," *The New York Times,* 26 Feb 2003)

You Tell Me: If you were to write an article on Smith for your college newspaper, what angle would you take? Explain what you would focus on. Do you think fans care about an athlete's political views? See if you can find examples of athletes who took stands on social or political issues.

Exercises

1. Study the coverage of the 2005 Congressional hearings on steroid use in baseball and summarize your findings on what you find.

2. Study the coverage of the denials and evasions about steroid use by athletes—for instance Jose Canseco said, "Because of my fear of future prosecution . . . I cannot be candid with this committee" and Mark McGwire said, "What I will not do is participate in naming names" (Richard Simon and Tim Brown, "Players Balk on Steroid Use," *Los Angeles Times,* 18 Mar 2005). Share what you find.

3. Discuss one of the following quotes about drugs and sports and offer three recommendations for how the news media should approach the subject:

   SEPP PLATTER, PRESIDENT OF FIFA, THE WORLD SOCCER FEDERATION: "Professional athletes are forced to take performance-enhancing drugs by the huge pressure to perform." (Quoted by Doug Rollins, "Competition and Drug Abuse," www.humanistsofutah.org).
   PRESIDENT BUSH: "The use of performance-enhancing drugs like steroids is dangerous, and it sends the wrong message – that there are shortcuts to accomplishment and that performance is more important than character" (State of the Union Address, January 2004).

Reprinted with the permission of Nike, Inc.

FIGURE 9.3
One of all-time superstars of sports—Michael Johnson. Photo by Nike, Inc.

Sports Stereotypes

Embedded in cultural attitudes are myths and stereotypes. This is as true in sports as in other aspects of our society. We know from Chapter 1 that stereotypes can act as an obstacle to clear thinking. This is as true in sports as the rest of society. We can tell a lot about such stereotypes by the nicknames athletes acquire. Some examples from professional sports are Hakeem ("the dream") Olajuwon, Julius ("Dr. J") Erving, Karl ("The Mailman") Malone, Michael ("Air") Jordan, Allen ("The Answer") Iverson, Dikembe ("Air Zaire") Mutombo, and Shaq O'Neal's nickname for himself ("The Big Aristotle"). The picture? Athletes are larger than life, powerhouses of strength, and with an almost indestructible might. See fig. 9.3.

Some think of athletes as heroes. Some think of them as role models. Psychologist Robert R. Butterworth, for instance, argues that athletes are role models, not heroes:

> Why is it so important for young people to be exposed to the feats of Olympic champions? Because of an absence of positive role models in our society, many young people grow up in the U.S. without the sense of the importance of hard work and discipline to reach one's goals.
>
> The Olympics show athletes competing and working hard towards a common goal and overcoming great odds in order to become winners. When teenagers are exposed

to these positive Olympic role models, it gives young people hope that they too can overcome obstacles in their own lives. These athletes show them by their deeds, not to give up when they are faced with frustration and doubt. ("Olympics—Powerful Role Models for Youth," www.prweb.com, 14 Aug. 2004)

Then there are myths. There's the myth of the lovable athlete who helps poor, disadvantaged children and the myth of the dedicated athlete, like Rocky, who keeps trying and finally comes out on top. There's the myth of the underdog who comes up from behind and surprises everyone. There are myths about perseverance being more important than talent. Then there are myths and superstitions what players do for good luck (such as wearing the same socks, doing things in a certain order, lucky bats or sports gear, and so on). Be on the lookout for myths and stereotypes around sports—and think about how they reflect on the society.

Group or Individual Exercise

Share your thoughts on the connection between our sense of heroes and sports figures:

1. What are the three or four main characteristics of a hero (or examples of heroes) in our culture?

2. What are the three or four main characteristics of a sports "superhero"?

3. Name three sports figures generally regarded as superheroes.

Sports and Morality

It is interesting to consider the assumptions and values we hold about sports. For example, we assume that winning the gold is considerably more meaningful than winning the silver or the bronze. We assume that a certain amount of violence is acceptable on and off the playing field. And so on. You add to the list. These assumptions and values shape a set of prescriptions about what we expect to see. They also tell us what we consider permissible behavior.

For every Yoda, there is a Darth Vader; for every hero, there is a villain. So too is this true in sports. Many sports stars become idols, worshipped by an adoring public. But that is not to say sports figures have to be perfect—hardly. We tolerate a certain amount of deviation from moral goodness. For example, the society puts up with some alcohol and substance abuse, unprofessional behavior on the court or field, and domestic violence on the part of athletic superstars. We tolerate moral weakness, particularly if there's an expression of remorse or steps are taken to get help to address "shortcomings." Babe Ruth's drinking problems and womanizing was tolerated, so long as he was still capable of success as a player. The public tolerated Michael Jordan's gambling weaknesses, Mike Tyson's rape conviction, and Daryl Strawberry's alcohol and substance abuse.

This tolerance may relate to our collective desire that our heroes not be found to be lacking the moral qualities we hold most dear. It may also show our awareness that even superstars are human and, at least to some degree, not that different from the rest of us. Of course, there are limits—times when the public has to assess athletes as public figures. For example, in the week the news broke about Magic Johnson's HIV status, 259 news articles, 18 front-page stories, and more lead stories on network news (8) than all other news about AIDS in the 11-year period 1985–96 appeared ("Covering the Epidemic," *Columbia Journalism Review,* July/Aug. 1996). See if you can find recent examples of athletes, such as Kobe Bryant (rape charge) or Damon Stoudamire (drug possession), who were subject to public scrutiny for some perceived failure or an affront to public morality.

The Global Dimension

The Disputed Olympic Gold: Yang Tae Young's "Loss" to Paul Hamm

Study the news coverage of the controversy around Paul Hamm's Olympic gold medal, which was disputed because of a scoring error. List the ways the controversy was covered, using distinctly different frames of reference including Hamm's point of view and the point of view of the gymnast, South Korea's Yang Tae Young, who would have won had the judge not made a mistake.

Exercises

1. Compare the coverage of the controversy surrounding Olympians Yang Tae Young and Paul Hamm with the controversy over Brazilian marathon runner Vanderlei de Lima's attack by a spectator (ex-priest Cornelius Horan) that resulted in de Lima falling out of first place and receiving the bronze medal. Note the degree to which Hamm being American affected the news coverage (at least from American news media).

2. What impact does the repeated use of the term "star" to refer to Kobe Bryant have in the following?

   DENVER (AP)—The judge in the Kobe Bryant case dealt a blow to the defense Wednesday, barring access to the medical records of the 19-year-old woman accusing the NBA **star** of rape. . . .

   Bryant, 25, faces four years to life in prison or 20 years to life on probation if convicted of felony sexual assault. The Los Angeles Lakers **star** has said he had consensual sex with the woman last summer at the Vail-area resort where she worked. . . .

   Bryant's attorneys have said in court filings they believed the woman's medical records could undermine her credibility and demonstrate she had a "scheme" to falsely accuse the Lakers **star.** (Associated Press, "Bryant Defense Barred from Accuser's Medical Records," 21 Apr 2004, emphasis mine)

3. Do a study of the news coverage of *any* professional athlete with respect to legal problems or moral shortcomings.

4. Do a study of the news coverage of any athlete with respect to issues around gender, race, or religion.

5. Save one week's worth of sports pages from the newspaper *and* watch at least one week's worth of sports programs on the nightly news. Answer the following and provide a copy of the most significant articles you utilize as an appendix to your discussion:

   a. What myths and stereotypes (about athletes, men and women, the audience, etc.) are found in the sports coverage?

   b. What do sportscasters and journalists *assume* on the part of the audience in terms of sports knowledge and interest? (Remember: an assumption is something taken as a given, as if it were a fact, without giving any evidence in support). List any such assumptions and note which are warranted and which are unwarranted.

   c. What does the sports coverage on TV and in the newspaper tell us about our society? Assume you are an anthropologist studying the society and all you have to go on are the sports pages and sports news coverage on TV.

CHAPTER TEN

Visions of the Real: Popular Culture

And we wept, Precious . . . We wept to be so alone. . . . And we forgot the taste of bread, the sound of trees, the softness of the wind. We even forgot our own name. My Precious . . .
—GOLLUM, *from Lord of the Rings: Return of the King*

Lord of the Rings, Return of the King introduces us to a character, Gollum (alias Smeagal) who epitomizes the struggle between altruism and self-interest—between good and evil. Gollum is in a running inner battle whether to be loyal to Frodo or to betray him so he can get the ring. His struggle has a price. While chomping into a foul, slimy fish, he laments all that he had forgotten. Gollum speaks for the many who have lost the way, forgotten their names, and struggled to make sense of who they are. Most of us can relate to Gollum's struggle. All the various aspects of popular culture that call up mythology put us in touch with that yearning, that quest for meaning. And, like Gollum, popular culture can act to strengthen the society—or to undermine it. Because of this we must be vigilant and put our critical thinking skills to work.

In the past, people read, sat around campfires sharing tall tales, and had nightly story-telling rituals at children's bedtime. Now the average person reads little, rarely sits around campfires, and mostly shares family stories at holidays, weddings, or funerals. But that doesn't mean we have lost touch with mythology, morality, and social issues. The images, the ideas, the stories unfolding in popular culture are often deeply connected to our cultural history and mythology. They resonate in our lives.

If the real world reflected the world we see and hear in popular culture, here's what we'd find: There would be many more males than females; vastly more whites than people of color; more people who are rich than poor; far fewer mothers, more attentive fathers, and children who seem to have no homework; many prostitutes, strippers, and nearly nude dancers holding onto poles; an astonishing number of serial rapists and murderers; a scattering of gorgeous women who end up victimized; and almost no one who is old, frail, or has disabilities other than blindness. We would also find a number of aliens, zombies, mutants, cyborgs, and vampires. The society would be ridden with conflicts resulting in a vast amount of gun-related violence, bombs, explosions, men leaping across rooftops, people falling through glass ceilings or through large windows, phones that don't work, lots of car accidents and speed chases, an inept or corrupt police force, and a lot of lone heroes who prevail in the face of extraordinary odds.

To judge by what we see, most people have very short workdays, plenty of cash, and lots of spare time. Those with social obligations or others to care for are rare. Few have money worries. Most live in nice homes and nice neighborhoods, except for marauding bands of gangs in the downtown area and "poor" neighborhoods. Social structures and relationships no longer resemble the idyllic portrayals of the past, but they aren't realistic either. Children often have doting fathers, but dead or missing mothers. At times we find fiercely protective mothers—while others forget their children altogether. Fathers and husbands tend to be loving, dependable, and strong, but some verge on the horrific. We see nuclear families, but we also find single-parent families, negligent or dysfunctional families—or orphaned children, old before their time.

When examining a work of popular culture, it pays to do a reality check. Some gloss over the dark side of ordinary life, some magnify, it some reflect or respond to the status quo, and so on. Look at the work—the "text"—as telling a story. You want to figure out what story is being told, its significance, and what messages it sends to us. Turn it over in your mind, looking at it as unique in itself. And see it also as a work embedded in context that also merits analysis.

The Big Picture

We can apply critical thinking to the different areas of popular culture and look at the underlying meaning, patterns, stereotypes, and both implicit and explicit messages about how to live and think. Philosopher Jean Beaudrillard, whose work influenced *The Matrix,* thinks we need to pay close attention to reality and images—and images of reality and images of images. These are not always easy to separate. For example, was Saddam Hussein found in a hole? Or was his capture staged to make us think well of the war effort? (See "Ex-Marine Says Public Version of Saddam Capture Fiction," United Press International, 9 Mar 2005). There are economic and political interests that may weigh in. Dan Rather observed that the media should have followed the money trail in the 2004 presidential campaign; so too ought we follow the money trail in popular culture. As we will see, other aspects figure in and, therefore, warrant attention.

You Tell Me Department

What Do Video Games Reveal about Us?

Are boys and men primarily brutes wanting to act out on the plane of violent imagery? Are girls and women primarily interested in sorting out social relationships and cracking puzzles? Here's one view:

> "In a game, there's really a problem, or set of problems, that we're selling," says Will Wright, one of the founding figures in the video game industry. "One way I think of games, as a designer, is the possibility space. What are the different states I can get into in that game, what are all the worlds I can experience?" Technological advances have greatly extended those possibilities. "Now these games are becoming more of a system through which people play out their own personalities," says Wright. Wright discusses male versus female consumers (players) of video games. He says:
>
> "Men are happy to sit there shooting the target over and over and over, blowing shit up," says Mr. Wright. "They have simple goal structures." Women, though, want more—not necessarily something different, just better. "They are more creatively driving the experience. They want a higher standard in interactive games," he says. "It doubles your market if you can start appealing to the other half of the people on the planet." ("Gamers Learn to Grow Up," *The Financial Times*, 1 Sep 2004)

You tell me: What would it take to convince you that Will Wright is right—that men want to blow up things, while women "want more" and have a higher standard? Share your thoughts.

Analyzing Popular Culture

We commonly find all types of arguments about aspects of popular culture. Here are key navigational tools to keep in mind:

- *Have your antennae out!* Pay close attention to arguments and examples.
- *The fact the topic is interesting does not mean the reasoning is sound!*
- *The fact you agree with the author's thesis does not mean the evidence is in place!*
- *Watch for details!* Backing up claims with relevant examples, statistics, and other forms of justification is crucial.
- *Be on the lookout for unwarranted assumptions, fallacies, and bias!* You've got the tools to sniff out problems—so put them to work.
- *Set out arguments in standard form to help see what's what!* Nothing like a systematic approach to keep things organized.
- *Watch for omissions or "holes" in the reasoning!* Don't fill in missing premises or make any assumptions that whitewash defective reasoning.
- *Watch for facts, opinions or speculation, and ideas!*
- *Watch for images and symbols! See Fig. 10.1.*
- *Watch for inferences!* Check to see if they are well founded.
- *Decide if arguments are inductive or deductive!* Proceed to determine the quality.

Media literacy, as Justin Lewis and Sut Jhally point out, should be about help-ing people become sophisticated *citizens* rather than sophisticated consumers:

> Media literacy, in short, is about more than the analysis of messages, it is about an awareness of why those messages are there. It is not enough to know that they are produced, or even how, in a technical sense, they are produced. To appreciate the significance of contemporary media, we need to know why they are produced, under what constraints and conditions, and by whom. (Justin Lewis and Sut Jhally, "The Struggle over Media Literacy," in Horace Newcomb, ed. *Television: A Critical View,* 6th ed.)

With the exception of music, popular culture tends to ignore economic class— white, Black, Asian, Latino, Native American, or otherwise. We may be interested to learn why this is the case in our quest for media literacy. Also of concern are

FIGURE **10.1**
The power of
the image:
Absolut makes
its mark in both
advertising and
popular culture.

ABSOLUT SELF-CONTROL.

the frame of reference, the intended audience, and the social context. In this chapter, we will also look at drawing inferences, constructing and deconstructing arguments, examining reviews, and applying different theories of interpretation.

Putting the Navigational Tools to Work—
Drawing Inferences

We are often put in the situation of observing, sorting and weighing perceptions or drawing inferences about different aspects of popular culture. This is especially true given the many awards, and rating systems: "thumbs up/thumbs down," "four out of five stars," and so on. From these various signals, we draw inferences. Sometimes those inferences are well supported; other times we find little evidence to back them up. Watch also for dubious assumptions. Consider alternative inferences that could be drawn.

Exercises

Directions: State what can you infer about men and women and their film interests by looking at the following poll results:

Top 10 Movies Chosen by Male Viewers

Rank	Title
1	*The Godfather* (1972)
2	*The Shawshank Redemption* (1994)
3	*Lord of the Rings: Return of the King* (2003)
4	*The Godfather: Part II* (1974)
5	*Schichinin no samurai* (1954)
6	*Casablanca* (1942)
7	*Star Wars* (1977)
8	*Schindler's List* (1993)
9	*Pulp Fiction* (1994)
10	*Lord of the Rings: Fellowship of the Ring* (2001)

Top 10 Movies Chosen by Female Viewers

Rank	Title
1	*Lord of the Rings: Return of the King* (2003)
2	*Lord of the Rings: The Two Towers* (2002)

3   *The Shawshank Redemption* (1994)

4   *Lord of the Rings: Fellowship of the Ring* (2001)

5   *Schindler's List* (1993)

6   *Le Fabuleux destin d'Amelie Poulain* (2001)

7   *The Usual Suspects* (1995)

8   *Pirates of the Caribbean: The Curse of the Black Pearl* (2003)

9   *Star Wars* (1977)

10   *Finding Nemo* (2003)

Source: www.imdb.com, 27 Sep 2004

The Global Dimension

Japanese Commentators on *Lost in Translation*

The movie *Lost in Translation*, about two people who become friends over the span of a few days in Tokyo, gave rise to comments about its representation of Japanese society. Read the two passages and then draw some inferences about the Japanese response to the film. Are the two speakers necessarily in conflict?

> **Commentator Yoko Akashi says:** In the film, the Japanese are always portrayed as inferior to the main (Anglo Saxon) characters . . . The Japanese are "funny," two-dimensional, cartoon-like characters who can't pronounce English words correctly and often mix "L" and "R" sounds . . . I also saw two bored and boring empty privileged Americans who can afford to stay and feel trapped for quite a long period of time in the most expensive hotel in Tokyo. (" 'Lost in Translation': A Japanese Woman's Reaction," *APA Film Buzz,* www.naatanet.org)

> **TV producer Mariko Fukuyuma says:** Having worked as a television producer as well as a translator and interpreter in Tokyo for more than 10 years, I say that Sofia Coppola's depiction of the obnoxious Japanese media entourage in *Lost in Translation* was pretty accurate, even from a Japanese point of view. I don't think Ms. Coppola's movie is racist or insulting; rather, it's similar to my everyday encounters in the United States: people refuse to pronounce my last name because it sounds obscene. Speaking of Ms. Coppola, I wonder what Italian people thought of her father's film *The Godfather.* (Letter to the Editor, *The New York Times,* 11 Jan 2004)

Group or Individual Exercise

Look over the list of top 20 grossing films in the United States as of fall 2004 and then answer the questions below.

2004 IMDB U.S. Box Office Top 20 Movies of All Time

1. *Titanic*
2. *Star Wars*
3. *Shrek 2*
4. *E.T.: The Extraterrestrial*
5. *Star Wars: Episode 1—the Phantom Menace*
6. *Spider-Man*
7. *Lord of the Rings: Return of the King*
8. *Spider-Man 2*
9. *The Passion of the Christ*
10. *Jurassic Park*
11. *Lord of the Rings: The Two Towers*
12. *Finding Nemo*
13. *Forrest Gump*
14. *The Lion King*
15. *Harry Potter and the Sorcerer's Stone*
16. *Lord of the Rings: The Fellowship of the Ring*
17. *Star Wars: Episode II—Attack of the Clones*
18. *Star Wars: Episode VI—Return of the Jedi*
19. *Independence Day*
20. *Pirates of the Caribbean: The Curse of the Black Pearl*

Answer the following:

1. What strikes you most about this list?
2. Why do you think films with mythological characters and themes are so popular?
3. Draw some inferences about the audience (or the audience's interests) given this list of profitable films.

FIGURE 10.2
Waits for the Bus
in Hollywood,
CA.

Photograph by Wanda Teays.

CASE STUDY

Drawing Inferences from Music Reviews

If you've ever turned to reviews, you know one thing if you know anything: Reviewers may agree in commending or criticizing a work, but it is more likely that they'll be all over the map. It's not as subjective as evaluating a culinary experiment (e.g., shrimps stir-fried with fruit or apple pie with hot chocolate sauce), but the assessment can vary widely. The perspective and criteria of evaluation are crucial. With a music or film review, we expect to see an assessment with some detailed explanation of the rating. Here are summary reviews and ratings of Tom Waits' *Real Gone* (See *Metacritic*, www.metacritic.com, 10 Oct 2004). See Fig. 10.2.

REVIEW #1: *Playlouder*

In *Real Gone's* fearsome complexity of rhythm, lyric and device, Tom Waits appropriates like a shoplifter without much time, and creates something entirely his own. A new music. RATING: 100.

REVIEW #2: *Entertainment Weekly*

Often riveting—and even a little gangsta. RATING: 83.

REVIEW #3: *Pitchfork*

It lurches along like a junk-heap jalopy, unsteady and unsafe, bits flying off in every direction, stopping, starting, and bouncing in pain. RATING: 80.

REVIEW #4: *PopMatters*

Real Gone leans on nail-bending percussion and swagger in a manner that recalls Bone Machine's metallic binge more than the recent theatrics of Alice or Blood Money. RATING: 80.

REVIEW #5: *The New York Times*

Like an altar built of barbed wire, scrap metal and broken glass, *Real Gone* hammers ungraceful materials into something like beauty. RATING: 70.

REVIEW #6: *Drowned In Sound*
Tough going and very samey, both in sonics and lyricism. Even if you enjoy the basic template, you may well run out of steam before the end. RATING: 50.

What do you see? The top rating mentions lyrics ("fearsome complexity"), as does the lowest rating ("tough going and very samey"). Are these contradictory? It may be that the qualities are similar (complex and fearsome versus tough going), but the value placed on that aspect is at issue. Except for the last review, the other five overlap ("gangsta" with "unsteady and unsafe," "metallic binge" and "barbed wire . . . ungraceful," "bouncing in pain" and "broken glass"). For that matter, look at Review #3 and Review #6: "lurches along like a junk-heap jalopy" which merits a rating of 80 compared to "tough going . . . may well run out of steam before the end" with a rating of 50. Reading further we discover:

Behind Review #3: Tom Waits is channeling frequencies that the rest of us cannot hear. . . . *Real Gone*, like most of Tom Waits' records, is teeming with all kinds of mysterious noises: clangs and spits, faceless hollers, squawks, irrational toots, not-quite-human coughs, vicious bangs, apologetic whispers.

Behind Review #6: He certainly deserves a chunk of respect . . . Waits assiduously avoids compromise. . . . [But] the album peaks, way too early, on the awe-inspiring, enormous, ten-minute 'Sins Of The Father.' This monster takes that blueprint to its limit, enveloping you in an extreme world of love and death and sin in one massive phlump. Sadly, Waits can't follow it. He's come too soon.

What this indicates: Going behind the review summary fleshes out the differences. The 50 rating in Review #6 is related to the reviewer's view of an early peak, leaving the rest of the CD hanging. In contrast, Review #3 seems to have no problems with the lurching and "mysterious noises" (that must not seem to sputter and fade away in this reviewer's assessment). This is at the crux of the disagreement. Consequently, by going deeper into the review itself, seeing what lies behind the summary and rating, we are able to grasp the reasons for the evaluation.

Applying the Navigational Tools to an Argument

When faced with an argument, stop and check out the reasoning. Set out the argument—state the conclusion and number each premise P_1, P_2, and so on. Then stack them, with the conclusion at the bottom. That makes the argument easy to read. We can then see how the premises work together to support the argument. If they don't offer sufficient support, we need to determine if there is a way to bolster the argument. For example,

It is critical to understand that male rappers did not invent sexism. Black practices have been openly sexist for a long time, and in this regard they keep solid company with many other highly revered dominant Western practices. Today's rappers are not alone in their symbolic objectification of Black women. They have lots of real live, and substantially more powerful, company, none of whom rap or make records. . . .

All manner of cultural practices and discourses that do not challenge the structures upon which these ideas are based wind up confirming them. Why, then, is the concern over rap lyrics so incredibly intense, particularly from Black middle-class guardians? Why not the same level of moral outrage over the life options that Black folks face in this country? It seems to me we need a censorship committee against poverty, sexism and racism. (Tricia Rose, "Black Texts/Black Contexts," in Gina Dent, ed. *Black Popular Culture*)

Let's set out the argument:

P_1:   Male rappers did not invent sexism.

P_2:   Black practices have been openly sexist for a long time.

P_3:   Black practices around sexism keep solid company with other highly revered dominant Western practices.

P_4:   These others outside of rap and music are more powerful.

P_5:   Many cultural practices and discourses that do not challenge the structures on which sexism is based end up confirming them.

P_6:   The concern over rap lyrics is disproportionately intense, especially from Black *middle-class guardians*.

C_1:   There ought to be the same level of moral outrage over the life options facing Blacks in this country.

From this argument, the author draws the further inference:

C_2:   There ought to be a censorship committee against poverty, sexism, and racism.

By highlighting each premise, we can look at each one singly and in combination to assess the strength of the reasoning. Tricia Rose starts with a claim about sexism not having its roots in male rappers and proceeds to point to other sexist practices in the dominant Western culture. In P_4 she asserts those outside music are more powerful—indicating the broader social context. If it is not self-evident, then Rose may need to elaborate. The next premise, P_5, asserts that cultural practices affirm sexism if they fail to challenge the structural basis of sexist practices. Perhaps this is also self-evident, though it may be true of all varieties of prejudice.

The premise most likely to raise questions is P_6, with the reference to "Black middle-class guardians." It might be stronger if Rose clarified and backed up this premise. Consider if the reference to Black middle-class guardians, supports or detracts from her point. Her concerns are important. She sees the issue raised about rap music as a red herring leading us away from greater societal problems.

Exercises

1. Set out the argument in the following excerpt about MTV and the Video Music Awards (VMA) show:

    As a cultural force, MTV doesn't have much going for it: second-rate reality shows, a few endlessly recycled videos by tired rappers and derivative rock bands. . . . Drowning in the conservative backwash after the debut of Janet Jackson's right nipple (shall we just call it the Jackson syndrome?) and banished to Miami so the Republican Party could turn New York into a facsimile of Kansas, this year's VMAs reflected, rather than enlivened, the state of 21st century American culture. They were banal, muzzled and garishly irrelevant. (Neva Chonin, "We Who Are about to Mock Salute You," *San Francisco Chronicle,* sfgate.com, 5 Sep 2004)

2. State the argument in this discussion of the TV series *The Sopranos* by setting out the premises and the conclusion:

Tony [the male lead] fails in his attempts at self-mastery and self-overcoming . . . He succumbs passively to the whims of his inner and outer fate while continuing to waver between raging resentment and absolute indifference. While the *external* villains in Tony's life change from season to season, the *internal* villain in his life remains ever-present: his inability to take account of *his own* moral decline, even while obsessing about the weakness of others. (Kevin L. Stoehr, " 'It's All a Big Nothing': The Nihilistic Vision of The Sopranos," in Richard Greene and Peter Vernezze, eds. *The Sopranos and Philosophy.*)

3. Read the excerpt below and identify the key claims professor Henry Jenkins cites (P_1, P_2, P_3, etc.,) to support his conclusion that "The availability of video games has *not* led to an epidemic of youth violence."

According to federal crime statistics, the rate of juvenile violent crime in the United States is at a 30-year low. . . . It's true that young offenders who have committed school shootings in America have also been game players. But young people in general are more likely to be gamers—90 percent of boys and 40 percent of girls play. The overwhelming majority of kids who play do NOT commit antisocial acts.

  According to a 2001 U.S. Surgeon General's report, the strongest risk factors for school shootings centered on mental stability and the quality of home life, not media exposure. The moral panic over violent video games is doubly harmful. It has led adult authorities to be more suspicious and hostile to many kids who already feel cut off from the system. It also misdirects energy away from eliminating the actual causes of youth violence and allows problems to continue to fester. (Henry Jenkins, "Reality Bytes: Myths about Video Games Debunked," www.pbs.org)

4. State the key claims in the following argument which concludes that a TV cartoon show could be a hit:

Just as "The Simpsons" essentially saved Fox Network 15 years ago, animated cartoons could become the small screen's pinch hitters, even if they've been benched for a while. "To a large degree, network programming has quit taking risks and is becoming the same thing over and over again," says Mike Lazzo, a senior vice president at Cartoon Network. "And I think that animation is just something different." While different, cartoons have also become more accepted, no longer sandwiched between Lucky Charms and Barbie advertisements on Saturday mornings. That generation has grown up—and they constitute a large chunk of the prime-time audience . . . an animated version of Aaron McGruder's subversive comic strip could spark interest. (Marie Ewald, "TV Gets Animated," *Christian Science Monitor,* 14 May 2004)

5. State the thesis and key claims in this discussion of hip-hop:

[H]ip-hop has a few things going for it after all. While a common complaint is that the industry is ruined because of a lack of support from "true hip-hop," the tastes of the average consumer are actually evolving: underground artists are actually eating now, gaining mainstream acceptance. . . . Kanye West, with the success of singles like "Jesus Walks" and "All Falls Down," has shown that rap artists don't have to talk about pimping and hoes to be successful. DJ Danger Mouse has had an underground name for years, but shook the world when he merged acapellas from Jay-Z's *Black Album* with the Beatles' *White Album*. . . . Artists can make fun songs—songs to dance to, songs to ride to, songs to get drunk to—without compromising their art. . . . If you don't like certain types of music, just don't support them . . . (William Ketchum III, "Is Hip-Hop Too Commercial?" *Ballerstatus,* www. ballerstatus.net, 10 Sep 2004)

6. State the key claims explaining the view that syndicated talk radio host Rush Limbaugh is a key factor in the rise of talk radio in popular culture:

According to *Talkers,* the country had about 125 talk-radio stations in 1987, the year before Limbaugh went national. Now the figure is closer to 1,200, or about one-tenth of all commercial radio stations in the United States.

Harrison said a number of factors laid the groundwork for the success of Limbaugh and talk radio. In the late '80s, AM stations were looking for a niche to stay in business, after losing music programming to their FM brethren. In addition, Harrison said many people felt disenfranchised by the mainstream media, and baby boomers . . . were ready to listen to something besides music. Also, advances in telephone and satellite technology made national talk radio programs more technically feasible, and finally, the repeal of the Federal Communications Commission's Fairness Doctrine "allowed radio to be controversial."

In 1987, the year before Limbaugh's national rollout, the regulatory agency eliminated its rule requiring broadcasters to air opposing viewpoints on controversial subjects. . . . And Limbaugh was ready to unleash talents he'd been honing since he was a 12-year-old in Cape Girardeau, Mo. (Steve Carney, "In Rush Limbaugh's World, He's Always Right," *Los Angeles Times,* 6 Aug 2003).

7. Set out Monique A. Levermore's concerns about children playing violent video games and watching violent TV shows and movies:

Many children in the United States view hours and hours of television filled with violent acts, deviant behaviors, warped reasoning, and a criminal code of ethics. Children are encouraged by our society, through television viewing, to glorify violent behavior, identify with the aggressor, and develop clever ways of engaging in deviant behavior without getting caught. They are exposed to violent cartoons, violent videogames, and a violent genre of action/adventure and horror films that are marked by gruesome murders. They glimpse into the psyche of killers and revel in character development that is flawless down to the last detail. (Monique A. Levermore, "Violent Media and Videogames, and Their Role in Creating Violent Youth," *Forensic Examiner,* Fall 2004).

8. Set out Henry Jenkin's argument *against* the claim that "Scientific evidence links violent game play with youth aggression":

Claims like this are based on the work of researchers who represent one relatively narrow school of research . . . But most of those studies are inconclusive . . . In these studies, media images are removed from any narrative context. Subjects are asked to engage with content that they would not normally consume and may not understand. Finally, the laboratory context is radically different from the environments where games would normally be played. Most studies found a correlation, not a causal relationship, which means the research could simply show that aggressive people like aggressive entertainment.

That's why the vague term "links" is used here. If there is a consensus emerging around this research, it is that violent video games may be one risk factor . . . which can contribute to anti-social behavior. But no research has found that video games are a primary factor or that violent video game play could turn an otherwise normal person into a killer. (Henry Jenkins, "Reality Bytes: Myths about Video Games Debunked," www.pbs.org)

Group or Individual Exercise

Assessing Arguments in Film Reviews: *The American President*

Let's take an argument and set it out in standard form. Our focus will be a (negative) review of *The American President* by John J. Pitney Jr. He argues that movies such as *The American President* show us that Hollywood thinks voters are stupid. Pitney's argument is as follows:

Premise 1: *The American President* concerns a chief executive (Michael Douglas) who is progressive yet practical. He says that gun control is hard to pass because people do not understand the link between guns and gun-related crime.

Premise 2: After he falls in love with an environmental lobbyist (Annette Bening), an evil senator (Richard Dreyfuss) turns the unthinking masses against the good President by making nasty comments about his new lady friend.

Premise 3: The President's approval ratings tumble, and the White House staff bemoans the people's willingness to believe anyone with a microphone.

Premise 4: At a climactic moment, the domestic policy advisor (Michael J. Fox) compares Americans to nomads who need a drink of water but get a glass of sand.

Premise 5: The President bitterly replies: "They drink the sand because they don't know the difference."

Premise 6: The image of a dumb, deluded electorate is hardly original with this movie; it is one of the film industry's moldiest clichés.

Premise 7: Many other films treat the electorate like idiots; for instance in *Mr. Smith Goes to Washington* (1939), ruthless thugs smash the young Smith with false charges and vicious news stories and the gullible public goes along.

Premise 8: In *Citizen Kane* (1941), Orson Welles plays a legendary newspaper publisher who can whip his readers into a war frenzy with far-fetched stories about Spanish galleons off the Jersey coast and thinks he can tell people what to think.

Premise 9: In *The Candidate* (1972), an idealistic Senate contender runs an issue-based campaign against a stodgy incumbent (with the stereotypical dark suit and short white hair) and seems doomed to lose until he starts speaking in platitudes and wins over the voters with mushy statements.

Premise 10: Political films show contempt for the people.

Conclusion: Hollywood thinks the voters are stupid.

Directions Read over Pitney's argument and then decide:

1. Is Pitney correct in his characterizations of the films he cites as treating voters with contempt? (If no one in the group has seen any of these four films, go on to question 2.)

2. Assuming Pitney's characterization of the movies is correct, is his sample of four political films sufficient to show that Hollywood thinks voters are stupid?

3. What are the strengths of his argument?

4. What would an opponent need to do to disprove Pitney's claims?

▓ Assessing Arguments

In assessing an argument it helps to have some guidelines to keep in mind (see Chapters 3 and 5 for a review of tools on assessing arguments).

Tips for Assessing Arguments

Check the factual claims. Are the claims made actually true? Do not assume the speaker is necessarily correct.

Check any assumptions. Determine if they are warranted or unwarranted. Unwarranted assumptions should be recognized and carefully examined.

Check for exaggeration. Are the claims made inflated or slanted to one side or another, when in fact another interpretation is possible?

Check for omissions. Has the reviewer left out relevant details that would offer another perspective or lead us to a different conclusion than the one being drawn?

Check for fallacious reasoning. If a sample is used, is it sufficient in number and representative? *Note:* If the sample group is too small, the speaker may have committed the fallacy of hasty generalization. If the sample group is biased toward one point of view or group, then the speaker may have committed the fallacy of biased statistics.

Check for details. Examples and illustrations can bring home a point and show how the work makes ideas concrete.

Check the strength of reasoning. Decide if the conclusion is sufficiently supported by the evidence given. The evidence lays the foundation for the conclusion, and it is important that this foundation is a solid one.

With these guidelines in mind, let's return to Pitney's argument. First, consider the claims of fact. He says *The American President* presents voters as dumb and deluded, that they "believe anyone with a microphone." Pitney doesn't talk about the end of the movie, or what happens after the president expresses his bitterness about the gullibility of the public.

We need to know: Did the "unthinking masses" come to see that the "good president" was *really* a good president and that they were wrong to believe his critics? Are voters "unthinking" if they are receptive to those who make nasty comments about presidents? Does listening to gossip imply a dumb or deluded mind?

Second, examine Pitney's assumptions. He assumes a familiarity with the other films he cites (*Mr. Smith Goes to Washington, Citizen Kane,* and *The Candidate*). Depending on the audience, this assumption may or may not be warranted.

Third, watch for exaggeration. It's a temptation to inflate key points for an extra boost. Assuming the public initially fell for the nasty comments about the president's new lady friend, does that necessarily mean they are "unthinking masses" or "a dumb, deluded electorate"?

Fourth, make sure nothing important has been omitted. Omissions often lead us to mistaken conclusions. Pitney stops at the president's bitter reply to his domestic policy advisor's comment about nomads getting sand instead of water to drink. We need to consider what happens after this. Decide if Pitney develops the implication that the public is deluded.

Next, watch for fallacious reasoning. Given all the films coming out of Hollywood, it is unlikely that only four of them make or imply judgments about voters. Pitney's collection ought to be a *representative* sample if we are going to draw conclusions from it. If not, his reasoning is not well founded.

As for details: Pitney offers a number of specifics in an attempt to clarify his points. Lastly, examine the connection between the premises and the conclusion. Consider whether Pitney's citation of four films made between 1939 and 1995 warrants the conclusion "Hollywood thinks voters are stupid." The conclusion should not say more than is warranted by the evidence.

You Tell Me Department

What Makes a TV Show "Great"?

We would likely vary in listing qualities that define "greatness" in a TV show and may be reluctant to label *any* TV show "great." However, some *do* make such assessments and recently two commentators argue that *The Wire* is the best show going.

> **TONY NORMAN:** No show comes close to *The Wire* in novelistic depth or authenticity of milieu. *The Wire* has a familiar story: West Baltimore has become an open-air drug market. The cops don't like it. . . . *The Wire* is a profound meditation on work in America, the importance of loyalty in the workplace and the pursuit of upward mobility through any means necessary. Drug dealers and cops are fleshed out human beings who, like most of us, are far more dependent on their colleagues' respect than they're comfortable acknowledging publicly. ("TV Show Wired Into The Human Condition," *Pittsburgh Post-Gazette,* www.post-gazette.com, 17 Sep 2004).

> **BRET MCCABE AND VAN SMITH:** The characters are the most instantly and constantly gratifying aspect of *The Wire* . . . On its surface *The Wire* is a cop show, the most stereotype-ridden of TV genres, yet nowhere in *The Wire* do stereotypes exist. There are no good guys and bad guys, merely men and women who work on opposites sides of the socially acceptable. *The Wire* treats both as people caught up in the same racial, class, and political tensions that afflict any American, and dramatizes them in manners that feel natural. ("Down to the Wire," *Baltimore City Paper,* www.citypaper.com, 12 Jan 2005)

You tell me: What stands out as definitive qualities of great TV?

Placing a Work of Popular Culture in Context

As you know from audience surveys at movie premieres, a great deal turns on the response of the target audience. And works that succeed in one context (e.g., urban areas) may fall flat in another. If we simply focus on the content and do what might be called a "textual analysis," we may not be able to grasp the bigger picture of how it shapes or is descriptive of society.

Content is to context like an egg is to the circumstances in which the egg is laid; for example, which hen laid the egg, whether the setting was a barnyard or an agribusiness, where this egg was one of hundreds gathered that day, and so on. When we look at content, we consider the various aspects of the work itself (e.g., plot or story line, characters, themes, visual and audio components, and so on). The context includes the time and place the work was created, audience response, the social and political setting, the target audience of any marketing, and the corporate backing.

Context and content are not always distinct. A case in point is a new reality TV show, "He's a Lady," that will showcase eleven "macho men" as they "learn"—for instance, by cross-dressing—what it's like to be a woman. To prevent us from muting out the ads and wandering off during commercials, the sponsor will use embedded ads and products. Specifically,

> Sponsoring the series is SC Johnson, which, in addition to product integration, receives tagged tune-in spots, on-air billboards, online exposure on the show's

microsite and logo placement in print ads. SC Johnson products, such as Edge Shaving Gel, Ziploc and Oust, will be creatively incorporated into the weekly competitions. (Press Release, "TBS Unveils Latest Adventure in Reality Television: HE'S A LADY," 27 Aug 2004).

What may speak to us at *this* time or *that* place might not succeed at another time or place. For example, films that did not open with a bang but now have a cult following include *Blade Runner, Groundhog Day,* and *Donnie Darko.* Some very influential films—such as *The Matrix*—received Academy Awards for sound, editing, and special effects, but not for the more noteworthy categories. *Blade Runner,* now regarded as a classic, received no nominations for an Academy Award other than Art Direction—and that award went to *Gandhi.* In hindsight, things often look different.

Also consider comic strips, which used to provide chuckles about life's foibles. Now comic strips are carving out political territory. Take a look at comics published on Sunday, October 3, 2004:

- *The Boondocks* features a honk-once-for-Kerry-twice-for-Bush piece;
- *La Cucaracha* plays off accusations about Senator Kerry ("flip-flops," "nuanced" positions, looks a little French).
- *Mallard Fillmore* throws a barb at Senator Kerry about the issue of the Vietnam War.
- *Non Sequitur* focuses on a piece on blood curdling screams during an election year.
- *Prickly City* finds common ground between Red America and Blue America—representatives of both wear signs that say, "Kick Me."
- *Opus* centers on journalists who question the mayor's office over a pothole-filling disaster and are met with denials and name-calling.
- *Doonesbury* addresses Secretary of Defense Donald Rumsfeld and the issue of responsibility for the atrocities at Abu Ghraib, the prison in Iraq where Americans abused and tortured detainees.

Group or Individual Exercise

Get a collection (five to six examples) of different comic strips that deal with political issues. You can find comics in print or on the Internet. Once you have your collection, answer the following:

1. What social role are the artists playing in raising political issues in the format of comics? Refer to your collection of comics.
2. Should an editor be able to censor any of these comics if they are considered in poor taste? Share your thoughts.

Exercises

1. *The Boondocks* creator Aaron McGruder writes about how 9/11 changed him as an artist: [After 9/11] Journalists stopped being journalists. All this cheerleading started. All of a sudden this lame president was being hailed as a bold national leader. No one was asking questions about how every system designed to protect this country failed . . . I was disgusted by the whole thing. And I thought, "What am I going to write about now? Puffy? That seems stupid now." I suddenly knew what I wanted to do . . . It was then I became a political cartoonist. (Quoted by Greg Braxton, "He's Gotta Fight the Power That Be," *Los Angeles Times Magazine,* 25 Apr 2004). Examine any two or three *Boondocks* comic strips and then give your assessment of the power of this art form to relay a political message. How does *Boondocks* reflect/describe one segment of the society that is angered about the war in Iraq and related social and political issues? Share your thoughts.

2. Argentinean cartoonist Maitena [my-tay-na] uses her art to look at men and women and their relations. She says, "To me an altered woman is one who has all of these battlefields open at the same time" and "We've got work, men, maternity, our body, our friends, our mothers, a whole bunch of things, and that's what puts us in an altered state, in which we can go from euphoria to a depressed crying jag in 15 minutes." (Larry Rohter, "A Sassy Appraisal of the Sexes," *The New York Times,* 23 Mar 2004).

Answer the following:

1. Do a study of any two or three female cartoonists (Roz Chast, Cathy Guisewite, Lynda Barry, Nicole Hollander, Lynn Johnston, etc.). (See happychaos.com/wci and www.cagle.slate.msn.com for examples. What topics or themes do you see?

2. Do you notice any differences between the subject matter of male versus female cartoonists?

Context

We can think of the relationship of context to content like that of background to foreground. Context provides us with the cultural roots, the audience and its receptivity, the sociotemporal framework and the economic and/or ideological thrust behind the work. It is the obverse of the work. A *contextual* analysis, therefore, takes us outside the work so we can see the other factors at work in how a piece of popular culture makes its mark.

The Global Dimension

Talk Radio in Iraq

Some think of talk radio as a venue for people to rant about politics. But that's not the only model a talk radio station could follow. Read about Radio Dijla in Baghdad:

> BAGHDAD—A housewife calls to talk about a broken sewer pipe. A student calls to talk about a lost love. . . . The station is one of the most listened-to in Baghdad, according to its employees, a claim that appears to have merit, judging by its broad following . . . The station receives an average of 185 calls an hour. Most calls are about the nuts and bolts of life. "Iraqi citizens have big problems but nobody listens to them," said Haidar al-Ameen . . . The station forces the government to make time. Local and federal officials come as guests and are grilled by listeners.
>
> Beyond easing the frustrations of daily life, the station provides a chance for Iraqis to talk publicly about politics for the first time in decades. Their calls open a window onto the lives of ordinary Iraqis, whose opinions often go unheard in the frantic pace of bombings, kidnappings and armed uprisings. . . . The station was started with seed money from the Swedish government. Its founder, Rakabi, the former chief of the U.S.-financed Iraqi Media Network, was born in 1969 in Prague, in what was then Czechoslovakia, after his family was forced to leave Iraq to escape political repression under Saddam.
>
> On the station's first day, Salim simply sat at the microphone and asked listeners what they wanted to talk about. Now, in addition to the government official call-in shows, the station has programs on which lawyers answer questions. (Sabrina Tavernise, "Talk Radio Gives Iraqis a Powerful New Voice," *International Herald Tribune*, www.iht.com, 31 Aug 2004)

Answer the following:

1. How might talk radio be used to strengthen free expression?
2. Do you think Radio Dijla has the potential to bring some of the qualities of democracy to Iraq?

Checklist for Examining Context

1. **Relative success:** What is its cultural "fit"? A hit? Moderately successful? A dud?
2. **Audience:** Who is the audience? Does it have broad appeal? Has it generated a narrow fan base?
3. **Sponsor(s):** Who are the work's sponsors? Private corporations? Public funding? Nonprofits?
4. **Marketing:** How is the work marketed—and to whom? What do the ads convey?
5. **Sociotemporal framework:** When and where was the work produced (time/place)?
6. **Social and political red flags:** Are there any relevant political or social factors (e.g., cultural currents in the 1960s, 70s, 90s or post-9/11 concerns).
7. **Show me the money:** Are economic interests at work? Any product placements?

8. **Response and reverberations:** What is or was the audience response? Have there been any continuing effects? Any critical acclaim?
9. **Ideological and political agendas:** Any political agenda at work? Conservative? Liberal? Religious? Marxist? For or against the status quo? And so on.
10. **Frame of reference:** From whose perspective—and values—is the work presented? That of the dominant society—or that of a minority or marginalized group?
11. **Missing pieces:** Whose voices are in—and whose are out? Whose *should* be in, given the work?
12. **Symmetry/asymmetry:** How do the society and/or relationships presented correspond to those of the audience? Is diversity represented? Is there a bias or imbalance when the work is compared to the "real" world?

Content

When we examine content, we undertake a *textual* analysis, deconstructing the work to see how it is structured, how its components work together and how to interpret the work through different lenses (such as social, political, ethical, spiritual, mythological).

Checklist for Examining Content

1. **Genre:** What genre most fits the work? Drama? Comedies? Thrillers? Horror? Documentaries? Animation? Rap? Hip-hop? Country? Folk? World music?
2. **Originality:** Is it a spin-off or a retread of an earlier work? Is it imitating or borrowing from another work? Is it unique or derivative?
3. **Focus or plot:** What is the work about? How could it be summarized in a few sentences?
4. **Characterization:** If there are characters, what is their significance? What role do the main characters play in the work as a whole?
5. **Narrative:** What is the impact, the power of the story, script, or lyrics? What stands out when looking at the level of the language, the story? What is memorable; for example, movie lines or quotes?
6. **Frame of reference:** What "voice" carries the work? From whose frame of reference or point of view is the work being presented? Does that perspective shift, or is it consistent?
7. **Levels of interpretation:** What are different ways of "reading" or interpreting the work? Does it have political or social aspects? Does it have an ethical or spiritual message? Could it be understood in terms of justice versus injustice?
8. **Lasting value:** Does the work stand out above the rest? Does it speak to the audience beyond mere entertainment? What stands out artistically?
9. **Total impact:** What is the verbal and/or visual message? Do they reinforce one another? Is music or sound effects a factor?

10. **Prescriptive versus descriptive aspects:** Does the work try to shape us, to tell us what we ought to think about one thing or another, or to set a direction for the audience? Does it reflect the society or aspects of society? Can we see ourselves in the work? Does it mirror the world we live in—or does it offer an alternative, a parallel world different from our own?

11. **Diversity:** Are the inhabits—the characters—representative of the real world? Is there a balance of different voices and diverse perspectives? Whose view is predominant?

12. **Power and influence:** Where do we see power and influence manifested in the work? Who are the leaders, the bosses, those who take control? Who are the followers?

Group or Individual Exercise

Drawing from the checklists for context and content, examine either an hour-long TV show or a movie. Some movies that might work well for this exercise are *The Manchurian Candidate*, *Million Dollar Baby*, *The Sea Inside*, *Osama* or any blockbuster such as *Spider-Man 2*, *Shrek 2* or *28 Days Later*.

Exercises

1. Use the checklists for context and content to study *one* of the following comedies: *Meet the Fockers*, *Man of the House*, *Diary of a Mad Black Woman*, *White Chicks*, or *Hitch*. Can you see the ways in which the film you selected functions as social commentary? Discuss.

2. Michael Eric Dyson says, "Rap music grew from its origins in New York's inner city over a decade ago as a musical outlet to creative cultural energies and to contest the invisibility of the ghetto in mainstream American society . . . [Rap tapped] into the cultural virtues and vices of the so-called underclass . . ." ("The Politics of Black Masculinity and the Ghetto in Black Film," in Carol Becker, ed., *The Subversive Imagination*). If film and TV ignore or downplay economic strife, rap music does not.

   Answer the following: Why do you think music is the main medium to examine class issues—particularly poverty and ghetto life?

3. Answer *one:*
   a. Find the lyrics to any rap song that demonstrates rap's ability to examine the gulf between the rich and the poor and the consequences of entrenched poverty on its victims.

You Tell Me Department

Does Barbie Have a Sense of Humor?

Just when you thought Barbie was going to retire and live in a guarded community with or without Ken, we find that an artist has used the doll in a satire. Read about this case and then answer the questions below:

SAN FRANCISCO—Mattel Inc. should have known it didn't have a shapely leg to stand on when it sued a Utah artist for his parody of the voluptuous cultural icon, Barbie. Now Barbie's corporate parent must pay artist Tom Forsythe's lawyer $1.8 million in fees and costs incurred defending against a copyright violation claim over his use of the doll to lambaste the "conventional beauty myth." U.S. District Judge Ronald S. W. Lew held that Mattel forced Forsythe "into costly litigation to discourage him from using Barbie's image in his artwork." Lew earlier dismissed the copyright, trademark and trade-dress violation claims against Forsythe.

Forsythe, a self-taught photographer from Kanab, Utah, produced a series of 78 photographs in 1997 that parodied Barbie dolls in various absurd and sexualized positions, often nude and being menaced by vintage kitchen appliances. "Malted Barbie" depicted the nude doll inside a vintage Hamilton Beach malt machine. "Barbie Enchiladas" portrayed the dolls wrapped in tortillas and covered with salsa in a casserole dish. The "Food Chain Barbie" series earned Forsythe just $3,659—and at least half the total sales were from purchases by Mattel's private investigators, according to court records. (Pamela A. MacLean, "$1.8M Fees in Barbie Case: The Toymaker Must Pay the Legal Costs of an Artist Who Satirized the Doll," *Daily Journal,* 25 Jun 2004)

You tell me: Is Barbie's image tarnished by such satirical treatments as wrapping the doll in a tortilla like she's an enchilada? What do you think are the strongest claims in support of Tom Forsythe's right to create satires on Barbie? If you were the judge, would you be inclined to rule for Tom Forsythe (the artist) or Mattel (the corporation)?

b. Find the lyrics to any rap song that demonstrates rap's ability to examine the collective despair or rage of those who are disenfranchised—that is, ignored or marginalized by a capitalistic society.

4. How has terrorism and the resulting terror it evokes impacted popular culture? Cite some examples.

The Interface of Pop Culture and Reality

Images can be extremely powerful. In *The Republic,* Plato expressed a similar idea much earlier. He argued that children are highly impressionable and, thus, we must guard against their exposure to works that might leave a lasting impact. He thought that images, music, and stories create an effect so powerful that it can't be eradicated. What Plato thought the case for children might today be considered true of many adults as well. Images, music, and stories have the power to latch hold of brain cells and never let go.

Think about it. There are horror movies that mutate into nightmares. But there are also scenes, characters, and even dialogue that make a mark—think of "Hasta la vista, baby," "You can't handle the truth," and "Here's looking at you, kid." These phrases have been incorporated into our thoughts and speech. Memorable dialog and pithy quotes from movies can take on a life of their own—long after the movie has faded from the public eye.

Exercises

1. In *Understanding Media* Marshall McLuhan says, "The movie is not only a supreme expression of mechanism, but paradoxically it offers as product the most magical of consumer commodities, namely dreams." Cite three examples of films that show we *can* (or, alternatively, *cannot*) escape from class roles and gender and ethnic stereotypes.

2. What is the social significance of horror films with their mutants, corpses, flesh-eating ghouls, vampires, and other undead? Set out three to four ideas explaining why audiences flock to horror films like *The Exorcist, Alien, 28 Days Later,* and *Night of the Living Dead.*

3. What factors help create a surprise hit on either TV or film? State what you see as the key factors. (Think of films like *Shrek 2, The Bourne Supremacy, Van Helsing* and *Dodgeball;* and hit TV shows *Alias,* the various *CSI* series, *Survivor, Will and Grace, Lost,* and *The Sopranos*).

4. Why are some films box office duds? If a film executive asked for your advice on why some films are total failures at the box office, what would you say? Share your thoughts.

5. Give your assessment of the following explanation for the popularity of Spider-Man:

   He [Spider-Man] really could be any one of us. To be Superman, you had to come from another planet. To be Wonder Woman you had to be born a mythological Amazon princess. But to be Spider-Man, you just had to be bitten by a radioactive spider. (Hey, it could happen.) You didn't have to be from a superhuman race. You just had to have it happen to you, and we all have things happen to us. (Danny Fingeroth, "Look Within: You'll Find a Spidey There," *Los Angeles Times,* 1 July 2004)

6. Does animé have a cult following? Research film reviews and audience reaction to *Steamboy, Akira, Tokyo Godfathers, Spirited Away,* and/or *Princess Mononoke* and share what you find to explain the rise of Japanese anime in its popularity with Western audiences. (Look for example at "External Reviews" of the films at www.imdb.com).

The Global Dimension

Hip-Hop from an Israeli Perspective

Ben Sisario reports that the influence of hip-hop on the Middle East is palpable (see "Hip-Hop from the Middle East Comes to Brooklyn," *The New York Times*, 8 July 2004). He says:

> With beats borrowed from Gang Starr and a Tribe Called Quest and lyrics inspired by the Beastie Boys and Tupac Shakur, Israeli rappers express a political urgency not often heard in hip-hop, whether in New York or any of the other corners of the world to which the music has spread. . . . [Israeli rapper T.N.] often lashes out against Israeli military tactics:
>
> > *You buried the parents*
> > *Under the stones of their own homes*
> > *And now you call me a terrorist?*
> > *Who is a terrorist?*
> > *You are a terrorist.*

Answer the following:

1. T.N. says, "My lyrics are with peace." He adds, "The question is which peace. Before you reach peace, you've got to have equality."

Discuss how his four lines above can be interpreted as a call for peace.

2. Why do you think rap music is such an important outlet for U.S. soldiers in Iraq. Read the following excerpt and share your thoughts:

> "Rap music, it seems, has been for many soldiers a bridge between their normal lives and the strange, surreal world of their Iraqi service. Their lives, they said, were changed dramatically by war, but their music helped them understand it. Rap, with its stories of crumbling neighborhoods, street violence, wild economic disparities and life-or-death swagger, helped them make sense of what they saw there. "When you start looking at the fighting between the Sunnis and the Shiites," said Drummond, 22, who finished four years of service in November after spending more than a year in Iraq, "it's at least as complicated as the fighting between the Bloods and the Crips back home." . . .
>
> "I don't know any other way to get my feelings out," Moncrief said. "I was scared over there, and frankly, I think if you weren't scared, there was something wrong with you. I rap because I feel it." (Monica Davey, "The War in Iraq, to the Rhythm of Rap," *The New York Times*, 22 Feb 2005).

7. Looking at the characters in *Ghost World*, *American Splendor* and *Napoleon Dynamite*, we might wonder what place do films about nerds or antiheroes have in our culture?

8. What do you think is the attraction of films about amnesia? Think of all the characters who have suffered traumatic memory loss—*The Bourne Identity*, *Memento*, *Vanilla Sky*, *Paycheck*, *50 First Dates*, *Eternal Sunshine of the Spotless Mind*, and so on. Why are so many films about losing contact with our former identity and struggling to deal with the consequences? Lev Gross says, "There's something profoundly sinister and infectious about the idea" ("Amnesia the Beautiful," *Time* magazine, 29 Mar 2004). Share your thoughts.

Group or Individual Exercise

Give your assessment of these famous movie lines—what makes them *memorable*?

1. "I'll be back."
2. "Life is like a box of chocolates."
3. "I'll make him an offer he can't refuse."
4. "Frankly my dear, I don't give a damn."
5. "Go ahead, make my day."
6. "I'm as mad as hell, and I'm not going to take this anymore!"
7. "Greed, for lack of a better word, is good."
8. "I'll have what she's having."
9. "Here's looking at you, kid."
10. "Show me the money!"
11. "You want answers?" "*I want the truth!*" "You can't handle the truth!"

Analyzing Reviews

Reviewers have a tricky job: They need to make their judgment clear to the reader, give a sense of the story line, and set out reasons for their rating. This must be done succinctly and in a readable and engaging way. Because the review presents the critic's assessment of the film, we need tools of analysis to see what the critic is saying and why.

As we discussed in Chapter 3 on argumentation, we need to set out and weigh the evidence, make sure the conclusion has sufficient support, consider alternative hypotheses, and watch for omissions, unwarranted assumptions, and biased or prejudicial language. Look at excerpts from a review of the movie *Shaun of the Dead,* paying attention to how the reviewer makes her case.

Review Highlights of *Shaun of the Dead:*
   Decaying flesh and strewn entrails don't usually equal funny. But "Shaun of the Dead," a remarkably fresh and inventive British import, transforms the unintentional camp of the zombie subgenre into full-on, hilarious comedy. "Shaun," already a huge hit in England, rounds things off nicely with romance, buddy hi-jinks and a coming-of-age story.
   That the coming-of-age story involves a 29-year-old is half the fun. Simon Pegg, an appealing everyman with crack comic timing, plays Shaun, an underachieving electronics salesman whose longtime girlfriend (Kate Ashfield) is still waiting to meet

his parents. Part of Shaun wants to grow up, but the other part is addicted to video games and getting wasted with his best pal and roommate Ed, played by a sublimely Neanderthal Nick Frost. It takes an attack of the walking dead to jostle Shaun out of his stupor. (Carla Meyer, "The Undead Meet Their Match: Brit Slackers," *San Francisco Chronicle*, 24 Sep 2004)

In a nutshell, these two opening paragraphs convey Meyer's argument about the movie. In the rest of her article, she goes into detail, summarizing the plot, noting the lead actors and discussing the quality of the performances. In her opening, we are briefly told the movie's strengths, her evaluation, and the genre in which the movie fits. This introduction has a lot packed into it.

Key Elements of a Film Review

Reviews are an interesting form of argument: They have to tell a story so as not to lose the audience and they have to present a position that is backed up by evidence and examples.

Key Elements of a Film Review

- A brief plot summary.
- An assessment of the acting.
- An evaluation or rating.
- Key evidence and assumptions.
- Detail laying out the argument.
- Concluding remarks reiterating the rating.

Our task is to evaluate the strength of that evidence. To do a good job, reviewers need to make their case. So, in analyzing the review, examine it as an argument and evaluate it. See if the evidence offered lends sufficient support for the conclusion the reviewer has drawn. Note that you can easily access film reviews and film criticism through Web sites like www.metacritic.com, www.imdb.com, filmlinc.com, www.filmcriticism.com, www.lib.berkeley.edu/MRC, and allmovie.com.

Exercises

1. A plot summary must be concise and clear—as with this one for *Steamboy*: Ray Steam is a cheeky young lad who receives a strange metal ball, which is dubbed a "steamball," from his grandfather, who must go into hiding. It contains a power that can preserve or destroy the human race, and he must protect it from an evil villain who has built an elaborate machine that will dominate London. (G. Allen Johnson, *San Francisco Chronicle*, www.sfgate.com, 18 Mar 2005). Write a plot summary of any TV episode *or* a film you've seen recently.

2. Compare and contrast these two reviews of *The Incredibles:*

Reviewer #1 (Liza Schwarzbaum of *Entertainment Weekly*):

Having previously explored the bonds of loyalty in his outstanding 1999 animated feature *The Iron Giant*, as well as in work on that perennial TV masterpiece *The Simpsons*, writer-director Brad Bird wants most of all to tell these truths: that being super is a right and a responsibility. That mutual trust and respect are not sitcom punchlines. And that family survival necessitates risk-taking valor, too. And so, with not a talking toy or animal in sight, *The Incredibles* makes adult philosophical points . . . Pixar has, once again, raised the level of excellence to which animated movies (and, why stop there, all movies) can aspire.

Reviewer #2 (Jessica Winter of *The Village Voice*):

The Incredibles brims with sly comic-book connoisseurship . . . Unfortunately, the delicious snatches of reflexive wit function as mere intermissions between the distended action sequences and Michael Bay–style megatonnage, which have earned Pixar its first ever PG rating. At the preview screening, a little boy burst into tears a few ammo rounds into an early auto chase, and the five-year-old to my left spent most of two hours cowering in her dad's lap. Pixar has never tiptoed around the young 'uns' fears and anxieties (see the nighttime terrors of *Monsters, Inc.* or the family-slaughter overture of *Finding Nemo*), but *The Incredibles* announces the studio's arrival in the vast yet overcrowded Hollywood lot of eardrum-bashing, metal-crunching action sludge. Given that its next film is called *Cars*, it seems it's opted for long-term parking.

3. Draw all the inferences you can from the comments reviewers made about *City of Angels*, excerpted below:

Reviewer #1 (Mark Peranson of the *Toronto Star*):

As an angel, Cage acts like he's hooked on methadone; after his fall, he's briefly a charming lout who very much conveys the joy of being alive. But [Meg] Ryan's character is pure Hollywood construct—the "doctor of the people" who bikes to work and makes house calls. . . . Despite overhead shots of LA and a powerful use of integrated special effects, the film aims as high as an empty Harlequin romance.

Reviewer # 2 (Shawn Levy of *The Oregonian*):

A melodramatic love story with a strong dose of New Age spiritual hooey, . . . The best thing by far is Cage. He's a genius of screen acting, able to give himself so wholly over to a part that he dissolves. His eyes are so calm and empathetic, his gaze so steady, his heart so plainly on his sleeve that he simply overwhelms you with earnestness. Late in the film, when he arrives on earth, he plays with unbridled comic gusto like a genie uncorked from a bottle. It's such a tremendous performance that he even makes Ryan look substantial.

4. State the conclusion and the premises in the following discussion about Satoshi Kon's animé, *Tokyo Godfathers:*

Tokyo Godfathers shows off Mr. Kon's graphic style at its subtlest and most evocative. Set in a fully imagined back-alley Tokyo on a snowy Christmas Eve, the film a avoids the bright colors usually associated with animation in favor of muted tones of brown, green and yellow, punctuated by pools of darkness. His images are formally exquisite compositions designed with a depth of field unusual for animé; movement is added sparingly. His films have a hushed, melancholy atmosphere and end-of-the-day reflectiveness that are rare in animé. (Dave Kehr, "New Contender for the Anime Throne," *The New York Times*, 11 Jan 2004)

5. Set out the argument and note any assumptions in the following discussion of film director Spike Lee and his film *Do the Right Thing*:

In an interview after the release of the film, Lee said that he was constantly amazed at people indignant over the destruction of property, but ignoring the black youth's death. Lee was initially concerned to interrogate the conditions that could lead to wanton killings of black youth . . . Thus, Lee seems to believe that violent protest is a legitimate response to the senseless killing of blacks, as would, presumably, Malcolm X himself. In a book on the making of *Do the Right Thing*, Lee remarks: "The character I play in *Do the Right Thing* is from the Malcolm X school of thought: 'An eye for an eye.' Fuck the turn-the-other-cheek shit. If we keep up that madness we'll be dead." (Douglas Kellner, "Spike Lee's Morality Tales," in Cynthia A. Freeland and Thomas E. Wartenberg, eds, *Philosophy and Film*)

6. Set out the argument and note any assumptions in the following from film critic, Kathy Maio:

If male filmmakers cared what I and other feminists thought about their work (and they most assuredly do not), I'd almost pity their predicament. They face what amounts to a no-win situation. If they leave women out of their movies, or use us only as trivialized support characters, damsels in distress, or beautiful objects of their male lust, they get blasted for their sexism. If they use us as major characters, we still love to pick holes in their portrayals of women, and we blast them anyway. Of course, all this blasting is done for good reason. It seems as though it matters little whether it's a bimbo bit part or a dramatic lead, male filmmakers can't seem to keep themselves from saying nasty things about women. (Kathy Maio, *Popcorn and Sexual Politics*)

7. Study a review of a recent film (these can be found at film Web sites under "External Reviews" or through a film journal or major newspaper).
   a. Briefly characterize (or set out) the key points of each review.
   b. Respond to *one* of the reviewers about the review. Include feedback on his or her argument, noting what you see as the key strengths and any room for improvement.

The Prescriptive versus Descriptive Debate

Some people think pop culture is prescriptive—that it sets down social and ethical guidelines for us to follow. For example, some think TV and film can inspire "copycat" behavior or otherwise corrupt the audience. Just look at the reaction to Janet Jackson's exposed breast during the half-time show of the 2004 Super Bowl.

Similarly, some think music and video games can have a powerful effect—thus the calls for stricter rating systems, parental controls, or censorship. Some worry also about the impact of a pop icon's behavior, such as when Madonna and Britney Spears kissed at an MTV awards show. We also saw the media storm on September 23, 2004 when Yusuf Islam (aka Cat Stevens) was barred from entering the United States for unspecified homeland security concerns. The government's actions reinforced the widely held view that musicians and other celebrities have power—and influence. On the other hand, some think popular culture is **descriptive,** in the sense that it reflects, or describes, our society. They would argue that, if a film or TV show touches a nerve, it's because the nerve was already there in the first place, pulsating away in our body politic.

Be careful, however, not to bifurcate (see the situation as "either/or" when other alternatives exist). A work of pop culture may be prescriptive and a catalyst for some action, while also being descriptive of other actions, people, or communities. Furthermore, it could serve other functions. For example, film and TV often convey myths and meaning not clearly originating from the individual director or producer. Political undercurrents may be afoot that they unconsciously incorporate. For that reason, being able to take different theoretical models to the work helps us interpret its significance and better understand it within the broader framework of art, society, and culture.

Theories of Interpretation

As you might imagine, if we examine a film using a religious perspective, we see one thing; if we use a political or social perspective, we see another. **Conceptual frameworks** are like mental headgear—lenses for the mind's eye—coloring what we focus on and how we interpret what we see. Commentators often refer to theories of interpretation using such frameworks by the German word, **"hermeneutics"** (pronounced her-meh-new-tics).

The interpretive framework we use shapes our understanding. Let's take a classic of its genre, *Die Hard,* and see how this works. We will use six interpretative models: mythological, social, ethical, justice/political, philosophical, and psychological.

Film theorists usually add a seventh component: namely, the filmic aspects like cinematography, color, sound, music, and film editing. They were omitted here because, without special training, assessing those areas has little value beyond mere opinion. That said let's look at the six categories in action, starting with a plot summary.

Dimensions of Interpretation

1. **Frame of Reference**

- From whose perspective is the story told?
- Are there any other relevant perspectives?
- What would change if we shifted the frame of reference?

2. **The Mythological Dimension**

- Are there links to earlier myths, fairy tales, folk tales, universally shared stories?
- What major archetypes (such as heroes, villains, trusty sidekicks, damsels in distress), characterizations, and patterns are presented?
- What mythic elements are in the film?

3. **The Social Dimension**

- How are factors of race, gender, age, nationality, class, and education expressed?
- What social issues are explicitly or implicitly addressed?
- How are issues like sexuality, relationships, and psychological conflicts presented?
- What are the political messages of the film?

4. **Ethical and Spiritual Dimension**

- What values and beliefs are expressed?
- Are there any religious messages or religious symbols?
- Would a shift of perspective affect the values portrayed?
- How are the issues of good versus evil dealt with?

5. **The Justice Dimension**

- What is expressed or implied about justice versus injustice?
- Are there any stereotypes in the portrayals of characters?
- Who has power, and is that power used in a just way?
- Are race relations realistically portrayed?

6. **Philosophical Dimension**

- What philosophical ideas and issues are raised?
- Are there any metaphysical concerns—such as the nature of the universe or the individual's place within a larger context?
- How is the existential dimension examined—such as the search for meaning, authenticity versus inauthenticity, despair, facing death?
- How are concepts such as free will, personal identity, social responsibility, or other philosophical themes treated?

CASE IN POINT: DIE HARD

Plot Summary

Die Hard is an action film about a terrorist takeover of a high rise in Los Angeles in which the terrorists are mostly German and the hostages are employees of an international corporation. Only one man can stop them: John McClane, an NYPD officer who is a bit of a renegade. However, he is vastly outnumbered and lacks the arsenal of weapons the terrorists have at their disposal. Among the hostages is his wife, Holly, from whom he has been estranged because of marital problems he has come to Los Angeles to address. A psychologically wounded but good-hearted black LAPD officer, Sgt. Al Powell, befriends him but is powerless to give much more than moral support until the very end. As a result, McClane has only his own wits and physical strength to draw from. The movie is that story.

Framework 1: Mythological Interpretation of *Die Hard*

Examining *Die Hard* as a myth, we have the hero or prince, the villain and his evil side-kicks, helper figures, the princess (the estranged wife, Holly), and the community (the hostages) the prince rescues. The hero, McClane, is called by force of circumstances to save the princess (his estranged wife) and restore order. He did not go into this intentionally; he is a bit of a fallen angel (drinking problems, suspended from the New York police force). However, he must rediscover parts of himself and develop his own inner strength.

Along the journey, our hero faces obstacles of mythic proportions. He sheds blood walking on glass, which represents his getting in touch with his heart. He is willing to sacrifice himself so others may live. He goes down the elevator shaft, symbolizing the descent into darkness. In the darkness, McClane confronts evil spirits and must be willing to face his own death. He plunges into the abyss (over the rooftop, where he hangs by a thread). It's definitely the dark night of the soul for him.

Before the hero can win the heart of his beloved, he must prove himself worthy. He must show that he is good, selfless, loving. There is no compromise with the devil; that much the hero knows. He also knows that no one else can take his place—he has been called by destiny to go forth on this journey. McClane proves he is up to it.

Framework 2: Social Interpretation of *Die Hard*

Here we look at stereotypes, racism, sexism, religious or other sorts of group bias, expressions of power, unwarranted assumptions, symbols and images that reinforce or challenge the status quo, and social impact. *Die Hard* presents us with an all-American (white) male hero named John and Nazi-like villains with names like Hans. The psychologically scarred black buddy figure (who is healed as the movie progresses) and a black limo driver down in the garage are outside the action; the Asian CEO is killed; and the woman Holly is silenced. She dares not speak so as not to be used to flush out her husband, McClane. She is also silenced in more subtle ways. Having resumed her birth name, Holly Gennero, she ends up willingly relinquishing her name (and a part of her identity) as a result of her eagerness to be together again.

Some of the stereotypes include the hero (courageous, honest, good at heart); the villain (cold, cunning, vicious, uncompromising); the loving wife (selfless, dependent, caring, supportive, protective); the news anchor (selfish, ruthless, obnoxious); the police, fire fighters; and other social institutions (worthless except to clean up); the buddy-sidekick (devoted, supportive, likeable); Germans (cold, analytical, technologically adept, good at planning and execution); the Latina housekeeper (maternal, caring, easily manipulated, weak).

Framework 3: Ethical Interpretation of *Die Hard*

To examine a movie using an ethical framework we should look at these elements: the concept of good (and examples of it in the film), the concept of evil (and examples in the film), trust, caring, forgiveness, sin and redemption, justice, and revenge.

Die Hard presents good versus evil as an either/or situation. The hero is unquestionably good; the villains are thoroughly evil. McClane, even with a shady past and a need to clear his record, is still a sympathetic figure. The terrorists deserve to die (or so it seems) and, thus, McClane's shooting to kill rather than maim is presented as the correct thing to do. The presentation of evil in *Die Hard* is fairly straightforward. The terrorists are unequivocally evil. The audience is not expected to identify with or care for the terrorists.

The notion of justice is simple and straightforward. There is good, there is evil; there is loyalty to family and country. Self-reliance is crucial, and if the societal institutions won't or can't uphold what is right and good, then the individual must be willing to do so, regardless of personal risk. Do not tolerate those who have no regard for the values we hold dear. Be cunning and strong to confront those who are evil. Stand up for what is right and be willing to look death in the eye.

Framework 4: Justice/Political Interpretation of *Die Hard*

The film, from this perspective, presents a kill-or-be-killed situation of Darwinian proportions. The un-American, can't be negotiated with, have-no-respect-for-life terrorists aren't receptive to dialogue. The hostages are unarmed and unable to escape. Both a hostage and a TV anchorman put others at risk for their own personal gain. This is not an image of people working together. The police are ineffective—they give no credence to our hero McClane's call. An attempt to bring out the fire department similarly fails. McClane is on his own inside a monolithic building facing well-armed opponents who have no respect for American values of justice.

We have, then, an updated Lone Ranger tale: A New York cop hero faces great odds to overcome evil. Limited support is offered by two men on the outside, a limo driver down in the parking garage and Sgt. Powell, the LAPD officer with emotional baggage of his own who drove to the building to investigate McClane's call. Powell especially provides moral support while McClane is battling the forces of destruction on the inside.

The journey is perilous. This is not an argument for gun control; there are bad guys out there and we need all the weapons at our disposal to arm ourselves against them. It's a brutish world; and it demands that our heroes be willing to act like brutes in order to set things right again.

Framework 5: Philosophical Interpretation of *Die Hard*

In approaching *Die Hard* using philosophical frameworks, we want to consider how the film helps us better grasp the big questions of life, the existential situation of this one man, alone in his quest to set things right, and alienated from his peers—his fellow cops, other than the black, unarmed buddy figure who is similarly alienated. He faces the absurdity of terrorists who have no respectable values (as Holly said, they are simple thieves). They cannot be reasoned with, they won't negotiate, and they are untrustworthy in any case. He is an outsider, a nonconformist, a rogue with an attitude who doesn't follow rules that appear to make no sense. He lives in the face of his own possible death. He is willing to die for his beliefs.

McClane undergoes a personal transformation in the course of stopping terrorists from killing dozens of hostages. Doing some serious values clarification, he grasps the importance of his family and reaffirms his commitment to fight for what is good. He realizes that he has behaved inauthentically in the past but gets back in touch with his own integrity. We watch him apply problem-solving and critical thinking skills to put a stop to the terrorists and to save the hostages.

Framework 6: Psychological Interpretation of *Die Hard*

Examining the film from a psychological (say Freudian) angle, the terrorists represent the violent, uncontrollable parts of the psyche that must be watched by the moral conscience. Without firm guidelines, all hell will break loose, as shown in the film. The terrorists symbolize those parts of ourselves that we have failed to face. Out of the depths, no matter how deep we bury our psychic garbage, come monsters (terrorists) that surface and cause destruction.

John McClane, symbolizing the good, but stern, hero/father (the Ego), has to regain control over the errant parts of his out-of-control passions (his unconscious, the Id). The bloody feet he gets in doing so represent the loss of innocence that the hero must undergo in order to assume power (and to experience full sexuality). That he tears his clothes along the way, revealing his masculinity (his muscles) shows that sexuality is fully a part of our becoming our own person. His estranged wife rediscovers her beloved, reawakens her own desire, and reunites with him at the end.

Exercises

Part One

1. Study the portrayal of heroes:
   a. Draw up a list of male heroes found in TV and film. Note what distinguishes them as heroes—their actions, personal characteristics, community positions, and the like.
   b. Draw up a list of female heroes found in TV and film. Note what distinguishes them as heroes—their actions, personal characteristics, community positions, and so forth.
   c. Compare your lists, noting any patterns. Draw some inferences about the society from your lists.

2. Recently films featuring African-American males who are neither buddies nor comics have been released (e.g., *Man on Fire, Ray, The Manchurian Candidate, I,Robot,* and *Collateral*). Discuss what this indicates about changing perceptions of black men in our society.

3. *Robots, Toy Story, Lilo and Stitch* and *Shrek 2* are relatively unthreatening films for children. In contrast, director Tim Burton added a frightening, almost ghoulish touch to *James and the Giant Peach*. How would you make a film or TV show based on a fairy tale or popular children's story? Assume you want to include political or social commentary in your film. In three to four paragraphs, sketch out your approach or ideas. State which fairy tale or children's story you are using as a base.

4. Discuss the portrayal of women in any two prime-time TV shows with female leads, indicating to what extent the portrayals are (a) positive, empowering; (b) negative, disempowering; and/or (c) realistic versus unrealistic.

5. Discuss the portrayal of men in any two prime-time TV shows with female leads and to what extent the portrayals are (a) positive, empowering; (b) negative, disempowering; and (c) sensitive to real-life issues.

6. Discuss ways to confront stereotypical or racist views of others using the media of film and TV. Cite any examples you can from recent movies or TV shows.

7. Pick two TV families (each from a different TV show) and compare and contrast the treatment of the family on television.
   a. Note the similarities and differences.
   b. Note any cultural stereotypes about the "typical" family. Look at such aspects as race, class, education, and family dynamics.

8. How has TV dealt with sexuality? Answer *one* of the following, citing specific examples from TV shows:
   a. Do a study of a show that is aimed at both teenagers and/or adults and assess how realistic you think it is.
   b. Given the widespread fear of AIDS, is it wise of producers to show so much unprotected sex on the screen?

Part Two

1. Does TV accurately portray the impact of racism, poverty, and oppression on the life of an individual? Make your case, citing examples.

2. Answer *one:*
   a. Give an argument for or against the claim: "TV should show a gay couple or an interracial couple raising a child, since it would reflect something that goes on in our society."

b. Give an argument for or against the claim: "Children should be shielded from TV shows that present gays and lesbians in a sympathetic way."

3. What can we infer about societal attitudes about disability by the portrayals on the screen?

4. What would be different if a film were presented from another character's frame of reference? Select either a classic or contemporary film OR a prime-time TV program and explain what would be different if the frame of reference were shifted.

Part Three

1. Do you think films that use vivid scenes of violence, like *Hostage, Kill Bill Vol. 1* and *Vol. 2*, and *Reservoir Dogs,* are descriptive (realistically portray the society)? Are they prescriptive (try to influence how things should be)? Are they both? Is there another way to interpret them?

2. Why have so many films been about vampires? Write three to four paragraphs setting out your theory about what vampires symbolize; that is, what they tell us about our society.

3. Respond to the concerns raised by Princeton University Professor Karen Beckman, who wrote in the *Journal of Criminal Justice and Popular Culture (JCJPC):*

Why does our society long to look at the bodies of dead women? How are we, as viewers and readers, implicated when we watch or read repeated scenes of female torture? Why do serial killer movies generally not show the murder of women, focusing instead on the dead bodies left at crime scenes? These questions seem crucial to any analysis of the genre in a socio-political context. ("Review of Philip Simpson, PsychoPaths: Tracking the Serial Killer through Contemporary American Fiction and Film," *JCJPC* 8, no. 1, 2001)

4. Do a study of the first 10 minutes of four different movies, drawing from any of the various frameworks (theories of interpretation).

5. Discuss the screen treatment of young women (for example, in *Thirteen, Mean Girls, Bend it Like Beckham, Joan of Arcadia, Degrassi Junior High*). Is the portrayal realistic?

6. Looking at either TV or film, answer *one* of the following:
   a. Compare and contrast the female villain with the male villain.
   b. How should class struggles and/or poverty be presented? (For example, look at *Maria Full of Grace, Barbershop, The Commitments, Set It Off, Do the Right Thing.*)
   c. Discuss the treatment of substance abuse (e.g., in films *Traffic, 28 Days, My Private Idaho,* or TV shows *The Wire* and *The Sopranos.*)

Group or Individual Exercise

Select any recent film out on DVD or *one* of these films to study: *Blade Runner, Thelma and Louise, Spirited Away, Lord of the Rings: Return of the King,* or *Ghost Dog.* Each group should study the film using the framework below and should then share their conclusions with the class:

Group 1:   Sociopolitical analysis of the film.
Group 2:   Psychological analysis of the film.
Group 3:   Mythological analysis of the film.
Group 4:   Race/class/gender analysis of the film.
Group 5:   Ethical analysis of the film.

▨ The Impact of Pop Culture

Any work of pop culture can obtain iconic status given the right combination of time, place, message, audience, and mythic power.

Film, however, plays a special role in pop culture. "The movie is the total realization of the medieval idea of change, in the form of an entertaining illusion," says Marshall McLuhan in *Understanding Media.* He says the business of the filmmaker is to transfer the viewer from one world to another so that those undergoing the experience accept it subliminally and without critical awareness. This is the transformative power of the work—how it lifts audience members out of their everyday reality into another realm. Producer Edward Zwick says, "There are no truths, only stories. In my life, art has meant narrative . . . Only narrative can reach us in a kind of limbic place where learning begins." ("The Campaign Celebration," *Harvard Magazine* 102, no. 6, July–August 2000).

Some "entertaining illusions" provide the viewer with an escape from reality. There's a reason comedy flourishes in times of societal upheaval and wartime—as *Shrek 2* and *The Incredibles* did in the summer and fall of 2004. In contrast, some films take us into realms found in nightmares. To some degree, people are drawn to thrillers and to horror films—as shown by the popularity of *28 Days Later, The Grudge, The Ring,* and *The Forgotten*—not to mention "classics" like *Psycho, Alien, Terminator,* and *Silence of the Lambs.*

Exercises

1. What are all the reasons for seeing a movie more than once? List them. Then share your response to Robert E. Yahnke's view that multiple viewings are necessary to understand a movie. He says "multiple viewings are required of films—in the same way as multiple readings of a novel or multiple viewings of a play. . . . [In his view] film was more aligned with art than it was with entertainment." (Robert E. Yahnke, "Growing Up on the Films of the 60s," www.tc.umn.edu).

2. Briefly summarize Eric Katz's claim that "The character that most obviously illustrates Plato's argument that the unjust life leads to nothing but unhappiness is Gollum, who is invariably described as a miserable creature, afraid of everything, friendless, homeless, constant seeking his 'precious' Ring. Gollum . . . seems almost completely corrupted by the desire for it—every action that he takes . . . is designed to regain the Ring" ("The Rings of Tolkien and Plato," in Eric Brassham and Eric Bronson, eds. *The Lord of the Rings and Philosophy*).

3. Examine the way the Internet is being used to market films. Share what you find.

4. Discuss Gordon Paddison describing fans as "film-making partners"—or whether you think there's a better way to think of fans in marketing films:

"We reverse-marketed," explains Gordon Paddison, New Line's senior vice-president of global interactive marketing. "I used to hate the internet," studio chief Ari Avad recently confessed to *USA Today*. "I thought it was just a place where people stole our ideas. But I see how influential the fans can be in building a consensus. I now consider them as film-making partners ("We are all nerds now," *Guardian Weekly*, film.guardian.co.uk, 12 Dec 2003).

Violence on the Screen

On one hand, people decry the amount of violence and, on the other hand, they rush to see it. *Basic Instinct,* with its ice-pick sex murderer, was a blockbuster. The two *Terminator* films propelled Arnold Schwarzenegger to fame and fortune. *Pulp Fiction, Mean Streets, Apocalypse Now,* and *Taxi Driver* are commonly viewed as great films. *Silence of the Lambs,* a movie about a serial killer who skinned his (female) victims, won the Academy Award for best picture. And don't forget the ad: "You don't have to go to Texas to see a Chainsaw Massacre."

Philosopher Sissela Bok recommends we pay close attention to the societal impact of film, particularly with respect to violence. Her book *Mayhem* recommends a more socially conscious approach. In contrast Andrew Klavan said: "Violence,

The Global Dimension

The Portrayal of Middle Easterners on Screen

We need to be attentive to racist and stereotypical portrayals. We need also to watch for religious intolerance. Share your response to these three main complaints about the portrayal of Middle Easterners in film (Daniel Mandel, "Muslims on the Silver Screen," *Middle East Quarterly* 8, no. 2 (Spring 2001), www.meforum.org). See if you can find evidence (looking at film or TV) to either support or disprove any of Mandel's claims.

1. **Complaint #1:** *Islamic violence is distorted.* One important issue is international terrorism. Muslims and Arabs are unfairly singled out.
2. **Complaint #2:** *Islamic terrorism is invented.* Research verifies that lurid and insidious depictions of Arabs as alien, violent strangers, intent upon battling nonbelievers, are staple fare.
3. **Complaint #3:** *Muslims and Arabs never appear in sympathetic roles.* Muslims and Arabs rarely appear as sympathetic, mainstream characters but turn up almost exclusively as fanatical, homicidal terrorists.

along with sex, is a part of entertainment because it is part of human experience." He goes on to say, Indeed, Mr. Schwarzenegger's oversized screen persona will strengthen my faith in the real Schwarzeneggers who have to fight our battles for us—so much greater than the screen image because they are so much smaller, so much braver because they are so mortal and fragile and afraid. (See "At the Movies, Losing Our Fears," *The New York Times,* 5 Oct. 2001).

Exercises

1. Share your thoughts on the sentiments expressed below:

   Richard Belzer: I believe that indiscriminate violence or excessive violence in film and television not only affects young but older people, too, and I think it desensitizes people and is dehumanizing, but I don't think it's the role of the government to discern at what point is violence dehumanizing. I think that's the discretion of producers and creative people to exercise their own taste, for parents and educators and critics and people in the arts to, if something does get created that is virulently dehumanizing, then people can speak out about it in the appropriate forums. ("Screen Violence and Youth," www.members.fortunecity.com)

2. Share your thoughts on the sentiments expressed below:

   Gregg Easterbrook: I'm not in favor of censorship and no sensible person is. But there is a difference between saying that and saying everything should be shown. The sensible position is to ask Hollywood and especially companies like Disney to voluntarily stop promoting this kind of thing, not to attempt to censor it, you couldn't anyway, simply for Hollywood to ask themselves, what do they want their own children seeing? (www.voa.gov)

CHAPTER ELEVEN

Web Sight: Critical Thinking and the Internet

Knowledge and Information are key drivers of human freedom, growth, well-being and progress. The Internet and other networked information technologies are capable of delivering this potential widely and effectively. They can help people listen, but can also help them speak and be heard.

—BERKMAN CENTER FOR INTERNET & SOCIETY, *Harvard University*

A mythic being central to the Laguna Pueblo Indians is Spiderwoman, who is so powerful that she can *think* things into being. She spins a web of stories that can transform the world. Language becomes prayer, ceremony, and ritual as she weaves the web linking people to ceremonies and to the earth. This is a positive force: "Their evil is mighty but it can't stand up to our stories."

We reaffirm this powerful link between people every time we access the Internet. We reach out into the universe when we use e-mail, go online for technical support, access a database or a library catalog, or use a uniform resource locator (**URL**) to call up a Web site. Each **www** we type reminds us that we are inextricably bound to one another in the World Wide Web. We are globally as one, tied by a web that allows us to traverse thousands of miles in a matter of seconds or minutes. It is truly an astonishing resource.

The Internet has fundamentally changed our lives. It has the potential to democratize knowledge by making available a seemingly limitless range of possibilities for investigation and the communication of ideas and information. It has no geographic boundaries: It doesn't matter if you live in a penthouse or a shack, the boondocks or a bustling metropolis, a fleabag motel or a swanky suite, a yurt on top of Mount Tamalpais or out of the backseat of your car in Fresno. It truly is a *worldwide* web. Whether you are in New York City or Montreal, Tijuana or Taiwan, Cape Dorset or Guadalajara, you can go online and access products and services, phone numbers, addresses, and directions from one place to another, along with a wealth of information.

The Internet has the potential to level the playing field by allowing us to expand our knowledge base and communicate across virtually all borders and boundaries. The exponential growth of its use is staggering:

- In 1994, there were approximately 10,000 Web servers.
- In 1999, there were an estimated 10 million Web servers and 146 million people connected to the Internet (see James Gillies and Robert Cailliau, *How the Web was Born*).
- In 2005 an estimated 218.4 million North Americans and 816.4 million people worldwide were Internet users (according to Nielson Net ratings).

Remember that this resource requires either a wireless hub or a reliable telephone line and electricity—and access to a computer. This means the Internet is not available to everyone. Witness the low Internet use by Africans and Appalachians alike. Once we can address these obstacles and create global access to the Internet, the resulting resource will be revolutionary in its scope.

Think of all we can access through the Internet. We can locate people and businesses, do library research, access professional journals, take a virtual tour of an art museum, and create a map from point A to point B. We can research photos at the National Archives, access military records, read the entire first edition of Marx's *Das Kapital* in either German or English, and check out the worldwide reaction to the Red Sox coming from three games behind to win the World Series in 2004. We can converse with specialists on health issues, compare the film scripts of *Alien* and *Alien vs. Predator,* examine political commentaries on virtually any topic you can name, and delve into newspaper archives. If it's communication we desire, we can enter a chat room and discuss current events and access a host of conspiracy theories about what was sticking out under President Bush's coat in the first 2004 presidential debate and what vets and non-vets think of John Kerry's war service. We can read reviews on movies and concerts, local blues artists, or virtually any topic under the sun.

Within our reach is a vast network linking us to religious organizations, political and social action groups, job opportunities, and medical services. Of course, there are also links to the Aryan Nation, white supremacists, and other extremist groups. There are links to quacks offering a range of health remedies and hucksters selling worthless products, not to mention pornographers and dubious characters who would like to meet some nice young person to molest.

Group or Individual Exercise

The World-Wide Encyclopedia

In its March, 2005 edition, *Wired* magazine had an article on Jimmy Wales, who gathered together an army of contributors to create a "library of the future," a Web encyclopedia called "Wikipedia." Read about his efforts; share your response and any ideas you have for other ways to democratize knowledge via the Internet:

> Four years ago (2001), a wealthy options trader named Jimmy Wales set out to build a massive online encyclopedia ambitious in purpose and unique in design. This encyclopedia would be freely available to anyone. And it would be created not by paid experts and editors, but by whoever wanted to contribute. With software called Wiki—which allows anybody with Web access to go to a site and edit, delete, or add to what's there—Wales and his volunteer crew would construct a repository of knowledge to rival the ancient library of Alexandria. In 2005, the nonprofit venture is the largest encyclopedia on the planet. Wikipedia offers 500,000 articles in English . . . and the total Wikipedia article count tops 1.3 million. (Daniel H. Pink, "The Book Stops Here," *Wired* magazine, March, 2005)

Imaging the Internet

The language used to describe this resource is very revealing. Think of terms like "World Wide Web," "Internet," and "cyberspace." All three (webs, nets, and spaces) have *physical correlates* that are instructive to contemplate. The Web may seem fragile, but it *is* a well-constructed series of links with almost limitless possibilities.

The **Internet** really *is* a kind of net. Just like fishing nets that pull in battered old shoes as well as nice rainbow trout, the Internet offers garbage as well as treasures, useless junk as well as valuable information, and access to weirdos as well as to experts. In spite of attempts to set some limits   such as protections for children who may be vulnerable to predators—much of the Internet is wide open territory.

In that sense, **cyberspace** really is a kind of space. People, as well as corporations, have staked out territory and attempted to set guidelines and enforce rules of conduct. Some have made claims about who owns what in cyberspace. Given the vastness of the enterprise, it is virtually impossible to control its growth, regardless of any attempts to rein it in. The result is a universe of ideas, information, products, services, texts, contacts, commentaries, speeches, images, audiovisual aides, movies, music, historical documents, political tracts, advertising, personal bios, family albums, and more.

It resembles the Wild West, with few laws and almost no way to enforce them. It's so easy to erect a Web site or sign up for an e-mail address that setting controls and keeping some semblance of order is exceedingly difficult. Plus, the Internet lacks a central authority. No one has to "certify" your page. There are neither Internet publishing bodies nor police, as are generally accepted in "real life" societies. This leads to conundrums such as how to deal with differences in different nations' laws—for example, Nazi material is illegal in Germany, whereas it is merely thought tasteless in the United States.

The sheer glut of what's out there is staggering. But navigating the Web can be frustrating and difficult. To a great extent, we are on our own. The host of search engines and techniques may or may not get us to where we want to go. As T. Matthew Ciolek wrote in his article, "The Six Quests for the Electronic Grail":

> [The Web] can be said to resemble a hall of mirrors, each reflecting a subset of the larger configuration. It is a spectacular place indeed, with some mirrors being more luminous, more innovative or more sensitive to the reflected lights and imagery than others. The result is a breathless and ever changing "information swamp" of visionary solutions, pigheaded stupidity and blunders, dedication and amateurishness, naivety as well as professionalism and chaos. (T. Mathew Ciolek, "The Six Quests for the Electronic Grail," www.ciolek.com)

True, there is often a sense of being in an "information swamp" It just may be difficult to find the way out of the swamp. Plus, rarely are there guides or guidelines to orchestrate order in the chaos or lead us through the mazes we encounter.

Given the inherent untidiness of the Internet—indeed, a kind of anarchy—we need to acquire tools to navigate the system. Librarians can help us steer the way, but there is no *one* source we can access that will put things in order for us. Rather, we have to rely on our own problem-solving skills and ability to follow leads (and links) to find what we are looking for.

Other issues about the Internet are interesting as well. As critical thinkers, we want to examine Internet-related issues of freedom of speech, privacy rights, intellectual property, and what content should be accessible.

Exercises

1. Does e-mail force us into a frantic state, thinking we have to respond immediately? Read the following comment and state whether or not you agree:

   The unhindered and massive flow of information in our time is about to fill all the gaps [in time], leading as a consequence to a situation where everything threatens to become a hysterical series of saturated moments, without a before-and-after, a here-and-there to separate them. Indeed, even the here-and-now is threatened since the next moment comes so quickly that it becomes difficult to live in the present . . . The consequences of this extreme hurriedness are overwhelming; both the past and the future as mental categories are threatened by the tyranny of the moment. (Thomas Hylland Eriksen, *Tyranny of the Moment: Fast and Slow Time in the Information Age*, www.studentaffairs.com)

2. Set out directions to someone who has never used the Internet on how to search for the following:

   a. A particular professor at a specific university (e.g., Dr. Alfred Newman at Mad University).

   b. An essay written by a particular author (e.g., "Still Crazy after All These Years" by Zooey Wild).

   c. How to get to the web site of a newspaper (e.g., the *Chicago Tribune*).

   d. How to get the requirements for a philosophy major at a particular university (e.g., at Oxford University in England, University of Texas at Austin, Santa Monica College).

   e. Directions from an airport to your university (e.g., from the Detroit Metro Airport to the University of Michigan Law Library in Ann Arbor, Michigan).

   f. The latest edition of *Wired* magazine, www.wired.com.

   g. Five different film reviews of a movie (e.g., *Hero, The Fast and the Furious*).

3. Explain to a beginning Internet-user how to find articles on a complex topic with three to four terms (e.g., *Marines* who refused *anthrax vaccinations* and faced a *court-martial*. The first term is "Marines," the second is "anthrax," the third is "vaccination," and the fourth is "court-martial.") *Hint:* Don't forget the usefulness of the plus sign and the minus sign in running a search. Be aware, however, that different search engines and databases use different mechanisms. Some include all terms automatically, for example

4. Using your Internet search skills, find out what you can about how to avoid a Web hoax (fake Web sites that look like the real thing—for example, martinlutherking.org was created by a white supremacy group). Write a summary of what you find on Web hoaxes and any suggestions to avoid getting trapped by them.

5. What does the following report from the Pew foundation tell you about the role of the Internet in the life of a student? Share your thoughts after reading this report summary:

Seventy-nine percent of college students reported that Internet use has had a positive impact on their college academic experience. Nearly half reported that e-mail enables them to express ideas to a professor that they would not have expressed in class. Many college students also reported using the Internet primarily to communicate socially, with friends. ("Reports: Education," Pew/Internet, www.pewinternet.org)

6. *Know thyself.* Do an Internet search on *one* of the following: your family name, one grandparent or godparent, your birthplace, your birth date (day in history), your dream getaway, or your favorite music. Try several search engines (such as www.google.com or www.metacrawler.com), and several search terms (e.g., type in your last name, your dream place, etc.). Summarize what you learned (and what you were *not* able to learn) in your study. Note also what you learned about Internet searches from your study.

Web Hoaxes

The Web lends itself to practical jokes and hoaxes, given the ease of constructing and dismantling bogus sites. For examples see the Gallery of Hoax Websites (www.museumofhoaxes.com) or Hoaxbusters (hoaxbusters.ciac.org). Some Web sites play on people's gullibility and curiosity, but are otherwise quite innocent. Some are actually pornography sites. Others try to manipulate users so they are forced to see alternative viewpoints from the one they were seeking.

Web Hoaxes, Parodies, and Spoofs

- www.martinlutherking.org (professional-looking, but a white supremacy site).
- www.onion.com (parody site with silly articles—some have thought them real and cited them).
- www.funnycrap.com (spoof site, creates fake sites).
- www.whitehouse.net (cartoon). Other URLS that include "white house" lead to porn sites; the real thing can be found at www.whitehouse.gov (see the link to kids).
- www.whirledbank.org (this alternative version of www.worldbank.org, has the motto "Our Dream Is a World Full of Poverty").
- www.gatt.org (counterfeit version of www.wpo.org [The World Presidents' Organization is a global organization of more than 3,300 individuals who are or have been chief executive officers of major business enterprises]—www.gatt.org is highly critical of the World Trade Organization).
- www.adbusters.org/spoofads (spoofs of advertising).
- www.improb.com (publishes the parody, The Annals of Improbable Research).
- www.improb.com/archives/classical/cat/cat.html (produced the now infamous article "Feline Reactions to Bearded Men").
- zapatopi.net/afdb.html (Aluminum Foil Deflector Beanies to combat Mind-Control).
- lme.mankato.msus.edu/akcj3/bmd.html (The Burmese Mountain Dog site).
- www.buydehydratedwater.com (Buy dehydrated water).

- online.coled.mankato.msus.edu/ded/webcred/Fredericton.html (Visit exciting Frederickton site).
- www.ihr.org (historical review—a front for Holocaust revisionism).
- www.cafeherpe.com (commercialized health care site—pushes their product).
- www.globalwarming.org (says global warming is a hoax).
- www.gwbush.com (fake Bush site; the real one is at www.georgewbush.com).
- homepages.udaytonedu/~ahern/rurindx.htm (a site for a fictitious country with games and simulations used at the University of Dayton).

Deceit and Trickery with Domain Names

Web hoaxes and parodies aren't the only potholes on the Internet. What about the debate over domain names? A person, business, or organization may have the same name as a much more famous person or organization or a similar name—thus leading to confusion on a user's part.

For example, people for the Ethical Treatment of Animals didn't like it that People Eating Tasty Animals had the domain name peta.org—and the original PETA sued to get it! Another example: The Islamic Society of North America, one of the biggest Islamic groups, does NOT own www.isna.org. This Web site is run by the Intersex Society of North America! And Southwest Airlines' URL is *not* swa.com (the home of Simpson Weather Associates). In addition, some have purchased domain names of celebrities and corporations—to the frustration of both those whose names have been used and those who look for information using the obvious URLS (to no avail).

This phenomenon is related to **cybersquatting**—where someone buys the name of a well-known company and then demands money to give it up. As noted by Susan Thea Posnock:

> Though the Internet presents a powerful new channel, it also enables individuals to encroach upon magazine brands, by registering domain names with the intent to sell the URL back to the publishers at a high cost or lure customers to their own sites. Publishers say the best way to avoid cybersquatters is to strike first by registering domain names early. "We typically don't write the business plan or get the money approved without securing the URL," says Ann Wilkins, vice president, Internet Strategy and Development, Penton Media. "Be proactive," she says. ("Conquering Cybersquatters," *Folio: The Magazine for Magazine Management,* Spring 2001).

Cybersquatting has created havoc for companies, groups, and individuals. In recognition of the greedy or malevolent acts of some cybersquatters, Congress enacted the Anti-cybersquatting Consumer Protection Act (ACPA) in 1999. This act allows publishers to take civil action against anyone with bad-faith intent to profit from use of an identical or confusingly similar domain name. Those who don't want to sue (due to time and the costs) can fight the cybersquatter using an international arbitration system created by the Internet Corporation of Assigned Names and Numbers.

According to the World Intellectual Property Organization (WIPO), in the years immediately following the enactment of ACPA in 1999, they were flooded with filings against cybersquatters. This has subsided a bit in the last few years. Here is their update:

> In 2003, the Center received 1,100 UDRP (Uniform Domain-Name Dispute-Resolution Policy) cases, averaging 3 cases per calendar day, similar to the daily filing rate during the previous year. . . . In addition to famous brands (recent WIPO (World Intellectual Property Organization) cases include the domain names pepsi-smash.com, calvinklein-watches.com, rolexgroup.com), celebrities continue to be targeted by cybersquatters. . . . In 2003, the Center received cases relating to movies, authors and books (jrrtolkien.com, thecatinthehat.com), pop stars (nsyncfilm.com, utadahikaru.com), television shows (oscartv.com, operaciontriunfo.tv), and movie stars (piercebrosnan.com, victoriarowell.com). Sports personalities (terrellowens.com) and sporting events (torino2006.net, madrid2012.org) were also the target of cybersquatters. ("WIPO Continues Efforts to Stamp Out Cybersquatting," World Intellectual Property Organization, www.wipo.int, 27 Jan 2004)

The ACPA law targeted those who sought to profit using the domain name of another. The trouble is, not every cybersquatter wants to make a profit. Some just want to make a political statement, parody a corporation or individual, poke fun, or wreak a little havoc in the system. This appeared to be the case for the lawyer who opened verizonsucks.com back in 2000 and for *2600* magazine, which purchased verizonreallysucks.com. Verizon's lawyers were not amused and took legal action. However,

> The problem for Verizon: *2600* didn't want to "profit" from verizonreallysucks.com. They just wanted to occasionally poke fun at a large company, which means that the anti-cybersquatting law does not apply.
>
> "Verizon intends to go after anyone who criticizes them on the Net, abusing the intent of this law to accomplish their goal. We cannot allow this. We call on INDIVIDUALS around the world to criticize Verizon on as many domain names as possible and to exercise your rights to free speech," *2600*'s Goldstein wrote in an open letter on his website. Just to prove his point, Goldstein then registered another domain name: VerizonShouldSpendMoreTimeFixingItsNetworkAndLessMoneyOnLawyers.com ("Real Cybersquatting Really Sucks," *Wired*, www.wired.com, 9 May 2000)

Group or Individual Exercises

1. Select a few spoof or hoax sites from the list above and study them. Try to figure out the source (author or group) of the site, its purpose, whether there are links that take you to the "mother site," and reveal the agenda behind the site; and the issues and concerns the site raises.

2. Find two to three examples of cybersquatting Web sites—sites that use the name of a company, group, or individual although they are not affiliated with that group or person. List the URL and explain what the site is really about (as opposed to its misleading name).

Hoax Busters.   Hoax-buster and scam-buster sites can be helpful resources. Paul Piper notes a number of such sites, including these:

- www.nonprofit.net/hoax/hoax.html
- www.fraud.org/welmes.htm (a consumer fraud center, including Internet fraud); www.scambusters.org
- ciac.llnl.gov/ciac (Computer Incident Advisory Center)

Of help when confronting problems with hoax sites are the American Library Association (www.ala.org) and the U.S. Department of Energy (ciac.llnl.gov/ciac/CIAHoaxes.html). Some Web sites offer advice on how to avoid fake sites:

- Virtual Chase, a guide to legal research on the Internet (www.virtualchase.com)
- Wolfgram University's links and references on evaluating Web sites (www2.widener.edu/Wolfgram-Memorial-Library/webevaluation/webeval.htm)

Web Research

You've procrastinated as long as possible, but you are running out of time and that essay deadline is looming. It's too late to go to the library; all you have is your computer for a research tool. Well, it is not generally as helpful a resource as a library, but there is a lot out there on the Web. Ask yourself:

Will you access good information?

This is a search question.

Can you distinguish higher-level from lower-quality Web sites and documents?

This is an evaluation question.

We need to look at both of these questions. The first one involves being able to search the Web. For that, you need to know how to use search engines, when to try more than one search engine, and other ways to access reference material. That can take time, which needs to be factored in as well. Also, we need to apply problem-solving and questioning techniques to optimize searches. The second question brings in the range of critical thinking skills set out in this chapter.

Whether you are a seasoned veteran of Internet research or a novice, there's still a lot to learn and, as more and more Web sites are developed, the number of sites out there in the cyber galaxy is increasing. Below are 10 pearls of wisdom of Web research that we should all keep in mind as we navigate cyberspace.

Ten Pearls of Wisdom of Web Research

1. **Research takes time:** Allow time to follow links and links within links to investigate the resources out there. If you do, you may find far more than you ever imagined possible.

2. **Think like a fox:** Maybe you'll win the lottery, maybe not. Maybe you'll find great stuff after your first search, maybe not. Try different search engines and different ways of formulating questions or search terms.

3. **Be imaginative:** Be crafty when phrasing search terms. If one doesn't work, try another. Try different search engines and electronic databases, approach the topic through various avenues, and consider different perspectives. You may hit the jackpot with one of them.

4. **Libraries are good things:** Use library Web sites and resources. Try local library resources (e.g., lapl.org), university library Web sites, the Library of Congress, and so on. These have a wide range of resource tools, links, and helpful databases for accessing a wide variety of sites including online dictionaries. And don't forget the Librarian's Index to the Internet (www.lii.org) and the American Library Association Web site (www.ala.org).

5. **Don't reinvent the wheel:** Investigate professional organizations. Remember laws and legal decisions are available online (e.g., U.S. Supreme Court site, www.supremecourtus.gov, the U.S. Supreme Court multimedia database, www.oyez.com, and the legal database, findlaw.com), as well as statistics, government documents, photo archives, historical papers, music and film reviews, and other hard-to-find resources.

6. **Know your friends:** Publishers' Web sites are good places to scout for documents; government sites can be a treasure trove, as can national archives, newspapers online, online journals, and meta-search engines.

7. **Consider unlikely suspects:** Go to sites that seem tangential. These may not directly relate to your search, but they may provide a back door to the topic or to links and resources that take you where you want to go.

8. **Network:** Communicate with those who are in the know: E-mail professionals, organizations, or other online contacts if you have questions or concerns that their expertise can help. Be as precise as you can in your request. Many experts are generous with their time and will answer and offer some leads or give you feedback.

9. **Ask questions:** Formulating your search as a question helps in navigating search engines and using search tools. Clarify the focus of your search and how you might be able to narrow down the topic should the need arise. Contacting reference persons or giving feedback to a site may demand good, clear questions.

10. **Keep an open mind:** Be receptive to new ideas and fresh perspectives. Try a variety of approaches. Think of your research as tackling an intellectual puzzle. The answer to our prayers may be staring us in the face, but we need to be perceptive and receptive to different ways of seeing the world.

Exercises

1. Choose any *two* government Web sites such as the FBI Web site
    www.fbi.gov; the NASA Web site, www.nasa.gov; the Internal Revenue
    Web site, www.irs.ustreas.gov; the Center for Disease Control Web site,
    www.cdc.gov, and the U.S. Postal Service Web site, www.usps.gov.
    a. Compare and contrast the quality of the resources.
    b. Compare the relative ease of navigating the sites.
2. Pick any *two* celebrities (e.g., movie stars, athletes, famous authors), and
    then compare and contrast the best Web site you found for each of your
    two figures.
3. How are people honored? Select *one* area (Grammy Awards, Pulitzer
    Prize, Booker Prize, Nobel Prize, Caldecott Medal, Academy Awards,
    Juno Awards, Gemini Awards, Emmy Awards, Nammy Awards, NBA
    Hall of Fame, the Olympics, Boston Marathon, etc.) and then evaluate the
    awarding organization's Web site.

Problem-Solving Skills are Vital

You know those sci-fi films where the ship lands (or crashes) on an alien planet?
Sometimes, as in *Contact,* the alien planet is wonderful to behold and a great place
to visit. Other times, as in *Alien* and *Aliens,* the alien planet is a place to escape
from, the sooner the better! So it is with travel in cyberspace.

There are a lot of helpful, even fantastic, Web sites out there. But, as we travel
to the outer reaches of the cyber galaxy, we may unknowingly land in hostile territory where we get trapped. We could land on a Web site graveyard filled with
dead links, dead-ends, and nonexistent "contacts." Or we could land on a Web
site junkyard, piled up with useless trivia, outdated relics, or once valuable treasures that are no longer relevant. Fortunately, our critical thinking skills can help
us steer our way through all this and hopefully get us to a Web site that either
meets our objective or provides valuable leads so we can continue our quest. As
we navigate, keep in mind the pearls of Web research noted above. Fundamental
to our success are problem-solving and questioning techniques.

Problem-solving skills involve the ability to define the problem (issue) we wish
to solve (search), decide upon the appropriate terms to launch the search, redefine
terms, and narrow down the search with combinations of search terms that we either want to find or want eliminated. They also involve knowing when to mention names or add in quotes when seeking specific passages.

Be prepared to experiment with search engines, search techniques, search
terms, navigating through poorly constructed Web sites, and dealing with hoaxes
and dirty tricks. The Internet is in many ways more complicated than finding

things in a library—the organizational system starts with running a search. The results depend to a great extent on the wording of the search itself.

The results are often organized by frequency of visitation (a sort of popularity contest). While having some benefits in research, we can't depend on the numbers of visitors to a site as a guarantee that the material posted there is of superior quality. Be prepared to dig through the search results to make sure you've found the best material to explore.

Results involving news searches are generally organized in descending order by date. This can be extremely useful, particularly if we are searching for information that is timely. However, if our quest is for specific sorts of information, regardless of the date, we may have some fishing to do. Fishing takes time. Allow for that.

Question techniques are also important. Being able to formulate different types of questions is crucial for using the Web. We need also to be able to ask questions to help access information, ideas, images, and Web documents. Just being able to ask ourselves exactly what it is we are looking for—and for what purpose and level of detail—can make all the difference in the terms we use to commence the search and where we go from there.

Group or Individual Exercises

1. Find the best Web site you can for those who study or collect *one* of the following: stamps, sports cars, insects, antique dolls, soccer jerseys, feathers, baseball cards, or beads from Tibet.

2. What is the ideal university Web site? Set out your ideas about what should and should not be on a university Web site (e.g., phone numbers of offices and staff, cafeteria menus, course schedules, courses required for each major, average SAT score, retention rate, campus safety, and so on).

Web Analysis

Let's assume we've arrived at a Web page that looks promising. There are two major areas of **web analysis.**

ONE: Assessing the Web page to determine credibility.
This focuses on the source of the information—the site itself and its legitimacy.

TWO: Assessing the quality of the article(s) found on a Web page or Web site.
This focuses on the content of the Web page—the quality of the reasoning found there.

The first issue is to get to a legitimate *source* of information and ideas—one where the authors have the appropriate qualifications or credentials and where the site itself is subject to review. The second issue is one of *content*. Here we are concerned with the quality of the reasoning set out in the articles and other material found at the site.

In addition to our own reasoning powers, the American Library Association (ALA) has produced helpful guidelines for evaluating the credibility of a Web site. As we know from those Web sites with strange inhabitants, anyone can publish almost anything on the Web. There is no Internet editor or cyber cop to weed out the oddities, the fringe, the threatening, the unpopular, and the cheesy. That has both advantages and disadvantages.

One advantage is that it makes it less likely that tyrannical governments exist without a channel for opposition. That is, the Internet not only provides access to information, it also allows networks to form and alliances to build. Anyone with Internet access is fairly free to search for a wide range of documents. We can also go through archives that might otherwise be eliminated because they are narrow in scope or of interest for only a small number of people.

Assessing the Source: Credible Web Pages

We cannot assume that everything we find on the Web is legitimate, well researched, or credible. Most documents have not been subject to a peer review, a professional organization, or an editorial staff. In addition, most are not held to any standard of excellence. This means we have to learn to evaluate sites and determine the value and legitimacy of the material we find.

A handy guide to locate credible Web sites is available from the American Library Association. The ALA sets out five criteria for evaluating the credibility of Web sites: (1) accuracy, (2) authority, (3) objectivity, (4) currency, and (5) coverage. These criteria are useful for navigating the Internet to ensure that the Web sites you use are credible and up to date.

ALA Tips for Assessing the Credibilty of a Web page

1. **Accuracy:** Who wrote the page and how can you contact them? What is the purpose of the document and why was it produced? Is this person qualified to write this document?
2. **Authority:** Who published the document? What is the domain of the document? Is an institutional affiliation listed?
3. **Objectivity:** What goals or objectives does this Web page meet? How detailed is the information? Does the author express any opinions? Is the Web page a mask for advertising? Do you detect any bias? Why was this written and who is the intended audience?
4. **Currency:** When was it produced? When was it updated? How up to date are the links (if any)? Are there any dead-links are on the page? Is any of the information out of date?
5. **Coverage:** Is the information presented cited correctly? Are there links to more detailed documents or related resources? What function do the visual images (or sound/videos) serve?

Exercises

Directions: In the questions below, focus on the legitimacy of the Web site itself, drawing from the ALA guidelines (above).

1. Select any controversial moral or social problem (animal rights, abortion, stem cell research, gay rights, and so on) and find *one* Web site whose *legitimacy* can be called into question and *one* Web site that appears credible.

2. Find a Web site that shows the author lacks the appropriate *authority* to be taken seriously or that the Web site is clearly self-serving.

3. Find a Web site that completely fails the *objectivity* test. Be sure to explain how it fails.

4. Find a Web site that passes the *objectivity* test. Be sure to explain how it succeeds in presenting balanced and objective material.

5. Find two examples with respect to *currency*—one Web site that is verifiably up to date and another that is hopelessly outdated.

6. Find a Web site that provides an excellent example of *coverage* on a current topic (such as prison reform, teens and alcohol abuse, choosing a college, good nutrition, child obesity, etc.).

7. Find a Web site with good *coverage* on any *one* of the following how-to topics: house-training a puppy, repairing a banjo, cooking shellfish, ostrich farming, painting with glazes, caring for an exotic pet, polishing an antique car, training for marathon-runners, or teaching a parrot to talk.

Assessing Content

Whether we surf the Web or dog paddle our way through a few Web sites, we need to be able to think critically about what we see and read. Not only do we have to deal with images, symbols, and text, but we also have to deal with advertising, dirty tricks, hoaxes, spoofs, being manipulated, or being sent to a pornographic hinterland or an advertising stranglehold that traps us until we shut down. And that's not even considering computer viruses that arrive through e-mail attachments or e-mail advertising that comes out of nowhere.

The legitimacy of the Web site itself cannot be assumed—thus the guidelines above. Once we've arrived at a credible Web site, we are ready for the second stage of Web analysis—that of examining the content and assessing the quality of the reasoning. For these tasks, the tools acquired in the first unit of this book are crucial.

Critical thinking skills are not just handy—they are essential to accessing information, evaluating Web sites, and analyzing the material obtained on the sites.

The range of critical thinking skills that apply to use of the Internet can be summarized as follows:

Content Checklist

1. **Assess thoroughness.** Ask yourself if the Web site does what it's supposed to do in terms of providing information and resources, as well as links and hyperlinks when appropriate.
2. **Determine frame of reference.** Consider other perspectives that might be taken on the situation and how things would change if other voices were heard.
3. **Examine reasoning.** Zero in on arguments and assess the strength of evidence cited in support of the conclusion. Pull out key claims and examine the structure of any arguments set out on the Web page or associated articles. Be aware of inductive and deductive arguments. Watch especially for use of analogies, reliance on statistical studies, and cause and effect reasoning.
4. **Analyze and evaluate.** Look at the quality of the arguments and assess their strengths and weaknesses. Check for warranted versus unwarranted assumptions, potential sources of bias or prejudice, stereotypical thinking, and the use of images and symbols.
5. **Check use of language.** Watch for loaded terms, biased language, asymmetrical descriptions, repetition, metaphors, and poetic expressions to convey an idea.
6. **Watch for fallacies.** The Internet is not immune from fallacious reasoning, so watch for some common fallacies: ad populum (appeal to the masses or to patriotism), ad verecundiam (irrelevant testimonial or improper appeal to authority), ad hominem (personal attack), ad hominem circumstantial (attack due to vested interests or affiliation) and question-begging epithets (slanted language biasing an interpretation). See Chapter 4 to review.
7. **Watch for diverse perspectives.** Examine the values and worldview implicitly presented. How narrow or broad is the Web site's understanding of the people or issues involved? See how inclusive the author is of alternative positions.
8. **Assess visual and verbal messages.** Check the presentation of information and the use of images/photographs. See if they are relevant to the topic— or if they are used for gratuitous means.
9. **Assess ads.** Figure out the ads' purpose and likely connection to the material on the Web page and the Web site in general. The ads may not just be helping pay the rent—they may be an indicator of a vested interest (and bias) by the author(s) of the material.
10. **Watch references and links.** Examine the use of references, documentation, citation, and associated links. The links can be as revealing as footnotes in terms of the quality of the research.

Exercises

1. Discuss the content of any *one* of these Web sites:
   - Smoke free movies (www.smokefreemovies.ucsf.edu)
   - Boston Athletic Association (www.bostonmarathon.org)
   - Revlon (www.revlon.com)
   - Barbie (www.barbie.com)
   - Porsche (www.porsche.com)
   - Kelloggs U.K. (www.kelloggs.co.uk)
   - MTV (www.mtv.org)
   - Coca Cola Company (www.cocacola.com)

2. Discuss the content of any *one* of these museum sites:
   - Getty Museum (www.getty.edu/museum)
   - National Museum of the American Indian (www.nmai.si.edu)
   - California African American Museum (www.caam.ca.gov)
   - Canada Technology and Science Museum (www.sciencetech. technomuses.ca/english)
   - NASA Museum (www.hightechscience.org/nasa_museum)

3. Analyze *one* TV news site (e.g., pbs.org, www.abcnews.com, www.cnn.com, www.nbc.com, etc.).

4. Compare the Web site for the president of the United States with the corresponding Web site in another country (e.g., the Web site for the Prime Minister of Canada).

5. Analyze *one* Web site on any topic in medicine (such as smallpox, AIDS advances, lasik eye surgery, finding an egg or sperm donor, alternative treatments for teenage acne, etc.) or law (such as legal services for the poor, positions by professional law groups on social issues, legal research sites, etc.). Focus especially on the site's use of graphics and assess the overall organization of the site.

6. Analyze a Web site of *one* of the following hate groups noted by the Southern Poverty Law Center (www.splcenter.org/intel/map/hate.jsp): Christian Identity, Racist Skinhead, Ku Klux Klan, Neo Nazis, Neo-Confederate Movement, American Front.

7. Compare and contrast the Web site of the Democratic National Committee with that of the Republican National Committee or the Web sites of Canadian political parties: the Conservatives, the Liberals, and the N.D.P.

8. Compare and contrast a small-town newspaper Web site with that of a large urban newspaper, such as the *Globe and Mail* (www.globeandmail.com), *The New York Times* (www.nytimes.com), *Washington Post* (www.washingtonpost.com), *Atlanta Journal-Constitution* (www.ajc.com), *The Oregonian* (www.oregonian.com), *Chicago Tribune* (www.chicagotribune.com), the *Los Angeles Times* (www.latimes.com), and the *Edmonton Journal* (www.edmontonjournal.com).

Spam

Spam is *not* a delicious treat to snack on while working on the computer. It is unwanted e-mail that is sent—usually on a mass scale—to email accounts of people who neither directly nor indirectly requested such e-mail. As anyone knows who has ever been spammed, such e-mails waste time, effort, and patience. In the early years of spam, recipients had the illusion that a "do not subscribe" reply would suffice to end the unsolicited material. If anything, replies made the situation worse—for then companies knew that *you exist and you opened their e-mail!* In some cases, that signaled unscrupulous agencies to send you more spam. Why? Well, if you read enough of the e-mail to find the response button, who knows? Maybe you'll read the next one and be interested.

Unfortunately spam-artists have become very clever about finding ways to send out their unwanted e-mails. They appear to have no qualms about using others' names and e-mail addresses as a mask for their underhanded, deceptive practices. This causes the recipient of an e-mail that appears to be from an actual person to open it.

Dirty Tricks

Yes there are hoax sites. Then there are *dirty tricks*. As anyone who uses the Web regularly knows, sometimes you click a link and end up at a pornography site. This is an example of what's been called "user manipulation." J. D. Biersdorfer cites a case in September 1999 in which people trying to get to 25 million popular Web pages were intentionally rerouted to pornography sites that trapped them—they could only escape by shutting down their computers. In that case, the FTC (Federal Trade Commission—www.ftc.gov) filed an injunction against those who were responsible.

But that's not the only dirty trick. Manipulators of the Web have also been known to disable the "back" button, keeping you stuck at the site in hopes that you'll look at its content and ads. Then there's *metatagging*. A **metatag** is a place in the HTML code where information about the site is listed. Putting popular terms (like "sex") in the metatags guarantees more surfers to that Web site. (See J. D. Biersdorfer, "Trapped in the Web without an Exit," *The New York Times,* 7 Oct. 1999).

Metatagging

Metatags are certainly not inherently evil. They were designed to better match computer users with the sites they seek. Some search engines rely on metatags to offer a description of the site. It is when Web designers include irrelevant words that users are deceived. Metatagging can be used for deceptive and sneaky purposes. For example, Biersdorfer notes that companies could embed names of the rival so if someone searches for the rival company, they get the manipulator also. If you've ever hunted for sites on controversial issues like abortion, you've also encountered metatagging. Searches for pro-choice sites bring up pro-life sites. Of

The Global Dimension

Australian Prime Minister Left with Spam on his Face

After Australian Prime Minister (yes Prime Minister!) John Howard was revealed to have funded a pre-election e-mail campaign, the spam hit the fan, so to speak. Evidently a company owned by Howard's son carried out the dirty deed. Read the reaction and then answer the questions below.

> Howard's conservative government recently outlawed Internet spam, but exempted political parties, charities and religious organizations.
>
> The opposition Labor Party also condemned Howard's spamming. "The prime minister has breached the spirit, if not the letter of anti-spam laws," the party's technology spokeswoman Kate Lundy said. "John Howard's government banned commercial spamming this year, but then the prime minister goes ahead and spams the public for political benefit—this is a clear case of double standards." (Associated Press, "Australian Prime Minister Admits Funding Pre-Election 'Spam' Campaign," 27 Aug 2004).

Answer the following:

1. Should an election by declared void if *one* of the candidates spams the voters with campaign e-mail "leaflets"?
2. Should e-mail recipients who get politician's spam have a right to recourse? What recourse might that be? Share your thoughts and ideas.

---

course, some supposedly "pro-choice" sites turn out to be sites where the woman's choice should be to be a mother and not get the abortion at all.

Warning Systems on the Internet

Life can be funny. Even when it comes to computer viruses, things can take a humorous turn. Take the example of the "naked wife" virus that evidently ran amok in May 2001. While the worm was chomping its way through victims' computer files, governmental officials were gnashing their teeth trying to find a way to warn people. Evidently they became victims of their own forethought. The very warnings they tried to send bounced back, censored, censored, censored. Here's the scoop:

> A recent example [of literal meanings that are frequently wrong or confusing] is the "naked wife" virus that spread rapidly through cyberspace a few months ago. The Department of Energy found it couldn't send out a warning about the virus because its prudish computer software interpreted "naked wife" literally—and censored the warning. (K. C. Cole, "Moving beyond the Boundaries of a Literal Meaning," *Los Angeles Times,* 14 May 2001)

According to CNN, the bug masqueraded as a Macromedia Flash movie, using the subject line "Fw: Naked Wife." The e-mail message stated: "My wife never looks like that! :-) Best Regards," and then adds the name of the sender. The worm spread by e-mailing itself to addresses listed in the user's Microsoft Outlook address book, clearly wreaking havoc.

You Tell Me Department

What About the "Naked Wife" Warning:

If the Department of Energy (DOE) could not use the term "naked wife" to send a warning, how might we alert the public about this virus? We may need to know whether it was the word "naked" that was objectionable, the word "wife" that caused the glitch, or the complex phrase "naked wife." It may be interesting to know if "naked husband" would have caused a similar reaction in the government's software.

You tell me: So what could the Department of Energy do to get around the software censorship? Offer some ideas and suggestions.

FIGURE 11.1
Attila the Hun shrinks into the background next to hackers and worms!

Assessing the Impact of Internet Use

Henry Jenkins, director of the Program in Comparative Media Studies at the Massachusetts Institute of Technology (MIT), thinks the public dialogue about the Internet has become *bifurcated*—split into a false dichotomy.

The Global Dimension

Growing Up Online

In a conference held at the University of London, participants from 40 different countries looked at the impact of new media on children. An important discussion concerned children "growing up online"—that is, with access to the Internet as a daily reality.

> A highlight of the conference was London School of Economics professor Sonia Livingstone's announcement of the preliminary findings of a major research initiative called UK Children Go Online.
>
> According to the study, children were neither as powerful nor as powerless as the two competing myths might suggest. As the Myth of the Digital Generation suggests, children and youth were using the Internet effectively as a resource for doing homework, connecting with friends, and seeking out news and entertainment. At the same time, as the Myth of the Columbine Generation might imply, the adults in these kids' lives tended to underestimate the problems their children encountered online, including the percentage who had unwanted access to pornography, had received harassing messages, or had given out personal information. (Henry Jenkins, "The Myths of Growing Up Online," *Technology Review,* www.technologyreview.com, 3 Sep 2004)

Answer the following:

1. Jenkins thinks the truth lies between these two extremes. Do you agree? In your experience, what do *you* think of the influence of the Internet on children?
2. How can either parents or schools play a role in helping children use the Internet in ways that are not potentially harmful to the users or those around them? (For example, should all schools install software to block certain types of Web sites?)

Evidently, one school of thought holds that there are two ways of looking at the Internet: that it breeds violence and social anarchy or that it liberates children from the confines of home and limitations of narrow-minded parents.

Jenkins expresses this polarization in terms of myths. The Myth of Columbine links school shootings to children's unfettered access to Internet pornography and violence. This myth is characterized by despair. The Myth of the Digital Generation, on the other hand, links online accessibility to the developing children's creative potential and making them better informed, socially connected people (See Henry Jenkins, "The Myths of Growing Up Online," *Technology Review,* www.technologyreview.com, 3 Sep 2004). Jenkins believes the truth lies somewhere between these two extremes.

Many children *do* have access to potentially disturbing, graphic images and text via the Internet—that much is true. However, children also have access to information and ideas that can transform their lives in terms of their education and personal growth. We ought not lose sight of this opportunity. For this reason, being able to apply critical thinking skills to use of the Internet is a necessity for even the youngest of users.

⊞ Blogs and More Blogs

Web logs or **blogs** are Web sites that function as online journals. Blogs can be about anything—and bloggers can be anyone. No one checks credentials for bloggers to get online. As *Time* magazine reports:

> A few years ago, Mathew Gross, 32, was a free-lance writer living in tiny Moab, Utah. Rob Malda, 28, was an underperforming undergraduate at a small Christian college in Michigan. Denis Dutton, 60, was a professor of philosophy in faraway Christchurch, New Zealand. Today they are some of the most influential media personalities in the world. You can be one too. (See Lev Grossman, "Meet Joe Blog," *Time* magazine, 21 June 2004)

Blogs tend to be narrowly focused (e.g., on recent advances in technology), while others are basically wide open. Many include links to commentary, news items, or other Web sites, making it easy for the audience to access the material the blogger cites (for instance see the Drudge Retort, www.drudge.com)

Just about any field you can name has a blogger or two sharing ideas, or opinions. Some blogs are great resources, with succinct summaries of what has been written on a topic. According to Lev Grossman, blogs existed under the radar until 2002. Then things changed:

> Most of America couldn't have cared less. Until December 2002, that is, when bloggers staged a dramatic show of force. The occasion was Strom Thurmond's 100th birthday party, during which Trent Lott made what sounded like a nostalgic reference to Thurmond's past segregationist leanings. The mainstream press largely glossed over the incident, but when regular journalists bury the lead, bloggers dig it right back up. "That story got ignored for three, four, five days by big papers and the TV networks while blogs kept it alive," says Joshua Micah Marshall, creator of talkingpointsmemo.com, one of a handful of blogs that stuck with the Lott story.
>
> Mainstream America wasn't listening, but Washington insiders and media honchos read blogs. Three days after the party, the story was on Meet the Press. Four days afterward, Lott made an official apology. (See Lev Grossman, "Meet Joe Blog," *Time* magazine, 21 June 2004)

According to *Adweek*, the audience of blogs is an ad agency's dream. To be specific,

> *Everybody Loves Raymond* they're not. Weblogs, still a fringe medium with an insider cred and a distaste for self-censorship, reach just 2 percent of some 70 million online households, according to Forrester Research. But it's who they're reaching, not how many, that is whetting the appetites of a few intrepid advertisers. Upscale, urbane and media-savvy trend-setters with money to burn—most between 26–35 and male— are online and reading blogs, which deal with everything from gossip (Quentin Tarantino's recent fistfight with French bouncers was a recent favorite) to informal product reviews. (Deanna Zammit, "In Blog Bonanza, Some See Fringe Benefits," *Adweek*, www.adweek.com, 17 May 2004)

You Tell Me Department

Forget Blogs—What about Text Messaging?

A new service from the Institute for Applied Autonomy (www.appliedautonomy.com), TxtMob, was introduced at the 2004 Democratic National Convention. It allowed more than 260 subscribers to automatically blast text messages to the mobile phones of every other subscriber. An article in *Wired* magazine about this new device reported that:

> "There were . . . a number of interesting uses that the system got put to" at the DNC, said John Henry, TxtMob's developer. "Police did arrest one protester, and there were not a lot of people around. Someone saw it happen, (sent a TxtMob message), and a hundred of that kid's friends were on the scene in minutes . . . to make sure" the police acted correctly. And because of concerns that police at the convention would run roughshod over them, some protesters found that TxtMob was useful for keeping each other apprised of police movements.
>
> For now, TxtMob is being used exclusively for political organizing. But Henry said once the technology has been fully proven after the conventions, he envisions it in any number of environments, including organized scavenger hunts, raves and even large companies that want to send out messages to widely dispersed work forces. According to Emily Turrettini, author of Textually.org, a blog about advances in text messaging, TxtMob could well prove to be a crucial tool for anyone trying to organize groups of people amid rapidly evolving circumstances. (Daniel Terdiman, "Text Messages for Critical Masses," *Wired* magazine, 12 Aug 2004).

You tell me:

1. Should TxtMob be available to those outside of law enforcement?
2. Does the potential benefit outweigh the risks?

Already advertisers are paying upwards of $375 a week to advertise on a Web log, Zammit notes. She says because of their uncensored nature, however, blogs have not become vehicles for mainstream online ads.

Blogs are more Wild West than High Society. As a result, some aspects of blogs are problematic—their anonymity means little or no accountability. According to graphic designer Steven Heller, blogs allow anonymous potshots that can be posted according to whim. The absence of accountability is the blog's great flaw ("Blog Me, Blog Me Not," *Print,* May–June 2004).

Grossman echoes this sentiment, saying, "In a way, blogs represent everything the Web was always supposed to be: a mass medium controlled by the masses, in which getting heard depends solely on having something to say and the moxie to say it. Unfortunately, there's a downside to this populist sentiment—that is, innocent casualties bloodied by a medium that trades in rumor, gossip and speculation without accountability." He cites as an example the rumors that hit blogs over Senator John Kerry having an affair with an intern—which both denied.

Blogs can be great resources, especially on current events or specialized topics. They have certainly had an enormous impact on mainstream media. But the lack of accountability or qualifications on the part of the blogger tells us this: Blogs must be viewed with care and occasionally caution. Watch for credibility on the part of the source and have your critical thinking tools at your disposal.

The Internet and Intellectual Freedom

One nice thing about the exposure to ideas is that it makes us think! Of course, not all ideas that we come across are noble or worth preserving. Some ideas are disturbing, disgusting, or detestable. On the other hand, some ideas are cathartic, inspiring, or groundbreaking. Some ideas have truly changed the world.

Access to ideas and information is necessary for a democracy to flourish—and we cannot take this for granted. Just look at the ongoing issues around works of fiction. In the last 30 years a number of novels have been banned from libraries or schools, including the *Harry Potter* series (by J. K. Rowling), *Death of a Salesman* (Arthur Miller), *The Color Purple* (Alice Walker), *Brave New World* (Aldous Huxley), *A Clockwork Orange* (Anthony Burgess), *The Diary of a Young Girl* (Anne Frank), *Forever* (Judy Blume), *Harriet the Spy* (Louise Fitzhugh), *1984* (George Orwell), *Of Mice and Men* (John Steinbeck), *One Flew over the Cuckoo's Nest* (Ken Kesey), *The Shining* (Stephen King), *Slaughterhouse Five* (Kurt Vonnegut, Jr.), *That was Then, This Is Now* (S. E. Hinton), *To Kill a Mockingbird* (Harper Lee), *Ulysses* (James Joyce). (For a fuller list and discussion, see the American Library Association Web site at www.ala.org)

Many of these works are considered classics of fiction. However, objections to them were raised for a variety of reasons such as profanity, undermining race relations, graphic language, immoral tone, lack of literary quality, violence, irreverence, explicit sexual content, demonic possession, vulgar language, Communist sympathies, and teaching children to lie, talk back, and curse, among others. For example, *To Kill a Mockingbird* has been accused of "undermining race relations," yet the novel was selected in August of 2001 as the *one* book that people in Chicago should read and discuss.

"Restriction of free thought and free speech is the most dangerous of all subversions. It is the one un-American act that could most easily defeat us," asserts Supreme Court Justice William O. Douglas ("The One Un-American Act." *Nieman Reports, 7,* no. 1, Jan. 1953). The American Library Association (ALA) seconds this view:

> The free expression of ideas as embodied in the First Amendment is a basic human right. As American citizens, we have the right to read what we want to read, hear what we want to hear, watch what we want to watch and think what we want to think. Intellectual freedom is the right to seek and receive information from all points of view, without restriction, even those ideas that might be highly controversial or offensive to others.
>
> As a personal liberty, intellectual freedom forms the foundation of our democracy. It is an essential part of government by the people. The right to vote is not enough— we also must be able to take part in forming public opinion by engaging in open and vigorous debate on controversial matters. Libraries allow people to be well-informed so they can make the decisions our Constitution says are ours to make. (See American Library Association, www.ala.org)

Incidentally, not all librarians agree with this position. One side of the controversy goes like this: What about the fact that libraries "discriminate" in what books and videos they purchase? One criterion for selecting what to buy is *quality*. Does the filtering process that libraries use in purchasing materials for the library have no parallel in the cyberworld? Some contend that filtering software is against the right to access information and ideas. They consider that any form of censorship has the potential to take us down a slippery slope, leading to the censorship of literature or ideas. That is why the ALA is fighting attempts to "protect" children by requiring filtering software in library computers.

On the other hand, many librarians and others argue that human filters have been in place since public libraries first opened. They note that we ordinarily set limits around what is socially permissible and have had no problems ejecting people from libraries if they cross the boundary of decency or acceptable behavior. It is important for us to look at both sides of this issue and apply our critical thinking skills.

Group or Individual Exercise

Read over the list of the 10 banned books recommended by the Independent Booksellers and the American Library Association's "Most Challenged Books of 2003." (see www.abffe.com)

Answer the following:

1. Why do you think these books were banned or challenged?

2. What concerns about these books might apply to the Internet?

The Ten Banned Books Recommended by the Independent Booksellers Fall 2004

To Kill a Mockingbird, by Harper Lee
King & King & Family, by Linda de Haan and Stern Nijland
Brave New World, by Aldous Huxley
I Knew Why the Caged Bird Sings, by Maya Angelou
The Adventures of Huckleberry Finn, by Mark Twain
Places I Never Meant to Be: Original Stories by Censored Writers, edited by
    Judy Blume
Fahrenheit 451, by Ray Bradbury
Fools Crow, by James Welch
*Kaffir Boy: The True Story of a Black Youth's Coming of Age in Apartheid
    South Africa,* by Mark Mathabane
Stones from the River, by Ursula Hegi

The Challenged Books of 2003 Noted by the American Library Association:

1. *Alice* series, for sexual content, using offensive language, and being unsuited to age group.
2. *Harry Potter* series, for its focus on wizardry and magic.
3. *Of Mice and Men* by John Steinbeck, for using offensive language.
4. *Arming America: The Origins of a National Gun Culture* by Michael A. Bellesiles, for inaccuracy.
5. *Fallen Angels* by Walter Dean Myers, for racism, sexual content, offensive language, drugs and violence.
6. *Go Ask Alice* by Anonymous, for drugs.
7. *It's Perfectly Normal* by Robie Harris, for homosexuality, nudity, sexual content, and sex education.
8. *We All Fall Down* by Robert Cormier, for offensive language and sexual content.
9. *King and King* by Linda de Haan, for homosexuality.
10. *Bridge to Terabithia* by Katherine Paterson, for offensive language and occult/satanism.

If we look over the list of challenged books, we see the following issues that are deemed objectionable: sexual content, offensive language, magic and wizardry, inaccuracies around the gun culture, racism, drugs and violence, homosexuality, and the occult/Satanism. Any number of these can evoke strong reactions. The question is where we should draw lines—both with regard to books and with regard to the Internet.

Censorship of the Internet

It's interesting to consider the censorship of the Internet alongside censorship of books. Obviously there are many similarities, but one key difference is how easy it is to access Internet sites in the privacy of your own room. Thus, unsupervised children may come upon (or seek out) material that parents would not normally allow them to access and libraries would not likely contain (e.g., pornography and hate speech). The question is whether those differences are sufficient to suggest a different policy for the Internet than for novels and other books.

Harry S. Truman remarked in 1950 that, "Once a government is committed to the principle of silencing the voice of opposition, it has only one way to go, and that is down the path of increasingly repressive measures, until it becomes a source of terror to all its citizens and creates a country where everyone lives in fear" (Special Message to the Congress on the Internal Security of the United States," www.trumanlibrary.org, 8 Aug 1950).

Group Exercise

Taking into consideration the proliferation of pornography, hate sites, and access to potentially offensive documents, answer the following:

1. State the three to four strongest arguments for and against censorship of the Internet.

2. Assume a mediation model. You can't have all or nothing when it comes to censorship, so what would you agree to let in? And what would you consider essential to be banned from the Internet? Make a decision.

3. State the strongest justification you can for what should be *included* or what should be *excluded* from the Internet. Focus on *one* group of users: (a) private users; (b) adults at public sites (cyber cafes, libraries, colleges, and universities); or (c) minors at public sites (schools, libraries, cyber cafes, etc.).

Conflicting Views of the Internet

As we can see from the anti–World Trade Organization Web sites (check them out!), many worry about the gap between the rich and the poor. Many of these sites are concerned about the ways in which technology like the Internet may be fueling that division, as we see in this statement on ethics and the Internet issued from the Vatican:

> One of the most important of these involves what today is called the digital divide—a form of discrimination dividing the rich from the poor, both within and among nations, on the basis of access, or lack of access, to the new information technology. . . . Individuals, groups, and nations must have access to the new technology in order to share in the promised benefits of globalization and development and not fall further behind. . . . Cyberspace ought to be a resource of comprehensive information and services available without charge to all, and in a wide range of languages. (Pontifical Council on Social Communications, The Vatican, www.vatican.va)

This raises important questions about economics and social justice and educational equity. The Internet, however, can also be used to fortify resistance, strengthen channels of communication, and share information—and it can do all this quickly and efficiently. And, although it provides channels for mega-corporations to expand their horizons, we also find Web sites allowing those in faraway places to survive.

Think of Benedictine monks illuminating manuscripts on Web pages (see the Vatican Web site at www.vatican.va). Think of Tibetans trying to sustain their culture, religion, and language (see the government of Tibet in exile at www.tibet.com). Think of all the Native American tribes whose Web sites are hubs of information (see for example, www.cherokee-nc.com, www.tlingit-haida.org, and www.navajo.org). Think of all the indigenous artists trying to sustain traditional arts and crafts by selling beadwork, weaving, and sculpture through Web sites. Such groups often lack the resources, contacts, financial backing, and channels to reach others. The Internet opens up a host of opportunities that can be transformative.

GROUP OR INDIVIDUAL EXERCISE

The FBI Wiretap System

The FBI has an Internet wiretapping system, initially called "Carnivore" and renamed DCS1000, that has been described as a PC Robocop. Like a pig sniffing for truffles, this system uses a "packet sniffer" during criminal investigations to sniff out data for the FBI. For instance, DCS1000 can be used to harvest information from e-mail messages (both ingoing and outgoing) much like tapping a phone line to trace the origin and destination of a suspect's calls. Supposedly it can capture and archive all traffic through an Internet service provider. Read the following excerpt and then answer the questions that follow.

The new system, which operates on off-the-shelf personal computers, takes advantage of one of the fundamental principles of the Internet: that virtually all such communications are broken up into "packets," or uniform chunks of data. Computers on the Internet break up e-mail messages, World Wide Website traffic and other information into pieces and route the packets across the global network, where they are reassembled on the other end.

FBI programmers devised a "packet sniffer" system that can analyze data flowing through computer networks to determine whether it is part of an e-mail message or some other piece of Web traffic.

The ability to distinguish between packets allows law enforcement officials to tailor their searches so that, for example, they can examine e-mail but leave alone a suspect's online shopping activities. The system could be tuned to do as little as monitoring how many e-mail messages the suspect sends and to whom they are addressed—the equivalent of a telephone "pen register," which takes down telephone numbers being called without grabbing the content of those calls (John Schwartz, "FBI's Internet Wiretaps Raise Privacy Concerns: New System Tracks Suspects Online," *Washington Post*, 11 July 2000).

Answer the following:

1. What do you think are the major concerns about DCS1000 (Carnivore)?
2. Do an Internet search and see what others consider Carnivore's strengths and weaknesses.
3. What should be done about this system that has the capabilities to scan private information and collect data on people (suspects and nonsuspects)?

FIGURE 11.2
Somebody knows you're a dog.

Surveillance and National Security Issues

Shortly after the 9/11 terrorist attacks on the United States using commercial aircraft, concerns surfaced about computer privacy. Fears were expressed that the FBI would seek to expand the steps taken with DCS1000/Carnivore:

> "I heard former President (George H. W.) Bush saying we've got to prepare to give up our civil liberties," said Erwin Chemerinsky, a constitutional law professor at the University of Southern California Law School in Los Angeles. "All of that sentiment is very dangerous at this point in time. I think there's going to be a real effort to give government more surveillance authority," he added.
>
> "When I heard (of) this (attack), I thought people are just going to trample the Bill of Rights into the dust," said Lance Cottrell, president of Anonymizer.com, which allows people to surf the Web anonymously. (Reuters, "Experts Say Digital Privacy May Suffer Amid Attacks," 13 Sep. 2001)

Terrorists in the 9/11 terrorist attacks, however, left a paper trail—they used credit cards, real names, and rental car receipts. Nevertheless, the wider issues that involve computer privacy versus government surveillance continue to be unresolved.

Finding a way to balance the competing concerns is not easy. For instance, in 2003 the federal government protected around 14 million documents, a 60 percent increase since 2001. The cost is high. Eric Lichtblau reports that, "Classifying and maintaining the nation's secrets amounted to $459 a memo—or $120 spent on maintaining secrets for each dollar spent to declassify and release them." Clearly it is a lot cheaper for the government to be open, rather than to have so many secrets.

The consequences are more than financial: Access to information has been stymied. As Lichtblau points out, "The resulting backlog at some agencies has delayed responses by up to four years. . . . At the same time, the Justice Department has made it easier for federal officials to refuse to release public records in the name of national security" (Eric Lichtblau, "Government by, for and Secret from

CHAPTER 11   Web Sight: Critical Thinking and the Internet   475

the People," *The New York Times,* 5 Sep 2004). Rep. Christopher Shays (Connecticut Republican) has this to say: "There are too many secrets." Others see it as the inevitable result of 9/11 and the "war on terror," particularly since e-mail has become a more prominent form of communication.

The Internet and Individual Privacy

This could be subtitled: *Big Brother is watching you!* See Fig. 11.2. The trend seems to be moving to the view that "less is more"—individuals should be willing to give up privacy rights in order to have a more security-conscious society. Between the USA Patriot Act and changes allowing the FBI to access e-mail from "public" servers, the concept of a right to privacy is being chipped away. This may be for the collective good, but it does have a price in terms of individual liberties.

According to the *Daily Journal,* the United States is funding a chat-room study to see if terrorists using the Internet to communicate could be monitored (and presumably stopped). Bulent Yener, a computer science professor at the Rensselaer Polytechnic Institute, hopes he can develop mathematical models to uncover structure within the scattershot traffic of online public forums. Yener will search for patterns, tracking the times messages were sent so he can create a statistical profile of the traffic. So if two people sent e-mail within seconds of each other, it may be that they are speaking to one another (Michael Hill, "U.S. Funds Chat-Room Study to Thwart Terrorist Plotters, *Daily Journal,* 12 Oct 2004).

Since they are focusing on chat-rooms, authorities are not violating constitutional rights to privacy, experts say. However, Johnathan Zittrain, Internet scholar at Harvard Law School, observed, "In a world in which you can embed your message in a pixel on a picture on a home page about tea cozies, I don't know whether if you're any better if you think chat would be any particular magnet." Mark Rasch, former head of the Justice Department's computer crimes unit, felt the system would bring us closer to the Pentagon's Terrorism Information Awareness program that was so roundly criticized. He said, "It's the ability to gather and analyze massive amounts of data that creates the privacy problem, even though no individual bit of data is particularly private" (as quoted by Michael Hill).

Have you ever opened your "preferences" on your Internet server to examine your list of "cookies" that enable access to Web sites? This can be an eye-opening experience, as it reveals how open your window is to the world. Attached to the cookies for the particular site are almost always a host of cookies enabling companies to track your use of the Internet (i.e., what Web sites you navigate to). This is of great interest to advertising agencies because it helps companies figure out where to invest their marketing dollar. That the practice comes at a price to your privacy does not cause the twinge of the corporate conscience that some would like to see. Consequently, consumers and privacy watchdog groups seek to address the issue of cookies. Law clerk William McGeveran offers this observation:

> It seems everyone subscribes to the famous aphorism from Justice Brandeis that describes "sunlight" as "the best of disinfectants." [That is, we ought to have as much openness as possible to avert corruption in a society.] This consensus persists despite

two countervailing legal trends. First, there is rising concern in nearly every other area of the law about information privacy. Scholars engage in lively discussion about its possible social, legal, and constitutional dimensions. Congress has enacted new protection for the confidentiality of records about an individual's health care, finances, and even video rentals.

Some of these initiatives encountered difficulties in implementation, but the trajectory of policy concern points consistently toward privacy. Information about campaign contributions is more easily available to the public than any of these other types of data, and perhaps more sensitive, yet there is little sign of commensurate concern about its privacy. (William McGeveran, "Mrs. McIntyre's Checkbook: Privacy Costs of Political Contribution Disclosure," as noted by Rich Hasen, electionlawblog.org, 17 Mar 2004)

Group or Individual Exercise

Following the Money Trail

You have awakened from your political slumber and decide to give money to a worthy political cause. Feeling very strongly about who should win the election, you dip into your life savings and give $200 to the League of Disaffected Voters. Your act of civic involvement has, unbeknownst to you, got your name on a fund raising tracking list. William McGeveran, as we know from the above quote, has concerns about this electronic foray into your once-private affairs. Perhaps you do as well, perhaps not. Read the following comments by Rick Hasen and then answer the questions below:

> I'm all for disclosure of major contributors and spenders in federal campaigns, but every once and a while I'm reminded of the privacy costs that come from disclosing the identity of small contributors. The last time was when I read William McGeveran's fine article on the topic. Now comes a link from the excellent website Political Wire (www.politicalwire.com) to Fundrace 2004's Neighbor Search. (www.fundrace.org/neighbors.php). Just plug in your home address and find all of your neighbors who have given as little as $200 to a presidential candidate. I found out a number of interesting things about my neighbors through this simple search. ("The Anonymity Costs of Disclosing Small Donations," posted by Rick Hasen, electionlawblog.org, 17 Mar 2004)

Answer the following:

1. Try out Fundrace's Neighbor Search to see how it posts names and addresses of contributors. State three to four possible uses that might be made of this information by political campaign organizers and/or advertising agencies.

2. Is this information that could be used in ways that violate individual liberties in general or you in particular would find offensive? Share your thoughts.

You Tell Me Department

How Can We Respect Privacy in Public Cases?

The rape case involving Lakers basketball star Kobe Bryant was dismissed, but it is an instance of what might be called trial by Internet. The case elicited a great deal of attention. Screw-ups on the part of the court only added to the reality that the Internet has changed our lives in many significant ways. As we all know, an error in what goes out as e-mail can have significant repercussions. This case showed that as well.

> In the Bryant case, court clerks have twice posted the name of Mr. Bryant's accuser, notwithstanding a court order to keep it secret. In addition, a court clerk mistakenly e-mailed a transcript of a secret hearing to seven news organizations, . . . Lawyers from Mr. Bryant's accuser say the mistakes have endangered her, done harm to her mental well-being, undermined her willingness to pursue the case and will discourage others from coming forward with allegations of sexual assault. (Adam Liptak, "Kobe Bryant's Accuser, Internet Victim," *The New York Times,* 15 Aug 2004)

You tell me: How can we balance the interests of the "public's right to know" and the rights of the news media with the individual's right to privacy in high-profile cases such as this one?

The Internet and Community

When it comes to the impact of computers in our lives, we face a range of concerns. Some relate to maximizing the beneficial options of this resource—look, for instance, at MIT putting up all of their course syllabi online. Others have shadow-sides that give rise to controversy—look, for instance, at the problems around e-mail privacy at the workplace or free speech issues around Internet pornography. Also, problems arise with hackers getting into corporate databases and wreaking havoc. In October 2004 UC Berkeley and Purdue University were both victimized by hackers. This caused them to notify students, faculty, and staff to change passwords and otherwise protect personal information.

Consider the degree to which the Internet has become a channel for communication on a large scale. News is sent around the world in a millisecond. Very quickly book groups can "chat" about their reactions to their latest read. In a flash of an eye, people can send out to the world their thoughts on political conventions, world events, neighborhood conflicts, and the like. This has both positive and negative aspects. One dark side is that hate groups can proliferate, given the almost otherworldly or underground quality to the Internet. A determined individual can do considerable harm with such a tool.

On the other hand, the Internet has an amazing positive side. This tool allows people to communicate without ever hearing the other's voice or seeing the other's handwriting. As Amy Harmon put it, "many of those who make an effort to take advantage of what it [the Web] has to offer say that the cultural impact of the Web lies not in its would-be alternative media outlets, but in the way it facilitates contact between individuals who would otherwise never have the benefit of each other's experience." ("Exploration of the World Wide Web Tilts from Eclectic to Mundane," *The New York Times,* 26 Aug 2001).

The Global Dimension

Landmine Victims in Central America

The U.S. State Department estimates that there are 60 to 70 million landmines in nearly 80 countries. Equally mind-boggling is that one kills or maims victims an average of every 22 minutes. According to the United Nations, 30 to 40 percent of these victims are children. More than 52 million stockpiled antipersonnel mines have been destroyed by 69 countries, including 4 million in 2003 ("Global Landmine Use Decreases, But Mine Ban Campaign Cautions against Complacency," www.icbl.org/news, 9 Sep 2003). In an article on innovative uses of online courses, Bonnie Rothman Morris tells the following story. Read it and then discuss the questions that follow:

> A medical worker in San Miguel, a city in eastern El Salvador, Mrs. Monge de Quintanilla toils daily . . . making and fitting prosthetic limbs for up to eight amputees daily, most of whom are victims of land mines. She acquired her skills as a prosthetist a decade ago through a military program during the war in El Salvador. In June she started an eight-month distance-education course intended to

train her in the latest prosthetic techniques. She is one of 23 prosthetists in El Salvador, Nicaragua and Guatemala who are taking the pilot program, which was developed by the Center for International Rehabilitation, a three-year-old organization in Chicago that works to help victims of landmines.

The lessons for the prosthetics course were developed at the Northwestern University Prosthetic Orthotic Center. (See Bonnie Rothman Morris, "Online Course Lets the Isolated Bring Their Medical Skills Up to Date," *The New York Times,* 30 Aug. 2001)

Answer the following:

1. Discuss the potential for using the Internet to help address other societal problems or tragedies.
2. Suggest ways of disseminating medical or other expertise, and any innovative ideas to help those who are short on money, resources, or personnel and yet face serious issues like the one Mrs. Monge de Quintanilla is trying to alleviate.

We saw the value of the Internet to help people in September 2004, when the biggest evacuation in Florida history was underway. Hurricane Frances was heading straight to Florida, and she was *not* in a good mood. Plus she was big (the size of the state of Texas). Thanks to the Internet, the state of Florida posted a list of services, emergency shelters, weather updates, the status of roads, Red Cross services and locations, and the like. Similarly, the Internet was instrumental in rallying help and money for tsunami victims after December, 2004.

Exercises

1. Select *one* issue, such as homelessness, poverty, access to health care, prisoners who claim innocence and seek DNA testing to make their case, teachers who are addressing literacy problems in the inner city, people with poor English language skills who are trying to access health care or education for their children, battered women and children trying to rebuild

their lives, teenagers struggling with substance abuse or alcohol, children with learning disabilities trying to make it through public schools. Then:

a. Write down all you think is being done to address this issue in our society.

b. Are you optimistic or pessimistic about how much we are doing to try to make a difference? Set down your thoughts.

c. Using *only* the Internet, see what is being done to address the issue you selected. Summarize your findings.

2. Select *one* of the following groups: the police, fire department, local churches, doctors/nurses, social workers, psychologists, lawyers, teachers, actors, musicians, airline employees, members of the military, Mothers Against Drunk Driving, Al Anon, and so on. Then:

a. Set out your ideas about what the group you selected is doing for community outreach or other ways it provides service for the community.

b. Try several searches (e.g., police and community outreach) to find information about the group you picked. Summarize the results and share whether or not you were surprised at your findings.

c. See what you can find on your group using community-networking Web sites such as www.scn.org and www.bev.net. Note that you can read about public libraries' role in providing community information at www.si.umich.edu/Community.

3. In light of the excerpt below, set out your three strongest arguments for or against allowing prisoners to use the Internet for online dating:

Online dating, the Web's largest trackable source of consumer dollars, drew $300 million last year. Prisons, one of America's largest industries, are worth an estimated $40 billion. . . . Convict matchmaking giants like prisonpenpals.com and jail-babes.com claim between 7,000 and 10,000 ads, and scores of competitors: from the straightforward (inmate.com) to the suggestive (ladiesofthepen.com). . . . Notoriety seems to almost guarantee mail—and proposals. . . . Last month, a personal ad on WriteAPrisoner.com by Susan Smith, the South Carolina mother who drove her two sons into a lake in 1994, drew an estimated 1 million e-mails and letters. . . .

Penpal sites make their money by charging inmates (roughly $40 to $75) to post their ads and print and forward any responses, or by charging pen pals (usually less than $10) for inmate addresses. Few US prisoners are allowed access to e-mail or the internet, so most never see their listings. Some sites boast pages of testimonials: from soon-to-be-released convicts who've found love to death-row inmates who say letter-writing has given them a way to come to peace with dying.

Some states take an active stand against the sites. In 2001, the Oklahoma Department of Corrections issued "misconduct" citations to 51 inmates for violating the department's policy that "inmates may not directly or indirectly use any Internet services." Last fall, on the other hand, a California judge overturned that state's DOC prohibition against inmates receiving mailed printouts from the Web, calling the policy "arbitrary." (Mary Wiltenburg, "Web's Largest Business Pairs up with Another Huge Industry: Prisons," *Christian Science Monitor*, www.csmonitor.com, 7 Aug 2003)

4. *You decide:* Convicted murderer Mumia Abu-Jamal (who says he was framed) has a number of Web sites supporting his release from jail (his legal appeals have thus far been denied). Convicted murderer Leonard Peltier (who asserts his innocence as well) also has Web sites presenting the case for his release. Examine at least one of the pro-Abu-Jamal Web sites *or* the pro-Peltier Web sites and then share your thoughts on how the Internet can (and should?) be used for political and personal causes.

5. What should be done to protect young people from sexual predators on the Internet? We keep reading about teenagers and children who are lured by a sexual predator posing as a "friend" in online chat rooms. Law enforcement agencies have stepped up Internet patrols, in light of the rising incidents. Read the following comments and then offer your suggestions about how to stop Internet predators of teenagers and children:

"There is no silver bullet," said Bob Weaver, the assistant special agent in charge of the New York Electronic Crimes Task Force, which is run by the Secret Service and harnesses the efforts of 45 law enforcement agencies. "Traditionally, law enforcement in general has a stovepipe approach," he said. "The primary focus is on arrests, prosecutions and convictions. Now you're getting into education. Now you make a difference. You're going to catch the kids before they have a problem."

Some pupils are told the story of an investigator in New Jersey who tracked down a girl he met online using the scant information she had given him, then warned the girl and her parents that others could do the same. "Some of them sit there and they're amazed," said Robert M. Sciarrone, a special agent in charge of the program. "We tell them not to give out personal information." (Elissa Gootman, "Stepping up Protection for Youths on Internet," *The New York Times*, 21 Aug 2001)

Hate Speech on the Web

The Web is no more immune from hate speech than any other vehicle of communication that does not have strict controls. The very existence of hate-filled Web sites creates a controversy around freedom of speech and freedom of information. Many think we should err on the side of freedom, letting the audience decide for themselves. On the other hand, some are alarmed at the rise of hate sites.

The White Supremacy (alias "White Nationalist") Web site called Stormfront is said to be the Web's first hate site and the most-visited white supremacist site on the Net. It was reported that more than 5,000 unduplicated visitors come to Stormfront daily, and several hundred a day (344,000 in two years) have visited the children's pages, called "White Pride for Kids." (See Tara McKelvey, "Father and Son Team on Hate Site, USAToday.com, 10 Aug 2001). At the kids' link of the Stormfront Web site is an image of an American flag morphing into a Confederate flag. We also find games, music, and other links to appeal to children.

The Anti-Defamation League (ADL) claims that Don Black, the creator of Stormfront, is behind another site called Bamboo Delight. According to the opening Web page, this combines "Aryan knowledge with Chinese Medicinal Exercises" (www.bamboo-delight.com). ADL reports that

> [A]nti-Semitism pervades the *Bamboo Delight* Web site. . . . The site hides downloadable anti-Semitic and racist computer programs behind the false front of a company selling "Tai Chi Chuan Chinese Exercise" materials. Looking past "Asian Health Philosophy" items such as the "Nine Treasure Exercises of Ancient China" videotape and the "Skinny Buddha Weight Loss Method" pamphlet, Web surfers find the downloadable computer programs "Jew Rats," "Police Patriots," "ZOG" and "Talmud." . . . "Jew Rats" is a multi-panel cartoon that depicts Jews as rats that kill Christians and encourage integration. Blacks are depicted as subhuman gorillas. ("Don Black: White Pride World Wide," The Anti-Defamation League, www.adl.org)

Other countries are starting to take action against Internet hate speech. For example, the Council of Europe has adopted a measure that would criminalize Internet hate speech, including hyperlinks to pages that contain offensive content. It bans "any written material, any image or any other representation of ideas or theories, which advocates, promotes or incites hatred, discrimination or violence, against any individual or group of individuals, based on race, colour, descent or national or ethnic origin, as well as religion if used as pretext for any of these factors" (Julia Scheeres, "Europeans Outlaw Net Hate Speech," *Wired* magazine, 9 Nov 2002).

Reaction on this side of the Atlantic has not been very supportive. American civil rights groups concerned about freedom of speech have condemned the European ban as "chilling" and/or "terrifying." The U.S. Justice Department has indicated it will not support broader restrictions because of potential incompatibility with First Amendment rights to free speech.

> "It's a terrifying prospect," says James Gattuso, a research fellow for the Heritage Foundation, a conservative think tank. "It's inherently dangerous for governments to define what appropriate speech is. You can't define or limit speech without chilling speech." The protocol is subject to interpretation, he notes. "If you have a cartoon criticizing French foreign policy, would the French government have recourse?" he asks. "I don't see anything that would exclude that."
> The treaty says Internet service providers would not be held responsible for simply hosting a Web site or chat room containing hate speech. However, if the Council of Europe member countries adopt laws that make it a crime to distribute such material to the public through e-mail or Web sites, this may negatively impact privacy and Internet use by Americans, say some civil liberties groups. (Michelle Madigan, "Internet Hate-Speech Ban Called 'Chilling'," *PC World*, 2 Dec 2002)

Exercise

On February 28, 2005 the husband and mother of a federal judge, Joan Humphrey Lefkow, were murdered execution-style. Speculation was that the murders may be tied to a decision unfavorable to a White Supremacist, Matt Hale. After the ruling, evidently some websites targeted Lefkow. Although the perpetrator appeared to have no ties to Matt Hale or to white supremacists, the case had a chilling effect on judges across the country. Here's why:

> The judge was once the target of a murder plot by a white nationalist, and postings praising the slayings on supremacist Web sites were accompanied by "RAHOWA!", meaning "racial holy war." . . . In a discussion on a white nationalist Web site in 2003, members had talked about the case against Hale and posted the Lefkows' home address. Anti-Defamation League official Mark Pitcavage said another white supremacist's short wave radio show last April had discussed killing the judge. . . . Judge Lefkow had been threatened by white supremacists since she ruled against them in a trademark case. ("Hate Groups Eyed in Judge Kin Slay," CBS News, www.cbsnews.com, 2 Mar 2005).

Answer the following:

1. List the key concerns for judges and lawyers prosecuting hate groups.
2. Make the strongest case you can for or against censoring websites that condone acts of violence in the name of a cause or political ideology.

Group or Individual Exercise

Poisoning the Web: Hate Speech

The Web has become a powerful tool of extremist groups. They can reach a vastly wider audience with significantly less cost than in the past. They usually target blacks, Jews, gays and lesbians, abortion providers, and others whose lives are deemed of little value. Groups like the Southern Poverty Law Center, the Anti-Defamation League, and many other civil rights groups and peace-oriented organizations have raised concerns about the harm done by hate Web sites. Some think we need to draw limits; others think Web censorship will end up hurting everyone by restricting free speech and the sharing of ideas.

Directions: Read the article below from the Anti-Defamation League and then write a three- to four-paragraph response, noting the issues and concerns raised in the article and whether or not you were persuaded by the reasoning here.

Poisoning the Web: The Internet as a Hate Tool

The Anti-Defamation League

For years hate groups have created written materials of every kind to spread their propaganda, including books, glossy magazines, newspapers, flyers and even graffiti. As communication technologies advanced, these groups have kept up. First, they used standard broadcast-band and short wave radio, audiotape, videotape and public access cable TV. More recently, bigots of all kinds recognized the Internet's power and rushed to use it to rally their supporters, preach to the unconverted, and intimidate those whom they perceive as their enemies.

Even before *Stormfront* appeared on the Web, extremists had begun exploiting other ways to use the Internet, and these practices continue today. Lively conversations take place on numerous extremist Internet Relay Chat channels, such as #Nazi and #Klan. The USENET, a collection of thousands of public discussion groups (or newsgroups) on which people write, read and respond to messages, attracts hundreds of thousands of participants each day, both active (those who write) and passive (those who simply read or "lurk"). Newsgroups have been compared to community bulletin boards. Haters of all sorts debate, rant, and insult their opponents on newsgroups with titles such as *alt.politics.white-power* and *alt.revisionism*.

Electronic mailing lists (or "listservs") flourish as well. Such lists are like private "bulletin boards" available only to subscribers. While some lists keep their subscription information confidential, most are easy to join. Postings to some of these lists are moderated (i.e., monitored by the list operator who applies certain standards of acceptability), but others are entirely unregulated. . . .

Extremists also use E-mail, which allows them to communicate with one another directly, their missives ostensibly hidden from public view. In fact, E-mail is not truly private: computer-savvy individuals can intercept and read private messages. Some users, nervous about eavesdroppers, now use cryptographic programs. Cryptography converts written material using a secret code, rendering it unreadable by anyone who does not have the means to decode it. With encrypted E-mail, extremists have found a secure forum in which to exchange ideas and plans. . . .

Though purveyors of hate make use of all the communication tools the Internet provides, the World Wide Web is their forum of choice. In addition to its multimedia capabilities and popularity with Internet users, the Web allows bigots to control their message. Organized haters complain about civil rights activists who critique their manifestoes in USENET newsgroups and other interactive forums. In contrast, haters can refuse to publish critical messages on their Websites, just as a TV station can refuse to broadcast another station's opinions over its airwaves.

Furthermore, it is impossible for someone surfing the Web to know if any particular organization, other than one with a national reputation, is credible. Both the reputable and the disreputable are on the Web, and many Web users lack the experience and knowledge to distinguish between them. Increasingly, Web development tools have made it simple for bigots to create sites that visually resemble those of reputable organizations. Consequently, hate groups using the Web can more easily portray themselves as legitimate voices of authority.

Source: Reprinted with the permission of the Anti-Defamation League

The Logic Connection

CHAPTER TWELVE

Wrestling with Big Questions:
Pinning Down Arguments

"I thought most of the civilians there were interpreters, but there were some civilians that I didn't know," Karpinski told me. "I called them the disappearing ghosts. I'd seen them once in a while at Abu Ghraib and then I'd see them months later."

—SEYMOUR HERSH, *The New Yorker*

There's an interesting villain in *Spider-Man 2:* Dr. Otto Octavius, who became his own experimental subject in a glorious moment of scientific progress. He ends up with gigantic metal tentacles fused onto his body. These tentacles have a "mind" of their own and proceed to cause a lot of death and destruction. The downward spiral from victor to victim and then from victim to villain unfolds as the movie progresses. It's not a pretty sight.

An unsuccessful attempt by a surgical team to remove the metal tentacles set in motion Dr. Octavius' descent into a living hell. He is doomed to spend the rest of his life trying to undo what he unleashed by pushing the limits of technology. Dr. Octavius, nicknamed "Dr. Octopus," is an example of an unusual sort of xenotransplant. Instead of using a pig liver or a baboon heart, however, our good doctor transplanted robotlike arms with the powers of an "intelligent machine." As the experiment runs amok, Dr. Octavius' life loses all semblance of normalcy as he becomes a robo-beast with a serious anger management problem. Mayhem ensues, until our hero, Peter (aka Spider-Man) convinces the mad doctor that enough is enough. Dr. Octavius quite literally puts an end to his disastrous foray into high-risk experimentation.

This seemingly fanciful tale may stretch reality. But there are parallels around us. We now have technological options that once were unthinkable—other than in science fiction. Dr. Octavius may have had advanced training and skills at his command, but he failed to think critically about the costs of what he was doing.

He lacked the street smarts to realize that ideas dreamed up in isolation should not be set loose without a public airing. And he made a big mistake forgetting to have a "Plan B" for the worst-case scenario. Dr. Octavius also slipped up on the value scale, wreaking havoc and harming others with his short-sighted and unreflective decision making.

It is important to develop—and use—the critical thinking tools we've been covering in this book. Remember that we are fallible and must be prepared to mop up any messes we make. Humility, a trait Dr. Otavius lacked, helps us keep things in perspective.

Real-life applications of our critical thinking skills are all around us. They pop up when we read the newspaper, turn on the TV, listen to the radio, talk to friends, look at Web sites, and glance up at billboards as we drive along the city streets. How we respond often reveals our notions of fairness or justice, our values, attitudes, and sense of obligation to those around us. We may think we know ourselves. But a decision, an action—or the failure to act—can cut to the quick of who we are. One such moment has the potential to strengthen—or unravel—the fabric of our lives.

In this chapter, we put our critical thinking tools to work by tackling longer articles. Our focus will be on articles where someone stakes out a position and then offers a justification in an attempt to persuade us to their way of thinking. Our goal is to dismantle the argument so we can analyze it and thereby assess its strength. This can be done in a number of ways; having a few techniques to draw from can be vital. Being able to organize the argument is a key step in the assessment process.

Here are some powerful methods for breaking down longer arguments:

First Method: The Flowchart
Second Method: The Highlighting of Key Phrases
Third Method: The Standard Form of the Argument
Fourth Method: The Traditional Outline
Fifth Method: The Bubble Outline

We will look at each method in action, to see how to use it. After all five methods are laid out, you can select from several articles to put any or all of these to use.

First Method: The Flowchart

The first method we'll look at is the flow chart. With a flowchart, we break down an article so we can see its structure. Once we get an overview of the structure, setting out the thesis and supporting evidence is a much less daunting task.

We will apply the method to an article that uses two parallel analogies. One analogy is between prisons and schools. The other is between what the author Paul Farley calls the "new slavery" (oppression of blacks today) and "old slavery" (oppression of blacks in the past). He argues that there is a link between the "new slavery" and the dual failure of urban schools and the prison system. Read the article and try to pull out the key point(s) of *each paragraph*.

Failing Schools, Prisons Produce People Doomed to Failure

Anthony Paul Farley

Daily Journal   June 14, 2004

Two million people are imprisoned in the United States. The majority of them are black. This is slavery in a new form, as is the scandalous quality of the educational resources meted out to the heirs of *Brown* v. *Board of Education*. The attack on freedom and the attack on literacy are related. Among the many thousands gone the way of incarceration are few, very few, who ever had the experience of a decent school.

Far too many of our urban schools resemble prisons. Visit one of these schools, and you will see how dreams are killed at an early age by educators who do not love the children that they have promised to educate. Dreams are killed by an educational-industrial complex that creates conditions that make such love impossible to imagine, as an ever-more-color-lined nation abandons altogether the twin dreams of education and emancipation.

Many, far too many, of these dreamless children find themselves leaving their loveless schools only to land in prison. Our failing schools, like our failing prisons, are overwhelmingly and unconscionably black. The failure of the school and the failure of the prison together create the color line. The new slavery—linked to the old by the color line—is the product of this two-stranded failure.

Failing schools produce illiteracy just as surely as failing prisons produce recidivism. In the antebellum South, the dream of the literate slave was always emancipation, just as the dream of the emancipated slave was always literacy. Reading and freedom have always been connected in the minds of former slaves and former slave masters in the United States.

We cannot forget that in the United States it was illegal to educate slaves, because the same people who were prisoners of the old slavery are prisoners of the new slavery. We cannot forget, because the same people who were forcibly kept illiterate then are kept illiterate now. Slavery is present today, in the prisons and in the schools.

Our schools fail. Our prisons fail. The former produce illiteracy while the latter produce recidivism—and both kill dreams of an emancipated future in the United States. When institutions fail year after year, we must re-examine what we mean by failure. When the reformers respond to this year's failure with last year's failed solutions, we must examine what we mean by reform. All these failed yet endlessly recycled reforms continue the color line's division of the United States into two nations: black and white, separate and unequal. And there seems to be no exit. What is to be done?

This is being done in Dorchester, Mass.: Since 1994, we have conducted a literature program for women and men who have been convicted in the Dorchester District Court for various offenses. The Dorchester experiment is part of a statewide program called Changing Lives Through Literacy, founded by professor Robert Waxler of the English department of the University of Massachusetts, Dartmouth, and by Judge Robert Kane. The founding Dorchester organizers include two judges, Sydney Hanlon and Thomas May; two college English professors, Ann Murphy and Taylor Stoehr; a law professor (me); six dedicated probation officers; and a number of Boston College law students.

The program has been an outstanding success. For many of the participants, it was the first time that they ever read a book from cover to cover. Many have confessed to me their late realization that reading can be liberating and enjoyable. They look back in anger at the ways that their schools succeeded in causing them to fail themselves by producing failing grades. They realize that they can read and that they have ideas about great literature. And this causes them to look forward with hope.

At the end of each term, we hold a voluntary graduation ceremony in the District Court. The graduates invite their family and friends. Most years, one or more of the graduates gives a short valedictory speech to the audience. Each graduate is presented with a diploma. Tears and applause always accompany the graduation ceremony. Afterwards everyone joins the judges in chambers for tea.

A literature program is just the beginning. If a university-level course can be taught as probation, then anything can be taught anywhere to anyone. Probation offices all over the nation can be transformed into schools. Prisons too can be transformed, into places of elementary, secondary, university and graduate education. And with success in the transformation of our failed prisons into successful schools must come success in the transformation of our failed schools.

Because our schools have become prisons, our prisons, and the urban schools that resemble them, are hated. They are hated because they show, more than any speeches or proclamations or court rulings or acts of legislation, the true attitude of the United States toward blacks and our dreams of education and emancipation. Our prisons, whatever they may be labeled, must be transformed into schools. If this seems like a dream, it is no less real than the nightmare we will live if our nation remains half slave and half free.

One program is not enough. All of our prisons need to become schools, and all of our schools need to become limitless palaces worthy of the boundless imaginations of youth. To break the color line, to save our bodies and souls from the nightmare we have manufactured, to renounce the past and create a decent society at long last, we must fight for literacy and emancipation as for bread and roses.

Which side are you on?

Source: Anthony Farley is an associate professor at Boston College Law School. Copyright 2004 *Daily Journal* Corp. Reprinted and/or posted with permission.

Setting Out the Flowchart

Let's break down the article with a flowchart to see Farley's thesis and support. Number each paragraph and briefly label what's in each paragraph in the middle column. In the third column, set out a *brief* overview. The point is to summarize, not to rewrite the paragraph. Here goes:

FLOWCHART Anthony Paul Farley's Article, "Failing Schools"

PARAGRAPH	FOCUS	OVERVIEW OF PARAGRAPH
Paragraph #1	Thesis: Prisons are like a new form of slavery. (Analogy)	*Thesis—links prison rates to literacy problems.* This is slavery in a new form, as is the scandalous quality of the
		(continued)

PARAGRAPH	FOCUS	OVERVIEW OF PARAGRAPH
		educational resources. The attack on freedom and the attack on literacy are related.
Paragraph #2:	**Parallel to slavery continued**	*Focus on schools:* Argument on the condition of urban schools and their effect on children.
Paragraph #3:	**Analogy between schools and prisons leads to "new slavery"**	*Analogy:* Poor schools linked to prisons— both fail our children. Resulting product (i.e. "the new slavery") is stipulated.
Paragraph #4:	**Schools/prisons analogy continued**	*Analogy continued:* Goes further on the links between schools and prisons and continues parallel to slavery ("Reading and freedom have always been connected in the minds of former slaves and former slave masters in the United States").
Paragraph #5:	**Illiteracy in prisons and schools (Analogy #2)**	*Illiteracy and slavery:* Slavery's connection to illiteracy— parallels with illiteracy in prisoners today. Posits slavery in both schools and prisons.
Paragraph #6:	**Failure of prisons and schools**	*Failure and failed reform:* Both schools and prisons continue to fail. Need to examine what we mean by "failure." Attempts at reform continue segregation mentality ("black and white, separate and unequal").
Paragraph #7:	**Solution: Introduction of Dorchester case**	*Recommendation:* "Turn the prisons into schools": Start with the probation system. *Case in point:* Dorchester, MA
Paragraph #8:	**Dorchester: Success Story**	*Dorchester case continued:* The program has been an outstanding success and cause for hope.
Paragraph #9:	**Success story continued**	*Dorchester case continued:* Success story continued

PARAGRAPH	FOCUS	OVERVIEW OF PARAGRAPH
Paragraph #10:	**Application**	*Applying the case:* Transforming prisons to schools/places of education. Predicted effect: Success in the transformation of prisons into successful schools must bring success in the transformation of schools.
Paragraph #11:	**Argument why schools are hated**	*Argument:* Schools are hated because they show the "true attitude of the United States toward blacks." *Recommendation:* "Our prisons, whatever they may be labeled, must be transformed into schools."
Paragraph #12:	**Recommendations**	*Recommendations continued:* Need more than one success story (the Dorchester case): "All of our prisons need to become schools, and all of our schools need to become limitless palaces worthy of the boundless imaginations of youth." *Reaffirms thesis:* We need the fight for literacy and emancipation to break the color line.
Paragraph #13:	**Call for action**	*Challenge to the reader:* Which side are you on? [You *should* be on this side.]

We can now examine the structure of Farley's argument. He starts with his thesis—prisons are parallel to schools in the "new slavery"—and then draws an analogy to the "old slavery." He then proceeds to set out his case, drawing from a successful case that he infers could work as a model for others. To analyze Farley's argument further, set out each analogy and assess it using the tools we learned in Chapter 7.

Using an analogy can be very persuasive, so that warrants our attention. Farley links together two big institutions (schools and prisons) and attempts to address the problems that they share. In so doing, he seeks to tackle social problems found in each institution and offer steps that are potentially transformative.

Second Method: Highlighting Key Words

What if you were a doctor or nurse who suspected that a patient was being abused—even tortured? Are you obligated to contact authorities? What if the authorities prefer you turn a blind eye to the torture? In the article below. M. Gregg Bloche considers it a duty of doctors and nurses to report abuses and not participate—even if the patient is a suspected terrorist. Read the article, keeping your eyes peeled for key words and phrases.

Physician, Turn Thyself In

M. Gregg Bloche

The New York Times, June 10, 2004

According to press reports, military doctors and nurses who examined prisoners at Abu Ghraib treated swollen genitals, prescribed painkillers, stitched wounds, and recorded evidence of the abuses going on around them. Under international law—as well as the standards of common decency—these medical professionals had a duty to tell those in power what they saw.

Instead, too often, they returned the victims of torture to the custody of their victimizers. Rather than putting a stop to torture, they tacitly abetted it, by patching up victims and staying silent.

The duty of doctors in such circumstances is clear. They must provide needed treatment; then do all they can to keep perpetrators from committing further abuse. This includes keeping detailed records of injuries and their likely causes, performing clinical tests to gather forensic evidence and reporting abuses to those with the will and power to act.

During the 1980's and 1990's, American human rights investigators traveled to many countries with oppressive governments, assembling evidence of medical complicity in torture. A pattern emerged in rogue regimes that claimed pride in their civility: doctors both contained and abetted torture—by treating its victims, returning them to perpetrators and then remaining silent.

I was one of these investigators. I vividly remember the Uruguayan military intelligence chief who spoke to me with contempt about Argentine "barbarians" who made tens of thousands disappear. By contrast, he boasted, in Uruguay the army kept doctors nearby to keep things from getting out of hand. Fewer than 200 Uruguayans died in detention while the army ruled.

Now the American military is essentially ruling Iraq—and it is urgent that we find out what our military doctors, nurses and medics know. They are likely to have kept records. Already, a medical assessment unearthed by investigators has given the lie to the Pentagon's claim that the former chief of Iraq's air force lost consciousness and died after saying he didn't feel well; the medical report said his death ensued from "asphyxia due to smothering and chest compression."

Congress and others investigating abuse of detainees in Iraq, Guantánamo Bay and elsewhere should quickly obtain all relevant medical records. They should ask independent experts to review these records—and to question military medical personnel about what they saw and heard. Independent doctors should also examine people who say they were abused, using state-of-the-art protocols for documentation of torture and other ill treatment. These protocols make it possible to find patterns of abuse.

Had military doctors come forward immediately with such evidence, brutal practices that have shamed us all could have been stopped at the outset. And had the perpetrators feared exposure through medical findings, they might have been dissuaded from their lawless course.

When guards and interrogators become torturers, doctors are first responders. International law demands that they act as such. In Iraq, it appears, a "don't ask, don't tell" ethic stood in the way. By staying silent for months, until an inquest began, doctors and nurses abandoned their patients. But these doctors and nurses probably saw enough to offer smoking-gun evidence of what went awry at Abu Ghraib and elsewhere. It is time for us to ask, and them to tell.

Source: M. Gregg Bloche teaches Law and Health Policy at Georgetown and Johns Hopkins Universities. Reprinted with the permission of M. Gregg Bloche. This article appeared in *The New York Times.*

Methodology for Highlighting Key Words

Let us now try to pin down the argument by highlighting the key words. Try these steps:

STEP ONE: Number each paragraph from the first to the last.
   Note: If one paragraph is more than five or six lines long, break up the paragraph. You want each numbered segment to be a manageable size.

STEP TWO: Go through each paragraph, underlining or highlighting the key terms. Include concepts and any reference to sources, names, or cases.

STEP THREE: Now read through what you have emphasized.

STEP FOUR: Summarize the argument in the article, drawing only from your list of terms and phrases. On a computer you can just delete anything that is *not* highlighted and then shape the remaining words and phrases into sentences.

STEP FIVE: From your summary, set out a statement of the argument.

Applying these steps to Bloche's article, we get a handle on the article's key points.

STEPS ONE AND TWO: Number and mark key words and phrases (in bold below).

1. According to press reports, **military doctors and nurses** who examined prisoners at **Abu Ghraib** treated swollen genitals, prescribed painkillers, stitched wounds, and recorded evidence of the abuses going on around them. **Under international law**—as well as the standards of common decency—these medical professionals **had a duty to tell those in power what they saw.**

2. **Instead,** too often, they returned the victims of torture to the custody of their victimizers. Rather than **putting a stop to torture, they tacitly abetted it,** by patching up victims and **staying silent.**

3. The **duty of doctors** in such circumstances is **clear.** They must **provide needed treatment,** then do all they can to keep perpetrators from committing further abuse. This includes **keeping detailed records** of injuries and their likely causes, performing clinical tests to gather forensic evidence and **reporting abuses** to those with the will and power to act.

4. During the **1980's and 1990's,** American **human rights** investigators traveled to many countries with oppressive governments, assembling **evidence of medical complicity** in torture. A **pattern** emerged in rogue regimes that claimed pride in their civility: **doctors both contained and abetted torture—** by treating its victims, returning them to perpetrators and then remaining silent.

5. I was one of these investigators. I vividly remember the **Uruguayan military intelligence** chief who spoke to me with contempt about Argentine "barbarians" who made tens of thousands disappear. By contrast, he **boasted,** in Uruguay the **army kept doctors nearby to keep things from getting out of hand.** Fewer than 200 Uruguayans died in detention while the army ruled.

6. Now the American military is essentially ruling **Iraq**—and it is urgent that we find out what our military **doctors, nurses and medics** know. They are **likely to have kept records.** Already, a medical assessment unearthed by investigators has given the lie to the Pentagon's claim that the **former chief of Iraq's air force** lost consciousness and **died** after saying he didn't feel well; the **medical report** said his death ensued from "**asphyxia** due to smothering and chest compression."

7. **Congress and others investigating abuse** of detainees in Iraq, Guantánamo Bay and elsewhere should quickly obtain all relevant medical records. They should **ask independent experts to review** these records—**and to question** military medical personnel about what they saw and heard. **Independent doctors should** also **examine people who say they were abused,** using state-of-the-art protocols for documentation of torture and other ill-treatment. These protocols make it possible to find patterns of abuse.

8. **Had military doctors come forward** immediately with such evidence, **brutal practices** that have shamed us all **could have been stopped at the outset.** And had the perpetrators feared exposure through medical findings, they might have been dissuaded from their lawless course.

9. When guards and interrogators become torturers, **doctors are first responders.** International law demands that they act as such. **In Iraq,** it appears, a "don't ask, don't tell" ethic stood in the way. By **staying silent** for months, until an inquest began, **doctors and nurses abandoned their patients.** But these **doctors and nurses probably saw enough to offer smoking-gun evidence** of what went awry at Abu Ghraib and elsewhere. It is **time for us to ask and them to tell.**

STEPS THREE AND FOUR: Read and summarize what we have. Pull out the highlighted words (or delete those not highlighted using your computer). Here's what we get:

1. Military doctors and nurses who examined prisoners at Abu Ghraib under international law had a duty to tell those in power what they saw.
2. Instead of putting a stop to torture, they tacitly abetted it, staying silent.
3. Duty of doctors is clear: provide needed treatment, keeping detailed records and reporting abuses.
4. 1980's and 1990's, human rights evidence of medical complicity. Pattern: doctors both contained and abetted torture.
5. I remember Uruguayan military intelligence boasted, army kept doctors nearby to keep things from getting out of hand.
6. Iraq—doctors, nurses and medics likely to have kept records. The former chief of Iraq's air force died—medical report said "asphyxia due to smothering."
7. Congress and others investigating abuse ask independent experts to review and to question. Independent doctors should examine people who say they were abused; protocols make it possible to find patterns of abuse.
8. Had military doctors come forward brutal practices could have been stopped at the outset.
9. Doctors are first responders. In Iraq, by staying silent doctors and nurses abandoned their patients. Doctors and nurses probably saw enough to offer smoking-gun evidence. It's time for us to ask and for them to tell.

Putting this together as a summary, we get:

M. Gregg Bloche, "Physician, Turn Thyself In"

Military doctors and nurses who examined prisoners at Abu Ghraib—under international law—had a duty to tell those who are in power what they saw. Instead of putting a stop to torture, they tacitly abetted it, staying silent. The duty of doctors is clear—providing needed treatment, keeping detailed records, and reporting abuses. In the 1980's and 1990's, evidence of human rights abuses showed medical complicity. The pattern: doctors both contained and abetted torture.

I remember Uruguayan military intelligence boasting that the army kept doctors nearby to keep things from getting out of hand. In Iraq doctors, nurses, and medics are likely to have kept records. For example, when the former chief of Iraq's air force died, the medical report said "asphyxia due to smothering."

Congress and others investigating abuse should ask independent experts to review—and to question. Independent doctors should examine people who say they were abused; protocols are possible to find patterns of abuse. Had military doctors come forward, brutal practices could have been stopped at the outset. Doctors are the first responders. In Iraq, by staying silent, doctors and nurses abandoned their patients. Doctors and nurses probably saw enough to offer smoking-gun evidence. It's time for us to ask and for them to tell.

In doing this summary, you should only have to make very minor additions (like "the" and "and") to smooth out the passage. You do not want to add anything of substance for risk of changing the author's intent. Your goal is to pluck out a summary using the author's own words.

STEP FIVE: Set out a statement of the argument. From our summary, we can see the author's thesis is this: Doctors and nurses at Abu Ghraib, Iraq, should come forward to report what they saw and did in the torture of detainees or prisoners. His argument can be set out as follows:

P_1: There is a duty under international law for doctors and nurses to tell those in power what they saw.

P_2: By staying silent, doctors and nurses abetted torture.

P_3: There is a clear duty to provide treatment, keep detailed records, and report abuses.

P_4: Evidence from the 1980s and 1990s showed medical complicity—the pattern of doctors both contained and abetted torture.

P_5: He saw such abuse and the role doctors played in enabling the abuse in Uruguay.

P_6: Iraq doctors likely kept records—as in the case of the Iraq air force chief who died by asphyxiation.

P_7: Congress should ask independent investigators to look into this.

P_8: Doctors are the first responders and could stop brutal practices.

P_9: By doctors and nurses staying silent, they abandon their patients.

P_{10}: Doctors and nurses likely have "smoking gun" evidence (i.e., proof of torture).

C: Doctors and nurses should step forward and tell what they know of the Abu Ghraib prison abuse.

This method has many virtues. The biggest virtue is that we end up with the argument clearly set out without doing much more than spotting key words and dropping out whatever is not highlighted—and then smoothing it out. This allows us to see the argument's basic form. Let us now turn to the next method of pinning down arguments.

▦ Third Method: Standard Form of an Argument

On January 24, 2003, the Public Broadcasting System (PBS) aired a discussion on *xenotransplants*—that is, transplanting animal organs into humans (but not metal arms as in *Spider-Man 2*). See Fig. 12.1 for one take on xenotransplants! The conversation included PBS correspondent Fred de Sam Lazaro, transplant surgeon Dr. David Cooper, and recipient of a fetal pig cell transplant, Parkinson's patient Jim Finn. Let's listen to some of their comments:

DE SAM LAZARO: Primates such as chimpanzees and baboons were once considered a potential organ source. But their organs are typically smaller than human ones, and because they live in the wild they may carry many unknown diseases. The less exotic pig has many advantages.

DR. COOPER: It is large enough to donate organs to the largest of humans. It breeds rapidly—10 or 12 in a litter. It's relatively easy and cheap to keep and house until you are ready to use the organs. Furthermore, we don't have so many ethical concerns about pigs. We actually slaughter 100 million pigs in the U.S. each year for food.

. . .

DE SAM LAZARO: Jim Finn, a Parkinson's patient for 20 years, was willing to take that risk. Six years ago, he participated in a clinical trial by the biotech firm Diacrin, which does extensive xenotransplantation research. Twelve million fetal pig cells were transplanted into his skull.

MR. FINN: It was a very simple procedure. They drill a hole in the skull. I think it's right here. A quarter of an inch hole. And they put a six-inch needle in your brain, filled with pig cells, and they inject these fetal brain pig cells. And they pump them into your brain and hope for the best.

DE SAM LAZARO: Before the transplant, Finn's condition had deteriorated so much he considered suicide.

. . .

MR. FINN: We are six years out from the surgery. If there were going to be anything, it would show up by now. It's been a miracle for me.

Reprinted with permission of Nik Scott, www.nikscott.com.

FIGURE 12.1
Any of you animals want to be a xenotransplant donor?

From the discussion, we may not realize the potential risks of the procedure. Patients like Jim Finn face any number of problems when 12 million fetal pig cells are injected into their brains. As Ben Wyld argues below, such procedures have broader issues of global import. Read his article and then we'll set out his argument in standard form.

As you may recall, an argument is in standard form if the premises are set out P_1, P_2, P_3, and so on like a stack of pancakes, with the conclusion at the bottom of the stack, below the last premise. This form is as follows:

Standard Form

P_1 Premise 1

P_2 Premise 2

P_3 Premise 3

. . .

$\underline{P_n\quad \text{Last Premise}}$

C   Conclusion

Keep this form in mind as you read Ben Wyld's argument. We will then set it out in standard form.

Animal Organs a Risk to Humans

Ben Wyld

Sydney Morning Herald, January 13, 2004

Fears that humans may be at risk of contracting diseases through animal organ transplants have been raised after a study revealed that human and animal DNA can fuse together naturally. Researchers from the Mayo Clinic in Rochester, Minnesota, found that pigs developed human and hybrid cells in their blood and organs after they were injected with human blood stem cells.

The hybrid cells were also found to contain the porcine endogenous retrovirus, a pig virus similar to HIV, which was able to transmit to normal human cells. The finding raises the possibility that xenotransplantation, a procedure in which organs from pigs are implanted into humans, could allow animal viruses to pass to the recipient's human cells.

Jack Sparrow, the chairman of the xenotransplantation working party within the National Health and Medical Research Council, said the risk of transfer of infection was a big concern. "The public health risks of any proposed animal to human xenotransplantation trial must be minimal and must be acceptable to the community," Dr. Sparrow said.

Scientists fear the movement of viruses from animals to humans could underlie some fatal diseases, with both AIDS and SARS recent examples where scientists believe the viruses crossed over from animal populations. Dr. Sparrow said the amount of xenotransplantation research being conducted in Australia was limited. "You have to keep in mind that any actual experimental work . . . will happen at the cellular level, then the tissue level before whole organ transplantation if, indeed, we ever get to that stage," he said.

But Peter Collignon, director of microbiology and infectious diseases at Canberra Hospital, said the study, reported in the online edition of a journal published by the Federation of American Societies for Experimental Biology, reinforced the dangers of xenotransplantation. "This is the very thing we're worried about, an animal virus adapting to people and spreading . . . this isn't just some science-fiction tale," Associate Professor Collignon said.

Xenotransplantation, thought to be a possible solution to the problem of donor shortages, increased the risk of possible infection, said Professor Collignon. Recipients need to have their immune system blocked by drugs to avoid rejecting the foreign tissue. Attention, he said, should instead focus on increasing organ donor rates. "This is a major red warning flag, and we need to be very careful about going down this path," he said.

Dr. Jeffrey Platt, director of the Mayo Clinic's Transplantation Biology Program, said the finding explained how a retrovirus could jump from one species to another and might help uncover the origin of AIDS and SARS.

Source: Sydney Morning Herald, Sydney AU, *www.smh.com.au,* 13 Jan 2004. Reprinted with the permission of Ben Wyld.

Setting out the Argument in Standard Form

Ben Wyld thinks it unwise at the present time to proceed with xenotransplants. His key concern is that humans may be at risk of contracting diseases through animal organ transplants (xenotransplants). As long as there are such concerns, we ought not allow xenotransplants. His argument is as follows:

Argument: Ben Wyld, "Animal Organs a Risk to Humans"

P_1: A Mayo clinic study found that pigs developed human and hybrid cells in their blood and organs after they were injected with human blood stem cells.

P_2: The hybrid cells were also found to contain the porcine endogenous retrovirus (PERV), a pig virus similar to HIV, which was able to transmit to normal human cells.

P_3: The finding raises the possibility that xenotransplantation could allow animal viruses to pass to the recipient's human cells.

P_4: Jack Sparrow, the chairman of the xenotransplantation working party within the National Health and Medical Research Council, said the risk of transfer of infection was a big concern.

P_5: We ought not allow xenotransplantation unless the public health risks are minimal.

P_6: Scientists fear the movement of viruses from animals to humans could underlie some fatal diseases, with both AIDS and SARS recent examples where scientists believe the viruses crossed over from animal populations.

P₇: Peter Collignon, director of microbiology and infectious diseases at Canberra Hospital, said the study, reported in the online edition of a journal published by the Federation of American Societies for Experimental Biology, reinforced the dangers of xenotransplantation. "This is the very thing we're worried about, an animal virus adapting to people and spreading . . . this isn't just some science-fiction tale," he said.

P₈: Xenotransplantation increased the risk of possible infection, said Professor Collignon. "This is a major red warning flag, and we need to be very careful about going down this path," he said.

P₉: Dr. Jeffrey Platt, director of the Mayo Clinic's Transplantation Biology Program, said the finding explained how a retrovirus could jump from one species to another and might help uncover the origin of AIDS and SARS.

C: We ought not undertake xenotransplants as long as there are such potential health risks.

Can you see how Wyld argued his case? He laid out reasons why xenotransplants put humans at risk for disease and presented the warnings as red flags. Unless such concerns are minimal, Wyld argues, we ought not allow xenotransplants. Since these concerns are not minimal at the present time, he opposes xenotransplants.

As you can see, setting out the argument in standard form has many virtues. The *biggest virtue* is that we end up with the premises laid out neatly above the conclusion. This allows us to easily look at any one premise and weigh its value as support for the conclusion—but we must identify all the premises and not omit any evidence. Err on the side of inclusion. When in doubt, list an idea or claim as a premise. You may end up with some background or packing material—but you won't risk eliminating a potentially key piece of evidence. However, be judicious. Otherwise you may have a much longer list of premises (or potential premises) than you need.

Fourth Method: The Traditional Outline

Some dilemmas we face today were unheard of a few decades ago. Some inspire sci-fi and horror films. Can't you picture *Dawn of the Pig-Men* on a double bill with *The DNA Dragnet Queen*? Fiction can't trump reality for mind-boggling uses of science and technology—such as cloning, stem cell research, fetal tissue brain transplants, and genetic engineering. Technology has opened up a Pandora's box of ethical, legal, and social controversies. And it's not over yet. California's Proposition 69, which passed in the 2004 election is this: Collection of DNA samples would be expanded to include people convicted of any felony plus those convicted or arrested for some other offenses. Criminal penalties, such as fees for traffic tickets, would go up to help pay for keeping track of more DNA samples. Let's look at the case of a DNA dragnet.

How would you feel if your father or brother (or yourself, if you are a male!) were asked to submit to DNA testing in a rape case? How would you feel if you were raped and the likely suspect lives in your neighborhood and the police think a DNA test might catch him? As you might imagine, both questions raise interesting moral and social concerns. Such concerns are not academic, either, as DNA testing in crimes is now a reality. This is the focus of our next article.

The wrestling technique for pinning down this argument is a classic. Just as the Terminator was able to quickly get the basics using its programmed assessment tools, we will use a traditional outline to pare down the argument to skeletal form. This involves using headings, subheadings, supporting examples, and details—all set out in a linear fashion that uses a nesting technique to package each of the component parts of the argument.

To keep the headings, subheadings, and supportive details straight, it is important to use a conventional format. A traditional outline format is like this:

I.

II.

III.   Headings

[Use capital roman numerals I, II, III, to indicate major claims.]

A.

B.

C.   Subheadings

[Use capital alphabetical letters A, B, C, etc. to indicate the main support under the heading/major claim in question.]

1.

2.

3.   Supportive detail

[Use numbers 1,2, 3, etc. to indicate supporting detail for the subheading in question.]

a.

b.

c.   Examples or more specific detail

[Use lower case alphabetical letters a, b, c, etc. to indicate examples or specific support of the detail under the subheading in question.]

i.

ii.

iii.   Elaboration of examples or specific detail

[Use lowercase Roman numerals i, ii, iii, iv, v, vi, etc.]

This outline breaks down the argument according to the categories "main headings/key claims," then under each are subheadings and under the subheadings the detailed support and examples. The result is nested boxes, like those little Chinese puzzle boxes or the Ukrainian dolls in which each doll fits inside the next larger one, and so on. With that in mind, read the article and then we'll go through a traditional outline.

DNA Dragnet in Search for Killer Raises Privacy Concerns

Jennifer L. Brown

Daily Journal, June 1, 2001

OKLAHOMA CITY—Police know who murdered Juli Busken. Not by name, but by the genetic code he left behind in the victim's car five years ago.

In their search for John Doe, police took blood from 200 men and compared their DNA to that of the man who left behind semen in Busken's car. There were no matches. Police plan to test 200 more men who either lived near the victim and have a criminal record of violence, resemble the police sketch or have been identified as a possible suspect.

There is a growing debate about whether innocent people should have to hand over their blood. Besides concern over unreasonable searches, even supporters of DNA testing say such large-scale genetic dragnets raise the possibility of police coercion.

For Busken's father, the answer is easy. Besides a rough sketch of someone who was seen with Busken before her death, a DNA match is about all he has to cling to in hopes of finding his daughter's killer. "If you don't want to give your DNA, you've got something to hide," said Bud Busken, who runs a golf course in Benton, Ark. "I'll stand by that until my dying day."

Busken, 21, had just finished her last semester at the University of Oklahoma when she was last seen on Dec. 20, 1996, and was about to drive home to Arkansas for Christmas vacation. Police believe she was abducted from the parking lot of her apartment building. Her body was found near a lake. The aspiring ballerina had been raped and shot in the head.

Cleveland County District Attorney Tim Kuykendall turned to the DNA testing last year.

Some of those tested gave DNA samples to exonerate themselves. Others were people associated with Busken, including fellow college dancers and even stagehands who worked at the university. Defense attorneys and civil libertarians call the sweeps an improper violation of the constitutional right to privacy.

A few such DNA dragnets have taken place in this country, but there's little precedent for determining their legality. Mass blood screenings are more common abroad, where the first was in 1987 in England when 5,000 people had their blood tested after two teen-agers were raped and murdered.

Fred Leatherman, chairman of the Forensic Evidence Committee of the National Association of Criminal Defense Lawyers, said he knew of no legal challenges to block mass screenings in the United States. He predicted they would be challenged, calling them "a clear violation of the right to privacy."

Critics fear what happens to DNA samples after they're collected. Some suspect they would be used in future investigations by forensic scientists who sometimes make errors, or that they might end up in the hands of health insurance companies that could see which diseases a person is predisposed to develop. "This is just horrendous, appalling," said Doug Parr, a board member of the Oklahoma Criminal Defense Lawyers Association. "It smacks of the kind of police state tactics that this country has gone to war against."

Most of the 200 men tested so far gave their blood voluntarily, but prosecutors obtained search warrants in a few cases where people declined to provide the sample. One of those was Dennis Stuermer, 23, who said his reputation has been tarnished because Oklahoma City police forced him to give a blood sample. Stuermer's photograph ran on the front page of the state's largest newspaper after a woman in jail who knew his family said he might be Busken's killer.

In the months it took to get the results of the DNA test, his landlord tried to evict him, a boss threatened to fire him and a few personal relationships deteriorated. "I was scared to death," he said. "I didn't have anything to be scared of, but people were breathing down my throat." Attorney Doug Wall said he and Stuermer, who has no criminal background,

may sue the police. "Police are basically saying, 'If we pop a needle into enough arms we're bound to get lucky sooner or later,'" Wall said.

Arthur Spitzer, a lawyer with the American Civil Liberties Union in Washington, said requiring people to give DNA samples without other evidence linking them to the crime would be an unconstitutional search and seizure. Attorney Barry Scheck, who cofounded The Innocence Project, a group that helps inmates challenge convictions with DNA evidence, said there are potential problems whenever so much testing is done.

Some people might feel coerced to give blood. "It's inherently coercive when a policeman comes to your door and says 'Give us a sample of your blood and if you don't give it to us, you're a suspect,'" he said. Bud Busken believes if authorities found his daughter's killer, it might stop the emotional roller coaster he and his wife have been on since that day. "Our life is never going to go back the way it was," he said.

Setting out the Traditional Outline

Now we can see what the argument looks like using a traditional outline. This can be helpful whether you are writing a paper or analyzing one. Go through each paragraph and break it down by headings, subheadings, and support. This works best when the article is well structured and neither rambles off on other topics nor jumps back and forth within the headings and subheadings. If the argument is set out in a fairly straightforward way, you can usually spot the main claims and their constituent parts. They can then be put in outline form. Most word processing software (e.g., Microsoft Word) has an outlining layout under "Format." You may find this useful to outline your article.

The trickiest part in Brown's article is what to do with the references to the Busken case and then later to the Stuermer case. The Busken case warrants treatment as a major claim, given that it opened the article. The second case (Stuermer) seems best handled as a subheading under the discussion of the legality of DNA searches. That is a judgment call. No great harm would be done to pull it out and treat it on the level of the Busken case, in light of the attention it received. The point of the outline is to pin down the argument—and there can be legitimate variations on how best to do that. With that in mind, let's look at the outline.

Outline: Jennifer L. Brown, "DNA Dragnet in Search for Killer Raises Privacy Concerns"

I.   Police know who murdered Juli Busken by the genetic code he left behind in the victim's car five years ago.

    A.   *In their search for John Doe, police took blood from 200 men.*

        1.   Police compared their DNA to that of the man who left behind semen in Busken's car.

           a.   There were no matches.

    B.   *Police plan to test 200 more men.*

        1.   They will test those who lived near the victim and have a criminal record of violence, resemble the police sketch, or have been identified as a possible suspect.

II.   There is a growing debate about whether innocent people should have to hand over their blood.

    A.   *There is concern over unreasonable searches.*

        1.   Even supporters of DNA testing say such large-scale genetic dragnets raise the possibility of police coercion.

        2.   For Busken's father, the answer is easy—do DNA searches.

           a.   A DNA match is about all he has to cling to in hopes of finding his daughter's killer.

              i.   All he has is a rough sketch of someone who was seen with Busken before her death.

    B.   *"If you don't want to give your DNA, you've got something to hide,"* Bud Busken said. *"I'll stand by that until my dying day."*

III.   The Busken case.

    A.   *Juli Busken, 21, had just finished her last semester at the University of Oklahoma when she was last seen on Dec. 20, 1996.*

        1.   She was about to drive home to Arkansas for Christmas vacation.

    B.   *Police believe she was abducted from the parking lot of her apartment building.*

        1.   Her body was found near a lake.

        2.   The aspiring ballerina had been raped and shot in the head.

    C.   *Cleveland County District Attorney Tim Kuykendall turned to the DNA testing last year.*

        1.   Some of those tested gave DNA samples to exonerate themselves.

2. Others were people associated with Busken, including fellow college dancers and even stagehands who worked at the university.

3. Defense attorneys and civil libertarians call the sweeps an improper violation of the constitutional right to privacy.

IV. A few such DNA dragnets have taken place in this country, but there's little precedent for determining their legality.

A. *Mass blood screenings are more common abroad.*

1. The first was in 1987 in England when 5,000 people had their blood tested after two teen-agers were raped and murdered.

B. *Fred Leatherman, chairman of the Forensic Evidence Committee of the National Association of Criminal Defense Lawyers, said he knew of no legal challenges to block mass screenings in the United States.*

1. He predicted they would be challenged.

a. He called them "a clear violation of the right to privacy."

C. *Critics fear what happens to DNA samples after they're collected.*

1. Some suspect they would be used in future investigations by forensic scientists who sometimes make errors,

2. They might end up in the hands of health insurance companies that could see which diseases a person is predisposed to develop.

3. "This is just horrendous, appalling," said Doug Parr, a board member of the Oklahoma Criminal Defense Lawyers Association.

a. "It smacks of the kind of police state tactics that this country has gone to war against."

D. *Most of the 200 men tested so far gave their blood voluntarily.*

E. *Prosecutors obtained search warrants in a few cases where people declined to provide the sample.*

V. The case of Dennis Stuermer, 23, who declined to give a DNA sample.

A. *Stuermer said his reputation has been tarnished because Oklahoma City police forced him to give a blood sample.*

1. Stuermer's photograph ran on the front page of the state's largest newspaper after a woman in jail who knew his family said he might be Busken's killer.

2. In the months it took to get the results of the DNA test, his landlord tried to evict him, a boss threatened to fire him, and a few personal relationships deteriorated.

3. "I was scared to death," he said. "I didn't have anything to be scared of, but people were breathing down my throat."

B. *Attorney Doug Wall said he and Stuermer, who had no criminal background, may sue the police.*

1. "Police are basically saying, "If we pop a needle into enough arms we're bound to get lucky sooner or later," Wall said.

VI. Requiring people to give DNA samples raises concerns.

   A. *Arthur Spitzer, a lawyer with the American Civil Liberties Union in Washington, said requiring people to give DNA samples without other evidence linking them to the crime would be an unconstitutional search and seizure.*

   B. *Attorney Barry Scheck, who co-founded The Innocence Project, a group that helps inmates challenge convictions with DNA evidence, said there are potential problems whenever so much testing is done.*

      1. Some people might feel coerced to give blood.

      2. "It's inherently coercive when a policeman comes to your door and says 'Give us a sample of your blood and if you don't give it to us, you're a suspect,'" he said.

   C. *Bud Busken brushes aside the concerns.*

      1. He believes if authorities found his daughter's killer, it might stop the emotional roller coaster he and his wife have been on since that day.

Once the argument is laid out in outline form, you can assess its strength. Be sure to check to see if anything is omitted. Examine the weight given to any aspect of the argument. For example, the outline shows quite a bit of attention given to the Stuermer case. It might be valuable to compare how the author treats—and links—the two cases (Busken and Stuermer). In the *first case,* the use of a DNA dragnet might reveal who the killer is—and, therefore, there would be a good result from the DNA dragnet, even if it has a coercive element.

In the *second case,* that of Stuermer, the refusal to give a DNA sample raised suspicions that Stuermer contends have harmed him. Brown's use of expert sources reinforces Stuermer's position. This case supports the view that the use of coercion to obtain DNA samples violates any number of rights (privacy, right against unlawful search and seizure, etc.). As a result, we see from the outline that, whereas Brown refers to the "debate" around DNA dragnets, her article presents a much more solid case *against* DNA dragnets.

By using an outline, we are able to get a better grasp of the argument. (See Fig. 12.2) This is as true for looking at our own arguments as it is for the arguments of others. So don't forget this tool when you want to see if your writing is cohesive.

Fifth Method: The Bubble Outline

As illustrated by the DNA dragnet case, some issues cry out for policies and guidelines. How do we make such decisions? Who decides, and on what set of criteria?

When we draw up policy guidelines, we are generalizing from our societal attitudes and norms. Often we bring to bear ethical or religious principles. Once we say, "You ought to do such and so," we are giving a *moral prescription.* That is, we are setting forth a recommendation for how others should think and behave.

FIGURE 12.2
It's good to find a
comfortable place
to think!

One such case that cries out for legal and ethical guidance is the selling of body parts. As you might imagine, there's a large market for organs and tissues, and the supply is relatively limited.

In the article below, Michele Goodwin discusses the controversy that arose over body parts in a recent scandal at UCLA and offers some recommendations. We will apply our fifth method of pinning down the argument—the bubble outline—to Goodwin's article. Read the article and then we'll put this technique to use.

Commerce in Cadavers an Open Secret

Michele Goodwin

Los Angeles Times Op-Ed   *March 11, 2004*

Are we shocked that a University of California official has been caught allegedly trading in body parts? We shouldn't be; UCLA is simply the canary in the coal mine. It's an open secret that there has long been a commercial trade in human bodies. An underground, illegal market has developed largely because of inconsistent federal policies and practices, including poor oversight of university hospitals, organ procurement organizations and biotechnology companies that engage in the exchange of body parts.

By and large, this black market serves a public good by supplying lifesaving and beneficial materials—such as heart valves and knees—to a demanding public. But without regulation and monitoring, it's not surprising that mistakes, fraud and abuse occur, as they did in the California case of infected tissues being sold to hospitals for knee transplants in 2002, or the 1997 scandal in which the Los Angeles coroner's office was found to have sold more than 500 pairs of corneas in one year to the Doheny Eye & Tissue Transplant Bank.

In the Doheny case, more than 80% of the donors, who were unwittingly placed in the stream of commerce, were black or Latino. The coroner's office received up to $335 per pair of corneas, which Doheny resold at $3,400 per pair. The coroner was not alone in this behavior; 29 states permitted the nonconsensual removal of eye tissues from cadavers. Most of the 29 still have presumed consent laws.

Currently, the Uniform Anatomical Gift Act and the National Organ Transplantation Act prohibit companies and private citizens from purchasing body parts from individuals. An individual cannot receive "payment" for donating an organ or other body part. Although hints of the existence of a market involving individual sellers are clearly apparent in sperm and ova sales, lawmakers have been slow to address this new, expanded marketplace. Such inaction drives the underground sales.

Although the laws allow "service" fees to be exchanged between hospitals and organ procurement organizations for body parts and cadavers used to promote research, those fees have come to resemble illegal payments. Hospitals, organ procurement organizations and universities have become middlemen in the human-parts supply industry, violating the spirit and legislative intent of the regulations, because they are selling body parts that will be used commercially and not for research. For-profit tissue banks and biotechnology firms engage in research, but their function is dual-purpose and, ultimately, they are beholden to shareholders who are interested in profits.

Federal oversight has been lax at best, and courts are seemingly unprepared to deal with the reality of a growing body market. State and circuit court decisions on the question of who owns the body have been inconsistent. Both individuals whose cell lines had been stolen and people who have donated family members' cadavers have sought legal remedies. State courts in Georgia and California have ruled against their claims for compensation for nonconsensual appropriation of body parts, while the federal 6th and 9th circuit courts have recognized at least a quasi property-right interest in the body.

In the UCLA case, do the sold body parts now belong to the tissue banks, UCLA or the new owners, or can they revert to the families? Can the families be compensated for their loss? Courts are stumped. Federal law proscribes individual ownership, yet a billion-dollar-a-year corporate industry thrives on buying, refashioning and selling body parts. From where, federal officials should ask, do they obtain the body parts?

Instead of ignoring the growing human-tissue industry, Congress, through the Food and Drug Administration, should regulate and monitor these exchanges. The essential elements of an informed system would include donor protections, an option for donor compensation, recourse for misrepresentation and mandatory annual reporting of donor/provider information, including race, gender and age data to prevent predatory practices. Finally, the federal government must also clarify its role in funding programs that sell body parts.

While the challenge to overhaul altruistic donations occupies lawmakers, private actors have developed a thriving black market. Thus the challenge, it seems, is whether to refashion altruism or introduce other supply alternatives with standards and regulations.

Source: Michele Goodwin is the director of the Health Law Institute, DePaul University College of Law. Reprinted with permission of Michele Goodwin.

Setting out the Bubble Outline

Now that we've read the article, we're ready to pin it down with the help of a bubble outline. Generally it is used for *brainstorming* more than for *breaking down* an argument that's already in place. But it also works as a tool of deconstruction.

The bubble outline is a form of aerial surveillance. It gives us the bird's eye view of the territory—flying across the country you see only the most prominent features of the land below. To your left you see mountains; in the middle you see roads and the traffic moving along them. Depending how high you are, you can spot houses, barns, and commercial buildings. Unless you are flying awfully low or coming in for a landing, you cannot see people, animals, or smaller objects. But you can still get a sense of the territory and see it in a way you'd never be able to see at eye level.

Look for the key words and try to see links and sublinks. That helps us set out a *nonlinear schema* of relationships between the different ideas and supporting detail. Think in terms of categories of issues, concerns raised, and how they are resolved (recommendations). Once you get a handle on this method, it is a useful way to set out an overview. *Think of answering this question as your goal:* How do the ideas in the article before you tie in with each other?

Figure 12.3 sets out a bubble outline for this article. The trickiest part here is to discern the sub-bubbles under the key ideas. Finding the *key points* helps us accomplish that goal. Once you clarify the main ideas, the back-up and examples are easier to spot.

A fascinating use of a bubble outline is the work of artist Mark Lombardi called "Global Networks." Lombardi did a series of drawings that consisted of bubbles linking individuals and corporations together over a span of time. His focus was global networks involving money trails (particularly banking scandals, shady oil money connections, drug cartels, and other corrupt or questionable undertakings). By using his bubble outline, he was able to demonstrate connections that would have been highly difficult, if not impossible, to figure out just by reading about it.

The visual schema of the bubble outline has an advantage like no other form of pinning down arguments. To illustrate how useful this method is, you may be interested to know that on October 17, 2001—five weeks after 9/11—an FBI agent contacted the Whitney Museum of American Art. It seems the FBI agent wanted to get a copy of one of Lombardi's drawings showing global connections in banking and oil. Among those Lombardi had on his "map" was Osama bin Laden (See Robert Hobbs, *Mark Lomardi Global Networks,* Independent Curators International).

FIGURE 12.3
A Bubble
Outline

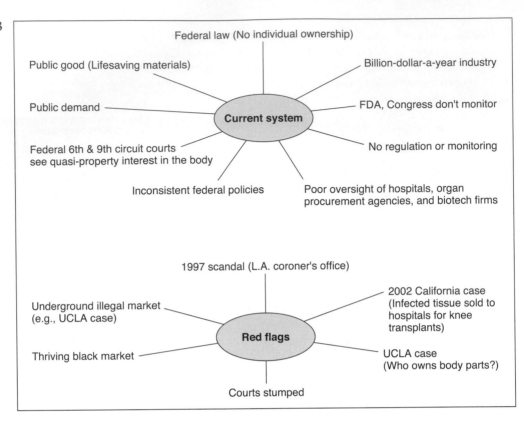

Exercises

Directions: Using any of the methods we covered in this chapter, analyze one of the two articles below.

Article #1: Crossing the Moral Boundary

Eminent Peruvian novelist, Mario Vargas Llosa, looks at the issue of the global trade in women. He reflects on the French justice system, which charged one of its citizens with having sex with children while vacationing in Thailand. As discussed in the article below, the French system does not require such a crime to have taken place within its own boundaries. It is this moral boundary that the article reflects upon.

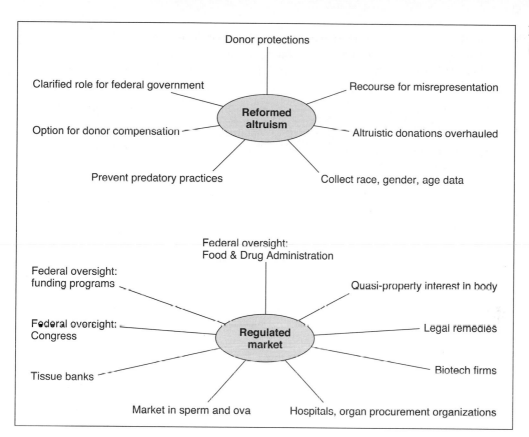

FIGURE 12.3
(continued)

Crossing the Moral Boundary

Mario Vargas Llosa

A model employee of the French public transport authority, according to his chiefs and workmates, the Parisian bachelor Amnon Chemouil, who is now 48, discovered one of Thailand's tourist attractions in 1992. Not its tropical landscape or its ancient civilization and Buddhist temples, but cheap and easy sex, one of the country's flourishing industries. At the resort of Pattaya, near Bangkok, he could have sex with very young prostitutes. He vacationed there again in 1993 and 1994.

On his third trip, he met in a bar at Pattaya another sex tourist, Viktor Michel, a Swiss cit-izen, who encouraged him to seek out even younger girls. Mr. Michel took care of everything: found the procuress and a hotel room. The woman appeared there with a niece who was 11 years of age, and Mr. Chemouil paid $20. All the doings in the hotel room at Pattaya were recorded on video by Viktor Michel, and upon returning to Paris and his job in the public transport system, Mr. Chemouil received a copy of this cassette from his friend and added it to his collection of pornographic videos.

Some time later Viktor Michel found himself in trouble with the Swiss police, much less tolerant than the Thai ones. Searching his home for illegal pornography as part of an investigation into a pedophile ring, they found the video from Pattaya. Under interrogation, the video hobbyist revealed the circumstances in which the video had been filmed and Mr. Chemouil's identity. A report was sent to the French police, who put it in the hands of a judge.

Here I must open a parenthesis in my story, to declare my admiration for French justice. Many things function poorly in France and deserve criticism, but justice functions very well. French courts and judges act with an independence and courage that are an example for all other democracies. They have brought to light countless cases of corruption at higher economic, administrative and political levels, and have sent to trial—and in some cases, to prison—people who by their wealth and influence would in other societies be untouchable. In matters of human rights, racial discrimination, and subversion and terrorism, justice in France is usually characterized by efficacy and prompt intervention.

This was not, we may assume, the impression felt by the surprised Amnon Chemouil when he was arrested and taken before a court in Paris to pay for having violated the penal code of 1994 by sexually violating a minor. The French penal law is applicable to all offenses committed by a French citizen "within or without" French territory, and a 1998 law authorizes the courts to try "sexual aggressions committed abroad" even when the deeds are not considered crimes in the country where they were committed.

The trial of Amnon Chemouil, which took place this fall, set a precedent. It was the first time an offense of "sex tourism" had come before a court in one of the wealthy countries where this sort of tourism typically originates. Several organizations that oppose sexual exploitation of children appeared as plaintiffs, among them the United Nations Children's Fund (*Unicef*), End Child Prostitution in Asian Tourism and a group in Thailand that was able to locate in Bangkok, seven years later, the aunt and girl of the story. The girl, now 18, went to Paris and testified, in private, to the judges, who also viewed a copy of Viktor Michel's video that was found in the search of Amnon Chemouil's house.

The accused, who said that in the eight months he had spent in prison awaiting trial he had experienced a mental cataclysm, admitted he had performed the acts in the video, begged the victim's pardon and asked the court to punish him. The sentence was seven years' imprisonment, instead of the 10 called for by the prosecutor.

Many conclusions may be drawn from this story. The first is that if France's example were followed by countries like Spain, Germany, Britain, Italy and the United States, which, with their high incomes, are among the principal practitioners of "sex tourism," then it is possible that the thousands of offenses of this type committed daily in the poorer countries—especially concerning the sexual exploitation of children—might at least diminish and that some of the perpetrators might be punished.

The precedent established by France is impeccable: a modern democracy cannot allow its citizens to be exonerated of legal responsibility if they sin cheerfully outside of national borders just because a foreign country has no juridical norms that prohibit the activity or because those norms are not enforced.

Hunger, the need for money, and extensive corruption and inefficiency in many poor countries have caused child prostitution to prosper spectacularly, with the indifference or open complicity of the authorities. As *Unicef* and its allies testified at the trial of Mr. Chemouil, the dimensions of the problem are multiple and growing. We need not entertain very high hopes of its eradication, of course, because the poverty and misery that lie behind it constitute an almost insurmountable obstacle.

But the trial in Paris shows a positive side to the new bete noire of the incorrigible enemies of modernity: globalization. If frontiers had not been fading away and, in many fields, disappearing, Amnon Chemouil would never have appeared before the court that tried and sentenced him, and would surely have spent many more vacations in Pattaya. The rigid, straitjacket conception of national sovereignty is being transformed, leading to attempts at wider justice like the detention of Augusto Pinochet in England for his crimes against humanity in Chile, and now this trial.

Globalization is not only the creation of world markets and transnational companies; it also means the extension of justice and democratic values into regions where barbarism still flourishes.

Source: Mario Vargas Llosa is a Peruvian novelist and winner of numerous awards, including the National Book Critics Circle Award, the Cervantes prize, and the Peace Prize of the German Book Trade. This article, which also appeared in *El Pais,* Madrid, was translated by James Brander. Reprinted with the permission of Mario Vargas Llosa.

Article #2: Vulgarities in "Friends" Case Get Supreme Court Airing

In our second article, Peter Blumberg reports on a Supreme Court case that centers on the workplace environment and whether the use of vulgar or lewd language constitutes sexual harassment. Using any one of our five methods, analyze the article. Note that this article presents a particular case in point and is not intended to be a position piece like we saw in our first article by Maria Vargas Lhosa. Nevertheless, any of our tools can be used to break down the article—so don't let the expository nature of the article slow you down.

Vulgarities in "Friends" Case Get Supreme Court Airing

Peter Blumberg

San Francisco Daily Journal, July 22, 2004

SAN FRANCISCO—In a case that pits freedom of speech against anti-discrimination laws, the California Supreme Court agreed Wednesday to decide whether the Hollywood studio that made the popular sitcom "Friends" can be sued for sexual harassment because the show's writers often made crude comments in mixed company. The high court unanimously agreed to consider whether the First Amendment offers a broad defense to allegations that the writers offended one of their assistants during script-writing sessions while making jokes and sharing fantasies about sex.

The media and entertainment industries urged the court to intervene after a Los Angeles appellate court revived the former employee's harassment lawsuit three months ago. A trial judge had earlier thrown out the suit, saying that the writers' discussions were a necessary part of the creative process. But the three-judge appellate panel held that a jury, not a judge, should decide whether the writers created a hostile work environment. The plaintiff, 31-year-old Amaani Lyle, who is black, also accused Warner Bros. of racial discrimination and wrongful termination. But the high court declined to take up her petition for review, which challenged the 2nd District Court of Appeal's conclusion that she was legitimately fired for poor performance after just four months on the job.

Los Angeles attorney Adam Levin, who represents Warner Bros., said Wednesday that anyone who works in a "communicative workplace," including writers, academics and artists, has a stake in how the Supreme Court resolves Lyle v. Warner Bros. "In those kinds of workplaces where free speech is an integral part of the business and necessary component of the job, the First Amendment is even more significant," said Levin, of Mitchell Silberberg & Knupp.

But for all the unions and associations representing creative types who have weighed in on Levin's side, the high court has also been barraged by amicus briefs from women's organizations and civil rights groups. They have warned the high court against giving a free pass to employees in certain occupations to assert that their offensive conduct is constitutionally protected. "The First Amendment is not absolute," said Nancy Solomon, a staff attorney with the California Women's Law Center. "You don't have an absolute privilege to say whatever you want whenever you want to."

California's primary law on harassment, the Fair Employment and Housing Act, already takes into account the context in which something is said that triggers a harassment or discrimination claim. But until now, the courts have not wrestled with whether speech in the workplace can constitute harassment when it's not directed at specific people. When Lyle's novel case reached the 2nd DCA, the panel ruled in her favor and found that "creative necessity" is not an affirmative defense to a sexual harassment complaint. Instead, the panel said, it should be up to a jury to decide the truth of the studio's claim that its writers needed to engage in frank and sometimes vulgar discussions of sex in order to do their jobs.

Lyle's job at Warner Bros. was to take notes while a team of writers developed ideas for "Friends," which treated viewers to a continuous fare of sexually-charged themes and dialogue throughout its lengthy run on NBC. In the complaint she filed in 2002, Lyle, who is the daughter of jazz musician Bobby Lyle, said that three male writers regularly engaged in lurid discussions, ranging from graphic descriptions of their own sexual exploits to fantasizing aloud about sex with "Friends" star Jennifer Aniston. At other times, she said, the writers drew pornographic sketches in coloring books or sat around pretending to masturbate. Lyle also complained that day after day, she was a captive audience to racist jokes mocking blacks. She further alleged that troubles with her employer began when she urged "Friends" staffers to add black members to the then-white cast.

The studio has not denied that the "Friends" writers engaged in crude conversation. But in court papers, Warner Bros. has steadfastly maintained that FEHA doesn't apply because none of the comments in question were directed at Lyle. "The show is about sex, that's undisputed," Levin said. "When you have writers talking about sex it's not because of gender or race. They joke about sex because that is their job. It doesn't reflect any animus against any group of people, whether it be women or African-Americans or Jews or anyone else."

The court Wednesday ordered attorneys to brief two issues: Can the use of coarse and vulgar language in the workplace constitute sexual harassment? And, would liability for that type of harassment infringe on the free speech clauses of the state or federal constitutions? Solomon said she's concerned a victory for Warner Bros. could set a dangerous precedent, allowing the First Amendment to become a shield against all kinds of workplace discrimination claims. "They're asking for carte blanche," she said. "We shouldn't have to go before a judge and jury to explain this conduct. We should be able to do whatever we want to—racial, sexual and religious minorities be damned."

But Tom Newton, general counsel of the California Newspaper Publishers Association, said he hopes the court will recognize that newsrooms would suffer with constraints on conversations among journalists. "It's a dangerous and disgusting world that we live in and in many cases it's an adult world that journalists are charged with covering," he said. "In the newsroom and other places where this creative process is undertaken, interesting and provocative and downright disgusting and obscene facts need to be discussed."

Source: Copyright 2004 *Daily Journal* Corp. Reprinted and/or posted with permission.

Article #3: Detainee Ethics: Terrorists as Research Subjects

In our third article, Prof. Jonathan D. Moreno examines the use of detainees for research in human experimentation. Using any one of our five methods, analyze the article. Note that

Moreno takes a position and sets out his argument that the detainees should have the right to be treated as research subjects.

Detainee Ethics: Terrorists as Research Subjects

Jonathan D. Moreno

The American Journal of Bioethics 3, no. 4

In his introduction to *The Nazi Doctors,* psychiatrist Robert Jay Lifton recalled a requirement imposed on him by the research ethics committee at Yale, where he was then on the faculty: Before beginning his interviews with the elderly physicians who had functioned in the racist bureaucracy of the Third Reich, Lifton would have to provide each of them with a consent form indicating that their participation in Lifton's research was voluntary and that they could withdraw at any time (Lifton 2000).

Though Lifton remarks on this incident almost in passing, it was for me a powerful and supremely ironic moment in his project, that some of the same individuals who contributed to the crimes that helped inspire modern research ethics should themselves be protected by the moral lessons learned. Yet consistency and principle seem to require no less than that ethical standards be applied without prejudice, in spite of the grotesqueries perpetrated by the individuals who are by virtue of their behavior objects of scientific interest. Our very humanity as moral agents is in this way affirmed, for the harder it is to apply ethical principles to persons whose conduct has violated the conditions of human decency, the more important it is to do so.

In our own time terrorism evokes its own cruel horror, and just as there is good reason to try to understand the mind of a racist thug, so there is also good reason to examine the processes that can drive an individual to wanton destruction of innocent human life. Since August 2002, behavioral scientists have been engaged in interviewing suspected al-Qaeda detainees at the U.S. Naval Base in Guantanamo Bay, Cuba. "We are trying to get more cultural knowledge and get into the minds of radical fundamentalists," one anonymous government official told the press. Sent by the FBI, the psychologists are reportedly attempting to learn about the detainees' personal lives and why they joined a terrorist organization, as well as their views of the United States (CBN News, 2002; BBC News, 2003; *Washington Times*, 2002).

The ultimate goal of these psychological profiles is of course to gain enough knowledge of the motivations of such people so that efforts to alter their views or at least anticipate their activities can be more targeted and effective. Behavioral scientists by no means agree that these kinds of assessments can help achieve these goals, especially under the circumstances in which the detainees are being held. But putting scientific legitimacy aside for the moment, it seems a sure bet that there has been no IRB [Institutional Review Board] review within the Justice Department of the psychological profiling project, in spite of the fact that "generalizable knowledge" about Islamic militants is the aim. From one perspective this is hardly surprising: Not only do the detainees occupy a fuzzy legal status that seems to disqualify them from the rights normally ascribed

to prisoners, it's hard to think of a group less likely to inspire sympathy among Americans than al-Qaeda fighters.

Nor are the detainees technically prisoners of war, because they are not associated with a state but rather with a criminal organization. Yet the Nazi war criminals were also characterized by American prosecutors as essentially a group of street toughs that happened to gain control of an important country, thereby justifying their prosecution without the immunity that was then commonly granted to national leaders. The National Socialist Party was identified by the prosecution as a "criminal organization" rather than a political party in the usual sense, which was a critical element of the case against individual party leaders (Taylor 1992). In these terms the Nazi Party and al-Qaeda analogy has some merit. Suppose, then, that the detainees should be treated as prisoners of war, as some legal commentators have argued in opposition to U.S. policy. In 1953, the Pentagon adopted the Nuremberg Code as its policy to govern human experiments, and added an eleventh rule: that prisoners of war should not be used as research subjects (Moreno 2001).

These inconvenient historical details at least suggest that, awkward as it might be, the detainees' right to be considered as human research subjects in the context of data-gathering interviews cannot easily be waved aside. Granted that the administration of a consent form at Guantanamo is about as likely an event as the current attorney general presiding over a gay marriage ceremony. Unlike the passions of the day, however, history tends to be less forgiving when governments ride roughshod over those values that are supposed to be among their most cherished. And the articulation of basic human rights following the victory over Nazi Germany is commonly taken to be one of the precious lessons of that carnage.

Finally, even the trump card of national security necessity is not so easily played. One of the Findings of the President's Advisory Committee on Human Experiments in 1995 was that "for the period 1944 to 1974 [the period within the Committee's purview] there is no evidence that any government statement or policy on research involving human subject contained a provision permitting a waiver of consent requirements for national security reasons" (Advisory Committee 1995). If the current administration has issued such a waiver, it would be without precedent.

Considering the circumstances of the detainees' incarceration not only direct ethical concerns about respect for persons, but also the indirect results of this behavioral research raise questions. It seems unlikely that these so-called interviews are benign chats over a pot of tea. Lack of cooperation could well convince authorities to extend the period of arrest and intensify the methods used to secure a more informative session. Research rules as they apply to prisoners of war or other miscreants in captivity are intended to prevent the putative scientific activity from becoming an opportunity for maltreatment.

If the war on terror continues indefinitely, as seems to be the case, this matter is sure to come up again. The Viet Cong were similarly examined during the Vietnam War, as were Communist prisoners during the Korean conflict. And then there are the unanswered questions about the very validity of such "research." Here is a radical suggestion: explaining to captives that our values include respecting their right not to be part of a scientific study might just elicit more cooperation than otherwise. In light of the stakes for both our survival and our decency it seems a hypothesis worth exploring.

References

Advisory Committee on Human Radiation Experiments. 1995. The Human Radiation Experiments, 501. New York: Oxford University Press.

BBC News. 2002. U.S. Delves into al-Qaeda Mindset. 9 August. Available from: Web (accessed August 8, 2003).

CBN News. 2002. FBI to Profile al-Qaida Detainees. 9 August. Available from: Web (accessed August 8, 2003).

Lifton, R. J. 2000. *The Nazi Doctors: Medical Killing and the Psychology of Genocide.* New York: Basic Books.

Moreno, J. D. 2001. *Undue Risk: Secret State Experiments on Humans.* New York: Routledge.

Taylor, T. 1992. *Anatomy of the Nuremberg Trials.* Boston: Little, Brown & Company.

The *Washington Times.* 2002. Psychological Profiles of al-Qaeda Suspects Sought. 10 August. Available from: Web (accessed August 8, 2003).

Source: Reprinted with the permission of Jonathan D. Moreno and Taylor Francis publishing.

CHAPTER THIRTEEN

Roll the Dice: Causal and Statistical Reasoning

Otto: *Apes don't read philosophy.*

Wanda: *Yes, they do Otto, they just don't understand it. Now let me correct you on a couple of things here. Aristotle was not Belgian. The central message of Buddhism is not 'every man for himself,' and the London Underground is not a political movement. Those are all mistakes, Otto. I looked them up. Now, you have just assaulted the one man who can keep you out of jail and make you rich. What are you going to do about it huh? What would an intellectual do? What would Plato do?*

—FROM *A Fish Called Wanda*

Between classes, you pop over to the cafeteria for some lunch and open your laptop to surf the Internet. You come across an article about the power of prayer. "Now that sounds worth reading," you think to yourself. According to the report, women getting in vitro fertilization (IVF) who had a prayer group were more successful at getting pregnant than those who had no organized group praying for them. Evidently, the women were not informed that others were praying for them, so it seems miraculous. Sounds like a bunch of hooey? Well, maybe so. But there it is in front of your eyes:

> Women who were prayed for had a 50 percent pregnancy rate, compared with 26 percent of women with no intercessory prayer. The 50 percent pregnancy rate was significantly higher than the success rate for the entire IVF program—which was also close to 26 percent—and the previous year's rate of 32.8 percent. One hundred ninety-nine women who were IVF candidates through embryo transfer at the Cha General Hospital in Seoul, Korea, between December 1998 and March 1999 were randomly assigned into two groups for the study. One group received no prayers. (Cindy Kuzma, "Pregnant on a Prayer," *Science & Spirit*, www.science-spirit.org)

How credible is this report? Two of the researchers are Columbia University physicians—and that is certainly impressive. Nothing like solid credentials to boost a research study. Unfortunately, Daniel Wirth, the third author of the study, pleaded guilty to embezzling $2 million from Adelphia Communications (via phony invoices) as well as conspiracy to commit mail fraud. That does not mean his research is faulty—but it definitely raises concerns.

Dr. Bruce Flamm, an obstetrician-gynecologist at Kaiser Permanente and clinical professor at UC Irvine, has raised question after question about the quality of the study. He asks, "If prayer were so powerful, why did the women need to use in vitro fertilization?" and "Why were the prayers to a Christian God?" He adds, "And was God punishing the women who didn't get pregnant?" (Jeff Gottlib, "Journal Silent after its Article on Power of Prayer Draws Criticism," *Los Angeles Times*, 17 Aug 2004). As you can see, this controversial experiment cries out for critical thinking tools to sort it all out.

One interesting element of the case is that it uses two important types of inductive reasoning: (1) causal reasoning and (2) statistical reasoning. You probably remember from Chapter 6, that **inductive reasoning** always involves an element of doubt—that the premises are not sufficient to guarantee the conclusion will be true.

By claiming that prayer positively increases a woman's chance of becoming pregnant using IVF, the researchers have offered a cause and effect argument. They bring in statistical reasoning in arguing that those in the sample group—who were prayed for—had a statistically greater chance of getting pregnant than those in the control group. They infer that praying for women who wish to get pregnant increases the probability of having the desired results. Both types of reasoning involve uncertainty and probability, even in the best of situations. However, the skepticism about both the statistical data and the causal claims in this case gives us food for thought!

In this chapter we will look at both of these key forms of inductive reasoning. We'll start with cause and effect arguments and turn to statistical reasoning in the second half of the chapter. A grounding in this area is very useful, as are tools for tackling inductive arguments, given how often people turn to cause-and-effect reasoning or statistics to try to persuade us. Since they can be highly persuasive, we need to use our critical thinking skills to examine both types of arguments.

▨ Cause-and-Effect Reasoning

Cause-and-effect reasoning is all around us. We see it when people look at the causes and effects of social problems (e.g., homelessness, crime, drug use, sexual behavior, and so on). It may be hard to think of such arguments as inductive rather than deductive because causal relationships are often presented as if they were certain. Nevertheless, there *are* uncertainties in causal reasoning.

There are inherent limitations on knowing all the possible causal factors of any given event. In addition, the interaction of causal factors may affect the outcome.

Be careful not to confuse correlation with cause. **Correlation** is a measure of the association between two things and how they are linked. The fact of a correlation between two events does *not* mean they are causally connected. For example, one pattern that has held for a number of years is that the direction of the Dow Jones Industrial Index predicts whether the AFC or the NFC will win the Super Bowl, but there is no causal connection between them.

CASE STUDY

Fetus May Signal the Birth Process

Around half a million babies are born prematurely every year in the United States alone. Of those, some do not survive and some suffer serious health problems. Read about a discovery by two scientists that may help change that reality and then answer the questions that follow.

Professor of Biochemistry and Obstetrics and Gynecology Carole R. Mendelson and her colleague Jennifer Condon found that fetal lungs produce a protein called surfactant protein A, or SP-A, to signal the mother that they are ready to begin breathing air. At the same time, it activates the release of infection-fighting white blood cells into the fluid-filled womb. The white blood cells then cause an inflammation in the uterus, which leads to labor. "We believe that labor is a cascade of events and that there is an initiating signal or trigger," says Mendelson. "We believe that the fetus, through the production of SP-A at the end of pregnancy, has the capacity to signal the mother when it's ready to be born."

When Mendelson and her team injected SP-A into the amniotic fluid of pregnant mice at a stage much earlier than it normally appears, the mice started labor early—at just 17 days instead of 19 days. When they injected pregnant mice with an antibody that blocks SP-A, the mice delivered late.

Mendelson hopes this research will have clinical uses for humans down the road, perhaps even in helping prevent preterm births. "We know that the same types of signals take place in the human womb," she says. "These signals are the same signals that seem to be involved in preterm labor. If one understands what they are in normal labor, then perhaps measures can be taken to use that knowledge to prevent labor prematurely." ("Triggering Birth," *ScienCentral News*, www.sciencentral.com, 15 Jun 2004)

Answer the following:

1. Clarify what Dr. Mendelson concluded from her study.
2. What do you consider the key evidence supporting her thesis?
3. To what extent does her study of mice fetuses apply to humans? Share any thoughts and concerns.

Group or Individual Exercise

Here's a medical mystery:

> Finland, a country of 5.4 million is among the wealthiest, least polluted, and most health-conscious in the world. Yet it has the highest rate of diabetes in the world, including insulin-dependent diabetics. Of the more than 180,000 Finns with diabetes, 30,000 are insulin-dependent. In other countries researchers found that breast-feeding helped inhibit diabetes; but Finland allows mothers to stay home with full pay and benefits for nine months, resulting in more breast-feeding than in other developed countries. However, Finland uses nitrates and nitrites in their farming and in cured meats, which are widely consumed. Finns are among the biggest consumers of coffee in all of Europe. (Carol J. Williams, "Researchers Struggle to Solve Mystery of Finland's High Diabetes Rate," *Los Angeles Times*, 30 July 2000).

Answer the following:

1. What can you infer from this information about Finland's problem with diabetes?
2. Speculate as to possible causes or solutions to this situation.

Basics of Cause and Effect Reasoning

Cause and effect arguments present us with probability, not certainty. The claim is that a stated condition will result in a particular effect—that the antecedent conditions, if true, cause the supposed effect to happen. How likely it is becomes the issue. We regularly see citations of cause and effect arguments. At times they seem reasonable; other times they seem questionable or far-fetched.

Take the case of the 2004 Boston Red Sox surprise win after being three games down. Did you realize that some suspected the turnabout was influenced by the players' *hair*? Yes, hair. According to Martin Miller, the sudden change of fortune for Johnny Damon (a Red Sox player) must be due to his hair. He adds, "Damon's hair must have known before Game 7 on Wednesday at Yankee Stadium that it was in danger of being sheared off by angry Beantown [that is, Boston] fans who'd watched the outfielder go 3 for 29 in the playoff series" (Martin Miller, "Bosox Secret? Only Their Hairdressers Know for Sure," *Los Angeles Times*, 23 Oct 2004).

Miller considers the hair of players Keven Mill, Manny Ramirez, and Pedro Martinez and notes that Beverly Hills stylist Rich Ohnmacht says, "To me their hair says they are hungry, they don't have time to have their hair cut. . . . It shows they are into the game. They are cavemen." That the hair made the difference in the game is arguable—we need to examine the causal reasoning involved.

Causal reasoning goes beyond sports. It is common in discussions of health and disease. For example, the ophthalmologist looks at your beet-red eye and says, "A virus probably caused your eye to get red—most likely someone coughed or sneezed into your eye." Dr. Littlefield is not absolutely certain; he is drawing an inference on the basis of the evidence before him. In eliminating one possible cause, he figures a virus is the culprit. *Prognoses* are, similarly, inductive. They are predictions based on the given facts of the case, along with what is known about analogous cases.

Causal reasoning is particularly important in scientific research, where empirical studies are an integral part of the research and theorizing. The fact that such reasoning is inductive does not mean it isn't taken seriously. The degree of probability may have an enormous impact on decisions people make. That is one reason doctors are required to inform you of possible risks before you consent to surgery or other kinds of medical treatment.

One way to address the uncertainty and probability of causal reasoning is to temper the claim. Instead of saying the stronger proposition "This is *the cause of* that," which attributes a single cause to a given effect, we could hedge our bets by saying, "This *is a causal factor* of that." For example consider the relationship between cigarette smoking and cancer:

> A series of authoritative reports by the U.S. Public Health Service and other international scientific organizations has conclusively documented a *causal relationship* between cigarette smoking and cancer of at least eight major sites (Shopland et al., 1991). These reports have uniformly identified smoking as a major cause of cancers of the lung, larynx, oral cavity, and esophagus—that is, cigarette smoking is responsible for a majority of the cases and deaths from cancer of these sites. These reports have also demonstrated that smoking substantially elevates the death rates for cancers of the bladder, kidney, and pancreas in both men and women, and, possibly, cervical cancer in women. A number of published reports have *suggested an association* between smoking and other cancers, including cancer of the stomach, liver, prostate, colon, and rectum. (Donald R. Shopland, "Cigarette Smoking as a Cause of Cancer," National Institutes of Health, rex.nci.nih.gov)

Let's see what it can mean to posit a **causal relationship.** First watch for any claims that there is a cause-and-effect relationship between two things. The word "cause" need not be present, by the way, so long as the relationship is made apparent. This can be done simply using the word "effect" or "effect of" or the equivalent. We can see the variation in the examples below.

CAUSAL CLAIM #1: Gulf vets with a host of strange symptoms "link" their ailments to vaccines intended to protect them against biochemical warfare.

CAUSAL CLAIM #2: Insomnia is correlated to drinking excessive amounts of caffeine, so you ought not to drink so many café lattes after dinner!

CAUSAL CLAIM #3: Workers at an atomic weapons factory who made uranium metal for nuclear bombs died at significantly younger ages and suffered a higher incidence of lung, intestinal, and blood cancers than the American population as a whole, according to an analysis of their medical records.

CAUSAL CLAIM #4: An Oxford University researcher theorized that AIDS might have entered the human population in a bizarre series of malaria

The Global Dimension

The SARS Epidemic in Toronto, Canada

Remember the movie *Outbreak*? There we find the story of an ebola-like epidemic that happened after an infected monkey was brought by ship for a pet store in Northern California. The monkey ends up escaping and the chase is on. This scenario is not as far-fetched as we might think. Overnight an epidemic can strike. All it takes is one host setting things in motion. This is what happened in the movie—and it also happened in 2003 when one infected person carried SARS (severe acute respiratory syndrome) into North America.

SARS surfaced in China in December 2002 and, thanks to global travel, quickly spread to other countries. In February 2003 a single traveler introduced SARS into Toronto, Canada. By April 249 cases had been reported and 14 people died. ("Epi-Update: Interim Report on the SARS outbreak in the Greater Toronto Area, Ontario, Canada April 24, 2003," *Health Canada,* www.hc-sc.gc.ca). Thanks to a quick health care response, the epidemic did not explode to a much bigger problem. Just as the *Outbreak* monkey spread the virus to those who infected others, SARS also quickly spread. Health Canada reported the stages of transmission as follows:

1. Spread of SARS infection within the family of the individual case.
2. Amplification of the SARS outbreak through hospital-based spread.
3. Transmission within immediate household members of the health care workers, patients, and visitors to these hospitals.
4. Isolated sporadic cases due to limited transmission in the workplace.
5. Transmission in an extended family and associated religious group.

Directions: Below is a list of individuals from each of the five categories of transmission. Put yourself in their position so you can more fully understand what they are going through. State the issues and concerns from "your" frame of reference and make recommendations to be included in a policy statement the government is putting together. Choose *one* as your frame of reference:

- Isabella del Rio, 25-year-old sister of SARS patient.
- Ruben Lopez, 34-year-old intern in the pediatrics ward where a baby has been checked in with SARS.
- Randy Parker, 19-year-old patient in the same hospital with a SARS patient. Rocky is in the hospital because of injuries sustained in a motorcycle accident (he lost his spleen and suffered two broken ribs and a fractured ankle).
- Mary Chung, 41-year-old lab assistant in the hospital wing where there are 14 SARS patients.
- Peter Tate, 28-year-old cousin of Nicola Tate, 23-year-old SARS patient.

experiments done between 1920 and the 1950s in which researchers innoculated themselves and prisoners with fresh blood from chimpanzees or mangabeys. Both chimpanzees and mangabeys are known to carry a virus similar to HIV2.

Notice the different ways of expressing cause-and-effect relationships. We don't want to overlook a causal argument just because we were only watching for the words "cause" and "effect." As you can see, we can express causation in a range of possible ways.

Exercises

Part One

Directions: List some possible causes of the effect or event mentioned.

1. Your neighbor's burglar alarm goes off and continues for over an hour. You bang on their door, but get no response, although both of their cars are on the street. Thirty minutes later it is quiet.

2. At 7:40 A.M. you go out to start your car and there is only a grating sound.

3. One evening you are sitting in your living room, watching TV, and you hear a loud sound in the direction of your backyard. You look out and realize there is a helicopter aiming a bright light at your yard and at the two neighbors' yards south of your house.

4. Over 300 people are on a flight from Halifax to Los Angeles. They stop in Detroit to refuel and bring on food. After landing, 158 people complain of dizziness, nausea, and vomiting. Upon investigating, the airline discovers everyone who felt ill had eaten the pressed turkey sandwich.

5. Ramona lives in a working-class neighborhood and attends an urban college where most students are commuters. She works part-time at a copy shop. One day Ramona left her class and discovered a deep scratch mark the entire length of her car.

6. Windows were shattered and obscene graffiti was left at a construction site for a mosque in Milpitas, California, near San Francisco. Police were summoned to the Montague Expressway site at about 7:45 P.M. Tuesday, said Lt. Sandy Holliday. There, they found windows shattered and belongings strewn about a construction trailer and camper parked behind a large industrial building that the Al-Hilaal Islamic Charitable Foundation plans to turn into a turreted masjid, or mosque. The graffiti included references to the devil and obscene phrases about Arabs.

7. The Health District received reports of acute gastrointestinal illness that occurred among children and staff at two jointly owned day care centers after a catered lunch. The lunch was served to 82 children age six or younger and to nine staff members; dietary histories were obtained for 80 people. Staff and all children aged four years old or older were interviewed directly; staff and parents were questioned for children younger than four years old. Of the 80 people, 67 ate the catered lunch. Fourteen people (21 percent) who ate the lunch became ill, compared with none of 13 who did not. Chicken fried rice prepared at a local restaurant was the only food significantly associated with illness; illness occurred in 14 of 48 persons (29 percent) who ate chicken fried rice, compared with none of 16 who did not; three of those who were not ill were uncertain if they had eaten the rice.

Other food items (peas and apple rings) were not available for analysis. (As noted in "Bacillus Cereus Food Poisoning," www.textbookofbacteriology.net.)

8. According to the results of a very small new study (10 patients), some people may experience migraine headaches due to wheat. By limiting gluten—a protein found in wheat, oats, barley and rye—seven of nine patients reduced their symptoms of severe headache. Evidently these patients had a sensitivity to gluten, and magnetic resonance imaging (MRI) scans suggested they had inflammation in the central nervous system. Nine of the 10 patients tried a gluten-free diet, and 7 stopped having headaches. Two other patients had some, but not complete, success by switching to a gluten-free diet. One patient did not follow the diet (Dr. Joseph Mercola, www.mercola.com).

Part Two

1. In the early 1980s in Woburn, Massachusetts, 14 children came down with leukemia. (This case was the basis for the novel and movie *A Civil Action*.) The families of the sick children got their water from the town wells G and H. The major industry near the neighborhood was the W.R. Grace Company. Barrels of the company's chemical waste were located near wells G and H. Grace employees testified that they had dumped the chemicals behind the plant into the ground or saw others do so. The Aberjona River was also located near the wells.

   Answer the following:
   a. What is the most likely cause of the effect cited?
   b. What are three alternatives to the probable cause you cited in *a*?
   c. What are two to three ideas for investigating further to determine the cause?

2. Fifteen thousand banana workers who work with pesticides and who are now sterile are suing companies (Dow Chemical, Shell Oil, Standard Fruit Co., and Chiquita Brands, Inc.) that manufacture and use a chemical DBCP (dibromochloropropane, a pesticide). Their lawyer asserts: "DBCP was developed by Dow and Shell to combat microscopic worms that attack banana plants. It was widely used in 1968. Banana workers who applied the chemicals had no protective clothes or gloves. The chemical was banned in the U.S. in 1979, but shipped to Central American countries, even though it was thought to cause sterilization. Eight thousand Costa Rican workers are apparently sterilized and they blame DBCP, which they worked with." (*Multinational Monitor*, July/August 1990).

   Answer the following:
   a. What is the most likely cause of the effect cited?
   b. What are three alternatives to the probable cause you cited in *a*?
   c. What are two to three ideas for investigating further to determine the cause?

3. The citizens of Europe and the Pentagon are taking a new look at the greatest danger such climate change (global warning) could produce for the northern hemisphere—a sudden shift into a new ice age. What they're finding is not at all comforting.

In quick summary, if enough cold, fresh water coming from the melting polar ice caps and the melting glaciers of Greenland flows into the northern Atlantic, it will shut down the Gulf Stream, which keeps Europe and northeastern North America warm. The worst-case scenario would be a full-blown return of the last ice age—in a period as short as 2 to 3 years from its onset—and the mid-case scenario would be a period like the "little ice age" of a few centuries ago that disrupted worldwide weather patterns leading to extremely harsh winters, droughts, worldwide desertification, crop failures, and wars around the world. (Thom Hartmann, "How Global Warming May Cause the Next Ice Age," Common Dreams News Center, www.commondreams.org, 30 Jan 2004)

Answer the following:

a. What is the worst-case scenario regarding global warming, according to this excerpt?

b. Does this worst-case scenario seem likely? Share your reaction, setting out your reasons.

c. What are two or three ideas for investigating further to determine if Hartmann's hypothesis is correct?

4. Six soldiers who have fallen ill since their return from Iraq said Friday that the Army ignored their complaints about uranium poisoning from U.S. weapons fired during combat. . . . "We were all healthy when we left home. Now, I suffer from headaches, fatigue, dizziness, blood in the urine, unexplained rashes," said Sgt. Jerry Ojeda, 28, who was stationed south of Baghdad with other National Guard members of the 442nd Military Police Company. He said symptoms also include shortness of breath, migraines and nausea. . . .

Five of the men said they also were recently tested independently by Dr. Asaf Durakovic, a former Army doctor and nuclear medicine expert, who found traces of depleted uranium in their bloodstream, with four registering high levels. . . . Since the start of the Iraq war, U.S. forces reportedly have fired at least 120 tons of shells packed with depleted uranium. Depleted uranium, which is left over from the process of enriching uranium for use as nuclear fuel, is an extremely dense material that the U.S. and British militaries use for tank armor and armor-piercing weapons. It is far less radioactive than natural uranium. (Associated Press, "Army Ignored Illness Complaints," 10 Apr 2004)

Answer the following:

a. If you were asked to speak for the Iraq war veterans who have suffered the symptoms noted above, what argument would you make to the U.S. government?

b. State what needs to be done before concluding that the depleted uranium is the source of the Iraq war veterans' health problems.

Part Three

1. On July 28, 2004, the Federal Communications Commission (FCC) reported on its intent to study the impact of media violence on children.

Read the following statement by the FCC and then answer the questions that follow:

What are the effects of viewing violent programming on children and other segments of the population? Much of the research within the public health and scientific communities suggests that exposure to media violence can be associated with certain negative effects. [The many different media and violence studies point to "a statistically significant connection between watching violence on television and behaving aggressively."]

Efforts have been made to establish a cause and effect relationship between the viewing of "violent" programming by children and subsequent aggressive behavior on the part of these individuals. Researchers have tended to focus on three possible harmful effects: (1) increased antisocial behavior, including imitations of aggression or negative interaction; (2) desensitization to violence and (3) increased fear of becoming a victim of violence.

Answer the following:

a. What questions would you like the FCC to answer before they consider taking action regarding the effects of media violence on children?
b. What alternatives might explain the perceived effects of antisocial behavior, desensitization, and so on rather than TV violence?

2. Read about a case of an altercation outside a store. Then answer the questions that follow.

A white man is suing the city because police failed to respond to his seven calls to 911 (emergency). An angry crowd gathered outside his store after he ran out of stereo speakers that were on sale. It seemed he only had five such items in stock. He offered to order more, but the crowd accused him of exploiting them (they were all Filipino) and started screaming. He claimed they made threats. The crowd dispersed after a half hour and no damage was done to his store. Nevertheless, the store owner is suing the city for $1 million. He insists the police's failure to respond put him at risk and he has suffered a nervous disorder ever since.

Answer the following:

a. If you were on the jury, what more would you need to know before you would consider the man deserving of any settlement?
b. What more would you want to know before you would rule in favor of the city?
c. What are the pros and cons of throwing out the case for insufficient evidence?

3. Set out the issues and concerns the following report raises on the increase of AIDS among blacks. Note if we need to obtain more information before declaring this a public health crisis:

Blacks now account for more than half of all new H.I.V. infections . . . Black women account for 72 percent of all new cases among women. During the decades that the

AIDS epidemic has spread, the number of people incarcerated has also soared, to nearly 2.1 million, according to the Bureau of Justice Statistics. Of that total, more than 40 percent are black. As the number of people living with H.I.V. increases, and with roughly 600,000 prisoners re-entering society each year, researchers are starting to address the two issues as intertwined epidemics requiring combined prevention and treatment strategies.

In North Carolina, African-Americans make up more than 70 percent of all existing H.I.V. and AIDS cases, and about 60 percent of the state's roughly 35,000 prisoners. James Thomas, a University of North Carolina epidemiologist . . . found "a robust correlation" between incarceration rates and the rates of H.I.V. and other sexually transmitted diseases. Doctors and social workers in the state say prison, either directly or indirectly, affects many of their H.I.V. patients. . . .

Many inmates enter prison already infected. The prevalence of confirmed AIDS cases in prisons is three times as high as it is in the general population, according to the Bureau of Justice Statistics. H.I.V. cases are harder to count, because only 19 states conduct mandatory H.I.V. testing of inmates. But many researchers believe the number of prisoners with H.I.V. to be far higher than the 1.9 percent most recently documented by the justice agency. (Lynette Clementson, "Links between Prison and the Spread of AIDS Affecting Blacks Inside and Out," *The New York Times*, The HIV Archive, www.natap.org, 6 Aug 2004)

Correlations and False Correlations

Sometimes people draw causal connections between events that are unrelated. We see it in **post hoc reasoning** where an inference is drawn that something causes another thing to happen just because it happened at an earlier time. The fact that one thing precedes another does not necessarily mean they are related. To infer they are linked without sufficient evidence is a **false correlation**. To assert such a relationship requires more evidence than the temporal sequence of when the two events happened. We need to show that there are causal—not just temporal—links between them.

Consider this unpublished study: In an attempt to explain the drop in crime in the 90s, researchers pointed out that it could be related to the legalization of abortion in 1973. They argue: "Many women whose children would have been most likely to commit crimes as young adults instead chose to abort their pregnancies. Because of that, a disproportionate number of would-be criminals in the 1990s were not born in the 1970s (as cited in "Study Links Dip in Crime to Abortions," *Los Angeles Times*, 9 Aug. 1999). Let's think about what has been argued here.

Look at the conclusions researchers drew. The drop in crime could relate to the fact that fewer would-be criminals were born 20 years earlier—but that could be

You Tell Me Department

What Is the Effect of Watching Music Videos?

Is watching music videos destructive for teenagers? See what Vishal Sharma has to say in this excerpt:

> "The sustained exposure to such uninhibited junk bodes ill for the overall health of the society. The rise in teenage pregnancies and reckless sexual behaviour are offshoots of the hedonistic lifestyles depicted on various television channels," says Chandigarh-based Dr. Vaibhav Bhola. "Reduced respect for each other, treating women merely as objects of sexual gratification and a dangerously liberal sexual lifestyle are often the results of constantly viewing pornographic material," he adds.

Dr Claudio Violato of the University of Calgary, Canada, found that constant exposure to porn and sexually explicit material leads to serious deviations in attitude towards intimate relationships. . . . "I have been inundated with complaints of students losing interest in studies, kids turning sexually active at a very tender age and trauma arising out of teenage pregnancies. I attribute all this to the degenerative impact that the media is making on young impressionable minds," says Sachin Sharma, a psychologist. (Vishal Sharma, "Sexed-up Music Videos," *The Tribune* (India), www.tribuneindia.com, 28 Aug 2004)

You tell me: Is it harmful for teens to watch music videos?

---

a false correlation. Perhaps there is a drop in crime because the society has changed, or perhaps because the educational system is better, or perhaps current sentencing laws are a deterrent. It may also be due to a rise in women breast-feeding their babies, making them more psychologically stable. And so on. Without more evidence linking abortion laws to crime statistics, the presumed correlation leaves a lot to the imagination.

Another example of a study attributing correlation looks at teenagers and the company they keep. An August 19, 2004, report from the National Center for Addiction and Substance Abuse at Columbia University (www.casacolumbia.org) stated that:

- Compared to teens with no sexually active friends, teens who report half or more of their friends are sexually active are more than six and one-half times likelier to drink; 31 times likelier to get drunk; 22.5 times likelier to have tried marijuana; and more than five and one-half times likelier to smoke.
- Teens who spend 25 or more hours a week with a boyfriend/girlfriend are two and one-half times likelier to drink; five times likelier to get drunk; 4.5 times likelier to have tried marijuana; and more than 2.5 times likelier to smoke than teens who spend less than 10 hours a week with a boyfriend/girlfriend.

Can we be certain it is the fault of the sexually active friends that teens become more sexually active or use alcohol or drugs? Could it be something the researchers overlooked or minimized in the study? Surely that is possible. But they have the results of their study of 1,000 teens and 500 parents to back them up, so their claim of a correlation warrants further attention.

The Global Dimension

Finland's Impressive Literacy Model

Finland may have shockingly high diabetes rates, but it's made quite a mark for its literacy rate. Finland is rated the world's best in educating children. Should we follow their lead in putting subtitles on TV shows? Read the following report and answer the questions below.

Imagine an educational system where children do not start school until they are 7, where spending is a paltry $5,000 a year per student, where there are no gifted programs and class sizes often approach 30. A prescription for failure, no doubt, in the eyes of many experts, but in this case a description of Finnish schools, which were recently ranked the world's best. Finland topped a respected international survey last year, coming in first in literacy and placing in the top five in math and science. . . .

Children here start school late on the theory that they will learn to love learning through play. Preschool for 6-year-olds is optional, although most attend. And since most women work outside the home in Finland, children usually go to day care after they turn one. At first, the 7-year-olds lag behind their peers in other countries in reading, but they catch up almost immediately and then excel. Experts cite several reasons: reading to children, telling folk tales and going to the library are activities cherished in Finland. Lastly, children grow up watching television shows and movies (many in English) with subtitles. So they read while they watch TV.

So long as schools stick to the core national curriculum, which lays out goals and subject areas, they are free to teach the way they want. They can choose their textbooks or ditch them altogether, teach indoors or outdoors, cluster children in small or large groups. (Lizette Alvarez, "Educators Flocking to Finland, Land of Literate Children," *Suutarila Journal,* 9 April 2004)

Answer the following:

1. From the report, what are the key causes attributed to the high literacy rate in Finland?
2. What is the strongest case to be made for adding subtitles to American TV shows?

Mill's Methods

Philosopher John Stuart Mill set forth a systematic way to look at cause-and-effect arguments. His method provides us with helpful tools for recognizing and assessing the basis for cause-and-effect reasoning. These methods are (1) the method of agreement; (2) the method of difference; (3) the joint method; and (4) the method of concomitant variation.

The Method of Agreement

Here we seek the cause of an event by examining all the cases where the event occurs and then looking for a common factor. For example, when a group of people becomes ill we often look for a common factor, such as exposure to a toxic chemical or spoiled food. If we can find a common factor, we may think we've solved the problem. In that case, we are using the **method of agreement,** which can set out as follows:

Method of Agreement

CASES	ANTECEDENT CONDITIONS	RESULT (OR EFFECT)
1	A, B, E, G, P	Event happens
2	C, D, K, P, W	Event happens
3	C, B, L, P, R, S	Event happens
. . .		
n	A, E, L, P, W, Z	Event happens

Note: In all the above cases, a common factor, "P," precedes the event. By the method of agreement, this means the probable cause of the event is P. One problem with the method of agreement is that we might overlook the real cause. Perhaps the real cause is something we ignored or didn't add to the list; so we fail to determine the most probable cause of the event.

This happened when people at a convention came down with symptoms that had the experts baffled. When those attending the conference in Philadelphia, Pennsylvania, started keeling over (some died), investigators completely overlooked the hotel ventilation system as a possible cause or causal factor of the problem. Several days transpired—and things got progressively worse—until investigators asked themselves if the air the folks breathed could have contributed to their being stricken with the disease. By the time it was over, 221 people at the convention had contracted the disease and 34 people had died. Since most of those who died were Legionnaires (an association for ex-military members), they called it "Legionnaires' disease." That was in 1976—the first time the disease was encountered—and it was after that date that warnings to keep air conditioners clean were issued. *Note* that window units do not pose this problem because they use refrigerated air instead of evaporated water. (See "Legionnaire's Disease," *Multiline,* www.multiline.com.au.)

Method of Difference

With the **method of difference** we compare two cases—one where an effect (or event) occurs and one where it doesn't occur. We then look at the antecedent conditions for these two cases to determine what is different. In light of the differences, we then select the probable cause.

For example, you buy two primroses and plant one in the sun and one in the shade. You put fertilizer on both of them and water them regularly. The primrose in the sun grows beautifully and has lots of blossoms. The primrose in the shade keels over and the leaves curl up. What do you think the problem is?

Let's see the method of difference set out in a diagram:

Method of Difference

CASES	ANTECEDENT CONDITIONS	EVENT
1	A, B, C, D, E	Effect occurs
2	A, B, C, E	Effect doesn't occur

Note: Only two cases are being compared—one when the event occurs and when it does not. The idea is to see what is *different* that might explain what caused the event to happen.

The problem with the method of difference is that we only look at two cases—one where the event occurs and another where it doesn't. This may not give enough data to draw a reliable conclusion. Also, we are only looking at *differences* and the points of agreement may also be instructive in terms of what causes something to happen.

The Joint Method

A more high-powered approach would be to combine the two methods, looking both at what is similar *and* what is different. This is what the *joint method* does. For example, you plant 20 fields of corn. Fifteen fields produce wonderful, tasty corn and five fields only have dried, shriveled corn that even a hungry cow would reject. After wiping away tears, you try to solve the problem. You discover the fields with the wonderful corn are next to a pasture. The five fields with crummy corn are not only near a chemical dump, but people walking by throw their trash into them. This suggests that the common location of the successful fields figures into getting good quality corn. Furthermore, both the chemical waste dump and the piles of trash landing on the struggling plants are differences that are significant enough to suggest a probable cause for these fields of corn doing so poorly. We can set out the joint method of agreement and difference in a diagram:

Joint Method

CASES	ANTECEDENT CONDITIONS	EFFECT
lst group	A, B, D, F, P, W	Event occurs
2nd group	A, B, F, X, Y	Event doesn't occur

Note: A, B, and F are common antecedent conditions. What is different is that in the first group we find conditions D, P, W and, in the second group, conditions X and Y. Note also that there are *groups* of cases, not just two cases. This means we are more likely to discover the cause than with *either* of the first two methods and, consequently, that this is a more powerful method than either of the first two.

You Tell Me Department

Does Only the Mummy Know for Sure?

King Tut, mummies, and pyramids have fascinated many people for decades. Look, for instance, at the 1932 film *The Mummy*, starring Boris Karloff, and all the mummy films since. Interest in King Tut seems to be a bug that has bitten an awful lot of people! The latest theory about how Tutankhamun died fuels that interest:

> Researchers continue to investigate the cause of Tutankhamun's premature death. Bob Brier, a mummy specialist from Long Island University, has been tracking down clues that indicate Tutankhamun may have been killed by his elderly chief advisor and successor, Ay. An X-ray of his skull revealed a calcified blood clot at its base. This could have been caused by a blow from a blunt implement, which eventually resulted in death. ("Tutankhamun, The Cause of His Death—Mysteries of Egypt," Canadian Museum of Civilization, www.civilization.ca)

You tell me: What sort of clues do you think Brier "tracked down" to arrive at his hypothesis? Do you know enough to be convinced? If not, what more do you need to conclude that Brier is probably right?

The Method of Concomitant Variation

This last method is for cases that are not all or nothing, but where an effect occurs in degrees. With the **method of concomitant variation** we might have increasing or decreasing amounts of some effect (like pollution in a city or disease patterns in a population). Although the effect always exists, its presence is a matter of percentage. We can set this out in the following diagram:

Method of Concomitant Variation

CASES	ANTECEDENT CONDITIONS	EFFECT
1st group	A, B, C, D	Event occurs (E)
2nd group	A, B, C, D+	E+ (or E−)
3rd group	A, B, C, D−	E (or E+)

Having more or less of some causal factors results in an increase or decrease of the effect (indicated by E+ and E− in the diagram). Note that the three different groups could be groups of individuals (say when a disease appears in a population), or it could be groups at different times (say when we are testing to see what happens when the air pollution goes up or down).

An example of the use of concomitant variation is the study of mosquito populations and health concerns. The West Nile virus is a potentially lethal disease transmitted by mosquitoes. The bite of an infected mosquito can be deadly for the victim. Since the West Nile virus appeared on the East Coast in 1999, it spread across the lower 48 states by summer 2004. So, in five years the disease has become a health concern beyond one state's borders. With the method of concomitant variation, researchers can study the varying rates of the spread of the disease.

Exercises

1. State the form of Mill's method of difference by filling in what is missing from the following:

Cases	Antecedent Circumstances	Event

2. State the *difference* in Mill's method of agreement and method of difference (be specific).

3. Explain why the joint method of agreement and difference is considered a more powerful tool than the method of difference.

4. State when you would likely use the method of concomitant variation.

5. State which of Mill's method to use in the following:

   On a recent trip to Kansas City, 53 bus passengers riding in the front of the bus felt itchy, broke out in hives and felt weak. The 45 passengers in the back of the bus were fine. It was found that a pesticide spray had been used in the first half of the bus, but not the second half.

6. State which of Mill's methods to use in the following:

   MIT Medical and Cambridge Hospital treated four MIT students and two members of the community for food poisoning last week . . . "This is the worst that any food company can experience," said Tony Vo, a vendor at Goosebeary's. Last Tuesday, four MIT students and two members of the community reported cases of food poisoning after eating at the Goosebeary's food truck. All six ordered chicken teriyaki. (Jeffrey Greenbaum, "Goosebeary's Closes after Food Poisoning," *The Tech*, www-tech.mit.edu)

6. State which of Mill's method to use in the following:

   Research being conducted by JoEllen Welsh, a professor of biological sciences at Notre Dame, is offering intriguing clues about the role vitamin D might play in breast cancer treatment and prevention. Studies by Welsh have indicated that vitamin D can stop the growth of cancer cells and shrink tumors in mice. Welsh studies genetically engineered "knockout" mice that lack the vitamin D receptor to help determine the substance's function in breast tissue. "In the absence of the receptor, the mammary gland grows more than in normal mice," she said. "This suggests that when vitamin D is present, it slows down cell growth." . . . "Treating cells with activators of the vitamin D receptor stops the growth of breast cancer cells and makes them undergo apoptosis, or cell death," she said. (William G. Gilroy, "Vitamin D May Help in Battle Against Breast Cancer," *University of Notre Dame News*, newsinfo.nd.edu, 1 Mar 2004)

7. State which of Mill's methods to use in the following:

   When Ryan had his first asthma attack, he stayed in bed, drank lots of fluids, ate lots of vitamin-rich foods, and used his inhaler. He felt better and breathed easier in five days. The second time Ryan had an asthma attack, he stayed in bed, drank lots of fluids, ate vitamin-rich foods, used his inhaler and took prednisone. His symptoms cleared up in two days.

8. State which of Mill's methods should be used:

   During the heat wave in the summer of 2004, there were eight smog alerts (dangerous levels of pollution) in southeastern Florida. One local hospital reported that patients with breathing problems increased by 24%. By September rates dropped back to around normal, and decreased by 11% in November after temperatures dropped to the mid-40s.

Group or Individual Exercise

A number of lawsuits against tobacco manufacturers have been filed by consumers who were long-time smokers and ended up with either lung cancer or emphysema. Select one to discuss:

1. If you were an advocate for the consumer suffering from lung disease, what steps should be taken to strengthen your claims against the company?

2. If you were a CEO at a tobacco company, what steps should the company take to strengthen its defense in these lawsuits?

3. If you were on the jury, what evidence would help you reach a decision about causation?

4. If you were a representative from the community on a committee reviewing the marketing of cigarettes, what sorts of warnings would you want to put on ads and packaging about the health risks of smoking?

Arguments Based on Statistical Studies

People frequently rely upon statistical data or study. **Arguments based on statistical studies** are inductive arguments since they draw an inference based on a sample group, where the evidence is partial at best. Statistical reasoning always entails a degree of probability—never certainty—in the relationship between the premises and the conclusion. We need to know how to properly use statistical studies to recognize strong arguments and avoid being fooled by the weak ones.

For instance, suppose someone said, "A study of 150 men at a Dallas university revealed that 54% had used recreational drugs; therefore, we can conclude that 54% of Americans have used recreational drugs." Is this good reasoning?

- If you said, "No," pat yourself on the back.
- If you said, "Yes," fear not, you can be helped, so read on.

A **statistical study** has two components: one, a **targeted population** about which we want information and, two, the **sample group** we intend to study as a a microcosm of the larger group. In certain sorts of statistical studies, such as medical experiments, psychological testing, or pharmaceutical studies, research protocol may call for a control group. This group is used to compare relative responses, for example, to a medical treatment or drug regimen, in order to eliminate other factors. In such cases, members of the control group are usually given some sort of placebo (e.g., a pill-like candy that has no medicinal value) to prevent the subjects from knowing whether or not they are in the control group or the experimental sample group.

Once we gather evidence from the sample study, we'll *generalize* to the larger, targeted population, allowing for a certain margin of error. The **margin of error** recognizes that the inference from the smaller, sample group to the targeted population is somewhat uncertain. The study sample may or may not be representative of the whole. In statistical studies, there are always uncertainties, even in the most elaborate, well-crafted cases. For this reason, instead of concluding that x percent of A is B, a margin of error is added: x plus-or-minus z percent of A is B, where z recognizes the uncertainty in generalizing from the sample group to the targeted population.

Word of Advice

If you really want to learn statistics, you need at least a semester-long course. However, we can get a general overview of statistical studies here.

Three Key Aspects of a Statistical Study

Date   What is the date of the study? Is it still relevant?

Size   How big was the sample group?

Diversity   How diverse is the sample population? Is it representative of the target population?

Importance of Date

A statistical study conducted 10 years ago is most likely out of date. Even the results of a study conducted five years ago could be worthless. Try to find current research for your data.

Think of AIDS research. A great deal has happened in the last 10 years. Recent studies are more likely to be reliable than ones done in the past. Also, think how much has shifted in terms of DNA research. And what about media research? Or research on methods of communication? Forty years ago many people did not own television sets. Personal computers, DVD players, and cell phones are relatively recent additions, but they have had an impact on our lives. And think how much has changed with e-mail access. This method of communication is far more powerful than telephones because we can ship documents, letters, essays, and the like around the world as attachments. Consequently, when examining statistical studies, pay attention to the date when they were conducted. Consider their relevance, as well as any potential obstacles that may decrease their currency.

Importance of Size

Next, is the issue of **sample size.** This is the number of subjects in the sample group used as the basis for an inference about a target population. If we have only a small sample population and generalize to an entire city, our results would be of negligible value.

For example, a study of 25 people in a city of 500,000 would have limited value. In fact, the fallacy of hasty generalization occurs when the sample size is too small. This happens, for instance, when people make generalizations about a type of ethnic food on the basis of one or two meals. A good study requires a large enough sample to avoid the problem of insufficient evidence.

Importance of Diversity

Last is the issue of **diversity.** The sample should be representative of the population in question. This means it should have sufficient diversity, preferably comparable to the diversity of the target population.

Two Major Ways to Get Sufficient Diversity in a Sample Study

1. **Representative sample.** A representative sample is obtained by trying to match the sample group with the target population. Try to keep a balance of the major aspects such as gender, age, race, religion, education, class, and geography.
2. **Random sample.** A random sample is *not* obtained by carefully constructing a sample group, taking into account the relevant factors such as age, gender, nationality, and class. Rather, in a random sample, each member of the target population has an equal chance of being studied. We get a random sample by using some numerical means (like polling every third person, stopping every sixth driver, or interviewing every tenth voter) combined with a sufficient quantity. Hopefully that process will generate enough diversity to reflect the target population.

For example, in the mid 1980s, a study of the San Pedro, California police found that officers pulled over a disproportionate number of people of color in checking for drunk drivers. The group had a striking absence of white and wealthy drivers. Concerned about possible racism underlying their method, the police department opted for random sampling, pulling over every sixth driver. Using this technique, *everyone* had an equal chance of being checked. The result was that those tested ranged across all racial groups, ages, and economic levels.

The Global Dimension

Early Call on the Venezuela Election

What should be done when a pollster calls the 2004 Venezuela election while the voting booths are still open—and the call is way off the mark? Set out what you think should be done to the U.S. firm responsible for publicizing their prediction four hours before the polls closed.

> A U.S. firm's exit poll that said President Hugo Chavez would lose a recall referendum has landed in the center of a controversy following his resounding victory. "Exit Poll Results Show Major Defeat for Chavez," the survey, conducted by Penn, Schoen & Berland Associates, asserted even as Sunday's voting was still on. But in fact, the opposite was true. Chavez ended up trouncing his enemies and capturing 59 percent of the vote.

> Any casual observer of the 2000 U.S. presidential elections knows exit polls can at times be unreliable. . . . Election officials banned publication or broadcast of any exit polls during the historic vote on whether to oust Chavez, a populist who has sought to help the poor and is reviled by the wealthy, who accuse him of stoking class divisions. But results of the Penn, Schoen & Berland survey were sent out by fax and e-mail to media outlets and opposition offices more than four hours before polls closed. It predicted just the opposite of what happened, saying 59 percent had voted in favor of recalling Chavez. (Andrew Selsky, "U.S. Polling firm lands in middle of Venezuelan Referendum dispute," Associated Press, 19 Aug 2004).

Fallacious Use of Statistics

Two types of fallacies frequently show up in statistical reasoning. (See Chapter 4 for a fuller discussion). These two fallacies are as follows:

- **Hasty generalization.** If the size is simply too small, a generalization from it could result in the fallacy of hasty generalization. This often underlies stereo-typical reasoning. If the sample size is not sufficient, avoid drawing a generalization.
- **Biased statistics.** If the size is sufficient, a random sample will likely result in a sample representative of the target population. For example, in studies of human behavior, such issues as gender, race, religion, class, age, education, and geography might be factored in to fulfill the diversity quotient. The failure to do this results in the fallacy called biased statistics.

Group or Individual Exercise

The following health tips rest on research using statistical studies. Discuss the issues and concerns for each health tip and what questions we'd want answered before concluding that the tip should be a guideline for good health. Which of the tips are most credible, most believable? List them from 1 (least credible) to 5 (most credible). Explain your rating. Note any reasoning you find questionable:

Health tip #1: Painkillers given to women during labor increase fivefold the likelihood of the child growing up to be a drug user. New research undertaken at Gothenburg University suggests that exposure in the womb to high-dose medication may be an important and preventable risk factor for later substance abuse (*Metro,* 19 Oct 2000, www.globalideasbank.org).

Health tip #2: Women who believe they are going to live for a long time are more likely than less optimistic women to give birth to sons, a new study suggests. Researchers reached the strange conclusion after completing a survey of British women who had recently become mothers. They found that for every extra year a woman thought she was going to live, the odds of her firstborn being a boy increased significantly . . . In the latest study, reported in the journal *Biology Letters,* 609 new mothers in Gloucestershire, southwest England, were asked, among other questions, to what age they expected to live (Ian Sample, "Optimists more likely to give birth to boys," *The Age,* www.theage.com.au, 5 Aug 2004).

Health tip #3: Smoking is bad for your gums: Results of a new study indicated that teenage smokers are nearly three times as likely as their nonsmoking peers to have gum disease in their mid-20s. According to the authors of the study, the longer teenagers smoked, the greater the extent of gum disease (*Community Dentistry and Oral Epidemiology,* www.coloradohealthnet.org).

Health tip #4: A survey by the National Sleep Foundation suggests that about half of American adults borrow from sleep to get more work done, watch late-night television, or surf the Internet. . . . The amount of sleep needed varies from person to person, but the *Harvard Heart Letter* notes that for most people, eight hours seems to be about right. Over the short term, not getting enough sleep increases blood pressure and stress hormone levels. Sleep deprivation makes it difficult for the body to process blood sugar and reduces levels of leptin, an appetite-depressing hormone. These two changes could lead to diabetes and weight gain. Lack of sleep also increases inflammation, thought to be a key element in the development of heart disease. Set your internal clock by establishing a regular bedtime schedule. Avoid alcohol. Although it may make you drowsy, it also makes you waken more easily later on. Regular exercise can aid a good night's sleep. Late afternoon activity seems to be best, but avoid exercising within three hours of bedtime. ("*Harvard Heart Letter* Examines the Costs of Not Getting Enough Sleep," *Harvard Health Publications,* www.health.harvard.edu, Aug 2004).

Health tip #5: A study by doctors at the University of Maryland has found that people who fail to raise a smile in stressful or uncomfortable situations may be more likely to develop heart problems. The researchers interviewed 150 people who had either suffered a heart attack or had undergone bypass surgery. Their attitudes were compared with 150 healthy people of the same age. Participants were asked how they would react to a number of uncomfortable everyday situations. These included arriving at a party to find somebody else wearing the same outfit and having a waiter spill a drink over them at a restaurant. The researchers found that people with a history of heart problems were more likely to get angry or hostile rather than laugh or use humor to overcome the embarrassment of the situation. People with previous heart conditions were also less likely to laugh even in positive situations. ("Laughter 'Protects the Heart,' " BBC News, www.news.bbc.co.uk, 15 Nov 2000).

Confronting Problems in Statistical Studies

If someone who had a heart attack is less likely to laugh, what should we infer? We may conclude, as in the tip, that the person's heart attack was the *result* of failing to laugh enough. However, it may be that the heart attack was *due* to an excessive amount of laughing and, thus, the victim has no desire to take up laughing to the degree prior to the cardiac arrest.

Alternatively, perhaps the heart attack victim finds a great deal hilarious afterward, but finds a few topics (e.g., death, heart failure, doctors, hospital gowns) not at all funny, thus lowering the patient's laugh-quotient and throwing off the statistical study. Without more information, it may be unwise to conclude that we should bring comedians into hospital cardiac wards. Statistical studies cannot always be taken at face value.

We might also question a study done of only 150 people. Was that a sufficient sample size? What race or ethnicity were the participants? Can we assume that a small size is adequate and that leaving out race and ethnicity is not a problem? These are questions we might want answered.

We may want to use a study that has some problems, in which case we need to decide what to do next. When the study is in doubt, basically we have these choices: (1) throw it out (in the event of serious concerns) or (2) examine the study's margin of error. Every study contains a margin of error. Because the inference from the sample study to the target population contains a wedge of doubt, the margin of error ought to be reflected in the conclusion; for example "x plus or minus z percent of As are Bs" (where z is some small number, usually 5 or lower).

The Margin of Error

The smaller the margin of error is, the better. In well-orchestrated studies like those we see in the Gallup Poll, the margin of error is usually 2 or 3 percent. A margin of error over 5 percent may indicate a less reliable study. Mathematician Matthew Delaney considers a 5 percent margin of error hard to achieve and, therefore, it may be unrealistic to think a study can achieve this level of accuracy.

Remember that the margin of error means the range goes from −z percent to +z percent, which is a range of 2z. This means if your margin of error is 3 percent, then the range is 6 percent and a margin of error of 5 percent will give a range

You Tell Me Department

What about Those Political Polls?

The CNN poll after John Kerry's acceptance of the Democratic nomination found Kerry running slightly ahead of Bush among registered voters but slightly behind among likely voters. Of the 1,011 adult Americans interviewed, 916 identified themselves as registered voters and 763 said they were likely voters. The registered voters surveyed favored Kerry over Bush 50–47, a slight change from 49–45 found in a similar poll conducted two weeks ago. The likely voters polled favored Bush 50–47, whereas two weeks earlier they had favored Kerry 49–47. (See "Poll: No 'Bounce' for Kerry so Far," CNN.com, www.cnn.com, 1 Aug 2004.)

You tell me: Twenty-five percent of those interviewed were evidently not likely to vote, by their own admission. Given this number of nonvoters, what do you make of the close call on the poll?

of 10 percent, which is a significant range. For example, 32 percent plus or minus 5 percent means the range goes from 27 percent to 37 percent—a range of 10 percentage points!

Two Forms of Statistical Arguments

Two forms of statistical arguments are prevalent: (1) statistical syllogisms and (2) inductive generalizations. Let's look at each of them.

Form of a Statistical Syllogism.

x% of A is a B.

p is an A.

Therefore, p is a B.

A *statistical syllogism* has two premises. The first asserts that a percentage of the subject class (A) has some predicated characteristic (B). Then we conclude (here's the inductive aspect of the reasoning) that what was said of class A applies to a specified individual member of the class. Of course, the wedge of doubt is whether the individual member is in the x percent of A with characteristic B or in the remaining 100 − x percent of A that don't have the characteristic B. Here are some examples of statistical syllogisms.

Example #1.

86% of women in Louisiana like shrimp creole.

Natalie is a woman living in Louisiana.

Therefore, Natalie likes shrimp creole.

Example #2.

65% of cats prefer birds to mice for dinner.

Prince is a cat.

Therefore, Prince prefers birds to mice for dinner.

The strength of a statistical syllogism is directly proportional to the percentage. The closer to 100 percent in an affirmative claim, the better the argument. Basically, 85 percent and up (the higher the better) is pretty strong. But the lower the percentage, the more questionable is the truth of the conclusion.

The second major kind of statistical argument is called an **inductive generalization**. In this case, we infer that what is true about the sample group is true in the targeted population as a whole. The wedge of doubt comes in the leap from the *sample* (about which we know some statistical data) to the *targeted population* the sample merely represents. As we know, the sample may not exactly resemble the whole group, so it is uncertain whether something true of the sample is really true of the larger group of which it is a part.

Form of an Inductive Generalization.

x% of As polled (or sampled) are Bs.

Therefore, x percent of all As are Bs.

In an inductive generalization we start with a sample study of the target population. We then infer that what was true of the sample group will also be true for the target population. Here are some examples of inductive generalizations.

Example #1.

48% of men polled outside the discount rug store in San Luis Obispo said they thought the president was doing a good job.

Therefore, 48% of American men think the president is doing a good job.

Example #2.

49% of those in the August 5, 2004 Investor's Business Daily poll think the U.S. military actions in Iraq have not made the world a better place.

Therefore, 49% of the people think the U.S. military actions in Iraq have not made the world a better place.

In a strong inductive generalization, watch for date, size, and diversity. Be sure the poll is recent, the size not too small, and the sample group representative of the target population. The issue of diversity (that the sample represents the larger group) is crucial.

A Word of Advice

Be aware that there is a lot more to statistics than the two inductive arguments discussed here. A thorough knowledge of statistical methods is vital for anyone going into math, business, psychology, sociology, economics, or clinical studies. Moreover, not all arguments using statistics are inductive. For example, "A toss of the coin will result in a 50% chance of getting heads. Joe tossed the coin. So, There's a 50% chance Joe will get heads." This argument is *deductive*, since the

The Global Dimension

Polls on How the United States Is Viewed

A poll by the British Broadcasting Corporation of 11 countries found negative attitudes about the United States. What should we make of these results? Read the following report on the poll and then answer the questions that follow:

> The survey gauged opinion towards U.S. military, economic, cultural, and political influence.
> COUNTRIES POLLED: Australia, Canada, Brazil, France, Indonesia, Israel, Jordan, Russia, South Korea, United Kingdom, the United States. Over half the sample felt that the U.S. was wrong to invade Iraq—this included 81% of Russian respondents, and 63% of the French response. Thirty-seven percent thought it right to invade—including 54% of the UK response, 74% of the U.S. response and 79% of the Israeli sample.
>
> Asked who is the more dangerous to world peace and stability, the United States was rated higher than al-Qaeda by respondents in both

Jordan (71%) and Indonesia (66%). America was also rated more dangerous than two countries considered as "rogue states" by Washington. It was rated more dangerous than Iran, by people in Jordan, Indonesia, Russia, South Korea and Brazil, and more dangerous than Syria by respondents in all the countries, except for Australia, Israel and the United States. The sample had over 11,000 respondents and was done during May and June 2003. ("Poll Suggests World Hostile to U.S.," *BBC News*, www.bbcnews.com, 16 Jun 2003)

Answer the following:

1. Looking at the list of countries, would you say this is sufficiently diverse to draw the inference about world attitudes? State your decision and share your reasons.

2. If you were hired by the State Department to give them suggestions for public relations, what advice would you offer, drawing from the poll results?

---

premises are sufficient for the conclusion and there is no wedge of doubt between the premises and the conclusion.

If you are familiar with these two inductive arguments based on statistics, you will be able to handle these two common forms, the statistical syllogism, and the inductive generalization. The exercises below will help you analyze these two forms of argument when you come across them.

Exercises

1. Here is an inductive generalization:

   <u>76% of seniors in the bank poll prefer tellers to ATM machines.</u>

   Therefore, 76% of seniors in the state prefer tellers to ATM machines.

   a. What would you need to know to determine whether or not this is a good inductive generalization? (What are the criteria?)
   b. What could you do to strengthen the argument, if you cannot take the poll again?

2. Discuss whether the following arguments are strong statistical syllogisms:

a. 82% of all women love sports cars.
   Evangelina is a woman.
   Therefore, Evangelina loves sports cars.

b. 95% of mechanics have mood swings.
   Harry is a mechanic.
   So, Harry has mood swings.

c. 67% of air traffic controllers have problems with stress.
   Tracy is an air traffic controller.
   So Tracy has problems with stress.

d. 81% of computer technicians have well-groomed hands.
   Yassir is a computer technician.
   So, Yassir has well-groomed hands.

e. 62% of electricians prefer incandescent to fluorescent lighting.
   Lenny is an electrician.
   So, Lenny prefers incandescent to fluorescent lighting.

f. 74% of gardeners prefer mulch to fertilizer.
   Elena is a gardener.
   So, Elena prefers mulch to fertilizer.

3. Give an example of a strong statistical syllogism and explain why it is strong.

4. Give an example of a fairly strong, but not extremely strong, statistical syllogism.

5. Give an example of a weak statistical syllogism, explaining why it is weak.

6. State if this a good inductive generalization and explain why. Note any concerns you may have about the sample group:

Just before Presidents Bush and Fox met in Washington to plot an amnesty for illegal aliens, FAIR released a national Harris poll it commissioned, confirming that the majority of Americans oppose an amnesty for illegal aliens in the United States. Based on a survey of over 1,000 voters, the poll found that Americans oppose an amnesty for illegal aliens by a 60 percent to 29 percent margin. Therefore we can conclude that 60 percent of voters oppose amnesty for illegal aliens. (www.freerepublic.com, 30 Aug 2001)

7. Give your assessment of the value of the poll results of this study:

Professor Whitaker wants to get out the vote of people in the under-30 age group. She took a poll of students at CSULB to see how many registered for the 2004 election and, of those, how many actually voted. Because her sample group had a disproportionately large number of Latinas in it compared to the number enrolled at the college, she calculated a margin of error of 8 percent.

8. What would you like to know in order to conclude whether the ABC News poll cited in the following report is reliable? What stands out in this news report? State your inferences:

Nearly three-quarters of Americans in an ABCNEWS poll say going on a very strict diet—eating one-third fewer calories—in order to live longer isn't worth it. In fact, most don't want to live to be extremely old under any circumstances: If it were possible, 65 percent say they wouldn't want to live to 120. And an overwhelming majority prefers to face those so-called golden years naturally, rather than take artificial measures to help roll back the clock. About nine in 10 or more say they're not interested in plastic surgery, Botox injections, or chemical peels to improve their appearance.

Men are more likely than women, by 40 percent to 27 percent, to want to live to 120, but men are no more likely to say they'd restrict their eating to get there. Seventy percent of men say they wouldn't eat fewer calories to live longer; 75 percent of women agree. Women, meanwhile, are more apt to express an interest in having cosmetic surgery and skin treatments such as chemical peels (yet still relatively few do so). This peaks among younger women: About two in 10 age 18–34 say they're personally interested in taking these measures to improve their appearance.

Methodology—This ABCNEWS poll was conducted by telephone August 14–18, 2002, among a random national sample of 1,023 adults. The results have a three-point error margin. (ABC News, www.abcnews.com)

9. What can you infer from the following poll results?

Americans by a 2–1 margin support stem cell research and say it should be funded by the federal government, despite controversy over its use of human embryos. Advocates of this research say it can produce new treatments for disease, while critics oppose using embryos in research. After hearing these competing views, 58 percent of Americans support stem cell research, while 30 percent oppose it, according to a new *ABCNEWS/Beliefnet* poll. Six in 10 also say the federal government should fund it. Catholics support it personally by a margin of 54 percent to 35 percent, and favor its federal funding by a slightly wider margin, 60 percent to 32 percent. . . . One of the groups that's least supportive of stem cell research is blacks—the most solidly Democratic group in the nation. Forty-four percent of blacks personally oppose stem cell research, 15 points higher than the level of opposition among whites. . . . Among all groups examined in this poll, opposition to stem cell research is highest—58 percent—among people who think abortion should be illegal in all cases (they account for one in five Americans). More moderate abortion opponents, who think abortion should be mostly, but not always, illegal, divide about evenly on stem cell research.

Among the three in 10 adults who oppose stem cell research, 42 percent say their religious beliefs had the most influence on their opinion—making religion the most significant factor in this opposition by a wide margin. Nonetheless, that still leaves a majority of opponents who cite other chief influences, including personal nonreligious beliefs (17 percent), news accounts (13 percent) and personal experiences (9 percent).

Methodology—This ABCNEWS/Beliefnet poll was conducted by telephone June 20–24, 2002, among a random national sample of 1,022 adults. The results have a three-point error margin. (*ABC News*, www.abcnews.com)

CHAPTER FOURTEEN

Handling Claims, Drawing Inferences

Dallas: *Something has attached itself to him. We have to get him to the infirmary right away.*

Ripley: *What kind of thing? I need a clear definition.*

Dallas: *An organism. Open the hatch.*

Ripley: *Wait a minute. If we let it in, the ship could be infected. You know the quarantine procedure. Twenty-four hours for decontamination.*

Dallas: *He could die in twenty-four hours. Open the hatch.*

Ripley: *Listen to me, if we break quarantine, we could all die.*

Lambert: *Could you open the god-damned hatch? We have to get him inside.*

Ripley: *No. I can't do that and if you were in my position, you'd do the same.*

—ALIEN

Feeling feverish, you head off to the UCLA Medical Center to have some blood drawn. You pick up the consent form and begin to read it. It looks like the same old six and seven, until the next to last paragraph. Tucked into the paragraph labeled "Teaching and Research Institution," you find the following: "I further understand that the University of California, including UCLA Health-care, may review and use medical information and specimens for teaching, study, and research purposes, including the development of potentially commercially useful products."

Your head bounces off the ceiling, as you leap up from your chair. As you pat the goose egg forming on the top of your skull, you try to decide: "Do I sign this and sign away all commercial rights to my DNA—or do I forget about this blood test for now and pay for my own blood test elsewhere?" In times like these you're glad you studied critical thinking. We need to know how to handle claims. Otherwise, we may come across an assertion and be unsure of what in the world it means. Also, we need to know what others might justifiably infer on the basis of *our* claims.

Consider two court cases of the last decade. On August 10, 2000, the conviction of Sandy Murphy and Rick Tabish for the murder of Las Vegas millionaire Ted Binion was called into question. It seems that juror #10, Joan Sanders, submitted to the court a potentially explosive sworn affidavit. She admitted that "I changed my vote to guilty when it was told to me by the other jurors, 'if you are in the house when a person dies, and do nothing to assist, that is murder.' " (See "Affidavit of Joan Sanders," Court TV, www.courttv.com.)

In another case, actress Kim Basinger was sued for breaking her contract for the movie *Boxing Helena*. The verdict favoring the producer was reversed by the appellate court—the court ruled that the jury instructions were simply ambiguous. Here's why: the jury instructions used the phrase "and/or" in asking the jury to determine whether it was Kim Basinger personally or her corporation, Mighty Wind, that entered into the contract.

We don't have to be trapped by logic to learn it. Knowing the tools of logic helps us work within systems already in place. It's sort of like x-ray vision: A firm grasp of logic gives us the ability to see how arguments are structured, to organize that reasoning, and to dismantle it so it can be evaluated. This is both useful and empowering. What we will do in this chapter is go deeper into analysis and critical thinking skills by examining different types of claims.

As you can see from the opening quote, the movie *Alien* shows us characters who are in a fight for survival after an alien creature was brought on board ship—attached to one of the crewmember's heads. Mind you, Ripley, our hero, refused to allow it, noting scientific protocol around contamination. But her claims were brushed aside. Their failure to give serious thought to the concerns she raises led to disastrous results. Fortunately, this does not always happen, but there is a moral (and cognitive) tale to the story. And we certainly learn of the value of drawing justifiable inferences. In this chapter, we'll cover techniques for building this skill.

Propositions

A **proposition** is a claim asserting that something is or is not the case. These are all propositions: "The car rolled into the street," "Chicago is in Illinois," "John Lennon was a Beatle." Propositions are not normally expressed as questions or exclamations, unless those are rhetorical forms of an assertion.

In classical logic, prescriptive or moral claims (like "You *ought* to eat spinach" or "Assault guns *should* be illegal") were not treated as propositions because of the difficulty in assigning them a truth value. This is also the case with aesthetic judgments, such as "Monet is the most impressive Impressionist ever!" That does not mean such claims are just a matter of opinion, since they may rest on a body of knowledge and research. But you cannot say they are true or false with the degree of certainty attached to empirical claims.

Different Kinds of Propositions

Ultimately, prescriptive and moral claims were allowed into logic, with the understanding that there may be disagreement over truth or falsity. This is also true of other value claims (such as "Redheads are sexier than blondes" or "A pear tart is a more elegant dessert than a Black Forest cake"). We proceed by *assuming* truth and then seeing the role a value claim will play in the argument. Since any proposition can be assigned a truth value, there are exactly three kinds of propositions.

The Three Kinds of Propositions

Tautologies: Propositions that are always true or true by definition.
Contradictions: Propositions that are always false or false by definition.
Contingent Claims: Propositions that are true or false according to the context. That is, they are dependent on what is going on in the world to determine the truth value. This would include claims for which the truth value is unknown.

Examples of Tautologies

Either you did or you did not hear a seal bark.
If B. B. King is the king of blues, then B. B. King is the king of blues.
It is false that my car has gas but it does not have gas.

Examples of Contradictions

Adam is a baby and is not a baby.
Peaches are fruit, but peaches are not fruit.
It is false that, if my car does not have gas, then my car does not have gas.

Examples of Contingent Claims

It is raining in Portland today.
If either Denzel Washington or Queen Latifah signs on, the film should do well.
My name is Geronimo.
If that is a beautiful sunset, Kenji is taking a photograph.

Most claims are *contingent,* since the context may vary, along with the parameters that determine whether the claim is true or false. For example, the claim, "It's roasting outside," is contingent because it may be true on one day, but not the next. Most of what we say is relative to a particular time and place, so such claims are contingent. We need also to be able to handle claims where the truth value is unknown. These are sentences whose truth value simply cannot be determined; for example, because we do not have the means or knowledge to ascertain if they are true or false as in the claim, "Intelligent life exists in other solar systems" or "Pig viruses will likely be even more destructive than AIDS." The evidence is not in yet on either one.

Propositions of *unknown truth value* are not useless, but there are limitations. We can use the propositions and draw inferences, but we cannot make any claims about the **soundness** of the argument. A sound argument has two characteristics: (1) the argument is valid, and (2) the premises are true. (See Chapter 6 for a review.) If we don't know if the premises are all true, we cannot declare that the argument is sound. Propositions of unknown truth value are relatives of contingent claims, but here we simply lack enough information to determine the truth value.

Structure of Propositions

A proposition is either simple or compound. A **simple proposition** is one at the atomic level—that is, it does not contain any of the *logical connectives* "and," "or", "not," "if . . . then," or "if and only if." A proposition that contains any of these five logical connectives is called a **compound proposition.**

Examples of Simple Propositions

Jasper chewed off some of the kitchen window.
Swiss cheese is awfully tasty.
Eighty-five percent of headache remedies have caffeine in them.

Examples of Compound Propositions

Jasper chewed off some of the kitchen window and then bit the computer cord.
Either Jasper popped keys off my laptop or he settled down and ate his corn.
If Jasper chewed off some of the kitchen window, then he's in trouble.
Jasper did not eat all the corn on his plate.
Jasper eats his corn if and only if it is warm.

The Five Types of Compound Propositions

1. *Conjunctions:*	Propositions of the form "A and B."
2. *Disjunctions:*	Propositions of the form "Either A or B."
3. *Negations:*	Propositions of the form "Not A."
4. *Conditional claims:*	Propositions of the form "If A then B" ("A is sufficient for B") or "B only if A" ("A is necessary for B")
5. *Biconditional claims (Equivalence):*	Propositions of the form "A if and only if B" ("A is both necessary and sufficient for B")

Conjunctions

These are propositions of the form "P and Q," where P and Q are each called **conjuncts**. A **conjunction** is a proposition that asserts two things are true at the same time. This means the conjunction is true only if *both* conjuncts are true. Otherwise, it is false.

Examples of Conjunctions

The Red Sox won and the Curse of the Bambino was lifted.
Both Jasper and Wellie are birds.
The 2004 Olympics were at Athens, but not everyone was happy about that.
The cinematography in *Collateral* was quite amazing, although the movie
    wasn't a blockbuster.

Alternative Constructions of Conjunctions.   A proposition does not have to contain "and" to be a conjunction. Watch for other words or phrases that function the same as "and," such as "but" and "however." When you spy an alternative, replace it with "and." That way, we will have a uniform way of setting up propositions—otherwise, it's too easy to make mistakes.

Alternative Indicators of Conjunctions

However	Although
But	In addition
Also	As well/as well as
Moreover	Furthermore
Additionally	Plus
Along with	We might add that

Disjunctions

These are propositions of the form "P or Q," where P and Q are each called **disjuncts**. A **disjunction** is a proposition that claims either one or the other, or both. For a disjunction to be true, at least one of the two disjuncts must be true.

Examples of Disjunctions

There is Ellen or someone who looks a lot like her.
Either squirrels or burglars are in the attic making noise.

Note: Disjunctions in logic are *inclusive*. This means a disjunction is true if either one *or both* of the two disjuncts are true. The "either/or *or both*" makes the claim an *inclusive or*. This contrasts with the everyday use of "either/or" which is treated as an exclusion not allowing both disjuncts to be true at the same time; for

FIGURE 14.1
Open-ended lists leave a
lot to the imagination.

instance, we see the exclusive "or" used in restaurant options. To the question,
"Do you want soup *or* salad?" if you say, "Both!" you'll probably be hit with an
extra charge.

Negations

These are of the form "not P." A negated proposition has the opposite truth value
of the original statement. A *negation* of a proposition is true only if the proposition itself is false.

Examples of Negations

The negation of: Galileo is the governor of Ohio.
It is not the case that Galileo is the governor of Ohio.
→ Galileo is not the governor of Ohio.

The negation of: Chocolate is not a health food.
It is not the case that chocolate is not a health food.
→ Chocolate is a health food.

If the original statement is negative, then the negation of it will be positive. In the
second example, the double negative leads to a positive. This will be discussed further below.

Special Constructions of Negations.   Two special forms of negations are the "neither/nor" and "not both." Basically, with a "neither/nor" claim both options are eliminated (i.e., "Not this *and* not that"). With "not both" one of the two options is eliminated (i.e., "Not this *or* not that"). As you can see, a "neither/nor" construction ends up being a conjunction ("not this and not that"). We will learn how to handle these later in the chapter, along with other types of negated propositions.

Conditional Claims

Conditional claims are of the form "If P then Q" or "Q only if P," where P is called the **antecedent** and Q is called the **consequent**. Conditional claims may also be expressed as "A is sufficient for B" and "A is necessary for B." **Sufficient conditions** are those that, if met, guarantee some effect will occur. This can be expressed in the form "If A then B"—where A represents the antecedent conditions and B represents the consequent effect. **Necessary conditions** are those that, if *not* met, guarantee the effect will *not* occur. This can be expressed in the form "B only if A" or "If not A then not B." That means that if B occurs, then A had to occur as well. Consequently, "If not A then not B" is equivalent to "If B then A." These can be set out as follows:

Sufficient and Necessary Conditions

A is *sufficient* for B:
If A occurs, B will occur as well.
→ "If A then B"
Being hungry is *sufficient* for Betty Jean to eat a donut.
→ If she is hungry, then Betty Jean will eat a donut.

A is *necessary* for B:
If A does not occur, B will not occur either.
→ "B only if A"
→ "If not A then not B"
→ "If B then A"
Having jelly inside is *necessary* for the donut to be tasty.
→ If there's no jelly inside, then the donut is not tasty.
→ If the donut is tasty, then there must be jelly inside.

Be careful: sometimes the "then" is omitted, so be sure to add it for clarification. A conditional claim is true in every case except when the antecedent is true and the consequent is false. For example, this is a false proposition: "If cows are animals {TRUE}, then elephants are rodents {FALSE}."

Examples of Conditional Claims

You'll feel stuffed if you eat too many tamales.
Rewrite as: If you eat too many tamales, then you'll feel stuffed.

Stan will go to Ottawa, if he can get plane tickets.
Rewrite as: If he can get plane tickets, then Stan will go to Ottawa.

Being able to climb Mt. Hood is sufficient to make Gary happy.
Rewrite as: If he is able to climb Mt. Hood, then Gary will be happy.

A sufficient condition of Fred's gaining weight is to eat an entire pizza.
Rewrite as: If he eats an entire pizza, then Fred will gain weight.

A necessary condition of Fred keeping his weight off is that he exercise.
Rewrite as: If he does not exercise then Fred won't keep his weight off.
Or: If Fred keeps his weight off, then he is exercising.

Alternative Constructions of Conditional Claims.   Other forms of conditional claims include "P only if Q," "Q is necessary for P," "A necessary condition of P is Q," "P unless Q," and "Without P, then Q." We will look at the "unless" and "without" forms later in the chapter.

The "Only If" Construction.   Propositions of the form "A only if B" assert that, "If B does not happen, then A won't happen either." In other words, "A only if B" can be rewritten "If not B then not A" or "If A then B."

The "only if" Construction

"P only if Q." P happens only if Q does.
→ "If not Q then not P."
   If you don't have Q, you won't have P.
→ "If P then Q."
   So, if P occurs, so must Q.

Examples of "only if" Claims

Jasper will go in his cage only if he's forced.
→ If he's not forced, Jasper will not go in his cage.
→ If the Jasper went in his cage, then he was forced.

Watering the pear tree is necessary for it to bear fruit.
→ If we don't water the pear tree, then it won't bear fruit.
→ If it bears fruit, then we watered the pear tree.

Handy Hints.   There are two parts to the conditional claim "If P then Q": the antecedent P and the consequent Q. Be aware that conditional claims can be expressed in a number of ways. Locate the "if" and the antecedent immediately follows. The consequent is what follows from the antecedent condition. It is located after the "then."

Be careful: The consequent is sometimes expressed *before* the antecedent. For example, "We will dance all night, *if* the band plays until dawn." The consequent is "we will dance all night." When this occurs, rewrite the sentence in the form of an "if . . . then" claim and locate the consequent after the "then."

Handling Alternative Constructions of Conditional Claims.   "P if Q," "Only if Q, then P," and "P only if Q," can all be rewritten in the "If . . . then" form. Be sure to make the necessary adjustments and add negatives when required. Below are some suggestions that should help clarify alternative constructions.

The Structure of a Conditional Claim

If <u>that is my pet bird, Jasper,</u> **then** <u>he will come down from the tree</u>.

         ↓   ↓

     Antecedent   Consequent

Locating the Antecedent and Consequent.   If we have a conditional claim, make sure it is in the "if . . . then" form and then you can easily locate the antecedent and consequent. We can see how to do this in the following proposition:

We'd better call 911 **if** someone is hurt in the accident.
Rewrite as:
If <u>someone is hurt in the accident</u> **then** <u>we'd better call 911</u>.

                ↓   ↓

      Antecedent   **Consequent**

Once we have restructured it as an "if . . . then" claim, reading the antecedent and consequent becomes much easier. The antecedent then can be found between the "if" and the "then," whereas the consequent is the proposition that follows the "then."

Equivalence (Biconditional Propositions)

Two propositions are **equivalent** if they assert the same thing. The resulting proposition is called a **biconditional**. "P is equivalent to Q" is the same as "If P then Q, and if Q then P." When that occurs, you can say "P if and only if Q."

Any two equivalent propositions have the same truth value; they are either both true or both false. The two sides are either true at the same time or false at the same time. It is impossible for A to be equivalent to B when A is true and B is false (or vice versa). *Note:* The term "equivalent to" can be expressed as an "if and only if" (sometimes abbreviated as "iff") statement.

Examples of Biconditional Claims

That Robert is addicted to caffeine is equivalent to his being physiologically dependent on it.
→ Robert is addicted to caffeine *if and only* if he is physiologically dependent on it.

→ If he is physiologically dependent on it, then Robert is addicted to caffeine, and if he is addicted to caffeine, then he is physiologically dependent on it.

Maria getting married is equivalent to ending her life as a single woman.
→ Maria ends her life as a single woman *if and only if* she gets married.
→ If Maria marries, then she ends her life as a single woman, and if she ends her life as a single woman, then Maria has gotten married.

We have now covered all five logical connectives. If a proposition contains none of these connectives, it is a simple proposition. If it contains at least one logical connective, it is called a compound proposition.

Categorical Propositions

For certain types of analysis, using categorical propositions is helpful. A **categorical proposition** begins with a quantifier ("all," "no," "some" or x percent) followed by the subject, a form of the verb "to be," and then the predicate. Negative propositions that are not all-or-nothing claims will have a "not" before the predicate (e.g., "Some cats are *not* milk-drinkers").

Expressing claims in the form of categorical propositions enables us to quickly determine if an argument is valid, as we'll see in the next chapter, Chapter 15; **valid** arguments are ones in which the premises provide sufficient support for drawing the conclusion. Here are the four different forms of categorical propositions:

The Forms of Categorical Propositions

All P is Q.	This is called an A claim.	All coyotes are animals.
No P is Q.	This is called an E claim.	No coyote is a squirrel.
Some P is Q.	This is called an I claim.	Some coyotes are rabid animals.
Some P is not Q.	This is called an O claim.	Some coyotes are not vicious beasts.

You probably wonder where we place claims like, "Charlie is a good ole boy" and "Fifty-four percent of toddlers prefer hot milk at bedtime." Propositions containing proper nouns as the subject are considered A or E claims, relative to being positive or negative. Propositions of the form "x% of A is B" (where x is neither 100 nor zero) are treated as I or O claims, relative to being positive or negative. So if you have a statistical claim that is not all-or-nothing, it will function as a particular claim (I or O).

Examples of Categorical Propositions

A claim:	All burnt muffins are inedible pastries.
E claim:	No burnt muffin is a tasty treat.
I claim:	Some burnt muffins are good breakfast food.
O claim:	Some burnt muffins are not good substitutes for hockey pucks.

Quantity.   The **quantity** of a proposition answers the question, "How much?" In other words, the quantity refers to how much of the subject class is said to have something predicated of it. The possible answer is "universal" or "particular" (i.e., all or some of it).

Quantity—Universal or Particular

Universal	All P is Q	All flies are irritating insects.
	No P is Q	No fly is a spider.
Particular	Some P is Q	Some vehicles are racecars.
	Some P is not Q.	Some vehicles are not pick-ups.

A and E	→	**Universal claims**
I and O	→	**Particular claims**

Quality.   The **quality** of a proposition answers, "Are you asserting that something *is* or *is not* the case?" You are either affirming that it is the case, so the quality of the proposition is positive, or denying it, so the quality of the proposition is negative.

Quality—Positive or Negative

Positive:	All P is Q	All chocolate is a delicious treat.
	Some P is Q	Some delicious treats are donuts.
Negative:	No P is Q	No airplane is a car.
	Some P is not Q	Some cars are not convertibles.

A and I	→	**Positive claims**
E and O	→	**Negative claims**

Examples

All football players are burly.
Anyone who can paint with watercolors is talented.

→ A claims are universal and A claims are positive.
→ These propositions are *universal positive*.

Fish are never good ingredients to put in a custard pie.
No wind instrument has strings.

→ E claims are universal and E claims are negative.
→ These propositions are *universal negative*.

Universal Positive Propositions.   There are many ways to say "all" or "none" to indicate we are referring to all the members of the subject class. These include

Every	*Any*
100 percent	*If . . . then . . .*

Without exception	The entire
Whatever	Whenever
Whoever	Whichever
Whomever	However (when used to mean "all the ways")

Universal Negative Propositions.   Propositions that are universal negative can take a number of different forms. Replace these with "no" and treat as E claims:

None	0 percent
Not any	If . . . then not . . .
All . . . are not	Not a one is
. . . is never . . .	Not even one
Whatever . . . is not . . .	Whenever . . . is not
Whoever . . . is not . . .	Whichever . . . is not

"Not Every" Propositions.   If I say, "Not every man is over six feet tall" I mean that *some men are not* over six feet tall. I do not mean that no man is over six feet tall. Therefore, when we see a "not every" construction, we need to be careful. "Not every . . . is . . ." is *not* the same as "No . . . is . . ." "Not every" is equivalent to "Some . . . are not . . ." For example, "Not every musician is talented" is equivalent to "Some musicians are not talented."

Special Constructions of Universal Claims.   A proposition that has a proper noun as the subject is treated as a universal claim.

Examples of Universal Claims

Shawn is an artist who can operate an airbrush.
→ Treat as a universal positive claim.
→ Classify as an A claim.

The Statue of Liberty is not in Rhode Island.
→ Treat as a universal negative claim.
→ Classify as an E claim.

Treat as Universal Claims.   Propositions that point to specific individuals usually function as universals, because they point to a particular subject in the same way a proper noun acts as an indicator.

This dog is an awfully strange looking beagle.
→ Treat as a universal positive claim (an A claim).

That little girl of yours is not a bashful child.
→ Treat as a universal negative claim (an E claim).

Particular Claims.   These are propositions that can be expressed in the form of "Some . . . are/are not . . ." These include the following:

Examples of Particular Claims

Most . . . are/are not . . .	A few . . . are/are not . . .
Lots of . . . are/are not . . .	Many . . . are/are not . . .
Much of . . . are/are not . . .	A bunch of . . . are/are not . . .
Several . . . are/are not . . .	Almost all . . . are/are not . . .
Not all . . . are . . .	More than a few of . . . are/are not . . .
Not every . . . are . . .	At least one of . . . are/are not . . .

Special Constructions of Particular Claims.   Most important, a proposition of the form "x% of P's are Q's" where x is neither 100% nor 0% would be treated as a particular claim. Even if the percentage is 99% it's not *all* and, therefore, cannot be considered a universal claim.

Examples

"59% of acrobats are bicyclists" is a particular positive proposition.
→ Classify as an I claim.

"82% of phone calls are not solicitations" is a particular negative proposition.
→ Classify as an O claim.

"96% of librarians are helpful people" is a particular positive proposition.
→ Classify as an I claim.

"75% of restaurant pies are not as delicious as a homemade pie" is a particular negative proposition.
→ Classify as an O claim.

Exercises

Part One

Directions: State the quantity and quality of the categorical propositions below and identify the proposition as A, E, I, or O.

1. All chocolate is a sinful food.
2. No dog is an animal that likes lettuce.
3. Some skunks are not animals that like mornings.

4. All fish are creatures with scales.

5. Some snakes are not poisonous reptiles.

6. Some macaws are sociable birds.

7. No raccoon is a native of Baffin Island.

8. All the mammals in Ruth's backyard are deer.

9. Some radiologists are not people who are scared of dentists.

10. No Shakespearean actor is a person who needs memory lessons.

11. Some wombats are vicious beasts when angered.

12. All diners who eat their peas with a knife are folks who like cornbread.

13. Some people who sing at the top of their lungs are courteous drivers.

14. All dogs are animals capable of eating slippers.

15. Some students are people who are fond of chimichangas.

16. Aki is an awfully well-behaved pup.

17. No well-behaved pup is a dog that shreds couches.

18. Some animals that shred couches are disobedient cats.

19. Some couch-shredders are children.

20. All photographers are people who like the unexpected.

Part Two

Directions: Rewrite the propositions below in categorical form and then state the quantity and quality.

1. Not all islanders know how to swim.

2. Most fish are relaxed in the water.

3. Lots of ice skaters have strong leg muscles.

4. A few baseball players chew tobacco.

5. Any Sumo wrestler likes a back rub.

6. Not all football players are fearless people.

7. Badminton players are not bodybuilders.

8. Most hawks have powerful beaks and piercing eyes.

9. Any woman who takes up snorkeling has a good sense of humor.

10. Several karate students were injured in the park.

11. A couple of hikers got frostbitten last night.

12. Whenever you go surfing watch out for jellyfish.

13. Much rock climbing is dangerous.

14. Almost all dancers are graceful.

15. Very few roller skaters are self-conscious.
16. Not one of the burly men ate the tortilla soup.
17. Some of the frostbitten hikers wore slippers to bed.
18. A few of the badminton players threw tantrums on the court.
19. Not every senior tolerates rambunctious boys.
20. Just about all horror movies disturb a sensitive woman.
21. Many a Sumo wrestler enjoys edamame beans and miso soup.
22. Most people who drive a car with a V8 engine put milk in their tea.
23. None of the dim sum was left in the dish.
24. Ginny Lou was not happy with the lumpy grits on her plate.
25. None of the snorkeling women got tangled up in the coral reefs.

Symbolizing Propositions

To analyze an argument, we need to see its structure. Logicians prefer a symbolic language using variables (letters of the alphabet) and logical connectives. The result is a kind of logical x-ray. It makes the structure explicit and provides a handy shorthand method so sentences and arguments can be examined easily and quickly.

LOGICAL CONNECTIVES	SYMBOL	EXPRESSION	ALTERNATIVES
and	&	P & Q	∧ and •
or	∨	P ∨ Q	none
if . . . then . . .	→	P → Q	⊃
if and only if . . .	≡	P ≡ Q	↔
not	~	~ P	none

Note: "P if and only if Q" could also be expressed "P is equivalent to Q," with the connective then referred to as equivalence.

Translations.   When symbolizing a sentence, mark all the *logical connectives*. Symbolize simple propositions with capital letters (A, B, C, etc.). Pick a letter that corresponds with a key word in the proposition in question; otherwise it's going to be hard to look at the finished translation and double check it for accuracy.

Steps to Translating a Proposition

Symbolizing a Proposition.   Translate the following proposition:

If I run out of gas, then my car will stop.

Step 1: Unpack the Structure.   We do this by examining the hierarchy of the connectives. This proposition's structure is straightforward because there is only one connective. The structure is:

> **If** (I run out of gas)   **then** (my car will stop).

This is a conditional claim, with the antecedent "I run out of gas" and consequent "my car will stop."

Step 2: Assign Variables to Component Propositions.   Replace the antecedent "I run out of gas" and consequent "my car will stop" with variables (A, B, C, etc.). Let the variables stand for the propositions.

> *Assign:*   R = I'll run out of gas.
> S = "my car will stop."

Be careful: Assign a different variable for one and only one proposition at a time. Never use the same variable for two different propositions, or the resulting translation will be incorrect. Pick something obvious.

Step 3: Replace Component Propositions with the Assigned Variable

> *Rewrite as:*   If R then S.

Step 4: Put Symbols in Place of All the Logical Connectives.   In this case, the $\rightarrow$ goes in the place where the "then" is located.

> *Translation:* R $\rightarrow$ S

Example of a Translation

Let us translate the sentence: "If I eat sausages and potatoes, then I'll either get sick or fat."

Step 1. Unpack the Structure.   We have:

> **If** (I eat <u>and</u> potatoes)   **then** (I'll either get sick <u>or</u> fat).

Note: the main connective in **bold** is the "if . . . then . . ." The antecedent is "I eat sausages and potatoes" and the consequent is "I'll either get sick or fat." Because both the antecedent and consequent are compound propositions, we have to mark those logical connectives too. Those are underlined above.

Step 2. Assign Variables to Component Propositions.

> *Assign:*   S = "I eat sausages" and P = "I eat potatoes."
> G = "I'll get sick" and   F = "I'll get fat."

We are now ready to substitute the variables into the proposition:

> **If** (I eat sausages and I eat potatoes) **then** (either I'll get sick or I'll get fat).

Step 3. Replace Component Propositions with the Assigned Variables.

Rewrite as: **If** (S and P) **then** (G or F).

Step 4. Replace Connectives with Their Symbols.   We are almost done! All we have to do is put in the symbols for the connectives and that's it.

Translation: (S & P) → (G ∨ F)

Recap: Faced with a compound proposition, locate all the logical connectives and look for the superstructure. Once you have the main connectives and subconnectives, you can assign variables to the individual propositions and complete the translation. So let's translate:

> "If men and boys prefer action films, then Uncle Ray will either like *Collateral* or *Bourne Supremacy*."

Note the connectives: "If, and, then, either, or." The main connective is the "if/then," and between the "if" and the "then" is the conjunction "and." After the "then" is the "either/or" construction. This can be set out as follows:

> **If** (men prefer action films <u>and</u> boys prefer action films) **then** (<u>either</u> Uncle Ray will like *Collateral* <u>or</u> Uncle Ray will like *Bourne Supremacy*).

The main connective "if/then" is in bold. Replace the connection words with symbols:

> Put → under the "then." Put in & for the "and" and the ∨ for the "or."

Using as our variables M, B, C, and S we are now ready to write out the translation.

Translation: (M & B) → (C ∨ S)

Punctuation and Precision

Being sloppy with punctuation can be a disaster. If we are not precise with the punctuation, we may end up with a proposition that can be misinterpreted and a translation saying something different than the original proposition. Because of this, we need to learn precision. Don't despair, though, because precision is not a snooty matter at all. It is a useful trait to have. In fact, it may prevent a crisis.

Think of it this way: Do you want a sloppy brain surgeon cutting into your cerebellum? Do you want a pilot who is not very precise with the controls when you are 33,000 feet up in the air? Do you want your car mechanic using imprecise calipers to adjust your car's brakes? Absolutely not! So we should be careful with punctuation. As a convention, start with parentheses, then use square brackets, then curly brackets. For example,

$$\{P \vee [Q \rightarrow (R \& S)]\}$$

This expresses the proposition of the form:

> **Either** P **or,**   <u>if</u> Q <u>then,</u>   both R *and* S.

This is the form of the claim:

> Either rats are in the walls or, if there are squirrels in the walls, then, they are awfully large and make high screeching sounds.

The superstructure of this proposition is a disjunction. The first disjunct is P and the second disjunct is "If Q then both R and S." We now have a convention that allows all of us to use the same packaging and easily read complex propositions.

Exercises

Part One

Directions: Translate the following sentences using variables and logical connectives. Use the letters indicated as your variables.

1. If I eat that sausage, I'll be poisoned. (E, P)
2. Both termites and butterflies are insects. (T, B)
3. It is not true that moths are carnivores. (M)
4. If another snail gets in my garden and chomps holes in the violets, then I will show no mercy. (S, C, M)
5. If Emmy Lou Harris cancels the concert, then Jody will be unhappy and listen to the Soggy Bottom Mountain Boys. (E, J, S)
6. Either the grasshoppers ate the begonia or something weird is going on. (G, W)
7. If the medfly returns and the city sprays pesticides, then we are in trouble. (M, C, T)
8. Jasper will get sick if he eats that centipede. (S, C)
9. Either the cat was stolen or it was carted off by the coyotes last night. (S, C)
10. If the files are sent and the computer crashes, we'll be in trouble. (F, C, T)
11. Chicken soup and vitamin C help fight a cold. (S, V)
12. If mosquitoes are in the room and keep buzzing, Carlos won't be able to sleep. (M, K, C)
13. Brazilian flamethrowers and violets are in bloom, but the poppies look dead. (B, V, P)
14. Chemistry is a useful subject, if you plan to be a doctor. (C, P)
15. If both Angie and Raphael quit fighting, then we can eat dinner. (A, R, D)
16. If Tina does more typing, her eyes will bulge and become bright red. (T, B, R)
17. If Anita sprays insecticide, the grasshoppers will die, but if she wants to avoid toxic chemicals, she'll kill them by hand. (S, G, W, K)

18. He is a famous movie star, but Georgina forgot his name. (M, G)

19. Although Ralph was not an android, he was unusual. (A, U)

20. It is not true that if Vera does not smoke, she won't get lung cancer. (V, L)

21. If Ernesto takes either physics or statistics next semester, he'll cut back on his part-time job at the courthouse. (P, S, C)

22. Either both Bruce and Ryan are wearing their costumes to the party, or they will stay home and make popcorn balls. (B, R, S, P)

23. If Robbie takes both physics and anthropology next semester, he'll quit his raquetball lessons. (P, A, Q)

24. Anita will either yank out the ivy and plant primroses, or she will dig up the wilted Peruvian lily and replace it with a potato vine. (I, P, D, R).

25. Only if Anita yanks out the ivy will Gary help her with the primroses. (A, G)

26. Gary helping with the primroses is necessary for Anita to be able to clear space before lunch. (G, A).

27. Ryan falling on the new potato vine was sufficient to make Anita unhappy and Gary frustrated. (R, A, G)

28. Evan planted loquat seeds in the yard, but Connolly showed no interest in gardening. (E, C)

29. If both Paul and Evan go to Chicago, then Laurel will be able to work only if she gets help with the baby. (P, E, L, H)

30. If the morning glories spread to the fence and overtake the roses, then we'll have to cut them back; but if they don't get invasive, the morning glories will do fine in the garden. (S, O, C, I, F)

Part Two

Directions: Using the variables indicated and logical connectives, symbolize the following more complex propositions.

1. If Josie stops complaining about the Yankees' loss to the Red Sox and Varoush gets off his soap box about air purifiers, then the two of them will either argue about politics or they'll gossip about Randy's search for the ideal woman. (J, V, P, G)

2. If both Mel Gibson and Michael J. Fox share their views of stem cell research, then Josie will be able to figure out how she wants to vote. (G, F, J)

3. Not just voters came to the Save Dolphins Against Tuna Cans concert. (V, C)

4. Unless the people in the Dolphin costumes get out of the road and they stop throwing empty tuna cans into the air, the mayor may get irritated with the demonstration. (D, T, M)

5. Either both Bruce Springsteen and Sheryl Crow are politically involved, or Matt was wrong when he said that all popular musicians are into politics these days. (B, S, M)

6. Sam and Dave will argue about Rap music, if they get the chance. (S, D, C)

7. If she reads three newspapers Keisha's eyes get red; however, she likes getting to see the news from different points of view and having something interesting to talk about with her best friend. (R, E, G, B)

8. If either Tim Robbins or Nicole Kidman speaks out on gun control, then, if Josie understands the arguments, then either she will know how to vote or she will have to read the campaign literature she received. (T, N, J, V, R)

9. If Keisha is not mistaken, then Ernie did not read the article on the face transplant controversy, but Varoush heard about it on the radio. (K, E, V)

10. Keeping up on world news is something not both Sam and Dave are interested in doing, but Dave plans to read either *The Guardian* or *Al Jazeera* to get an alternative perspective. (S, D, G, A).

11. Being informed helps Kenji understand the fine print of Proposition 64; however not all his fellow students will be attending the demonstration. (I, U, F, A)

12. Ray is voting "No" on Prop. 120; in addition, he plans to protest by either wearing a skeleton costume or by releasing 50 black balloons over downtown Louisville. (R, W, B).

13. Not any protestor carried red balloons to the rally against Prop. 120. (P, R)

14. Not all the protestors in Dolphin suits were handing out the leaflets; yet the mayor took the time to come out of his office and talk with them. (P, H, C, T)

15. Whenever Josie and Varoush eat tuna, they argue about the dolphins, but it was Ray who joined the protest. (J, V, A, R)

Rules of Replacement for Ordinary Language

Here are some techniques for treating different sentence structures that we commonly encounter. We will be looking at 12 different rules for replacing one claim with a logically equivalent form.

Rules of Replacement for Ordinary Language

Here are some techniques for treating different sentence structures that we commonly encounter. We will be looking at 12 different rules for replacing one claim with a logically equivalent form.

There are seven rules of replacement for ordinary language. They are: (1) Only, (2) The only, (3) Unless, (4) Sufficient, (5) Necessary, (6) The "evers" (Whatever, Whenever, etc.), and (7) Negation. Let's look at each one of these rules.

1. *Only.* "Only" functions as an exclusion, narrowing down the territory of the predicate class. Any proposition of the form "Only P is Q" can be rewritten as "If not P, then not Q." This is also equivalent to "All Q is P." Propositions of the form "Only P is Q" are symbolized as follows:

   Forms of "Only P Is Q" $(\sim P \to \sim Q) \equiv (Q \to P)$

   Only P is Q
   $\to$ If it's not P then, it's not Q.
   $\to$ If it's a Q, then it's a P.
   $\to$ All Q is P.

   Examples

   Only Americans eat hamburgers.
   $\to$ If they are not Americans, they won't eat hamburgers.
   $\to$ If they eat hamburgers, they are Americans.
   $\to$ All people who eat hamburgers are Americans.
   Translation: $\sim A \to \sim H$ *(Form 1)* or $H \to A$ *(Form 2).*

   Only skinny women can be models.
   $\to$ If she's not skinny, she can't be a model.
   $\to$ If she is a model, then she is skinny.
   $\to$ All models are skinny.
   Translation: $\sim S \to \sim M$ *(Form 1)* or $M \to S$ *(Form 2).*

See how the exclusion works? In the first example, the use of "only" narrows down those who eat hamburgers to Americans—everyone else is excluded. In the second example, "only" limits those who can be models to skinny women; everyone else is excluded.

2. *The only.* Another exclusion is "the only." Here it is the subject being restricted, not the predicate as above. Any proposition of the form "The only P is Q" can be rewritten: "If not Q then not P." It is also equivalent to "All P is Q."

   Propositions of the form "The only P is Q" are symbolized as follows:

   Forms of "The Only P Is Q" $(\sim Q \to \sim P) \equiv (P \to Q)$

   The only P is Q
   $\to$ If it's not Q then, it's not P.

→ If it's a P, then it's a Q.
→ All P is Q.

Examples

The only woman for Romeo is Juliet.
→ If she's not Juliet, then she's not the woman for Romeo.
→ If she's the woman for Romeo, then she's Juliet.
Translation: ~J → ~W (*Form 1*) or W → J (*Form 2*).

The only outer gear the Count owns is a cape.
→ If it's not a cape, it's not outer gear the count owns.
→ If it's outer gear the count owns, then it's a cape.
→ All the outer gear the count owns are capes.
Translation: ~C → ~O (*Form 1*) or O → C (*Form 2*)

See how the exclusion works? In the first example, "The only" limits women for Romeo to Juliet; all other women are excluded. In the second example, "The only" limits outer gear the Count owns to capes; everything else is excluded.

The Connection between "only" and "the only."

We can change an "only" claim to one that starts with "the only." If we focus on the object, we can see how they relate. Look at this example:

The only woman for Romeo is Juliet. *This is the same as:*

Only Juliet is the woman for Romeo.

Do you see what happened? In both cases, the object of Romeo's affection is Juliet. This can be expressed using either "the only" or "only," but the terms are switched. In other words:

The only P is Q   *is equivalent to*   **Only Q is P.**

So we can move back and forth between them, but need to switch the order of the terms, P and Q, in doing so.

3. *Unless.* Propositions of the form "P unless Q" can be expressed as either a conditional claim or a disjunction. As a conditional claim it can be written, "If not Q then P." The restricted condition Q is the one thing that can stop P from happening. In other words, if you *don't* have Q, then P occurs. The second way to write "P unless Q" is in the form, "*Either* P or Q." To get to this second construction, just toss out the "unless" and replace it with "or" (or "either/or") and you are done.

Forms of "P unless Q" $(\sim Q \rightarrow \sim P) \equiv (P \vee Q)$

P unless Q
→ If not Q then P.
→ Either P or Q.

Examples

We will go on a picnic unless it rains.
→ If it does not rain, we will go on a picnic.
→ Either we went on a picnic or it rained.
Translation: ~R → P (*Form 1*) or R ∨ P (*Form 2*).

Unless Joe stops the car, he's going to hit the moose.
→ If Joe does not stop the car, he's going to hit the moose.
→ Either Joe stops the car or he's going to hit the moose.
Translation: ~S → M (*Form 1*) or S ∨ M (*Form 2*).

Alternatives to "Unless."   An alternative to unless is *without*. It is treated exactly the same as unless, so it would be rewritten in either form (the conditional or the disjunction). So, you would translate "Without ice cream, pie is bland," as "If you do not have ice cream, your pie will be bland."

4. *Sufficient.* "P is sufficient for Q" asserts that Q will happen whenever P occurs. In other words, "P is sufficient for Q" is equivalent to "If P then Q." This is symbolized as P → Q.

Form of "P Is Sufficient for Q"   P → Q

P is sufficient for Q
→ If P then Q.
Translation: P → Q

Examples

Traveling to Montreal is sufficient for seeing maple leaves.
→ If you travel to Montreal, then you will see maple leaves.
Translation: T → S

Getting free airfare to Tokyo would be sufficient for my going there.
→ If I get free airfare to Tokyo, I will go there.
Translation: F → G

Alternatives to "Sufficient."   Another phrase that functions the same as "sufficient" is *provided that*. So, you would translate "I'll take flute lessons, provided that you take up the electric guitar" as "If you take up the electric guitar, then I'll take flute lessons."

5. *Necessary.* "P is necessary for Q" asserts that Q won't happen without P. That is, if you don't have P, you won't have Q. So if you have Q, you must also have P.

Forms of "P Is Necessary for Q"   (~P → ~Q) ≡ (Q → P)

P is necessary for Q.
→ If not P then not Q.
→ If Q then P Put the arrow → in place of the "then."
Translation: Q → P or the logically equivalent form: ~P → ~Q.

Examples

Oxygen is necessary to stay alive.
→ If you do not have oxygen, you cannot live.
→ If you live, then you had oxygen.
Translation: ~O → ~L (*Form 1*) or L → O (*Form 2*).

Gas in the tank is necessary for my car to be driven to work.
→ If I don't have gas in the tank, I won't be able to drive to work.
→ If I am able to drive to work, then I had gas in the tank.
Translation: ~G → ~D (*Form 1*) or D → G (*Form 2*).

Relationship between "Necessary" and "Only." If we say something is necessary for something else, we are saying the second thing will happen *only* if the first one does. In other words, "P is necessary for Q" is the same as "Q only if P." So, if not P, then not Q (if P is not the case, then Q is not the case). This means, as the equivalent expressions in the examples showed us, that "Q only if P" can also be written "If Q then P."

6. *The evers: whenever, whoever, whatever, wherever, and special constructions of however.* Any proposition with the "—ever" construction should be treated as a universal claim. These propositions can be rewritten as conditional claims. This is symbolized P → Q.

Forms of the "Evers"   P → Q

Whenever P is Q.
→ If P then Q.
Translation: P → Q

Note: This also applies to whatever, whoever, wherever constructions. It applies to "however" constructions in the form of "whatever way," rather than functioning as a conjunction. It does not apply to "never" (see "Negations," below).

Examples

Whenever you go on your vacation, it rains.
→ If you go on your vacation, then it rains.

Whoever is hiding behind the tree is making grunting sounds.
→ If someone is hiding behind the tree, then that person is making grunting sounds.

However you tie the bow, it looks silly.
→ If you tie the bow, then it looks silly.

7. Negations: "P is never Q," "It is not true that P," "Not only P is Q," "Not just P is Q," "It is false that P."

Form of a Double Negative

It is not true that P is not the case.
→ P is the case.
Translation: P

Form of "Never"

P is never Q
→ No P is Q.
→ If P then not Q.
Translation: P → ~Q

Example

Men can never experience pregnancy.
→ If the person is a man, then he cannot experience pregnancy.
→ No man can experience pregnancy.

Form of "Not all"

Not all P is Q.
→ Some P is not Q.
Translation: P & ~Q

Example

Not all comedians are ticklish people.
→ Some comedians are not ticklish people.

Not every joke is funny.
→ Some things are jokes and they are not funny.

Form of "Not None"

It is not the case that no P is Q.
→ Some P is Q.
Translation: P & Q

Basically this is a double negative. If there is not none, there are some. For example, if it's not true that no cat bites its owner, then there are some cats that bite their owners.

Examples

It is false that no sauces are fattening.
→ Some sauces are fattening.

It's not true that no one can sing the national anthem.
→ Some people can sing the national anthem.

Form of "Not Only"

Not only P is Q.
→ Some Q is not P.

Note: With "not only" the order of the P and Q switch in the translation.

Examples

Not only turnips are vegetables.
→ Some vegetables are not turnips.

Not only models are thin people.
→ Some thin people are not models.

Form of "Not Just"

Not just P is Q.
→ Some Q is not P
Note: Treat this form exactly the same as a "not only" claim.

Example

Not just sculptors are artists.
→ Some artists are not sculptors.

Form of "Not If/Then"

It's not true that if P then Q.
→ Some P are not Q.
Note: Treat this form exactly the same as a "not all" claim.

Example

It's not true that if babies are thrown in the water they will swim.
→ Some babies are thrown in the water and they do not swim.

Rules of Replacement for Ordinary Language

1. ONLY	*Form 1*	Only P is Q	If it's not P, then it's not Q.
	Form 2	Only P is Q	All Q is P.
2. THE ONLY	*Form 1*	The only P is Q	If it's not Q, then it's not P.
	Form 2	The only P is Q	All P is Q.
3. UNLESS	*Form 1*	P unless Q	If it's not Q, then P.
	Form 2	P unless Q	Either P or Q.
4. SUFFICIENT		P is sufficient for Q	If P then Q.
5. NECESSARY	*Form 1*	P is necessary for Q	If not P then not Q.
	Form 2	P is necessary for Q	If Q then P.
6. WHEN/WHAT/HOW/WHERE/WHOEVER			
Form 1	When/what/how/where/whoever P is Q.		If P then Q.
Form 2	When/what/how/where/whoever P is Q.		All P is Q.
7. NEGATIONS			
P is never Q		*Form 1:* No P is Q.	
		Form 2: If P then not Q.	
Not All P is Q		Some P is not Q.	
Not None/not no one of P is Q		Some P is Q.	
Not only P is Q		Some Q is not P.	
Not just P is Q		P and not Q.	
It is not true that, if P then Q		Some P is not Q.	

▦ Formal Rules of Replacement

The remaining rules of replacement are not simply focused on replacing one expression in ordinary English with an equivalent one, but on logical structure. These rules provide the means to translate from one logical form to another equivalent form.

8. *DeMorgan's Laws:* These are two special forms of negations. With the "not both" construction, one of the choices is being denied—either the first option or the second one. With a "neither . . . nor . . ." construction, *both* options are being denied: the first choice *and* the second one. This can be expressed as follows:

DeMorgan's Law #1: Not Both $\sim (P \,\&\, Q) \equiv (\sim P \vee \sim Q)$

Not both P and Q.
→ It is not true that both P and Q is the case.
→ *Either* P is *not* the case *or* Q is *not* the case.

DeMorgan's Law #2: Neither/Nor $\sim (P \vee Q) \equiv (\sim P \,\&\, \sim Q)$

Neither P *nor* Q.
→ It is not true that either P or Q is the case.
→ P is *not* the case *and* Q is *not* the case.

Example of Not Both

Not both Kung Pao beef and lasagna are Chinese food.
→ Either Kung Pao beef is not Chinese food or lasagna is not Chinese food.

Jamie does not like both blue grass and jazz.
→ Either Jamie does not like blue grass or she does not like jazz.

Examples of Neither/Nor

Neither frogs nor salamanders are in the water.
→ Frogs are not in the water and salamanders are not in the water.

Ben likes neither octopus nor squid.
→ Ben does not like octopus and Ben does not like squid.

9. *Transposition:* The rule of transposition allows us to flip the antecedent and consequent in a conditional claim—but doing so requires the terms to change to their opposites (positive/negative). In other words, transposing the antecedent and consequent is only acceptable if you also change the quality of each one at the same time. (In short, flip and switch.) This rule can be expressed as follows:

Form of Transposition $(P \rightarrow Q) \equiv (\sim Q \rightarrow \sim P)$

If P then Q.
→ If *not* Q then *not* P.

Examples of Transposition

If Lisa doesn't hurry, then she will be late to school.
→ If she was not late to school, then Lisa hurried.

If Homer eats another plate of shrimp, then his stomach will burst.
→ If Homer's stomach doesn't burst, then he didn't eat another plate of shrimp.

10. *Material implication.* Material implication allows you to go from a conditional claim (if/then) to a disjunction (either/or), with one proviso. When we make the switch the first term is negated. In other words, "If there's mud, we need galoshes" can change to the disjunction, "Either there's *not* mud or we need galoshes." Do you see why the "not" had to be interjected?

Form of Material Implication $(P \rightarrow Q) \equiv (\sim P \lor Q)$

If P then Q ≡ Either not P or Q.

Note: You can go from the conditional "if/then" to the disjunction "either/or" and vice versa.

Examples of Material Implication

If Casey does not stop screaming, then Christina will plug her ears.
→ Either Casey stopped screaming or Christina plugged her ears.

Either the basement flooded or the sandbags worked.
→ If the basement did not flood, then the sandbags worked.

11. *Exportation.* Any conditional claim with a conjunction in the antecedent can be rewritten as an "if/then" chain (and vice versa). The form of exportation is this:

Form of Exportation $[(A \ \& \ B) \rightarrow C] \equiv [A \rightarrow (B \rightarrow C)]$

If A and B, then C.
→ If A then, if B then C.

Note: Do you see how the second conjunct in the antecedent was shipped back to the consequent?

Examples of Exportation

If he spills paint and doesn't wipe it up, then there will be a mess.
→ If he spills paint, then, if he doesn't wipe it up, there will be a mess.

If the flashlight's on, then, if we aim it in the cave, the bats fly out.
→ If the flashlight's on and we aim it in the cave, the bats fly out.

12. *Equivalence.* This is also known as a biconditional or an "if and only if" claim. This rule allows us to set out the two component parts of a biconditional claim in two different ways.

Forms of Biconditional Propositions

"P if and only if Q" can be written in two equivalent forms:
→ If P then Q, and, if Q then P.
→ If P then Q, and, if not P then not Q.
Translation of form 1:   (P → Q) & (Q → P)
Translation of form 2:   (P → Q) & (~P → ~Q)

Example of Equivalence

Fish can swim *if and only if* they are in the water.
→ If fish are in the water then they can swim, and if fish can swim then they
  are in the water.
→ If fish are in the water then they can swim, and if fish are not in the
  water then they cannot swim.
Translation of form 1:   (F → W) & (W → F)
Translation of form 2:   (F → W) & (~F → ~W)

Exercises to Practice

Directions: Rewrite in an equivalent form using the rules.

1. Unless that's Adam, don't set out the toys.
2. Only a DVD can fit in the machine.
3. Not only maple leaves change colors in the fall.
4. Avocados are necessary to make guacamole.
5. Not both Ari and Moosh like raisin cookies.
6. Neither Moosh nor Ari like morning swims.
7. Barking puppies are sufficient to turn the pet store into chaos.
8. Unless the spare tire has air in it, we are going to need some help.
9. Not both Ivana and Hank like to wear baseball caps.
10. Taking the 8:00 A.M. plane is sufficient to get to Albuquerque for lunch.
11. Unless that's your mother watering the plants, we should call the police.
12. Marissa is not amused by either mud wrestling or snake charming.
13. Nicole is not thrilled by both bungie jumping and the luge.
14. Neither a raft nor a boat can make it over the waterfall.
15. Unless Max makes chicken pot pie, grandpa will be upset.
16. Getting into the toy box is sufficient to keep Jasper busy.
17. Li Ming will make dim sum unless she makes tamales.
18. Not only sunsets are beautiful things in nature.

19. A warm day is necessary to have a good pool party.
20. Only if that's corn chowder will Carolyn come to dinner.
21. Ivana is not both a fan of watercolors and oil painting.
22. Neither watermelon nor cantaloupe is a vegetable.
23. A wet suit is necessary for surfers to keep warm in the water.
24. A noisy helicopter is sufficient to irritate King Kong.
25. Not only scary movies cause nightmares.

Exercises

Part One

Directions: Rewrite the following, without the underlined word or phrase, using the appropriate rule.

1. <u>Only</u> blizzards stop Kerry from working out at the gym.
2. <u>Unless</u> the fog rolls in, Peter is going with Linda to the movie.
3. <u>Neither</u> hurricanes <u>nor</u> floods bother Omar.
4. <u>Only if</u> there's an earthquake will Cubby be scared.
5. <u>Whenever</u> there's a tornado, Zenon sleeps downstairs.
6. <u>The only time</u> Grandma screams is when she sees a dead possum.
7. <u>Not both</u> Percy and Ubu like liver.
8. Eating escargot is <u>sufficient</u> to disgust me.
9. Being tall <u>is necessary</u> for joining the basketball team.
10. <u>Neither</u> football <u>nor</u> soccer involves swimming.
11. <u>Only if</u> you shout, can I find you in the cave.
12. <u>Unless</u> there's mustard on the sandwich, the boys won't touch it.
13. <u>Whenever</u> the baby throws food on the floor, the pup wolfs it down.
14. <u>Without</u> chocolate, peanut butter isn't real tasty.
15. Candle light is <u>necessary</u> for a romantic evening.
16. Squeak eats crunchies, <u>provided that</u> he doesn't get liver.
17. <u>Without</u> a friend, the little pony is sad and lonely.
18. Not both bagels and croissants are French pastries.
19. <u>It is not the case that</u> all enchiladas are made with meat.
20. A letter from home is <u>sufficient</u> to make Alex excited.

21. Rewrite the following sentences as categorical propositions:
    a. Most surfers are both tan and muscular.
    b. Only nudity should be banned from the beach.
    c. Not all books are worth reading.
    d. Nobody is both ornery and easygoing.
    e. Whatever ate a hole in the sweater made grandpa angry.
    f. Being a swimmer is necessary to be a lifeguard.
    g. Being a belly dancer is sufficient to be exotic.
    h. The only time Michiko sings is in the shower.

22. Rewrite the following: It is not true that if you can drive a car you can tap dance.

23. Rewrite the following: Not just oatmeal sticks to your stomach.

24. Rewrite the following: Not only a howling wind creates atmosphere.

25. Rewrite the following: It is false that if you can dance, you can swim.

Part Two

Directions: Rewrite the following using the Rule of Replacement as indicated.

1. Using DeMorgan's Law rewrite: Not both Oaxaca and Toronto are in Canada.

2. Using DeMorgan's Law rewrite: Neither Taos nor Minneapolis are in Mexico.

3. Using material implication rewrite: Either snakes are taking over Guam or the news show exaggerated.

4. Using transposition rewrite: If that's jello, then it's not protoplasm.

5. Using transposition rewrite: If that's Fatso, then it's not Casper.

6. Using DeMorgan's Law rewrite: Not both novels and poetry are on the shelf.

7. Using DeMorgan's Law rewrite: Neither drama nor action films interest Jamal.

8. Using exportation rewrite: If the book is stolen and she can't read the assignment, Keisha will not be able to finish her homework.

9. Using material implication rewrite: If the tire's not flat, then we can go home.

10. Using material implication rewrite: Either the deliveryman is sick or his car is not working again.

11. Using material implication rewrite: If the pilots walk out, we can't make it to Lexington.

12. Write out using equivalence: The workers will organize if and only if they have a leader.

13. Write out using equivalence: The doctors will strike if and only if the nurses walk out.

14. Using transposition rewrite: If Luis gets a new car, he'll sell his hot rod.

15. Using exportation rewrite: If that's not Greg and is a burglar, then we better run out the backdoor.

16. Using material implication rewrite: If that's a burglar, then it's not Greg.

17. Using DeMorgan's Law rewrite: Neither Hector nor Salazar is lonely.

18. Using DeMorgan's Law rewrite: Not both Russ and Dorothy eat shrimp.

Part Three

1. Name the rule of replacement used below:
   a. If the dog eats George's burger, George will be upset. So, if George is not upset, then the dog did not eat George's burger.
   b. Not both Lenny and Maria like poetry. So either Lenny does not like poetry or Maria does not like poetry.
   c. Either the dog ate Tori's lunch or someone stole it. So, if the dog did not eat Tori's lunch, then someone stole it.
   d. We can make it on time if and only if the bridge is down. So, if we make it on time, the bridge is down, and if we do not make it on time, then the bridge was not down.
   e. The dog did not eat Tori's fruit salad and he did not eat Carl's tofu. So, the dog ate neither Tori's fruit salad nor Carl's Tofu.
   f. If the dog ate Rose's ham salad sandwich, he might not have gone for George's burger. So either the dog did not eat Rose's ham salad sandwich or he might not have gone for George's burger.
   g. If we get lost and run out of gas, it doesn't matter if the bridge is down. So, if we get lost then, if we run out of gas, then it doesn't matter if the bridge is down.

2. Rewrite this without the "only":

   Only sore feet keep grandpa from his morning walk.

3. Rewrite in two ways without the "unless":

   Unless Kineisha can handle a staple gun, she can't put up the posters.

4. Rewrite without the "whenever":

   Whenever Brad thinks of Malibu, he thinks of home.

5. Name the rule of replacement below:
   a. Either the creek is dry or we can dunk our toes in the water. This is equivalent to: If the creek is not dry, then we can dunk our toes in the water.
   b. If Ginny Lou does not stop singing at the top of her lungs, she'll wake the neighbors. This is equivalent to: If Ginny Lou did not wake the neighbors, then she stopped singing at the top of her lungs.
   c. Not both Sylvester and Tweetie are birds. This means, either Sylvester is not a bird or Tweetie is not a bird.

6. Rewrite using transposition:

   If the painter keeps leaving lids off paint cans, his boss will be upset.

7. Rewrite without the "only if":

   Only if Alex learns to hold the hammer will he quit hitting his thumb.

Part Four

Directions: Rewrite the following sentences without the underlined word (and then symbolize if you can).

1. <u>Only</u> Indiana Jones and Wonder Woman know the secret code.
2. June will come to the spring dance <u>provided that</u> she gets a ride.
3. A <u>necessary condition</u> for peace accord is that both sides must stop bio-warfare production.
4. Elizabeth will go see her parents <u>only if</u> she can go with them to the Garth Brooks concert.
5. It is <u>sufficient</u> for my cat to have fleas for me to bathe him today.
6. A <u>necessary condition</u> for giving Big Dog a bath is that he is dirty.
7. <u>Unless</u> Big Dog leaves the skunk alone, he's going to be very sorry.
8. <u>Without</u> proper nutrition, your body will disintegrate.
9. <u>Whenever</u> Araceli stays up too late, her eyes are red and puffy.
10. <u>Only when</u> John plays racquetball, does he feel in top shape.
11. <u>Only</u> a truck driver would enjoy my cooking.
12. Seeing a tarantula is <u>sufficient</u> for a jolt to the system.
13. Soaking in the tub is <u>necessary</u> to make Louie relax.
14. <u>Neither</u> fishing <u>nor</u> hunting got the little boy excited.
15. <u>Only</u> if Jim finds a pencil can he solve the crossword puzzle.
16. <u>It is not the case that</u> some chocolate is good for your teeth.
17. <u>Unless</u> Nguyen gets a radio, he can't listen to the ballgame.
18. <u>Without</u> shoes, you shouldn't go in the restaurant.
19. Studying logic is <u>necessary</u> for Audrey to feel powerful.
20. Studying logic is <u>sufficient</u> for Ernie to be self-confident.
21. <u>Unless</u> Alice has a nap, she fees deprived.
22. <u>It is false that</u> all dentists are into torture.
23. <u>Not only</u> clams are slimy foods.
24. <u>Not any</u> squid I've eaten is tasty.

Part Five

1. Translate the following argument using logical connectives and variables:

    If George smokes and drinks too much, then he doesn't sleep well. (S, D, W) If he doesn't sleep well or doesn't eat well, then George feels rotten. (E, R) If George feels rotten, then he does not clean his room and does not do his homework. (C, H) George drinks too much. Therefore, George does not do his homework.

2. Translate the following argument using variables and logical connectives:

   There are ghouls in my basement, but no vampires. (G, V) Only if there are vampires in my basement will I get angry. (A) If there are ghouls in my basement, then I'm not both dialing 911 and calling an exterminator. (D, E) I didn't dial 911. Therefore, I will get angry, but there are no ghouls in my basement.

3. Translate this argument:

   If I watch *Alien,* I'll be scared, but if I don't watch *Alien,* I'll be bored. (W, S, B) If I am bored, I get listless and start chopping onions. (L, C) If I start chopping onions, then my eyes water and my mascara runs. (E, M) If I'm scared, I'll pull my hair and bite my fingernails. (P, F) If I bite my fingernails, my hands won't be beautiful. (H) I watched *Alien.* Therefore, my hands won't be beautiful.

4. Translate this argument:

   There are marshmallows in the kitchen, but no chocolate. (M, C) Only if there are marshmallows and chocolate, can I rest easy. (E) If either I rest easy or I do breathing exercises, then I can both sleep peacefully and not have nightmares. (B, S, N). I don't sleep peacefully, if it's raining outside; however, if it's not raining, my dog barks. (R, D) Therefore, I will rest easy if I don't have nightmares, but my dog barks.

5. Translate this argument:

   If Ubu is sick, either he was chasing Jasper or he ate the meatball. (S, C, A) Ubu was chasing Jasper only if Jasper was out of his cage. (O) If Jasper was out of his cage then Silvio was home. (S) If Silvio was home then he wasn't working.(W) Silvio was working, but Ubu is sick. Therefore, Ubu ate the meatball.

6. Translate this argument:

   Either George ate the lemon pie or a thief broke into the house and stole it. (G, B, S) If George ate the lemon pie, then Keisha will be furious.(K) If a thief broke into the house, then either we should call the police or plan a way to trap the thief. (C, P) Keisha is not furious, but we will not plan a way to trap the thief. Therefore, we should call the police.

7. Translate this argument:

   If Jasper is out of his cage, then either the cats will start chasing him or he'll perch up on top of the cabinets. (O, C, P) If Jasper perches on top of the cabinets and is safe from the cats, then we can relax. (S, R) The cats will start chasing Jasper only if they are not napping. (N) Jasper is out of his cage and is safe from the cats, and the cats are napping. Therefore, we can relax.

8. Translate this argument:

   If the butler told the truth, then the window was closed; and if the gardener told the truth, then the automatic sprinkler system was not operating on the evening of the murder. (B, W, G, A) If neither the butler nor the gardener is telling the truth, then a conspiracy must exist to protect someone in the house and there would have been a little pool of water on the floor just inside the window. (C, P) The window was not closed. There was a little pool of water on the floor just inside the window. So, if there is a conspiracy to protect someone in the house, then the gardener did not tell the truth.

▓ Square of Opposition

The ability to draw inferences is not only useful, it is powerful because we go from knowing one thing to many other things. The square of opposition sets out vital relationships between the different categorical propositions. Once we know the truth value of one proposition, we can use these relationships to derive other truth values.

Contrary

Two propositions are contraries if they cannot both be true, but could both be false. If one is true, then the other one is necessarily false. The truth of the A or E claim forces the contrary to be false. Only universal claims can be contraries.

Examples of Contraries

If it is true that "All drummers are musicians."
→ "No drummer is a musician" must be false.
If it is true that "No dog has wings."
→ "All dogs have wings" must be false.

Be careful: If an A or E claim is false, it need not mean the corresponding E or A claim is then true. For instance, the claim "All cats are tigers" is false, but "No cats are tigers" is also false.

Subcontrary

Two propositions are subcontraries if they cannot both be false but could both be true. This is true of the two particular claims. If one is false then the other must be true.

Examples of Subcontraries

If it is false that "Some dogs are fish."
→ "Some dogs are not fish" is true.
If it is false that "Some mice are not rodents"
→ "Some mice are rodents" is true.

Remember: This only applies when the particular claim is *false*. It could very well be the case that they are *both* true. For instance, "Some dogs are not chihuahuas" is true and "Some dogs are chihuahuas" is also true.

Contradictory

Two propositions are contradictories if they cannot both be true *and* they cannot both be false. All the categorical propositions have contradictories. "All P is Q"

is opposite in truth value to "Some P is not Q." "No P is Q" has an opposite truth
value to "Some P is Q."

Examples of Contradictories

If it is true that "All horses are mammals."
→ "Some horses are not mammals" must be false.
If it is true that "Some birds are hawks."
→ "No bird is a hawk" must be false.

Subaltern

When a universal claim is true *and* the subject class is not empty of members, we
can conclude that the corresponding particular claim is also true. This is called the
subaltern. The process of going from the universal claim to its corresponding particular claim is called *subalternation.*

Examples of Subalterns

If it is true that "All Persians are cats" *and* we know there exist Persians,
→ "Some Persians are cats" must be true.
If it is true that "All flying saucers are UFOs," but we don't know that flying
   saucers actually exist then:
→ "Some flying saucers are UFOs" cannot be inferred as true.

We can summarize these four inferences in a diagram that shows their relationship as follows:

The Square of Opposition

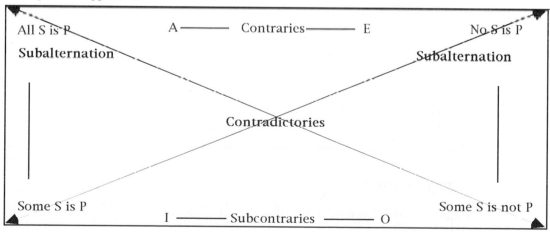

Exercises

Directions: Draw the inferences and truth values (if unknown, just say so).

1. State the subaltern and its truth value of "No novels are tax statements."

2. State the subcontrary and its truth value of the false proposition: "Some dinosaurs were insects."

3. State the contrary and its truth value of the false proposition: "No hawks are birds."

4. State the subaltern and its truth value of the true proposition: "All werewolves are monsters."

5. State the subcontrary and its truth value of the true proposition: "Some animals are ferocious."

6. State the contrary and its truth value of the true proposition: "All sewer rats are rodents."

7. State the contradictory and its truth value of the false proposition: "Some poisonous lizards make nice pets."

8. State the contrary and its truth value of the true proposition: "No well-trained animal bites its owner."

9. State the contradictory and its truth value of the true proposition: "All trapeze artists are daring people."

10. Given "All cocaine smugglers use airplanes for transport" is false:
    a. State the contrary and its truth value.
    b. State the contradictory and its truth value.
    c. State the subaltern and its truth value.

11. State the contradictory and its truth value of the true proposition: "No skyscraper is a small building."

12. Given the true proposition: "No cheese is a vegetable":
    a. State the contrary and its truth value.
    b. State the contradictory and its truth value.
    c. State the subaltern and its truth value.

13. Given the false proposition: "Some chocolate fudge sundaes are nonfattening":
    a. State the subcontrary and its truth value.
    b. State the contradictory and its truth value.

14. Given the true proposition: "All Martians are aliens":
    a. State the contrary and its truth value.
    b. State the subaltern and its truth value.
    c. State the contradictory and its truth value.

15. State everything you can infer from the true proposition: "No illegal alien is a U.S. citizen."

▦ The Obverse, Converse, and Contrapositive

There are three other key moves you can make to draw inferences. These are the obverse, the converse, and the contrapositive. For these we need to know one more thing: the complement of a class.

Complement

The complement of a class A is the class of those things *not* in A. So, for instance, the complement of the set of voters is the set of nonvoters. The complement of the set of noncitizens is the set of citizens. So, given any set A, the complement is the set non-A. Similarly, given any set non-B, the complement is the set B. (Think of a non-non-B as a double negative, that takes us back to set B). Examples of complements: farmworkers/nonfarmworkers; snake stompers/non–snake stompers; nonworkers/workers.

Obverse

The obverse of a proposition involves two steps: First, change the quality (from positive to negative or vice versa); then change the predicate to its complement. The result is the obverse. It has the same truth value as the original claim. If the original proposition is true, so is the obverse. If it is false, then the obverse is false. The obverse can be taken on any proposition.

Examples of the Obverse

All slugs are repulsive creatures.
→ No slug is a nonrepulsive creature.
Some men are not noncommunicative.
→ Some men are communicative people.

Converse

The converse of a proposition is obtained by switching the subject and the predicate, when possible. We can take a converse on an E or I claim. However, the converse of an A claim is known as *converse by limitation,* for we must step down to an I claim. We can't take the converse of an O claim.

Examples of the Converse

No scuba divers are nonswimmers.
→ No nonswimmers are scuba divers.
Some ice-skaters are hockey players.
→ Some hockey players are ice-skaters.
All pilots are daredevils.
→ <u>Some</u> daredevils are pilots.

Some hikers are not fond of heights.
→ Does not exist (no converse of an O claim!).

Contrapositive

To take the contrapositive of a proposition, follow these two steps: First, replace the subject with the complement of the predicate. Second, replace the predicate with the complement of the subject. The contrapositive cannot be taken on an I claim; it applies only to A, E, and O claims. The E claim is *contrapositive by limitation*: Step down to an O claim. Don't be surprised with a strange-looking result. Once you verify that the original sentence is A, O, or E, then just flip the subject and predicate, changing each one to the complement when you do the switch and, in the case of the E claim, move it down to an O claim.

Examples of Contrapositives

All trout are fish.
→ All nonfish are nontrout.
All non-citizens are nonvoters.
→ All voters are citizens.
Some citizens are not nonvoters.
→ Some voters are not noncitizens.
No FBI agent is in the CIA
→ Some nonpeople in the CIA are not non-FBI agents.
(*Note:* Change the E claim to an O claim in contrapositives).

Neither the converse nor the contrapositive changes the quality of the original proposition. Negatives stay negative and positives stay positive. Only the obverse changes the quality: Be sure with the obverse to change positive to negative claims and vice versa. Also, the converse is the only one of these three techniques that does NOT involve a complement. So be sure that you do *not* introduce it. We can summarize all this as follows:

Converse, Obverse, and Contrapositive

CONVERSE: A, E, AND I (NOTE: WE CAN'T TAKE THE CONVERSE ON THE O CLAIM)
One Step: Switch subject and predicate
Note: Converse of an A goes to an I

FORMS OF THE CONVERSE

No P is Q.	Converse is	No Q is P.
Some P is Q.	Converse is	Some Q is P.
All P is Q.	Converse is	Some Q is P.
Some P is not Q.	No converse	N/A

OBVERSE: A, E, I, O (ALL CLAIMS)
Two steps: Change quality (positive to negative and vice versa).
Change predicate to its complement.

FORMS OF THE OBVERSE

All P is Q.	Obverse is	No P is non-Q.
No P is Q.	Obverse is	All P is non-Q.
Some P is Q.	Obverse is	Some P is not non-Q.
Some P is not Q.	Obverse is	Some P is non-Q.

CONTRAPOSITIVE: A, E AND O (WE CAN'T TAKE THE CONTRAPOSITIVE ON I CLAIM)
Two steps: Replace subject with the complement of the predicate.
                  Replace predicate with the complement of the subject.
Note: Contrapositive of an E goes to an O.

FORMS OF THE CONTRAPOSITIVE

All P is Q.	Contrapositive is	All non-Q is non-P.
No P is Q.	Contrapositive is	Some non-Q is not non-P.
Some P is not Q.	Contrapositive is	Some non-Q is not non-P.
Some P is Q.	No contrapositive	N/A

Exercises

1. What is the converse of "All dinosaurs are extinct animals"?

2. What is the obverse of "Some aliens are androids"?

3. What is the contrapositive of "No electricians are scatterbrained"?

4. What is the obverse of "No sane woman would marry a murderer"?

5. What is the contradictory of "Some wild women are body builders"?

6. What is the converse of the subcontrary of "Some snake swallowers are not overweight"? (*Hint:* Take the subcontrary first, then take the converse of what you get.)

7. What is the contradictory of the obverse of "No woman who shaves her head is boring"? (*Hint:* Take the obverse first and then the contradictory of what you get.)

8. What is the contrapositive of the contrary of "All men with tattoos are adventurous"?

9. Given it is true that "All drummers are musicians," state and give the truth value of each of the following:
    a. The contrary
    b. The subaltern
    c. The contradictory
    d. The converse

10. Draw the inferences below:
    a. What is the converse of "No snakes are mammals"?
    b. What is the converse of "All mathematicians are witty people"?
    c. What is the obverse of "Some women are not citizens"?
    d. What is the obverse of the converse of "No friend of Damon's is a burglar"?
    e. What is the contrapositive of the obverse of "Some voters are Republicans"?
    f. Take the obverse of the contrapositive of "No slimy creature is a nonvoter."

11. Draw the inference and then give the inference's truth value.
    a. The contrapositive of "All rodents are nonfish." (True)
    b. The obverse of "Some non reptiles are not rodents." (True)
    c. The contrapositive of "No noninsects are grasshoppers." (True)
    d. The converse of "All nonandroids are nonvoters." (False)
    e. The subcontrary of "Some reptiles are mammals." (False)

12. Given this is true: "All robbers are thieves," draw all the inferences you can.

13. Given this is true: "No nun is a priest," draw these inferences and give the truth value of those inferences:
    a. The obverse
    b. The contradictory
    c. The converse
    d. The contrary
    e. The subaltern
    f. The contrapositive
    g. The contradictory of the obverse

14. Given it is false that: "Some pit bulls are not dogs," draw these inferences and state their truth values:
    a. The obverse
    b. The contradictory
    c. The contrary
    d. The subaltern
    e. The contrapositive
    f. The subcontrary

CHAPTER FIFTEEN

Syllogisms

'Twas brillig, and the slithy toves did gyre and gimble in the wabe: All mimsy were the borogoves, And the mome raths outgrabe.

—LEWIS CARROLL from *Jabberwocky*

You are having dinner with your family when you realize your father is serving your brother twice as many mashed potatoes as he gave your sister. You ask why. Your dad says, "Boys need to eat more than girls, that's why." Is your father's argument defensible? Well, let's see. His argument is this: "All boys need to eat more than girls. Your brother is a boy. So, your brother needs to eat more than your sister."

You probably have no trouble with the second premise, "Your brother is a boy." By definition your brother is a male and the only dispute might be whether he is young enough to warrant being called a "boy." So, you turn to the tricky premise, the first one. Is it true that "All boys need to eat more than girls"? If your sister were an Olympic athlete and your brother a receptionist, your sister would probably need more food. If, however, she is tiny and in a physically undemanding job and he is 6'7" and jogs to work, then she may need less. But it is not patently obvious that any given boy will need more food than any particular girl. We would need to know more about the individuals concerned. In that respect, the first premise is **contingent** on the specific circumstances and is neither certainly true nor certainly false. Consequently, your father's argument could not be said to be a sound one, given that the premises are not clearly true.

▓ Introduction to Syllogisms

What your dad has done is to offer a **syllogism.** This is a three-line argument with two premises and one conclusion in which there are only three terms. In the argument above the terms are: "boys," "your brother," and "people who need more food than girls." If we were to replace the terms with variables, letting B = boys, Y = your brother, and P = people who need more food than girls, then the argument can be written as:

> All B is P.
> (All) Y is B.
> Therefore, (All) Y is P.

Now we can examine the form of the argument and study the relationship between the premises and the conclusion. As we know from Chapter 6, this is a **deductive argument.** That is, the premises are claimed to provide sufficient support for the conclusion. We want to know: Is the argument valid? Is it sound? In this chapter, we will learn how to examine syllogisms in order to determine if they are valid or invalid.

▓ Validity and Soundness

Your father's argument is well constructed. The problem has to do with the truth of the premises, not whether or not the premises offer sufficient support for the conclusion. If it were true that all B is P and that all Y is B, then it would follow that all Y is P. No problem there. The concern isn't the structure of the argument, but the truth of the claims. This gives rise to two key issues—validity and soundness.

First, **validity.** The argument is structurally correct (*if* the premises were true, the conclusion could not be false). This means the argument is valid. It does *not* mean that the premises are necessarily true. This is crucial to imprint on our brains. Validity is a structural problem, not a truth problem—contrary to how people commonly use the word "valid" to mean "good" or "true."

Next there is the issue of **soundness.** You may remember the two criteria for sound arguments: (1) the argument is valid and (2) the premises are actually true. If an argument has both these characteristics, it is called a *sound* argument.

Validity

Only deductive arguments can be considered valid or invalid. Validity is an issue about the relationship between the premises and the conclusion—not about whether any statements are *actually* true or not. The question is: Do the premises, if they were assumed to be true, fully support the conclusion?

With **inductive arguments,** the truth of the premises would not *necessarily* force the truth of the conclusion because there are missing pieces in the evidence. Thus, the wedge of doubt that resides with inductive reasoning.

In **valid deductive arguments,** however, the premises could not be true and the conclusion false. This is slam-dunk reasoning. In a valid argument, the conclusion comes right out of the premises, leaving no doubt in our minds. Look at these examples of *valid syllogisms:*

Examples

All reptiles are covered in feathers.

<u>All lizards are reptiles.</u>

Therefore, all lizards are covered in feathers.

If dessert is not a chocolate cake, then Nick will be disappointed.

<u>Nick was not disappointed.</u>

Therefore, dessert was a chocolate cake.

In both of these arguments, if the premises were true, the conclusion would have to be true—it could not be false.

We can determine the validity of a syllogism. Note that a syllogism is an argument with two premises and a conclusion, containing three terms (called the major term, the minor term, and the middle term). We'll see how to locate the three terms shortly. First, we will set out our argument.

Universal versus Particular Propositions

Basically, propositions fall into one of two categories, as we saw in Chapter 14. They could be **universal,** which means something is being predicated about *all* members of the subject class (i.e., that they either have or lack some characteristic). The "all" here may refer to the collective or to "each and every one" or "any" of the subject. The result is all-or-nothing claims, such as "All hawks are birds" and "No chickens are dogs." This includes propositions in which something is being affirmed or denied about a class with only one member (e.g., a person, a city, this particular thing, etc.).

Basic Forms of Universal Claims:

Form 1:	"All A is B."	→ Universal positive	"All cockatoos are birds that can talk."
Form 2:	"No A is B."	→ Universal negative	"No cockatoo is a duck."
Form 3:	"A is/is not B."	→ Universal positive/ negative	"Denver is not an overwhelming city."
		→ *Where A has only one member*	"That baby cockatoo is an awfully darling bird!"

Universal Claims Are All-or-Nothing Claims

- All farmhands like a big breakfast.
- That little boy is really out of control.
- No weight lifter likes salad for lunch.
- Any person who can drive a forklift is talented.
- Every member of the film group liked *Groundhog Day.*
- New Mexico is a magical place.
- Ripley never liked Ash.
- The U.S. Constitution is an important document.
- 100 percent of Carla's savings was spent on her trip to Scotland.

On the other hand, a proposition could be *particular.* In the case of a particular proposition, some trait is being predicated about some (but not all or none) of the subject class. This includes statistical propositions of the form x% of A is B, where x ≠ 100 and x ≠ 0. Particular claims are about *some,* not all. Particular claims are never all-or-nothing propositions.

Basic Forms of Particular Claims

Form 1:	"Some A is B"	→ Particular positive	"Some chefs are good bakers."
Form 2:	"Some A is not B"	→ Particular negative	"Some truffles are not a chocolate candy."
Form 3:	"x% of A is/is not B"	→ Particular positive or negative	"64% of women are tea drinkers."
		→ *Where* x≠ 100 or 0.	"86% of soccer players are men."

Particular Claims Refer to at Least One, but Not All

- Some Italian food does not use tomatoes.
- Many people in North Carolina are fond of lamb.
- Most travelers to Nova Scotia bring digital cameras.
- A few Apache at the filming of the last scene did not agree with the director.
- Not all Turkish desserts contain honey.
- Ninety-two percent of southern desserts are topped with ice cream.

🔲 Categorical Propositions

A standardized approach provides a technique for simplifying the terms of the argument, so we can evaluate the syllogism more quickly. In analyzing a syllogism, it's usually best to rewrite the premises and the conclusion in the form of categorical propositions. These are as follows:

The Four Categorical Propositions

Mood	Categorical Proposition	Example
A	All P are Q.	All basketball players are athletes.
E	No P is Q.	No violinist is a football player.
I	Some P is Q.	Some third basemen are film-lovers.
O	Some P is not Q.	Some mountain climbers are not stamp collectors.

Variations of the Categorical Propositions

1. *Proper nouns as subject:* Remember, if you use specific individuals or proper names, like Andrea, Chicago, or the Eiffel tower, then the claim is universal and will be either an A or an E claim, depending on whether the sentence is positive or negative. (For example, "Lisa is a wild woman" is an A claim, whereas "Kobe is not a short man" is an E claim).
2. *Statistical claims:* If you have statistical claims in which x% of A is B, (where $x \neq 100$ or 0), then that claim is treated as an I or O claim (depending upon whether it's positive or negative). So "82% of donuts are greasy" is an I claim and "19% of chocolate is not addictive" is an O claim.

These forms (A, E, I, O) are called *categorical propositions* and are useful to provide a kind of uniformity, so we can quickly organize a syllogism and see if it is valid or invalid. See Chapter 14 for a review.

Categorical Syllogisms

A **categorical syllogism** is a syllogism in which the premises and the conclusion are **categorical** claims. The **standard form of a categorical syllogism** is what we have when we set out the syllogism in a particular order: major premise, minor premise, and then the conclusion. We will learn how to do this, starting with the different terms of the syllogism.

The standard form of the syllogism always starts with the **major premise**. This is the premise that contains the *predicate* term (major term) found in the conclusion. The second premise is called the **minor premise,** and it contains the *subject* term (minor term) found in the conclusion. This means the premise nearest to the conclusion should contain the minor term (the subject of the conclusion). Both premises have a linking term (the middle term) that does not appear in the conclusion. The **middle term** is the term that is found only in the premises. Here's an example:

Most cows are relatively calm.

Jerseys are cows.

Therefore, Jerseys are relatively calm animals.

Let us rewrite this argument so each proposition is in *standard form*. Express both of the premises and the conclusion in one of these four forms (abbreviated as A, E, I, O). Making things as uniform as possible helps streamline the process. The argument above in standard form is:

Some cows are relatively calm animals.

<u>All Jerseys are cows.</u>

Therefore, all Jerseys are relatively calm animals.

Notice that we had to change "*Most* cows are relatively calm animals" to "*Some* cows are relatively calm animals." Not only did we add the quantifier "some," we also constructed a predicate class ("relatively calm animals"). Note also that "all" was added before "Jerseys" to make it explicit that the claim is universal. You need to do this to get the sentence into categorical form. It makes a big difference in a speedy assessment of arguments and makes errors less likely.

Why Bother

This system of analyzing syllogisms is not only a time saver; it lessens the chance of error. If you were like the Tom Hanks character in *Cast Away*, you might prefer taking a *very* long time to puzzle through the problems you face. On the other hand, you may prefer the jet propulsion model of reasoning, where speed and accuracy is of the essence. *Think about it:* What if your house is on fire, you've just hit an ice slick on the road, or you're on a reality TV show and stand to make your fortune if you can think quickly on your feet? The ability to dismantle and evaluate syllogistic arguments quickly and correctly is more valuable than you may realize.

▦ The Three Terms of the Syllogism

Once we have the premises and conclusion expressed in standard form, we can take the next step. This is to locate the three terms. The *major term* is the predicate of the conclusion. In the example above, the major term is "relatively calm animals." The *minor term* is the subject of the conclusion. In the example above it is "Jerseys." And the *middle term* is the term that is only found in the two premises; here it is "cows."

Example of the Three Terms:

Some easily irritated creatures are watchdogs.

<u>All badgers are easily irritated creatures.</u>

So, some badgers are watchdogs.

Major term → Predicate of the conclusion, "watchdogs"
Minor term → Subject of the conclusion, "badgers"
Middle term → Term only in the premises, "easily irritated creatures"

Exercises

Directions: Name the *major, minor,* and *middle* terms in the syllogisms below.

1. All plutonium is a dangerous substance.
   <u>No dangerous substance is a thing that should be legal.</u>
   Thus, no plutonium is a thing that should be legal.

2. Some snakes are poisonous animals.
   <u>All poisonous animals are things to be avoided.</u>
   So, some things to be avoided are snakes.

3. No good driver is a person who drives drunk.
   <u>No drunk driver is a person worthy of respect.</u>
   Therefore, all persons worthy of respect are good drivers.

4. No sound engineer likes blaring music.
   <u>Trent is a sound engineer.</u>
   So Trent is not someone who likes blaring music.

5. All attractive men are people who can wink.
   <u>Big Mike is a person who can wink.</u>
   So, Big Mike is an attractive man.

6. Some archaeologists are Celtics fans.
   <u>No Celtics fan is an introvert.</u>
   So, some introverts are not archaeologists.

7. All Dolphins fans are people who like Miami.
   <u>Some people who like Miami are graphic artists.</u>
   Therefore, some graphic artists are Dolphins fans.

8. No electrical engineer is a person who finds the Houston Rockets boring.
   All people who find the Houston Rockets boring are people who like to read
   <u>Kafka.</u>
   Therefore, no one who likes to read Kafka is an electrical engineer.

9. Some belly dancers are Rangers fans.
   <u>Some people who like to wear caps and eat hot dogs are Rangers fans.</u>
   Therefore, Some people who like to wear caps and eat hot dogs are belly
   dancers.

10. All Nobel Prize winners are unusual people.
    <u>Jorge Luis Borges is a Nobel Prize winner.</u>
    Therefore, Jorge Luis Borges is an unusual person.

11. Some movies are things that waste money and time.

   Akira is a movie.

   So, *Akira* is a thing that wastes money and time.

12. Some people who can eat a whole pizza are not neurotic people.

   No person who can eat a whole pizza is a backup singer for a rock band.

   Therefore, no backup singers for a rock band are neurotic people.

13. Some radiologists are people who love to snorkel.

   Some people who love to snorkel are drifters.

   Therefore, some drifters are radiologists.

14. All x-ray technicians are risk takers.

   Some risk takers are exotic and mysterious people.

   Therefore, some exotic and mysterious people are x-ray technicians.

15. No flat-footed weasel is a well-behaved pet.

   All guinea pigs are well-behaved pets.

   Therefore, some guinea pigs are not flat-footed weasels.

16. Some birds are not scared of cats.

   All mice are scared of cats.

   Therefore, no mice are birds.

17. All football players are big and burly.

   Some big and burly people are couch potatoes.

   Therefore, some couch potatoes are football players.

18. All chefs are fond of hats.

   No small child is fond of hats.

   Therefore, no small child is a chef.

19. Some truck drivers are country music fans.

   All country music fans are from Kentucky.

   Therefore, some people from Kentucky are truck drivers.

20. Some short men are Oregonians.

   Kareem is not a short man.

   Therefore, Kareem is not an Oregonian.

Major and Minor Premises

Order is everything in the world of syllogisms. If we are testing a syllogism, we must first set out the argument. Our first step is to locate the conclusion. If we don't know the conclusion, we won't know where the person is headed.

Our next step is to examine the conclusion to determine which term is the major term and which is the minor term. The predicate is the **major term** and, once you know this, you also know the major premise. The **major premise** is the premise containing the major term. The subject of the conclusion is the **minor term** and, once you know this, you also know the **minor premise.** The minor premise is the premise containing the minor term. The **middle term** is the term found only in the premises (*not* in the conclusion).

Standard Form of a Syllogism

Major Premise	→	Contains the major and middle terms
Minor Premise	→	Contains the minor and middle terms
Conclusion	→	Contains the minor and major terms

Remember: *Minor term* = Subject of the conclusion
Major term = Predicate of the conclusion
Middle term = Term found in both premises

The first premise should contain the major term and the middle term. The second premise should contain the minor term and the middle term. The conclusion contains the major and minor terms. The argument must be exactly in this order to be in standard form.

Always double check: The premise *closest* to the conclusion should contain the minor term. If not, rearrange the premises. The major term should be in the first premise, and the minor term in the second premise. *Remember:* The major term is the last term of the conclusion—its predicate.

Be sure to express each proposition in *categorical form:*

QUANTIFIER	SUBJECT	IS/ARE	PREDICATE
All	cats	are	animals.
No	cats	are	dogs.
Some	cats	are	picky eaters.
Some	cats	are not	ill-mannered beasts.

If the proposition does not have a quantifier, then we have to decide if it is universal or particular. For instance, "Skunks should be approached carefully" and "Scoundrels are immoral" would be rewritten, "All skunks are animals that should be approached carefully" and "All scoundrels are immoral people."

In contrast, "Muffins were eaten at breakfast" would be rewritten: "Some muffins were food eaten at breakfast." And "Nights can get cold in Alaska" would be rewritten: "Some nights are times that can get cold in Alaska." *Remember:* A universal claim is saying more than a particular claim because it has a wider scope.

Expressing Arguments in Standard Form

Let us practice working with what we know so far. Put this argument in standard form:

Cobras are snakes.

A lot of snakes are disgusting.

Therefore, cobras are disgusting.

First, express the propositions in categorical form—in the form of A, E, I, or O claims. Then label the proposition (A, E, I, O) on the left, for easy reference:

A   All cobras are snakes.

I   Some snakes are disgusting animals.

A   Therefore, all cobras are disgusting animals.

The next step is to look at the conclusion. The predicate of the conclusion is "disgusting animals." That is the major term. The major premise must contain that term, so look at the premises and locate it. The major premise then is "Some snakes are disgusting animals." This premise—the major premise—must be listed first. The remaining premise is the minor premise, containing the minor term "cobras." We can now put the argument in order:

Major premise: Some snakes are disgusting animals.

Minor premise: All cobras are snakes.

Conclusion: All cobras are disgusting animals.

The argument is now in standard form.

Exercises

Directions: Put the following arguments in standard form, with each sentence expressed as a categorical proposition. Name the major, minor, and middle terms.

1. Every woman loves a challenge. All those who love a challenge are daredevils. As a result, all women are daredevils.

2. Many sports fans are men. All sports fans are people who like to discuss sports. Therefore, most sports fans are men.

3. A lot of children are afraid of the dark. Therefore, many children scream loudly, because most people afraid of the dark scream loudly.

4. No animal you can take for granted is a crocodile. Every pet is an animal you can take for granted. Consequently, no crocodile is a pet.

5. Some dogs are revolting creatures, because many dogs eat with their mouth open, and, any animal that eats with its mouth wide open is revolting.

6. All moths can fly. This is true because some insects are moths and most insects are creatures that can fly.

7. Count Dracula sucks blood. All vampires suck blood. Therefore, Count Dracula is a vampire.

8. No fruit is a vegetable. Some fruits are members of the citrus family. Therefore, some members of the citrus family are not vegetables.

9. Opossums are smarter than most people think. A large number of animals that are smarter than most people think are birds. Therefore, some birds are opossums.

10. Any earthquake is a scary thing to experience. Many scary things to experience are tornadoes. Therefore, a few earthquakes are tornadoes.

11. Lots of movie stars are people who give to charity. Wimpy is not a movie star. So, Wimpy is not someone who gives to charity.

12. A few things recognized for their artistic merit are TV shows. *Jeopardy* is a TV show. Therefore, *Jeopardy* is a TV show that has been recognized for its artistic merit.

13. A fair amount of dental work is something unpleasant to experience. No dental work is something to anticipate with glee. Therefore, no thing to anticipate with glee is something unpleasant to experience.

14. All dreams about being swallowed whole are nightmares. Many dreams about sharks are dreams about being swallowed whole. Therefore, almost every dream about sharks is a nightmare.

15. Most enjoyable moments are good to note in your scrapbook. Wrestling down the alligator was not an enjoyable moment. Thus wrestling down the alligator is not good to note in your scrapbook.

16. No hockey game is a boring sport. Many badminton games are boring. Therefore, no hockey game is a badminton game.

17. All scary movies are things that frighten Carl. Many things that Carl avoids are things that frighten him. Therefore, all scary movies are things Carl avoids.

18. A bunch of children were running around the yard. Most children are people who eat a lot of peanuts. Therefore, some people running around the yard are people who eat a lot of peanuts.

19. Every tall animal is able to look over fences. Lots of animals able to look over fences are not warthogs. Therefore, a large number of warthogs are not tall animals.

20. Not one donut hole is a filling snack. All popcorn is a filling snack. Therefore, not any donut hole is popcorn.

⧉ The Mood of a Syllogism

The **mood of a syllogism** is the list of the types of claims (A, E, I, and O) of the major premise, minor premise, and conclusion (in that order). Because there are two premises and one conclusion, we will use three letters to indicate the categorical propositions that constitute the syllogism. For example, the syllogism below is in standard form:

> All wallpaper with paisleys is something that is tiring on the eyes.
> <u>Some people have wallpaper with paisleys.</u>
> Therefore, some people have wallpaper that is tiring on the eyes.

The mood of this syllogism can then be read as AII (The major premise is an A claim, the minor premise is an I claim, and the conclusion is an I claim).

Handy Abbreviations

P = *Predicate* of the conclusion   →   Major term
S = *Subject* of the conclusion   →   Minor term
M = Linking term in both premises   →   Middle term

⧉ Figure of the Syllogism

The *figure* of a syllogism is the placement of the middle term in the two premises. Let P = major term, S = minor term, and M = middle term. To determine the figure, we need to see where the middle term is located. There are four possible locations of the middle term in any syllogism.

Once the syllogism is in standard categorical form, the major term P should be in the first premise, the minor term S will be in the second premise, and the middle term is in both premises. The arrangement of the middle term reveals the figure.

The Figures of the Syllogism

FIGURE 1	FIGURE 2	FIGURE 3	FIGURE 4
M ↘ P	P M ↑	M ↓ P	P ↗ M
<u>S</u> <u>M</u>	<u>S</u> <u>M</u>	<u>M</u> <u>S</u>	<u>M</u> <u>S</u>
S P	S P	S P	S P
FIGURE 1	FIGURE 2	FIGURE 3	FIGURE 4
M's step down right	M's on right	M's on left	M's step up left

Examples of the different figures:

Mood and figure EIO –(1)

    No **M** is P

    Some S is **M**

So,   Some S is not P

For example:

No cars are trucks.

Some Toyotas are cars.

So, some Toyotas are not trucks.

Mood and figure AOA –(2)

    All P is **M**

    Some S is not **M**

So,   Some S is not P

For example:

All Corvettes are cars.

Some vehicles are not cars.

Some vehicles are not Corvettes.

Mood and figure AEE –(3)

    All **M** is P

    No **M** is S

So,   No S is P

For example:

All Lexus cars are luxury vehicles.

No Lexus car is a BMW.

So, No BMW is a luxury car.

Mood and figure AIA—(4)

    All P is **M**

    Some **M** is S

So,   All S is P.

For example:

All Land Rovers are all-terrain vehicles.

Some all-terrain vehicles are jeeps.

All jeeps are Land Rovers.

Exercises

Directions: Put the following syllogisms in standard form and then state the mood and figure.

1. No nurse is afraid to touch people. John is afraid to touch people. So John is not a nurse.

2. Some architects love Korean barbeques. Rick is a person who loves Korean barbeques. So Rick is an architect.

3. Surgeons are people with a mind for details. A number of people with a mind for details are people who love to do their taxes. Therefore, all people who love to do their taxes are surgeons.

4. No Rolls Royce mechanic is afraid to get messy. Some cooks are not Rolls Royce mechanics. Therefore, some cooks are afraid to get messy.

5. Many purchasing agents like to do paperwork. No person who likes to do paperwork is a hair stylist. Therefore, no hair stylist is a purchasing agent.

6. All photographers have a highly developed visual sense. All photographers are artists. Therefore, some artists have a highly developed visual sense.

7. Some welders have a talent for fine metalwork. All jewelers have a talent for fine metalwork. Therefore, some welders are jewelers.

8. All lawyers are analytical people. Some analytical people are not fond of playing jokes on others. Therefore, some lawyers are not fond of playing jokes on others.

9. Some people with a sardonic sense of humor are judges. All people who liked *Fargo* are people with a sardonic sense of humor. Therefore, some people who liked *Fargo* are judges.

10. Some people over 6 feet tall are not gymnasts. Some gymnasts do great back flips. Therefore, some people who do great back flips are not over 6 feet tall.

11. The vast majority of waitresses are courteous. Some waitresses are crazy about stamp collecting. So, many courteous people are crazy about stamp collecting.

12. Anyone who loves the blues is familiar with Jelly Roll Morton. All guitar players are people who are familiar with Jelly Roll Morton. Therefore, all guitar players love the blues.

13. Whoever likes comedy knows about the Marx Brothers. Will Smith likes comedy, so he must know about the Marx Brothers.

14. Some people who watch MTV are computer hackers. This is because many computer hackers are people who enjoy music videos. Also, everyone who enjoys music videos likes to watch MTV.

15. Most elderly folks enjoy playing Scrabble. A few elderly folks enjoy going to the racetrack. Therefore, a lot of people who enjoy going to the racetrack will enjoy playing Scrabble.

16. Children under 10 will like *The Never-Ending Story*. Here's why: All children under 10 like tales about flying creatures. *The Never-Ending Story* is a tale about a flying creature.

17. Just about all rabbits are furry animals. Not all furry animals are nice to pet. It follows that lots of rabbits are nice to pet.

18. Everyone who is a friend of mine has a good sense of humor. Chris Rock has a good sense of humor. Consequently, Chris Rock is a friend of mine.

▓ Checking for Validity

Before we can test the syllogism for validity, we need to know how to tell if a term is distributed. Distribution involves the question of how much. If your brother asked you to distribute a stack of leaflets, you'd know that he wants you to pass them all out. Distribution of a term is similar, in the sense that a distributed term includes all its members.

Distribution

When we talk distribution, we are talking about the number of members of the class in question. If the term is meant to apply to *all* members of the class it defines, then it is called **distributed.** If it applies to only an indefinite part of those members, it's called *undistributed.* To grasp this concept, it helps to see the term "distribution" in operation. We will look at the key ways to test for distribution and then run through some examples. For any given proposition there are only two terms to examine to determine distribution—the subject and the predicate. The subject is distributed in any *universal* claim and the predicate is distributed in any *negative* claim. Let's look at this in more detail.

Distribution of Terms

Checking distribution of terms involves two steps:

Step 1: Check the location of the term (is it the *subject* or the *predicate* of the proposition?).

Step 2: According to the location, check either the quality or the quantity of the proposition. If the term is in the subject place, then check if the proposition is universal (A or E). If so, the subject is distributed. If the term is in the predicate place, check if the proposition is negative (E or O). If so then the predicate is distributed.

Distribution Table

PROPOSITION	DISTRIBUTED TERM
All P is Q	subject
No P is Q	subject *and* predicate
Some P is Q	nothing
Some P is not Q	predicate

Subject Distributed.   If the proposition is *universal,* the subject is distributed, because you are saying that all the members of the subject class either have or don't have some characteristic.

Example 1

All opossums are slow-moving creatures.
→ Claim is universal. Subject is distributed in universal propositions. Subject "opossums" is distributed.

Example 2

Some possums are animals that like cat food.
→ Claim is particular (*not* universal). Subject is not distributed in particular propositions. "Possums" is not distributed.

Note: The term "some possums" tells us nothing about *all* possums in terms of liking cat food. Thus the term "possums" is not distributed. For instance, "All pajamas are comfortable to wear" is talking about *all* pajamas, not just some of them. Similarly, "No bathtub is a good place to fall asleep in," is talking about *all* bathtubs and saying that they are *not* places you'd want to sleep in. So *both A and E propositions have a distributed subject.*

Checking the Subject for Distribution

Check the *quantity* of the proposition.
→ See if the proposition is *universal.* The subject is distributed in A and E claims.

Examples

No cats are dogs.
→ Check the *quantity* of the proposition. The proposition is universal (E claim). Subject is distributed in an E claim. Subject "cats" is distributed.
Some cats are not Persians.
→ Check the *quantity* of the proposition. The proposition is particular (O claim). Subject is not distributed in an O claim. Subject "cats" is not distributed.

Predicate Distributed.   If the claim is *negative,* the predicate is distributed. This is because a negative is excluding the subject class (some or all of it) from having the characteristic set out in the predicate.

Examples

No rattlesnake is a well-mannered animal.
→ Check the *quality* of the proposition. The proposition is negative (E claim). Predicate is distributed in an E claim. Predicate "Well-mannered animal" is distributed.
All rattlesnakes are creatures that like the sun.
→ Check the *quality* of the proposition. The proposition is positive (A claim). Predicate is not distributed in an A claim. Predicate "creatures that like the sun" is not distributed.

Note: There are creatures that like the sun (e.g., land turtles, hummingbirds, giraffes, elephants, etc.) that are not rattlesnakes.
    For instance, if someone says, "No octopus can climb a tree," they are saying that the class of animals that can climb trees does NOT contain *any* octopi —they

are ALL excluded from the tree-climber class. Similarly, if you heard, "Some tall people are not basketball players," you would know that the term "basketball players" does not cover all tall people—it excludes *all* those in the subject class. Therefore, the term "basketball players" is distributed. *So both E and O claims distribute the predicate.*

Determining if the Predicate is Distributed

Check the *quality* of the proposition.
→ See if the claim is *negative*. The predicate is distributed in E and O claims.

Example 1

All wolfhounds are dogs.
→ Check the *quality* of the proposition. The proposition is positive (A claim).
  Predicate is not distributed in an A claim. Predicate "dogs" is not distributed.

Example 2

Some dogs are not chihuahuas.
→ Check the *quality* of the proposition. The proposition is negative (O claim).
  Predicate is distributed in an O claim. Predicate "chihuahuas" is distributed.

Summary of Distribution

Checking Subjects: To test a subject for distribution, look at the *quantity* (universal versus particular) of the proposition.
→ If the proposition is universal, the subject *is* distributed.
→ If the proposition is particular, the subject *is not* distributed.

Checking Predicates: To test a predicate for distribution, look at the *quality* (positive versus negative) of the proposition.
→ If the proposition is negative, the predicate *is* distributed.
→ If the proposition is positive, the predicate *is not* distributed.

We can see how the terms are distributed in the table below:

Distribution

TYPE OF CLAIM	SUBJECT DISTRIBUTED?	PREDICATE DISTRIBUTED?
A	Yes	No
E	Yes	Yes
I	No	No
O	No	Yes

So, for example, in the claim "All novels are books," the term "novels" is distributed. In the claim, "No screenplay is a novel," both "screenplay" and "novel" are distributed. In the claim, "Some math textbooks are not great literature" the term "great literature" is distributed. But in the claim, "Some poetry is an inspiration," neither term is distributed.

▦ Testing the Validity of a Syllogism: Two Methods

You know how to put a syllogism in standard form. You know how to find the mood and the figure. The next step is to test for validity. The quickest way is to use the rules of the syllogism. However, an alternative method is to use Venn diagrams. We'll start with the rules of the syllogism and go through the method of testing validity. Then we'll turn to Venn diagrams and go through that method. If you learn both methods, you can then decide which one works best for you.

Rules of the Syllogism

Any syllogism that satisfies each of the rules is valid. Test for validity simply by running through each rule and seeing if the syllogism checks out on each one.

Testing a Syllogism for Validity

Let's now test some syllogisms to determine validity. We will start with one in standard form.

Example 1
All psychologists are insightful people.
<u>Some gardeners are insightful people.</u>
So, some gardeners are psychologists.

Look at each claim and set out the mood and figure. It is AII—(2). Run through the rules of the syllogism to see if AII—(2) is valid.

The first rule (about the middle term) is violated: Look at the middle term ("insightful people"). In the first premise, it is in the predicate. To be distributed, the predicate must be negative—but this claim is positive. So the term is not distributed in the major premise. Check the minor premise: The minor premise is an I claim and nothing is distributed. That means this syllogism has an undistributed middle and, thus, it is invalid. If you check all the other rules you will see that they are fine (rule 2 doesn't apply because nothing is distributed in the conclusion; rules 3 and 4 have to do with negatives and there are no negatives here; and rule 5 doesn't apply because we do not have two universal premises or a universal conclusion).

Rules of the Syllogism

Rule 1: The middle term must be distributed at least once.

Rule 2: If a term is distributed in the conclusion, it must also be distributed in its corresponding premise.

- *Illicit major:* When the major term is distributed in the conclusion, but is not distributed in the major premise.
- *Illicit minor:* When the minor term is distributed in the conclusion, but is not distributed in the minor premise.

Note: A valid syllogism does not require the conclusion to have distributed terms. But *if* a term is distributed in the conclusion, then it must also be distributed in its corresponding premise.

Rule 3: At least one premise must be positive (two negative premises = invalid argument).

Rule 4: If the syllogism has a negative premise, there must be a negative conclusion, and vice versa.

Rule 5: If both of the premises are universal, the conclusion must also be universal, and vice versa.

Example 2

Some dogs are Siberian huskies.

No dog is liked by geese.

So, no goose likes Siberian huskies.

First, make sure that it is in standard form and the claims are expressed as categorical propositions. Put it into categorical propositions and then we will get it in standard form. Rewriting the argument, we get:

Some dogs are Siberian huskies.

<u>No dog is a creature liked by geese.</u>

So, no Siberian husky is a creature liked by geese.

Now, put it in standard form. The predicate of the conclusion (major term) is "a creature liked by geese." The major premise contains the major term and that means the major premise is "No dog is a creature liked by geese." That leaves the other premise, "Some dogs are Siberian huskies," as the minor premise. Note that it contains the minor term, "Siberian husky." Putting the syllogism in order (major premise, minor premise, conclusion), we get:

No dog is a creature liked by geese.

<u>Some dogs are Siberian huskies.</u>

So, no Siberian husky is a creature liked by geese.

Now we can test the syllogism. Note that the mood and figure of this argument is EIE—(3). Let us go through each rule, to see if the syllogism obeys each rule. Rule 1 is OK, because the major premise is negative and the middle term ("dog") is therefore distributed. Now check rule 2. The conclusion is an E claim and that means both the major and minor terms are distributed, so we must check each premise to see that it is distributed in its corresponding premise. The major term is

OK because the major premise is a universal negative. However, the minor term "Siberian husky" is not distributed in the minor premise, because the claim is an I claim, where nothing is distributed. This means we have an illicit minor. It also violates rule 5 (the universal conclusion requires two universal premises). Therefore the syllogism is invalid. The other rules are fine (rules 3 and 4 are not violated). The problem is that both rule 2 and rule 5 are violated. So the syllogism is invalid.

Not all syllogistic arguments are invalid, though. Many are valid. For instance, if someone argued the following, they'd be giving a valid argument.

Example 3

All swimmers love summer.

All people who love summer enjoy fireworks.

So, all swimmers enjoy fireworks.

First, express the premises as categorical propositions and then put the argument in standard form. Expressing the propositions in categorical form, we get:

All swimmers are people who love summer.

All people who love summer are people who enjoy fireworks.

So, all swimmers are people who enjoy fireworks.

Because "people who enjoy fireworks" is the major term (predicate of the conclusion), the major premise is "All people who love summer are people who enjoy fireworks." So, we need to switch the order of the premises and then the argument will be in standard form. Our argument is now:

All people who love summer are people who enjoy fireworks.

All swimmers are people who love summer.

So, all swimmers are people who enjoy fireworks.

Now test for validity. The mood and figure is AAA—(1). Rule 1 is satisfied, because the middle term "people who love summer" is distributed in the first premise, the major premise. Rule 2 is fine, because the conclusion does have the minor term "swimmers" distributed, but it is also distributed in its corresponding premise (the minor premise). Rules 3 and 4 don't apply because there are no negatives. Rule 5 is satisfied because we do have two universal premises, but we also have a universal conclusion. So our argument is valid!

Remember, a valid argument isn't necessarily sound. To be sound it would have to be both valid *and* have all its premises true, which isn't clearly the case here (the premises are not obviously true). Let's try one more syllogism.

Testing for Validity Knowing Only the Mood and Figure

If an argument is given in the form of mood and figure, just write it out using P for the major term, S for the minor term, and M for the middle term and then test. For instance, AEA—(4). This can be written:

All P is M.

<u>No M is S.</u>

So, all S is P.

Running through the rules we find: Rule 1 is fine, because the minor premise is an E claim (and everything is distributed in an E claim). Rule 2 is satisfied because the term S that is distributed in the conclusion is also distributed in its corresponding premise (the minor premise, which is negative). Because the P (the major term) is not distributed in the conclusion, you don't have to test it. Rule 3 is our problem. We have a negative premise and, therefore, need a negative conclusion. That means the syllogism is invalid. (Rules 4 and 5 are fine, because neither rule is violated). The trouble is with rule 3. So the syllogism is invalid.

We don't have to actually know the specific major, minor, and middle terms in order to assess validity. If we know the mood and figure of the syllogism, we can use the five rules of the syllogism to test the argument. Let's see how this is done.

If you know only the mood and figure, you can still test for validity. Just use S, P, and M for the minor, major, and middle terms (respectively) and set it up and then test it. For example, test EAE—(3). Figure 3 means the middle term is on the left so the argument can be expressed:

No M is P.

<u>All M is S.</u>

No S is P.

Remember: P, the major term, must be in the first premise; S, the minor term, in the second premise; and M, the middle term, in both premises.

Now test the argument. Rule 1 is fine because the first premise is an E claim and distributes everything. Rule 2 must be checked because both the subject and predicate of the conclusion are distributed. P is also distributed in the major premise (predicate of a negative claim is distributed), but S is not distributed in the minor premise (because S is in the predicate, the claim needs to be negative). This means we have an illicit minor, so the syllogism is invalid. Rules 3 and 4 are both OK (they don't have two negatives, and a negative premise and a negative conclusion satisfies rule 4), and so is rule 5 (because we have two universal premises and a universal conclusion). Because of the illicit minor, the argument, is invalid.

Constructing Valid Arguments

Say you wanted a valid argument for the conclusion, "Some vampires are bloodthirsty." Because it is an I claim, we don't have to worry about rule 2 (because nothing in the conclusion is distributed, there is no problem here).

We just need to avoid problems with the other rules. Rule 1 means we need to have the middle term distributed. Because the conclusion is positive, we do not want any negatives in the premises (or we would violate rule 4) and with no negatives in the premises we won't violate rule 3.

FIGURE 15.1
The Cat and
Trans Fat.
All cats that
eat trans fat are
creatures that
feel queasy.
All creatures that
feel queasy roll
their eyes and say
"Agkh!"
Therefore, all cats
that eat trans fat
roll their eyes and
say "Agkh! Mood
and figure:
AAA—(1).
Valid argument!

Credit: Greg Perry, Artist/Illustrator. Reprinted with the permission of Greg Perry, www.perryink.com.

That means we need one of the premises to be a universal positive claim, distributing the middle term. This forces the middle term to be in the subject place (because if it was in the predicate, the claim would have to be negative). The other premise cannot be universal, or we'd violate rule 5. And, because it cannot be negative (or we would violate rule 4), that means it must be an I claim. Once we distribute the middle term in the A claim, it will not matter where the middle term is in the I claim. That means we have several options. Our conclusion is: "Some vampires are bloodthirsty creatures." This means "vampires" is the minor term and "bloodthirsty creatures" the major term.

So the possible valid arguments are any of these forms: AII—(1), AII—(3), IAI—(3), or IAI—(4). These distribute the middle term and violate none of our rules of the syllogism. So we can just pick one and set up our valid argument. If we pick AII—(1), our argument then is:

All M are bloodthirsty creatures.

Some vampires are M.

So, some vampires are bloodthirsty creatures.

Now all we have to do is make up an M and we are done. Let M = vampire bats. This means our valid argument is:

All vampire bats are bloodthirsty creatures.

<u>Some vampires are vampire bats.</u>

So, some vampires are bloodthirsty creatures.

A Historical Note

One of the more famous logicians in history is Lewis Carroll (alias Rev. C. L. Dodgson), author of *Alice in Wonderland* and the opening quote of this chapter. Most of his examples are imaginative and humorous. Some, however, are so offensive because of his anti-Semitism, that a 1977 edition to honor his work contained a note to the reader from the editor and publisher asking the reader to put such examples in their "historical setting." Never assume, even in what appears as straightforward and objective as syllogistic reasoning, that we should let down our guard.

Exercises

Part One

1. Test these three arguments (they are in standard form) for validity. Note any rules violated, if invalid.
   a. All marathon runners are people who like a challenge. Some marathon runners are alien life forms. Therefore, some people who like a challenge are alien life forms.
   b. Anyone who blows bubbles is a person who likes chewing gum. All babies are people who blow bubbles. So, all babies are people who like chewing gum.
   c. No football player is an astronaut. All football players are strong people. So, no astronaut is a strong person.

2. Put in standard form and then give mood and figure: Many cartoonists are zany people. All zany people are unpredictable. So, some cartoonists are unpredictable.

3. Test the argument in 2 for validity and, if invalid, note any rules violated.

4. Using the rules, decide if the following arguments are valid. Note any rules violated, if invalid:
   a. AEE—(3)
   b. EIO—(2)
   c. OIO—(1)
   d. AII—(4)

5. Using the rules, decide if the following arguments are valid. Note any rules violated, if invalid:
   a. AOA—(2)
   b. IAI—(3)
   c. AEA—(4)

6. Put the following in standard form and note the major, minor, and middle terms, then test for validity. If invalid, name all the rules violated:
   a. Whenever Bernie sees a rainbow, tears come to her eyes. Consequently, whenever Bernie sees a rainbow, she needs tissues. This is the case because all the times tears come to Bernie's eyes are times she needs tissues.
   b. No woman who likes dirt between her toes should garden barefoot. Every woman who likes dirt between her toes needs a pedicure. Therefore, most women who garden barefoot are people who need a pedicure.
   c. Rabid animals are dangerous. Anything dangerous should be avoided. That means we should avoid rabid animals.

7. Put the following in standard form and note the major, minor, and middle terms, then test for validity. If invalid, name all the rules violated:
   a. Most donuts are exquisite morsels. All donuts are greasy. So, some exquisite morsels are greasy.
   b. No vehicles capable of climbing Mount Hood are jeeps. Some vehicles capable of crossing creeks are jeeps. Therefore, some vehicles capable of crossing creeks are not capable of climbing Mount Hood.
   c. A lot of tomatoes taste like cardboard. All things that taste like cardboard are bad for your health. Therefore, some tomatoes are bad for your health.
   d. No puppy is unlovable. All puppies are furry. Therefore, no unlovable thing is furry.

8. Test for validity and name any rules broken if invalid:
   a. Every marshmallow is white. Most ghosts are white. Therefore, some ghosts are marshmallows.
   b. No gorilla is a desirable pet. All gorillas like to be touched. Therefore, some animals that like to be touched are not desirable pets.
   c. Most chimpanzees enjoy bananas. Some well-behaved animals are chimpanzees. Thus, many well-behaved animals are creatures that enjoy bananas.
   d. Lots of people like to go to the movies. Everyone who likes to go to the movies eats popcorn. Therefore, almost everyone eats popcorn.

9. Put the following argument in standard form and then test for validity:
   a. No bird is a lizard. Some lizards are not poisonous. Thus, some poisonous creatures are not birds.
   b. Most sandwiches are not spicy. Anything with mustard is spicy. Therefore, some sandwiches do not contain mustard.

c. All chocolate lovers are interesting people. Some interesting people are weight lifters. Therefore, all weight lifters are chocolate lovers.

10. Give an example of a syllogism that has an undistributed middle, but violates no other rule. Use "weight lifters" for the major term, "chefs" for the minor term, and "caffeine addicts" for the middle term.

11. Give an example of syllogisms in the following mood and figure:
a. AEE—(1)
b. EOE—(3)
c. AOA—(4)
d. AII—(2)

12. Give a VALID argument for the conclusion "Therefore, no bank robber is someone to trust." Show that your argument is valid.

13. Put in standard form and then test for validity using the rules:
Any man who can lift a refrigerator is a powerhouse.
All men who are powerhouses are sexy.
Thus, all sexy men can lift a refrigerator.

14. An example of an argument in AIO—(3) is (state one you make up):

15. Give an invalid argument with an illicit minor for the conclusion, "All music lovers are discriminating people." Show that it is invalid. (It's OK to violate other rules of the syllogism.)

16. Give an invalid argument with an illicit major for the conclusion: "No pizza is a lightweight snack." Show that it is invalid. (It's OK to violate other rules of the syllogism.)

17. Give a valid argument for the conclusion: "All mathematicians are careful thinkers." Show that it is valid.

18. Give an invalid argument that has an undistributed middle for the conclusion: "All vampires are fond of capes." (It's OK to violate other rules of the syllogism.)

19. Give an invalid argument that has an illicit major and violates rule 5 for the conclusion: "Some trout fishermen are not pranksters."

20. Give an example of a syllogism with mood and figure EIO—(4). Use the major term "daredevils" the minor term "economists," and the middle term "trumpet players."

21. Give an example of a syllogism with mood and figure EAE—(2) with the major term "paleontologists," the minor term "wrestlers," and the middle term "skinny people."

22. Give an example of a syllogism with mood and figure AOI—(3) with the major term "carrot lovers," the minor term "rabbit," and the middle term "vegetarians."

Part Two

1. Give a valid argument for the conclusion: "No vegetarian is a meat-eater." Show that it is valid.

2. Give an invalid argument that has an illicit major and an undistributed middle.

3. Why can't an argument with an A conclusion have an illicit major?

4. Give an example of an argument in mood and figure EOA—(3), with the major term "rodents," the minor term "pests," and the middle term "squirrels." Test your argument to see if it's valid.

5. Why can't a syllogism with an I conclusion have an illicit minor?

6. Why can't a syllogism with an E claim in either premise have an undistributed middle?

Venn Diagrams

An alternative approach to testing syllogisms for validity is to use Venn diagrams. These provide a handy way for us actually to see if the conclusion follows from the premises. We will start with categorical propositions and see how to express them using Venn diagrams. Then we can proceed to assessing arguments.

Basically, **Venn diagrams** are intersecting circles that are used to indicate the relationship between terms of propositions. We need as many intersecting circles as the number of terms we are dealing with. If we have two terms (e.g., the subject class and the predicate class), we need to use two intersecting circles. If we have three terms, then we need three intersecting circles. This will be the case when testing a syllogism—remember a syllogism has three terms (major, minor, and middle).

Universal Positive Claims.   The A claim "All A is B" asserts that every member of A is also in B (e.g., "All tigers are cats"). In terms of the Venn diagrams, this means the area outside the intersection of A and B is *empty*. We indicate this by shading it in (shaded = empty).

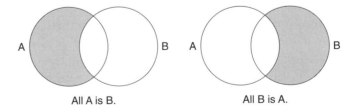

All A is B.   All B is A.

Universal Negative Claims.   With E claims (No P is Q), the diagram needs to indicate that there is no element in the first set that is also in the second. Since there's nothing in common between A and B, the intersection of the two will be empty (shaded).

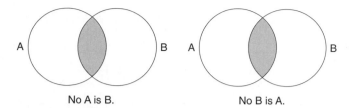

No A is B.   No B is A.

If nothing is in common between two sets, then their intersection will be empty so shade the entire intersection of the two sets in question. Be careful to shade nothing else.

Particular Positive Claims. The I claim "Some A is B," asserts that there's at least one member of A that is also in B (e.g., some cats are tigers). Because nothing is said about *all* members x of A, we cannot presume more than we know. Therefore, we cannot shade in any area like we do with universal claims. Use an X to indicate that at least one A is a B.

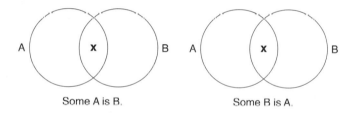

Some A is B.   Some B is A.

Remember: "Some" means "at least one." To indicate "at least one," we use an X to mark the spot. Because it is asserted that some members of the first set are in the second, we put an X in the intersection.

Particular Negative Claims. The O claim "Some A is not B" asserts that at least one member of A is not a member of B (e.g., some cats are not tigers). Here we also use an X to indicate that at least one A is not in B and thus lies outside the intersection.

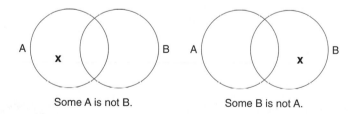

Some A is not B.   Some B is not A.

Remember: Because at least one member of the first set is not in the second, we put an X outside of the intersection.

Exercises

1. Express the following propositions using Venn diagrams:
   a. Some M is not P.
   b. All P is S.
   c. No M is S.
   d. Some M is P.
   e. All S is P.
   f. No P is M.
   g. Some P is S.
   h. Some P is not M.
   i. All P is M.
   j. No S is M.
   k. Some S is M.
   l. All M is P.

2. Express the following propositions using Venn diagrams (*Hint*: first write them in categorical form):
   a. Most cowboys like to nap.
   b. No animal trainer is scared of dogs.
   c. All computer technicians like puzzles.
   d. Some lion tamers are nervous people.
   e. Some rap artists are not conservative.
   f. All chefs are fond of banana bread.
   g. No janitor is a cynic.
   h. A few Italians do not like pasta.
   i. Many paramedics are fond of bingo.

Venn Diagrams: Handling Three Terms.   We're now ready to complicate our lives! Instead of using two intersecting circles (for the two terms), we will now use three circles (for three terms). In the four groupings that follow, we see the two universal claims (A and E) and the two particular claims (I and O) set out using Venn diagrams employing three terms.

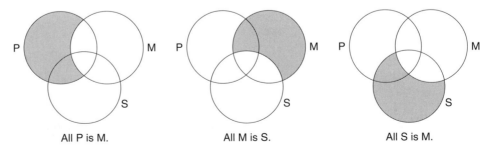

All P is M.   All M is S.   All S is M.

Note: If everything in one set is contained in another set, then the area outside their intersection will be empty (shaded in).

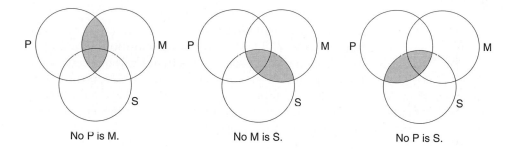

No P is M. No M is S. No P is S.

If nothing is in common between two sets, then their intersection will be empty (so shade the entire intersection of the two sets in question). Don't let the third circle confuse you.

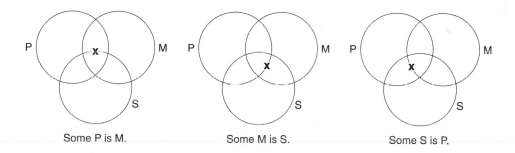

Some P is M. Some M is S. Some S is P.

If there is at least one element that is common to both sets, indicate this by marking an X in the intersection of the two. If we do not know whether the element is in the third set and that third set is not empty, then simply straddle it on the fence.

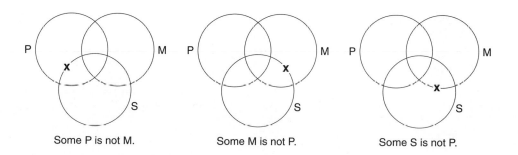

Some P is not M. Some M is not P. Some S is not P.

In all three cases, it is asserted that there is at least one element in the first set but not in the second one. So we have to mark that with an X outside of the intersection of the two sets. If we do not know where it lies in the big crescent, then it has to straddle the fence.

Venn Diagrams: Three Terms, Two Propositions.   The first thing to remember when you have three terms to deal with and, thus, two propositions to put up on the diagrams is this: *Always* do universal propositions first. Universal claims have a greater scope and, thus, they need to be placed first. If both propositions are universal, then take your pick—the order only matters if you have one universal and one particular claim. If you have two propositions of the same quantity (both universal or both particular), the order is irrelevant.

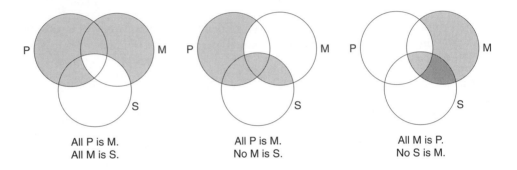

All P is M.   All P is M.   All M is P.
All M is S.   No M is S.   No S is M.

Remember, shaded areas are empty areas. So if *all* of one set is in another, leave the big area outside the intersection in the dark. If there's *nothing* in common between the two sets, then it is the shared area (the intersection) that is in the dark.

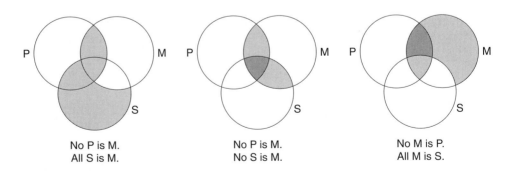

No P is M.   No P is M.   No M is P.
All S is M.   No S is M.   All M is S.

If nothing is in common between two sets, then their intersection will be empty so shade the entire intersection of the two sets in question. Be careful to shade nothing else. For the second premise, be careful to shade only what is empty and not to shade too much.

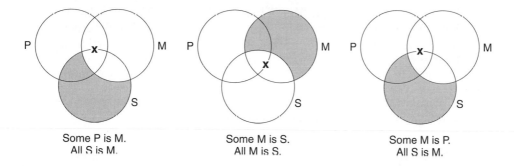

Some P is M.
All S is M.

Some M is S.
All M is S.

Some M is P.
All S is M.

Remember: Diagram universal claims first, shading in the big crescent area of the subject set that lies outside the intersection of the two sets.

For particular positive claims (I claims), X lies somewhere in the intersection of the two sets. The key is whether the X could be a member of the third set.

There are three possible placements here: The X could lie in the intersection with the third set, it could be only in the intersection area of the two sets that excludes the third set, or it could straddle the fence. If the third set is empty, however, the X cannot straddle the fence—leaving only the first two options open as to possible location of the X. If the X is in one set but not in the second one, then that means the X must be placed *outside* of the intersection of the two sets.

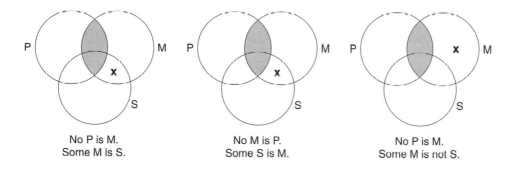

No P is M.
Some M is S.

No M is P.
Some S is M.

No P is M.
Some M is not S.

Always put up the universal claims first. Then turn to the particular claims. Be careful where you put the X. The only time it would *not* straddle the fence is when the fence is the border of a shaded (empty) area. *Remember:* an X cannot straddle the fence of an empty (shaded) area. The reason it is sitting on the fence in the first place is that it could be on either side. But if one side is *empty,* then nothing can possibly be there. So in the case of the Venn diagrams on the far right, first put up "No P is M." We then see that the X for "Some M is not S" cannot be on the fence between the intersection and the big crescent remaining in the P circle. That means the X has to lie in the area outside of S *and* outside P.

Using Venn Diagrams to Check Validity.   We are now ready to use Venn diagrams to determine whether the argument is valid.

> *First Step.* Identify the major, minor, and middle terms (*remember:* The major term is the predicate of the conclusion, the minor term is the subject of the conclusion, and the middle term only appears in the premises).
>
> *Second Step.* Put the argument in standard categorical form. This is as follows:

> Major premise (the premise containing the major term).
>
> Minor premise (the premise containing the minor term).
>
> Therefore, conclusion.

> *Third Step.* Set out the premises using Venn diagrams, remembering to put up universal claims before any particular claims.
>
> *Fourth Step.* See if you can read the conclusion without doing anything extra to the diagrams. It should be right there in front of your eyes—if not, the argument is *invalid.* In other words, the argument is *valid* only if the conclusion is expressed in the Venn diagrams of the two premises. If the conclusion can be read from the Venn diagrams of the two premises, → The argument is valid. If the conclusion cannot be read from the Venn diagrams of the two premises, → The argument is invalid.

If the conclusion cannot be read from the diagrams, the argument is invalid and, therefore, unsound. If you have to manipulate the diagrams to get the conclusion to appear, the argument fails.

> ***Example 1.*** AEE-2 (in categorical form):
>
> All P is M.
>
> No S is M.
>
> So, no S is P.

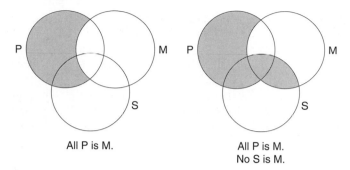

All P is M.

All P is M.
No S is M.

Since both premises are universal, start with either of them. The Venn diagram for "All P is M" is on the left. The Venn diagram for the universal claim "All P is M" and the minor premise "No S is M" is on the right. If the argument is valid, we should be able to read the conclusion right from the Venn diagram. Let's see if we can. The conclusion "No S is P" would require that the entire intersection of S and P be shaded in. As we can see, this *is* the case. Therefore, the argument is *valid*.

Example 2. AII-3. (in categorical form):

All M is P.

Some M is S.

So, some S is P.

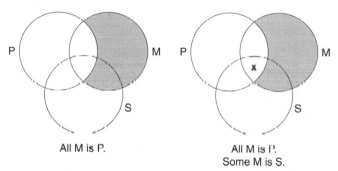

All M is P.

All M is P.
Some M is S.

Handle the universal claim first. If we put up "All M is P," the result is shown on the diagram on the left. Now let's put up "Some M is S." Because we cannot put an X straddling the fence of an area that is shaded, we only have the very center (the intersection of all three) where the X can be. This we see on the Venn diagram on the right (above). Both premises are now diagrammed. If the argument is valid, we should be able to read the conclusion. The conclusion "Some S is P" would require that the intersection of S and P have an X in it. As we can see, this *is* the case. Therefore, the argument is *valid*.

Exercises

1. Test for validity:
   a. AEA—(1)
   b. EIO—(2)
   c. AOO—(3)
   d. IEO—(4)
   e. AAA—(3)
   f. IAI—(4)

2. Put in standard form and then test with Venn diagrams:
   a. All hamburgers are greasy. All donuts are greasy. Therefore, all donuts are hamburgers.
   b. No hamburger is a vegetable. All vegetables are good for your health. Therefore, no hamburger is good for your health.
   c. All anthropologists eat hamburgers. Some anthropologists are lonely people. Therefore, some lonely people eat hamburgers.
   d. No carrots are purple. Some purple things are violets. Therefore, no violet is a carrot.
   e. Every gardener is a nature lover. All nature lovers enjoy yodeling. Therefore, all who yodel are gardeners.

3. Put in standard form and then test with Venn diagrams:
   a. Most rude people are tired. No tired person is happy. Therefore, no rude person is happy.
   b. All happy people get a good night's rest. A lot of nurses do not get a good night's rest. Therefore, many happy people are not nurses.
   c. No puppy is ugly. All puppies are furry. Therefore, no furry thing is ugly.
   d. Most wild dogs are in the forest. No creature in the forest is an African elephant. Therefore, no African elephants are wild dogs.

4. For extra practice, test the following using the rules and/or Venn diagrams:
   a. EOO—(1)
   b. AIO—(2)
   c. IAI—(3)
   d. AEA—(3)
   e. EIO—(2)
   f. AAA—(4)
   g. AEA—(1)

CHAPTER SIXTEEN

Patterns of Deductive Reasoning: Rules of Inference

When you have eliminated the impossible, whatever remains, however improbable, must be the truth.

—SHERLOCK HOLMES, from *The Sign of Four*

Y ou are driving to school when you hear a "thump, thump, thump" and it is much harder to steer the car. "Gad," you think "another flat tire." A man in a pickup drives up and stops to help you. "Hey, you gotta flat!" he points out. Further demonstrating his reasoning skills, he says, "If you don't have good tires, you get a flat. You have a flat, so you must not have had good tires on your car. In fact, I'd say you were taken for a sucker!"

Is this an example of good thinking on his part? If you said "No," pat yourself on the back and read on to learn the type of mistake he made. If you said, "Yes," you need help, so keep reading. Think of it: What can cause your tire to go flat? You could have old tread, you could have run over a nail, your tire could have been slashed, you could have hit a pothole, to name a few. Having a flat does *not* necessarily mean you have bad tires, you are a cheapskate or you got ripped off when you bought the tire. The existence of a flat tire does not, in itself, point to one potential cause. We need more information; we cannot eliminate possible causes in one wave of the arm.

There is a name for this fellow's faulty reasoning. We may remember it from Chapter 4; namely, the **fallacy of affirming the consequent.** We will examine this and other faulty reasoning in this chapter. Most of our attention, though, will be on **valid arguments** forms. In valid arguments the premises are sufficient support for the conclusion—if we assume the premises are all true, then the conclusion could not be false. For a review, see Chapter 6.

The most common valid argument forms have specific names and are included in the rules of inference (because they indicate what can be safely inferred from the premises). Knowing the correct forms will make it easier to use correct reasoning when constructing our own arguments.

Whereas rules of replacement focus on propositions, rules of inference focus on arguments. A familiarity with both the rules of replacement and rules of inference give us the tools to reformulate propositions and draw inferences. Once we learn the rules of inference, we can spot poorly reasoned arguments like that of the roadside helper and be able to construct well-reasoned, defensible arguments.

Advantages of Learning the Techniques of Logic

Some people question the value of these conventional ways of doing logic because it puts analytical tools above the experiential and emotional, and it requires a level of precision that requires us to be attentive to fine details.

With logic we can hone certain argumentative skills and techniques. Perfecting the techniques acquired through a study of logic can be enormously useful—and satisfying. Logic can be used as a tool for problem solving and analysis. Having a facility with logic gives us the techniques to examine and evaluate the many kinds of arguments we confront. This does not help us develop moral fiber, but it does help us develop *mental dexterity*. Being good at logic is only part of being good at critical thinking, but it is both useful and empowering. With that in mind, let's go deeper into the terrain of logic.

Valid Argument Forms

An argument is **valid** if the conclusion follows directly from the premises and could not be false if the premises were assumed true. This does not mean the premises have to be true! *Repeat:* A valid argument does *not* have to have true premises, even if that seems like a bunch of hooey. But it does mean that, if we assume they were true, the conclusion would necessarily be true as well.

The propositions making up the argument could be *entirely false* and yet the argument is valid. This is because the *focus in validity is on the form itself*, not the substance of the claims. For example, this is a valid argument: "All sheep can fly like a bird. Anything that can fly like a bird has wings. Therefore, all sheep have wings." However, preposterous this sounds; the conclusion could not be false if the two premises were true.

Studying validity is like examining x-rays, in that the focus is the structure of the argument. If there are problems with the structure (the bones) then the argument won't be able to stand on its own two feet.

The rules of inference function like patterns of good reasoning: Anything that fits the pattern, regardless of the subject matter, is a valid argument. We can assess the validity of a deductive argument by examining the structure of the argument. Nothing else is necessary at this stage.

▦ Rules of Inference

You are changing the tire when a woman comes by, walking her dog. She offers *her* argument: "If the tire only has a nail in it, then it can be repaired. Oh, look, that is just a nail. Good—your tire can be repaired." What do you think of *her* reasoning?

Her argument is a valid one, because *if* we assume the two premises are true, then she is right to suggest the tire can be repaired. Her reasoning is, therefore, correct. That does not mean the argument is sound, unless we know the premises are actually true. *Remember:* a sound argument is a valid argument that has true premises. That is, soundness goes one step beyond validity—it requires truth, as well as a good, solid structure.

If you just have a nail in your tire, she is probably right to say the tire can be fixed—though this is not certain. Your tire may be destined for the recycling bin. However, the woman has proven that she can construct a valid argument. The name of her argument is called *modus ponens*. **Modus ponens** is a valid argument form that argues: "If this then that. This; therefore, that."

Modus Ponens

The term "modus ponens" is Latin for *mode that affirms*. Given a conditional claim (if *this* then *that*), if we can affirm that *this* is true, then *that* must be true as well.

Form of Modus Ponens

If A then B.

A is true.

Therefore, B is true as well.

The first premise is a conditional claim. The second premise affirms that the antecedent happened. The conclusion then is that the consequent must also have happened. So, whether the antecedent is positive or negative, it gets repeated in the second premise.

Examples

If that's an alligator, you better get out of the swamp.

That is an alligator.

So, you better get out of the swamp.

If you've got the room cleaned and you have no homework, *then* we can either go to a movie or try out the skates I found in the shed.

You've got the room cleaned and you have no homework.

So, we can either go to a movie or try out the skates I found in the shed.

Note: In this last case, the antecedent was compound (a conjunction, A and B) and, therefore, the second premise has to repeat the entire conjunction. Note also that the consequent is compound (a disjunction, A or B). Nevertheless, the form of the argument is still modus ponens.

Modus Tollens

Our next valid argument form is called **modus tollens.** The term "modus tollens" is Latin for *mode that denies.* The first premise is a conditional claim. The second premise denies the consequent by saying it did not happen. The conclusion is then that the antecedent could not have happened either.

Here we introduce opposites. That is, where modus ponens just repeats the antecedent in the second premise, in modus tollens the second premise is the opposite of the consequent. The form it takes is this: "If this then that. Not that, therefore, not this."

For example, a police officer stopped to see how you were doing with your flat tire. He says, "If you cannot get the car lifted, then your jack is no good. Your jack looks good, so you'll be able to get the car lifted." Do you see what the officer did in his argument? Look at the first premise and then look at the second. What shifted? The consequent from the first premise ("Your jack is no good") has been changed to its opposite and is now the second premise ("Your jack looks good"). What follows then is the negated antecedent (so, you *can* get the car lifted). This is a strong argument. It is called modus tollens.

Form of Modus Tollens

If A then B.

B is not the case.

Therefore, A is not the case either.

Examples

If Michigan State does not beat North Carolina, then they'll have a shot at the championship.

Michigan State has a shot at the championship.

Therefore, they beat North Carolina.

Only if we put air in the tires, can we make it to Sacramento.

We did not put air in the tires.

Therefore, we did not make it to Sacramento.

Note: The "only if" claim can be rewritten: "If we make it to Sacramento, then we put air in the tires." The second premise denies the consequent and allows the conclusion (the denial of the antecedent) to pop out according to modus tollens.

Hypothetical Syllogism

The valid argument form of **hypothetical syllogism** sets out a chain of conditional claims: If *this* then *that*, if *that* then *such-and-such*. Therefore, if *this* then *such-and-such*." The chain is this: The first term leads to a second term, the second to a third; so the first must lead to the third. It's like cutting out the middleman and going direct from the first to the third.

Suppose you are at home (your tire fixed!) and the phone rings. It is your mother, who has been calling all morning. She is relieved you are OK and says, "If you have another flat tire, then call me. If you call me, then I won't worry. So, if you have another flat tire, I won't worry." Your mother may be a worrywart, but her reasoning is valid. The name of her argument is called the hypothetical syllogism. As you can see, it is composed entirely of conditional (hypothetical) claims.

Form of the Hypothetical Syllogism

If A then B.

If B then C.

Therefore, if A then C.

It is crucial that the linking term, B, connecting A and C together be the consequent of the first premise and the antecedent of the second one. Otherwise there's a break in the chain and the argument will be invalid.

Example 1

If that's a cockroach in the kitchen, then either call an exterminator or set out poison.

If we either call an exterminator or set out poison, then we can solve the problem.

Therefore, if that's a cockroach in the kitchen, then we can solve the problem.

Note: You can see that this example of a hypothetical syllogism involves a *compound term* (the consequent in the first premise is the antecedent in the second premise). The superstructure, however, is still in the form of a hypothetical syllogism and, thus, it's still as valid as if it had been less complex.

Example 2

Unless he studies hard, Danny will have trouble with the GRE exam.

If he has trouble with the GRE exam, then Danny may not get into Ohio State.

Therefore, unless he studies hard, Danny may not get into Ohio State.

Note: The first sentence has an "unless"—this is the same as an "If not." So "unless he studies hard" means "If he does not study hard." We can, thus, treat this as a conditional claim.

Exercises

Part One

1. Using *modus tollens,* finish the argument that starts with: "If he can clone the mouse embryo, Dr. White will file for a patent."

2. Using *hypothetical syllogism,* finish the argument that starts with: "If Dr. White clones the mouse, he'll clone a small mammal."

3. Using *modus ponens* finish the argument that starts with: "If there's pink fluid under the car, it may be wise to check the transmission."

4. Using *hypothetical syllogism,* finish the argument that starts with: "If she gets another x-ray, she'll glow in the dark."

5. Using *modus tollens* finish each of the following arguments that start with:
   a. If Jason uses an earpiece with his cell phone, he'll be a better driver.
   b. If Anthea hears screaming from the attic, she'll think there's a poltergeist.
   c. If there are poltergeists in the house and they're causing trouble, Bruce will hold a séance.
   d. If Ryan hears about the séance, he will study his book on Egyptology.

6. Using *modus ponens* finish each of the following arguments that start with:
   a. If the mouse embryo is cloned, then the lab experiment worked.
   b. If the lab experiments work, then people will want to clone their pets.
   c. If people clone their pets, they will want to try cloning either their children or themselves.
   d. If people clone themselves and are happy with the results, they will rethink their views of death.

7. Using *hypothetical syllogism* finish the following arguments that start with:
   a. If Silvio gets a speeding ticket, he'll go to traffic school.
   b. If we drive out the poltergeists, we can sell the story to *E-Extra!*
   c. If the pink ooze in the sewer system is not transmission fluid, the police have a problem.
   d. If the Curse of the Bambino is lifted from Boston Red Sox, they could win for years to come.

Part Two

Directions: Name the argument forms in the following statements. Each statement involves one of the following forms: modus ponens, modus tollens, or hypothetical syllogism.

1. If it keeps snowing, the skiing will be great. The skiing was not great, so it didn't keep snowing.

2. If the sun stays out, the snow will melt and the slopes will be muddy. If the snow melts and the slopes are muddy, then we can't ski. Therefore, if the sun stays out, then we can't ski.

3. If Chris Rock runs for public office, he'll get a lot of votes. Chris Rock did not get a lot of votes, so he must not have run for public office.

4. If we play Stevie Nicks albums all night, then we won't finish our homework. We finished our homework. Therefore, we did not play Stevie Nicks albums all night.

5. If you are not consistent, then you can't train a puppy. I see your puppy is trained, so you must have been consistent.

6. If neither the police nor the fire truck arrives, we may wish we picked somewhere else to live. Neither the police nor the fire truck arrived. So we may wish we picked somewhere else to live.

7. If the police helicopter lands in the yard, Virginia's vegetable garden will be flattened. If her vegetable garden is flattened, she will sue the city. So if the police helicopter lands in the yard, Virginia will sue the city.

8. If the part-time job works out and you finally get some money coming in, then we can plan a weekend getaway to the desert. The part-time job worked out and you finally got money coming in, so we can plan a weekend getaway to the desert.

9. If Sandie keeps lying in the sun, she'll get burned. Sandie did not get burned. We can conclude that Sandie did not keep lying in the sun.

10. If Steve gets everyone in the car by 3 A.M., they should be able to get to Winslow, Arizona, by evening. If they get to Winslow, Arizona, by evening, they can make it to Tulsa by Thursday afternoon. So, if Steve gets everyone in the car by 3 A.M., they can make it to Tulsa by Thursday afternoon.

Disjunctive Syllogism

There is nothing like a **disjunctive syllogism**. In this valid argument form, we start with a **disjunction** (an "either/or" claim) and then the second premise is a denial of one of the disjuncts. This forces the conclusion to be the remaining disjunct. Basically it is like this: "This or that. Not this, therefore that." You have a choice between two options and one choice is eliminated—leaving you with the other choice.

For example, your brother finds something weird on his plate. He picks it up and turns it over and over. He finally says, "Either this is someone's false eyelashes or they got some of the cowhide in the hamburger. This is not false eyelashes, so there's cowhide in the hamburger." Your brother shows his potential as a logician and you feel downright smug in telling him that his valid argument is called the disjunctive syllogism.

Form of the Disjunctive Syllogism

Either A or B.

A is not the case   (or B is not the case).

Therefore, B is the case   (or A is the case).

The first premise is a choice between two options. The second premise eliminates one of the options. That leaves us with the conclusion that the remaining option must then be the case. Let's look at some examples of disjunctive syllogism.

Examples

Either a wolf is howling or the wind is in the trees.

There's no wind tonight.

Therefore, it must be a wolf howling.

Either Tim and Rita sort out their relationship or they are in for more conflict.

Tim and Rita are not in for more conflict.

So, they sorted out their relationship.

Note: The first premise has a compound first disjunct. The superstructure is still a disjunctive syllogism, so proceed in the same way as with the simpler cases.

Conjunction

This valid argument form is very straightforward: Two claims that are each true are true in combination—*this* is true, *that* is true and so "*this and that*" are true together. The rule of **conjunction** asserts that if we have two claims that we know to be true, then they are both true together.

Form of Conjunction

A is true.

B is also true.

Therefore, both A and B are true.

Examples

Omar was happy to see Lamu again when he went to Kenya.

He was sorry he didn't make it to Nairobi.

Therefore, Omar was happy to see Lamu again when he went to Kenya, but he was sorry he didn't make it to Nairobi.

A good book deserves two readings.

Molloy is a good book.

Therefore, a good book deserves two readings and *Molloy* is a good book.

Simplification

Another valid form of argument starts with two things given together in conjunction. If both together are true, then it follows that each proposition is individually true. This is called **simplification.** Here's how it goes: Both *this* and *that* are true. Therefore, *this* is true and *that* is true.

For example, if someone said that both the Democrats and the Republicans have a plan for an improved health care system, then it would follow that the Democrats have a plan for an improved health care system. It also follows that the Republicans have a plan.

Form of Simplification

A and B are true together.

Therefore, A is true as well (or B is also true).

In other words, knowing that the collective, A and B, is true, it follows that each conjunct individually is true as well.

Examples

The reviewer liked both *Shaun of the Dead* and *Sideways*.

Therefore, the reviewer liked *Shaun of the Dead*. [Or: The reviewer liked *Sideways*.]

Neither skunks nor raccoons are easy to have as pets.

Therefore, skunks are not easy to have as pets. [Or: Raccoons are not easy to have as pets.]

Note: Remember from DeMorgan's laws that you can change the "neither/nor" claim to "Skunks are not easy to have as pets and raccoons are not easy to have as pets."

Logical Addition

Our next rule of inference has a name that seems counterintuitive. It is called **logical addition.** This valid argument form asserts that if we know any one proposition is true, then a disjunction made up of this true proposition and any other proposition is necessarily true as well. The form it takes is: "A is true. Therefore A or any other proposition is also true." If *this* is true, then the disjunction "*This* and *that*" is forced to be true—no matter what "*that*" is.

The name "logical addition" is a bit misleading, because the addition here occurs by use of an "or" not an "and."

Form of Logical Addition

A is true.

Therefore, either A or B is true.

In this valid argument form, you can infer from anything that is true to a disjunction consisting of the true claim and any other proposition. Let's see some examples of logical addition.

Examples

<u>The basement flooded after the rain.</u>

Therefore, either the basement flooded after the rain or I had a nightmare last night.

<u>Seaweed contains a lot of minerals and is good for your health.</u>

Therefore, either seaweed has a lot of minerals in it and is good for your health, or that nutrition book I read gave the wrong information.

Note: Did you see how this example has a *compound* first premise? We can still apply the rule of logical addition.

Exercises

Part One

Directions: Complete the arguments using the rule indicated.

1. Using *logical addition:* "Skydiving is never boring."
2. Using *simplification:* "Both Batman and Spider-man wear snug-fitting clothing."
3. Using *disjunctive syllogism:* "Either I heard a coyote or that's the neighbor's shepherd pup."
4. Using *hypothetical syllogism:* "If you go barefoot, people will stare at you."
5. Using *conjunction:* "Jasper enjoys peas any time of the day. Jasper won't eat spaghetti."
6. Using *modus tollens:* "If Tony smells a rat, the game is up."
7. Using *logical addition:* "Canned fruit tastes slimy."
8. Using *simplification:* "A good pie is warm and has ice cream on top."
9. Using *logical addition:* "The Boston marathon is not for the weak-willed."
10. Using *conjunction:* "The fire jumped the freeway. The houses and cars were in danger."
11. Using *modus ponens:* "If you take up martial arts, you'll need comfortable clothing."
12. Using *simplification:* "April does not like small rodents and she doesn't care much for large rodents either."

Part Two

Directions: Name the following rules used in the arguments below.

1. If you are an art lover, then you will enjoy pottery. If you enjoy pottery, then you'll love the Zuni pots at the Southwest Museum. Therefore, if you are an art lover, then you'll love the Zuni pots at the Southwest Museum.

2. If you do not enjoy race car driving, then you are not a daredevil. Jackie Chan is a daredevil. Therefore, he may enjoy race car driving.

3. Ed did not take the chihuahuas out for a walk. Jack did not play flamenco music. Therefore, Ed did not take the chihuahuas out for a walk and Jack did not play flamenco music.

4. If we want to see a classic film, we will watch *Wings of Desire*. Bruno wanted to see a classic film, so he'll watch *Wings of Desire*.

5. Carla didn't think *Paulie* was as good as *Babe*. Therefore, either my memory is shot or Carla didn't think *Paulie* was as good as *Babe*.

6. Either Frank will watch *Without a Trace* or he'll read Plato. Frank didn't read Plato. Therefore, he watched *Without a Trace*.

7. Will went to see *Blood Curdling Screams* and he sat in front of a girl who kicked the back of his seat. Therefore Will sat in front of a girl who kicked the back of his seat.

8. If Lyndsay eats too much popcorn, she'll feel sick and won't enjoy the movie. Lyndsay ate too much popcorn. So she felt sick and didn't enjoy the movie.

9. Either we'll see *Shawshank Redemption* for the hundredth time or we'll see *The Eye*. We didn't see *Shawshank Redemption* for the hundredth time, so we saw *The Eye*.

10. *The Vanishing* was an awfully creepy movie. Therefore, either *The Vanishing* was an awfully creepy movie or I'm just squeamish.

11. If you don't like to be scared, don't see *Night of the Living Dead*. If you don't see *Night of the Living Dead*, you might as well forget about watching *28 Days Later*. Therefore, if you don't like to be scared, you might as well forget about watching *28 Days Later*.

12. Provided that he enjoys animation and stories about heroes, Amman will like *The Incredibles*. Amman enjoys animation and stories about heroes, so he liked *The Incredibles*.

Constructive Dilemma

In ancient Greece, they used to talk about being stuck on the horns of a *dilemma*. This means being faced with two choices where each choice has serious consequences; yet you have to pick. So you choose one and then have to deal with the set of consequences that follow. The **constructive dilemma** is a valid argument that starts with two conditional propositions and one or the other antecedent is true. Consequently, either one or the other of the two consequents must also be true. Think of it as a choice between two options, where each option leads to some consequences. Either you'll pick the first choice or the second. So either you'll have to deal with the first set of consequences or the second set.

For example, what if your best friend said, "I'm in love"? You ask him what he is going to do and he says: "If I tell my parents, they'll want me to get married, but if I don't tell them, then our relationship will really suffer." Either he's going to tell his folks, or he's not. So either of the two consequences will then follow.

Form of Constructive Dilemma

If A then B, and if C then D.

Either A or C.

Therefore, either B or D.

If you look closely at the constructive dilemma, you will see it is like a compound modus ponens, which we can see by stretching it out:

	If A then B	and	if C then D
	A	or	C
Therefore,	B	or	D

The second premise is a disjunction of the two antecedents from the first premise, and the conclusion is a disjunction of the two consequents.

Examples

If the computer crashes again, Irasema will have to reinstall the software; but if the computer quits crashing, Irasema will be able to finish her assignment for bioethics.

Either the computer crashed or it quit crashing.

So, either Irasema will have to reinstall the software or she'll be able to finish her assignment for bioethics.

If the band goes by bus, the concert may have to be delayed, but if the band takes the plane, the profits will be small.

Either the band will go by bus or they'll take a plane.

So either the concert may be delayed or the profits will be small.

Destructive Dilemma

There is another dilemma besides the constructive dilemma. It is called the **destructive dilemma.** Here we start with two conditional claims and we are told that either the first consequent is not true or the second consequent is not true. We can then conclude that either the first antecedent is not true or the second antecedent is not true. *Think of it* as a choice between two options, each leading to a set of consequences. Either you don't have to deal with one set of consequences or you don't have to deal with the other. So either you did not choose the first option or you did not choose the second option.

Destructive dilemma is like a compound modus tollens. Here's an example: "If you study math, it'll help you with the sciences but if you study literature, you'll be strong in the humanities. Either you are not going to be helped in the sciences or you won't be strong in the humanities. Therefore, either you didn't study math or you didn't study literature."

Form of the Destructive Dilemma

If A then B, and if C then D.

Either B is not the case or D is not the case.

Therefore, either A is not the case or C is not the case.

Examples

If the lotus flowers are in bloom, the crowds will come to Silver Lake, but if the flowers haven't yet opened, it'll be easy to find parking.

Either the crowds haven't come to Silver Lake or it won't be easy to find parking.

So, either the lotus flowers are not in bloom or the flowers have opened.

If Lisa takes accounting, she'll get promoted, but if she doesn't work overtime, she can spend more time with Charlie.

Either Lisa did not get promoted or she can't spend more time with Charlie.

So, either Lisa did not take accounting or she did not work overtime.

Absorption

With the rule of absorption we start with a conditional claim. We then infer that the antecedent can be repeated in the consequent. The form of absorption is: "If *this* then *that*; therefore, if *this* then *this* and *that*." Absorption allows us to repeat the antecedent by putting it in conjunction with the consequent.

Start with a conditional claim, such as "If it rains, the roads will be muddy." We can then infer, "If it rains, then it rains and the roads will be muddy." The antecedent gets absorbed (think *repeated*) into the consequent when you replace the consequent with the conjunction of the antecedent and the consequent.

Form of the Rule of Absorption

If A then B.

Therefore, if A, then both A and B.

Do you see how this goes? It may look like mere repetition, but it can be particularly handy for certain situations. Think of it like a Phillips head screwdriver: you don't need it very often, but when you do nothing else works nearly as well.

Examples

If the Pistons go to the play-offs, their fans will go nuts.

Therefore, if the Pistons go to the play-offs, then the Pistons go to the play-offs and their fans will go nuts.

Note: The entire antecedent had to move back to the consequent. Whatever the antecedent is—simple or compound—the whole thing has to get absorbed into (placed in conjunction with) the consequent.

If we can make it to a Vancouver Canucks game, then we won't go to the museum.

Therefore, if we can make it to a Vancouver Canucks game, then we can make it to a Vancouver Canucks game and won't go to the museum.

Exercises

Directions: Drawing from the constructive dilemma, the destructive dilemma, and absorption, name the rule of inference in the following:

1. If the hurricane moves up from Florida, Paula and Ted will hit the road. Therefore, if the hurricane moves up from Florida, then the hurricane moved up from Florida and Paula and Ted will hit the road.

2. If Lisa drives the Jeep, Charlie will have to take the bus. Subsequently, if Lisa drives the jeep, then she'll drive the jeep and Charlie will have to take the bus.

3. Either the billboard got blown away during the tornado, or someone removed it overnight. If the billboard got blown away during the tornado, then we'll have a view of the lake, but if someone removed it overnight, then they must be planning construction on the new lot. Therefore, either we'll have a view of the lake or they must be planning construction on the new lot.

4. If the lightning hits the trees, there could be a fire. If the lightning misses the trees, then it could strike one of the cows. Either there was not a fire or none of the cows got struck by lightning, therefore either the lightning did not hit the trees or the lightning did not miss the trees.

5. If Choug drives through the night, she'll get out of the storm. Therefore, if Choug drives through the night, then she drove through the night and got out of the storm.

6. If the lightning hits the jeep, it could melt the steering wheel; but if it misses the jeep, Lisa won't have to worry about getting a new car. Either the steering wheel was not melted or Lisa did have to worry about getting a new car. Therefore, either the lightning did not hit the jeep or it did not miss it.

7. Either the weather report is wrong or the storm is going to strike. If the weather report is wrong, then Jamal and Sam can make it to the Star Trek conference. If the storm strikes, they'll have to stay home. Therefore, either Jamal and Sam made it to the Star Trek conference or they'll have to stay home.

8. If the rain doesn't stop, the roads will be flooded, but if the rain stops, we can drive to Moose Jaw. Either the rain didn't stop or it did. Therefore either the roads will be flooded or we can drive to Moose Jaw.

9. If Laura gets back from Saskatoon, then Darin will be happy. Therefore, if Laura gets back from Saskatoon then she got back from Saksatoon and Darin is happy.

10. If the storm blows the roof off the garage, Nick's new VW convertible will get drenched; but if the storm moves on to the East, Nick can relax. Either the storm blew the roof off the garage or the storm moved on to the East. Therefore, either Nick's new VW convertible got drenched or Nick could relax.

Reminder on Validity and Soundness

All the **rules of inference** are valid argument forms. That means any argument in any of these forms is *valid*. So if we assume the premises are true, the conclusion would be forced to be true as well. The conclusion can't be false whenever a valid argument has true premises.

Be aware though, that in a valid argument the evidence fully supports the conclusion. So, if we *assume* the premises to be true in any of these rules of inference, then the conclusion will follow as true. *But it doesn't mean the premises are necessarily true.* That's another issue altogether. To be *sound* the argument must be valid, but it must also have true premises. Don't confuse validity and soundness—soundness is more stringent in its requirements.

We want also to have our antennae out for the formal fallacies, so we don't accidentally mistake a fallacy for either modus ponens or modus tollens, both valid argument forms.

▓ Formal Fallacies

Fallacies are always invalid arguments, whether or not they have true premises. They are incorrect forms of reasoning, no matter how persuasive they may be. People are regularly persuaded by bad reasoning—but that doesn't change the fact that the reasoning is still bad. Our task is to spot that bad reasoning and cut it off at its knees, so to speak!

There are two key formal fallacies. They are called **formal fallacies** because the error is with a misuse of form, or structure. Even if the premises were true, the conclusion would not follow as true because of the structural problems. These two fallacies are, basically, mutations of modus ponens and modus tollens. But where both modus ponens and modus tollens are valid argument forms, the two formal fallacies are both invalid and unsound. The two major formal fallacies are the fallacy of denying the antecedent and the fallacy of affirming the consequent.

Valid Argument Forms versus Formal Fallacies

We know that two famous valid argument forms are *modus ponens* and *modus tollens,* as set out below:

Modus ponens—A *valid* argument form (*not* a fallacy)

If A then B.

A is true.

So, B is true.

Example

If the peach pie has ice cream on it, Ginny Lou will be pleased.

The peach pie did have ice cream on it.

So, Ginny Lou was pleased.

Modus Tollens—A *valid* argument form (*not* a fallacy)

If A then B.

B is not the case.

So, A is not case.

Example

If the shark chomps off part of Ray's new surfboard, he won't be very happy.

Ray is happy.

Therefore, the shark did not chomp off part of Ray's new surfboard.

Note: If the two premises are true, the conclusion has to be true as well—it couldn't be false. This makes the argument valid.

If we see that an argument fits either of the valid argument patterns above, we can relax. However, that may not happen. Instead, we may be staring at a fallacy. Our job is to examine the form of the argument to make that determination.

Fallacy of Denying the Antecedent

The **fallacy of denying the antecedent** asserts a causal relationship between the antecedent condition (A) and the consequent (B). The fallacy occurs when the person claims that, because the antecedent doesn't happen, the consequent can't happen either. However, there may be many things that cause the consequent to happen.

The conclusion does not automatically follow if the premises are true—unless a one-to-one ("if and only if") connection between the antecedent cause A, and the effect B is given. The fact that one possible cause does not occur does not preclude some other factor causing the effect.

For example, "If the bank robber is hiding in the college mailroom, then we had better call the FBI." This fallacy occurs when it is argued, "The bank robber is not hiding in the college mailroom; therefore, we don't need to call the FBI." The reason this is fallacious is that, even if there is not a bank robber in the college mailroom, we may still need to contact the FBI. We might, for instance, realize that, instead of the bank robber, three agents from the old KGB are camped out in the woodshed, plotting the overthrow of the Uzbekistan government. Or perhaps an escapee from the nearest prison is lurking in the backyard. Or it may be that we've found evidence of an e-mail scam targeting people on welfare. Simply because there's no bank robber in the college mailroom doesn't mean the consequent ("We had better call the FBI") is not the case.

Form of the Fallacy of Denying the Antecedent

If A then B.

<u>A is not the case.</u>

Therefore, B is not the case.

Note: A and B could be either positive or negative claims, and they could be compound propositions as well.

Examples

If another snail crawls under the door, I'm pouring salt around the house.

<u>Another snail did not crawl under the door.</u>

So I didn't pour salt around the house.

Note: I might pour salt simply as a preventative measure or to cut down on the number of slugs and mealy bugs crawling up to the door.

- If Wimpy jogs around the block, then he'll get in shape. Wimpy didn't jog around the block, so he didn't get in shape. → There are many ways to work out; jogging is but one of them.

- If George chases that skunk, he may be very sorry. George did not chase the skunk, so he was not sorry. → George could be sorry for other reasons, such as losing his wallet.

Fallacy of Affirming the Consequent

This **fallacy of affirming the consequent** is faulty reasoning that takes the form: "If A then B. B is true (the consequent happens) and, therefore, A is true (the antecedent happens also)." As with the fallacy of denying the antecedent, having a causal connection does not make it a one-to-one ("if and only if") connection. That must be specified. If it is not stated (if A then B *and* if B then A), then the fact that B is true does not mean that A has to be true as well. There could be a number of causal factors independently causing an event.

For example, suppose someone said to you, "If the coyotes get in the backyard, the primroses will be crushed. The primroses were crushed. Therefore, there must have been coyotes in the back yard." What's wrong with this reasoning? Well, coyotes aren't the only things that can crush primroses. For example, dogs could have run through, or the maintenance men could have stomped on the primroses when they were fixing the fence in the back, and so forth.

Form of the Fallacy of Affirming the Consequent

If A then B.

B is the case.

Therefore, A is the case as well.

Note: A and B could be either positive or negative claims and either or both could be compound propositions.

Examples

If the road is muddy, it will be hard to go hiking.

It was hard to go hiking.

Therefore the road was muddy.

Note: Many factors make it difficult to hike; muddy roads are only one.

If the driver in the blue Cadillac sneaks into the carpool lane, she will get a ticket.

The driver in the blue Cadillac got a ticket.

So she must have sneaked into the carpool lane.

Note: She could have gotten a ticket for speeding, for drunk driving, or something else besides sneaking into the carpool lane.

More Examples

If Big Mike gets stuck in the mud, he'll be late to the party. Big Mike was late to the party, so he must have gotten stuck in the mud. → Big Mike could have been late because he stopped at the bank or because he took a nap.

Exercises

Directions: Name the formal fallacy or valid argument (either modus ponens or modus tollens) below:

1. If Ray doesn't study logic, he'll go to the gym. Ray didn't study logic, so he must be at the gym.

2. If Max gets another Loreena McKennitt album, we will get a new speaker system. We got a new speaker, so Max must have gotten another Loreena McKennitt record.

3. If Ray becomes an aerobics instructor, he won't have time to study logic. Ray didn't become an aerobics instructor, so he must have time to study logic.

4. If Pinky feels better, he can go home and take his dog Blue for a walk. Pinky did not go home or take his dog Blue for a walk, so he must not feel better.

5. If Shannon doesn't make it to dinner, then she'll just eat takeout as she drives. Shannon made it to dinner, so she won't have to eat takeout as she drives.

6. If Amelia decides to go to law school, then she will have to take the LSAT. Amelia did not take the LSAT. Therefore, she didn't decide to go to law school.

7. If the virus comes in as an attachment and you open it, all heck will break loose. I'm glad to hear you did not open the attachment with the Melissa virus in it. Therefore, you don't have to worry about heck breaking loose on your computer!

8. If the worm gets into Mark's address book, he'll need to get an antivirus program. The worm got into Mark's address book, so he'll need to get an antivirus program.

9. If you burn the potatoes and cremate the onions, the frittata won't be very tasty. Alice did not both burn the potatoes and cremate the onions, so she must have made a tasty frittata.

10. If the virus infects your e-mail system, you might as well erase your hard disk and start over. A virus infected Mark's e-mail program. As a result, he might as well erase his hard disk and start over.

11. If a cook lacks the right ingredients, he won't be able to make a good soufflé. Claude wasn't able to make a good soufflé, so he must not have had the right ingredients.

12. If Max keeps practicing his Chinese drums, he will drive Maria crazy. Max did not keep practicing his Chinese drums. So he did not drive Maria crazy.

Overview

At this point, we've covered a lot of territory in terms of the valid argument forms and the two formal fallacies. The following table is a summary of the area we've covered.

Rules of Inference—Valid Argument Forms

Modus ponens	If A then B. A. Therefore B.
Modus tollens	If A then B. Not B. Therefore not A.
Hypothetical syllogism	If A then B. If B then C. Therefore, if A then C.
Disjunctive syllogism	Either A or B. Not A. Therefore, B.
Constructive dilemma	If A then B, and, if C then D. Either A or C. Thus, either B or D.
Destructive dilemma	If A then B, and, if C then D. Either not B or not D. Therefore, either not A or not C.
Simplification	A and B. Therefore, A. (Or: Therefore, B.)
Logical addition	A. Therefore, either A or B.
Conjunction	A. B. Therefore, A and B.
Absorption	If A then B. Therefore, If A, then (both A and B).

RULES OF REPLACEMENT

DeMorgan's Laws

Not both	Not both A and B ≡ Not A or not B.
Neither/nor	Neither A nor B ≡ Not A and not B.
Material implication	"If A then B" is equivalent to "Either not A or B."
Transposition	"If A then B" is equivalent to "If not B then not A."
Exportation	"If (A and B) then C" is equivalent to "If A then, (if B then C)."
Equivalence	"A if and only if B" is equivalent to "If A then B, and if B then A."

FORMAL FALLACIES

Fallacy of affirming the consequent	If A then B. B. Therefore, A.
Fallacy of denying the antecedent	If A then B. Not A. Therefore, not B.

Exercises

Part One

Directions: Using the rule indicated complete the argument or give an equivalent sentence.

1. *Destructive dilemma:* If truth is stranger than fiction, then they'll want to hear the truth, whereas if art imitates life, then they will have stories to tell.

2. *Material implication:* Either Julie told the truth or she deceived her friend.

3. *Modus tollens:* If he doesn't get an Austin Mini, then Scott will buy an Audi.

4. *Logical addition:* A marathon runner leaped over the car.

5. *Exportation:* If the slugs get on the lilies and eat the leaves, Ruben will not be happy.

6. *Absorption:* If Ruben is happy, then his lilies must be OK.

7. *Hypothetical syllogism:* If Carla serves chili, Jamal will bring chips and salsa.

8. *Material implication:* If the band needs a sound engineer, they will call Trent.

9. *Transposition:* If Ed's fever does not break, he will go to the doctor.

10. *DeMorgan's laws:*
    a. Neither opera nor jazz comforts a bluegrass lover.
    b. David is not guilty of both eating the tamales and gobbling up the flan.

11. *Conjunction:* Pulling weeds is good for stress. Nothing beats getting rid of deadwood.

12. *Constructive dilemma:* If they have a long talk, things will improve; but if they refuse to speak, we better put on some soul music.

13. *Simplification:* Omar enjoys discussing politics and is a serious Lakers fan.

14. *Modus ponens:* If the rumors spread, there will be trouble.

15. *Constructive dilemma:* If the Jazz lose again, Jerry will throw a fit, but if they win, then Jerry will have to make good on his bet.

16. *Hypothetical syllogism:* If the Pistons win, then Anna will gloat.

17. *Disjunctive syllogism:* Either Madeleine is from Topeka or she's from Boulder.

18. *Absorption:* If that's a Harvard woman, then ask her about the Peabody Museum.

19. *Modus tollens:* If the pizza doesn't arrive on time, Fred will eat the fudge brownies.

20. *Conjunction:* He's been to Machias, Maine. He knows about Helen's Pies.

Part Two

Directions: Name the rule of inference used below. If more than one rule is used, name both.

1. Only warm bread makes Louie happy after he loses at Scrabble. Louie lost at Scrabble, so he'll want to have warm bread.

2. If something eats beef it is carnivorous. John is not a carnivore. So John is not a beef-eater.

3. John does not eat beef. John enjoys seafood. Thus, John does not eat beef and he enjoys seafood.

4. Either Bobo gets his steak rare or he'll get a hamburger. Bobo did not get a hamburger, so he got his steak rare.

5. All steak-eaters revolt Veronica. All those who revolt Veronica won't be invited to her party. So all steak-eaters won't be invited to Veronica's party.

6. Brooke likes to eat at Farfalla. If Brooke does not like meatballs on her spaghetti, then she won't like to eat at Farfalla. Thus, Brooke likes meatballs on top of her spaghetti.

7. April does not like reptiles and she doesn't care much for insects either. Therefore, April does not care much for insects.

8. Skateboarders enjoy leaping into the air and surfers like to stand on waves. Therefore, skateboarders enjoy leaping into the air.

9. Bungie jumping is not good for those who are prone to squeamishness. Therefore either bungie jumping is not good for those who are prone to squeamishness or the sky is made of blue wallpaper paste.

10. Small alligators can be unpleasant and so can small badgers. Therefore, small alligators can be unpleasant.

11. If the transmission goes, Ernie will get out his cell phone and sit down on the curb. The transmission went, so Ernie got out his cell phone and sat down on the curb.

12. If Leon can fix the transmission by himself, Harry will start on the radiator. Leon could fix the transmission by himself. So Harry can start on the radiator.

Part Three

Directions: Name the rule of inference, rule of replacement, or formal fallacy below. *Be careful:* Not all the sentences are in standard form so translate them first and then check for the rules.

1. Unless you come with me, I won't go to see Dr. Gutierrez. I didn't go to see Dr. Gutierrez. Therefore, you came with me.

2. I will talk with that Elvis impersonator if he stops teasing me. The Elvis impersonator stopped teasing me; therefore I talked with him.

3. If the operation is a success, Frank won't have to put up with a plug in his neck. The operation was not a success, so Frank will have to put up with a plug in his neck.

4. If the doctor operates and leaves in a sponge, then there'll be a lawsuit. This is equivalent to "If the doctor operates, then, if she leaves in a sponge, there'll be a lawsuit."

5. If that's a badger, it may be wise to stay inside the car. It was wise to stay inside the car; therefore, it must be a badger out there.

6. If the farmer sees another two-headed dog, then he can sell his story to a tabloid. This means if the farmer did not sell his story to a tabloid, then he did not see another two-headed dog.

7. Tod says a UFO beamed a barbequed chicken down to him. Therefore, either Tod says a UFO beamed a barbequed chicken down to him or I had another nightmare.

8. If the Elvis impersonator sings "Jailhouse Rock" one more time, the news media will not come; but if the Elvis impersonator marries the Marilyn impersonator, the news media will be there. Either news media is there or not there. As a result, either the Elvis impersonator did not sing "Jailhouse Rock" another time or the Elvis impersonator did not marry the Marilyn impersonator.

9. Una will go with Tim to the dance contest, if she doesn't have to wear her leopard tights. Una had to wear leopard tights. So she did not go with Tim to the dance contest.

10. A mudslide is a sufficient condition to mess up the freeway. If the freeway is messed up, traffic will be a tad slow. So if there's a mudslide, traffic will be a tad slow.

11. Either there's a banana slug in the kitchen or Grandpa spilled some of the linguini. Grandpa did not spill any linguini. So there's a banana slug in the kitchen.

12. Whenever Jim hears Otis Redding music, he sings at the top of his lungs. Whenever Jim sings at the top of his lungs, Nancy puts a pillow over her head. Therefore, whenever Jim hears Otis Redding music, Nancy puts a pillow over her head.

13. If Jack is squeamish, he might find riding the roller coaster a bit disturbing. Jack is not squeamish, so he shouldn't be disturbed riding the roller coaster.

14. Neither Vin Diesel nor J. Lo eat at my local diner. So, Vin Diesel does not eat at my local diner and J. Lo doesn't eat at my local diner.

15. LaToya will knit another afghan if she can get the right color yarn. LaToya knitted another afghan. So she got the right color yarn.

16. If the insecticidal soap doesn't work, Anita will go after the aphids by hand. Therefore, if the insecticidal soap doesn't work, then the insecticidal soap didn't work and Anita will go after the aphids by hand.

17. If the eggs come with grits, then we won't need potatoes. This means, if we need potatoes, then the eggs did not come with grits.

18. John: "For economic issues, I rely on logic. For political issues, I rely on logic or on gut instinct. For moral issues, I never rely on logic." What follows?
    a. If John relies on logic, he may be responding to a moral issue.
    b. If John relies on logic, he is not responding to an economic issue.
    c. If John does not rely on logic, he is responding to a political issue.
    d. If John does not rely on logic, he must be responding to an economic issue.
    e. If John does not rely on logic, he might be responding to a political issue.

Part Four

Directions: More practice with the rules. Name the rule of inference or replacement below. If it's a fallacy, name it.

1. If Nazreen sees *The Exorcist*, she will have to sleep with the lights on. Nazreen did not sleep with the lights on. Therefore, she did not see *The Exorcist*.

2. Neither *Open Water* nor *Saw* disturbed Carlos. That means *Open Water* did not disturb Carlos and *Saw* did not disturb Carlos.

3. If the alien makes meatloaf of the predator, then the audience will cheer. This is equivalent to "If the audience did not cheer, then the alien did not make meatloaf of the predator."

4. There's an android drooling over that pit of slime and there's T-X changing her arm into a metal hook. Therefore, there's an android drooling over that pit of slime.

5. If Frankenstein could get better fitting shoes, he'd find walking easier. Frankenstein didn't find walking easier, so he must not have gotten better fitting shoes.

6. Either that's the Wolfman or it's Ryan in his gorilla costume. That's not Ryan in his gorilla costume, so it must be the Wolfman.

7. Whenever the moon is full, there are strange noises in the forest near the old mill. Whenever there are strange noises in the forest near the old mill, the coyotes start to howl. Therefore, whenever the moon is full, the coyotes start to howl.

8. If that werewolf leers at me another moment, then I'll dial 911, and if that werewolf does not leer at me another moment, then I can sit down and read my new novel. Either the werewolf leered at me another moment or he didn't. Consequently, either I dialed 911 or I sat down and read my new novel.

9. Either that's the house that dripped blood or our vacation cottage is haunted. That is not the house that dripped blood, so our vacation cottage is haunted.

10. If that's not Spider-man, then I'm confused about Peter's ability to walk on walls. That is Spider-man. So I'm not confused about his ability to walk on walls.

11. Waving a garlic clove is sufficient to deter a ghoul from getting within 3 feet of a human. The ghoul came up to the UPS deliveryman, so he must not have waved the garlic clove.

12. If that's not an extraterrestrial, then he might work as a bouncer. Therefore, if he doesn't work as a bouncer, then he's an extraterrestrial.

13. Unless that's Dr. Lecter, your threats will mean nothing. He's not Dr. Lecter, so your threats meant nothing.

14. There goes one of those pod people from that invasion last week in West Hollywood. Therefore, either that's one of the pod people from the invasion last week in West Hollywood or it's that troubled young man who works at Astro's Coffee Shop.

15. Either that's the Blob or it's slime left over from a Halloween party. That's not the Blob. Therefore, that's slime left over from a Halloween party.

16. Either that's an insurance salesman or it's an extra from *The Interpreter*. Thus, if it's not an insurance salesman, then it's an extra from *The Interpreter*.

17. If the new stereo arrives, Lulu won't leave her house. Lulu left her house; therefore, the new stereo didn't arrive.

18. Provided that that's not the electrician, it must be an insurance salesman. This means, if it's not an insurance salesman, then it's an electrician.

19. Either there's a family of mice hiding in the bag of dog food or something weird is going on. Something weird is not going on. Therefore, there's a family of mice hiding in the bag of dog food.

20. If she doesn't cook the meat, it will taste strange. This means, if the meat doesn't taste strange, so she must have cooked it.

21. If you get a cape with fake fur lining, then you can use it as a couch cover when you aren't wearing it. Anna got a cape with fake fur lining, so she can use it as a couch cover when she isn't wearing it.

22. Not both Harry and Leon thought the problem was with the fuel pump. Therefore, either Harry did not think the problem was with the fuel pump or Leon did not think the problem was with the fuel pump.

Part Five

Directions: Name the rule or fallacy.

1. **Boss:** Hey Gloria, what are you doing digging in my desk drawer?

   Gloria: Oh, Mr. Munoz, did I ever tell you how much the secretaries respect you? They think you are so much fun to work with and we love when you do imitations of Bruce Springsteen. I bet your family just adores you!

2. If the journalist digs in the trash, she will find incriminating evidence about the mayor's brother. The journalist dug in the trash, so she found incriminating evidence about the mayor's brother.

3. Spencer makes rich cheesecake and he spent a lot of money on the ingredients. Therefore, he makes rich cheesecake.

4. Either that's Keanu Reeves on the phone or someone is playing a trick on her. This means, if that's not Keanu Reeves on the phone, then someone's playing a trick on her.

5. If you are a cynic and only see problems, then life won't be easy for you. This is the same as, If you are a cynic, then, if you only see problems, life won't be easy for you.

6. In a study of teens in South Central, it was found that 83 percent of them preferred rhythm and blues to country music. This means 83 percent of all Americans prefer rhythm & blues to country music.

7. Laura is not both a cynic nor a pessimist. That means either Laura's not a cynic or she's not a pessimist.

8. If you don't like to gather pods and stones, you won't like camping. The boys liked camping, so they must like to gather pods and stones.

9. Dr. Green, you should carry more of the load in the Philosophy Department. If you don't I will tell your son, Evan, that there's no Easter Bunny and it's you, not Santa, who gave him that bicycle last year.

10. If Jasper eats both peas and corn, he won't want zucchini. Jasper did not want any zucchini, so he must have eaten both peas *and corn*.

11. Nicole said never to lie, so I should tell Dr. Teays that all those stories about her bird waste precious time in our class! Plus, I should tell her that her new hairdo makes her look like a Dutch boy!

12. If Prince eats another bird, we'll have to keep him indoors, but if Prince eats up his crunchies, we'll have to go get more cat food. Either Prince ate another bird or he ate up his crunchies. So, either we'll have to keep Prince indoors or we'll have to go get more cat food.

Glossary

Absorption. One of the rules of inference and thus a valid form of argument. It is of the form: "If A then B. Therefore, if A then (A and B)."

Accent. One of the fallacies of ambiguity. This fallacy occurs when accent (the emphasis of a word or phrase) leads us to draw an incorrect conclusion.

Accident. Fallacy that occurs when a general rule or principle is applied to a special case in which, by reason of its special or atypical characteristics, the rule simply does not apply. This fallacy might be a misapplication of a moral principle, a rule from work, or a general pronouncement made by a family member or friend. The unwarranted assumption is that the rule applies to all cases, without exception.

Accountability. The extent to which an individual or institution could be held responsible for a decision, policy, or action.

Ad Baculum. Fallacy that occurs when force, the threat of force, or coercion is used to persuade someone to a conclusion. This includes verbal or sexual harassment, blackmail, extortion, and threat of violence used to "persuade" someone to a position. A variation is bribery, where the coercion comes in the form of a promise, offer, money, or position.

Ad Hominem. Fallacy that involves an attack on the character or traits of the person making an argument, rather than their ideas or argument. We see ad hominem when someone is discredited because of such traits as race, gender, nationality, or age.

Ad Hominem Circumstantial. Fallacy that involves an attack on an opponent because of their special circumstances or vested interests, rather than focusing on their ideas or arguments. We see ad hominem circumstantial fallacy when someone is criticized because of the person's membership in a group or professional, religious, cultural, or political associations.

Ad Ignorantiam. Fallacy that occurs when someone argues that something must be the case true or false) because you cannot prove otherwise. This is the "if you can't prove me wrong, then I must be right!" defense. The person argues on the basis of a lack of proof to the contrary. However, a failure to disprove something does not mean the opposite is true. And when it comes to legal matters, a *presumption* of innocence is quite different than *proof* of innocence.

Ad Misericordiam. One of the fallacies of relevance; this fallacy occurs when there is an attempt to persuade on the basis of an appeal to pity or someone's unfortunate circumstances rather than on the basis of evidence.

Ad Populum. One of the fallacies of relevance in which there is an attempt to persuade on the basis of an appeal to the majority, snob appeal, mass sentiment or patriotism.

Ad Verecundiam. One of the fallacies of relevance; this fallacy occurs when there is an attempt to persuade on the basis of the testimony or appeal to a public figure or celebrity who is not an expert in the field in question.

Addition.   Addition is one of the rules of inference and thus a valid form of argument. It is of the form: "A. Therefore, either A or B."

Ah-ha effect.   A mental breakthrough—when we finally get something.

Ambiguity.   A lack of clarity in the use of language either by accident or intent, resulting in a confusion that may lead to an incorrect conclusion being drawn. Problems can occur when words, grammar, or sentence structure create an ambiguity or a variety of interpretations.

Amphiboly.   Fallacy that occurs when the sentence structure or use of grammar creates an ambiguity, leading to an incorrect conclusion being drawn.

Analysis.   The process of gathering evidence, weighing premises, sorting out warranted from unwarranted assumptions, structuring arguments, evaluating the strength of an inductive argument, and assessing the validity and soundness of deductive arguments. The central task of analysis is the evaluation of an argument to determine its strength.

Analytical Tools.   Ways to weigh evidence, construct or dismantle arguments, analyze the various aspects of reasoning, acquire a facility for both inductive and deductive reasoning, and determine the strength of the reasoning holding the argument together.

Antecedent.   The condition that is claimed to lead to a certain effect (known as the "consequent"). The antecedent lies between the "if" and the "then" in a conditional claim.

Antonyms.   Words that are opposite in meaning (e.g., hot and cold, tall and short).

Application of a Rule.   Using a set of criteria to draw a conclusion, as with: "Rule X applies to any cases with characteristics A, B, C, and D. Individual case P has characteristics A, B, C, and D. Therefore, rule X applies to case P."

Argument.   A set of propositions that consists of a conclusion and the premises (evidence). The premises act as supporting evidence for the conclusion. An argument consists of *only one* conclusion and *at least one* premise.

Argument based on statistical studies.   An inductive argument consisting of one or more inferences about a targeted population drawn on the basis of a sample group. There are two components to a statistical study: The targeted population about which we want information and the sample group to be studied as a microcosm of the larger group.

Argument from Analogy.   An inductive argument that rests on a comparison that claims a characteristic true of the one term in the equation will also be true of the other. In law this usually involves the application of a precedent or legal principle.

Assessment Tools.   Ways to gather information, consider options, organize data using a set of criteria, sort warranted from unwarranted assumptions, sort into relevant categories, and break down an argument in order to evaluate the quality of the reasoning.

Assumption.   Something that is taken for granted or supposed to be the case without proof. An assumption is usually unstated.

Asymmetrical Descriptions.   When members of one group are referred to, valued, or described in ways that would not be used for a different group. An asymmetry usually indicates a double standard—generally resulting in one group being treated with more leniency or given higher status.

Asymmetry.   When a set of criteria applied to one group results in distinctly different results than when applied to a parallel (seemingly similar) group. In other words, two asymmetrical things simply do not match up. For example, newspaper descriptions of one ethnic group or gender are often dissimilar from descriptions of the dominant ethnic group or gender.

Attitudes and Dispositions of a Critical Thinker. The key attitudes and dispositions of a clear thinker—such as being receptive, flexible, open-minded, a careful listener, attentive to detail, observant, questioning, and willing to persevere. Personal traits include being willing to take risks and able to look at problems from different vantage points.

Authenticity. That which forms the basis for personal integrity and self-respect, including being true to oneself.

Authority (of a Web Page). The source of a document or Web page. Concerns around authority center on legitimacy and credibility.

Begging the Question (Petitio Principii). Fallacy that involves circular reasoning, whereby the speaker assumes what she or he is trying to prove. The conclusion is drawn on the basis of evidence containing a restatement of the conclusion itself. What is concluded must come out of the premises and not be a restatement of them.

Beyond a Reasonable Doubt. The standard of proof in criminal trials—that the evidence offers sufficient support for the conclusion so an alternative explanation is highly unlikely or impossible. This is a higher standard than that of civil trials, which rests on the preponderance of the evidence.

Bias. Functions as a kind of blinder or filter, slanting our thinking one way or another. It must be set aside if we want to think clearly, formulate strong arguments, and act out of a sense of justice. Prejudice and bias have to do with attitudes and states of mind—oppression involves action.

Biased Statistics. Fallacy that occurs when a statistical study is used to draw an inference about a target population, but the sample group is not diverse enough.

Biconditional. A proposition in the form "A if and only if B" or "A is equivalent to B." These can be expressed in either form: "If A then B, and if B then A" and "If A then B, and if not A then not B."

Bifurcation (Also Known as "False Dichotomy" or "Excluded Middle"). Fallacy that involves the presentation of an either/or situation having more than two options. This occurs when two choices are presented as complete and absolute (i.e., uncompromising contrasts).

Bloated Claims. A variation of eulogisms that includes exaggeration, grandiose promises, or predictions to offer possibilities that are too good to be true.

Blogs. Web logs; that is, web sites that function as online journals usually compromised of links and postings in reverse chronological order (most recent is first).

Bubble outline. Method of organizing a text or laying out an argument using circles ("bubbles") of varying size. The larger circles indicate key ideas or concepts and the smaller ones related concepts or examples of the key idea to which they are joined.

Buzzwords (See Jargon). A newly coined word or an old word used in a new way or used in a totally different context for an intended effect.

Categorical Proposition. Propositions that are expressed in one of four forms: "All A is B," "No A is B," "Some (or x% of) A is B" and "Some (or x% of) A is not B," where x ≠ 0 or 100. For example, "All cockatoos are birds" and "75% of cockatoos are animals that enjoy cantaloupe."

Categorical Syllogisms. Three-line arguments (or chains of them), consisting of two premises and a conclusion, with all the propositions in the form of categorical propositions. The resulting argument consists of three terms that make up the subjects and predicates. These terms are called the major term (predicate of the conclusion), the minor term (subject of the conclusion), and the middle term (the remaining term found in each of the premises).

Categories (See Labels).   Words used to characterize something or someone. Categories can be neutral or imbued with meaning (positive or negative).

Causal Claim.   A proposition of the form "A causes B," "A is caused by B," or "B is the effect of A."

Cause-and-Effect Reasoning.   A kind of inductive argument that argues that a particular event or effect occurs on the basis of specific antecedent conditions said to be the causal factor or factors.

Censorship.   Editing of a creation or performance or prohibiting any part of it to be seen or otherwise exhibited—presumably because of aspects deemed offensive to the public taste or morality.

Circumstantial Evidence.   Evidence that does not singularly or collectively definitively support a particular conclusion, but alternative explanations seem unlikely. This occurs when we have no hard evidence one way or the other, but the evidence points to the one conclusion. No amount of circumstantial evidence can provide certainty. What gives circumstantial evidence its weight is the lack of an alternative explanation.

Cogent.   Synonymous with "clear and convincing." A cogent argument is convincing because of the quality and persuasive force of the evidence supporting the conclusion. A cogent argument is well reasoned and clearly structured so we can follow the argument, seeing how the evidence lays the foundation for the conclusion.

Complement.   The set of all elements that are not contained in a given set. The complement of a set A is non-A. For example, the complement of "voters" is "non-voters."

Complex Question.   Fallacy that consists of two questions rolled into one, so the complex question cannot be answered without answering the previous, unasked question. The result is that the person is asked to give a simple answer to a multi-part (a complex) question, where the hidden question is potentially incriminating.

Composition.   Fallacy that occurs when it is argued that what is true of the parts or members must then be true of the whole or organization. Each of the parts or members may have some characteristic (say being lightweight), but that does not mean the whole group or object will be lightweight. The characteristics of the parts do *not* necessarily transfer to the entity as a whole.

Compound Proposition.   A proposition that contains at least one logical connective (i.e., "not," "and," "or," "if . . . then," and "if and only if"). For example, "Jasper loves corn and pine nuts."

Conceptual.   A type of question that draws upon knowledge of key terms and concepts and asks students to think on a more abstract level.

Conceptual framework.   A worldview or way of thinking that shapes an interpretation. The conceptual framework acts as a way to define the terms of an inquiry, arrive at a set of criteria for evaluating evidence and slants the ways in which decisions are made and justified.

Conclusion.   The proposition said to follow from at least one piece of evidence. Arguments consist of a set of premises (evidence) and one conclusion.

Conclusion-indicator.   A word or phrase that often precedes a conclusion. If you can replace the term with "therefore" without changing the argument, the term is a conclusion-indicator (for example: "thus," "hence," "consequently," "it follows that," and so on).

Conditional Claim.   A proposition that can be expressed in the form "If A then B." It is sometimes referred to as a hypothetical proposition, since we may not know whether the antecedent, A, is actually true in order to assert "If A then B."

Conjunct.   A term found in a conjunction. The terms "A" and "B" are both conjuncts for the conjunction "A and B."

Conjunction.   Any proposition that can be written in the form "A and B." Note: conjunctions could have terms that are equivalent to "and," such as "plus," "also," "moreover," and "but." The rule of conjunction asserts that if A is true and if B is also true, then the claim "A and B" is then true.

Connotation.   An issue of semantics that has to do with what words signify. The *connotation* is what the word suggests, implies, or conjures up in our minds, whereas the *denotation* of a word is the literal meaning.

Consequent.   What is said to follow if some antecedent condition is assumed true. In an "if . . . then" claim, the consequent follows the "then."

Constructive Dilemma.   A valid deductive argument of the form: If A then B, and if C then D. Either A or C. Therefore, either B or D. In other words, there's a choice between two options, where each option leads to some effect and you have to pick between either of the two options. The constructive dilemma is often referred to as a compound *modus ponens*.

Context.   The time and place in which a work was created, including audience response, the social and political setting, the target audience, and corporate backing.

Context of Discovery.   The framework within which the problem is named and how evidence will be sought and weighed leave as it is.

Context of Justification.   The framework within which the proof or argument and its evidence will be assessed or justified.

Contingent Claim.   A proposition that is either true or false, depending upon its component variables. In other words, contingent claims are neither tautologies (always true) nor contradictions (always false). For example, "Today is Sunday" is a contingent claim.

Contradiction.   A proposition that is always false, or false by definition (for example, any proposition of the form "A and not A," such as "The sky is blue but it is not blue").

Contrapositive.   The resulting proposition after the subject is replaced by the complement of the predicate and the predicate is replaced by the complement of the subject. The contrapositive cannot be taken on an I claim such as "Some A is B." The contrapositive of the E claim "No A is B" is the O claim "Some non-B is not non-A." For example, the contrapositive of "All painters are artists" is "All nonartists are nonpainters."

Contraries.   Propositions that cannot both be true, but could both be false. For example, A (universal positive) and E (universal negative) propositions are contraries since they cannot both be true, but could both be false.

Converse.   The resulting proposition after the subject and predicate are interchanged. The converse cannot be taken on an O claim. No change in the quality is required, except in the case of the A claim ("All A is B," which requires the converse to be changed to the I claim "Some B is A"). For example, the converse of "No cowhands are lonely people" is "No lonely people are cowhands."

Correlation.   A measure of the association between two things and how they are linked.

Corroborating Evidence.   A form of reinforcement, in the sense that the corroborating evidence strengthens the case by mutually supporting other evidence. When evidence poses no clear conflicts or contradictions if we assume it is actually true, we have *corroborating* evidence.

Credible Sources.   Sources considered to be legitimate, authentic, reliable, genuine, respectable. Jurors (and judges!) are regularly put in the position of having to assess the credibility of expert witnesses. Sizing up credibility is not always easy.

Critical Thinking Tools.   The means by which we accomplish the various tasks of critical thinking. There are four basic kinds of tools. (1) surveillance tools; (2) analytical tools; (3) assessment tools; and (4) synthesis tools.

Culturally Defined Uses of Language.   Norms around who can say what to whom, who can speak and in what order, and who gets the first and last word. We find these norms in public gatherings or in family dynamics. Our society and culture shape our use of language.

Currency.   The time a web page was last updated. Concerns around currency center on whether the page is up-to-date or outdated.

Cybersquatting.   When someone buys up the name of a well-known company and then demands money or simply refuses to give it up.

Deadly Triad.   The status quo *plus* habit *plus* stereotypical thinking. This triad is formed by the mindset of the dominant culture, the habitual ways of doing things, and belief systems that lock attitudes and stereotypical ways of thinking into place. Think of this deadly triad as conceptual snow goggles.

Deconstruction of an Ad.   Assessing its verbal message and visual message and the role of symbols and images in an attempt to analyze the various elements making up the ad.

Deductive Argument.   An argument in which the premises are claimed to be sufficient for drawing the conclusion. This assumes there are no missing pieces. In that sense, a deductive argument is a closed set. Examples of valid deductive arguments are modus ponens, modus tollens, disjunctive syllogism, and the hypothetical syllogism.

Definiendum.   The word or phrase that is being clarified or the meaning being sought.

Definiens.   The words meaning the same as the word or phrase in question (the explanation, the definition).

Definition.   A two-part explanation: first, the word or phrase to define or clarify. This is called the *definiendum*. Second is the explanation—words meaning the same as the word or phrase in question. This is called the *definiens*. *Synonym*s are words that are similar in meaning (e.g., warm and toasty), whereas *antonyms* are words that are opposite in meaning (e.g., hot and cold).

Denotation.   An issue of semantics. The *denotation* of a word is the literal meaning, whereas the *connotation* is what the word suggests, implies, or conjures up in our minds.

Description.   A statement about what is or is not the case pertaining to something or someone. Generally, each item in a description is either true or false and could be verified by examination.

Destructive Dilemma.   One of the rules of inference and thus a valid form of argument. It is of the form "If A then B, and if C then D. Either not B or not D. Therefore, either not A or not C." It is often referred to as a compound modus tollens.

Disjunction.   A proposition in the form of "Either A or B." The terms A and B are called *disjuncts*. For example, "Either pudding is a vegetable or it is a creamy dessert."

Disjunctive Syllogism.   A valid deductive argument of the form: "Either A or B. Not A (or not B). Therefore, B (or therefore, A)."

Distribution.   When all the members of a class have a certain predicated characteristic. Determining distribution rests on two things: the location of the term (subject or predicate) and (2) the proposition's quality (in the case of the subject) or quantity (in the case of the predicate). Only universal propositions have a distributed subject and only negative propositions have a distributed predicate. In universal negative propositions, both terms are distributed.

Diversity of the sample.   The extent to which a sample group in a statistical study is representative of the targeted population in terms of key factors such as race or ethnicity, age, gender, education-level, and so on.

Double Standard.   When rules are applied unfairly to different groups, resulting in one group being treated with higher or lower status than the other.

Dyslogism.   A variation of begging the question that uses highly slanted language such as name-calling to bias an argument against someone or something.

Embedded advertising   Product placement. This is a form of marketing that places products in scenes, art, or scenarios that are not ostensibly advertising. For example, the movie *ET* has the protagonist using a particular brand of candy in various scenes.

Equivocation.   Fallacy that occurs when there is a shift of meaning in a word or phrase leading to an incorrect conclusion being drawn.

Ethical and Spiritual Dimension of Popular Culture.   The aspects of popular culture that relate to religion, faith, values, and morality.

Evaluation Question.   Referring to the Internet, a question that focuses on distinguishing the quality of the Web page or Web site and checking for any of the following: accuracy, authority, coverage, currency, and objectivity.

Exaggeration.   Inflating or distorting something (e.g., stretching the truth) in order to achieve a desired effect.

Euphemism.   A variation of begging the question that uses highly slanted language to bias an argument in favor of someone or something.

Equivalent.   Two propositions that have the same logical meaning, even if their form may differ. "A is equivalent to B" entails "If A then B" and "If B than A."

Fact.   Something known to be true or that could be confirmed by empirical or other means. Facts are actually the case, known by observation or reliable testimony, rather than inferred or surmised. Statements of fact include all that we can say is "true" or are true by definition.

Factual Judgments: An inference generally drawn from earlier observations (the factual picture). A factual judgment is made on the basis of a set of facts about the issue in question. Because the judgment is one step removed from the fact, this means that the inference drawn on the basis of the fact is not necessarily true—it must be scrutinized so we are not misled. For example, to assess the impact of a new law on your economic interests as a student, you would arrive at a factual judgment by seeing how those interests fit into the entire factual picture surrounding the new law.

Fallacies of Ambiguity   (Also known as Linguistic Fallacies). Fallacies that center on the use of language in terms of emphasis, interpretation, sentence structure, or the relationship between the parts and the whole. The ambiguity results in an incorrect conclusion being drawn, causing the fallacy. The names of the fallacies relate to the form the flawed reasoning takes.

Fallacies of Presumption.   Fallacies that rest upon an unwarranted assumption, that leads to an incorrect conclusion being drawn. The names of the fallacies relate to the form the flawed reasoning takes.

Fallacies of Relevance.   Fallacies in which the premises simply fail to support the conclusion. So they are irrelevant. The names of the fallacies relate to the form the flawed reasoning takes.

Fallacy.   A deceptive or misleading argument that may persuade us, but is nevertheless unsound. A fallacy may take many different forms, but they all share a common trait—namely, they are poorly reasoned arguments, however persuasive they seem on the surface. Every fallacy contains a fundamental flaw in reasoning.

Fallacy of Affirming the Consequent.   One of the formal fallacies. It takes the form: "If A then B. B. Therefore, A."

Fallacy of Complex Question.   Fallacy that consists of two questions rolled into one, so the complex question cannot be answered without answering the previous, unasked question. The result is that the person is asked to give a simple answer to a multi-part (a complex) question. It is this first, hidden, question that is incriminating and carries a presumption of guilt that is then attached to the second, stated, question. For example, "Have you still a slob?" assumes that "you" are guilty of having been a slob in the past.

Fallacy of Denying the Antecedent.   One of the formal fallacies. It takes the form: "If A then B. A is not the case. Therefore, B is not the case either."

Fallacy of Misleading Vividness.   A fallacy of presumption that occurs when strong evidence is overlooked because of a striking counter example.

False Analogy.   Fallacy that draws an inference resting on a comparison between two terms having no real similarities, other than trivial ones. The form it takes is this: "A is like B and A has property P. Therefore, B has property P as well." The problem is the comparison of A and B is seriously flawed.

False correlation.   Inference that one thing that precedes another is causally related to it despite insufficient evidence.

Figure.   In a syllogism, determined by the location of the middle term. There are four possible figures. Knowing the figure is crucial for assessing the validity of a syllogism.

Film review.   A commentary on a film that includes some or all of the following: plot, character development, evaluation or rating, justification for assessing the film or its components (such as the acting), and a detailed argument about the film.

First Amendment   (of the U.S. Constitution). Guarantees freedom of speech.

Flowchart.   Method of organizing a text or laying out an argument using numbered labels (or boxes). Each label has a description of the numbered paragraph in the text or argument.

Formal Fallacies.   Fallacies that occur because of a structural error. As a result, the very form of the reasoning is incorrect. The different names of the formal fallacies refer to the pattern of that flawed reasoning, such as the fallacy of denying the antecedent and the fallacy of affirming the consequent.

Forms of argument.   Two categories of arguments (as determined by logicians): deductive and inductive.

Frame of reference   A particular vantage point (point of view) that could be used to examine a given issue. The frame of reference influences the ways issues are presented and potentially "stacks the deck." This framework is shaped by our prior knowledge, assumptions, values, language or notation, among others.

Habit.   Routines that may act as blinders or restrictions on perceiving the world and evaluating what is seen and that therefore should be scrutinized as a potential obstacle to clear thinking.

Hasty Generalization.   Fallacy in which a statistical study is used as the basis for an inference, but the sample size is too small or atypical. This fallacy is commonly seen in stereotypical reasoning based on a sample of one or two. If the sample size is not sufficient, avoid drawing a generalization.

Hate Crimes.   One of the most odious expressions of prejudice. The American Psychological Association says of hate crime that not only is it an attack on one's physical self, but it is also an attack on one's very identity.

Hedging.   Undercutting a claim or raising doubts about it by the use of language. Hedging can take two forms: (1) it can indicate a shift from one position to a much weaker one; or (2) it can suggest a negative connotation of a phrase or claim.

Hermeneutics.   A German word meaning "theories of interpretation." According to the framework used in assessing a "text" (a film or work of art or literature), we arrive at different sorts of interpretations.

Higher-Order Thinking Skills.   Comprehension skills, that include application, synthesis, drawing inferences, comparison or contrast, justification, analysis, evaluation, moral reasoning, and using inductive and deductive reasoning.

Hoax-Buster.   A resource or Web site intended to help users identify Web sites that are hoaxes or spoofs.

Human Interest Story.   A news story intended to appeal to the general reader because of its focus on a particular case (such as a moving story about an individual or group of individuals).

Hypothetical Case (Alias Hypo).   A law case that presents a scenario or story with the task of deciding how it is to be evaluated given existing laws and precedents. This is an important application of analogical reasoning, requiring lawyers and law students to be both astute and imaginative in assessing the hypothetical cases.

Hypothetical Syllogism.   A valid deductive argument of the form: "If A then B. If B then C. Therefore, if A then C."

Ideas.   Solutions, intentions, plans of action, or theories. The ancient roots of the word go back to a general or ideal form, pattern, or standard by which things are measured. More commonly now, we use it to refer to insights, purposes, or recommendations.

Independent Evidence.   One piece of evidence that is sufficient in and of itself (singularly) to establish the conclusion.

Inductive.   An argument in which the conclusion can only be said to follow with probability or likelihood even if the premises are assumed to be true. The conclusion of an inductive never follows with certainty. Examples include predictions, cause and effect arguments, statistical reasoning, and arguments from analogy.

Inductive Generalization.   An argument of the form: "x% of As polled (or sampled) are Bs. Therefore, x% of all As are Bs."

Inference.   A conclusion drawn on the basis of some evidence or observations. An inference is an answer to the question, "What's it about? What story does this tell?"

Interdependent Evidence.   When a conclusion could not be established by any one of the premises but the premises together support the conclusion. In other words, the evidence works as a unit, not singularly, to establish the conclusion.

Invalid.   An argument in which the assumed truth of the premises does not guarantee that the conclusion is also true. In other words, if the premises could be true while the conclusion was false, the argument would be invalid. Invalid arguments are always unsound.

Jargon.   The language of a particular group or profession or the specialized technical terminology coined for a specific purpose or effect.

Joint Method.   Combining the method of agreement and the method of difference to determine the cause of an event. This method, then, looks both at what was the same *and* what was different in the event's antecedent conditions.

Labels.   Words used to characterize something or someone—such as a person, group, or set of objects. Labels can be neutral or imbued with meaning (positive or negative).

Legal Precedent.   A previous legal case used as an analogy to draw an inference to another case. We are implicitly asserting that the similarities allow for the ruling of the precedent-setting case to apply to the case at hand.

Liberatory voice.   Works of inspiration that have a transformative effect on the audience. Think of those who have stood up against injustice and raised their voices in opposition.

Linguistic fallacy.   Also known as a fallacy of ambiguity (because of the lack of clarity leading to a mistaken conclusion due to the use of language). The three key linguistic fallacies are equivocation (where there's a shift of meaning in a word or phrase leading to an incorrect conclusion), accent (where the emphasis of a word or phrase leads us to an incorrect conclusion), and amphiboly (where the sentence structure or use of grammar creates an ambiguity, leading to an incorrect conclusion).

Loaded Language.   Value-laden language that creates either a positive or negative bias. The use of loaded terms tends to unfairly prejudge the case. Loaded language is to be distinguished from colorful, or figurative, language. With the latter, striking images (from ugly to funny to beautiful) are evoked because of the vivid use of language, but it does not function as a means of persuasion for a particular conclusion.

Logical Addition (a.k.a. Addition).   One of the rules of inference and thus a valid form of argument. It is of the form "A. Therefore, either A or B."

Lower-Order Thinking Skills.   Thinking skills that are at a more basic, rather than advanced level. This includes observation, gathering data, comparison, and contrast.

Major Premise: The premise of a syllogism containing the major term (the predicate of the conclusion).

Major Term: The predicate of the conclusion in a syllogism.

Margin of Error.   Recognizes that the inference from the smaller, sample group to the targeted population contains a degree of probability, which is indicated by the range of the margin of error plus-or-minus z. The margin of error means the range goes from $-z\%$ to $+z\%$, which is a range of 2z. This means that if your margin of error is 3%, then the range is 6%, and a margin of error of 5% will give a range of 10%, which is a significant range. The smaller the margin of error z, the better.

Metaphor.   The application of a word or phrase to draw a comparison or indicate a similarity (e.g., "she is a shrew and he's a snake").

Metatag.   A metatag is a place in the HTML code where information about the site is listed.

Method of Agreement.   A way to determine the cause of an event by examining all the cases where the event occurs and then looking for a common factor among the antecedent conditions.

Mood of a syllogism.   The list of types of proposition (A, E, I, O) of the major premise, minor premise, and conclusion (as expressed in standard form). Since there are three propositions to a syllogism, the mood consists of some combination of A's, E's, I's, and O's. Typically, the mood is stated before the figure, as we see with mood and figure OAO-(3).

Method of Concomitant Variation   A way to determine the cause of an event by examining situations in which more or less of some causal factor(s) result in an increase or decrease of the effect.

Method of Difference.   A way to determine the cause of an event by examining all the cases where the event occurs and where it doesn't in order to determine what was different and therefore identify the cause.

Middle Term: The term that only appears in the two premises of a syllogism.

Minor Premise: The premise of a syllogism containing the minor term.

Minor Term: The subject of the conclusion in a syllogism.

Modus Ponens.   A valid deductive argument of the form "If A then B. A. Therefore B."

Modus Tollens.   A valid deductive argument of the form "If A then B. Not B. Therefore not A."

Necessary.   A condition P is necessary for Q if Q could not occur without P. This means, if Q is true, then P is also true. "P is necessary for Q" is the same as "If not P then not Q," or the equivalent proposition, "If Q then P."

Netspeak.   A mode of communication over the Internet that uses abbreviations (e.g., CUL8R, RUOK).

News Media.   The institutions in charge of producing news and commentary, including both print media (newspapers or newsletters), electronic media (online news sources), and TV news.

Objectivity.   Being fair and balanced in an assessment or presentation. The contrast is subjectivity, which points to a vested interest or possible bias.

Obverse.   Proposition that results after two steps: (1) change the quality of the proposition to its opposite (positive to negative or vice versa) and then (2) replace the predicate by its complement. The obverse can be taken of any categorical proposition. For example, the obverse of "No snakes are lizards" is "All snakes are nonlizards" and the obverse of "Some cows are Jerseys" is "Some cows are not non-Jerseys."

Opinions.   (1) Statements of belief or conjecture, for example, "The best music is rhythm and blues" and "Practicing verb drills is a drag." (2) Statement of perception, individual taste, or emotion. This gives rise to the refrain, "Well, that's just a matter of opinion." (3) Legal opinion. In a legal context, opinions may be expressed as a formal statement, a ruling, or considered advice. Court opinions, for example, function as an explanation for a decision that becomes law.

Particular Claim.   A proposition that could be expressed in the form "Some A are (or are not) B." This includes statistical claims of the form "x% of A is/is not B," where x is neither 100% nor zero. A particular claim is to be contrasted with a universal claim, which is an all-or-nothing claim.

Passive Voice.   Making the object of an action into the subject of a sentence, as in "The chicken was eaten by the coyote." Passive constructions can be spotted by looking for a form of "to be" followed by a past participle. One effect of the passive voice is that it avoids calling attention to the one performing an action (the coyote); rather, its focus is upon the recipient of the action (the chicken).

Post Hoc Fallacy.   Fallacious argument in which it is claimed "A causes B" on the basis of "A" happening before "B." The fact are event occurs before another does not reson they are causally related.

Predictions.   An argument about the future based on past or present evidence. A prediction is an inductive argument.

Premise.   A proposition offered or assumed as evidence in support of a particular conclusion.

Unstated assumptions may function as premises, so it is important for all premises to be articulated when analyzing an argument.

Premise-Indicator.   A word or phrase that precedes a premise. If a word can be replaced with "because," (for example: "given that," "in light of the fact that," "whereas," and so on) it is a premise-indicator.

Prescription.   A recommendation. Prescriptions can be written in the form of "This *ought to* be done" or "This *ought not* to be done" or related claims (such as "X ought or ought not do Y").

Problem-solving skills.   The analytical skills required to guide an investigation, arrive at an answer, or come to a resolution (e.g., of a dilemma). The include questioning-skills, observation-skills, the ability to sort and weigh evidence, the ability to use a framework or shift information into categories, and the ability to draw inferences on the strength of available evidence.

Prognoses.   Predictions based on the given facts of the case, along with what is known about analogous cases. Prognoses entail inductive reasoning because of the lack of certainty.

Propaganda.   Use of words and images to shape public consciousness, to predispose people to certain ideas, policies and actions—and to manipulate them to think, vote, and act in ways in sync with the propaganda machine. Propaganda can come from all directions—left, right, and center—it is the substance, not the source that marks propaganda.

Proposition.   An assertion that is either true or false. Declarations and rhetorical questions may operate as propositions, in order to clarify what's being asserted. A proposition can always be expressed in the form in which something (called the predicate) is either affirmed or denied about something else (called the subject).

Quality.   Answers, "Are you asserting something *is* or *is not* the case?" You are either af-

firming that it is the case (the quality is positive) or denying it (the quality is negative); therefore, the quality of a proposition is always either *positive* or *negative*.

Quantifier.   A term that indicates "how much"; such as the universal quantifiers "all" or "no" and the particular quantifier "some." Statistical propositions of the form x percent of A is B (x is neither 0 nor 100) are treated as particular propositions.

Quantity.   Answers the question, "How much?" In other words, the quantity refers to how much of the subject class is said to have something predicated of it. The possible answer, are "universal" or "particular" (i.e., all or some of it).

Propaganda.   Material (words or images) used deceptively in order to persuade an audience to a particular way of thinking (e.g., about politics, society, the government, or the like). Propaganda can take a number of forms.

Question-Begging Epithet.   Fallacy that occurs when language is biased so that it stacks the deck in either a positive or negative direction and leads to an incorrect conclusion. This results from the slanted language causing us to unfairly prejudge the case.

Question Techniques.   Methods that focus the inquiry, narrow down the territory under consideration to eliminate false leads or irrelevant material.

Red Herring.   Fallacy that occurs when an irrelevant line of reasoning is intentionally used to divert people away from the topic at hand. We see this when someone purposely shifts the subject of the conversation to avoid an incriminating line of questioning or to deceive someone. It's called a red herring, because a stinking little herring (fish) is an effective way to lead the hound dogs off the scent.

Retrodiction.   An inductive argument about the past based on present evidence.

Rule of Inference. A valid deductive argument form that allows us to draw an inference on the basis of the structure of the argument. Examples include modus ponens, modus tollens, disjunctive syllogism, hypothetical syllogism, constructive dilemma, simplification, and conjunction.

Rule of Replacement. Rule that allows us to restate a proposition into an equivalent form. Examples include DeMorgan's Laws, material implication, transposition, and exportation.

Rules of the Syllogism. Conditions that must be met in order for the syllogism to be valid. There are 5 rules of the syllogism.

Sample Group: A microcosm of a larger group, the targeted population, that we study in order to generalize about the larger group.

Search Question. Keywords or description in order to obtain a list of links on a particular topic using Internet software.

Sample Size. The number of subjects in the sample group used as the basis for an inference about a target population. The fallacy of hasty generalization occurs when the sample size is too small and the fallacy of biased statistics occurs when the sample size is not diverse enough.

Semantics. The meaning of words, what they signify in contrast to syntax, which focuses on the use of grammar, sentence structure, and punctuation, which are structural issues.

Simple Proposition. An assertion that does not contain any logical connectives ("and," "or," "not," "if . . . then," and "if and only if"). For example, "Pudding is a tasty dessert" is a simple proposition; whereas "Pudding is not good for your diet" is a compound proposition.

Simplification. One of the rules of inference and thus a valid form of argument. It is of the form: "A and B. Therefore, A (or: Therefore, B)."

Slippery Slope. Fallacy that involves an argument against something on the basis that, if it is allowed, it will lead to something worse, which in turn leads to something even worse and so on (down the slippery slope). The unstated assumption is that the first in the causal chain leads to the second and that leads to the third, and so on. The connection is incorrectly assumed and not proven. *Note:* Not all propositions that involve causal chains are slippery slopes. The fallacy occurs when the chain is asserted, but not proven.

Slogan. The jingle or sales line that is meant to be memorable and identify that product with this manufacturer.

Sound. A valid argument with true premises. Only deductive arguments can be sound (inductive arguments can't be sound because they could never be valid).

Spam. Unsolicited email—the web equivalent of junk mail.

Speculation. A form of guesswork. We normally use the term "speculation" to apply to hypotheses that have little, if any, evidence to back them up. There may be a kernel of evidence, but not enough to draw a solid conclusion.

Square of Opposition. Diagram indicating the relationship between categorical propositions: universal claims are contraries, particular claims are subcontraries, universal positive claims are contradictories of particular negative claims, universal negative claims are contradictories of particular positive claims, the two particular claims are subalterns of the two universal claims that are of the same quality (positive or negative).

Standard Form of a Proposition. A proposition expressed as one of these forms: "All A is B," "No A is B," "Some A are/are not B," or "x% of A are/are not B."

Standard Form of a Categorical Syllogism. A syllogism in which the propositions are all expressed in the form of an A, E, I, or O claim ("All A is B," "No A is B," "Some A is B,"

Some A is not B," and the syllogism is ordered: major premises, minor premise, conclusion.

Standard Outline.   Method of organizing a text or laying out an argument using traditional outline form consisting of alphabetical letters, roman numerals, and numbers to indicate main themes, sub-themes, explanations, and examples.

Statistical Reasoning.   When an inference is drawn about a target population on the basis of what is said to be true of a sample group. Key factors in statistical reasoning are the size of the sample, the diversity of the sample, and the date the study is done.

Statistical Syllogism.   An inductive argument in the form: "X% of A is B. p is an A. Therefore, p is a B" and where x is neither 100 nor zero. For example, "85% of women like men with a good sense of humor. Ursula is a woman. Therefore, Ursula will like men with a good sense of humor."

Strategy for Setting out Arguments.   (1) State the conclusion (thesis/hypothesis); (2) List the premises (reasons/evidence) one by one; (3) Examine the premises (reasons/evidence) to see if it is sufficient to support the conclusion.

Straw Man Fallacy.   Fallacy that presents an opponent's position as so extreme that it's indefensible. We are then steered toward another, more moderate or appealing position which is offered as the alternative. The image of the "straw man" (scarecrow) is that of something so flimsy that it will go up in smoke if we put a match near it. With the straw man fallacy, the opposition is usually painted as much more extreme than it actually is and the speaker's own position is offered as the better alternative.

Subaltern.   A particular proposition that can be inferred from the truth of the universal proposition, where we know the subject class is not empty. For example, the subaltern of "All tigers are cats" is "Some tigers are cats."

Subalternation.   The process of inferring from the universal claim to its corresponding particular claim.

Subcontraries.   Propositions that cannot both be false, but could both be true. For example, I (particular positive) and O (particular negative) propositions are subcontraries, since they cannot both be false, but could both be true.

Sufficient.   The minimal conditions for the truth of a proposition. This is expressed as follows: "P is sufficient for Q" is equivalent to "If P then Q" or "If not Q then not P." All three expressions are equivalent.

Surveillance Tools.   Perceive problems; recognize unsupported opinions versus facts and supported claims; spot prejudicial or biased modes of thinking, recognize the different uses of language; and watch for what is not said, omitted, downplayed or discarded.

Syllogism.   Three-line argument with two premises and one conclusion in which there are only three terms (called the major term, the minor term, and the middle term). The major term is the predicate of the conclusion, the minor term is the subject of the conclusion, and the middle term is the remaining term found only in the premises.

Synonyms.   Words that are similar in meaning (e.g., warm and toasty).

Syntax.   Sentence structure, grammar, and punctuation, in contrast to semantics, which focuses on the meaning, or significance, of words.

Synthesis Tools.   Articulate goals and decisions using a defensible set of criteria; resolve personal conflicts and professional dilemmas; recognize the role of ideas and creativity in problemsolving; evaluate decisions, plans, and policies; summarize arguments and synthesize information; and examine our own thinking processes and decision-making strategies.

Systemic Violence.   Violence that is found throughout a work or performance, as opposed to being present in one scene or aspect of the work.

Tabloidism.   Journalism that uses titillation, exaggeration, shock, disgust, or graphic photographs or details to attract an audience.

Targeted Population: The group about which we seek information in a statistical study by generalizing from the characteristics of a sample group.

Tautology.   A tautology is a proposition that is always true, or true by definition (for example, "Either that's a bowl of pudding or it's not a bowl of pudding").

Thematic Approach.   Presents an analysis of a film of TV program within a particular framework or theme (such as justice versus injustice, good versus evil, psychology, existentialism, etc.). When doing a thematic approach, our goal is to be single-mindedly focused on the central theme and to go into depth, citing examples to back up points.

Thesis.   The position being argued by an author. In an argument it functions as the conclusion for which the premises (evidence) are offered as support.

Transition Words.   Act to amplify, emphasize, introduce, illustrate, or contrast. Examples are "moreover," "to restate," "primarily," "in simpler terms," "notably," "in fact," alternatively," "on the other hand," and so on. Transition words are neither premise-indicators nor conclusion-indicators.

Tu Quo.   Fallacy that occurs when there's an attempt to discredit those whose actions are not in keeping with their words or who don't "practice what they preach."

Universal Claim.   A claim that can be expressed in the form "All A is B" or "No A is B." In contrast, particular claims assert or deny a predicated characteristic of only some (neither all nor none) of the subject class.

Unsound Argument.   An argument that has one or both of these traits: (1) it is not valid, (2) it does not have true premises.

URL.   A Web address. For example the URL of the *Washington Post* is http:www.washington-post.com.

Valid.   An argument in which the premises certainly support the conclusion. This means that, if we assume the premises are true, the conclusion would be forced to be true as well. The conclusion cannot be false and the premises true in a valid argument. A valid argument is not necessarily sound; soundness requires that the argument be valid *and* the premises actually true. Validity does not apply to inductive arguments—only to deductive ones.

Value Claims.   Express some kind of moral, social, or aesthetic judgment and, thus, are not normally presented as either true or false. They may be used as evidence, but they should be handled carefully. Value claims are usually expressed in sentences that assert a judgment or a recommendation.

Variable.   A letter (A, B, C, or p, q, r) used to stand for propositions. For example, "If pudding is on the menu, then George will order it" could be rewritten using variables P = pudding is on the menu and G = George will order it. The proposition then would be written: "If P then G."

Venn Diagrams.   Intersecting circles that are used to indicate the relationship between terms of propositions or to assess validity. The diagram must contain as many intersecting circles as the number of terms involved.

Verbal message.   What is being said in ads in terms of the text (or copy).

Visual Message.   The use of color or black and white, symbols, images, "characters," and the layout of an ad.

Watchdog.   An individual, group of individuals, or association whose job or duty it is to observe and report on someone or something for the welfare of the general public.

Weasel Words.   Slippery terms that are used in manipulative ways, twisting the meaning of words or phrases to create a certain effect.

Web Analysis.   Analysis of a Web page or document on a Web site. The American Library Association sets out five aspects to Web analysis: authority, accuracy, coverage, currency, and objectivity.

w.w.w.   Abbreviation for "World Wide Web."

Index